Drawn by J. Thurston. Engraved by W. Finden.

GEOFFREY CHAUCER.

From a Limning in Occleve's De Regimine Principis, *preserved in the Harleian Library.*

EDITED FOR POPULAR PERUSAL WITH CURRENT ILLUSTRATIONS

AND EXPLANATORY NOTES

BY

D. LAING PURVES

Wm W. SWAYNE,
BROOKLYN & NEW YORK

CONTENTS.

PREFACE.

The object of this volume is to place before the general reader our two early poetic masterpieces—The Canterbury Tales and The Faerie Queen; to do so in a way that will render their "popular perusal" easy in a time of little leisure and unbounded temptations to intellectual languor; and, on the same conditions, to present a liberal and fairly representative selection from the less important and familiar poems of Chaucer and Spenser. There is, it may be said at the outset, peculiar advantage and propriety in placing the two poets side by side in the manner now attempted for the first time. Although two centuries divide them, yet Spenser is the direct and really the immediate successor to the poetical inheritance of Chaucer. Those two hundred years, eventful as they were, produced no poet at all worthy to take up the mantle that fell from Chaucer's shoulders; and Spenser does not need his affected archaisms, nor his frequent and reverent appeals to "Dan Geffrey," to vindicate for himself a place very close to his great predecessor in the literary history of England. If Chaucer is the "Well of English undefiled," Spenser is the broad and stately river that yet holds the tenure of its very life from the fountain far away in other and ruder scenes.

The Canterbury Tales, so far as they are in verse, have been printed without any abridgment or designed change in the sense. But the two Tales in prose —Chaucer's Tale of Meliboeus, and the Parson's long Sermon on Penitence— have been contracted, so as to exclude thirty pages of unattractive prose, and to admit the same amount of interesting and characteristic poetry. The gaps thus made in the prose Tales, however, are supplied by careful outlines of the omitted matter, so that the reader need be at no loss to comprehend the whole scope and sequence of the original. With The Faerie Queen a bolder course has been pursued. The great obstacle to the popularity of Spenser's splendid work has lain less in its language than in its length. If we add together the three great poems of antiquity—the twenty-four books of the Iliad, the twenty-four books of the Odyssey, and the twelve books of the Æneid—we get at the dimensions of only one-half of The Faerie Queen. The *six* books, and the fragment of a seventh, which alone exist of the author's contemplated twelve, number about 35,000 verses; the *sixty* books of Homer and Virgil number no more than

37,000. The mere bulk of the poem, then, has opposed a formidable barrier to its popularity; to say nothing of the distracting effect produced by the numberless episodes, the tedious narrations, and the constant repetitions, which have largely swelled that bulk. In this volume the poem is compressed into two-thirds of its original space, through the expedient of representing the less interesting and more mechanical passages by a condensed prose outline, in which it has been sought as far as possible to preserve the very words of the poet. While deprecating a too critical judgment on the bare and constrained *précis* standing in such trying juxtaposition, it is hoped that the labour bestowed in saving the reader the trouble of wading through much that is not essential for the enjoyment of Spenser's marvellous allegory, will not be unappreciated.

As regards the manner in which the text of the two great works, especially of The Canterbury Tales, is presented, the Editor is aware that some whose judgment is weighty will differ from him. This volume has been prepared "for popular perusal;" and its very *raison d'être* would have failed, if the ancient orthography had been retained. It has often been affirmed by editors of Chaucer in the old forms of the language, that a little trouble at first would render the antiquated spelling and obsolete inflections a continual source, not of difficulty, but of actual delight, for the reader coming to the study of Chaucer without any preliminary acquaintance with the English of his day—or of his copyists' days. Despite this complacent assurance, the obvious fact is, that Chaucer in the old forms has *not* become popular, in the true sense of the word; he is *not* "understanded of the vulgar." In this volume, therefore, the text of Chaucer has been presented in nineteenth-century garb. But there has been not the slightest attempt to "modernise" Chaucer, in the wider meaning of the phrase; to replace his words by words which he did not use; or, following the example of some operators, to translate him into English of the modern spirit as well as the modern forms. So far from that, in every case where the old spelling or form seemed essential to metre, to rhyme, or meaning, no change has been attempted. But, wherever its preservation was not essential, the spelling of the monkish transcribers—for the most ardent purist must now despair of getting at the spelling of Chaucer himself—has been discarded for that of the reader's own day. It is a poor compliment to the Father of English Poetry, to say that by such treatment the *bouquet* and individuality of his works must be lost. If his masterpiece is valuable for one thing more than any other, it is the vivid distinctness with which English men and women of the fourteenth century are there painted, for the study of all the centuries to follow. But we wantonly balk the artist's own purpose, and discredit his labour, when we keep before his picture the screen of dust and cobwebs which, for the English people in these days, the crude forms of the infant language have practically become. Shakespeare has not suffered by similar changes; Spenser has not suffered; it would be surprising if Chaucer should suffer, when the loss of popular comprehension and favour in his case are necessarily all the greater for his remoteness from our day. In a much smaller degree—since previous labours in the same direction had left far less to do—the same work has been performed for the spelling of Spenser; and the whole endeavour in this department of the Editor's task has been, to present a text plain and easily intelligible to the modern reader, without rendering any injustice to the old poet. It would be presumptuous to believe that in every case both ends have been achieved together; but the *laudatores temporis acti*—the students who may differ most from the plan pursued in this volume—will best appreciate the difficulty of the enterprise, and most leniently regard any failure in the details of its accomplishment.

With all the works of Chaucer, outside The Canterbury Tales, it would have been absolutely impossible to deal within the scope of this volume. But nearly one hundred pages (200–292), have been devoted to his minor poems; and, by dint of careful selection and judicious abridgment—a connecting outline of the story in all such cases being given—the Editor ventures to hope that he has presented fair and acceptable specimens of Chaucer's workmanship in all styles. The preparation of this part of the volume has been a laborious task; no similar attempt on the same scale has been made; and, while here also the truth of the text in matters essential has been in nowise sacrificed to mere ease of perusal, the general reader will find opened up for him a new view of Chaucer and his works. Before a perusal of these hundred pages, will melt away for ever the lingering tradition or prejudice that Chaucer was only, or characteristically, a coarse buffoon, who pandered to a base and licentious appetite by painting and exaggerating the lowest vices of his time. In these selections—made without a thought of taking only what is to the poet's credit from a wide range of poems in which hardly a word is to his discredit—we behold Chaucer as he was; a courtier, a gallant, pure-hearted gentleman, a scholar, a philosopher, a poet of gay and vivid fancy, playing around themes of chivalric convention, of deep human interest, or broad-sighted satire. In The Canterbury Tales, we see, not Chaucer, but Chaucer's times and neighbours; the artist has lost himself in his work. To show him honestly and without disguise, as he lived his own life and sung his own songs at the brilliant Court of Edward III., is to do his memory a moral justice far more material than any literary wrong that can ever come out of spelling. As to the minor poems of Spenser, which follow The Faerie Queen, the choice has been governed by the desire to give at once the most interesting, and the most characteristic of the poet's several styles; and, save in the case of the Sonnets, the poems so selected are given entire.

It is manifest that the endeavours to adapt this volume for popular use, which have been already noticed, would imperfectly succeed without the aid of notes and glossary, to explain allusions that have become obsolete, or antiquated words which it was necessary to retain. An endeavour has been made to render each page self-explanatory, by placing on it all the glossarial and illustrative notes required for its elucidation, or—to avoid repetitions that would have occupied space—the references to the spot where information may be found. The great advantage of such a plan to the reader, is the measure of its difficulty for the editor. It permits much more flexibility in the choice of glossarial explanations or equivalents; it saves the distracting and time-consuming labour of reference to the end or the beginning of the book; but, at the same time, it largely enhances the liabilities to error. The Editor is conscious that in the 12,000 or 13,000 notes, as well as in the innumerable minute points of spelling, accentuation, and rhythm, he must now and again be found tripping; he can only ask any reader who may detect all that he could himself point out as being amiss, to set off against inevitable mistakes and misjudgments, the conscientious labour bestowed on the book, and the broad consideration of its fitness for the object contemplated.

The Editor, working frequently under disadvantages, has incurred the sole responsibility for the issue of the undertaking. From books he has derived valuable help; as from Mr Cowden Clarke's revised modern text of The Canterbury Tales, published in Mr Nimmo's Library Edition of the English Poets; from Mr Wright's scholarly edition of the same work; from the indispensable Tyrwhitt; from Mr Bell's edition of Chaucer's Poems; from Professor Craik's "Spenser and his Poetry," published twenty-five years ago by Charles Knight; and from many others. In the abridgment of The Faerie Queen, the plan may at first sight seem to be modelled on the lines of Mr Craik's painstaking condensation; but the coincidences are either inevitable or involuntary. Many of the notes, especially of those explaining classical references and those attached to the minor poems of Chaucer, have been prepared specially for this edition. The Editor leaves his task with the hope that his attempt to remove artificial obstacles to the popularity of England's earliest great poets, will not altogether miscarry.

D. LAING PURVES.

LONDON, *December* 7, 1869.

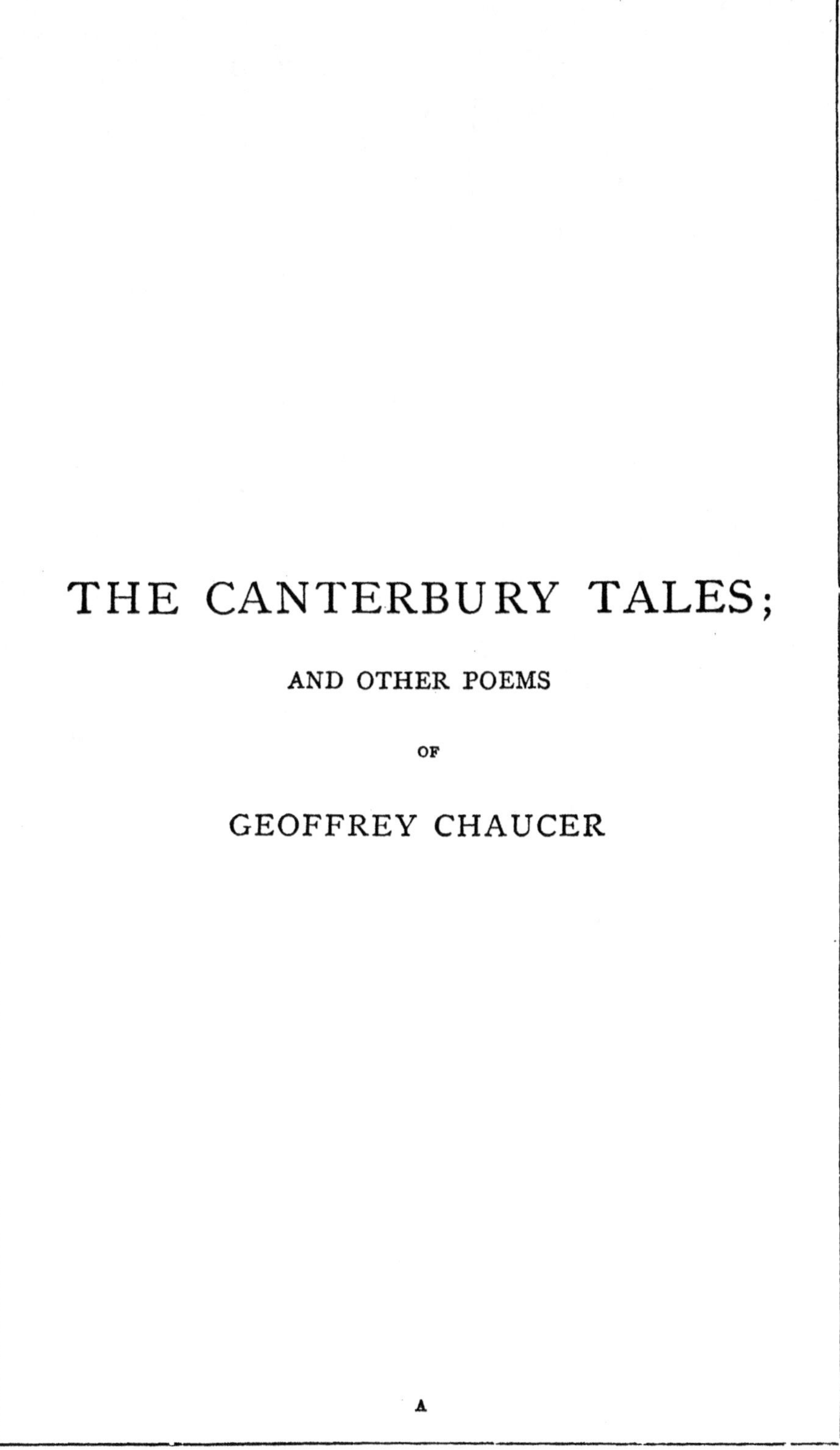

THE CANTERBURY TALES;

AND OTHER POEMS

OF

GEOFFREY CHAUCER

LIFE OF GEOFFREY CHAUCER.

Not in point of genius only, but even in point of time, Chaucer may claim the proud designation of "first" English poet. He wrote "The Court of Love" in 1346, and "The Romaunt of the Rose," if not also "Troilus and Cressida," probably within the next decade: the dates usually assigned to the poems of Laurence Minot extend from 1335 to 1355, while "The Vision of Piers Plowman" mentions events that occurred in 1360 and 1362—before which date Chaucer had certainly written "The Assembly of Fowls" and his "Dream." But, though they were his contemporaries, neither Minot nor Langland (if Langland was the author of the Vision) at all approached Chaucer in the finish, the force, or the universal interest of their works; and the poems of earlier writers, as Layamon and the author of the "Ormulum," are less English than Anglo-Saxon or Anglo-Norman. Those poems reflected the perplexed struggle for supremacy between the two grand elements of our language, which marked the twelfth and thirteenth centuries; a struggle intimately associated with the political relations between the conquering Normans and the subjugated Anglo-Saxons. Chaucer found two branches of the language; that spoken by the people, Teutonic in its genius and its forms; that spoken by the learned and the noble, based on the French. Yet each branch had begun to borrow of the other—just as nobles and people had been taught to recognise that each needed the other in the wars and the social tasks of the time; and Chaucer, a scholar, a courtier, a man conversant with all orders of society, but accustomed to speak, think, and write in the words of the highest, by his comprehensive genius cast into the simmering mould a magical amalgamant which made the two half-hostile elements unite and interpenetrate each other. Before Chaucer wrote, there were two tongues in England, keeping alive the feuds and resentments of cruel centuries; when he laid down his pen, there was practically but one speech—there was, and ever since has been, but one people.

Geoffrey Chaucer, according to the most trustworthy traditions—for authentic testimonies on the subject are wanting—was born in 1328; and London is generally believed to have been his birth-place. It is true that Leland, the biographer of England's first great poet who lived nearest to his time, not merely speaks of Chaucer as having been born many years later than the date now assigned, but mentions Berkshire or Oxfordshire as the scene of his birth. So great uncertainty have some felt on the latter score, that elaborate parallels have been drawn between Chaucer, and Homer—for whose birth-place several cities contended, and whose descent was traced to the demigods. Leland may seem to have had fair opportunities of getting at the truth about Chaucer's birth—for Henry VIII. had commissioned him, at the suppression of the monasteries throughout England, to search for records of public interest the archives of the religious houses. But it may be questioned whether he was likely to find many authentic particulars regarding the personal history of the poet in the quarters which he explored; and Leland's testimony seems to be set aside by Chaucer's own evidence as to his birthplace, and by the contemporary references which make him out an aged man for years preceding the accepted date of his death. In one of his prose works, "The Testament of Love," the poet speaks of himself in terms that strongly confirm the claim of London to the honour of giving him birth; for he there mentions "the city of London, that is to me so dear and sweet, in which I was forth growen; and more kindly love," says he, "have I to that place than to any other in earth; as every kindly creature hath full appetite to that *place of his kindly engendrure*, and to will rest and peace in that place to abide." This tolerably direct evidence is supported—so far as it can be at such an interval of time—by the learned Camden; in his Annals of Queen Elizabeth, he describes Spenser, who (see page 295) was certainly born in London, as being a fellow-citizen of Chaucer's—"*Edmundus Spenserus, patriâ* Londinensis, *Musis adeo arridentibus natus, ut omnes Anglicos superioris ævi poetas, ne* Chaucero *quidem* concive *excepto, superaret.*" The records of the time notice more than one person of the name of Chaucer, who held honourable positions about the Court; and though we cannot distinctly trace the poet's relationship with any of these namesakes or antecessors, we find excellent ground for belief that his family or friends stood well at Court, in the ease with which Chaucer made his way there, and in his subsequent career.

Like his great successor, Spenser, it was the fortune of Chaucer to live under a splendid, chivalrous, and high-spirited reign. 1328 was the second year of Edward III.; and, what with Scotch wars, French expeditions, and the strenuous and costly struggle to hold England in a worthy place among the States of Europe, there was sufficient bustle, bold achievement, and high ambition in the period to inspire a poet who was prepared to catch the spirit of the day. It was an age of elaborate courtesy, of high-paced gallantry, of courageous venture, of noble disdain for mean tranquillity; and Chaucer, on the whole a man of peaceful avocations, was penetrated to the depth of his consciousness with the lofty and lovely civil side of that brilliant and restless military period. No record of his youthful years, however, remains to us; if we believe that at the age of eighteen he was a student of Cambridge, it is only on the strength of a reference in his "Court of Love" (page 206), where the narrator is made to say that his name is Philogenet, "of Cambridge clerk;" while he had (page 201) already told us that when he was stirred to seek the Court of Cupid he was "at eighteen year of age." According to Leland, however, he was educated at Oxford, proceeding thence to France and the Netherlands, to finish his studies; but there remains no certain evidence of his having belonged to either University. At the same time, it is not doubted that his family was of good condition; and, whether or not we accept the assertion that his father held the rank of knighthood—rejecting the hypotheses that make him a merchant, or a vintner "at the corner of Kirton Lane"—it is plain, from Chaucer's whole career, that he had introductions to public life, and recommendations to courtly favour, wholly independent of his genius. We have the clearest testimony that his mental training was of wide range and thorough excellence, altogether rare for a mere courtier in those days: his poems attest his intimate acquaintance with the divinity, the philosophy, and the scholarship of his time, and show him to have had the sciences, as then developed and taught, "at his fingers' ends." Another proof of Chaucer's good birth and fortune would be found in the statement that, after his University career was completed, he entered the Inner Temple—the expenses of which could be borne only by men of noble and opulent families; but although there is a story that he was once fined two shillings for thrashing a Franciscan friar in Fleet Street, we have no direct authority for believing that the poet devoted himself to the uncongenial study of the law. No special display of knowledge on that subject appears in his works; yet in the sketch of the Manciple, in the Prologue to the Canterbury Tales (page 23), may be found indications of his familiarity with the internal economy of the Inns of Court; while numerous legal phrases and references hint that his comprehensive information was not at fault on legal matters. Leland says that he quitted the University "a ready logician, a smooth rhetorician, a pleasant poet, a grave philosopher, an ingenious mathematician, and a holy divine;" and by all accounts, when Geoffrey Chaucer comes before us authentically for the first time, at the age of thirty-one, he was possessed of knowledge and accomplishments far beyond the common standard of his day.

Chaucer at this period possessed also other qualities fitted to recommend him to favour in a Court like that of Edward III. Urry describes him, on the authority of a portrait, as being then "of a fair beautiful complexion, his lips red and full, his size of a just medium, and his port and air graceful and majestic. So," continues the ardent biographer,—"so that every ornament that could claim the approbation of the great and fair, his abilities to record the valour of the one, and celebrate the beauty of the other, and his wit and gentle behaviour to converse with both, conspired to make him a complete courtier." If we believe that his "Court of Love" had received such publicity as the literary media of the time allowed in the somewhat narrow and select literary world—not to speak of "Troilus and Cressida," which, as Lydgate mentions it first among Chaucer's works, some have supposed to be a youthful production—we find a third and not less powerful recommendation to the favour of the great co-operating with his learning and his gallant bearing. Elsewhere (page 281) reasons have been shown for doubt whether "Troilus and Cressida" should not be assigned to a later period of Chaucer's life; but very little is positively known about the dates and sequence of his various works. In the year 1386, being called as witness with regard to a contest on a point of heraldry between Lord Scrope and Sir Robert Grosvenor, Chaucer deposed that he entered on his military career in 1359. In that year Edward III. invaded France, for the third time, in pursuit of his claim to the French crown; and we may fancy that, in describing the embarkation of the knights in "Chaucer's Dream" (pages 277–278), the poet gained some of the vividness and stir of his picture from his recollections of the embarkation of the splendid and well-appointed royal host at Sandwich, on board the eleven hundred transports provided for the enterprise. In this expedition the laurels of Poitiers were flung on the ground; after vainly attempting Rheims and Paris, Edward was constrained, by cruel weather and lack of provisions, to retreat toward his ships; the fury of the elements made the retreat more disastrous than an overthrow in pitched battle; horses and men perished by thousands, or fell into the hands of the pursuing French. Chaucer, who had been made prisoner at the siege of Retters, was among the captives in the possession of France when the treaty of Bretigny—the "great peace"—was concluded, in May, 1360. Returning to England, as we may suppose, at the peace, the poet, ere long, fell into another and a pleasanter captivity; for his marriage is generally believed to have taken place shortly after his release from foreign durance. He had already gained the personal friendship and favour of John of Gaunt, Duke of Lancaster, the King's son; the Duke, while Earl of Richmond, had courted, and won to wife after a certain delay, Blanche, daughter and co-heiress of Henry Duke of Lancaster; and Chaucer is by some believed to have written "The Assembly of Fowls" to celebrate the wooing, as he wrote "Chaucer's Dream" to celebrate the wedding, of his patron. The marriage took place in 1359, the year of Chaucer's expedition to

France ; and as, in "The Assembly of Fowls," the formel or female eagle, who is supposed to represent the Lady Blanche, begs that her choice of a mate may be deferred for a year, 1358 and 1359 have been assigned as the respective dates of the two poems already mentioned. In the "Dream," Chaucer prominently introduces his own lady-love, to whom, after the happy union of his patron with the Lady Blanche, he is wedded amid great rejoicing; and various expressions in the same poem show that not only was the poet high in favour with the illustrious pair, but that his future wife had also peculiar claims on their regard. She was the younger daughter of Sir Payne Roet, a native of Hainault, who had, like many of his countrymen, been attracted to England by the example and patronage of Queen Philippa. The favourite attendant on the Lady Blanche was her elder sister Katherine: subsequently married to Sir Hugh Swynford, a gentleman of Lincolnshire; and destined, after the death of Blanche, to be in succession governess of her children, mistress of John of Gaunt, and lawfully-wedded Duchess of Lancaster. It is quite sufficient proof that Chaucer's position at Court was of no mean consequence, to find that his wife, the sister of the future Duchess of Lancaster, was one of the royal maids of honour, and even, as Sir Harris Nicolas conjectures, a god-daughter of the Queen—for her name also was Philippa.

Between 1359, when the poet himself testifies that he was made prisoner while bearing arms in France, and September 1366, when Queen Philippa granted to her former maid of honour, by the name of Philippa Chaucer, a yearly pension of ten marks, or £6, 13s. 4d., we have no authentic mention of Chaucer, express or indirect. It is plain from this grant that the poet's marriage with Sir Payne Roet's daughter was not celebrated later than 1366; the probability is, that it closely followed his return from the wars. In 1367, Edward III. settled upon Chaucer a life-pension of twenty marks, "for the good service which our beloved Valet—*dilectus Valettus noster*—Geoffrey Chaucer has rendered, and will render in time to come." Camden explains *Valettus hospitii* to signify a Gentleman of the Privy Chamber; Selden says that the designation was bestowed "upon young heirs designed to be knighted, or young gentlemen of great descent and quality." Whatever the strict meaning of the word, it is plain that the poet's position was honourable and near to the King's person, and also that his worldly circumstances were easy, if not affluent—for it need not be said that twenty marks in those days represented twelve or twenty times the sum in these. It is believed that he found powerful patronage, not merely from the Duke of Lancaster and his wife, but from Margaret Countess of Pembroke, the King's daughter. To her Chaucer is supposed to have addressed the "Goodly Ballad" (page 289), in which the lady is celebrated under the image of the daisy; her he is by some understood to have represented under the title of Queen Alcestis, in the "Court of Love" and the Prologue to "The Legend of Good Women;" and in her praise we may read his charming descriptions and eulogies of the daisy—French, "*Marguerite*," the name of his Royal patroness. To this period of Chaucer's career we may probably attribute the elegant and courtly, if somewhat conventional, poems of "The Flower and the Leaf," "The Cuckoo and the Nightingale," &c. "The Lady Margaret," says Urry, ". . . would frequently compliment him upon his poems. But this is not to be meant of his Canterbury Tales, they being written in the latter part of his life, when the courtier and the fine gentleman gave way to solid sense and plain descriptions. In his love-pieces he was obliged to have the strictest regard to modesty and decency; the ladies at that time insisting so much upon the nicest punctilios of honour, that it was highly criminal to depreciate their sex, or do anything that might offend virtue." Chaucer, in their estimation, had sinned against the dignity and honour of womankind by his translation of the French "Roman de la Rose," and by his

"Troilus and Cressida"—assuming it to have been among his less mature works; and to atone for those offences the Lady Margaret (though other and older accounts say that it was the first Queen of Richard II., Anne of Bohemia), prescribed to him the task of writing "The Legend of Good Women" (see introductory note, page 281). About this period, too, we may place the composition of Chaucer's A.B.C., or The Prayer of Our Lady (page 287), made at the request of the Duchess Blanche, a lady of great devoutness in her private life. She died in 1369; and Chaucer, as he had allegorised her wooing, celebrated her marriage, and aided her devotions, now lamented her death, in a poem entitled "The Book of the Duchess; or, the Death of Blanche.[1]

In 1370, Chaucer was employed on the King's service abroad; and in November 1372, by the title of "*Scutifer noster*"—our Esquire or Shield-bearer—he was associated with "Jacobus Pronan," and "Johannes de Mari civis Januensis," in a royal commission, bestowing full powers to treat with the Duke of Genoa, his Council, and State. The object of the embassy was to negotiate upon the choice of an English port at which the Genoese might form a commercial establishment; and Chaucer, having quitted England in December, visited Genoa and Florence, and returned to England before the 22d of November 1373—for on that day he drew his pension from the Exchequer in person. The most interesting point connected with this Italian mission is the question, whether Chaucer visited Petrarch at Padua. That he did, is unhesitatingly affirmed by the old biographers; but the authentic notices of Chaucer during the years 1372-1373, as shown by the researches of Sir Harris Nicolas, are confined to the facts already stated; and we are left to answer the question by the probabilities of the case, and by the aid of what faint light the poet himself affords. We can scarcely fancy that Chaucer, visiting Italy for the first time, in a capacity which opened for him easy access to the great and the famous, did not embrace the chance of meeting a poet whose works he evidently knew in their native tongue, and highly esteemed. With Mr Wright, we are strongly disinclined to believe "that Chaucer did not profit by the opportunity . . . of improving his acquaintance with the poetry, if not the poets, of the country he thus visited, whose influence was now being felt on the literature of most countries of Western Europe." That Chaucer was familiar with the Italian language appears not merely from his repeated selection as Envoy to Italian States, but by many passages in his poetry, from "The Assembly of Fowls" to "The Canterbury Tales." In the opening of the first poem (as pointed out in note 37, page 217) there is a striking parallel to Dante's inscription on the gate of Hell. The first Song of Troilus, in "Troilus and Cressida" (page 250), is a nearly literal translation of Petrarch's 88th Sonnet. In the Prologue to "The Legend of Good Women" (see note 10, page 285), there is a reference to Dante which can hardly have reached the poet at second-hand. And in Chaucer's great work—as in The Wife of Bath's Tale (see note 22, page 81), and The Monk's Tale (see note 13, page 164)—direct reference by name is made to Dante, "the wise poet of Florence," "the great poet of Italy," as the source whence the author has quoted. When we consider the poet's high place in literature and at Court, which could not fail to make him free of the hospitalities of the brilliant little Lombard States; his familiarity with the tongue and the works

[1] Called in the editions before 1597 "The Dream of Chaucer"—and inadvertently mentioned under that name in note 31, page 60. The poem, which is not included in the present edition, does indeed, like many of Chaucer's smaller works, tell the story of a dream, in which a knight, representing John of Gaunt, is found by the poet mourning the loss of his lady; but the true "Dream of Chaucer," in which he celebrates the marriage of his patron, was published for the first time by Speght in 1597. John of Gaunt, in the end of 1371, married his second wife, Constance, daughter to Pedro the Cruel of Spain; so that "The Book of the Duchess" must have been written between 1369 and 1371.

of Italy's greatest bards, dead and living; the reverential regard which he paid to the memory of great poets, of which we have examples in "The House of Fame," and at the close of "Troilus and Cressida";[1] along with his own testimony in the Prologue to The Clerk's Tale, we cannot fail to construe that testimony as a declaration that the Tale was actually told to Chaucer by the lips of Petrarch, in 1373, the very year in which Petrarch translated it into Latin, from Boccaccio's "Decameron."[2] Mr Bell notes the objection to this interpretation, that the words are put into the mouth, not of the poet, but of the Clerk; and meets it by the counter-objection, that the Clerk, being a purely imaginary personage, could not have learned the story at Padua from Petrarch—and therefore that Chaucer must have departed from the dramatic assumption maintained in the rest of the dialogue. Instances could be adduced from Chaucer's writings to show that such a sudden "departure from the dramatic assumption" would not be unexampled: witness the "aside" in The Wife of Bath's Prologue, where, after the jolly Dame has asserted that "half so boldly there can no man swear and lie as a woman can" (page 73), the poet hastens to interpose, in his own person, these two lines:

"I say not this by wivës that be wise,
But if it be when they them misadvise."

And again, in the Prologue to the "Legend of Good Women," from a description of the daisy—

"She is the clearness and the very light,
That in this darkë world me guides and leads,"

the poet, in the very next lines, slides into an address to his lady:

"The heart within my sorrowful heart *you* dreads
And loves so sore, that *ye* be, verily,
The mistress of my wit, and nothing I," &c.[3]

When, therefore, the Clerk of Oxford is made to say that he will tell a tale—

"The which that I
Learn'd at Padova of a worthy clerk,
As proved by his wordës and his werk.
He is now dead, and nailed in his chest,
I pray to God to give his soul good rest.
Francis Petrarc', the laureate poéte,
Hightë this clerk, whose rhetoric so sweet
Illumin'd all Itaile of poetry. . . .
But forth to tellen of this worthy man,
That taughtë me this tale, as I began." . . .

we may without violent effort believe that Chaucer speaks in his own person, though dramatically the words are on the Clerk's lips. And the belief is not impaired by the sorrowful way in which the Clerk lingers on Petrarch's death—which would be less intelligible if the fictitious narrator had only read the story in the Latin translation, than if we suppose the news of Petrarch's death at Arquà in July 1374 to have closely followed Chaucer to England, and to have cruelly and irresistibly mingled itself with our poet's personal recollections of his great Italian contemporary. Nor must we regard as without significance the manner in which the Clerk is made to distinguish between the "body" of Petrarch's tale, and the fashion in which it was set forth in writing, with a proem that seemed "a thing impertinent," save

[1] Where (page 273) he bids his "little book"

"Subject be unto all poesy,
And kiss the steps, where as thou seest space,
Of Virgil, Ovid, Homer, Lucan, Stace."

[2] See note 13, page 93.

[3] See note 16, page 282.

that the poet had chosen in that way to "convey his matter"—told, or "taught," so much more directly and simply by word of mouth. It is impossible to pronounce positively on the subject; the question whether Chaucer saw Petrarch in 1373 must remain a moot-point, so long as we have only our present information; but fancy loves to dwell on the thought of the two poets conversing under the vines at Arquà; and we find in the history and the writings of Chaucer nothing to contradict, a good deal to countenance, the belief that such a meeting occurred.

Though we have no express record, we have indirect testimony, that Chaucer's Genoese mission was discharged satisfactorily; for on the 23d of April 1374, Edward III. grants at Windsor to the poet, by the title of "our beloved squire"—*dilecto Armigero nostro—unum pycher. vini*, "one pitcher of wine" daily, to be "perceived" in the port of London; a grant which, on the analogy of more modern usage, might be held equivalent to Chaucer's appointment as Poet Laureate. When we find that soon afterwards the grant was commuted for a money payment of twenty marks per annum, we need not conclude that Chaucer's circumstances were poor; for it may be easily supposed that the daily "perception" of such an article of income was attended with considerable prosaic inconvenience. A permanent provision for Chaucer was made on the 8th of June 1374, when he was appointed Controller of the Customs in the Port of London, for the lucrative imports of wools, skins or "wool-fells," and tanned hides—on condition that he should fulfil the duties of that office in person and not by deputy, and should write out the accounts with his own hand. We have what seems evidence of Chaucer's compliance with these terms in "The House of Fame" (page 235), where, by the mouth of the eagle, the poet describes himself, when he has finished his labour and made his reckonings, as not seeking rest and news in social intercourse, but going home to his own house, and there, "all so dumb as any stone," sitting "at another book," until his look is dazed; and again, in the record that in 1376 he received a grant of £71, 4s. 6d., the amount of a fine levied on one John Kent, whom Chaucer's vigilance had frustrated in the attempt to ship a quantity of wool for Dordrecht without paying the duty. The seemingly derogatory condition, that the Controller should write out the accounts or rolls ("*rotulos*") of his office with his own hand, appears to have been designed, or treated, as merely formal; no records in Chaucer's handwriting are known to exist—which could hardly be the case if, for the twelve years of his Controllership (1374–1386), he had duly complied with the condition; and during that period he was more than once employed abroad, so that the condition was evidently regarded as a formality even by those who had imposed it. Also in 1374, the Duke of Lancaster, whose ambitious views may well have made him anxious to retain the adhesion of a man so capable and accomplished as Chaucer, changed into a joint life-annuity remaining to the survivor, and charged on the revenues of the Savoy, a pension of £10 which two years before he settled on the poet's wife—whose sister was then the governess of the Duke's two daughters, Philippa and Elizabeth, and the Duke's own mistress. Another proof of Chaucer's personal reputation and high Court favour at this time, is his selection (1375) as ward to the son of Sir Edmond Staplegate of Bilsynton, in Kent; a charge on the surrender of which the guardian received no less a sum than £104.

We find Chaucer in 1376 again employed on a foreign mission. In 1377, the last year of Edward III., he was sent to Flanders with Sir Thomas Percy, afterwards Earl of Worcester, for the purpose of obtaining a prolongation of the truce; and in January 1378, he was associated with Sir Guichard d'Angle and other Commissioners, to pursue certain negotiations for a marriage between Princess Mary of France and the young King Richard II., which had been set on foot before the death of Edward III. The negotiation, however, proved fruitless; and in May 1378,

Chaucer was selected to accompany Sir John Berkeley on a mission to the Court of Bernardo Visconti, Duke of Milan, with the view, it is supposed, of concerting military plans against the outbreak of war with France. The new King, meantime, had shown that he was not insensible to Chaucer's merit—or to the influence of his tutor and the poet's patron, the Duke of Lancaster; for Richard II. confirmed to Chaucer his pension of twenty marks, along with an equal annual sum, for which the daily pitcher of wine granted in 1374 had been commuted. Before his departure for Lombardy, Chaucer—still holding his post in the Customs—selected two representatives or trustees, to protect his estate against legal proceedings in his absence, or to sue in his name defaulters and offenders against the imposts which he was charged to enforce. One of these trustees was called Richard Forrester; the other was John Gower, the poet, the most famous English contemporary of Chaucer, with whom he had for many years been on terms of admiring friendship—although, from the strictures passed on certain productions of Gower's in the Prologue to The Man of Law's Tale,[1] it has been supposed that in the later years of Chaucer's life the friendship suffered some diminution. To the "moral Gower" and "the philosophical Strode," Chaucer "directed" or dedicated his "Troilus and Cressida;"[2] while, in the "Confessio Amantis," Gower introduces a handsome compliment to his greater contemporary, as the "disciple and the poet" of Venus, with whose glad songs and ditties, made in her praise during the flowers of his youth, the land was filled everywhere. Gower, however—a monk and a Conservative—held to the party of the Duke of Gloucester, the rival of the Wycliffite and innovating Duke of Lancaster, who was Chaucer's patron, and whose cause was not a little aided by Chaucer's strictures on the clergy; and thus it is not impossible that political differences may have weakened the old bonds of personal friendship and poetic esteem. Returning from Lombardy early in 1379, Chaucer seems to have been again sent abroad; for the records exhibit no trace of him between May and December of that year. Whether by proxy or in person, however, he received his pensions regularly until 1382, when his income was increased by his appointment to the post of Controller of Petty Customs in the port of London. In November 1384, he obtained a month's leave of absence on account of his private affairs, and a deputy was appointed to fill his place; and in February of the next year he was permitted to appoint a permanent deputy—thus at length gaining relief from that close attention to business which probably curtailed the poetic fruits of the poet's most powerful years.[3]

[1] See page 61, and note 9.

[2] "Written," says Mr Wright, "in the sixteenth year of the reign of Richard II. (1392–1393);" a powerful confirmation of the opinion that this poem was really produced in Chaucer's mature age. See the introductory notes to it (page 248) and to the Legend of Good Women (page 281).

[3] The old biographers of Chaucer, founding on what they took to be autobiographic allusions in "The Testament of Love," assign to him between 1384 and 1389 a very different history from that here given on the strength of authentic records explored and quoted by Sir H. Nicolas. Chaucer is made to espouse the cause of John of Northampton, the Wycliffite Lord Mayor of London, whose re-election in 1384 was so vehemently opposed by the clergy, and who was imprisoned in the sequel of the grave disorders that arose. The poet, it is said, fled to the Continent, taking with him a large sum of money, which he spent in supporting companions in exile; then, returning by stealth to England in quest of funds, he was detected and sent to the Tower, where he languished for three years, being released only on the humiliating condition of informing against his associates in the plot. The public records show, however, that, all the time of his alleged exile and captivity, he was quietly living in London, regularly drawing his pensions in person, sitting in Parliament, and discharging his duties in the Customs until his dismissal in 1386. It need not be said, further, that although Chaucer freely handled the errors, the ignorance, and vices of the clergy, he did so rather as a man of sense and of conscience, than as a Wycliffite—and there is no evidence that he espoused the opinions

Chaucer is next found occupying a post which has not often been held by men gifted with his peculiar genius—that of a county member. The contest between the Dukes of Gloucester and Lancaster, and their adherents, for the control of the Government, was coming to a crisis; and when the recluse and studious Chaucer was induced to offer himself to the electors of Kent as one of the knights of their shire—where presumably he held property—we may suppose that it was with the view of supporting his patron's cause in the impending conflict. The Parliament in which the poet sat assembled at Westminster on the 1st of October, and was dissolved on the 1st of November, 1386. Lancaster was fighting and intriguing abroad, absorbed in the affairs of his Castilian succession; Gloucester and his friends at home had everything their own way; the Earl of Suffolk was dismissed from the woolsack, and impeached by the Commons; and although Richard at first stood out courageously for the friends of his uncle Lancaster, he was constrained, by the refusal of supplies, to consent to the proceedings of Gloucester. A commission was wrung from him, under protest, appointing Gloucester, Arundel, and twelve other Peers and prelates, a permanent council to inquire into the condition of all the public departments, the courts of law, and the royal household, with absolute powers of redress and dismissal. We need not ascribe to Chaucer's Parliamentary exertions in his patron's behalf, nor to any malpractices in his official conduct, the fact that he was among the earliest victims of the commission.[1] In December 1386, he was dismissed from both his offices in the port of London; but he retained his pensions, and drew them regularly twice a year at the Exchequer until 1388. In 1387, Chaucer's political reverses were aggravated by a severe domestic calamity: his wife died, and with her died the pension which had been settled on her by Queen Philippa in 1366, and confirmed to her at Richard's accession in 1377. The change made in Chaucer's pecuniary position, by the loss of his offices and his wife's pension, must have been very great. It would appear that during his prosperous times he had lived in a style quite equal to his income, and had no ample resources against a season of reverse; for, on the 1st of May 1388, less than a year and a half after being dismissed from the Customs, he was constrained to assign his pensions, by surrender in Chancery, to one John Scalby.

In May 1389, Richard II., now of age, abruptly resumed the reins of government, which, for more than two years, had been ably but cruelly managed by Gloucester. The friends of Lancaster were once more supreme in the royal councils, and Chaucer speedily profited by the change. On the 12th of July he was appointed Clerk of the King's Works at the Palace of Westminster, the Tower, the royal manors of Kennington, Eltham, Clarendon, Sheen, Byfleet, Childern Langley, and Feckenham, the castle of Berkhamstead, the royal lodge of Hathenburgh in the New Forest, the lodges in the parks of Clarendon, Childern Langley, and Feckenham, and the mews for the King's falcons at Charing Cross; he received a salary of two shillings per day, and was allowed to perform the duties by deputy. For

of the zealous Reformer, far less played the part of an extreme and self-regardless partisan of his old friend and college-companion.

[1] "The Commissioners appear to have commenced their labours with examining the accounts of the officers employed in the collection of the revenue; and the sequel affords a strong presumption that the royal administration [under Lancaster and his friends] had been foully calumniated. We hear not of any frauds discovered, or of defaulters punished, or of grievances redressed." Such is the testimony of Lingard (chap. iv., 1386), all the more valuable for his aversion from the Wycliffite leanings of John of Gaunt. Chaucer's department in the London Customs was in those days one of the most important and lucrative in the kingdom; and if mercenary abuse of his post could have been proved, we may be sure that his and his patron's enemies would not have been content with simple dismissal, but would have heavily amerced or imprisoned him.

some reason unknown, Chaucer held this lucrative office[1] little more than two years, quitting it before the 16th of September 1391, at which date it had passed into the hands of one John Gedney. The next two years and a half are a blank, so far as authentic records are concerned; Chaucer is supposed to have passed them in retirement, probably devoting them principally to the composition of The Canterbury Tales. In February 1394, the King conferred upon him a grant of £20 a year for life; but he seems to have had no other source of income, and to have become embarrassed by debt, for frequent memoranda of small advances on his pension show that his circumstances were, in comparison, greatly reduced. Things appear to have grown worse and worse with the poet; for in May 1398 he was compelled to obtain from the King letters of protection against arrest, extending over a term of two years. Not for the first time, it is true—for similar documents had been issued at the beginning of Richard's reign; but at that time Chaucer's missions abroad, and his responsible duties in the port of London, may have furnished reasons for securing him against annoyance or frivolous prosecution, which were wholly wanting at the later date. In 1398, fortune began again to smile upon him; he received a royal grant of a tun of wine annually, the value being about £4. Next year, Richard II. having been deposed by the son of John of Gaunt[2]—Henry of Bolingbroke, Duke of Lancaster—the new King, four days after his accession, bestowed on Chaucer a grant of forty marks (£26, 13s. 4d.) per annum, in addition to the pension of £20 conferred by Richard II. in 1394. But the poet, now seventy-one years of age, and probably broken down by the reverses of the past few years, was not destined long to enjoy his renewed prosperity. On Christmas Eve of 1399, he entered on the possession of a house in the garden of the Chapel of the Blessed Mary of Westminster—near to the present site of Henry VII.'s Chapel—having obtained a lease from Robert Hermodesworth, a monk of the adjacent convent, for fifty-three years, at the annual rent of four marks (£2, 13s. 4d.) Until the 1st of March 1400, Chaucer drew his pensions in person; then they were received for him by another hand; and on the 25th of October, in the same year, he died, at the age of seventy-two. The only lights thrown by his poems on his closing days are furnished in the little ballad called "Good Counsel of Chaucer,"[3]—which, though said to have been written when "upon his death-bed lying in his great anguish," breathes the very spirit of courage, resignation, and philosophic calm; and by the "Retractation" at the end of The Canterbury Tales,[4] which, if it was not foisted in by monkish transcribers, may be supposed the effect of Chaucer's regrets and self-reproaches on that solemn review of his life-work which the close approach of death compelled. The poet was buried in Westminster Abbey;[5] and not many years after his death a slab was

[1] The salary was £36, 10s. per annum; the salary of the Chief Judges was £40, of the Puisne Judges about £27. Probably the Judges—certainly the Clerk of the Works—had fees or perquisites besides the stated payment.

[2] Chaucer's patron had died earlier in 1399, during the exile of his son (then Duke of Hereford) in France. The Duchess Constance had died in 1394; and the Duke had made reparation to Katherine Swynford—who had already borne him four children—by marrying her in 1396, with the approval of Richard II., who legitimated the children, and made the eldest son of the poet's sister-in-law Earl of Somerset. From this long-illicit union sprang the house of Beaufort—that being the surname of the Duke's children by Katherine, after the name of the castle in Anjou (Belfort, or Beaufort) where they were born.

[3] Page 291.

[4] Page 199, and note 4.

[5] Of Chaucer's two sons by Philippa Roet, his only wife, the younger, Lewis, for whom he wrote the Treatise on the Astrolabe, died young. The elder, Thomas, married Maud, the second daughter and co-heiress of Sir John Burghersh, brother of the Bishop of Lincoln, the Chancellor and Treasurer of England. By this marriage Thomas Chaucer acquired great estates in Oxfordshire and elsewhere; and he figured prominently in the second rank of courtiers for many years. He was Chief Butler to Richard II.; under Henry IV. he was Constable of Wallingford Castle, Steward of the Honours of Wallingford and St Valery, and of the

placed on a pillar near his grave, bearing the lines, taken from an epitaph or eulogy made by Stephanus Surigonus of Milan, at the request of Caxton :

> "*Galfridus Chaucer, vates, et fama poesis*
> *Maternæ, hâc sacrâ sum tumulatus humo.*"

About 1555, Mr Nicholas Brigham, a gentleman of Oxford who greatly admired the genius of Chaucer, erected the present tomb, as near to the spot where the poet lay, "before the chapel of St Benet," as was then possible by reason of the "cancelli," which the Duke of Buckingham subsequently obtained leave to remove, that room might be made for the tomb of Dryden. On the structure of Mr Brigham, besides a full-length representation of Chaucer, taken from a portrait drawn by his "scholar" Thomas Occleve, was—or is, though now almost illegible—the following inscription :—

M. S.
QUI FUIT ANGLORUM VATES TER MAXIMUS OLIM,
GALFRIDUS CHAUCER CONDITUR HOC TUMULO ;
ANNUM SI QUÆRAS DOMINI, SI TEMPORA VITÆ,
ECCE NOTÆ SUBSUNT, QUÆ TIBI CUNCTA NOTANT.
25 OCTOBRIS 1400.
ÆRUMNARUM REQUIES MORS.
N. BRIGHAM HOS FECIT MUSARUM NOMINE SUMPTUS
1556.

Concerning his personal appearance and habits, Chaucer has not been reticent in his poetry. Urry sums up the traits of his aspect and character fairly thus : "He was of a middle stature, the latter part of his life inclinable to be fat and corpulent, as appears by the Host's bantering him in the journey to Canterbury, and comparing shapes with him.[1] His face was fleshy, his features just and regular, his complexion fair, and somewhat pale, his hair of a dusky yellow, short and thin ; the hair of his beard in two forked tufts, of a wheat colour ; his forehead broad and smooth ; his eyes inclining usually to the ground, which is intimated by the Host's words ; his whole face full of liveliness, a calm, easy sweetness, and a studious venerable aspect. . . . As to his temper, he had a mixture of the gay, the modest, and the grave. The sprightliness of his humour was more distinguished by his writings than by his appearance ; which gave occasion to Margaret Countess of Pembroke often to rally him upon his silent modesty in company, telling him, that his absence was more agreeable to her than his conversation, since the first was productive of agreeable pieces of wit in his writings,[2] but the latter was filled with a modest deference, and a too distant respect. We see nothing merry or jocose in his behaviour with his pilgrims, but a silent attention to their mirth, rather than any mixture of his own. . . . When disengaged from public affairs, his time was entirely spent in study and reading ; so agreeable to him was this exercise, that he

Chiltern Hundreds ; and the queen of Henry IV. granted him the farm of several of her manors, a grant subsequently confirmed to him for life by the King, after the Queen's death. He sat in Parliament repeatedly for Oxfordshire, was Speaker in 1414, and in the same year went to France as commissioner to negotiate the marriage of Henry V. with the Princess Katherine. He held, before he died in 1434, various other posts of trust and distinction ; but he left no heirs-male. His only child, Alice Chaucer, married twice ; first Sir John Philip ; and afterwards the Duke of Suffolk—attainted and beheaded in 1450. She had three children by the Duke ; and her eldest son married the Princess Elizabeth, sister of Edward IV. The eldest son of this marriage, created Earl of Lincoln, was declared by Richard III. heir-apparent to the throne, in case the Prince of Wales should die without issue ; but the death of Lincoln himself, at the battle of Stoke in 1487, destroyed all prospect that the poet's descendants might succeed to the crown of England ; and his family is now believed to be extinct.

[1] See the Prologue to Chaucer's Tale of Sir Thopas, page 146.

[2] See the "Goodly Ballad of Chaucer," seventh stanza, page 290.

says he preferred it to all other sports and diversions.[1] He lived within himself, neither desirous to hear nor busy to concern himself with the affairs of his neighbours. His course of living was temperate and regular; he went to rest with the sun, and rose before it; and by that means enjoyed the pleasures of the better part of the day, his morning walk and fresh contemplations. This gave him the advantage of describing the morning in so lively a manner as he does everywhere in his works. The springing sun glows warm in his lines, and the fragrant air blows cool in his descriptions; we smell the sweets of the bloomy haws, and hear the music of the feathered choir, whenever we take a forest walk with him. The hour of the day is not easier to be discovered from the reflection of the sun in Titian's paintings, than in Chaucer's morning landscapes. . . . His reading was deep and extensive, his judgment sound and discerning. . . . In one word, he was a great scholar, a pleasant wit, a candid critic, a sociable companion, a steadfast friend, a grave philosopher, a temperate economist, and a pious Christian."

Chaucer's most important poems are "Troilus and Cressida," "The Romaunt of the Rose," and "The Canterbury Tales." Of the first, containing 8246 lines, an abridgment, with a prose connecting outline of the story, is given in this volume—pages 247–274. With the second, consisting of 7699 octosyllabic verses, like those in which "The House of Fame" is written, it was found impossible to deal in the present edition. The poem is a curtailed translation from the French "Roman de la Rose"—commenced by Guillaume de Lorris, who died in 1260, after contributing 4070 verses, and completed, in the last quarter of the thirteenth century, by Jean de Meun, who added some 18,000 verses. It is a satirical allegory, in which the vices of courts, the corruptions of the clergy, the disorders and inequalities of society in general, are unsparingly attacked, and the most revolutionary doctrines are advanced; and though, in making his translation, Chaucer softened or eliminated much of the satire of the poem, still it remained, in his verse, a caustic exposure of the abuses of the time, especially those which discredited the Church.

The Canterbury Tales are presented in this edition with as near an approach to completeness as regard for the popular character of the volume permitted. The 17,385 verses, of which the poetical Tales consist, have been given without abridgment or purgation—save in a single couplet; but, the main purpose of the volume being to make the general reader acquainted with the "poems" of Chaucer and Spenser, the Editor has ventured to contract the two prose Tales—Chaucer's Tale of Melibœus, and the Parson's Sermon or Treatise on Penitence—so as to save about thirty pages for the introduction of Chaucer's minor pieces. At the same time, by giving prose outlines of the omitted parts, it has been sought to guard the reader against the fear that he was losing anything essential, or even valuable. It is almost needless to describe the plot, or point out the literary place, of the Canterbury Tales. Perhaps in the entire range of ancient and modern literature there is no work that so clearly and freshly paints for future times the picture of the past; certainly no Englishman has ever approached Chaucer in the power of fixing for ever the fleeting traits of his own time. The plan of the poem had been adopted before Chaucer chose it; notably in the "Decameron" of Boccaccio—although, there, the circumstances under which the tales were told, with the terror of the plague hanging over the merry company, lend a grim grotesqueness to the narrative, unless we can look at it abstracted from its setting. Chaucer, on the other hand, strikes a perpetual key-note of gaiety whenever he mentions the word "pilgrimage;" and at

[1] See the opening of the Prologue to "The Legend of Good Women," page 282; and the poet's account of his habits in "The House of Fame," page 235.

every stage of the connecting story we bless the happy thought which gives us incessant incident, movement, variety, and unclouded but never monotonous joyousness. The poet, the evening before he starts on a pilgrimage to the shrine of St Thomas at Canterbury, lies at the Tabard Inn, in Southwark, curious to know in what companionship he is destined to fare forward on the morrow. Chance sends him "nine and twenty in a company," representing all orders of English society, lay and clerical, from the Knight and the Abbot down to the Ploughman and the Sompnour. The jolly Host of the Tabard, after supper, when tongues are loosened and hearts are opened, declares that "not this year" has he seen such a company at once under his roof-tree, and proposes that, when they set out next morning, he should ride with them and make them sport. All agree, and Harry Bailly unfolds his scheme: each pilgrim, including the poet, shall tell two tales on the road to Canterbury, and two on the way back to London; and he whom the general voice pronounces to have told the best tale, shall be treated to a supper at the common cost—and, of course, to mine Host's profit—when the cavalcade returns from the saint's shrine to the Southwark hostelry. All joyously assent; and early on the morrow, in the gay spring sunshine, they ride forth, listening to the heroic tale of the brave and gentle Knight, who has been gracefully chosen by the Host to lead the spirited competition of story-telling.

To describe thus the nature of the plan, and to say that when Chaucer conceived, or at least began to execute it, he was between sixty and seventy years of age, is to proclaim that The Canterbury Tales could never be more than a fragment. Thirty pilgrims, each telling two tales on the way out, and two more on the way back—that makes 120 tales; to say nothing of the prologue, the description of the journey, the occurences at Canterbury, "and all the remnant of their pilgrimage," which Chaucer also undertook. No more than twenty-three of the 120 stories are told in the work as it comes down to us; that is, only twenty-three of the thirty pilgrims tell the first of the two stories on the road to Canterbury; while of the stories on the return journey we have not one, and nothing is said about the doings of the pilgrims at Canterbury—which would, if treated like the scene at the Tabard, have given us a still livelier "picture of the period." But the plan was too large; and although the poet had some reserves, in stories which he had already composed in an independent form, death cut short his labour ere he could even complete the arrangement and connection of more than a very few of the Tales. Incomplete as it is, however, the *magnum opus* of Chaucer was in his own time received with immense favour; manuscript copies are numerous even now—no slight proof of its popularity; and when the invention of printing was introduced into England by William Caxton, The Canterbury Tales issued from his press in the year after the first English-printed book, "The Game of the Chesse," had been struck off. Innumerable editions have since been published; and it may fairly be affirmed, that few books have been so much in favour with the reading public of every generation as this book, which the lapse of every generation has been rendering more unreadable.

Apart from "The Romaunt of the Rose," no really important poetical work of Chaucer's is omitted from or unrepresented in the present edition. Of "The Legend of Good Women," the Prologue only is given—but it is the most genuinely Chaucerian part of the poem. Of "The Court of Love," three-fourths are here presented; of "The Assembly of Fowls," "The Cuckoo and the Nightingale," "The Flower and the Leaf," all; of "Chaucer's Dream," one-fourth; of "The House of Fame," two-thirds; and of the minor poems such a selection as may give an idea of Chaucer's power in the "occasional" department of verse. Necessarily, no space whatever could be given to Chaucer's prose works—his translation of Boethius' Treatise on the Consolation of Philosophy; his Treatise on the Astrolabe, written for the use of his son Lewis; and his "Testament of Love," composed in his later years, and reflecting the troubles that then beset the poet. If, after studying in a simplified form the salient works of England's first great bard, the reader is tempted to regret that he was not introduced to a wider acquaintance with the author, the purpose of the Editor will have been more than attained.

The plan of the volume does not demand an elaborate examination into the state of our language when Chaucer wrote, or the nice questions of grammatical and metrical structure which conspire with the obsolete orthography to make his poems a sealed book for the masses. The most important element in the proper reading of Chaucer's verses—whether written in the decasyllabic or heroic metre, which he introduced into our literature, or in the octosyllabic measure used with such animated effect in "The House of Fame," "Chaucer's Dream," &c.—is the sounding of the terminal "e" where it is now silent. That letter is still valid in French poetry; and Chaucer's lines can be scanned only by reading them as we would read Racine's or Molière's. The terminal "e" played an important part in grammar; in many cases it was the sign of the infinitive—the "n" being dropped from the end; at other times it pointed the distinction between singular and plural, between adjective and adverb. The pages that follow, however, being prepared from the modern English point of view, necessarily no account is taken of those distinctions; and the now silent "e" has been retained in the text of Chaucer only when required by the modern spelling, or by the exigencies of metre. In the latter case, which occurs in almost every line, the Editor has followed the plan adopted in Mr Nimmo's Library Edition of The Canterbury Tales, by marking with the sign of diæresis (as "ë") the terminal mute "e" that should be sounded; for example, in these five lines from the opening of The Canterbury Tales:—

"Whĕn Zē | phy̆rūs | ĕke wīth | hĭs swŏo | të̆ | breāth,
Ĭnspī | rĕd hāth | ĭn ēve | ry̆ hōlt | ănd hēath
Thĕ tēn | dĕr crōp | pë̆s, ānd | thĕ yōun | gë̆ sūn
Hăth īn | thĕ Rām | hĭs hāl | fë̆ cōurse | y̆-rūn,
Ănd smāl | lë̆ fōw | lë̆s mā | kë̆ mē | lŏdy̆."

Before a word beginning with a vowel, or with the letter "h," the final "e" was almost without exception mute; and in such cases, in the plural forms and infinitives of verbs, the terminal "n" is generally retained for the sake of euphony. The only other mark employed in this edition is the acute accent, used to show where the accentuation of Chaucer's time differed from that of ours—as in the words "Natúre," "couráge," "creatúre," "mannére" (manner), "sciénce," &c.; and to signify that the termination of such words as "natión," "salvatión," "opinión," should be pronounced as a dissyllable. No reader who is acquainted with the French language will find it hard to fall into Chaucer's accentuation; while, for such as are not, a simple perusal of the text according to the rules of modern verse, with attention to the nowise formidable accentual marks, should remove every difficulty.

THE POEMS OF GEOFFREY CHAUCER.

THE CANTERBURY TALES.

THE PROLOGUE.

WHEN that Aprilis, with his showers swoot,[1]
The drought of March hath pierced to the root,
And bathed every vein in such licóur,
Of which virtúe engender'd is the flower;
When Zephyrus eke with his swootë breath
Inspired hath in every holt[2] and heath
The tender croppës,[3] and the youngë sun
Hath in the Ram[4] his halfë course y-run,
And smallë fowlës makë melody,
That sleepen all the night with open eye,
(So pricketh them natúre in their corâges[5]);
Then longë folk to go on pilgrimages,
And palmers[6] for to seekë strangë strands,
To fernë hallows couth[7] in sundry lands;
And specially, from every shirë's end
Of Engleland, to Canterbury they wend,
The holy blissful Martyr for to seek,
That them hath holpen, when that they were sick.
  Befell that, in that season on a day,
In Southwark at the Tabard[8] as I lay,
Ready to wenden on my pilgrimage
To Canterbury with devout coráge,
At night was come into that hostelry
Well nine and twenty in a company
Of sundry folk, by áventure y-fall
In fellowship,[9] and pilgrims were they all,
That toward Canterbury wouldë ride.
The chambers and the stables werë wide,
And well we weren eased at the best.[10]
And shortly, when the sunnë was to rest,
So had I spoken with them every one,
That I was of their fellowship anon,
And madë forword[11] early for to rise,
To take our way there as I you devise.[12]
  But natheless, while I have time and space,
Ere that I farther in this talë pace,
Me thinketh it accordant to reasón,
To tell you allë the condition
Of each of them, so as it seemed me,
And which they weren, and of what degree;
And eke in what array that they were in:
And at a Knight then will I first begin.
  A KNIGHT there was, and that a worthy man,
That from the timë that he first began
To riden out, he loved chivalry,
Truth and honoúr, freedom and courtesy.
Full worthy was he in his Lordë's war,
And thereto had he ridden, no man farre,[13]
As well in Christendom as in Heatheness,
And ever honour'd for his worthiness.
At Alisandre[14] he was when it was won.

1 Sweet. 2 Grove, forest. 3 Twigs, boughs.

4 Tyrwhitt points out that "the Bull" should be read here, not "the Ram," which would place the time of the pilgrimage in the end of March; whereas, in the Prologue to the Man of Law's Tale, the date is given as the "eight and twenty day Of April, that is messenger to May."

5 Hearts, inclinations.

6 Dante, in the "Vita Nuova," distinguishes three classes of pilgrims: *palmieri*, palmers, who go beyond sea to the East, and often bring back staves of palm-wood; *peregrini*, who go to the shrine of St Jago in Galicia; *Romei*, who go to Rome. Sir Walter Scott, however, says that palmers were in the habit of passing from shrine to shrine, living on charity; pilgrims, on the other hand, made the journey to any shrine only once, and immediately returned to their ordinary avocations. Chaucer uses "palmer" of all pilgrims.

7 To distant saints known, renowned, in sundry lands. "Hallows" survives, in the meaning here given, in All-Hallows—All-Saints'—Day. "Couth," past participle of "conne" to know, exists in "uncouth."

8 The Tabard—the sign of the inn—was a sleeveless coat, worn by heralds. The name of the inn was, some three centuries after Chaucer, changed to the Talbot.

9 Who had by chance fallen into company. In "y-fall," "y" is a corruption of the Anglo-Saxon "ge" prefixed to participles of verbs; it is used by Chaucer merely to help the metre. In German, "y-fall," or "y-falle," would be "gefallen;" "y-run," or "y-ronne," would be "geronnen."

10 And we were well accommodated with the best.

11 Foreword, covenant, promise.

12 Describe, relate. 13 Farther.

14 Alexandria, in Egypt, captured by Pierre de Lusignan, king of Cyprus, in 1365, but abandoned immediately afterwards. Thirteen years before, the same prince had taken Satalie, the ancient Attalia, in Anatolia; and in 1367, he won Layas, in Armenia, both places named just below.

Full often time he had the board begun
Aboven allë natións in Prusse.[1]
In Lettowe had he reysed,[2] and in Russe,
No Christian man so oft of his degree.
In Grenade at the siege eke had he be
Of Algesir,[3] and ridden in Belmarie.[3]
At Leyës was he, and at Satalie,
When they were won ; and in the Greatë Sea[3]
At many a noble army had he be.
At mortal battles had he been fifteen,
And foughten for our faith at Tramissene[3]
In listës thriës, and aye slain his foe.
This ilkë[4] worthy knight had been also
Some timë with the lord of Palatie,[3]
Against another heathen in Turkie:
And evermore he had a sovereign price.[5]
And though that he was worthy he was wise,
And of his port as meek as is a maid.
He never yet no villainy[6] ne said
In all his life, unto no manner wight.
He was a very perfect gentle knight.
But for to tellë you of his array,
His horse was good, but yet he was not gay.
Of fustian he weared a gipon,
Allë besmotter'd with his habergeon,[7]
For he was late y-come from his voyáge,
And wentë for to do his pilgrimáge.

With him there was his son, a youngë SQUIRE,
A lover, and a lusty bacheler,
With lockës crulle[8] as they were laid in press.
Of twenty year of age he was I guess.
Of his statúre he was of even length,
And wonderly deliver,[9] and great of strength.
And he had been some time in chevachie,[10]
In Flanders, in Artois, and Picardie,
And borne him well, as of so little space,[11]
In hope to standen in his lady's grace.
Embroider'd was he, as it were a mead
All full of freshë flowers, white and red.
Singing he was, or fluting all the day ;
He was as fresh as is the month of May.
Short was his gown, with sleevës long and wide.
Well could he sit on horse, and fairë ride.
He couldë songës make, and well indite,
Joust, and eke dance, and well pourtray and write.
So hot he loved, that by nightertale[12]
He slept no more than doth the nightingale.
Courteous he was, lowly, and serviceable,
And carv'd before his father at the table.[13]

A YEOMAN had he, and servánts no mo'
At that timë, for him list ridë so ;[14]
And he was clad in coat and hood of green.
A sheaf of peacock arrows[15] bright and keen
Under his belt he bare full thriftily.
Well could he dress his tackle yeomanly :
His arrows drooped not with feathers low ;
And in his hand he bare a mighty bow.
A nut-head[16] had he, with a brown viságe :
Of wood-craft coud[17] he well all the uságe :
Upon his arm he bare a gay bracér,[18]
And by his side a sword and a bucklér,
And on that other side a gay daggere,
Harnessed well, and sharp as point of spear :
A Christopher[19] on his breast of silver sheen.
An horn he bare, the baldric was of green :
A forster[20] was he soothly[21] as I guess.

There was also a Nun, a PRIORESS,
That of her smiling was full simple and coy ;
Her greatest oathë was but by Saint Loy ;[22]
And she was cleped[23] Madame Eglentine.
Full well she sang the servicë divine,
Entuned in her nose full seemëly ;[24]
And French she spake full fair and fetisly[25]
After the school of Stratford attë Bow,
For French of Paris was to her unknow.
At meatë was she well y-taught withal ;
She let no morsel from her lippës fall,
Nor wet her fingers in her saucë deep.
Well could she carry a morsel, and well keep,
That no droppë ne fell upon her breast.
In courtesy was set full much her lest.[26]
Her over-lippë wiped she so clean,
That in her cup there was no farthing[27] seen
Of greasë, when she drunken had her draught ;
Full seemëly after her meat she raught :[28]
And sickerly she was of great disport,[29]
And full pleasánt, and amiable of port,
And pained her to counterfeitë cheer

1 Been placed at the head of the table, above knights of all nations, in Prussia, whither warriors from all countries were wont to repair, to aid the Teutonic Order in their continual conflicts with their heathen neighbours in "Lettowe" or Lithuania (German, "Litthauen"), Russia, &c.

2 Journeyed, ridden, made campaigns ; German, "reisen," to travel.

3 Algesiras, taken from the Moorish king of Grenada, in 1344 : the Earls of Derby and Salisbury took part in the siege. Belmarie is supposed to have been a Moorish state in Africa ; but "Palmyrie" has been suggested as the correct reading. The Great Sea, or perhaps the Greek sea, is the Eastern Mediterranean. Tramissene, or Tremessen, is enumerated by Froissart among the Moorish kingdoms in Africa. Palatie, or Palathia, in Anatolia, was a fief held by the Christian knights after the Turkish conquests—the holders paying tribute to the infidel. Our knight had fought with one of those lords against a heathen neighbour.

4 Ilkë, same ; compare the Scottish phrase "of that ilk,"—that is, of the estate which bears the same name as its owner's title.

5 He was held in very high esteem.

6 Nothing unbecoming a gentleman.

7 He wore a short doublet, all soiled by the contact of his coat of mail.

8 Curled. 9 Wonderfully nimble.

10 Engaged in cavalry expeditions or raids into the enemy's country.

11 Considering the short time he had had.

12 Night-time.

13 It was the custom for squires of the highest degree to carve at their fathers' tables.

14 For it pleased him so to ride.

15 Large arrows, with peacocks' feathers.

16 With nut-brown hair ; or, round like a nut, the hair being cut short. 17 Knew.

18 Shield for an archer's arm, still called a "bracer," from the French "bras," arm.

19 A figure of St Christopher, used as a brooch, and supposed to possess the power of charming away danger.

20 Forester. 21 Certainly. 22 St Eligius, or Eloy.

23 Called. 24 In seemly fashion.

25 Properly ; Chaucer sneers at the debased Anglo-Norman then taught as French in England.

26 Pleasure. 27 Not the least speck.

28 Reached out her hand.

29 Assuredly she was of a lively disposition.

Of court,[1] and be estately of mannére,
And to be holden digne[2] of reverence.
  But for to speaken of her conscience,
She was so charitable and so pitous,[3]
She wouldë weep if that she saw a mouse
Caught in a trap, if it were dead or bled.
Of smallë houndës had she, that she fed
With roasted flesh, and milk, and wastel bread.[4]
But sore she wept if one of them were dead,
Or if men smote it with a yardë[5] smart:
And all was conscience and tender heart.
Full seemly her wimple y-pinched was;
Her nose tretis;[6] her eyen gray as glass;[7]
Her mouth full small, and thereto soft and red;
But sickerly she had a fair forehéad.
It was almost a spannë broad I trow;
For hardily she was not undergrow.[8]
Full fetis[9] was her cloak, as I was ware.
Of small corál about her arm she bare
A pair of beadës, gauded all with green;[10]
And thereon hung a brooch of gold full sheen,
On which was first y-written a crown'd A,
And after, *Amor vincit omnia.*
Another NUN also with her had she,
[That was her chapelléine, and PRIESTËS three.]

  A MONK there was, a fair for the mast'ry,[11]
An out-rider, that loved venery;[12]
A manly man, to be an abbot able.
Full many a dainty horse had he in stable:
And when he rode, men might his bridle hear
Jingeling[13] in a whistling wind as clear,
And eke as loud, as doth the chapel bell,
There as this lord was keeper of the cell.
The rule of Saint Maur and of Saint Benet,[14]
Because that it was old and somedeal[15] strait,
This ilkë[16] monk let oldë thingës pace,
And held after the newë world the trace.
He gave not of the text a pulled hen,[17]
That saith, that hunters be not holy men;
Ne that a monk, when he is cloisterless;
Is like to a fish that is waterless;
This is to say, a monk out of his cloister.
This ilkë text held he not worth an oyster;
And I say his opinion was good.
Why should he study, and make himselfë
    wood,[18]
Upon a book in cloister always pore,
Or swinken[19] with his handës, and labour,
As Austin bit?[20] how shall the world be served?
Let Austin have his swink to him reserved.
Therefore he was a prickasour aright:[21]
Greyhounds he had as swift as fowl of flight:
Of pricking[22] and of hunting for the hare
Was all his lust,[23] for no cost would he spare.
I saw his sleevës purfil'd at the hand
With gris,[24] and that the finest of the land.
And for to fasten his hood under his chin,
He had of gold y-wrought a curious pin:
A love-knot in the greater end there was.
His head was bald, and shone as any glass,
And eke his face, as it had been anoint;
He was a lord full fat and in good point;
His eyen steep,[25] and rolling in his head,
That steamed as a furnace of a lead.
His bootës supple, his horse in great estate,
Now certainly he was a fair preláte;
He was not pale as a forpined[26] ghost;
A fat swan lov'd he best of any roast.
His palfrey was as brown as is a berry.

  A FRIAR there was, a wanton and a merry,
A limitour,[27] a full solemnë man.
In all the orders four is none that can[28]
So much of dalliance and fair language.
He had y-made full many a marriáge
Of youngë women, at his owen cost.
Unto his order he was a noble post;
Full well belov'd, and familiár was he
With franklins over all[29] in his country,
And eke with worthy women of the town:
For he had power of confessión,
As said himselfë, more than a curáte,
For of his order he was licentiate.
Full sweetëly heard he confession,
And pleasant was his absolution.
He was an easy man to give penánce,
There as he wist to have a good pittánce:[30]
For unto a poor order for to give
Is signë that a man is well y-shrive.[31]
For if he gave, he durstë make avant,[32]
He wistë that the man was repentant.
For many a man so hard is of his heart,
He may not weep although him sorë smart.
Therefore instead of weeping and prayéres,
Men must give silver to the poorë freres.
  His tippet was aye farsed[33] full of knives,
And pinnës, for to give to fairë wives;
And certainly he had a merry note:
Well could he sing and playen on a rote;[34]
Of yeddings[35] he bare utterly the prize.
His neck was white as is the fleur-de-lis.

1 Took pains to assume a courtly air.
2 Worthy; French, "digne."
3 Piteous; full of pity.
4 Bread of finest flour.
5 Staff, rod.
6 Well-formed.
7 Gray eyes appear to have been a mark of female beauty in Chaucer's time.
8 Certainly she was not of low stature.
9 Neat.
10 A string of beads having the drops, or gaudies, green.
11 Fair above all others; "for the mastery" was applied to medicines in the sense of "sovereign," as we now apply it to a remedy.
12 A bold rider, fond of hunting—a proclivity of the monks in those days, that occasioned much complaint and satire.
13 It was fashionable to hang bells on horses' bridles.
14 St Benedict was the first founder of a spiritual order in the Roman Church. Maurus, Abbot of Fulda from 822 to 842, did much to re-establish the discipline of the Benedictines on a true Christian basis.
15 Somewhat.
16 Same.
17 He cared nothing for the text.
18 Mad; Scottish, "wud." Felix says to Paul, "Too much learning hath made thee mad."
19 Toil hard.
20 As the rules of St Augustine prescribe.
21 A right hard rider.
22 Riding.
23 Pleasure.
24 Worked at the edge with a fur called "gris," or gray.
25 Deep-set.
26 Wasted.
27 A friar with licence or privilege to beg, or exercise other functions, within a certain district: as "the limitour of Holderness."
28 Knows, understands.
29 Everywhere; German, "ueberall."
30 Where he knew that a liberal dole would be given him.
31 Has well made confession.
32 Vaunt, boast.
33 Stuffed.
34 By rote; from memory.
35 A kind of song; from the Saxon "geddian," to sing.

Thereto he strong was as a champion,
And knew well the tavérns in every town.
And every hosteler and gay tapstére,
Better than a lazar[1] or a beggére,
For unto such a worthy man as he
Accordeth not, as by his faculty,
To havë with such lazars acquaintánce.
It is not honest, it may not advance,
As for to dealë with no such pouraille,[2]
But all with rich, and sellers of vitaille.
And ov'r all there as[3] profit should arise,
Courteous he was, and lowly of service;
There n'as no man nowhere[4] so virtuous.
He was the bestë beggar in all his house:
And gave a certain farmë[5] for the grant,
None of his bretheren came in his haunt.
For though a widow haddë but one shoe,
So pleasant was his *In principio*,[6]
Yet would he have a farthing ere he went;
His purchase was well better than his rent.
And rage he could and play as any whelp,
In lovëdays;[7] there could he muchel help.[8]
For there was he not like a cloisterer,
With threadbare cope, as is a poor scholer,
But he was like a master or a pope.
Of double worsted was his semicope,[9]
That rounded was as a bell out of press.
Somewhat he lisped for his wantonness,
To make his English sweet upon his tongue;
And in his harping, when that he had sung,
His eyen twinkled in his head aright,
As do the starrës in a frosty night.
This worthy limitour was call'd Hubérd.

A Merchant was there with a forked beard,
In motley, and high on his horse he sat,
Upon his head a Flandrish beaver hat.
His bootës clasped fair and fetisly.[10]
His reasons aye spake he full solemnly,
Sounding alway th' increase of his winning.
He would the sea were kept[11] for any thing
Betwixtë Middleburg and Orëwell.[12]
Well could he in exchangë shieldës[13] sell.
This worthy man full well his wit beset;[14]
There wistë no wight that he was in debt,
So estately was he of governance[15]
With his bargáins, and with his chevisance.[16]
For sooth he was a worthy man withal,
But sooth to say, I n'ot[17] how men him call.

A Clerk there was of Oxenford[18] also,
That unto logic haddë long y-go.[19]
As leanë was his horse as is a rake,
And he was not right fat, I undertake;
But looked hollow,[20] and thereto soberly.[21]
Full threadbare was his overest courtepy,[22]
For he had gotten him yet no benefice,
Ne was not worldly, to have an office.
For him was lever[23] have at his bed's head
Twenty bookës, clothed in black or red,
Of Aristotle, and his philosophy,
Than robës rich, or fiddle, or psalt'ry.
But all be that he was a philosópher,
Yet haddë he but little gold in coffer,
But all that he might of his friendës hent,[24]
On bookës and on learning he it spent,
And busily gan for the soulës pray
Of them that gave him wherewith to scholay.[25]
Of study took he mostë care and heed.
Not one word spake he morë than was need;
And that was said in form and reverence,
And short and quick, and full of high senténce.
Sounding in moral virtue was his speech,
And gladly would he learn, and gladly teach.

A Sergeant of the Law, wary and wise,
That often had y-been at the Parvis,[26]
There was also, full rich of excellence.
Discreet he was, and of great reverence:
He seemed such, his wordës were so wise,
Justice he was full often in assize,
By patent, and by plein[27] commission;
For his sciénce, and for his high renown,
Of fees and robës had he many one.
So great a purchaser was nowhere none.
All was fee simple to him, in effect
His purchasing might not be in suspect.[28]
Nowhere so busy a man as he there was,
And yet he seemed busier than he was.
In termës had he case' and doomës[29] all,
That from the time of King Will. werë fall.
Thereto he could indite, and make a thing,
There couldë no wight pinch at his writing.[30]
And every statute coud[31] he plain by rote.
He rode but homely in a medley[32] coat,
Girt with a seint[33] of silk, with barrës small;
Of his array tell I no longer tale.

A Frankëlin[34] was in this company;
White was his beard, as is the daïsy.
Of his complexión he was sanguíne.
Well lov'd he in the morn a sop in wine.

1 A leper.
2 Offal, refuse; from the French "pourrir," to rot.
3 In every place where.
4 Was nowhere any man.
5 Rent; that is, he paid a premium for his licence to beg.
6 The first words of Genesis and John, employed in some part of the mass.
7 At meetings appointed for friendly settlement of differences; the business was often followed by sports and feasting.
8 He was of much service. 9 Half or short cloak.
10 Neatly.
11 He would for anything that the sea were guarded. "The old subsidy of tonnage and poundage," says Tyrwhitt, "was given to the king 'pour la saufgarde et custodie del mer,'" for the safeguard and keeping of the sea (12 E. IV., c. 3).
12 Middleburg, at the mouth of the Scheldt, in Holland; Orwell, a seaport in Essex.
13 Crowns, so called from the shields stamped on them; French, "écu;" Italian, "scudo."
14 Employed.
15 In such a dignified way did he manage.
16 Merchandising; conduct of trade; agreement to borrow money. 17 Know not; wot not. 18 Oxford.
19 Had long gone, devoted himself. 20 Thin.
21 Poorly. 22 His uppermost short cloak.
23 Liefer; rather. 24 Obtain.
25 To study, attend school; poor scholars at the universities used then to go about begging for money to maintain them at their studies.
26 The portico of St Paul's, which lawyers frequented to meet their clients.
27 Full. 28 In suspicion. 29 Judgments.
30 Pick a flaw in what he wrote. 31 Knew.
32 Mixed in colour; French, "mêler," to mix.
33 Cincture, sash, girdle; usually ornamented with bars or stripes.
34 A large freeholder; a country gentleman.

To liven in delight was ever his won,[1]
For he was Epicurus' owen son,
That held opinion, that plein[2] delight
Was verily felicity perfíte.
An householder, and that a great, was he;
Saint Julian[3] he was in his countrý.
His bread, his ale, was alway after one;[4]
A better envined[5] man was nowhere none;
Withouten bake-meat never was his house,
Of fish and flesh, and that so plentëous,
It snowed in his house of meat and drink,
Of allë dainties that men couldë think.
After the sundry seasons of the year,
So changed he his meat and his soupére.
Full many a fat partridge had he in mew,[6]
And many a bream, and many a luce in stew.[7]
Woe was his cook, but if[8] his saucë were
Poignant and sharp, and ready all his gear.
His table dormant[9] in his hall alway
Stood ready cover'd all the longë day.
At sessions there was he lord and sire.
Full often time he was knight of the shire.
An anlace, and a gipciere[10] all of silk,
Hung at his girdle, white as morning milk.
A sheriff had he been, and a countour.[11]
Was nowhere such a worthy vavasour.[12]

An HABERDASHER, and a CARPENTER,
A WEBBE,[13] a DYER, and a TAPISER,[14]
Were with us eke, cloth'd in one livery,
Of a solémn and great fraternity.
Full fresh and new their gear y-picked[15] was.
Their knivës were y-chaped[16] not with brass,
But all with silver wrought full clean and well,
Their girdles and their pouches every deal.[17]
Well seemed each of them a fair burgéss,
To sitten in a guild-hall, on the dais.[18]
Evereach, for the wisdom that he can,[19]
Was shapely[20] for to be an alderman.
For chattels haddë they enough and rent,
And eke their wivës would it well assent:
And ellës certain they had been to blame.
It is full fair to be y-clep'd madáme,
And for to go to vigils all before,
And have a mantle royally y-bore.[21]

A COOK they haddë with them for the nones,[22]
To boil the chickens and the marrow bones,
And powder merchant tart and galingale.[23]
Well could he know a draught of London ale.
He couldë roast, and seethe, and broil, and fry,
Makë mortrewës,[24] and well bake a pie.
But great harm was it, as it thoughtë me,
That on his shin a mormal[25] haddë he.
For blanc manger,[26] that made he with the best.

A SHIPMAN was there, wonned far by West:[27]
For ought I wot, he was of Dartëmouth.
He rode upon a rouncy, as he couth,[28]
All in a gown of falding[29] to the knee.
A dagger hanging by a lace had he
About his neck under his arm adown;
The hot summer had made his hue all brown;
And certainly he was a good felláw.
Full many a draught of wine he had y-draw
From Bourdeaux-ward, while that the chapmen sleep;
Of nicë consciénce took he no keep.
If that he fought, and had the higher hand,
By water he sent them home to every land.
But of his craft to reckon well his tides,
His streamës and his strandës him besides,
His herberow,[30] his moon, and lodemanage,[31]
There was none such, from Hull unto Carthage.
Hardy he was, and wise, I undertake:
With many a tempest had his beard been shake.
He knew well all the havens, as they were,
From Scotland to the Cape of Finisterre,
And every creek in Bretagne and in Spain:
His barge y-cleped was the Magdelain.

With us there was a DOCTOR OF PHYSIC;
In all this worldë was there none him like
To speak of physic, and of surgery:
For he was grounded in astronomy.
He kept his patiént a full great deal
In hourës by his magic natural.
Well could he fortunë[32] the áscendent
Of his imáges for his patiént.
He knew the cause of every malady,
Were it of cold, or hot, or moist, or dry,
And where engender'd, and of what humoúr.
He was a very perfect practisour.
The cause y-know,[33] and of his harm the root,
Anón he gave to the sick man his boot.[34]
Full ready had he his apothecaries,
To send his druggës and his lectuaries,
For each of them made other for to win:
Their friendship was not newë to begin.
Well knew he the old Esculapius,

1 Wont, custom. 2 Full.
3 The patron saint of hospitality, celebrated for supplying his votaries with good lodging and good cheer. 4 Constantly being pressed on one.
5 Stored with wine.
6 In cage; the place behind Whitehall, where the king's hawks were encaged, was called the Mews.
7 Many a pike in his fish-pond; in those Catholic days, when much fish was eaten, no gentleman's mansion was complete without a "stew."
8 Unless. 9 Fixed, always ready.
10 A dagger and a purse.
11 Probably a steward or accountant in the county court.
12 A landholder of consequence; holding of a duke, marquis, or earl, and ranking below a baron.
13 Weaver; German, "Weber."
14 Tapestry-maker; French, "tapissier."
15 Spruce. 16 Mounted. 17 In every part.
18 On the raised platform at the end of the hall, where sat at meat or in judgment those high in authority, rank, or honour; in our days the worthy craftsmen might have been described as "good platform men." 19 Knew. 20 Fitted.
21 To take precedence over all in going to the evening service of the Church, or to festival meetings, to which it was the fashion to carry rich cloaks or mantles against the home-coming.
22 The nonce, occasion.
23 "Poudre marchand tart," some now unknown ingredient used in cookery; "galingale," sweet or long-rooted cyprus.
24 A rich soup made by stamping flesh in a mortar.
25 Gangrene, ulcer.
26 Not what is now known by the name; one part of it was the brawn of a capon.
27 A seaman who dwelt far to the West.
28 On a hack, as he could. 29 Coarse cloth.
30 Harbourage.
31 Pilotage; from Anglo-Saxon "ladman," a leader, guide, or pilot; hence "lodestar," "lodestone."
32 Make fortunate. 33 Known. 34 Remedy.

And Dioscorides, and eke Rufus;
Old Hippocras, Hali, and Gallien;
Serapion, Rasis, and Avicen;
Averrois, Damascene, and Constantin;
Bernard, and Gatisden, and Gilbertin.[1]
Of his diet measúrable was he,
For it was of no superfluity,
But of great nourishing, and digestible.
His study was but little on the Bible.
In sanguine and in perse[2] he clad was, all
Lined with taffata, and with sendall.[3]
And yet he was but easy of dispence:
He kept that he won in the pestilence.[4]
For gold in physic is a cordial;
Therefore he loved gold in special.

A good WIFE was there OF besidë BATH,
But she was somedeal deaf, and that was scath.[5]
Of cloth-making she haddë such an haunt,[6]
She passed them of Ypres, and of Gaunt.
In all the parish wifë was there none,
That to the off'ring[7] before her should gon,
And if there did, certain so wroth was she,
That she was out of allë charity.
Her coverchiefs[8] werë full fine of ground;
I durstë swear, they weighedë ten pound
That on the Sunday were upon her head.
Her hosen weren of fine scarlet red,
Full strait y-tied, and shoes full moist[9] and new.
Bold was her face, and fair and red of hue.
She was a worthy woman all her live,
Husbands at the church door had she had five,
Withouten other company in youth;
But thereof needeth not to speak as nouth.[10]
And thrice had she been at Jerusalem;
She haddë passed many a strangë stream;
At Romë she had been, and at Bologne,[11]
In Galice at Saint James,[12] and at Cologne;
She coudë[13] much of wand'ring by the way,
Gat-toothed[14] was she, soothly for to say.
Upon an ambler easily she sat,
Y-wimpled well, and on her head an hat
As broad as is a buckler or a targe.
A foot-mantle about her hippës large,
And on her feet a pair of spurrës sharp.
In fellowship well could she laugh and carp.[15]
Of remedies of love she knew perchance,
For of that art she coud[13] the oldë dance.

A good man there was of religión,
That was a poorë PARSON of a town:
But rich he was of holy thought and werk:[16]
He was also a learned man, a clerk,
That Christë's gospel truly wouldë preach.
His parishens devoutly would he teach.
Benign he was, and wonder diligent,
And in adversity full patient:
And such he was y-proved often sithes.[17]
Full loth were him to cursë for his tithes,
But rather would he given out of doubt,
Unto his poorë parishens about,
Of his off'ring, and eke of his substánce.
He could in little thing have suffisance.[18]
Wide was his parish, and houses far asunder,
But he ne left not, for no rain nor thunder,
In sickness and in mischief to visit
The farthest in his parish, much and lit,[19]
Upon his feet, and in his hand a staff.
This noble ensample to his sheep he gaf,[20]
That first he wrought, and afterward he taught.
Out of the gospel he the wordës caught,
And this figúre he added yet thereto,
That if gold rustë, what should iron do?
For if a priest be foul, on whom we trust,
No wonder is a lewëd[21] man to rust:
And shame it is, if that a priest take keep,
To see a shitten shepherd and clean sheep:
Well ought a priest ensample for to give,
By his own cleanness, how his sheep should live.
He settë not his benefice to hire,
And left his sheep encumber'd in the mire,
And ran unto London, unto Saint Poul's,
To seekë him a chantery[22] for souls,
Or with a brotherhood to be withold:[23]
But dwelt at home, and keptë well his fold,
So that the wolf ne made it not miscarry.
He was a shepherd, and no mercenary.
And though he holy were, and virtuous,
He was to sinful men not dispitous[24]
Nor of his speechë dangerous nor dign,[25]
But in his teaching díscreet and benign.
To drawen folk to heaven, with fairness,
By good ensample, was his business:
But it were[26] any person obstinate,
What so he were of high or low estate,
Him would he snibbë[27] sharply for the nonës.[28]
A better priest I trow that nowhere none is.
He waited after no pomp nor reverence,
Nor maked him a spiced consciénce,[29]
But Christë's lore, and his apostles' twelve,
He taught, and first he follow'd it himselve.

With him there was a PLOUGHMAN, was his brother,

1 The authors mentioned here were the chief medical text-books of the middle ages. The names of Galen and Hippocrates were then usually spelt "Gallien" and "Hypocras" or "Ypocras."
2 In red and blue.
3 A fine silk stuff.
4 He spent but moderately, keeping the money he had made during the visitation of the plague.
5 Damage; pity.
6 Skill. The west of England, especially around Bath, was the seat of the cloth-manufacture, as were Ypres and Ghent in Flanders.
7 The offering at mass.
8 Head-dresses; Chaucer here satirises the fashion of the time, which piled bulky and heavy waddings on ladies' heads.
9 Used in the sense of fresh or new; as in Latin, "mustum" signifies new wine; and Chaucer elsewhere speaks of "moisty ale" as opposed to "old."
10 Now.
11 Bologna in Italy.
12 At the shrine of St Jago of Compostella in Spain.
13 Knew.
14 Buck-toothed; goat-toothed, to signify her wantonness; or gap-toothed—with gaps between her teeth.
15 Jest, talk.
16 Work.
17 Oftentimes.
18 He was satisfied with very little.
19 Great and small.
20 Gave.
21 Unlearned.
22 An endowment to sing masses for the soul of the donor.
23 Detained.
24 Severe.
25 Disdainful.
26 But if it were.
27 Reprove; hence our modern "snub."
28 Nonce, occasion.
29 Double or artificial conscience.

That had y-laid of dung full many a fother.[1]
A truë swinker [2] and a good was he,
Living in peace and perfect charity.
God loved he bestë with all his heart
At allë timës, were it gain or smart,[3]
And then his neighëbour right as himselve.
He wouldë thresh, and thereto dike,[4] and delve,
For Christë's sake, for every poorë wight,
Withouten hire, if it lay in his might.
His tithës payed he full fair and well,
Both of his proper swink, and his chattel.[5]
In a tabard [6] he rode upon a mere.
There was also a Reeve, and a Millere,
A Sompnour, and a Pardoner also,
A Manciple, and myself, there were no mo'.

The **Miller** was a stout carle for the nones,
Full big he was of brawn, and eke of bones;
That proved well, for ov'r all where [7] he came,
At wrestling he would bear away the ram.[8]
He was short-shouldered, broad, a thickë gnarr,[9]
There was no door, that he n'old heave off bar,
Or break it at a running with his head.
His beard as any sow or fox was red,
And thereto broad, as though it were a spade.
Upon the cop [10] right of his nose he had
A wart, and thereon stood a tuft of hairs
Red as the bristles of a sowë's ears.
His nosë-thirlës [11] blackë were and wide.
A sword and buckler bare he by his side.
His mouth as widë was as a furnáce.
He was a jangler, and a goliardais,[12]
And that was most of sin and harlotries.
Well could he stealë corn, and tollë thrice.
And yet he had a thumb of gold, pardie.[13]
A white coat and a blue hood weared he.
A baggëpipe well could he blow and soun',
And therewithal he brought us out of town.

A gentle **Manciple** [14] was there of a temple,
Of which achatours [15] mightë take ensample
For to be wise in buying of vitaille.
For whether that he paid, or took by taile,[16]
Algate [17] he waited so in his achate,[18]
That he was aye before in good estate.
Now is not that of God a full fair grace
That such a lewed mannë's wit shall pace [19]
The wisdom of an heap of learned men?
Of masters had he more than thriës ten,
That were of law expert and curious:
Of which there was a dozen in that house,
Worthy to be stewárds of rent and land
Of any lord that is in Engleland,
To makë him live by his proper good,
In honour debtless, but if he were wood,[20]
Or live as scarcely as him list desire;
And able for to helpen all a shire
In any case that mightë fall or hap;
And yet this Manciple set their aller cap.[21]

The **Reevë** [22] was a slender choleric man,
His beard was shav'd as nigh as ever he can.
His hair was by his earës round y-shorn;
His top was docked like a priest beforn.
Full longë were his leggës, and full lean,
Y-like a staff, there was no calf y-seen.
Well could he keep a garner and a bin:[23]
There was no auditor [24] could on him win.
Well wist he by the drought, and by the rain,
The yielding of his seed and of his grain.
His lordë's sheep, his neat,[25] and his dairy.
His swine, his horse, his store, and his poultry,
Were wholly in this Reevë's governing,
And by his cov'nant gave he reckoning,
Since that his lord was twenty year of age;
There could no man bring him in arrearáge.
There was no bailiff, herd, nor other hine,[26]
That he ne knew his sleight and his covine:[27]
They were adrad [28] of him, as of the death.
His wonning [29] was full fair upon an heath,
With greenë trees y-shadow'd was his place.
He couldë better than his lord purchase.
Full rich he was y-stored privily.
His lord well could he pleasë subtilly,
To give and lend him of his owen good,
And have a thank, and yet [30] a coat and hood.
In youth he learned had a good mistére.[31]
He was a well good wright, a carpentére.
This Reevë sate upon a right good stot,[32]
That was all pomely [33] gray, and hightë [34] Scot.
A long surcoat of perse [35] upon he had,
And by his side he bare a rusty blade.
Of Norfolk was this Reeve, of which I tell,
Beside a town men clepen Baldeswell.
Tucked he was, as is a friar, about,
And ever rode the hinderest of the rout.[36]

A **Sompnour** [37] was there with us in that place,
That had a fire-red cherubinnës face,
For sausëfleme [38] he was, with eyen narrow.
As hot he was and lecherous as a sparrow,
With scalled browës black, and pilled [39] beard:
Of his viságe children were sore afeard.

1 Properly a ton; generally, any large quantity.
2 Hard worker. 3 Pain, loss. 4 Ditch, dig.
5 Both of his own labour and his goods.
6 Jacket without sleeves. 7 Wheresoever.
8 The usual prize at wrestling matches.
9 Stub or knot in a tree; it describes a thickset strong man. 10 Head; German, "Kopf."
11 Nostrils; from the Anglo-Saxon, "thirlian," to pierce; hence the word "drill," to bore.
12 A babbler and a buffoon; Golias was the founder of a jovial sect called by his name.
13 The proverb says that every honest miller has a thumb of gold; probably Chaucer means that this one was as honest as his brethren.
14 A Manciple—Latin, "manceps," a purchaser or contractor—was an officer charged with the purchase of victuals for inns of court or colleges.
15 Buyers; French, "acheteurs." 16 On trust.
17 Always. 18 Purchase. 19 Surpass.
20 Unless he were mad.
21 Outwitted, made a fool of, them all.
22 A land-steward; still called "grieve"—Anglo-Saxon, "gerefa"—in some parts of Scotland.
23 A store-place for grain.
24 Examiner of accounts. 25 Cattle.
26 Hind, servant. 27 His tricks and cheating.
28 In dread. 29 Abode. 30 Also.
31 Mystery; trade, handicraft.
32 For "stod," a stallion, or steed. 33 Dapple.
34 Was called. 35 Blue-gray, or sky-blue.
36 The hindermost in the troop or procession.
37 Summoner, apparitor, who cited delinquents to appear in ecclesiastical courts.
38 Red or pimply. 39 Scanty.

There n' as quicksilver, litharge, nor brimstone,
Boras, ceruse, nor oil of tartar none,
Nor ointëment that wouldë cleanse or bite,
That him might helpen of his whelkës [1] white,
Nor of the knobbës [2] sitting on his cheeks.
Well lov'd he garlic, oniôns, and leeks,
And for to drink strong wine as red as blood.
Then would he speak, and cry as he were wood;
And when that he well drunken had the wine,
Then would he speakë no word but Latin.
A fewë termës knew he, two or three,
That he had learned out of some decree;
No wonder is, he heard it all the day.
And eke ye knowen well, how that a jay
Can clepen [3] "Wat," as well as can the Pope.
But whoso would in other thing him grope,[4]
Then had he spent all his philosophy,
Aye, *Questio quid juris*,[5] would he cry.
He was a gentle harlot [6] and a kind;
A better fellow should a man not find.
He wouldë suffer, for a quart of wine,
A good fellôw to have his concubine
A twelvemonth, and excuse him at the full.
Full privily a finch eke could he pull.[7]
And if he found owhere [8] a good felláw,
He wouldë teachë him to have none awe
In such a case of the archdeacon's curse;
But if [9] a mannë's soul were in his purse;
For in his purse he should y-punished be.
"Purse is the archëdeacon's hell," said he.
But well I wot, he lied right indeed:
Of cursing ought each guilty man to dread,
For curse will slay right as assoiling [10] saveth;
And also 'ware him of a *significavit*.[11]
In danger had he at his owen guise [12]
The youngë girlës of the diocese,
And knew their counsel, and was of their rede.[13]
A garland had he set upon his head,
As great as it were for an alëstake:[14]
A buckler had he made him of a cake.

With him there rode a gentle PARDONERE [15]
Of Ronceval, his friend and his compere,
That straight was comen from the court of Romë.
Full loud he sang, "Come hither, lovë, tó me."
This Sompnour bare to him a stiff burdoun,[16]
Was never trump of half so great a soun'.
This Pardoner had hair as yellow as wax,
But smooth it hung, as doth a strike [17] of flax:
By ounces hung his lockës that he had,
And therewith he his shoulders overspread.
Full thin it lay, by culpons [18] one and one,
But hood, for jollity, he weared none,
For it was trussed up in his wallét.
Him thought he rode all of the newë get,[19]
Dishevel, save his cap, he rode all bare.
Such glaring eyen had he, as an hare.
A vernicle [20] had he sew'd upon his cap.
His wallet lay before him in his lap,
Bretful [21] of pardon come from Rome all hot.
A voice he had as small as hath a goat.
No beard had he, nor ever one should have.
As smooth it was as it were new y-shave;
I trow he were a gelding or a mare.
But of his craft, from Berwick unto Ware,
Ne was there such another pardonere.
For in his mail [22] he had a pillowbere,[23]
Which, as he saidë, was our Lady's veil:
He said, he had a gobbet [24] of the sail
That Saintë Peter had, when that he went
Upon the sea, till Jesus Christ him hent.[25]
He had a cross of latoun [26] full of stones,
And in a glass he haddë piggë's bones.
But with these relics, whennë that he fond
A poorë parson dwelling upon lond,
Upon a day he got him more money
Than that the parson got in moneths tway;
And thus with feigned flattering and japes,[27]
He made the parson and the people his apes.
But truëly to tellen at the last,
He was in church a noble ecclesiast.
Well could he read a lesson or a story,
But alderbest [28] he sang an offertóry:[29]
For well he wistë, when that song was sung,
He mustë preach, and well afile his tongue,[30]
To winnë silver, as he right well could:
Therefore he sang full merrily and loud.

Now have I told you shortly in a clause
Th' estate, th' array, the number, and eke the cause
Why that assembled was this company
In Southwark at this gentle hostelry,
That hightë the Tabard, fast by the Bell.[31]
But now is timë to you for to tell
How that we baren us that ilkë night,[32]
When we were in that hostelry alight.
And after will I tell of our voyáge,
And all the remnant of our pilgrimage.
But first I pray you of your courtesy,
That ye arette it not my villainy,[33]
Though that I plainly speak in this mattére.
To tellen you their wordës and their cheer;
Not though I speak their wordës properly.
For this ye knowen all so well as I,
Whoso shall tell a tale after a man,

1 Pustules, weals. 2 Buttons. 3 Call.
4 Search. 5 A cant law-Latin phrase.
6 A low, ribald fellow; the word was used of both sexes; it comes from the Anglo-Saxon verb to hire.
7 "Fleece" a man; "pluck a pigeon."
8 Anywhere. 9 Unless.
10 Absolving. 11 An ecclesiastical writ.
12 Within his jurisdiction had he at his own pleasure the young people (of both sexes) in the diocese.
13 Counsel.
14 The post of an alehouse sign; a May pole.
15 A seller of pardons or indulgences.
16 Sang the bass. 17 Streak, strip.
18 Locks, shreds, little heaps.
19 The new gait, or fashion; "gait" is still used in this sense in some parts of the country.
20 An image of Christ; so called from St Veronica, who gave the Saviour a napkin to wipe the sweat from His face as He bore the Cross, and received it back with an impression of His countenance upon it.
21 Brimful.
22 Packet, baggage; French, "malle," a trunk.
23 Pillow-case. 24 Piece. 25 Took hold of him.
26 Copper, latten. 27 Jests.
28 Alderbest, altherbest, allerbest—best of all.
29 An anthem sung while the congregation made the offering.
30 Polish well his tongue; speak smoothly.
31 Apparently another Southwark tavern; Stowe mentions a "Bull" as being near the Tabard.
32 How we bore ourselves—what we did—that same night. 33 Account it not rudeness in me.

He must rehearse, as nigh as ever he can,
Every word, if it be in his charge,
All speak he[1] ne'er so rudely and so large;
Or ellës he must tell his tale untrue,
Or feignë things, or findë wordës new.
He may not spare, although he were his brother;
He must as well say one word as another.
Christ spake Himself full broad in Holy Writ,
And well ye wot no villainy is it.
Eke Plato saith, whoso that can him read,
The wordës must be cousin to the deed.
Also I pray you to forgive it me,
All have I[2] not set folk in their degree,
Here in this tale, as that they shoulden stand:
My wit is short, ye may well understand.

Great cheerë made our Host us every one,
And to the supper set he us anon:
And served us with victual of the best.
Strong was the wine, and well to drink us lest.[3]
A seemly man our Hostë was withal
For to have been a marshal in an hall.
A largë man he was with eyen steep,[4]
A fairer burgess is there none in Cheap:[5]
Bold of his speech, and wise and well y-taught,
And of manhoodë lacked him right naught.
Eke thereto was he right a merry man,
And after supper playen he began,
And spake of mirth amongës other things,
When that we haddë made our reckonings;
And saidë thus; "Now, lordingës, truly
Ye be to me welcome right heartily:
For by my troth, if that I shall not lie,
I saw not this year such a company
At once in this herberow,[6] as is now.
Fain would I do you mirth, an[7] I wist how.
And of a mirth I am right now bethought,
To do you ease,[8] and it shall costë nought.
Ye go to Canterbury; God you speed,
The blissful Martyr quitë you your meed;
And well I wot, as ye go by the way,
Ye shapen you[9] to talken and to play:
For truëly comfórt nor mirth is none
To ridë by the way as dumb as stone:
And therefore would I makë you disport,
As I said erst, and do you some comfórt.
And if you liketh all[10] by one assent
Now for to standen at my judgëment,
And for to worken as I shall you say
To-morrow, when ye riden on the way,
Now by my father's soulë that is dead,
But ye be merry, smiteth off[11] mine head.
Hold up your hands withoutë morë speech."
Our counsel was not longë for to seech:[12]
Us thought it was not worth to make it wise,[13]
And granted him withoutë more avise,[14]
And bade him say his verdict, as him lest.
"Lordings (quoth he), now hearken for the best;
But take it not, I pray you, in disdain;
This is the point, to speak it plat[15] and plain.
That each of you, to shorten with your way
In this voyáge, shall tellen talës tway,
To Canterbury-ward, I mean it so,
And homeward he shall tellen other two,
Of aventúres that whilom have befall.
And which of you that bear'th him best of all,
That is to say, that telleth in this case
Talës of best senténce and most solace,
Shall have a supper at your aller cost[16]
Here in this placë, sitting by this post,
When that ye come again from Canterbury.
And for to makë you the morë merry,
I will myselfë gladly with you ride,
Right at mine owen cost, and be your guide.
And whoso will my judgëment withsay,
Shall pay for all we spenden by the way.
And if ye vouchësafe that it be so,
Tell me anon withoutë wordës mo',[17]
And I will early shapë me therefore."
This thing was granted, and our oath we swore
With full glad heart, and prayed him also,
That he would vouchësafe for to do so,
And that he wouldë be our governour,
And of our talës judge and reportour,
And set a supper at a certain price;
And we will ruled be at his device,
In high and low: and thus by one assent,
We be accorded to his judgëment.
And thereupon the wine was fet[18] anon.
We drunken, and to restë went each one,
Withouten any longer tarrying.
A-morrow, when the day began to spring,
Up rose our host, and was our aller cock,[19]
And gather'd us together in a flock,
And forth we ridden all a little space,
Unto the watering of Saint Thomas:[20]
And there our host began his horse arrest,
And saidë; "Lordës, hearken if you lest.
Ye weet your forword,[21] and I it record.
If even-song and morning-song accord,
Let see now who shall tellë the first tale.
As ever may I drinkë wine or ale,
Whoso is rebel to my judgëment,
Shall pay for all that by the way is spent.
Now draw ye cuts, ere that ye farther twin.[22]
He which that hath the shortest shall begin."
"Sir Knight (quoth he), my master and my lord,
Now draw the cut, for that is mine accord.
Come near (quoth he), my Lady Prioress,
And ye, Sir Clerk, let be your shamefastness,
Nor study not: lay hand to, every man."
Anon to drawen every wight began,
And shortly for to tellen as it was,
Were it by áventure, or sort, or cas,[23]
The sooth is this, the cut fell to the Knight,
Of which full blithe and glad was every wight;

1 Let him speak. 2 Although I have.
3 List, pleased. 4 Deep-set.
5 Cheapside, then inhabited by the richest and most prosperous citizens of London.
6 Lodging, inn; German, "Herberge." 7 If.
8 Pleasure. 9 Prepare yourselves, intend.
10 If it please you all.
11 If ye be not merry, smite off. 12 Seek.

13 To make it matter of deliberation; to weigh the proposal carefully. 14 Consideration. 15 Flat.
16 At the cost of you all. 17 More. 18 Fetched.
19 Was the cock to awaken us all.
20 At the second milestone on the old Canterbury road. 21 Know your promise.
22 Draw lots ere ye go farther.
23 Lot (Latin, "sors"), or chance (Latin, "casus").

And tell he must his tale as was reasón,
By forword, and by composition,
As ye have heard; what needeth wordës mo'?
And when this good man saw that it was so,
As he that wise was and obediént
To keep his forword by his free assent,
He said; "Sithen [1] I shall begin this game,
Why, welcome be the cut in Goddë's name.
Now let us ride, and hearken what I say."
  And with that word we ridden forth our way;
And he began with right a merry cheer
His tale anon, and said as ye shall hear.

THE KNIGHT'S TALE.[2]

WHILOM,[3] as oldë stories tellen us,
There was a duke that hightë [4] Theseus.
Of Athens he was lord and governor,
And in his timë such a conqueror
That greater was there none under the sun.
Full many a richë country had he won.
What with his wisdom and his chivalry,
He conquer'd all the regne of Feminie,[5]
That whilom was y-cleped Scythia;
And weddedë the Queen Hippolyta,
And brought her home with him to his country
With muchel [6] glory and great solemnity,
And eke her youngë sister Emily,
And thus with vict'ry and with melody
Let I this worthy Duke to Athens ride,
And all his host, in armës him beside.
  And certes, if it n'ere [7] too long to hear,
I would have told you fully the mannére,
How wonnen [8] was the regne of Feminie,
By Theseus, and by his chivalry;
And of the greatë battle for the nonce
Betwixt Athenës and the Amazons;
And how assieged was Hippolyta,
The fairë hardy queen of Scythia;
And of the feast that was at her wedding,
And of the tempest at her homecoming.
But all these things I must as now forbear.
I have, God wot, a largë field to ear; [9]
And weakë be the oxen in my plough;
The remnant of my tale is long enow.
I will not letten eke none of this rout.[10]
Let every fellow tell his tale about,
And let see now who shall the supper win.
There as I left,[11] I will again begin.

This Duke, of whom I makë mentioún,
When he was come almost unto the town,
In all his weal [12] and in his mostë pride,
He was ware, as he cast his eye aside,
Where that there kneeled in the highë way
A company of ladies, tway and tway,
Each after other, clad in clothës black:
But such a cry and such a woe they make,
That in this world n'is creatúre living,
That heardë such another waimenting.[13]
And of this crying would they never stenten,[14]
Till they the reinës of his bridle henten.[15]
"What folk be ye that at mine homecoming
Perturben so my feastë with crying?"
Quoth Theseus; "Have ye so great envý
Of mine honoúr, that thus complain and cry?
Or who hath you misboden,[16] or offended?
Do tellë me, if it may be amended;
And why that ye be clad thus all in black?"
  The oldest lady of them all then spake,
When she had swooned, with a deadly cheer,[17]
That it was ruthë [18] for to see or hear.
She saidë; "Lord, to whom fortúne hath given
Vict'ry, and as a conqueror to liven,
Nought grieveth us your glory and your honoúr;
But we beseechen mercy and succóur.
Have mercy on our woe and our distress;
Some drop of pity, through thy gentleness,
Upon us wretched women let now fall.
For certës, lord, there is none of us all
That hath not been a duchess or a queen;
Now be we caitives,[19] as it is well seen:
Thanked be Fortune, and her falsë wheel,
That none estate ensureth to be wele.[20]
And certes, lord, t' abiden your presénce
Here in this temple of the goddess Clemence
We have been waiting all this fortënight:
Now help us, lord, since it lies in thy might.
  "I, wretched wight, that weep and wailë thus,
Was whilom wife to king Capaneus,
That starf [21] at Thebes, cursed be that day:
And allë we that be in this array,
And maken all this lamentatioún,
We losten all our husbands at that town,
While that the siegë thereabouten lay.
And yet the oldë Creon, wellaway!
That lord is now of Thebes the city,
Fulfilled of ire and of iniquity,
He for despite, and for his tyranny,
To do the deadë bodies villainy,[22]

1 Since.

2 For the plan and principal incidents of the "Knight's Tale," Chaucer was indebted to Boccaccio, who had himself borrowed from some prior poet, chronicler, or romancer. Boccaccio speaks of the story as "very ancient;" and, though that may not be proof of its antiquity, it certainly shows that he took it from an earlier writer. The "Tale" is more or less a paraphrase of Boccaccio's "Theseida;" but in some points the copy has a distinct dramatic superiority over the original. The "Theseida" contained ten thousand lines; Chaucer has condensed it into less than one-fourth of the number. The "Knight's Tale" is supposed to have been at first composed as a separate work; it is undetermined whether Chaucer took it direct from the Italian of Boccaccio, or from a French translation.

3 Once on a while; formerly.

4 Was called; from the Anglo-Saxon, "hatan," to bid or call; German, "heissen," "heisst."

5 The "Royaume des Femmes"—kingdom of the Amazons. Gower, in the "Confessio Amantis," styles Penthesilea the "Queen of Feminie."

6 Mickle, great.

7 If it were not.

8 Won, conquered; German, "gewonnen."

9 To plough; Latin, "arare." "I have abundant matter for discourse." The first, and half of the second, of Boccaccio's twelve books are disposed of in the few lines foregoing.

10 Nor will I hinder any of this company.

11 Where I left off.

12 Prosperity, wealth.

13 Bewailing, lamenting; German, "wehklagen."

14 Stint, cease, desist.

15 Seize.

16 Wronged.

17 Aspect, countenance.

18 Pity.

19 Captives or slaves; hence it means generally in wretched circumstances.

20 That assures no continuance of prosperous estate.

21 Died; German, "sterben," "starb."

22 Outrage, insult.

Of all our lordës, which that been y-slaw,[1]
Hath all the bodies on an heap y-draw,
And will not suffer them by none assent
Neither to be y-buried, nor y-brent,[2]
But maketh houndës eat them in despite."
And with that word, withoutë more respite
They fallen groff,[3] and cryden piteously;
"Have on us wretched women some mercy,
And let our sorrow sinken in thine heart."
 This gentle Duke down from his courser start
With heartë piteous, when he heard them speak.
Him thoughtë that his heart would all to-break,
When he saw them so piteous and so mate,[4]
That whilom weren of so great estate.
And in his armës he them all up hent,[5]
And them comfórted in full good intent,
And swore his oath, as he was truë knight,
He wouldë do so farforthly his might[6]
Upon the tyrant Creon them to wreak,[7]
That all the people of Greecë shouldë speak,
How Creon was of Theseus y-served,
As he that had his death full well deserved.
And right anon withoutë more abode[8]
His banner he display'd, and forth he rode
To Thebes-ward, and all his host beside:
No ner[9] Athenës would he go nor ride,
Nor take his easë fully half a day,
But onward on his way that night he lay:
And sent anon Hippolyta the queen,
And Emily her youngë sister sheen[10]
Unto the town of Athens for to dwell:
And forth he rit;[11] there is no more to tell.
 The red statúe of Mars with spear and targe
So shineth in his whitë banner large,
That all the fieldës glitter up and down:
And by his banner borne is his pennon
Of gold full rich, in which there was y-beat[12]
The Minotaur[13] which that he slew in Crete.
Thus rit this Duke, thus rit this conquerour,
And in his host of chivalry the flower,
Till that he came to Thebes, and alight
Fair in a field, there as he thought to fight.
But shortly for to speaken of this thing,
With Creon, which that was of Thebes king,
He fought, and slew him manly as a knight
In plain batáille, and put his folk to flight:
And by assault he won the city after,
And rent adown both wall, and spar, and rafter;
And to the ladies he restored again
The bodies of their husbands that were slain,
To do obséquies, as was then the guise.[14]
 But it were all too long for to devise[15]
The greatë clamour, and the waimenting,[16]
Which that the ladies made at the brenning[17]
Of the bodiës, and the great honour
That Theseus the noble conqueror
Did to the ladies, when they from him went:
But shortly for to tell is mine intent.
 When that this worthy Duke, this Theseus,
Had Creon slain, and wonnen Thebés thus,
Still in the field he took all night his rest,
And did with all the country as him lest.[18]
To ransack in the tas[19] of bodies dead,
Them for to strip of harness and of weed,[20]
The pillers[21] did their business and cure,
After the battle and discomfiture.
And so befell, that in the tas they found,
Through girt with many a grievous bloody wound,
Two youngë knightës ligging by and by[22]
Both in one armës,[23] wrought full richëly:
Of whichë two, Arcita hight that one,
And he that other hightë Palamon.
Not fully quick, nor fully dead they were,
But by their coat-armoúr, and by their gear,
The heralds knew them well in speciál,
As those that weren of the blood royál
Of Thebes, and of sistren two y-born.[24]
Out of the tas the pillers have them torn,
And have them carried soft unto the tent
Of Theseus, and he full soon them sent
To Athens, for to dwellen in prisón
Perpetually, he n'oldë no ranson.[25]
And when this worthy Duke had thus y-done,
He took his host, and home he rit anon
With laurel crowned as a conquerour;
And there he lived in joy and in honour
Term of his life;[26] what needeth wordës mo'?
And in a tower, in anguish and in woe,
Dwellen this Palamon, and eke Arcite,
For evermore, there may no gold them quite.[27]
 Thus passed year by year, and day by day,
Till it fell onës in a morn of May
That Emily, that fairer was to seen
Than is the lily upon his stalkë green,
And fresher than the May with flowers new
(For with the rosë colour strove her hue;
I n'ot[28] which was the finer of them two),
Ere it was day, as she was wont to do,
She was arisen, and all ready dight,[29]
For May will have no sluggardy a-night;
The season pricketh every gentle heart,
And maketh him out of his sleep to start,
And saith, "Arise, and do thine óbservance."
 This maketh Emily have rémembrance
To do honoúr to May, and for to rise.
Y-clothed was she fresh for to devise;
Her yellow hair was braided in a tress,
Behind her back, a yardë long I guess.
And in the garden at the sun uprist[30]
She walketh up and down where as her list.
She gathereth flowers, party[31] white and red,

1 Slain. 2 Burnt.
3 Flat on the ground; grovelling on the earth.
4 Abased, dejected, consumed away.
5 Raised, took.
6 As far as his power went; all that in him lay.
7 Avenge. 8 Delay.
9 "Ner" or "nerre," is used as the comparative of "ner," near, instead of "nerer."
10 Bright, lovely. 11 Rode. 12 Stamped.
13 The monster, half-man and half-bull, which yearly devoured a tribute of fourteen Athenian youths and maidens, until it was slain by Theseus.
14 Custom. 15 Describe. 16 Lamenting.
17 Burning. 18 List, pleased.
19 Heap; French, "tas."
20 Of armour and clothing.
21 Pillagers, strippers; French, "pilleurs."
22 Lying side by side.
23 Armour of the same fashion.
24 Born of two sisters.
25 He would take no ransom.
26 For the rest of his life. 27 Set free.
28 Wot not, know not. 29 Decked, dressed.
30 Sunrise. 31 Mingled.

To make a sotel[1] garland for her head,
And as an angel heavenly she sung.
The greatë tower, that was so thick and strong,
Which of the castle was the chief dungeón[2]
(Where as these knightës weren in prisón,
Of which I toldë you, and tellë shall),
Was even joinant[3] to the garden wall,
There as this Emily had her playing.
Bright was the sun, and clear that morrowning,
And Palamon, this woful prisoner,
As was his wont, by leave of his gaoler,
Was ris'n, and roamed in a chamber on high,
In which he all the noble city sigh,[4]
And eke the garden, full of branches green,
There as this fresh Emelia the sheen
Was in her walk, and roamed up and down.
This sorrowful prisoner, this Palamon
Went in his chamber roaming to and fro,
And to himself complaining of his woe:
That he was born, full oft he said, Alas!
And so befell, by áventure or cas,[5]
That through a window thick of many a bar
Of iron great, and square as any spar,
He cast his eyes upon Emelia,
And therewithal he blent[6] and cried, Ah!
As though he stungen were unto the heart.
And with that cry Arcite anon up start,
And saidë, "Cousin mine, what aileth thee,
That art so pale and deadly for to see?
Why cried'st thou? who hath thee done offence?
For Goddë's love, take all in patience
Our prison,[7] for it may none other be.
Fortune hath giv'n us this adversity.
Some wick'[8] aspéct or dispositión
Of Saturn, by some constellatión,
Hath giv'n us this, although we had it sworn,
So stood the heaven when that we were born,
We must endure; this is the short and plain."
This Palamon answér'd, and said again:
"Cousin, forsooth of this opinión
Thou hast a vain imaginatión.
This prison caused me not for to cry;
But I was hurt right now thorough mine eye
Into mine heart; that will my banë[9] be.
The fairness of the lady that I see
Yond in the garden roaming to and fro,
Is cause of all my crying and my woe.
I n'ot whe'r[10] she be woman or goddéss.
But Venus is it, soothly[11] as I guess."
And therewithal on knees adown he fill,
And saidë: "Venus, if it be your will
You in this garden thus to transfigúre,
Before me sorrowful wretched creatúre,
Out of this prison help that we may scape.
And if so be our destiny be shape
By etern word to dien in prisón,
Of our lineage have some compassión,
That is so low y-brought by tyranny."
And with that word Arcita gan espy[12]
Where as this lady roamed to and fro.
And with that sight her beauty hurt him so,
That if that Palamon was wounded sore,
Arcite is hurt as much as he, or more.
And with a sigh he saidë piteously:
"The freshë beauty slay'th me suddenly
Of her that roameth yonder in the place.
And but[13] I have her mercy and her grace,
That I may see her at the leastë way,
I am but dead; there is no more to say."
This Palamon, when he these wordës heard,
Dispiteously[14] he looked, and answér'd:
"Whether say'st thou this in earnest or in play?"
"Nay," quoth Arcite, "in earnest, by my fay.[15]
God help me so, me lust full ill to play."[16]
This Palamon gan knit his browës tway.
"It were," quoth he, "to thee no great honoúr
For to be false, nor for to be traitoúr
To me, that am thy cousin and thy brother
Y-sworn full deep, and each of us to other,
That never for to dien in the pain,[17]
Till that the death departen shall us twain,
Neither of us in love to hinder other,
Nor in none other case, my levë[18] brother;
But that thou shouldest truly farther me
In every case, as I should farther thee.
This was thine oath, and mine also certáin;
I wot it well, thou dar'st it not withsayn.[19]
Thus art thou of my counsel out of doubt.
And now thou wouldest falsely be about
To love my lady, whom I love and serve,
And ever shall, until mine heartë sterve.[20]
Now certes, false Arcite, thou shalt not so.
I lov'd her first, and toldë thee my woe
As to my counsel, and my brother sworn
To farther me, as I have told beforn.
For which thou art y-bounden as a knight
To helpë me, if it lie in thy might,
Or ellës art thou false, I dare well sayn."
This Arcita full proudly spake again:
"Thou shalt," quoth he, "be rather[21] false than I,
And thou art false, I tell thee utterly;
For *par amour* I lov'd her first ere thou.
What wilt thou say? thou wist it not right now[22]
Whether she be a woman or goddéss.
Thine is affectión of holiness,
And mine is love, as to a creatúre:
For which I toldë thee mine áventure

1 Subtle, well-arranged.
2 The donjon was originally the central tower or "keep" of feudal castles; it was employed to detain prisoners of importance. Hence the modern meaning of the word dungeon.
3 Adjoining. 4 Saw. 5 Chance.
6 Stop, start aside. 7 Imprisonment.
8 Wicked; Saturn, in the old astrology, was a most unpropitious star to be born under.
9 Ruin, destruction. 10 Know not whether.
11 Assuredly, truly. 12 Began to look forth.
13 Unless. 14 Despitefully, angrily.
15 By my faith; Spanish, "fé; French, "foi."
16 I am in no humour for jesting.
17 To die in the pain was a proverbial expression in the French, used as an alternative to enforce a resolution or a promise. Edward III., according to Froissart, declared that he would either succeed in the war against France or die in the pain—"Ou il mourroit en la peine." It was the fashion in those times to swear oaths of friendship and brotherhood; and hence, though the fashion has long died out, we still speak of "sworn friends."
18 Loved, dear; German, "lieber."
19 Gainsay, deny. 20 Die. 21 Sooner.
22 Even now thou knowest not.

As to my cousin, and my brother swórn.
I posë,[1] that thou loved'st her beforn:
Wost[2] thou not well the oldë clerkë's saw,[3]
That who shall give a lover any law?
Love is a greater lawë, by my pan,[4]
Than may be giv'n to any earthly man:
Therefore positive law, and such decree,
Is broke alway for love in each degree.
A man must needës love, maugré his head.[5]
He may not flee it, though he should be dead,
All be she[6] maid, or widow, or else wife.
And eke it is not likely all thy life
To standen in her grace, no more than I:
For well thou wost thyselfë verily,
That thou and I be damned to prisón
Perpetual, us gaineth no ranson.
We strive, as did the houndës for the bone;
They fought all day, and yet their part was none.
There came a kite, while that they were so wroth,
And bare away the bone betwixt them both.
And therefore at the kingë's court, my brother,
Each man for himselfë, there is none other.
Love if thee list; for I love and aye shall:
And soothly, levë brother, this is all.
Here in this prison musten we endure,
And each of us takë his áventúre."
Great was the strife and long betwixt them tway,
If that I haddë leisure for to say;
But to the effect: it happen'd on a day
(To tell it you as shortly as I may),
A worthy duke that hight Perithous,
That fellow was to this Duke Theseus[7]
Since thilkë[8] day that they were children lite,[9]
Was come to Athéns, his fellow to visite,
And for to play, as he was wont to do;
For in this world he loved no man so:
And he lov'd him as tenderly again.
So well they lov'd, as oldë bookës sayn,
That when that one was dead, soothly to tell,
His fellow went and sought him down in hell:
But of that story list me not to write.
Duke Perithous loved well Arcite,
And had him known at Thebes year by year:
And finally at réquest and prayére
Of Perithous, withoutë ransón
Duke Theseus him let out of prisón,
Freely to go, where him list over all,
In such a guise, as I you tellen shall.
This was the forword,[10] plainly to indite,
Betwixtë Theseus and him Arcite:
That if so were, that Arcite were y-found
Ever in his life, by day or night, one stound[11]
In any country of this Theseus,
And he were caught, it was accorded thus,
That with a sword he shouldë lose his head;
There was none other remedy nor rede.[12]
But took his leave, and homeward he him sped;
Let him beware, his neckë lieth to wed.[13]
How great a sorrow suff'reth now Arcite!
The death he feeleth through his heartë smite;
He weepeth, waileth, crieth piteously;
To slay himself he waiteth privily.
He said; "Alas the day that I was born!
Now is my prison worsë than beforn:
Now is me shape[14] eternally to dwell
Not in purgatory, but right in hell.
Alas! that ever I knew Perithous.
For ellës had I dwelt with Theseus
Y-fettered in his prison evermo'.
Then had I been in bliss, and not in woe.
Only the sight of her, whom that I serve,
Though that I never may her grace deserve,
Would have sufficed right enough for me.
O dearë cousin Palamon," quoth he,
"Thine is the vict'ry of this áventúre,
Full blissfully in prison to endure:
In prison? nay certes, in paradise.
Well hath fortúne y-turned thee the dice,
That hast the sight of her, and I th' absénce.
For possible is, since thou hast her presénce,
And art a knight, a worthy and an able,
That by some cas,[15] since fortune is changeáble,
Thou may'st to thy desire sometime attain.
But I that am exiled, and barrén
Of allë grace, and in so great despair,
That there n'is earthë, water, fire, nor air,
Nor creature, that of them maked is,
That may me helpë nor comfort in this,
Well ought I sterve in wanhope[16] and distress.
Farewell my life, my lust,[17] and my gladnéss.
Alas, why plainen men so in commúne
Of purveyance of God,[18] or of Fortúne,
That giveth them full oft in many a guise
Well better than they can themselves devise?
Some man desireth for to have richéss,
That cause is of his murder or great sicknéss,
And some man would out of his prison fain,
That in his house is of his meinie[19] slain.
Infinite harmës be in this mattére.
We wot never what thing we pray for here,
We fare as he that drunk is as a mouse.
A drunken man wot well he hath an house,
But he wot not which is the right way thither,
And to a drunken man the way is slither.[20]
And certes in this world so farë we.
We seekë fast after felicity,
But we go wrong full often truëly.

1 Suppose. 2 Know'st.
3 The saying of the old scholar—Boethius, in his treatise "De Consolatione Philosophiæ," which Chaucer translated, and from which he has freely borrowed in his poetry. The words are
"Quis legem det amantibus?
Major lex amor est sibi."
4 Head. 5 In spite of his head.
6 Whether the woman he loves be.
7 "Perithous" and "Theseus" must, for the metre, be pronounced as words of four and three syllables respectively—the vowels at the end not being diphthongated, but enunciated separately, as if the words were printed "Perithöüs," "Theseüs." The same rule applies in such words as "creature" and "conscience," which are trisyllables.
8 That. 9 Little. 10 Covenant, promise.
11 Moment, short space of time; from Anglo-Saxon, "stund;" akin to which is German, "Stunde," an hour. 12 Counsel. 13 In pledge, pawn.
14 It is shaped, decreed, fixed for me.
15 Chance.
16 Die in despair; in want of hope. 17 Pleasure.
18 Why do men so often complain of God's providence?
19 Household; menials, or servants, &c., dwelling together in a house; from an Anglo-Saxon word meaning a crowd. Compare German, "Menge," multitude. 20 Or "slider," slippery.

Thus we may sayen all, and namely[1] I,
That ween'd,[2] and had a great opinión,
That if I might escapë from prisón
Then had I been in joy and perfect heal,
Where now I am exiled from my weal.
Since that I may not see you, Emily,
I am but dead; there is no remedy."
Upon that other sidë, Palamon,
When that he wist Arcita was agone,
Such sorrow maketh, that the greatë tower
Resounded of his yelling and clamoúr.
The purë fetters[3] on his shinnës great
Were of his bitter saltë tearës wet.
"Alas!" quoth he, "Arcita, cousin mine,
Of all our strife, God wot, the fruit is thine.
Thou walkest now in Thebes at thy large,
And of my woe thou givest little charge.[4]
Thou mayst, since thou hast wisdom and man-head,[5]
Assemble all the folk of our kindréd,
And make a war so sharp on this countrý,
That by some áventure, or some treatý,
Thou mayst have her to lady and to wife,
For whom that I must needës lose my life.
For as by way of possibility,
Since thou art at thy large, of prison free,
And art a lord, great is thine ávantage,
More than is mine, that sterve[6] here in a cage.
For I must weep and wail, while that I live,
With all the woe that prison may me give,
And eke with pain that love me gives also,
That doubles all my torment and my woe."
Therewith the fire of jealousy upstart
Within his breast, and hent him by the heart
So woodly,[7] that he like was to behold
The box-tree, or the ashes dead and cold.
Then said; "O cruel goddess, that govérn
This world with binding of your word etern,[8]
And writen in the table of adamant
Your parlement[9] and your eternal grant,
What is mankind more unto you y-hold[10]
Than is the sheep, that rouketh[11] in the fold!
For slain is man, right as another beast,
And dwelleth eke in prison and arrest,
And hath sicknéss, and great adversity,
And oftentimës guiltëless, pardie.[12]
What governance is in your prescience,
That guiltëless tormenteth innocence?
And yet increaseth this all my penance,
That man is bounden to his observance
For Goddë's sake to letten of his will,[13]
Whereas a beast may all his lust[14] fulfil.
And when a beast is dead, he hath no pain;
But man after his death must weep and plain,
Though in this worldë he have care and woe:
Withoutë doubt it mayë standen so.
"The answer of this leave I to divinës,
But well I wot, that in this world great pine[15] is:
Alas! I see a serpent or a thief
That many a truë man hath done mischief,
Go at his large, and where him list may turn.
But I must be in prison through Saturn,
And eke through Juno, jealous and eke wood,[16]
That hath well nigh destroyed all the blood
Of Thebes, with his wastë wallës wide.
And Venus slay'th me on that other side
For jealousy, and fear of him, Arcite."
Now will I stent[17] of Palamon a lite,[18]
And let him in his prison stillë dwell,
And of Arcita forth I will you tell.
The summer passeth, and the nightës long
Increasë double-wise the painës strong
Both of the lover and the prisonére.
I n'ot[19] which hath the wofuller mistére.[20]
For, shortly for to say, this Palamon
Perpetually is damned to prisón,
In chainës and in fetters to be dead;
And Arcite is exiled on his head[21]
For evermore as out of that country,
Nor never more he shall his lady see.
You lovers ask I now this question,[22]
Who hath the worse, Arcite or Palamon?
The one may see his lady day by day,
But in prison he dwellë must alway.
The other where him list may ride or go,
But see his lady shall he never mo'.
Now deem all as you listë, ye that can,
For I will tell you forth as I began.
When that Arcite to Thebes comen was,
Full oft a day he swelt,[23] and said, "Alas!"
For see his lady shall he never mo'.
And shortly to concluden all his woe,
So much sorrow had never creatúre
That is or shall be while the world may dure.
His sleep, his meat, his drink is him byraft,[24]
That lean he wex,[25] and dry as any shaft.[26]
His eyen hollow, grisly to behold,
His hue fallow,[27] and pale as ashes cold,
And solitary he was, ever alone,
And wailing all the night, making his moan.
And if he heardë song or instrument,
Then would he weepen, he might not be stent.[28]
So feeble were his spirits, and so low,
And changed so, that no man couldë know
His speech, neither his voice, though men it heard.
And in his gear[29] for all the world he far'd
Not only like the lovers' malady
Of Eros, but rather y-like maníe,[30]

1 Especially I; I for instance. 2 Thought.
3 The very fetters. The Greeks used καθαρος, the Romans "purus," in the same sense.
4 Takest little heed. 5 Manhood, courage.
6 Perish, die. 7 Seized so madly upon his heart.
8 Eternal. 9 Consultation.
10 More by you esteemed.
11 Lie huddled together, sleep.
12 Par Dieu—by God.
13 Restrain his desire. 14 Pleasure.
15 Pain, trouble; French, "peine." 16 Mad.
17 Stint, pause. 18 Little. 19 Know not.
20 Condition. 21 On peril of his head.
22 In the mediæval courts of love, to which allusion is probably made forty lines before, in the word "parlement," or "parliament," questions like that here proposed were seriously discussed.
23 Fainted, died. 24 Bereft, taken away, from him.
25 Became, waxed.
26 Arrow. The phrase is equivalent to our "dry as a bone."
27 Yellow; old spelling "falwe," French "fauve," tawny-coloured. Some editions have "sallow."
28 Stinted, stopped.
29 Behaviour, fashion, dress; but, by another reading, the word is "gyre," and means fit, trance—from the Latin, "gyro," I turn round.
30 Mania, madness.

Engender'd of humoúrs meláncholic,
Before his head in his cell fántastic.[1]
And shortly turned was all upside down,
Both habit and eke dispositioún,
Of him, this woful lover Dan[2] Arcite.
Why should I all day of his woe indite?
When he endured had a year or two
This cruel torment, and this pain and woe,
At Thebes, in his country, as I said,
Upon a night in sleep as he him laid,
Him thought how that the winged god Mercúry
Before him stood, and bade him to be merry.
His sleepy yard[3] in hand he bare upright;
A hat he wore upon his hairës bright.
Arrayèd was this god (as he took keep)[4]
As he was when that Argus[5] took his sleep;
And said him thus: "To Athens shalt thou wend;[6]
There is thee shapen[7] of thy woe an end."
And with that word Arcite woke and start.
"Now truëly how sore that e'er me smart,"
Quoth he, "to Athens right now will I fare.
Nor for no dread of death shall I not spare
To see my lady that I love and serve;
In her presénce I reckë not to sterve."[8]
And with that word he caught a great mirrór,
And saw that changed was all his colór,
And saw his visage all in other kind.
And right anon it ran him in his mind,
That since his facë was so disfigúr'd
Of malady the which he had endúr'd,
He mightë well, if that he bare him low,[9]
Live in Athenës evermore unknow,
And see his lady wellnigh day by day.
And right anon he changed his array,
And clad him as a poorë labourer.
And all alone, save only a squiér,
That knew his privity[10] and all his cas,[11]
Which was disguised poorly as he was,
To Athens is he gone the nextë[12] way.
And to the court he went upon a day,
And at the gate he proffer'd his service,
To drudge and draw, what so men would devise.[13]
And, shortly of this matter for to sayn,
He fell in office with a chamberlain,
The which that dwelling was with Emily.
For he was wise, and couldë soon espy
Of every servant which that served her.
Well could he hewë wood, and water bear,
For he was young and mighty for the nones,[14]
And thereto he was strong and big of bones
To do that any wight can him devise.
A year or two he was in this servíce,
Page of the chamber of Emily the bright;
And Philostrate he saidë that he hight.
But half so well belov'd a man as he
Ne was there never in court of his degree.
He was so gentle of conditioún,
That throughout all the court was his renown.
They saidë that it were a charity
That Theseus would énhance his degree,[15]
And put him in some worshipful servíce,
There as he might his virtue exercise.
And thus within a while his namë sprung
Both of his deedës, and of his good tongue,
That Theseus hath taken him so near,
That of his chamber he hath made him squire,
And gave him gold to máintain his degree;
And eke men brought him out of his country
From year to year full privily his rent.
But honestly and slyly[16] he it spent,
That no man wonder'd how that he it had.
And three year in this wise his life he lad,[17]
And bare him so in peace and eke in werre,[18]
There was no man that Theseus had so derre.[19]
And in this blissë leave I now Arcite,
And speak I will of Palamon a lite.[20]
In darkness horrible, and strong prisón,
This seven year hath sitten Palamon,
Forpined,[21] what for love, and for distress.
Who feeleth double sorrow and heaviness
But Palamon? that love distraineth[22] so,
That wood[23] out of his wits he went for woe,
And eke thereto he is a prisonére
Perpetual, not only for a year.
Who couldë rhyme in English properly
His martyrdom? forsooth, it am not I;[24]
Therefore I pass as lightly as I may.
It fell that in the seventh year, in May
The thirdë night (as oldë bookës sayn,
That all this story tellen morë plain),
Were it by áventure or destiny
(As, when a thing is shapen[25] it shall be),
That, soon after the midnight, Palamon
By helping of a friend brake his prisón,
And fled the city fast as he might go,
For he had given drink his gaoler so
Of a clary,[26] made of a certain wine,
With narcotise and opie[27] of Thebes fine,
That all the night, though that men would him shake,
The gaoler slept, he mightë not awake:
And thus he fled as fast as ever he may.
The night was short, and fastë by the day
That needës cast he must[28] himself to hide.
And to a grovë fastë there beside
With dreadful foot then stalked Palamon.
For shortly this was his opinión,
That in the grove he would him hide all day,
And in the night then would he take his way

1 In front of his head in his fantastic cell. "The division of the brain into cells, according to the different sensitive faculties," says Mr Wright, "is very ancient, and is found depicted in mediæval manuscripts." In a manuscript in the Harleian Library, it is stated, "Certum est in prora cerebri esse fantasiam, in medio rationem discretionis, in puppi memoriam"—a classification not materially differing from that of modern phrenologists. 2 "Dominus," Lord; Spanish, "Don."
3 Rod; the "caduceus." 4 Heed, notice.
5 Argus was employed by Juno to watch Io with his hundred eyes; but he was set to sleep by the flute of Mercury, who then cut off his head.
6 Go. 7 Fixed, prepared. 8 Die.
9 Lived in lowly fashion.
10 His secret, his private history. 11 Fortune.
12 Nearest; German, "nächste." 13 Order, direct.
14 Nonce, occasion, purpose.
15 Elevate him in rank. 16 Prudently, discreetly.
17 Led. 18 War. 19 Dear. 20 Little.
21 Pined, wasted away.
22 Whom love so distresses or afflicts.
23 Mad. 24 In truth, I am not the man to do it.
25 Settled, decreed.
26 Hippocras wine made with spices.
27 Narcotics and opiates, or opium.
28 Close at hand was the day, during which he must cast about, or contrive, to conceal himself.

To Thebes-ward, his friendës for to pray
On Theseus to help him to warray.[1]
And shortly either he would lose his life,
Or winnen Emily unto his wife.
This is th' effect, and his intention plain.
Now will I turn to Arcita again,
That little wist how nighë was his care,
Till that Fortúne had brought him in the snare.
The busy lark, the messenger of day,
Saluteth in her song the morning gray;
And fiery Phœbus riseth up so bright,
That all the orient laugheth at the sight,
And with his streamës[2] drieth in the greves[3]
The silver droppës, hanging on the leaves;
And Arcite, that is in the court royál
With Theseus, his squier principal,
Is ris'n, and looketh on the merry day.
And for to do his óbservance to May,
Remembering the point[4] of his desire,
He on his courser, starting as the fire,
Is ridden to the fieldës him to play,
Out of the court, were it a mile or tway.
And to the grove, of which I have you told,
By áventure his way began to hold,
To makë him a garland of the greves,[3]
Were it of woodbine, or of hawthorn leaves,
And loud he sang against the sun so sheen.[5]
"O May, with all thy flowers and thy green,
Right welcome be thou, fairë freshë May,
I hope that I some green here getten may."
And from his courser, with a lusty heart,
Into the grove full hastily he start,
And in a path he roamed up and down,
There as by áventure this Palamon
Was in a bush, that no man might him see,
For sore afeared of his death was he.
Nothing ne knew he that it was Arcite;
God wot he would have trowed it full lite.[6]
But sooth is said, gone since full many years,[7]
The field hath eyen, and the wood hath ears.
It is full fair a man to bear him even,[8]
For all day meeten men at unset steven.[9]
Full little wot Arcite of his felláw,
That was so nigh to hearken óf his saw,[10]
For in the bush he sitteth now full still.
When that Arcite had roamed all his fill,
And sungen all the roundel[11] lustily,
Into a study he fell suddenly,
As do those lovers in their quaintë gears,[12]
Now in the crop, and now down in the breres,[13]
Now up, now down, as bucket in a well.
Right as the Friday, soothly for to tell,
Now shineth it, and now it raineth fast,
Right so can geary[14] Venus overcast
The heartës of her folk, right as her day
Is gearful,[14] right so changeth she array.
Seldom is Friday all the weekë like.
When Arcite had y-sung, he gan to sike,[15]
And sat him down withouten any more:
"Alas!" quoth he, "the day that I was bore!
How longë, Juno, through thy cruelty
Wilt thou warrayen[16] Thebes the city?
Alas! y-brought is to confusion
The blood royál of Cadm' and Amphion:
Of Cadmus, which that was the firstë man,
That Thebes built, or first the town began,
And of the city first was crowned king.
Of his lineáge am I, and his offspring
By very line, as of the stock royál;
And now I am so caitiff and so thrall,[17]
That he that is my mortal enemy,
I serve him as his squiër poorëly.
And yet doth Juno me well morë shame,
For I dare not beknow[18] mine owen name,
But there as I was wont to hight Arcite,
Now hight I Philostrate, not worth a mite.
Alas! thou fell Mars, and alas! Juno,
Thus hath your ire our lineage all fordo'.[19]
Save only me, and wretched Palamon,
That Theseus martýreth in prisón.
And over all this, to slay me utterly,
Love hath his fiery dart so brenningly[20]
Y-sticked through my truë careful heart,
That shapen was my death erst than my shert.[21]
Ye slay me with your eyen, Emily;
Ye be the causë wherefore that I die.
Of all the remnant of mine other care
Ne set I not the mountance of a tare,[22]
So that I could do aught to your pleasance."
And with that word he fell down in a trance
A longë time; and afterward upstart
This Palamon, that thought thorough his heart
He felt a cold sword suddenly to glide:
For ire he quoke,[23] no longer would he hide.
And when that he had heard Arcite's tale,
As he were wood,[24] with facë dead and pale,
He start him up out of the bushes thick,
And said: "False Arcita, false traitor wick',[25]
Now art thou hent,[26] that lov'st my lady so,
For whom that I have all this pain and woe,
And art my blood, and to my counsel sworn,
As I full oft have told thee herebeforn,
And hast bejaped[27] here Duke Theseus,
And falsely changed hast thy namë thus;
I will be dead, or ellës thou shalt die.
Thou shalt not love my lady Emily,
But I will love her only and no mo';
For I am Palamon thy mortal foe.
And though I have no weapon in this place,
But out of prison am astart[28] by grace,

1 To make war; French, "guerroyer," to molest; hence, perhaps, "to worry."
2 Beams, rays. 3 Groves. 4 Object.
5 Shining, bright. 6 Full little believed it.
7 It is an old and true saying.
8 To be always of the same demeanour; on his guard.
9 Every day men meet at unexpected time. To "set a steven," is to fix a time, make an appointment.
10 Saying, speech.
11 Roundelay; song coming round again to the words with which it opened. 12 Odd fashions.
13 Now in the tree-top, now in the briars. "Crop and root," top and bottom, is used to express the perfection or totality of anything.
14 Changeful, full of "gears" or humours, inconstant.
15 Sigh. 16 Torment.
17 So wretched and enslaved.
18 Avow, acknowledge; German, "bekennen."
19 Undone, ruined. 20 Burningly.
21 My death was decreed before my shirt was shaped—that is, before any clothes were made for me, before my birth.
22 The value of a tare or a straw.
23 Or "quook," from "quake," as "shook" from "shake." 24 Mad.
25 Wicked. 26 Caught.
27 Deceived, imposed upon. 28 Escaped.

I dreadë[1] not that either thou shalt die,
Or else thou shalt not loven Emily.
Choose which thou wilt, for thou shalt not astart."
This Arcite then, with full dispiteous[2] heart,
When he him knew, and had his talë heard,
As fierce as lion pulled out a swerd,
And saidë thus; "By God that sitt'th above,
N'ere it[3] that thou art sick, and wood for love,
And eke that thou no weap'n hast in this place,
Thou should'st never out of this grovë pace,
That thou ne shouldest dien of mine hand.
For I defy the surety and the band,
Which that thou sayest I have made to thee.
What? very fool, think well that love is free;
And I will love her maugré[4] all thy might.
But, for thou art a worthy gentle knight,
And wilnest to darraine her by bataille,[5]
Have here my troth, to-morrow I will not fail,
Without weeting[6] of any other wight,
That here I will be founden as a knight,
And bringë harness[7] right enough for thee;
And choose the best, and leave the worst for me.
And meat and drinkë this night will I bring
Enough for thee, and clothes for thy bedding.
And if so be that thou my lady win,
And slay me in this wood that I am in,
Thou may'st well have thy lady as for me."
This Palamon answér'd, "I grant it thee."
And thus they be departed till the morrow,
When each of them hath laid his faith to borrow.[8]
O Cupid, out of allë charity!
O Regne[9] that wilt no fellow have with thee!
Full sooth is said, that love nor lordëship
Will not, his thanks,[10] have any fellowship.
Well finden that Arcite and Palamon.
Arcite is ridd anon unto the town,
And on the morrow, ere it were daylight,
Full privily two harness hath he dight,[11]
Both suffisant and meetë to darraine[12]
The battle in the field betwixt them twain.
And on his horse, alone as he was born,
He carrieth all this harness him beforn;
And in the grove, at time and place y-set,
This Arcite and this Palamon be met.
Then changë gan the colour of their face;
Right as the hunter in the regne[13] of Thrace
That standeth at a gappë[14] with a spear
When hunted is the lion or the bear,
And heareth him come rushing in the greves,[15]
And breaking both the boughës and the leaves,
Thinketh, "Here comes my mortal enemy,
Withoutë fail, he must be dead or I;
For either I must slay him at the gap;
Or he must slay me, if that me mishap:"
So fared they, in changing of their hue
As far as either of them other knew.[16]
There was no good day, and no saluting,
But straight, withoutë wordës rehearsing,
Evereach of them holp to arm the other,
As friendly, as he were his owen brother.
And after that, with sharpë spearës strong
They foined[17] each at other wonder long.
Thou mightest weenë,[18] that this Palamon
In his fighting were as a wood[19] lion,
And as a cruel tiger was Arcite:
As wildë boars gan they together smite,
That froth as white as foam, for irë wood.[20]
Up to the ancle fought they in their blood.
And in this wise I let them fighting dwell,
And forth I will of Theseus you tell.
The Destiny, minister general,
That executeth in the world o'er all
The purveyánce,[21] that God hath seen beforn;
So strong it is, that though the world had sworn
The contrary of a thing by yea or nay,
Yet some time it shall fallen on a day
That falleth not eft[22] in a thousand year.
For certainly our appetitës here,
Be it of war, or peace, or hate, or love,
All is this ruled by the sight[23] above.
This mean I now by mighty Theseus,
That for to hunten is so desirous—
And namëly[24] the greatë hart in May—
That in his bed there daweth him no day
That he n'is clad, and ready for to ride
With hunt and horn, and houndës him beside.
For in his hunting hath he such delight,
That it is all his joy and appetite
To be himself the greatë hartë's bane;[25]
For after Mars he serveth now Diane.
Clear was the day, as I have told ere this,
And Theseus, with allë joy and bliss,
With his Hippolyta, the fairë queen,
And Emily, y-clothed all in green,
On hunting be they ridden royally.
And to the grove, that stood there fastë by,
In which there was an hart, as men him told,
Duke Theseus the straightë way doth hold,
And to the laund[26] he rideth him full right,
There was the hart y-wont to have his flight,
And over a brook, and so forth on his way.
This Duke will have a course at him or tway
With houndës, such as him lust[27] to command.
And when this Duke was comë to the laund,
Under the sun he looked, and anon
He was ware of Arcite and Palamon,
That foughtë breme,[28] as it were bullës two.
The brightë swordës wentë to and fro
So hideously, that with the leastë stroke
It seemed that it wouldë fell an oak,
But what they werë, nothing yet he wote.
This Duke his courser with his spurrës smote,
And at a start[29] he was betwixt them two,

1 Doubt. 2 Wrathful.
3 Were it not. 4 Despite.
5 Wilt challenge, reclaim, her by combat.
6 Knowledge. 7 Armour, arms.
8 Had pledged his faith.
9 Queen; French, "Reine;" Venus is meant. The common reading, however, is "regne," reign or power.
10 Thanks to him; with his goodwill.
11 Prepared two suits of armour. 12 Contest.
13 Realm, kingdom. 14 Gap, opening.
15 Groves.
16 When they recognised each other afar off.
17 Thrust. 18 Think. 19 Mad.
20 For anger mad.
21 Providence, foreordination.
22 Again. 23 Eye; intelligence, power.
24 Especially. 25 Torment, destruction.
26 Plain. Compare modern English, "lawn," and French, "Landes"—flat, bare marshy tracts in the south of France.
27 Pleased. 28 Fiercely.
29 In a moment, on a sudden.

And pulled out a sword and cried, "Ho!
No more, on pain of losing of your head.
By mighty Mars, he shall anon be dead
That smiteth any stroke, that I may see!
But tell to me what mister[1] men ye be,
That be so hardy for to fightë here
Withoutë judge or other officer,
As though it were in listës[2] royally."
This Palamon answered hastily,
And saidë: "Sir, what needeth wordës mo'?
We have the death deserved bothë two,
Two woful wretches be we, and caitíves,
That be accumbered[3] of our own lives,
And as thou art a rightful lord and judge,
So give us neither mercy nor refuge.
And slay me first, for saintë charity,
But slay my fellow eke as well as me.
Or slay him first; for, though thou know it lite,[4]
This is thy mortal foe, this is Arcite,
That from thy land is banisht on his head,
For which he hath deserved to be dead.
For this is he that came unto thy gate
And saidë, that he hightë Philostrate.
Thus hath he japed[5] thee full many a year,
And thou hast made of him thy chief esquiér;
And this is he, that loveth Emily.
For since the day is come that I shall die
I makë pleinly[6] my confessión,
That I am thilkë[7] woful Palamon,
That hath thy prison broken wickedly.
I am thy mortal foe, and it am I
That so hot loveth Emily the bright,
That I would die here present in her sight.
Therefore I askë death and my jewise.[8]
But slay my fellow eke in the same wise,
For both we have deserved to be slain."
This worthy Duke answér'd anon again,
And said, "This is a short conclusión.
Your own mouth, by your own confessión
Hath damned you, and I will it record;
It needeth not to pain you with the cord;
Ye shall be dead, by mighty Mars the Red."[9]
The queen anon for very womanhead
Began to weep, and so did Emily,
And all the ladies in the company.
Great pity was it, as it thought them all,
That ever such a chancë should befall,
For gentle men they were, of great estate,
And nothing but for love was this debate;
They saw their bloody woundës wide and sore,
And cried all at once, both less and more,
"Have mercy, Lord, upon us women all."
And on their barë knees adown they fall,
And would have kiss'd his feet there as he stood,
Till at the last aslaked was his mood[10]
(For pity runneth soon in gentle heart);
And though at first for ire he quoke and start,
He hath consider'd shortly in a clause
The trespass of them both, and eke the cause:
And although that his ire their guilt accused,
Yet in his reason he them both excused;
As thus; he thoughtë well that every man
Will help himself in love if that he can,
And eke deliver himself out of prison.
And eke his heartë had compassión
Of women, for they wepten ever-in-one:[11]
And in his gentle heart he thought anon,
And soft unto himself he saidë: "Fie
Upon a lord that will have no mercy,
But be a lion both in word and deed,
To them that be in répentance and dread,
As well as to a proud dispiteous[12] man
That will maintainë what he first began.
That lord hath little of discretión,
That in such case can no división:[13]
But weigheth pride and humbless after one."[14]
And shortly, when his ire is thus agone,
He gan to look on them with eyen light,[15]
And spake these samë wordës all on height.[16]
"The god of love, ah! *benedicite*,[17]
How mighty and how great a lord is he!
Against his might there gainë[18] none obstácles,
He may be call'd a god for his mirácles.
For he can maken at his owen guise
Of every heart, as that him list devise.
Lo here this Arcite, and this Palamon,
That quietly were out of my prisón,
And might have lived in Thebes royally,
And weet[19] I am their mortal enemy,
And that their death li'th in my might also,
And yet hath love, maugré their eyen two,[20]
Y-brought them hither bothë for to die.
Now look ye, is not this an high folly?
Who may not be a fool, if but he love?
Behold, for Goddë's sake that sits above,
See how they bleed! be they not well array'd?
Thus hath their lord, the god of love, them paid
Their wages and their fees for their servíce;
And yet they weenë for to be full wise,
That servë love, for ought that may befall.
But this is yet the bestë game[21] of all,
That she, for whom they have this jealousy,
Can them therefor as muchel thank as me.
She wot no more of all this hotë fare,[22]
By God, than wot a cuckoo or an hare.
But all must be assayed hot or cold;
A man must be a fool, or young or old;
I wot it by myself full yore agone:[23]
For in my time a servant was I one.

1 Manner, kind; German, "Muster," sample, model.
2 In the lists, prepared for such single combats between champion and accuser, &c.
3 Wearied, burdened. 4 Little.
5 Deceived. 6 Fully, unreservedly.
7 Contracted from "the ilke," the same; that.
8 Doom, judgment; from the Latin, "judicium."
9 Referring to the ruddy colour of the planet, to which was doubtless due the transference to it of the name of the God of War. In his "Republic," enumerating the seven planets, Cicero speaks of the propitious and beneficent light of Jupiter: "Tum (fulgor) rutilus horribilisque terris, quem Martium dicitis"—"Then the red glow, horrible to the nations, [which you say to be that of Mars." Boccaccio opens the "Theseida" by an invocation to "rubicondo Marte."
10 His anger was appeased.
11 Continually; perhaps another reading, "every one," is the better. 12 Unpitying, disdainful.
13 Can make no distinction.
14 Alike. 15 Gentle, lenient.
16 Aloud; he had just been speaking to himself.
17 Bless ye him. 18 Avail, conquer. 19 Know.
20 "In spite of their eyes."
21 The best joke of all—the best of the joke.
22 Behaviour. 23 Long ago; years ago.

And therefore since I know of lovë's pain,
And wot how sore it can a man distrain,[1]
As he that oft hath been caught in his las,[2]
I you forgivë wholly this trespáss,
At réquest of the queen that kneeleth here,
And eke of Emily, my sister dear.
And ye shall both anon unto me swear,
That never more ye shall my country dere,[3]
Nor makë war upon me night nor day,
But be my friends in allë that ye may.
I you forgive this trespass every deal."[4]
And they him sware his asking[5] fair and well,
And him of lordship and of mercy pray'd,
And he them granted grace, and thus he said:
"To speak of royal lineage and richéss,
Though that she were a queen or a princess,
Each of you both is worthy doubtëless
To weddë when time is; but natheless
I speak as for my sister Emily,
For whom ye have this strife and jealousy,
Ye wot yourselves, she may not wed the two
At once, although ye fight for evermo':
But one of you, all be him loth or lief,[6]
He must go pipe into an ivy leaf:[7]
This is to say, she may not have you both,
All be ye never so jealous, nor so wroth.
And therefore I you put in this degree,
That each of you shall have his destiny
As him is shape;[8] and hearken in what wise;
Lo hear your end of that I shall devise.
My will is this, for plain conclusión
Withouten any replicatión,[9]
If that you liketh, take it for the best,
That evereach of you shall go where him lest,[10]
Freely withoutë ransom or dangér;
And this day fifty weekës, farre ne nerre,[11]
Evereach of you shall bring an hundred knights,
Armed for listës up at allë rights
All ready to darraine[12] her by bataille,
And this behete[13] I you withoutë fail
Upon my troth, and as I am a knight,
That whether of you bothë that hath might,
That is to say, that whether he or thou
May with his hundred, as I spake of now,
Slay his contráry, or out of listës drive,
Him shall I given Emily to wive,
To whom that fortune gives so fair a grace.
The listës shall I make here in this place.
And God so wisly on my soulë rue,[14]
As I shall even judgë be and true.
Ye shall none other endë with me maken
Than one of you shallë be dead or taken.
And if you thinketh this is well y-said,
Say your advice,[15] and hold yourselves apaid.[16]
This is your end, and your conclusión."
Who looketh lightly now but Palamon?
Who springeth up for joyë but Arcite?
Who could it tell, or who could it indite,
The joyë that is maked in the place
When Theseus hath done so fair a grace?
But down on knees went every manner[17] wight,
And thanked him with all their heartës' might,
And namëly[18] these Thebans oftë sithe.[19]
And thus with good hope and with heartë blithe
They take their leave, and homeward gan they ride
To Thebes-ward, with his old wallës wide.
I trow men wouldë deem it negligence,
If I forgot to tellë the dispence[20]
Of Theseus, that went so busily
To maken up the listës royally,
That such a noble theatre as it was,
I dare well say, in all this world there n'as.[21]
The circuít a milë was about,
Walled of stone, and ditched all without.
Round was the shape, in manner of compáss,
Full of degrees,[22] the height of sixty pas,[23]
That when a man was set on one degree
He letted[24] not his fellow for to see.
Eastward there stood a gate of marble white,
Westward right such another opposite.
And, shortly to concludë, such a place
Was never on earth made in so little space,
For in the land there was no craftës-man,
That geometry or arsmetrikë can,[25]
Nor pourtrayor,[26] nor carver of imáges,
That Theseus ne gave him meat and wages
The theatre to make and to devise.
And for to do his rite and sacrifice
He eastward hath upon the gate above,
In worship of Venus, goddess of love,
Done[27] make an altar and an oratory;
And westward, in the mind and in memory
Of Mars, he maked hath right such another,
That costë largëly of gold a fother.[28]
And northward, in a turret on the wall,
Of alabaster white and red corál
An oratory richë for to see,
In worship of Diane of chastity,
Hath Theseus done[27] work in noble wise.
But yet had I forgotten to devise[29]
The noble carving, and the portraitures,
The shape, the countenance of the figúres
That weren in these oratories three.
First in the temple of Venus may'st thou see
Wrought on the wall, full piteous to behold,
The broken sleepës, and the sikës[30] cold,
The sacred tearës, and the waimentings,[31]
The fiery strokës of the desirings,
That Lovë's servants in this life endure;
The oathës, that their covenants assure.
Pleasance and Hope, Desire, Foolhardiness,
Beauty and Youth, and Bawdry and Richéss,
Charms and Sorc'ry, Leasings[32] and Flattery,

1 Distress, torment.
2 Lace, leash, noose; snare; from Latin, "laqueus."
3 Injure. 4 Completely. 5 What he asked.
6 Will he, nill he. 7 "He must go whistle."
8 As is decreed, prepared, for him.
9 Reply. 10 Where he pleases.
11 Neither farther nor nearer.
12 Contend for. 13 Promise.
14 May God as surely have mercy on my soul.
15 Opinion. 16 Satisfied. 17 Kind of. 18 Especially.
19 Oftentimes; the Thebans are the rival lovers.
20 Expenditure. 21 Was not.
22 Steps, benches, as in the ancient amphitheatre.
23 Either the building was sixty paces high; or, more probably, there were sixty of the steps or benches.
24 Hindered. 25 Arithmetic.
26 Painter of figures or portraits.
27 Caused. 28 A great amount, heap.
29 Describe. 30 Sighs.
31 Lamentings. 32 Falsehoods.

Dispencë, Business, and Jealousy,
That wore of yellow goldës[1] a garland,
And had a cuckoo sitting on her hand,
Feasts, instruments, and carolës and dances,
Lust and array, and all the circumstánces
Of Love, which I reckon'd and reckon shall
In order, werë painted on the wall,
And more than I can make of mentión.
For soothly all the mount of Citheron,[2]
Where Venus hath her principal dwelling,
Was showed on the wall in pourtraying,
With all the garden, and the lustiness.[3]
Nor was forgot the porter Idleness,
Nor Narcissus the fair of yore agone,[4]
Nor yet the folly of King Solomon,
Nor yet the greatë strength of Hercules,
Th' enchantments of Medea and Circés,
Nor of Turnus the hardy fierce courâge,
The richë Crœsus caitif in servâge.[5]
Thus may ye see, that wisdom nor richéss,
Beauty, nor sleight, nor strength, nor hardiness,
Ne may with Venus holdë champartie,[6]
For as her listë the world may she gie.[7]
Lo, all these folk so caught were in her las[8]
Till they for woe full often said, Alas!
Sufficë these ensamples one or two,
Although I could reckon a thousand mo'.
  The statue of Venus, glorious to see
Was naked floating in the largë sea,
And from the navel down all cover'd was
With wavës green, and bright as any glass.
A citole[9] in her right hand haddë she,
And on her head, full seemly for to see,
A rosë garland fresh, and well smelling,
Above her head her dovës flickering.
Before her stood her sonë Cupido,
Upon his shoulders wingës had he two;
And blind he was, as it is often seen;
A bow he bare, and arrows bright and keen.
  Why should I not as well eke tell you all
The portraiture, that was upon the wall
Within the temple of mighty Mars the Red?
All painted was the wall in length and brede[10]
Like to the estres[11] of the grisly place
That hight the great Temple of Mars in Thrace,
In thilkë[12] cold and frosty región,
There as Mars hath his sovereign mansión.
First on the wall was painted a forést,
In which there dwelled neither man nor beast,
With knotty gnarry[13] barren treës old
Of stubbës sharp and hideous to behold;
In which there ran a rumble and a sough,[14]
As though a storm should bursten every bough:
And downward from an hill under a bent,[15]
There stood the temple of Mars Armipotent,
Wrought all of burnish'd steel, of which th' entry
Was long and strait, and ghastly for to see.
And thereout came a rage and such a vise,[16]
That it made all the gatës for to rise.
The northern light in at the doorë shone,
For window on the wallë was there none
Through which men mighten any light discern.
The doors were all of adamant etern,
Y-clenched overthwart and endëlong[17]
With iron tough, and, for to make it strong,
Every pillar the temple to sustain
Was tunnë-great,[18] of iron bright and sheen.
There saw I first the dark imagining
Of felony, and all the compassing;
The cruel ire, as red as any glede,[19]
The pickëpurse,[20] and eke the palë dread;
The smiler with the knife under the cloak,
The shepen[21] burning with the blackë smoke;
The treason of the murd'ring in the bed,
The open war, with woundës all be-bled;
Conteke[22] with bloody knife, and sharp menace.
All full of chirking[23] was that sorry place.
The slayer of himself eke saw I there,
His heartë-blood had bathed all his hair:
The nail y-driven in the shode[24] at night,
The coldë death, with mouth gaping upright.
Amiddës of the temple sat Mischance,
With discomfórt and sorry countenance;
Eke saw I Woodness[25] laughing in his rage,
Armed Complaint, Outhees,[26] and fierce Outrage;
The carrain[27] in the bush, with throat y-corve,[28]
A thousand slain, and not of qualm y-storve;[29]
The tyrant, with the prey by force y-reft;
The town destroy'd, that there was nothing left.
Yet saw I brent the shippës hoppësteres,[30]
The hunter strangled with the wildë bears:
The sow freting[31] the child right in the cradle;
The cook scalded, for all his longë ladle.
Nor was forgot, by th' infortune of Mart[32]
The carter overridden with his cart;
Under the wheel full low he lay adown.

1 The flower turnsol, or girasol, which turns with and seems to watch the sun, as a jealous lover his mistress.
2 The isle of Venus, Cythēra, in the Ægean Sea; now called Cerigo: not, as Chaucer's form of the word might imply, Mount Cithæron, in the south-west of Bœotia, which was appropriated to other deities than Venus—to Jupiter, to Bacchus, and the Muses.
3 Pleasantness. 4 Olden time.
5 Abased into slavery. It need not be said that Chaucer pays slight heed to chronology in this passage, where the deeds of Turnus, the glory of King Solomon, and the fate of Crœsus are made memories of the far past in the time of fabulous Theseus, the Minotaur-slayer.
6 Divided power or possession; an old law-term, signifying the maintenance of a person in a suit on the condition of receiving part of the property in dispute, if recovered.
7 Or "guy;" guide, rule. 8 Snare.
9 A kind of dulcimer. 10 Breadth.
11 Interior, chambers. 12 That. 13 Gnarled.
14 Groaning noise. 15 Slope.
16 Such a furious voice.
17 Crossways and lengthways. 18 Thick as a tun.
19 Live coal.
20 The plunderers that followed armies, and gave to war a horror all their own.
21 Stable; Anglo-Saxon, "scypen;" the word "sheppon" still survives in provincial parlance.
22 Contention, discord. 23 Creaking, jarring noise.
24 Hair of the head; the line, perhaps, refers to the deed of Jael. 25 Madness. 26 Outcry.
27 Carrion, corpse. 28 Slashed, cut.
29 Not dead of sickness.
30 The meaning is dubious. We may understand "the dancing ships," the ships that "hop" on the waves; "steres" being taken as the feminine adjectival termination: or we may, perhaps, read, with one of the manuscripts, "the ships upo the steres"—that is, even as they are being steered, or on the open sea—a more picturesque notion.
31 Devouring; the Germans use "fressen" to describe eating by animals, "essen" by men.
32 Through the misfortune of war.

There were also of Mars' division,
The armourer, the bowyer,[1] and the smith,
That forgeth sharpë swordës on his stith.[2]
And all above depainted in a tower
Saw I Conquest, sitting in great honoúr,
With thilkë [3] sharpë sword over his head
Hanging by a subtle y-twined thread.
Painted the slaughter was of Julius,[4]
Of cruel Nero, and Antonius:
Although at that time they were yet unborn,
Yet was their death depainted there beforn,
By menacing of Mars, right by figúre,
So was it showed in that portraitúre,
As is depainted in the stars above,
Who shall be slain, or ellës dead for love.
Sufficeth one ensample in stories old,
I may not reckon them all, though I wo'ld.
The statue of Mars upon a cartë [5] stood
Armed, and looked grim as he were wood,[6]
And over his head there shonë two figúres
Of starrës, that be cleped in scriptures,
That one Puella, that other Rubeus.[7]
This god of armës was arrayed thus:
A wolf there stood before him at his feet
With eyen red, and of a man he eat:
With subtle pencil painted was this story,
In redouting [8] of Mars and of his glory.
Now to the temple of Dian the chaste
As shortly as I can I will me haste,
To tellë you all the descriptioun.
Depainted be the wallës up and down
Of hunting and of shamefast chastity.
There saw I how woful Calistope,[9]
When that Dian aggrieved was with her,
Was turned from a woman till a bear,
And after was she made the lodëstar:[10]
Thus was it painted, I can say no far;[11]
Her son is eke a star as men may see.
There saw I Danë [12] turn'd into a tree,
I meanë not the goddess Dianë,
But Peneus' daughter, which that hight Danë.
There saw I Actæon an hart y-maked,[13]
For vengeance that he saw Dian all naked:
I saw how that his houndës have him caught,
And freten [14] him, for that they knew him not.
Yet painted was, a little farthermore,
How Atalanta hunted the wild boar,
And Meleager, and many other mo',
For which Diana wrought them care and woe.
There saw I many another wondrous story,
The which me list not drawen to memóry.
This goddess on an hart full high was set,[15]
With smallë houndës all about her feet,
And underneath her feet she had a moon,
Waxing it was, and shouldë wanë soon.
In gaudy green her statue clothed was,
With bow in hand, and arrows in a case.[16]
Her eyen castë she full low adown,
Where Pluto hath his darkë regioun.
A woman travailing was her beforn,
But, for her child so longë was unborn,
Full piteously Lucina [17] gan she call,
And saidë; "Help, for thou may'st best of all."
Well could he paintë lifelike that it wrought;
With many a florin he the hues had bought.
Now be these listës made, and Theseus,
That at his greatë cost arrayed thus
The temples, and the theatre every deal,[18]
When it was done, him liked wonder well.
But stint [19] I will of Theseus a lite,[20]
And speak of Palamon and of Arcite.
The day approacheth of their returning,
That evereach an hundred knights should bring,
The battle to darraine [21] as I you told;
And to Athens, their covenant to hold,
Hath ev'reach of them brought an hundred knights,
Well armed for the war at allë rights.
And sickerly [22] there trowed [23] many a man,
That never, sithen [24] that the world began,
For to speaken of knighthood of their hand,
As far as God hath maked sea and land,
Was, of so few, so noble a company.[25]
For every wight that loved chivalry,
And would, his thankës,[26] have a passant[27] name,
Had prayed, that he might be of that game,
And well was him, that thereto chosen was.
For if there fell to-morrow such a case,
Ye knowë well, that every lusty knight,
That loveth par amour, and hath his might,
Were it in Engleland, or ellëswhere,
They would, their thankës, willen to be there,
T' fight for a lady; *benedicite*,
It were a lusty [28] sightë for to see.
And right so fared they with Palamon;
With him there wentë knightës many one.
Some will be armed in an habergeon,
And in a breast-plate, and in a gipon;[29]

1 Maker of bows. 2 Stithy, anvil. 3 That.
4 Julius Cæsar. 5 Chariot. 6 Mad.
7 Puella and Rubeus were two figures in geomancy, representing two constellations—the one signifying Mars retrograde, the other Mars direct.
8 In reverence, fear.
9 Or Callisto: daughter of Lycaon, seduced by Jupiter, turned into a bear by Diana, and placed afterwards, with her son, as the Great Bear among the stars.
10 Polestar. 11 Farther; for "farre" or "ferre."
12 Daphne, daughter of the river-god Peneus, in Thessaly; she was beloved by Apollo, but to avoid his pursuit, she was, at her own prayer, changed into a laurel-tree.
13 Made. 14 Devour. 15 Seated. 16 Quiver.
17 As the goddess of Light, or the goddess who brings to light, Diana—as well as Juno—was invoked by women in child-birth: so Horace, Odes iii. 22, says:—
"Montium custos nemorumque, Virgo,
Quæ laborantes utero puellas
Ter vocata audis adimisque leto, Diva triformis."
18 In every part: "deal" corresponds to the German "Theil," a portion.
19 Cease speaking. 20 Little.
21 Set in array; contest.
22 Surely; German, "sicher;" Scotch, "sikkar," certain. When Robert Bruce had escaped from England to assume the Scottish crown, he stabbed Comyn before the altar at Dumfries; and, emerging from the church, was asked by his friend Kirkpatrick if he had slain the traitor. "I doubt it," said Bruce. "Doubt," cried Kirkpatrick. "I 'll mak sikkar;" and he rushed into the church, and despatched Comyn with repeated thrusts of his dagger.
23 Believed. 24 Since.
25 Never since the world began was there assembled from every part of the earth, in proportion to the smallness of the number, such a brave and noble company of knights.
26 With his good-will; thanks to his own efforts.
27 Surpassing. 28 Pleasing. 29 Short doublet.

And some will have a pair of platës[1] large;
And some will have a Prussë[2] shield, or targe;
Some will be armed on their leggës weel;[3]
Some have an axe, and some a mace of steel.
There is no newë guise,[4] but it was old.
Armed they weren, as I have you told,
Evereach after his opinión.

There may'st thou see coming with Palamon
Licurgus himself, the great king of Thrace:
Black was his beard, and manly was his face.
The circles of his eyen in his head
They glowed betwixtë yellow and red,
And like a griffin looked he about,
With kemped[5] hairës on his browës stout;
His limbs were great, his brawns were hard and strong,
His shoulders broad, his armës round and long.
And as the guisë[4] was in his country,
Full high upon a car of gold stood he,
With fourë whitë bullës in the trace.
Instead of coat-armour on his harness,
With yellow nails, and bright as any gold,
He had a bearë's skin, coal-black for old.[6]
His long hair was y-kempt behind his back,
As any raven's feather it shone for black.
A wreath of gold arm-great,[7] of hugë weight,
Upon his head sate, full of stonës bright,
Of finë rubies and clear diamánts.
About his car there wentë white alauns,[8]
Twenty and more, as great as any steer,
To hunt the lion or the wildë bear,
And follow'd him, with muzzle fast y-bound,
Collars of gold, and torettes[9] filed round.
An hundred lordës had he in his rout,[10]
Armed full well, with heartës stern and stout.

With Arcita, in stories as men find,
The great Emetrius the king of Ind,
Upon a steedë bay,[11] trapped in steel,
Cover'd with cloth of gold diápred[12] well,
Came riding like the god of armës, Mars.
His coat-armoúr was of a cloth of Tars,[13]
Couched[14] with pearlës white and round and great.
His saddle was of burnish'd gold new beat;
A mantëlet on his shoulders hanging
Bretful[15] of rubies red, as fire sparkling.
His crispë hair like ringës was y-run,[16]
And that was yellow, glittering as the sun.
His nose was high, his eyen bright citrine,[17]
His lips were round, his colour was sanguine,
A fewë fracknes in his face y-sprent,[18]
Betwixt yellow and black somedeal y-ment,[19]
And as a lion he his looking cast.[20]
Of five and twenty year his age I cast.[21]
His beard was well begunnen for to spring;
His voice was as a trumpet thundering.
Upon his head he wore of laurel green
A garland fresh and lusty to be seen;
Upon his hand he bare, for his delight,
An eagle tame, as any lily white.
An hundred lordës had he with him there,
All armed, save their heads, in all their gear,
Full richëly in allë manner things.
For trust ye well, that earlës, dukes, and kings
Were gather'd in this noble company,
For love, and for increase of chivalry.
About this king there ran on every part
Full many a tame lión and leopart.
And in this wise these lordës all and some[22]
Be on the Sunday to the city come
Aboutë prime,[23] and in the town alight.

This Theseus, this Duke, this worthy knight,
When he had brought them into his city,
And inned[24] them, ev'reach at his degree,
He feasteth them, and doth so great laboúr
To easen them,[25] and do them all honoúr,
That yet men weenë[26] that no mannë's wit
Of none estatë could amenden[27] it.
The minstrelsy, the service at the feast,
The greatë giftës to the most and least,
The rich array of Theseus' paláce,
Nor who sate first or last upon the dais,[28]
What ladies fairest be, or best dancing,
Or which of them can carol best or sing,
Or who most feelingly speaketh of love;
What hawkës sitten on the perch above,
What houndës liggen[29] on the floor adown,
Of all this now make I no mentioun;
But of th' effect; that thinketh me the best;
Now comes the point, and hearken if you lest.[30]

The Sunday night, ere day began to spring,
When Palamon the larkë heardë sing,
Although it were not day by hourës two,
Yet sang the lark, and Palamon right tho[31]
With holy heart, and with an high courágе,
Arose, to wenden[32] on his pilgrimage
Unto the blissful Cithera benign,
I meanë Venus, honourable and digne.[33]
And in her hour[34] he walketh forth a pace
Unto the listës, where her temple was,
And down he kneeleth, and with humble cheer[35]
And heartë sore, he said as ye shall hear.

"Fairest of fair, O lady mine Venus,
Daughter to Jove, and spouse of Vulcanus,
Thou gladder of the mount of Citheron![36]
For thilkë[37] love thou haddest to Adon[38]

1 Back and front armour. 2 Prussian.
3 Well-greaved; like Homer's εὐκνημιδες Αχαιοι.
4 Fashion.
5 Combed; the word survives in "unkempt."
6 Age. 7 As thick as a man's arm.
8 Greyhounds, mastiffs; from the Spanish word "Alano," signifying a mastiff. 9 Rings.
10 Retinue, company. 11 Bay horse.
12 Diversified with flourishes or figures.
13 A kind of silk. 14 Trimmed.
15 Brimful, covered with.
16 His curled hair ran down into ringlets.
17 Pale yellow colour.
18 A few freckles sprinkled on his face.
19 Somewhat mixed; German, "mengen," to mix.
20 Cast about his eyes.
21 Reckon; as we now speak of "casting a sum."
22 All and sundry.
23 The time of early prayers, between six and nine in the morning. 24 Lodged; whence "inn."
25 Give them pleasure, make them comfortable.
26 Think. 27 Improve. 28 See note 18, page 21.
29 Lie. 30 Please. 31 Then. 32 Go. 33 Worthy.
34 In the hour of the day which, under the astrological system that apportioned the twenty-four among the seven ruling planets, was under the influence of Venus.
35 Demeanour. 36 See note 2, page 36. 37 That.
38 Adonis, a beautiful youth beloved of Venus, whose death by the tusk of a boar she deeply mourned.

Have pity on my bitter tearës' smart,
And take mine humble prayer to thine heart.
Alas! I havë no languáge to tell
Th' effectë, nor the torment of mine hell;
Mine heartë may mine harmës not betray;
I am so cónfused, that I cannot say.
But mercy, lady bright, that knowest well
My thought, and seest what harm that I feel.
Consider all this, and rue upon[1] my sore,
As wisly[2] as I shall for evermore
Enforce my might, thy true servant to be,
And holdë war alway with chastity:
That make I mine avow,[3] so ye me help.
I keepë not of armës for to yelp,[4]
Nor ask I not to-morrow to have victóry,
Nor rénown in this case, nor vainë glory
Of prize of armës,[5] blowing up and down,
But I would have fully possessioun
Of Emily, and die in her service;
Find thou the manner how, and in what wise.
I reckë not but[6] it may better be
To have vict'ry of them, or they of me,
So that I have my lady in mine arms.
For though so be that Mars is god of arms,
Your virtue is so great in heaven abóve,
That, if you list, I shall well have my love.
Thy temple will I worship evermo',
And on thine altar, where I ride or go,
I will do sacrifice, and firës bete.[7]
And if ye will not so, my lady sweet,
Then pray I you, to-morrow with a spear
That Arcita me through the heartë bear.
Then reck I not, when I have lost my life,
Though that Arcita win her to his wife.
This is th' effect and end of my prayére,—
Give me my love, thou blissful lady dear."
When th' orison was done of Palamon,
His sacrifice he did, and that anon,
Full piteously, with allë circumstances,
All tell I not as now[8] his observánces.
But at the last the statue of Venus shook,
And made a signë, whereby that he took[9]
That his prayér accepted was that day.
For though the signë shewed a delay,[10]
Yet wist he well that granted was his boon;
And with glad heart he went him home full soon.
The third hour unequál[11] that Palamon
Began to Venus' temple for to gon,
Up rose the sun, and up rose Emily,
And to the temple of Dian gan hie.
Her maidens, that she thither with her lad,[12]
Full readily with them the fire they had,
Th' incense, the clothës, and the remnant all
That to the sacrifice belongë shall,
The hornës full of mead, as was the guise;
There lacked nought to do her sacrifice.
Smoking[13] the temple full of clothës fair,
This Emily with heartë debonnair[14]
Her body wash'd with water of a well.
But how she did her rite I dare not tell;
But[15] it be any thing in general;
And yet it were a game[16] to hearen all;
To him that meaneth well it were no charge:
But it is good a man to be at large.[17]
Her bright hair combed was, untressed all.
A coronet of green oak cerrial[18]
Upon her head was set full fair and meet.
Two firës on the altar gan she bete,
And did her thingës, as men may behold
In Stace[19] of Thebes, and these bookës old.
When kindled was the fire, with piteous cheer
Unto Dian she spake as ye may hear.
"O chastë goddess of the woodës green,
To whom both heav'n and earth and sea is seen,
Queen of the realm of Pluto dark and low,
Goddess of maidens, that mine heart hast know
Full many a year, and wost[20] what I desire,
So keep me from the vengeance of thine ire,
That Actæon aboughtë[21] cruelly:
Chastë goddéss, well wottest thou that I
Desire to be a maiden all my life,
Nor never will I be no love nor wife.
I am, thou wost,[20] yet of thy company,
A maid, and love hunting and venery,[22]
And for to walken in the woodës wild,
And not to be a wife, and be with child.
Nought will I know the company of man.
Now help me, lady, since ye may and can,
For those three formës[23] that thou hast in thee.
And Palamon, that hath such love to me,
And eke Arcite, that loveth me so sore,
This grace I prayë thee withoutë more,
As sendë love and peace betwixt them two:
And from me turn away their heartës so,
That all their hotë love, and their desire,
And all their busy torment, and their fire,
Be queint,[24] or turn'd into another place.
And if so be thou wilt do me no grace,
Or if my destiny be shapen so
That I shall needës have one of them two,
So send me him that most desireth me.
Behold, goddess of cleanë chastity,
The bitter tears that on my cheekës fall.
Since thou art maid, and keeper of us all,

1 Take pity on.
2 Certainly, truly; German, "gewiss."
3 Vow, promise.
4 Care not to boast of feats of arms.
5 Praise, esteem for valour.
6 Whether.
7 Make, kindle.
8 Although I tell not now.
9 Understood.
10 Was not immediately vouchsafed.
11 In the third planetary hour; Palamon had gone forth in the hour of Venus, two hours before daybreak; the hour of Mercury intervened; the third hour was that of Luna, or Diana. "Unequal" refers to the astrological division of day and night, whatever their duration, into twelve parts, which of necessity varied in length with the season.
12 Led.
13 Draping; hence the word "smock;" "smokless," in Chaucer, means naked.
14 Gentle.
15 Except.
16 Pleasure.
17 Do as he will.
18 Of the species of oak which Pliny, in his "Natural History," calls "cerrus."
19 Statius, the Roman poet, who embodied in the twelve books of his "Thebaid" the ancient legends connected with the war of the Seven against Thebes.
20 Knowest.
21 Earned; suffered from.
22 Field sports.
23 Diana was Luna in heaven, Diana on earth, and Hecate in hell; hence the direction of the eyes of her statue to "Pluto's dark region." Her statue was set up where three ways met, so that with a different face she looked down each of the three; from which she was called Trivia. See the quotation from Horace. note 17, page 37.
24 Quenched.

My maidenhead thou keep and well conserve,
And, while I live, a maid I will thee serve."
The firës burn upon the altar clear,
While Emily was thus in her prayére :
But suddenly she saw a sightë quaint.[1]
For right anon one of the firës queint
And quick'd [2] again, and after that anon
That other fire was queint, and all agone :
And as it queint, it made a whisteling,
As doth a brandë wet in its burning.
And at the brandës end outran anon
As it were bloody droppës many one :
For which so sore aghast was Emily,
That she was well-nigh mad, and gan to cry,
For she ne wistë what it signified;
But onëly for fearë thus she cried,
And wept, that it was pity for to hear.
And therewithal Diana gan appear
With bow in hand, right as an hunteress,
And saidë; "Daughter, stint [3] thine heaviness.
Among the goddës high it is affirm'd,
And by eternal word writ and confirm'd,
Thou shalt be wedded unto one of tho [4]
That have for thee so muchë care and woe :
But unto which of them I may not tell.
Farewell, for here I may no longer dwell.
The firës which that on mine altar brenn,[5]
Shall thee declaren, ere that thou go henne,[6]
Thine áventure of love, as in this case."
And with that word, the arrows in the case [7]
Of the goddess did clatter fast and ring,
And forth she went, and made a vanishing,
For which this Emily astonied was,
And saidë; "What amounteth this,[8] alas !
I put me under thy protectión,
Diane, and in thy dispositión."
And home she went anon the nextë [9] way.
This is th' effect, there is no more to say.
The nextë hour of Mars following this
Arcite to the temple walked is
Of fiercë Mars, to do his sacrifice
With all the ritës of his pagan guise.
With piteous [10] heart and high devotión.
Right thus to Mars he said his orison.
"O strongë god, that in the regnës [11] cold
Of Thracë honoured art, and lord y-hold,[12]
And hast in every regne, and every land
Of armës all the bridle in thine hand,
And them fortúnest as thee list devise,[13]
Accept of me my piteous sacrifice.
If so be that my youthë may deserve,
And that my might be worthy for to serve
Thy godhead, that I may be one of thine,
Then pray I thee to rue upon my pine,[14]
For thilkë [15] pain, and thilkë hotë fire,
In which thou whilom burned'st for desire
Whennë that thou usedest [16] the beauty
Of fairë youngë Venus, fresh and free,
And haddest her in armës at thy will :
And though thee onës on a time misfill,[17]
When Vulcanus had caught thee in his las,[18]
And found thee ligging [19] by his wife, alas !
For thilkë sorrow that was in thine heart,
Have ruth [20] as well upon my painë's smart.
I am young and unconning, [21] as thou know'st,
And, as I trow,[22] with love offended most,
That e'er was any living creature:
For she, that doth [23] me all this woe endure,
Ne recketh ne'er whether I sink or fleet.[24]
And well I wot, ere she me mercy hete,[25]
I must with strengthë win her in the place :
And well I wot, withoutë help or grace
Of thee, ne may my strengthë not avail :
Then help me, lord, to-morr'w in my bataille,
For thilkë fire that whilom burned thee,
As well as this fire that now burneth me;
And do [26] that I to-morr'w may have victóry.
Mine be the travail, all thine be the glory.
Thy sovereign temple will I most honoúr
Of any place, and alway most laboúr
In thy pleasance and in thy craftës strong.
And in thy temple I will my banner hong,[27]
And all the armës of my company,
And evermore, until that day I die,
Eternal fire I will before thee find.
And eke to this my vow I will me bind :
My beard, my hair that hangeth long adown,
That never yet hath felt offensión [28]
Of razor nor of shears, I will thee give,
And be thy truë servant while I live.
Now, lord, have ruth upon my sorrows sore,
Give me the victory, I ask no more."
The prayer stint [29] of Arcita the strong,
The ringës on the temple door that hong,
And eke the doorës, clattered full fast,
Of which Arcita somewhat was aghast.
The firës burn'd upon the altar bright,
That it gan all the temple for to light;
A sweetë smell anon the ground up gaf,[30]
And Arcita anon his hand up haf,[31]
And more incénse into the fire he cast,
With other ritës more, and at the last
The statue of Mars began his hauberk ring;
And with that sound he heard a murmuring
Full low and dim, that saidë thus, "Victóry."
For which he gave to Mars honour and glory.
And thus with joy, and hopë well to fare,
Arcite anon unto his inn doth fare,
As fain [32] as fowl is of the brightë sun.
And right anon such strife there is begun
For thilkë granting,[33] in the heav'n above,
Betwixtë Venus the goddéss of love,
And Mars the sternë god armipotent,
That Jupiter was busy it to stent : [34]

1 Strange. 2 Went out and revived. 3 Cease.
4 Those. 5 Burn. 6 Hence. 7 Quiver.
8 To what does this amount? 9 Nearest.
10 Imploring, pious. 11 Realms. 12 Held.
13 Sendest fortune at thy pleasure.
14 Pity my anguish. 15 That.
16 Didst enjoy; Latin, "utor."
17 Thou wert unlucky.
18 Net, snare; the invisible toils in which Hephæstus caught Ares and the faithless Aphrodite, and exposed them to the "inextinguishable laughter" of Olympus.
19 Lying. 20 Pity. 21 Ignorant, simple.
22 Believe. 23 Causeth. 24 Float, swim.
25 Promise, vouchsafe. 26 Cause.
27 Hang. 28 The offence, indignity.
29 Ended. 30 Arose from the ground.
31 Heaved, lifted. 32 Glad.
33 That concession of Arcite's prayer. 34 Stop.

Till that the palë Saturnus the cold,[1]
That knew so many of adventures old,
Found in his old experience such an art,
That he full soon hath pleased every part.
As sooth is said, eld[2] hath great advantage,
In eld is bothë wisdom and uságe:[3]
Men may the old out-run, but not out-rede.[4]
Saturn anon, to stint the strife and drede,
Albeit that it is against his kind,
Of all this strife gan a remédy find.
"My dearë daughter Venus," quoth Saturn,
"My course,[5] that hath so widë for to turn,
Hath morë power than wot any man.
Mine is the drowning in the sea so wan;
Mine is the prison in the darkë cote,[6]
Mine the strangling and hanging by the throat,
The murmur, and the churlish rebelling,
The groyning,[7] and the privy poisoning.
I do vengeance and plein[8] correctión,
While I dwell in the sign of the lión.
Mine is the ruin of the highë halls,
The falling of the towers and the walls
Upon the miner or the carpenter:
I slew Samson in shaking the pillar:
Mine also be the maladiës cold,
The darkë treasons, and the castës[9] old:
My looking is the father of pestilence.
Now weep no more, I shall do diligence
That Palamon, that is thine owen knight,
Shall have his lady, as thou hast him hight.[10]
Though Mars shall help his knight, yet natheless
Betwixtë you there must sometime be peace:
All be ye not of one complexión,
That each day causeth such división.
I am thine ayel,[11] ready at thy will;
Weep now no more, I shall thy lust[12] fulfil."
Now will I stenten[13] of the gods above,
Of Mars, and of Venus, goddess of love,
And tellë you as plainly as I can
The great effect, for which that I began.
Great was the feast in Athens thilkë[14] day;
And eke the lusty season of that May
Made every wight to be in such pleasance,
That all that Monday jousten they and dance,
And spenden it in Venus' high servíce.
But by the causë that they shouldë rise
Early a-morrow for to see that fight,
Unto their restë wentë they at night.
And on the morrow, when the day gan spring,
Of horse and harness[15] noise and clattering
There was in the hostelries all about:
And to the palace rode there many a rout[16]
Of lordës, upon steedës and palfreys.
There mayst thou see devising of harness
So uncouth[17] and so rich, and wrought so weel
Of goldsmithry, of brouding,[18] and of steel;
The shieldës bright, the testers,[19] and trappures;[20]
Gold-hewen helmets, hauberks, coat-armures;
Lordës in parements[21] on their courséres,
Knightës of retinue, and eke squiérs,
Nailing the spears, and helmës buckëling,
Gniding[22] of shieldës, with lainers[23] lacing;
There as need is, they werë nothing idle:
The foamy steeds upon the golden bridle
Gnawing, and fast the armourers also
With file and hammer pricking to and fro;
Yeomen on foot, and knavës[24] many one
With shortë stavës, thick as they may gon;[25]
Pipës, trumpets, nakéres,[26] and clariouns,
That in the battle blowë bloody souns;
The palace full of people up and down,
Here three, there ten, holding their questioun,[27]
Divining[28] of these Theban knightës two.
Some saiden thus, some said it shall be so;
Some helden with him with the blackë beard,
Some with the ballëd,[29] some with the thick-hair'd;
Some said he lookëd grim, and wouldë fight:
He had a sparth[30] of twenty pound of weight.
Thus was the hallë full of divining[28]
Long after that the sunnë gan up spring.
The great Theseus that of his sleep is waked
With minstrelsy, and noisë that was maked,
Held yet the chamber of his palace rich,
Till that the Theban knightës both y-lich[31]
Honoúred were, and to the palace fet.[32]
Duke Theseus is at a window set,
Array'd right as he were a god in throne:
The people presseth thitherward full soon
Him for to see, and do him reverence,
And eke to hearken his hest[33] and his sentence.[34]
An herald on a scaffold made an O,[35]
Till the noise of the people was y-do:[36]
And when he saw the people of noise all still,
Thus shewed he the mighty Dukë's will.
"The lord hath of his high discretión
Considered that it were destructión
To gentle blood, to fighten in the guise
Of mortal battle now in this emprise:
Wherefore to shapë[37] that they shall not die,
He will his firstë purpose modify.
No man therefore, on pain of loss of life,
No manner[38] shot, nor poleaxe, nor short knife
Into the lists shall send, or thither bring.
Nor short sword for to stick with point biting
No man shall draw, nor bear it by his side.
And no man shall unto his fellow ride

1 Here, as in "Mars the Red," we have the person of the deity endowed with the supposed quality of the planet called after his name.
2 Age. 3 Experience.
4 Surpass in counsel; outwit.
5 Orbit; the astrologers ascribed great power to Saturn, and predicted "much debate" under his ascendancy; hence it was "against his kind" to compose the heavenly strife.
6 Cottage, cell. 7 Discontent. 8 Full.
9 Contrivances, plots. 10 Promised.
11 Grandfather; French, "aïeul." 12 Pleasure.
13 Cease speaking. 14 That. 15 Armour.
16 Train, retinue. 17 Rare. 18 Embroidering.
19 Head-pieces, helmets; from the French, "teste," "tête," head. 20 Trappings.
21 Ornamental garb; French, "parer," to deck.
22 Rubbing, polishing; Anglo-Saxon "gnidan," to rub.
23 Thongs; compare "lanyards." 24 Servants.
25 As close as they can walk.
26 Drums, used in the cavalry: Boccaccio's word is "nachere." 27 Conversation. 28 Conjecturing.
29 Bald. 30 Double-headed axe; Latin, "bipennis."
31 Alike. 32 Fetched, brought.
33 Behest, command. 34 Discourse.
35 "Ho! ho!" to command attention; like "Oyez," the call for silence in law-courts or before proclamations.
36 Done. 37 Arrange, contrive. 38 Kind of.

But one course, with a sharp y-grounden spear:
Foin[1] if him list on foot, himself to wear.[2]
And he that is at mischief[3] shall be take,
And not slain, but be brought unto the stake,
That shall be ordained on either side;
Thither he shall by force, and there abide.
And if so fall[4] the chiefëtain be take
On either side, or ellës slay his make,[5]
No longer then the tourneying shall last.
God speedë you; go forth and lay on fast.
With long sword and with macë fight your fill.
Go now your way; this is the lordë's will."
The voice of the people touched the heaven,
So loudë criëd they with merry steven:[6]
"God savë such a lord that is so good,
He willeth no destructión of blood."
Up go the trumpets and the melody,
And to the listës rode the company
By ordinance,[7] throughout the city large,
Hanged with cloth of gold, and not with sarge.[8]
Full like a lord this noble Duke gan ride,
And these two Thebans upon either side:
And after rode the queen and Emily,
And after them another company
Of one and other, after their degree.
And thus they passed thorough that city,
And to the listës camë they by time:
It was not of the day yet fully prime.[9]
When set was Theseus full rich and high,
Hippolyta the queen, and Emily,
And other ladies in their degrees about,
Unto the seatës presseth all the rout.
And westward, through the gatës under Mart,
Arcite, and eke the hundred of his part,
With banner red, is enter'd right anon;
And in the selvë[10] moment Palamon
Is, under Venus, eastward in the place,
With banner white, and hardy cheer[11] and face.
In all the world, to seeken up and down,
So even[12] without variatioún
There were such companiës never tway.
For there was none so wise that couldë say
That any had of other ávantáge
Of worthiness, nor of estate, nor age,
So even were they chosen for to guess.
And in two ranges fairë they them dress.[13]
When that their namës read were every one,
That in their number guilë[14] were there none,
Then were the gatës shut, and cried was loud;
"Do now your dévoir, youngë knights proud!"
The heralds left their pricking[15] up and down.
Now ring the trumpet loud and clarioun.
There is no more to say, but east and west
In go the spearës sadly[16] in the rest;
In go the sharpë spurs into the side.
There see men who can joust, and who can ride.
There shiver shaftës upon shieldës thick;
He feeleth through the heartë-spoon[17] the prick.
Up spring the spearës twenty foot on height;
Out go the swordës as the silver bright.
The helmës they to-hewen, and to-shred;[18]
Out burst the blood, with sternë streamës red.
With mighty maces the bones they to-brest.[19]
He through the thickest of the throng gan threst.[20]
There stumble steedës strong, and down go all.
He rolleth under foot as doth a ball.
He foineth[21] on his foe with a trunchoun,
And he him hurtleth with his horse adown.
He through the body hurt is, and sith take,[22]
Maugré his head, and brought unto the stake,
As forword[23] was, right there he must abide.
Another led is on that other side.
And sometime doth[24] them Theseus to rest,
Them to refresh, and drinken if them lest.[25]
Full oft a day have thilkë[26] Thebans two
Together met, and wrought each other woe:
Unhorsed hath each other of them tway.[27]
There was no tiger in the vale of Galaphay,[28]
When that her whelp is stole, when it is lite,[29]
So cruel on the hunter, as Arcite
For jealous heart upon this Palamon:
Nor in Belmarie[30] there is no fell lión,
That hunted is, or for his hunger wood,[31]
Nor of his prey desireth so the blood,
As Palamon to slay his foe Arcite.
The jealous strokes upon their helmets bite;
Out runneth blood on both their sidës red,
Sometime an end there is of every deed.
For ere the sun unto the restë went,
The strongë king Emetrius gan hent[32]
This Palamon, as he fought with Arcite,
And made his sword deep in his flesh to bite,
And by the force of twenty is he take,
Unyielding, and is drawn unto the stake.
And in the rescue of this Palamon
The strongë king Licurgus is borne down:
And king Emetrius for all his strength
Is borne out of his saddle a sword's length,
So hit him Palamon ere he were take:
But all for nought; he was brought to the stake:
His hardy heartë might him helpë naught,
He must abidë, when that he was caught,
By force, and eke by compositión.[33]
Who sorroweth now but woful Palamon
That must no morë go again to fight?
And when that Theseus had seen that sight,
Unto the folk that foughtë thus each one,
He cried, "Ho! no more, for it is done!
I will be truë judge, and not party.
Arcite of Thebes shall have Emily,
That by his fortune hath her fairly won."

1 Fence, thrust. 2 Defend.
3 In peril or distress. 4 Happen.
5 His equal, match. 6 Sound.
7 In orderly array. 8 Serge, woollen cloth.
9 First quarter, between six and nine A.M.
10 Same, self-same; German, "derselbe."
11 Bold demeanour. 12 Equal.
13 Arrange themselves in two ranks or rows.
14 Fraud. 15 Spurring, riding.
16 Steadily.
17 Concave part of breast, where lower ribs join cartilago ensiformis.
18 Strike in pieces; "to" before a verb implies extraordinary violence in the action denoted.
19 Burst, shatter.
20 Push his way; "he" refers impersonally to any of the combatants. 21 Thrusteth.
22 Afterwards taken. 23 Covenant. 24 Caused.
25 Pleased. 26 Those. 27 Twice.
28 Galapha, in Mauritania. 29 Little.
30 See note 3, page 18. 31 Mad.
32 Seize, assail.
33 By the bargain, that whoever was brought to the stake, or barrier, should be out of the fight.

Anon there is a noise of people gone,
For joy of this, so loud and high withal,
It seemed that the listës shouldë fall.
What can now fairë Venus do above?
What saith she now? what doth this queen of love?
But weepeth so, for wanting of her will,
Till that her tearës in the listës fill:[1]
She said: "I am ashamed doubtëless."
Saturnus saidë: "Daughter, hold thy peace.
Mars hath his will, his knight hath all his boon,
And by mine head thou shalt be eased[2] soon."
The trumpeters with the loud minstrelsy,
The heralds, that full loudë yell and cry,
Be in their joy for weal of Dan[3] Arcite.
But hearken me, and stintë noise a lite,[4]
What a miràcle there befell anon.
This fierce Arcite hath off his helm y-done,
And on a courser for to shew his face
He pricketh endëlong[5] the largë place,
Looking upward upon this Emily;
And she again him cast a friendly eye
(For women, as to speaken in commúne,[6]
They follow all the favour of fortúne),
And was all his in cheer,[7] as his in heart.
Out of the ground a fire infernal start,
From Pluto sent, at réquest of Saturn,
For which his horse for fear began to turn,
And leap aside, and founder[8] as he leap:
And ere that Arcite may take any keep,[9]
He pight him on the pummel[10] of his head,
That in the place he lay as he were dead,
His breast to-bursten with his saddle-bow.
As black he lay as any coal or crow,
So was the blood y-run into his face.
Anon he was y-borne out of the place
With heartë sore, to Theseus' palace.
Then was he carven[11] out of his harnéss,
And in a bed y-brought full fair and blive,[12]
For he was yet in mem'ry and alive,
And always crying after Emily.
Duke Theseus, with all his company,
Is comë home to Athens his city,
With allë bliss and great solemnity.
Albeit that this áventure was fall,[13]
He wouldë not discómfortë[14] them all.
Men saíd eke, that Arcite should not die,
He should be healed of his malady.
And of another thing they were as fain,[15]
That of them allë was there no one slain,
All[16] were they sorely hurt, and namely[17] one,
That with a spear was thirled[18] his breast-bone.
To other woundës, and to broken arms,
Some hadden salvës, and some hadden charms:
And pharmacies of herbs, and ekë save[19]
They dranken, for they would their livës have.
For which this noble Duke, as he well can,
Comfórteth and honoúreth every man,
And madë revel all the longë night,
Unto the strangë lordës, as was right.
Nor there was holden no discomforting,
But as at jousts or at a tourneying;
For soothly there was no discomfiture,
For falling is not but an áventure.[20]
Nor to be led by force unto a stake
Unyielding, and with twenty knighs y-take
One person all alone, withouten mo',
And harried[21] forth by armës, foot, and toe,
And eke his steedë driven forth with staves,
With footmen, bothë yeomen and eke knaves,[22]
It was aretted[23] him no villainy:
There may no man clepen it cowardy.[24]
For which anon Duke Theseus let cry,—[25]
To stenten[26] allë rancour and envy,—
The gree[27] as well on one side as the other,
And either side alike, as other's brother:
And gave them giftës after their degree,
And held a feastë fully dayës three:
And conveyed the kingës worthily
Out of his town a journée[28] largëly.
And home went every man the rightë way,
There was no more but "Farewell, Have good day."
Of this batáille I will no more indite,
But speak of Palamon and of Arcite.
Swelleth the breast of Arcite, and the sore
Increaseth at his heartë more and more.
The clotted blood, for any leachë-craft,[29]
Corrupteth, and is in his bouk y-laft,[30]
That neither veinë-blood nor ventousing,[31]
Nor drink of herbes may be his helping.
The virtue expulsive or animal,
From thilkë virtue called natural,
Nor may the venom voidë, nor expel.
The pipës of his lungs began to swell,
And every lacert[32] in his breast adown
Is shent[33] with venom and corruptioún.
Him gaineth[34] neither, for to get his life,
Vomit upwárd, nor downward laxative;
All is to-bursten thilkë región;
Nature hath now no dominatión.
And certainly where nature will not wirch,[35]
Farewell physíc; go bear the man to chirch.[36]
This all and some is, Arcite must die.
For which he sendeth after Emily,
And Palamon, that was his cousin dear.
Then said he thus, as ye shall after hear.
"Nought may the woful spirit in mine heart
Declare one point of all my sorrows' smart
To you, my lady, that I love the most;
But I bequeath the service of my ghost[37]
To you aboven every creature,
Since that my life ne may no longer dure.
Alas the woe! alas, the painës strong
That I for you have suffered, and so long!
Alas the death! alas, mine Emily!

1 Fell. 2 Contented. 3 Lord. 4 Keep silence. 5 Rides from end to end. 6 Generally speaking. 7 Countenance, outward show. 8 Stumble. 9 Care. 10 Pitched him on the top. 11 Cut. 12 Quickly; "belive" is still used in Scotland to mean by and by, immediately. 13 Befallen. 14 Discourage. 15 Glad. 16 Although. 17 Especially. 18 Pierced. 19 The herb sage; Latin, "salvia."

20 Chance, accident. 21 Dragged, hurried. 22 Servants. 23 Imputed to him as no disgrace. 24 Call it cowardice. 25 Caused to be proclaimed. 26 Stop. 27 Prize, merit. 28 Day's journey. 29 Surgical skill. 30 Left in his body. 31 Neither opening veins nor cupping; French, "ventouser," to cup. 32 Sinew, muscle. 33 Destroyed. 34 Availeth. 35 Work. 36 Church. 37 Spirit.

Alas departing[1] of our company!
Alas, mine heartë's queen! alas, my wife!
Mine heartë's lady, ender of my life!
What is this world? what askë men to have?
Now with his love, now in his coldë grave
Alone, withouten any company.
Farewell, my sweet, farewell, mine Emily,
And softly take me in your armës tway,
For love of God, and hearken what I say.
I have here with my cousin Palamon
Had strife and rancour many a day agone,
For love of you, and for my jealousy.
And Jupiter so wis my soulë gie,[2]
To speaken of a servant properly,
With allë circumstances truëly,
That is to say, truth, honour, and knighthead,
Wisdom, humbless,[3] estate, and high kindred,
Freedom, and all that longeth to that art,
So Jupiter have of my soulë part,
As in this world right now I know not one,
So worthy to be lov'd as Palamon,
That serveth you, and will do all his life.
And if that you shall ever be a wife,
Forget not Palamon, the gentle man."
  And with that word his speech to fail began.
For from his feet up to his breast was come
The cold of death, that had him overnome.[4]
And yet moreover in his armës two
The vital strength is lost, and all ago.[5]
Only the intellect, withoutë more,
That dwelled in his heartë sick and sore,
Gan failë, when the heartë feltë death;
Dusked[6] his eyen two, and fail'd his breath.
But on his lady yet he cast his eye;
His lastë word was; "Mercy, Emily!"
His spirit changed house, and wentë there,
As I came never I cannot tell where.[7]
Therefore I stent,[8] I am no divinístor;[9]
Of soulës find I nought in this regíster.
Ne me list not th' opinions to tell
Of them, though that they writen where they dwell;
Arcite is cold, there Mars his soulë gie.[10]
Now will I speakë forth of Emily.
  Shriek'd Emily, and howled Palamon,
And Theseus his sister took anon
Swooning, and bare her from the corpse away.
What helpeth it to tarry forth the day,
To tellë how she wept both eve and morrow?
For in such cases women have such sorrow,
When that their husbands be from them y-go,[11]
That for the morë part they sorrow so,
Or ellës fall into such malady,
That at the lastë certainly they die.
Infinite be the sorrows and the tears
Of oldë folk, and folk of tender years,
In all the town, for death of this Theban:
For him there weepeth bothë child and man.
So great a weeping was there none certáin,
When Hector was y-brought, all fresh y-slain,
To Troy: alas! the pity that was there,
Scratching of cheeks, and rending eke of hair.
"Why wouldest thou be dead?" these women cry,
"And haddest gold enough, and Emily."
  No manner man might gladden Theseus,
Saving his oldë father Egeus,
That knew this worldë's transmutatioun,
As he had seen it changen up and down,
Joy after woe, and woe after gladness;
And shewed him example and likeness.
"Right as there diëd never man," quoth he,
"That he ne liv'd in earth in some degree,[12]
Right so there lived never man," he said,
"In all this world, that sometime he not died.
This world is but a throughfare full of woe,
And we be pilgrims, passing to and fro:
Death is an end of every worldly sore."
And over all this said he yet much more
To this effect, full wisely to exhort
The people, that they should them recomfórt.
  Duke Theseus, with all his busy cure,[13]
Casteth about,[14] where that the sepulture
Of good Arcite may best y-maked be,
And eke most honourable in his degree.
And at the last he took conclusión,
That there as first Arcite and Palamon
Haddë for love the battle them between,
That in that selvë[15] grovë, sweet and green,
There as he had his amorous desires,
His cómplaint, and for love his hotë fires,
He wouldë make a fire,[16] in which th' office
Of funeral he might all áccomplice;
And let anon command[17] to hack and hew
The oakës old, and lay them on a rew[18]
In culpons,[19] well arrayed for to brenne.[20]
His officers with swiftë feet they renne[21]
And ride anon at his commandëment.
And after this, Duke Theseus hath sent
After a bier, and it all oversprad
With cloth of gold, the richest that he had;
And of the samë suit he clad Arcite.
Upon his handës were his glovës white,
Eke on his head a crown of laurel green,
And in his hand a sword full bright and keen.
He laid him bare the visage[22] on the bier,
Therewith he wept, that pity was to hear.
And, for the people shouldë see him all,
When it was day he brought them to the hall,
That roareth of the crying and the soun'.[23]
Then came this woful Theban, Palamon,
With sluttery beard, and ruggy ashy hairs,[24]
In clothës black, y-dropped all with tears,
And (passing over weeping Emily)

1 The severance. 2 So surely guide my soul. 3 Humility. 4 Overtaken, overcome. 5 Gone. 6 Grew dim.
7 Went whither I cannot tell you, as I was never there.
8 Refrain. Tyrwhitt thinks that Chaucer is sneering at Boccaccio's pompous account of the passage of Arcite's soul to heaven. Up to this point, the description of the death-scene is taken literally from the "Theseida." 9 Diviner; or divine.
10 Guide. 11 Gone. 12 Rank, condition.

13 Care; Latin, "cura." 14 Deliberates. 15 Self-same. 16 A funeral pyre.
17 Caused orders straightway to be given.
18 Row. 19 Logs, pieces. 20 Well arranged to burn. 21 Run.
22 With face uncovered.
23 Made by the people who saw him lie in state.
24 With neglected beard, and rough hair strewn with ashes. "Flotery" is the general reading; but "sluttery" seems to be more in keeping with the picture of abandonment to grief.

The ruefullest of all the company.
And inasmuch as[1] the servíce should be
The more noble and rich in its degree,
Duke Theseus let forth three steedës bring,
That trapped were in steel all glittering.
And covered with the arms of Dan Arcite.
Upon these steedës, that were great and white,
There sattë folk, of whom one bare his shield,
Another his spear in his handës held;
The thirdë bare with him his bow Turkeis,[2]
Of brent[3] gold was the case[4] and the harness:
And ridë forth a pace with sorrowful cheer[5]
Toward the grove, as ye shall after hear.
The noblest of the Greekës that there were
Upon their shoulders carried the bier,
With slackë pace, and eyen red and wet,
Throughout the city, by the master street,[6]
That spread was all with black, and wondrous high
Right of the same is all the street y-wrie.[7]
Upon the right hand went old Egeus,
And on the other side Duke Theseus,
With vessels in their hand of gold full fine,
All full of honey, milk, and blood, and wine;
Eke Palamon, with a great company;
And after that came woful Emily,
With fire in hand, as was that time the guise,[8]
To do th' offíce of funeral servíce.
High labour, and full great appareling[9]
Was at the service, and the pyre-making,
That with its greenë top the heaven raught,[10]
And twenty fathom broad its armës straught:[11]
This is to say, the boughës were so broad.
Of straw first there was laid many a load.
But how the pyre was maked up on height,
And eke the namës how the treës hight,[12]
As oak, fir, birch, asp,[13] alder, holm, poplére,
Will'w, elm, plane, ash, box, chestnut, lind,[14] laurére,
Maple, thorn, beech, hazel, yew, whipul tree,
How they were fell'd, shall not be told for me;
Nor how the goddës[15] rannen up and down
Disherited of their habitatioún,
In which they wonned[16] had in rest and peace,
Nymphës, Faunës, and Hamadryadës;
Nor how the beastës and the birdës all
Fledden for fearë, when the wood gan fall;
Nor how the ground aghast[17] was of the light,
That was not wont to see the sunnë bright;
Nor how the fire was couched[18] first with stre,[19]
And then with dry stickës cloven in three,
And then with greenë wood and spicery,[20]
And then with cloth of gold and with pierrie,[21]
And garlands hanging with full many a flower,
The myrrh, the incense with so sweet odoúr;
Nor how Arcita lay among all this,
Nor what richéss about his body is;
Nor how that Emily, as was the guise,
Put in[22] the fire of funeral servíce;
Nor how she swooned when she made the fire,
Nor what she spake, nor what was her desire;
Nor what jewels men in the fire then cast
When that the fire was great and burned fast;
Nor how some cast their shield, and some their spear,
And of their vestiments, which that they wear,
And cuppës full of wine, and milk, and blood,
Into the fire, that burnt as it were wood;[23]
Nor how the Greekës with a hugë rout[24]
Three timës riden all the fire about
Upon the left hand, with a loud shouting,
And thriës with their spearës clattering;
And thriës how the ladies gan to cry;
Nor how that led was homeward Emily;
Nor how Arcite is burnt to ashes cold;
Nor how the lykë-wakë[25] was y-hold
All thilkë[26] night, nor how the Greekës play
The wakë-plays,[27] ne keep[28] I not to say:
Who wrestled best naked, with oil anoint,
Nor who that bare him best in no disjoint.[29]
I will not tell eke how they all are gone
Home to Athenës when the play is done;
But shortly to the point now will I wend,[30]
And maken of my longë tale an end.
By process and by length of certain years
All stinted[31] is the mourning and the tears
Of Greekës, by one general assent.
Then seemed me there was a parlement[32]
At Athens, upon certain points and cas:[33]
Amongës the which points y-spoken was
To have with certain countries álliánce,
And have of Thebans full obeisánce.
For which this noble Theseus anon
Let[34] send after the gentle Palamon,
Unwist[35] of him what the cause and why:
But in his blackë clothes sorrowfully
He came at his commandment on hie;[36]
Then sentë Theseus for Emily.
When they were set,[37] and hush'd was all the place
And Theseus abided[38] had a space
Ere any word came from his wisë breast

1 In order that. 2 Turkish.
3 Burnished. 4 Quiver.
5 They ride out slowly—at a foot pace—with sorrowful air.
6 Main street; so Froissart speaks of "le souverain carrefour."
7 Covered, hid; Anglo-Saxon, "wrigan," to veil.
8 Custom. 9 Preparation. 10 Reached.
11 Stretched. 12 Were called. 13 Aspen.
14 Linden, lime. 15 The forest deities. 16 Dwelt.
17 Terrified. 18 Laid. 19 Straw.
20 Spices. 21 Precious stones; French, "pierreries."
22 Applied the funeral torch. The "guise" was, among the ancients, for the nearest relative of the deceased to do this, with averted face. 23 Mad.
24 Procession. It was the custom for soldiers to march thrice around the funeral pile of an emperor or general; "on the left hand" is added, in reference to the belief that the left hand was propitious—the Roman augur turning his face southward, and so placing on his left hand the east, whence good omens came. With the Greeks, however, their augurs facing the north, it was just the contrary. The confusion, frequent in classical writers, is complicated here by the fact that Chaucer's description of the funeral of Arcite is taken from Statius' "Thebaid"—from a Roman's account of a Greek solemnity.
25 Watching by the remains of the dead; from Anglo-Saxon, "lice," a corpse; German, "Leichnam."
26 That. 27 Funeral games. 28 Care.
29 In any danger, contest. 30 Come. 31 Ended.
32 Assembly for consultation. 33 Cases, incidents.
34 Caused. 35 Unknown. 36 In haste.
37 Seated. 38 Waited.

His eyen set he there as was his lest,[1]
And with a sad viságe he sighed still,
And after that right thus he said his will.
"The firstë mover of the cause above
When he first made the fairë chain of love,
Great was th' effect, and high was his intent;
Well wist he why, and what thereof he meant:
For with that fairë chain of love he bond[2]
The fire, the air, the water, and the lond
In certain bondës, that they may not flee:[3]
That samë prince and mover eke," quoth he,
"Hath stablish'd, in this wretched world adown,
Certain of dayës and duratión
To all that are engender'd in this place,
Over the whichë day they may not pace,[4]
All[5] may they yet their dayës well abridge.
There needeth no authority to allege
For it is proved by experience;
But that me list declarë my senténce.[6]
Then may men by this order well discern,
That thilkë[7] mover stable is and etern.
Well may men know, but that it be a fool,
That every part deriveth from its whole.
For nature hath not ta'en its beginning
Of no partie nor cantle[8] of a thing,
But of a thing that perfect is and stable,
Descending so, till it be corruptáble.
And therefore of his wisë purveyance[9]
He hath so well beset[10] his ordinance,
That species of things and progressións
Shallen endurë by successións,
And not etern, withouten any lie:
This mayst thou understand and see at eye.
Lo th' oak, that hath so long a nourishing
From the time that it 'ginneth first to spring,
And hath so long a life, as ye may see,
Yet at the last y-wasted is the tree.
Consider eke, how that the hardë stone
Under our feet, on which we tread and gon,[11]
Yet wasteth, as it lieth by the way.
The broadë river some time waxeth drey.[12]
The greatë townës see we wane and wend.[13]
Then may ye see that all things have an end.
Of man and woman see we well also,
That needës in one of the termës two,—
That is to say, in youth or else in age,—
He must be dead, the king as shall a page;
Some in his bed, some in the deepë sea,
Some in the largë field, as ye may see:
There helpeth nought, all go that ilkë[14] way:
Then may I say that allë thing must die.
What maketh this but Jupiter the king?
The which is prince, and cause of allë thing,
Converting all unto his proper will,
From which it is derived, sooth to tell.
And hereagainst no creature alive,
Of no degree, availeth for to strive.

1 He fixed his eyes where it pleased him.
2 Bound.
3 Chaucer here borrows from Boethius, who says:
"Hanc rerum seriem ligat,
Terras ac pelagus regens,
Et cœlo imperitans, amor."
4 Pass. 5 Although. 6 Sentiment, opinion.
7 This same. 8 No part or piece.
9 Providence; "He" is the "first mover."
10 Arranged, ordered. 11 Walk. 12 Dry.
13 Go, disappear. 14 The same.

Then is it wisdom, as it thinketh me,
To make a virtue of necessity,
And take it well, that we may not eschew,[15]
And namëly what to us all is due.
And whoso grudgeth[16] ought, he doth folly,
And rebel is to him that all may gie.[17]
And certainly a man hath most honoúr
To dien in his excellence and flower,
When he is sicker[18] of his goodë name.
Then hath he done his friend, nor him,[19] no shame;
And gladder ought his friend be of his death,
When with honoúr is yielded up his breath,
Than when his name appalled is for age;[20]
For all forgotten is his vassalage.[21]
Then is it best, as for a worthy fame,
To dien when a man is best of name.
The contrary of all this is wilfulness.
Why grudgë we, why have we heaviness,
That good Arcite, of chivalry the flower,
Departed is, with duty and honoúr,
Out of this foulë prison of this life?
Why grudgë here his cousin and his wife
Of his welfare, that loved him so well?
Can he them thank?—nay, God wot, never a deal,—[22]
That both his soul and eke themselves offend,[23]
And yet they may their lustës not amend.[24]
What may I cónclude of this longë série,[25]
But after sorrow I rede[26] us to be merry,
And thankë Jupiter for all his grace?
And ere that we departë from this place,
I redë that we make of sorrows two
One perfect joyë lasting evermo':
And look now where most sorrow is herein,
There will I first amenden and begin.
"Sister," quoth he, "this is my full assent,
With all th' advice here of my parlement,
That gentle Palamon, your owen knight,
That serveth you with will, and heart, and might,
And ever hath, since first time ye him knew,
That ye shall of your grace upon him rue,[27]
And take him for your husband and your lord:
Lend me your hand, for this is our accord.
Let see[28] now of your womanly pity.
He is a kingë's brother's son, pardie.[29]
And though he were a poorë bachelére,
Since he hath served you so many a year,
And had for you so great adversity,
It mustë be considered, 'lieveth me.[30]
For gentle mercy oweth to passen right."[31]
Then said he thus to Palamon the knight;
"I trow there needeth little sermoning
To makë you assentë to this thing.
Come near, and take your lady by the hand."
Betwixtë them was made anon the band,
That hight matrimony or marriáge,

15 Escape, avoid. 16 Murmurs at.
17 Direct, guide. 18 Certain. 19 Himself.
20 Grown pale, decayed, by old age.
21 Valour, prowess, service. 22 Never a jot, whit.
23 Hurt.
24 Cannot control or amend their desires.
25 Series; string of remarks. 26 Counsel.
27 Have pity. 28 Make display.
29 By God. 30 Believe me.
31 Ought to be rightly directed; "oweth" is the present tense, as "ought" is the past, of "owe."

By all the counsel of the baronage.
And thus with allë bliss and melody
Hath Palamon y-wedded Emily.
And God, that all this widë world hath wrought,
Send him his love, that hath it dearly bought.
For now is Palamon in all his weal,
Living in bliss, in riches, and in heal;[1]
And Emily him loves so tenderly,
And he her serveth all so gentilly,
That never was there wordë them between
Of jealousy, nor of none other teen,[2]
Thus endeth Palamon and Emily;
And God save all this fairë company.

THE MILLER'S TALE.

THE PROLOGUE.

WHEN that the Knight had thus his talë told,
In all the rout was neither young nor old,
That he not said it was a noble story,
And worthy to be drawen to memóry;[3]
And namëly the gentles every one.[4]
Our Host then laugh'd and swore, "So may I gon,[5]
This goes aright; unbuckled is the mail;[6]
Let see now who shall tell another tale:
For truëly this game is well begun.
Now telleth ye, Sir Monk, if that ye conne,[7]
Somewhat, to quiten[8] with the Knightë's tale."
The Miller that fordrunken was all pale,[9]
So that unnethes[10] upon his horse he sat,
He would avalen[11] neither hood nor hat,
Nor abide[12] no man for his courtesy,
But in Pilatë's voice[13] he gan to cry,
And swore by armës, and by blood, and bones,
"I can a noble talë for the nones,[14]
With which I will now quite[8] the Knightë's tale."
Our Host saw well how drunk he was of ale,
And said; "Robin, abide, my levë[15] brother,
Some better man shall tell us first another:
Abide, and let us workë thriftily."[16]
"By Goddë's soul," quoth he, "that will not I,
For I will speak, or ellës go my way!"
Our Host answer'd; "Tell on a devil way;[17]
Thou art a fool; thy wit is overcome."
"Now hearken," quoth the Miller, "all and some:
But first I make a protestatioún.
That I am drunk, I know it by my soun':
And therefore if that I misspeak or say,
Wite[18] it the ale of Southwark, I you pray:
For I will tell a legend and a life
Both of a carpenter and of his wife,
How that a clerk hath set the wrightë's cap."[19]
The Reeve answér'd and saidë, "Stint thy clap,[20]
Let be thy lewëd drunken harlotry.
It is a sin, and eke a great folly
To apeiren[21] any man, or him defame,
And eke to bringë wives in evil name.
Thou may'st enough of other thingës sayn."
This drunken Miller spake full soon again,
And saidë, "Levë brother Osëwold,
Who hath no wifë, he is no cuckóld.
But I say not therefore that thou art one;
There be full goodë wivës many one.
Why art thou angry with my talë now?
I have a wife, pardie, as well as thou,
Yet n'old[22] I, for the oxen in my plough,
Taken upon me morë than enough,
To deemen[23] of myself that I am one;
I will believë well that I am none.
An husband should not be inquisitive
Of Goddë's privity, nor of his wife.
So he may findë Goddë's foison[24] there,
Of the remnant needeth not to enquére."
What should I more say, but that this Millére
He would his wordës for no man forbear,
But told his churlish[25] tale in his mannére;
Me thinketh, that I shall rehearse it here.
And therefore every gentle wight I pray,
For Goddë's love to deem not that I say
Of evil intent, but that I must rehearse
Their talës all, be they better or worse,
Or ellës falsen[26] some of my mattére.
And therefore whoso list it not to hear,
Turn o'er the leaf, and choose another tale;
For he shall find enough, both great and smale,
Of storial[27] thing that toucheth gentiless,
And eke morality and holiness.
Blamë not me, if that ye choose amiss.
The Miller is a churl, ye know well this,—
So was the Reeve, with many other mo',
And harlotry[28] they toldë bothë two.
Avise you[29] now, and put me out of blame;
And eke men should not make earnest of game.[30]

THE TALE.

Whilom there was dwelling in Oxenford
A richë gnof,[31] that guestës held to board,[32]
And of his craft he was a carpentér.
With him there was dwelling a poor scholér,
Had learned art, but all his fantasy
Was turned for to learn astrology.
He coude[33] a certain of conclusions

1 Health; German, "Heil."
2 Cause of anger, vexation. 3 Recorded.
4 All the gentler members of the company, in especial. 5 Prosper. 6 The budget is opened.
7 Know how. 8 Match, requite.
9 Was all pale with drunkenness.
10 Hardly, with difficulty. 11 Unveil, uncover.
12 Await, give way to.
13 Pilate, an unpopular personage in the mystery-plays of the middle ages, was probably represented as having a gruff, harsh voice. 14 Occasion.
15 Dear. 16 Prudently, civilly.
17 Devil take thee! an oath of impatience.
18 Blame; in Scotland, "to bear the wyte," is to bear the blame. 19 Befooled him.
20 Hold thy tongue; stop thy noisy talk, which is like the clapper of thy mill. 21 Injure, abuse.
22 Would not. 23 Judge. 24 Abundance.
25 Boorish, rude. 26 Falsify.
27 Historical, true things.
28 Ribald, rough jesting tale.
29 Consider; be advised. 30 Jest, fun.
31 Miser; perhaps from Anglo-Saxon, "gnafan," to gnaw. 32 Took in boarders. 33 Knew.

To deemë [1] by interrogations,
If that men asked him in certain hours,
When that men should have drought or ellës show'rs:
Or if men asked him what shouldë fall
Of everything, I may not reckon all.
This clerk was called Hendy [2] Nicholas;
Of dernë [3] love he knew and of solace;
And therewith he was sly and full privy,
And like a maiden meekë for to see.
A chamber had he in that hostelry
Alone, withouten any company,
Full fetisly y-dight [4] with herbës swoot,[5]
And he himself was sweet as is the root
Of liquorice, or any setewall.[6]
His Almagest,[7] and bookës great and small,
His astrolabe,[8] belonging to his art,
His augrim stonës,[9] layed fair apart
On shelvës couched [10] at his beddë's head,
His press y-cover'd with a falding [11] red.
And all above there lay a gay psalt'ry
On which he made at nightës melody,
So sweetëly, that all the chamber rang:
And *Angelus ad virginem* [12] he sang.
And after that he sung the kingë's note;
Full often blessed was his merry throat.
And thus this sweetë clerk his timë spent
After his friendës finding and his rent.[13]
This carpenter had wedded new a wife,
Which that he loved morë than his life:
Of eighteen year, I guess, she was of age.
Jealous he was, and held her narr'w in cage,
For she was wild and young, and he was old,
And deemed himself bélike [14] a cuckóld.
He knew not Cato,[15] for his wit was rude,
That bade a man wed his similitude.
Men shouldë wedden after their estate,
For youth and eld [16] are often at debate.
But since that he was fallen in the snare,
He must endure (as other folk) his care.
Fair was this youngë wife, and therewithal
As any weasel her body gent [17] and small.
A seint [18] she weared, barred all of silk,
A barm-cloth [19] eke as white as morning milk
Upon her lendës,[20] full of many a gore.[21]
White was her smock,[22] and broider'd all before,
And eke behind, on her collar about
Of coal-black silk, within and eke without.
The tapës [23] of her whitë volupere [24]
Were of the samë suit of her collére;
Her fillet broad of silk, and set full high:
And sickerly [25] she had a likerous [26] eye.
Full small y-pulled were her browës two,
And they were bent,[27] and black as any sloe.
She was well morë blissful on to see [28]
Than is the newë perjenetë [29] tree;
And softer than the wool is of a wether.
And by her girdle hung a purse of leather,
Tassel'd with silk, and pearlëd with latoun.[30]
In all this world to seeken up and down
There is no man so wise, that coudë thenche [31]
So gay a popelot,[32] or such a wench.
Full brighter was the shining of her hue,
Than in the Tower the noble [33] forged new.
But of her song, it was as loud and yern,[34]
As any swallow chittering on a bern.[35]
Thereto [36] she couldë skip, and make a game,[37]
As any kid or calf following his dame.
Her mouth was sweet as braket,[38] or as methe,[39]
Or hoard of apples, laid in hay or heath.
Wincing [40] she was as is a jolly colt,
Long as a mast, and upright as a bolt.
A brooch she bare upon her low collére,
As broad as is the boss of a bucklére.
Her shoon were laced on her leggës high;
She was a primerole,[41] a piggesnie,[42]
For any lord t' have ligging [43] in his bed,
Or yet for any good yeoman to wed.
Now, sir, and eft [44] sir, so befell the case,
That on a day this Hendy [45] Nicholas
Fell with this youngë wife to rage and play,[46]
While that her husband was at Oseney,[47]
As clerkës be full subtle and full quaint.
And privily he caught her by the queint,
And said; "Y-wis,[48] but if I have my will,
For dernë [49] love of thee, leman,[50] I spill." [51]

1 Determine. 2 Gentle, handsome.
3 Secret, earnest. 4 Neatly decked.
5 Sweet. 6 Valerian, setwall.
7 The book of Ptolemy the astronomer, which formed the canon of astrological science in the middle ages.
8 "Astrelagour," "astrelabore;" a mathematical instrument for taking the altitude of the sun or stars.
9 "Augrim" is a corruption of algorithm, the Arabian term for numeration; "augrim stones," therefore, were probably marked with numerals, and used as counters. 10 Laid, set. 11 Coarse cloth.
12 The Angel's salutation to Mary; Luke i. 28. It was the "Ave Maria" of the Catholic Church service.
13 Attending to his friends, and providing for the cost of his lodging. 14 Perhaps.
15 Though Chaucer may have referred to the famous Censor, more probably the reference is merely to the "Moral Distichs," which go under his name, though written after his time; and in a supplement to which the quoted passage may be found.
16 Age. 17 Slim, neat. 18 Girdle, with silk stripes.
19 Apron; from Anglo-Saxon "barme," bosom or lap.
20 Loins. 21 Plait, fold.
22 Not the underdress, but the robe or gown.
23 Strings.
24 Head-gear, kerchief; from French, "envelopper," to wrap up. 25 Certainly.
26 Lascivious, liquorish. 27 Arched.
28 Pleasant to look upon. 29 Young pear-tree.
30 Brass, latten, in the shape of pearls.
31 Could fancy, think of.
32 Puppet; butterfly; young wench.
33 The noble new coined in the Tower, where was the Mint; nobles were gold coins of especial purity and brightness; "Ex auro nobilissimi, unde nobilis vocatus," says Vossius.
34 Shrill, lively; German, "gern," willingly, cheerfully.
35 Barn. 36 In addition to all this. 37 Romp.
38 Bragget, a sweet drink made of honey, spices, &c. In some parts of the country, a drink made from honeycomb, after the honey is extracted, is still called "bragwort." 39 Metheglin, mead.
40 Wanton, skittish. 41 Primrose.
42 A fond term, like "my duck;" from Anglo-Saxon, "piga," a young maid; but Tyrwhitt associates it with the Latin, "ocellus," little eye, a fondling term, and suggests that the "pig's-eye," which is very small, was applied in the same sense. Davenport and Butler both use the word pigsnie, the first for "darling," the second literally for "eye;" and Bishop Gardner, "On True Obedience," in his address to the reader, says: "How softly she was wont to chirpe him under the chin, and kiss him; how prettily she could talk to him (how doth my sweet heart, what saith now pig's-eye)."
43 Lying. 44 Again.
45 Courteous. 46 Toy; play the rogue.
47 A once well-known abbey near Oxford.
48 Assuredly. 49 Earnest, cruel.
50 My mistress. 51 Die, perish.

And heldë her fast by the haunchë bones,
And saidë, "Leman, love me well at once,
Or I will dien, all so God me save."
And she sprang as a colt doth in the trave:[1]
And with her head she writhed fast away,
And said; "I will not kiss thee, by my fay.[2]
Why let be," quoth she, "let be, Nicholas,
Or I will cry out harow and alas![3]
Do away your handës, for your courtesy."
This Nicholas gan mercy for to cry,
And spake so fair, and proffer'd him so fast,
That she her love him granted at the last,
And swore her oath by Saint Thomas of Kent,
That she would be at his commandement,
When that she may her leisure well espy.
"My husband is so full of jealousy,
That but[4] ye waitë well, and be privy,
I wot right well I am but dead," quoth she.
"Ye mustë be full derne[5] as in this case."
"Nay, thereof care thee nought," quoth Nicholas:
"A clerk had litherly beset his while,[6]
But if[4] he could a carpenter beguile."
And thus they were accorded and y-sworn
To wait a time, as I have said beforn.
When Nicholas had done thus every deal,[7]
And thwacked her about the lendës well,
He kiss'd her sweet, and taketh his psalt'ry
And playeth fast, and maketh melody.
Then fell it thus, that to the parish church,
Of Christë's owen workës for to wirch,[8]
This good wife went upon a holy day:
Her forehead shone as bright as any day,
So was it washen, when she left her werk.
Now was there of that church a parish clerk,
The which that was y-cleped Absolon.
Curl'd was his hair, and as the gold it shone,
And strutted[9] as a fannë large and broad;
Full straight and even lay his jolly shode.[10]
His rode[11] was red, his eyen grey as goose,
With Paulë's windows carven[12] on his shoes.
In hosen red he went full fetisly.[13]
Y-clad he was full small and properly,
All in a kirtle[14] of a light waget;[15]
Full fair and thickë be the pointës set.
And thereupon he had a gay surplice,
As white as is the blossom on the rise.[16]
A merry child he was, so God me save;
Well could he letten blood, and clip, and shave,
And make a charter of land, and a quittance.
In twenty manners could he trip and dance,
After the school of Oxenfordë tho,[17]
And with his leggës castë to and fro;
And playen songës on a small ribible;[18]
Thereto he sung sometimes a loud quinible.[19]
And as well could he play on a gitérn.[20]
In all the town was brewhouse nor tavérn,
That he not visited with his solas,[21]
There as that any gaillard tapstere[22] was.
But sooth to say he was somedeal squaimous[23]
Of farting, and of speechë dangerous.
This Absolon, that jolly was and gay,
Went with a censer on the holy day,
Censing[24] the wivës of the parish fast;
And many a lovely look he on them cast,
And namëly[25] on this carpénter's wife:
To look on her him thought a merry life.
She was so proper, and sweet, and likerous.
I dare well say, if she had been a mouse,
And he a cat, he would her hent anon.[26]
This parish clerk, this jolly Absolon,
Hath in his heartë such a love-longing!
That of no wife took he none offering;
For courtesy he said he wouldë none.
The moon at night full clear and brightë shone,
And Absolon his gitern hath y-taken,
For paramours he thoughtë for to waken,
And forth he went, jolif[27] and amorous,
Till he came to the carpentérë's house,
A little after the cock had y-crow,
And dressed him[28] under a shot[29] window,
That was upon the carpentérë's wall.
He singeth in his voice gentle and small;
"*Now, dear lady, if thy will be,*
I pray that ye will rue[30] *on me;*"
Full well accordant to his giterning.
This carpenter awoke, and heard him sing,
And spake unto his wife, and said anon,
"What, Alison, hear'st thou not Absolon,
That chanteth thus under our bower[31] wall?"
And she answer'd her husband therewithal;
"Yes, God wot, John, I hear him every deal."
This passeth forth; what will ye bet[32] than well?
From day to day this jolly Absolon
So wooeth her, that him is woebegone.
He waketh all the night, and all the day,
To comb his lockës broad, and make him gay.
He wooeth her by means and by brocage,[33]
And swore he wouldë be her owen page.
He singeth brokking[34] as a nightingale.
He sent her piment,[35] mead, and spiced ale,
And wafers[36] piping hot out of the glede:[37]
And, for she was of town, he proffer'd meed.[38]

1 Travise; a frame in which unruly horses were shod. 2 Faith.
3 Haro! an old Norman cry for redress or aid. The "Clameur de Haro" was lately raised, under peculiar circumstances, as the prelude to a legal protest, in Jersey.
4 Unless. 5 Secret. 6 Ill spent his time.
7 Whit. 8 Work. 9 Stretched.
10 Head of hair. 11 Complexion.
12 His shoes ornamented like the windows of St Paul's, especially like the old rose-window.
13 Daintily, neatly.
14 A gown girt around the waist.
15 Sky colour.
16 Twig, bush; German, "Reis," a twig; "Reisig," a copse.
17 Then; Chaucer satirises the dancing of Oxford as he did the French of Stratford at Bow. See note 25, page 18.
18 Rebeck, a kind of fiddle.
19 Treble. 20 Guitar. 21 Mirth, sport.
22 Gay, licentious girl that served in a tavern.
23 Somewhat squeamish. 24 Burning incense for.
25 Above all. 26 Have soon caught.
27 Jolly, joyous. 28 Stationed himself.
29 Projecting or bow window, whence it was possible to shoot at any one approaching the door.
30 Take pity. 31 Chamber. 32 Better.
33 By presents and by agents, pimping, or brokerage.
34 Quavering.
35 A drink made with wine, honey, and spices.
36 Cakes. 37 Red-hot coal.
38 Because she was town-bred, he offered wealth, or money reward, for her love.

For some folk will be wonnen for richéss,
And some for strokes, and some with gentiless.
Sometimes, to show his lightness and mast'ry,
He playeth Herod [1] on a scaffold high.
But what availeth him as in this case?
So loveth she the Hendy Nicholas,
That Absolon may blow the buckë's horn: [2]
He had for all his labour but a scorn.
And thus she maketh Absolon her ape,
And all his earnest turneth to a jape.[3]
Full sooth is this provérb, it is no lie;
Men say right thus alway; the nighë sly
Maketh oft time the far lief to be loth.[4]
For though that Absolon be wood [5] or wroth
Becausë that he far was from her sight,
This nigh Nicholas stood still in his light.
Now bear thee well, thou Hendy Nicholas,
For Absolon may wail and sing "Alas!"
  And so befell, that on a Saturday
This carpenter was gone to Oseney,
And Hendy Nicholas and Alisón
Accorded were to this conclusión,
That Nicholas shall shapë him a wile [6]
The silly jealous husband to beguile;
And if so were the gamë went aright,
She shouldë sleepen in his arms all night;
For this was her desire and his also.
And right anon, withoutë wordës mo',
This Nicholas no longer would he tarry,
But doth full soft unto his chamber carry
Both meat and drinkë for a day or tway.
And to her husband bade her for to say,
If that he asked after Nicholas,
She shouldë say, "She wist [7] not where he was;
Of all the day she saw him not with eye;
She trowed [8] he was in some maladý,
For no cry that her maiden could him call
He would answer, for nought that might befall."
Thus passed forth all thilkë [9] Saturday,
That Nicholas still in his chamber lay,
And ate, and slept, and diddë what him list
Till Sunday, that the sunnë went to rest.[10]
This silly carpenter had great marvail [11]
Of Nicholas, or what thing might him ail,
And said; "I am adrad,[12] by Saint Thomas!
It standeth not aright with Nicholas:
God shieldë [13] that he died suddenly.
This world is now full tickle [14] sickerly.[15]
I saw to-day a corpse y-borne to chirch,
That now on Monday last I saw him wirch.[16]
"Go up," quod he unto his knave,[17] "anon;
Clepe [18] at his door, or knockë with a stone:
Look how it is, and tell me boldëly."
This knavë went him up full sturdily,
And, at the chamber door while that he stood,
He cried and knocked as that he were wood: [5]
"What how? what do ye, Master Nicholay?
How may ye sleepen all the longë day?"
But all for nought, he heardë not a word.
An hole he found full low upon the board,
There as [19] the cat was wont in for to creep,
And at that hole he looked in full deep,
And at the last he had of him a sight.
This Nicholas sat ever gaping upright,
As he had kyked [20] on the newë moon.
Adown he went, and told his master soon,
In what array he saw this ilkë [21] man.
  This carpenter to blissen him [22] began,
And said: "Now help us, Saintë Frideswide.[23]
A man wot [24] little what shall him betide.
This man is fall'n with his astronomy
Into some woodness [25] or some agony.
I thought aye well how that it shouldë be.
Men should know nought of Goddë's privity.[26]
Yea, blessed be alway a lewëd [27] man,
That nought but only his believë can.[28]
So far'd another clerk with astrónomý:
He walked in the fieldës for to pry
Upon [29] the starrës, what there should befall,
Till he was in a marlë pit y-fall.[30]
He saw not that. But yet, by Saint Thomas!
Me rueth sore of [31] Hendy Nicholas:
He shall be rated of his studying,[32]
If that I may, by Jesus, heaven's king!
Get me a staff, that I may underspore [33]
While that thou, Robin, heavest off the door:
He shall out of his studying, as I guess."
And to the chamber door he gan him dress.[34]
His knavë was a strong carl for the nonce,
And by the hasp [35] he heav'd it off at once;
Into the floor the door fell down anon.
This Nicholas sat aye as still as stone,
And ever he gap'd upward into the air.
The carpenter ween'd [36] he were in despair,
And hent [37] him by the shoulders mightily,
And shook him hard, and cried spitously; [38]
"What, Nicholas? what how, man? look adown:
Awake, and think on Christë's passioún.
I crouchë thee [39] from elvës, and from wights."[40]
Therewith the night-spell said he anon rights,[41]
On the four halvës [42] of the house about,
And on the threshold of the door without.
"Lord Jesus Christ, and Saintë Benedight,
Blessë this house from every wicked wight,

1 Parish-clerks, like Absolon, had leading parts in the mysteries or religious plays; Herod was one of these parts, which may have been an object of competition among the amateurs of the period.
2 "May go whistle." 3 Jest.
4 The cunning one near at hand oft makes the loving one afar off to be odious. 5 Mad.
6 Devise a stratagem. 7 Knew. 8 Believed.
9 That. 10 Till Sunday evening.
11 Wondered greatly. 12 Afraid, in dread.
13 Heaven forefend! 14 Ticklish, fickle, uncertain.
15 Surely. 16 Work. 17 Servant.
18 Call. 19 Where.
20 Looked; "keek" is still used in some parts in the sense of "peep."
21 Same. 22 To bless, cross himself.
23 Saint Frideswide, the patroness of a considerable priory at Oxford, and held there in high repute.
24 Knows. 25 Madness.
26 Secret counsel. 27 Unlearned.
28 Knows no more than his "credo."
29 Watch, keep watch on.
30 Till he fell into a marl-pit. Plato, in his "Theatetus," tells this story of Thales; but it has since appeared in many other forms.
31 I am very sorry for.
32 Chidden, rated, for his devotion to study.
33 Heave up the door by a lever beneath.
34 Apply himself.
35 Lock; from the Anglo-Saxon, "hæpsian," to lock, fasten; German, "Hespe."
36 Thought. 37 Caught. 38 Angrily.
39 Protect thee, by signing the sign of the Cross.
40 Witches, who were not of the feminine gender only.
41 In due form. 42 Corners, parts.

From the night mare, the white Pater-noster;
Where wonnest[1] thou now, Saintë Peter's sister?"
And at the last this Hendy Nicholas
Gan for to sigh full sore, and said; "Alas!
Shall all the world be lost eftsoonës [2] now?"
This carpenter answér'd; "What sayest thou?
What? think on God, as we do, men that swink."[3]
This Nicholas answer'd; "Fetch me a drink;
And after will I speak in privity
Of certain thing that toucheth thee and me:
I will tell it no other man certain."
This carpenter went down, and came again,
And brought of mighty ale a largë quart;
And when that each of them had drunk his part,
This Nicholas his chamber door fast shet,[4]
And down the carpentér by him he set,
And saidë; "John, mine host full lief [5] and dear,
Thou shalt upon thy truthë swear me here,
That to no wight thou shalt my counsel wray:[6]
For it is Christë's counsel that I say,
And if thou tell it man, thou art forlore:[7]
For this vengeance thou shalt have therefor,
That if thou wrayë [6] me, thou shalt be wood."[8]
"Nay, Christ forbid it for his holy blood!"
Quoth then this silly man; "I am no blab,[9]
Nor, though I say it, am I lief to gab.[10]
Say what thou wilt, I shall it never tell
To child or wife, by him that harried Hell."[11]
"Now, John," quoth Nicholas, "I will not lie;
I have y-found in my astrology,
As I have looked in the moonë bright,
That now on Monday next, at quarter night,
Shall fall a rain, and that so wild and wood,[8]
That never half so great was Noë's flood.
This world," he said, "in less than half an hour
Shall all be dreint,[12] so hideous is the shower:
Thus shall mankindë drench,[13] and lose their life."
This carpenter answér'd; "Alas, my wife!
And shall she drench? alas, mine Alisoún!"
For sorrow of this he fell almost adown,
And said; "Is there no remedy in this case?"
"Why, yes, for God," quoth Hendy Nicholas;
"If thou wilt worken after lore and rede;[14]
Thou may'st not worken after thine own head.
For thus saith Solomon, that was full true:
Work all by counsel, and thou shalt not rue.[15]
And if thou workë wilt by good counseil,
I undertake, withoutë mast or sail,
Yet shall I savë her, and thee, and me.
Hast thou not heard how saved was Noë,
When that our Lord had warned him beforn,
That all the world with water should be lorn?"[16]
"Yes," quoth this carpenter, "full yore ago."[17]
"Hast thou not heard," quoth Nicholas, "also
The sorrow of Noë, with his fellowship,
That he had ere he got his wife to ship?[18]
Him had been lever,[19] I dare well undertake,
At thilkë [20] time, than all his wethers black,
That she had had a ship herself alone.
And therefore know'st thou what is best to be done?
This asketh haste, and of an hasty thing
Men may not preach or makë tarrying.
Anon go get us fast into this inn[21]
A kneading trough, or else a kemelin,[22]
For each of us; but look that they be large,
In whichë we may swim as in a barge:
And have therein vitaillë suffisant
But for one day; fie on the remenant;
The water shall aslake [23] and go away
Aboutë prime [24] upon the nextë day.
But Robin may not know of this, thy knave,[25]
Nor eke thy maiden Gill I may not save:
Ask me not why: for though thou askë me
I will not tellë Goddë's privity.
Sufficeth thee, but if thy wit be mad,[26]
To have as great a grace as Noë had;
Thy wife shall I well saven out of doubt.
Go now thy way, and speed thee hereabout.
But when thou hast for her, and thee, and me,
Y-gotten us these kneading tubbës three,
Then shalt thou hang them in the roof full high,
So that no man our purveyance [27] espy:
And when thou hast done thus as I have said,
And hast our vitaille fair in them y-laid,
And eke an axe to smite the cord in two
When that the water comes, that we may go,
And break an hole on high upon the gable
Into the garden-ward, over the stable,
That we may freely passë forth our way,
When that the greatë shower is gone away.
Then shalt thou swim as merry, I undertake,
As doth the whitë duck after her drake:
Then will I clepe,[28] 'How, Alison? how, John?
Be merry: for the flood will pass anon.'
And thou wilt say, 'Hail, Master Nicholay,
Good-morrow, I see thee well, for it is day.'
And then shall we be lordës all our life
Of all the world, as Noë and his wife.
But of one thing I warnë thee full right,
Be well advised, on that ilkë [29] night,
When we be enter'd into shippë's board,
That none of us not speak a single word,
Nor clepe nor cry, but be in his prayére,
For that is Goddë's owen hestë [30] dear.
Thy wife and thou must hangen far atween,[31]
For that betwixtë you shall be no sin,

1 Dwellest. 2 Forthwith, immediately. 3 Labour. 4 Shut. 5 Loved. 6 Betray. 7 Lost; German, "verloren." 8 Mad. 9 Talker. 10 Fond of prating.
11 Wasted or subdued Hell: in the middle ages, some very active exploits against the Prince of Darkness and his powers were ascribed by the monkish tale-tellers to the Saviour after He had "descended into Hell." 12 Drenched, drowned. 13 Drown.
14 Learning and counsel. 15 Repent.
16 Should perish. 17 Long since.
18 According to the old mysteries, Noah's wife refused to come into the ark, and bade her husband row forth and get him a new wife, because he was leaving her gossips in the town to drown. Shem and his brothers got her shipped by main force; and Noah, coming forward to welcome her, was greeted with a box on the ear.
19 He would have given all his black wethers, if she had had an ark to herself. 20 That. 21 House.
22 Brewing-tub. 23 Slacken, abate.
24 Early forenoon. 25 Servant.
26 Unless thou be out of thy wits.
27 Foresight, providence. 28 Call out.
29 Same. 30 Command.
31 Asunder.

No more in looking than there shall in deed.
This ordinance is said: go, God thee speed.
To-morrow night, when men be all asleep,
Into our kneading tubbës will we creep,
And sittë there, abiding Goddë's grace.
Go now thy way, I have no longer space
To make of this no longer sermoning:
Men say thus: Send the wise, and say nothing:
Thou art so wise, it needeth thee nought teach.
Go, save our lives, and that I thee beseech."
  This silly carpenter went forth his way,
Full oft he said, "Alas! and Well-a-day!"
And to his wife he told his privity,
And she was ware, and better knew than he
What all this quaintë cast was for to say.[1]
But natheless she fear'd as she would dey,[2]
And said: "Alas! go forth thy way anon.
Help us to scape, or we be dead each one.
I am thy true and very wedded wife;
Go, dearë spouse, and help to save our life."
Lo, what a great thing is affectión!
Men may die of imaginatión,
So deeply may impressión be take.
This silly carpenter begins to quake:
He thinketh verily that he may see
This newë flood come weltering as the sea
To drenchen[3] Alison, his honey dear.
He weepeth, waileth, maketh sorry cheer;[4]
He sigheth, with full many a sorry sough.[5]
He go'th, and getteth him a kneading trough,
And after that a tub, and a kemelin,
And privily he sent them to his inn:
And hung them in the roof full privily.
With his own hand then made he ladders three,
To climbë by the ranges and the stalks[6]
Unto the tubbës hanging in the balks;[7]
And victualed them, kemelin, trough, and tub,
With bread and cheese, and good ale in a jub,[8]
Sufficing right enough as for a day.
But ere that he had made all this array,
He sent his knave, and eke his wench[9] also,
Upon his need[10] to London for to go.
And on the Monday, when it drew to night,
He shut his door withoutë candle light,
And dressed[11] every thing as it should be.
And shortly up they climbed all the three.
They sattë stillë well a furlong way.[12]
"Now, *Pater noster*, clum,"[13] said Nicholay,
And "clum," quoth John; and "clum," said Alison:
This carpenter said his devotión,
And still he sat and bidded his prayére,
Awaiting on the rain, if he it hear.
The deadë sleep, for weary business,
Fell on this carpenter, right as I guess,
About the curfew-time,[14] or little more,
For travail of his ghost[15] he groaned sore,
And eft he routed, for his head mislay.[16]
Adown the ladder stalked Nicholay;
And Alison full soft adown she sped.
Withoutë wordës more they went to bed,
There as[17] the carpenter was wont to lie:
There was the revel, and the melody.
And thus lay Alison and Nicholas,
In business of mirth and in solace,
Until the bell of *laudes*[18] gan to ring,
And friars in the chancel went to sing.
  This parish clerk, this amorous Absolon,
That is for love alway so woebegone,
Upon the Monday was at Oseney
With company, him to disport and play;
And asked upon cas[19] a cloisterer[20]
Full privily after John the carpenter;
And he drew him apart out of the church,
And said, "I n'ot;[21] I saw him not here wirch[22]
Since Saturday; I trow that he be went
For timber, where our abbot hath him sent.
For he is wont for timber for to go,
And dwellen at the Grange a day or two:
Or else he is at his own house certain.
Where that he be, I cannot soothly sayn."[23]
This Absolon full jolly was and light,
And thought, "Now is the time to wake all night,
For sickerly[24] I saw him not stirring
About his door, since day began to spring.
So may I thrive, but I shall at cock crow
Full privily go knock at his windów,
That stands full low upon his bower wall:[25]
To Alison then will I tellen all
My lovë-longing; for I shall not miss
That at the leastë way I shall her kiss.
Some manner comfort shall I have, parfay,[26]
My mouth hath itched all this livelong day:
That is a sign of kissing at the least.
All night I mette[27] eke I was at a feast.
Therefore I will go sleep an hour or tway,
And all the night then will I wake and play."
When that the first cock crowed had, anon
Up rose this jolly lover Absolon,
And him arrayed gay, at point devise.[28]
But first he chewed grains[29] and liquorice,
To smellë sweet, ere he had combed his hair.
Under his tongue a truë love[30] he bare,
For thereby thought he to be gracious.
Then came he to the carpentérë's house,
And still he stood under the shot window;

1 What all the strange contrivance meant.
2 Pretended to fear that she would die.
3 Drown.
4 A dismal countenance.
5 Groaning.
6 Rungs and uprights, or sides.
7 Beams, joists.
8 Jug, bottle.
9 His servant and serving-maid.
10 Business.
11 Prepared.
12 As long as it might take to walk a furlong.
13 "Clum," like "mum," a note of silence; but otherwise explained as the humming sound made in repeating prayers; from the Anglo-Saxon, "clumian," to mutter, speak in an under-tone, keep silence.
14 Eight in the evening, when, by the law of William the Conqueror, all people were, on ringing of a bell, to extinguish fire and candle, and go to rest; hence the word curfew, from French, "couvre-feu," cover-fire.
15 Spirit.
16 Then he snored, for his head lay awry.
17 Where.
18 Matins, or morning song, at three in the morning.
19 Occasion.
20 Cloistered monk.
21 Know not.
22 Work.
23 Say certainly.
24 Sure enough.
25 Chamber wall; the window, it has been said, projected over the door.
26 By my faith.
27 Dreamt.
28 With exact care.
29 Grains of Paris, or Paradise; a favourite spice.
30 Some sweet herb: another reading, however, is "a true love-knot," which may have been of the nature of a charm.

Unto his breast it raught,[1] it was so low;
And soft he coughed with a semisoún'.[2]
"What do ye, honeycomb, sweet Alisoún?
My fairë bird, my sweet cinamomé,[3]
Awaken, leman[4] mine, and speak to me.
Full little thinkë ye upon my woe,
That for your love I sweat there as[5] I go.
No wonder is that I do swelt[6] and sweat.
I mourn as doth a lamb after the teat.
Y-wis,[7] leman, I have such love-longíng,
That like a turtle true is my mourníng.
I may not eat, no morë than a maid."
"Go from the window, thou jack fool," she said:
"As help me God, it will not be, come ba me.[8]
I love another, else I were to blamë,
Well better than thee, by Jesus, Absolon.
Go forth thy way, or I will cast a stone;
And let me sleep; a twenty devil way."[9]
"Alas!" quoth Absolon, "and well away!
That true love ever was so ill beset:
Then kiss me, since that it may be no bet,[10]
For Jesus' love, and for the love of me."
"Wilt thou then go thy way therewith?" quoth she.
"Yea, certes, leman," quoth this Absolon.
"Then make thee ready," quoth she, "I come anon."
[And unto Nicholas she said full still:[11]
"Now peace, and thou shalt laugh anon thy fill."]
This Absolon down set him on his knees,
And said; "I am a lord at all degrees:
For after this I hope there cometh more;
Leman, thy grace, and, sweetë bird, thine ore."[12]
The window she undid, and that in haste.
"Have done," quoth she, "come off, and speed thee fast,
Lest that our neighëbours should thee espy."
Then Absolon gan wipe his mouth full dry.
Dark was the night as pitch or as the coal,
And at the window she put out her hole,
And Absolon him fell ne bet ne werse,[13]
But with his mouth he kiss'd her naked erse
Full savourly. When he was ware of this,
Aback he start, and thought it was amiss,
For well he wist a woman hath no beard.
He felt a thing all rough, and long y-hair'd,
And saidë; "Fy, alas! what have I do?"
"Te he!" quoth she, and clapt the window to;
And Absolon went forth at sorry pace.
"A beard, a beard," said Hendy Nicholas;
"By God's *corpus*, this game went fair and well."
This silly Absolon heard every deal,[14]
And on his lip he gan for anger bite;
And to himself he said, "I shall thee quite.[15]
Who rubbeth now, who frotteth[16] now his lips
With dust, with sand, with straw, with cloth, with chips,
But Absolon? that saith full oft, "Alas!
My soul betake I unto Sathanas,
But me were lever[17] than all this town," quoth he,
"Of this despite awroken[18] for to be.
Alas! alas! that I have been y-blent."[19]
His hotë love is cold, and all y-quent.[20]
For from that time that he had kiss'd her erse,
Of paramours he settë not a kers,[21]
For he was healed of his malady;
Full often paramours he gan defy,
And weep as doth a child that hath been beat.
A softë pace he went over the street
Unto a smith, men callen Dan[22] Gerveis,
That in his forgë smithed plough-harnéss;
He sharped share and culter busily.
This Absolon knocked all easily,
And said; "Undo, Gerveis, and that anon."
"What, who art thou?" "It is I, Absolon."
"What? Absolon, what? Christë's sweetë tree,[23]
Why rise so rath?[24] hey! *benedicite*,
What aileth you? some gay girl,[25] God it wote,
Hath brought you thus upon the virëtote:[26]
By Saint Neot, ye wot well what I mean."
This Absolon he raughtë[27] not a bean
Of all his play; no word again he gaf,[28]
For he had morë tow on his distaff[29]
Than Gerveis knew, and saidë; "Friend so dear,
That hotë culter in the chimney here
Lend it to me, I have therewith to don:[30]
I will it bring again to thee full soon."
Gerveis answered; "Certes, were it gold,
Or in a pokë[31] nobles all untold,
Thou shouldst it have, as I am a true smith.
Hey! Christë's foot, what will ye do therewith?"
"Thereof," quoth Absolon, "be as be may;
I shall well tell it thee another day:"
And caught the culter by the coldë stele.[32]
Full soft out at the door he gan to steal,
And went unto the carpentérë's wall.
He coughed first, and knocked therewithal
Upon the window, right as he did ere.[33]

1 Reached. 2 Low tone. 3 Cinnamon.
4 Mistress. 5 Wherever.
6 Faint, swelter; hence "sultry."
7 Certainly. 8 Come ba, or kiss, me.
9 Twenty devils fly away with thee! 10 Better.
11 In a low voice. The two lines within brackets are not in most of the editions: they are taken from Urry; whether he supplied them or not, they serve the purpose of a necessary explanation. 12 Favour.
13 Neither better nor worse befell.
14 Every word. 15 Requite, pay off, be even with.
16 Rubbeth; French, "frotter." 17 Rather.
18 Revenged; from "wreak," "awreak."
19 Deceived, befooled. 20 Quenched.
21 Cared not a rush: "kers" is the modern "cress."
22 Master.
23 Cross. 24 Early.
25 As applied to a young woman of light manners, this euphemistic phrase has enjoyed a wonderful vitality.
26 Urry reads "meritote," and explains it from Spelman as a game in which children made themselves giddy by whirling on ropes. In French, "virer" means to turn; and the explanation may, therefore, suit either reading. In modern slang parlance, Gerveis would probably have said, "on the rampage," or "on the swing"—not very far from Spelman's rendering.
27 Recked, cared. 28 Gave.
29 A proverbial saying: he was playing a deeper game, had more serious business on hand.
30 Something to do. 31 Bag.
32 Handle. 33 Before; German, "eher."

This Alison answered; "Who is there
That knocketh so? I warrant him a thief."
"Nay, nay," quoth he, "God wot, my sweetë lefe,[1]
I am thine Absolon, my own darling.
Of gold," quoth he, "I have thee brought a ring,
My mother gave it me, so God me save!
Full fine it is, and thereto well y-grave:[2]
This will I give to thee, if thou me kiss."
Now Nicholas was risen up to piss,
And thought he would amenden all the jape;[3]
He shouldë kiss his erse ere that he scape:
And up the window did he hastily,
And out his erse he put full privily
Over the buttock, to the haunchë bone.
And therewith spake this clerk, this Absolon,
"Speak, sweetë bird, I know not where thou art."
This Nicholas anon let fly a fart,
As great as it had been a thunder dent,[4]
That with the stroke he was well nigh y-blent;[5]
But he was ready with his iron hot,
And Nicholas amid the erse he smote.
Off went the skin an handbreadth all about.
The hotë culter burned so his tout,[6]
That for the smart he weened[7] he would die;
As he were wood,[8] for woe he gan to cry,
"Help! water, water, help for Goddë's heart!"
This carpenter out of his slumber start,
And heard one cry "Water," as he were wood,[8]
And thought, "Alas! now cometh Noë's flood."
He sat him up withoutë wordës mo',
And with his axe he smote the cord in two;
And down went all; he found neither to sell
Nor bread nor ale,[9] till he came to the sell,[10]
Upon the floor, and there in swoon he lay.
Up started Alison and Nicholay,
And cried out an "harow!"[11] in the street.
The neighbours allë, bothë small and great
In rannë, for to gauren[12] on this man,
That yet in swoonë lay, both pale and wan:
For with the fall he broken had his arm.
But stand he must unto his owen harm,
For when he spake, he was anon borne down
With Hendy Nicholas and Alisoún.
They told to every man that he was wood;[8]
He was aghastë[13] so of Noë's flood,
Through phantasy, that of his vanity
He had y-bought him kneading-tubbës three,
And had them hanged in the roof above;
And that he prayed them for Goddë's love
To sitten in the roof for company.
The folk gan laughen at his phantasy.
Into the roof they kyken,[14] and they gape,
And turned all his harm into a jape.[15]
For whatsoe'er this carpenter answér'd,
It was for nought, no man his reason heard.
With oathës great he was so sworn adown,
That he was holden wood in all the town.
For every clerk anon right held with other;
They said, "The man was wood, my levë[16] brother;"
And every wight gan laughen at his strife.
Thus swived[17] was the carpentérë's wife,
For all his keeping[18] and his jealousy;
And Absolon hath kiss'd her nether eye;
And Nicholas is scalded in the tout.
This tale is done, and God save all the rout.[19]

THE REEVE'S TALE.

THE PROLOGUE.

When folk had laughed all at this nice case
Of Absolon and Hendy Nicholas,
Diversë folk diversëly they said,
But for the morë part they laugh'd and play'd;[20]
And at this tale I saw no man him grieve,
But it were only Osëwold the Reeve.
Because he was of carpentérë's craft,
A little ire is in his heartë laft;[21]
He gan to grudge[22] and blamed it a lite.[23]
"So thé I,"[24] quoth he, "full well could I him quite[25]
With blearing[26] of a proudë miller's eye,
If that me list to speak of ribaldry.
But I am old; me list not play for age;[27]
Grass time is done, my fodder is now forάge.
This whitë top[28] writeth mine oldë years;
Mine heart is also moulded[29] as mine hairs;
And I do fare as doth an open-erse;[30]
That ilkë[31] fruit is ever longer werse,
Till it be rotten in mullok or in stre.[32]
We oldë men, I dread, so farë we;
Till we be rotten, can we not be ripe;
We hop[33] alway, while that the world will pipe;
For in our will there sticketh aye a nail,
To have an hoary head and a green tail,
As hath a leek; for though our might be gone,
Our will desireth folly ever-in-one:[34]
For when we may not do, then will we speak,
Yet in our ashes cold does firë reek.[35]
Four gledës[36] have we, which I shall devise,[37]
Vaunting, and lying, anger, covetíse.[38]
These fourë sparks belongen unto eld.
Our oldë limbës well may be unweld,[39]
But will shall never fail us, that is sooth.
And yet have I alway a coltë's tooth,[40]
As many a year as it is passed and gone

1 Dear, love. 2 Engraved. 3 Improve the jest.
4 Peal, clap. 5 Blinded. 6 Breech.
7 Thought. 8 Mad.
9 Found nothing to stop him.
10 Sill of the door, threshold; French, "seuil," Latin, "solum," the ground.
11 See note 3, page 49.
12 Stare. 13 Terrified.
14 Peep, look. 15 Jest. 16 Dear.
17 Enjoyed. 18 Care. 19 Company.
20 Were diverted. 21 Left. 22 Murmur.
23 Little.
24 Or "so the ik," so may I thrive.
25 Match, recompense.
26 Dimming his eye; playing off a joke on him.
27 Age takes away my zest for drollery. 28 Head.
29 Grown mouldy. 30 Medlar. 31 Same.
32 On the ground or in the straw. 33 Dance.
34 Continually.
35 Smoke. "Ev'n in our ashes live their wonted fires."
36 Glowing coals (of passion). 37 Relate, describe.
38 Covetousness. 39 Unwieldy.
40 A wanton humour, a relish for pleasure.

Since that my tap of life began to run;
For sickerly,[1] when I was born, anon
Death drew the tap of life, and let it gon:
And ever since hath so the tap y-run,
Till that almost all empty is the tun.
The stream of life now droppeth on the chimb.[2]
The silly tonguë well may ring and chime
Of wretchedness, that passed is full yore: [3]
With oldë folk, save dotage, is no more." [4]
When that our Host had heard this sermoning,
He gan to speak as lordly as a king,
And said; "To what amounteth all this wit?
What? shall we speak all day of holy writ?
The devil made a Reevë for to preach,
As of a souter [5] a shipman, or a leach.[6]
Say forth thy tale, and tarry not the time:
Lo here is Deptford, and 't is half past prime: [7]
Lo Greenwich, where many a shrew is in.
It were high time thy talë to begin."
"Now, sirs," quoth then this Osëwold the Reeve,
"I pray you all that none of you do grieve,
Though I answér, and somewhat set his hove,[8]
For lawful is force off with force to shove.[9]
This drunken miller hath y-told us here
How that beguiled was a carpentére,
Paráventure in scorn,—for I am one:
And, by your leave, I shall him quite anon.
Right in his churlish termës will I speak,—
I pray to God his neckë might to-break.
He can well in mine eyë see a stalk,[10]
But in his own he cannot see a balk."

THE TALE.[11]

At Trompington, not far from Cantebrig,[12]
There goes a brook, and over that a brig,
Upon the whichë brook there stands a mill:
And this is very sooth that I you tell.
A miller was there dwelling many a day,
As any peacock he was proud and gay:
Pipen he could, and fish, and nettës bete,[13]
And turnë cups, and wrestle well, and shete.[14]
Aye by his belt he bare a long pavade,[15]
And of his sword full trenchant was the blade.
A jolly popper [16] bare he in his pouch;
There was no man for peril durst him touch.
A Sheffield whittle bare he in his hose.
Round was his face, and camuse [17] was his nose.
As pilled [18] as an apë's was his skull.
He was a market-beter at the full.[19]
There durstë no wight hand upon him legge,[20]
That he ne swore anon he should abegge.[21]
A thief he was, for sooth, of corn and meal,
And that a sly, and used well to steal.
His name was hoten deinous Simekin.[22]
A wife he haddë, come of noble kin:
The parson of the town her father was.
With her he gave full many a pan of brass,
For that Simkin should in his blood ally.
She was y-foster'd in a nunnery:
For Simkin wouldë no wife, as he said,
But she were well y-nourish'd, and a maid,
To saven his estate and yeomanry:
And she was proud, and pert as is a pie.[23]
A full fair sight it was to see them two;
On holy days before her would he go
With his tippét [24] y-bound about his head;
And she came after in a gite [25] of red,
And Simkin haddë hosen of the same.
There durstë no wight call her aught but Dame:
None was so hardy, walking by that way,
That with her either durstë rage or play,[26]
But if [27] he would be slain by Simekin
With pavade, or with knife, or bodëkin.
For jealous folk be per'lous evermo':
Algate [28] they would their wivës wendë so.[29]
And eke for she was somewhat smutterlich,[30]
She was as dign [31] as water in a ditch,
And all so full of hoker,[32] and bismare.[33]
Her thoughtë that a lady should her spare,[34]
What for her kindred, and her nortelrie [35]
That she had learned in the nunnery.
One daughter haddë they betwixt them two
Of twenty year, withouten any mo,
Saving a child that was of half year age,
In cradle it lay, and was a proper page.[36]
This wenchë thick and well y-growen was,
With camuse nose, and eyen gray as glass;
With buttocks broad, and breastës round and high;
But right fair was her hair, I will not lie.
The parson of the town, for she was fair,[37]
In purpose was to make of her his heir
Both of his chattels and his messuage,
And strange he made it of [38] her marriáge.
His purpose was for to bestow her high
Into some worthy blood of ancestry.

1 Certainly.
2 The rim of the barrel where the staves project beyond the head.
3 Long.
4 Dotage is all that is left them; that is, they can only dwell fondly, dote, on the past.
5 Cobbler; Scotticé, "sutor;" from Latin, "suere," to sew.
6 Surgeon. "Ex sutore medicus" and "ex sutore nauclerus"—seaman or pilot—were both proverbial expressions in the Middle Ages.
7 Half-way between prime and tierce; about half-past seven in the morning.
8 Like "set their caps;" see note 21, page 23. "Hove" or "houfe," means "hood;" and the phrase signifies to be even with, outwit.
9 To repel force by force.
10 The illustration of the mote and the beam, from Matthew.
11 The incidents of this tale were much relished in the Middle Ages, and are found under various forms. Boccaccio has told them in the ninth day of his "Decameron."
12 Cambridge.
13 Prepare.
14 Shoot.
15 Poniard.
16 Dagger.
17 Flat; French, "camus," snub-nose.
18 Peeled, bald.
19 A brawler, bully, in full or open market.
20 Lay.
21 Suffer the penalty.
22 Called "Disdainful Simkin," or little Simon.
23 Magpie.
24 Hood, or head-gear.
25 Gown or coat; French, "jupe."
26 Use freedom.
27 Unless.
28 Always.
29 So behave themselves.
30 Dirty.
31 Nasty; akin to "dung."
32 Ill-nature.
33 Scandal, abusive speech.
34 Should not judge her hardly.
35 Nurturing, education.
36 Boy.
37 Because of her beauty.
38 He made it matter of consequence or difficulty.

For holy Church's good may be dispended [1]
On holy Church's blood that is descended.
Therefore he would his holy blood honoúr,
Though that he holy Churchë should devour.
Great soken [2] hath this miller, out of doubt,
With wheat and malt, of all the land about;
And namëly [3] there was a great collége
Men call the Soler Hall at Cantebrege, [4]
There was their wheat and eke their malt y-ground.
And on a day it happed in a stound, [5]
Sick lay the manciple [6] of a malady,
Men weened wisly [7] that he shouldë die.
For which this miller stole both meal and corn
An hundred timës morë than beforn.
For theretofore he stole but courteously,
But now he was a thief outrageously.
For which the warden chid and madë fare, [8]
But thereof set the miller not a tare; [9]
He crack'd his boast, [10] and swore it was not so.
Then were there youngë poorë scholars two,
That dwelled in the hall of which I say;
Testif [11] they were, and lusty for to play;
And only for their mirth and revelry
Upon the warden busily they cry,
To give them leave for but a little stound, [12]
To go to mill, and see their corn y-ground:
And hardily [13] they durstë lay their neck,
The miller should not steal them half a peck
Of corn by sleight, nor them by force bereave. [14]
And at the last the warden give them leave:
John hight the one, and Alein hight the other,
Of one town were they born, that hightë Strother, [15]
Far in the North, I cannot tell you where.
This Alein he made ready all his gear,
And on a horse the sack he cast anon:
Forth went Alein the clerk, and also John,
With good sword and with buckler by their side.
John knew the way, him needed not no guide,
And at the mill the sack adown he lay'th.
Alein spake first; "All hail, Simón, in faith,
How fares thy fairë daughter, and thy wife?"
"Alein, welcome," quoth Simkin, "by my life,
And John also: how now, what do ye here?"
"By God, Simón," quoth John, "need has no peer. [16]
Him serve himself behoves that has no swain, [17]
Or else he is a fool, as clerkës sayn.
Our manciple I hope [18] he will be dead,
So workës aye the wangës [19] in his head:
And therefore is I come, and eke Alein,
To grind our corn and carry it home again:
I pray you speed us hence as well ye may."
"It shall be done," quoth Simkin, "by my fay.
What will ye do while that it is in hand?"
"By God, right by the hopper will I stand,"
Quoth John, "and see how that the corn goes in.
Yet saw I never, by my father's kin,
How that the hopper waggës to and fro."
Alein answered, "John, and wilt thou so?
Then will I be beneathë, by my crown,
And see how that the mealë falls adown
Into the trough, that shall be my disport: [20]
For, John, in faith I may be of your sort;
I is as ill a miller as is ye."
This miller smiled at their nicéty, [21]
And thought, "All this is done but for a wile.
They weenen [22] that no man may them beguile,
But by my thrift yet shall I blear their eye, [23]
For all the sleight in their philosophy.
The morë quaintë knackës [24] that they make,
The morë will I steal when that I take.
Instead of flour yet will I give them bren. [25]
The greatest clerks are not the wisest men,
As whilom to the wolf thus spake the mare: [26]
Of all their art ne count I not a tare."
Out at the door he went full privily,
When that he saw his timë, softëly.
He looked up and down, until he found
The clerkës' horse, there as he stood y-bound
Behind the mill, under a levesell: [27]
And to the horse he went him fair and well,
And stripped off the bridle right anon.
And when the horse was loose, he gan to gon
Toward the fen, where wildë marës run,
Forth, with "Wehee!" through thick and eke through thin.
This miller went again, no word he said,
But did his note, [28] and with these clerkës play'd, [29]
Till that their corn was fair and well y-ground.
And when the meal was sacked and y-bound,
Then John went out, and found his horse away,
And gan to cry, "Harow, and well-away!
Our horse is lost: Alein, for Goddë's bones,
Step on thy feet; come off, man, all at once:
Alas! our warden has his palfrey lorn." [30]
This Alein all forgot, both meal and corn;
All was out of his mind his husbandry: [31]
"What, which way is he gone?" he gan to cry.
The wife came leaping inward at a renne, [32]
She said; "Alas! your horse went to the fen
With wildë mares, as fast as he could go.

1 Spent. 2 Toll taken for grinding; custom.
3 Especially.
4 The hall or college at Cambridge with the gallery or upper storey; supposed to have been Clare Hall.
5 Suddenly. 6 Steward; provisioner of the hall.
7 Thought certainly. 8 Ado.
9 Cared the miller not a rush. 10 Talked big.
11 Headstrong, wild-brained; French, "entêté."
12 Short time. 13 Boldly. 14 Take away.
15 Tyrwhitt points to Anstruther, in Fife: Mr Wright to the Vale of Langstroth, in the West Riding of Yorkshire. Chaucer has given the scholars a dialect that may have belonged to either district, although it more immediately suggests the more northern of the two.
16 Equal. 17 Servant. 18 Expect.
19 Grinders, cheek-teeth; Anglo-Saxon, "wang," the cheek; German, "Wange."
20 Amusement. 21 Simplicity.
22 Think. 23 See note 26, page 54.
24 Odd little tricks. 25 Bran.
26 In the "Cento Novelle Antiche," the story is told of a mule, which pretends that his name is written on the bottom of his hind foot. The wolf attempts to read it, the mule kills him with a kick in the forehead; and the fox, looking on, remarks that "every man of letters is not wise." A similar story is told in "Reynard the Fox."
27 An arbour; Anglo-Saxon, "lefe-setl," leafy seat.
28 Business; German, "Noth," necessity. 29 Jested.
30 Lost. 31 Careful watch over the corn. 32 Run.

Unthank[1] come on his hand that bound him so,
And his that better should have knit the rein."
"Alas!" quoth John, "Alein, for Christë's pain
Lay down thy sword, and I shall mine also.
I is full wight,[2] God wate,[3] as is a roe.
By Goddë's soul he shall not scape us bathe.[4]
Why n' had thou put the capel[5] in the lathe?[6]
Ill hail, Alein, by God thou is a fonne."[7]
These silly clerkës have full fast y-run
Toward the fen, both Alein and eke John;
And when the miller saw that they were gone,
He half a bushel of their flour did take,
And bade his wife go knead it in a cake.
He said; "I trow, the clerkës were afeard,
Yet can a miller make a clerkë's beard,[8]
For all his art: yea, let them go their way!
Lo where they go! yea, let the children play:
They get him not so lightly, by my crown."
These silly clerkës runnen up and down
With "Keep, keep; stand, stand; jossa,[9] warderere.
Go whistle thou, and I shall keep[10] him here."
But shortly, till that it was very night
They couldë not, though they did all their might,
Their capel catch, he ran alway so fast:
Till in a ditch they caught him at the last.
Weary and wet, as beastës in the rain,
Comes silly John, and with him comes Alein.
"Alas," quoth John, "the day that I was born!
Now are we driv'n till hething[11] and till scorn.
Our corn is stol'n, men will us fonnës[7] call,
Both the wardén, and eke our fellows all,
And namëly[12] the miller, well-away!"
Thus plained John, as he went by the way
Toward the mill, and Bayard[13] in his hand.
The miller sitting by the fire he fand.[14]
For it was night, and forther[15] might they not,
But for the love of God they him besought
Of herberow and easë,[16] for their penny.[17]
The miller said again, "If there be any,
Such as it is, yet shall ye have your part.
Mine house is strait, but ye have learned art;
Ye can by arguments maken a place
A milë broad, of twenty foot of space.
Let see now if this placë may suffice,
Or make it room with speech, as is your guise."[18]
"Now, Simon," said this John, "by Saint Cuthberd
Aye is thou merry, and that is fair answér'd.
I have heard say, man shall take of two things,
Such as he findës, or such as he brings.
But specially I pray thee, hostë dear,
Gar[19] us have meat and drink, and make us cheer,
And we shall pay thee truly at the full:
With empty hand men may not hawkës tull.[20]
Lo here our silver ready for to spend."
This miller to the town his daughter send
For ale and bread, and roasted them a goose,
And bound their horse, he should no more go loose:
And them in his own chamber made a bed,
With sheetës and with chalons[21] fair y-spread,
Not from his owen bed ten foot or twelve:
His daughter had a bed all by herselve,
Right in the samë chamber by and by:[22]
It might no better be, and causë why,—
There was no roomer herberow[23] in the place.
They suppen, and they speaken of solace,
And drinken ever strong ale at the best.
Aboutë midnight went they all to rest.
Well had this miller varnished his head;
Full pale he was, fordrunken, and nought red.[24]
He yoxed,[25] and he spake thorough the nose,
As he were in the quakke,[26] or in the pose.[27]
To bed he went, and with him went his wife,
As any jay she light was and jolife,[28]
So was her jolly whistle well y-wet.
The cradle at her beddë's feet was set,
To rock, and eke to give the child to suck.
And when that drunken was all in the crock[29]
To beddë went the daughter right anon,
To beddë went Alein, and also John.
There was no morë; needed them no dwale.[30]
This miller had so wisly[31] bibbed ale,
That as a horse he snorted in his sleep,
Nor of his tail behind he took no keep.[32]
His wife bare him a burdoun,[33] a full strong;
Men might their routing[34] hearen a furlong.
The wenchë routed eke for company.
Alein the clerk, that heard this melody,
He poked John, and saidë: "Sleepest thou?
Heardest thou ever such a song ere now?
Lo what a compline[35] is y-mell[36] them all.
A wildë fire upon their bodies fall,
Who hearken'd ever such a ferly[37] thing?
Yea, they shall have the flow'r of ill ending!
This longë night there tidës[38] me no rest.
But yet no force,[39] all shall be for the best.
For, John," said he, "as ever may I thrive,
If that I may, yon wenchë will I swive.[40]
Some easëment has law y-shapen[41] us.
For, John, there is a law that sayeth thus,
That if a man in one point be aggriev'd,

1 Ill luck, a curse. 2 Swift.
3 Knows. 4 Both; Scotticé, "baith."
5 Horse; French, "cheval;" Italian, "cavallo," from Latin, "cavallus." 6 Barn. 7 Fool.
8 Cheat a scholar; French, "faire la barbe;" and Boccaccio uses the proverb in the same sense.
9 Turn. 10 Catch, intercept; Scotticé, "kep."
11 Mockery. 12 Especially.
13 The bay horse. 14 Found.
15 Proceed on their way.
16 Lodging and entertainment.
17 Payment. 18 Fashion.
19 "Gar" is Scotch for "cause;" some editions read, however, "get us some." 20 Allure.
21 Blankets, coverlets, made at Chalons.
22 Side by side. 23 Roomier lodging.
24 Drunk, and without his wits about him.
25 Hiccuped.
26 Inarticulate sound accompanying bodily exertion.
27 Catarrh. 28 Jolly.
29 Pitcher, cruse; Anglo-Saxon, "crocca;" Germane "Krug;" hence "crockery."
30 Night-shade, *solanum somniferum*, given to caus, sleep. 31 Certainly. 32 Heed.
33 Bass; "burden" of a song. It originally means the drone of a bagpipe; French, "bourdon." 34 Snoring.
35 Even-song in the Church service; chorus.
36 Among.
37 Strange. In Scotland, a "ferlie" is an unwonted or remarkable sight. 38 Comes to me.
39 Matter. 40 Enjoy carnally.
41 Some satisfaction, pleasure, has law provided.

That in another he shall be reliev'd.
Our corn is stol'n, soothly it is no nay,
And we have had an evil fit to-day.
And since I shall have none amendëment
Against my loss, I will have easëment:
By Goddë's soul, it shall none other be:"
This John answér'd; "Alein, avisë thee:[1]
The miller is a perilous man," he said,
"And if that he out of his sleep abraid,[2]
He mightë do us both a villainy."[3]
Alein answér'd; "I count him not a fly."
And up he rose, and by the wench he crept.
This wenchë lay upright, and fast she slept,
Till he so nigh was, ere she might espy,
That it had been too latë for to cry:
And, shortly for to say, they were at one.
Now play, Alein, for I will speak of John.
  This John lay still a furlong way or two,[4]
And to himself he madë ruth[5] and woe.
"Alas!" quoth he, "this is a wicked jape;[6]
Now may I say, that I is but an ape.
Yet has my fellow somewhat for his harm;
He has the miller's daughter in his arm:
He auntred[7] him, and hath his needës sped,
And I lie as a draff-sack in my bed;
And when this jape is told another day,
I shall be held a daffe[8] or a cockenay:[9]
I will arise, and auntre it, by my fay:
Unhardy is unsely,[10] as men say."
And up he rose, and softëly he went
Unto the cradle, and in his hand it hent,[11]
And bare it soft unto his beddë's feet.
Soon after this the wife her routing lete,[12]
And gan awake, and went her out to piss,
And came again, and gan the cradle miss,
And groped here and there, but she found none.
"Alas!" quoth she, "I had almost misgone,
I had almost gone to the clerkës' bed.
Ey! *benedicite*, then had I foul y-sped."
And forth she went, till she the cradle fand.
She groped alway farther with her hand,
And found the bed, and thoughtë not but good,[13]
Becausë that the cradle by it stood,
And wist not where she was, for it was derk;
But fair and well she crept in by the clerk,
And lay full still, and would have caught a sleep.
Within a while this John the clerk up leap,
And on this goodë wife laid on full sore;
So merry a fit had she not had full yore.[14]
He pricked hard and deep, as he were mad.
  This jolly life have these two clerkës lad,
Till that the thirdë cock began to sing.
Alein wax'd weary in the morrowing,
For he had swonken[15] all the longë night,
And saidë; "Farewell, Malkin, my sweet wight.
The day is come, I may no longer bide,
But evermore, where so I go or ride,
I is thine owen clerk, so have I hele."[16]
"Now, dearë leman,"[17] quoth she, "go, farewele:
But ere thou go, one thing I will thee tell.
When that thou wendest homeward by the mill,
Right at the entry of the door behind
Thou shalt a cake of half a bushel find,
That was y-maked of thine owen meal,
Which that I help'd my father for to steal.
And, goodë leman, God thee save and keep."
And with that word she gan almost to weep.
Alein uprose and thought, "Ere the day daw
I will go creepen in by my felláw:"
And found the cradle with his hand anon.
"By God!" thought he, "all wrong I have misgone:
My head is totty of my swink[18] to-night,
That maketh me that I go not aright.
I wot well by the cradle I have misgo';
Here lie the miller and his wife also."
And forth he went a twenty devil way
Unto the bed, there as the miller lay.
He ween'd[19] t' have creeped by his fellow John,
And by the miller in he crept anon,
And caught him by the neck, and gan him shake,
And said; "Thou John, thou swinë's-head, awake
For Christë's soul, and hear a noble game!
For by that lord that called is Saint Jame,
As I have thriës in this shortë night
Swived the miller's daughter bolt-upright,
While thou hast as a coward lain aghast."[20]
  "Thou falsë harlot," quoth the miller, "hast?
Ah, falsë traitor, falsë clerk," quoth he,
"Thou shalt be dead, by Goddë's dignity,
Who durstë be so bold to disparáge[21]
My daughter, that is come of such lineáge?"
And by the throatë-ball[22] he caught Alein,
And he him hent[23] dispiteously[24] again,
And on the nose he smote him with his fist;
Down ran the bloody stream upon his breast:
And in the floor with nose and mouth all broke
They wallow, as do two pigs in a poke.
And up they go, and down again anon,
Till that the miller spurned[25] on a stone,
And down he backward fell upon his wife,
That wistë nothing of this nicë strife:
For she was fall'n asleep a little wight[26]
With John the clerk, that waked had all night:
And with the fall out of her sleep she braid.[27]
"Help, holy cross of Bromëholm,"[28] she said;
"*In manus tuas!* Lord, to thee I call.
Awake, Simón, the fiend is on me fall;
Mine heart is broken; help; I am but dead:
There li'th one on my womb and on mine head.
Help, Simkin, for these falsë clerks do fight."
This John start up as fast as e'er he might,

[1] Have a care. [2] Awaked. [3] Mischief.
[4] See note 12, page 52. [5] Wail.
[6] Trick, befooling. [7] Adventured.
[8] A coward, blockhead.
[9] A term of contempt, probably borrowed from the kitchen; a cook, in base Latin, being termed "coquinarius." Compare French "coquin," rascal.
[10] The cowardly is unlucky; "nothing venture, nothing have;" German, "unselig," unhappy.
[11] Took. [12] Left off. [13] Had no suspicion.
[14] Long. [15] Laboured. [16] Health.
[17] Sweetheart; the word was used of either sex.
[18] Giddy, tottering, with my hard work.
[19] Thought. [20] Afraid.
[21] Disgrace, do indignity to.
[22] The protuberance in the throat, called "Adam's apple." [23] Seized. [24] Angrily.
[25] Stumbled. [26] While. [27] Woke.
[28] A common adjuration at that time; the cross or rood of the priory of Bromholm, in Norfolk, was said to contain part of the real cross, and therefore held in high esteem.

And groped by the wallës to and fro
To find a staff; and she start up also,
And knew the estres[1] better than this John,
And by the wall she took a staff anon:
And saw a little shimmering of a light,
For at an hole in shone the moonë bright,
And by that light she saw them both the two,
But sickerly[2] she wist not who was who,
But as she saw a white thing in her eye.
And when she gan this whitë thing espy,
She ween'd[3] the clerk had wear'd a volupere;[4]
And with the staff she drew aye nere and nere,[5]
And ween'd to have hit this Alein at the full,
And smote the miller on the pilled[6] skull,
That down he went, and cried, "Harow! I die."
These clerkës beat him well, and let him lie,
And greithen[7] them, and take their horse anon,
And eke their meal, and on their way they gon:
And at the mill door eke they took their cake
Of half a bushel flour, full well y-bake.
Thus is the proudë miller well y-beat,
And hath y-lost the grinding of the wheat,
And payed for the supper every deal[8]
Of Alein and of John, that beat him well;
His wife is swived, and his daughter als;[9]
Lo, such it is a miller to be false.
And therefore this proverb is said full sooth,
"Him thar[10] not winnen[11] well that evil do'th;
A guiler shall himself beguiled be:"
And God that sitteth high in majesty
Save all this company, both great and smale.
Thus have I quit[12] the Miller in my tale.

THE COOK'S TALE.

THE PROLOGUE.

The Cook of London, while the Reeve thus spake,
For joy he laugh'd and clapp'd him on the back:
"Aha!" quoth he, "for Christë's passión,
This Miller had a sharp conclusión,
Upon this argument of herbergage.[13]
Well saidë Solomon in his languáge,
Bring thou not every man into thine house,
For harbouring by night is periloús.
Well ought a man avised for to be[14]
Whom that he brought into his privity.
I pray to God to give me sorrow and care
If ever, since I hightë[15] Hodge of Ware,
Heard I a miller better set a-werk;[16]
He had a jape[17] of malice in the derk.
But God forbid that we should stintë[18] here,
And therefore if ye will vouchsafe to hear
A tale of me, that am a poorë man,
I will you tell as well as e'er I can
A little jape that fell in our city."
Our Host answér'd and said; "I grant it thee.
Roger, tell on; and look that it be good,
For many a pasty hast thou letten blood,
And many a Jack of Dover[19] hast thou sold,
That had been twicë hot and twicë cold.
Of many a pilgrim hast thou Christë's curse,
For of thy parsley yet fare they the worse,
That they have eaten in thy stubble goose:
For in thy shop doth many a fly go loose.
Now tell on, gentle Roger, by thy name,
But yet I pray thee be not wroth for game;[20]
A man may say full sooth in game and play."
"Thou sayst full sooth," quoth Roger, "by my
fay;
But sooth play quad play,[21] as the Fleming saith,
And therefore, Harry Bailly, by thy faith,
Be thou not wroth, else we departë[22] here,
Though that my tale be of an hostelére.[23]
But natheless, I will not tell it yet,
But ere we part, y-wis[24] thou shalt be quit."
And therewithal he laugh'd and madë cheer,[25]
And told his tale, as ye shall after hear.

THE TALE.

A prentice whilom dwelt in our city,
And of a craft of victuallers was he:
Gaillard[26] he was, as goldfinch in the shaw,[27]
Brown as a berry, a proper short felláw:
With lockës black, combed full fetisly.[28]
And dance he could so well and jollily,
That he was called Perkin Revellour.
He was as full of love and paramour,
As is the honeycomb of honey sweet;
Well was the wenchë that with him might meet.
At every bridal would he sing and hop;
He better lov'd the tavern than the shop.
For when there any riding was in Cheap,[29]
Out of the shoppë thither would he leap,
And, till that he had all the sight y-seen,
And danced well, he would not come again;
And gather'd him a meinie of his sort,[30]
To hop and sing, and makë such disport:
And there they settë steven[31] for to meet
To playen at the dice in such a street.
For in the townë was there no prentíce
That fairer couldë cast a pair of dice
Than Perkin could; and thereto he was free
Of his dispence, in place of privity.[32]
That found his master well in his chaffare,[33]
For oftentime he found his box full bare.

1 Apartment. 2 Certainly. 3 Supposed. 4 Night-cap. 5 Nearer and nearer. 6 Bald. 7 Make ready, dress. 8 Every bit. 9 Also. 10 It behoves; from the Anglo-Saxon, "thearfian," to be obliged. 11 Gain; obtain good. 12 Made myself quits with, paid off. 13 Lodging. 14 A man should take good heed. 15 Since my name was. 16 Better handled. 17 Trick. 18 Stop. 19 An article of cookery. 20 Be not angry with my jesting. 21 True jest no jest. 22 Else we part company. 23 Innkeeper.

24 Assuredly. It may be remembered that each pilgrim was bound to tell two stories; one on the way to Canterbury, the other returning. 25 French, "fit bonne mine;" put on a pleasant countenance. 26 Lively, gay. 27 Shade, grove. 28 Daintily. 29 Cheapside, where jousts were sometimes held, and which was the great scene of city revels and processions. 30 Company of fellows like himself. 31 Made appointment. 32 And, moreover, he spent money liberally in places where he could do so without being observed. 33 Wares, merchandise.

For, soothëly, a prentice revelloúr,
That haunteth dice, riot, and paramoúr,
His master shall it in his shop abie,[1]
All[2] have he no part of the minstrelsy.
For theft and riot they be convertible,
All[2] can they play on gitern or ribible.[3]
Revel and truth, as in a low degree,
They be full wroth[4] all day, as men may see.
This jolly prentice with his master bode,
Till he was nigh out of his prenticehood,
All[2] were he snubbed[5] both early and late,
And sometimes led with revel to Newgate.
But at the last his master him bethought,
Upon a day when he his paper[6] sought,
Of a proverb, that saith this samë word;
Better is rotten apple out of hoard,
Than that it should rot all the remenánt:
So fares it by a riotous servánt;
It is well lessë harm to let him pace,[7]
Than he shend[8] all the servants in the place.
Therefore his master gave him a quittánce,
And bade him go, with sorrow and mischance.
And thus this jolly prentice had his leve:[9]
Now let him riot all the night, or leave.[10]
And, for there is no thief without a louke,[11]
That helpeth him to wasten and to souk[12]
Of that he bribë can, or borrow may,
Anon he sent his bed and his array
Unto a compere[13] of his owen sort,
That loved dice, and riot, and disport;
And had a wife, that held for countenance[14]
A shop, and swived[15] for her sustenance.
. . . . . .[16]

THE MAN OF LAW'S TALE.

THE PROLOGUE.

Our Hostë saw well that the brightë sun
Th' arc of his artificial day had run
The fourthë part, and half an hourë more;
And, though he were not deep expert in lore,
He wist it was the eight-and-twenty day
Of April, that is messenger to May;
And saw well that the shadow of every tree
Was in its length of the same quantity
That was the body erect that caused it;
And therefore by the shadow he took his wit,[17]
That Phœbus, which that shone so clear and bright,
Degrees was five-and-forty clomb on height;
And for that day, as in that latitude,
It was ten of the clock, he gan conclude;
And suddenly he plight[18] his horse about.
"Lordings," quoth he, "I warn you all this rout,[19]
The fourthë partie of this day is gone.
Now for the love of God and of Saint John
Losë no time, as farforth as ye may.
Lordings, the timë wasteth night and day,
And steals from us, what privily sleepíng,
And what through negligence in our wakíng,
As doth the stream, that turneth never again,
Descending from the mountain to the plain.
Well might Senec, and many a philosópher,
Bewailë timë more than gold in coffer.
For loss of chattels may recover'd be,
But loss of timë shendeth[20] us, quoth he.
It will not come again, withoutë dread,[21]
No morë than will Malkin's maidenhead,[22]
When she hath lost it in her wantonness.
Let us not mouldë thus in idleness.
Sir Man of Law," quoth he, "so have ye bliss,
Tell us a tale anon, as forword is.[23]
Ye be submitted through your free assent
To stand in this case at my judgëment.
Acquit you now, and holdë your behest;[24]
Then have ye done your dévoir[25] at the least."
"Hostë," quoth he, "*de par dieux jeo assente;*[26]
To breakë forword is not mine intent.
Behest is debt, and I would hold it fain,
All my behest; I can no better sayn.
For such law as a man gives another wight,
He should himselfë usen it by right.
Thus will our text: but natheless certáin
I can right now no thrifty[27] talë sayn,
But Chaucer (though he can but lewëdly[28]
On metres and on rhyming craftily)
Hath said them, in such English as he can,
Of oldë time, as knoweth many a man.
And if he have not said them, levë[29] brother,
In one book, he hath said them in another
For he hath told of lovers up and down,
More than Ovidë made of mentioun[30]
In his Epistolæ, that be full old.
Why should I tellë them, since they be told?
In youth he made of Ceyx and Alcyon,[31]

1 Suffer for. 2 Although. 3 Guitar or rebeck.
4 At variance. 5 Rebuked.
6 Certificate of completed apprenticeship.
7 Pass, go. 8 Corrupt.
9 What he loved, his desire. 10 Refrain.
11 The precise meaning of the word is unknown, but it is doubtless included in the cant term "pal."
12 Suck, consume, spend. 13 Comrade.
14 For the sake of appearances.
15 Prostituted herself.
16 The Cook's Tale is unfinished in all the manuscripts; but in some, of minor authority, the Cook is made to break off his tale, because "it is so foul," and to tell the story of Gamelyn, on which Shakespeare's "As You Like It" is founded. The story is not Chaucer's, and is different in metre, and inferior in composition to the Tales. It is supposed that Chaucer expunged the Cook's Tale for the same reason that made him on his death-bed lament that he had written so much "ribaldry."
17 Knowledge.
18 Pulled; the word is an obsolete past tense from "pluck." 19 Company.
20 Destroys. 21 Doubt.
22 A proverbial saying; which, however, had obtained fresh point from the Reeve's Tale, to which the Host doubtless refers.
23 According to our bargain.
24 Keep your promise. 25 Duty.
26 It is characteristic that the somewhat pompous Sergeant of Law should couch his assent in the semi-barbarous French, then familiar in law procedure.
27 Worthy.
28 Understands but imperfectly.
29 Dear. 30 Made mention of.
31 In the introduction to the poem called "The Dream of Chaucer;" or, "The Book of the Duchess." It relates to the death of Blanche, wife of John of Gaunt, Duke of Lancaster, the poet's patron, and afterwards his connexion by marriage.

And since then hath he spoke of every one
These noble wivës, and these lovers eke.
Whoso that will his largë volume seek
Called the Saintës' Legend of Cupíd:[1]
There may he see the largë woundës wide
Of Lucrece, and of Babylon Thisbé;
The sword of Dido for the false Enée;
The tree of Phillis for her Demophon;
The plaint of Diane, and of Hermion,
Of Ariadne, and Hypsipilé;
The barren islë standing in the sea;
The drown'd Leander for his fair Heró;
The tearës of Heléne, and eke the woe
Of Briseïs, and Laodamia;
The cruelty of thee, Queen Medeá,
Thy little children hanging by the halse,[2]
For thy Jason, that was of love so false.
O Hypermnestra, Pénelop', Alcest',
Your wifehood he commendeth with the best.
But certainly no wordë writeth he
Of thilkë wick'[3] example of Canacé,
That loved her own brother sinfully;
(Of all such cursed stories I say, Fy),
Or else of Tyrius Apollonius,
How that the cursed king Antiochus
Bereft his daughter of her maidenhead;
That is so horrible a tale to read,
When he her threw upon the pavëment.
And therefore he, of full avisëment,[4]
Would never write in none of his sermons
Of such unkind[5] abominatións;
Nor I will none rehearse, if that I may.
But of my tale how shall I do this day?
Me were loth to be liken'd doubtëless
To Muses, that men call Pieridés[6]
(*Metamorphoseos*[7] wot what I mean),
But natheless I reckë not a bean,
Though I come after him with hawëbake;[8]
I speak in prose, and let him rhymës make."
And with that word, he with a sober cheer
Began his tale, and said as ye shall hear.

THE TALE.[9]

O scatheful harm, condition of povérty,
With thirst, with cold, with hunger so confounded,
To askë help thee shameth in thine heartë;
If thou none ask, so sore art thou y-wounded,
That very need unwrappeth all thy wound hid.
Maugré thine head thou must for indigence
Or steal, or beg, or borrow thy dispence.[10]

Thou blamest Christ, and sayst full bitterly,
He misdeparteth[11] riches temporal;
Thy neighëbour thou witest[12] sinfully,
And sayst, thou hast too little, and he hath all:
"Parfay (sayst thou) sometime he reckon shall,
When that his tail shall brennen in the glede,[13]
For he not help'd the needful in their need."

Hearken what is the sentence of the wise:
Better to die than to have indigence.
Thy selvë neighëbour[14] will thee despise,
If thou be poor, farewell thy reverence.
Yet of the wisë man take this senténce,
Allë the days of poorë men be wick',[15]
Beware therefore ere thou come to that prick.[16]

If thou be poor, thy brother hateth thee,
And all thy friendës flee from thee, alas!
O richë merchants, full of wealth be ye,
O noble, prudent folk, as in this case,
Your baggës be not fill'd with ambës ace,[17]
But with six-cinque,[18] that runneth for your chance;
At Christenmass well merry may ye dance.

Ye seekë land and sea for your winníngs,
As wisë folk ye knowen all th' estate
Of regnës;[19] ye be fathers of tidings,
And talës, both of peace and of debate:[20]
I were right now of talës desolate,[21]
But that a merchant, gone in many a year,
Me taught a tale, which ye shall after hear.

In Syria whilom dwelt a company
Of chapmen rich, and thereto sad[22] and true,
That widëwherë[23] sent their spicery,
Clothës of gold, and satins rich of hue.
Their chaffare[24] was so thriftly[25] and so new,
That every wight had dainty[26] to chaffare[27]
With them, and eke to sellë them their ware.

Now fell it, that the masters of that sort
Have shapen them[28] to Romë for to wend,
Were it for chapmanhood[29] or for disport,
None other message would they thither send,
But come themselves to Rome, this is the end:
And in such place as thought them ávantage
For their intent, they took their herbergage.[30]

Sojourned have these merchants in that town

1 Now called "The Legend of Good Women." The names of eight ladies mentioned here are not in the "Legend" as it has come down to us; while those of two ladies in the "Legend"—Cleopatra and Philomela—are here omitted.

2 Neck. 3 That wicked.

4 Deliberately, advisedly. 5 Unnatural.

6 Not the Muses, who had their surname from the place near Mount Olympus where the Thracians first worshipped them; but the nine daughters of Pierus, king of Macedonia, whom he called the nine Muses, and who, being conquered in a contest with the genuine sisterhood, were changed into birds. 7 Ovid's.

8 Hawbuck, country lout; the common proverbial phrase, "to put a rogue above a gentleman," may throw light on the reading here, which is difficult.

9 This Tale is believed by Tyrwhitt to have been taken, with no material change, from the "Confessio Amantis" of John Gower, who was contemporary with Chaucer, though somewhat his senior. In the prologue, the references to the stories of Canace, and of Apollonius Tyrius, seem to be an attack on Gower, who had given those tales in his book; whence Tyrwhitt concludes that the friendship between the two poets suffered some interruption in the latter part of their lives. Gower was not the inventor of the story, which he found in old French romances; and it is not improbable that Chaucer may have gone to the same source as Gower, though the latter undoubtedly led the way.

10 Expense. 11 Allots amiss. 12 Blamest.

13 Burn in the fire.

14 That same neighbour of thine.

15 Wicked, evil. 16 Point. 17 Two aces.

18 Six-five. 19 Kingdoms.

20 Contention, war. 21 Barren, empty.

22 Grave, steadfast. 23 To distant parts.

24 Wares. 25 Cheap, advantageous.

26 To "have dainty," is to take pleasure in or esteem a thing. 27 Deal.

28 Determined, prepared. 29 Trading.

30 Lodging.

A certain time, as fell to their pleasance:
And so befell, that th' excellent renown
Of th' emperorë's daughter, Dame Constance,
Reported was, with every circumstance,
Unto these Syrian merchants in such wise,
From day to day, as I shall you devise.[1]

This was the common voice of every man:
"Our emperor of Romë, God him see,[2]
A daughter hath, that since the world began,
To reckon as well her goodness as beautý,
Was never such another as is she:
I pray to God in honour her sustene,
And would she were of all Európe the queen.

"In her is highë beauty without pride,
And youth withoutë greenhood[3] or follý:
To all her workës virtue is her guide;
Humbless hath slain in her all tyranny:
She is the mirror of all courtesy,
Her heart a very chamber of holiness,
Her hand minister of freedom for almess."[4]

And all this voice was sooth, as God is true;
But now to purpose[5] let us turn again.
These merchants have done freight[6] their shippës new,
And when they have this blissful maiden seen,
Homë to Syria then they went full fain,
And did their needës,[7] as they have done yore,[8]
And liv'd in weal;[9] I can you sáy no more.

Now fell it, that these merchants stood in grace[10]
Of him that was the Soudan[11] of Syrie:
For when they came from any strangë place
He would of his benignë courtesy
Make them good cheer, and busily espy[12]
Tidings of sundry regnës,[13] for to lear[14]
The wonders that they mightë see or hear.

Amongës other thingës, speciálly
These merchants have him told of Dame Constance'
So great nobless, in earnest so royálly,
That this Soudan hath caught so great pleasance
To have her figure in his remembránce,
That all his lust,[15] and all his busy cure,[16]
Was for to love her while his life may dure.

Paráventure in thilkë[17] largë book,
Which that men call the heaven, y-written was
With starrës, when that he his birthë took,
That he for love should have his death, alas!
For in the starrës, clearer than is glass,
Is written, God wot, whoso could it read,
The death of every man withoutë dread.[18]

In starrës many a winter therebeforn
Was writ the death of Hector, Achilles,
Of Pompey, Julius, ere they were born;
The strife of Thebes; and of Hercules,
Of Samson, Turnus, and of Socrates
The death; but mennë's wittës be so dull,
That no wight can well read it at the full.

This Soudan for his privy council sent,
And, shortly of this matter for to pace,[19]
He hath to them declared his intent,
And told them certain, but[20] he might have grace
To have Constance, within a little space,
He was but dead; and charged them in hie[21]
To shapë[22] for his life some remedy.

Diversë men diversë thingës said;
And arguments they casten up and down;
Many a subtle reason forth they laid;
They speak of magic, and abusión;[23]
But finally, as in conclusión,
They cannot see in that none ávantage,
Nor in no other way, save marriáge.

Then saw they therein such difficulty
By way of reason, for to speak all plain,
Because that there was such diversity
Between their bothë lawës, that they sayn,
They trowë[24] that no Christian prince would fain[25]
Wedden his child under our lawë sweet,
That us was given by Mahound[26] our prophéte.

And he answered: "Rather than I lose
Constance, I will be christen'd doubtëless:
I must be hers, I may none other choose,
I pray you hold your arguments in peace,[27]
Savë my life, and be not reckëless
To gettë her that hath my life in cure,[28]
For in this woe I may not long endure."

What needeth greater dilatation?
I say, by treaty and ambassadry,
And by the Popë's mediation,
And all the Church, and all the chivalry,
That in destruction of Mah'metry,[29]
And in increase of Christë's lawë dear,
They be accorded[30] so as ye may hear;

How that the Soudan, and his baronage,
And all his lieges, shall y-christen'd be,
And he shall have Constance in marriáge,
And certain gold, I n'ot[31] what quantity,
And hereto find they suffisant suretý.
The same accord is sworn on either side;
Now, fair Constance, Almighty God thee guide!

Now wouldë some men waiten, as I guess,
That I should tellen all the purveyance,[32]
The which the emperor of his nobless
Hath shapen[33] for his daughter, Dame Constance.
Well may men know that so great ordinance
May no man tellen in a little clause,
As was arrayed for so high a cause.

Bishops be shapen[33] with her for to wend,[34]
Lordës, ladíes, and knightës of renown,
And other folk enough, this is the end.
And notified is throughout all the town,
That every wight with great devotioún

1 Relate. 2 Save; look on with favour. 3 Childishness, immaturity. 4 Liberality for deeds of charity. 5 To our discourse, tale; French, "propos." 6 Caused to be laden. 7 Business. 8 Formerly. 9 Prosperity. 10 Favour. 11 Sultan. 12 Inquire. 13 Realms. 14 Learn. 15 Pleasure. 16 Care.

17 That. 18 Doubt. 19 To pass briefly by. 20 Unless. 21 Haste. 22 Contrive. 23 Deception, stratagem. 24 Believe. 25 Willingly. 26 Mahomet. 27 "Peace" rhymed with "lese" and "chese," the old forms of "lose" and "choose." 28 Keeping. 29 Mahometanism. 30 Agreed. 31 Know not. 32 Provision. 33 Prepared. 34 Go.

Should pray to Christ, that he this marriáge
Receive in gree,[1] and speedë this voyáge.

The day is comen of her départing,—
I say the woful fatal day is come,
That there may be no longer tarrying,
But forward they them dressen[2] all and some.
Constance, that was with sorrow all o'ercome,
Full pale arose, and dressed her to wend,
For well she saw there was no other end.

Alas! what wonder is it though she wept,
That shall be sent to a strange natión
From friendës, that so tenderly her kept,
And to be bound under subjectión
Of one, she knew not his conditión?
Husbands be all good, and have been of yore,[3]
That knowë wivës; I dare say no more.

"Father," she said, "thy wretched child Constance,
Thy youngë daughter, foster'd up so soft,
And you, my mother, my sov'reign pleasance
Over all thing, out-taken[4] Christ on loft,[5]
Constance your child her recommendeth oft
Unto your grace; for I shall to Syrie,
Nor shall I ever see you more with eye.

"Alas! unto the barbarous natión
I must anon, since that it is your will:
But Christ, that starf[6] for our redemptión,
So give me grace his hestës[7] to fulfil.
I, wretched woman, no force though I spill![8]
Women are born to thraldom and penánce,
And to be under mannë's governance."

I trow at Troy when Pyrrhus brake the wall,
Or Ilion burnt, or Thebes the city,
Nor at Rome for the harm through Hannibal,
That Romans hath y-vanquish'd timës three,
Was heard such tender weeping for pitý,
As in the chamber was for her partíng;
But forth she must, whether she weep or sing.

O firstë moving cruel Firmament,[9]
With thy diurnal sway that crowdest[10] aye,
And hurtlest all from East till Occident
That naturally would hold another way;
Thy crowding set the heav'n in such array
At the beginning of this fierce voyáge,
That cruel Mars hath slain this marriáge.

Unfortunate ascendant tortuous,
Of which the lord is helpless fall'n, alas!
Out of his angle into the darkest house.
O Mars, O Atyzar,[11] as in this case;
O feeble Moon, unhappy is thy pace.[12]
Thou knittest thee where thou art not receiv'd,[13]
Where thou wert well, from thennës art thou weiv'd.[14]

Imprudent emperor of Rome, alas!
Was there no philosóphen in all thy town?
Is no time bet[15] than other in such case?
Of voyage is there none electión,
Namely[16] to folk of high conditión,
Not when a root is of a birth y-know?[17]
Alas! we be too lewëd,[18] or too slow.

To ship was brought this woeful fairë maid
Solemnëly, with every circumstance:
"Now Jesus Christ be with you all," she said.
There is no more, but "Farewell, fair Constance."
She pained her[19] to make good countenance.
And forth I let her sail in this mannér,
And turn I will again to my mattér.

The mother of the Soudan, well of vices,
Espied hath her sonë's plain intent,
How he will leave his oldë sacrifices:
And right anon she for her council sent,
And they be come, to knowë what she meant,
And when assembled was this folk in fere,[20]
She sat her down, and said as ye shall hear.

"Lordës," she said, "ye knowen every one,
How that my son in point is for to lete[21]
The holy lawës of our Alkaron,[22]
Given by God's messenger Mahométe:
But one avow to greatë God I hete,[23]
Life shall rather out of my body start,
Than Mahomet's law go out of mine heart.

"What should us tiden[24] of this newë law,
But thraldom to our bodies, and penánce,
And afterward in hell to be y-draw,
For we renied Mahound our creance?[25]
But, lordës, will ye maken assurance,
As I shall say, assenting to my lore?[26]
And I shall make us safe for evermore."

They sworen and assented every man
To live with her and die, and by her stand:
And every one, in the best wise he can,
To strengthen her shall all his friendës fand.[27]
And she hath this emprise taken in hand,
Which ye shall hearë that I shall devise;[28]
And to them all she spake right in this wise.

"We shall first feign us Christendom to take;[29]
Cold water shall not grieve us but a lite:[30]
And I shall such a feast and revel make,
That, as I trow, I shall the Soudan quite.[31]
For though his wife be christen'd ne'er so white,
She shall have need to wash away the red,
Though she a fount of water with her led."

O Soudaness,[32] root of iniquity,
Virago thou, Semiramis the secónd!
O serpent under femininity,
Like to the serpent deep in hell y-bound!
O feigned woman, all that may confound

1 With good will, favour. 2 Prepare to set out.
3 Of old. 4 Except. 5 On high. 6 Died.
7 Commands. 8 No matter though I perish.
9 According to Middle Age writers there were two motions of the first heaven; one moving everything always from east to west above the stars; the other moving the stars against the first motion, from west to east, on two other poles.
10 Pushest together, drivest.
11 The meaning of this word is not known; but "occifer," murderer, has been suggested instead by Urry, on the authority of a marginal reading on a manuscript. 12 Progress.
13 Thou joinest thyself where thou art rejected, and art declined or departed from the place where thou wert well. The Moon portends the fortunes of Constance. 14 Waived, declined.
15 Better. 16 Especially.
17 When the nativity is known.
18 Ignorant. 19 Made an effort.
20 Together. 21 Forsake.
22 Koran. 23 Promise. 24 Betide, befall.
25 For denying Mahomet our belief. 26 Advice.
27 Endeavour; from Anglo-Saxon, "fandian," to try.
28 Relate. 29 To embrace Christianity.
30 Little. 31 Requite, match. 32 Sultaness.

Virtue and innocence, through thy malice,
Is bred in thee, as nest of every vice!

O Satan envious! since thilkë day
That thou wert chased from our heritage,
Well knowest thou to woman th' oldë way.
Thou madest Eve to bring us in scrvâge:[1]
Thou wilt fordo[2] this Christian marriâge:
Thine instrument so (well-away the while!)
Mak'st thou of women when thou wilt beguile.

This Soudaness, whom I thus blame and warray,[3]
Let privily her council go their way:
Why should I in this talë longer tarry?
She rode unto the Soudan on a day,
And said him, that she would reny her lay,[4]
And Christendom of priestës' handës fong,[5]
Repenting her she heathen was so long;

Beseeching him to do her that honoûr,
That she might have the Christian folk to feast:
"To pleasë them I will do my laboûr."
The Soudan said, "I will do at your hest,"[6]
And kneeling, thanked her for that request;
So glad he was, he wist[7] not what to say.
She kiss'd her son, and home she went her way.

Arrived be these Christian folk to land
In Syria, with a great solemnë rout,
And hastily this Soudan sent his sond,[8]
First to his mother, and all the realm about,
And said, his wife was comen out of doubt,
And pray'd them for to ride again[9] the queen,
The honour of his regnë[10] to sustene.

Great was the press, and rich was the array
Of Syrians and Romans met in fere.[11]
The mother of the Soudan rich and gay
Received her with all so glad a cheer[12]
As any mother might her daughter dear:
And to the nextë city there beside
A softë pace solemnëly they ride.

Nought, trow I, the triûmph of Julius,
Of which that Lucan maketh such a boast,
Was royaller, or morë curious,
Than was th' assembly of this blissful host:
But O this scorpion, this wicked ghost,[13]
The Soudaness, for all her flattering
Cast[14] under this full mortally to sting.

The Soudan came himself soon after this,
So royally, that wonder is to tell,
And welcomed her with all joy and bliss.
And thus in mirth and joy I let them dwell.
The fruit of this mattér is that I tell;
When the time came, men thought it for the best
That revel stint,[15] and men go to their rest.

The time is come that this old Soudaness
Ordained hath the feast of which I told,
And to the feast the Christian folk them dress
In general, yea, bothë young and old.

There may men feast and royalty behold,
And dainties more than I can you devise;
But all too dear they bought it ere they rise.

O sudden woe, that ev'r art successoûr
To worldly bliss! sprent[16] is with bitterness
Th' end of our joy, of our worldly laboûr:
Woe occupies the fine[17] of our gladness.
Hearken this counsel, for thy sickerness:[18]
Upon thy gladë days have in thy mind
The unware[19] woe of harm, that comes behind.

For, shortly for to tell it at a word,
The Soudan and the Christians every one
Were all to-hewn and sticked at the board,[20]
But it were only Dame Constance alone.
This oldë Soudaness, this cursed crone,
Had with her friendës done this cursed deed,
For she herself would all the country lead.

Nor there was Syrian that was converted,
That of the counsel of the Soudan wot,[21]
That was not all to-hewn, ere he asterted:[22]
And Constance have they ta'en anon foot-hot,[23]
And in a ship all steerëless,[24] God wot,
They have her set, and bid her learn to sail
Out of Syria again-ward to Itale.[25]

A certain treasure that she thither lad,[26]
And, sooth to say, of victual great plenty,
They have her giv'n, and clothës eke she had,
And forth she sailed in the saltë sea:
O my Constance, full of benignity,
O emperorë's youngë daughter dear,
He that is lord of fortune be thy steer![27]

She bless'd herself, and with full piteous voice
Unto the cross of Christ thus saidë she;
"O dear, O wealful[28] altar, holy cross,
Red of the Lambë's blood, full of pity,
That wash'd the world from old iniquity,
Me from the fiend and from his clawës keep,
That day that I shall drenchen[29] in the deep.

"Victorious tree, protection of the true,
That only worthy werë for to bear
The King of Heaven, with his woundës new,
The whitë Lamb, that hurt was with a spear;
Flemer[30] of fiendës out of him and her
On which thy limbës faithfully extend,[31]
Me keep, and give me might my life to mend."

Yearës and days floated this creature
Throughout the sea of Greece, unto the strait
Of Maroc,[32] as it was her âventure:
On many a sorry meal now may she bait,
After her death full often may she wait,[33]
Ere that the wildë wavës will her drive
Unto the place there as[34] she shall arrive.

Men mighten askë, why she was not slain?
Eke at the feast who might her body save?
And I answer to that demand again,
Who saved Daniel in the horrible cave,

1 Bondage. 2 Ruin. 3 Oppose, censure.
4 Renounce her creed, profession.
5 Take; Anglo-Saxon, "fengian;" German, "fangen."
6 Desire, command. 7 Knew. 8 Message.
9 To meet. 10 Realm. 11 In company.
12 Face. 13 Spirit. 14 Contrived. 15 Cease.
16 Sprinkled. 17 Seizes the end.
18 Security. 19 Unforeseen.

20 Cut in pieces and stabbed at table. 21 Knew.
22 Escaped. 23 Immediately, in haste.
24 Without rudder. 25 Back to Italy.
26 Led, took. 27 Rudder, guide.
28 Blessed, beneficent.
29 Drown. 30 Banisher, driver out.
31 Out of those who in faith wear the crucifix.
32 Morocco; Gibraltar. 33 Expect.
34 Where.

Where every wight, save he, master or knave,[1]
Was with the lion frett,[2] ere he astart?[3]
No wight but God, that he bare in his heart.

God list[4] to shew his wonderful mirácle
In her, that we should see his mighty workës:
Christ, which that is to every harm triácle,[5]
By certain meanës oft, as knowë clerkës,[6]
Doth thing for certain endë, that full derk is
To mannë's wit, that for our ignorance
Ne cannot know his prudent purveyance.[7]

Now since she was not at the feast y-slaw,[8]
Who keptë her from drowning in the sea?
Who keptë Jonas in the fish's maw,
Till he was spouted up at Nineveh?
Well may men know, it was no wight but he
That kept the Hebrew people from drowníng,
With dryë feet throughout the sea passing.

Who bade the fourë spirits of tempést,[9]
That power have t' annoyë land and sea,
Both north and south, and also west and east,
Annoyë neither sea, nor land, nor tree?
Soothly the cómmander of that was he
That from the tempest aye this woman kept,
As well when she awoke as when she slept.

Where might this woman meat and drinkë have?
Three year and more how lasted her vitaille?[10]
Who fed the Egyptian Mary in the cave
Or in desért? no wight but Christ *sans faille*.[11]
Five thousand folk it was as great marvaille
With loavës five and fishës two to feed:
God sent his foison[12] at her greatë need.

She drived forth into our oceán
Throughout our wildë sea, till at the last
Under an hold,[13] that nempnen[14] I not can,
Far in Northumberland, the wave her cast,
And in the sand her ship sticked so fast,
That thennës would it not in all a tide:[15]
The will of Christ was that she should abide.

The Constable of the castle down did fare[16]
To see this wreck, and all the ship he sought,[17]
And found this weary woman full of care;
He found also the treasure that she brought:
In her languágë mercy she besought,
The life out of her body for to twin,[18]
Her to deliver of woe that she was in.

A manner Latin corrupt[19] was her speech,
But algate[20] thereby was she understond.
The Constable, when him list no longer seech,[21]
This woeful woman brought he to the lond.
She kneeled down, and thanked Goddë's sond;[22]
But what she was she would to no man say
For foul nor fair, although that she should dey.[23]

She said, she was so mazed in the sea,
That she forgot her mindë, by her truth.
The Constable had of her so great pity
And eke his wifë, that they wept for ruth:[24]
She was so diligent withoutë slouth
To serve and please every one in that place,
That all her lov'd, that looked in her face.

The Constable and Dame Hermegild his wife
Were Pagans, and that country every where;
But Hermegild lov'd Constance as her life;
And Constance had so long sojourned there
In orisons, with many a bitter tear,
Till Jesus had converted through His grace
Dame Hermegild, Constábless of that place.

In all that land no Christians durstë rout;[25]
All Christian folk had fled from that countrý
Through Pagans, that conquered all about
The plages[26] of the North by land and sea.
To Wales had fled the Christianity
Of oldë Britons,[27] dwelling in this isle;
There was their refuge for the meanëwhile.

But yet n'ere[28] Christian Britons so exiled,
That there n'ere[28] some which in their privity
Honoured Christ, and heathen folk beguiled;
And nigh the castle such there dwelled three:
And one of them was blind, and might not see,
But[29] it were with thilk[30] eyen of his mind,
With which men mayë see when they be blind.

Bright was the sun, as in a summer's day,
For which the Constable, and his wife also,
And Constance, have y-take the rightë way
Toward the sea, a furlong way or two,
To playen, and to roamë to and fro;
And in their walk this blindë man they met,
Crooked and old, with eyen fast y-shet.[31]

"In the name of Christ," criéd this blind Britón,
"Dame Hermegild, give me my sight again!"
This lady wax'd afrayed of that soun',[32]
Lest that her husband, shortly for to sayn,
Would her for Jesus Christë's love have slain,
Till Constance made her bold, and bade her wirch[33]
The will of Christ, as daughter of holy Church.

The Constable wax'd abashed[34] of that sight,
And saidë; "What amounteth all this fare?"[35]
Constance answered; "Sir, it is Christ's might,
That helpeth folk out of the fiendë's snare:"
And so farforth[36] she gan our law declare,
That she the Constable, ere that it were eve,
Converted, and on Christ made him believe.

This Constable was not lord of the place
Of which I speak, there as he Constance fand,[37]
But kept it strongly many a winter space,
Under Allá, king of Northumberland,
That was full wise, and worthy of his hand

1 Servant. 2 Devoured.
3 Escaped. 4 It pleased.
5 Treacle; remedy, salve. 6 Scholars.
7 Foresight. 8 Slain.
9 The four angels who held the four winds of the earth, and to whom it was given to hurt the earth and the sea (Rev. vii. 1, 2). 10 Victuals.
11 Without fail. 12 Abundance.
13 Castle. 14 Name.
15 Thence would it not move for long, at all.
16 Go. 17 Searched. 18 Divide.
19 A kind of bastard Latin.
20 Nevertheless. 21 Search (in the ship).
22 Thanked God for what He had sent.
23 Die. 24 Pity.
25 Assemble. 26 Regions, coasts.
27 Such of the old Britons as were Christians.
28 Were not. 29 Except. 30 Those.
31 Closed, shut. 32 Was alarmed by that cry.
33 Work. 34 Astonished.
35 What means all this ado?
36 So far, with such effect. 37 Found.

Against the Scotës, as men may well hear;
But turn I will again to my mattére.

Satan, that ever us waiteth to beguile,
Saw of Constance all her perfectioún,
And cast[1] anon how he might quite her while;[2]
And made a young knight, that dwelt in that town,
Love her so hot of foul affectioún,
That verily him thought that he should spill[3]
But[4] he of her might onës have his will.

He wooed her, but it availed nought;
She wouldë do no sinnë by no way:
And for despite, he compassed his thought
To makë her a shameful death to dey;[5]
He waiteth when the Constable is away,
And privily upon a night he crept
In Hermegilda's chamber while she slept.

Weary, forwaked[6] in her orisons,
Sleepeth Constance, and Hermegild also.
This knight, through Satanas' temptatións,
All softëly is to the bed y-go,[7]
And cut the throat of Hermegild in two,
And laid the bloody knife by Dame Constance,
And went his way, there God give him mischance.

Soon after came the Constable home again,
And eke Allá that king was of that land,
And saw his wife dispiteously[8] slain,
For which full oft he wept and wrung his hand;
And in the bed the bloody knife he fand
By Dame Constance: Alas! what might she say?
For very woe her wit was all away.

To King Allá was told all this mischance,
And eke the time, and where, and in what wise,
That in a ship was founden this Constance,
As here before ye have me heard devise:[9]
The kingë's heart for pity gan agrise,[10]
When he saw so benign a creature
Fall in disease[11] and in misáventure.

For as the lamb toward his death is brought,
So stood this innocent before the king:
This falsë knight, that had this treason wrought,
Bore her in hand[12] that she had done this thing:
But natheless there was great murmuring
Among the people, that say they cannot guess
That she had done so great a wickedness.

For they had seen her ever virtuoús,
And loving Hermegild right as her life:
Of this bare witness each one in that house,
Save he that Hermegild slew with his knife:
This gentle king had caught a great motife[13]
Of this witness, and thought he would inquere
Deeper into this case, the truth to lear.[14]

Alas! Constance, thou has no champión,
Nor fightë canst thou not, so well-away!
But he that starf[15] for our redemptión,
And bound Satán, and yet li'th where he lay,[16]
So be thy strongë champion this day:
For, but Christ upon thee mirácle kithe,[17]
Withoutë guilt thou shalt be slain as swithe.[18]

She set her down on knees, and thus she said;
"Immortal God, that savedest Susanne
From falsë blame; and thou merciful maid,
Mary I mean, the daughter to Saint Anne,
Before whose child the angels sing Osanne,[19]
If I be guiltless of this felony,[20]
My succour be, or ellës shall I die."

Have ye not seen sometime a palë face
(Among a press) of him that hath been lad[21]
Toward his death, where he getteth no grace,
And such a colour in his face hath had,
Men mightë know him that was so bestad[22]
Amongës all the faces in that rout?
So stood Constance, and looked her about.

O queenës living in prosperity,
Duchesses, and ye ladies every one,
Havë some ruth[23] on her adversity!
An emperor's daughtér, she stood alone;
She had no wight to whom to make her moan.
O blood royál, that standest in this drede,[24]
Far be thy friendës in thy greatë need!

This king Allá had such compassióun,
As gentle heart is full filled of pitý,
That from his eyen ran the water down.
"Now hastily do fetch a book," quoth he;
"And if this knight will swearë, how that she
This woman slew, yet will we us advise[25]
Whom that we will that shall be our justíce."[26]

A Briton book, written with Evangiles,[27]
Was fetched, and on this book he swore anon
She guilty was; and, in the meanëwhiles,
An hand him smote upon the neckë bone,
That down he fell at once right as a stone:
And both his eyen burst out of his face
In sight of ev'rybody in that place.

A voice was heard, in general audience,
That said; "Thou hast deslander'd guiltëless
The daughter of holy Church in high presence;
Thus hast thou done, and yet hold I my peace?"[28]
Of this marvel aghast was all the press,
As mazed folk they stood every one
For dread of wreakë,[29] save Constance alone.

Great was the dread and eke the repentánce
Of them that haddë wrong suspición
Upon this sely[30] innocent Constance;
And for this miracle, in conclusión,
And by Constance's mediatión,
The king, and many another in that place,
Converted was, thanked be Christë's grace!

This falsë knight was slain for his untruth
By judgëment of Alla hastily;
And yet Constance had of his death great ruth;[31]
And after this Jesus of his mercý

1 Deliberated, contrived.
2 Repay her labour, revenge himself on her.
3 Perish.
4 Unless.
5 Die.
6 Having been long awake.
7 Gone.
8 Cruelly.
9 Describe.
10 To be grieved, to tremble.
11 Distress.
12 Accused her falsely.
13 Been greatly moved by the evidence.
14 Learn.
15 Died.
16 That lieth yet where he was laid.
17 Show.
18 Immediately.
19 Hosanna.
20 Cruelty, wickedness.
21 Led.
22 Bested, situated.
23 Pity.
24 Dread, danger.
25 Consider.
26 Judge.
27 The Gospels.
28 And shall I be silent?
29 Vengeance.
30 Simple, harmless.
31 Compassion.

Made Alla weddë full solemnëly
This holy woman, that is so bright and sheen,
And thus hath Christ y-made Constance a queen.

But who was woeful, if I shall not lie,
Of this wedding but Donegild, and no mo',
The kingë's mother, full of tyranny?
Her thought her cursed heart would burst in two;
She would not that her son had donë so;
Her thought it a despite that he should take
So strange a creature unto his make.[1]

Me list not of the chaff nor of the stre[2]
Makë so long a tale, as of the corn.
What should I tellen of the royalty
Of this marriáge, or which course goes beforn,
Who bloweth in a trump or in an horn?
The fruit of every tale is for to say;
They eat and drink, and dance, and sing, and play.

They go to bed, as it was skill[3] and right;
For though that wivës be full holy things,
They mustë take in patience at night
Such manner[4] necessaries as be pleasings
To folk that have y-wedded them with rings,
And lay a lite[5] their holiness aside
As for the time, it may no better betide.

On her he got a knavë[6] child anon,
And to a Bishop and to his Constable eke
He took his wife to keep, when he is gone
To Scotland-ward, his foemen for to seek.
Now fair Constance, that is so humble and meek,
So long is gone with childë till that still
She held her chamb'r, abiding Christë's will.

The time is come, a knavë child she bare;
Mauricius at the font-stone they him call.
This Constable doth forth come[7] a messenger,
And wrote unto his king that clep'd was All',
How that this blissful tiding is befall,
And other tidings speedful for to say.
He[8] hath the letter, and forth he go'th his way.

This messenger, to do his ávantage,[9]
Unto the kingë's mother rideth swithe,[10]
And salueth[11] her full fair in his languáge.
"Madame," quoth he, "ye may be glad and blithe,
And thankë God an hundred thousand sithe;[12]
My lady queen hath child, withoutë doubt,
To joy and bliss of all this realm about.

"Lo, here the letter sealed of this thing,
That I must bear with all the haste I may:
If ye will aught unto your son the king,
I am your servant both by night and day."
Donegild answér'd, "As now at this time, nay;
But here I will all night thou take thy rest,
To-morrow will I say thee what me lest."[13]

This messenger drank sadly[14] ale and wine,
And stolen were his letters privily
Out of his box, while he slept as a swine;
And counterfeited was full subtilly
Another letter, wrote full sinfully,
Unto the king, direct of this mattére
From his Constable, as ye shall after hear.

This letter said, the queen deliver'd was
Of so horrible a fiendlike creatúre,
That in the castle none so hardy[15] was
That any while he durst therein endure:
The mother was an elf by áventure
Become,[16] by charmës or by sorcery,
And every man hated her company.

Woe was this king when he this letter had seen,
But to no wight he told his sorrows sore,
But with his owen hand he wrote again;
"Welcome the sond[17] of Christ for evermore
To me, that am now learned in this lore:[18]
Lord, welcome be thy lust[19] and thy pleasance,
My lust I put all in thine ordinance.

"Keepë[20] this child, all be it foul or fair,
And eke my wife, unto mine homecoming:
Christ when him list may send to me an heir,
More agreeáble than this to my liking."
This letter he sealed, privily weeping,
Which to the messenger was taken soon,
And forth he went, there is no more to do'n.[21]

O messenger full fill'd of drunkenness,
Strong is thy breath, thy limbës falter aye,
And thou betrayest allë secretness;
Thy mind is lorn,[22] thou janglest as a jay;
Thy face is turned in a new array;[23]
Where drunkenness reigneth in any rout,[24]
There is no counsel hid, withoutë doubt.

O Donegild, I have none English dign[25]
Unto thy malice, and thy tyranny:
And therefore to the fiend I thee resign,
Let him indite of all thy treachery.
Fy, mannish,[26] fy! O nay, by God I lie;
Fy, fiendlike spirit! for I dare well tell,
Though thou here walk, thy spirit is in hell.

This messenger came from the king again,
And at the kingë's mother's court he light,[27]
And she was of this messenger full fain,[28]
And pleased him in all that e'er she might.
He drank, and well his girdle underpight;[29]
He slept, and eke he snored in his guise
All night, until the sun began to rise.

Eft[30] were his letters stolen every one,
And counterfeited letters in this wise:
The king commanded his Constable anon,
On pain of hanging and of high jewíse,[31]
That he should suffer in no manner wise
Constance within his regne[32] for to abide
Three dayës, and a quarter of a tide;[33]

But in the samë ship as he her fand,
Her and her youngë son, and all her gear,

1 Mate, consort. 2 Straw. 3 Reasonable. 4 Kind of. 5 Little. 6 Male; German, "Knabe," boy. 7 Caused to come forth. 8 The messenger. 9 Promote his own interest. 10 Swiftly. 11 Greets. 12 Times. 13 Pleases. 14 Steadily. 15 Bold, brave. 16 Had by ill-chance become an elf, a witch.

17 The will, sending. 18 By his conversion. 19 Will, pleasure. 20 Preserve. 21 Do. 22 Lost. 23 Aspect. 24 Company. 25 Worthy. 26 Unwomanly woman. 27 Alighted. 28 Glad. 29 Packed, stuffed his belt, stowed away liquor under his girdle. 30 Again. 31 Judgment, doom. 32 Kingdom. 33 A fourth of the time.

He shouldë put, and crowd[1] her from the land,
And charge her, that she never eft come there.
O my Constance, well may thy ghost[2] have fear,
And sleeping in thy dream be in penánce,[3]
When Donëgild cast[4] all this ordinance.[5]

This messenger, on morrow when he woke,
Unto the castle held the nextë[6] way,
And to the Constable the letter took;
And when he this dispiteous[7] letter sey,[8]
Full oft he said, "Alas, and well-away!
Lord Christ," quoth he, "how may this world endure?
So full of sin is many a creature.

"O mighty God, if that it be thy will,
Since thou art rightful judge, how may it be
That thou wilt suffer innocence to spill,[9]
And wicked folk reign in prosperity?
Ah! good Constance, alas! so woe is me,
That I must be thy tormentór, or dey[10]
A shameful death, there is no other way."

Wept bothë young and old in all that place,
When that the king this cursed letter sent;
And Constance, with a deadly palë face,
The fourthë day toward her ship she went:
But natheless she took in good intent
The will of Christ, and kneeling on the strond[11]
She saidë, "Lord, aye welcome be thy sond.[12]

"He that me keptë from the falsë blame,
While I was in the land amongës you,
He can me keep from harm and eke from shame
In the salt sea, although I see not how:
As strong as ever he was, he is yet now,
In him trust I, and in his mother dear;
That is to me my sail and eke my stere."[13]

Her little child lay weeping in her arm,
And, kneeling, piteously to him she said,
"Peace, little son, I will do thee no harm:"
With that her kerchief off her head she braid,[14]
And over his little eyen she it laid,
And in her arm she lulled it full fast,
And unto heav'n her eyen up she cast.

"Mother," quoth she, "and maiden bright, Marý,
Sooth is, that through a woman's eggement[15]
Mankind was lorn,[16] and damned aye to die;
For which thy child was on a cross y-rent:[17]
Thy blissful eyen saw all his torment,
Then is there no comparison between
Thy woe, and any woe man may sustene.

"Thou saw'st thy child y-slain before thine eyen,
And yet now lives my little child, parfay:[18]
Now, lady bright, to whom the woeful cryen,
Thou glory of womanhood, thou fairë may,[19]
Thou haven of refuge, bright star of day,
Rue[20] on my child, that of thy gentleness
Ruest on every rueful[21] in distress.

"O little child, alas! what is thy guilt,
That never wroughtest sin as yet, pardie?[22]
Why will thine hardë[23] father have thee spilt?[24]
O mercy, dearë Constable," quoth she,
"And let my little child here dwell with thee:
And if thou dar'st not savë him from blame,
So kiss him onës in his father's name."

Therewith she looked backward to the land,
And saidë, "Farewell, husband ruthëless!"[25]
And up she rose, and walked down the strand
Toward the ship, her following all the press:[26]
And ever she pray'd her child to hold his peace,
And took her leave, and with an holy intent
She blessed her, and to the ship she went.

Victualed was the ship, it is no drede,[27]
Abundantly for her a full long space:
And other necessaries that should need[28]
She had enough, heried[29] be Goddë's grace:
For wind and weather, Almighty God purchase,[30]
And bring her home; I can no better say;
But in the sea she drived forth her way.

Allá the king came home soon after this
Unto the castle, of the which I told,
And asked where his wife and his child is;
The Constable gan about his heart feel cold,
And plainly all the matter he him told
As ye have heard; I can tell it no better;
And shew'd the king his seal, and eke his letter

And saidë; "Lord, as ye commanded me
On pain of death, so have I done certáin."
The messenger tormented[31] was, till he
Mustë beknow,[32] and tell it flat and plain,
From night to night in what place he had lain;
And thus, by wit and subtle inquiring,
Imagin'd was by whom this harm gan spring.

The hand was known that had the letter wrote,
And all the venom of the cursed deed;
But in what wise, certáinly I know nót.
Th' effect is this, that Alla, out of drede,[33]
His mother slew, that may men plainly read,
For that she traitor was to her liegeánce:[34]
Thus ended oldë Donegild with mischance.

The sorrow that this Alla night and day
Made for his wife, and for his child also,
There is no tonguë that it tellë may.
But now will I again to Constance go,
That floated in the sea in pain and woe
Five year and more, as liked Christë's sond,[35]
Ere that her ship approached to the lond.[36]

Under an heathen castle, at the last,
Of which the name in my text I not find,
Constance and eke her child the sea upcast.
Almighty God, that saved all mankind,
Have on Constance and on her child some mind,
That fallen is in heathen hand eftsoon[37]
In point to spill,[38] as I shall tell you soon!

Down from the castle came there many a wight

1 Push. 2 Spirit. 3 Pain, trouble. 4 Contrived. 5 Plan, plot. 6 Nearest. 7 Cruel. 8 Saw. 9 Be destroyed. 10 Die. 11 Strand, shore. 12 Thy will; whatever Thou sendest. 13 Rudder; guide. 14 Took, drew. 15 Incitement, egging on. 16 Lost. 17 Torn, pierced. 18 By my faith. 19 Maid. 20 Take pity. 21 Sorrowful. 22 Par Dieu; by God.

23 Cruel, stern. 24 Destroyed. 25 Pitiless. 26 Multitude. 27 Doubt. 28 Be needed. 29 Honoured, praised; from Anglo-Saxon, "herian." Compare German, "herrlich," glorious, honourable. 30 Provide. 31 Tortured. 32 Confess; German, "bekennen." 33 Doubt. 34 Allegiance. 35 Decree, command. 36 Land. 37 Again. 38 In danger of perishing.

To gauren [1] on this ship, and on Constance:
But shortly from the castle, on a night,
The lordë's steward,—God give him mischance,—
A thief that had renied our creance,[2]
Came to the ship alone, and said he would
Her leman [3] be, whether she would or n'ould.[4]

Woe was this wretched woman then begone;
Her child cri'd, and she cried piteously:
But blissful Mary help'd her right anon,
For, with her struggling well and mightily,
The thief fell overboard all suddenly,
And in the sea he drenched [5] for vengeánce,
And thus hath Christ unwemmed [6] kept Constánce.

O foul lust of luxúry! lo thine end!
Not only that thou faintest [7] mannë's mind,
But verily thou wilt his body shend.[8]
Th' end of thy work, or of thy lustës blind,
Is cómplaining: how many may men find,
That not for work, sometimes, but for th' intent
To do this sin, be either slain or shent?

How may this weakë woman have the strength
Her to defend against this renegate?
O Góliath, unmeasurable of length,
How mightë David makë thee so mate? [9]
So young, and of armoúr so desolate,[10]
How durst he look upon thy dreadful face?
Well may men see it was but Goddë's grace.

Who gave Judith couráge or hardiness
To slay him, Holofernes, in his tent,
And to deliver out of wretchedness
The people of God? I say for this intent,
That right as God spirit of vigour sent
To them, and saved them out of mischance,
So sent he might and vigour to Constance.

Forth went her ship throughout the narrow mouth
Of Jubaltare and Septe,[11] driving alway,
Sometimë west, and sometime north and south,
And sometime east, full many a weary day:
Till Christë's mother (blessed be she aye)
Had shapen [12] through her endëless goodness
To make an end of all her heaviness.

Now let us stint of Constance but a throw,[13]
And speak we of the Roman emperor,
That out of Syria had by letters know
The slaughter of Christian folk, and dishonór
Done to his daughter by a false traitór,—
I mean the cursed wicked Soudaness,
That at the feast let [14] slay both more and less.

For which this emperor had sent anon
His senator, with royal ordinance,
And other lordës, God wot, many a one,
On Syrians to takë high vengeánce:
They burn and slay, and bring them to mischance
Full many a day: but shortly this is th' end,
Homeward to Rome they shaped them to wend.

This senator repaired with victóry
To Romë-ward, sailing full royally,
And met the ship driving, as saith the story,
In which Constancë sat full piteously:
And nothing knew he what she was, nor why
She was in such array; nor she will say
Of her estate, although that she should dey.[15]

He brought her unto Rome, and to his wife
He gave her, and her youngë son also:
And with the senator she led her life.
Thus can our Lady bringen out of woe
Woeful Constance, and many another mo':
And longë time she dwelled in that place,
In holy works ever, as was her grace.

The senatorë's wife her auntë was,
But for all that she knew her ne'er the more:
I will no longer tarry in this case,
But to King Alla, whom I spake of yore,
That for his wifë wept and sighed sore,
I will return, and leave I will Constance
Under the senatorë's governance.

King Alla, which that had his mother slain,
Upon a day fell in such repentánce,
That, if I shortly tell it shall and plain,
To Rome he came to receive his penánce,
And put him in the Popë's ordinance
In high and low, and Jesus Christ besought
Forgive his wicked works that he had wrought.

The fame anon throughout the town is borne,
How Alla king shall come on pilgrimage,
By harbingers that wentë him beforn,
For which the senator, as was uságe,
Rode him again,[16] and many of his lineáge,
As well to show his high magnificence,
As to do any king a reverence.

Great cheerë [17] did this noble senator
To King Allá, and he to him also;
Each of them did the other great honór;
And so befell, that in a day or two
This senator did to King Alla go
To feast, and shortly, if I shall not lie,
Constance's son went in his company.

Some men would say,[18] at réquest of Constance
This senator had led this child to feast:
I may not tellen every circumstance,
Be as be may, there was he at the least:
But sooth is this, that at his mother's hest [19]
Before Allá, during the meatë's space,[20]
The child stood, looking in the kingë's face.

This Alla king had of this child great wonder,
And to the senator he said anon,
"Whose is that fairë child that standeth yonder?"
"I n'ot,"[21] quoth he, "by God and by Saint John;
A mother he hath, but father hath he none,
That I of wot:" and shortly in a stound [22]
He told to Alla how this child was found.

"But God wot," quoth this senator also,
"So virtuous a liver in all my life
I never saw, as she, nor heard of mo'
Of worldly woman, maiden, widow or wife:

1 Gaze, stare. 2 Denied our faith. 3 Illicit lover. 4 Would not. 5 Was drowned. 6 Unblemished. 7 Weakenest. 8 Destroy. 9 Abashed, overthrown. 10 Devoid. 11 Gibraltar and Ceuta. 12 Resolved, arranged.

13 A short time; as long as a cast of the dice. 14 Caused. 15 Die. 16 To meet him. 17 Courtesy, profession of welcome. 18 The poet here refers to Gower's version of the story. 19 Command. 20 Meal time. 21 Know not. 22 Short time.

I dare well say she haddë lever [1] a knife
Throughout her breast, than be a woman wick',[2]
There is no man could bring her to that prick.[3]

Now was this child as like unto Constance
As possible is a creature to be:
This Alla had the face in remembránce
Of Dame Constance, and thereon mused he,
If that the childë's mother were aught she [4]
That was his wife; and privily he sight,[5]
And sped him from the table that he might.[6]

"Parfay,"[7] thought he, "phantom [8] is in mine head.
I ought to deem, of skilful judgëment,[9]
That in the saltë sea my wife is dead."
And afterward he made his argument,
"What wot I, if that Christ have hither sent
My wife by sea, as well as he her sent
To my country, from thennës that she went?"

And, after noon, home with the senator
Went Alla, for to see this wondrous chance.
This senator did Alla great honór,
And hastily he sent after Constance:
But trustë well, her listë not to dance.
When that she wistë wherefore was that sond,[10]
Unneth [11] upon her feet she mightë stand.

When Alla saw his wife, fair he her gret,[12]
And wept, that it was ruthë for to see,
For at the firstë look he on her set
He knew well verily that it was she:
And she, for sorrow, as dumb stood as a tree:
So was her heartë shut in her distress,
When she remember'd his unkindëness.

Twicë she swooned in his owen sight,
He wept and him excused piteously:
"Now God," quoth he, "and all his hallows [13] bright
So wisly [14] on my soulë have mercy,
That of your harm as guiltëless am I,
As is Mauríce my son, so like your face,
Else may the fiend me fetch out of this place."

Long was the sobbing and the bitter pain,
Ere that their woeful heartës mightë cease;
Great was the pity for to hear them plain,[15]
Through whichë plaintës gan their woe increase.
I pray you all my labour to release,
I may not tell all their woe till to-morrow,
I am so weary for to speak of sorrow.

But finally, when that the sooth is wist,[16]
That Alla guiltless was of all her woe,
I trow an hundred timës have they kiss'd,
And such a bliss is there betwixt them two,
That, save the joy that lasteth evermo',
There is none like, that any creatúre
Hath seen, or shall see, while the world may dure.

Then prayed she her husband meekëly
In the relief of her long piteous pine,[17]
That he would pray her father specially,
That of his majesty he would incline
To vouchësafe some day with him to dine:
She pray'd him eke, that he should by no way
Unto her father no word of her say.

Some men would say, how that the child Mauríce
Did this messáge unto the emperor:
But, as I guess, Alla was not so nice,[18]
To him that is so sovereign of honór
As he that is of Christian folk the flow'r,
Send any child, but better 'tis to deem
He went himself; and so it may well seem.

This emperor hath granted gentilly
To come to dinner, as he him besought:
And well rede [19] I, he looked busily
Upon this child, and on his daughter thought.
Alla went to his inn, and as him ought
Arrayed [20] for this feast in every wise,
As farforth as his cunning [21] may suffice.

The morrow came, and Alla gan him dress,[22]
And eke his wife, the emperor to meet:
And forth they rode in joy and in gladness,
And when she saw her father in the street,
She lighted down and fell before his feet.
"Father," quoth she, "your youngë child Constance
Is now full clean out of your rémembránce.

"I am your daughter, your Constance," quoth she,
"That whilom ye have sent into Syrie;
It am I, father, that in the salt sea
Was put alone, and damned [23] for to die.
Now, goodë father, I you mercy cry,
Send me no more into none heatheness,
But thank my lord here of his kindëness."

Who can the piteous joyë tellen all,
Betwixt them three, since they be thus y-met?
But of my talë make an end I shall,
The day goes fast, I will no longer let.[24]
These gladdë folk to dinner be y-set;
In joy and bliss at meat I let them dwell,
A thousand fold well more than I can tell.

This child Maurice was since then emperór
Made by the Pope, and lived Christianly,
To Christë's Churchë did he great honór:
But I let all his story passë by,
Of Constance is my tale especially,
In the oldë Roman gestës [25] men may find
Mauríce's life, I bear it not in mind.

This King Alla, when he his timë sey,[26]
With his Constance, his holy wife so sweet,
To England are they come the rightë way,
Where they did live in joy and in quiét.
But little while it lasted, I you hete,[27]
Joy of this world for time will not abide,
From day to night it changeth as the tide.

Who liv'd ever in such delight one day,
That him not moved either conscience,
Or ire, or talent, or some kind affray,[28]

1 Rather. 2 Wicked. 3 Point.
4 Could by any chance be she. 5 Sighed.
6 Fast as he could. 7 By my faith.
8 A phantasm, mere fancy.
9 I should be certain. 10 Message, summons.
11 Not easily, with difficulty. 12 Greeted.
13 Saints. 14 Surely. 15 Mourn, complain.
16 Truth is known. 17 Sorrow.
18 Rude, foolish. 19 Guess, know. 20 Prepared.
21 So far as his skill. 22 Make ready.
23 Condemned, doomed. 24 Hinder.
25 "Res gestæ;" histories, exploits.
26 Saw. 27 Promise.
28 Disturbance.

Envy, or pride, or passion, or offence?
I say but for this endë this senténce,[1]
That little while in joy or in pleasance
Lasted the bliss of Alla with Constance.

For death, that takes of high and low his rent,
When passed was a year, even as I guess,
Out of this world this King Alla he hent,[2]
For whom Constance had full great heaviness.
Now let us pray that God his soulë bless:
And Dame Constancë, finally to say,
Toward the town of Romë went her way.

To Rome is come this holy creature,
And findeth there her friendës whole and sound:
Now is she scaped all her áventure:
And when that she her father hath y-found,
Down on her kneës falleth she to ground,
Weeping for tenderness in heartë blithe
She herieth[3] God an hundred thousand sithe.[4]

In virtue and in holy almës-deed
They liven all, and ne'er asunder wend;
Till death departeth them, this life they lead:
And fare now well, my tale is at an end.—
Now Jesus Christ, that of his might may send
Joy after woe, govérn us in his grace,
And keep us allë that be in this place.

THE WIFE OF BATH'S TALE.

THE PROLOGUE.[5]

EXPERIENCE, though none authority[6]
Were in this world, is right enough for me
To speak of woe that is in marriáge:
For, lordings, since I twelve year was of age,
(Thanked be God that is etern on live),[7]
Husbands at the church door have I had five,[8] —
For I so often have y-wedded be,—
And all were worthy men in their degree.
But me was told, not longë timë gone is,
That sithen[9] Christë went never but onës
To wedding, in the Cane[10] of Galilee,
That by that ilk[11] example taught he me,
That I not wedded shouldë be but once.
Lo, hearken eke a sharp word for the nonce,[12]
Beside a wellë Jesus, God and man,
Spake in reproof of the Samaritan:
"Thou hast y-had five husbandës," said he;
"And thilkë[13] man, that now hath wedded thee,
Is not thine husband:"[14] thus said he certáin;
What that he meant thereby, I cannot sayn.
But that I askë, why the fifthë man
Was not husband to the Samaritan?
How many might she have in marriáge?
Yet heard I never tellen in mine age[15]
Upon this number definitioún.
Men may divine, and glosen[16] up and down;
But well I wot, express without a lie,
God bade us for to wax and multiply;
That gentle text can I well understand.
Eke well I wot, he said, that mine husbánd
Should leave father and mother, and take to me;
But of no number mentión made he,
Of bigamy or of octogamy;
Why then should men speak of it villainy?[17]

Lo here, the wisë king Dan[18] Solomon,
I trow that he had wivës more than one;
As would to God it lawful were to me
To be refreshed half so oft as he!
What gift[19] of God had he for all his wivës?
No man hath such, that in this world alive is.
God wot, this noble king, as to my wit,[20]
The first night had many a merry fit
With each of them, so well was him on live.[21]
Blessed be God that I have wedded five!
Welcome the sixth whenever that he shall.
For since I will not keep me chaste in all,
When mine husband is from the world y-gone,
Some Christian man shall weddë me anon.
For then th' apostle saith that I am free
To wed, a' God's half,[22] where it liketh me.
He saith, that to be wedded is no sin;
Better is to be wedded than to brin.[23]
What recketh me[24] though folk say villainy[25]
Of shrewed[26] Lamech, and his bigamy?
I wot well Abraham was a holy man,
And Jacob eke, as far as ev'r I can.[27]
And each of them had wivës more than two;
And many another holy man also.
Where can ye see, in any manner age,[28]
That highë God defended[29] marriáge
By word express? I pray you tell it me;
Or where commanded he virginity?
I wot as well as you, it is no dread,[30]
Th' apostle, when he spake of maidenhead,

1 Judgment, opinion. 2 Snatched.
3 Praises. 4 Times.
5 Among the evidences that Chaucer's great work was left incomplete, is the absence of any link of connexion between the Wife of Bath's Prologue and Tale, and what goes before. This deficiency has in some editions caused the Squire's and the Merchant's Tales to be interposed between those of the Man of Law and the Wife of Bath; but in the Merchant's Tale there is internal proof that it was told after the jolly Dame's. Several manuscripts contain verses designed to serve as a connexion; but they are evidently not Chaucer's, and it is unnecessary to give them here. Of this Prologue, which may fairly be regarded as a distinct autobiographical tale, Tyrwhitt says: "The extraordinary length of it, as well as the vein of pleasantry that runs through it, is very suitable to the character of the speaker. The greatest part must have been of Chaucer's own invention, though one may plainly see that he had been reading the popular invectives against marriage and women in general; such as the 'Roman de la Rose,' 'Valerius ad Rufinum, De non Ducendâ Uxore,' and particularly 'Hieronymus contra Jovinianum.'" St Jerome, among other things designed to discourage marriage, has inserted in his treatise a long passage from "Liber Aureolus Theophrasti de Nuptiis."
6 Authorities, written opinions, texts.
7 Lives eternally.
8 Great part of the marriage service used to be performed in the church-porch. 9 Since. 10 Cana.
11 Same. 12 Occasion. 13 That.
14 John iv. 13. 15 In my life.
16 Comment, make glosses.
17 As if it were a disgrace.
18 Lord; "dominus." Another reading is "the wisë man, king Solomon."
19 What special favour or licence.
20 As I understand, as I take it.
21 So well went things with him in his life.
22 On God's part. 23 Burn. 24 What care I.
25 Evil. 26 Impious, wicked.
27 Know. 28 In any period.
29 Forbade; French, "defendre," to prohibit.
30 Doubt.

He said, that precept thereof had he none:
Men may counsél a woman to be one,[1]
But counseling is no commandëment;
He pút it in our owen judgëment.
For, haddë God commanded maidenhead,
Then had he damned[2] wedding out of dread;[3]
And certes, if there were no seed y-sow,[4]
Virginity then whereof should it grow?
Paul durstë nót commanden, at the least,
A thing of which his Master gave no hest.[5]
The dart[6] is set up for virginity;
Catch whoso may, who runneth best let see.
But this word is not ta'en of every wight,
But there as[7] God will give it of his might.
I wot well that th' apostle was a maid,
But natheless, although he wrote and said,
He would that every wight were such as he,
All is but counsel to virginitý.
And, since to be a wife he gave me leave
Of indulgence, so is it no repreve[8]
To weddë me, if that my make[9] should die,
Without exceptión[10] of bigamy;
All were it[11] good no woman for to touch
(He meant as in his bed or in his couch),
For peril is both fire and tow t' assemble;
Ye know what this example may resemble.
This is all and some, he held virginity
More profit than wedding in fraïlty:[12]
(Frailty clepe I, but if[13] that he and she
Would lead their livës all in chastity),
I grant it well, I have of none envý
Who maidenhead prefer to bigamy;
It liketh them t' be clean in body and ghost;[14]
Of mine estate[15] I will not make a boast.
For, well ye know, a lord in his household
Hath not every vessel all of gold;[16]
Some are of tree, and do their lord servíce.
God calleth folk to him in sundry wise,
And each one hath of God a proper gift,
Some this, some that, as liketh him to shift.[17]
Virginity is great perfectión,
And continence eke with devotión:
But Christ, that of perfection is the well,[18]
Bade not every wight he should go sell
All that he had, and give it to the poor,
And in such wise follow him and his lore:[19]
He spake to them that would live perfectly,—
And, lordings, by your leave, that am not I;
I will bestow the flower of mine age
In th' acts and in the fruits of marriáge.
Tell me also, to what conclusión[20]
Were members made of generatión,
And of so perfect wise a wight[21] y-wrought?
Trust me right well, they were nót made for nought.
Glose whoso will, and say both up and down,
That they were made for the purgatioún
Of urine, and of other thingës smale,
And eke to know a female from a male:
And for none other causë? say ye no?
Experience wot well it is not so.
So that the clerkës[22] be not with me wroth,
I say this, that they werë made for both,
That is to say, for office,[23] and for ease[24],
Of engendrure, there we God not displease.
Why should men ellës in their bookës set,
That man shall yield unto his wife her debt?
Now wherewith should he make his payëment,
If he us'd not his silly instrument?
Then were they made upon a creature
To purge urine, and eke for engendrure.
But I say not that every wight is hold,[25]
That hath such harness[26] as I to you told,
To go and usë them in engendrure;
Then should men take of chastity no cure.[27]
Christ was a maid, and shapen[28] as a man,
And many a saint, since that this world began,
Yet ever liv'd in perfect chastity.
I will not vie[29] with no virginity.
Let them with bread of pured[30] wheat be fed,
And let us wivës eat our barley bread.
And yet with barley bread, Mark tell us can,[31]
Our Lord Jesus refreshed many a man.
In such estate as God hath cleped us,[32]
I'll persevere, I am not precious,[33]
In wifehood I will use mine instrument
As freely as my Maker hath it sent.
If I be dangerous[34] God give me sorrow;
Mine husband shall it have, bot[illegible] and morrow,
When that him list come forth and pay his debt.
A husband will I have, I will no let,[35]
Which shall be both my debtor and my thrall,[36]
And have his tribulatión withal
Upon his flesh, while that I am his wife.
I have the power during all my life
Upon his proper body, and not he;
Right thus th' apostle told it unto me,
And bade our husbands for to love us well;
All this senténce me liketh every deal.—[37]
Up start the Pardoner, and that anon;
"Now, Dame," quoth he, "by God and by Saint John,
Ye are a noble preacher in this case.
I was about to wed a wife, alas!
What? should I bie[38] it on my flesh so dear?
Yet had I lever[39] wed no wife this year."
"Abide,"[40] quoth she; "my tale is not begun.
Nay, thou shalt drinken of another tun
Ere that I go, shall savour worse than ale.
And when that I have told thee forth my tale
Of tribulatión in marriáge,
Of which I am expert in all mine age,

1 A maid. 2 Condemned.
3 Doubt. 4 Sown. 5 Command.
6 The goal; a spear or dart was set up to mark the point of victory. 7 Except where.
8 Scandal, reproach. 9 Mate, husband.
10 Charge, reproach. 11 Although it were.
12 Frailty. 13 Frailty I call it, unless.
14 Spirit. 15 Condition.
16 "But in a great house there are not only vessels of gold and silver, but also of wood and of earth; and some to honour, and some to dishonour."—2 Tim. ii. 20.
17 Appoint, distribute. 18 Fountain.
19 Doctrine. 20 End, purpose. 21 Being.
22 Scholars. 23 Duty. 24 Pleasure.
25 Held bound, obliged. 26 Weapons. 27 Care.
28 Fashioned. 29 Contend. 30 Purified.
31 Mark vi. 41, 42. 32 Called us to,
33 Scrupulous, dainty, over-nice.
34 Sparing, or difficult, of my favours.
35 I will bear no hindrance. 36 Slave.
37 Whit. 38 Suffer for,
39 Rather, 40 Wait in patience.

(This is to say, myself hath been the whip),[1]
Then mayest thou choose whether thou wilt sip
Of thilkë tunnë,[2] that I now shall broach.
Beware of it, ere thou too nigh approach,
For I shall tell examples more than ten:
Whoso will not beware by other men,
By him shall other men corrected be:
These samë wordës writeth Ptolemý;
Read in his Almagest, and take it there."
"Dame, I would pray you, if your will it were,"
Saidë this Pardoner, "as ye began,
Tell forth your tale, and sparë for no man,
And teach us youngë men of your practique."
"Gladly," quoth she, "since that it may you
like.
But that I pray to all this company,
If that I speak after my fantasy,
To takë nought agrief[3] what I may say;
For mine intent is only for to play.—
Now, Sirs, then will I tell you forth my tale.
As ever may I drinkë wine or ale
I shall say sooth; the husbands that I had
Three of them werë good, and two were bad.
The three were goodë men, and rich, and old.
Unnethes[4] mightë they the statute hold[5]
In which that they were bounden unto me.
Yet wot well what I mean of this, pardie.[6]
As God me help, I laugh when that I think
How piteously at night I made them swink,[7]
But, by my fay,[8] I told of it no store:[9]
They had me giv'n their land and their treasór,
Me needed not do longer diligence
To win their love, or do them reverence.
They loved me so well, by God above,
That I toldë no dainty[10] of their love.
A wise woman will busy her ever-in-one[11]
To get their lovë, where that she hath none.
But, since I had them wholly in my hand,
And that they had me given all their land,
Why should I takë keep[12] them for to please,
But[13] it were for my profit, or mine ease?
I set them so a-workë, by my fay,
That many a night they sangë, well-away!
The bacon was not fetched for them, I trow,
That some men have in Essex at Dunmow.[14]
I govern'd them so well after my law,
That each of them full blissful was and fawe[15]
To bringë me gay thingës from the fair.
They were full glad when that I spake them fair,
For, God it wot, I chid them spiteously.[16]
Now hearken how I bare me properly.
Ye wisë wivës, that can understand,
Thus should ye speak, and bear them wrong on
hand,[17]
For half so boldëly can there no man
Swearen and lien as a woman can.
(I say not this by wivës that be wise,
But if it be when they them misadvise.)[18]
A wisë wife, if that she can[19] her good,
Shall bearë them on hand the cow is wood,[20]
And takë witness of her owen maid
Of their assent: but hearken how I said.
"Sir oldë kaynard,[21] is this thine array?
Why is my neighëbourë's wife so gay?
She is honour'd over all where[22] she go'th,
I sit at home, I have no thrifty cloth.[23]
What dost thou at my neighëbourë's house?
Is she so fair? art thou so amoroús?
What rown'st[24] thou with our maid? *ben'dicite,*
Sir oldë lechour, let thy japës[25] be.
And if I have a gossip, or a friend
(Withoutë guilt), thou chidest as a fiend,
If that I walk or play unto his house.
Thou comest home as drunken as a mouse,
And preachest on thy bench, with evil prefe:[26]
Thou say'st to me, it is a great mischief
To wed a poorë woman, for costáge:[27]
And if that she be rich, of high paráge,[28]
Then say'st thou, that it is a tormentry
To suffer her pride and meláncholy.
And if that she be fair, thou very knave,
Thou say'st that every holour[29] will her have;
She may no while in chastity abide,
That is assailed upon every side.
Thou say'st some folk desire us for richéss,
Some for our shape, and some for our fairness,
And some, for she can either sing or dance,
And some for gentiless and dalliance,
Some for her handës and her armës smale:
Thus goes all to the devil, by thy tale;
Thou say'st, men may not keep a castle wall
That may be so assailed over all.[30]
And if that she be foul, thou say'st that she
Coveteth every man that she may see;
For as a spaniel she will on him leap,
Till she may findë some man her to cheap;[31]
And none so grey goose goes there in the lake,
(So say'st thou) that will be without a make.[32]
And say'st, it is a hard thing for to weld[33]
A thing that no man will, his thankës,[34] held.[35]
Thus say'st thou, lorel,[36] when thou go'st to bed,
And that no wise man needeth for to wed,
Nor no man that intendeth unto heaven.
With wildë thunder dint[37] and fiery leven[38]
Motë[39] thy wicked neckë be to-broke.
Thou say'st, that dropping houses, and eke
smoke,
And chiding wivës, makë men to flee

1 The instrument of administering torture.
2 That tun.
3 Not to be offended by, not to take to heart.
4 With difficulty. 5 Fulfil the law.
6 By God, in God's name. 7 Labour.
8 Faith. 9 Held it of no account.
10 Cared nothing for, set no value on.
11 Constantly. 12 Care. 13 Unless.
14 At Dunmow prevailed the custom of giving, amid much merry-making, a flitch of bacon to the married pair who had lived together for a year without quarrel or regret. The same custom prevailed of old in Bretagne. 15 Happy and fain. 16 Angrily.
17 Make them believe falsely.
18 Unless they have acted unadvisedly. 19 Know.
20 Delude them into believing that the cow is mad—or is made of wood.
21 "Cagnard," or "Caignard," a French term of reproach, originally derived from "canis," a dog.
22 Wheresoever. 23 Good clothing.
24 Whisperest. 25 Buffooneries, tricks.
26 Proof. 27 Expense.
28 Birth, kindred; from Latin, "pario," I beget.
29 Whoremonger.
30 Everywhere, on all sides. 31 Buy.
32 Mate. 33 Wield, govern. 34 With his good will.
35 Hold. 36 Good-for-nothing.
37 Stroke. 38 Lightning. 39 May.

Out of their own house; ah! *ben'dicite,*
What aileth such an old man for to chide?
Thou say'st, we wivës will our vices hide,
Till we be fast,[1] and then we will them shew.
Well may that be a proverb of a shrew.[2]
Thou say'st, that oxen, asses, horses, hounds,
They be assayed at diversë stounds,[3]
Basons and lavers, ere that men them buy,
Spoonës, stoolës, and all such husbandry,
And so be pots, and clothës, and array,[4]
But folk of wivës makë none assay,
Till they be wedded,—oldë dotard shrew!—
And then, say'st thou, we will our vices shew.
Thou say'st also, that it displeaseth me,
But if[5] that thou wilt praisë my beauty,
And but[5] thou pore alway upon my face,
And call me fairë dame in every place;
And but[5] thou make a feast on thilkë[6] day
That I was born, and make me fresh and gay;
And but thou do to my norice[7] honoúr,
And to my chamberere[8] within my bow'r,
And to my father's folk, and mine allies;[9]
Thus sayest thou, old barrel full of lies.
And yet also of our prentice Jenkin,
For his crisp hair, shining as gold so fine,
And for he squireth me both up and down,
Yet hast thou caught a false suspicioún:
I will him not, though thou wert dead to-morrow.
But tell me this, why hidest thou, with sorrow,[10]
The keyës of thy chest away from me?
It is my good[11] as well as thine, pardie.
What, think'st to make an idiot of our dame?
Now, by that lord that called is Saint Jame,[12]
Thou shalt not both, although that thou wert wood,[13]
Be master of my body, and my good,
The one thou shalt forego, maugré[14] thine eyen.
What helpeth it of me t' inquire and spyen?
I trow thou wouldest lock me in thy chest.
Thou shouldest say, 'Fair wife, go where thee lest;[15]
Take your disport; I will believe no tales;
I know you for a truë wife, Dame Ales.'[16]
"We love no man, that taketh keep[17] or charge
Where that we go; we will be at our large.
Of allë men most blessed may he be,
The wise astrologer Dan[18] Ptolemy,
That saith this proverb in his Almagest:
'Of allë men his wisdom is highést,
That recketh not who hath the world in hand.'
By this proverb thou shalt well understand,
Have thou enough, what thar[19] thee reck or care
How merrily that other folkës fare?
For certes, oldë dotard, by your leave,
Ye shall have [pleasure] right enough at eve.
He is too great a niggard that will werne[20]
A man to light a candle at his lantérn;
He shall have never the less light, pardie.
Have thou enough, thee thar[19] not plainë[21] thee.
Thou say'st also, if that we make us gay
With clothing and with precious array,
That it is peril of our chastity.
And yet,—with sorrow!—thou enforcest thee,
And say'st these words in the apostle's name:
'In habit made with chastity and shame[22]
Ye women shall apparel you,' quoth he,
'And not in tressed hair and gay perrie,[23]
As pearlës, nor with gold, nor clothës rich.'
After thy text nor after thy rubrich
I will not work as muchel as a gnat.
Thou say'st also, I walk out like a cat;
For whoso wouldë singe the cattë's skin,
Then will the cattë well dwell in her inn;[24]
And if the cattë's skin be sleek and gay,
She will not dwell in housë half a day,
But forth she will, ere any day be daw'd,
To shew her skin, and go a caterwaw'd.[25]
This is to say, if I be gay, sir shrew,
I will run out, my borel[26] for to shew.
Sir oldë fool, what helpeth thee to spyen?
Though thou pray Argus with his hundred eyen
To be my wardécorps,[27] as he can best,
In faith he shall not keep me, but me lest:[28]
Yet could I make his beard,[29] so may I thé.[30]
"Thou sayest eke, that there be thingës three,
Which thingës greatly trouble all this earth,
And that no wightë may endure the ferth:[31]
O lefe[32] sir shrew, may Jesus short[33] thy life.
Yet preachest thou, and say'st, a hateful wife
Y-reckon'd is for one of these mischances.
Be there none other manner resembláncés[34]
That ye may liken your parables unto,
But if a silly wife be one of tho?[35]
Thou likenest a woman's love to hell;
To barren land, where water may not dwell.
Thou likenest it also to wild fire;
The more it burns, the more it hath desire
To cónsume every thing that burnt will be.
Thou sayest, right as wormës shend[36] a tree,
Right so a wife destroyeth her husbond;
This know they well that be to wivës bond."
Lordings, right thus, as ye have understand,
Bare I stiffly mine old husbands on hand,[37]
That thus they saiden in their drunkenness;
And all was false, but that I took witness
On Jenkin, and upon my niece also.
O Lord! the pain I did them, and the woe,
Full guiltëless, by Goddë's sweetë pine;[38]
For as a horse I couldë bite and whine;
I couldë plain,[39] an'[40] I was in the guilt,

1 Wedded. 2 Ill-tempered wretch.
3 Proved at various seasons. 4 Raiment.
5 Unless. 6 That.
7 Nurse; French, "nourrice."
8 Chamber-maid. 9 Relations.
10 Sorrow on thee! 11 Property.
12 St Jago of Compostella. 13 Furious.
14 Spite of. 15 Pleases.
16 Alice, Alison. 17 Care.
18 Lord. This and the previous quotation from Ptolemy are due to the Dame's own fancy.
19 Needs, behoves. 20 Forbid. 21 Complain.
22 Modesty. See 1 Tim. ii. 9.
23 Precious stones, jewels. 24 House.
25 Caterwauling. 26 Apparel, fine clothes.
27 "Gardecorps," body-guard.
28 Unless it please me.
29 Make a jest of him.
30 Thrive. 31 Fourth. 32 Pleasant.
33 Shorten. 34 No other kind of comparisons.
35 Those. 36 Destroy.
37 Made them believe. 38 Pain.
39 Complain.
40 Even though.

Or ellës oftentime I had been spilt.[1]
Whoso first cometh to the mill, first grint;[2]
I plained first, so was our war y-stint.[3]
They were full glad to excuse them full blive[4]
Of things that they never aguilt their live.[5]
Of wenches would I bearë them on hand,[6]
When that for sickness scarcely might they stand,
Yet tickled I his heartë for that he
Ween'd[7] that I had of him so great cherté:[8]
I swore that all my walking out by night
Was for to éspy wenches that he dight:[9]
Under that colour had I many a mirth.
For all such wit is given us at birth;
Deceit, weeping, and spinning, God doth give
To women kindly,[10] while that they may live.
And thus of one thing I may vauntë me,
At th' end I had the better in each degree,
By sleight, or force, or by some manner thing,
As by continual murmur or grudging,[11]
Namely[12] a-bed, there haddë they mischance,
There would I chide, and do them no pleasance:
I would no longer in the bed abide,
If that I felt his arm over my side,
Till he had made his ransom unto me,
Then would I suffer him do his nicety.[13]
And therefore every man this tale I tell,
Win whoso may, for all is for to sell;
With empty hand men may no hawkës lure;
For winning would I all his will endure,
And makë me a feigned appetite,—
And yet in bacon[14] had I never delight:
That made me that I ever would them chide.
For, though the Pope had sitten them beside,
I would not spare them at their owen board,
For, by my troth, I quit[15] them word for word.
As help me very God omnipotent,
Though I right now should make my testament,
I owe them not a word, that is not quit,
I brought it so aboutë by my wit,
That they must give it up, as for the best,
Or ellës had we never been in rest.
For, though he looked as a wood[16] lión,
Yet should he fail of his conclusión.
Then would I say, "Now, goodë lefe,[17] take keep[18]
How meekly looketh Wilken ourë sheep!
Come near, my spouse, and let me ba[19] thy cheek.
Ye shouldë be all patient and meek,
And have a sweet y-spiced[20] conscience,
Since ye so preach of Jobë's patience.
Suffer alway, since ye so well can preach,
And but[21] ye do, certáin we shall you teach
That it is fair to have a wife in peace.
One of us two must bowë[22] doubtëless:
And since a man is more reasónable
Than woman is, ye must be suff'rable.
What aileth you to grudgë[23] thus and groan?
Is it for ye would have my [love] alone?
Why, take it all: lo, have it every deal.[24]
Peter![25] I shrew[26] you but ye love it well.
For if I wouldë sell my *bellë chose*,
I couldë walk as fresh as is a rose,
But I will keep it for your owen tooth.
Ye be to blame, by God, I say you sooth."
Such manner wordës haddë we on hand.
Now will I speaken of my fourth husbánd.
My fourthë husband was a revellour;
This is to say, he had a paramour,
And I was young and full of ragerie,[27]
Stubborn and strong, and jolly as a pie.
Then could I dancë to a harpë smale,
And sing, y-wis,[28] as any nightingale,
When I had drunk a draught of sweetë wine.
Metellius, the foulë churl, the swine,
That with a staff bereft his wife of life
For[29] she drank wine, though I had been his wife,
Never should he have daunted me from drink:
And, after wine, of Venus most I think.
For all so sure as cold engenders hail,
A liquorish mouth must have a liquorish tail.
In woman vinolent[30] is no defence,[31]
This knowë lechours by experience.
But, lord Christ, when that it remembr'reth me
Upon my youth, and on my jollity,
It tickleth me about mine heartë-root;
Unto this day it doth mine heartë boot,[32]
That I have had my world as in my time.
But age, alas! that all will envenime,[33]
Hath me bereft my beauty and my pith:[34]
Let go; farewell; the devil go therewith.
The flour is gone, there is no more to tell,
The bran, as I best may, now must I sell.
But yet to be right merry will I fand.[35]
Now forth to tell you of my fourth husband.
I say, I in my heart had great despite,
That he of any other had delight;
But he was quit,[36] by God and by Saint Joce:[37]
I made for him of the same wood a cross;
Not of my body in no foul mannére,
But certainly I madë folk such cheer,
That in his owen grease I made him fry
For anger, and for very jealousy.
By God, in earth I was his purgatory,
For which I hope his soul may be in glory.
For, God it wot, he sat full oft and sung,
When that his shoe full bitterly him wrung.[38]
There was no wight, save God and he, that wist
In many wise how sore I did him twist.
He died when I came from Jerusalem,

1 Ruined. 2 Is ground. 3 Stopped.
4 Quickly. 5 Were never guilty of in their lives.
6 Falsely accuse them. 7 Thought.
8 Affection; from French, "cher," dear.
9 Adorned; took to himself. 10 Naturally.
11 Complaining. 12 Especially.
13 Folly; French, "niaiserie."
14 The bacon of Dunmow. 15 Requited, repaid.
16 Furious. 17 Dear. 18 Heed, notice.
19 Kiss; from French, "baiser."
20 Tender, nice. 21 Unless.
22 Bend, give way. 23 Murmur. 24 Whit.

25 By Saint Peter! a common adjuration, like Marie! from the Virgin's name. 26 Curse.
27 Wantonness. 28 Certainly.
29 Because. 30 Full of wine. 31 Resistance.
32 Good. 33 Poison, embitter. 34 Vigour.
35 Try. 36 Requited.
37 Or Judocus, a saint of Ponthieu, in France.
38 Pinched. "An allusion," says Mr Wright, "to the story of the Roman sage who, when blamed for divorcing his wife, said that a shoe might appear outwardly to fit well, but no one but the wearer knew where it pinched."

And lies in grave under the roodë beam:[1]
Although his tomb is not so curious
As was the sepulchre of Darius,
Which that Apelles wrought so subtlely.
It is but waste to bury them preciously.
Let him fare well, God give his soulë rest,
He is now in his grave and in his chest.
Now of my fifthë husband will I tell:
God let his soul never come into hell.
And yet was he to me the mostë shrew;[2]
That feel I on my ribbës all by rew,[3]
And ever shall, until mine ending day.
But in our bed he was so fresh and gay,
And therewithal so well he could me glose,[4]
When that he wouldë have my *bellë chose*,
Though he had beaten me on every bone,
Yet could he win again my love anon.
I trow, I lov'd him better, for that he
Was of his love so dangerous[5] to me.
We women have, if that I shall not lie,
In this mattér a quaintë fantasy.
Whatever thing we may not lightly have,
Thereafter will we cry all day and crave.
Forbid us thing, and that desirë we;
Press on us fast, and thennë will we flee.
With danger[6] utter we all our chaffare;[7]
Great press at market maketh dearë ware,
And too great cheap is held at little price;
This knoweth every woman that is wise.
My fifthë husband, God his soulë bless,
Which that I took for love and no richéss,
He some time was a clerk of Oxenford,[8]
And had left school, and went at home to board
With my gossip, dwelling in ourë town:
God have her soul, her name was Alisoun.
She knew my heart, and all my privity,
Bet than our parish priest, so may I thé.[9]
To her betrayed I my counsel all;
For had my husband pissed on a wall,
Or done a thing that should have cost his life,
To her, and to another worthy wife,
And to my niece, which that I loved well,
I would have told his counsel every deal.[10]
And so I did full often, God it wot,
That made his face full often red and hot
For very shame, and blam'd himself, for he
Had told to me so great a privity.[11]
And so befell that onës in a Lent
(So oftentimes I to my gossip went,
For ever yet I loved to be gay,
And for to walk in March, April, and May
From house to house, to hearë sundry tales),
That Jenkin clerk, and my gossíp, Dame Ales,
And I myself, into the fieldës went.
Mine husband was at London all that Lent;
I had the better leisure for to play,
And for to see, and eke for to be sey[12]
Of lusty folk; what wist I where my grace[13]
Was shapen[14] for to be, or in what place?
Therefore made I my visitatións
To vigilies,[15] and to processións,
To preachings eke, and to these pilgrimáges,
To plays of miracles, and marriáges,
And weared upon me gay scarlet gites.[16]
These wormës, nor these mothës, nor these mites
On my apparel frett[17] them never a deal[18]
And know'st thou why? for they were used[19] well.
Now will I tellë forth what happen'd me:
I say, that in the fieldës walked we,
Till truëly we had such dalliance,
This clerk and I, that of my purveyance[20]
I spake to him, and told him how that he,
If I were widow, shouldë weddë me.
For certainly, I say for no bobance,[21]
Yet was I never without purveyance[20]
Of marriage, nor of other thingës eke:
I hold a mouse's wit not worth a leek,
That hath but one hole for to startë to,[22]
And if that failë, then is all y-do.[23]
[I bare him on hand[24] he had enchanted me
(My damë taughtë me that subtilty);
And eke I said, I mette[25] of him all night,
He would have slain me, as I lay upright,
And all my bed was full of very blood;
But yet I hop'd that he should do me good;
For blood betoken'd gold, as me was taught.
And all was false, I dream'd of him right naught,
But as I follow'd aye my damë's lore,
As well of that as of other things more.]
But now, sir, let me see, what shall I sayn?
Aha! by God, I have my tale again.
When that my fourthë husband was on bier,
I wept algate[26] and made a sorry cheer,[27]
As wivës must, for it is the uságe;
And with my kerchief covered my viságe;
But, for I was provided with a make,[28]
I wept but little, that I undertake.[29]
To churchë was mine husband borne a-morrow
With neighëbours that for him madë sorrow,
And Jenkin, ourë clerk, was one of tho:[30]
As help me God, when that I saw him go
After the bier, methought he had a pair
Of leggës and of feet so clean and fair,
That all my heart I gave unto his hold.[31]
He was, I trow, a twenty winter old,
And I was forty, if I shall say sooth,
But yet I had always a coltë's tooth.
Gat-toothed[32] I was, and that became me well,
I had the print of Saintë Venus' seal.
[As help me God, I was a lusty one,
And fair, and rich, and young, and well be-gone:[33]

1 Cross. 2 Cruel, ill-tempered. 3 In a row. 4 Flatter. 5 Sparing, difficult. 6 Difficulty. 7 Merchandise. 8 A scholar of Oxford. 9 Thrive. 10 Jot. 11 Secret. 12 Seen. 13 Favour. 14 Appointed. 15 Festival-eves. See note 21, page 21. 16 Gowns. 17 Fed. 18 Whit. 19 Worn. 20 Foresight.
21 Boasting; Ben Jonson's braggart, in "Every Man in his Humour," is named Bobadil.
22 A very old proverb in French, German, and Latin. "Startë," to escape. 23 Done.
24 Falsely assured him. 25 Dreamed. 26 Always. 27 Countenance. 28 Mate. 29 Promise. 30 Those. 31 Keeping.
32 Gap-toothed; goat-toothed; or cat- or separate toothed. See note 14, page 22.
33 In a good way. The lines in brackets are only in some of the manuscripts.

For certes I am all venerian
In feeling, and my heart is martian;[1]
Venus me gave my lust and liquorishness,
And Mars gave me my sturdy hardiness.]
Mine áscendant was Taure,[2] and Mars there-in:
Alas, alas, that ever love was sin!
I follow'd aye mine inclinatión
By virtue of my constellatión:
That made me that I couldë not withdraw
My chamber of Venus from a good felláw.
[Yet have I Martë's mark upon my face,
And also in another privy place.
For God so wisly[3] be my salvatión,
I loved never by discretión,
But ever follow'd mine own appetite,
All[4] were he short, or long, or black, or white,
I took no keep,[5] so that he liked me,
How poor he was, neither of what degree.]
What should I say? but that at the month's end
This jolly clerk Jenkin, that was so hend,[6]
Had wedded me with great solemnity,
And to him gave I all the land and fee
That ever was me given therebefore:
But afterward repented me full sore.
He wouldë suffer nothing of my list.[7]
By God, he smote me onës with his fist,
For that I rent out of his book a leaf,
That of the stroke mine earë wax'd all deaf.
Stubborn I was, as is a lioness,
And of my tongue a very jangleress,[8]
And walk I would, as I had done beforn,
From house to house, although he had it sworn:[9]
For which he oftentimës wouldë preach,
And me of oldë Roman gestës[10] teach.
How that Sulpitius Gallus left his wife,
And her forsook for term of all his life,
For nought but open-headed[11] he her say.[12]
Looking out at his door upon a day.
Another Roman[13] told he me by name,
That, for his wife was at a summer game
Without his knowing, he forsook her eke.
And then would he upon his Bible seek
That ilkë[14] proverb of Ecclesiast,
Where he commandeth, and forbiddeth fast,
Man shall not suffer his wife go roll about.
Then would he say right thus withoutë doubt:
"*Whoso that buildeth his house all of sallows,*[15]
And pricketh his blind horse over the fallows,
And suff'reth his wife to go seekë hallows,[16]
Is worthy to be hanged on the gallows."
But all for nought; I settë not a haw[17]
Of his provérbs, nor of his oldë saw;
Nor would I not of him corrected be.
I hate them that my vices tellë me,
And so do more of us (God wot) than I.
This máde him wood[18] with me all utterly;
I wouldë not forbear[19] him in no case.
Now will I say you sooth, by Saint Thomas,
Why that I rent out of his book a leaf,
For which he smote me, so that I was deaf.
He had a book, that gladly night and day
For his disport he would it read alway;
He call'd it Valerie,[20] and Theophrast,
And with that book he laugh'd alway full fast.
And eke there was a clerk sometime at Rome,
A cardinal, that hightë Saint Jerome,
That made a book against Jovinian,
Which book was there; and eke Tertullian,
Chrysippus, Trotula, and Heloïse,
That was an abbess not far from Paris;
And eke the Parables[21] of Solomon,
Ovidë's Art,[22] and bourdës[23] many one;
And allë these were bound in one volume.
And every night and day was his custume
(When he had leisure and vacatión
From other worldly occupatión)
To readen in this book of wicked wives.
He knew of them more legends and more lives
Than be of goodë wivës in the Bible.
For, trust me well, it is an impossíble
That any clerk will speakë good of wives,
(But if[24] it be of holy saintës' lives)
Nor of none other woman never the mo'.
Who painted the lión, tell it me, who?
By God, if women haddë written stories,
As clerkës have within their oratóries,
They would have writ of men more wickedness
Than all the mark of Adam[25] may redress.
The children of Mercury and of Venus,[26]
Be in their working full contrarious.
Mercury loveth wisdom and sciénce,
And Venus loveth riot and dispence.[27]
And for their diverse dispositión,
Each falls in other's exaltatión.[28]
As thus, God wot, Mercúry is desolate
In Pisces, where Venus is exaltáte,
And Venus falls where Mercury is raised.
Therefore no woman by no clerk is praised.
The clerk, when he is old, and may not do
Of Venus' works not worth his oldë shoe,
Then sits he down, and writes in his dotage,
That women cannot keep their marriáge.
But now to purpose, why I toldë thee
That I was beaten for a book, pardie.
Upon a night Jenkin, that was our sire,[29]
Read on his book, as he sat by the fire,
Of Eva first, that for her wickedness
Was all mankind brought into wretchedness,
For which that Jesus Christ himself was slain,

1 Under the influence of Mars.
2 Taurus, the Bull. 3 Certainly. 4 Whether.
5 Heed. 6 Handsome, courteous. 7 Pleasure.
8 Prater. 9 Had sworn to prevent it.
10 Stories. 11 Bare-headed. 12 Saw.
13 Sempronius Sophus, of whom Valérius Maximus tells in his sixth book. 14 Same. 15 Willows.
16 Make pilgrimages to shrines of saints.
17 Cared not a straw.
18 Furious. 19 Endure, bear with.
20 The tract of Walter Mapes against marriage, published under the title of "Epistola Valerii ad Rufinum."
21 Proverbs. 22 "Ars Amoris."
23 Jests. 24 Unless.
25 All who bear the mark of Adam—all men.
26 Those born under the influence of the respective planets. 27 Expense.
28 A planet, according to the old astrologers, was in "exaltation" when in the sign of the Zodiac in which it exerted its strongest influence; the opposite sign, in which it was weakest, was called its "dejection." Venus being strongest in Pisces, was weakest in Virgo; but in Virgo Mercury was in "exaltation."
29 Goodman.

That bought us with his heartë-blood again.
Lo here express of women may ye find
That woman was the loss of all mankind.
Then read he me how Samson lost his hairs
Sleeping, his leman cut them with her shears,
Through whichë treason lost he both his eyen.
Then read he me, if that I shall not lien,
Of Hercules, and of his Dejanire,
That caused him to set himself on fire.
Nothing forgot he of the care and woe
That Socrates had with his wivës two;
How Xantippe cast piss upon his head.
This silly man sat still, as he were dead,
He wip'd his head, and no more durst he sayn,
But, "Ere the thunder stint[1] there cometh rain."
Of Phasiphaë, that was queen of Crete,
For shrewedness[2] he thought the talë sweet.
Fy, speak no more, it is a grisly thing,
Of her horrible lust and her liking.
Of Clytemnestra, for her lechery
That falsely made her husband for to die,
He read it with full good devotión.
He told me eke, for what occasión
Amphiorax at Thebes lost his life:
My husband had a legend of his wife
Eryphilé, that for an ouche[3] of gold
Had privily unto the Greekës told,
Where that her husband hid him in a place,
For which he had at Thebes sorry grace.
Of Luna told he me, and of Lucie;
They bothë made their husbands for to die,
That one for love, that other was for hate.
Luna her husband on an ev'ning late
Empoison'd had, for that she was his foe:
Lucia liquorish lov'd her husband so,
That, for he should always upon her think,
She gave him such a manner[4] lovë-drink,
That he was dead before it were the morrow:
And thus algatës[5] husbands haddë sorrow.
Then told he me how one Latumeus
Complained to his fellow Arius
That in his garden growed such a tree,
On which he said how that his wivës three
Hanged themselves for heart dispiteous.
"O leve[6] brother," quoth this Arius,
"Give me a plant of thilkë[7] blessed tree,
And in my garden planted shall it be."
Of later date of wivës hath he read,
That some have slain their husbands in their bed,
And let their lechour dight them all the night,
While that the corpse lay on the floor upright:
And some have driven nails into their brain,
While that they slept, and thus they have them slain:
Some have them given poison in their drink:
He spake more harm than heartë may bethink.
And therewithal he knew of more provérbs,
Than in this world there groweth grass or herbs.
"Better (quoth he) thine habitatión
Be with a lion, or a foul dragón,
Than with a woman using for to chide.
Better (quoth he) high in the roof abide,
Than with an angry woman in the house,
They be so wicked and contrarioús:
They hatë that their husbands loven aye."
He said, "A woman cast her shame away
When she cast off her smock;" and farthermo',
"A fair woman, but[8] she be chaste also,
Is like a gold ring in a sowë's nose."
Who couldë ween,[9] or who couldë suppose
The woe that in mine heart was, and the pine?[10]
And when I saw that he would never fine[11]
To readen on this cursed book all night,
All suddenly three leavës have I plight[12]
Out of his book, right as he read, and eke
I with my fist so took him on the cheek,
That in our fire he backward fell adown.
And he up start, as doth a wood lión,
And with his fist he smote me on the head,
That on the floor I lay as I were dead.
And when he saw how still that there I lay,
He was aghast, and would have fled away,
Till at the last out of my swoon I braid,[13]
"Oh, hast thou slain me, thou false thief?" I said,
"And for my land thus hast thou murder'd me?
Ere I be dead, yet will I kissë thee."
And near he came, and kneeled fair adown,
And saidë, "Dearë sister Alisoun,
As help me God, I shall thee never smite:
That I have done it is thyself to wite,[14]
Forgive it me, and that I thee beseek."[15]
And yet eftsoons[16] I hit him on the cheek,
And saidë, "Thief, thus much am I awreak.[17]
Now will I die, I may no longer speak."
But at the last, with muchë care and woe
We fell accorded[18] by ourselvës two:
He gave me all the bridle in mine hand
To have the governance of house and land,
And of his tongue, and of his hand also.
I made him burn his book anon right tho.[19]
And when that I had gotten unto me
By mast'ry all the sovereignëty,
And that he said, "Mine owen truë wife,
Do as thee list,[20] the term of all thy life,
Keep thine honoúr, and eke keep mine estate;"
After that day we never had debate.
God help me so, I was to him as kind
As any wife from Denmark unto Ind,
And also true, and so was he to me:
I pray to God that sits in majesty
So bless his soulë, for his mercy dear.
Now will I say my tale, if ye will hear.—

The Friar laugh'd when he had heard all this:
"Now, Dame," quoth he, "so have I joy and bliss,
This is a long preamble of a tale."
And when the Sompnour heard the Friar gale,[21]
"Lo," quoth this Sompnour, "Goddë's armës two,

1 Ceases. 2 Wickedness. 3 Clasp, collar. 4 Sort of. 5 Always. 6 Dear. 7 That. 8 Except. 9 Think. 10 Pain. 11 Have done, end. 12 Plucked. 13 Woke. 14 Blame. 15 Beseech. 16 Immediately; again. 17 Avenged. 18 Agreed. 19 Then. 20 Pleases thee. 21 Speak, flout; "chaff."

A friar will intermete[1] him evermo':
Lo, goodë men, a fly and eke a frere
Will fall in ev'ry dish and eke mattére.
What speak'st thou of perambulatioún?[2]
What? amble or trot; or peace, or go sit down:
Thou lettest[3] our disport in this mattére."
"Yea, wilt thou so, Sir Sompnour?" quoth the Frere;
"Now by my faith I shall, ere that I go,
Tell of a Sompnour such a tale or two,
That all the folk shall laughen in this place."
"Now do, else, Friar, I beshrew[4] thy face,"
Quoth this Sompnour; "and I beshrewë me,
But if[5] I tellë talës two or three
Of friars, ere I come to Sittingbourne,
That I shall make thine heartë for to mourn:
For well I wot thy patience is gone."
Our Hostë criëd, "Peace, and that anon;"
And saidë, "Let the woman tell her tale.
Ye fare[6] as folk that drunken be of ale.
Do, Dame, tell forth your tale, and that is best."
"All ready, sir," quoth she, "right as you lest,[7]
If I have licence of this worthy Frere."
"Yes, Dame," quoth he, "tell forth, and I will hear."

THE TALE.[8]

In oldë dayës of the king Arthoúr,
Of which that Britons speakë great honoúr,
All was this land full fill'd of faërie;[9]
The Elf-queen, with her jolly company,
Danced full oft in many a green mead.
This was the old opinion, as I read;
I speak of many hundred years ago;
But now can no man see none elvës mo',
For now the great charitý and prayéres
Of limitours,[10] and other holy freres,
That search every land and ev'ry stream,
As thick as motës in the sunnë-beam,
Blessing halls, chambers, kitchenës, and bowers,
Cities and burghës, castles high and towers,
Thorpës[11] and barnës, shepens[12] and dairies,
This makes that there be now no faëries:
For there as[13] wont to walkë was an elf,
There walketh now the limitour himself,
In undermelës[14] and in morrownings,
And saith his matins and his holy things,
As he goes in his limitatioún.[15]
Women may now go safely up and down,
In every bush, and under every tree;
There is none other incubus[16] but he;
And he will do to them no dishonoúr.

And so befell it, that this king Arthoúr
Had in his house a lusty bachelér,
That on a day came riding from rivér:[17]
And happen'd, that, alone as she was born,
He saw a maiden walking him beforn,
Of which maiden anon, maugré[18] her head,
By very force he reft her maidenhead:
For which oppressión was such clamoúr,
And such pursuit unto the king Arthoúr,
That damned[19] was this knight for to be dead
By course of law, and should have lost his head;
(Parâventure such[20] was the statute tho),[21]
But that the queen and other ladies mo'
So long they prayed the king of his grace,
Till he his life him granted in the place,
And gave him to the queen, all at her will
To choose whether she would him save or spill.[22]
The queen thanked the king with all her might;
And, after this, thus spake she to the knight,
When that she saw her time upon a day.
"Thou standest yet," quoth she, "in such array,[23]
That of thy life yet hast thou no suretý;
I grant thee life, if thou canst tell to me
What thing is it that women most desiren:
Beware, and keep thy neck-bone from the iron.[24]
And if thou canst not tell it me anon,
Yet will I give thee leavë for to gon
A twelvemonth and a day, to seek and lear[25]
An answer suffisant[26] in this mattére.
And surety will I have, ere that thou pace,[27]
Thy body for to yielden in this place."
Woe was the knight, and sorrowfully siked;[28]
But what? he might not do all as him liked.
And at the last he chose him for to wend,[29]
And come again, right at the yearë's end,
With such answér as God would him purvey:[30]
And took his leave, and wended forth his way.
He sought in ev'ry house and ev'ry place,
Where as he hoped for to findë grace,
To learnë what thing women love the most:
But he could not arrive in any coast,
Where as he mightë find in this mattére
Two creaturës according in fere.[31]
Some said that women loved best richéss,
Some said honoúr, and some said jolliness,
Some rich array, and some said lust[32] a-bed,
And oft time to be widow and be wed.
Some said, that we are in our heart most eased
When that we are y-flatter'd and y-praised.
He went full nigh the sooth,[33] I will not lie;
A man shall win us best with flattery;

1 Interpose; French, "entremettre."
2 Preamble. Some editions print "preambulation," but the word in the text seems meant to show up the ignorance of the clergy, as Chaucer lost no occasion of doing. 3 Hinderest. 4 Curse.
5 Unless. 6 Behave. 7 Please.
8 It is not clear whence Chaucer derived this tale. Tyrwhitt thinks it was taken from the story of Florent, in the first book of Gower's "Confessio Amantis;" or perhaps from an older narrative from which Gower himself borrowed. Chaucer has condensed and otherwise improved the fable, especially by laying the scene, not in Sicily, but at the court of our own King Arthur. 9 Fairies; French, "féerie."
10 Begging friars. See note 27, page 19.
11 Villages. Compare German, "Dorf."
12 Stables, sheep-pens. 13 Where.
14 Evening-tides, afternoons; "undern" signifies the evening; and "mele," corresponds to the German "Mal" or "Mahl," time. 15 Begging district.
16 An evil spirit supposed to do violence to women; a nightmare.
17 Where he had been hawking after waterfowl. Froissart says that any one engaged in this sport "alloit en rivière." 18 Spite of.
19 Condemned. 20 For as it happened, such.
21 Then. 22 Execute, destroy.
23 In such a position. 24 The executioner's axe.
25 Learn. 26 Satisfactory.
27 Go. 28 Sighed. 29 Depart.
30 Provide him with. 31 Agreeing together.
32 Pleasure. 33 Came very near the truth.

And with attendance, and with business
Be we y-liméd,[1] bothë more and less.
And some men said that we do love the best
For to be free, and do right as us lest,[2]
And that no man reprove us of our vice,
But say that we are wise, and nothing nice,[3]
For truly there is none among us all,
If any wight will claw us on the gall,[4]
That will not kick, for that he saith us sooth:
Assay,[5] and he shall find it, that so do'th.
For be we never so vicioús within,
We will be held both wise and clean of sin.
And some men said, that great delight have we
For to be held stable and eke secré,[6]
And in one purpose steadfastly to dwell,
And not bewray a thing that men us tell.
But that tale is not worth a rakë-stele.[7]
Pardie, we women cannë nothing hele,[8]
Witness on Midas; will ye hear the tale?
Ovid, amongës other thingës smale,[9]
Saith, Midas had, under his longë hairs,
Growing upon his head two ass's ears;
The whichë vice he hid, as best he might,
Full subtlely from every man's sight,
That, save his wife, there knew of it no mo';
He lov'd her most, and trusted her also;
He prayed her, that to no creature
She wouldë tellen of his disfigúre.[10]
She swore him, nay, for all the world to win,
She would not do that villainy or sin,
To make her husband have so foul a name:
She would not tell it for her owen shame.
But natheless her thoughtë that she died,
That she so longë should a counsel hide;
Her thought it swell'd so sore about her heart,
That needës must some word from her astart;
And, since she durst not tell it unto man,
Down to a marish fast thereby she ran,
Till she came there, her heart was all afire:
And, as a bittern bumbles [11] in the mire,
She laid her mouth unto the water down.
"Bewray me not, thou water, with thy soun'," [12]
Quoth she, "to thee I tell it, and no mo',
Mine husband hath long ass's earës two!
Now is mine heart all whole; now is it out;
I might no longer keep it, out of doubt."
Here may ye see, though we a time abide,
Yet out it must, we can no counsel hide.
The remnant of the tale, if ye will hear,
Read in Ovíd, and there ye may it lear.[13]
This knight, of whom my tale is specially,
When that he saw he might not come thereby,—
That is to say, what women love the most,—
Within his breast full sorrowful was his ghost.[14]
But home he went, for he might not sojourn,
The day was come, that homeward he must turn.
And in his way it happen'd him to ride,
In all his care,[15] under a forest side,
Where as he saw upon a dancë go
Of ladies four-and-twenty, and yet mo'.
Toward this ilkë[16] dance he drew full yern,[17]
In hope that he some wisdom there should learn;
But certainly, ere he came fully there,
Y-vanish'd was this dance, he knew not where;
No creaturë saw he that bare life,
Save on the green he sitting saw a wife,—
A fouler wight there may no man devise.[18]
Against [19] this knight this old wife gan to rise,
And said, "Sir Knight, hereforth[20] lieth no way.
Tell me what ye are seeking, by your fay.[21]
Paráventure it may the better be:
These oldë folk know muchë thing," quoth she.
"My levë [22] mother," quoth this knight, "certáin,
I am but dead, but if [23] that I can sayn
What thing it is that women most desire:
Could ye me wiss,[24] I would well quite your hire." [25]
"Plight me thy troth here in mine hand," quoth she,
"The nextë thing that I require of thee
Thou shalt it do, if it be in thy might,
And I will tell it thee ere it be night."
"Have here my trothë," quoth the knight; "I grant."
"Thennë," quoth she, "I dare me well avaunt,[26]
Thy life is safe, for I will stand thereby,
Upon my life the queen will say as I:
Let see, which is the proudest of them all,
That wears either a kerchief or a caul,
That dare say nay to that I shall you teach.
Let us go forth withoutë longer speech."
Then rowned she a pistel [27] in his ear,
And bade him to be glad, and have no fear.
When they were come unto the court, this knight
Said, he had held his day, as he had hight,[28]
And ready was his answer, as he said.
Full many a noble wife, and many a maid,
And many a widow, for that they be wise,—
The queen herself sitting as a justíce,—
Assembled be, his answer for to hear,
And afterward this knight was bid appear.
To every wight commanded was silénce,
And that the knight should tell in audience,
What thing that worldly women love the best.
This knight he stood not still, as doth a beast,
But to this questión anon answér'd
With manly voice, that all the court it heard,
"My liegë lady, generally," quoth he,
"Women desire to have the sovereignty
As well over their husband as their love,
And for to be in mast'ry him above.
This is your most desire, though ye me kill,
Do as you list, I am here at your will."
In all the court there was no wife nor maid,

1 Caught, as birds with lime.
2 Pleases. 3 Foolish; French, "niais."
4 Fret the sore. Compare, "Let the galled jade wince." 5 Try.
6 Secret, good at keeping confidence.
7 Rake-handle.
8 From Anglo-Saxon, "helan," to hide, conceal.
9 Small. 10 Deformity, disfigurement.
11 Makes a humming noise.
12 Sound. 13 Learn. 14 Spirit.
15 Trouble, anxiety. 16 Same.
17 Eagerly; German, "gern." 18 Imagine, tell.
19 To meet. 20 Forth from hence.
21 Faith. 22 Dear. 23 Unless.
24 Instruct; German, "weisen," to show or counsel.
25 Pay your reward. 26 Boast, affirm,
27 Whispered a secret, a lesson.
28 Promised.

Nor widow, that contráried what he said,
But said, he worthy was to have his life.
And with that word up start that oldë wife
Which that the knight saw sitting on the green.
"Mercy," quoth she, "my sovereign lady queen,
Ere that your court departë, do me right.
I taughtë this answér unto this knight,
For which he plighted me his trothë there,
The firstë thing I would of him requere,
He would it do, if it lay in his might.
Before this court then pray I thee, Sir Knight,"
Quoth she, "that thou me take unto thy wife,
For well thou know'st that I have kept[1] thy life.
If I say false, say nay, upon thy fay."[2]
This knight answér'd, "Alas, and well-away!
I know right well that such was my behest.[3]
For Goddë's lovë choose a new request:
Take all my good, and let my body go."
"Nay, then," quoth she, "I shrew[4] us bothë two,
For though that I be old, and foul, and poor,
I n'ould[5] for all the metal nor the ore,
That under earth is grave,[6] or lies above,
But if thy wife I were and eke thy love."
"My love?" quoth he, "nay, my damnatión,
Alas! that any of my natión
Should ever so foul disparáged be."
But all for nought; the end is this, that he
Constrained was, that needs he must her wed,
And take this oldë wife, and go to bed.
Now wouldë some men say paráventure,[7]
That for my negligence I do no cure[8]
To tell you all the joy and all th' array
That at the feast was made that ilkë[9] day.
To which thing shortly answeren I shall:
I say there was no joy nor feast at all,
There was but heaviness and muchë sorrow:
For privily he wed her on the morrow;
And all day after hid him as an owl,
So woe was him, his wifë look'd so foul.
Great was the woe the knight had in his thought
When he was with his wife to bed y-brought;
He wallow'd, and he turned to and fro.
This oldë wife lay smiling evermo',
And said, "Dear husband, *benedicite,*
Fares every knight thus with his wife as ye?
Is this the law of king Arthoúrë's house?
Is every knight of his thus dangerous?[10]
I am your owen love, and eke your wife,
I am she, which that saved hath your life,
And certes yet did I you ne'er unright.
Why fare ye thus with me this firstë night?
Ye farë like a man had lost his wit.
What is my guilt? for God's love tell me it,
And it shall be amended, if I may."
"Amended!" quoth this knight; "alas! nay, nay,
It will not be amended, never mo';
Thou art so loathly, and so old also,
And thereto[11] comest of so low a kind,
That little wonder though I wallow and wind;[12]
So wouldë God, mine heartë wouldë brest!"[13]
"Is this," quoth she, "the cause of your unrest?"
"Yea, certainly," quoth he; "no wonder is."
"Now, Sir," quoth she, "I could amend all this,
If that me list, ere it were dayës three,
So well ye mightë bear you unto me.[14]
But, for ye speaken of such gentleness
As is descended out of old richéss,
That therefore shallë ye be gentlemen;
Such arrogancy is not worth a hen.[15]
Look who that is most virtuous alway,
Prive and apert,[16] and most intendeth aye
To do the gentle deedës that he can;
And take him for the greatest gentleman.
Christ will,[17] we claim of him our gentleness,
Nót of our elders[18] for their old richéss.
For though they gave us all their heritage,
For which we claim to be of high parage,[19]
Yet may they not bequeathë, for no thing,
To none of us, their virtuous living
That made them gentlemen called to be,
And bade us follow them in such degree.
Well can the wisë poet of Florence,
That hightë Dante, speak of this senténce:[20]
Lo, in such manner[21] rhyme is Dante's tale.
'Full seld' upriseth by his branches smale
Prowess of man, for God of his goodness
Wills that we claim of him our gentleness;'[22]
For of our elders may we nothing claim
But temp'ral things that man may hurt and maim.
Eke every wight knows this as well as I,
If gentleness were planted naturally
Unto a certain lineage down the line,
Prive and apert, then would they never fine[23]
To do of gentleness the fair office;
Then might they do no villainy nor vice.
Take fire, and bear it to the darkest house
Betwixt this and the mount of Caucasus,
And let men shut the doorës, and go thenne,[24]
Yet will the fire as fair and lightë brenne[25]
As twenty thousand men might it behold;
Its office natural aye will it hold,[26]—
On peril of my life,—till that it die.
Here may ye see well how that gentery[27]
Is not annexed to possessión,
Since folk do not their operatión
Alway, as doth the fire, lo, in its kind.[28]
For, God it wot, men may full often find
A lordë's son do shame and villainy.
And he that will have price[29] of his gent'ry,
For[30] he was boren of a gentle house,
And had his elders noble and virtuoús,
And will himselfë do no gentle deedës,
Nor follow his gentle ancestry, that dead is,
He is not gentle, be he duke or earl;
For villain sinful deedës make a churl.

1 Preserved. 2 Faith. 3 Promise.
4 Curse. 5 Would not. 6 Buried.
7 Perhaps. 8 Take no pains. 9 Same.
10 Fastidious, niggardly. 11 In addition.
12 Writhe, turn about. 13 Burst.
14 If you could conduct yourself well towards me.
15 Is only to be despised. See note 17, page 19.
16 In private and in public. 17 Wills, requires.
18 Ancestors. 19 Birth, descent. 20 Sentiment.
21 Kind of. 22 Dante, "Purgatorio," vii. 121.
23 Cease. 24 Thence. 25 Burn.
26 It will perform its natural function.
27 Gentility, nobility. 28 From its very nature.
29 Esteem, honour. 30 Because.

For gentleness is but the renomée [1]
Of thine ancéstors, for their high bounté,[2]
Which is a strangë thing to thy persón:
Thy gentleness cometh from God alone.
Then comes our very [3] gentleness of grace;
It was no thing bequeath'd us with our place.
Think how noble, as saith Valerius,
Was thilkë [4] Tullius Hostilius,
That out of povert' rose to high nobless.
Read in Senec, and read eke in Boece,
There shall ye see express, that it no drede [5] is,
That he is gentle that doth gentle deedës.
And therefore, levë [6] husband, I conclude,
Albeit that mine ancestors were rude,
Yet may the highë God,—and so hope I,—
Grant me His grace to live virtuously:
Then am I gentle, when that I begin
To live virtuously, and waivë [7] sin.
"And whereas ye of povert' me repreve,[8]
The highë God, on whom that we believe,
In wilful povert' chose to lead his life:
And certes, every man, maiden, or wife
May understand that Jesus, heaven's king,
Ne would not choose a vicious living.
Glad povert' [9] is an honest thing, certáin;
This will Senec and other clerkës [10] sayn.
Whoso that holds him paid of [11] his povért',
I hold him rich, though he had not a shirt.
He that covéteth is a poorë wight,
For he would have what is not in his might.
But he that nought hath, nor covéteth t' have,
Is rich, although ye hold him but a knave.[12]
Very povért' is sinnë, properly.[13]
Juvenal saith of povert' merrily:
The poorë man, when he goes by the way,
Before the thievës he may sing and play.[14]
Povért' is hateful good;[15] and, as I guess,
A full great bringer out of business;[16]
A great amender eke of sapience
To him that taketh it in patience.
Povert' is this, although it seem elenge,[17]
Possessión that no wight will challénge.
Povert' full often, when a man is low,
Makes him his God and eke himself to know:
Povert' a spectacle is,[18] as thinketh me,
Through which he may his very [3] friendës see.
And, therefore, Sir, since that I you not grieve,
Of my povert' no morë me repreve.
"Now, Sir, of eldë [19] ye reprevë me:
And certes, Sir, though none authority [20]
Were in no book, ye gentles of honoúr
Say, that men should an oldë wight honoúr,
And call him father, for your gentleness;
And authors shall I finden, as I guess.
Now there ye say that I am foul and old,
Then dread ye not to be a cokëwold.[21]
For filth, and eldë, all so may I thé,[22]
Be greatë wardens upon chastity.
But natheless, since I know your delight,
I shall fulfil your worldly appetite.
Choose now," quoth she, "one of these thingës
tway,
To have me foul and old till that I dey,[23]
And be to you a truë humble wife,
And never you displease in all my life:
Or elles will ye have me young and fair,
And take your áventure of the repair [24]
That shall be to your house because of me,—
Or in some other place, it may well be?
Now choose yourselfë whether that you liketh."
This knight adviseth [25] him, and sore he siketh,[26]
But at the last he said in this mannére;
"My lady and my love, and wife so dear,
I put me in your wisë governance,
Choose for yourself which may be most pleasance
And most honoúr to you and me also;
I do no force [27] the whether of the two:
For as you liketh, it sufficeth me."
"Then have I got the mastery," quoth she,
"Since I may choose and govern as me lest."[28]
"Yea, certes, wife," quoth he, "I hold it best."
"Kiss me," quoth she, "we are no longer
wroth,[29]
For by my troth I will be to you both;
This is to say, yea, bothë fair and good.
I pray to God that I may stervë wood,[30]
But [31] I to you be all so good and true,
As ever was wife, since the world was new;
And but [31] I be to-morrow as fair to seen,
As any lady, emperess, or queen,
That is betwixt the East and eke the West,
Do with my life and death right as you lest.[28]
Cast up the curtain, and look how it is."
And when the knight saw verily all this,
That she so fair was, and so young thereto,
For joy he hent [32] her in his armës two:
His heartë bathed in a bath of bliss,
A thousand times on row [33] he gan her kiss:
And she obeyed him in every thing
That mightë do him pleasance or liking.
And thus they live unto their livës' end
In perfect joy; and Jesus Christ us send
Husbandës meek and young, and fresh in bed,
And grace to overlive them that we wed.
And eke I pray Jesus to short their lives,
That will not be govérned by their wives.
And old and angry niggards of dispence,[34]
God send them soon a very pestilence!

1 French, "renommée," renown.
2 Goodness, worth. 3 True. 4 That.
5 Doubt. 6 Dear. 7 Forsake.
8 Reproach.
9 Poverty endured with contentment.
10 Scholars.
11 Holds himself satisfied with, is content with.
12 A slave, abject wretch.
13 Properly, the only true poverty is sin.
14 "Cantabit vacuus coram latrone viator."—"Satires," x. 22.
15 In a fabulous conference between the Emperor Adrian and the philosopher Secundus, reported by Vincent of Beauvais, occurs the passage which Chaucer here paraphrases:—"Quid est Paupertas? Odibile bonum; sanitatis mater; remotio curarum; sapientiæ repertrix; negotium sine damno; possessio absque calumnia; sine sollicitudine felicitas."
16 Deliverer from care and trouble.
17 Strange; from French, "eloigner," to remove.
18 Is a spying-glass, pair of spectacles.
19 Age. 20 Text, dictum. 21 Cuckold.
22 Thrive. 23 Die. 24 Resort.
25 Considered. 26 Sighed.
27 Set no value, care not. 28 Pleases.
29 At variance. 30 Die mad. 31 Unless.
32 Took. 33 In succession.
34 Grudgers of expense.

THE FRIAR'S TALE.[1]

THE PROLOGUE.

THIS worthy limitour, this noble Frere,
He made always a manner louring cheer[2]
Upon the Sompnour; but for honesty[3]
No villain word as yet to him spake he:
But at the last he said unto the Wife:
"Damë," quoth he, "God give you right good life,
Ye have here touched, all so may I thé,[4]
In school matter a greatë difficulty.
Ye have said muchë thing right well, I say;
But, Damë, here as we ride by the way,
Us needeth not but for to speak of game,
And leave authorities, in Goddë's name,
To preaching, and to school eke of clergy.
But if it like unto this company,
I will you of a Sompnour tell a game;
Pardie, ye may well knowë by the name,
That of a Sompnour may no good be said;
I pray that none of you be evil paid;[5]
A Sompnour is a runner up and down
With mandements[6] for fornicatioún,
And is y-beat at every townë's end."
Then spake our Host; "Ah, Sir, ye should be hend[7]
And courteous, as a man of your estate;
In company we will have no debate:
Tell us your tale, and let the Sompnour be."
"Nay," quoth the Sompnour, "let him say by me
What so him list; when it comes to my lot,
By God, I shall him quiten[8] every groat!
I shall him tellë what a great honoúr
It is to be a flattering limitour,
And his office I shall him tell y-wis."[9]
Our Host answered, "Peace, no more of this."
And afterward he said unto the Frere,
"Tell forth your tale, mine owen master dear."

THE TALE.

Whilom[10] there was dwelling in my countrý
An archdeacon, a man of high degree,
That boldëly did executión,
In punishing of fornicatión,
Of witchëcraft, and eke of bawdery,
Of defamation, and adultery,
Of churchë-reevës,[11] and of testaments,
Of contracts, and of lack of sacraments,
And eke of many another manner[12] crime,
Which needeth not rehearsen at this time,
Of usury, and simony also;
But, certes, lechours did he greatest woe;
They shouldë singen, if that they were hent;[13]
And smallë tithers[14] werë foul y-shent,[15]
If any person would on them complain;
There might astert them no pecunial pain.[16]
For smallë tithës, and small offering,
He made the people piteously to sing;
For ere the bishop caught them with his crook,
They weren in the archëdeacon's book;
Then had he, through his jurisdictión,
Power to do on them correctión.
He had a Sompnour ready to his hand,
A slier boy was none in Engleland;
For subtlely he had his espiaille,[17]
That taught him well where it might aught avail.
He couldë spare of lechours one or two,
To teachë him to four and twenty mo'.
For,—though this Sompnour wood[18] be as a hare,—
To tell his harlotry I will not spare,
For we be out of their correctión,
They have of us no jurisdictión,
Ne never shall have, term of all their lives.
"Peter, so be the women of the stives,"[19]
Quoth this Sompnoúr, "y-put out of our cure."[20]
"Peace, with mischance and with misáventure,"
Our Hostë said, "and let him tell his tale.
Now tellë forth, and let the Sompnour gale,[21]
Nor sparë not, mine owen master dear."
This falsë thief, the Sompnour (quoth the Frere),
Had always bawdës ready to his hand,
As any hawk to lure in Engleland,
That told him all the secrets that they knew,—
For their acquaintance was not come of new;
They werë his approvers[22] privily.
He took himself a great profit thereby:
His master knew not always what he wan.[23]
Withoutë mandement, a lewëd[24] man
He could summon, on pain of Christë's curse,
And they were inly glad to fill his purse,
And make him greatë feastës at the nale.[25]
And right as Judas haddë purses smale,[26]
And was a thief, right such a thief was he,
His master had but half his duëty.[27]
He was (if I shall givë him his laud)
A thief, and eke a Sompnour, and a bawd.
And he had wenches at his retinue,

[1] On the Tale of the Friar, and that of the Sompnour which follows, Tyrwhitt has remarked that they "are well engrafted upon that of the Wife of Bath. The ill-humour which shows itself between those two characters is quite natural, as no two professions at that time were at more constant variance. The regular clergy, and particularly the mendicant friars, affected a total exemption from all ecclesiastical jurisdiction, except that of the Pope, which made them exceedingly obnoxious to the bishops, and of course to all the inferior officers of the national hierarchy." Both tales, whatever their origin, are bitter satires on the greed and worldliness of the Romish clergy.
[2] A kind of gloomy countenance.
[3] Good manners. [4] Thrive. [5] Dissatisfied.
[6] Mandates, summonses. [7] Civil, gentle.
[8] Pay him off. [9] Assuredly.
[10] Once on a time. [11] Churchwardens.
[12] Sort of. [13] Caught.
[14] People who did not pay their full tithes. Mr Wright remarks that "the sermons of the friars in the fourteenth century were most frequently designed to impress the absolute duty of paying full tithes and offerings." [15] Troubled, put to shame.
[16] They got off with no mere pecuniary punishment.
[17] Espionage. [18] Furious, mad.
[19] Stews. [20] Care. [21] Whistle; bawl.
[22] Informers. [23] Won. [24] Ignorant.
[25] Ale-house; inn-ale, a house for ale. [26] Small.
[27] What was owing him.

That whether that Sir Robert or Sir Hugh,
Or Jack, or Ralph, or whoso that it were
That lay by them, they told it in his ear.
Thus were the wench and he of one assent;
And he would fetch a feigned mandement,
And to the chapter summon them both two,
And pill[1] the man, and let the wenchë go.
Then would he say, "Friend, I shall for thy sake
Do strike thee[2] out of ourë letters blake;[3]
Thee thar[4] no more as in this case travail;
I am thy friend where I may thee avail."
Certain he knew of bribers many mo'
Than possible is to tell in yearës two:
For in this world is no dog for the bow,[5]
That can a hurt deer from a wholë know,
Bet[6] than this Sompnour knew a sly lechour,
Or an adult'rer, or a paramour:
And, for that was the fruit of all his rent,
Therefore on it he set all his intent.
  And so befell, that once upon a day
This Sompnour, waiting ever on his prey,
Rode forth to summon a widow, an old ribibe,[7]
Feigning a cause, for he would have a bribe.
And happen'd that he saw before him ride
A gay yeoman under a forest side:
A bow he bare, and arrows bright and keen,
He had upon a courtepy[8] of green,
A hat upon his head with fringes blake.
"Sir," quoth this Sompnour, "hail, and well o'ertake."
"Welcome," quoth he, "and every good felláw;
Whither ridést thou under this green shaw?"[9]
Saidë this yeoman; "wilt thou far to-day?"
This Sompnour answer'd him, and saidë, "Nay.
Here fastë by," quoth he, "is mine intent
To ridë, for to raisen up a rent,
That longeth to my lordë's duëty."
"Ah! art thou then a bailiff?" "Yea," quoth he.
He durstë not for very filth and shame
Say that he was a Sompnour, for the name.
"*De par dieux*,"[10] quoth this yeoman, "levë[11] brother,
Thou art a bailiff, and I am another.
I am unknowen, as in this countrý.
Of thine acquaintance I will prayë thee,
And eke of brotherhood, if that thee list.[12]
I have gold and silver lying in my chest;
If that thee hap to come into our shire,
All shall be thine, right as thou wilt desire."
"*Grand mercy*,"[13] quoth this Sompnour, "by my faith."
Each in the other's hand his trothë lay'th,
For to be swornë brethren till they dey.[14]
In dalliance they ridë forth and play.
  This Sompnour, which that was as full of jangles,[15]
As full of venom be those wariangles,[16]
And ev'r inquiring upon every thing,
"Brother," quoth he, "where is now your dwelling,
Another day if that I should you seech?"[17]
This yeoman him answered in soft speech;
"Brother," quoth he, "far in the North countrý,[18]
Where as I hope some time I shall thee see.
Ere we depart I shall thee so well wiss,[19]
That of mine housë shalt thou never miss."
"Now, brother," quoth this Sompnour, "I you pray,
Teach me, while that we ridë by the way,
(Since that ye be a bailiff as am I,)
Some subtilty, and tell me faithfully
In mine offíce how that I most may win.
And sparë not[20] for conscience or for sin,
But, as my brother, tell me how do ye."
"Now by my trothë, brother mine," said he,
"As I shall tell to thee a faithful tale:
My wages be full strait and eke full smale;
My lord is hard to me and dangerous,[21]
And mine offíce is full laborious;
And therefore by extortión I live,
Forsooth I take all that men will me give.
Algate[22] by sleightë, or by violence,
From year to year I win all my dispence;
I can no better tell thee faithfully."
"Now certes," quoth this Sompnour, "so fare[23] I;
I sparë not to takë, God it wot,
But if[24] it be too heavy or too hot.
What I may get in counsel privily,
No manner conscience of that have I.
N'ere[25] mine extortión, I might not live,
Nor of such japës[26] will I not be shrive.[27]
Stomach nor consciencë know I none;
I shrew[28] these shriftë-fathers[29] every one.
Well be we met, by God and by St Jame.
But, levë brother, tell me then thy name,"
Quoth this Sompnour. Right in this meanë while
This yeoman gan a little for to smile.
  "Brother," quoth he, "wilt thou that I thee tell?
I am a fiend, my dwelling is in hell,
And here I ride about my purchasing,
To know where men will give me any thing.
My purchase is th' effect of all my rent.[30]
Look how thou ridest for the same intent
To winnë good, thou reckest never how,
Right so fare I, for ridë will I now
Unto the worldë's endë for a prey."

1 Plunder, pluck.
2 Cause thee to be struck.
3 Black.
4 It is needful.
5 Dog attending a huntsman with bow and arrow.
6 Better.
7 The name of a musical instrument; applied to an old woman because of the shrillness of her voice.
8 Wore a short doublet.
9 Shade.
10 By the gods.
11 Dear.
12 Please.
13 Great thanks.
14 Die. See note 17, page 28.
15 Chattering.
16 Butcher-birds; which are very noisy and ravenous, and tear in pieces the birds on which they prey; the thorn on which they do this was said to become poisonous.
17 Seek, visit.
18 Mediæval legends located hell in the North.
19 Inform.
20 Conceal nothing from me.
21 Niggardly.
22 Whether.
23 Do.
24 Unless.
25 Were it not for.
26 Tricks.
27 Confessed, shriven.
28 Curse.
29 Confessors.
30 What I can gain is my sole revenue.

"Ah," quoth this Sompnour, "*benedicite!* what say y'?
I weened[1] ye were a yeoman truly.
Ye have a mannë's shape as well as I.
Have ye then a figúre determinate
In hellë, where ye be in your estate?"[2]
"Nay, certainly," quoth he, "there have we none,
But when us liketh we can take us one.
Or ellës make you seem[3] that we be shape
Sometimë like a man, or like an ape;
Or like an angel can I ride or go;
It is no wondrous thing though it be so,
A lousy juggler can deceivë thee,
And, pardie, yet can[4] I more craft[5] than he."
"Why," quoth the Sompnour, "ride ye then or gon
In sundry shapes, and not always in one?"
"For we," quoth he, "will us in such form make,
As most is able our prey for to take."
"What maketh you to have all this labóur?"
"Full many a causë, levë Sir Sompnoúr,"
Saidë this fiend. "But all thing hath a time;
The day is short, and it is passed prime,
And yet have I won nothing in this day;
I will intend[6] to winning, if I may,
And not intend our thingës to declare:
For, brother mine, thy wit is all too bare
To understand, although I told them thee.
But for[7] thou askest, why laboúrë we:
For sometimes we be Goddë's instruments
And meanës to do his commandëments,
When that him list, upon his creatures,
In divers acts and in divérs figúres:
Withoutë him we have no might, certain,
If that him list to standë thereagain.[8]
And sometimes, at our prayer, have we leave
Only the body, not the soul, to grieve:
Witness on Job, whom that we did full woe.
And sometimes have we might on both the two,—
This is to say, on soul and body eke.
And sometimes be we suffer'd for to seek
Upon a man, and do his soul unrest
And not his body, and all is for the best.
When he withstandeth our temptatión,
It is a cause of his salvatión,
Albeit that it was not our intent
He should be safe, but that we would him hent.[9]
And sometimes be we servants unto man,
As to the archibishop Saint Dunstan,
And to th' apostle servant eke was I."
"Yet tell me," quoth this Sompnour, "faithfully,
Make ye you newë bodies thus alway
Of th' elements?" The fiend answered, "Nay:
Sometimes we feign, and sometimes we arise
With deadë bodies, in full sundry wise,
And speak as reas'nably, and fair, and well,
As to the Pythoness[10] did Samuel:
And yet will some men say it was not he.
I do no force of[11] your divinity.
But one thing warn I thee, I will not jape,[12]
Thou wilt algatës[13] weet[14] how we be shape:
Thou shalt hereafterward, my brother dear,
Come, where thee needeth not of me to lear.[15]
For thou shalt by thine own experience
Conne in a chair to rede of this senténce,[16]
Better than Virgil, while he was alive,
Or Dante also.[17] Now let us ride blive,[18]
For I will holdë company with thee,
Till it be so that thou forsakë me."
"Nay," quoth this Sompnour, "that shall ne'er betide.
I am a yeoman, that is known full wide;
My trothë will I hold, as in this case;
For though thou wert the devil Satanas,
My trothë will I hold to thee, my brother,
As I have sworn, and each of us to other,
For to be truë brethren in this case,
And both we go abouten our purchase.[19]
Take thou thy part, what that men will thee give,
And I shall mine, thus may we bothë live.
And if that any of us have more than other,
Let him be true, and part it with his brother."
"I grantë," quoth the devil, "by my fay."
And with that word they rodë forth their way,
And right at th' ent'ring of the townë's end,
To which this Sompnour shope[20] him for to wend,[21]
They saw a cart, that charged was with hay,
Which that a carter drove forth on his way.
Deep was the way, for which the cartë stood:
The carter smote, and cried as he were wood,[22]
"Heit Scot! heit Brok! what, spare ye for the stones?
The fiend (quoth he) you fetch body and bones,
As farforthly[23] as ever ye were foal'd,
So muchë woe as I have with you tholed.[24]
The devil have all, horses, and cart, and hay."
The Sompnour said, "Here shall we have a prey;"
And near the fiend he drew, as nought ne were,[25]
Full privily, and rowned[26] in his ear:
"Hearken, my brother, hearken, by thy faith,
Hearest thou not, how that the carter saith?
Hent[27] it anon, for he hath giv'n it thee,
Both hay and cart, and eke his capels[28] three."
"Nay," quoth the devil, "God wot, never a deal,[29]
It is not his intent, trust thou me well;

1 Thought. 2 At home; in your natural state. 3 Make it seem to you. 4 Know. 5 Skill, cunning. 6 Apply myself. 7 Because. 8 Against it. 9 Catch.
10 The witch, or woman, possessed with a prophesying spirit; from the Greek, Πυθια. Chaucer of course refers to the raising of Samuel's spirit by the Witch of Endor. 11 Set no value upon. 12 Jest. 13 Assuredly. 14 Know. 15 Learn.
16 Learn to understand what I have said.
17 Both poets who had in fancy visited hell.
18 Briskly. 19 Seeking what we may pick up.
20 Shaped, resolved. 21 Go.
22 Mad. 23 As sure.
24 Suffered, endured; "thole" is still used in Scotland in the same sense.
25 As if nothing were the matter. 26 Whispered.
27 Seize. 28 Horses. 29 Whit.

Ask him thyself, if thou not trowest[1] me,
Or ellës stint[2] a while and thou shalt see."
The carter thwack'd his horses on the croup,
And they began to drawen and to stoop.
"Heit now," quoth he; "there, Jesus Christ you bless,
And all his handiwork, both more and less!
That was well twight,[3] mine owen liart,[4] boy,
I pray God save thy body, and Saint Loy!
Now is my cart out of the slough, pardie."
"Lo, brother," quoth the fiend, "what told I thee?
Here may ye see, mine owen dearë brother,
The churl spake one thing, but he thought another.
Let us go forth abouten our voyáge;
Here win I nothing upon this carriáge."
When that they came somewhat out of the town,
This Sompnour to his brother gan to rown;
"Brother," quoth he, "here wons[5] an old rebeck,[6]
That had almost as lief to lose her neck.
As for to give a penny of her good.
I will have twelvepence, though that she be wood,[7]
Or I will summon her to our offíce;
And yet, God wot, of her know I no vice.
But for thou canst not, as in this countrý,
Winnë thy cost, take here example of me."
This Sompnour clapped at the widow's gate:
"Come out," he said, "thou oldë very trate;[8]
I trow thou hast some friar or priest with thee."
"Who clappeth?" said this wife; "*ben'dicite,*
God save you, Sir, what is your sweetë will?"
"I have," quoth he, "of summons here a bill.
Up[9] pain of cursing, lookë that thou be
To-morrow before our archdeacon's knee,
To answer to the court of certain things."
"Now Lord," quoth she, "Christ Jesus, king of kings,
So wisly[10] helpë me, as I not may.[11]
I have been sick, and that full many a day.
I may not go so far," quoth she, "nor ride,
But I be dead, so pricketh[12] it my side.
May I not ask a libel, Sir Sompnoúr,
And answer there by my procúratoúr
To such thing as men would apposë[13] me?"
"Yes," quoth this Sompnour, "pay anon, let see,
Twelvepence to me, and I will thee acquit.
I shall no profit have thereby but lit:[14]
My master hath the profit and not I.
Come off, and let me ridë hastily;
Give me twelvepence, I may no longer tarry."
"Twelvepence!" quoth she; "now lady Saintë Mary
So wisly[10] help me out of care and sin,
This widë world though that I should it win,
Ne have I not twelvepence within my hold.
Ye know full well that I am poor and old;
Kithë your almës[15] upon me poor wretch."
"Nay then," quoth he, "the foulë fiend me fetch,
If I excuse thee, though thou should'st be spilt."[16]
"Alas!" quoth she, "God wot, I have no guilt."
"Pay me," quoth he, "or, by the sweet Saint Anne,
As I will bear away thy newë pan
For debtë, which thou owest me of old,—
When that thou madest thine husbánd cuck-óld,—
I paid at home for thy correctión."
"Thou liest," quoth she, "by my salvatión;
Never was I ere now, widow or wife,
Summon'd unto your court in all my life;
Nor never I was but of my body true.
Unto the devil rough and black of hue
Give I thy body and my pan also."
And when the devil heard her cursë so
Upon her knees, he said in this mannére;
"Now, Mabily, mine owen mother dear,
Is this your will in earnest that ye say?"
"The devil," quoth she, "so fetch him ere he dey,[17]
And pan and all, but[18] he will him repent."
"Nay, oldë stoat,[19] that is not mine intent,"
Quoth this Sompnour, "for to repentë me
For any thing that I have had of thee;
I would I had thy smock and every cloth."
"Now, brother," quoth the devil, "be not wroth;
Thy body and this pan be mine by right.
Thou shalt with me to hellë yet to-night,
Where thou shalt knowen of our privity[20]
More than a master of divinity."
And with that word the foulë fiend him hent.[21]
Body and soul, he with the devil went,
Where as the Sompnours have their heritage;
And God, that maked after his imáge
Mankindë, save and guide us all and some,
And let this Sompnour a good man become.
Lordings, I could have told you (quoth this Frere),
Had I had leisure for this Sompnour here,
After the text of Christ, and Paul, and John,
And of our other doctors many a one,
Such painës, that your heartës might agrise,[22]
Albeit so, that no tongue may devise,—[23]
Though that I might a thousand winters tell,—
The pains of thilkë[24] cursed house of hell.
But for to keep us from that cursed place
Wake we, and pray we Jesus, of his grace,

1 Believest. 2 Stop.
3 Pulled; for "twitched."
4 Gray; elsewhere applied by Chaucer to the hairs of an old man. So Burns, in the "Cotter's Saturday Night," speaks of the gray temples of "the sire"—"His lyart haffets wearing thin and bare." 5 Dwells.
6 Used like "ribibe,"—as a nickname for a shrill old scold. 7 Mad.
8 Trot; a contemptuous term for an old woman who has trotted about much, or who moves with quick short steps. 9 Upon. 10 Surely.
11 Cannot help myself. 12 Paineth.
13 Question me about, lay to my charge.
14 Little. 15 Show your charity.
16 Ruined, put to death. 17 Die.
18 Unless. 19 Polecat. 20 Secrets.
21 Seized. 22 Frighten, horrify.
23 Relate. 24 That.

So keep us from the tempter, Satanas.
Hearken this word, beware as in this case.
The lion sits in his await[1] alway
To slay the innocent, if that he may.
Disposen aye your heartës to withstond
The fiend, that would you makë thrall and bond;
He may not temptë you over your might,
For Christ will be your champion and your knight;
And pray, that this our Sompnour him repent
Of his misdeeds, ere that the fiend him hent.[2]

THE SOMPNOUR'S TALE.

THE PROLOGUE.

THIS Sompnour in his stirrups high he stood,
Upon this Friar his heartë was so wood,[3]
That like an aspen leaf he quoke[4] for ire:
"Lordings," quoth he, "but one thing I desire;
I you beseech, that of your courtesy,
Since ye have heard this falsë Friar lie,
As suffer me I may my talë tell.
This Friar boasteth that he knoweth hell,
And, God it wot, that is but little wonder,
Friars and fiends be but little asunder.
For, pardie, ye have often time heard tell,
How that a friar ravish'd was to hell
In spirit onës by a visioún,
And, as an angel led him up and down,
To shew him all the painës that there were,
In all the placë saw he not a frere;
Of other folk he saw enough in woe.
Unto the angel spake the friar tho;[5]
'Now, Sir,' quoth he, 'have friars such a grace,
That none of them shall come into this place?'
'Yes,' quoth the angel, 'many a millioún:'
And unto Satanas he led him down.
'And now hath Satanas,' said he, 'a tail
Broader than of a carrack[6] is the sail.
Hold up thy tail, thou Satanas,' quoth he,
'Shew forth thine erse, and let the friar see
Where is the nest of friars in this place.'
And less than half a furlong way of space,[7]
Right so as bees swarmen out of a hive,
Out of the devil's erse there gan to drive
A twenty thousand friars on a rout.[8]
And throughout hell they swarmed all about,
And came again, as fast as they may gon,
And in his erse they creeped every one:
He clapt his tail again, and lay full still.
This friar, when he looked had his fill
Upon the torments of that sorry place,
His spirit God restored of his grace
Into his body again, and he awoke;
But natheless for fearë yet he quoke,
So was the devil's erse aye in his mind;
That is his heritage, of very kind.[9]
God save you allë, save this cursed Frere;
My prologue will I end in this mannére.

THE TALE.

Lordings, there is in Yorkshire, as I guess,
A marshy country called Holderness,
In which there went a limitour about
To preach, and eke to beg, it is no doubt.
And so befell that on a day this frere
Had preached at a church in his mannére,
And speciálly, above every thing,
Excited he the people in his preaching
To trentals,[10] and to give, for Goddë's sake,
Wherewith men mightë holy houses make,
There as divinë service is honoúr'd,
Not there as it is wasted and devoúr'd,
Nor where it needeth not for to be given,
As to possessioners,[11] that may liven,
Thanked be God, in wealth and abundánce.
"Trentals," said he, "deliver from penánce
Their friendës' soulës, as well old as young,
Yea, when that they be hastily y-sung,—
Not for to hold a priest jolly and gay,
He singeth not but one mass in a day.
Deliver out," quoth he, "anon the souls.
Full hard it is, with flesh-hook or with owls
To be y-clawed, or to burn or bake:[12]
Now speed you hastily, for Christë's sake."
And when this friar had said all his intent,
With *qui cum patre*[13] forth his way he went,
When folk in church had giv'n him what them lest;[14]
He went his way, no longer would he rest,
With scrip and tipped staff, y-tucked high:[15]
In every house he gan to pore[16] and pry,
And begged meal and cheese, or ellës corn.
His fellow had a staff tipped with horn,
A pair of tables[17] all of ivory,
And a pointel[18] y-polish'd fetisly,[19]
And wrote alway the namës, as he stood,
Of all the folk that gave them any good,
Askauncë[20] that he wouldë for them pray.

1 On the watch; French, "aux aguets."
2 Seize.
3 Furious.
4 Quaked, trembled.
5 Then.
6 A great ship of burden used by the Portuguese; the name is from the Italian, "cargare," to load.
7 Immediately.
8 In a company, crowd.
9 By his very nature.
10 The money given to the priests for performing thirty masses for the dead, either in succession or on the anniversaries of their death; also the masses themselves, which were very profitable to the clergy.
11 The regular religious orders, who had lands and fixed revenues; while the friars, by their vows, had to depend on voluntary contributions, though their greed suggested many modes of evading the prescription.
12 In Chaucer's day the most material notions about the tortures of hell prevailed, and were made the most of by the clergy, who preyed on the affection and fear of the survivors, through the ingenious doctrine of purgatory. Old paintings and illuminations represent the dead as torn by hooks, roasted in fires, boiled in pots, and subjected to many other physical torments.
13 The closing words of the final benediction pronounced at mass.
14 Pleased.
15 With his gown tucked up high.
16 Peer, gaze curiously.
17 Writing tablets.
18 A style, or pencil.
19 Daintily.
20 The word now means sideways or asquint; here it means "as if;" and its force is probably to suggest that the second friar, with an ostentatious stealthiness, noted down the names of the liberal, to make them believe that they would be remembered in the holy beggars' orisons.

"Give us a bushel wheat, or malt, or rey,[1]
A Goddë's kichel,[2] or a trip[3] of cheese,
Or ellës what you list, we may not chese;[4]
A Goddë's halfpenny, or a mass penny;
Or give us of your brawn, if ye have any;
A dagon[5] of your blanket, levë dame,
Our sister dear,—lo, here I write your name,—
Bacon or beef, or such thing as ye find."
A sturdy harlot[6] went them aye behind,
That was their hostë's man, and bare a sack,
And what men gave them, laid it on his back.
And when that he was out at door, anon
He planed away the namës every one,
That he before had written in his tables:
He served them with nifles[7] and with fables.—
"Nay, there thou liest, thou Sompnour," quoth the Frere.
"Peace," quoth our Host, "for Christë's mother dear;
Tell forth thy tale, and spare it not at all."
"So thrive I," quoth this Sompnour, "so I shall."—
So long he went from house to house, till he
Came to a house, where he was wont to be
Refreshed more than in a hundred places.
Sick lay the husband man, whose that the place is,
Bedrid upon a couchë low he lay:
"*Deus hic,*"[8] quoth he; "O Thomas friend, good day,"
Said this friár, all courteously and soft.
"Thomas," quoth he, "God yield it you,[9] full oft
Have I upon this bench fared full well,
Here have I eaten many a merry meal."
And from the bench he drove away the cat,
And laid adown his potent[10] and his hat,
And eke his scrip, and sat himself adown:
His fellow was y-walked into town
Forth with his knave,[11] into that hostelry
Where as he shopë[12] him that night to lie.
"O dearë master," quoth this sickë man,
"How have ye fared since that March began?
I saw you not this fortënight and more."
"God wot," quoth he, "laboúr'd have I full sore;
And specially for thy salvatión
Have I said many a precious orison,
And for mine other friendës, God them bless.
I have this day been at your church at mess,[13]
And said sermón after my simple wit,
Not all after the text of Holy Writ;
For it is hard to you, as I suppose,
And therefore will I teach you aye the glose.[14]
Glosing is a full glorious thing certáin,
For letter slayeth, as we clerkës[15] sayn.
There have I taught them to be charitable,
And spend their good where it is reasonable.
And there I saw our damë; where is she?"
"Yonder I trow that in the yard she be,"
Saidë this man; "and she will come anon."
"Hey master, welcome be ye by Saint John,"
Saidë this wife; "how fare ye heartily?"
This friar riseth up full courteously,
And her embraceth in his armës narrow,[16]
And kiss'th her sweet, and chirketh as a sparrow
With his lippës: "Damë," quoth he, "right well,
As he that is your servant every deal.[17]
Thanked be God, that gave you soul and life,
Yet saw I not this day so fair a wife
In all the churchë, God so savë me."
"Yea, God amend defaultës, Sir," quoth she;
"Algatës[18] welcome be ye, by my fay."
"*Grand mercy*, Dame; that have I found alway.
But of your greatë goodness, by your leave,
I wouldë pray you that ye not you grieve,
I will with Thomas speak a little throw:[19]
These curates be so negligent and slow
To gropë tenderly a conscience.
In shrift[20] and preaching is my diligence
And study in Peter's wordës and in Paul's;
I walk and fishë Christian mennë's souls,
To yield our Lord Jesus his proper rent;
To spread his word is allë mine intent."
"Now by your faith, O dearë Sir," quoth she,
"Chide him right well, for saintë charity.
He is aye angry as is a pismire,
Though that he have all that he can desire,
Though I him wrie[21] at night, and make him warm,
And ov'r him lay my leg and eke mine arm,
He groaneth as our boar that lies in sty:
Other disport of him right none have I,
I may not please him in no manner case."[22]
"O Thomas, *je vous dis*, Thomas, Thomas,
This maketh the fiend,[23] this must be amended.
Ire is a thing that high God hath defended,[24]
And thereof will I speak a word or two."
"Now, master," quoth the wife, "ere that I go,
What will ye dine? I will go thereabout."
"Now, Damë," quoth he, "*je vous dis sans doute*,
Had I not of a capon but the liver,
And of your whitë bread not but a shiver,[25]
And after that a roasted piggë's head,
(But I would that for me no beast were dead,)
Then had I with you homely suffisánce.
I am a man of little sustenánce.
My spirit hath its fost'ring in the Bible.
My body is aye so ready and penible[26]
To wakë,[27] that my stomach is destroy'd.
I pray you, Dame, that ye be not annoy'd,
Though I so friendly you my counsel shew;
By God, I would have told it but to few."
"Now, Sir," quoth she, "but one word ere I go;
My child is dead within these weekës two,
Soon after that ye went out of this town."

1 Rye. 2 Little cake, given for God's sake. 3 Small piece. 4 Choose. 5 Slip, remnant.
6 Hired servant; from Anglo-Saxon, "hyran," to hire; the word was commonly applied to males.
7 Trifles, silly tales.
8 God be in this place; the formula of benediction at entering a house.
9 God recompense you therefor.
10 Staff; French, "potence," crutch, gibbet.
11 Servant. 12 Shaped; purposed.
13 Mass. 14 Comment, gloss. 15 Scholars.
16 Closely. 17 Whit. 18 Always.
19 A little while. 20 Confession.
21 Cover. 22 By any sort of chance.
23 This is the fiend's work. 24 Forbidden.
25 Thin slice. 26 Painstaking. 27 Watch.

"His death saw I by revelatioún,"
Said this friar, "at home in our dortour.[1]
I dare well say, that less than half an hour
After his death, I saw him borne to bliss
In minë vision, so God me wiss.[2]
So did our sexton, and our fermerere,[3]
That have been truë friars fifty year,—
They may now, God be thanked of his love,
Makë their jubilee, and walk above.[4]
And up I rose, and all our convent eke,
With many a tearë trilling on my cheek,
Withoutë noise or clattering of bells,
Te Deum was our song, and nothing else,
Save that to Christ I bade an orison,
Thanking him of my revelatión.
For, Sir and Damë, trustë me right well,
Our orisons be more effectuel,
And more we see of Christë's secret things,
Than borel folk,[5] although that they be kings.
We live in povert', and in abstinence,
And borel folk in riches and dispence
Of meat and drink, and in their foul delight.
We have this worldë's lust [6] all in despight.[7]
Lazar and Dives lived diversely,
And diverse guerdon haddë they thereby.
Whoso will pray, he must fast and be clean,
And fat his soul, and keep his body lean.
We fare as saith th' apostle ; cloth [8] and food
Suffice us, although they be not full good.
The cleanness and the fasting of us freres
Maketh that Christ accepteth our prayéres.
Lo, Moses forty days and forty night
Fasted, ere that the high God full of might
Spake with him in the mountain of Sinái:
With empty womb of fasting many a day
Received he the lawë, that was writ
With Goddë's finger ; and Eli,[9] well ye wit,[10]
In Mount Horeb, ere he had any speech
With highë God, that is our livës' leech,[11]
He fasted long, and was in contemplánce.
Aaron, that had the temple in governánce,
And eke the other priestës every one,
Into the temple when they shouldë gon
To prayë for the people, and do service,
They wouldë drinken in no manner wise
No drinkë, which that might them drunken make,
But there in abstinencë pray and wake,[12]
Lest that they diëd : take heed what I say—
But [13] they be sober that for the people pray—
Ware that, I say—no more : for it sufficeth.
Our Lord Jesus, as Holy Writ deviseth,[14]
Gave us example of fasting and prayéres:

1 Dormitory ; French, "dortoir."
2 Direct. 3 Infirmary-keeper.
4 The rules of St Benedict granted peculiar honours and immunities to monks who had lived fifty years—the jubilee period—in the order. The usual reading of the words ending the two lines is "loan" or "lone," and "alone;" but to walk alone does not seem to have been any peculiar privilege of a friar, while the idea of precedence, or higher place at table and in processions, is suggested by the reading in the text.
5 Laymen, people who are not learned; "borel" was a kind of coarse cloth.
6 Pleasure. 7 Contempt. 8 Clothing.
9 Elijah (1 Kings, xix.) 10 Know.
11 Physician, healer. 12 Watch. 13 Unless.
14 Narrates. 15 Simple, lowly.

Therefore we mendicants, we sely [15] freres,
Be wedded to povert' and continence,
To charity, humbless, and abstinence,
To persecutión for righteousness,
To weeping, misericorde,[16] and to cleannéss.
And therefore may ye see that our prayéres
(I speak of us, we mendicants, we freres),
Be to the highë God more acceptable
Than yourës, with your feastës at your table.
From Paradise first, if I shall not lie,
Was man out chased for his gluttony,
And chaste was man in Paradise certáin.
But hark now, Thomas, what I shall thee sayn;
I have no text of it, as I suppose,
But I shall find it in a manner glose;[17]
That speciálly our sweet Lord Jesus
Spake this of friars, when he saidë thus,
'Blessed be they that poor in spirit be.'
And so forth all the gospel may ye see,
Whether it be liker our professión,
Or theirs that swimmen in possessión;
Fy on their pomp, and on their gluttony,
And on their lewëdness! I them defy.
Me thinketh they be like Jovinian,[18]
Fat as a whale, and walking as a swan;
All vinolent as bottle in the spence;[19]
Their prayer is of full great reverence;
When they for soulës say the Psalm of David,
Lo, 'Buf' they say, *Cor meum eructavit.*[20]
Who follow Christë's gospel and his lore [21]
But we, that humble be, and chaste, and pore,[22]
Workers of Goddë's word, not auditoúrs?[23]
Therefore right as a hawk upon a sours [24]
Up springs into the air, right so prayéres
Of charitable and chaste busy freres
Makë their sours to Goddë's earës two.
Thomas, Thomas, so may I ride or go,
And by that lord that called is Saint Ive,
N'ere thou our brother, shouldest thou not thrive;[25]
In our chapíter pray we day and night
To Christ, that he thee sendë health and might,
Thy body for to wieldë hastily." [26]
"God wot," quoth he, "nothing thereof feel I;
So help me Christ, as I in fewë years
Have spended upon divers manner freres [27]
Full many a pound, yet fare I ne'er the bet;[28]
Certain my good have I almost beset:[29]
Farewell my gold, for it is all ago."[30]
The friar answér'd, "O Thomas, dost thou so?
What needest thou diversë friars to seech?[31]
What needeth him that hath a perfect leech,

16 Compassion. 17 A kind of comment.
18 An emperor Jovinian was famous in the mediæval legends for his pride and luxury. 19 Store-room.
20 Literally, "My heart has belched forth;" in our translation, "My heart is inditing a goodly matter." (Ps. xlv. 1.) "Buf" is meant to represent the sound of an eructation, and to show the "great reverence" with which "those in possession," the monks of the rich monasteries, performed divine service.
21 Doctrine. 22 Poor. 23 Hearers.
24 Upon the "soar," or rise.
25 If thou wert not of our brotherhood, thou shouldst have no hope of recovery.
26 Soon to be able to move thy body freely.
27 Friars of various sorts. 28 Better.
29 Spent. 30 Gone. 31 Seek, beseech.

To seeken other leeches in the town?
Your inconstánce is your confusioún.
Hold ye then me, or ellës our convént,
To prayë for you insufficiént?
Thomas, that jape[1] it is not worth a mite;
Your malady is for we have too lite.[2]
Ah, give that convent half a quarter oats;
And give that convent four and twenty groats;
And give that friar a penny, and let him go!
Nay, nay, Thomas, it may no thing be so.
What is a farthing worth parted on twelve?
Lo, each thing that is oned[3] in himselve
Is morë strong than when it is y-scatter'd.
Thomas, of me thou shalt not be y-flatter'd,
Thou wouldest have our labour all for nought.
The highë God, that all this world hath wrought,
Saith, that the workman worthy is his hire.
Thomas, nought of your treasure I desire
As for myself, but that all our convént
To pray for you is aye so diligent:
And for to buildë Christë's owen church.
Thomas, if ye will learnë for to wirch,[4]
Of building up of churches may ye find
If it be good, in Thomas' life of Ind.
Ye lie here full of anger and of ire,
With which the devil sets your heart on fire,
And chidë here this holy innocent
Your wife, that is so meek and patiént.
And therefore trow[5] me, Thomas, if thee lest,[6]
Ne strive not with thy wife, as for the best.
And bear this word away now, by thy faith,
Touching such thing, lo, what the wise man saith:
'Within thy housë be thou no lión;
To thy subjécts do none oppressión;
Nor make thou thine acquaintance for to flee.'
And yet, Thomas, eftsoonës[7] charge I thee,
Beware from ire that in thy bosom sleeps,
Ware from the serpent, that so slily creeps
Under the grass, and stingeth subtilly.
Beware, my son, and hearken patiently,
That twenty thousand men have lost their lives
For striving with their lemans[8] and their wives.
Now since ye have so holy and meek a wife,
What needeth you, Thomas, to makë strife?
There is, y-wis,[9] no serpent so cruél,
When men tread on his tail, nor half so fell,[10]
As woman is, when she hath caught an ire;
Very[11] vengeánce is then all her desire.
Ire is a sin, one of the greatë seven,[12]
Abominable to the God of heaven,
And to himself it is destructión.
This every lewëd[13] vicar and parsón
Can say, how ire engenders homicide;
Ire is in sooth th' executor[14] of pride.
I could of ire you say so muchë sorrow,
My talë shouldë last until to-morrow.
And therefore pray I God both day and night,
An irous[15] man God send him little might.
It is great harm, and certes great pitý
To set an irous man in high degree.
"Whilom[16] there was an irous potestatë,[17]
As saith Senec, that during his estate[18]
Upon a day out rodë knightës two;
And, as fortunë would that it were so,
The one of them came home, the other not.
Anon the knight before the judge is brought,
That saidë thus; 'Thou hast thy fellow slain,
For which I doom thee to the death certáin.'
And to another knight commanded he;
'Go, lead him to the death, I chargë thee.'
And happened, as they went by the way
Toward the placë where as he should dey,[19]
The knight came, which men weened[20] had been dead.
Then thoughtë they it was the bestë rede[21]
To lead them both unto the judge again.
They saidë, 'Lord, the knight hath not y-slain
His fellow; here he standeth whole alive.'
'Ye shall be dead,' quoth he, 'so may I thrive,
That is to say, both one, and two, and three.'
And to the firstë knight right thus spake he:
'I damned thee, thou must algate[22] be dead:
And thou also must needës lose thine head,
For thou the cause art why thy fellow dieth.'
And to the thirdë knight right thus he sayeth,
'Thou hast not done that I commanded thee.'
And thus he did do slay them[23] allë three.
Irous Cambyses was eke dronkelew,[24]
And aye delighted him to be a shrew.[25]
And so befell, a lord of his meinie,[26]
That loved virtuous moralitý,
Said on a day betwixt them two right thus:
'A lord is lost, if he be vicious.
[An irous man is like a frantic beast,
In which there is of wisdom none arrest[27]];
And drunkenness is eke a foul record
Of any man, and namely[28] of a lord.
There is full many an eye and many an ear
Awaiting on[29] a lord, he knows not where.
For Goddë's love, drink more attemperly:[30]
Wine maketh man to losë wretchedly
His mind, and eke his limbës every one.'
'The réverse shalt thou see,' quoth he, 'anon,
And prove it by thine own experience,
That winë doth to folk no such offence.
There is no wine bereaveth me my might
Of hand, nor foot, nor of mine eyen sight.'
And for despite he drankë muchë more
A hundred part[31] than he had done before,
And right anon this cursed irous wretch
This knightë's sonë let[32] before him fetch,
Commanding him he should before him stand:
And suddenly he took his bow in hand,
And up the string he pulled to his ear,
And with an arrow slew the child right there.
'Now whether have I a sicker[33] hand or non?'[34]
Quoth he; 'Is all my might and mind agone?

1 Trick.
2 Because we have too little.
3 Made one, united. 4 Work. 5 Believe.
6 If it please thee. 7 Again. 8 Mistresses.
9 Certainly. 10 Fierce. 11 Pure; only.
12 The seven cardinal sins. 13 Ignorant.
14 Executioner. 15 Passionate. 16 Once.
17 Chief magistrate or judge; Latin, "potestas;" Italian, "podesta." Seneca relates the story of Cornelius Piso; "De Ira," i. 16. 18 Term of office.
19 Die. 20 Thought. 21 Counsel.
22 At all events. 23 Caused them to be slain.
24 A drunkard. 25 Vicious, ill-tempered.
26 Suite. 27 No decree, control. 28 Especially.
29 Watching. 30 Temperately. 31 Times.
32 Caused. 33 Sure. 34 Not.

Hath wine bereaved me mine eyen sight?'
Why should I tell the answer of the knight?
His son was slain, there is no more to say.
Beware therefore with lordës how ye play,[1]
Sing *Placebo;*[2] and I shall if I can,
But if[3] it be unto a poorë man:
To a poor man men should his vices tell,
But not t' a lord, though he should go to hell.
Lo, irous Cyrus, thilkë[4] Persian,
How he destroy'd the river of Gisen,[5]
For that a horse of his was drowned therein,
When that he wentë Babylon to win:
He madë that the river was so small,
That women mightë wade it over all.[6]
Lo, what said he, that so well teachë can?
'Be thou no fellow to an irous man,
Nor with no wood[7] man walkë by the way,
Lest thee repent;' I will no farther say.
"Now, Thomas, levë[8] brother, leave thine ire,
Thou shalt me find as just as is a squire;
Hold not the devil's knife aye at thine heart;
Thine anger doth thee all too sorë smart;[9]
But shew to me all thy confessión."
"Nay," quoth the sickë man, "by Saint Simón
I have been shriven[10] this day of my curáte;
I have him told all wholly mine estate.
Needeth no more to speak of it, saith he,
But if me list of mine humility."
"Give me then of thy good to make our cloister,"
Quoth he, "for many a mussel and many an oyster,
When other men have been full well at ease,
Hath been our food, our cloister for to rese:[11]
And yet, God wot, unneth[12] the foundement[13]
Performed is, nor of our pavëment
Is not a tilë yet within our wones:[14]
By God, we owë forty pound for stones.
Now help, Thomas, for him that harrow'd hell,[15]
For ellës must we ourë bookës sell,
And if ye lack our predicatión,
Then goes this world all to destructión.
For whoso from this world would us bereave,
So God me savë, Thomas, by your leave,
He would bereave out of this world the sun.
For who can teach and worken as we conne?[16]
And that is not of little time (quoth he),
But since Elijah was, and Elisée,[17]
Have friars been, that find I of record,
In charity, y-thanked be our Lord.
Now, Thomas, help for saintë charity."
And down anon he set him on his knee.
This sick man waxed well nigh wood[18] for ire,
He wouldë that the friar had been a-fire
With his falsë dissimulatión.
"Such thing as is in my possessión,"
Quoth he, "that may I give you and none other:
Ye say me thus, how that I am your brother."
"Yea, certes," quoth this friar, "yea, trustë well;
I took our Dame the letter of our seal."[19]
"Now well," quoth he, "and somewhat shall I give
Unto your holy convent while I live;
And in thine hand thou shalt it have anon,
On this conditión, and other none,
That thou depart[20] it so, my dearë brother,
That every friar have as much as other:
This shalt thou swear on thy professión,
Withoutë fraud or cavillatión."[21]
"I swear it," quoth the friar, "upon my faith."
And therewithal his hand in his he lay'th;
"Lo here my faith, in me shall be no lack."
"Then put thine hand adown right by my back,"
Saidë this man, "and gropë well behind,
Beneath my buttock, therë thou shalt find
A thing, that I have hid in privity."
"Ah," thought this friar, "that shall go with me."
And down his hand he launched to the clift,
In hopë for to findë there a gift.
And when this sickë man feltë this frere
About his tailë groping there and here,
Amid his hand he let the friar a fart;
There is no capel[22] drawing in a cart,
That might have let a fart of such a soun'.
The friar up start, as doth a wood[23] lioún:
"Ah, falsë churl," quoth he, "for Goddë's bones,
This hast thou in despite done for the nones:[24]
Thou shalt abie[25] this fart, if that I may."
His meinie,[26] which that heard of this affray,
Came leaping in, and chased out the frere,
And forth he went with a full angry cheer[27]
And fetch'd his fellow, there as lay his store:
He looked as it were a wildë boar,
And groundë with his teeth, so was he wroth.
A sturdy pace down to the court he go'th,
Where as there wonn'd[28] a man of great honoúr,
To whom that he was always confessoúr:
This worthy man was lord of that villáge.
This friar came, as he were in a rage,
Where as this lord sat eating at his board:
Unnethës[29] might the friar speak one word,
Till at the last he saidë, "God you see."[30]
This lord gan look, and said, "*Ben'dicite!*
What? Friar John, what manner world is this?
I see well that there something is amiss;
Ye look as though the wood were full of thievës.
Sit down anon, and tell me what your grieve[31] is,

1 Use freedom.
2 An anthem of the Roman Church, from Psalm cxvi. 9, which in the Vulgate reads, "Placebo Domino in regione virorum"—"I will please the Lord."
3 Unless.
4 That.
5 Seneca calls it the Gyndes; Sir John Mandeville tells the story of the Euphrates. "Gihon" was the name of one of the four rivers of Eden (Gen. ii. 13).
6 Everywhere.
7 Furious.
8 Dear.
9 Pain.
10 Confessed.
11 Raise, build.
12 Scarcely.
13 Foundation.
14 Habitation.
15 For Christ's sake that ravaged hell; see note 11, page 51.
16 Know how to do.
17 Elisha.
18 Mad.
19 Mr Wright says that "it was a common practice to grant under the conventual seal to benefactors and others a brotherly participation in the spiritual good works of the convent, and in their expected reward after death."
20 Divide.
21 Quibbling.
22 Horse.
23 Fierce.
24 Purpose.
25 Suffer.
26 Servants.
27 Countenance.
28 Dwelt.
29 With difficulty.
30 Save.
31 Grievance, grief.

And it shall be amended, if I may."
"I have," quoth he, "had a despite to-day,
God yieldë you,[1] adown in your villáge,
That in this world is none so poor a page,
That would not have abominatioún
Of that I have received in your town:
And yet ne grieveth me nothing so sore,
As that the oldë churl, with lockës hoar,
Blasphemed hath our holy convent eke."
"Now, master," quoth this lord, "I you beseek"——
"No master, Sir," quoth he, "but servitoúr,
Though I have had in schoolë that honoúr.
God liketh not, that men us Rabbi call,
Neither in market, nor in your large hall."
"No force,"[2] quoth he; "but tell me all your grief."
"Sir," quoth this friar, "an odious mischíef
This day betid[3] is to mine order and me,
And so *par consequence* to each degree
Of holy churchë, God amend it soon."
"Sir," quoth the lord, "ye know what is to doon:[4]
Distemp'r you not,[5] ye be my confessoúr.
Ye be the salt of th' earth, and the savoúr;
For Goddë's love your patiénce now hold;
Tell me your grief." And he anon him told
As ye have heard before, ye know well what.
The lady of the house aye stillë sat,
Till she had heardë what the friar said.
"Hey, Goddë's mother," quoth she, "blissful maid,
Is there ought ellës? tell me faithfully."
"Madame," quoth he, "how thinketh you thereby?"
"How thinketh me?" quoth she; "so God me speed,
I say, a churl hath done a churlish deed.
What should I say? God let him never thé;[6]
His sickë head is full of vanity;
I hold him in a manner phrenesy."[7]
"Madame," quoth he, "by God, I shall not lie,
But I in other wise may be awreke,[8]
I shall diffame him ov'r all there[9] I speak;
This falsë blasphemoúr, that charged me
To partë that will not departed be,
To every man alikë, with mischance."
The lord sat still, as he were in a trance,
And in his heart he rolled up and down,
"How had this churl imaginatioún
To shewë such a problem to the frere.
Never ere now heard I of such mattére;
I trow[10] the Devil put it in his mind.
In all arsmetrik[11] shall there no man find,
Before this day, of such a questión.
Who shouldë make a demonstratión,
That every man should have alike his part
As of the sound and savour of a fart?
O nicë[12] proudë churl, I shrew[13] his face.
Lo, Sirës," quoth the lord, "with hardë grace,[14]
Who ever heard of such a thing ere now?
To every man alikë? tell me how.
It is impossible, it may not be.
Hey, nicë[12] churl, God let him never thé.[6]
The rumbling of a fart, and every soun',
Is but of air reverberatioún,
And ever wasteth lite and lite[15] away;
There is no man can deemen,[16] by my fay,
If that it were departed[17] equally.
What? lo, my churl, lo yet how shrewedly[18]
Unto my confessoúr to-day he spake;
I hold him certain a demoniac.
Now eat your meat, and let the churl go play,
Let him go hang himself a devil way!"
Now stood the lordë's squiër at the board,
That carv'd his meat, and heardë word by word
Of all this thing, which that I have you said.
"My lord," quoth he, "be ye not evil paid,[19]
I couldë tellë, for a gownë-cloth,[20]
To you, Sir Friar, so that ye be not wroth,
How that this fart should even[21] dealed be
Among your convent, if it liked thee."
"Tell," quoth the lord, "and thou shalt have anon
A gownë-cloth, by God and by Saint John."
"My lord," quoth he, "when that the weather is fair,
Withoutë wind, or perturbíng of air,
Let[22] bring a cart-wheel here into this hall,
But lookë that it have its spokës all;
Twelve spokës hath a cart-wheel commonly;
And bring me then twelve friars, know ye why?
For thirteen is a convent as I guess;[23]
Your confessór here, for his worthiness,
Shall perform up[24] the number of his convént.
Then shall they kneel adown by one assent,
And to each spokë's end, in this mannére,
Full sadly[25] lay his nosë shall a frere;
Your noble confessór there, God him save,
Shall hold his nose upright under the nave.
Then shall this churl, with belly stiff and tought[26]
As any tabour,[27] hither be y-brought;
And set him on the wheel right of this cart
Upon the nave, and make him let a fart,
And ye shall see, on peril of my life,
By very proof that is demonstrative,
That equally the sound of it will wend,[28]
And eke the stink, unto the spokës' end,
Save that this worthy man, your confessoúr
(Because he is a man of great honoúr),
Shall have the firstë fruit, as reason is;
The noble uságe of friars yet it is,
The worthy men of them shall first be served,
And certainly he hath it well deserved;
He hath to-day taught us so muchë good
With preaching in the pulpit where he stood,
That I may vouchësafe, I say for me,

1 Reward you. 2 No matter. 3 Befallen.
4 Do. 5 Be not impatient, out of temper.
6 Thrive. 7 Sort of frenzy. 8 Revenged.
9 Speak discreditably of him everywhere.
10 Believe. 11 Arithmetic.
12 Foolish; French, "niais." 13 Curse.
14 Ill-favour attend him (the churl).
15 Little. 16 Judge, decide. 17 Divided.
18 Impiously, wickedly. 19 Displeased.
20 Cloth for a gown. 21 Equally. 22 Cause.
23 The regular number of monks or friars in a convent was fixed at twelve, with a superior, in imitation of the apostles and their Master; and large religious houses were held to consist of so many convents.
24 Complete. 25 Carefully, steadily.
26 Tight. 27 Drum. 28 Go.

He had the firstë smell of fartës three;
And so would all his brethren hardily;
He beareth him so fair and holily."
The lord, the lady, and each man, save the frere,
Saidë, that Jankin spake in this mattére
As well as Euclid, or as Ptolemy.
Touching the churl, they said that subtilty
And high wit made him speaken as he spake;
He is no fool, nor no demoniac.
And Jankin hath y-won a newë gown;
My tale is done, we are almost at town.

THE CLERK'S TALE.

THE PROLOGUE.

"SIR Clerk of Oxenford," our Hostë said,
"Ye ride as still and coy, as doth a maid
That were new spoused, sitting at the board:
This day I heard not of your tongue a word.
I trow ye study about some sophime:[1]
But Solomon saith, every thing hath time.
For Goddë's sakë, be of better cheer,[2]
It is no timë for to study here.
Tell us some merry talë, by your fay;[3]
For what man that is entered in a play,
He needës must unto that play assent.
But preachë not, as friars do in Lent,
To make us for our oldë sinnës weep,
Nor that thy talë make us not to sleep.
Tell us some merry thing of áventures.
Your terms, your colourës, and your figúres,
Keep them in store, till so be ye indite
High style, as when that men to kingës write.
Speakë so plain at this time, I you pray,
That we may understandë what ye say."
This worthy Clerk benignëly answér'd;
"Hostë," quoth he, "I am under your yerd,[4]
Ye have of us as now the governánce,
And therefore would I do you obeisánce,
As far as reason asketh, hardily:[5]
I will you tell a talë, which that I
Learn'd at Padova of a worthy clerk,
As proved by his wordës and his werk.
He is now dead, and nailed in his chest,
I pray to God to give his soul good rest.
Francis Petrarc', the laureate poét,[6]
Hightë[7] this clerk, whose rhetoric so sweet
Illumin'd all Itále of poetry,
As Linian[8] did of philosophy,
Or law, or other art particulére:
But death, that will not suffer us dwell here
But as it were a twinkling of an eye,
Them both hath slain, and allë we shall die.
"But forth to tellen of this worthy man,
That taughtë me this tale, as I began,
I say that first he with high style inditeth
(Ere he the body of his talë writeth)
A proem, in the which describeth he
Piedmont, and of Saluces[9] the countrý,
And speaketh of the Pennine hillës high,
That be the bounds of all West Lombardy:
And of Mount Vesulus in special,
Where as the Po out of a wellë small
Taketh his firstë springing and his source,
That eastward aye increaseth in his course
T' Emilia-ward,[10] to Ferrare, and Veníce,
The which a long thing werë to devise.[11]
And truëly, as to my judgëment,
Me thinketh it a thing impertinent,[12]
Save that he would conveyë his mattére:
But this is the tale, which that ye shall hear."

THE TALE.[13]

Pars Prima.

There is, right at the west side of Itále,
Down at the root of Vesulus[14] the cold,
A lusty[15] plain, abundant of vitáille;
There many a town and tow'r thou may'st behold,
That founded were in time of fathers old,
And many another délectáble sight;
And Saluces this noble country hight.

A marquis whilom lord was of that land,
As were his worthy elders[16] him before,
And obedient, aye ready to his hand,
Were all his lieges, bothë less and more:
Thus in delight he liv'd, and had done yore,[17]
Belov'd and drad,[18] through favour of fortúne,
Both of his lordës and of his commúne.[19]

Therewith he was, to speak of lineage,
The gentilest y-born of Lombardy,
A fair persón, and strong, and young of age,
And full of honour and of courtesy:
Discreet enough his country for to gie,[20]
Saving in some things that he was to blame;
And Walter was this youngë lordë's name.

I blame him thus, that he consider'd not

1 Sophism. 2 Livelier mien. 3 Faith.
4 Rod; as the emblem of government or direction.
5 Boldly, truly.
6 Francesco Petrarca, born 1304, died 1374; for his Latin epic poem on the career of Scipio, called "Africa," he was solemnly crowned with the poetic laurel in the Capitol of Rome, on Easter-day of 1341.
7 Was called.
8 An eminent jurist and philosopher, now almost forgotten, who died four or five years after Petrarch.
9 Saluzzo, a district of Savoy; its marquises were celebrated during the Middle Ages.
10 The region called Æmilia, across which ran the Via Æmilia—made by M. Æmilius Lepidus, who was consul at Rome B.C. 187. It continued the Flaminian Way from Ariminum (Rimini) across the Po at Placentia to Mediolanum (Milan), traversing Cisalpine Gaul.
11 Narrate. 12 Irrelevant.
13 Petrarch, in his Latin romance, "De obedientiâ et fide uxoriâ Mythologia," translated the charming story of "the patient Grizel" from the Italian of Boccaccio's "Decameron;" and Chaucer has closely followed Petrarch's translation, made in 1373, the year before that in which he died. The fact that the embassy to Genoa, on which Chaucer was sent, took place in 1372-73, has lent countenance to the opinion that the English poet did actually visit the Italian bard at Padua, and hear the story from his own lips. This, however, is only a probability; for it is a moot point whether the two poets ever met.
14 Monte Viso, a lofty peak at the junction of the Maritime and Cottian Alps; from two springs on its east side rises the Po. 15 Pleasant.
16 Ancestors. 17 Long.
18 Held in reverence. 19 Commonalty.
20 Guide, rule.

In timë coming what might him betide,
But on his present lust[1] was all his thought,
And for to hawk and hunt on every side;
Well nigh all other carës let he slide,
And eke he would (that was the worst of all)
Weddë no wife for aught that might befall.

Only that point his people bare so sore,
That flockmel[2] on a day to him they went,
And one of them, that wisest was of lore
(Or ellës that the lord would best assent
That he should tell him what the people meant,
Or ellës could he well shew such mattére),
He to the marquis said as ye shall hear.

"O noble Marquis! your humanity
Assureth us and gives us hardiness,
As oft as time is of necessity,
That we to you may tell our heaviness:
Acceptë, Lord, now of your gentleness,
What we with piteous heart unto you plain,[3]
And let your ears my voicë not disdain.

"All[4] have I nought to do in this mattére
More than another man hath in this place,
Yet forasmuch as ye, my Lord so dear,
Have always shewed me favour and grace,
I dare the better ask of you a space
Of audience, to shewen our request,
And ye, my Lord, to do right as you lest.[5]

"For certes, Lord, so well us likë you
And all your work, and ev'r have done, that we
Ne couldë not ourselves devisë how
We mightë live in more felicity:
Save one thing, Lord, if that your will it be,
That for to be a wedded man you lest;
Then were your people in sovereign heart's rest.[6]

"Bowë your neck under the blissful yoke
Of sovereignty, and not of servíce,
Which that men call espousal or wedlóck:
And thinkë, Lord, among your thoughtës wise,
How that our dayës pass in sundry wise;
For though we sleep, or wake, or roam, or ride,
Aye fleeth time, it will no man abide.

"And though your greenë youthë flow'r as yet,
In creepeth age always as still as stone,
And death menáceth every age, and smit[7]
In each estate, for there escapeth none:
And all so certain as we know each one
That we shall die, as uncertáin we all
Be of that day when death shall on us fall.

"Acceptë then of us the true intent,[8]
That never yet refused yourë hest,[9].
And we will, Lord, if that ye will assent,
Choose you a wife, in short time at the lest,[10]
Born of the gentilest and of the best
Of all this land, so that it ought to seem
Honour to God and you, as we can deem.

"Deliver us out of all this busy dread,[11]
And take a wife, for highë Goddë's sake:
For if it so befell, as God forbid,
That through your death your lineage should slake,[12]
And that a strange successor shouldë take
Your heritage, oh! woe were us on live:[13]
Wherefore we pray you hastily to wive."

Their meekë prayer and their piteous cheer
Madë the marquis for to have pitý.
"Ye will," quoth he, "mine owen people dear,
To that I ne'er ere[14] thought constrainë me.
I me rejoiced of my liberty,
That seldom time is found in marriáge;
Where I was free, I must be in servåge![15]

"But natheless I see your true intent,
And trust upon your wit, and have done aye:
Wherefore of my free will I will assent
To weddë me, as soon as e'er I may.
But whereas ye have proffer'd me to-day
To choosë me a wife, I you release
That choice, and pray you of that proffer cease.

"For God it wot, that children often been
Unlike their worthy elders them before,
Bounté[16] comes all of God, not of the strene[17]
Of which they be engender'd and y-bore:
I trust in Goddë's bounté, and therefore
My marriage, and mine estate and rest,
I him betake;[18] he may do as him lest.

"Let me alone in choosing of my wife;
That charge upon my back I will endure:
But I you pray, and charge upon your life,
That what wife that I take, ye me assure
To worship[19] her, while that her life may dure,
In word and work both here and ellëswhere,
As she an emperorë's daughter were.

"And farthermore this shall ye swear, that ye
Against my choice shall never grudge[20] nor strive.
For since I shall forego my liberty
At your request, as ever may I thrive,
Where as mine heart is set, there will I wive
And but[21] ye will assent in such mannére,
I pray you speak no more of this mattére."

With heartly will they sworen and assent'
To all this thing, there said not one wight nay:
Beseeching him of grace, ere that they went,
That he would grantë them a certain day
Of his espousal, soon as e'er he may,
For yet always the people somewhat dread[22]
Lest that the marquis wouldë no wife wed.

He granted them a day, such as him lest,
On which he would be wedded sickerly,[23]
And said he did all this at their request;
And they with humble heart full buxomly,[24]
Kneeling upon their knees full reverently,
Him thanked all; and thus they have an end
Of their intent, and home again they wend.

And hereupon he to his officers
Commanded for the feastë to purvey.[25]
And to his privy knightës and squiérs

1 Pleasure.
2 All in a flock or body.
3 Complain of.
4 Although.
5 As pleaseth you.
6 Completely satisfied, at ease.
7 Smiteth.
8 Mind, desire.
9 Command.
10 Least.
11 Doubt.
12 Cease, become extinct.
13 Alive.
14 Before.
15 Servitude.
16 Goodness.
17 Stock, race.
18 Commend to him.
19 Honour.
20 Murmur.
21 Unless.
22 Were in fear or doubt.
23 Certainly.
24 Obediently; Anglo-Saxon, "bogsom," old English, "boughsome," that can be easily bent or bowed; German, "biegsam," pliant, obedient.
25 Provide.

Such charge he gave, as him list on them lay:
And they to his commandëment obey,
And each of them doth all his diligence
To do unto the feast all reverence.

Pars Secunda.

Not far from thilkë[1] palace honouráble,
Where as this marquis shope[2] his marriáge,
There stood a thorp,[3] of sightë délectáble,
In which the poorë folk of that villáge
Haddë their beastës and their harbourage,[4]
And of their labour took their sustenance,
After the earthë gave them ábundánce.

Among this poorë folk there dwelt a man
Which that was holden poorest of them all;
But highë God sometimës sendë can
His grace unto a little ox's stall;
Janicola men of that thorp him call.
A daughter had he, fair enough to sight,
And Griseldis this youngë maiden hight.

But for to speak of virtuous beauty,
Then was she one the fairest under sun:
Full poorëly y-foster'd up was she;
No likerous lust[5] was in her heart y-run;
Well ofter of the well than of the tun[6]
She drank, and, for[7] she wouldë virtue please,
She knew well labour, but no idle ease.

But though this maiden tender were of age,
Yet in the breast of her virginity
There was inclos'd a sad and ripe coráge;[8]
And in great reverence and charity
Her oldë poorë father foster'd she.
A few sheep, spinning, on the field she kept,
She wouldë not be idle till she slept.

And when she homeward camë, she would bring
Wortës,[9] and other herbës, timës oft,
The which she shred and seeth'd for her livíng,
And made her bed full hard, and nothing soft:
And aye she kept her father's life on loft[10]
With ev'ry obeisánce and diligence,
That child may do to father's reverence.

Upon Griselda, this poor creatúre,
Full often sithes[11] this marquis set his eye,
As he on hunting rode, paráventure:[12]
And when it fell that he might her espy,
He not with wanton looking of follý
His eyen cast on her, but in sad[13] wise
Upon her cheer[14] he would him oft advise;[15]

Commending in his heart her womanhead,
And eke her virtue, passing any wight
Of so young age, as well in cheer as deed.
For though the people have no great insight
In virtue, he considered full right
Her bounté,[16] and disposed that he would
Wed only her, if ever wed he should.

The day of wedding came, but no wight can
Tellë what woman that it shouldë be;
For which marvail wonder'd many a man,
And saidë, when they were in privity,
"Will not our lord yet leave his vanity?
Will he not wed? Alas, alas the while!
Why will he thus himself and us beguile?"

But natheless this marquis had done[17] make
Of gemmës, set in gold and in azúre,
Brooches and ringës, for Griselda's sake,
And of her clothing took he the measúre
Of a maiden like unto her statúre,
And eke of other ornamentës all
That unto such a wedding shouldë fall.[18]

The time of undern[19] of the samë day
Approached, that this wedding shouldë be,
And all the palace put was in array,
Both hall and chamber, each in its degree,
Houses of office stuffed with plenty
There may'st thou see of dainteous vitáille,
That may be found, as far as lasts Itále.

This royal marquis, richëly array'd,
Lordës and ladies in his company,
The which unto the feastë werë pray'd,
And of his retinue the bach'lerý,
With many a sound of sundry melody,
Unto the village, of the which I told,
In this array the right way did they hold.

Griseld' of this (God wot) full innocent,
That for her shapen[20] was all this array,
To fetchë water at a well is went,
And home she came as soon as e'er she may.
For well she had heard say, that on that day
The marquis shouldë wed, and, if she might,
She fain would have seen somewhat of that sight.

She thought, "I will with other maidens stand,
That be my fellows, in our door, and see
The marchioness; and therefore will I fand[21]
To do at home, as soon as it may be,
The labour which belongeth unto me,
And then I may at leisure her behold,
If she this way unto the castle hold."

And as she would over the threshold gon,
The marquis came and gan for her to call,
And she set down her water-pot anon
Beside the threshold, in an ox's stall,
And down upon her knees she gan to fall,
And with sad[22] countenancë kneeled still,
Till she had heard what was the lordë's will.

The thoughtful marquis spake unto the maid
Full soberly, and said in this mannére:
"Where is your father, Griseldis?" he said.
And she with reverence, in humble cheer,[23]
Answered, "Lord, he is all ready here."
And in she went withoutë longer let,[24]
And to the marquis she her father fet.[25]

He by the hand then took the poorë man,
And saidë thus, when he him had aside:
"Janicola, I neither may nor can
Longer the pleasance of mine heartë hide;
If that thou vouchësafe, whatso betide,

1 That. 2 Prepared; resolved on. 3 Hamlet. 4 Dwelling. 5 Luxurious pleasure. 6 Of water than of wine. 7 Because. 8 Steadfast and mature spirit. 9 Plants, cabbages. 10 Up, aloft. 11 Times. 12 By chance. 13 Serious.

14 Countenance, demeanour. 15 Consider. 16 Goodness. 17 Caused. 18 Befit. 19 Afternoon, or evening; see note 14, page 79. 20 Prepared, designed. 21 Strive. 22 Steady. 23 With humble air. 24 Delay. 25 Fetched.

Thy daughter will I take, ere that I wend,[1]
As for my wife, unto her lifë's end.

"Thou lovest me, that know I well certáin,
And art my faithful liegëman y-bore,[2]
And all that liketh me, I dare well sayn
It liketh thee; and specially therefore
Tell me that point, that I have said before,—
If that thou wilt unto this purpose draw,
To takë me as for thy son-in-law."

This sudden case[3] the man astonied so,
That red he wax'd, abash'd,[4] and all quaking
He stood; unnethës[5] said he wordës mo',
But only thus; "Lord," quoth he, "my willing
Is as ye will, nor against your liking
I will no thing, mine owen lord so dear;
Right as you list governë this mattére."

"Then will I," quoth the marquis softëly,
"That in thy chamber I, and thou, and she,
Have a collatión;[6] and know'st thou why?
For I will ask her, if her will it be
To be my wife, and rule her after me:
And all this shall be done in thy presénce,
I will not speak out of thine audience."[7]

And in the chamber while they were about
The treaty, which ye shall hereafter hear,
The people came into the house without,
And wonder'd them in how honést mannére
And tenderly she kept her father dear;
But utterly Griseldis wonder might,
For never erst[8] ne saw she such a sight.

No wonder is though that she be astoned,[9]
To see so great a guest come in that place,
She never was to no such guestës woned;[10]
For which she looked with full palë face.
But shortly forth this matter for to chase,[11]
These are the wordës that the marquis said
To this benignë, very,[12] faithful maid.

"Griseld'," he said, "ye shall well understand,
It liketh to your father and to me
That I you wed, and eke it may so stand,
As I suppose ye will that it so be:
But these demandës ask I first," quoth he,
"Since that it shall be done in hasty wise;
Will ye assent, or ellës you advise?[13]

"I say this, be ye ready with good heart
To all my lust,[14] and that I freely may,
As me best thinketh, do[15] you laugh or smart,
And never ye to grudgë,[16] night nor day,
And eke when I say Yea, ye say not Nay,
Neither by word, nor frowning countenance?
Swear this, and here I swear our álliance."

Wond'ring upon this word, quaking for dread,
She saidë; "Lord, indigne and unworthy
Am I to this honoúr that ye me bede,[17]
But as ye will yourself, right so will I:
And here I swear, that never willingly
In work or thought I will you disobey,
For to be dead; though me were loth to dey."[18]

"This is enough, Griselda mine," quoth he.
And forth he went with a full sober cheer,
Out at the door, and after then came she,
And to the people he said in this mannére:
"This is my wife," quoth he, "that standeth here.
Honoúrë her, and love her, I you pray,
Whoso me loves; there is no more to say."

And, for that nothing of her oldë gear
She shouldë bring into his house, he bade
That women should despoilë[19] her right there;
Of which these ladies werë nothing glad
To handle her clothës wherein she was clad:
But natheless this maiden bright of hue
From foot to head they clothed have all new.

Her hairës have they comb'd that lay untress'd[20]
Full rudëly, and with their fingers small
A crown upon her head they havë dress'd,
And set her full of nouches[21] great and small:
Of her array why should I make a tale?
Unneth[5] the people her knew for her fairnéss,
When she transmuted was in such richéss.

The marquis hath her spoused with a ring
Brought for the samë cause, and then her set
Upon a horse snow-white, and well ambling,
And to his palace, ere he longer let[22]
(With joyful people, that her led and met),
Conveyed her; and thus the day they spend
In revel, till the sunnë gan descend.

And, shortly forth this talë for to chase,
I say, that to this newë marchioness
God hath such favour sent her of his grace,
That it ne seemed not by likeliness
That she was born and fed in rudëness,—
As in a cot, or in an ox's stall,—
But nourish'd in an emperorë's hall.

To every wight she waxen[23] is so dear
And worshipful, that folk where she was born,
That from her birthë knew her year by year,
Unnethës trowed[24] they, but durst have sworn,
That to Janicol' of whom I spake before,
She was not daughter, for by conjectúre
Them thought she was another creatúre.

For though that ever virtuous was she,
She was increased in such excellence
Of thewës[25] good, y-set in high bounté,
And so discreet, and fair of eloquence,
So benign, and so digne[26] of reverence,
And couldë so the people's heart embrace,
That each her lov'd that looked on her face.

Not only of Saluces in the town
Published was the bounté of her name,
But eke besides in many a regioún;
If one said well, another said the same:
So spread of herë high bounté the fame,

1 Go. 2 Born.
3 Event. 4 Amazed. 5 Scarcely.
6 Conference. 7 Hearing.
8 Before. 9 Astonished.
10 Accustomed, wont. 11 Push on, pursue.
12 True; French, "vraie." 13 Consider.
14 Pleasure. 15 Cause. 16 Murmur.
17 Offer. 18 Die.
19 Strip. 20 Loose, unplaited.
21 Ornaments of some kind not precisely known; some editions read "ouches," studs, brooches.
22 Delayed. 23 Grown.
24 Scarcely believed. 25 Qualities.
26 Worthy.

That men and women, young as well as old,
Went to Saluces, her for to behold.

Thus Walter lowly,—nay, but royally,—
Wedded with fortunate honesteté,[1]
In Goddë's peace lived full easily
At home, and outward grace enough had he:
And, for he saw that under low degree
Was honest virtue hid, the people him held
A prudent man, and that is seen full seld'.[2]

Not only this Griseldis through her wit
Couth all the feat[3] of wifely homeliness,
But eke, when that the case required it,
The common profit couldë she redress:[4]
There n'as discord, rancoúr, nor heaviness
In all the land, that she could not appease,
And wisely bring them all in rest and ease.

Though that her husband absent were or non,[5]
If gentlemen, or other of that country,
Were wroth,[6] she wouldë bringë them at one,
So wise and ripë wordës haddë she,
And judgëment of so great equity,
That she from heaven sent was, as men wend,[7]
People to save, and every wrong t' amend.

Not longë time after that this Grisild'
Was wedded, she a daughter had y-bore;
All she had lever[8] borne a knavë[9] child,
Glad was the marquis and his folk therefore;
For, though a maiden child came all before,
She may unto a knavë child attain
By likelihood, since she is not barrén.

Pars Tertia.

There fell, as falleth many timës mo',
When that his child had sucked but a throw,[10]
This marquis in his heartë longed so
To tempt his wife, her sadness[11] for to know,
That he might not out of his heartë throw
This marvellous desire his wife t' assay;[12]
Needless,[13] God wot, he thought her to affray.[14]

He had assayed her anough before,
And found her ever good; what needed it
Her for to tempt, and always more and more?
Though some men praise it for a subtle wit,
But as for me, I say that evil it sit[15]
T' assay a wife when that it is no need,
And puttë her in anguish and in dread.

For which this marquis wrought in this manére:
He came at night alone there as she lay,
With sternë face and with full troubled cheer,
And saidë thus; "Griseld'," quoth he, "that day
That I you took out of your poor array,
And put you in estate of high nobléss,
Ye have it not forgotten, as I guess.

"I say, Griseld', this present dignity,
In which that I have put you, as I trow[16]
Maketh you not forgetful for to be
That I you took in poor estate full low,
For any weal you must yourselfë know.
Take heed of every word that I you say,
There is no wight that hears it but we tway.[17]

"Ye know yourself well how that ye came here
Into this house, it is not long ago;
And though to me ye be right lefe[18] and dear,
Unto my gentles[19] ye be nothing so:
They say, to them it is great shame and woe
For to be subject, and be in serváge,
To thee, that born art of small lineage.

"And namely[20] since thy daughter was y-bore
These wordës have they spoken doubtëless;
But I desire, as I have done before,
To live my life with them in rest and peace:
I may not in this case be reckëless;
I must do with thy daughter for the best,
Not as I would, but as my gentles lest.[21]

"And yet, God wot, this is full loth[22] to me:
But natheless withoutë your weeting[23]
I will nought do; but this will I," quoth he,
"That ye to me assenten in this thing.
Shew now your patience in your working,
That ye me hight[24] and swore in your villáge
The day that maked was our marriáge."

When she had heard all this, she not amev'd[25]
Neither in word, in cheer, nor countenance
(For, as it seemed, she was not aggriev'd);
She saidë; "Lord, all lies in your pleasánce,
My child and I, with hearty obeisánce
Be yourës all, and ye may save or spill[26]
Your owen thing: work then after your will.

"There may no thing, so God my soulë save,
Likë to[27] you, that may displeasë me:
Nor I desirë nothing for to have,
Nor dreadë for to lose, save only ye:
This will is in mine heart, and aye shall be,
No length of time, nor death, may this deface,
Nor change my corage[28] to another place."

Glad was the marquis for her answering,
But yet he feigned as he were not so;
All dreary was his cheer and his looking
When that he should out of the chamber go.
Soon after this, a furlong way or two,[29]
He privily hath told all his intent
Unto a man, and to his wife him sent.

A manner sergeant[30] was this private man,[31]
The which he faithful often founden had
In thingës great, and eke such folk well can
Do executión in thingës bad:
The lord knew well, that he him loved and drad.[32]
And when this sergeant knew his lordë's will,
Into the chamber stalked he full still.

"Madam," he said, "ye must forgive it me,

1 Virtue. 2 Seldom.
3 Knew, understood, all the duty or performance.
4 She could well labour for the public advantage.
5 Not. 6 At feud. 7 Weened, imagined.
8 Though she had rather. 9 Male.
10 Little while. 11 Steadfastness, endurance.
12 Try. 13 Causelessly. 14 Alarm, disturb.
15 It ill became him. 16 Believe. 17 Two.
18 Pleasant, loved. 19 Nobles, gentlefolk.
20 Especially. 21 Please. 22 Odious.
23 Knowing. 24 Promised. 25 Changed.
26 Destroy. 27 Be pleasing. 28 Spirit, heart.
29 About as much time as one might take to walk a furlong or two; a short space.
30 A kind of squire. 31 Confidant, trusty tool.
32 Dreaded.

Though I do thing to which I am constrain'd;
Ye be so wise, that right well knowë ye
That lordës' hestës may not be y-feign'd;[1]
They may well be bewailed and complain'd,
But men must needs unto their lust[2] obey;
And so will I, there is no more to say.

"This child I am commanded for to take."
And spake no more, but out the child he hent[3]
Dispiteously,[4] and gan a cheer to make[5]
As though he would have slain it ere he went.
Griseldis must all suffer and consent:
And as a lamb she sat there meek and still,
And let this cruel sergeant do his will.

Suspicious[6] was the diffame[7] of this man,
Suspect his face, suspect his word also,
Suspect the time in which he this began:
Alas! her daughter, that she loved so,
She weened[8] he would have it slain right tho,[9]
But natheless she neither wept nor siked,[10]
Conforming her to what the marquis liked.

But at the last to speakë she began,
And meekly she unto the sergeant pray'd,
So as he was a worthy gentle man,
That she might kiss her child, ere that it died:
And in her barme[11] this little child she laid,
With full sad face, and gan the child to bless,[12]
And lulled it, and after gan it kiss.

And thus she said in her benignë voice:
"Farewell, my child, I shall thee never see;
But, since I have thee marked with the cross,
Of that father y-blessed may'st thou be
That for us died upon a cross of tree:
Thy soul, my little child, I him betake,[13]
For this night shalt thou dien for my sake."

I trow[14] that to a norice[15] in this case
It had been hard this ruthë[16] for to see:
Well might a mother then have cried, "Alas!"
But natheless so sad steadfást was she,
That she endured all adversity,
And to the sergeant meekëly she said,
"Have here again your little youngë maid.

"Go now," quoth she, "and do my lord's behest.
And one thing would I pray you of your grace,
But if[17] my lord forbade you at the least,
Bury this little body in some place,
That neither beasts nor birdës it arace."[18]
But he no word would to that purpose say,
But took the child and went upon his way.

The sergeant came unto his lord again,
And of Griselda's words and of her cheer[19]
He told him point for point, in short and plain,
And him presented with his daughter dear.
Somewhat this lord had ruth in his mannére,
But natheless his purpose held he still,
As lordës do, when they will have their will;

And bade this sergeant that he privily
Shouldë the child full softly wind and wrap,
With allë circumstances tenderly,
And carry it in a coffer, or in lap;
But, upon pain his head off for to swap,[20]
That no man shouldë know of his intent,
Nor whence he came, nor whither that he went;

But at Bologna, to his sister dear,
That at that time of Panic'[21] was Countéss,
He should it take, and shew her this mattére,
Beseeching her to do her business
This child to foster in all gentleness,
And whosë child it was he bade her hide
From every wight, for aught that might betide.

The sergeant went, and hath fulfill'd this thing.
But to the marquis now returnë we;
For now went he full fast imagining
If by his wifë's cheer he mightë see,
Or by her wordës apperceive, that she
Were changed; but he never could her find,
But ever-in-one[22] alikë sad[23] and kind.

As glad, as humble, as busy in servíce,
And eke in love, as she was wont to be,
Was she to him, in every manner wise;[24]
And of her daughter not a word spake she;
No accident for no adversity[25]
Was seen in her, nor e'er her daughter's name
She named, or in earnest or in game.

Pars Quarta.

In this estate there passed be four year
Ere she with childë was; but, as God wo'ld,
A knavë[26] child she bare by this Waltére,
Full gracious and fair for to behold;
And when that folk it to his father told,
Not only he, but all his country, merry
Were for this child, and God they thank and hery.[27]

When it was two year old, and from the breast
Departed[28] of the norice, on a day
This marquis caughtë yet another lest[29]
To tempt his wife yet farther, if he may.
Oh! needless was she tempted in assay;[30]
But wedded men not connen no measúre,[31]
When that they find a patient creatúre.

"Wife," quoth the marquis, "ye have heard ere this
My people sickly bear[32] our marriáge;
And namely[33] since my son y-boren is,
Now is it worse than ever in all our age:
The murmur slays mine heart and my coráge,
For to mine ears cometh the voice so smart,[34]
That it well nigh destroyed hath mine heart.

"Now say they thus, 'When Walter is y-gone,

1 It will not do merely to feign compliance with a lord's commands. 2 Pleasure. 3 Seized. 4 Unpityingly. 5 To make a show, assume an aspect. 6 Ominous. 7 Reputation, evil fame. 8 Thought. 9 Then. 10 Sighed. 11 Lap, bosom. 12 Cross. 13 Commit unto him. 14 Believe. 15 Nurse. 16 Pitiful case, sight. 17 Unless. 18 Tear; French, "arracher." 19 Demeanour.

20 Strike. 21 Panico. 22 Constantly. 23 Steadfast. 24 Sort of way. 25 No change of humour resulting from her affliction. 26 Male, boy. 27 Praise. 28 Taken, weaned. 29 Was seized by yet another desire. 30 Trial. 31 Know no moderation. 32 Do not regard with pleasure. Compare the Latin phrase, "ægre ferre." 33 Especially. 34 Sorely, painfully.

Then shall the blood of Janicol' succeed,
And be our lord, for other have we none:'
Such wordës say my people, out of drede.[1]
Well ought I of such murmur takë heed,
For certainly I dread all such senténce,[2]
Though they not plainen in mine audiénce.[3]

"I wouldë live in peace, if that I might;
Wherefore I am disposed utterly,
As I his sister served ere[4] by night,
Right so think I to serve him privily.
This warn I you, that ye not suddenly
Out of yourself for no woe should outraie;[5]
Be patient, and thereof I you pray."

"I have," quoth she, "said thus, and ever shall,
I will no thing, nor n'ill no thing, certáin,
But as you list; not grieveth me at all
Though that my daughter and my son be slain
At your commandëment; that is to sayn,
I have not had no part of children twain,
But first sicknéss, and after woe and pain.

"Ye be my lord, do with your owen thing
Right as you list, and ask no rede[6] of me;
For, as I left at home all my clothing
When I came first to you, right so," quoth she,
"Left I my will and all my liberty,
And took your clothing: wherefore I you pray,
Do your pleasánce, I will your lust[7] obey.

"And, certes, if I haddë prescience
Your will to know, ere ye your lust[7] me told,
I would it do withoutë negligence:
But, now I know your lust, and what ye wo'ld,
All your pleasancë firm and stable I hold;
For, wist I that my death might do you ease,
Right gladly would I dien you to please.

"Death may not makë no comparisoún
Unto your love." And when this marquis say[8]
The constance of his wife, he cast adown
His eyen two, and wonder'd how she may
In patience suffer all this array;
And forth he went with dreary countenance;
But to his heart it was full great pleasánce.

This ugly sergeant, in the samë wise
That he her daughter caught, right so hath he
(Or worse, if men can any worse devise,)
Y-hent[9] her son, that full was of beauty:
And ever-in-one[10] so patient was she,
That she no cheerë made of heaviness,
But kiss'd her son, and after gan him bless.

Save this she prayed him, if that he might,
Her little son he would in earthë grave,[11]
His tender limbës, delicate to sight,
From fowlës and from beastës for to save.
But she none answer of him mightë have;
He went his way, as him nothing ne raught,[12]
But to Bologna tenderly it brought.

The marquis wonder'd ever longer more
Upon her patience; and, if that he
Not haddë soothly knowen therebefore
That perfectly her children loved she,
He would have ween'd[13] that of some subtilty,
And of malíce, or for cruel corage,[14]
She haddë suffer'd this with sad[15] viságe.

But well he knew, that, next himself, certáin
She lov'd her children best in every wise.
But now of women would I askë fain,
If these assayës mightë not suffice?
What could a sturdy[16] husband more devise
To prove her wifehood and her steadfastness,
And he continuing ev'r in sturdiness?

But there be folk of such conditión,
That, when they have a certain purpose take,
They cannot stint[17] of their intentión,
But, right as they were bound unto a stake,
They will not of their firstë purpose slake:[18]
Right so this marquis fully hath purpós'd
To tempt his wife, as he was first dispos'd.

He waited, if by word or countenance
That she to him was changed of coráge:[19]
But never could he findë variance,
She was aye one in heart and in viságe,
And aye the farther that she was in age,
The morë true (if that it were possíble)
She was to him in love, and more penible.[20]

For which it seemed thus, that of them two
There was but one will; for, as Walter lest,[21]
The same pleasáncë was her lust also;
And, God be thanked, all fell for the best.
She shewed well, for no worldly unrest,
A wife as of herself no thingë should
Will, in effect, but as her husband would.

The sland'r of Walter wondrous widë sprad,
That of a cruel heart he wickedly,
For[22] he a poorë woman wedded had,
Had murder'd both his children privily:
Such murmur was among them commonly.
No wonder is: for to the people's ear
There came no word, but that they murder'd were.

For which, whereas his people therebefore
Had lov'd him well, the sland'r of his diffame[23]
Made them that they him hated therëfore.
To be a murd'rer is a hateful name.
But natheless, for earnest or for game,
He of his cruel purpose would not stent;[24]
To tempt his wife was set all his intent.

When that his daughter twelve year was of age,
He to the Court of Rome, in subtle wise
Informed of his will, sent his message,[25]
Commanding him such bullës to devise
As to his cruel purpose may suffice,
How that the Popë, for his people's rest,
Bade him to wed another, if him lest.[26]

I say he bade they shouldë counterfeit
The Pope's bullës, making mentión
That he had leave his firstë wife to lete,[27]
As by the Popë's dispensatión,

1 Doubt. 2 Expression of opinion. 3 Complain in my hearing. 4 Before. 5 Become outrageous, rave. 6 Advice. 7 Will. 8 Saw. 9 Seized. 10 Unvaryingly. 11 Bury. 12 Recked, cared. 13 Thought. 14 Disposition. 15 Steadfast, unmoved. 16 Stubborn, stern.

17 Cease. 18 Slacken, abate. 19 Spirit. 20 Devoted, full of painstaking in duty. 21 Pleased. 22 Because. 23 Evil repute, reproach. 24 Desist, stop. 25 Messenger; for French "messager." 26 Pleased. 27 Leave.

To stintë[1] rancour and dissensión
Betwixt his people and him : thus spake the bull,
The which they havë published at full.

The rudë people, as no wonder is,
Weened[2] full well that it had been right so :
But, when these tidings came to Griseldis,
I deemë that her heart was full of woe;
But she, alikë sad[3] for evermo',
Disposed was, this humble creatúre,
Th' adversity of fortune all t' endure;

Abiding ever his lust and his pleasánce,
To whom that she was given, heart and all,
As to her very worldly suffisance.[4]
But, shortly if this story tell I shall,
The marquis written hath in special
A letter, in which he shewed his intent,
And secretly it to Bologna sent.

To th' earl of Panico, which haddë tho[5]
Wedded his sister, pray'd he specially
To bringë home again his children two
In honourable estate all openly:
But one thing he him prayed utterly,
That he to no wight, though men would inquere,
Shouldë not tell whose children that they were,

But say, the maiden should y-wedded be
Unto the marquis of Salúce anon.
And as this earl was prayed, so did he,
For, at day set, he on his way is gone
Toward Salúce, and lordës many a one
In rich array, this maiden for to guide,—
Her youngë brother riding her beside.

Arrayed was toward[6] her marriáge
This freshë maiden, full of gemmës clear;
Her brother, which that seven year was of age,
Arrayed eke full fresh in his mannére:
And thus, in great nobléss, and with glad cheer,
Toward Saluces shaping their journéy,
From day to day they rode upon their way.

Pars Quinta.

Among all this,[7] after his wick' uságe,
The marquis, yet his wife to temptë more
To the uttermost proof of her coráge,
Fully to have experience and lore[8]
If that she were as steadfast as before,
He on a day, in open audience,
Full boisterously said her this senténce:

"Certes, Griseld', I had enough pleasánce
To have you to my wife, for your goodness,
And for your truth, and for your obeisánce,
Not for your lineage, nor for your richéss;
But now know I, in very soothfastness,
That in great lordship, if I well advise,
There is great servitude in sundry wise.

"I may not do as every ploughman may:
My people me constraineth for to take
Another wife, and cryeth day by day;
And eke the Popë, rancour for to slake,
Consenteth it, that dare I undertake:

And truëly, thus much I will you say,
My newë wife is coming by the way.

"Be strong of heart, and void anon[9] her place;
And thilkë[10] dower that ye brought to me,
Take it again, I grant it of my grace.
Returnë to your father's house," quoth he;
"No man may always have prosperity;
With even heart I rede[11] you to endure
The stroke of fortune or of áventúre."

And she again answér'd in patience:
"My Lord," quoth she, "I know, and knew alway,
How that betwixtë your magnificence
And my povert' no wight nor can nor may
Makë comparison, it is no nay;[12]
I held me never digne[13] in no mannére
To be your wife, nor yet your chamberére.[14]

"And in this house, where ye me lady made,
(The highë God take I for my witness,
And all so wisly[15] he my soulë glade),
I never held me lady nor mistress,
But humble servant to your worthiness,
And ever shall, while that my life may dure,
Aboven every worldly creatúre.

"That ye so long, of your benignity,
Have holden me in honour and nobley,[16]
Where as I was not worthy for to be,
That thank I God and you, to whom I pray
Foryield[17] it you; there is no more to say:
Unto my father gladly will I wend,[18]
And with him dwell, unto my lifë's end,

"Where I was foster'd as a child full small;
Till I be dead my life there will I lead,
A widow clean in body, heart, and all.
For since I gave to you my maidenhead,
And am your truë wife, it is no dread,[19]
God shieldë[20] such a lordë's wife to take
Another man to husband or to make.[21]

"And of your newë wife, God of his grace
So grant you weal and all prosperity:
For I will gladly yield to her my place,
In which that I was blissful wont to be.
For since it liketh you, my Lord," quoth she,
"That whilom weren all mine heartë's rest,
That I shall go, I will go when you lest.

"But whereas ye me proffer such dowaire
As I first brought, it is well in my mind,
It was my wretched clothës, nothing fair,
The which to me were hard now for to find.
O goodë God! how gentle and how kind
Ye seemed by your speech and your viságe,
The day that maked was our marriáge!

"But sooth is said,—algate[22] I find it true,
For in effect it proved is on me,—
Love is not old as when that it is new.
But certes, Lord, for no adversity,
To dien in this case, it shall not be
That e'er in word or work I shall repent
That I you gave mine heart in whole intent.

1 Put an end to.
2 Thought, believed.
3 Steadfast.
4 To the utmost extent of her power.
5 Then.
6 As if for.
7 While all this was going on.
8 Knowledge.
9 Immediately make vacant.
10 That.
11 Counsel.
12 Not to be denied.
13 Worthy.
14 Chamber-maid.
15 Surely.
16 Nobility.
17 Recompense, reward.
18 Go.
19 Doubt.
20 Forbid.
21 Mate.
22 At all events.

"My Lord, ye know that in my father's place
Ye did me strip out of my poorë weed,[1]
And richëly ye clad me of your grace;
To you brought I nought ellës, out of dread,
But faith, and nakedness, and maidenhead;
And here again your clothing I restore,
And eke your wedding ring for evermore.

"The remnant of your jewels ready be
Within your chamber, I dare safely sayn:
Naked out of my father's house," quoth she,
"I came, and naked I must turn again.
All your pleasáncë would I follow fain:[2]
But yet I hope it be not your intent
That smockless[3] I out of your palace went.

"Ye could not do so dishonést[4] a thing,
That thilkë[5] womb, in which your children lay,
Shouldë before the people, in my walking,
Be seen all bare: and therefore I you pray,
Let me not like a worm go by the way:
Remember you, mine owen Lord so dear,
I was your wife, though I unworthy were.

"Wherefore, in guerdon[6] of my maidenhead,
Which that I brought and not again I bear,
As vouchësafe to give me to my meed[6]
But such a smock as I was wont to wear,
That I therewith may wrie[7] the womb of her
That was your wife: and here I take my leave
Of you, mine owen Lord, lest I you grieve."

"The smock," quoth he, "that thou hast on thy back,
Let it be still, and bear it forth with thee."
But well unnethës[8] thilkë word he spake,
But went his way for ruth and for pitý.
Before the folk herselfë stripped she,
And in her smock, with foot and head all bare,
Toward her father's house forth is she fare.[9]

The folk her follow'd weeping on her way,
And fortune aye they cursed as they gon:[10]
But she from weeping kept her eyen drey,[11]
Nor in this timë wordë spake she none.
Her father, that this tiding heard anon,
Cursed the day and timë, that natúre
Shope[12] him to be a living creatúre.

For, out of doubt, this oldë poorë man
Was ever in suspéct of her marriáge:
For ever deem'd he, since it first began,
That when the lord fulfill'd had his coráge,[13]
He wouldë think it were a disparáge[14]
To his estate, so low for to alight,
And voidë[15] her as soon as e'er he might.

Against[16] his daughter hastily went he
(For he by noise of folk knew her coming),
And with her oldë coat, as it might be,
He cover'd her, full sorrowfully weepíng:
But on her body might he it not bring,[17]
For rudë was the cloth, and more of age
By dayës fele[18] than at her marriáge.

Thus with her father for a certain space
Dwelled this flow'r of wifely patience,
That neither by her words nor by her face,
Before the folk nor eke in their absence,
Ne shewed she that her was done offence,
Nor of her high estate no rémembránce
Ne haddë she, as by[19] her countenance.

No wonder is, for in her great estate
Her ghost[20] was ever in plein[21] humility;
No tender mouth, no heartë delicate,
No pomp, and no semblánt of royalty;
But full of patient benignity,
Discreet and pridëless, aye honouráble,
And to her husband ever meek and stable.

Men speak of Job, and most for his humbléss,
As clerkës, when them list, can well indite,
Namely[22] of men; but, as in soothfastness,
Though clerkës praisë women but a lite,[23]
There can no man in humbless him acquite
As women can, nor can be half so true
As women be, but it be fall of new.[24]

Pars Sexta.

From Bologn' is the earl of Panic' come,
Of which the fame up sprang to more and less;
And to the people's earës all and some
Was known eke, that a newë marchioness
He with him brought, in such pomp and richéss
That never was there seen with mannë's eye
So noble array in all West Lombardy.

The marquis, which that shope[25] and knew all this,
Ere that the earl was come, sent his messáge[26]
For thilkë poorë sely[27] Griseldis;
And she, with humble heart and glad viságe,
Nor with no swelling thought in her coráge,[28]
Came at his hest,[29] and on her knees her set,
And rev'rently and wisely she him gret.[30]

"Griseld'," quoth he, "my will is utterly,
This maiden, that shall wedded be to me,
Received be to-morrow as royally
As it possíble is in my house to be;
And eke that every wight in his degree
Have his estate[31] in sitting and servíce,
And in high pleasance, as I can devise.

"I have no women sufficient, certáin,
The chambers to array in ordinance
After my lust;[32] and therefore would I fain
That thine were all such manner governance:
Thou knowest eke of old all my pleasánce;
Though thine array be bad, and ill besey,[33]
Do thou thy dévoir at the leastë way."[34]

"Not only, Lord, that I am glad," quoth she,
"To do your lust, but I desire also
You for to serve and please in my degree,
Withoutë fainting, and shall evermo':
Nor ever for no weal, nor for no woe,
Ne shall the ghost[35] within mine heartë stent[36]
To love you best with all my true intent."

1 Raiment. 2 Cheerfully. 3 Naked. 4 Dishonourable. 5 That. 6 Reward. 7 Cover. 8 With difficulty. 9 Gone. 10 Go. 11 Dry. 12 Formed, ordained. 13 Had gratified his inclination. 14 Disparagement. 15 Dismiss, get rid of. 16 To meet. 17 Cause it to meet.

18 Many; German, "viel." 19 To judge from. 20 Spirit. 21 Full. 22 Particularly. 23 Little. 24 Unless it has lately come to pass. 25 Arranged. 26 Messenger. 27 Innocent. 28 Mind. 29 Command. 30 Greeted. 31 What befits his condition. 32 Pleasure. 33 Poor to look on. 34 In the quickest manner. 35 Spirit. 36 Cease.

And with that word she gan the house to dight,[1]
And tables for to set, and beds to make,
And pained her[2] to do all that she might,
Praying the chamberéres for Goddë's sake
To hasten them, and fastë sweep and shake,
And she the most servíceable of all
Hath ev'ry chamber arrayed, and his hall.

Abouten undern[3] gan the earl alight,
That with him brought these noble children tway;
For which the people ran to see the sight
Of their array, so richëly besey;[4]
And then at erst[5] amongës them they say,
That Walter was no fool, though that him lest[6]
To change his wife; for it was for the best.

For she is fairer, as they deemen[7] all,
Than is Griseld', and more tender of age,
And fairer fruit between them shouldë fall,
And morë pleasant, for her high lineage:
Her brother eke so fair was of viságe,
That them to see the people hath caught pleasánce,
Commending now the marquis' governance.

"O stormy people, unsad[8] and ev'r untrue,
And undiscreet, and changing as a vane,
Delighting ev'r in rumour that is new,
For like the moon so waxë ye and wane:
Aye full of clapping, dear enough a jane,[9]
Your doom[10] is false, your constance evil preveth,[11]
A full great fool is he that you believeth."

Thus saidë the sad[12] folk in that city,
When that the people gazed up and down;
For they were glad, right for the novelty,
To have a newë lady of their town.
No more of this now make I mentioún,
But to Griseld' again I will me dress,
And tell her constancy and business.

Full busy was Griseld' in ev'ry thing
That to the feastë was appertinent;
Right nought was she abash'd[13] of her clothing,
Though it were rude, and somedeal eke torent;[14]
But with glad cheer unto the gate she went
With other folk, to greet the marchioness,
And after that did forth her business.

With so glad cheer his guestës she receiv'd
And so conningly[15] each in his degree,
That no defaultë no man apperceiv'd,
But aye they wonder'd what she mightë be
That in so poor array was for to see,
And coudë[16] such honoúr and reverence;
And worthily they praisë her prudence.

In all this meanë while she not stent[17]
This maid, and eke her brother, to commend
With all her heart in full benign intent,
So well, that no man could her praise amend:
But at the last, when that these lordës wend[18]
To sittë down to meat, he gan to call
Griseld', as she was busy in the hall.

"Griseld'," quoth he, as it were in his play,
"How liketh thee my wife, and her beauty?"
"Right well, my Lord," quoth she, "for, in good fay,[19]
A fairer saw I never none than she:
I pray to God give you prosperity;
And so I hope, that he will to you send
Pleasance enough unto your livës' end.

"One thing beseech I you, and warn also,
That ye not prickë with no tórmentíng
This tender maiden, as ye have done mo:[20]
For she is foster'd in her nourishing
More tenderly, and, to my supposing,
She mightë not adversity endure
As could a poorë foster'd creatúre."

And when this Walter saw her patience,
Her gladdë cheer, and no malíce at all,
And[21] he so often had her done offence,
And she aye sad[22] and constant as a wall,
Continuing ev'r her innocence o'er all,
The sturdy marquis gan his heartë dress[23]
To rue upon her wifely steadfastness.

"This is enough, Griselda mine," quoth he,
"Be now no more aghast, nor evil paid,[24]
I have thy faith and thy benignity
As well as ever woman was, assay'd,
In great estate and poorëly array'd:
Now know I, dearë wife, thy steadfastness;"
And her in arms he took, and gan to kiss.

And she for wonder took of it no keep;[25]
She heardë not what thing he to her said:
She far'd as she had start out of a sleep,
Till she out of her mazedness abraid.[26]
"Griseld'," quoth he, "by God that for us died,
Thou art my wifë, none other I have,
Nor ever had, as God my soulë save.

"This is thy daughter, which thou hast suppos'd
To be my wife; that other faithfully
Shall be mine heir, as I have aye dispos'd;
Thou bare them of thy body truëly:
At Bologna kept I them privily:
Take them again, for now may'st thou not say
That thou hast lorn[27] none of thy children tway.

"And folk, that otherwise have said of me,
I warn them well, that I have done this deed
For no malíce, nor for no cruelty,
But to assay in thee thy womanhead:
And not to slay my children (God forbid),
But for to keep them privily and still,
Till I thy purpose knew, and all thy will."

1 Arrange. 2 Took all pains, used every exertion. 3 Eventide, or afternoon; though by some "undern" is understood as dinner-time—9 A.M. 4 So rich to behold. 5 For the first time. 6 Pleased. 7 Think. 8 Variable. 9 A small coin of little value. 10 Judgment. 11 Proveth. 12 Sedate. 13 Ashamed. 14 Torn. 15 Cleverly, skilfully. 16 Knew, understood how to do.

17 Ceased. 18 Thought. 19 Faith. 20 Me. "This is one of the most licentious corruptions of orthography," says Tyrwhitt, "that I remember to have observed in Chaucer;" but such liberties were common among the European poets of his time, when there was an extreme lack of certainty in orthography. 21 Although. 22 Steadfast. 23 Prepare, incline. 24 Afraid nor displeased. 25 Notice, heed. 26 Awoke. 27 Lost.

When she this heard, in swoon adown she falleth
For piteous joy ; and after her swooning,
She both her youngë children to her calleth,
And in her armës piteously weeping
Embraced them, and tenderly kissing,
Full like a mother, with her saltë tears
She bathed both their visage and their hairs.

O, what a piteous thing it was to see
Her swooning, and her humble voice to hear!
"*Grand mercy*, Lord, God thank it you," quoth she,
"That ye have saved me my children dear;
Now reck[1] I never to be dead right here;
Since I stand in your love, and in your grace,
No force of[2] death, nor when my spirit pace.[3]

"O tender, O dear, O young children mine,
Your woeful mother weened steadfastly[4]
That cruel houndës, or some foul vermíne,
Had eaten you; but God of his mercy,
And your benignë father, tenderly
Have done you keep:"[5] and in that samë stound,[6]
All suddenly she swapt[7] down to the ground.

And in her swoon so sadly[8] holdeth she
Her children two, when she gan them embrace,
That with great sleight[9] and great difficulty
The children from her arm they can arace,[10]
O! many a tear on many a piteous face
Down ran of them that stoodë her beside,
Unneth[11] aboutë her might they abide.

Walter her gladdeth, and her sorrow slaketh:[12]
She riseth up abashed[13] from her trance,
And every wight her joy and feastë maketh,
Till she hath caught again her countenance.
Walter her doth so faithfully pleasánce,
That it was dainty for to see the cheer
Betwixt them two, since they be met in fere.[14]

The ladies, when that they their timë sey,[15]
Have taken her, and into chamber gone,
And stripped her out of her rude array,
And in a cloth of gold that brightly shone,
And with a crown of many a richë stone
Upon her head, they into hall her brought:
And there she was honoúred as her ought.

Thus had this piteous day a blissful end;
For every man and woman did his might
This day in mirth and revel to dispend,
Till on the welkin[16] shone the starrës bright:
For more solémn in every mannë's sight
This feastë was, and greater of costage,[17]
Than was the revel of her marriáge.

Full many a year in high prosperity
Lived these two in concord and in rest;
And richëly his daughter married he
Unto a lord, one of the worthiest
Of all Itále; and then in peace and rest
His wifë's father in his court he kept,
Till that the soul out of his body crept.

His son succeeded in his heritage,
In rest and peace, after his father's day:
And fortunate was eke in marriáge,
All[18] he put not his wife in great assay:
This world is not so strong, it is no nay,[19]
As it hath been in oldë timës yore;
And hearken what this author saith, therefore:

This story is said,[20] not for that wivës should
Follow Griselda in humility,
For it were importáble[21] though they would;
But for that every wight in his degree
Shouldë be constant in adversity,
As was Griselda; therefore Petrarch writeth
This story, which with high style he inditeth.

For, since a woman was so patient
Unto a mortal man, well more we ought
Receiven all in gree[22] that God us sent.
For great skill is he proved that he wrought:[23]
But he tempteth no man that he hath bought,
As saith Saint James, if ye his 'pistle read;
He proveth folk all day, it is no dread.[24]

And suffereth us, for our exercise,
With sharpë scourges of adversity
Full often to be beat in sundry wise;
Not for to know our will, for certes he,
Ere we were born, knew all our frailty;
And for our best is all his governance;
Let us then live in virtuous sufferance.

But one word, lordings, hearken, ere I go:
It were full hard to findë now-a-days
In all a town Griseldas three or two:
For, if that they were put to such assays,
The gold of them hath now so bad allays[25]
With brass, that though the coin be fair at eye,[26]
It wouldë rather break in two than ply.[27]

For which here, for the Wifë's love of Bath,—
Whose life and all her sex may God maintain
In high mast'rý, and ellës were it scath,[28]—
I will, with lusty heartë fresh and green,
Say you a song to gladden you, I ween:
And let us stint of earnestful mattére.
Hearken my song, that saith in this mannére.

L'Envoy of Chaucer.

"Griseld' is dead, and eke her patience,
And both at once are buried in Itále:
For which I cry in open audience,
No wedded man so hardy be t' assail
His wifë's patience, in trust to find
Griselda's, for in certain he shall fail.

"O noble wivës, full of high prudence,
Let no humility your tonguës nail:
Nor let no clerk have cause or diligence
To write of you a story of such marvail,

1 Care. 2 No matter for. 3 Departs.
4 Believed firmly. 5 Caused you to be preserved.
6 Instant. 7 Fell. 8 Firmly.
9 Art. 10 Pluck away, withdraw.
11 Scarcely. 12 Assuages. 13 Astonished.
14 Together. 15 Saw. 16 Firmament.
17 Expense; sumptuousness. 18 Although.

19 Not to be denied.
20 The fourteen lines that follow are translated almost literally from Petrarch's Latin.
21 Impossible; not to be borne. 22 Good-will.
23 For it is most reasonable that He should prove or test that which He made. 24 Doubt. 25 Alloys.
26 To view. 27 Bend. 28 Damage, pity.

As of Griselda patient and kind,
Lest Chichëvache[1] you swallow in her entrail.

"Follow Echo, that holdeth no silence,
But ever answereth at the countertail;[2]
Be not bedaffed[3] for your innocence,
But sharply take on you the governail;[4]
Imprintë well this lesson in your mind,
For common profit, since it may avail.

"Ye archiwivës,[5] stand aye at defence,
Since ye be strong as is a great camail,[6]
Nor suffer not that men do you offence.
And slender wivës, feeble in battail,
Be eager as a tiger yond in Ind;
Aye clapping as a mill, I you counsail.

"Nor dread them not, nor do them reverence;
For though thine husband armed be in mail,
The arrows of thy crabbed eloquence
Shall pierce his breast, and eke his aventail;[7]
In jealousy I rede[8] eke thou him bind,
And thou shalt make him couch[9] as doth a quail.

"If thou be fair, where folk be in presénce
Shew thou thy visage and thine apparail:
If thou be foul, be free of thy dispence;
To get thee friendës aye do thy travail:
Be aye of cheer as light as leaf on lind,[10]
And let him care, and weep, and wring, and wail."

THE MERCHANT'S TALE.

THE PROLOGUE.[11]

"WEEPING and wailing, care and other sorrow,
I have enough, on even and on morrow,"
Quoth the Merchánt, "and so have other mo',
That wedded be; I trow[12] that it be so;
For well I wot it fareth so by me.
I have a wife, the worstë that may be,
For though the fiend to her y-coupled were,
She would him overmatch, I dare well swear.
Why should I you rehearse in speciál
Her high malíce? she is a shrew at all.[13]
There is a long and largë difference
Betwixt Griselda's greatë patience,
And of my wife the passing cruelty.
Were I unbounden, all so may I thé,[14]
I wouldë never eft[15] come in the snare.
We wedded men live in sorrow and care;
Assay it whoso will, and he shall find
That I say sooth, by Saint Thomas of Ind,
As for the morë part; I say not all,—
God shieldë[16] that it shouldë so befall.
Ah! good Sir Host, I have y-wedded be
These moneths two, and morë not, pardie;
And yet I trow[12] that he that all his life
Wifeless hath been, though that men would him rive
Into the heartë, could in no mannére
Tellë so much sorrów, as I you here
Could tellen of my wifë's cursedness."[17]

"Now," quoth our Host, "Merchánt, so God you bless,
Since ye so muchë knowen of that art,
Full heartily I pray you tell us part."

"Gladly," quoth he; "but of mine owen sore,
For sorry heart, I tellë may no more."

THE TALE.[18]

Whilom there was dwelling in Lombardy
A worthy knight, that born was at Pavie,
In which he liv'd in great prosperity;
And forty years a wifeless man was he,
And follow'd aye his bodily delight
On women, where as was his appetite,
As do these foolës that be seculeres.[19]
And, when that he was passed sixty years,
Were it for holiness, or for dotáge,
I cannot say, but such a great coráge[20]
Haddë this knight to be a wedded man,

1 Chichevache, in old popular fable, was a monster that fed only on good women, and was always very thin from scarcity of such food; a corresponding monster, Bycorne, fed only on obedient and kind husbands, and was always fat. The origin of the fable was French; but Lydgate has a ballad on the subject. "Chichevache" literally means "niggardly" or "greedy cow."

2 Counter-tally or counter-foil; something exactly corresponding. 3 Befooled. 4 Helm.

5 Wives of rank. 6 Camel.

7 Forepart of a helmet, vizor. 8 Advise.

9 Submit, shrink. 10 Linden, lime-tree.

11 Though the manner in which the Merchant takes up the closing words of the Envoy to the Clerk's Tale, and refers to the patience of Griselda, seems to prove beyond doubt that the order of the Tales in the text is the right one, yet in some manuscripts of good authority the Franklin's Tale follows the Clerk's, and the Envoy is concluded by this stanza:—

"This worthy Clerk when ended was his tale,
Our Hostë said, and swore by cockë's bones
'Me lever were than a barrel of ale
My wife at home had heard this legend once;
This is a gentle talë for the nonce;
As to my purpose, wistë ye my will.
But thing that will not be, let it be still.'"

In other manuscripts of less authority, the Host proceeds, in two similar stanzas, to impose a Tale on the Franklin; but Tyrwhitt is probably right in setting them aside as spurious, and in admitting the genuineness of the first only, if it be supposed that Chaucer forgot to cancel it when he had decided on another mode of connecting the Merchant's with the Clerk's Tale.

12 Believe.

13 Thoroughly, in everything, wicked.

14 So may I thrive! 15 Again.

16 Guard, forbid. 17 Wickedness, shrewishness.

18 If, as is probable, this Tale was translated from the French, the original is not now extant. Tyrwhitt remarks that the scene "is laid in Italy, but none of the names, except Damian and Justin, seem to be Italian, but rather made at pleasure; so that I doubt whether the story be really of Italian growth. The adventure of the pear-tree I find in a small collection of Latin fables, written by one Adolphus, in elegiac verses of his fashion, in the year 1315. . . . Whatever was the real origin of the Tale, the machinery of the fairies, which Chaucer has used so happily, was probably added by himself; and, indeed, I cannot help thinking that his Pluto and Proserpina were the true progenitors of Oberon and Titania; or rather, that they themselves have, once at least, deigned to revisit our poetical system under the latter names."

19 Of the laity; but perhaps, since the word is of twofold meaning, Chaucer intends a hit at the secular clergy, who, unlike the regular orders, did not live separate from the world, but shared in all its interests and pleasures—all the more easily and freely, that they had not the civil restraint of marriage.

20 Inclination.

That day and night he did all that he can
To espy where that he might wedded be;
Praying our Lord to grantë him, that he
Mightë once knowen of that blissful life
That is betwixt a husband and his wife,
And for to live under that holy bond
With which God firstë man and woman bond.
"None other life," said he, "is worth a bean;
For wedlock is so easy, and so clean,
That in this world it is a paradise."
Thus said this oldë knight, that was so wise.
And certainly, as sooth[1] as God is king,
To take a wife it is a glorious thing,
And namely[2] when a man is old and hoar,
Then is a wife the fruit of his treasór;
Then should he take a young wife and a fair,
On which he might engender him an heir,
And lead his life in joy and in solace;[3]
Whereas these bachelors singen "Alas!"
When that they find any adversity
In love, which is but childish vanity.
And truëly it sits[4] well to be so,
That bachelors have often pain and woe:
On brittle ground they build, and brittleness
They findë, when they weenë sickerness:[5]
They live but as a bird or as a beast,
In liberty, and under no arrest;[6]
Whereas a wedded man in his estate
Liveth a life blissful and ordinate,
Under the yoke of marriáge y-bound;
Well may his heart in joy and bliss abound.
For who can be so buxom[7] as a wife?
Who is so true, and eke so áttentíve
To keep[8] him, sick and whole, as is his make?[9]
For weal or woe she will him not forsake:
She is not weary him to love and serve,
Though that he lie bedrid until he sterve.[10]
And yet some clerkës say it is not so;
Of which he, Theophrast, is one of tho:[11]
What force[12] though Theophrast list for to lie?
"Takë no wife," quoth he, "for husbandry,[13]
As for to spare in household thy dispence;
A truë servant doth more diligence
Thy good to keep, than doth thine owen wife,
For she will claim a half part all her life.
And if that thou be sick, so God me save,
Thy very friendës, or a truë knave,[14]
Will keep thee bet[15] than she, that waiteth aye
After[16] thy good, and hath done many a day."
This sentence, and a hundred timës worse,
Writeth this man, there God his bonës curse.
But take no keep[17] of all such vanity,
Defy[18] Theóphrast, and hearken to me.
A wife is Goddë's giftë verily;
All other manner giftës hardily,[19]
As landës, rentës, pasture, or commúne,[20]
Or mebles,[21] all be giftës of fortúne,
That passen as a shadow on the wall:
But dread[22] thou not, if plainly speak I shall,
A wife will last, and in thine house endure,
Well longer than thee list, paráventure.[23]
Marriage is a full great sacrament;
He which that hath no wife, I hold him shent;[24]
He liveth helpless, and all desolate
(I speak of folk in secular estate[25]):
And hearken why,—I say not this for nought,—
That woman is for mannë's help y-wrought.
The highë God, when he had Adam maked,
And saw him all alonë belly naked,
God of his greatë goodness saidë then,
Let us now make a help unto this man
Like to himself; and then he made him Eve.
Here may ye see, and hereby may ye preve,[26]
That a wife is man's help and his comfórt,
His paradise terrestre and his disport.
So buxom[27] and so virtuous is she,
They mustë needës live in unity;
One flesh they be, and one blood, as I guess,
With but one heart in weal and in distress.
A wife? Ah! Saint Marý, *ben'dicite*,
How might a man have any adversity
That hath a wife? certes I cannot say
The bliss the which that is betwixt them tway,
There may no tongue it tell, or heartë think.
If he be poor, she helpeth him to swink;[28]
She keeps his good, and wasteth never a deal;[29]
All that her husband list, her liketh[30] well;
She saith not onës Nay, when he saith Yea;
"Do this," saith he; "All ready, Sir," saith she.
O blissful order, wedlock precioús!
Thou art so merry, and eke so virtuous,
And so commended and approved eke,
That every man that holds him worth a leek
Upon his barë knees ought all his life
To thank his God, that him hath sent a wife;
Or ellës pray to God him for to send
A wife, to last unto his lifë's end.
For then his life is set in sickerness,[31]
He may not be deceived, as I guess,
So that he work after his wifë's rede;[32]
Then may he boldëly bear up his head,
They be so true, and therewithal so wise.
For which, if thou wilt worken as the wise,
Do alway so as women will thee rede.[32]
Lo how that Jacob, as these clerkës read,
By good-counsel of his mother Rebecc'
Boundë the kiddë's skin about his neck;
For which his father's benison[33] he wan.
Lo Judith, as the story tellë can,
By good counsel she Goddë's people kept,
And slew him, Holofernes, while he slept.
Lo Abigail, by good counsél, how she
Saved her husband Nabal, when that he
Should have been slain. And lo, Esther also

1 True. 2 Especially.
3 Mirth, delight. 4 Becomes, befits.
5 Think that there is security.
6 Check, control. 7 Obedient.
8 Care for, attend to. 9 Mate.
10 Die. 11 Those. 12 What matter.
13 Thrift. This and the next eight lines are taken from the "Liber aureolus Theophrasti de nuptiis," quoted by Hieronymus, "Contra Jovinianum," and thence again by John of Salisbury.
14 Servant. 15 Better.
16 Waits on, longs to have. 17 Heed, notice.
18 Distrust. 19 Truly. 20 Common land.
21 Movables, furniture, &c.; French, "meubles."
22 Doubt. 23 Perhaps. 24 Ruined.
25 Who are not of the clergy. 26 Prove.
27 Obedient, complying. 28 Labour.
29 Whit. 30 Pleaseth.
31 Security. 32 Counsel.
33 Benediction.

By counsel good deliver'd out of woe
The people of God, and made him, Mardoché,
Of Assuere enhanced [1] for to be.
There is nothing in gree superlative [2]
(As saith Senec) above a humble wife.
Suffer thy wifë's tongue, as Cato bit; [3]
She shall command, and thou shalt suffer it,
And yet she will obey of courtesy.
A wife is keeper of thine husbandry:
Well may the sickë man bewail and weep,
There as there is no wife the house to keep.
I warnë thee, if wisely thou wilt wirch, [4]
Love well thy wife, as Christ loveth his church:
Thou lov'st thyself, if thou lovest thy wife.
No man hateth his flesh, but in his life
He fost'reth it; and therefore bid I thee
Cherish thy wife, or thou shalt never thé. [5]
Husband and wife, what so men jape or play, [6]
Of worldly folk holdë the sicker [7] way;
They be so knit, there may no harm betide,
And namëly [8] upon the wifë's side.
For which this January, of whom I told,
Consider'd hath, within his dayës old,
The lusty life, the virtuous quiét,
That is in marriágë honey-sweet.
And for his friends upon a day he sent
To tell them the effect of his intent.
With facë sad, [9] his tale he hath them told:
He saidë, "Friendës, I am hoar and old,
And almost (God wot) on my pittë's [10] brink,
Upon my soulë somewhat must I think.
I have my body foolishly dispended,
Blessed be God that it shall be amended;
For I will be certáin a wedded man,
And that anon in all the haste I can,
Unto some maiden, fair and tender of age;
I pray you shapë [11] for my marriáge
All suddenly, for I will not abide:
And I will fond [12] to éspy, on my side,
To whom I may be wedded hastily.
But forasmuch as ye be more than I,
Ye shallë rather [13] such a thing espy
Than I, and where me best were to ally.
But one thing warn I you, my friendës dear,
I will none old wife have in no mannére:
She shall not passë sixteen year certáin.
Old fish and youngë flesh would I have fain.
Better," quoth he, "a pike than a pickerel, [14]
And better than old beef is tender veal.
I will no woman thirty year of age,
It is but beanëstraw and great forágе.
And eke these oldë widows (God it wot)
They connë [15] so much craft on Wadë's boat, [16]
So muchë brookë harm [17] when that them lest, [18]
That with them should I never live in rest.
For sundry schoolës makë subtle clerkës;
Woman of many schoolës half a clerk is.
But certainly a young thing men may guy, [19]
Right as men may warm wax with handës ply. [20]
Wherefore I say you plainly in a clause,
I will none old wife have, right for this cause.
For if so were I haddë such mischance,
That I in her could havë no pleasance,
Then should I lead my life in avoutrie, [21]
And go straight to the devil when I die.
Nor children should I none upon her getten:
Yet were me lever [22] houndës had me eaten
Than that mine heritagë shouldë fall
In strangë hands: and this I tell you all.
I doubtë not I know the causë why
Men shouldë wed: and farthermore know I
There speaketh many a man of marriáge
That knows no more of it than doth my page,
For what causes a man should take a wife.
If he ne may not livë chaste his life,
Take him a wife with great devotión,
Because of lawful procreatión
Of children, to th' honoúr of God above,
And not only for paramour or love;
And for they shouldë lechery eschew,
And yield their debtë when that it is due:
Or for that each of them should help the other
In mischief, [23] as a sister shall the brother,
And live in chastity full holily.
But, Sirës, by your leave, that am not I,
For, God be thanked, I dare make avaunt, [24]
I feel my limbës stark [25] and suffisant
To do all that a man belongeth to:
I wot myselfë best what I may do.
Though I be hoar, I fare as doth a tree,
That blossoms ere the fruit y-waxen [26] be;
The blossomy tree is neither dry nor dead;
I feel me nowhere hoar but on my head.
Mine heart and all my limbës are as green
As laurel through the year is for to seen. [27]
And, since that ye have heard all mine intent,
I pray you to my will ye would assent."
Diversë men diversëly him told
Of marriáge many examples old;
Some blamed it, some praised it, certáin;
But at the lastë, shortly for to sayn
(As all day [28] falleth altercatión
Betwixtë friends in disputatión),
There fell a strife betwixt his brethren two,
Of which that one was called Placebo,
Justinus soothly called was that other.
Placebo said; "O January, brother,
Full little need have ye, my lord so dear,
Counsel to ask of any that is here:
But that ye be so full of sapience,
That you not liketh, for your high prudénce,

1 Advanced in dignity.
2 To be esteemed in the highest degree.
3 Bade. 4 Work. 5 Thrive.
6 Let men jest and laugh as they will.
7 Sure. 8 Especially. 9 Grave, earnest.
10 Grave's. 11 Arrange, contrive. 12 Try.
13 Sooner. 14 Young pike. 15 Know.
16 "Wade's boat" was called Guingelot; and in it, according to the old romance, the owner underwent a long series of wild adventures, and performed many strange exploits. The romance is lost, and therefore the exact force of the phrase in the text is uncertain; but Mr Wright seems to be warranted in supposing that Wade's adventures were cited as examples of craft and cunning—that the hero, in fact, was a kind of Northern Ulysses. It is possible that to the same source we may trace the proverbial phrase, found in Chaucer's "Remedy of Love," to "bear Watti's pack"—signifying to be duped or beguiled.
17 So much mischief can they perform, employ.
18 Pleases. 19 Guide. 20 Bend, mould.
21 Adultery. 22 I would rather. 23 Trouble.
24 Boast. 25 Strong. 26 Grown.
27 See. 28 Constantly, every day.

To waivë [1] from the word of Solomon.
This word said he unto us every one;
Work allë thing by counsel,—thus said he,—
And thennë shalt thou not repentë thee.
But though that Solomon spake such a word,
Mine owen dearë brother and my lord,
So wisly [2] God my soulë bring at rest,
I hold your owen counsel is the best.
For, brother mine, take of me this motive; [3]
I have now been a court-man all my life,
And, God it wot, though I unworthy be,
I havë standen in full great degree
Aboutë lordës of full high estate;
Yet had I ne'er with none of them debate;
I never them contráried truëly.
I know well that my lord can [4] more than I;
What that he saith, I hold it firm and stable,
I say the same, or else a thing semblâble.
A full great fool is any counsellor
That serveth any lord of high honoúr,
That dare presume, or onës thinken it,
That his counsel should pass his lordë's wit.
Nay, lordës be no foolës, by my fay.
Ye have yourselfë shewed here to-day
So high senténce, [5] so holily and well,
That I consent, and cónfirm every deal [6]
Your wordës all, and your opinioún.
By God, there is no man in all this town
Nor in Itále, could better have y-said:
Christ holds him of this counsel well apaid. [7]
And truëly it is a high couráge
Of any man that stopen [8] is in age,
To take a young wife, by my father's kin;
Your heartë hangeth on a jolly pin.
Do now in this matter right as you lest,
For finally I hold it for the best."
Justinus, that aye stillë sat and heard,
Right in this wise to Placebo answér'd.
"Now, brother mine, be patient I pray,
Since ye have said, and hearken what I say.
Senec, among his other wordës wise,
Saith, that a man ought him right well advise, [9]
To whom he gives his land or his chattél.
And since I ought advisë me right well
To whom I give my good away from me,
Well more I ought advisë me, pardie,
To whom I give my body: for alway
I warn you well it is no childë's play
To take a wife without advisëment.
Men must inquirë (this is mine assent)
Whe'er she be wise, or sober, or dronkelew, [10]
Or proud, or any other ways a shrew,
A chidester, [11] or a waster of thy good,
Or rich or poor; or else a man is wood. [12]
Albeit so, that no man findë shall
None in this world, that trotteth whole in all, [13]
Nor man, nor beast, such as men can devise, [14]
But natheless it ought enough suffice
With any wife, if so were that she had

1 Depart, deviate. 2 Surely.
3 Advice, encouragement. 4 Knows.
5 Judgment, sentiment.
6 In every point. 7 Satisfied.
8 Advanced; past participle of "step." Elsewhere "y-stept in age" is used by Chaucer.
9 Consider.

More goodë thewës [15] than her vices bad:
And all this asketh leisure to inquére.
For, God it wot, I have wept many a tear
Full privily, since I have had a wife.
Praise whoso will a wedded mannë's life,
Certes, I find in it but cost and care,
And observánces of all blisses bare.
And yet, God wot, my neighëbours about,
And namëly [16] of women many a rout, [17]
Say that I have the mostë steadfast wife,
And eke the meekest one, that beareth life.
But I know best where wringeth [18] me my shoe.
Ye may for me right as you likë do.
Advisë you, ye be a man of age,
How that ye enter into marriáge;
And namely [16] with a young wife and a fair.
By him that madë water, fire, earth, air,
The youngest man that is in all this rout [17]
Is busy enough to bringen it about
To have his wife alonë, trustë me:
Ye shall not please her fully yearës three,
This is to say, to do her full pleasánce.
A wife asketh full many an observánce.
I pray you that ye be not evil apaid." [19]
"Well," quoth this January, "and hast thou said?
Straw for thy Senec, and for thy provérbs,
I countë not a pannier full of herbs
Of schoolë termës; wiser men than thou,
As thou hast heard, assented here right now
To my purpose: Placebo, what say ye?"
"I say it is a cursed [20] man," quoth he,
"That letteth [21] matrimony, sickerly."
And with that word they rise up suddenly,
And be assented fully, that he should
Be wedded when him list, and where he would.
High fantasy and curious business
From day to day gan in the soul impress [22]
Of January about his marriáge.
Many a fair shape, and many a fair viság
There passed through his heartë night by night.
As whoso took a mirror polish'd bright,
And set it in a common market-place,
Then should he see many a figure pace
By his mirrór; and in the samë wise
Gan January in his thought devise
Of maidens, which that dweltë him beside:
He wistë not where that he might abide. [23]
For if that one had beauty in her face,
Another stood so in the people's grace
For her sadness [24] and her benignity,
That of the people greatest voice had she:
And some were rich and had a baddë name.
But natheless, betwixt earnest and game,
He at the last appointed him on one,
And let all others from his heartë gon,
And chose her of his own authority;
For love is blind all day, and may not see.
And when that he was into bed y-brought,

10 Given to drink. 11 A scold.
12 Mad. 13 Sound in every point.
14 Describe, tell. 15 Qualities. 16 Especially.
17 Company. 18 Pinches. 19 Displeased.
20 Ill-natured, wicked. 21 Hindereth.
22 Imprint themselves. 23 Stay, fix his choice.
24 Sedateness.

He pourtray'd in his heart and in his thought
Her freshë beauty, and her agë tender,
Her middle small, her armës long and slender,
Her wisë governance, her gentleness,
Her womanly bearíng, and her sadnéss.[1]
And when that he on her was condescended,[2]
He thought his choicë might not be amended;
For when that he himself concluded had,
He thought each other mannë's wit so bad,
That impossíble it werë to reply
Against his choice; this was his fantasy.
His friendës sent he to, at his instánce,
And prayed them to do him that pleasánce,
That hastily they would unto him come;
He would abridge their labour all and some:
Needed no more for them to go nor ride,[3]
He was appointed where he would abide.[4]
 Placebo came, and eke his friendës soon,
And alderfirst [5] he bade them all a boon,[6]
That none of them no arguments would make
Against the purpose that he had y-take:
Which purpose was pleasánt to God, said he,
And very ground of his prosperity.
He said, there was a maiden in the town,
Which that of beauty haddë great renown;
All[7] were it so she were of small degree,
Sufficed him her youth and her beautý;
Which maid, he said, he would have to his wife,
To lead in ease and holiness his life;
And thanked God, that he might have her all,
That no wight with his blissë partë [8] shall;
And prayed them to labour in this need,
And shapë that he failë not to speed:
For then, he said, his spirit was at ease.
"Then is," quoth he, "nothing may me displease,
Save one thing pricketh in my conscience,
The which I will rehearse in your presénce.
I have," quoth he, "heard said, full yore [9] ago,
There may no man have perfect blisses two,
This is to say, on earth and eke in heaven.
For though he keep him from the sinnës seven,
And eke from every branch of thilkë tree,[10]
Yet is there so perfect felicity,
And so great ease and lust,[11] in marriáge,
That ev'r I am aghast,[12] now in mine age
That I shall lead now so merry a life,
So delicate, withoutë woe or strife,
That I shall have mine heav'n on earthë here.
For since that very heav'n is bought so dear,
With tribulatión and great penánce,
How should I then, living in such pleasánce
As allë wedded men do with their wivës,
Come to the bliss where Christ etern on live is?[13]
This is my dread;[14] and ye, my brethren tway,
Assoilë[15] me this question, I you pray."
 Justinus, which that hated his follý,
Answér'd anon right in his japery;[16]
And, for he would his longë tale abridge,
He wouldë no authority[17] allege,
But saidë; "Sir, so there be none obstácle
Other than this, God of his high mirácle,
And of his mercy, may so for you wirch,[18]
That, ere ye have your rights of holy church,
Ye may repent of wedded mannë's life,
In which ye say there is no woe nor strife:
And ellës God forbid, but if [19] he sent
A wedded man his grace him to repent
Well often, rather than a single man.
And therefore, Sir, the bestë rede I can,[20]
Despair you not, but have in your memóry,
Parâventure she may be your purgatóry;
She may be Goddë's means, and Goddë's whip;
And then your soul shall up to heaven skip
Swifter than doth an arrow from a bow.
I hope to God hereafter ye shall know
That there is none so great felicity
In marriáge, nor ever more shall be,
That you shall let[21] of your salvatión;
So that ye use, as skill is and reasón,
The lustës [22] of your wife attemperly,[23]
And that ye please her not too amorously,
And that ye keep you eke from other sin.
My tale is done, for my wit is but thin.
Be not aghast[12] hereof, my brother dear,
But let us waden out of this mattére.
The Wife of Bath, if ye have understand,
Of marriáge, which ye have now in hand,
Declared hath full well in little space;
Fare ye now well, God have you in his grace."
 And with this word this Justin' and his brother
Have ta'en their leave, and each of them of other.
And when they saw that it must needës be,
They wroughtë so, by sleight and wise treatý,
That she, this maiden, which that Maius hight,[24]
As hastily as ever that she might,
Shall wedded be unto this Januáry.
I trow it were too longë you to tarry,
If I told you of every script and band[25]
By which she was feoffed in his land;
Or for to reckon of her rich array.
But finally y-comen is the day
That to the churchë bothë be they went,
For to receive the holy sacrament.
Forth came the priest, with stole about his neck,
And bade her be like Sarah and Rebecc'
In wisdom and in truth of marriáge;
And said his orisons, as is uságe,
And crouched[26] them, and bade[27] God should them bless,
And made all sicker[28] enough with holiness.
 Thus be they wedded with solemnity;
And at the feastë sat both he and she,
With other worthy folk, upon the dais.
All full of joy and bliss is the paláce,
And full of instruments, and of vitáille,
The mostë dainteous[29] of all Itále.

1 Sedateness. 2 Had selected her.
3 In quest of a wife for him, as they had promised.
4 He had definitively made his choice.
5 First of all. 6 Asked a favour, made a request.
7 Although. 8 Have a share. 9 Long.
10 That tree of original sin, of which the special sins are the branches. 11 Comfort and pleasure.
12 Alarmed, afraid. 13 Lives eternally.
14 Doubt. 15 Resolve, answer.
16 Mockery, jesting way. 17 Written texts.
18 Work. 19 Unless.
20 This is the best counsel that I know.
21 Hinder. 22 Pleasures. 23 Moderately.
24 Was named. 25 Writing and bond.
26 Crossed. 27 Prayed that.
28 Secure. 29 Delicate.

Before them stood such instruments of soun',
That Orpheus, nor of Thebes Amphioún,
Ne madë never such a melody.
At every course came in loud minstrelsy,
That never Joab trumped for to hear,
Nor he, Theodomas, yet half so clear
At Thebes, when the city was in doubt.
Bacchus the wine them skinked[1] all about.
And Venus laughed upon every wight
(For January was become her knight,
And wouldë both assayë his courâge
In liberty, and eke in marriâge),
And with her firebrand in her hand about
Danced before the bride and all the rout.
And certainly I dare right well say this,
Hyméneus, that god of wedding is,
Saw never his life so merry a wedded man.
Hold thou thy peace, thou poet Marcian,[2]
That writest us that ilkë[3] wedding merry
Of her Philology and him Mercúry,
And of the songës that the Muses sung;
Too small is both thy pen, and eke thy tongue,
For to describen of this marriâge.
When tender youth hath wedded stooping age,
There is such mirth that it may not be writ;
Assay it yourëself, then may ye wit[4]
If that I lie or no in this mattére.

Maius, that sat with so benign a cheer,[5]
Her to behold it seemed faërie;
Queen Esther never look'd with such an eye
On Assuere, so meek a look had she;
I may you not devise all her beauty;
But thus much of her beauty tell I may,
That she was like the bright morrow of May
Full filled of all beauty and pleasánce.
This January is ravish'd in a trance,
At every time he looked in her face;
But in his heart he gan her to menace,
That he that night in armës would her strain
Harder than ever Paris did Heléne.
But natheless yet had he great pitý
That thilkë night offendë her must be,
And thought, "Alas, O tender creatúre,
Now wouldë God ye mightë well endure
All my courâge, it is so sharp and keen;
I am aghast[6] ye shall it not sustene.
But God forbid that I did all my might.
Now wouldë God that it were waxen night,
And that the night would lasten evermo'.
I would that all this people were y-go."[7]
And finally he did all his laboúr,
As he best mightë, saving his honoúr,
To haste them from the meat in subtle wise.

The timë came that reason was to rise;
And after that men dance, and drinkë fast,
And spices all about the house they cast,
And full of joy and bliss is every man,
All but a squire, that hightë Damian,
Who carv'd before the knight full many a day;
He was so ravish'd on his lady May,
That for the very pain he was nigh wood;[8]
Almost he swelt[9] and swooned where he stood,
So sore had Venus hurt him with her brand,
As that she bare it dancing in her hand.
And to his bed he went him hastily;
No more of him as at this time speak I;
But there I let him weep enough and plain,[10]
Till freshë May will rue upon his pain.
O perilous fire, that in the bedstraw breedeth!
O foe familiar,[11] that his service bedeth![12]
O servant traitor, O false homely hewe,[13]
Like to the adder in bosom sly untrue,
God shield us allë from your acquaintánce!
O January, drunken in pleasánce
Of marriage, see how thy Damian,
Thine owen squiër and thy boren[14] man,
Intendeth for to do thee villainy:[15]
God grantë thee thine homely foe[16] t' espy.
For in this world is no worse pestilence
Than homely foe, all day in thy presénce.

Performed hath the sun his arc diurn,[17]
No longer may the body of him sojourn
On the horizon, in that latitude:
Night with his mantle, that is dark and rude,
Gan overspread the hemisphere about:
For which departed is this lusty rout[18]
From January, with thank on every side.
Home to their houses lustily they ride,
Where as they do their thingës as them lest,
And when they see their time they go to rest.
Soon after that this hasty[19] Januáry
Will go to bed, he will no longer tarry.
He drankë hippocras, clarre,[20] and vernage[21]
Of spices hot, to increase his courâge;
And many a lectuary had he full fine,
Such as the cursed monk Dan Constantine[22]
Hath written in his book *de Coitu;*
To eat them all he would nothing eschew:
And to his privy friendës thus said he:
"For Goddë's love, as soon as it may be,
Let voiden all this house in courteous wise."
And they have done right as he will devise.
Men drinken, and the travers[23] draw anon;
The bride is brought to bed as still as stone;
And when the bed was with the priest y-bless'd,
Out of the chamber every wight him dress'd,
And January hath fast in arms y-take
His freshë May, his paradise, his make.[24]
He lulled her, he kissed her full oft;
With thickë bristles of his beard unsoft,

1 Poured out; from Anglo-Saxon, "scencan."

2 Marcianus Capella, who wrote a kind of philosophical romance, "De Nuptiis Mercurii et Philologiæ." "Her" and "him," two lines after, like "he" applied to Theodomas, are prefixed to the proper names for emphasis, according to the Anglo-Saxon usage.

3 That same, that. 4 Know. 5 Countenance. 6 Afraid. 7 Gone away. 8 Mad. 9 Fainted. 10 Bewail.

11 Domestic; belonging to the "familia," or household. 12 Offers.

13 Domestic servant; from Anglo-Saxon, "hiwa." Tyrwhitt reads "false of holy hue;" but Mr Wright has properly restored the reading adopted in the text.

14 Born; owing to January faith and loyalty because born in his household. 15 Dishonour, outrage.

16 Enemy in the household.

17 Diurnal. 18 Pleasant company.

19 Eager. 20 Spiced wine.

21 A wine believed to have come from Crete, although its name—Italian, "Vernaccia"—seems to be derived from Verona.

22 A medical author who wrote about 1080; his works were printed at Basle in 1536. 23 Curtains.

24 Mate, consort.

Like to the skin of houndfish,[1] sharp as brere [2]
(For he was shav'n all new in his mannére),
He rubbed her upon her tender face,
And saidë thus; "Alas! I must trespace
To you, my spouse, and you greatly offend,
Ere timë come that I will down descend.
But natheless consider this," quoth he,
"There is no workman, whatsoe'er he be,
That may both workë well and hastily:
This will be done at leisure perfectly.
It is no force[3] how longë that we play;
In truë wedlock coupled be we tway;
And blessed be the yoke that we be in,
For in our actës may there be no sin.
A man may do no sinnë with his wife,
Nor hurt himselfë with his owen knife;
For we have leave to play us by the law."
Thus labour'd he, till that the day gan daw,
And then he took a sop in fine clarré,
And upright in his beddë then sat he.
And after that he sang full loud and clear,
And kiss'd his wife, and madë wanton cheer.
He was all coltish, full of ragerie[4]
And full of jargon as a flecked pie.
The slackë skin about his neckë shaked,
While that he sang, so chanted he and craked.[5]
But God wot what that May thought in her heart,
When she him saw up sitting in his shirt
In his night-cap, and with his neckë lean:
She praised not his playing worth a bean.
Then said he thus; "My restë will I take
Now day is come, I may no longer wake;
And down he laid his head and slept till prime.
And afterward, when that he saw his time,
Up rosë January, but freshë May
Heldë her chamber till the fourthë day,
As usage is of wivës for the best.
For every labour some time must have rest,
Or ellës longë may he not endure;
This is to say, no life of creature,
Be it of fish, or bird, or beast, or man.
Now will I speak of woeful Damian,
That languisheth for love, as ye shall hear;
Therefore I speak to him in this mannére.
I say; "O silly Damian, alas!
Answér to this demand, as in this case,
How shalt thou to thy lady, freshë May,
Tellë thy woe? She will alway say nay;
Eke if thou speak, she will thy woe bewray;[6]
God be thine help, I can no better say.
This sickë Damian in Venus' fire
So burned that he diëd for desire;
For which he put his life in áventure,[7]
No longer might he in this wise endure;
But privily a penner[8] gan he borrow,
And in a letter wrote he all his sorrow,
In manner of a cómplaint or a lay,
Unto his fairë freshë lady May.
And in a purse of silk, hung on his shirt,
He hath it put, and laid it at his heart.
The moonë, that at noon was thilkë[9] day
That January had wedded freshë May,
In ten of Taure, was into Cancer glided;[10]
So long had Maius in her chamber abided,
As custom is unto these nobles all.
A bridë shall not eaten in the hall
Till dayës four, or three days at the least,
Y-passed be; then let her go to feast.
The fourthë day complete from noon to noon,
When that the highë massë was y-done,
In hallë sat this January, and May,
As fresh as is the brightë summer's day.
And so befell, how that this goodë man
Remember'd him upon this Damian.
And saidë; "Saint Marý, how may this be,
That Damian attendeth not to me?
Is he aye sick? or how may this betide?"
His squiërs, which that stoodë there beside,
Excused him, because of his sickness,
Which letted[11] him to do his business:
None other causë mightë make him tarry.
"That me forthinketh,"[12] quoth this January;
"He is a gentle squiër, by my truth;
If that he died, it were great harm and ruth.
He is as wise, as díscreet, and secré,[13]
As any man I know of his degree,
And thereto manly and eke serviceáble,
And for to be a thrifty man right able.
But after meat, as soon as ever I may
I will myself visit him, and eke May,
To do him all the comfort that I can."
And for that word him blessed every man,
That of his bounty and his gentleness
He wouldë so comfórten in sickness
His squiër, for it was a gentle deed.
"Dame," quoth this January, "take good heed,
At after meat, ye with your women all
(When that ye be in chamb'r out of this hall),
That all ye go to see this Damian:
Do him disport, he is a gentle man;
And tellë him that I will him visíte,
Have I nothing but rested me a lite:[14]
And speed you fastë, for I will abide
Till that ye sleepë fastë by my side."
And with that word he gan unto him call
A squiër, that was marshal of his hall,
And told him certain thingës that he wo'ld.
This freshë May hath straight her way y-hold,
With all her women, unto Damian.
Down by his beddë's sidë sat she than,[15]
Comfórting him as goodly as she may.
This Damian, when that his time he say,[16]
In secret wise his purse, and eke his bill,
In which that he y-written had his will,

1 Dogfish. 2 Briar.
3 No matter. 4 Wantonness.
5 Quavered in his singing.
6 Discover, betray. 7 Risk.
8 Writing-case, carried about by clerks or scholars.
9 That.
10 Nearly all the manuscripts read "in two of Taure;" but Tyrwhitt has shown that, setting out from the second degree of Taurus, the moon, which in the four complete days that Maius spent in her chamber could not have advanced more than fifty-three degrees, would only have been at the twenty-fifth degree of Gemini—whereas, by reading "ten," she is brought to the third degree of Cancer.
11 Hindered. 12 Grieves, causes uneasiness.
13 Secret, trusty.
14 When only I have rested me a little.
15 Then. 16 Saw.

Hath put into her hand withoutë more,
Save that he sighed wondrous deep and sore,
And softëly to her right thus said he:
"Mercy, and that ye not discover me:
For I am dead if that this thing be kid."[1]
The pursë hath she in her bosom hid,
And went her way; ye get no more of me;
But unto January come is she,
That on his beddë's sidë sat full soft.
He took her, and he kissed her full oft,
And laid him down to sleep, and that anon.
She feigned her as that she mustë gon
There as ye know that every wight must need;
And when she of this bill had taken heed,
She rent it all to cloutës[2] at the last,
And in the privy softëly it cast.
Who studieth[3] now but fairë freshë May?
Adown by oldë January she lay,
That sleptë, till the cough had him awaked:
Anon he pray'd her strippë her all naked,
He would of her, he said, have some pleasánce;
And said her clothës did him incumbránce.
And she obey'd him, be her lefe or loth.[4]
But, lest that precious[5] folk be with me wroth,
How that he wrought I dare not to you tell,
Or whether she thought it paradise or hell;
But there I let them worken in their wise
Till even-song ring, and they must arise.
Were it by destiny, or áventure,
Were it by influence, or by natúre,
Or constellation, that in such estate
The heaven stood at that time fortunate
As for to put a bill of Venus' works
(For allë thing hath time, as say these clerks),
To any woman for to get her love,
I cannot say; but greatë God above,
That knoweth that none act is causëless,
He deem[6] of all, for I will hold my peace.
But sooth is this, how that this freshë May
Hath taken such impressión that day
Of pity on this sickë Damian,
That from her heartë she not drivë can
The remembráncë for to do him ease.[7]
"Certain," thought she, "whom that this thing displease
I reckë not, for here I him assure,
To love him best of any creature,
Though he no morë haddë than his shirt."
Lo, pity runneth soon in gentle heart.
Here may ye see, how excellent franchise[8]
In women is when they them narrow advise.[9]
Some tyrant is,—as there be many a one,—
That hath a heart as hard as any stone,
Which would have let him sterven[10] in the place
Well rather than have granted him her grace;
And then rejoicen in her cruel pride.
And reckon not to be a homicide.
This gentle May, full filled of pitý,
Right of her hand a letter maked she,
In which she granted him her very grace;
There lacked nought, but only day and place,
Where that she might unto his lust suffice:
For it shall be right as he will devise.
And when she saw her time upon a day
To visit this Damían went this May,
And subtilly this letter down she thrust
Under his pillow, read it if him lust.
She took him by the hand, and hard him twist'
So secretly, that no wight of it wist,
And bade him be all whole; and forth she went
To January, when he for her sent.
Up rosë Damian the nextë morrow,
All passed was his sickness and his sorrow.
He combed him, he proined[11] him and picked,
He did all that unto his lady liked;
And eke to January he went as low
As ever did a doggë for the bow.[12]
He is so pleasant unto every man
(For craft is all, whoso that do it can),
That every wight is fain to speak him good;
And fully in his lady's grace he stood.
Thus leave I Damian about his need,
And in my talë forth I will proceed.
Some clerkës[13] holdë that felicitý
Stands in delight; and therefore certain he,
This noble January, with all his might
In honest wise as longeth to a knight,
Shope[14] him to livë full deliciously:
His housing, his array, as honestly[15]
To his degree was maked as a king's.
Amongës other of his honest things
He had a garden walled all with stone;
So fair a garden wot I nowhere none.
For out of doubt I verily suppose
That he that wrote the Romance of the Rose[16]
Could not of it the beauty well devise;[17]
Nor Priapus[18] mightë not well suffice,
Though he be god of gardens, for to tell
The beauty of the garden, and the well[19]
That stood under a laurel always green.
Full often time he, Pluto, and his queen
Proserpina, and all their faërie,
Disported them and madë melody
About that well, and danced, as men told.
This noble knight, this January old,
Such dainty[20] had in it to walk and play,
That he would suffer no wight to bear the key,
Save he himself, for of the small wickét
He bare always of silver a clikét,[21]
With which, when that him list, he it unshet.[22]
And when that he would pay his wifë's debt,
In summer season, thither would he go,
And May his wife, and no wight but they two;
And thingës which that were not done in bed,

1 Or "kidde," past participle of "kythe" or "kithe," to show or discover.
2 Fragments.
3 Is thoughtful.
4 Whether she were willing or reluctant.
5 Precise, over-nice; French, "precieux," affected.
6 Let him judge.
7 To satisfy his desire.
8 Generosity.
9 Closely consider.
10 Die.
11 Or "pruned;" carefully trimmed and dressed himself. The word is used in falconry of a hawk when she picks and trims her feathers.
12 A dog attending a hunter with the bow.
13 Writers, scholars.
14 Prepared, arranged.
15 Honourably, suitably.
16 Which opens with the description of a beautiful garden.
17 Tell, describe.
18 Son of Bacchus and Venus; he was regarded as the promoter of fertility in all agricultural life, vegetable and animal; while not only gardens, but fields, flocks, bees—and even fisheries—were supposed to be under his protection.
19 Fountain.
20 Pleasure.
21 Key.
22 Unshut, opened.

He in the garden them perform'd and sped.
And in this wisë many a merry day
Lived this January and fresh May,
But worldly joy may not always endure
To January, nor to no creatúre.
O sudden hap! O thou fortúne unstable!
Like to the scorpión so deceiváble,[1]
That flatt'rest with thy head when thou wilt sting;
Thy tail is death, through thine envenoming.
O brittle joy! O sweetë poison quaint![2]
O monster, that so subtilly canst paint
Thy giftës, under hue of steadfastness,
That thou deceivest bothë more and less![3]
Why hast thou January thus deceiv'd,
That haddest him for thy full friend receiv'd?
And now thou hast bereft him both his eyen,
For sorrow of which desireth he to dien.
Alas! this noble January free,
Amid his lust[4] and his prosperity
Is waxen blind, and that all suddenly.
He weeped and he wailed piteously;
And therewithal the fire of jealousy
(Lest that his wife should fall in some follý)
So burnt his heartë, that he wouldë fain,
That some man bothë him and her had slain;
For neither after his death, nor in his life,
Ne would he that she were no love nor wife,
But ever live as widow in clothës black,
Sole as the turtle that hath lost her make.[5]
But at the last, after a month or tway,
His sorrow gan assuagë, sooth to say.
For, when he wist it might none other be,
He patiently took his adversity:
Save out of doubtë he may not foregon
That he was jealous evermore-in-one:[6]
Which jealousy was so outrageoús,
That neither in hall, nor in none other house,
Nor in none other place never the mo'
He wouldë suffer her to ride or go,
But if[7] that he had hand on her alway.
For which full often weptë freshë May,
That loved Damian so burningly
That she must either dien suddenly,
Or ellës she must have him as her lest:[8]
She waited[9] when her heartë wouldë brest.[10]
Upon that other sidë Damian
Becomen is the sorrowfullest man
That ever was; for neither night nor day
He mightë speak a word to freshë May,
As to his purpose, of no such mattére,
But if[7] that January must it hear,
That had a hand upon her evermo'.
But natheless, by writing to and fro,
And privy signës, wist he what she meant,
And she knew eke the fine[11] of his intent.
O January, what might it thee avail,
Though thou might see as far as shippës sail?
For as good is it blind deceiv'd to be,
As be deceived when a man may see.
Lo, Argus, which that had a hundred eyen,
For all that ever he could pore or pryen,
Yet was he blent;[12] and, God wot, so be mo',
That weenë wisly[13] that it be not so:
Pass over is an ease, I say no more.
This freshë May, of which I spakë yore,
In warm wax hath imprinted the clikét[14]
That January bare of the small wickét
By which into his garden oft he went;
And Damian, that knew all her intent,
The cliket counterfeited privily;
There is no more to say, but hastily
Some wonder by this cliket shall betide,
Which ye shall hearen, if ye will abide.
O noble Ovid, sooth say'st thou, God wot,
What sleight is it, if love be long and hot,
That he 'll not find it out in some mannére?
By Pyramus and Thisbe may men lear;[15]
Though they were kept full long and strait o'er all,
They be accorded,[16] rowning[17] through a wall,
Where no wight could have found out such a sleight.
But now to purpose; ere that dayës eight
Were passed of the month of July, fill[18]
That January caught so great a will,
Through egging[19] of his wife, him for to play
In his gardén, and no wight but they tway,
That in a morning to this May said he:
"Rise up, my wife, my love, my lady free;
The turtle's voice is heard, mine owen sweet;
The winter is gone, with all his rainës weet.[20]
Come forth now with thine eyen columbine.[21]
Well fairer be thy breasts than any wine.
The garden is enclosed all about;
Come forth, my whitë spouse; for, out of doubt,
Thou hast me wounded in mine heart, O wife:
No spot in thee was e'er in all thy life.
Come forth, and let us taken our disport;
I choose thee for my wife and my comfórt."
Such oldë lewëd wordës used he.
On Damian a signë madë she,
That he should go beforë with his cliket.
This Damian then hath opened the wicket,
And in he start, and that in such mannére
That no wight might him either see or hear;
And still he sat under a bush. Anon
This January, as blind as is a stone,
With Maius in his hand, and no wight mo',
Into this freshë garden is y-go,
And clapped to the wicket suddenly.
"Now, wife," quoth he, "here is but thou and I;
Thou art the creature that I bestë love:
For, by that Lord that sits in heav'n above,
Lever[22] I had to dien on a knife,
Than thee offendë, dearë truë wife.
For Goddë's sakë, think how I thee chees,[23]
Not for no covetisë[24] doubtëless,
But only for the love I had to thee.

1 Deceitful.
2 Strange.
3 Both great and small.
4 Pleasure.
5 Mate.
6 He could not cease to be jealous continually.
7 Unless.
8 Pleased.
9 Expected.
10 Burst.
11 End, aim.
12 Deceived; by Mercury, see note 5, page 31.
13 Think confidently.
14 Taken an impression of the key.
15 Learn.
16 They exchanged the assurances of their love; came to an agreement.
17 Whispering.
18 It befell, it happened.
19 Inciting.
20 Wet. See Song of Solomon, chap. ii.
21 Dove's eyes.
22 Rather.
23 Chose.
24 Covetousness.

And though that I be old, and may not see,
Be to me true, and I will tell you why.
Certes three thingës shall ye win thereby:
First, love of Christ, and to yourself honoúr,
And all mine heritagë, town and tow'r.
I give it you, make charters as you lest;
This shall be done to-morrow ere sun rest,
So wisly[1] God my soulë bring to bliss!
I pray you, on this covenant me kiss.
And though that I be jealous, wite[2] me not;
Ye be so deep imprinted in my thought,
That when that I consider your beautý,
And therewithal th' unlikely[3] eld of me,
I may not, certes, though I shouldë die,
Forbear to be out of your company,
For very love; this is withoutë doubt:
Now kiss me, wife, and let us roam about."
This freshë May, when she these wordës heard,
Benignëly to January answér'd;
But first and forward she began to weep:
"I have," quoth she, "a soulë for to keep
As well as ye, and also mine honoúr,
And of my wifehood thilkë tender flow'r
Which that I have assured in your hond,
When that the priest to you my body bond:
Wherefore I will answer in this mannére,
With leave of you, mine owen lord so dear.
I pray to God, that never dawn the day
That I ne sterve,[4] as foul as woman may,
If e'er I do unto my kin that shame,
Or ellës I impairë so my name,
That I be false; and if I do that lack,
Do[5] strippë me, and put me in a sack,
And in the nextë river do[5] me drench:[6]
I am a gentle woman, and no wench.
Why speak ye thus? but men be e'er untrue,
And women have reproof of you aye new.
Ye know none other dalliance, I believe,
But speak to us of untrust and repreve."[7]
And with that word she saw where Damian
Sat in the bush, and coughë she began;
And with her finger signë madë she,
That Damian should climb upon a tree
That charged was with fruit; and up he went:
For verily he knew all her intent,
And every signë that she couldë make,
Better than January her own make.[8]
For in a letter she had told him all
Of this mattér, how that he workë shall.
And thus I leave him sitting in the perry,[9]
And January and May roaming full merry.
Bright was the day, and blue the firmament;
Phœbus of gold his streamës down had sent
To gladden every flow'r with his warmnéss;
He was that time in *Geminis*, I guess,
But little from his declinatión
Of Cancer, Jovë's exaltatión.
And so befell, in that bright morning-tide,
That in the garden, on the farther side,
Pluto, that is the king of Faërie,
And many a lady in his company
Following his wife, the queen Proserpina,—
Which that he ravished out of Ethna,[10]
While that she gather'd flowers in the mead
(In Claudian ye may the story read,
How in his grisly chariot he her fet[11]),—
This king of Faërie adown him set
Upon a bank of turfës fresh and green,
And right anon thus said he to his queen.
"My wife," quoth he, "there may no wight say nay,[12]—
Experience so proves it every day,—
The treason which that woman doth to man.
Ten hundred thousand stories tell I can
Notáble of your untruth and brittleness.[13]
O Solomon, richest of all richéss,
Full fill'd of sapience and worldly glory,
Full worthy be thy wordës of memóry
To every wight that wit and reason can.[14]
Thus praised he yet the bounté[15] of man:
'Among a thousand men yet found I one,
But of all women found I never none.'[16]
Thus said this king, that knew your wickedness;
And Jesus, *Filius* Sirach,[17] as I guess,
He spake of you but seldom reverénce.
A wildë fire and córrupt pestilence
So fall upon your bodies yet to-night!
Ne see ye not this honourable knight?
Because, alas! that he is blind and old,
His owen man shall makë him cuckóld.
Lo, where he sits, the lechour, in the tree.
Now will I granten, of my majesty,
Unto this oldë blindë worthy knight,
That he shall have again his eyen sight,
When that his wife will do him villainy;
Then shall he knowen all her harlotry,
Both in reproof of her and other mo'."
"Yea, Sir," quoth Proserpine, "and will ye so?
Now by my mother Ceres' soul I swear
That I shall give her suffisant answér,
And allë women after, for her sake;
That though they be in any guilt y-take,
With facë bold they shall themselves excuse,
And bear them down that wouldë them accuse.
For lack of answer, none of them shall dien.
All[18] had ye seen a thing with both your eyen,
Yet shall we visage it[19] so hardily,
And weep, and swear, and chidë subtilly,
That ye shall be as lewëd[20] as be geese.
What recketh me of your authorities?
I wot well that this Jew, this Solomon,
Found of us women foolës many one:
But though that he foundë no good womán,
Yet there hath found many another man
Women full good, and true, and virtuoús;
Witness on them that dwelt in Christë's house;

1 Surely. 2 Blame. 3 Dissimilar, incompatible. 4 Die not. 5 Cause. 6 Drown. 7 Reproof. 8 Mate. 9 Pear-tree.
10 "That fair field
Of Enna, where Proserpine, gath'ring flowers,
Herself a fairer flow'r, by gloomy Dis
Was gather'd."
—MILTON, "Paradise Lost," iv. 268.

11 Fetched. 12 Deny. 13 Inconstancy. 14 Knows. 15 Goodness. 16 See Ecclesiastes vii. 28.
17 Jesus, the son of Sirach, to whom is ascribed one of the books of the Apocrypha—that called the "Wisdom of Jesus the Son of Sirach, or Ecclesiasticus;" in which, especially in the ninth and twenty-fifth chapters, severe cautions are given against women. 18 Although.
19 Confront it, face it out. 20 Ignorant, confounded.

With martyrdom they proved their constánce,
The Roman gestës[1] makë remembránce
Of many a very truë wife also.
But, Sirë, be not wroth, albeit so,
Though that he said he found no good womán,
I pray you take the sentence[2] of the man:
He meant thus, that in sovereign bounté[3]
Is none but God, no, neither he nor she.[4]
Hey, for the very God that is but one,
Why makë ye so much of Solomon?
What though he made a temple, Goddë's house?
What though he werë rich and glorioús?
So made he eke a temple of false goddës;
How might he do a thing that more forbode[5] is?
Pardie, as fair as ye his name emplaster,[6]
He was a lechour, and an idolaster,[7]
And in his eld he very[8] God forsook.
And if that God had not (as saith the book)
Spared him for his father's sake, he should
Have lost his regnë[9] rather[10] than he would.
I settë not, of[11] all the villainy
That he of women wrote, a butterfly.
I am a woman, needës must I speak,
Or ellës swell until mine heartë break.
For since he said that we be jangleresses,[12]
As ever may I brookë[13] whole my tresses,
I shall not sparë for no courtesy
To speak him harm, that said us villainy."
"Dame," quoth this Pluto, "be no longer wroth;
I give it up: but, since I swore mine oath
That I would grant to him his sight again,
My word shall stand, that warn I you certáin:
I am a king, it sits[14] me not to lie."
"And I," quoth she, "am queen of Faërie.
Her answer she shall have, I undertake,
Let us no morë wordës of it make.
Forsooth, I will no longer you contráry."
Now let us turn again to January,
That in the garden with his fairë May
Singeth well merrier than the popinjay:[15]
"You love I best, and shall, and other none."
So long about the alleys is he gone,
Till he was comë to that ilkë perry,[16]
Where as this Damian sattë full merry
On high, among the freshë leavës green.
This freshë May, that is so bright and sheen,
Gan for to sigh, and said, "Alas my side!
Now, Sir," quoth she, "for aught that may betide,
I must have of the pearës that I see,
Or I must die, so sorë longeth me
To eaten of the smallë pearës green;
Help, for her love that is of heaven queen!
I tell you well, a woman in my plight
May have to fruit so great an appetite,
That she may dien, but[17] she of it have."
"Alas!" quoth he, "that I had here a knave[18]
That couldë climb; alas! alas!" quoth he,
"For I am blind." "Yea, Sir, no force,"[19] quoth she;
"But would ye vouchësafe, for Goddë's sake,
The perry in your armës for to take
(For well I wot that ye mistrustë me),
Then would I climbë well enough," quoth she,
"So I my foot might set upon your back."
"Certes," said he, "therein shall be no lack,
Might I you helpë with mine heartë's blood."
He stooped down, and on his back she stood,
And caught her by a twist,[20] and up she go'th.
(Ladies, I pray you that ye be not wroth,
I cannot glose,[21] I am a rudë man):
And suddenly anon this Damian
Gan pullen up the smock, and in he throng.[22]
And when that Pluto saw this greatë wrong,
To January he gave again his sight,
And made him see as well as ever he might.
And when he thus had caught his sight again,
Was never man of anything so fain:
But on his wife his thought was evermo'.
Up to the tree he cast his eyen two,
And saw how Damian his wife had dress'd,
In such mannére, it may not be express'd,
But if[23] I wouldë speak uncourteously.
And up he gave a roaring and a cry,
As doth the mother when the child shall die;
"Out! help! alas! harow!" he gan to cry;
"O strongë, lady, stowre![24] what dost thou?"
And she answered: "Sir, what aileth you?
Have patience and reason in your mind,
I have you help'd on both your eyen blind.
On peril of my soul, I shall not lien,
As me was taught to helpë with your eyen,
Was nothing better for to make you see,
Than struggle with a man upon a tree:
God wot, I did it in full good intent."
"Struggle!" quoth he, "yea, algate in it went.
God give you both one shamë's death to dien!
He swived thee; I saw it with mine eyen;
And ellës be I hanged by the halse."[25]
"Then is," quoth she, "my medicine all false;
For certainly, if that ye mightë see,
Ye would not say these wordës unto me.
Ye have some glimpsing,[26] and no perfect sight."
"I see," quoth he, "as well as ever I might,
(Thanked be God!) with both mine eyen two,
And by my faith me thought he did thee so."
"Ye maze, ye mazë,[27] goodë Sir," quoth she;
"This thank have I for I have made you see:
Alas!" quoth she, "that e'er I was so kind."
"Now, Dame," quoth he, "let all pass out of mind;

1 Histories; such as those of Lucretia, Porcia, &c.
2 Opinion, real meaning.
3 Perfect goodness.
4 Man nor woman.
5 Forbidden.
6 Plaster over, "whitewash."
7 Idolater.
8 The true.
9 Kingdom.
10 Sooner.
11 Care not for, value not.
12 Praters.
13 Enjoy the use of, preserve.
14 Becomes, befits.
15 Parrot.
16 That same pear-tree.
17 Unless.
18 Servant.
19 No matter.
20 Twig, bough.
21 Mince matters.
22 At this point, and again some twenty lines below, several verses of a very coarse character had been inserted in later manuscripts; but they are evidently spurious, and are omitted in the best editions.
23 Unless.
24 "Store" is the general reading here, but its meaning is not obvious. "Stowre" is found in several manuscripts; it signifies "struggle" or "resist;" and both for its own appropriateness, and for the force which it gives the word "stronge," the reading in the text seems the better.
25 Neck.
26 Glimmering.
27 Rave, are confused.

Come down, my lefe,[1] and if I have missaid,
God help me so, as I am evil apaid.[2]
But, by my father's soul, I ween'd have seen
How that this Damian had by thee lain,
And that thy smock had lain upon his breast."
"Yea, Sir," quoth she, "ye may ween as you lest:[3]
But, Sir, a man that wakes out of his sleep,
He may not suddenly well takë keep[4]
Upon a thing, nor see it perfectly,
Till that he be adawed[5] verily.
Right so a man, that long hath blind y-be,
He may not suddenly so well y-see,
First when his sight is newë come again,
As he that hath a day or two y-seen.
Till that your sight establish'd be a while,
There may full many a sightë you beguile.
Beware, I pray you, for, by heaven's king,
Full many a man weeneth to see a thing,
And it is all another than it seemeth;
He which that misconceiveth oft misdeemeth."[6]
And with that word she leapt down from the tree.
This January, who is glad but he?
He kissed her, and clipped[7] her full oft,
And on her womb he stroked her full soft;
And to his palace home he hath her lad.[8]
Now, goodë men, I pray you to be glad.
Thus endeth here my tale of Januáry,
God bless us, and his mother, Saintë Mary.

THE SQUIRE'S TALE.

THE PROLOGUE.

"Hey! Goddë's mercy!" said our Hostë tho,[9]
"Now such a wife I pray God keep me fro'.
Lo, suchë sleightës and subtilities
In women be; for aye as busy as bees
Are they us silly men for to deceive,
And from the soothë[10] will they ever weive,[11]
As this Merchantë's tale it proveth well.
But natheless, as true as any steel,
I have a wife, though that she poorë be;
But of her tongue a labbing[12] shrew is she;
And yet[13] she hath a heap of vices mo'.
Thereof no force;[14] let all such thingës go.
But wit[15] ye what? in counsel[16] be it said,
Me rueth sore I am unto her tied;
For, an'[17] I shouldë reckon every vice
Which that she hath, y-wis[18] I were too nice;[19]
And causë why, it should reported be
And told her by some of this companý
(By whom, it needeth not for to declare,
Since women connen utter such chaffáre[20]),
And eke my wit sufficeth not thereto
To tellen all; wherefore my tale is do.[21]
Squiër, come near, if it your willë be,
And say somewhat of love, for certes ye
Connë thereon[22] as much as any man."
"Nay, Sir," quoth he; "but such thing as I can,
With hearty will,—for I will not rebel
Against your lust,[23]—a talë will I tell.
Have me excused if I speak amiss;
My will is good; and lo, my tale is this."

THE TALE.[24]

Pars Prima.

At Sarra, in the land of Tartary,
There dwelt a king that warrayed[25] Russie,
Through which there died many a doughty man;
This noble king was called Cambuscan,[26]
Which in his time was of so great renown,
That there was nowhere in no regioún
So excellent a lord in allë thing:
Him lacked nought that longeth to a king,
As of the sect of which that he was born.
He kept his law to which he was y-sworn,
And thereto[27] he was hardy, wise, and rich,
And piteous and just, always y-lich;[28]
True of his word, benign and honouráble;
Of his coráge as any centre stable;[29]
Young, fresh, and strong, in armës desiroús
As any bachelor of all his house.
A fair persón he was, and fortunate,
And kept alway so well his royal estate,
That there was nowhere such another man.
This noble king, this Tartar Cambuscan,
Haddë two sons by Elfeta his wife,
Of which the eldest hightë Algarsife,
The other was y-called Camballó.
A daughter had this worthy king also,
That youngest was, and hightë Canacé:
But for to tellë you all her beautý,
It lies not in my tongue, nor my conníng;[30]
I dare not undertake so high a thing:
Mine English eke is insufficient,
It mustë be a rhetor[31] excellent,

1 Dear. 2 Grieved.
3 Think as you please. 4 Notice.
5 Awakened. 6 Who mistakes oft misjudges.
7 Embraced. 8 Led.
9 Then. 10 Truth. 11 Swerve, depart.
12 Blabbing, prating. 13 Moreover.
14 No matter. 15 Know.
16 Secret, confidence. 17 If.
18 Certainly. 19 Foolish.
20 Are adepts at giving circulation to such wares. The Host evidently means that his wife would be sure to hear of his confessions from some female member of the company. 21 Done.
22 Know of it. 23 Pleasure.
24 The Squire's Tale has not been found under any other form among the literary remains of the Middle Ages; and it is unknown from what original it was derived, if from any. The Tale is unfinished, not because the conclusion has been lost, but because the author left it so.
25 Made war upon; the Russians and Tartars waged constant hostilities between the thirteenth and sixteenth centuries.
26 In the best manuscripts the name is "Cambynskan," and thus, no doubt, it should strictly be read. But it is a most pardonable offence against literal accuracy to use the word which Milton has made classical, in "Il Penseroso," speaking of "him that left half-told the story of Cambuscan bold." Surely the admiration of Milton might well seem to the spirit of Chaucer to condone a much greater transgression on his domain than this verbal change—which to both eye and ear is an unquestionable improvement on the uncouth original.
27 Moreover, besides. 28 Alike, in even mood.
29 Firm, immovable of spirit. 30 Skill. 31 Orator.

That couth his colours longing for that art,[1]
If he should her describen any part;
I am none such, I must speak as I can.
And so befell, that when this Cambuscan
Had twenty winters borne his diadem,
As he was wont from year to year, I deem,
He let the feast of his nativity
Do cryë,[2] throughout Sarra his citý,
The last Idus of March, after the year.
Phœbus the sun full jolly was and clear,
For he was nigh his exaltatión
In Martë's face, and in his mansión[3]
In Aries, the choleric hot sign:
Full lusty[4] was the weather and benign;
For which the fowls against the sunnë sheen,[5]
What for the season and the youngë green,
Full loudë sangë their affectións:
Them seemed to have got protectións
Against the sword of winter keen and cold.
This Cambuscan, of which I have you told,
In royal vesture, sat upon his dais,
With diadem, full high in his palace;
And held his feast so solemn and so rich,
That in this worldë was there none it lich.[6]
Of which if I should tell all the array,
Then would it occupy a summer's day;
And eke it needeth not for to devise[7]
At every course the order of servíce.
I will not tellen of their strangë sewes,[8]
Nor of their swannës, nor their heronsews.[9]
Eke in that land, as tellë knightës old,
There is some meat that is full dainty hold,
That in this land men reck of[10] it full small:
There is no man that may reporten all.
I will not tarry you, for it is prime,
And for it is no fruit, but loss of time;
Unto my purpose[11] I will have recourse.
And so befell that, after the third course,
While that this king sat thus in his nobley,[12]
Hearing his ministrelës their thingës play
Before him at his board deliciously,
In at the hallë door all suddenly
There came a knight upon a steed of brass,
And in his hand a broad mirrór of glass;
Upon his thumb he had of gold a ring,
And by his side a naked sword hangíng:
And up he rode unto the highë board.
In all the hall was there not spoke a word,
For marvel of this knight; him to behold
Full busily they waited,[13] young and old.
This strangë knight, that came thus suddenly,
All armed, save his head, full richëly,
Saluted king, and queen, and lordës all,
By order as they satten in the hall,
With so high reverence and óbservánce,
As well in speech as in his countenánce,
That Gawain[14] with his oldë courtesý,
Though he were come again out of Faerie,
Him couldë not amendë with a word.[15]
And after this, before the highë board,
He with a manly voice said his messáge,
After the form used in his languáge,
Withoutë vice[16] of syllable or letter.
And, for his talë shouldë seem the better,
Accordant to his wordës was his cheer,[17]
As teacheth art of speech them that it lear.[18]
Albeit that I cannot sound his style,
Nor cannot climb over so high a stile,
Yet say I this, as to commúne intent,[19]
Thus much amounteth[20] all that ever he meant,
If it so be that I have it in mind.
He said; "The king of Araby and Ind,
My liegë lord, on this solemnë day
Saluteth you as he best can and may,
And sendeth you, in honour of your feast,
By me, that am all ready at your hest,[21]
This steed of brass, that easily and well
Can in the space of one day naturel
(This is to say, in four-and-twenty hours),
Whereso you list, in drought or else in show'rs,
Bearë your body into every place
To which your heartë willeth for to pace,[22]
Withoutë wem[23] of you, through foul or fair.
Or if you list to fly as high in air
As doth an eagle, when him list to soar,
This samë steed shall bear you evermore
Withoutë harm, till ye be where you lest[24]
(Though that ye sleepen on his back, or rest),
And turn again, with writhing[25] of a pin.
He that it wrought, he coudë[26] many a gin;[27]
He waited[28] many a constellatión,
Ere he had done this operatión,
And knew full many a seal[29] and many a bond.
This mirror eke, that I have in mine hond,
Hath such a might, that men may in it see
When there shall fall any adversitý
Unto your realm, or to yourself also,
And openly who is your friend or foe.
And over all this, if any lady bright
Hath set her heart on any manner wight,
If he be false, she shall his treason see,
His newë love, and all his subtlety,
So openly that there shall nothing hide.
Wherefore, against this lusty summer-tide,
This mirror, and this ring that ye may see,
He hath sent to my lady Canacé,

1 Well skilled in using the colours—the word-painting—belonging to his art.
2 Caused his birthday festival to be proclaimed, ordered by proclamation.
3 Aries was the mansion of Mars—to whom "his" applies. Leo was the mansion of the Sun.
4 Pleasant. 5 Bright. 6 Like. 7 Relate.
8 Dishes, or soups. The precise force of the word is uncertain; but it may be connected with "seethe," to boil; and it seems to describe a dish in which the flesh was served up amid a kind of broth or gravy. The "sewer," taster or assayer of the viands served at great tables, probably derived his name from the verb to "say" or "assay;" though Tyrwhitt would connect the two words, by taking both from the French, "asseoir," to place—making the arrangement of the table the leading duty of the "sewer," rather than the testing of the food.
9 Young herons; French, "heronneaux."
10 Care for. 11 Story, discourse; French, "propos."
12 Noble, brave array. 13 Watched.
14 Celebrated in mediæval romance as the most courteous among King Arthur's knights.
15 Could not better him by one word.
16 Fault. 17 Demeanour. 18 Learn.
19 The general sense or meaning.
20 This is the sum of. 21 Command.
22 Pass, go. 23 Hurt, injury.
24 It pleases you. 25 Twisting. 26 Knew.
27 Contrivance; trick; snare. Compare Italian, "inganno," deception; and our own "engine."
28 Observed.
29 Mr Wright remarks that "the making and arrangement of seals was one of the important operations of mediæval magic."

Your excellentë daughter that is here.
The virtue of this ring, if ye will hear,
Is this, that if her list it for to wear
Upon her thumb, or in her purse it bear,
There is no fowl that flyeth under heaven,
That she shall not well understand his steven,[1]
And know his meaning openly and plain,
And answer him in his languáge again:
And every grass that groweth upon root
She shall eke know, to whom it will do boot,[2]
All be his woundës ne'er so deep and wide.
This naked sword, that hangeth by my side,
Such virtue hath, that what man that it smite,
Throughout his armour it will carve and bite,
Were it as thick as is a branched oak:
And what man is y-wounded with the stroke
Shall ne'er be whole, till that you list, of grace,
To stroke him with the flat in thilkë[3] place
Where he is hurt; this is as much to sayn,
Ye mustë with the flattë sword again
Stroke him upon the wound, and it will close.
This is the very sooth, withoutë glose;[4]
It faileth not, while it is in your hold."
And when this knight had thus his talë told,
He rode out of the hall, and down he light.
His steedë, which that shone as sunnë bright,
Stood in the court as still as any stone.
The knight is to his chamber led anon,
And is unarmed, and to meat y-set.[5]
These presents be full richëly y-fet,[6]—
This is to say, the sword and the mirroúr,—
And borne anon into the highë tow'r,
With certain officers ordain'd therefor;
And unto Canacé the ring is bore
Solemnëly, where she sat at the table;
But sickerly, withouten any fable,
The horse of brass, that may not be remued.[7]
It stood as it were to the ground y-glued;
There may no man out of the place it drive
For no engíne of windlass or polive;[8]
And causë why, for they can not the craft;[9]
And therefore in the place they have it laft,
Till that the knight hath taught them the mannére
To voidë[10] him, as ye shall after hear.
Great was the press, that swarmed to and fro
To gauren[11] on this horse that stoodë so:
For it so high was, and so broad and long,
So well proportioned for to be strong,
Right as it were a steed of Lombardy;
Therewith so horsely, and so quick of eye,
As it a gentle Poileis[12] courser were:
For certes, from his tail unto his ear
Nature nor art ne could him not ámend
In no degree, as all the people wend.[13]
But evermore their mostë wonder was
How that it couldë go, and was of brass;
It was of Faerie, as the people seem'd.
Diversë folk diversëly they deem'd;
As many heads, as many wittës been.
They murmured, as doth a swarm of been,[14]
And madë skills[15] after their fantasies,
Rehearsing of the oldë poetries,
And said that it was like the Pegasé,[16]
The horse that haddë wingës for to flee;
Or else it was the Greekë's horse Sinon,[17]
That broughtë Troyë to destructión,
As men may in the oldë gestës[18] read.
"Mine heart," quoth one, "is evermore in dread;
I trow some men of armës be therein,
That shapë them[19] this city for to win:
It were right good that all such thing were know."
Another rowned[20] to his fellow low,
And said, "He lies; for it is rather like
An ápparéncë made by some magíc,
As jugglers playen at these feastës great."
Of sundry doubts they jangle thus and treat.
As lewëd[21] people deemë commonly
Of thingës that be made more subtilly
Than they can in their lew'dness comprehend;
They deemë gladly to the badder end.[22]
And some of them wonder'd on the mirroúr,
That borne was up into the master tow'r,[23]
How men might in it suchë thingës see.
Another answér'd and said, it might well be
Naturallý by compositións
Of angles, and of sly reflectións;
And saidë that in Rome was such a one.
They speak of Alhazen and Vitellon,[24]
And Aristotle, that wrote in their lives
Of quaintë[25] mirrors, and of próspectives,
As knowë they that have their bookës heard.
And other folk have wonder'd on the swerd,
That wouldë piercë throughout every thing;
And fell in speech of Telephus the king,
And of Achilles for his quaintë spear,
For he could with it bothë heal and dere,[26]
Right in such wise as men may with the swerd
Of which right now ye have yourselvës heard.
They spake of sundry hard'ning of metál,
And spake of medicínës therewithal,
And how, and when, it shouldë harden'd be,
Which is unknowen algate[27] unto me.
Then spakë they of Canacéë's ring,
And saiden all, that such a wondrous thing

1 Speech, sound. 2 Remedy. 3 The same.
4 Deceit. 5 Seated at table. 6 Fetched.
7 Removed; French, "remuer," to stir.
8 Pulley.
9 Know not the cunning of the mechanism.
10 Remove. 11 Gaze.
12 Apulian. The horses of Apulia—in old French "Poille," in Italian "Puglia"—were held in high value. 13 Weened, thought.
14 Bees. 15 Reasons. 16 Pegasus.
17 The wooden horse of the Greek Sinon, introduced into Troy by the stratagem of its maker.
18 Narratives of exploits and adventures.
19 Design, prepare. 20 Whispered.
21 Ignorant. 22 Are ready to think the worst.
23 Chief tower; as, in the Knight's Tale, the principal street is called the "master street." See note 6, page 45.
24 Two writers on optics, the first supposed to have lived about 1100; the other about 1270. Tyrwhitt says that their works were printed at Basle in 1572, under the title "Alhazeni et Vitellonis Opticæ."
25 Curious.
26 Wound. Telephus, a son of Hercules, reigned over Mysia when the Greeks came to besiege Troy, and he sought to prevent their landing. But, by the art of Dionysus, he was made to stumble over a vine, and Achilles wounded him with his spear. The oracle informed Telephus that the hurt could be healed only by him, or by the weapon, that inflicted it; and the king, seeking the Grecian camp, was healed by Achilles with the rust of the charmed spear. 27 However.

Of craft of ringës heard they never none,
Save that he, Moses, and King Solomon,
Hadden a name of conning [1] in such art.
Thus said the people, and drew them apart.
But natheless some saidë that it was
Wonder to maken of fern ashes glass,
And yet is glass nought like ashes of fern;
But, for [2] they have y-knowen it so ferne,[3]
Therefore ceaseth their jangling and their wonder.
As sorë wonder some on cause of thunder,
On ebb and flood, on gossamer and mist,
And on all thing, till that the cause is wist.[4]
Thus jangle they, and deemen and devise,
Till that the king gan from his board arise.
Phœbus had left the angle meridional,
And yet ascending was the beast royál,
The gentle Lion, with his Aldrian,[5]
When that this Tartar king, this Cambuscan,
Rose from his board, there as he sat full high:
Before him went the loudë minstrelsy,
Till he came to his chamber of parëments,[6]
There as they sounded divers instruments,
That it was like a heaven for to hear.
Now danced lusty Venus' children dear:
For in the Fish [7] their lady sat full high,
And looked on them with a friendly eye.
This noble king is set upon his throne;
This strangë knight is fetched to him full sone,[8]
And on the dance he goes with Canacé.
Here is the revel and the jollity,
That is not able a dull man to devise: [9]
He must have knowen love and his servíce,
And been a feastly [10] man, as fresh as May,
That shouldë you devisë such array.
Who couldë tellë you the form of dances
So úncouth,[11] and so freshë countenances,[12]
Such subtle lookings and dissimulings
For dread of jealous men's appérceivíngs?
No man but Launcelot,[13] and he is dead.
Therefore I pass o'er all this lustihead;[14]
I say no more, but in this jolliness
I leave them, till to supper men them dress.
The steward bids the spices for to hie [15]
And eke the wine, in all this melodý;
The ushers and the squiërs be y-gone,
The spices and the wine is come anon:
They eat and drink, and when this hath an end,
Unto the temple, as reason was, they wend;
The service done, they suppen all by day.
What needeth you rehearsë their array?
Each man wot well, that at a kingë's feast
Is plenty, to the most [16] and to the least,
And dainties more than be in my knowíng.
At after supper went this noble king
To see the horse of brass, with all a rout
Of lordës and of ladies him about.
Such wond'ring was there on this horse of brass,
That, since the greatë siege of Troyë was,
There as men wonder'd on a horse also,
Ne'er was there such a wond'ring as was tho.[17]
But finally the king asked the knight
The virtue of this courser, and the might,
And prayed him to tell his governance.[18]
The horse anon began to trip and dance,
When that the knight laid hand upon his rein,
And saidë, "Sir, there is no more to sayn,
But when you list to riden anywhere,
Ye mustë trill [19] a pin, stands in his ear,
Which I shall tellë you betwixt us two;
Ye mustë name him to what place also,
Or to what country that you list to ride.
And when ye comë where you list abide,
Bid him descend, and trill another pin
(For therein lies th' effect of all the gin [20]),
And he will down descend and do your will,
And in that place he will abidë still;
Though all the world had the contráry swore,
He shall not thence be throwen nor be bore.
Or, if you list to bid him thennës gon,
Trill this pin, and he will vaních anon
Out of the sight of every manner wight,
And come again, be it by day or night,
When that you list to clepë [21] him again
In such a guise, as I shall to you sayn
Betwixtë you and me, and that full soon.
Ride [22] when you list, there is no more to do'n."
Informed when the king was of the knight,
And had conceived in his wit aright
The manner and the form of all this thing,
Full glad and blithe, this noble doughty king
Repaired to his revel as beforn.
The bridle is into the tower borne,
And kept among his jewels lefe [23] and dear;
The horse vanish'd, I n'ot [24] in what mannére,
Out of their sight; ye get no more of me:
But thus I leave in lust and jollitý
This Cambuscan his lordës feastying,[25]
Until well nigh the day began to spring.

Pars Secunda.

The norice [26] of digestión, the sleep,
Gan on them wink, and bade them takë keep,[27]
That muchë mirth and labour will have rest:
And with a gaping [28] mouth them all he kest,[29]
And said, that it was timë to lie down,
For blood was in his dominatioún:
"Cherish the blood,[30] natúrë's friend," quoth he.

1 Had a reputation for knowledge.
2 Because.
3 Before; a corruption of "forne," from Anglo-Saxon, "foran."
4 Known.
5 Or Alderan; a star in the neck of the constellation Leo.
6 Presence-chamber, or chamber of state, full of splendid furniture and ornaments. The same expression is used in French and Italian.
7 In Pisces, Venus was said to be at her exaltation or greatest power. See note 28, page 77.
8 Soon.
9 Tell, describe.
10 Merry, gay.
11 Unfamiliar, strange; from "conne," to know. See note 7, page 17.
12 The pantomimic gestures of the dance.
13 Arthur's famous knight, so accomplished and courtly, that he was held the very pink of chivalry.
14 Pleasantness.
15 Haste.
16 Greatest.
17 Then.
18 Mode of managing him.
19 Turn; akin to "thirl," "drill."
20 Contrivance.
21 Call.
22 Another reading is "bide," alight or remain.
23 Cherished.
24 Know not.
25 Entertaining; French, "festoyer," to feast.
26 Nurse.
27 Heed.
28 Yawning.
29 Kissed.
30 The old physicians held that blood dominated in the human body late at night and in the early morning. Galen says that the domination lasts for seven hours.

They thanked him gaping, by two and three;
And every wight gan draw him to his rest,
As sleep them bade, they took it for the best.
Their dreamës shall not now be told for me;
Full were their headës of fumosity,[1]
That caused dreams of which there is no charge.[2]
They sleptë till that it was primë large,[3]
The mostë part, but[4] it were Canacé;
She was full measuráble,[5] as women be.
For of her father had she ta'en her leave,
To go to rest, soon after it was eve;
Her listë not appalled[6] for to be,
Nor on the morrow unfeastly for to see;[7]
And slept her firstë sleep, and then awoke.
For such a joy she in her heartë took
Both of her quaintë[8] ring and her mirroúr,
That twenty times she changed her coloúr;
And in her sleep, right for th' impressión
Of her mirrór, she had a visión.
Wherefore, ere that the sunnë gan up glide,
She call'd upon her mistress'[9] her beside,
And saidë, that her listë for to rise.
These oldë women, that be gladly wise,
As are her mistresses, answér'd anon,
And said; "Madamë, whither will ye gon
Thus early? for the folk be all in rest."
"I will," quoth she, "arisë, for me lest
No longer for to sleep, and walk about."
Her mistresses call'd women a great rout,
And up they rosë, well a ten or twelve;
Up rosë freshë Canacé herselve,
As ruddy and bright as is the youngë sun
That in the Ram is four degrees y-run;
No higher was he, when she ready was;
And forth she walked easily a pace,
Array'd after the lusty[10] season swoot,[11]
Lightëly for to play, and walk on foot,
Nought but with five or six of her meinie;[12]
And in a trench[13] forth in the park went she.
The vapour, which up from the earthë glode,[14]
Madë the sun to seem ruddy and broad:
But, natheless, it was so fair a sight
That it made all their heartës for to light,[15]
What for the season, and the morrowning,
And for the fowlës that she heardë sing.
For right anon she wistë[16] what they meant
Right by their song, and knew all their intent.
The knottë,[17] why that every tale is told,
If it be tarried[18] till the lust[19] be cold
Of them that have it hearken'd after yore,[20]
The savour passeth ever longer more,
For fulsomeness of the prolixitý:
And by that samë reason thinketh me
I should unto the knottë condescend,
And maken of her walking soon an end.
Amid a tree fordry,[21] as white as chalk,
As Canacé was playing in her walk,
There sat a falcon o'er her head full high,
That with a piteous voice so gan to cry,
That all the wood resounded of her cry,
And beat she had herself so piteouslý
With both her wingës, till the reddë blood
Ran endëlong[22] the tree, there as she stood.
And ever-in-one[23] alway she cried and shright,[24]
And with her beak herselfë she so pight,[25]
That there is no tiger, nor cruel beast,
That dwelleth either in wood or in forést,
But would have wept, if that he weepë could,
For sorrow of her, she shriek'd alway so loud.
For there was never yet no man alive,
If that he could a falcon well descrive,[26]
That heard of such another of fairnéss
As well of plumage, as of gentleness,
Of shape, of all that mightë reckon'd be.
A falcon peregrinë seemed she,
Of fremdë[27] land; and ever as she stood
She swooned now and now for lack of blood,
Till well-nigh is she fallen from the tree.
This fairë kingë's daughter Canacé,
That on her finger bare the quaintë[8] ring,
Through which she understood well every thing
That any fowl may in his leden[28] sayn,
And could him answer in his leden again,
Hath understoodë what this falcon said,
And well-nigh for the ruth[29] almost she died;
And to the tree she went full hastily,
And on this falcon looked piteously,
And held her lap abroad, for well she wist
The falcon mustë fallë from the twist[30]
When that she swooned next, for lack of blood.
A longë while to waitë her she stood,
Till at the last she spake in this mannére
Unto the hawk, as ye shall after hear.
"What is the cause, if it be for to tell,
That ye be in this furial[31] pain of hell?"
Quoth Canacé unto this hawk above;
"Is this for sorrow of death, or loss of love?
For, as I trow,[32] these be the causes two,
That causë most a gentle heartë woe.
Of other harm it needeth not to speak.
For ye yourself upon yourself awreak,[33]
Which proveth well, that either ire or dread[34]
Must be occasion of your cruel deed,
Since that I see none other wight you chase.
For love of God, as do yourselfë grace,[35]
Or what may be your help? for, west nor east,
I never saw ere now no bird nor beast
That fared with himself so piteously.
Ye slay me with your sorrow verily,
I have of you so great compassioún.
For Goddë's love come from the tree adown;
And, as I am a kingë's daughter true,

1 Fumes of wine rising from the stomach to the head.
2 Which are of no significance.
3 Broad forenoon, dinner-time.
4 Except.
5 Moderate.
6 She did not choose to be made pale.
7 To look sad, depressed.
8 Curious.
9 Tutoresses, governesses.
10 Pleasant.
11 Sweet.
12 Servants, household.
13 A path cut out.
14 Glided.
15 Be lightened, gladdened.
16 Knew.
17 Nucleus, chief matter.
18 Delayed.
19 Inclination, zest.
20 For a long time.
21 Thoroughly dried up.
22 From top to bottom of.
23 Incessantly.
24 Shrieked.
25 Picked, wounded.
26 Describe.
27 Foreign, strange; German, "fremd;" in the northern dialects, "frem," or "fremmed," is used in the same sense.
28 Language, dialect; from Anglo-Saxon, "leden" or "læden," a corruption from "Latin."
29 Pity.
30 Twig, bough.
31 Raging, furious.
32 Believe.
33 Revenge.
34 Fear.
35 Have mercy on yourself.

If that I verily the causes knew
Of your disease,[1] if it lay in my might,
I would amend it, ere that it were night,
So wisly [2] help me the great God of kind.[3]
And herbës shall I right enoughë find,
To healë with your hurtës hastily."
Then shriek'd this falcon yet more piteously
Than ever she did, and fell to ground anon,
And lay aswoon, as dead as lies a stone,
Till Canacé had in her lap her take,
Unto that time she gan of swoon awake:
And, after that she out of swoon abraid,[4]
Right in her hawkë's leden thus she said:
"That pity runneth soon in gentle heart
(Feeling his simil'tude in painë's smart),
Is proved every day, as men may see,
As well by work as by authority;[5]
For gentle heartë kitheth [6] gentleness.
I see well, that ye have on my distress
Compassión, my fairë Canacé,
Of very womanly benignity
That nature in your principles hath set.
But for no hopë for to fare the bet,[7]
But for t' obey unto your heartë free,
And for to make others aware by me,
As by the whelp chastis'd [8] is the lión,
Right for that cause and that conclusión,
While that I have a leisure and a space,
Mine harm I will confessen ere I pace."[9]
And ever while the one her sorrow told,
The other wept, as she to water wo'ld,[10]
Till that the falcon bade her to be still,
And with a sigh right thus she said her till:[11]
"Where I was bred (alas that ilkë [12] day!)
And foster'd in a rock of marble gray
So tenderly, that nothing ailed me,
I wistë not what was adversitý,
Till I could flee full high under the sky.
Then dwell'd a tercëlet [13] me fastë by,
That seem'd a well of allë gentleness;
All were he [14] full of treason and falsenéss,
It was so wrapped under humble cheer,[15]
And under hue of truth, in such mannére,
Under pleasánce, and under busy pain,
That no wight weened that he couldë feign,
So deep in grain he dyed his coloúrs.
Right as a serpent hides him under flow'rs,
Till he may see his timë for to bite,
Right so this god of lovë's hypocrite
Did so his ceremonies and obeisánces,
And kept in semblance all his óbservánces,
That sounden unto [16] gentleness of love.
As on a tomb is all the fair above,
And under is the corpse, which that ye wot,
Such was this hypocrite, both cold and hot;
And in this wise he served his intent,
That, save the fiend, none wistë what he meant:
Till he so long had weeped and complain'd,
And many a year his service to me feign'd,
Till that mine heart, too piteous and too nice,[17]
All innocent of his crowned malíce,
Forfeared of his death,[18] as thoughtë me,
Upon his oathës and his surëtý
Granted him love, on this conditioún,
That evermore mine honour and renown
Were saved, bothë privy and apert;[19]
This is to say, that, after his desert,
I gave him all my heart and all my thought
(God wot, and he, that other wayës nought [20]),
And took his heart in change of mine for aye.
But sooth is said, gone since many a day,
A true wight and a thiefë think not one.[21]
And when he saw the thing so far y-gone,
That I had granted him fully my love,
In such a wise as I have said above,
And given him my truë heart as free
As he swore that he gave his heart to me,
Anon this tiger, full of doubleness,
Fell on his knees with so great humbleness,
With so high reverence, as by his cheer,[22]
So like a gentle lover in mannére,
So ravish'd, as it seemed, for the joy,
That never Jason, nor París of Troy,—
Jason? certes, nor ever other man,
Since Lamech was, that alderfirst [23] began
To lovë two, as writë folk beforn,
Nor ever since the firstë man was born,
Couldë no man, by twenty thousand part,
Counterfeit the sophimës [24] of his art;
Nor worthy were t' unbuckle his galoche,[25]
Where doubleness of feigning should approach,
Nor could so thank a wight, as he did me.
His manner was a heaven for to see
To any woman, were she ne'er so wise;
So painted he and kempt,[26] at point devise,[27]
As well his wordës as his countenánce.
And I so lov'd him for his obeisánce,
And for the truth I deemed in his heart,
That, if so were that any thing him smart,[28]
All were it ne'er so lite,[29] and I it wist,
Methought I felt death at my heartë twist.
And shortly, so farforth this thing is went,[30]
That my will was his willë's instrumént;
That is to say, my will obey'd his will
In allë thing, as far as reason fill,[31]
Keeping the boundës of my worship ever;
And never had I thing so lefe, or lever,[32]
As him, God wot, nor never shall no mo'.
"This lasted longer than a year or two,
That I supposed of him naught but good.

1 Distress. 2 Surely. 3 Nature. 4 Awoke.
5 By experience as by text or doctrine.
6 Sheweth. 7 Better. 8 Instructed, corrected.
9 Depart. 10 As if she would dissolve into water.
11 To her. 12 Same.
13 The "tassel," or male of any species of hawk; so called, according to Cotgrave, because he is one-third ("tiers") smaller than the female.
14 Although he was.
15 Under an aspect, mien, of humility.
16 Are consonant to. 17 Foolish, simple.
18 Greatly afraid lest he should die.
19 Both privately and in public.
20 In no other way, on no other terms.
21 Do not think alike. 22 Mien.
23 First of all. "And Lamech took unto him two wives: the name of the one Adah, and the name of the other Zillah" (Gen. iv. 19).
24 Sophistries, beguilements.
25 Shoe; it seems to have been used in France, of a "sabot," or wooden shoe. The reader cannot fail to recall the same illustration in John i. 27, where the Baptist says of Christ: "He it is, who coming after me is preferred before me; whose shoe's latchet I am not worthy to unloose." 26 Combed, studied.
27 With perfect precision. 28 Pained.
29 Little. 30 So far did this go.
31 Fell; allowed. 32 So dear, or dearer.

But finally, thus at the last it stood,
That fortune wouldë that he mustë twin[1]
Out of that placë which that I was in.
Whe'er[2] me was woe, it is no questión;
I cannot make of it descriptión.
For one thing dare I tellë boldëly,
I know what is the pain of death thereby;
Such harm I felt, for he might not byleve.[3]
So on a day of me he took his leave,
So sorrowful eke, that I ween'd verily,
That he had felt as muchë harm as I,
When that I heard him speak, and saw his hue.
But natheless, I thought he was so true,
And eke that he repairë should again
Within a little whilë, sooth to sayn,
And reason would eke that he mustë go
For his honoúr, as often happ'neth so,
That I made virtue of necessitý,
And took it well, since that it mustë be.
As I best might, I hid from him my sorrow,
And took him by the hand, Saint John to borrow,[4]
And said him thus; 'Lo, I am yourës all;
Be such as I have been to you, and shall.'
What he answér'd, it needs not to rehearse;
Who can say bet[5] than he, who can do worse?
When he had all well said, then had he done.
Therefore behoveth him a full long spoon,
That shall eat with a fiend; thus heard I say.
So at the last he mustë forth his way,
And forth he flew, till he came where him lest.
When it came him to purpose for to rest,
I trow that he had thilkë text in mind,
That allë thing repairing to his kind
Gladdeth himself;[6] thus say men, as I guess;
Men love of [proper] kind newfangleness,[7]
As birdës do, that men in cages feed.
For though thou night and day take of them heed,
And strew their cagë fair and soft as silk,
And give them sugar, honey, bread, and milk,
Yet, right anon as that his door is up,[8]
He with his feet will spurnë down his cup,
And to the wood he will, and wormës eat;
So newëfangle be they of their meat,
And lovë novelties, of proper kind;
No gentleness of bloodë may them bind.
So far'd this tercëlet, alas the day!
Though he were gentle born, and fresh, and gay,
And goodly for to see, and humble, and free,
He saw upon a time a kitë flee,
And suddenly he loved this kite so,
That all his love is clean from me y-go:
And hath his trothë falsed in this wise.
Thus hath the kite my love in her servíce,
And I am lorn[9] withoutë remedy."
  And with that word this falcon gan to cry,
And swooned eft[10] in Canacéë's barme.[11]
Great was the sorrow, for that hawkë's harm,
That Canacé and all her women made;
They wist not how they might the falcon glade.[12]
But Canacé home bare her in her lap,
And softëly in plasters gan her wrap,
There as she with her beak had hurt herselve.
Now cannot Canacé but herbës delve
Out of the ground, and makë salvës new
Of herbës precioús and fine of hue,
To healë with this hawk; from day to night
She did her business, and all her might.
And by her beddë's head she made a mew,[13]
And cover'd it with velouettës blue,[14]
In sign of truth that is in woman seen;
And all without the mew is painted green,
In which were painted all these falsë fowls,
As be these tidifes,[15] tercëlets, and owls;
And piës, on them for to cry and chide,
Right for despite were painted them beside.
  Thus leave I Canacé her hawk keeping.
I will no more as now speak of her ring,
Till it come eft[16] to purpose for to sayn
How that this falcon got her love again
Repentant, as the story telleth us,
By mediatión of Camballus,
The kingë's son of which that I you told.
But hencëforth I will my process hold
To speak of áventures, and of battailes,
That yet was never heard so great marvailles.
First I will tellë you of Cambuscan,
That in his timë many a city wan;
And after will I speak of Algarsife,
How he won Theodora to his wife,
For whom full oft in great períl he was,
N' had he[17] been holpen by the horse of brass.
And after will I speak of Camballó,[18]
That fought in listës with the brethren two
For Canacé, ere that he might her win;
And where I left I will again begin.

. . . .

1 Depart, separate. 2 Whether.
3 Stay; another form is "bleve;" from Anglo-Saxon, "belifan," to remain. Compare German, "bleiben."
4 Witness, pledge. 5 Better.
6 This sentiment, as well as the illustration of the bird which follows, is taken from the third book of Boethius, "De Consolatione Philosophiæ," *metrum* 2. It has thus been rendered in Chaucer's translation: "All things seek aye to their proper course, and all things rejoice on their returning again to their nature."
7 Men, by their own—their very—nature, are fond of novelty, and prone to inconstancy.
8 Immediately on his door being opened.
9 Lost, undone. 10 Again.
11 Lap. 12 Gladden.
13 Cage.
14 Blue velvets. Blue was the colour of truth, as green was that of inconstancy. In John Stowe's additions to Chaucer's works, printed in 1561, there is "A balade whiche Chaucer made against women inconstaunt," of which the refrain is, "In stede of blew, thus may ye were al grene."
15 Supposed to be the titmouse.
16 Again, presently. 17 Had he not.
18 Unless we suppose this to be a namesake of the Camballo who was Canacé's brother—which is not at all probable—we must agree with Tyrwhitt that there is a mistake here; which no doubt Chaucer would have rectified, if the tale had not been "left half-told." One manuscript reads "Caballo;" and though not much authority need be given to a difference that may be due to mere omission of the mark of contraction over the "a," there is enough in the text to show that another person than the king's younger son is intended. The Squire promises to tell the adventures that befell each member of Cambuscan's family; and in thorough consistency with this plan, and with the canons of chivalric story, would be "the marriage of Canacé to some knight who was first obliged to fight for her with her two brethren; a method of courtship," adds Tyrwhitt, "very consonant to the spirit of ancient chivalry."

THE FRANKLIN'S TALE.

THE PROLOGUE.[1]

"In faith, Squiër, thou hast thee well acquit,
And gentilly; I praisë well thy wit,"
Quoth the Franklin; "considering thy youthë
So feelingly thou speak'st, Sir, I aloue[2] thee,
As to my doom,[3] there is none that is here
Of eloquencë that shall be thy peer,
If that thou live; God give thee goodë chance,
And in virtúe send thee continuánce,
For of thy speaking I have great daintý.[4]
I have a son, and, by the Trinitý,
It were me lever[5] than twenty pound worth land,
Though it right now were fallen in my hand,
He were a man of such discretión
As that ye be: fy on possessión,
But if[6] a man be virtuous withal.
I have my sonë snibbed,[7] and yet shall,
For he to virtue listeth not t' intend,[8]
But for to play at dice, and to dispend,
And lose all that he hath, is his uságe;
And he had lever talkë with a page,
Than to commune with any gentle wight,
There he might learen gentilless aright."
"Straw for your gentillessë!" quoth our Host.
"What? Frankëlin, pardie, Sir, well thou wost[9]
That each of you must tellen at the least
A tale or two, or breakë his behest."[10]
"That know I well, Sir," quoth the Frankëlin;
"I pray you havë me not in disdain,
Though I to this man speak a word or two."
"Tell on thy tale, withoutë wordës mo'."
"Gladly, Sir Host," quoth he, "I will obey
Unto your will; now hearken what I say;
I will you not contráry in no wise,
As far as that my wittës may suffice.
I pray to God that it may pleasë you,
Then wot I well that it is good enow.
"These oldë gentle Bretons, in their days,
Of divers áventúrës madë lays,[11]
Rhymeden in their firstë Breton tongue;
Which layës with their instruments they sung,
Or ellës readë them for their pleasánce;
And one of them have I in remembránce,
Which I shall say with good will as I can.
But, Sirs, because I am a borel[12] man,
At my beginning first I you beseech
Have me excused of my rudë speech.
I learned never rhetoric, certáin;
Thing that I speak, it must be bare and plain.
I slept never on the mount of Parnassó,
Nor learned Marcus Tullius Cicero.
Coloúrës know I none, withoutë dread,[13]
But such coloúrs as growen in the mead,
Or ellës such as men dye with or paint;
Coloúrs of rhetoric be to me quaint;[14]
My spirit feeleth not of such mattére.
But, if you list, my talë shall ye hear."

THE TALE.

In Armoric', that called is Bretagne,
There was a knight, that lov'd and did his pain[15]
To serve a lady in his bestë wise;
And many a labour, many a great emprise,
He for his lady wrought, ere she were won:
For she was one the fairest under sun,
And eke thereto come of so high kindréd,
That well unnethës[16] durst this knight, for dread,
Tell her his woe, his pain, and his distress.
But, at the last, she for his worthiness,
And namëly[17] for his meek obeisánce,
Hath such a pity caught of his penánce,[18]
That privily she fell of his accord
To take him for her husband and her lord
(Of such lordship as men have o'er their wives);
And, for to lead the more in bliss their lives,
Of his free will he swore her as a knight,
That never in all his life he day nor night
Should take upon himself no mastery
Against her will, nor kithe[19] her jealousy,
But her obey, and follow her will in all,
As any lover to his lady shall;
Save that the name of sovereignëty
That would he have, for shame of his degree.
She thanked him, and with full great humbléss
She saidë; "Sir, since of your gentleness
Ye proffer me to have so large a reign,
Ne wouldë God never betwixt us twain,
As in my guilt, were either war or strife:[20]
Sir, I will be your humble truë wife,
Have here my troth, till that my heartë brest."[21]
Thus be they both in quiet and in rest.
For one thing, Sirës, safely dare I say,
That friends ever each other must obey,
If they will longë hold in company.
Love will not be constrain'd by mastery.
When mast'ry comes, the god of love anon
Beateth[22] his wings, and, farewell, he is gone.

1 In the older editions, the verses here given as the prologue were prefixed to the Merchant's Tale, and put into his mouth. Tyrwhitt was abundantly justified, by the internal evidence afforded by the lines themselves, in transferring them to their present place.
2 Allow, approve. 3 So far as my judgment goes.
4 Value, esteem.
5 It were dearer to me; I would rather.
6 Unless. 7 Rebuked; "snubbed."
8 Apply himself. 9 Knowest. 10 Promise.
11 The "Breton Lays" were an important and curious element in the literature of the Middle Ages; they were originally composed in the Armorican language, and the chief collection of them extant was translated into French verse by a poetess calling herself "Marie," about the middle of the thirteenth century. But though this collection was the most famous, and had doubtless been read by Chaucer, there were other British or Breton lays, and from one of those the Franklin's Tale is taken. Boccaccio has dealt with the same story in the "Decameron" and the "Philocopo," altering the circumstances to suit the removal of its scene to a southern clime.
12 Rude, unlearned. 13 Doubt. 14 Strange.
15 Devoted himself, strove.
16 Hardly, for fear that she would not entertain his suit. 17 Especially.
18 Suffering, distress. 19 Show.
20 Would to God there may never be war or strife between us, through my fault. 21 Burst.
22 Perhaps the true reading is "beteth"—prepares, makes ready, his wings for flight.

Love is a thing as any spirit free.
Women of kind[1] desirë liberty,
And not to be constrained as a thrall;[2]
And so do men, if soothly I say shall.
Look who that is most patiént in love,
He is at his advantage all above.[3]
Patience is a high virtúe certáin,
For it vanquísheth, as these clerkës sayn,
Thingës that rigour never should attain.
For every word men may not chide or plain.
Learnë to suffer, or, so may I go,[4]
Ye shall it learn whether ye will or no.
For in this world certáin no wight there is,
That he not doth or saith sometimes amiss.
Ire, or sicknéss, or constellatión,[5]
Wine, woe, or changing of complexión,
Causeth full oft to do amiss or speaken:
On every wrong a man may not be wreaken.[6]
After[7] the timë must be temperance
To every wight that can of[8] governance.
And therefore hath this worthy wisë knight
(To live in easë) suff'rance her behight;[9]
And she to him full wisly[10] gan to swear
That never should there be default in her.
Here may men see a humble wife accord;
Thus hath she ta'en her servant and her lord,
Servant in love, and lord in marriáge.
Then was he both in lordship and servage?
Servage? nay, but in lordship all above,
Since he had both his lady and his love:
His lady certes, and his wife also,
The which that law of love accordeth to.
And when he was in this prosperity,
Home with his wife he went to his country,
Not far from Penmark,[11] where his dwelling was,
And there he liv'd in bliss and in solace.[12]
Who couldë tell, but[13] he had wedded be,
The joy, the ease, and the prosperity,
That is betwixt a husband and his wife?
A year and more lasted this blissful life,
Till that this knight, of whom I spakë thus,
That of Cairrud[14] was call'd Arviragus,
Shope[15] him to go and dwell a year or twain
In Engleland, that call'd was eke Britáin,
To seek in armës worship and honoúr
(For all his lust[16] he set in such laboúr);
And dwelled there two years; the book saith thus.
Now will I stint[17] of this Arviragus,
And speak I will of Dorigen his wife,
That lov'd her husband as her heartë's life.
For his abséncë weepeth she and siketh,[18]
As do these noble wivës when them liketh;
She mourneth, waketh, waileth, fasteth, plaineth;
Desire of his presénce her so distraineth,
That all this widë world she set at nought.
Her friendës, which that knew her heavy thought,
Comfórtë her in all that ever they may;
They preachë her, they tell her night and day,
That causëless she slays herself, alas!
And every comfort possible in this case
They do to her, with all their business,[19]
And all to make her leave her heaviness.
By process, as ye knowen every one,
Men may so longë graven in a stone,
Till some figúre therein imprinted be:
So long have they comfórted her, till she
Received hath, by hope and by reasón,
Th' imprinting of their consolatión,
Through which her greatë sorrow gan assuage;
She may not always duren in such rage.
And eke Arviragus, in all this care,
Hath sent his letters home of his welfare,
And that he will come hastily again,
Or ellës had this sorrow her hearty-slain.
Her friendës saw her sorrow gin to slake,[20]
And prayed her on knees for Goddë's sake
To come and roamen in their company,
Away to drive her darkë fantasy;
And finally she granted that request,
For well she saw that it was for the best.
Now stood her castle fastë by the sea,
And often with her friendës walked she,
Her to disport upon the bank on high,
Where as she many a ship and bargë sigh,[21]
Sailing their courses, where them list to go.
But then was that a parcel[22] of her woe,
For to herself full oft, "Alas!" said she,
"Is there no ship, of so many as I see,
Will bringë home my lord? then were my heart
All warish'd[23] of this bitter painë's smart."
Another timë would she sit and think,
And cast her eyen downward from the brink;
But when she saw the grisly rockës blake,[24]
For very fear so would her heartë quake,
That on her feet she might her not sustene:
Then would she sit adown upon the green,
And piteously into the sea behold,[25]
And say right thus, with careful sikës[26] cold:
"Eternal God! that through thy purveyánce
Leadest this world by certain governance,
In idle,[27] as men say, ye nothing make;
But, Lord, these grisly fiendly rockës blake,
That seem rather a foul confusión
Of work, than any fair creatión
Of such a perfect wisë God and stable,
Why have ye wrought this work unreasonáble?
For by this work, north, south, or west, or east,
There is not foster'd man, nor bird, nor beast:
It doth no good, to my wit, but annoyeth.[28]
See ye not, Lord, how mankind it destroyeth?
A hundred thousand bodies of mankind

1 By nature. 2 Slave.
3 Enjoys the highest advantages of all.
4 Prosper. 5 The influence of the planets.
6 Revenged. 7 According to.
8 Is capable of. 9 Promised. 10 Surely.
11 On the west coast of Brittany, between Brest and L'Orient. The name is composed of two British words, "pen," mountain, and "mark," region; it therefore means the mountainous country.
12 Delight. 13 Unless.
14 "The red city;" it is not known where it was situated. 15 Prepared, arranged.
16 Pleasure. 17 Cease speaking.
18 Sigheth. 19 Assiduity.
20 To diminish, slacken. 21 Saw. 22 Part.
23 Cured; French, "guérir," to heal, or recover from sickness.
24 Black. 25 Look out on the sea.
26 Painful sighs. 27 Idly, in vain.
28 Works mischief; from Latin, "noceo," I hurt.

Have rockës slain, all be they not in mind;[1]
Which mankind is so fair part of thy work,
Thou madest it like to thine owen mark.[2]
Then seemed it ye had a great cherté[3]
Toward mankind; but how then may it be
That ye such meanës make it to destroy?
Which meanës do no good, but ever annoy.
I wot well, clerkës will say as them lest,[4]
By arguments, that all is for the best,
Although I can the causes not y-know;
But thilke[5] God that made the wind to blow,
As keep my lord, this is my conclusión:
To clerks leave I all disputatión:
But would to God that all these rockës blake
Were sunken into hellë for his sake!
These rockës slay mine heartë for the fear."
Thus would she say, with many a piteous tear.
Her friendës saw that it was no disport
To roamë by the sea, but discomfórt,
And shope them for to playë somewhere else.
They leadë her by rivers and by wells,
And eke in other places delectábles;
They dancen, and they play at chess and tables.
So on a day, right in the morning-tide,
Unto a garden that was there beside,
In which that they had made their ordinance[6]
Of victual, and of other purveyánce,
They go and play them all the longë day:
And this was on the sixth morrow of May,
Which May had painted with his softë show'rs
This garden full of leavës and of flow'rs:
And craft of mannë's hand so curiously
Arrayed had this garden truëly,
That never was there garden of such price,[7]
But if it were the very Paradise.
Th' odoúr of flowers, and the freshë sight,
Would havë maked any heartë light
That e'er was born, but if[8] too great sicknéss
Or too great sorrow held it in distress;
So full it was of beauty and pleasánce.
And after dinner they began to dance
And sing also, save Dorigen alone,
Who made alway her cómplaint and her moan,
For she saw not him on the dancë go
That was her husband, and her love also;
But natheless she must a time abide,
And with good hopë let her sorrow slide.
Upon this dance, amongës other men,
Danced a squiër before Dorigen,
That fresher was, and jollier of array,
As to my doom,[9] than is the month of May.
He sang and danced, passing any man
That is or was since that the world began;
Therewith he was, if men should him descrive,
One of the bestë faring[10] men alive,
Young, strong, and virtuous, and rich, and wise,
And well belov'd, and holden in great price.[11]
And, shortly if the sooth I tellë shall,
Unweeting[12] of this Dorigen at all,
This lusty squiër, servant to Venús,
Which that y-called was Aurelius,
Had lov'd her best of any creatúre
Two year and more, as was his áventúre;[13]
But never durst he tell her his grievánce;
Withoutë cup he drank all his penánce.
He was despaired, nothing durst he say,
Save in his songës somewhat would he wray[14]
His woe, as in a general cómplainíng;
He said, he lov'd, and was belov'd nothing.
Of suchë matter made he many lays,
Songës, complaintës, roundels, virëlays;[15]
How that he durstë not his sorrow tell,
But languished, as doth a Fury in hell;
And die he must, he said, as did Echo
For Narcissus, that durst not tell her woe.
In other manner than ye hear me say,
He durstë not to her his woe bewray,
Save that paráventure sometimes at dances,
Where youngë folkë keep their óbservánces,
It may well be he looked on her face
In such a wise, as man that asketh grace,
But nothing wistë she of his intent.
Nath'less it happen'd, ere they thennës[16] went,
Becausë that he was her neighëbour,
And was a man of worship and honoúr,
And she had knowen him of timë yore,[17]
They fell in speech, and forth aye more and more
Unto his purpose drew Aurelius;
And when he saw his time, he saidë thus:
"Madam," quoth he, "by God that this world made,
So that I wist it might your heartë glade,[18]
I would, that day that your Arviragus
Went over sea, that I, Aurelius,
Had gone where I should never come again;
For well I wot my service is in vain.
My guerdon[19] is but bursting of mine heart.
Madamë, rue upon my painë's smart,
For with a word ye may me slay or save.
Here at your feet God would that I were grave.[20]
I havë now no leisure more to say:
Have mercy, sweet, or you will do me dey."[21]
She gan to look upon Aurelius;
"Is this your will," quoth she, "and say ye thus?
Ne'er erst,"[22] quoth she, "I wistë what ye meant:
But now, Aurelius, I know your intent.
By thilkë[5] God that gave me soul and life,
Never shall I be an untruë wife
In word nor work, as far as I have wit;
I will be his to whom that I am knit;
Take this for final answer as of me."
But after that in play[23] thus saidë she.
"Aurelius," quoth she, "by high God above,
Yet will I grantë you to be your love
(Since I you see so piteously complain);

1 Though they are forgotten. 2 Image.
3 Love, affection; from French, "cher," dear.
4 Pleaseth. 5 That.
6 Provision, arrangement.
7 So much to be valued or praised.
8 Unless. 9 In my judgment.
10 Most accomplished, best mannered.
11 Esteem, value.
12 Without the knowledge.
13 Fortune. 14 Betray.
15 Ballads; the "virelai" was an ancient French poem of two rhymes. 16 Thence; from the garden.
17 For a long time. 18 Gladden.
19 Reward. 20 Buried.
21 Cause me to die. 22 Before.
23 Playfully, in jest.

Lookë, what day that endëlong[1] Bretágne
Ye remove all the rockës, stone by stone,
That they not lettë[2] ship nor boat to gon,
I say, when ye have made this coast so clean
Of rockës, that there is no stonë seen,
Then will I love you best of any man;
Have here my troth, in all that ever I can;
For well I wot that it shall ne'er betide.
Let such follý out of your heartë glide.
What dainty[3] should a man have in his life
For to go love another mannë's wife,
That hath her body when that ever him liketh?"
Aurelius full often sorë siketh;[4]
"Is there none other grace in you?" quoth he,
"No, by that Lord," quoth she, "that maked me."
Woe was Aurelius when that he this heard,
And with a sorrowful heart he thus answér'd.
"Madame," quoth he, "this were an impossíble.
Then must I die of sudden death horríble."
And with that word he turned him anon.
Then came her other friends many a one,
And in the alleys roamed up and down,
And nothing wist of this conclusión,
But suddenly began to revel new,
Till that the brightë sun had lost his hue,
For th' horizón had reft the sun his light
(This is as much to say as it was night);
And home they go in mirth and in solace;
Save only wretch'd Aurelius, alas!
He to his house is gone with sorrowful heart.
He said, he may not from his death astart.[5]
Him seemed, that he felt his heartë cold.
Up to the heav'n his handës gan he hold,
And on his kneës bare he set him down,
And in his raving said his orisoún.[6]
For very woe out of his wit he braid;[7]
He wist not what he spake, but thus he said;
With piteous heart his plaint hath he begun
Unto the gods, and first unto the Sun.
He said; "Apollo! God and governoúr
Of every plantë, herbë, tree, and flow'r,
That giv'st, after thy declinatión,
To each of them his time and his seasón,
As thine herberow[8] changeth low and high;
Lord Phœbus! cast thy merciable[9] eye
On wretch'd Aurelius, which that am but lorn.[10]
Lo, lord, my lady hath my death y-sworn,
Withoutë guilt, but[11] thy benignity
Upon my deadly heart have some pitý.
For well I wot, Lord Phœbus, if you lest,[12]
Ye may me helpë, save my lady, best.
Now vouchësafe, that I may you devise[13]
How that I may be holp,[14] and in what wise.
Your blissful sister, Lucina the sheen,[15]
That of the sea is chief goddéss and queen,—
Though Neptunus have deity in the sea,
Yet emperess abovë him is she;—
Ye know well, lord, that, right as her desire
Is to be quick'd[16] and lighted of your fire,
For which she followeth you full busily,
Right so the sea desireth naturally
To follow her, as she that is goddéss
Both in the sea and rivers more and less.
Wherefore, Lord Phœbus, this is my request,
Do this miracle, or do[17] mine heartë brest;[18]
That now, next at this opposition,
Which in the sign shall be of the Lión,
As prayë her so great a flood to bring,
That five fathóm at least it overspring
The highest rock in Armoric' Bretágne,
And let this flood endurë yearës twain:
Then certes to my lady may I say,
"Holdë your hest,[19] the rockës be away."
Lord Phœbus, this miracle do for me,
Pray her she go no faster course than ye;
I say this, pray your sister that she go
No faster course than ye these yearës two:
Then shall she be even at full alway,
And spring-flood lastë bothë night and day.
And but she[20] vouchësafe in such mannére
To grantë me my sov'reign lady dear,
Pray her to sink every rock adown
Into her owen darkë regioún
Under the ground, where Pluto dwelleth in
Or nevermore shall I my lady win.
Thy temple in Delphos will I barefoot seek.
Lord Phœbus! see the tearës on my cheek
And on my pain have some compassioún."
And with that word in sorrow he fell down,
And longë time he lay forth in a trance.
His brother, which that knew of his penánce,[21]
Up caught him, and to bed he hath him brought.
Despaired in this torment and this thought
Let I this woeful creatúrë lie;
Choose he for me whe'er[22] he will live or die.
Arviragus with health and great honoúr
(As he that was of chivalry the flow'r)
Is comë home, and other worthy men.
Oh, blissful art thou now, thou Dorigen!
Thou hast thy lusty husband in thine arms,
The freshë knight, the worthy man of arms,
That loveth thee as his own heartë's life:
Nothing list him to be imaginatif[23]
If any wight had spoke, while he was out,
To her of love; he had of that no doubt;[24]
He not intended[25] to no such mattére,
But danced, jousted, and made merry cheer.
And thus in joy and bliss I let them dwell,
And of the sick Aurelius will I tell.
In languor and in torment furious
Two year and more lay wretch'd Aurelius,
Ere any foot on earth he mightë gon;
Nor comfort in this timë had he none,
Save of his brother, which that was a clerk.[26]
He knew of all this woe and all this work;
For to none other creatúre certáin
Of this matter he durst no wordë sayn;
Under his breast he bare it more secré
Than e'er did Pamphilus for Galatee.[27]

1 From end to end of. 2 Prevent. 3 Value, pleasure. 4 Sigheth. 5 Escape. 6 Prayer. 7 Wandered, went. 8 Dwelling, situation. 9 Compassionate. 10 Undone. 11 Unless. 12 Pleaseth. 13 Tell, explain. 14 Helped. 15 Diana the bright. See note 17, page 37.

16 Quickened. 17 Cause. 18 Burst. 19 Promise. 20 If she do not. 21 Distress. 22 Whether. 23 He cared not to fancy. 24 Fear, suspicion. 25 Occupied himself with. 26 Scholar, man in holy orders. 27 In a Latin poem, very popular in Chaucer's time, Pamphilus relates his amour with Galatea, setting

His breast was whole withoutë for to seen,
But in his heart aye was the arrow keen,
And well ye know that of a sursanure[1]
In surgery is perilous the cure,
But[2] men might touch the arrow or come thereby.
His brother wept and wailed privily,
Till at the last him fell in rémembránce,
That while he was at Orleans[3] in France,—
As youngë clerkës, that be likerous[4]
To readen artës that be curious,
Seeken in every halk and every hern[5]
Particular sciénces for to learn,—
He him remember'd, that upon a day
At Orleans in study a book he say[6]
Of magic natural, which his felláw,
That was that time a bachelor of law,
All[7] were he there to learn another craft,
Had privily upon his desk y-laft;
Which book spake much of operatións
Touching the eight-and-twenty mansións
That longë to the Moon, and such follý
As in our dayës is not worth a fly;
For holy church's faith, in our believe,[8]
Us suff'reth none illusión to grieve.
And when this book was in his rémembránce,
Anon for joy his heart began to dance,
And to himself he saidë privily;
"My brother shall be warish'd[9] hastily:
For I am sicker[10] that there be sciénces,
By which men makë divers apparences,
Such as these subtle tregetourës[11] play.
For oft at feastës have I well heard say,
That tregetours, within a hallë large,
Have made come in a water and a barge,
And in the hallë rowen up and down.
Sometimes hath seemed come a grim lioún,
And sometimes flowers spring as in a mead;
Sometimes a vine, and grapës white and red;
Sometimes a castle all of lime and stone;
And, when them liked, voided[12] it anon:
Thus seemed it to every mannë's sight.
Now then conclude I thus; if that I might
At Orleans some oldë fellow find,
That hath these Moonë's mansións in mind,
Or other magic natural above,
He should well make my brother have his love.
For with an áppearánce a clerk[13] may make,
To mannë's sight, that all the rockës blake
Of Brétagne werë voided[12] every one,
And shippës by the brinkë come and gon,
And in such form endure a day or two;
Then were my brother warish'd[9] of his woe,
Then must she needës holdë her behest,[14]
Or ellës he shall shame her at the least."
Why should I make a longer tale of this?
Unto his brother's bed he comen is,
And such comfórt he gave him, for to gon
To Orleans, that he upstart anon,
And on his way forth-ward then is he fare,[15]
In hope for to be lissed[16] of his care.
When they were come almost to that citý,
But if it were[17] a two furlong or three,
A young clerk roaming by himself they met,
Which that in Latin thriftily[18] them gret.[19]
And after that he said a wondrous thing;
"I know," quoth he, "the cause of your comíng;"
And ere they farther any footë went,
He told them all that was in their intent.
The Breton clerk him asked of felláws
The which he haddë known in oldë daws,[20]
And he answér'd him that they deadë were,
For which he wept full often many a tear.
Down off his horse Aurelius light anon,
And forth with this magician is he gone
Home to his house, and made him well at ease;
Them lacked no vitáil that might them please.
So well-array'd a house as there was one,
Aurelius in his life saw never none.
He shewed him, ere they went to suppére,
Forestës, parkës, full of wildë deer.
There saw he hartës with their hornës high,
The greatest that were ever seen with eye.
He saw of them an hundred slain with hounds,
And some with arrows bleed of bitter wounds.
He saw, when voided[21] were the wildë deer,
These falconers upon a fair rivére,
That with their hawkës have the heron slain.
Then saw he knightës jousting in a plain.
And after this he did him such pleasánce,
That he him shew'd his lady on a dance,
On which himselfë danced, as him thought.
And when this master, that this magic wrought,
Saw it was time, he clapp'd his handës two,
And farewell, all the revel is y-go.[22]
And yet remov'd they never out of the house,
While they saw all the sightës marvelloús;
But in his study, where his bookës be,
They sattë still, and no wight but they three.
To him this master called his squiér,
And said him thus, "May we go to suppér?
Almost an hour it is, I undertake,
Since I you bade our supper for to make,
When that these worthy men wentë with me
Into my study, where my bookës be."
"Sir," quoth this squiër, "when it liketh you,
It is all ready, though ye will right now."
"Go we then sup," quoth he, "as for the best;
These amorous folk some timë must have rest."
At after supper fell they in treatý
What summë should this master's guerdon be,

out with the idea adopted by our poet in the lines that follow.

1 A wound healed on the surface, but festering beneath. 2 Except.

3 Where was a celebrated and very famous university, afterwards eclipsed by that of Paris. It was founded by Philip le Bel in 1312.

4 Eager, curious.

5 Every nook and corner. Anglo-Saxon, "healc," a nook; "hyrn," a corner. 6 Saw. 7 Though.

8 Belief, creed. 9 Cured. 10 Certain.

11 Tricksters, jugglers. The word is probably derived —in "treget," deceit or imposture—from the French "trebuchet," a military machine; since it is evident that much and elaborate machinery must have been employed to produce the effects afterwards described. Another derivation is from the Low Latin, "tricator," a deceiver. 12 Vanished, removed.

13 Learned man.

14 Keep her promise. 15 Gone.

16 Eased of, released from; another form of "less" or "lessen." 17 All but. 18 Civilly.

19 Greeted. 20 Days. 21 Gone, removed.

22 Passed away.

To remove all the rockës of Bretágne,
And eke from Gironde[1] to the mouth of Seine.
He made it strange,[2] and swore, so God him save,
Less than a thousand pound he would not have,
Nor gladly for that sum he would not gon.[3]
Aurelius with blissful heart anon
Answered thus; "Fie on a thousand pound!
This widë world, which that men say is round,
I would it give, if I were lord of it.
This bargain is full-driv'n, for we be knit;[4]
Ye shall be payed truly by my troth.
But lookë, for no negligence or sloth,
Ye tarry us here no longer than to-morrow."
"Nay," quoth the clerk, "have here my faith to borrow."[5]
To bed is gone Aurelius when him lest,
And well-nigh all that night he had his rest,
What for his labour, and his hope of bliss,
His woeful heart of penance had a liss.[6]
Upon the morrow, when that it was day,
Unto Bretágne they took the rightë way,
Aurelius and this magicián beside,
And be descended where they would abide:
And this was, as the bookës me remember,
The coldë frosty season of December.
Phœbus wax'd old, and huëd like latoun,[7]
That in his hotë declinatioûn
Shone as the burned gold, with streamës[8] bright;
But now in Capricorn adown he light,
Where as he shone full pale, I dare well sayn.
The bitter frostës, with the sleet and rain,
Destroyed have the green in every yard.[9]
Janus sits by the fire with double beard,
And drinketh of his bugle horn the wine:
Before him stands the brawn of tusked swine,
And "nowel"[10] crieth every lusty man.
Aurelius, in all that ev'r he can,
Did to his master cheer and reverence,
And prayed him to do his diligence
To bringë him out of his painë's smart,
Or with a sword that he would slit his heart.
This subtle clerk such ruth[11] had on this man,
That night and day he sped him, that he can,
To wait a time of his conclusión;
This is to say, to make illusión,
By such an áppearánce of jugglery
(I know no termës of astrology),
That she and every wight should ween and say,
That of Bretágne the rockës were away,
Or else they werë sunken under ground.
So at the last he hath a timë found
To make his japës[12] and his wretchedness
Of such a superstitious cursedness.[13]
His tables Toletanës[14] forth he brought,
Full well corrected, that there lacked nought,
Neither his collect, nor his expanse years,
Neither his rootës, nor his other gears,
As be his centres, and his arguments,
And his proportional conveniénts
For his equatións in everything.
And by his eightë spheres in his workíng,
He knew full well how far Alnath[15] was shove
From the head of that fix'd Aries above,
That in the ninthë sphere consider'd is.
Full subtilly he calcul'ed all this.
When he had found his firstë mansión,
He knew the remnant by proportión;
And knew the rising of his moonë well,
And in whose fa e, and term, and every deal;
And knew full well the moonë's mansión
Accordant to his operatión;
And knew also his other observánces,
For such illusións and such meschances,[16]
As heathen folk used in thilkë days.
For which no longer made he delays;
But through his magic, for a day or tway,[17]
It seemed all the rockës were away.
Aurelius, which yet despaired is
Whe'er[18] he shall have his love, or fare amiss,
Awaited night and day on this mirácle:
And when he knew that there was none obstácle,
That voided[19] were these rockës every one,
Down at his master's feet he fell anon,
And said; "I, woeful wretch'd Aurelius,
Thank you, my Lord, and lady mine Venús,
That me have holpen from my carës cold."
And to the temple his way forth hath he hold',
Where as he knew he should his lady see.
And when he saw his time, anon right he
With dreadful[20] heart and with full humble cheer[21]
Saluted hath his sovereign lady dear.
"My rightful Lady," quoth this woeful man,
"Whom I most dread, and love as I best can,
And lothest were of all this world displease,
Were 't not that I for you have such disease,[22]
That I must die here at your foot anon,
Nought would I tell how me is woebegone.
But certes either must I die or plain;[23]
Ye slay me guiltëless for very pain.
But of my death though that ye have no ruth,
Advisë you, ere that ye break your truth:
Repentë you, for thilkë God above,
Ere ye me slay because that I you love.
For, Madame, well ye wot what ye have hight;[24]
Not that I challenge anything of right
Of you, my sovereign lady, but of grace;

[1] The river, formed by the union of the Dordogne and Garonne, on which Bourdeaux stands.
[2] A matter of difficulty. See note 38, page 55.
[3] And even for that sum he would not willingly go to work.
[4] Agreed.
[5] I pledge my faith on it.
[6] Had a respite, relief, from anguish.
[7] Coloured like copper or latten.
[8] Beams.
[9] Court-yard, garden.
[10] "Noël," the French for Christmas—derived from "natalis," and signifying that on that day Christ was born—came to be used as a festive cry by the people on solemn occasions.
[11] Pity.
[12] Tricks.
[13] Detestable villany.
[14] Toledan tables; the astronomical tables composed by order of Alphonso II., King of Castile, about 1250, and so called because they were adapted to the city of Toledo.
[15] "Alnath," says Mr Wright, was "the first star in the horns of Aries, whence the first mansion of the moon is named."
[16] Wicked devices.
[17] Another and better reading is "a week or two."
[18] Whether.
[19] Removed.
[20] Fearful.
[21] Mien.
[22] Distress, affliction.
[23] Bewail.
[24] Promised.

But in a garden yond', in such a place,
Ye wot right well what ye behightë me,
And in mine hand your trothë plighted ye,
To love me best; God wot ye saidë so,
Albeit that I unworthy am thereto;
Madame, I speak it for th' honoúr of you,
More than to save my heartë's life right now;
I have done so as ye commanded me,
And if ye vouchësafe, ye may go see.
Do as you list, have your behest in mind,
For, quick or dead, right there ye shall me find;
In you lies all to do [1] me live or dey; [2]
But well I wot the rockës be away."
He took his leave, and she astonish'd stood;
In all her face was not one drop of blood:
She never ween'd t' have come in such a trap.
"Alas!" quoth she, "that ever this should hap!
For ween'd I ne'er, by possibility,
That such a monster or marváil might be;
It is against the process of natúre."
And home she went a sorrowful creatúre;
For very fear unnethës [3] may she go.
She weeped, wailed, all a day or two,
And swooned, that it ruthë was to see:
But why it was, to no wight toldë she,
For out of town was gone Arviragus.
But to herself she spake, and saidë thus,
With facë pale, and full sorrowful cheer,
In her complaint, as ye shall after hear.
"Alas!" quoth she, "on thee, Fortúne, I plain, [4]
That unware hast me wrapped in thy chain,
From which to scapë, wot I no succoúr,
Save only death, or ellës dishonoúr;
One of these two behoveth me to choose.
But natheless, yet had I lever [5] lose
My life, than of my body havë shame,
Or know myselfë false, or lose my name;
And with my death I may be quit y-wis. [6]
Hath there not many a noble wife, ere this,
And many a maiden, slain herself, alas!
Rather than with her body do trespass?
Yes, certes; lo, these stories bear witnéss. [7]
When thirty tyrants full of cursedness [8]
Had slain Phidon in Athens at the feast,
They cómmanded his daughters to arrest,
And bringë them before them, in despite,
All naked, to fulfil their foul delight;
And in their father's blood they made them dance
Upon the pavement,—God give them mischance.
For which these woeful maidens, full of dread,
Rather than they would lose their maidenhead,
They privily be start [9] into a well,
And drowned themselves, as the bookës tell.
They of Messenë let inquire and seek
Of Lacedæmon fifty maidens eke,
On which they wouldë do their lechery:
But there was none of all that company
That was not slain, and with a glad intent
Chose rather for to die, than to assent
To be oppressed [10] of her maidenhead.
Why should I then to dien be in dread?
Lo, eke the tryrant Aristoclides,
That lov'd a maiden hight Stimphalides,
When that her father slain was on a night,
Unto Diana's temple went she right,
And hent [11] the image in her handës two,
From which imáge she wouldë never go;
No wight her handës might off it arace, [12]
Till she was slain right in the selfë [13] place.
Now since that maidens haddë such despite
To be defouled with man's foul delight,
Well ought a wife rather herself to slé, [14]
Than be defouled, as it thinketh me.
What shall I say of Hasdrubalë's wife,
That at Carthage bereft herself of life?
For, when she saw the Romans win the town,
She took her children all, and skipt adown
Into the fire, and rather chose to die,
Than any Roman did her villainý.
Hath not Lucretia slain herself, alas!
At Romë, when that she oppressed [15] was
Of Tarquin? for her thought it was a shame
To livë, when she haddë lost her name.
The seven maidens of Milesie also
Have slain themselves for very dread and woe,
Rather than folk of Gaul them should oppress.
More than a thousand stories, as I guess,
Could I now tell as touching this mattére.
When Abradate was slain, his wife so dear [16]
Herselfë slew, and let her blood to glide
In Abradatë's woundës, deep and wide,
And said, 'My body at the leastë way
There shall no wight defoul, if that I may.'
Why should I more examples hereof sayn?
Since that so many have themselvës slain,
Well rather than they would defouled be,
I will conclude that it is bet [17] for me
To slay myself, than be defouled thus.
I will be true unto Arviragus,
Or ellës slay myself in some mannére,
As did Demotionë's daughter dear,
Because she wouldë not defouled be.
O Sedasus, it is full great pitý
To readë how thy daughters died, alas!
That slew themselves for suchë manner cas. [18]
As great a pity was it, or well more,
The Theban maiden, that for Nicanór
Herselfë slew, right for such manner woe.
Another Theban maiden did right so;
For one of Macedon had her oppress'd,
She with her death her maidenhead redress'd. [19]

1 Cause. 2 Die. 3 Scarcely.
4 Complain. 5 Sooner, rather.
6 I may certainly purchase my exemption.
7 They are all taken from the book of St Jerome "Contra Jovinianum," from which the Wife of Bath drew so many of her ancient instances. See note 5, page 71.
8 Wickedness.
9 Suddenly leaped. 10 Forcibly bereft.
11 Caught, clasped.
12 Pluck away by force. 13 Same.
14 Slay. 15 Ravished.
16 Panthea. Abradatas, King of Susa, was an ally of the Assyrians against Cyrus; and his wife was taken at the conquest of the Assyrian camp. Struck by the honourable treatment she received at the captor's hands, Abradatas joined Cyrus, and fell in battle against his former allies. His wife, inconsolable at his loss, slew herself immediately.
17 Better.
18 In circumstances of the same kind.
19 Avenged, vindicated.

What shall I say of Niceratus' wife,
That for such case bereft herself her life?
How true was eke to Alcibiades
His love, that for to dien rather chese,[1]
Than for to suffer his body unburied be?
Lo, what a wife was Alcesté?" quoth she.
"What saith Homér of good Penelope?
All Greecë knoweth of her chastity.
Pardie, of Laodamía is written thus,
That when at Troy was slain Protesilaus,[2]
No longer would she live after his day.
The same of noble Porcia tell I may;
Withoutë Brutus couldë she not live,
To whom she did all whole her heartë give.[3]
The perfect wifehood of Artemisie[4]
Honoúred is throughout all Barbarie.
O Teuta[5] queen, thy wifely chastitý
To allë wivës may a mirror be."[6]
Thus plained Dorigen a day or tway,
Purposing ever that she wouldë dey;[7]
But natheless upon the thirdë night
Home came Arviragus, the worthy knight,
And asked her why that she wept so sore?
And she gan weepen ever longer more.
"Alas," quoth she, "that ever I was born!
Thus have I said," quoth she; "thus have I sworn."
And told him all, as ye have heard before:
It needeth not rehearse it you no more.
This husband with glad cheer,[8] in friendly wise,
Answér'd and said, as I shall you devise.[9]
"Is there aught ellës, Dorigen, but this?"
"Nay, nay," quoth she, "God help me so, as wis[10]
This is too much, an'[11] it were Goddë's will."
"Yea, wife," quoth he, "let sleepë what is still,
It may be well par'venture yet to-day.
Ye shall your trothë holdë, by my fay.
For, God so wisly[12] have mercý on me,
I had well lever sticked for to be,[13]
For very lovë which I to you have,
But if ye should your trothë keep and save.
Truth is the highest thing that man may keep."
But with that word he burst anon to weep,
And said; "I you forbid, on pain of death,
That never, while you lasteth life or breath,
To no wight tell ye this misáventúre;
As I may best, I will my woe endure,
Nor make no countenance of heaviness,
That folk of you may deemë harm, or guess."
And forth he call'd a squiër and a maid.
"Go forth anon with Dorigen," he said,
"And bringë her to such a place anon."
They take their leave, and on their way they gon:
But they not wistë why she thither went;
He would to no wight tellë his intent.
This squiër, which that hight Aurelius,
On Dorigen that was so amorous,
Of áventúrë happen'd her to meet
Amid the town, right in the quickest[14] street,
As she was bound[15] to go the way forthright
Toward the garden, there as she had hight.[16]
And he was to the garden-ward also;
For well he spiëd when she wouldë go
Out of her house, to any manner place;
But thus they met, of áventúre or grace,
And he saluted her with glad intent,
And asked of her whitherward she went.
And she answered, half as she were mad,
"Unto the garden, as my husband bade,
My trothë for to hold, alas! alas!"
Aurelius gan to wonder on this case,
And in his heart had great compassión
Of her, and of her lamentatión,
And of Arviragus, the worthy knight,
That bade her hold all that she haddë hight;
So loth him was his wife should break her truth.
And in his heart he caught of it great ruth,[17]
Considering the best on every side,
That from his lust yet were him lever[18] abide,
Than do so high a churlish wretchedness[19]
Against franchise,[20] and allë gentleness;
For which in fewë words he saidë thus;
"Madame, say to your lord Arviragus,
That since I see the greatë gentleness
Of him, and eke I see well your distress,
That him were lever[18] have shame (and that were ruth[17])
Than ye to me should breakë thus your truth,
I had well lever aye to suffer woe,
Than to depart[21] the love betwixt you two.
I you release, Madame, into your hond,
Quit ev'ry surëment[22] and ev'ry bond,
That ye have made to me as herebeforn,
Since thilkë timë that ye werë born.
Have here my truth, I shall you ne'er repreve[23]
Of no behest;[24] and here I take my leave,
As of the truest and the bestë wife
That ever yet I knew in all my life.
But every wife beware of her behest;
On Dorigen remember at the least.
Thus can a squiër do a gentle deed,
As well as can a knight, withoutë drede."[25]

1 Chose.

2 Her husband. She begged the gods, after his death, that but three hours' converse with him might be allowed her; the request was granted; and when her dead husband, at the expiry of the time, returned to the world of shades, she bore him company.

3 The daughter of Cato of Utica, Porcia married Marcus Brutus, the friend and the assassin of Julius Cæsar; when her husband died by his own hand after the battle of Philippi, she committed suicide, it is said, by swallowing live coals—all other means having been removed by her friends.

4 Artemisia, Queen of Caria, who built to her husband, Mausolus, the splendid monument which was accounted among the wonders of the world; and who mingled her husband's ashes with her daily drink. "Barbarie" is used in the Greek sense, to designate the non-Hellenic peoples of Asia.

5 Queen of Illyria, who, after her husband's death, made war on and was conquered by the Romans, B.C. 228.

6 At this point, in some manuscripts, occur the following two lines:—

"The samë thing I say of Bilia,
Of Rhodogone and of Valeria."

7 Die. 8 Demeanour. 9 Relate. 10 Assuredly. 11 If. 12 Certainly. 13 I had rather be slain. 14 Readiest.

15 Prepared; going. To "boun" or "bown" is a good old word, whence comes our word "bound," in the sense of "on the way." 16 Promised. 17 Pity. 18 Rather. 19 Rude outrage. 20 Generosity. 21 Sunder, split up. 22 Surety. 23 Reproach. 24 Of no (breach of) promise. 25 Doubt.

She thanked him upon her kneës bare,
And home unto her husband is she fare,[1]
And told him all, as ye have heardë said;
And, trustë me, he was so well apaid,[2]
That it were impossíble me to write.
Why should I longer of this case indite?
Arviragus and Dorigen his wife
In sov'reign blissë leddë forth their life;
Ne'er after was there anger them between;
He cherish'd her as though she were a queen,
And she was to him true for evermore;
Of these two folk ye get of me no more.
Aurelius, that his cost had all forlorn,[3]
Cursed the time that ever he was born.
"Alas!" quoth he, "alas that I behight[4]
Of pured[5] gold a thousand pound of weight
To this philosopher! how shall I do?
I see no more, but that I am fordo.[6]
Mine heritagë must I needës sell,
And be a beggar; here I will not dwell,
And shamen all my kindred in this place,
But[7] I of him may gettë better grace.
But natheless I will of him assay
At certain dayës year by year to pay,
And thank him of his greatë courtesy.
My trothë will I keep, I will not lie."
With heartë sore he went unto his coffer,
And broughtë gold unto this philosópher,
The value of five hundred pound, I guess,
And him beseeched, of his gentleness,
To grant him dayës of[8] the remenant;
And said; "Master, I dare well make avaunt,
I failed never of my truth as yet.
For sickerly my debtë shall be quit
Towardës you, how so that e'er I fare
To go a-begging in my kirtle bare:
But would ye vouchësafe, upon suretý,
Two year, or three, for to respitë me,
Then were I well, for ellës must I sell
Mine heritage; there is no more to tell."
This philosópher soberly[9] answér'd,
And saidë thus, when he these wordës heard;
"Have I not holden covenant to thee?"
"Yes, certes, well and truëly," quoth he.
"Hast thou not had thy lady as thee liked?"
"No, no," quoth he, and sorrowfully siked.[10]
"What was the causë? tell me if thou can."
Aurelius his tale anon began,
And told him all as ye have heard before,
It needeth not to you rehearse it more.
He said, "Arviragus of gentleness
Had lever[11] die in sorrow and distress,
Than that his wife were of her trothë false."
The sorrow of Dorigen he told him als',[12]
How loth her was to be a wicked wife,
And that she lever had lost that day her life;
And that her troth she swore through innocence;
She ne'er erst[13] had heard speak of apparénce;[14]
That made me have of her so great pitý,
And right as freely as he sent her to me,
As freely sent I her to him again:
This is all and some, there is no more to sayn."
The philosópher answer'd; "Levë[15] brother,
Evereach of you did gently to the other;
Thou art a squiër, and he is a knight,
But God forbiddë, for his blissful might,
But if a clerk could do a gentle deed
As well as any of you, it is no drede.[16]
Sir, I releasë thee thy thousand pound,
As thou right now were crept out of the ground,
Nor ever ere now haddest knowen me.
For, Sir, I will not take a penny of thee
For all my craft, nor naught for my travail;[17]
Thou hast y-payed well for my vitáille;
It is enough; and farewell, have good day."
And took his horse, and forth he went his way.
Lordings, this question would I askë now,
Which was the mostë free,[18] as thinketh you?
Now tellë me, ere that ye farther wend.
I can[19] no more, my tale is at an end.

THE DOCTOR'S TALE.[20]

THE PROLOGUE.

["Yea, let that passë," quoth our Host, "as now.
Sir Doctor of Physík, I prayë you,
Tell us a tale of some honést mattére."
"It shall be done, if that ye will it hear,"
Said this Doctór; and his tale gan anon.
"Now, good men," quoth he, "hearken every one."]

THE TALE.

There was, as telleth Titus Livius,[21]
A knight, that called was Virginius,
Full filled of honoúr and worthiness,
And strong of friendës, and of great richéss.
This knight one daughter haddë by his wife;
No children had he more in all his life.
Fair was this maid in excellent beautý
Aboven ev'ry wight that man may see:
For nature had with sov'reign diligence
Y-formed her in so great excellence,
As though she wouldë say, "Lo, I, Natúre,

1 Gone. 2 Satisfied. 3 Utterly lost.
4 Promised. 5 Purified, refined.
6 Ruined, undone. 7 Unless.
8 Time to pay up. 9 Gravely. 10 Sighed.
11 Rather. 12 Also. 13 Before.
14 Such an ocular deception, or apparition—more properly, disappearance—as the removal of the rocks.
15 Dear. 16 Doubt.
17 Labour, pains.
18 Generous, liberal; the same question is stated at the end of Boccaccio's version of the story in the "Philocopo," where the queen determines in favour of Arviragus. The question is evidently one of those which it was the fashion to propose for debate in the mediæval "courts of love." 19 Know, can tell.
20 The authenticity of the prologue is questionable. It is found in one manuscript only; other manuscripts give other prologues, more plainly not Chaucer's than this; and some manuscripts have merely a colophon to the effect that "Here endeth the Franklin's Tale and beginneth the Physician's Tale without a prologue." The Tale itself is the well-known story of Virginia, with several departures from the text of Livy. Chaucer probably followed the "Romance of the Rose" and Gower's "Confessio Amantis," in both of which the story is found. 21 Livy, Book iii. cap. 44, *et seqq.*

Thus can I form and paint a creatúre,
When that me list; who can me counterfeit?
Pygmalion? not though he aye forge and beat,
Or grave, or paintë: for I dare well sayn,
Apelles, Zeuxis, shouldë work in vain,
Either to grave, or paint, or forge, or beat,
If they presumed me to counterfeit.
For he that is the former principal,
Hath madë me his vicar-general
To form and painten earthly creatúrës
Right as me list, and all thing in my cure[1] is,
Under the moonë, that may wane and wax.
And for my work right nothing will I ax;[2]
My lord and I be full of one accord.
I made her to the worship[3] of my lord;
So do I all mine other creatúres,
What colour that they have, or what figúres."
Thus seemeth me that Nature wouldë say.

This maiden was of age twelve year and tway,
In which that Nature haddë such delight.
For right as she can paint a lily white,
And red a rosë, right with such paintúre
She painted had this noble creatúre,
Ere she was born, upon her limbës free,
Where as by right such colours shouldë be:
And Phœbus dyed had her tresses great,
Like to the streamës[4] of his burned heat.
And if that excellent was her beauty,
A thousand-fold more virtuous was she.
In her there lacked no conditión,
That is to praise, as by discretión.
As well in ghost[5] as body chaste was she:
For which she flower'd in virginity,
With all humility and abstinence,
With allë temperance and patience,
With measure[6] eke of bearing and array.
Discreet she was in answering alway,
Though she were wise as Pallas, dare I sayn;
Her faconde[7] eke full womanly and plain,
No counterfeited termës haddë she
To seemë wise; but after her degree
She spake, and all her wordës more and less
Sounding in virtue and in gentleness.
Shamefast she was in maiden's shamefastness,
Constant in heart, and ever in business[8]
To drive her out of idle sluggardy:
Bacchus had of her mouth right no mast'ry.
For wine and slothë[9] do Venus increase,
As men in fire will casten oil and grease.
And of her owen virtue, unconstrain'd,
She had herself full often sick y-feign'd,
For that she wouldë flee the company,
Where likely was to treaten of folly,
As is at feasts, at revels, and at dances,
That be occasións of dalliánces.
Such thingës makë children for to be
Too soonë ripe and bold, as men may see,
Which is full perilous, and hath been yore;[10]
For all too soonë may she learnë lore
Of boldëness, when that she is a wife.

And ye mistrésses,[11] in your oldë life
That lordës' daughters have in governánce,
Takë not of my wordës displeasánce:
Thinkë that ye be set in governings
Of lordës' daughters only for two things;
Either for ye have kept your honesty,
Or else for ye have fallen in frailty
And knowë well enough the oldë dance,
And have forsaken fully such meschance[12]
For evermore; therefore, for Christë's sake,
To teach them virtue look that ye not slake.[13]
A thief of venison, that hath forlaft[14]
His lik'rousness,[15] and all his oldë craft,
Can keep a forest best of any man;
Now keep them well, for if ye will ye can.
Look well, that ye unto no vice assent,
Lest ye be damned for your wick'[16] intent,
For whoso doth, a traitor is certáin;
And takë keep[17] of that I shall you sayn;
Of allë treason, sov'reign pestilence
Is when a wight betrayeth innocence.
Ye fathers, and ye mothers eke also,
Though ye have children, be it one or mo',
Yours is the charge of all their surveyance,[18]
While that they be under your governance.
Beware, that by example of your living,
Or by your negligence in chastising,
That they not perish: for I dare well say,
If that they do, ye shall it dear abeye.[19]
Under a shepherd soft and negligent
The wolf hath many a sheep and lamb to-rent.
Sufficë this example now as here,
For I must turn again to my mattére.

This maid, of which I tell my tale express,
She kept herself, her needed no mistréss;
For in her living maidens mightë read,
As in a book, ev'ry good word and deed
That longeth to a maiden virtuous;
She was so prudent and so bounteous.
For which the fame out sprang on every side
Both of her beauty and her bounté[20] wide:
That through the land they praised her each one
That loved virtue, save envy alone,
That sorry is of other mannë's weal,
And glad is of his sorrow and unheal.[21]—
The Doctor maketh this descriptioún.[22]—
This maiden on a day went in the town
Toward a temple, with her mother dear,
As is of youngë maidens the mannére.
Now was there then a justice in that town,
That governor was of that regioún:
And so befell, this judge his eyen cast
Upon this maid, avising[23] her full fast,
As she came forth by where this judgë stood;
Anon his heartë changed and his mood,
So was he caught with beauty of this maid
And to himself full privily he said,

1 Care.
2 Ask.
3 Glory.
4 Beams, rays.
5 Mind, spirit.
6 Moderation.
7 Utterance, speech; from Latin, "facundia," eloquence.
8 Diligent, eager.
9 Other readings are "thought" and "youth."
10 Of old.
11 Governesses, duennas.
12 Wickedness; French, "méchanceté."
13 Be slack, fail.
14 Forsaken, left.
15 Gluttony.
16 Wicked, evil.
17 Heed.
18 Oversight.
19 Pay for, suffer for.
20 Goodness.
21 Misfortune.
22 This line seems to be a kind of aside thrown in by Chaucer himself.
23 Observing.

"This maiden shall be mine for any man."
Anon the fiend into his heartë ran,
And taught him suddenly, that he by sleight
This maiden to his purpose winnë might.
For certes, by no force, nor by no meed,[1]
Him thought he was not able for to speed;
For she was strong of friendës, and eke she
Confirmed was in such sov'reign bounté,
That well he wist he might her never win,
As for to make her with her body sin.
For which, with great deliberatioún,
He sent after a clerk [2] was in the town,
The which he knew for subtle and for bold.
This judge unto this clerk his talë told
In secret wise, and made him to assure
He shouldë tell it to no creatúre,
And if he did, he shouldë lose his head.
And when assented was this cursed rede,[3]
Glad was the judge, and made him greatë cheer,
And gave him giftës precioús and dear.
When shapen [4] was all their conspiracy
From point to point, how that his lechery
Performed shouldë be full subtilly,
As ye shall hear it after openly,
Home went this clerk, that hightë Claudius.
This falsë judge, that hightë Appius,—
(So was his namë, for it is no fable,
But knowen for a storial [5] thing notáble;
The sentence[6] of it sooth [7] is out of doubt);—
This falsë judgë went now fast about
To hasten his delight all that he may.
And so befell, soon after on a day,
This falsë judge, as telleth us the story,
As he was wont, sat in his consistóry,
And gave his doomës [8] upon sundry case';
This falsë clerk came forth a full great pace,[9]
And saidë; "Lord, if that it be your will,
As do me right upon this piteous bill,[10]
In which I plain upon Virginius.
And if that he will say it is not thus,
I will it prove, and findë good witnéss,
That sooth is what my billë will express."
The judge answér'd, "Of this, in his absénce,
I may not give definitive senténce.
Let do [11] him call, and I will gladly hear;
Thou shalt have allë right, and no wrong here."
Virginius came to weet [12] the judgë's will,
And right anon was read this cursed bill;
The sentence of it was as ye shall hear:
"To you, my lord, Sir Appius so dear,
Sheweth your poorë servant Claudius,
How that a knight called Virginius,
Against the law, against all equity,
Holdeth, express against the will of me,
My servant, which that is my thrall [13] by right,
Which from my house was stolen on a night,
While that she was full young; I will it preve [14]
By witness, lord, so that it you not grieve; [15]
She is his daughter not, what so he say.
Wherefore to you, my lord the judge, I pray,
Yield me my thrall, if that it be your will."
Lo, this was all the sentence of the bill.
Virginius gan upon the clerk behold;
But hastily, ere he his talë told,
And would have proved it, as should a knight,
And eke by witnessing of many a wight,
That all was false that said his adversary,
This cursed [16] judgë would no longer tarry,
Nor hear a word more of Virginius,
But gave his judgëment, and saidë thus:
"I deem [17] anon this clerk his servant have;
Thou shalt no longer in thy house her save.
Go, bring her forth, and put her in our ward;
The clerk shall have his thrall: thus I award."
And when this worthy knight, Virginius,
Through sentence of this justice Appius,
Mustë by force his dearë daughter give
Unto the judge, in lechery to live,
He went him home, and sat him in his hall,
And let anon his dearë daughter call;
And with a facë dead as ashes cold
Upon her humble face he gan behold,
With father's pity sticking [18] through his heart,
All [19] would he from his purpose not convert.[20]
"Daughter," quoth he, "Virginia by name,
There be two wayës, either death or shame,
That thou must suffer,—alas that I was bore!
For never thou deservedest wherefore
To dien with a sword or with a knife.
O dearë daughter, ender of my life,
Whom I have foster'd up with such pleasánce
That thou were ne'er out of my remembrance;
O daughter, which that art my lastë woe,
And in this life my lastë joy also,
O gem of chastity, in patiénce
Take thou thy death, for this is my senténce:
For love and not for hate thou must be dead;
My piteous hand must smiten off thine head.
Alas, that ever Appius thee say! [21]
Thus hath he falsely judged thee to-day."
And told her all the case, as ye before
Have heard; it needeth not to tell it more.
"O mercy, dearë father," quoth the maid.
And with that word she both her armës laid
About his neck, as she was wont to do,
(The tearës burst out of her eyen two),
And said, "O goodë father, shall I die?
Is there no grace? is there no remedy?"
"No, certes, dearë daughter mine," quoth he.
"Then give me leisure, father mine," quoth she,
"My death for to complain [22] a little space:
For, pardie, Jephthah gave his daughter grace
For to complain, ere he her slew, alas! [23]

1 Bribe, reward.
2 The various readings of this word are "churl," or "cherl," in the best manuscripts; "client" in the common editions; and "clerk," supported by two important manuscripts. "Client" would perhaps be the best reading, if it were not awkward for the metre; but between "churl" and "clerk" there can be little doubt that Mr Wright chose wisely when he preferred the second.
3 Counsel, plot.
4 Arranged.
5 Historical, authentic.
6 Discourse, account.
7 True.
8 Judgments.
9 In haste.
10 Petition.
11 Cause.
12 Know, learn.
13 Slave.
14 Prove.
15 Be not displeasing.
16 Villainous.
17 Pronounce, determine.
18 Piercing.
19 Although.
20 Swerve, turn aside.
21 Saw.
22 Bewail.
23 Judges xi. 37, 38. "And she said unto her father, Let . . . . me alone two months, that I may go up and down upon the mountains, and bewail my virginity, I and my fellows. And he said, Go."

And, God it wot, nothing was her trespáss,[1]
But for she ran her father first to see,
To welcome him with great solemnity."
And with that word she fell a-swoon anon;
And after, when her swooning was y-gone,
She rose up, and unto her father said:
"Blessed be God, that I shall die a maid.
Give me my death, ere that I havë shame;
Do with your child your will, in Goddë's name."
And with that word she prayed him full oft
That with his sword he wouldë smite her soft;
And with that word, a-swoon again she fell.
Her father, with full sorrowful heart and fell,[2]
Her head off smote, and by the top it hent,[3]
And to the judge he went it to present,
As he sat yet in doom[4] in consistóry.
And when the judge it saw, as saith the story,
He bade to take him, and to hang him fast.
But right anon a thousand people in thrast[5]
To save the knight, for ruth and for pitý,
For knowen was the false iniquity.
The people anon had súspect[6] in this thing,
By manner of the clerkë's challengíng,
That it was by th' assent of Appius;
They wistë well that he was lecherous.
For which unto this Appius they gon,
And cast him in a prison right anon,
Where as he slew himself: and Claudius,
That servant was unto this Appius,
Was doomed for to hang upon a tree;
But that Virginius, of his pitý,
So prayed for him, that he was exil'd;
And ellës certes had he been beguil'd;[7]
The remenant were hanged, more and less,
That were consenting to this cursedness.[8]
Here men may see how sin hath his meríte:[9]
Beware, for no man knows how God will smite
In no degree, nor in which manner wise
The worm of consciéncë may agrise
Of[10] wicked life, though it so privy be,
That no man knows thereof, save God and he;
For be he lewëd man or ellës lear'd,[11]
He knows not how soon he shall be afear'd;
Therefore I redë[12] you this counsel take,
Forsakë sin, ere sinnë you forsake.

THE PARDONER'S TALE.

THE PROLOGUE.

OUR Hostë gan to swear as he were wood;[13]
"Harow!" quoth he, "by nailës and by blood,[14]
This was a cursed thief, a false justíce.
As shameful death as heartë can devise
Come to these judges and their advoca's.[15]
Algate[16] this sely[17] maid is slain, alas!
Alas! too dearë bought[18] she her beautý.
Wherefore I say, that all day man may see
That giftës of fortúne and of natúre
Be cause of death to many a creatúre.
Her beauty was her death, I dare well sayn;
Alas! so piteously as she was slain.
[Of bothë giftës, that I speak of now,
Men have full often morë harm than prow.[19]]
But truëly, mine owen master dear,
This was a piteous talë for to hear;
But natheless, pass over; 'tis no force.[20]
I pray to God to save thy gentle corse,[21]
And eke thine urinals, and thy jordans,
Thine Hippocras, and eke thy Galliens,[22]
And every boist[23] full of thy lectuary,
God bless them, and our lady Saintë Mary.
So may I thé,[24] thou art a proper man,
And like a prelate, by Saint Ronian;
Said I not well? can I not speak in term?[25]
But well I wot, thou dost[26] mine heart to erme,[27]
That I have almost caught a cardiácle:[28]
By *corpus Domini*, but[29] I have triácle,[30]
Or else a draught of moist and corny[31] ale,
Or but[20] I hear anon a merry tale,
Mine heart is brost[32] for pity of this maid.
Thou *bel ami*, thou Pardoner," he said,
"Tell us some mirth of japës[33] right anon."
"It shall be done," quoth he, "by Saint Ronion.
But first," quoth he, "here at this alë-stake[34]
I will both drink, and biten on a cake."
But right anon the gentles gan to cry,
"Nay, let him tell us of no ribaldry.
Tell us some moral thing, that we may lear[35]
Some wit,[36] and thennë will we gladly hear."
"I grant y-wis,"[37] quoth he; "but I must think
Upon some honest thing while that I drink."

THE TALE.[38]

Lordings (quoth he), in churchë when I preach,
I painë me[39] to have an hautein[40] speech,
And ring it out, as round as doth a bell,
For I know all by rotë that I tell.
My theme is always one, and ever was;
Radix malorum est cupiditas.[41]
First I pronouncë whencë that I come,
And then my bullës shew I all and some;

1 Offence. 2 Stern, cruel. 3 Took.
4 Judgment. 5 Thrust. 6 Suspicion.
7 "Cast into gaol," according to Urry's explanation; though we should probably understand that, if Claudius had not been sent out of the country, his death would have been secretly contrived through private detestation. 8 Villainy. 9 Desert.
10 Cause a man to tremble because of.
11 Illiterate or learned. 12 Advise. 13 Mad.
14 The nails and blood of Christ, by which it was then a fashion to swear.
15 Counsellors; those who aid their undertakings.
16 Nevertheless. 17 Innocent.
18 Paid for, suffered for. 19 Profit.
20 No matter. 21 Body.
22 See note 1, page 22.
23 Box; French, "boîte," old form "boiste."
24 Thrive. 25 In set form. 26 Makest.
27 Grieve; from Anglo-Saxon, "earme," wretched.
28 Heartache; from Greek, κάρδιαλγια.
29 Unless. 30 A remedy.
31 New and strong, nappy. As to "moist," see note 9, page 22. 32 Broken, burst. 33 Jokes.
34 Ale-house sign. 35 Learn.
36 Wisdom, sense. 37 Surely.
38 The outline of this Tale is to be found in the "Cento Novelle Antiche," but the original is now lost. As in the case of the Wife of Bath's Tale, there is a long prologue, but in this case it has been treated as part of the Tale.
39 Take pains, make an effort.
40 Loud, lofty; from French, "hautain."
41 "The love of money is the root of all evil" (1 Tim. vi. 10).

Our liegë lordë's seal on my patént,
That shew I first, my body to warrent,[1]
That no man be so hardy, priest nor clerk,
Me to disturb of Christë's holy werk.
And after that then tell I forth my tales.
Bullës of popës, and of cardinales,
Of patriarchs, and of bishóps I shew,
And in Latín I speak a wordës few,
To savour with my predicatión,
And for to stir men to devotión
Then shew I forth my longë crystal stones,
Y-crammed full of cloutës[2] and of bones;
Relics they be, as weenë they[3] each one.
Then have I in latoun[4] a shoulder-bone
Which that was of a holy Jewë's sheep.
"Good men," say I, "take of my wordës keep;[5]
If that this bone be wash'd in any well,
If cow, or calf, or sheep, or oxë swell,
That any worm hath eat, or worm y-stung,
Take water of that well, and wash his tongue,
And it is whole anon; and farthermore
Of pockës, and of scab, and every sore
Shall every sheep be whole, that of this well
Drinketh a draught; take keep[5] of that I tell.
"If that the goodman, that the beastës oweth,[6]
Will every week, ere that the cóck him croweth,
Fasting, y-drinken of this well a draught,
As thilkë holy Jew our elders taught,
His beastës and his store shall multiply.
And, Sirs, also it healeth jealousy;
For though a man be fall'n in jealous rage,
Let makë with this water his pottáge,
And never shall he more his wife mistrist,[7]
Though he the sooth of her defaultë wist;
All[8] had she taken priestës two or three.
Here is a mittain[9] eke, that ye may see;
He that his hand will put in this mittáin,
He shall have multiplying of his grain,
When he hath sowen, be it wheat or oats,
So that he offer pence, or ellës groats.
And, men and women, one thing warn I you;
If any wight be in this churchë now
That hath done sin horríble, so that he
Dare not for shame of it y-shriven[10] be;
Or any woman, be she young or old,
That hath y-made her husband cokëwold,[11]
Such folk shall have no power nor no grace
To offer to my relics in this place.
And whoso findeth him out of such blame,
He will come up and offer in God's name;
And I assoil him by the authority
Which that by bull y-granted was to me."
By this gaud[12] have I wonnë year by year
A hundred marks, since I was pardonére.
I standë like a clerk in my pulpit,
And when the lewëd[13] people down is set,
I preachë so as ye have heard before,
And tellë them a hundred japës[14] more.
Then pain I me to stretchë forth my neck,
And east and west upon the people I beck,
As doth a dovë, sitting on a bern;[15]
My handës and my tonguë go so yern,[16]
That it is joy to see my business.
Of avarice and of such cursedness[17]
Is all my preaching, for to make them free
To give their pence, and namely[18] unto me.
For mine intent is not but for to win,
And nothing for correctión of sin.
I reckë never, when that they be buried,
Though that their soulës go a blackburied.[19]
For certes many a predicatión
Cometh oft-time of evil intentión;[20]
Some for pleasánce of folk, and flattery,
To be advanced by hypocrisy;
And some for vainglory, and some for hate.
For, when I dare not otherwise debate,
Then will I sting him with my tónguë smart[21]
In preaching, so that he shall not astart[22]
To be defamed falsely, if that he
Hath trespass'd[23] to my brethren or to me.
For, though I tellë not his proper name,
Men shall well knowë that it is the same
By signës, and by other circumstánces.
Thus quite I[24] folk that do us displeasánces:
Thus spit I out my venom, under hue
Of holiness, to seem holy and true.
But, shortly mine intent I will devise,
I preach of nothing but of covetise.
Therefore my theme is yet, and ever was,—
Radix malorum est cupiditas.
Thus can I preach against the samë vice
Which that I use, and that is avarice.
But though myself be guilty in that sin,
Yet can I maken other folk to twin[25]
From avarice, and sorë them repent.
But that is not my principal intent;
I preachë nothing but for covetise.
Of this mattére it ought enough suffice.
Then tell I them examples many a one,
Of oldë stories longë timë gone;
For lewëd[26] people lovë talës old;
Such thingës can they well report and hold.
What? trowë ye, that whilës I may preach
And winnë gold and silver for[27] I teach,
That I will live in povert' wilfully?
Nay, nay, I thought it never truëly.
For I will preach and beg in sundry lands;
I will not do no labour with mine hands,
Nor makë baskets for to live thereby,
Because I will not beggen idlely.
I will none of the apostles counterfeit;[28]
I will have money, wool, and cheese, and wheat,
All[8] were it given of the poorest page,
Or of the poorest widow in a villáge:
All[8] should her children stervë[29] for famíne.
Nay, I will drink the liquor of the vine,
And have a jolly wench in every town.
But hearken, lordings, in conclusioún;

1 For the protection of my person.
2 Rags, fragments. 3 As my auditors think.
4 Brass. 5 Heed. 6 Owneth.
7 Mistrust. 8 Although. 9 Glove, mitten.
10 Confessed. 11 Cuckold. 12 Jest, trick.
13 Ignorant. 14 Jests. 15 Barn.
16 Briskly. 17 Wickedness. 18 Especially.
19 The meaning of this is not very clear, but it is probably a periphrastic and picturesque way of indicating damnation.
20 Preaching is often inspired by evil motives.
21 Sharply. 22 Escape. 23 Offended.
24 Am I revenged on. 25 Depart.
26 Unlearned. 27 Because.
28 In respect of the poverty enjoined on and practised by them. 29 Die.

Your liking is, that I shall tell a tale.
Now I have drunk a draught of corny ale,
By God, I hope I shall you tell a thing
That shall by reason be to your liking;
For though myself be a full vicious man,
A moral tale yet I you tellë can,
Which I am wont to preachë, for to win.
Now hold your peace, my tale I will begin.

In Flanders whilom was a company
Of youngë folkës, that haunted folly,
As riot, hazard, stewës, and tavérns;
Where as with lutës, harpës, and gitérns,[1]
They dance and play at dice both day and night,
And eat also, and drink over their might;
Through which they do the devil sacrifice
Within the devil's temple, in cursed wise,
By superfluity abominable.
Their oathës be so great and so damnáble,
That it is grisly[2] for to hear them swear.
Our blissful Lordë's body they to-tear;[3]
Them thought the Jewës rent him not enough;
And each of them at other's sinnë lough.[4]
And right anon in comë tombesteres[5]
Fetis[6] and small, and youngë fruitesteres.[7]
Singers with harpës, baudës,[8] waferers,[9]
Which be the very devil's officers,
To kindle and blow the fire of lechery,
That is annexed unto gluttony.
The Holy Writ take I to my witnéss,
That luxury is in wine and drunkenness.[10]
Lo, how that drunken Lot unkindëly[11]
Lay by his daughters two unwittingly,
So drunk he was he knew not what he wrought.
Heródes, who so well the stories sought,[12]
When he of wine replete was at his feast,
Right at his owen table gave his hest[13]
To slay the Baptist John full guiltëless.
Seneca saith a good word, doubtëless:
He saith he can no differencë find
Betwixt a man that is out of his mind,
And a man whichë that is drunkelew:[14]
But that woodnéss,[15] y-fallen in a shrew,[16]
Persevereth longer than drunkenness.
O gluttony, full of all cursedness;
O causë first of our confusión,
Original of our damnatión,
Till Christ had bought us with his blood again!
Lookë, how dearë, shortly for to sayn,
Abought[17] was first this cursed villainy:
Corrupt was all this world for gluttony.
Adam our father, and his wife also,
From Paradise, to labour and to woe,
Were driven for that vice, it is no dread.[18]
For while that Adam fasted, as I read,
He was in Paradise; and when that he
Ate of the fruit defended[19] of the tree,
Anon he was cast out to woe and pain.
O gluttony! well ought us on thee plain.
Oh! wist a man how many maladies
Follow of éxcess and of gluttonies,
He wouldë be the morë measuráble[20]
Of his dietë, sitting at his table.
Alas! the shortë throat, the tender mouth,
Maketh that east and west, and north and south,
In earth, in air, in water, men do swink[21]
To get a glutton dainty meat and drink.
Of this mattére, O Paul! well canst thou treat.
Meat unto womb, and womb eke unto meat,
Shall God destroyë both, as Paulus saith.[22]
Alas! a foul thing is it, by my faith,
To say this word, and fouler is the deed,
When man so drinketh of the white and red,[23]
That of his throat he maketh his privy
Through thilkë cursed superfluity.
The apostle saith,[24] weeping full piteously,
There walk many, of which you told have I,—
I say it now weeping with piteous voice,—
That they be enemies of Christë's crois;[25]
Of which the end is death; womb is their God.
O womb, O belly, stinking is thy cod,[26]
Full fill'd of dung and of corruptioún;
At either end of thee foul is the soun'.
How great laboúr and cost is thee to find![27]
These cookës how they stamp, and strain, and grind,
And turnë substance into accident,
To fúlfil all thy likerous talent!
Out of the hardë bonës knockë they
The marrow, for they castë naught away
That may go through the gullet soft and swoot;[28]
Of spicery and leaves, of bark and root,
Shall be his sauce y-maked by delight,
To make him have a newer appetite.
But, certes, he that haunteth such delices
Is dead while that he liveth in those vices.
A lecherous thing is wine, and drunkenness
Is full of striving and of wretchedness.
O drunken man! disfigur'd is thy face,[29]
Sour is thy breath, foul art thou to embrace:
And through thy drunken nose sowneth the soun',
As though thou saidest aye, Samsoún! Samsoún!
And yet, God wot, Samson drank never wine.

1 Guitars.
2 Dreadful; fitted to "agrise" or horrify the listener.
3 See note 18, page 42. Mr Wright says: "The common oaths in the Middle Ages were by the different parts of God's body; and the popular preachers represented that profane swearers tore Christ's body by their imprecations." The idea was doubtless borrowed from the passage in Hebrews (vi. 6), where apostates are said to "crucify to themselves the Son of God afresh, and put Him to an open shame."
4 Laughed.
5 Female dancers or tumblers; from Anglo-Saxon, "tumban," to dance.
6 Dainty.
7 Fruit-girls.
8 Revellers.
9 Cake-sellers.
10 "Be not drunk with wine, wherein is excess" (Eph. v. 18).
11 Unnaturally.
12 The reference is probably to the diligent inquiries he made at the time of Christ's birth. See Matt. ii. 4-8.
13 Command.
14 A drunkard. "Perhaps," says Tyrwhitt, "Chaucer refers to Epist. lxxxiii., 'Extende in plures dies illum ebrii habitum; nunquid de furore dubitabis? nunc quoque non est minor sed brevior.'"
15 Madness.
16 One evil-tempered.
17 Atoned for.
18 Doubt.
19 Forbidden. St Jerome, in his book against Jovinian, says that so long as Adam fasted, he was in Paradise; he ate, and he was thrust out.
20 Moderate.
21 Labour.
22 "Meats for the belly, and the belly for meats; but God shall destroy both it and them." (1 Cor. vi. 13).
23 Wine.
24 See Phil. iii. 18, 19.
25 Cross; French, "croix."
26 Bag; Anglo-Saxon, "codde;" hence peas-cod, pin-cod (pin-cushion), &c.
27 Supply.
28 Sweet.
29 Compare with the lines which follow, the picture of the drunken messenger in the Man of Law's Tale, page 67.

Thou fallest as it were a sticked swine;
Thy tongue is lost, and all thine honest cure;[1]
For drunkenness is very sepultúre
Of mannë's wit and his discretión.
In whom that drink hath dominatión,
He can no counsel keep, it is no dread.[2]
Now keep you from the white and from the red,
And namely[3] from the whitë wine of Lepe,[4]
That is to sell in Fish Street[5] and in Cheap.
This wine of Spainë creepeth subtilly
In other winës growing fastë by,
Of which there riseth such fumosity,
That when a man hath drunken draughtës three,
And weeneth that he be at home in Cheap,
He is in Spain, right at the town of Lepe,
Not at the Róchelle, nor at Bourdeaux town;
And thennë will he say, Samsoún! Samsoún!
But hearken, lordings, one word, I you pray,
That all the sov'reign actës, dare I say,
Of victories in the Old Testament,
Through very God that is omnipotent,
Were done in abstinence and in prayére:
Look in the Bible, and there ye may it lear.[6]
Look, Attila, the greatë conqueror,
Died in his sleep,[7] with shame and dishonór,
Bleeding aye at his nose in drunkenness:
A captain should aye live in soberness.
And o'er all this, advisë[8] you right well
What was commanded unto Lemuel;
Not Samuel, but Lemuel, say I.
Readë the Bible,[9] and find it expresslý
Of wine giving to them that have justíce.
No more of this, for it may well suffice.
And, now that I have spoke of gluttony,
Now will I you defendë hazardry.[10]
Hazárd is very mother of leasíngs,[11]
And of deceit, and cursed forswearíngs:
Blasphem' of Christ, manslaughter, and waste also
Of chattel[12] and of time; and furthermo'
It is repreve,[13] and contrar' of honoúr,
For to be held a common hazardoúr.
And ever the higher he is of estate,
The morë he is holden desolate.[14]
If that a princë usë hazardry,
In allë governance and policy
He is, as by commón opinión,
Y-hold the less in reputatión.
Chilon, that was a wise ambassador,
Was sent to Corinth with full great honór
From Lacedæmon,[15] to make álliánce;
And when he came, it happen'd him, by chance,
That all the greatest that were of that land,
Y-playing attë hazard he them fand.
For which, as soon as that it mightë be,
He stole him home again to his countrý.
And saidë there, "I will not lose my name,
Nor will I take on me so great diffame,[16]
You to ally unto no hazardors.[17]
Sendë some other wise ambassadors,
For, by my troth, me werë lever[18] die,
Than I should you to hazardors ally.
For ye, that be so glorious in honoúrs,
Shall not ally you to no hazardoúrs,
As by my will, nor as by my treatý."
This wisë philosópher thus said he.
Look eke how to the King Demetrius
The King of Parthes, as the book saith us,
Sent him a pair of dice of gold in scorn,
For he had used hazard therebeforn:
For which he held his glory and renown
At no valúe or reputatioún.
Lordës may finden other manner play
Honest enough to drive the day away.
Now will I speak of oathës false and great
A word or two, as oldë bookës treat.
Great swearing is a thing abominâble,
And false swearing is morë reprovâble.
The highë God forbade swearing at all;
Witness on Matthew:[19] but in special
Of swearing saith the holy Jeremie,[20]
Thou shalt swear sooth thine oathës, and not lie:
And swear in doom,[21] and eke in righteousness;
But idle swearing is a cursedness.[22]
Behold and see, there in the firstë table
Of highë Goddë's hestës[23] honouráble,
How that the second hest of him is this,
Take not my name in idle[24] or amiss.
Lo, rather[25] he forbiddeth such swearíng,
Than homicide, or many a cursed thing;
I say that as by order thus it standeth;
This knoweth he that his hests understandeth,
How that the second hest of God is that.
And farthermore, I will thee tell all plat,[26]
That vengeance shall not partë from his house,
That of his oathës is outrageoús.
"By Goddë's precious heart, and by his nails,[27]
And by the blood of Christ, that is in Hailes,[28]
Seven is my chance, and thine is cinque and trey:
By Goddë's armës, if thou falsely play,
This dagger shall throughout thine heartë go."
This fruit comes of the bicched[29] bonës two,
Forswearing, ire, falseness, and homicide.
Now, for the love of Christ that for us died,

[1] Care. [2] Doubt. [3] Especially.
[4] A town near Cadiz, whence a stronger wine than the Gascon vintages afforded was imported to England.
[5] Another reading is "Fleet Street." [6] Learn.
[7] He was suffocated in the night by a hæmorrhage, brought on by a debauch, when he was preparing a new invasion of Italy, in 453. [8] Consider, bethink.
[9] Prov. xxxi. 4, 5: "It is not for kings, O Lemuel, it is not for kings to drink wine, nor for princes strong drink; lest they drink, and forget the law, and pervert the judgment of any of the afflicted."
[10] Forbid gaming. [11] Lies. [12] Property.
[13] Reproach. [14] Undone, worthless.
[15] Most manuscripts, evidently in error, have "Stilbon" and "Calidone" for Chilon and Lacedæmon. Chilon was one of the seven sages of Greece, and flourished about B.C. 590. According to Diogenes Laertius, he died, under the pressure of age and joy, in the arms of his son, who had just been crowned victor at the Olympic games. [16] Reproach.
[17] Gamesters. [18] Rather.
[19] "Swear not at all;" Christ's words in Matt. v. 34.
[20] Jeremiah iv. 2. [21] Judgment.
[22] Wickedness. [23] Commandments.
[24] In vain. [25] Sooner. [26] Flatly, plainly.
[27] The nails that fastened Christ on the cross, which were regarded with superstitious reverence.
[28] An abbey in Gloucestershire, where, under the designation of "the blood of Hailes," a portion of Christ's blood was preserved.
[29] A term of opprobrious reprobation, applied to the dice.

Leavë your oathës, bothë great and smale.
But, Sirs, now will I ell you forth my tale.
These riotoúrës hree, of which I tell,
Long erst than[1] primë rang of any bell,
Were set them in a tavern for to drink;
And as they sat, they heard a bellë clink
Before a corpse, was carried to the grave.
That one of them gan callë to his knave,[2]
"Go bet,"[3] quoth he, "and askë readily
What corpse is this, that passeth here forth by;
And look that thou report his namë well."
"Sir," quoth the boy, "it needeth never a deal;[4]
It was me told ere ye came here two hours;
He was, pardie, an old fellów of yours,
And suddenly he was y-slain to-night;
Fordrunk[5] as he sat on his bench upright,
There came a privy thief, men clepë Death,
That in this country all the people slay'th,
And with his spear he smote his heart in two,
And went his way withoutë wordës mo'.
He hath a thousand slain this pestilence;
And, master, ere you come in his presénce,
Me thinketh that it were full necessary
For to beware of such an adversary;
Be ready for to meet him evermore.
Thus taughtë me my dame; I say no more."
"By Saintë Mary," said the tavernére,
"The child saith sooth, for he hath slain this year,
Hence ov'r a mile, within a great villáge,
Both man and woman, child, and hind, and page;
I trow his habitatión be there;
To be advised[6] great wisdóm it were,
Ere[7] that he did a man a dishonoúr."
"Yea, Goddë's armës," quoth this riotoúr,
"Is it such peril with him for to meet?
I shall him seek, by stile and eke by street.
I make a vow, by Goddë's dignë[8] bones.
Hearken, fellóws, we three be allë ones:[9]
Let each of us hold up his hand to other,
And each of us become the other's brother,
And we will slay this falsë traitor Death;
He shall be slain, he that so many slay'th,
By Goddë's dignity, ere it be night."
Together have these three their trothë plight
To live and die each one of them for other
As though he were his owen boren[10] brother.
And up they start, all drunken, in this rage,
And forth they go towárdës that villáge
Of which the taverner had spoke beforn,
And many a grisly[11] oathë have they sworn,
And Christë's blessed body they to-rent;[12]
"Death shall be dead, if that we may him hent."[13]
When they had gone not fully half a mile,
Right as they would have trodden o'er a stile,
An old man and a poorë with them met.
This oldë man full meekëly them gret,[14]
And saidë thus; "Now, lordës, God you see!"[15]
The proudest of these riotoúrës three
Answér'd again; "What? churl, with sorry grace,
Why art thou all forwrapped[16] save thy face?
Why livest thou so long in so great age?"
This oldë man gan look on his viságe,
And saidë thus; "For that I cannot find
A man, though that I walked unto Ind,
Neither in city, nor in no villáge,
That wouldë change his youthë for mine age;
And therefore must I have mine agë still
As longë time as it is Goddë's will.
And Death, alas! he will not have my life.
Thus walk I like a restëless caitífe,[17]
And on the ground, which is my mother's gate,
I knockë with my staff, early and late,
And say to her, 'Leve[18] mother, let me in.
Lo, how I wanë, flesh, and blood, and skin;
Alas! when shall my bonës be at rest?
Mother, with you I wouldë change my chest,
That in my chamber longë time hath be,
Yea, for an hairy clout to wrap in me.'[19]
But yet to me she will not do that grace,
For which full pale and welked[20] is my face.
But, Sirs, to you it is no courtesy
To speak unto an old man villainy,
But[21] he trespass in word or else in deed.
In Holy Writ ye may yourselvës read;
'Against[22] an old man, hoar upon his head,
Ye should arisë:' therefore I you rede,[23]
Ne do unto an old man no harm now,
No morë than ye would a man did you
In age, if that ye may so long abide.
And God be with you, whether ye go or ride.
I must go thither as I have to go."
"Nay, oldë churl, by God thou shalt not so,"
Saidë this other hazardor anon;
"Thou partest not so lightly, by Saint John.
Thou spakest right now of that traitor Death,
That in this country all our friendës slay'th;
Have here my troth, as thou art his espy;[24]
Tell where he is, or thou shalt it abie,[25]
By God and by the holy sacrament;
For soothly thou art one of his assent
To slay us youngë folk, thou falsë thief."
"Now, Sirs," quoth he, "if it be you so lief[26]
To findë Death, turn up this crooked way,
For in that grove I left him, by my fay,
Under a tree, and there he will abide;
Nor for your boast he will him nothing hide.
See ye that oak? right there ye shall him find.
God savë you, that bought again mankind,
And you amend!" Thus said this oldë man;
And evereach of these riotoúrës ran,
Till they came to the tree, and there they found
Of florins fine, of gold y-coined round,
Well nigh a seven bushels, as them thought.
No longer as then after Death they sought;
But each of them so glad was of the sight,
For that the florins were so fair and bright,
That down they sat them by the precious hoard.
The youngest of them spake the firstë word:

1 Before. 2 Servant.
3 A hunting phrase; apparently its force is, "go beat up the game." 4 Whit. 5 Completely drunk.
6 Watchful, on one's guard. 7 Lest, in case.
8 Worthy. 9 At one.
10 Born; a better reading is "sworen." 11 Dreadful.
12 See note 3, page 135. 13 Catch.
14 Greeted. 15 Preserve, look upon graciously.
16 Closely wrapt up. 17 Miserable wretch.
18 Dear. 19 To wrap myself in. 20 Withered.
21 Except. 22 To meet. 23 Advise.
24 Spy. 25 Suffer for. 26 Desired a thing.

"Brethren," quoth he, "take keep what I shall say;
My wit is great, though that I bourde[1] and play.
This treasure hath Fortúne unto us given
In mirth and jollity our life to liven;
And lightly as it comes, so will we spend.
Hey! Goddë's precious dignity! who wend[2]
To-day that we should have so fair a grace?
But might this gold be carried from this place
Home to my house, or ellës unto yours
(For well I wot that all this gold is ours),
Then werë we in high felicitý.
But truëly by day it may not be;
Men wouldë say that we were thievës strong,
And for our owen treasure do us hong.[3]
This treasure mustë carried be by night,
As wisely and as slily as it might.
Wherefore I rede,[4] that cut[5] among us all
We draw, and let see where the cut will fall:
And he that hath the cut, with heartë blithe
Shall run unto the town, and that full swithe,[6]
And bring us bread and wine full privily:
And two of us shall keepë subtilly
This treasure well: and if he will not tarry,
When it is night, we will this treasure carry,
By one assent, where as us thinketh best."
Then one of them the cut brought in his fist,
And bade them draw, and look where it would fall;
And it fell on the youngest of them all;
And forth toward the town he went anon.
And all so soon as that he was y-gone,
The one of them spake thus unto the other;
"Thou knowest well that thou art my sworn brother,
Thy profit[7] will I tell thee right anon.
Thou knowest well that our fellów is gone,
And here is gold, and that full great plentý,
That shall departed[8] be among us three.
But natheless, if I could shape[9] it so
That it departed were among us two,
Had I not done a friendë's turn to thee?"
Th' other answér'd, "I n'ot[10] how that may be;
He knows well that the gold is with us tway.
What shall we do? what shall we to him say?"
"Shall it be counsel?"[11] said the firstë shrew;[12]
"And I shall tell to thee in wordës few
What we shall do, and bring it well about."
"I grantë," quoth the other, "out of doubt,
That by my truth I will thee not bewray."
"Now," quoth the first, "thou know'st well we be tway,
And two of us shall stronger be than one.
Look, when that he is set,[13] thou right anon
Arise, as though thou wouldest with him play;
And I shall rive him through the sidës tway,
While that thou strugglest with him as in game;
And with thy dagger look thou do the same.
And then shall all this gold departed be,
My dearë friend, betwixtë thee and me:
Then may we both our lustës[14] all fulfil,
And play at dice right at our owen will."
And thus accorded[15] be these shrewës[12] tway
To slay the third, as ye have heard me say.
The youngest, which that wentë to the town,
Full oft in heart he rolled up and down
The beauty of these florins new and bright.
"O Lord!" quoth he, "if so were that I might
Have all this treasure to myself alone,
There is no man that lives under the throne
Of God, that shouldë live so merry as I."
And at the last the fiend our enemy
Put in his thought, that he should poison buy,
With which he mightë slay his fellows twy.[16]
For why, the fiend found him in such livíng,[17]
That he had leave to sorrow him to bring.
For this was utterly his full intent
To slay them both, and never to repent.
And forth he went, no longer would he tarry,
Into the town to an apothecáry,
And prayed him that he him wouldë sell
Some poison, that he might his rattës quell,[18]
And eke there was a polecat in his haw,[19]
That, as he said, his capons had y-slaw:[20]
And fain he would him wreak,[21] if that he might,
Of vermin that destroyed him by night.
Th' apothecary answer'd, "Thou shalt have
A thing, as wisly[22] God my soulë save,
In all this world there is no creatúre
That eat or drank hath of this cónfectúre,
Not but the mountance[23] of a corn of wheat,
That he shall not his life anon forlete;[24]
Yea, sterve[25] he shall, and that in lessë while
Than thou wilt go a pace[26] nought but a mile:
This poison is so strong and violent."
This cursed man hath in his hand y-hent[27]
This poison in a box, and swift he ran
Into the nextë street, unto a man,
And borrow'd of him largë bottles three;
And in the two the poison poured he;
The third he keptë clean for his own drink,
For all the night he shope him[28] for to swink[29]
In carrying off the gold out of that place.
And when this riotoúr, with sorry grace,
Had fill'd with wine his greatë bottles three,
To his fellóws again repaired he.
What needeth it thereof to sermon[30] more?
For, right as they had cast[31] his death before,
Right so they have him slain, and that anon.
And when that this was done, thus spake the one;
"Now let us sit and drink, and make us merry,
And afterward we will his body bury."
And with that word it happen'd him *par cas*[32]
To take the bottle where the poison was,

1 Joke, frolic. 2 Weened, thought.
3 Cause us to be hanged.
4 My advice is. 5 Lots. 6 Quickly.
7 What is for thine advantage. 8 Divided.
9 Contrive. 10 Know not.
11 Secret, in confidence. 12 Wicked wretch.
13 Sat down. 14 Pleasures.
15 Agreed. 16 Two; German, "zwei."
17 Leading such a (bad) life.
18 Kill, destroy, his rats.
19 Farm-yard, hedge. Compare the French, "haie."
20 Slain. 21 Revenge. 22 Surely.
23 Amount. 24 Lay down, quit. 25 Die.
26 At a pace, quickly; so, on several occasions, Chaucer speaks of "a furlong," or one or two furlongs, when he means to denote a brief lapse of time. See note 12, page 52, for an instance. 27 Taken.
28 Purposed. 29 Labour.
30 Talk, discourse. 31 Contrived, plotted.
32 By chance.

And drank, and gave his fellow drink also,
For which anon they sterved[1] both the two.
But certes I suppose that Avicen
Wrote never in no canon, nor no fen,[2]
More wondrous signës of empoisoning,
Than had these wretches two ere their ending.
Thus ended be these homicidës two,
And eke the false empoisoner also.
O cursed sin, full of all cursedness!
O trait'rous homicide! O wickedness!
O glutt'ny, luxury, and hazárdry!
Thou blasphemer of Christ with villainy,[3]
And oathës great, of usage and of pride!
Alas! mankindë, how may it betide,
That to thy Creatór, which that thee wrought,
And with his precious heartë-blood thee bought,
Thou art so false and so unkind,[4] alas!
  Now, good men, God forgive you your trespáss,
And ware[5] you from the sin of avaríce.
Mine holy pardon may you all warice,[6]
So that ye offer nobles or sterlings,[7]
Or ellës silver brooches, spoons, or rings.
Bowë your head under this holy bull.
Come up, ye wives, and offer of your will;
Your names I enter in my roll anon;
Into the bliss of heaven shall ye gon;
I you assoil[8] by minë high powére,
You that will offer, as clean and eke as clear
As ye were born. Lo, Sirës, thus I preach;
And Jesus Christ, that is our soulës' leech,[9]
So grantë you his pardon to receive;
For that is best, I will you not deceive.
  But, Sirs, one word forgot I in my tale;
I have relícs and pardon in my mail,
As fair as any man in Engleland,
Which were me given by the Popë's hand.
If any of you will of devotión
Offer, and have mine absolutión,
Come forth anon, and kneelë here adown,
And meekëly receivë my pardoún.
Or ellës takë pardon, as ye wend,[10]
All new and fresh at every townë's end,
So that ye offer, always new and new,
Nobles or pence which that be good and true.
'Tis an honoúr to evereach that is here,
That ye have a suffisant pardonére
T' assoilë[8] you in country as ye ride,
For áventúrës which that may betide.
Parâventure there may fall one or two
Down of his horse, and break his neck in two.
Look, what a surety is it to you all,
That I am in your fellowship y-fall,
That may assoil you bothë more and lass,[11]
When that the soul shall from the body pass.
I redë[12] that our Hostë shall begin,
For he is most enveloped in sin.
Come forth, Sir Host, and offer first anon,
And thou shalt kiss the relics every one,
Yea, for a groat; unbuckle anon thy purse.

  "Nay, nay," quoth he, "then have I Christë's curse!
Let be," quoth he, "it shall not be, so thé 'ch.[13]
Thou wouldest make me kiss thine oldë breech,
And swear it were a relic of a saint,
Though it were with thy fundament depaint'.
But, by the cross which that Saint Helen fand,[14]
I would I had thy coilons in mine hand,
Instead of relics, or of sanctuary.
Let cut them off, I will thee help them carry;
They shall be shrined in a hoggë's tord."
The Pardoner answered not one word;
So wroth he was, no wordë would he say.
  "Now," quoth our Host, "I will no longer play
With thee, nor with none other angry man."
But right anon the worthy Knight began
(When that he saw that all the people lough[15]),
"No more of this, for it is right enough.
Sir Pardoner, be merry and glad of cheer;
And ye, Sir Host, that be to me so dear,
I pray you that ye kiss the Pardoner;
And, Pardoner, I pray thee draw thee ner,[16]
And as we diddë, let us laugh and play."
Anon they kiss'd, and rodë forth their way.

THE SHIPMAN'S TALE.[17]

THE PROLOGUE.

Our Host upon his stirrups stood anon,
And saidë; "Good men, hearken every one,
This was a thrifty[18] talë for the nones.
Sir Parish Priest," quoth he, "for Goddë's bones,
Tell us a tale, as was thy forword yore:[19]
I see well that ye learned men in lore
Can[20] muchë good, by Goddë's dignity."
The Parson him answér'd, "*Ben'dicite!*
What ails the man, so sinfully to swear?"
Our Host answér'd, "O Jankin, be ye there?
Now, good men," quoth our Host, "hearken to me.
I smell a Lollard[21] in the wind," quoth he.

1 Died.
2 Avicen, or Avicenna, was among the distinguished physicians of the Arabian school in the eleventh century, and very popular in the Middle Ages. His great work was called "Canon Medicinæ," and was divided into "fens," "fennes," or sections.
3 Outrage, impiety. 4 Unnatural.
5 Guard, keep. 6 "Warish," heal.
7 Sterling money.
8 Absolve. Compare the Scotch law-term "assoilzie," to acquit. 9 Physician of souls.
10 Go. 11 Both great and small.
12 Would counsel. 13 So thé ich—so may I thrive.
14 Saint Helen, according to Sir John Mandeville, found the cross of Christ deep below ground, under a rock, where the Jews had hidden it; and she tested the genuineness of the sacred tree, by raising to life a dead man laid upon it. 15 Laughed. 16 Nearer.
17 In this Tale Chaucer seems to have followed an old French story, which also formed the groundwork of the first story in the eighth day of the "Decameron." The Prologue here given was transferred by Tyrwhitt from the place, preceding the Squire's Tale, which it had formerly occupied; the Shipman's Tale having no Prologue in the best manuscripts.
18 Discreet, profitable. 19 Thy promise formerly.
20 Know, are capable of telling.
21 A contemptuous name for the followers of Wyckliffe; presumably derived from the Latin, "lolium," tares, as if they were the tares among the Lord's wheat; so, a few lines below, the Shipman intimates his fear lest the Parson should "spring cockle in our clean corn."

"Abide, for Goddë's dignë[1] passión,
For we shall have a predicatión:
This Lollard here will preachen us somewhat."
"Nay, by my father's soul, that shall he not,
Saidë the Shipman; "Here shall he not preach,
He shall no gospel glosë[2] here nor teach.
We all believe in the great God," quoth he.
"He wouldë sowë some difficultý,
Or springë cockle[3] in our cleanë corn.
And therefore, Host, I warnë thee beforn,
My jolly body shall a talë tell,
And I shall clinkë you so merry a bell,
That I shall waken all this company;
But it shall not be of philosophy,
Nor of physíc, nor termës quaint of law;
There is but little Latin in my maw."[4]

THE TALE.

A Merchant whilom dwell'd at Saint Deníse,
That richë was, for which men held him wise.
A wife he had of excellent beautý,
And companiable and revellous[5] was she,
Which is a thing that causeth more dispence
Than worth is all the cheer and reverence
That men them do at feastës and at dances.
Such salutatións and countenánces
Passen, as doth the shadow on the wall;
But woe is him that payë must for all.
The sely[6] husband algate[7] he must pay,
He must us[8] clothe and he must us array
All for his owen worship richëly:
In which array we dancë jollily.
And if that he may not, paráventure,
Or ellës list not such dispence endure,
But thinketh it is wasted and y-lost,
Then must another payë for our cost,
Or lend us gold, and that is perilous.
  This noble merchant held a noble house;
For which he had all day so great repair,[9]
For his largesse, and for his wife was fair,
That wonder is; but hearken to my tale.
Amongës all these guestës great and smale,
There was a monk, a fair man and a bold,
I trow a thirty winter he was old,
That ever-in-one[10] was drawing to that place.
This youngë monk, that was so fair of face,
Acquainted was so with this goodë man,
Since that their firstë knowledgë began,
That in his house as familiár was he
As it is possible any friend to be.
And, for as muchel as this goodë man,
And eke this monk of which that I began,
Were both the two y-born in one villáge,
The monk him claimed, as for cousinage,[11]
And he again him said not oncë nay,
But was as glad thereof as fowl of day;
For to his heart it was a great pleasánce.
Thus be they knit with etern' alliánce,
And each of them gan other to assure
Of brotherhood while that their life may dure.
Free was Dan[12] John, and namely[13] of dispence,
As in that house, and full of diligence
To do pleasánce, and also great costáge;[14]
He not forgot to give the leastë page
In all that house; but, after their degree,
He gave the lord, and sithen[15] his meinie,[16]
When that he came, some manner honest thing;
For which they were as glad of his comíng
As fowl is fain when that the sun upriseth.
No more of this as now, for it sufficeth.
  But so befell, this merchant on a day
Shope[17] him to makë ready his array
Toward the town of Bruges for to fare,
To buyë there a portión of ware;[18]
For which he hath to Paris sent anon
A messenger, and prayed hath Dan John
That he should come to Saint Denís, and play[19]
With him, and with his wife, a day or tway,
Ere he to Bruges went, in allë wise.
This noble monk, of which I you devise,[20]
Had of his abbot, as him list, licence,
(Because he was a man of high prudence,
And eke an officer out for to ride,
To see their granges and their barnës wide[21]);
And unto Saint Denis he came anon.
Who was so welcome as my lord Dan John,
Our dearë cousin, full of courtesy?
With him he brought a jub[22] of malvesie,[23]
And eke another full of fine vernage,[23]
And volatile,[24] as aye was his uságe:
And thus I let them eat, and drink, and play,
This merchant and this monk, a day or tway.
The thirdë day the merchant up ariseth,
And on his needës sadly him adviseth;[25]
And up into his countour-house[26] went he,
To reckon with himself as well may be,
Of thilkë[27] year, how that it with him stood,
And how that he dispended had his good,
And if that he increased were or non.
His bookës and his baggës many a one
He laid before him on his counting-board.
Full richë was his treasure and his hoard;
For which full fast his countour door he shet;
And eke he would that no man should him let[28]
Of his accountës, for the meanë time:
And thus he sat, till it was passed prime.
  Dan John was risen in the morn also,
And in the garden walked to and fro,
And had his thingës said full courteously.

1 Worthy. 2 Comment upon.
3 Tares, weeds; the "agrostemma githago" of Linnæus; perhaps named from the Anglo-Saxon, "ceocan," because it "chokes" the corn. 4 Belly.
5 Fond of society and merry-making.
6 Simple. 7 Always; or, however.
8 So in all the manuscripts; and from this and the following lines it may be inferred that Chaucer had intended to put the Tale into the mouth of a female speaker. 9 Resort of visitors. 10 Constantly.
11 Claimed cousinship, kindred, with him.
12 A title bestowed on priests and scholars; from "Dominus," like the Spanish, "Don."
13 Especially. 14 Liberal outlay. 15 Afterwards.
16 Household, servants. 17 Resolved, arranged.
18 Merchandise. Bruges was in Chaucer's time the great emporium of European commerce.
19 Enjoy himself. 20 Tell.
21 To inspect and manage the rural property of the monastery. 22 Jar.
23 Malvesie or Malmesy wine derived its name from Malvasia, a region of the Morea near Cape Malea, where it was made—as it also was on Chios and some other Greek islands. As to vernage, see note 21, p. 109.
24 Wild fowl, birds for the table; French, "volatille," "volaille." 25 Seriously deliberated on his affairs.
26 Counting-house; French, "comptoir."
27 That. 28 Detain from, hinder.

The good wife came walking full privily
Into the garden, where he walked soft,
And him saluted, as she had done oft;
A maiden child came in her companý,
Which as her list she might govérn and gie,[1]
For yet under the yardë[2] was the maid.
"O dearë cousin mine, Dan John," she said,
"What aileth you so rath[3] for to arise?"
"Niecë," quoth he, "it ought enough suffice
Five hourës for to sleep upon a night;
But[4] it were for an old appalled[5] wight,
As be these wedded men, that lie and dare,[6]
As in a formë sits a weary hare,
Allë forstraught[7] with houndës great and smale;
But, dearë niecë, why be ye so pale?
I trowë certes that our goodë man
Hath you laboúred, since this night began,
That you were need to restë hastily."
And with that word he laugh'd full merrily,
And of his owen thought he wax'd all red.
This fairë wife gan for to shake her head,
And saidë thus; "Yea, God wot all," quoth she.
"Nay, cousin mine, it stands not so with me;
For by that God, that gave me soul and life,
In all the realm of France is there no wife
That lessë lust hath to that sorry play;
For I may sing alas and well-away!
That I was born; but to no wight," quoth she,
"Dare I not tell how that it stands with me.
Wherefore I think out of this land to wend,
Or ellës of myself to make an end,
So full am I of dread and eke of care."
This monk began upon this wife to stare,
And said, "Alas! my niecë, God forbid
That ye for any sorrow, or any dread,
Fordo[8] yourself: but tellë me your grief,
Parâventure I may, in your mischíef,[9]
Counsel or help; and therefore tellë me
All your annoy, for it shall be secré.
For on my portos[10] here I make an oath,
That never in my life, for lief nor loth,[11]
Ne shall I of no counsel you bewray."
"The same again to you," quoth she, "I say.
By God and by this portos I you swear,
Though men me woulden all in pieces tear,
Ne shall I never, for[12] to go to hell,
Bewray one word of thing that ye me tell,
Not for no cousinage, nor alliânce,
But verily for love and affiânce."[13]
Thus be they sworn, and thereupon they kiss'd,
And each of them told other what them list.
"Cousin," quoth she, "if that I haddë space,
As I have none, and namely[14] in this place,
Then would I tell a legend of my life,
What I have suffer'd since I was a wife
With mine husbánd, all[15] be he your cousín.
"Nay," quoth this monk, "by God and Saint Martín,
He is no morë cousin unto me,
Than is the leaf that hangeth on the tree;
I call him so, by Saint Denis of France,
To have the morë cause of âcquaintânce
Of you, which I have loved specially
Aboven allë women sickerly,[16]
This swear I you on my professioún;[17]
Tell me your grief, lest that he come adown,
And hasten you, and go away anon."
"My dearë love," quoth she, "O my Dan John,
Full lief[18] were me this counsel for to hide,
But out it must, I may no more abide.
My husband is to me the worstë man
That ever was since that the world began;
But since I am a wife, it sits[19] not me
To tellë no wight of our privity,
Neither in bed, nor in none other place;
God shield[20] I shouldë tell it for his grace;
A wifë shall not say of her husbánd
But all honoúr, as I can understand;
Save unto you thus much I tellë shall;
As help me God, he is nought worth at all,
In no degree, the value of a fly.
But yet me grieveth most his niggardý.[21]
And well ye wot, that women naturally
Desirë thingës six, as well as I.
They wouldë that their husbands shouldë be
Hardy,[22] and wise, and rich, and thereto free,
And buxom[23] to his wife, and fresh in bed.
But, by that ilkë[24] Lord that for us bled,
For his honoúr myself for to array,
On Sunday next I mustë needës pay
A hundred francs, or ellës am I lorn.[25]
Yet were me lever[26] that I were unborn,
Thân me were done slander or villainý.
And if mine husband eke might it espy,
I were but lost; and therefore I you pray,
Lend me this sum, or ellës must I dey.[27]
Dan John, I say, lend me these hundred francs;
Pardie, I will not failë you, my thanks,[28]
If that you list to do that I you pray;
For at a certain day I will you pay,
And do to you what pleasance and servíce
That I may do, right as you list devise.
And but[4] I do, God take on me vengeânce,
As foul as e'er had Ganilion[29] of France."
This gentle monk answér'd in this mannére;
"Now truëly, mine owen lady dear,
I have," quoth he, "on you so greatë ruth,[30]
That I you swear, and plightë you my truth,
That when your husband is to Flanders fare,[31]
I will deliver you out of this care,
For I will bringë you a hundred francs."
And with that word he caught her by the flanks,

1 Guide.
2 Rod; in pupillage; a phrase properly used of children, but employed by the Clerk in the prologue to his tale. See note 4, page 93.
3 Early.
4 Unless.
5 Pallid, wasted.
6 Stare.
7 Distracted, confounded.
8 Ruin.
9 Distress.
10 Breviary.
11 Willing or unwilling.
12 Though the alternative should be.
13 Confidence, promise.
14 Especially.
15 Although.
16 Assuredly.
17 By my vows of religion.
18 Pleasant.
19 Becomes.
20 Forbid.
21 Stinginess.
22 Brave.
23 Yielding, obedient.
24 Same.
25 Ruined, undone.
26 I would rather.
27 Die.
28 With my good-will; if I can help it.
29 Genelon, Ganelon, or Ganilion; one of Charlemagne's officers, whose treachery was the cause of the disastrous defeat of the Christians by the Saracens at Roncevalles; he was torn to pieces by four horses.
30 Pity.
31 Gone.

And her embraced hard, and kiss'd her oft.
"Go now your way," quoth he, "all still and soft,
And let us dine as soon as that ye may,
For by my calendar 'tis prime of day;
Go now, and be as true as I shall be."
"Now ellës God forbiddë, Sir," quoth she;
And forth she went, as jolly as a pie,
And bade the cookës that they should them hie,[1]
So that men mightë dine, and that anon.
Up to her husband is this wifë gone,
And knocked at his contour boldëly.
"*Qui est la?*"[2] quoth he. "Peter! it am I,"
Quoth she; "What, Sir, how longë will ye fast?
How longë time will ye reckon and cast
Your summës, and your bookës, and your things?
The devil have part of all such reckonings!
Ye have enough, pardie, of Goddë's sond.[3]
Come down to-day, and let your baggës stond.
Ne be ye not ashamed, that Dan John
Shall fasting all this day elengë[4] gon?
What? let us hear a mass, and go we dine."
"Wife," quoth this man, "little canst thou divine
The curious businessë that we have;
For of us chapmen, all so God me save,
And by that lord that cleped is Saint Ive,
Scarcely amongës twenty, ten shall thrive
Continually, lasting unto our age.
We may well makë cheer and good viságe,
And drivë forth the world as it may be,
And keepen our estate in privity,
Till we be dead, or ellës that we play
A pilgrimage, or go out of the way.
And therefore have I great necessity
Upon this quaint[5] world to advisë[6] me.
For evermorë must we stand in dread
Of hap and fortune in our chapmanhead.[7]
To Flanders will I go to-morrow at day,
And come again as soon as e'er I may:
For which, my dearë wife, I thee beseek
As be to every wight buxom[8] and meek,
And for to keep our good be curious,
And honestly governë well our house.
Thou hast enough, in every manner wise,
That to a thrifty household may suffice.
Thee lacketh none array, nor no vitail;
Of silver in thy purse thou shalt not fail."
And with that word his contour door he shet,[9]
And down he went; no longer would he let;[10]
And hastily a mass was therë said,
And speedily the tables werë laid,
And to the dinner fastë they them sped,
And richëly this monk the chapman fed.
And after dinner Dan John soberly
This chapman took apart, and privily
He said him thus: "Cousin, it standeth so,
That, well I see, to Bruges ye will go;
God and Saint Austin speedë you and guide.
I pray you, cousin, wisely that ye ride:
Governë you also of your diét
Attemperly,[11] and namely[12] in this heat.
Betwixt us two needeth no strangë fare;[13]
Farewell, cousín, God shieldë you from care.
If any thing there be, by day or night,
If it lie in my power and my might,
That ye me will command in any wise,
It shall be done, right as ye will devise.
But one thing ere ye go, if it may be;
I wouldë pray you for to lend to me
A hundred frankës, for a week or twy,
For certain beastës that I mustë buy,
To storë with[14] a placë that is ours
(God help me so, I would that it were yours);
I shall not failë surely of my day,
Not for a thousand francs, a milë way.
But let this thing be secret, I you pray;
For yet to-night these beastës must I buy.
And fare now well, mine owen cousin dear;
Grand mercy[15] of your cost and of your cheer."
This noble merchant gentilly[16] anon
Answér'd and said, "O cousin mine, Dan John,
Now sickerly this is a small request:
My gold is yourës, when that it you lest,
And not only my gold, but my chaffare;[17]
Take what you list, God shieldë that ye spare.[18]
But one thing is, ye know it well enow
Of chapmen, that their money is their plough.
We may creancë[19] while we have a name,
But goldless for to be it is no game.
Pay it again when it lies in your ease;
After my might full fain would I you please."
These hundred frankës set he forth anon,
And privily he took them to Dan John;
No wight in all this world wist of this loan,
Saving the merchant and Dan John alone.
They drink, and speak, and roam a while, and play,
Till that Dan John rode unto his abbay.
The morrow came, and forth this merchant rideth
To Flanders-ward, his prentice well him guideth,
Till he came unto Bruges merrily.
Now went this merchant fast and busily
About his need, and buyed and creanced;
He neither played at the dice, nor danced;
But as a merchant, shortly for to tell,
He led his life; and there I let him dwell.
The Sunday next[20] the merchant was y-gone,
To Saint Denís y-comen is Dan John,
With crown and beard all fresh and newly shave.
In all the house was not so little a knave,[21]
Nor no wight ellës, that was not full fain
For that my lord Dan John was come again.
And, shortly to the point right for to gon,
This fairë wife accorded with Dan John,
That for these hundred francs he should all night

1 Haste. 2 Who is there? 3 Sending, gifts.
4 From French, "eloigner," to remove; it may mean either the lonely, cheerless condition of the priest, or the strange behaviour of the merchant in leaving him to himself. 5 Strange. 6 Consider.
7 Trading. 8 Civil, courteous. 9 Shut.
10 Hinder, delay. 11 Moderately.
12 Particularly. 13 Ado, ceremony.
14 With which to store. 15 Great thanks.
16 Handsomely, like a gentleman.
17 Merchandise.
18 God forbid that you should take too little.
19 Obtain credit; French, "créance," credit.
20 After. 21 Servant-boy.

Havë her in his armës bolt upright;
And this accord performed was in deed.
In mirth all night a busy life they lead,
Till it was day, that Dan John went his way,
And bade the meinie[1] "Farewell; have good day."
For none of them, nor no wight in the town,
Had of Dan John right no suspicioún;
And forth he rodë home to his abbay,
Or where him list; no more of him I say.
The merchant, when that ended was the fair,
To Saint Denís he gan for to repair,
And with his wife he madë feast and cheer,
And toldë her that chaffare[2] was so dear,
That needës must he make a chevisance;[3]
For he was bound in a recognisance
To payë twenty thousand shields[4] anon.
For which this merchant is to Paris gone,
To borrow of certain friendës that he had
A certain francs, and some with him he lad.[5]
And when that he was come into the town,
For great cherté[6] and great affectioún
Unto Dan John he wentë first to play;
Not for to borrow of him no monéy,
But for to weet[7] and see of his welfare,
And for to tellë him of his chaffare,
As friendës do, when they be met in fere.[8]
Dan John him madë feast and merry cheer;
And he him told again full specially,
How he had well y-bought and graciously
(Thanked be God) all whole his merchandise;
Save that he must, in allë manner wise,
Maken a chevisance, as for his best;
And then he shouldë be in joy and rest.
Dan John answered, "Certes, I am fain[9]
That ye in health be comë home again:
And if that I were rich, as have I bliss,
Of twenty thousand shields should ye not miss,
For ye so kindëly the other day
Lentë me gold, and as I can and may
I thankë you, by God and by Saint Jame.
But natheless I took unto our Dame,
Your wife at home, the samë gold again,
Upon your bench; she wot it well, certáin,
By certain tokens that I can her tell.
Now, by your leave, I may no longer dwell;
Our abbot will out of this town anon,
And in his company I mustë gon.
Greet well our Dame, mine owen niecë sweet,
And farewell, dearë cousin, till we meet."
This merchant, which that was full ware and wise,
Creanced hath, and paid eke in París
To certain Lombards ready in their hond
The sum of gold, and got of them his bond,
And home he went, merry as a popinjay.
For well he knew he stood in such array
That needës must he win in that voyáge[10]
A thousand francs, above all his costáge.[11]
His wife full ready met him at the gate,
As she was wont of old uságe algate;[12]
And all that night in mirthë they beset;[13]
For he was rich, and clearly out of debt.
When it was day, the merchant gan embrace
His wife all new, and kiss'd her in her face,
And up he went, and maked it full tough.
"No more," quoth she, "by God ye have enough;"
And wantonly again with him she play'd,
Till at the last this merchant to her said.
"By God," quoth he, "I am a little wroth
With you, my wife, although it be me loth;
And wot ye why? by God, as that I guess,
That ye have made a manner strangëness[14]
Betwixtë me and my cousín, Dan John.
Ye should have warned me, ere I had gone,
That he you had a hundred frankës paid
By ready token; he held him evil apaid[15]
For that I to him spake of chevisance,[16]
(Me seemed so as by his countenance);
But natheless, by God of heaven king,
I thoughtë not to ask of him no thing.
I pray thee, wife, do thou no morë so.
Tell me alway, ere that I from thee go,
If any debtor hath in mine absénce
Y-payed thee, lest through thy negligence
I might him ask a thing that he hath paid."
This wife was not afeared nor afraid,
But boldëly she said, and that anon;
"Mary! I defy that falsë monk Dan John,
I keep[17] not of his tokens never a deal:[18]
He took me certain gold, I wot it well.—
What? evil thedom[19] on his monkë's snout!—
For, God it wot, I ween'd withoutë doubt
That he had given it me, because of you,
To do therewith mine honour and my prow,[20]
For cousinage, and eke for *bellë* cheer
That he hath had full oftentimë here.
But since I see I stand in such disjoint,[21]
I will answér you shortly to the point.
Ye have more slackë debtors than am I;
For I will pay you well and readily,
From day to day, and if so be I fail,
I am your wife, score it upon my tail,
And I shall pay as soon as ever I may.
For, by my troth, I have on mine array,
And not in waste, bestow'd it every deal.
And, for I have bestowed it so well,
For your honoúr, for Goddë's sake I say,
As be not wroth, but let us laugh and play.
Ye shall my jolly body have to wed;[22]
By God, I will not pay you but in bed;
Forgive it me, mine owen spousë dear;
Turn hitherward, and makë better cheer."
The merchant saw none other remedy;
And for to chide, it were but a follý,
Since that the thing might not amended be.
"Now, wife," he said, "and I forgive it thee;
But by thy lifë be no more so large;[23]

1 Servants. 2 Merchandise.
3 Raise money by means of a borrowing agreement; from French, "achever," to finish; the general meaning of the word is a bargain, an agreement.
4 Crowns; French, "écu." 5 Took.
6 Love. 7 Know. 8 Company. 9 Glad.
10 By his journey to Bruges. 11 Expenses.
12 Always. 13 Spent.
14 A kind of estrangement, coolness.
15 Was displeased. 16 Borrowing.
17 Care. 18 Whit.
19 Thriving, success; from the verb "thé," thrive.
20 Profit, advantage. 21 Danger, awkward position.
22 In pledge. 23 Liberal, lavish.

Keep better my good, this give I thee in charge."
Thus endeth now my tale ; and God us send
Taling enough, unto our livës' end!

THE PRIORESS'S TALE.

THE PROLOGUE.

"WELL said, by *corpus Domini*," quoth our Host;
"Now longë may'st thou sailë by the coast,
Thou gentle Master, gentle Marinére.
God give the monk a thousand last quad year! [1]
Aha! fellows, beware of such a jape.[2]
The monk put in the mannë's hood an ape,[3]
And in his wifë's eke, by Saint Austin.
Drawë no monkës more into your inn.
But now pass over, and let us seek about,
Who shall now tellë first of all this rout
Another tale;" and with that word he said,
As courteously as it had been a maid;
"My Lady Prioressë, by your leave,
So that I wist I shouldë you not grieve,[4]
I wouldë deemë [5] that ye tellë should
A talë next, if so were that ye would.
Now will ye vouchësafe, my lady dear?"
"Gladly," quoth she; and said as ye shall hear.

THE TALE.[6]

O Lord our Lord! thy name how marvellous
Is in this largë world y-spread![7] (quoth she)
For not only thy laudë [8] precious
Performed is by men of high degree,
But by the mouth of children thy bounté
Performed is, for on the breast sucking
Sometimës showë they thy herying.[9]

Wherefore in laud, as I best can or may
Of thee, and of the whitë lily flow'r
Which that thee bare, and is a maid alway,
To tell a story I will do my labour;
Not that I may increasë her honour,
For she herselven is honour and root
Of bounté,[10] next her son, and soulës' boot.[11]

O mother maid, O maid and mother free![12]
O bush unburnt, burning in Moses' sight,
That ravished'st down from the deity,
Through thy humbless, the ghost that in thee light;[13]
Of whose virtúe, when he thine heartë light,[14]
Conceived was the Father's sapience;
Help me to tell it to thy reverence.

Lady! thy bounty, thy magnificence,
Thy virtue, and thy great humility,
There may no tongue express in no science:
For sometimes, Lady! ere men pray to thee,
Thou go'st before, of thy benignity,
And gettest us the light, through thy prayére,
To guiden us unto thy son so dear.

My conning [15] is so weak, O blissful queen,
For to declarë thy great worthiness,
That I not may the weight of it sustene;
But as a child of twelvemonth old, or less,
That can unnethës [16] any word express,
Right so fare I; and therefore, I you pray,
Guidë my song that I shall of you say.

There was in Asia, in a great citý,
Amongës Christian folk, a Jewery,[17]
Sustained by a lord of that countrý,
For foul usure, and lucre of villainy,
Hateful to Christ, and to his company;
And through the street men mightë ride and wend,[18]
For it was free, and open at each end.

A little school of Christian folk there stood
Down at the farther end, in which there were
Children an heap y-come of Christian blood,
That learned in that schoolë year by year
Such manner doctrine as men used there;
This is to say, to singen and to read,
As smallë children do in their childhead.

Among these children was a widow's son,
A little clergion,[19] seven year of age,
That day by day to scholay was his won,[20]
And eke also, whereso he saw th' imáge
Of Christë's mother, had he in uságe,
As him was taught, to kneel adown, and say
Ave Maria, as he went by the way.

Thus had this widow her little son y-taught
Our blissful Lady, Christë's mother dear,
To worship aye, and he forgot it not;
For sely [21] child will always soonë lear.[22]
But aye when I remember on this mattére,
Saint Nicholas [23] stands ever in my presence;
For he so young to Christ did reverence.

This little child his little book learníng,
As he sat in the school at his primére,

1 Ever so much evil. "Last" means a load, "quad," bad (see note 21, page 59); and literally we may read "a thousand weight of bad years." The Italians use "mal anno" in the same sense.
2 Trick.
3 To put an ape in one's hood, on one's head, is to befool or deceive him.
4 Offend. 5 Judge, decide.
6 Tales of the murder of children by Jews were frequent in the Middle Ages, being probably designed to keep up the bitter feeling of the Christians against the Jews. Not a few children were canonised on this account; and the scene of the misdeeds was laid anywhere and everywhere, so that Chaucer could be at no loss for material.
7 Psalms viii. 1, "Domine, dominus noster, quàm admirabile est nomen tuum in universâ terrâ.".
8 Praise.
9 Glory. "Out of the mouths of babes and sucklings hast Thou ordained strength" (Ps. viii. 2).
10 Goodness. 11 Help. 12 Bounteous.
13 The spirit that on thee alighted; the Holy Ghost through whose power Christ was conceived.
14 Lightened, gladdened.
15 Skill, ability. 16 Scarcely.
17 A quarter which the Jews were permitted to inhabit; the Old Jewry in London got its name in this way. 18 Go, walk. 19 A young clerk or scholar.
20 To study, go to school, was his wont.
21 Simple, innocent. 22 Learn.
23 Who, even in his swaddling clothes—so says the "Breviarium Romanum"—gave promise of extraordinary virtue and holiness; for, though he sucked freely on other days, on Wednesdays and Fridays he applied to the breast only once, and that not until the evening.

He *Alma redemptoris*[1] heardë sing,
As children learned their antiphonere;[2]
And as he durst, he drew him nere and nere,[3]
And hearken'd aye the wordës and the note,
Till he the firstë verse knew all by rote.

Nought wist he what this Latin was to say,[4]
For he so young and tender was of age;
But on a day his fellow gan he pray
To éxpound him this song in his languáge,
Or tell him why this song was in uságe:
This pray'd he him to construe and declare,
Full oftentime upon his kneës bare.

His fellow, which that elder was than he,
Answér'd him thus: "This song, I have heard say,
Was maked of our blissful Lady free,
Her to salute, and ekë her to pray
To be our help and succour when we dey.[5]
I can no more expound in this mattére:
I learnë song, I know but small grammére."

"And is this song y-made in reverence
Of Christë's mother?" said this innocent;
Now certes I will do my diligence
To conne[6] it all, ere Christëmas be went;
Though that I for my primer shall be shent,[7]
And shall be beaten thriës in an hour,
I will it conne, our Lady to honoúr."

His fellow taught him homeward[8] privily
From day to day, till he coud[9] it by rote,
And then he sang it well and boldëly
From word to word according with the note;
Twice in a day it passed through his throat;
To schoolë-ward, and homeward when he went;
On Christ's mother was set all his intent.

As I have said, throughout the Jewery,
This little child, as he came to and fro,
Full merrily then would he sing and cry,
O Alma redemptoris, evermo';
The sweetness hath his heartë pierced so
Of Christë's mother, that to her to pray
He cannot stint[10] of singing by the way.

Our firstë foe, the serpent Satanas,
That hath in Jewës' heart his waspë's nest,
Upswell'd and said, "O Hebrew people, alas!
Is this to you a thing that is honést,[11]
That such a boy shall walken as him lest
In your despite, and sing of such senténce,
Which is against your lawë's reverence?"

From thencëforth the Jewës have conspired
This innocent out of the world to chase;
A homicidë thereto have they hired,
That in an alley had a privy place,
And, as the child gan forth by for to pace,
This cursed Jew him hent,[12] and held him fast,
And cut his throat, and in a pit him cast.

I say that in a wardrobe[13] they him threw,
Where as the Jewës purged their entrail.
O cursed folk! O Herodës all new!
What may your evil intentë you avail?
Murder will out, certáin it will not fail,
And namely[14] where th' honoúr of God shall spread;
The blood out crieth on your cursed deed.

O martyr souded[15] to virginity,
Now may'st thou sing, and follow ever-in-one[16]
The whitë Lamb celestial (quoth she),
Of which the great Evangelist Saint John
In Patmos wrote, which saith that they that gon
Before this Lamb, and sing a song all new,
That never fleshly woman they ne knew.[17]

This poorë widow waited all that night
After her little child, but he came not;
For which, as soon as it was dayë's light,
With facë pale, in dread and busy thought,
She hath at school and ellëswhere him sought,
Till finally she gan so far espy,
That he was last seen in the Jewerý.

With mother's pity in her breast enclosed,
She went, as she were half out of her mind,
To every placë, where she hath supposed
By likelihood her little child to find:
And ever on Christ's mother meek and kind
She cried, and at the lastë thus she wrought,
Among the cursed Jewës she him sought.

She freined,[18] and she prayed piteously
To every Jew that dwelled in that place,
To tell her, if her childë went thereby;
They saidë, "Nay;" but Jesus of his grace
Gave in her thought, within a little space,
That in that place after her son she cried,
Where he was cast into a pit beside.

O greatë God, that pérformest thy laud
By mouth of innocents, lo here thy might!
This gem of chastity, this emeraud,[19]
And eke of martyrdom the ruby bright,
Where he with throat y-carven[20] lay upright,
He *Alma redemptoris* gan to sing
So loud, that all the place began to ring.

The Christian folk, that through the streetë went,
In camë, for to wonder on this thing:
And hastily they for the provost sent.
He came anon withoutë tarrying,
And heried[21] Christ, that is of heaven king,
And eke his mother, honour of mankind;
And after that the Jewës let[22] he bind.

With torment, and with shameful death each one
The provost did[22] these Jewës for to sterve[23]
That of this murder wist, and that anon;
He wouldë no such cursedness observe;[24]
Evil shall have, that evil will deserve;
Therefore with horses wild he did them draw,
And after that he hung them by the law.

The child, with piteous lamentatión,

1 "O Alma Redemptoris Mater;" the beginning of a hymn to the Virgin.
2 Book of anthems, or psalms, chanted in the choir by alternate verses. 3 Nearer. 4 Meant.
5 Die. 6 Learn; con.
7 Disgraced. 8 On the way home.
9 Knew. 10 Cease.
11 Creditable, becoming. 12 Seized.
13 French, "garderobe," a privy. 14 Especially.
15 Confirmed; from French, "soulde;" Latin, "solidatus." 16 Continually. 17 See Revelations xiv. 3, 4.
18 Asked, inquired; from Anglo-Saxon, "frinan," "frægnian." Compare German, "fragen."
19 Emerald. 20 Cut. 21 Praised.
22 Caused. 23 Die.
24 Countenance, overlook.

Was taken up, singing his song alway:
And with honoúr and great processión,
They carry him unto the next abbay.
His mother swooning by the bierë lay;
Unnethës [1] might the people that were there
This newë Rachel bringë from his bier.

Upon his bierë lay this innocent
Before the altar while the massë last'; [2]
And, after that, th' abbót with his convént
Have sped them for to bury him full fast;
And when they holy water on him cast,
Yet spake this child, when sprinkled was the water,
And sang, *O Alma redemptoris mater!*

This abbot, which that was a holy man,
As monkës be, or ellës ought to be,
This youngë child to conjure he began,
And said; "O dearë child! I halsë [3] thee,
In virtue of the holy Trinity;
Tell me what is thy causë for to sing,
Since that thy throat is cut, to my seeming."

"My throat is cut unto my neckë-bone,"
Saidë this child, "and, as by way of kind, [4]
I should have diëd, yea long time agone;
But Jesus Christ, as ye in bookës find,
Will that his glory last and be in mind;
And, for the worship [5] of his mother dear,
Yet may I sing *O Alma* loud and clear.

"This well [6] of mercy, Christë's mother sweet,
I loved alway, after my conning: [7]
And when that I my lifë should forlete, [8]
To me she came, and bade me for to sing
This anthem verily in my dying,
As ye have heard; and, when that I had sung,
Me thought she laid a grain upon my tongue.

"Wherefore I sing, and sing I must certáin,
In honour of that blissful maiden free,
Till from my tongue off taken is the grain.
And after that thus saidë she to me;
'My little child, then will I fetchë thee,
When that the grain is from thy tonguë take:
Be not aghast, [9] I will thee not forsake.'"

This holy monk, this abbot him mean I,
His tongue out caught, and took away the grain;
And he gave up the ghost full softëly.
And when this abbot had this wonder seen,
His saltë tearës trickled down as rain:
And groff [10] he fell all flat upon the ground,
And still he lay, as he had been y-bound.

The convent [11] lay eke on the pavëment
Weeping, and herying [12] Christ's mother dear.
And after that they rose, and forth they went,
And took away this martyr from his bier,
And in a tomb of marble stonës clear
Enclosed they his little body sweet;
Where he is now, God lene [13] us for to meet.

O youngë Hugh of Lincoln! [14] slain also
With cursed Jewës,—as it is notáble,
For it is but a little while ago,—
Pray eke for us, we sinful folk unstable,
That, of his mercy, God so merciáble [15]
On us his greatë mercy multiply,
For reverence of his mother Marý.

CHAUCER'S TALE OF SIR THOPAS.

THE PROLOGUE. [16]

When said was this miràcle, every man
As sober [17] was, that wonder was to see,
Till that our Host to japen [18] he began,
And then at erst [19] he looked upon me,
And saidë thus; "What man art thou?" quoth he;
"Thou lookest as thou wouldest find an hare,
For ever on the ground I see thee stare.

"Approachë near, and look up merrily.
Now ware you, Sirs, and let this man have place.
He in the waist is shapen as well as I; [20]
This were a puppet in an arm t' embrace
For any woman small and fair of face.
He seemeth elvish [21] by his countenánce,
For unto no wight doth he dalliánce.

"Say now somewhat, since other folk have said;
Tell us a tale of mirth, and that anon."
"Hostë," quoth I, "be not evil apaid, [22]
For other talë certes can [23] I none,
But of a rhyme I learned yore [24] agone."
"Yea, that is good," quoth he; "now shall we hear
Some dainty thing, me thinketh by thy cheer." [25]

THE TALE. [26]

Listen, lordings, in good intent,
And I will tell you *verament* [27]
Of mirth and of solas, [28]
All of a knight was fair and gent, [29]

1 Scarcely. 2 Lasted.
3 Embrace or salute; implore; from Anglo-Saxon, "hals," the neck. 4 In course of nature.
5 Glory. 6 Fountain. 7 Knowledge.
8 Leave. 9 Afraid.
10 Prostrate. See note 3, page 27.
11 The monks that composed the convent. See note 23, page 92. 12 Praising. 13 Grant; lend.
14 A boy said to have been slain by the Jews at Lincoln in 1255, according to Matthew Paris. Many popular ballads were made about the event, which the diligence of the Church doubtless kept fresh in mind at Chaucer's day. 15 Merciful.
16 This Prologue is interesting, for the picture which it gives of Chaucer himself; riding apart from and indifferent to the rest of the pilgrims, with eyes fixed on the ground, and an "elvish," morose, or rather self-absorbed air; portly, if not actually stout, in body; and evidently a man out of the common, as the closing words of the Host imply. 17 Serious.
18 Talk lightly. 19 For the first time.
20 Referring to the poet's corpulency.
21 Surly, morose. 22 Dissatisfied. 23 Know.
24 Long. 25 Expression, mien.
26 "The Rhyme of Sir Thopas," as it is generally called, is introduced by Chaucer as a satire on the dull, pompous, and prolix metrical romances then in vogue. It is full of phrases taken from the popular rhymesters in the vein which he holds up to ridicule; if, indeed—though of that there is no evidence—it be not actually part of an old romance which Chaucer selected and reproduced to point his assault on the prevailing taste in literature. 27 Truly.
28 Delight, solace. 29 Gentle.

In battle and in tournament,
His name was Sir Thopas.
Y-born he was in far countrý,
In Flanders, all beyond the sea,
At Popering[1] in the place;
His father was a man full free,
And lord he was of that countrý,
As it was Goddë's grace.
Sir Thopas was a doughty swain,
White was his face as paindemain,[2]
His lippës red as rose.
His rode[3] is like scarlét in grain,
And I you tell in good certáin
He had a seemly nose.
His hair, his beard, was like saffroún,
That to his girdle reach'd adown,
His shoes of cordëwane;[4]
Of Bruges were his hosen brown;
His robë was of ciclatoún,[5]
That costë many a jane.[6]
He couldë hunt at the wild deer,
And ride on hawking for rivére[7]
With gray goshawk on hand:
Thereto he was a good archére,
Of wrestling was there none his peer,
Where any ram[8] should stand.
Full many a maiden bright in bow'r
They mourned for him *par amour*,
When them were better sleep;
But he was chaste, and no lechoúr,
And sweet as is the bramble flow'r
That beareth the red heep.[9]
And so it fell upon a day,
For sooth as I you tellë may,
Sir Thopas would out ride;
He worth[10] upon his steedë gray,
And in his hand a launcëgay,[11]
A long sword by his side.
He pricked through a fair forést,
Wherein is many a wildë beast,
Yea, bothë buck and hare;
And as he pricked north and east,
I tell it you, him had almest
Betid[12] a sorry care.
There sprangë herbës great and small,
The liquorice and the setëwall,[13]
And many a clove-gilofre,[14]
And nutëmeg to put in ale,
Whether it be moist[15] or stale,
Or for to lay in coffer.
The birdës sang, it is no nay,
The sperhawk[16] and the popinjay,
That joy it was to hear;
The throstle-cock made eke his lay,
The woodë-dove upon the spray
She sang full loud and clear.
Sir Thopas fell in love-longíng
All when he heard the throstle sing,
And prick'd as he were wood;[17]
His fairë steed in his pricking
So sweated, that men might him wring,
His sidës were all blood.
Sir Thopas eke so weary was
For pricking on the softë grass,
So fierce was his coráge,[18]
That down he laid him in that place,
To makë his steed some solace,
And gave him good foráge.
"Ah, Saint Marý, *ben'dicite*,
What aileth thilkë[19] love at me
To bindë me so sore?
Me dreamed all this night, pardie,
An elf-queen shall my leman[20] be,
And sleep under my gore.[21]
An elf-queen will I love, y-wis,[22]
For in this world no woman is
Worthy to be my make
In town;
All other women I forsake,
And to an elf-queen I me take
By dale and eke by down."
Into his saddle he clomb anon,
And pricked over stile and stone
An elf-queen for to spy,
Till he so long had ridden and gone,
That he found in a privy wonne[23]
The country of Faerý,
So wild;
For in that country was there none
That to him durstë ride or gon,
Neither wife nor child.
Till that there came a great giaunt,
His namë was Sir Oliphaunt,[24]
A perilous man of deed;
He saidë, "Child,[25] by Termagaunt,[26]
But if[27] thou prick out of mine haunt,
Anon I slay thy steed
With mace.
Here is the Queen of Faëry,
With harp, and pipe, and symphony,
Dwelling in this place."
The Child said, "All so may I thé,[28]
To-morrow will I meetë thee,
When I have mine armór;

1 Poppering, or Poppeling, a parish in the marches of Calais, of which the famous antiquary Leland was once Rector.

2 Either "pain de matin," morning bread; or "pain de Maine," because it was made best in that province; a kind of fine white bread.

3 Or "rudde;" complexion.

4 Cordovan; fine Spanish leather, so called from the name of the city where it was prepared.

5 A rich Oriental stuff of silk and gold, of which was made the circular robe of state called a "ciclaton," from the Latin, "cyclas." The word is French.

6 A Genoese coin, of small value; in our old statutes called "gallihalpens," or galley half-pence.

7 For river-fowl. See note 17, page 79.

8 The usual prize of wrestling contests. See note 8, page 23.

9 Fruit of the dog-rose, hip.

10 Mounted.

11 Spear; "azagay" is the name of a Moorish weapon, and the identity of termination is singular.

12 Befallen.

13 Valerian.

14 Clove-gilliflower; "caryophyllus hortensis."

15 New. See note 9, page 22.

16 Sparrowhawk.

17 Mad.

18 Inclination, spirit.

19 This.

20 Mistress.

21 Shirt, garment.

22 Assuredly.

23 Haunt.

24 Literally, "Sir Elephant;" Sir John Mandeville calls those animals "Olyfauntes."

25 Young man.

26 A pagan or Saracen deity, otherwise named Tervagan, and often mentioned in Middle Age literature. His name has passed into our language, to denote a ranter or blusterer, as he was represented to be.

27 Unless.

28 Thrive.

And yet I hopë, *par ma fay*,
That thou shalt with this launcëgay
Abyen[1] it full sore;
Thy maw[2]
Shall I pierce, if I may,
Ere it be fully prime of day,
For here thou shalt be slaw."[3]
Sir Thopas drew aback full fast;
This giant at him stonës cast
Out of a fell staff sling:
But fair escaped Child Thopas,
And all it was through Goddë's grace,
And through his fair bearíng.
Yet listen, lordings, to my tale,
Merrier than the nightingale,
For now I will you rown,[4]
How Sir Thopas, with sidës smale,
Pricking over hill and dale,
Is come again to town.
His merry men commanded he
To makë him both game and glee;
For needës must he fight
With a giánt with headës three,
For paramour and jollity
Of one that shone full bright.
"Do[5] come," he saidë, "my minstrâles
And gestours[6] for to tellë tales
Anon in mine armíng,
Of rómances that be royáls,[7]
Of popës and of cardinals,
And eke of love-longíng."
They fetch'd him first the sweetë wine,
And mead eke in a maseline,[8]
And royal spicery;
Of ginger-bread that was full fine,
And liquorice and eke cumin,
With sugar that is trie.[9]
He diddë,[10] next his whitë lere,[11]
Of cloth of lakë[12] fine and clear,
A breech and eke a shirt;
And next his shirt an haketon,[13]
And over that an habergeon,[14]
For piercing of his heart;
And over that a fine hauberk,[15]
Was all y-wrought of Jewës'[16] werk,
Full strong it was of plate;
And over that his coat-armoúr,[17]
As white as is the lily flow'r,
In which he would debate.[18]
His shield was all of gold so red,
And therein was a boarë's head,
A charboucle[19] beside;
And there he swore on ale and bread,
How that the giant should be dead,
Betide whatso betide.
His jambeaux[20] were of cuirbouly,[21]
His swordë's sheath of ivory,
His helm of latoun[22] bright,
His saddle was of rewel[23] bone,
His bridle as the sunnë shone,
Or as the moonëlight.
His spearë was of fine cypress,
That bodeth war, and nothing peace;
The head full sharp y-ground.
His steedë was all dapple gray,
It went an amble in the way
Full softëly and round
In land.
Lo, Lordës mine, here is a fytt;[24]
If ye will any more of it,
To tell it will I fand.[25]

Now hold your mouth for charity,
Bothë knight and lady free,
And hearken to my spell;[26]
Of battle and of chivalry,
Of ladies' love and druerie,[27]
Anon I will you tell.
Men speak of rómances of price[28]
Of Horn Child, and of Ipotis,
Of Bevis, and Sir Guy,[29]
Of Sir Libeux,[30] and Pleindamour,
But Sir Thopas, he bears the flow'r
Of royal chivalry.
His goodë steed he all bestrode,
And forth upon his way he glode,[31]
As sparkle out of brand;[32]
Upon his crest he bare a tow'r,
And therein stick'd a lily flow'r;
God shield his corse from shand![33]
And, for he was a knight auntroús,[34]
He wouldë sleepen in none house,
But liggen[35] in his hood,
His brightë helm was his wangér,[36]
And by him baited his destrér[37]
Of herbës fine and good.
Himself drank water of the well,
As did the knight Sir Percivel,[38]
So worthy under weed;
Till on a day —— . . . . . .

1 Suffer for. 2 Belly. 3 Slain. 4 Whisper. 5 Cause.
6 Tellers of tales of adventure and chivalry.
7 So called because they related to Charlemagne and his family. 8 Drinking-bowl of maple.
9 Tried, refined. 10 Put on, donned.
11 Skin. 12 Fine lawn. 13 Cassock.
14 Sleeves and gorget of mail. 15 Plate-armour.
16 Magicians'. 17 Knight's surcoat. 18 Fight.
19 Carbuncle; French, "escarboucle;" a heraldic device.
20 Boots; from French, "jambe," the leg.
21 "Cuir bouilli," French, boiled or prepared leather; also used to cover shields, &c.
22 Brass, or latten.
23 No satisfactory explanation has been furnished of this word, used to describe some material from which rich saddles were made.
24 Division of a metrical romance. 25 Try.
26 Tale, discourse; from Anglo-Saxon, "spellian," to declare, tell a story.
27 Gallantry. 28 Worth, esteem.
29 Sir Bevis of Hampton, and Sir Guy of Warwick, two knights of great renown.
30 One of Arthur's knights, called "Ly beau desconus," "the fair unknown."
31 Glowed, shone, as he rode. 32 Torch.
33 Harm. 34 Adventurous. 35 Lie.
36 Pillow; from Anglo-Saxon, "wangere," because the "wanges;" or cheeks, rested on it.
37 "Destrier," French, a war-horse; in Latin, "dextrarius," as if led by the right hand.
38 Sir Percival de Galis, whose adventures were written in more than 60,000 verses by Chrétien de Troyes, one of the oldest and best French romancers, in 1191.

CHAUCER'S TALE OF MELIBŒUS.

THE PROLOGUE.

"No more of this, for Goddë's dignity!"
Quoth ourë Hostë; "for thou makest me
So weary of thy very lewëdness,[1]
That, all so wisly[2] God my soulë bless,
Mine earës achë for thy drafty[3] speech.
Now such a rhyme the devil I beteche:[4]
This may well be rhyme doggerel," quoth he.
"Why so?" quoth I; "why wilt thou lettë[5] me
More of my tale than any other man,
Since that it is the best rhyme that I can?"
"By God!" quoth he, "for, plainly at one word,
Thy drafty rhyming is not worth a tord:
Thou dost naught ellës but dispendest[6] time.
Sir, at one word, thou shalt no longer rhyme.
Let see whe'er[7] thou canst tellen aught in gest,[8]
Or tell in prosë somewhat, at the least,
In which there be some mirth or some doctríne."[9]
"Gladly," quoth I, "by Goddë's sweetë pine,[10]
I will you tell a little thing in prose,
That oughtë likë you,[11] as I suppose,
Or else certés ye be too dangerous.[12]
It is a moral talë virtuous,
All be it[13] told sometimes in sundry wise
By sundry folk, as I shall you devise.
As thus, ye wot that ev'ry Evangelist,
That telleth us the pain[14] of Jesus Christ,
He saith not all thing as his fellow doth;
But natheless their sentence is all soth,[15]
And all accorden as in their senténce,[16]
All be there in their telling differénce;
For some of them say more, and some say less,
When they his piteous passión express;
I mean of Mark and Matthew, Luke and John;
But doubtëless their sentence is all one.
Therefore, lordingës all, I you beseech,
If that ye think I vary in my speech,
As thus, though that I tellë somedeal more
Of proverbës, than ye have heard before
Comprehended in this little treatise here,
T' enforcë with[17] the effect of my mattére,
And though I not the samë wordës say
As ye have heard, yet to you all I pray
Blamë me not; for as in my senténce
Shall ye nowhere findë no differénce
From the senténce of thilkë[18] treatise lite,[19]
After the which this merry tale I write.
And therefore hearken to what I shall say,
And let me tellen all my tale, I pray."

THE TALE.[20]

A young man called Meliboeus, mighty and rich, begat upon his wife, that called was Prudence, a daughter which that called was Sophia. Upon a day befell, that he for his disport went into the fields him to play. His wife and eke his daughter hath he left within his house, of which the doors were fast shut. Three of his old foes have it espied, and set ladders to the walls of his house, and by the windows be entered, and beaten his wife, and wounded his daughter with five mortal wounds, in five sundry places; that is to say, in her feet, in her hands, in her ears, in her nose, and in her mouth; and left her for dead, and went away. When Meliboeus returned was into his house, and saw all this mischief, he, like a man mad, rending his clothes, gan weep and cry. Prudence his wife, as farforth as she durst, besought him of his weeping for to stint: but not forthy[21] he gan to weep and cry ever longer the more.

This noble wife Prudence remembered her upon the sentence of Ovid, in his book that called is the "Remedy of Love,"[22] where he saith: He is a fool that disturbeth the mother to weep in the death of her child, till she have wept her fill, as for a certain time; and then shall a man do his diligence with amiable words

1 Illiterateness, stupidity. Chaucer crowns the satire on the romancists by making the very landlord of the Tabard cry out in indignant disgust against the stuff which he had heard recited—the good Host ascribing to sheer ignorance the string of pompous platitudes and prosaic details which Chaucer had uttered.
2 Surely.
3 Worthless, vile; no better than draff or dregs; from the Anglo-Saxon, "drifan," to drive away, expel.
4 Commend to.
5 Prevent.
6 Spendest, wastest.
7 Whether.
8 By way of narrative.
9 Some amusement or instruction.
10 Suffering.
11 Ought to please you.
12 Fastidious.
13 Although it be.
14 Agony, passion.
15 Sooth, true.
16 Meaning.
17 With which to enforce.
18 That.
19 Little.
20 The Tale of Meliboeus is literally translated from a French story, or rather "treatise," in prose, entitled "Le Livre de Melibée et de Dame Prudence;" of which two manuscripts, both dating from the fifteenth century, are preserved in the British Museum. Tyrwhitt, justly enough, says of it that it is indeed, as Chaucer called it in the prologue, "'a moral talë virtuous,' and was probably much esteemed in its time; but, in this age of levity, I doubt some readers will be apt to regret that he did not rather give us the remainder of Sir Thopas." It has been remarked that in the earlier portion of the Tale, as it left the hand of the poet, a number of blank verses were intermixed; though this peculiarity of style, noticeable in any case only in the first 150 or 200 lines, has necessarily all but disappeared by the changes of spelling made in the modern editions. The Editor's purpose being to present to the public not "The Canterbury Tales" merely, but "The Poems" of Chaucer, so far as may be consistent with the limits of this volume, he has condensed the long reasonings and learned quotations of Dame Prudence into a mere outline, connecting those portions of the Tale wherein lies so much of story as it actually possesses; and the general reader will probably not regret the sacrifice, made in the view of retaining so far as possible the completeness of the Tales, while lessening the intrusion of prose into a volume of poems. The good wife of Meliboeus literally overflows with quotations from David, Solomon, Jesus the Son of Sirach, the Apostles, Ovid, Cicero, Seneca, Cassiodorus, Cato, Petrus Alphonsus—the converted Spanish Jew, of the twelfth century, who wrote the "Disciplina Clericalis"—and other authorities; and in some passages, especially where husband and wife debate the merits or demerits of women, and where Prudence dilates on the evils of poverty, Chaucer only reproduces much that had been said already in the Tales that preceded—such as the Merchant's and the Man of Law's.
21 Notwithstanding.
22 "Quis matrem, nisi mentis inops, in funere nati
Flere vetet? non hoc illa monenda loco.
Cum dederit lacrymas, animumque expleverit ægrum,
Ille dolor verbis emoderandus erit."
—"Remed. Amor.," 127-131.

her to recomfort and pray her of her weeping for to stint.[1] For which reason this noble wife Prudence suffered her husband for to weep and cry, as for a certain space; and when she saw her time, she said to him in this wise: "Alas! my lord," quoth she, "why make ye yourself for to be like a fool? For sooth it appertaineth not to a wise man to make such a sorrow. Your daughter, with the grace of God, shall warish[2] and escape. And all[3] were it so that she right now were dead, ye ought not for her death yourself to destroy. Seneca saith, 'The wise man shall not take too great discomfort for the death of his children, but certes he should suffer it in patience, as well as he abideth the death of his own proper person.'"

Meliboeus answered anon and said: "What man," quoth he, "should of his weeping stint, that hath so great a cause to weep? Jesus Christ, our Lord, himself wept for the death of Lazarus his friend." Prudence answered, "Certes, well I wot, attempered[4] weeping is nothing defended[5] to him that sorrowful is, among folk in sorrow, but it is rather granted him to weep. The Apostle Paul unto the Romans writeth, 'Man shall rejoice with them that make joy, and weep with such folk as weep.' But though temperate weeping be granted, outrageous weeping certes is defended. Measure of weeping should be conserved,[6] after the lore[7] that teacheth us Seneca. 'When that thy friend is dead,' quoth he, 'let not thine eyes too moist be of tears, nor too much dry: although the tears come to thine eyes, let them not fall. And when thou hast forgone[8] thy friend, do diligence to get again another friend: and this is more wisdom than to weep for thy friend which that thou hast lorn,[8] for therein is no boot.'[9] And therefore if ye govern you by sapience, put away sorrow out of your heart. Remember you that Jesus Sirach saith, 'A man that is joyous and glad in heart, it him conserveth flourishing in his age: but soothly a sorrowful heart maketh his bones dry.' He saith eke thus, 'that sorrow in heart slayeth full many a man.' Solomon saith, 'that right as moths in the sheep's fleece annoy[10] to the clothes, and the small worms to the tree, right so annoyeth sorrow to the heart of man.' Wherefore us ought as well in the death of our children, as in the loss of our goods temporal, have patience. Remember you upon the patient Job, when he had lost his children and his temporal substance, and in his body endured and received full many a grievous tribulation, yet said he thus: 'Our Lord hath given it to me, our Lord hath bereft it me; right as our Lord would, right so be it done; blessed be the name of our Lord.'"

To these foresaid things answered Meliboeus unto his wife Prudence: "All thy words," quoth he, "be true, and thereto[11] profitable, but truly mine heart is troubled with this sorrow so grievously, that I know not what to do." "Let call," quoth Prudence, "thy true friends all, and thy lineage, which be wise, and tell to them your case, and hearken what they say in counselling, and govern you after their sentence.[12] Solomon saith, 'Work all things by counsel, and thou shall never repent.'" Then, by counsel of his wife Prudence, this Meliboeus let call[13] a great congregation of folk, as surgeons, physicians, old folk and young, and some of his old enemies reconciled (as by their semblance) to his love and to his grace; and therewithal there come some of his neighbours, that did him reverence more for dread than for love, as happeneth oft. There come also full many subtle flatterers, and wise advocates learned in the law. And when these folk together assembled were, this Meliboeus in sorrowful wise showed them his case, and by the manner of his speech it seemed that in heart he bare a cruel ire, ready to do vengeance upon his foes, and suddenly desired that the war should begin, but nevertheless yet asked he their counsel in this matter. A surgeon, by licence and assent of such as were wise, up rose, and to Meliboeus said as ye may hear. "Sir," quoth he, "as to us surgeons appertaineth, that we do to every wight the best that we can, where as we be withholden,[14] and to our patient that we do no damage; wherefore it happeneth many a time and oft, that when two men have wounded each other, one same surgeon healeth them both; wherefore unto our art it is not pertinent to nurse war, nor parties to support.[15] But certes, as to the warishing[16] of your daughter, albeit so that perilously she be wounded, we shall do so attentive business from day to night, that, with the grace of God, she shall be whole and sound, as soon as is possible." Almost right in the same wise the physicians answered, save that they said a few words more: that right as maladies be cured by their contraries, right so shall man warish war [by peace]. His neighbours full of envy, his feigned friends that seemed reconciled, and his flatterers, made semblance of weeping, and impaired and agregged much of this matter,[17] in praising greatly Meliboeus of might, of power, of riches, and of friends, despising the power of his adversaries: and said utterly, that he anon should wreak him on his foes, and begin war.

Up rose then an advocate that was wise, by leave and by counsel of other that were wise, and said, "Lordings, the need[18] for which we be assembled in this place, is a full heavy thing, and an high matter, because of the wrong and of the wickedness that hath been done, and eke by reason of the great damages that in time coming be possible to fall for the same cause,

1 Cease. 2 Be healed. 3 Although.
4 Moderate. 5 Forbidden.
6 Moderation should be kept or observed.
7 Doctrine. 8 Lost. 9 Advantage, remedy.
10 Do injury. 11 Also. 12 Opinion.
13 Caused to be summoned.
14 Employed, retained.
15 To take sides in a quarrel. 16 Healing.
17 Made worse and aggravated the matter.
18 Business.

and eke by reason of the great riches and power of the parties both; for which reasons, it were a full great peril to err in this matter. Wherefore, Meliboeus, this is our sentence;[1] we counsel you, above all things, that right anon thou do thy diligence in keeping of thy body, in such a wise that thou want no espy[2] nor watch thy body to save. And after that, we counsel that in thine house thou set sufficient garrison, so that they may as well thy body as thy house defend. But, certes, to move war, or suddenly to do vengeance, we may not deem[3] in so little time that it were profitable. Wherefore we ask leisure and space to have deliberation in this case to deem; for the common proverb saith thus; 'He that soon deemeth, soon shall repent.' And eke men say, that that judge is wise, that soon understandeth a matter, and judgeth by leisure. For albeit so that all tarrying be annoying, algates[4] it is no reproof[5] in giving of judgment, nor in vengeance taking, when it is sufficient and reasonable. And that shewed our Lord Jesus Christ by example; for when that the woman that was taken in adultery was brought in his presence to know what should be done with her person, albeit that he wist well himself what he would answer, yet would he not answer suddenly, but he would have deliberation, and in the ground he wrote twice. And by these causes we ask deliberation; and we shall then by the grace of God counsel the thing that shall be profitable."

Up started then the young folk anon at once, and the most part of that company have scorned these old wise men, and begun to make noise and said, "Right as while that iron is hot men should smite, right so men should wreak their wrongs while that they be fresh and new:" and with loud voice they cried, "War! War!" Up rose then one of these old wise, and with his hand made countenance[6] that men should hold them still, and give him audience. "Lordings," quoth he, "there is full many a man that crieth, 'War! war!' that wot full little what war amounteth. War at his beginning hath so great an entering and so large, that every wight may enter when him liketh, and lightly[7] find war: but certes what end shall fall thereof, it is not light to know. For soothly when war is once begun, there is full many a child unborn of his mother, that shall sterve[8] young, by cause of that war, or else live in sorrow and die in wretchedness; and therefore, ere that any war be begun, men must have great counsel and great deliberation." And when this old man weened[9] to enforce his tale by reasons, well-nigh all at once began they to rise, for to break his tale, and bid him full oft his words abridge. For soothly he that preacheth to them that list not hear his words, his sermon them annoyeth. For Jesus Sirach saith, that music in weeping is a noyous[10] thing. This is to say, as much availeth to speak before folk to whom his speech annoyeth, as to sing before him that weepeth. And when this wise man saw that him wanted audience, all shamefast he sat him down again. For Solomon saith, "Where as thou mayest have no audience, enforce thee not to speak." "I see well," quoth this wise man, "that the common proverb is sooth, that good counsel wanteth, when it is most need." Yet[11] had this Meliboeus in his council many folk, that privily in his ear counselled him certain thing, and counselled him the contrary in general audience. When Meliboeus had heard that the greatest part of his council were accorded[12] that he should make war, anon he consented to their counselling, and fully affirmed their sentence.[13]

[Dame Prudence, seeing her husband's resolution thus taken, in full humble wise, when she saw her time, begins to counsel him against war, by a warning against haste in requital of either good or evil. Meliboeus tells her that he will not work by her counsel, because he should be held a fool if he rejected for her advice the opinion of so many wise men; because all women are bad; because it would seem that he had given her the mastery over him; and because she could not keep his secret, if he resolved to follow her advice. To these reasons Prudence answers that it is no folly to change counsel when things, or men's judgments of them, change—especially to alter a resolution taken on the impulse of a great multitude of folk, where every man crieth and clattereth what him liketh; that if all women had been wicked, Jesus Christ would never have descended to be born of a woman, nor have showed himself first to a woman after his resurrection—and that when Solomon said he had found no good woman, he meant that God alone was supremely good;[14] that her husband would not seem to give her the mastery by following her counsel, for he had his own free choice in following or rejecting it; and that he knew well and had often tested her great silence, patience, and secrecy. And whereas he had quoted a saying, that in wicked counsel women vanquish men, she reminds him that she would counsel him against doing a wickedness on which he had set his mind, and cites instances to show that many women have been and yet are full good, and their counsel wholesome and profitable. Lastly, she quotes the words of God himself, when he was about to make woman as an help meet for man; and promises that, if her husband will trust her counsel, she will restore to him his daughter whole and sound, and make him have honour in this case. Meliboeus answers that because of his wife's sweet words, and also because he has proved and

1 Opinion.
2 Observation, looking out.
3 Determine.
4 Nevertheless.
5 Subject for reproach.
6 A sign, gesture.
7 Easily.
8 Die.
9 Thought, intended.
10 Troublesome.
11 Besides, further.
12 Agreed.
13 Opinion, judgment.
14 See the conversation between Pluto and Proserpine, *ante*, pp. 113 and 114.

assayed her great wisdom and her great truth, he will govern him by her counsel in all things. Thus encouraged, Prudence enters on a long discourse, full of learned citations, regarding the manner in which counsellors should be chosen and consulted, and the times and reasons for changing a counsel. First, God must be besought for guidance. Then a man must well examine his own thoughts, of such things as he holds to be best for his own profit; driving out of his heart anger, covetousness, and hastiness, which perturb and pervert the judgment. Then he must keep his counsel secret, unless confiding it to another shall be more profitable; but, in so confiding it, he shall say nothing to bias the mind of the counsellor toward flattery or subserviency. After that he should consider his friends and his enemies, choosing of the former such as be most faithful and wise, and eldest and most approved in counselling; and even of these only a few. Then he must eschew the counselling of fools, of flatterers, of his old enemies that be reconciled, of servants who bear him great reverence and fear, of folk that be drunken and can hide no counsel, of such as counsel one thing privily and the contrary openly; and of young folk, for their counselling is not ripe. Then, in examining his counsel, he must truly tell his tale; he must consider whether the thing he proposes to do be reasonable, within his power, and acceptable to the more part and the better part of his counsellors; he must look at the things that may follow from that counselling, choosing the best and waiving all besides; he must consider the root whence the matter of his counsel is engendered, what fruits it may bear, and from what causes they be sprung. And having thus examined his counsel and approved it by many wise folk and old, he shall consider if he may perform it and make of it a good end; if he be in doubt, he shall choose rather to suffer than to begin; but otherwise he shall prosecute his resolution steadfastly till the enterprise be at an end. As to changing his counsel, a man may do so without reproach, if the cause cease, or when a new case betides, or if he find that by error or otherwise harm or damage may result, or if his counsel be dishonest or come of dishonest cause, or if it be impossible or may not properly be kept; and he must take it for a general rule, that every counsel which is affirmed so strongly, that it may not be changed for any condition that may betide, that counsel is wicked. Meliboeus, admitting that his wife has spoken well and suitably as to counsellors and counsel in general, prays her to tell him in especial what she thinks of the counsellors whom they have chosen in their present need. Prudence replies that his counsel in this case could not properly be called a counselling, but a movement of folly; and points out that he has erred in sundry wise against the rules which he had just laid down. Granting that he has erred, Meliboeus says that he is all ready to change his counsel right as she will devise; for, as the proverb runs, to do sin is human, but to persevere long in sin is work of the Devil. Prudence then minutely recites, analyses, and criticises the counsel given to her husband in the assembly of his friends. She commends the advice of the physicians and surgeons, and urges that they should be well rewarded for their noble speech and their services in healing Sophia; and she asks Meliboeus how he understands their proposition that one contrary must be cured by another contrary. Meliboeus answers, that he should do vengeance on his enemies, who had done him wrong. Prudence, however, insists that vengeance is not the contrary of vengeance, nor wrong of wrong, but the like; and that wickedness should be healed by goodness, discord by accord, war by peace. She proceeds to deal with the counsel of the lawyers and wise folk that advised Meliboeus to take prudent measures for the security of his body and of his house. First, she would have her husband pray for the protection and aid of Christ; then commit the keeping of his person to his true friends; then suspect and avoid all strange folk, and liars, and such people as she had already warned him against; then beware of presuming on his strength, or the weakness of his adversary, and neglecting to guard his person—for every wise man dreadeth his enemy; then he should evermore be on the watch against ambush and all espial, even in what seems a place of safety; though he should not be so cowardly, as to fear where is no cause for dread; yet he should dread to be poisoned, and therefore shun scorners, and fly their words as venom. As to the fortification of his house, she points out that towers and great edifices are costly and laborious, yet useless unless defended by true friends that be old and wise; and the greatest and strongest garrison that a rich man may have, as well to keep his person as his goods, is, that he be beloved by his subjects and by his neighbours. Warmly approving the counsel that in all this business Meliboeus should proceed with great diligence and deliberation, Prudence goes on to examine the advice given by his neighbours that do him reverence without love, his old enemies reconciled, his flatterers that counselled him certain things privily and openly counselled him the contrary, and the young folk that counselled him to avenge himself and make war at once. She reminds him that he stands alone against three powerful enemies, whose kindred are numerous and close, while his are fewer and remote in relationship; that only the judge who has jurisdiction in a case may take sudden vengeance on any man; that her husband's power does not accord with his desire; and that, if he did take vengeance, it would only breed fresh wrongs and contests. As to the causes of the wrong done to him, she holds that God, the causer of all things, has permitted him to suffer because he has drunk so much honey[1] of sweet temporal riches, and

[1] "Thy name," she says, "is Meliboeus; that is to say, a man that drinketh honey."

delights, and honours of this world, that he is drunken, and has forgotten Jesus Christ his Saviour; the three enemies of mankind, the flesh, the fiend, and the world, have entered his heart by the windows of his body, and wounded his soul in five places—that is to say, the deadly sins that have entered into his heart by the five senses; and in the same manner Christ has suffered his three enemies to enter his house by the windows, and wound his daughter in the five places before specified. Meliboeus demurs, that if his wife's objections prevailed, vengeance would never be taken, and thence great mischiefs would arise; but Prudence replies that the taking of vengeance lies with the judges, to whom the private individual must have recourse. Meliboeus declares that such vengeance does not please him, and that, as Fortune has nourished and helped him from his childhood, he will now assay her, trusting, with God's help, that she will aid him to avenge his shame. Prudence warns him against trusting to Fortune, all the less because she has hitherto favoured him, for just on that account she is the more likely to fail him; and she calls on him to leave his vengeance with the Sovereign Judge, that avengeth all villainies and wrongs. Meliboeus argues that if he refrains from taking vengeance he will invite his enemies to do him further wrong, and he will be put and held over low; but Prudence contends that such a result can be brought about only by the neglect of the judges, not by the patience of the individual. Supposing that he had leave to avenge himself, she repeats that he is not strong enough, and quotes the common saw, that it is madness for a man to strive with a stronger than himself, peril to strive with one of equal strength, and folly to strive with a weaker. But, considering his own defaults and demerits—remembering the patience of Christ and the undeserved tribulations of the saints, the brevity of this life with all its trouble and sorrow, the discredit thrown on the wisdom and training of a man who cannot bear wrong with patience—he should refrain wholly from taking vengeance. Meliboeus submits that he is not at all a perfect man, and his heart will never be at peace until he is avenged; and that as his enemies disregarded the peril when they attacked him, so he might, without reproach, incur some peril in attacking them in return, even though he did a great excess in avenging one wrong by another. Prudence strongly deprecates all outrage or excess; but Meliboeus insists that he cannot see that it might greatly harm him though he took vengeance, for he is richer and mightier than his enemies, and all things obey money. Prudence thereupon launches into a long dissertation on the advantages of riches, the evils of poverty, the means by which wealth should be gathered, and the manner in which it should be used; and concludes by counselling her husband not to move war and battle through trust in his riches, for they suffice not to maintain war, the battle is not always to the strong or the numerous, and the perils of conflict are many. Meliboeus then curtly asks her for her counsel how he shall do in this need; and she answers that certainly she counsels him to agree with his adversaries and have peace with them. Meliboeus on this cries out that plainly she loves not his honour or his worship, in counselling him to go and humble himself before his enemies, crying mercy to them that, having done him so grievous wrong, ask him not to be reconciled. Then Prudence, making semblance of wrath, retorts that she loves his honour and profit as she loves her own, and ever has done; she cites the Scriptures in support of her counsel to seek peace; and says she will leave him to his own courses, for she knows well he is so stubborn, that he will do nothing for her. Meliboeus then relents; admits that he is angry and cannot judge aright; and puts himself wholly in her hands, promising to do just as she desires, and admitting that he is the more held to love and praise her, if she reproves him of his folly.]

Then Dame Prudence discovered all her counsel and her will unto him, and said: "I counsel you," quoth she, "above all things, that ye make peace between God and you, and be reconciled unto him and to his grace; for, as I have said to you herebefore, God hath suffered you to have this tribulation and disease[1] for your sins; and if ye do as I say you, God will send your adversaries unto you, and make them fall at your feet, ready to do your will and your commandment. For Solomon saith, 'When the condition of man is pleasant and liking to God, he changeth the hearts of the man's adversaries, and constraineth them to beseech him of peace and of grace.' And I pray you let me speak with your adversaries in privy place, for they shall not know it is by your will or your assent; and then, when I know their will and their intent, I may counsel you the more surely." "Dame," quoth Meliboeus, "do your will and your liking, for I put me wholly in your disposition and ordinance."

Then Dame Prudence, when she saw the goodwill of her husband, deliberated and took advice in herself, thinking how she might bring this need[2] unto a good end. And when she saw her time, she sent for these adversaries to come unto her into a privy place, and showed wisely unto them the great goods that come of peace, and the great harms and perils that be in war; and said to them, in goodly manner, how that they ought have great repentance of the injuries and wrongs that they had done to Meliboeus her lord, and unto her and her daughter. And when they heard the goodly words of Dame Prudence, then they were surprised and ravished, and had so great joy of her, that wonder was to tell. "Ah lady!" quoth they, "ye have showed unto us the blessing of sweetness, after the saying of David the prophet; for the reconciling which we be not worthy to have in no manner, but we ought require it with great

1 Distress, trouble.

2 Affair, emergency.

contrition and humility, ye of your great goodness have presented unto us. Now see we well, that the science and conning[1] of Solomon is full true; for he saith, that sweet words multiply and increase friends, and make shrews[2] to be debonair[3] and meek. Certes we put our deed, and all our matter and cause, all wholly in your goodwill, and be ready to obey unto the speech and commandment of my lord Meliboeus. And therefore, dear and benign lady, we pray you and beseech you as meekly as we can and may, that it like unto your great goodness to fulfil in deed your goodly words. For we consider and acknowledge that we have offended and grieved my lord Meliboeus out of measure, so far forth that we be not of power to make him amends; and therefore we oblige and bind us and our friends to do all his will and his commandment. But peradventure he hath such heaviness and such wrath to usward, because of our offence, that he will enjoin us such a pain[4] as we may not bear nor sustain; and therefore, noble lady, we beseech to your womanly pity to take such advisement[5] in this need, that we, nor our friends, be not disinherited and destroyed through our folly."

"Certes," quoth Prudence, "it is an hard thing, and right perilous, that a man put him all utterly in the arbitration and judgment and in the might and power of his enemy. For Solomon saith, 'Believe me, and give credence to that that I shall say: to thy son, to thy wife, to thy friend, nor to thy brother, give thou never might nor mastery over thy body, while thou livest.' Now, since he defendeth[6] that a man should not give to his brother, nor to his friend, the might of his body, by a stronger reason he defendeth and forbiddeth a man to give himself to his enemy. And nevertheless, I counsel you that ye mistrust not my lord: for I wot well and know verily, that he is debonair and meek, large, courteous, and nothing desirous nor covetous of good nor riches: for there is nothing in this world that he desireth save only worship and honour. Furthermore I know well, and am right sure, that he shall nothing do in this need without counsel of me; and I shall so work in this case, that by the grace of our Lord God ye shall be reconciled unto us." Then said they with one voice, "Worshipful lady, we put us and our goods all fully in your will and disposition, and be ready to come, what day that it like unto your nobleness to limit us or assign us, for to make our obligation and bond, as strong as it liketh unto your goodness, that we may fulfil the will of you and of my lord Meliboeus."

When Dame Prudence had heard the answer of these men, she bade them go again privily, and she returned to her lord Meliboeus, and told him how she found his adversaries full repentant, acknowledging full lowly their sins and trespasses, and how they were ready to suffer all pain, requiring and praying him of mercy and pity. Then said Meliboeus, "He is well worthy to have pardon and forgiveness of his sin, that excuseth not his sin, but acknowledgeth, and repenteth him, asking indulgence. For Seneca saith, 'There is the remission and forgiveness, where the confession is; for confession is neighbour to innocence.' And therefore I assent and confirm me to have peace, but it is good that we do naught without the assent and will of our friends." Then was Prudence right glad and joyful, and said, "Certes, Sir, ye be well and goodly advised; for right as by the counsel, assent, and help of your friends ye have been stirred to avenge you and make war, right so without their counsel shall ye not accord you, nor have peace with your adversaries. For the law saith, 'There is nothing so good by way of kind,[7] as a thing to be unbound by him that it was bound.'"

And then Dame Prudence, without delay or tarrying, sent anon her messengers for their kin and for their old friends, which were true and wise; and told them by order, in the presence of Meliboeus, all this matter, as it is above expressed and declared; and prayed them that they would give their advice and counsel what were best to do in this need. And when Meliboeus' friends had taken their advice and deliberation of the foresaid matter, and had examined it by great business and great diligence, they gave full counsel for to have peace and rest, and that Meliboeus should with good heart receive his adversaries to forgiveness and mercy. And when Dame Prudence had heard the assent of her lord Meliboeus, and the counsel of his friends, accord with her will and her intention, she was wondrous glad in her heart, and said: "There is an old proverb that saith, 'The goodness that thou mayest do this day, do it, and abide not nor delay it not till to-morrow:' and therefore I counsel you that ye send your messengers, such as be discreet and wise, unto your adversaries, telling them on your behalf, that if they will treat of peace and of accord, that they shape[8] them, without delay or tarrying, to come unto us." Which thing performed was indeed. And when these trespassers and repenting folk of their follies, that is to say, the adversaries of Meliboeus, had heard what these messengers said unto them, they were right glad and joyful, and answered full meekly and benignly, yielding graces and thanks to their lord Meliboeus, and to all his company; and shaped them without delay to go with the messengers, and obey to the commandment of their lord Meliboeus. And right anon they took their way to the court of Meliboeus, and took with them some of their true friends, to make faith for them, and for to be their borrows.[9]

And when they were come to the presence of Meliboeus, he said to them these words; "It stands thus," quoth Meliboeus, "and sooth it

1 Knowledge.
2 The ill-natured or angry.
3 Gentle, courteous.
4 Penalty.
5 Consideration.
6 Forbiddeth.
7 Nature.
8 Prepare.
9 Sureties.

is, that ye causeless, and without skill and reason, have done great injuries and wrongs to me, and to my wife Prudence, and to my daughter also; for ye have entered into my house by violence, and have done such outrage, that all men know well that ye have deserved the death: and therefore will I know and weet of you, whether ye will put the punishing and chastising, and the vengeance of this outrage, in the will of me and of my wife, or ye will not?" Then the wisest of them three answered for them all, and said; "Sir," quoth he, "we know well, that we be unworthy to come to the court of so great a lord and so worthy as ye be, for we have so greatly mistaken us, and have offended and aguilt[1] in such wise against your high lordship, that truly we have deserved the death. But yet for the great goodness and debonairté[2] that all the world witnesseth of your person, we submit us to the excellence and benignity of your gracious lordship, and be ready to obey to all your commandments, beseeching you, that of your merciable[3] pity ye will consider our great repentance and low submission, and grant us forgiveness of our outrageous trespass and offence; for well we know, that your liberal grace and mercy stretch them farther into goodness, than do our outrageous guilt and trespass into wickedness; albeit that cursedly[4] and damnably we have aguilt[1] against your high lordship." Then Melibœus took them up from the ground full benignly, and received their obligations and their bonds, by their oaths upon their pledges and borrows,[5] and assigned them a certain day to return unto his court for to receive and accept sentence and judgment, that Melibœus would command to be done on them, by the causes aforesaid; which things ordained, every man returned home to his house.

And when that Dame Prudence saw her time, she freined[6] and asked her lord Melibœus, what vengeance he thought to take of his adversaries. To which Melibœus answered, and said; "Certes," quoth he, "I think and purpose me fully to disinherit them of all that ever they have, and for to put them in exile for evermore." "Certes," quoth Dame Prudence, "this were a cruel sentence, and much against reason. For ye be rich enough, and have no need of other men's goods; and ye might lightly[7] in this wise get you a covetous name, which is a vicious thing, and ought to be eschewed of every good man: for, after the saying of the Apostle, covetousness is root of all harms. And therefore it were better for you to lose much good of your own, than for to take of their good in this manner. For better it is to lose good with worship,[8] than to win good with villainy and shame. And every man ought to do his diligence and his business to get him a good name. And yet[9] shall he not only busy him in keeping his good name, but he shall also enforce him alway to do some thing by which he may renew his good name; for it is written, that the old good los[10] of a man is soon gone and passed, when it is not renewed. And as touching that ye say, that ye will exile your adversaries, that thinketh me much against reason, and out of measure,[11] considered the power that they have given you upon themselves. And it is written, that he is worthy to lose his privilege, that misuseth the might and the power that is given him. And I set case[12] ye might enjoin them that pain by right and by law (which I trow ye may not do), I say, ye might not put it to execution peradventure, and then it were like to return to the war, as it was before. And therefore if ye will that men do you obeisance, ye must deem[13] more courteously, that is to say, ye must give more easy sentences and judgments. For it is written, 'He that most courteously commandeth, to him men most obey.' And therefore I pray you, that in this necessity and in this need ye cast you[14] to overcome your heart. For Seneca saith, that he that overcometh his heart, overcometh twice. And Tullius saith, 'There is nothing so commendable in a great lord, as when he is debonair and meek, and appeaseth him lightly.'[7] And I pray you, that ye will now forbear to do vengeance, in such a manner, that your good name may be kept and conserved, and that men may have cause and matter to praise you of pity and of mercy; and that ye have no cause to repent you of thing that ye do. For Seneca saith, 'He overcometh in an evil manner, that repenteth him of his victory.' Wherefore I pray you let mercy be in your heart, to the effect and intent that God Almighty have mercy upon you in his last judgment; for Saint James saith in his Epistle, 'Judgment without mercy shall be done to him, that hath no mercy of another wight.'"

When Melibœus had heard the great skills[15] and reasons of Dame Prudence, and her wise information and teaching, his heart gan incline to the will of his wife, considering her true intent, he conformed him anon and assented fully to work after her counsel, and thanked God, of whom proceedeth all goodness and all virtue, that him sent a wife of so great discretion. And when the day came that his adversaries should appear in his presence, he spake to them full goodly, and said in this wise; "Albeit so, that of your pride and high presumption and folly, and of your negligence and unconning,[16] ye have misborne[17] you, and trespassed[18] unto me, yet forasmuch as I see and behold your great humility, and that ye be sorry and repentant of your guilts, it constraineth me to do you grace and mercy. Wherefore I receive you into my grace, and forgive you utterly all

1 Incurred guilt. 2 Courtesy, gentleness. 3 Merciful. 4 Wickedly. 5 Sureties. 6 Inquired. 7 Easily. 8 Honour. 9 Further.
10 Reputation; from the past participle of the Anglo-Saxon, "hlisan," to celebrate. Compare Latin, "laus."
11 Moderation. 12 If I assume.
13 Decide.
14 Endeavour, devise a way.
15 Arguments, reasons. 16 Ignorance.
17 Misbehaved. 18 Done injury.

the offences, injuries, and wrongs, that ye have done against me and mine, to this effect and to this end, that God of his endless mercy will at the time of our dying forgive us our guilts, that we have trespassed to him in this wretched world; for doubtless, if we be sorry and repentant of the sins and guilts which we have trespassed in the sight of our Lord God, he is so free and so merciable,[1] that he will forgive us our guilts, and bring us to the bliss that never hath end." Amen.

THE MONK'S TALE.

THE PROLOGUE.

When ended was my tale of Melibee,
And of Prudénce and her benignity,
Our Hostë said, "As I am faithful man,
And by the precious *corpus Madrian*,[2]
I had lever[3] than a barrel of ale,
That goodë lefe[4] my wife had heard this tale;
For she is no thing of such patiénce
As was this Meliboeus' wife Prudénce.
By Goddë's bonës! when I beat my knaves
She bringeth me the greatë clubbed staves,
And crieth, 'Slay the doggës every one,
And break of them both back and ev'ry bone.'
And if that any neighëbour of mine
Will not in church unto my wife incline,[5]
Or be so hardy to her to trespace,[6]
When she comes home she rampeth[7] in my face,
And crieth, 'Falsë coward, wreak[8] thy wife:
By *corpus Domini*, I will have thy knife,
And thou shalt have my distaff, and go spin.'
From day till night right thus she will begin.
'Alas!' she saith, 'that ever I was shape[9]
To wed a milksop, or a coward ape,
That will be overlad[10] with every wight!
Thou darest not stand by thy wifë's right.'
"This is my life, but if[11] that I will fight;
And out at door anon I must me dight,[12]
Or ellës I am lost, but if that I
Be, like a wildë lion, fool-hardy̆.
I wot well she will do[13] me slay some day
Some neighëbour, and thennë go my way;[14]
For I am perilous with knife in hand,
Albeit that I dare not her withstand;
For she is big in armës, by my faith!
That shall he find, that her misdoth or saith.[15]
But let us pass away from this mattére.
My lord the Monk," quoth he, "be merry of cheer,
For ye shall tell a talë truëly̆.
Lo, Rochester stands herë fastë by.
Ride forth, mine owen lord, break not our game.
But by my troth I cannot tell your name;
Whether shall I call you my lord Dan John,
Or Dan Thomas, or ellës Dan Albon?
Of what house be ye, by your father's kin?
I vow to God, thou hast a full fair skin;
It is a gentle pasture where thou go'st;
Thou art not like a penant[16] or a ghost.
Upon my faith thou art some officer,
Some worthy sexton, or some cellarer.
For by my father's soul, as to my dome,[17]
Thou art a master when thou art at home;
No poorë cloisterer, nor no novíce,
But a govérnor, both wily and wise,
And therewithal, of brawnës[18] and of bones,
A right well-faring person for the nonce.
I pray to God give him confusión
That first thee brought into religión.
Thou would'st have been a treadë-fowl[19] aright;
Hadst thou as greatë leave, as thou hast might,
To perform all thy lust in engendrure,
Thou hadst begotten many a creatúre.
Alas! why wearest thou so wide a cope?[20]
God give me sorrow, but, an'[21] I were pope,
Not only thou, but every mighty man,
Though he were shorn full high upon his pan,[22]
Should have a wife; for all this world is lorn;[23]
Religión hath ta'en up all the corn
Of treading, and we borel[24] men be shrimps:[25]
Of feeble trees there comë wretched imps.[26]
This maketh that our heirës be so slender
And feeble, that they may not well engender.
This maketh that our wivës will assay
Religious folk, for they may better pay
Of Venus' payëmentës than may we:
God wot, no lushëburghës[27] payë ye.
But be not wroth, my lord, though that I play;
Full oft in game a sooth have I heard say."
This worthy Monk took all in patiénce,
And said, "I will do all my diligence,
As far as souneth unto honesty,[28]
To tellë you a tale, or two or three.
And if you list to hearken hitherward,
I will you say the life of Saint Edward;
Or ellës first tragédies I will tell,
Of which I have an hundred in my cell.
Tragédy is to say[29] a certain story,
As oldë bookës maken us memóry,
Of him that stood in great prosperity̆,

1 Merciful.
2 The body of St Maternus, of Treves.
3 Rather. 4 Dear. 5 Bow.
6 Bold enough to offend her. 7 Leaps, springs.
8 Avenge. 9 Destined.
10 Overborne, imposed upon. 11 Unless.
12 Betake myself. 13 Make.
14 Take to flight.
15 That does or says anything to displease her.
16 One doing penance.
17 In my judgment; for "doom."
18 Sinews. 19 A cock.
20 An ecclesiastical vestment covering all the body like a cloak. 21 If.
22 Crown; though he were tonsured, as the clergy are. 23 Undone, ruined. 24 Lay, unlettered.
25 Puny, contemptible creatures.
26 Shoots, branches; from Anglo-Saxon, "impian," German, "impfen," to implant, ingraft. The word is now used in a very restricted sense, to signify the progeny, children, of the devil.
27 Base or counterfeit coins; so called because struck at Luxemburg. A great importation of them took place during the reigns of the earlier Edwards, and they caused much annoyance and complaint, till in 1351 it was declared treason to bring them into the country.
28 Is in harmony with good manners. 29 Means.

And is y-fallen out of high degree
In misery, and endeth wretchedly.
And they be versifiëd commonly
Of six feet, which men call hexámetron;
In prose eke be indited many a one,
And eke in metre, in many a sundry wise.
Lo, this declaring ought enough suffice.
Now hearken, if ye likë for to hear.
But first I you beseech in this mattére,
Though I by order tellë not these things,
Be it of popës, emperors, or kings,
After their ages,[1] as men written find,
But tell them some before and some behind,
As it now cometh to my remembránce,
Have me excused of mine ignorance."

THE TALE.[2]

I will bewail, in manner of tragédy,
The harm of them that stood in high degree,
And fellë so, that there was no remédy
To bring them out of their adversitý.
For, certain, when that Fortune list to flee,
There may no man the course of her wheel hold:
Let no man trust in blind prosperity;
Beware by these examples true and old.

At LUCIFER, though he an angel were,
And not a man, at him I will begin.
For though Fortúnë may no angel dere,[3]
From high degree yet fell he for his sin
Down into hell, where as he yet is in.
O Lucifer! brightest of angels all,
Now art thou Satanas, that may'st not twin[4]
Out of the misery in which thou art fall.

Lo ADAM, in the field of Damascene[5]
With Goddë's owen finger wrought was he,
And not begotten of man's sperm unclean;
And welt[6] all Paradise saving one tree:
Had never worldly man so high degree
As Adam, till he for misgovernance[7]
Was driven out of his prosperity
To labour, and to hell, and to mischance.

Lo SAMPSON, which that was annunciate
By the angel, long ere his nativity;[8]
And was to God Almighty consecrate,
And stood in nobless while that he might see;
Was never such another as was he,
To speak of strength, and thereto hardiness;[9]
But to his wivës told he his secré,
Through which he slew himself for wretchedness.

Sampson, this noble and mighty champión,
Withoutë weapon, save his handës tway,
He slew and all to-rentë[10] the lión,
Toward his wedding walking by the way.
His falsë wife could him so please, and pray,
Till she his counsel knew; and she, untrue,
Unto his foes his counsel gan bewray,
And him forsook, and took another new.

Three hundred foxes Sampson took for ire,
And all their tailës he together band,
And set the foxes' tailës all on fire,
For he in every tail had knit a brand,
And they burnt all the cornës of that land,
And all their olivéres[11] and vinës eke.
A thousand men he slew eke with his hand,
And had no weapon but an ass's cheek.

When they were slain, so thirsted him, that he
Was well-nigh lorn,[12] for which he gan to pray
That God would on his pain have some pitý,
And send him drink, or ellës must he die;
And of this ass's cheek, that was so dry,
Out of a wang-tooth[13] sprang anon a well,
Of which he drank enough, shortly to say.
Thus help'd him God, as *Judicum*[14] can tell.

By very force, at Gaza, on a night,
Maugré the Philistines of that citý,
The gatës of the town he hath up plight,[15]
And on his back y-carried them hath he
High on an hill, where as men might them see.
O noble mighty Sampson, lefe[16] and dear,
Hadst thou not told to women thy secré,
In all this world there had not been thy peer.

This Sampson never cider drank nor wine,
Nor on his head came razor none nor shear,
By precept of the messenger divine;
For all his strengthës in his hairës were;
And fully twenty winters, year by year,
He had of Israel the governance;
But soonë shall he weepë many a tear,
For women shall him bringë to mischance.

Unto his leman[17] Dalila[18] he told,
That in his hairës all his strengthë lay;
And falsely to his foemen she him sold,
And sleeping in her barme[19] upon a day
She made to clip or shear his hair away,
And made his foemen all his craft espien.
And when they foundë him in this array,
They bound him fast, and put out both his eyen.

But, ere his hair was clipped or y-shave,
There was no bond with which men might him bind;
But now is he in prison in a cave,
Where as they made him at the quernë[20] grind.
O noble Sampson, strongest of mankind!
O whilom judge in glory and richéss!
Now may'st thou weepë with thine eyen blind,
Since thou from weal art fall'n to wretchedness.

1 According to the dates at which they lived.
2 The Monk's Tale is founded in its main features on Boccaccio's work, "De Casibus Virorum Illustrium;" but Chaucer has taken the separate stories of which it is composed from different authors, and dealt with them after his own fashion.
3 Hurt. 4 Depart.
5 Boccaccio opens his book with Adam, whose story is told at much greater length than here. Lydgate, in his translation from Boccaccio, speaks of Adam and Eve as made "of slime of the erth in Damascene the felde."
6 Wielded, had at his command.
7 Misbehaviour.
8 Judges xiii. 3. Boccaccio also tells the story of Samson; but Chaucer seems, by his quotation a few lines below, to have taken his version direct from the sacred book.
9 Courage. 10 Tore all to pieces.
11 Olive trees; French, "oliviers."
12 Was near to perishing. 13 Cheek-tooth.
14 "Liber Judicum," the Book of Judges; chap. xv.
15 Plucked, wrenched. 16 Loved. 17 Mistress.
18 Chaucer writes it "Dalida." 19 Lap.
20 Mill; from Anglo-Saxon, "cyrran," to turn, "cweorn," a mill.

Th' end of this caitiff[1] was as I shall say;
His foemen made a feast upon a day,
And made him as their fool before them play;
And this was in a temple of great array.
But at the last he made a foul affray,
For he two pillars shook, and made them fall,
And down fell temple and all, and there it lay,
And slew himself and eke his foemen all;

This is to say, the princes every one;
And eke three thousand bodies were there slain
With falling of the great temple of stone.
Of Sampson now will I no morë sayn;
Beware by this example old and plain,
That no man tell his counsel to his wife
Of such thing as he would have secret fain,
If that it touch his limbës or his life.

Of HERCULES the sov'reign conqueroúr
Singë his workës' laud and high renown;
For in his time of strength he bare the flow'r.
He slew and reft the skin of the lioún;
He of the Centaurs laid the boast adown;
He Harpies[2] slew, the cruel birdës fell;
He golden apples reft from the dragón;
He drew out Cerberus the hound of hell.

He slew the cruel tyrant Busirus,[3]
And made his horse to fret[4] him flesh and bone;
He slew the fiery serpent venomous;
Of Achelous' two hornës brake he one.
And he slew Cacus in a cave of stone;
He slew the giant Antæus the strong;
He slew the grisly boar, and that anon;
And bare the heav'n upon his neckë long.[5]

Was never wight, since that the world began,
That slew so many monsters as did he;
Throughout the widë world his namë ran,
What for his strength, and for his high bounté;
And every realmë went he for to see;
He was so strong that no man might him let;
At both the worldë's ends, as saith Trophee,[6]
Instead of boundës he a pillar set.

A leman had this noble champión,
That hightë Dejanira, fresh as May;
And, as these clerkës makë mentión,
She hath him sent a shirtë fresh and gay;
Alas! this shirt, alas and well-away!
Envenomed was subtilly withal,
That ere that he had worn it half a day,
It made his flesh all from his bonës fall.

But natheless some clerkës her excuse
By one, that hightë Nessus, that it maked;
Be as be may, I will not her accuse;
But on his back this shirt he wore all naked,
Till that his flesh was for the venom blaked.[7]

And when he saw none other remedy,
In hotë coals he hath himselfë raked,
For with no venom deigned he to die.

Thus starf[8] this worthy mighty Hercules.
Lo, who may trust on Fortune any throw?[9]
For him that followeth all this world of pres,[10]
Ere he be ware, is often laid full low;
Full wise is he that can himselfë know.
Bèware, for when that Fortune list to glose,
Then waiteth she her man to overthrow,
By such a way as he would least suppose.

The mighty throne, the precious treasór,
The glorious sceptre, and royal majesty,
That had the king NABUCHODONOSOR,
With tongue unnethës[11] may described be.
He twice won Jerusalem the citý,
The vessels of the temple he with him lad;[12]
At Babylonë was his sov'reign see,[13]
In which his glory and delight he had.

The fairest children of the blood royál
Of Israel he did do[14] geld anon,
And maked each of them to be his thrall.[15]
Amongës others Daniel was one,
That was the wisest child of every one;
For he the dreamës of the king expounded,
Where in Chaldæa clerkë was there none
That wistë to what fine[16] his dreamës sounded.

This proudë king let make a statue of gold
Sixty cubitës long, and seven in bread',
To which imagë bothë young and old
Commanded he to lout,[17] and have in dread,
Or in a furnace, full of flamës red,
He should be burnt that wouldë not obey:
But never would assentë to that deed
Daniel, nor his youngë fellows tway.

This king of kingës proud was and elate;
He ween'd[18] that God, that sits in majesty,
Mightë him not bereave of his estate;
But suddenly he lost his dignity,
And like a beast he seemed for to be,
And ate hay as an ox, and lay thereout
In rain, with wildë beastës walked he,
Till certain timë was y-come about.

And like an eagle's feathers wax'd his hairs,
His nailës like a birdë's clawës were,
Till God released him at certain years,
And gave him wit; and then with many a tear
He thanked God, and ever his life in fear
Was he to do amiss, or more trespace:
And till that time he laid was on his bier,
He knew that God was full of might and grace.

His sonë, which that hightë BALTHASAR,
That held the regne[19] after his father's day,

1 Wretched man.
2 The Stymphalian Birds, which fed on human flesh.
3 Busiris, king of Egypt, was wont to sacrifice all foreigners coming to his dominions. Hercules was seized, bound, and led to the altar by his orders, but the hero broke his bonds and slew the tyrant.
4 Devour.
5 A long time. The feats of Hercules here recorded are not all those known as the "twelve labours;" for instance, the cleansing of the Augean stables, and the capture of Hippolyte's girdle, are not in this list,—other and less famous deeds of the hero taking their place. For this, however, we must accuse not Chaucer, but Boethius, whom he has almost literally translated, though with some change of order.
6 One of the manuscripts has a marginal reference to "Tropheus vates Chaldæorum;" but it is not known what author Chaucer meant—unless the reference is to a passage in the "Filostrato" of Boccaccio, on which Chaucer founded his "Troilus and Cressida," and which Lydgate mentions, under the name of "Trophe," as having been translated by Chaucer.
7 Blackened.
8 Died.
9 For a moment.
10 Near; French, "pres;" the meaning seems to be, this nearer, lower world.
11 Scarcely.
12 Took away.
13 Seat.
14 Caused.
15 Slave.
16 End.
17 Bow down, do honour.
18 Thought.
19 Possessed the kingdom.

He by his father couldë not beware,
For proud he was of heart and of array;
And eke an idolaster was he aye.
His high estate assured[1] him in pride;
But Fortune cast him down, and there he lay,
And suddenly his regnë gan divide.

A feast he made unto his lordës all
Upon a time, and made them blithë be,
And then his officérës gan he call;
"Go, bringë forth the vessels," saidë he,
"Which that my father in his prosperity
Out of the temple of Jerusalem reft,
And to our highë goddës thankë we
Of honour, that our elders[2] with us left."

His wife, his lordës, and his concubines
Aye drankë, while their appetites did last,
Out of these noble vessels sundry wines.
And on a wall this king his eyen cast,
And saw an hand, armless, that wrote full fast;
For fear of which he quaked, and sighed sore.
This hand, that Balthasar so sore aghast,[3]
Wrote *Mane, tekel, phares*, and no more.

In all that land magician was there none
That could expoundë what this letter meant.
But Daniel expounded it anon,
And said, "O King, God to thy father lent
Glory and honour, regnë, treasure, rent;[4]
And he was proud, and nothing God he drad;[5]
And therefore God great wreche[6] upon him
sent,
And him bereft the regnë that he had.

"He was cast out of mannë's company;
With asses was his habitatión;
And ate hay, as a beast, in wet and dry,
Till that he knew by grace and by reasón
That God of heaven hath dominatión
O'er every regne, and every creatúre;
And then had God of him compassión,
And him restor'd his regne and his figúre.

"Eke thou, that art his son, art proud also,
And knowest all these thingës verily;
And art rebel to God, and art his foe.
Thou drankest of his vessels boldëly;
Thy wife eke, and thy wenches, sinfully
Drank of the samë vessels sundry winës,
And heried[7] falsë goddës cursedly;[8]
Therefore to thee y-shapen[9] full great pine[10] is.

"This hand was sent from God, that on the
wall
Wrote *Mane, tekel, phares*, trustë me;
Thy reign is done; thou weighest naught at all;
Divided is thy regne, and it shall be
To Medës and to Persians giv'n," quoth he.
And thilkë samë night this king was slaw;[11]
And Darius occupied his degree,
Though he thereto had neither right nor law.

Lordings, example hereby may ye take,
How that in lordship[12] is no sickerness;[13]
For when that Fortune will a man forsake,
She bears away his regne and his richéss,
And eke his friendës bothë more and less.
For what man that hath friendës through
fortúne,
Mishap will make them enemies, I guess;
This proverb is full sooth, and full commúne.

ZENOBIA, of Palmyrie the queen,[14]
As writë Persians of her nobléss,
So worthy was in armës, and so keen,
That no wight passed her in hardiness,
Nor in lineáge, nor other gentleness.[15]
Of the king's blood of Perse[16] is she descended;
I say not that she haddë most fairnéss,
But of her shape she might not be amended.

From her childhood I findë that she fled
Office of woman, and to woods she went,
And many a wildë hartë's blood she shed
With arrows broad that she against them sent;
She was so swift, that she anon them hent.[17]
And when that she was older, she would kill
Lions, leopárds, and bearës all to-rent,
And in her armës wield them at her will.

She durst the wildë beastës' dennës seek,
And runnen in the mountains all the night,
And sleep under a bush; and she could eke
Wrestle by very force and very might
With any young man, were he ne'er so wight;[18]
There mightë nothing in her armës stond.
She kept her maidenhood from every wight,
To no man deigned she for to be bond.

But at the last her friendës have her married
To Odenate,[19] a prince of that country;
All were it so, that she them longë tarried.
And ye shall understandë how that he
Haddë such fantasies as haddë she;
But natheless, when they were knit in fere,[20]
They liv'd in joy, and in felicity,
For each of them had other lefe[21] and dear.

Save one thing, that she never would assent,
By no way, that he shouldë by her lie
But onës, for it was her plain intent
To have a child, the world to multiply;
And all so soon as that she might espy
That she was not with childë by that deed,
Then would she suffer him do his fantasy
Eftsoon,[22] and not but onës, out of dread.[23]

And if she were with child at thilkë cast,
No morë should he playë thilkë game
Till fully forty dayës werë past;
Then would she once suffer him do the same.
All[24] were this Odenatus wild or tame,
He got no more of her; for thus she said,
It was to wivës lechery and shame
In other case[25] if that men with them play'd.

Two sonës by this Odenate had she,
The which she kept in virtue and lettrure.[26]
But now unto our talë turnë we;

1 Confirmed. 2 Forefathers. 3 Dismayed.
4 Revenue. 5 Dreaded. 6 Vengeance.
7 Praised. 8 Impiously.
9 Decreed. 10 Punishment.
11 Slain. 12 Power. 13 Security.
14 Chaucer has taken the story of Zenobia from Boccaccio's work "De Claris Mulieribus."
15 Noble qualities. 16 Persia.
17 Caught. 18 Active, nimble.
19 Odenatus, who, for his services to the Romans, received from Gallienus the title of "Augustus;" he was assassinated in A.D. 266—not, it was believed, without the connivance of Zenobia, who succeeded him on the throne. 20 Together. 21 Loved.
22 Again. 23 Doubt. 24 Whether.
25 On other terms, in other wise. 26 Learning.

I say, so worshipful a creatúre,
And wise therewith, and largë with measúre,[1]
So penible[2] in the war, and courteous eke,
Nor morë labour might in war endure,
Was none, though all this worldë men should seek.

Her rich array it mightë not be told,
As well in vessel[3] as in her clothíng:
She was all clad in pierrie[4] and in gold,
And eke she leftë not,[5] for no huntíng,
To have of sundry tonguës full knowíng,
When that she leisure had, and for t' intend[6]
To learnë bookës was all her likíng,
How she in virtue might her life dispend.

And, shortly of this story for to treat,
So doughty was her husband and eke she,
That they conquered many regnës great
In th' Orient, with many a fair city
Appertinent unto the majesty
Of Rome, and with strong handë held them fast,
Nor ever might their foemen do[7] them flee,
Aye while that Odenatus' dayës last'.

Her battles, whoso list them for to read,
Against Sapor the king,[8] and other mo',
And how that all this process fell in deed,
Why she conquér'd, and what title thereto,
And after of her mischief[9] and her woe,
How that she was besieged and y-take,
Let him unto my master Petrarch go,
That writes enough of this, I undertake.

When Odenate was dead, she mightily
The regnë held, and with her proper hand
Against her foes she fought so cruelly,
That there n'as[10] king nor prince in all that land,
That was not glad, if he that gracë fand
That she would not upon his land warray;[11]
With her they maden álliánce by bond,
To be in peace, and let her ride and play.

The emperor of Romë, Claudius,
Nor, him before, the Roman Gallien,
Durstë never be so courageoús,
Nor no Armenian, nor Egyptien,
Nor Syrian, nor no Arabien,
Within the fieldë durstë with her fight,
Lest that she would them with her handës slén,[12]
Or with her meinie[13] puttë them to flight.

In kingës' habit went her sonës two,
As heirës of their father's regnës all;
And Herëmanno and Timolaó
Their namës were, as Persians them call.
But aye Fortúne hath in her honey gall;
This mighty queenë may no while endure;
Fortune out of her regnë made her fall
To wretchedness and to misádventúre.

Aurelian, when that the governánce
Of Romë came into his handës tway,[14]
He shope[15] upon this queen to do vengeánce;
And with his legións he took his way
Toward Zenobie, and, shortly for to say,
He made her flee, and at the last her hent,[16]
And fetter'd her, and eke her children tway,
And won the land, and home to Rome he went.

Amongës other thingës that he wan,
Her car, that was with gold wrought and pierrie,
This greatë Roman, this Aurelian
Hath with him led, for that men should it see.
Before in his triumphë walked she
With giltë chains upon her neck hangíng;
Crowned she was, as after[17] her degree,
And full of pierrie charged[18] her clothíng.

Alas, Fortúnë! she that whilom was
Dreadful to kingës and to emperoúrs,
Now galeth[19] all the people on her, alas!
And she that helmed was in starkë stowres,[20]
And won by forcë townës strong and tow'rs,
Shall on her head now wear a vitremite;[21]
And she that bare the sceptre full of flow'rs
Shall bear a distaff, her cost for to quite.[22]

Although that NERO were as vicious
As any fiend that lies full low adown,
Yet he, as telleth us Suetonius,[23]
This widë world had in subjectioún,
Both East and West, South and Septentrioún.
Of rubies, sapphires, and of pearlës white
Were all his clothes embroider'd up and down,
For he in gemmës greatly gan delight.

More delicate, more pompous of array,
More proud, was never emperor than he;
That ilkë cloth[24] that he had worn one day,
After that time he would it never see;
Nettës of gold thread had he great plentý,
To fish in Tiber, when him list to play;
His lustës were as law, in his degree,
For Fortune as his friend would him obey.

He Romë burnt for his délicacý;[25]
The senators he slew upon a day,
To hearë how that men would weep and cry;
And slew his brother, and by his sister lay.
His mother made he in piteous array;
For he her wombë slittë, to behold
Where he conceived was; so well-away!
That he so little of his mother told.[26]

No tear out of his eyen for that sight
Came; but he said, a fair woman was she.
Great wonder is, how that he could or might
Be doomësman[27] of her deadë beautý:
The wine to bringë him commanded he,
And drank anon; none other woe he made.

1 Bountiful with due moderation. 2 Laborious.
3 Plate; French, "vaisselle."
4 Precious stones. 5 Did not neglect.
6 Apply. 7 Make.
8 Of Persia, who made the Emperor Valerian prisoner, conquered Syria, and was pressing triumphantly westward, when he was met and defeated by Odenatus and Zenobia.
9 Misfortune. 10 Was not.
11 Make war. 12 Slay. 13 Troops.
14 In A.D. 270. 15 Resolved, prepared.
16 Took. 17 According to. 18 Loaded.
19 Yelleth, shouteth.
20 Wore helmet in obstinate battles.
21 The signification of this word, which is spelled in several ways, is not known. Skinner's explanation, "another attire," founded on the spelling "autremite," is obviously insufficient.
22 To spin for her maintenance.
23 Great part of this "tragedy" of Nero is really borrowed, however, from the "Romance of the Rose."
24 Same robe.
25 Pleasure. 26 So little valued.
27 Judge, critic.

When might is joined unto cruelty,
Alas! too deepë will the venom wade.

In youth a master had this emperoúr,
To teachë him lettrure[1] and courtesy;
For of morality he was the flow'r,
As in his timë, but if[2] bookës lie.
And while this master had of him mast'rý,
He madë him so conning and so souple,[3]
That longë time it was ere tyrannÿ,
Or any vicë, durst in him uncouple.[4]

This Seneca, of which that I devise,[5]
Because Nero had of him suchë dread,
For he from vices would him aye chastise
Discreetly, as by word, and not by deed;
"Sir," he would say, "an emperor must need
Be virtuous, and hatë tyranny."
For which he made him in a bath to bleed
On both his armës, till he mustë die.

This Nero had eke of a custumance[6]
In youth against his master for to rise;[7]
Which afterward he thought a great grievánce;
Therefore he made him dien in this wise.
But natheless this Seneca the wise
Chose in a bath to die in this mannére,
Rather than have another tormentise;[8]
And thus hath Nero slain his master dear.

Now fell it so, that Fortune list no longer
The highë pride of Nero to cherice;[9]
For though he werë strong, yet was she stronger.
She thoughtë thus; "By God, I am too nice[10]
To set a man, that is full fill'd of vice,
In high degree, and emperor him call!
By God, out of his seat I will him trice![11]
When he least weeneth,[12] soonest shall he fall."

The people rose upon him on a night,
For his default; and when he it espied,
Out of his doors anon he hath him dight[13]
Alone, and where he ween'd t' have been allied,[14]
He knocked fast, and aye the more he cried
The faster shuttë they their doorës all;
Then wist he well he had himself misgied,[15]
And went his way, no longer durst he call.

The people cried and rumbled up and down,
That with his earës heard he how they said;
"Where is this falsë tyrant, this Neroún?"
For fear almost out of his wit he braid,[16]
And to his goddës piteously he pray'd
For succour, but it mightë not betide;
For dread of this he thoughtë that he died,
And ran into a garden him to hide.

And in this garden found he churlës tway,
That sattë by a firë great and red;
And to these churlës two he gan to pray
To slay him, and to girden[17] off his head,
That to his body, when that he were dead,
Were no despitë done for his defame.[18]
Himself he slew, he coud no better rede;[19]
Of which Fortúnë laugh'd and haddë game.[20]

Was never capitain under a king,
That regnës more put in subjectioún,
Nor stronger was in field of allë thing
As in his time, nor greater of renown,
Nor more pompous in high presumptioún,
Than HOLOFERNES, whom Fortúne aye kiss'd
So lik'rously, and led him up and down,
Till that his head was off ere that he wist.

Not only that this world had of him awe,
For losing of richéss and liberty;
But he made every man reny his law.[21]
Nabuchodónosór was God, said he;
None other Goddë should honoúred be.
Against his hest[22] there dare no wight trespace,
Save in Bethulia, a strong citý,
Where Eliáchim priest was of that place.

But take keep[23] of the death of Holofern;
Amid his host he drunken lay at night
Within his tentë, large as is a bern;[24]
And yet, for all his pomp and all his might,
Judith, a woman, as he lay upright
Sleeping, his head off smote, and from his tent
Full privily she stole from every wight,
And with his head unto her town she went.

What needeth it of king ANTIOCHUS[25]
To tell his high and royal majesty,
His great pride, and his workës venomous?
For such another was there none as he;
Readë what that he was in Maccabee.
And read the proudë wordës that he said,
And why he fell from his prosperity,
And in an hill how wretchedly he died.

Fortúne him had enhanced so in pride,
That verily he ween'd he might attain
Unto the starrës upon every side,
And in a balance weighen each mountáin,
And all the floodës of the sea restrain.
And Goddë's people had he most in hate;
Them would he slay in torment and in pain,
Weening that God might not his pride abate.

And for that Nicanor and Timothee
With Jewës werë vanquish'd mightily,[26]
Unto the Jewës such an hate had he,
That he bade graith his car[27] full hastily,
And swore and saidë full dispiteously,
Unto Jerusalem he would eftsoon,[28]
To wreak his ire on it full cruelly;
But of his purpose was he let[29] full soon.

God for his menace him so sorë smote,
With invisíble wound incurable,
That in his guttës carf it so and bote,[30]

1 Learning, letters. 2 Unless.
3 So intelligent and pliable.
4 Let itself loose, like a hound released from the leash.
5 Tell. 6 Habit.
7 To rise up in his master's presence, out of respect.
8 Torture. 9 Cherish. 10 Foolish.
11 Thrust; from Anglo-Saxon, "thriccan."
12 Expecteth. 13 Betaken himself.
14 Regarded with friendship.
15 Misguided, misled. 16 Went.
17 Strike. 18 Infamy.
19 He knew no better counsel; there was no other resource.
20 Made merry, was amused by the sport.
21 Renounce his religion; so, in the Man of Law's Tale, the Sultaness promises her son that she will "reny her lay;" see page 64. 22 Commandment.
23 Notice. 24 Barn.
25 As the "tragedy" of Holofernes is founded on the Book of Judith, so is that of Antiochus on the Second Book of the Maccabees, chap. ix.
26 By the insurgents under the leadership of Judas Maccabeus; 2 Macc. chap. viii.
27 Prepare his chariot. 28 Immediately.
29 Prevented.
30 It so cut and gnawed in his entrails.

Till that his painës were importable;[1]
And certainly the wreche[2] was reasonable,
For many a mannë's guttës did he pain;
But from his purpose, curs'd[3] and damnable,
For all his smart he would him not restrain;
But bade anon apparailë[4] his host.
And suddenly, ere he was of it ware,
God daunted all his pride, and all his boast;
For he so sorë fell out of his chare,[5]
That it his limbës and his skin to-tare,
So that he neither mightë go nor ride;
But in a chairë men about him bare,
Allë forbruised bothë back and side.

The wreche[2] of God him smote so cruelly,
That through his body wicked wormës crept,
And therewithal he stank so horribly
That none of all his meinie[6] that him kept,
Whether so that he woke or ellës slept,
Ne mightë not of him the stink endure.
In this mischíef he wailed and eke wept,
And knew God Lord of every creatúre.

To all his host, and to himself also,
Full wlatsom[7] was the stink of his carráin;[8]
No mannë might him bearë to and fro.
And in this stink, and this horríble pain,
He starf[9] full wretchedly in a mountáin.
Thus hath this robber, and this homicide,
That many a mannë made to weep and plain,
Such guerdon[10] as belongeth unto pride.

The story of ALEXANDER is so commúne,
That ev'ry wight that hath discretioún
Hath heard somewhat or all of his fortúne.
This widë world, as in conclusioún,[11]
He won by strength; or, for his high renown,
They werë glad for peace to him to send.
The pride and boast of man he laid adown,
Whereso he came, unto the worldë's end.

Comparison yet[12] never might be maked
Between him and another conqueroúr;
For all this world for dread of him had quaked;
He was of knighthood and of freedom flow'r:
Fortúne him made the heir of her honoúr.
Save wine and women, nothing might assuage
His high intent in armës and laboúr,
So was he full of leonine courâge.

What praise were it to him, though I you told
Of Darius, and a hundred thousand mo',
Of kingës, princes, dukes, and earlës bold,
Which he conquér'd, and brought them into woe?
I say, as far as man may ride or go,
The world was his, why should I more devise?[13]
For, though I wrote or told you evermo',
Of his knighthood it mightë not suffice.

Twelve years he reigned, as saith Maccabee;
Philippë's son of Macedon he was,
That first was king in Greecë the countrý.
O worthy gentle[14] Alexander, alas
That ever should thee fallë such a case!
Empoison'd of thine owen folk thou were;
Thy six[15] Fortúne hath turn'd into an ace,
And yet for thee she weptë never a tear.

Who shall me givë tearës to complain
The death of gentiléss, and of franchise,[16]
That all this worldë had in his demaine,[17]
And yet he thought it mightë not suffice,
So full was his coráge[18] of high emprise?
Alas! who shall me helpë to indite
Falsë Fortúne, and poison to despise?
The whichë two of all this woe I wite.[19]

By wisdom, manhood, and by great laboúr,
From humbleness to royal majesty
Up rose he, JULIUS the Conqueroúr,
That won all th' Occident,[20] by land and sea,
By strength of hand or ellës by treatý,
And unto Romë made them tributáry;
And since[21] of Rome the emperor was he,
Till that Fortúnë wax'd his adversáry.

O mighty Cæsar, that in Thessaly
Against POMPEIUS, father thine in law,[22]
That of th' Oriént had all the chivalry,
As far as that the day begins to daw,
That through thy knighthood hast them take and slaw,[23]
Save fewë folk that with Pompeius fled;
Through which thou put all th' Orient in awe;
Thankë Fortúnë that so well thee sped.

But now a little while I will bewail
This Pompeius, this noble governór
Of Romë, which that fled at this battaile;
I say, one of his men, a false traitór,
His head off smote, to winnë him favór
Of Julius, and him the head he brought;
Alas! Pompey, of th' Orient conquerór,
That Fortune unto such a fine[24] thee brought!

To Rome again repaired Julius,
With his triumphë laureate full high;
But on a time Brutus and Cassius,
That ever had of his estate envý,
Full privily have made conspiracý
Against this Julius in subtle wise;
And cast[25] the place in which he shouldë die,
With bodëkins,[26] as I shall you devise.[27]

This Julius to the Capitôlë went
Upon a day, as he was wont to gon;
And in the Capitol anon him hent[28]
This falsë Brutus, and his other fone,
And sticked him with bodëkins anon
With many a wound, and thus they let him lie.
But never groan'd he at no stroke but one,
Or else at two, but if[29] the story lie.

So manly was this Julius of heart,
And so well lov'd estately honesty,[30]
That, though his deadly woundës sorë smert,[31]
His mantle o'er his hippës castë he,
That no man shouldë see his privity.

1 Unendurable. 2 Vengeance. 3 Impious.
4 Prepare. 5 Chariot. 6 Servants.
7 Loathsome; from Anglo-Saxon, "wlætan," to loathe. 8 Body. 9 Died.
10 Recompense. 11 To sum up his career.
12 Moreover. 13 Tell. 14 Noble.
15 The highest cast on a dicing-cube; here representing the highest favour of fortune. 16 Generosity.
17 Government, dominion. 18 Spirit.
19 Blame. 20 West. 21 Afterwards.
22 He had married his daughter Julia to Cæsar; but she died six years before Pompey's final overthrow.
23 Slain; at the battle of Pharsalia, B.C. 48.
24 End. 25 Arranged. 26 Daggers.
27 Relate. 28 Assailed. 29 Unless.
30 Dignified propriety. 31 Pained him.

And as he lay a-dying in a trance,
And wistë verily that dead was he,
Of honesty yet had he remembránce.

Lucan, to thee this story I recommend,
And to Sueton', and Valerie also,
That of this story writë word and end;[1]
How that to these great conqueróres two
Fortune was first a friend, and since[2] a foe.
No mannë trust upon her favour long,
But have her in await[3] for evermo';
Witness on all these conqueróres strong.

The richë CRŒSUS, whilom king of Lyde,—
Of which Crœsus Cyrus him sorë drad,[4]—
Yet was he caught amiddës all his pride,
And to be burnt men to the fire him lad;[5]
But such a rain down from the welkin shad,[6]
That slew the fire, and made him to escape:
But to beware no gracë yet he had,
Till fortune on the gallows made him gape.

When he escaped was, he could not stint[7]
For to begin a newë war again;
He weened well, for[8] that Fortúne him sent
Such hap, that he escaped through the rain,
That of his foes he mightë not be slain.
And eke a sweven[9] on a night he mette,[10]
Of which he was so proud, and eke so fain,[11]
That he in vengeance all his heartë set.

Upon a tree he was set, as he thought,
Where Jupiter him wash'd, both back and side,
And Phœbus eke a fair towél him brought
To dry him with; and therefore wax'd his pride.
And to his daughter that stood him beside,
Which he knew in high science to abound,
He bade her tell him what it signified;
And she his dream began right thus expound.

"The tree," quoth she, "the gallows is to mean,
And Jupiter betokens snow and rain,
And Phœbus, with his towel clear and clean,
Those be the sunnë's streamës,[12] sooth to sayn;
Thou shalt y-hanged be, father, certáin;
Rain shall thee wash, and sunnë shall thee dry."
Thus warned him full plat and eke full plain
His daughter, which that called was Phaníe.

And hanged was Crœsus the proudë king;
His royal thronë might him not avail.
Tragédy is none other manner thing,
Nor can in singing crien nor bewail,
But for that Fortune all day will assail
With unware stroke the regnës[13] that be proud:
For when men trustë her, then will she fail,
And cover her bright facë with a cloud.

O noble, O worthy PEDRO,[14] glory OF SPAIN,
Whom Fortune held so high in majesty,
Well oughtë men thy piteous death complain.
Out of thy land thy brother made thee flee,
And after, at a siege, by subtlety,
Thou wert betray'd, and led unto his tent,
Where as he with his owen hand slew thee,
Succeeding in thy regne and in thy rent.[15]

The field of snow, with th' eagle of black therein,
Caught with the lion, red-colour'd as the glede,[16]
He brew'd this cursedness,[17] and all this sin;
The wicked nest was worker of this deed;
Not Charlës' Oliver,[18] that took aye heed
Of truth and honour, but of Armorike
Ganilion Oliver, corrupt for meed,
Broughtë this worthy king in such a brike.[19]

O worthy PETRO, King OF CYPRE,[20] also,
That Alisandre won by high mast'ry,
Full many a heathen wroughtest thou full woe,
Of which thine owen lieges had envý;
And, for no thing but for thy chivalry,
They in thy bed have slain thee by the morrow;
Thus can Fortúne her wheel govérn and gie,[21]
And out of joy bringë men into sorrow.

Of Milan greatë BARNABO VISCOUNT,
God of delight, and scourge of Lombardy,
Why should I not thine infortúne account,[22]
Since in estate thou clomben wert so high?
Thy brother's son, that was thy double allý,
For he thy nephew was and son-in-law,
Within his prison madë thee to die,
But why, nor how, n'ot[23] I that thou were slaw.[24]

1 Apparently a corruption of the Anglo-Saxon phrase, "ord and end," meaning the whole, the beginning and the end.
2 Afterwards.
3 Ever be watchful against her.
4 At the opening of the story of Crœsus, Chaucer has copied from his own translation of Boethius; but the story is mainly taken from the "Romance of the Rose."
5 Led.
6 Shed, poured.
7 Refrain.
8 Because.
9 Dream.
10 Dreamed.
11 Glad.
12 Rays.
13 Kingdoms. "This reflection," says Tyrwhitt, "seems to have been suggested by one which follows soon after the mention of Crœsus in the passage just cited from Boethius. 'What other thing bewail the cryings of tragedies but only the deeds of fortune, that with an awkward stroke overturneth the realms of great nobley?'"—In some manuscripts, the four "tragedies" that follow are placed between those of Zenobia and Nero; but although the general reflection with which the "tragedy" of Crœsus closes might most appropriately wind up the whole series, the general chronological arrangement which is observed in the other cases, recommends the order followed in the text. Besides, since, like several other Tales, the Monk's tragedies were cut short by the impatience of the auditors, it is more natural that the Tale should close abruptly, than by such a rhetorical finish as these lines afford.
14 Pedro the Cruel, King of Aragon, against whom his brother Henry rebelled. He was by false pretences inveigled into his brother's tent, and treacherously slain. Mr Wright has remarked that "the cause of Pedro, though he was no better than a cruel and reckless tyrant, was popular in England from the very circumstance that Prince Edward (the Black Prince) had embarked in it."
15 Thy kingdom and revenues.
16 Burning coal.
17 Wickedness, villainy.
18 Not the Oliver of Charlemagne—but a traitorous Oliver of Armorica, corrupted by a bribe. Ganilion was the betrayer of the Christian army at Roncesvalles (see note 29, p. 141); and his name appears to have been for a long time used in France to denote a traitor. Duguesclin, who betrayed Pedro into his brother's tent, seems to be intended by the term "Ganilion Oliver," but if so, Chaucer has mistaken his name, which was Bertrand—perhaps confounding him, as Tyrwhitt suggests, with Oliver de Clisson, another illustrious Breton of those times, who was also Constable of France, after Duguesclin. The arms of the latter are supposed to be described a little above.
19 Breach, ruin.
20 Pierre de Lusignan, King of Cyprus, who captured Alexandria in 1365 (see note 14, p. 17). He was assassinated in 1369.
21 Guide.
22 Reckon.
23 Know not.
24 Bernabo Visconti, Duke of Milan, was deposed and

Of th' Earl HUGOLIN OF PISE the languoúr[1]
There may no tonguë tellë for pitý.
But little out of Pisa stands a tow'r,
In whichë tow'r in prison put was he,
And with him be his little children three;
The eldest scarcely five years was of age;
Alas! Fortúne, it was great cruelty
Such birdës for to put in such a cage.

Damned was he to die in that prisón;
For Roger, which that bishop was of Pise,
Had on him made a false suggestión,
Through which the people gan upon him rise,
And put him in prisón, in such a wise
As ye have heard; and meat and drink he had
So small, that well unneth[2] it might suffice,
And therewithal it was full poor and bad.

And on a day befell, that in that hour
When that his meatë wont was to be brought,
The jailor shut the doorës of the tow'r;
He heard it right well, but he spakë nought.
And in his heart anon there fell a thought,
That they for hunger wouldë do him dien;[3]
"Alas!" quoth he, "alas that I was wrought!"[4]
Therewith the tearës fellë from his eyen.

His youngest son, that three years was of age,
Unto him said, "Father, why do ye weep?
When will the jailor bringen our pottáge?
Is there no morsel bread that ye do keep?
I am so hungry, that I may not sleep.
Now wouldë God that I might sleepen ever!
Then should not hunger in my wombë creep;
There is no thing, save bread, that me were lever."[5]

Thus day by day this child began to cry,
Till in his father's barme[6] adown he lay,
And saidë, "Farewell, father, I must die;"
And kiss'd his father, and died the samë day.
And when the woeful father did it sey,[7]
For woe his armës two he gan to bite,
And said, "Alas! Fortúne, and well-away!
To thy false wheel my woe all may I wite."[8]

His children ween'd[9] that it for hunger was
That he his armës gnaw'd, and not for woe,
And saidë, "Father, do not so, alas!
But rather eat the flesh upon us two.
Our flesh thou gave us, our flesh take us fro',
And eat enough;" right thus they to him said.
And after that, within a day or two,
They laid them in his lap adown, and died.

Himself, despaired, eke for hunger starf.[10]
Thus ended is this mighty Earl of Pise;
From high estate Fortúne away him carf.[11]
Of this tragédy it ought enough suffice;
Whoso will hear it in a longer wise,[12]
Readë the greatë poet of Itále,
That Dante hight, for he can it devise[13]
From point to point, not one word will he fail.

THE NUN'S PRIEST'S TALE.

THE PROLOGUE.

"Ho!" quoth the Knight, "good sir, no more of this;
That ye have said is right enough, y-wis,[14]
And muchë more; for little heaviness
Is right enough to muchë folk, I guess.
I say for me, it is a great disease,[15]
Where as men have been in great wealth and ease,
To hearen of their sudden fall, alas!
And the contráry is joy and great solas,[16]
As when a man hath been in poor estate,
And climbeth up, and waxeth fortunate,
And there abideth in prosperity;
Such thing is gladsome, as it thinketh me,
And of such thing were goodly for to tell."
"Yea," quoth our Hostë, "by Saint Paulë's bell,
Ye say right sooth; this monk hath clapped[17] loud;
He spake how Fortune cover'd with a cloud
I wot not what, and als' of a tragédy
Right now ye heard: and pardie no remédy
It is for to bewailë, nor complain
That that is done, and also it is pain,
As ye have said, to hear of heaviness.
Sir Monk, no more of this, so God you bless;
Your tale annoyeth all this company;
Such talking is not worth a butterfly,
For therein is there no disport nor game;
Therefore, Sir Monkë, Dan Piers by your name,
I pray you heart'ly, tell us somewhat else,
For sickerly, n'ere clinking of your bells,[18]
That on your bridle hang on every side,
By heaven's king, that for us allë died,
I should ere this have fallen down for sleep,
Although the slough had been never so deep;
Then had your talë been all told in vain.
For certainly, as thesë clerkës sayn,
Where as a man may have no audience,
Nought helpeth it to tellë his senténce.
And well I wot the substance is in me,
If anything shall well reported be.
Sir, say somewhat of hunting,[19] I you pray."
"Nay," quoth the Monk, "I have no lust to play;[20]
Now let another tell, as I have told."
Then spake our Host with rudë speech and bold,
And said unto the Nunnë's Priest anon,

imprisoned by his nephew, and died a captive in 1385. His death is the latest historical fact mentioned in the Tales; and thus it throws the date of their composition to about the sixtieth year of Chaucer's age.

1 Agony. 2 With difficulty. 3 Cause him to die. 4 Made, born. 5 Dearer. 6 Lap. 7 See. 8 Blame, impute. 9 Thought. 10 Died. 11 Cut off. 12 More at length.

13 Relate. The story of Ugolino is told in the 33d canto of the "Inferno." 14 Of a surety.
15 Source of distress, annoyance.
16 Delight, comfort. 17 Talked.
18 Were it not for the jingling of your bridle-bells. See note 13, page 19.
19 The request is justified by the description of the Monk in the Prologue as "an out-rider, that loved venery;" see page 19.
20 I have no fondness for jesting.

"Come near, thou Priest, come hither, thou Sir John,[1]
Tell us such thing as may our heartës glade.[2]
Be blithe, although thou ride upon a jade.
What though thine horse be bothë foul and lean?
If he will serve thee, reck thou not a bean;
Look that thine heart be merry evermo'."
"Yes, Host," quoth he, "so may I ride or go,
But[3] I be merry, y-wis I will be blamed."
And right anon his tale he hath attamed;[4]
And thus he said unto us every one,
This sweetë priest, this goodly man, Sir John.

THE TALE.[5]

A poor widow, somedeal y-stept[6] in age,
Was whilom dwelling in a poor cottáge,
Beside a grovë, standing in a dale.
This widow, of which I tellë you my tale,
Since thilkë day that she was last a wife,
In patiénce led a full simple life,
For little was her chattel and her rent.[7]
By husbandry[8] of such as God her sent,
She found[9] herself, and eke her daughters two.
Three largë sowës had she, and no mo';
Three kine, and eke a sheep that hightë Mall.
Full sooty was her bow'r,[10] and eke her hall,
In which she ate full many a slender meal.
Of poignant saucë knew she never a deal.[11]
No dainty morsel passed through her throat;
Her diet was accordant to her cote.[12]
Repletión her madë never sick;
Attemper[13] diet was all her physíc,
And exercise, and heartë's suffisance.[14]
The goutë let her nothing[15] for to dance,
Nor apoplexy shentë[16] not her head.
No winë drank she, neither white nor red:
Her board was served most with white and black,
Milk and brown bread, in which she found no lack,
Seind[17] bacon, and sometimes an egg or tway;
For she was as it were a manner dey.[18]
A yard[19] she had, enclosed all about
With stickës, and a dryë ditch without,
In which she had a cock, hight Chanticleer;
In all the land of crowing n'as[20] his peer.[21]
His voice was merrier than the merry orgón,[22]
On massë days that in the churches gon.
Well sickerer[23] was his crowing in his lodge,
Than is a clock, or an abbáy horloge.[24]
By nature he knew each ascensioún
Of th' equinoctial in thilkë town;
For when degrees fifteenë were ascended,
Then crew he, that it might not be amended.
His comb was redder than the fine corál,
Embattell'd[25] as it were a castle wall.
His bill was black, and as the jet it shone;
Like azure were his leggës and his tone;[26]
His nailës whiter than the lily flow'r,
And like the burnish'd gold was his coloúr.
This gentle cock had in his governánce
Sev'n hennës, for to do all his pleasánce,
Which were his sisters and his paramours,
And wondrous like to him as of coloúrs.
Of which the fairest-hued in the throat
Was called Damosellë Partelote.
Courteous she was, discreet, and debonair,
And cómpaniáble,[27] and bare herself so fair,
Sincë the day that she sev'n night was old,
That truëly she had the heart in hold
Of Chanticleer, locked in every lith;[28]
He lov'd her so, that well was him therewith.
But such a joy it was to hear them sing,
When that the brightë sunnë gan to spring,
In sweet accord, "My lefe[29] is fare[30] in land."[31]
For at that time, as I have understand,
Beastës and birdës couldë speak and sing.
And so befell, that in a dawëning,
As Chanticleer among his wivës all
Sat on his perchë, that was in the hall,
And next him sat this fairë Partelote,
This Chanticleer gan groanen in his throat,
As man that in his dream is dretched[32] sore.
And when that Partelote thus heard him roar,
She was aghast,[33] and saidë, "Heartë dear,
What aileth you to groan in this mannére?
Ye be a very sleeper, fy for shame!"
And he answér'd and saidë thus; "Madame,
I pray you that ye take it not agrief;[34]

1 On this Tyrwhitt remarks: "I know not how it has happened, that in the principal modern languages, John, or its equivalent, is a name of contempt, or at least of slight. So the Italians use 'Gianni,' from whence 'Zani;' the Spaniards 'Juan,' as 'Bobo Juan,' a foolish John; the French 'Jean,' with various additions; and in English, when we call a man 'a John,' we do not mean it as a title of honour." The title of "Sir" was usually given by courtesy to priests.
2 Gladden.
3 Unless.
4 Commenced, broached. Compare French, "entamer," to cut the first piece off a joint; thence to begin.
5 The Tale of the Nun's Priest is founded on the fifth chapter of an old French metrical "Romance of Renard;" the same story forming one of the Fables of Marie, the translator of the Breton Lays. (See note 11, page 122.) Although Dryden was in error when he ascribed the Tale to Chaucer's own invention, still the materials on which he had to operate were out of comparison more trivial than the result.
6 Somewhat advanced.
7 Her goods and her income.
8 Thrifty management.
9 Maintained.
10 Chamber.
11 Whit.
12 In keeping with her cottage.
13 Moderate.
14 Contentment of heart.
15 No wise prevented her.
16 Hurt, destroyed.
17 Singed.
18 Kind of day labourer. Tyrwhitt quotes two statutes of Edward III., in which "deys" are included among the servants employed in agricultural pursuits; the name seems to have originally meant a servant who gave his labour by the day, but afterwards to have been appropriated exclusively to one who superintended or worked in a dairy.
19 Court-yard, farm-yard.
20 Was not.
21 Equal.
22 Licentiously used for the plural, "organs" or "orgons," corresponding to the plural verb "gon" in the next line.
23 More punctual.
24 Clock; French, "horloge."
25 Indented on the upper edge like the battlements of a castle.
26 Toes.
27 Sociable.
28 Limb.
29 Love.
30 Gone.
31 This seems to have been the refrain of some old song, and its precise meaning is uncertain. It corresponds in cadence with the morning salutation of the cock; and may be taken as a greeting to the sun, which is beloved of Chanticleer, and has just come upon the earth—or in the sense of a more local boast, as vaunting the fairness of his favourite hen above all others in the country round.
32 Oppressed.
33 Afraid.
34 Amiss, in umbrage.

By God, me mette[1] I was in such mischief,[2]
Right now, that yet mine heart is sore affright'.
Now God," quoth he, "my sweven[3] read aright,
And keep my body out of foul prisoún.
Me mette,[1] how that I roamed up and down
Within our yard, where as I saw a beast
Was like an hound, and would have made arrest[4]
Upon my body, and would have had me dead.
His colour was betwixt yellow and red;
And tipped was his tail, and both his ears,
With black, unlike the remnant of his hairs.
His snout was small, with glowing eyen tway;
Yet of his look almost for fear I dey;[5]
This caused me my groaning doubtëless."
"Away,"[6] quoth she, "fy on you, heartëless![7]
Alas!" quoth she, "for, by that God above!
Now have ye lost my heart and all my love;
I cannot love a coward, by my faith.
For certes, what so any woman saith,
We all desiren, if it mightë be,
To have husbandës hardy, wise, and free,
And secret, and no niggard nor no fool,
Nor him that is aghast[8] of every tool,[9]
Nor no avantour,[10] by that God above!
How durstë ye for shame say to your love
That anything might makë you afear'd?
Have ye no mannë's heart, and have a beard?
Alas! and can ye be aghast of swevenës?[11]
Nothing but vanity, God wot, in sweven is.
Swevens engender of[12] repletións,
And oft of fume, and of complexións,
When humours be too abundant in a wight.
Certes this dream, which ye have mette to-night,
Cometh of the great superfluity
Of yourë redë *cholera*,[13] pardie,
Which causeth folk to dreaden in their dreams
Of arrows, and of fire with redë beams,
Of redë beastës, that they will them bite,
Of conteke,[14] and of whelpës great and lite;[15]
Right as the humour of meláncholy
Causeth full many a man in sleep to cry,
For fear of bullës, or of bearës blake,
Or ellës that black devils will them take.
Of other humours could I tell also,
That workë many a man in sleep much woe;
But I will pass as lightly as I can.
Lo Cato, which that was so wise a man,
Said he not thus, 'Ne do no force of[16] dreams.'
Now, Sir," quoth she, "when we fly from these beams,[17]
For Goddë's love, as take some laxatife;
On peril of my soul, and of my life,
I counsel you the best, I will not lie,
That both of choler, and meláncholy,
Ye purgë you; and, for ye shall not tarry,
Though in this town is no apothecáry,
I shall myself two herbës teachë you,
That shall be for your health, and for your prow;[18]
And in our yard the herbës shall I find,
The which have of their property by kind[19]
To purgë you beneath, and eke above.
Sirë, forget not this, for Goddë's love;
Ye be full choleric of complexión;
Ware that the sun, in his ascensión,
You findë not replete of humours hot;
And if it do, I dare well lay a groat,
That ye shall have a fever tertiane,
Or else an ague, that may be your bane.
A day or two ye shall have digestives
Of wormës, ere ye take your laxatives,
Of laurel, centaury,[20] and fumetére,[21]
Or else of elder-berry, that groweth there,
Of catapuce,[22] or of the gaitre-berries,[23]
Or herb ivy growing in our yard, that merry is:
Pick them right as they grow, and eat them in.
Be merry, husband, for your father's kin;
Dreadë no dream; I can say you no more."
"Madame," quoth he, "*grand mercy* of your lore.
But natheless, as touching Dan Catoún,
That hath of wisdom such a great renown,
Though that he bade no dreamës for to dread,
By God, men may in oldë bookës read
Of many a man more of authority
Than ever Cato was, so may I thé,[24]
That all the reversë say of his senténce,[25]
And have well founden by experience
That dreamës be significatións
As well of joy, as tribulatións
That folk enduren in this life presént.
There needeth make of this no argument;
The very prevë[26] sheweth it indeed.
One of the greatest authors that men read[27]
Saith thus, that whilom two fellówës went
On pilgrimage in a full good intent;
And happen'd so, they came into a town
Where there was such a congregatioún
Of people, and eke so strait of herbergage,[28]
That they found not as much as one cottáge
In which they bothë might y-lodged be:
Wherefore they musten of necessity,
As for that night, departë company;
And each of them went to his hostelry,[29]
And took his lodging as it wouldë fall.
The one of them was lodged in a stall,

1 I dreamed. 2 Peril, trouble.
3 Dream, vision. 4 Seizure. 5 Die.
6 "Avoi!" is the word here rendered "away!" It was frequently used in the French fabliaux, and the Italians employ the word "via!" in the same sense.
7 Coward. 8 Frightened.
9 Rag, clout, trifle. 10 Braggart.
11 Dreams. 12 Are produced by.
13 Choler, bile. 14 Contention. 15 Little.
16 Attach no consequence to; "Somnia ne cures," Cato "De Moribus," l. ii. dist. 32.
17 The rafters of the hall, on which they were perched.
18 Profit, advantage. 19 Nature.
20 The herb so called because by its virtue the Centaur Chiron was healed when the poisoned arrow of Hercules had accidentally wounded his foot.
21 The herb "fumitory."
22 Spurge; a plant of purgative qualities. To its name in the text correspond the Italian "catapuzza," and French "catapuce"—words the origin of which is connected with the effects of the plant.
23 Dog-wood berries.
24 Thrive. 25 Opinion.
26 Trial, experience.
27 Cicero, who in his book "De Divinatione" tells this and the following story, though in contrary order and with many differences.
28 Lodging. 29 Inn.

Far in a yard, with oxen of the plough;
That other man was lodged well enow,
As was his âventúre, or his fortúne,
That us govérneth all, as in commúne.
And so befell, that, long ere it were day,
This man mette[1] in his bed, there as he lay,
How that his fellow gan upon him call,
And said, 'Alas! for in an ox's stall
This night shall I be murder'd, where I lie.
Now help me, dearë brother, or I die;
In allë hastë come to me,' he said.
This man out of his sleep for fear abraid;[2]
But when that he was wak'd out of his sleep,
He turned him, and took of this no keep;
He thought his dream was but a vanity.
Thus twiës in his sleeping dreamed he.
And at the thirdë time yet[3] his fellâw
Came, as he thought, and said, 'I am now slaw;[4]
Behold my bloody woundës, deep and wide.
Arise up early, in the morning tide,
And at the west gate of the town,' quoth he,
'A cartë full of dung there shalt thou see,
In which my body is hid privily.
Do thilkë cart arrestë[5] boldëly.
My gold caused my murder, sooth to sayn.'
And told him every point how he was slain,
With a full piteous face, and pale of hue.
"And, trustë well, his dream he found full true;
For on the morrow, as soon as it was day,
To his fellôwë's inn he took his way;
And when that he came to this ox's stall,
After his fellow he began to call.
The hostelére answered him anon,
And saidë, 'Sir, your fellow is y-gone,
As soon as day he went out of the town.'
This man gan fallen in suspicioún,
Rememb'ring on his dreamës that he mette,[1]
And forth he went, no longer would he let,[6]
Unto the west gate of the town, and fand
A dung cart, as it went for to dung land,
That was arrayed in the samë wise
As ye have heard the deadë man devise;[7]
And with an hardy heart he gan to cry,
'Vengeance and justice of this felony:
My fellow murder'd is this samë night,
And in this cart he lies, gaping upright.
I cry out on the ministers,' quoth he,
'That shouldë keep and rulë this city;
Harow! alas! here lies my fellow slain.'
What should I more unto this talë sayn?
The people out start, and cast the cart to ground,
And in the middle of the dung they found
The deadë man, that murder'd was all new.
O blissful God! that art so good and true,
Lo, how that thou bewray'st murder alway.
Murder will out, that see we day by day.
Murder is so wlatsom[8] and abominable
To God, that is so just and reasonable,
That he will not suffer it heled[9] be;
Though it abide a year, or two, or three,
Murder will out, this is my conclusioún.
And right anon, the ministers of the town
Have hent[10] the carter, and so sore him pined,[11]
And eke the hostelére so sore engined,[12]
That they beknew[13] their wickedness anon,
And werë hanged by the neckë bone.
"Here may ye see that dreamës be to dread.
And certes in the samë book I read,
Right in the nextë chapter after this
(I gabbë[14] not, so have I joy and bliss),
Two men that would have passed over sea,
For certain cause, into a far countrý,
If that the wind not haddë been contráry,
That made them in a city for to tarry,
That stood full merry upon an haven side;
But on a day, against the even-tide,
The wind gan change, and blew right as them lest.[15]
Jolly and glad they wentë to their rest,
And castë[16] them full early for to sail.
But to the one man fell a great marvail.
That one of them, in sleeping as he lay,
He mette[1] a wondrous dream, against the day:
He thought a man stood by his beddë's side,
And him commanded that he should abide;
And said him thus; 'If thou to-morrow wend,[17]
Thou shalt be drown'd; my tale is at an end.'
He woke, and told his fellow what he mette,
And prayed him his voyage for to let;[18]
As for that day, he pray'd him to abide.
His fellow, that lay by his beddë's side,
Gan for to laugh, and scorned him full fast.
'No dream,' quoth he, 'may so my heart aghast,[19]
That I will lettë for to do my things.[20]
I settë not a straw by thy dreamíngs,
For swevens[21] be but vanities and japes.[22]
Men dream all day of owlës and of apes,
And eke of many a mazë[23] therewithal;
Men dream of thing that never was, nor shall.
But since I see that thou wilt here abide,
And thus forslothë[24] wilfully thy tide,[25]
God wot, it rueth me;[26] and have good day.'
And thus he took his leave, and went his way.
But, ere that he had half his coursë sail'd,
I know not why, nor what mischance it ail'd,
But casually[27] the ship's bottom rent,
And ship and man under the water went,
In sight of other shippës there beside
That with him sailed at the samë tide.[25]
"And therefore, fairë Partelote so dear,
By such examples oldë may'st thou lear,[28]
That no man shouldë be too reckëless
Of dreamës, for I say thee doubtëless,
That many a dream full sore is for to dread.
Lo, in the life of Saint Kenelm[29] I read,

1 Dreamed. 2 Awoke, started. 3 Again.
4 Slain. 5 Cause that cart to be stopped.
6 Delay. 7 Describe. 8 Loathsome.
9 Or hylled; from Anglo-Saxon, "helan;" hid, concealed. 10 Seized.
11 Tortured. 12 Racked. 13 Confessed.
14 I am not prating idly, or lying.
15 As they wished. 16 Prepared, resolved.
17 Depart. 18 Delay. 19 Dismay.
20 Transact my business. 21 Dreams.
22 Tricks. 23 Incoherent, wild imagining.
24 Spend or lose in sloth, loiter away.
25 Time. 26 I am sorry for thee.
27 By an accident. 28 Learn.
29 Kenelm succeeded his father as king of the Saxon realm of Mercia in 811, at the age of seven years;

That was Kenulphus' son, the noble king
Of Mercenrike,[1] how Kenelm mette a thing.
A little ere he was murder'd on a day,
His murder in his visión he say.[2]
His norice[3] him expounded every deal[4]
His sweven, and bade him to keep[5] him well
For treason; but he was but seven years old,
And therefore little talë hath he told[6]
Of any dream, so holy was his heart.
By God, I haddë lever than my shirt
That ye had read his legend, as have I.
Dame Partelote, I say you truëly,
Macrobius, that wrote the visión
In Afric' of the worthy Scipion,[7]
Affirmeth dreamës, and saith that they be
Warnings of thingës that men after see.
And furthermore, I pray you lookë well
In the Old Testament, of Daniél,
If he held dreamës any vanity.
Read eke of Joseph, and there shall ye see
Whether dreams be sometimes (I say not all)
Warnings of thingës that shall after fall.
Look of Egypt the king, Dan Pharaóh,
His baker and his buteler also,
Whether they feltë none effect[8] in dreams.
Whoso will seek the acts of sundry remes[9]
May read of dreamës many a wondrous thing.
Lo Crœsus, which that was of Lydia king,
Mette he not that he sat upon a tree,
Which signified he shouldë hanged be?[10]
Lo here, Andromaché, Hectorë's wife,
That day that Hector shouldë lose his life,
She dreamed on the samë night beforn,
How that the life of Hector should be lorn,[11]
If thilkë day he went into battaile;
She warned him, but it might not avail;
He wentë forth to fightë natheless,
And was y-slain anon of Achillés.
But thilkë tale is all too long to tell;
And eke it is nigh day, I may not dwell.
Shortly I say, as for conclusión,
That I shall have of this avisión
Adversity; and I say furthermore,
That I ne tell of laxatives no store,[12]
For they be venomous, I wot it well;
I them defy,[13] I love them never a del.[14]
"But let us speak of mirth, and stint[15] all this;
Madamë Partelote, so have I bliss,
Of one thing God hath sent me largë[16] grace;
For when I see the beauty of your face,
Ye be so scarlet-hued about your eyen,
It maketh all my dreadë for to dien,
For, all so sicker[17] as *In principio*,[18]
Mulier est hominis confusio.[19]
(Madam, the sentence[20] of this Latin is,
Woman is mannë's joy and mannë's bliss.)
For when I feel at night your softë side,—
Albeit that I may not on you ride,
For that our perch is made so narrow, alas!—
I am so full of joy and of solas,[21]
That I defy both sweven and eke dream."
And with that word he flew down from the beam,
For it was day, and eke his hennës all;
And with a chuck he gan them for to call,
For he had found a corn, lay in the yard.
Royal he was, he was no more afear'd;
He feather'd Partelotë twenty time,
And as oft trode her, ere that it was prime.
He looked as it were a grim lioún,
And on his toes he roamed up and down;
He deigned not to set his feet to ground;
He chucked, when he had a corn y-found,
And to him rannë then his wivës all.
Thus royal, as a prince is in his hall,
Leave I this Chanticleer in his pastúre;
And after will I tell his áventúre.

When that the month in which the world began,
That hightë March, when God first maked man,
Was cómplete, and y-passed were also,
Sincë March ended, thirty days and two,
Befell that Chanticleer in all his pride,
His seven wivës walking him beside,
Cast up his eyen to the brightë sun,
That in the sign of Taurus had y-run
Twenty degrees and one, and somewhat more;
He knew by kind,[22] and by none other lore,[23]
That it was prime, and crew with blissful steven.[24]
"The sun," he said, "is clomben up in heaven
Twenty degrees and one, and more y-wis.[25]
Madamë Partelote, my worldë's bliss,
Hearken these blissful birdës how they sing,
And see the freshë flowers how they spring;
Full is mine heart of revel and solace."
But suddenly him fell a sorrowful case;[26]
For ever the latter end of joy is woe:
God wot that worldly joy is soon y-go:
And, if a rhetor[27] couldë fair indite,
He in a chronicle might it safely write,

but he was slain by his ambitious aunt Quendrada. The place of his burial was miraculously discovered, and he was subsequently elevated to the rank of a saint and martyr. His life is in the English "Golden Legend."

1 The kingdom of Mercia; Anglo-Saxon, "Myrcnarice. Compare the second member of the compound in the German, "Frankreich," France; "Oesterreich," Austria.

2 Saw. 3 Nurse.

4 In all points. 5 Guard.

6 Little significance has he attached to.

7 Cicero ("De Republicâ," lib. vi.) wrote the Dream of Scipio, in which the Younger relates the appearance of the Elder Africanus, and the counsels and exhortations which the shade addressed to the sleeper. Macrobius wrote an elaborate "Commentary on the Dream of Scipio,"—a philosophical treatise much studied and relished during the Middle Ages. 8 Significance.

9 Realms. 10 See the Monk's Tale, page 163.

11 Lost. Andromache's dream will not be found in Homer; it is related in the book of the fictitious Dares Phrygius, the most popular authority during the Middle Ages for the history of the Trojan War.

12 Hold laxatives of no value. 13 Distrust.

14 Not a whit. 15 Cease. 16 Liberal.

17 Certain. 18 See note 6, page 20.

19 This line is taken from the same fabulous conference between the Emperor Adrian and the philosopher Secundus, whence Chaucer derived some of the arguments in praise of poverty employed in the Wife of Bath's Tale proper. See note 15, page 82. The passage transferred to the text is the commencement of a description of woman. "Quid est mulier? hominis confusio," &c. 20 Meaning. 21 Delight.

22 Natural instinct. 23 Learning.

24 Voice. 25 Assuredly. 26 Casualty.

27 Rhetorician, orator.

As for a sov'reign notability.[1]
Now every wise man, let him hearken me;
This story is all as true, I undertake,
As is the book of Launcelot du Lake,
That women hold in full great reverence.
Now will I turn again to my senténce.
A col-fox,[2] full of sly iniquity,
That in the grove had wonned[3] yearës three,
By high imaginatión forecast,
The samë night thorough the hedges brast[4]
Into the yard, where Chanticleer the fair
Was wont, and eke his wivës, to repair;
And in a bed of wortës[5] still he lay,
Till it was passed undern[6] of the day,
Waiting his time on Chanticleer to fall:
As gladly do these homicidës all,
That in awaitë lie to murder men.
O falsë murd'rer! rouking[7] in thy den!
O new Iscariot, new Ganilion![8]
O false dissimuler, O Greek Sinón,[9]
That broughtest Troy all utterly to sorrow!
O Chanticleer! accursed be the morrow
That thou into thy yard flew from the beams;[10]
Thou wert full well y-warned by thy dreams
That thilkë day was perilous to thee.
But what that God forewot[11] must needës be,
After th' opinion of certain clerkës.
Witness on him that any perfect clerk is,
That in school is great altercatión
In this matter, and great disputatión,
And hath been of an hundred thousand men.
But I ne cannot boult it to the bren,[12]
As can the holy doctor Augustine,
Or Boece, or the bishop Bradwardine,[13]
Whether that Goddë's worthy foreweeting[14]
Straineth me needly[15] for to do a thing
(Needly call I simple necessity),
Or ellës if free choice be granted me
To do that samë thing, or do it not,
Though God forewot[11] it ere that it was wrought;
Or if his weeting[16] straineth[17] never a deal,[18]
But by necessity conditionel.
I will not have to do of such mattére;
My tale is of a cock, as ye may hear,
That took his counsel of his wife, with sorrow,
To walken in the yard upon the morrow
That he had mette the dream, as I you told.
Womenë's counsels be full often cold;[19]
Womanë's counsel brought us first to woe,
And made Adám from Paradise to go,
There as he was full merry and well at ease.
But, for I n'ot[20] to whom I might displease
If I counsél of women wouldë blame,
Pass over, for I said it in my game.[21]
Read authors, where they treat of such mattére,
And what they say of women ye may hear.
These be the cockë's wordës, and not mine;
I can no harm of no woman divine.[22]
Fair in the sand, to bathe[23] her merrily,
Lies Partelote, and all her sisters by,
Against the sun, and Chanticleer so free
Sang merrier than the mermaid in the sea;
For Physiologus saith sickerly,[24]
How that they singë well and merrily.[25]
And so befell that, as he cast his eye
Among the wortës,[5] on a butterfly,
He was ware of this fox that lay full low.
Nothing ne list him thennë[26] for to crow,
But cried anon "Cock! cock!" and up he start,
As man that was affrayed in his heart.
For naturally a beast desireth flee
From his contráry,[27] if he may it see,
Though he ne'er erst[28] had seen it with his eye
This Chanticleer, when he gan him espy,
He would have fled, but that the fox anon
Said, "Gentle Sir, alas! why will ye gon?
Be ye afraid of me that am your friend?
Now, certes, I were worse than any fiend,
If I to you would harm or villainy.
I am not come your counsel to espy.
But truëly the cause of my coming
Was only for to hearken how ye sing;
For truëly ye have as merry a steven,[29]
As any angel hath that is in heaven;
Therewith ye have of music more feeling,
Than had Boece, or any that can sing.
My lord your father (God his soulë bless)
And eke your mother of her gentleness,
Have in mine housë been, to my great ease:[30]
And certes, Sir, full fain would I you please.
But, for men speak of singing, I will say,
So may I brookë[31] well mine eyen tway,
Save you, I heardë never man so sing
As did your father in the morrowning.
Certes it was of heart all that he sung.
And, for to make his voice the morë strong,
He would so pain him,[32] that with both his eyen
He mustë wink, so loud he wouldë cryen,
And standen on his tiptoes therewithal,
And stretchë forth his neckë long and small.

1 A thing supremely notable.
2 A blackish fox, so called from its likeness to coal, according to Skinner; though more probably the prefix has a reproachful meaning, and is in some way connected with the word "cold," as, some forty lines afterwards, it is applied to the prejudicial counsel of women, and as frequently it is used to describe "sighs" and other tokens of grief, and "cares" or "anxieties."
3 Dwelt. 4 Burst. 5 Cabbages.
6 In this case, the meaning of "evening" or "afternoon" can hardly be applied to the word, which must be taken to signify some early hour of the forenoon. 7 Crouching, lurking.
8 See note 29, page 141; and note 18, page 163.
9 See note 17, page 117. 10 Rafters.
11 Foreknows.
12 Examine the matter thoroughly; a metaphor taken from the sifting of meal, to divide the fine flour from the bran.
13 Thomas Bradwardine, Archbishop of Canterbury in the thirteenth century, who wrote a book, "De Causâ Dei," in controversy with Pelagius; and also numerous other treatises, among them one on predestination. 14 Foreknowledge.
15 Of inevitable necessity. 16 Knowledge.
17 Constrains, necessitates. 18 Not at all.
19 Mischievous, unwise. 20 Know not.
21 Jest. 22 Conjecture, imagine.
23 Bask. 24 Certainly.
25 In a popular metrical Latin treatise by one Theobaldus, entitled "Physiologus de Naturis XII. Animalium," Sirens are described as skilled in song, and drawing unwary mariners to destruction by the sweetness of their voices.
26 Then he had no inclination. 27 Enemy.
28 Never before. 29 Voice.
30 Satisfaction. 31 Enjoy, possess, or use.
32 Make such an exertion.

And eke he was of such discretión,
That there was no man, in no región,
That him in song or wisdom mightë pass.
I have well read in Dan Burnel the Ass,[1]
Among his verse, how that there was a cock
That, for[2] a priestë's son gave him a knock
Upon his leg, while he was young and nice,[3]
He made him for to lose his benefice.
But certain there is no comparisón
Betwixt the wisdom and discretión
Of yourë father, and his subtilty.
Nŏw singë, Sir, for saintë charity,
Let see, can ye your father counterfeit?"
This Chanticleer his wings began to beat,
As man that could not his treasón espy,
So was he ravish'd with his flattery.
Alas! ye lordës, many a false flattour[4]
Is in your court, and many a losengeour,[5]
That pleasë you well morë, by my faith,
Than he that soothfastness[6] unto you saith.
Read in Ecclesiast of flattery;
Beware, ye lordës, of their treachery.
This Chanticleer stood high upon his toes,
Stretching his neck, and held his eyen close,
And gan to crowë loudë for the nonce:[7]
And Dan Russel[8] the fox start up at once,
And by the gargat hentë[9] Chanticleer,
And on his back toward the wood him bare.
For yet was there no man that him pursu'd.
O destiny, that may'st not be eschew'd![10]
Alas, that Chanticleer flew from the beams!
Alas, his wifë raughtë[11] nought of dreams!
And on a Friday fell all this mischance.
O Venus, that art goddess of pleasánce,
Since that thy servant was this Chanticleer,
And in thy service did all his powére,
More for delight, than the world to multiply,
Why wilt thou suffer him on thy day to die?
O Gaufrid, dearë master sovereign,
That, when thy worthy king Richárd was slain[12]
With shot, complainedest his death so sore,
Why n' had I now thy sentence and thy lore,
The Friday for to chiden, as did ye?
(For on a Friday, soothly, slain was he),
Then would I shew you how that I could plain
For Chanticleerë's dread, and for his pain.
Certes such cry nor lamentatión
Was ne'er of ladies made, when Ilión
Was won, and Pyrrhus[13] with his straightë swerd,
When he had hent king Priam by the beard,
And slain him (as saith us *Eneidos*),
As maden all the hennës in the close,[14]
When they had seen of Chanticleer the sight.
But sov'reignly[15] Dame Partelotë shright,[16]
Full louder than did Hasdrubalë's wife,
When that her husband haddë lost his life,
And that the Romans had y-burnt Cartháge;
She was so full of torment and of rage,
That wilfully into the fire she start,
And burnt herselfë with a steadfast heart.
O woeful hennës! right so criëd ye,
As, when that Nero burned the citý
Of Romë, cried the senatorës' wives,
For that their husbands losten all their lives;
Withoutë guilt this Nero hath them slain.
Now will I turn unto my tale again;
The sely[17] widow, and her daughters two,
Heardë these hennës cry and makë woe,
And at the doors out started they anon,
And saw the fox toward the wood is gone,
And bare upon his back the cock away:
They criëd, "Out! harow! and well-away!
Aha! the fox!" and after him they ran,
And eke with stavës many another man;
Ran Coll our dog, and Talbot, and Garlánd;
And Malkin, with her distaff in her hand;
Ran cow and calf, and eke the very hoggës,
So fear'd they were for barking of the doggës,
And shouting of the men and women eke.
They rannë so, them thought their hearts would break.
They yelled as the fiendës do in hell;
The duckës criëd as men would them quell;[18]
The geese for fearë flewen o'er the trees,
Out of the hivë came the swarm of bees,
So hideous was the noise, *ben'dicite!*
Certes he, Jackë Straw,[19] and his meinie,[20]
Ne madë never shoutës half so shrill,

1 "Nigellus Wireker," says Urry's Glossary, "a monk and precentor of Canterbury, wrote a Latin poem intituled 'Speculum Speculorum,' dedicated to William Longchamp, Bishop of Ely, and Lord Chancellor; wherein, under the fable of an Ass (which he calls 'Burnellus') that desired a longer tail, is represented the folly of such as are not content with their own condition. There is introduced a tale of a cock, who having his leg broke by a priest's son (called Gundulfus) watched an opportunity to be revenged; which at last presented itself on this occasion: A day was appointed for Gundulfus's being admitted into holy orders at a place remote from his father's habitation; he therefore orders the servants to call him at first cock-crowing, which the cock overhearing did not crow at all that morning. So Gundulfus overslept himself, and was thereby disappointed of his ordination; the office being quite finished before he came to the place." Wireker's satire was among the most celebrated and popular Latin poems of the Middle Ages. The Ass was probably, as Tyrwhitt suggests, called "Burnel," or "Brunel," from his brown colour; as, a little below, the reddish fox is called "Russel."

2 Because. 3 Foolish.

4 Flatterer; French, "flatteur."

5 Deceiver, cozener; the word had analogues in the French "losengier," and the Spanish "lisongero." It is probably connected with "leasing," falsehood, which has been derived from Anglo-Saxon "hlisan," to celebrate—as if it meant the spreading of a false renown.

6 Truth. 7 Occasion.

8 Master Russet; a name given to the fox, from his reddish colour.

9 Seized him by the throat.

10 Escaped. 11 Recked, regarded.

12 Geoffrey de Vinsauf was the author of a well-known mediæval treatise on composition in various poetical styles, of which he gave examples. Chaucer's irony is here directed against some grandiose and affected lines on the death of Richard I., intended to illustrate the pathetic style, in which Friday is addressed as "O Veneris lachrymosa dies!"

13 "[Priamum] altaria ad ipsa trementem
Traxit, et in multo lapsantem sanguine nati;
Implicuitque comam lævâ, dextrâque coruscum
Extulit, ac lateri capulo tenus abdidit ensem.
Haec finis Priami fatorum."
—Virgil, Æneid. ii. 550.

14 Yard, enclosure. 15 Above all others.

16 Shrieked. 17 Simple, honest.

18 Kill, destroy.

19 The leader of a Kentish rising, in the reign of Richard II., in 1381, by which the Flemish merchants in London were great sufferers. 20 Followers.

When that they woulden any Fleming kill,
As thilkë day was made upon the fox.
Of brass they broughtë beamës [1] and of box,
Of horn and bone, in which they blew and pooped,[2]
And therewithal they shrieked and they hooped;
It seemed as the heaven shouldë fall.
Now, goodë men, I pray you hearken all;
Lo, how Fortúnë turneth suddenly
The hope and pride eke of her enemy.
This cock, that lay upon the fox's back,
In all his dread unto the fox he spake,
And saidë, "Sir, if that I were as ye,
Yet would I say (as wisly [3] God help me),
'Turn ye again, ye proudë churlës all; [4]
A very pestilence upon you fall.
Now am I come unto the woodë's side,
Maugré your head, the cock shall here abide;
I will him eat, in faith, and that anon.'"
The fox answér'd, "In faith it shall be done:"
And, as he spake the word, all suddenly
The cock brake from his mouth deliverly,[5]
And high upon a tree he flew anon.
And when the fox saw that the cock was gone,
"Alas!" quoth he, "O Chanticleer, alas!
I have," quoth he, "y-done to you trespass,[6]
Inasmuch as I maked you afear'd,
When I you hent,[7] and brought out of your yard;
But, Sir, I did it in no wick' intent;
Come down, and I shall tell you what I meant.
I shall say sooth to you, God help me so."
"Nay then," quoth he, "I shrew [8] us both the two,
And first I shrew myself, both blood and bones,
If thou beguile me oftener than once.
Thou shalt no morë through thy flattery
Do [9] me to sing and winkë with mine eye;
For he that winketh when he shouldë see,
All wilfully, God let him never thé." [10]
"Nay," quoth the fox; "but God give him mischance
That is so indiscreet of governánce,
That jangleth [11] when that he should hold his peace."
Lo, what it is for to be reckëless
And negligent, and trust on flattery.
But ye that holdë this tale a folly,
As of a fox, or of a cock or hen,
Take the morality thereof, good men.
For Saint Paul saith, That all that written is,
To our doctríne [12] it written is y-wis.[13]
Takë the fruit, and let the chaff be still.
Now goodë God, if that it be thy will,
As saith my Lord,[14] so make us all good men;
And bring us all to thy high bliss. *Amen.*

"Sir Nunnë's Priest," our Hostë said anon,
"Y-blessed be thy breech, and every stone;
This was a merry tale of Chanticleer.
But by my truth, if thou wert seculére,[15]
Thou wouldest be a treadëfowl [16] aright;
For if thou have courágе as thou hast might,
Thee werë need of hennës, as I ween,
Yea more than seven timës seventeen.
See, whatë brawnës [17] hath this gentle priest,
So great a neck, and such a largë breast!
He looketh as a sperhawk with his eyen;
Him needeth not his colour for to dyen
With Brazil, nor with grain of Portugale.
But, Sirë, fairë fall you for your tale."
And, after that, he with full merry cheer
Said to another, as ye shallë hear.[18]

. . . . . .

THE SECOND NUN'S TALE.[19]

THE minister and norice [20] unto vices,
Which that men call in English idleness,
The porter at the gate is of delices; [21]
T' eschew, and by her contrar' her oppress,—
That is to say, by lawful business,[22]—
Well oughtë we to do all our intent,[23]
Lest that the fiend through idleness us hent.[24]

For he, that with his thousand cordës sly
Continually us waiteth to beclap,[25]
When he may man in idleness espy,
He can so lightly catch him in his trap,

1 Trumpets; Anglo-Saxon, "bema."
2 Made a popping or tooting noise.
3 Surely.
4 Addressing the pursuers.
5 Nimbly.
6 Offence.
7 Took.
8 Curse.
9 Cause.
10 Thrive.
11 Prateth.
12 For our instruction. See 2 Tim. iii. 16.
13 Certainly.
14 A marginal note on a manuscript indicates that some Archbishop of Canterbury is here quoted.
15 A layman.
16 Cock.
17 The brawny parts of the body.
18 The sixteen lines appended to the Tale of the Nun's Priest seem, as Tyrwhitt observes, to commence the prologue to the succeeding Tale—but the difficulty is to determine which that Tale should be. In earlier editions, the lines formed the opening of the prologue to the Manciple's Tale; but most of the manuscripts acknowledge themselves defective in this part, and give the Nun's Tale after that of the Nun's Priest. In the Harleian manuscript, followed by Mr Wright, the second Nun's Tale, and the Canon's Yeoman's Tale, are placed after the Franklin's Tale; and the sixteen lines above are not found—the Manciple's prologue coming immediately after the "Amen" of the Nun's Priest. In two manuscripts, the last line of the sixteen runs thus: "Said unto the Nun as ye shall hear;" and six lines more, evidently forged, are given to introduce the Nun's Tale. All this confusion and doubt only strengthen the certainty, and deepen the regret, that "The Canterbury Tales" were left at Chaucer's death not merely very imperfect as a whole, but destitute of many finishing touches that would have made them complete so far as the conception had actually been carried into performance.
19 This Tale was originally composed by Chaucer as a separate work, and as such it is mentioned in the "Legend of Good Women" under the title of "The Life of Saint Cecile." Tyrwhitt quotes the line in which the author calls himself an "unworthy son of Eve," and that in which he says, "Yet pray I you, that readë what I *write*" (see note 17, page 172), as internal evidence that the insertion of the poem among the Canterbury Tales was the result of an afterthought; while the whole tenor of the introduction confirms the belief that Chaucer composed it as a writer or translator—not, dramatically, as a speaker. The story is almost literally translated from the Life of St Cecilia in the "Legenda Aurea."
20 Nurse.
21 Delights.
22 Occupation, activity.
23 Endeavour, apply ourselves.
24 Seize.
25 Entangle, bind.

Till that a man be hent right by the lappe,[1]
He is not ware the fiend hath him in hand;
Well ought we work, and idleness withstand.

And though men dreaded never for to die,
Yet see men well by reason, doubtëless,
That idleness is root of sluggardý,
Of which there cometh never good increase;
And see that sloth them holdeth in a leas,[2]
Only to sleep, and for to eat and drink,
And to devouren all that others swink.[3]

And, for to put us from such idleness,
That cause is of so great confusión,
I have here done my faithful business,
After the Legend, in translatión
Right of thy glorious life and passión,—
Thou with thy garland wrought of rose and lily,
Thee mean I, maid and martyr, Saint Cecílie.

And thou, thou art the flow'r of virgins all,
Of whom that Bernard list so well to write,[4]
To thee at my beginning first I call;
Thou comfort of us wretches, do me indite
Thy maiden's death, that won through her merite
Th' eternal life, and o'er the fiend victóry,
As man may after readen in her story.

Thou maid and mother, daughter of thy Son,
Thou well of mercy, sinful soulës' cure,
In whom that God of bounté chose to won;[5]
Thou humble and high o'er every creatúre,
Thou nobilest, so far forth our natúre,[6]
That no disdain the Maker had of kind,[7]
His Son in blood and flesh to clothe and wind.[8]

Within the cloister of thy blissful sidës
Took mannë's shape th' eternal love and peace,
That of the trinë compass[9] Lord and guide is;
Whom earth, and sea, and heav'n, out of release,[10]
Aye hery;[11] and thou, Virgin wemmëless,[12]
Bare of thy body, and dweltest maiden pure,
The Creatór of every creatúre.

Assembled is in thee magnificence[13]
With mercy, goodness, and with such pitý,
That thou, that art the sun of excellence,
Not only helpest them that pray to thee,
But oftentime, of thy benignity,
Full freely, ere that men thine help beseech,
Thou go'st before, and art their livës' leech.[14]

Now help, thou meek and blissful fairë maid,
Me, flemed[15] wretch, in this desért of gall;
Think on the woman Cananée, that said
That whelpës eat some of the crumbës all
That from their Lordë's table be y-fall;[16]
And though that I, unworthy son of Eve,[17]
Be sinful, yet acceptë my believe.[18]

And, for that faith is dead withoutë werkës,
So for to workë give me wit and space,
That I be quit from thennes that most derk is;[19]
O thou, that art so fair and full of grace,
Be thou mine advocate in that high place,
Where as withouten end is sung Osanne,
Thou Christë's mother, daughter dear of Anne.

And of thy light my soul in prison light,
That troubled is by the contagión
Of my bodý, and also by the weight
Of earthly lust and false affectión;
O hav'n of refuge, O salvatión
Of them that be in sorrow and distress,
Now help, for to my work I will me dress.

Yet pray I you, that readë what I write,[17]
Forgive me that I do no diligence
This ilkë[20] story subtilly t' indite.
For both have I the wordës and senténce
Of him that at the saintë's reverence
The story wrote, and follow her legénd;
And pray you that you will my work amend.

First will I you the name of Saint Cecílie
Expound, as men may in her story see.
It is to say in English, Heaven's lily,[21]
For purë chasteness of virginity;
Or, for she whiteness had of honesty,[22]
And green of consciénce, and of good fame
The sweetë savour, Lilie was her name.

Or Cecilie is to say, the way of blind;[23]
For she example was by good teachíng;
Or else Cecilie, as I written find,
Is joined by a manner conjoiníng
Of heaven and *Lia*,[24] and herein figuríng
The heaven is set for thought of holiness,
And *Lia* for her lasting business.

Cecilie may eke be said in this mannére,
Wanting of blindness, for her greatë light
Of sapience, and for her thewes[25] clear.
Or ellës, lo, this maiden's namë bright
Of heaven and *Leos* comes, for which by right
Men might her well the heaven of people call,
Example of good and wisë workës all;

For *Leos* people[26] in English is to say;[27]
And right as men may in the heaven see
The sun and moon, and starrës every way,
Right so men ghostly,[28] in this maiden free,
Sawen of faith the magnanimitý,
And eke the clearness whole of sapiénce,
And sundry workës bright of excellence.

And right so as these philosóphers write,
That heav'n is swift and round, and eke burning,
Right so was fairë Cecilíe the white
Full swift and busy in every good workíng,
And round and whole[29] in good persévering,

1 Skirt, or lappet, of a garment.
2 Leash, snare; the same as "las," oftener used in Chaucer.
3 For which others labour.
4 The nativity and assumption of the Virgin Mary formed the themes of some of St Bernard's most eloquent sermons.
5 Dwell.
6 Thou noblest one, as far as our nature admitted.
7 Nature.
8 Wrap.
9 The Trinity.
10 Without remission, unceasingly.
11 Praise.
12 Without blemish.
13 Compare with this stanza the fourth stanza of the Prioress's Tale, page 144, the substance of which is the same.
14 Healer, saviour.
15 Banished, outcast.
16 Matthew xv. 26, 27.
17 See note 19, page 171.
18 Faith.
19 Delivered from that place where is outer darkness.
20 Same.
21 Latin, "Cœli lilium." Such punning derivations of proper names were very much in favour in the Middle Ages. The explanations of St Cecilia's name are literally taken from the prologue to the Latin legend.
22 Purity.
23 Latin, "Cæci via."
24 From "Cœlum," and "ligo," I bind.
25 Qualities.
26 Greek, λαος, ληος (Ion.) λεως (Att.), the people.
27 Signifies.
28 Spiritually.
29 The passage suggests Horace's description of the

And burning ever in charity full bright;
Now have I you declared what she hight.[1]

This maiden bright Cecile, as her life saith,
Was come of Romans, and of noble kind,
And from her cradle foster'd in the faith
Of Christ, and bare his Gospel in her mind:
She never ceased, as I written find,
Of her prayére, and God to love and dread,
Beseeching him to keep her maidenhead.

And when this maiden should unto a man
Y-wedded be, that was full young of age,
Which that y-called was Valerian,
And comë was the day of marriáge,
She, full devout and humble in her coráge,[2]
Under her robe of gold, that sat full fair,
Had next her flesh y-clad her in an hair.[3]

And while the organs madë melody,
To God alone thus in her heart sang she;
"O Lord, my soul and eke my body gie[4]
Unwemmed,[5] lest that I confounded be."
And, for his love that died upon the tree,
Every second or third day she fast',
Aye bidding[6] in her orisons full fast.

The night came, and to beddë must she gon
With her husbánd, as it is the mannére;
And privily she said to him anon;
"O sweet and well-beloved spousë dear,
There is a counsel,[7] an'[8] ye will it hear,
Which that right fain I would unto you say,
So that ye swear ye will it not bewray."

Valerian gan fast unto her swear
That for no case nor thing that mightë be,
He never should to none bewrayen her;
And then at erst[9] thus to him saidë she;
"I have an angel which that loveth me,
That with great love, whether I wake or sleep,
Is ready aye my body for to keep;

"And if that he may feelen, out of dread,[10]
That ye me touch or love in villainy,
He right anon will slay you with the deed,
And in your youthë thus ye shouldë die.
And if that ye in cleanë love me gie,[11]
He will you love as me, for your cleannéss,
And shew to you his joy and his brightnéss."

Valerian, corrected as God wo'ld,
Answer'd again, "If I shall trustë thee,
Let me that angel see, and him behold;
And if that it a very angel be,
Then will I do as thou hast prayed me;
And if thou love another man, forsooth
Right with this sword then will I slay you both."

Cecile answér'd anon right in this wise;
"If that you list, the angel shall ye see,
So that ye trow[12] on Christ, and you baptise;
Go forth to Via Appia," quoth she,
"That from this townë[13] stands but milës three,

And to the poorë folkës that there dwell
Say them right thus, as that I shall you tell.

"Tell them, that I, Cecile, you to them sent,
To shewë you the good Urban the old,
For secret needës,[14] and for good intent;
And when that ye Saint Urban have behold,
Tell him the wordës which I to you told;
And when that he hath purged you from sin,
Then shall ye see that angel ere ye twin."[15]

Valerian is to the placë gone;
And, right as he was taught by her learning,
He found this holy old Urban anon
Among the saintës' burials louting;[16]
And he anon, withoutë tarrying,
Did his messáge, and when that he it told,
Urban for joy his handës gan uphold.

The tearës from his eyen let he fall;
"Almighty Lord, O Jesus Christ," quoth he,
"Sower of chaste counsél, herd[17] of us all;
The fruit of thilkë[18] seed of chastity
That thou hast sown in Cecile, take to thee:
Lo, like a busy bee, withoutë guile,
Thee serveth aye thine owen thrall[19] Cecile.

"For thilkë spousë, that she took but new,[20]
Full like a fierce lión, she sendeth here,
As meek as e'er was any lamb to ewe."
And with that word anon there gan appear
An old man, clad in whitë clothës clear,
That had a book with letters of gold in hand,
And gan before Valerian to stand.

Valerian, as dead, fell down for dread,
When he him saw; and he up hent[21] him tho,[22]
And on his book right thus he gan to read;
"One Lord, one faith, one God withoutë mo',
One Christendom, one Father of all alsó,
Aboven all, and over all everywhere."
These wordës all with gold y-written were.

When this was read, then said this oldë man,
"Believ'st thou this or no? say yea or nay."
"I believe all this," quoth Valerian,
"For soother[23] thing than this, I dare well say,
Under the heaven no wight thinkë may."
Then vanish'd the old man, he wist not where;
And Pope Urban him christened right there.

Valerian went home, and found Cecílie
Within his chamber with an angel stand;
This angel had of roses and of lily
Coronës[24] two, the which he bare in hand,
And first to Cecile, as I understand,
He gave the one, and after gan he take
The other to Valerian her make.[25]

"With body clean, and with unwemmed[5] thought,
Keep aye well these coronës two," quoth he;
"From Paradise to you I have them brought,
Nor ever morë shall they rotten[26] be,
Nor lose their sweetë savour, trustë me,

wise man, who, among other things, is "in se ipso totus, teres, atque rotundus."—"Satires," 2, vii. 86.
1 Why she had her name. 2 Heart.
3 Garment of hair-cloth. 4 Guide, keep.
5 Unspotted, blameless. 6 Praying.
7 Secret. 8 If.
9 For the first time.
10 Doubt. 11 Govern, dispose of.
12 Believe. 13 Rome.

14 Business. 15 Depart.
16 Lingering, or lying concealed, among the burial-places of the saints; the Latin original has "inter sepulchra martyrum *latitantem*."
17 Shepherd, keeper. 18 That.
19 Servant, handmaid. 20 But lately, newly.
21 Took, lifted. 22 Then. 23 Truer.
24 Crowns. 25 Mate, husband.
26 Decayed.

Nor ever wight shall see them with his eye,
But[1] he be chaste, and hatë villainy.
"And thou, Valerian, for thou so soon
Assented hast to good counsél, also
Say what thee list, and thou shalt have thy boon."[2]
"I have a brother," quoth Valerian tho,[3]
"That in this world I lovë no man so;
I pray you that my brother may have grace
To know the truth, as I do in this place."
The angel said, "God liketh thy request,
And bothë, with the palm of martyrdom,
Ye shallë come unto his blissful rest."
And, with that word, Tiburce his brother come.
And when that he the savour undernome[4]
Which that the roses and the lilies cast,
Within his heart he gan to wonder fast;
And said; "I wonder, this time of the year,
Whencë that sweetë savour cometh so
Of rose and lilies, that I smellë here;
For though I had them in mine handës two,
The savour might in me no deeper go;
The sweetë smell, that in my heart I find,
Hath changed me all in another kind."[5]
Valerian said, "Two crownës here have we,
Snow-white and rosë-red, that shinë clear,
Which that thine eyen have no might to see;
And, as thou smellest them through my prayére,
So shalt thou see them, levë[6] brother dear,
If it so be thou wilt withoutë sloth
Believe aright, and know the very troth."[7]
Tiburce answéred, "Say'st thou this to me
In soothness, or in dreamë hear I this?"
"In dreamës," quoth Valerian, "have we be
Unto this timë, brother mine, y-wis:[8]
But now at erst[9] in truth our dwelling is."
"How know'st thou this," quoth Tiburce; "in what wise?"
Quoth Valerián, "That shall I thee devise.[10]
"The angel of God hath me the truth y-taught,
Which thou shalt see, if that thou wilt reny[11]
The idols, and be clean, and ellës nought."
[[12]And of the mirácle of these crownës tway
Saint Ambrose in his preface list to say;
Solemnëly this noble doctor dear
Commendeth it, and saith in this mannére:
"The palm of martyrdom for to receive,
Saint Cecilie, full filled of God's gift,
The world and eke her chamber gan to weive;[13]
Witness Tiburce's and Cecilie's shrift,[14]
To which God of his bounty wouldë shift[15]
Coronës two, of flowers well smellíng,
And made his angel them the crownës bring.
"The maid hath brought these men to bliss above;
The world hath wist what it is worth, certáin,
Devotión of chastity to love."]
Then showed him Cecile all open and plain,
That idols all are but a thing in vain,
For they be dumb, and thereto[16] they be deave;[17]
And charged him his idols for to leave.
"Whoso that trow'th[18] not this, a beast he is,"
Quoth this Tiburce, "if that I shall not lie."
And she gan kiss his breast when she heard this,
And was full glad he could the truth espy:
"This day I takë thee for mine ally,"[19]
Saidë this blissful fairë maiden dear;
And after that she said as ye may hear.
"Lo, right so as the love of Christ," quoth she,
"Made me thy brother's wife, right in that wise
Anon for mine allý here take I thee,
Since that thou wilt thine idolës despise.
Go with thy brother now and thee baptise,
And make thee clean, so that thou may'st behold
The angel's face, of which thy brother told."
Tiburce answér'd, and saidë, "Brother dear,
First tell me whither I shall, and to what man?"
"To whom?" quoth he, "come forth with goodë cheer,
I will thee lead unto the Pope Urbán."
"To Urban? brother mine Valerián,"
Quoth then Tiburce; "wilt thou me thither lead?
Me thinketh that it were a wondrous deed.
"Meanest thou not that Urban," quoth he tho,[3]
"That is so often damned to be dead,
And wons[20] in halkës[21] always to and fro,
And dare not onës puttë forth his head?
Men should him brennen[22] in a fire so red,
If he were found, or if men might him spy:
And us also, to bear him companý.
"And while we seekë that Divinity
That is y-hid in heaven privily,
Algatë[23] burnt in this world should we be."
To whom Cecilie answer'd boldëly;
"Men mightë dreadë well and skilfully[24]
This life to lose, mine owen dearë brother,
If this were living only, and none other.
"But there is better life in other place,
That never shall be lostë, dread thee nought;
Which Goddë's Son us toldë through his grace,
That Father's Son which allë thingës wrought;
And all that wrought is with a skilful[25] thought,
The Ghost,[26] that from the Father gan proceed,
Hath souled[27] them, withouten any drede.[28]
"By word and by mirácle, high God's Son,
When he was in this world, declared here,
That there is other life where men may won."[29]

1 Unless. 2 Request. 3 Then.
4 Perceived.
5 Into another being or nature.
6 Beloved. 7 Truth. 8 Verily.
9 For the first time. 10 Tell. 11 Renounce.
12 The fourteen lines within brackets are supposed to have been originally an interpolation in the Latin legend, from which they are literally translated. They awkwardly interrupt the flow of the narration.

13 Forsake. 14 Confession.
15 Allot, appropriate. 16 Moreover.
17 Deaf. 18 Believeth.
19 Chosen friend.
20 Dwelleth. 21 Corners.
22 Burn. 23 Nevertheless.
24 Reasonably. 25 Reasonable.
26 Spirit. 27 Endowed them with a soul.
28 Doubt. 29 Dwell.

To whom answẃer'd Tiburce, "O sister dear,
Saidest thou not right now in this mannére,
There was but one God, Lord in soothfastness,[1]
And now of three how may'st thou bear witnéss?"

"That shall I tell," quoth she, "ere that I go.
Right as a man hath sapiénces three,
Memory, engine,[2] and intellect also,
So in one being of divinity
Three personës there mayë right well be."
Then gan she him full busily to preach
Of Christë's coming, and his painës teach,

And many pointës of his passión;
How Goddë's Son in this world was withhold[3]
To do mankindë plein[4] remissión,
That was y-bound in sin and carës cold.[5]
All this thing she unto Tiburcë told,
And after this Tiburce, in good intent,
With Valerián to Pope Urban he went;

That thanked God, and with glad heart and light
He christen'd him, and made him in that place
Perféct in his learníng, and Goddë's knight.
And after this Tiburcë got such grace,
That every day he saw in time and space
Th' angel of God, and every manner boon[6]
That he God asked, it was sped[7] full soon.

It were full hard by order for to sayn
How many wonders Jesus for them wrought.
But at the last, to tellë short and plain,
The sergeants of the town of Rome them sought,
And them before Almach the prefect brought,
Which them appos'd,[8] and knew all their intent,
And to th' image of Jupiter them sent;

And said, "Whoso will not do sacrifice,
Swap[9] off his head, this is my sentence here."
Anon these martyrs, that I you devise,[10]
One Maximus, that was an officére
Of the preféct's, and his corniculére,[11]
Them hent,[12] and when he forth the saintës lad,[13]
Himself he wept for pity that he had.

When Maximus had heard the saintës' lore,[14]
He got him of the tormentorës leave,
And led them to his house withoutë more;
And with their preaching, ere that it were eve,
They gonnen[15] from the tórmentors to reave,[16]
And from Maxim', and from his folk each one,
The falsë faith, to trow[17] in God alone.

Cecilia came, when it was waxen night,
With priestës, that them christen'd all in fere;[18]
And afterward, when day was waxen light,
Cecile them said with a full steadfast cheer,[19]
"Now, Christë's owen knightës lefe[20] and dear,
Cast all away the workës of darknéss,
And armë you in armour of brightnéss.

"Ye have forsooth y-done a great battaile;
Your course is done,[21] your faith have ye conserved;
Go to the crown of life that may not fail;
The rightful Judgë, which that ye have served,
Shall give it you, as ye have it deserved."
And when this thing was said, as I devise,[22]
Men led them forth to do the sacrifice.

But when they were unto the placë brought,
To tellë shortly the conclusión,
They would incénse nor sacrifice right nought.
But on their knees they settë them adown,
With humble heart and sad[23] devotión,
And lostë both their headës in the place;[24]
Their soulës wentë to the King of grace.

This Maximus, that saw this thing betide,
With piteous tearës told it anon right,
That he their soulës saw to heaven glide
With angels, full of clearness and of light;
And with his word converted many a wight.
For which Almachius did him to-beat[25]
With whip of lead, till he his life gan lete.[26]

Cecile him took, and buried him anon
By Tiburce and Valerian softëly,
Within their burying-place, under the stone.
And after this Almachius hastily
Bade his minísters fetchen openly
Cecile, so that she might in his presénce
Do sacrifice, and Jupiter incénse.[27]

But they, converted at her wisë lore,[28]
Weptë full sore, and gavë full credénce
Unto her word, and criëd more and more;
"Christ, Goddë's Son, withoutë difference,
Is very God, this is all our senténce,[29]
That hath so good a servant him to serve:
Thus with one voice we trowë,[30] though we sterve."[31]

Almachius, that heard of this doíng,
Bade fetch Cecilie, that he might her see;
And alderfirst,[32] lo, this was his askíng;
"What manner woman artë thou?" quoth he.
"I am a gentle woman born," quoth she.
"I askë thee," quoth he, "though it thee grieve,
Of thy religion and of thy believe."

"Ye have begun your question foolishly,"
Quoth she, "that wouldest two answérs conclude
In one demand? ye askë lewëdly."[33]
Almach answér'd to that similitude,
"Of whencë comes thine answering so rude?"
"Of whencë?" quoth she, when that she was freined,[34]
"Of consciénce, and of good faith unfeigned."

1 Truth.
2 Wit; the devising or constructive faculty; Latin, "ingenium."
3 Employed.
4 Full.
5 Distressful, wretched. See note 2, page 169.
6 Request, favour.
7 Granted, successful.
8 Questioned.
9 Strike.
10 Of whom I tell you.
11 The secretary or registrar who was charged with publishing the acts, decrees, and orders of the prefect.
12 Seized.
13 Led.
14 Doctrine, teaching.
15 Began.
16 To wrest, root out.
17 Believe.
18 In a company.
19 Mien.
20 Beloved.
21 See 2 Tim. iv. 7, 8; "I have fought a good fight, I have finished my course, I have kept the faith," &c.
22 Relate.
23 Steadfast.
24 On the spot.
25 Caused him to be cruelly or fatally beaten; the force of the "to" is intensive.
26 Quit.
27 Burn incense to.
28 Teaching.
29 Opinion.
30 Believe.
31 Die.
32 First of all.
33 Ignorantly.
34 Asked.

Almachius saidë; "Takest thou no heed
Of my powér?" and she him answer'd this;
"Your might," quoth she, "full little is to dread;
For every mortal mannë's power is
But like a bladder full of wind, y-wis;[1]
For with a needle's point, when it is blow',
May all the boast of it be laid full low."

"Full wrongfully begunnest thou," quoth he,
"And yet in wrong is thy persévéránce.
Know'st thou not how our mighty princes free
Have thus commanded and made ordinánce,
That every Christian wight shall have penánce,[2]
But if that he his Christendom withsay,[3]
And go all quit, if he will it renay?"[4]

"Your princes erren, as your nobley[5] doth,"
Quoth then Cecile, "and with a wood[6] senténce[7]
Ye make us guilty, and it is not sooth:[8]
For ye that knowë well our innocence,
Forasmuch as we do aye reverence
To Christ, and for we bear a Christian name,
Ye put on us a crime and eke a blame.

"But we that knowë thilkë namë so
For virtuous, we may it not withsay."
Almach answered, "Choose one of these two,
Do sacrifice, or Christendom renay,
That thou may'st now escapë by that way."
At which the holy blissful fairë maid
Gan for to laugh, and to the judgë said;

"O judge, confused in thy nicety,[9]
Wouldest thou that I rény innocence?
To makë me a wicked wight," quoth she,
"Lo, he dissimuleth[10] here in audience;
He stareth and woodeth[11] in his adverténce."[12]
To whom Almachius said, "Unsely[13] wretch,
Knowest thou not how far my might may stretch?

"Have not our mighty princes to me given
Yea bothë power and eke authority
To makë folk to dien or to liven?
Why speakest thou so proudly then to me?"
"I speakë not but steadfastly," quoth she,
Not proudly, for I say, as for my side,
We hatë deadly[14] thilkë vice of pride.

"And, if thou dreadë not a sooth[15] to hear,
Then will I shew all openly by right,
That thou hast made a full great leasing[16] here.
Thou say'st thy princes have thee given might
Both for to slay and for to quick[17] a wight,—
Thou that may'st not but only life bereave;
Thou hast none other power nor no leave.

"But thou may'st say, thy princes have thee maked
Minister of death; for if thou speak of mo',
Thou liest; for thy power is full naked."
"Do away[18] thy boldness," said Almachius tho,[19]
"And sacrifice to our gods, ere thou go.
I reckë not what wrong that thou me proffer,
For I can suffer it as a philosópher.

"But thosë wrongës may I not endure,
That thou speak'st of our goddës here," quoth he.
Cecile answér'd, "O nicë[20] creatúre,
Thou saidest no word, since thou spake to me,
That I knew not therewith thy nicety,[21]
And that thou wert in every manner wise[22]
A lewëd[23] officer, a vain justíce.

"There lacketh nothing to thine outward eyen
That thou art blind; for thing that we see all
That it is stone, that men may well espyen,
That ilkë[24] stone a god thou wilt it call.
I rede[25] thee let thine hand upon it fall,
And taste[26] it well, and stone thou shalt it find;
Since that thou see'st not with thine eyen blind.

"It is a shamë that the people shall
So scornë thee, and laugh at thy follý;
For commonly men wot it well over all,[27]
That mighty God is in his heaven high;
And these imáges, well may'st thou espy,
To thee nor to themselves may not profíte,
For in effect they be not worth a mite."

These wordës and such others saidë she,
And he wax'd wroth, and bade men should her lead
Home to her house; "And in her house," quoth he,
"Burn her right in a bath, with flamës red."
And as he bade, right so was done the deed;
For in a bath they gan her fastë shetten,[28]
And night and day great fire they under betten.[29]

The longë night, and eke a day also,
For all the fire, and eke the bathë's heat,
She sat all cold, and felt of it no woe,
It made her not one droppë for to sweat;
But in that bath her lifë she must lete.[30]
For he, Almachius, with full wick' intent,
To slay her in the bath his sondë[31] sent.

Three strokës in the neck he smote her tho,[19]
The tórmentor,[32] but for no manner chance
He might not smite her fairë neck in two:
And, for there was that time an ordinance
That no man shouldë do man such penánce,[33]
The fourthë stroke to smitë, soft or sore,
This tórmentor he durstë do no more;

But half dead, with her neckë carven[34] there
He let her lie, and on his way is went.
The Christian folk, which that about her were,
With sheetës have the blood full fair y-hent;[35]
Three dayës lived she in this tormént,
And never ceased them the faith to teach,
That she had foster'd them, she gan to preach.

1 Certainly. 2 Punishment. 3 Deny. 4 Renounce. 5 Nobility. 6 Mad. 7 Judgment. 8 True. 9 Confounded in thy folly. 10 Dissembles. 11 Grows mad, furious. 12 Thought, consideration. 13 Unhappy. 14 Mortally. 15 Truth. 16 Falsehood. 17 Give life to. 18 Cease, have done with. 19 Then. 20 Foolish. 21 Folly. 22 Every sort of way.

23 Ignorant. 24 Very, selfsame. 25 Advise. 26 Examine, test. 27 Everywhere; or, above all things. 28 Shut, confine. 29 Kindled, applied. 30 Leave. 31 Message, order. 32 Executioner. 33 Cause such torture, exercise such severity of punishment. 34 Mangled, gashed. 35 Received, caught up.

And them she gave her mebles[1] and her thing,
And to the Pope Urban betook[2] them tho;[3]
And said, "I askë this of heaven's king,
To have respite three dayës and no mo',
To recommend to you, ere that I go,
These soulës, lo; and that I might do wirch[4]
Here of mine house perpetually a church."
Saint Urban, with his deacons, privily
The body fetch'd, and buried it by night
Among his other saintës honestly;[5]
Her house the church of Saint Cecilie hight;[6]
Saint Urban hallow'd it, as he well might;
In which unto this day, in noble wise,
Men do to Christ and to his saint service.

THE CANON'S YEOMAN'S TALE.[7]

THE PROLOGUE.

WHEN ended was the life of Saint Cecile,
Ere we had ridden fully fivë mile,[8]
At Boughton-under-Blee us gan o'ertake
A man, that clothed was in clothës black,
And underneath he wore a white surplice.
His hackenay,[9] which was all pomely-gris,[10]
So sweated, that it wonder was to see;
It seem'd as he had pricked[11] milës three.
The horse eke that his yeoman rode upon
So sweated, that unnethës[12] might he gon.
About the peytrel[13] stood the foam full high;
He was of foam as flecked[14] as a pie.
A mailë twyfold[15] on his crupper lay;
It seemed that he carried little array;
All light for summer rode this worthy man.
And in my heart to wonder I began
What that he was, till that I understood
How that his cloak was sewed to his hood;
For which, when I had long advised[16] me,
I deemed him some Canon for to be.
His hat hung at his back down by a lace,[17]
For he had ridden more than trot or pace;
He haddë pricked like as he were wood.[18]
A clote-leaf[19] he had laid under his hood,
For sweat, and for to keep his head from heat.
But it was joyë for to see him sweat;
His forehead dropped as a stillatory[20]
Were full of plantain or of paritory.[21]
And when that he was come, he gan to cry,
"God save," quoth he, "this jolly company.
Fast have I pricked," quoth he, "for your sake,
Becausë that I would you overtake,
To riden in this merry company."
His Yeoman was eke full of courtesy,
And saidë, "Sirs, now in the morning tide
Out of your hostelry I saw you ride,
And warned here my lord and sovereign,
Which that to ridë with you is full fain,
For his disport; he loveth dalliance."
"Friend, for thy warning God give thee good chance,"[22]
Said ourë Host; "certáin it wouldë seem
Thy lord were wise, and so I may well deem;
He is full jocund also, dare I lay;
Can he aught tell a merry tale or tway,
With which he gladden may this company?"
"Who, Sir? my lord? Yea, Sir, withoutë lie,
He can[23] of mirth and eke of jollity
Not but[24] enough; also, Sir, trustë me,
An'[25] ye him knew all so well as do I,
Ye would wonder how well and craftily
He couldë work, and that in sundry wise.
He hath take on him many a great emprise,
Which were full hard for any that is here
To bring about, but[26] they of him it lear.[27]
As homely as he rides amongës you,
If ye him knew, it would be for your prow:[28]
Ye wouldë not forego his ácquaintánce
For muchë good, I dare lay in balance
All that I have in my possessión.
He is a man of high discretión.
I warn you well, he is a passing[29] man."
"Well," quoth our Host, "I pray thee tell me than,
Is he a clerk,[30] or no? Tell what he is."
"Nay, he is greater than a clerk, y-wis,"[31]
Saidë this Yeoman; "and, in wordës few,
Host, of his craft somewhat I will you shew.
I say, my lord can[23] such a subtlety
(But all his craft ye may not weet[32] of me,
And somewhat help I yet to his working),
That all the ground on which we be riding
Till that we come to Canterbury town,
He could all cleanë turnen up so down,
And pave it all of silver and of gold."
And when this Yeoman had this talë told
Unto our Host, he said; "*Ben'dicite!*
This thing is wonder marvellous to me,
Since that thy lord is of so high prudénce,

1 Goods, moveables. 2 Commended. 3 Then.
4 Cause to be established or made.
5 Honourably, decorously. 6 Is called.
7 "The introduction," says Tyrwhitt, "of the Canon's Yeoman to tell a Tale at a time when so many of the original characters remain to be called upon, appears a little extraordinary. It should seem that some sudden resentment had determined Chaucer to interrupt the regular course of his work, in order to insert a satire against the alchemists. That their pretended science was much cultivated about this time, and produced its usual evils, may fairly be inferred from the Act, which was passed soon after, 5 H. IV. c. iv., to make it felony 'to multiply gold or silver, or to use the art of multiplication.'" Tyrwhitt finds in the prologue some colour for the hypothesis that this Tale was intended by Chaucer to begin the return journey from Canterbury; but against this must be set the fact that the Yeoman himself expressly speaks of the distance *to* Canterbury yet to be ridden.
8 From some place which the loss of the Second Nun's Prologue does not enable us to identify.
9 Nag. 10 Dapple-gray.
11 Spurred. 12 Scarcely.
13 The breast-plate of a horse's harness; French, "poitrail." 14 Spotted.
15 A double valise; a wallet hanging across the crupper on either side of the horse.
16 Considered. 17 Cord. 18 Mad.
19 Burdock-leaf. 20 Still. 21 Wall-flower.
22 Fortune. 23 Knows. 24 Not less than.
25 If. 26 Unless. 27 Learn.
28 Advantage. 29 Surpassing, extraordinary.
30 A scholar, or a man in holy orders.
31 Certainly.
32 Learn, know.

Because of which men should him reverence,
That of his worship[1] recketh he so lite;[2]
His overest slop[3] it is not worth a mite
As in effect to him, so may I go;[4]
It is all baudy[5] and to-tore also.
Why is thy lord so sluttish, I thee pray,
And is of power better clothes to bey,[6]
If that his deed accordeth with thy speech?
Tellë me that, and that I thee beseech."
"Why?" quoth this Yeoman, "whereto ask ye me?
God help me so, for he shall never thé[7]
(But I will not avowë[8] that I say,
And therefore keep it secret, I you pray);
He is too wise, in faith, as I believe.
Thing that is overdone, it will not preve[9]
Aright, as clerkës say; it is a vice;
Wherefore in that I hold him lew'd[10] and nice.[11]
For when a man hath over great a wit,
Full oft him happens to misusen it;
So doth my lord, and that me grieveth sore.
God it amend; I can say now no more."
"Thereof no force,[12] good Yeoman," quoth our Host;
"Since of the conning[13] of thy lord thou know'st,
Tell how he doth, I pray thee heartilý,
Since that he is so crafty and so sly.[14]
Where dwellë ye, if it to tellë be?"
"In the suburbës of a town," quoth he,
"Lurking in hernës[15] and in lanës blind,
Where as these robbers and these thieves by kind[16]
Holdë their privy fearful residence,
As they that darë not shew their presénce,
So farë we, if I shall say the soothë."[17]
"Yet," quoth our Hostë, "let me talkë tó thee;
Why art thou so discolour'd of thy face?"
"Peter!"[18] quoth he, "God give it hardë grace,[19]
I am so us'd the hotë fire to blow,
That it hath changed my coloúr, I trow;
I am not wont in no mirrór to pry,
But swinkë[20] sore, and learn to multiply.[21]
We blunder[22] ever, and poren[23] in the fire,
And, for all that, we fail of our desire;
For ever we lack our conclusión.
To muchë folk we do[24] illusión,
And borrow gold, be it a pound or two,
Or ten or twelve, or many summës mo',
And make them weenen,[25] at the leastë way,
That of a poundë we can makë tway.
Yet is it false; and aye we have good hope
It for to do, and after it we grope:[26]
But that sciénce is so far us beforn,
That we may not, although we had it sworn,
It overtake, it slides away so fast;
It will us makë beggars at the last."
While this Yeomán was thus in his talkíng,
This Canon drew him near, and heard all thing
Which this Yeomán spake, for suspición
Of mennë's speech ever had this Canón:
For Cato saith, that he that guilty is,
Deemeth all things be spoken of him y-wis;[27]
Because of that he gan so nigh to draw
To his Yeomán, that he heard all his saw;[28]
And thus he said unto his Yeoman tho;[29]
"Hold thou thy peace, and speak no wordës mo':
For if thou do, thou shalt it dear abie.[30]
Thou slanderest me here in this companý,
And eke discoverest that thou shouldest hide."
"Yea," quoth our Host, "tell on, whatso betide;
Of all his threatening reck not a mite."
"In faith," quoth he, "no more I do but lite."[2]
And when this Canon saw it would not be
But his Yeoman would tell his privitý,
He fled away for very sorrow and shame.
"Ah!" quoth the Yeoman, "here shall rise a game;[31]
All that I can anon I will you tell,
Since he is gone; the foulë fiend him quell![32]
For ne'er hereafter will I with him meet,
For penny nor for pound, I you behete.[33]
He that me broughtë first unto that game,
Ere that he die, sorrow have he and shame.
For it is earnest[34] to me, by my faith;
That feel I well, what so any man saith;
And yet for all my smart, and all my grief,
For all my sorrow, labour, and mischíef,[35]
I couldë never leave it in no wise.
Now would to God my wittë might suffice
To tellen all that longeth to that art!
But natheless yet will I tellë part;
Since that my lord is gone, I will not spare;
Such thing as that I know, I will declare."

THE TALE.[36]

With this Canón I dwelt have seven year,
And of his science am I ne'er the near:[37]
All that I had I havë lost thereby,
And, God wot, so have many more than I.
Where I was wont to be right fresh and gay
Of clothing, and of other good array
Now may I wear an hose upon mine head;

1 Honour, reputation. 2 Little. 3 Upper garment; breeches. 4 Prosper. 5 Soiled, slovenly. 6 Buy. 7 Thrive. 8 Own (to him). 9 Stand the test or proof. 10 Ignorant, stupid. 11 Foolish. 12 No matter. 13 Skill, knowledge. 14 Wise. 15 Corners. 16 Nature. 17 Truth. 18 By Saint Peter! 19 An exclamation of dislike and ill-will; "confound it!" 20 Labour. 21 Transmute metals, in the attempt to multiply gold and silver by chemistry. 22 Toil. 23 Pore, peer anxiously. 24 Cause. 25 Fancy. 26 Search, strive. 27 Surely. "Conscius ipse sibi de se putat omnia dici"—"De Moribus," l. i. dist. 17.

28 Saying. 29 Then. 30 Pay dear for it. 31 Some diversion. 32 Destroy. 33 Promise. 34 A serious matter. 35 Trouble, injury. 36 The Tale of the Canon's Yeoman, like those of the Wife of Bath and the Pardoner, is made up of two parts; a long general introduction, and the story proper. In the case of the Wife of Bath, the interruptions of other pilgrims, and the autobiographical nature of the discourse, recommend the separation of the prologue from the Tale proper; but in the other cases the introductory or merely connecting matter ceases wholly where the opening of "The Tale" has been marked in the text. 37 Nearer.

And where my colour was both fresh and red,
Now is it wan, and of a leaden hue
(Whoso it useth, sore shall he it rue);
And of my swink[1] yet bleared is mine eye;[2]
Lo what advantage is to multiply!
That sliding[3] science hath me made so bare,
That I have no good,[4] where that ever I fare;
And yet I am indebted so thereby
Of gold, that I have borrow'd truëly,
That, while I live, I shall it quitë[5] never;
Let every man beware by me for ever.
What manner man that casteth[6] him thereto,
If he continue, I hold his thrift y-do;[7]
So help me God, thereby shall he not win,
But empty his purse, and make his wittës thin.
And when he, through his madness and follý,
Hath lost his owen good through jupartie,[8]
Then he exciteth other men thereto,
To lose their good as he himself hath do'.
For unto shrewës[9] joy it is and ease
To have their fellows in pain and disease.[10]
Thus was I onës learned of a clerk;
Of that no charge;[11] I will speak of our work.
When we be there as we shall exercise
Our elvish[12] craft, we seemë wonder wise,
Our termës be so clergial and quaint.[13]
I blow the fire till that mine heartë faint.
Why should I tellen each proportión
Of thingës, whichë that we work upon,
As on five or six ounces, may well be,
Of silver, or some other quantitý?
And busy me to tellë you the names,
As orpiment, burnt bonës, iron squames,[14]
That into powder grounden be full small?
And in an earthen pot how put is all,
And salt y-put in, and also peppére,
Before these powders that I speak of here,
And well y-cover'd with a lamp of glass?
And of much other thing which that there was?
And of the pots and glasses engluting,[15]
That of the air might passen out no thing?
And of the easy[16] fire, and smart[17] also,
Which that was made? and of the care and woe
That we had in our matters súbliming,
And in amalgaming, and calcining
Of quicksilver, called mercúry crude?
For all our sleightës we can not conclude.
Our orpiment, and súblim'd mercurý,
Our ground litharge[18] eke on the porphyrý,
Of each of these of ounces a certáin,[19]
Not helpeth us, our labour is in vain.
Nor neither our spirits' ascensioún,
Nor our mattérs that lie all fix'd adown,
May in our working nothing us avail;
For lost is all our labour and traváil,
And all the cost, a twenty devil way,
Is lost also, which we upon it lay.
There is also full many another thing
That is unto our craft appértaining,
Though I by order them not rehearsë can,
Becausë that I am a lewëd[20] man;
Yet will I tell them as they come to mind,
Although I cannot set them in their kind,
As bol-armoniac, verdigris, boráce;
And sundry vessels made of earth and glass;
Our urinalës, and our descensories,[21]
Phials, and croslets,[22] and sublímatories,
Cucurbitës,[23] and álembikës[24] eke,
And other suchë, dear enough a leek,[25]
It needeth not for to rehearse them all.
Waters rubifying, and bullës' gall,
Arsenic, sal-armoniac, and brimstóne,
And herbës could I tell eke many a one,
As egremoine,[26] valerian, and lunáry,[27]
And other such, if that me list to tarry;
Our lampës burning bothë night and day,
To bring about our craft if that we may;
Our furnace eke of calcinatión,
And of waters albificatión,
Unslaked lime, chalk, and glair of an ey,[28]
Powders divérse, ashes, dung, piss, and clay,
Seared pokettes,[29] saltpetre, and vitriol;
And divers firës made of wood and coal;
Sal-tartar, alkali, salt preparáte,
And combust matters, and coaguláte;
Clay made with horse and mannë's hair, and oil
Of tartar, alum, glass, barm, wort, argoil,[30]
Rosalgar,[31] and other matters imbibing;
And eke of our mattérs encorporing,[32]
And of our silver citrinatión,[33]
Our cémenting, and fermentatión,
Our ingots,[34] tests, and many thingës mo'.
I will you tell, as was me taught also,
The fourë spirits, and the bodies seven,
By order, as oft I heard my lord them neven.[35]
The first spirit Quicksilver called is;

1 By my labour.
2 My sight is grown dim; perhaps the phrase has also the metaphorical sense of being deceived or befooled. See note 26, page 54.
3 Slippery, deceptive.
4 Property.
5 Repay.
6 Betaketh; designeth to occupy him in that art.
7 His prosperity at an end.
8 Jeopardy, hazard. In Froissart's French, "à jeu parti" is used to signify a game or a contest in which the chances were exactly equal for both sides.
9 Wicked folk.
10 Trouble.
11 No matter.
12 Fantastic, wicked.
13 Learned and strange.
14 Scales; Latin, "squamæ."
15 Cementing, sealing up.
16 Slow.
17 Quick.
18 White lead.
19 A certain number or proportion.
20 Unlearned.
21 Vessels for distillation "per descensum;" they were placed under the fire, and the spirit to be extracted was thrown downwards.
22 Crucibles; French, "creuset."
23 Retorts; distilling-vessels; so called from their likeness in shape to a gourd—Latin, "cucurbita."
24 Stills, limbecs.
25 At the price of, in exchange for, a leek.
26 Agrimony.
27 Moon-wort.
28 White of egg, glair; French, "glaire;" German, "Ey," an egg.
29 The meaning of this phrase is obscure; but if we take the reading "cered poketts," from the Harleian manuscript, we are led to the supposition that it signifies receptacles—bags or pokes—prepared with wax for some process. Latin, "cera," wax.
30 Potter's clay, used for luting or closing vessels in the laboratories of the alchemists; Latin, "argilla;" French, "argile."
31 Flowers of antimony.
32 Incorporating.
33 Turning to a citrine colour, or yellow, by chemical action; that was the colour which proved the philosopher's stone.
34 Not, as in its modern meaning, the masses of metal shaped by pouring into moulds; but the moulds themselves into which the fused metal was poured. Compare Dutch, "ingieten," part. "inghehoten," to infuse; German, "eingiessen," part. "eingegossen," to pour in.
35 Name.

The second Orpiment; the third, y-wis,
Sal-Armoniac, and the fourth Brimstóne.
The bodies sev'n eke, lo them here anon.
Sol gold is, and Luna silvér we threpe;[1]
Mars iron, Mercury quícksilver we clepe;[2]
Saturnus lead, and Jupiter is tin,
And Venus copper, by my father's kin.
This cursed craft whoso will exercise,
He shall no good have that him may suffice;
For all the good he spendeth thereabout,
He losë shall, thereof have I no doubt.
Whoso that list to utter[3] his follý,
Let him come forth and learn to multiply:
And every man that hath aught in his coffer,
Let him appear, and wax a philosópher;
Ascauncë[4] that craft is so light to lear.[5]
Nay, nay, God wot, all be he monk or frere,
Priest or canón, or any other wight;
Though he sit at his book both day and night;
In learning of this elvish nicë[6] lore,
All is in vain; and pardie muchë more,
Is to learn a lew'd[7] man this subtletý;
Fie! speak not thereof, for it will not be.
And conne he letterure,[8] or conne he none,
As in effect, he shall it find all one;
For bothë two, by my salvatión,
Concluden in multiplicatión[9]
Alikë well, when they have all y-do;
This is to say, they failë bothë two.
Yet forgot I to makë rehearsále
Of waters corrosive, and of limáile,[10]
And of bodies' mollificatión,
And also of their induratión,
Oilës, ablutións, metál fusíble,
To tellen all, would passen any Bible
That owhere[11] is; wherefore, as for the best,
Of all these namës now will I me rest;
For, as I trow, I have you told enough
To raise a fiend, all look he ne'er so rough.[12]
Ah! nay, let be; the philosópher's stone,
Elixir call'd, we seekë fast each one;
For had we him, then were we sicker[13] enow;
But unto God of heaven I make avow,[14]
For all our craft, when we have all y-do,
And all our sleight, he will not come us to.
He hath y-made us spendë muchë good,
For sorrow of which almost we waxed wood,[15]
But that good hopë creeped in our heart,
Supposing ever, though we sorë smart,
To be relieved by him afterward.
Such súpposing and hope is sharp and hard.
I warn you well it is to seeken ever.
That future *temps*[16] hath madë men dissever,
In trust thereof, from all that ever they had,
Yet of that art they cannot waxë sad,[17]
For unto them it is a bitter sweet;
So seemeth it; for had they but a sheet
Which that they mightë wrap them in at night,
And a bratt[18] to walk in by dayëlight,
They would them sell, and spend it on this craft;
They cannot stint,[19] until no thing be laft.
And evermore, wherever that they gon,
Men may them knowë by smell of brimstóne;
For all the world they stinken as a goat;
Their savour is so rammish and so hot,
That though a man a milë from them be,
The savour will infect him, trustë me.
Lo, thus by smelling and threadbare array,
If that men list, this folk they knowë may.
And if a man will ask them privily,
Why they be clothed so unthriftily,[20]
They right anon will rownen[21] in his ear,
And sayen, if that they espied were,
Men would them slay, because of their sciénce:
Lo, thus these folk betrayen innocence!
Pass over this; I go my tale unto.
Ere that the pot be on the fire y-do[22]
Of metals, with a certain quantity
My lord them tempers,[23] and no man but he
(Now he is gone, I dare say boldëly);
For as men say, he can do craftily,
Algate[24] I wot well he hath such a name,
And yet full oft he runneth into blame;
And know ye how? full oft it happ'neth so,
The pot to-breaks, and farewell! all is go'.[25]
These metals be of so great violence,
Our wallës may not make them résistence,
But if[26] they werë wrought of lime and stone;
They piercë so, that through the wall they gon;
And some of them sink down into the ground
(Thus have we lost by timës many a pound),
And some are scatter'd all the floor about;
Some leap into the roof withoutë doubt.
Though that the fiend not in our sight him shew,
I trowë that he be with us, that shrew;[27]
In hellë, where that he is lord and sire,
Is there no morë woe, rancoúr, nor ire.
When that our pot is broke, as I have said,
Every man chides, and holds him evil apaid.[28]
Some said it was long on[29] the fire-making;
Some saidë nay, it was on the blowíng
(Then was I fear'd, for that was mine offíce);
"Straw!" quoth the third, "ye be lewëd and nice,[30]
It was not temper'd[31] as it ought to be."
"Nay," quoth the fourthë, "stint[32] and hearken me;
Because our fire was not y-made of beech,
That is the cause, and other none, so thé 'ch.[33]
I cannot tell whereon it was along,
But well I wot great strife is us among."

1 Name; from Anglo-Saxon, "threapian."
2 Call.
3 Publish, display.
4 As if. See note 20, page 87.
5 Easy to learn.
6 Fantastic foolish.
7 Ignorant.
8 Know he letters—be he learned.
9 Come to the same result in the pursuit of the art of making gold.
10 Metal filings; French, "limaille."
11 Anywhere.
12 Though he look never so grim or fierce.
13 Secure.
14 Confession.
15 Mad.
16 Time.
17 Repentant.
18 Coarse cloak; Anglo-Saxon, "bratt." The word is still used in Lincolnshire, and some parts of the north, to signify a coarse kind of apron.
19 Cease.
20 Shabbily.
21 Whisper.
22 Placed.
23 Adjusts the proportions.
24 Although.
25 Gone, lost.
26 Unless.
27 Impious wretch.
28 Dissatisfied.
29 In consequence of; the modern vulgar phrase "all along of," or "all along on," best conveys the force of the words in the text.
30 Ignorant and foolish.
31 Mixed in due proportions.
32 Stop.
33 So thé ich—so may I thrive.

"What?" quoth my lord, "there is no more
to do'n,
Of these perils I will beware eftsoon.[1]
I am right sicker[2] that the pot was crazed.[3]
Be as be may, be ye no thing amazed.[4]
As usage is, let sweep the floor as swithe;[5]
Pluck up your heartës and be glad and blithe."
The mullok[6] on a heap y-sweeped was,
And on the floor y-cast a canëvas,
And all this mullok in a sieve y-throw,
And sifted, and y-picked many a throw.[7]
"Pardie," quoth one, "somewhat of our metál
Yet is there here, though that we have not all.
And though this thing mishapped hath as now,[8]
Another time it may be well enow.
We mustë put our good in ádventúre;[9]
A merchant, pardie, may not aye endúre,
Trustë me well, in his prosperity:
Sometimes his good is drenched[10] in the sea,
And sometimes comes it safe unto the land."
"Peace," quoth my lord; "the next time I
will fand[11]
To bring our craft all in another plight,[12]
And but I do, Sirs, let me have the wite;[13]
There was default in somewhat, well I wot."
Another said, the fire was over hot.
But be it hot or cold, I dare say this,
That we concluden evermore amiss;
We fail alway of that which we would have;
And in our madness evermore we rave.
And when we be together every one,
Every man seemeth a Solomon.
But all thing, which that shineth as the gold,
It is not gold, as I have heard it told;
Nor every apple that is fair at eye,
It is not good, what so men clap[14] or cry.
Right so, lo, fareth it amongës us.
He that the wisest seemeth, by Jesús,
Is most fool, when it cometh to the prefe;[15]
And he that seemeth truest, is a thief.
That shall ye know, ere that I from you wend;
By that I of my tale have made an end.
There was a canon of religioún
Amongës us, would ínfect all a town,
Though it as great were as was Ninevéh,
Rome, Alisandre,[16] Troy, or other three.
His sleightës[17] and his infinite falsenéss
There couldë no man writen, as I guess,
Though that he mightë live a thousand year;
In all this world of falseness n'is[18] his peer.
For in his termës he will him so wind,
And speak his wordës in so sly a kind,
When he commúnë shall with any wight,
That he will make him doat[19] anon aright,
But[20] it a fiendë be, as himself is.
Full many a man hath he beguil'd ere this,
And will, if that he may live any while;
And yet men go and ride many a mile
Him for to seek, and have his ácquaintánce,
Not knowing of his falsë governánce.[21]
And if you list to give me audiénce,
I will it tellë here in your presénce.
But, worshipful canóns religioús,
Ne deemë not that I slander your house,
Although that my tale of a canon be.
Of every order some shrew is,[22] pardie;
And God forbid that all a company
Should rue a singular[23] mannë's folly.
To slander you is no thing mine intent;
But to correct that is amiss I meant.
This talë was not only told for you,
But eke for other more; ye wot well how
That amongës Christë's apostlës twelve
There was no traitor but Judas himselve;
Then why should all the remenant have blame,
That guiltless were? By you I say the same.
Save only this, if ye will hearken me,
If any Judas in your convent be,
Removë him betimës, I you rede,[24]
If shame or loss may causen any dread.
And be no thing displeased, I you pray;
But in this casë hearken what I say.
In London was a priest, an annualére,[25]
That therein dwelled haddë many a year,
Which was so pleasant and so serviceáble
Unto the wife, where as he was at table,
That she would suffer him no thing to pay
For board nor clothing, went he ne'er so gay;
And spending silver had he right enow;
Thereof no force;[26] I will proceed as now,
And tellë forth my tale of the canón,
That brought this priestë to confusión.
This falsë canon came upon a day
Unto the priestë's chamber, where he lay,
Beseeching him to lend him a certáin
Of gold, and he would quit it him again.
"Lend me a mark," quoth he, "but dayës three,
And at my day I will it quitë thee.
And if it so be that thou find me false,
Another day hang me up by the halse."[27]
This priest him took a mark, and that as swithe,[28]
And this canón him thanked often sithe,[29]
And took his leave, and wentë forth his way;
And at the thirdë day brought his monéy;
And to the priest he took his gold again,
Whereof this priest was wondrous glad and
fain.[30]
"Certes," quoth he, "nothing annoyeth me[31]
To lend a man a noble, or two, or three,
Or what thing were in my possessión,
When he so true is of conditión,
That in no wise he breakë will his day;

1 Again, another time. 2 Sure.
3 Cracked; from French, "écraser," to crack or crush. 4 Confounded. 5 Quickly.
6 Rubbish. 7 Time.
8 Has gone amiss at present.
9 Risk our property. 10 Drowned, sunk.
11 Endeavour.
12 To bring our enterprise into a better condition—to a better issue. 13 Blame.
14 Assert, affirm noisily. 15 Proof, test.
16 Alexandria. 17 Cunning tricks.
18 Is not.
19 Contract an excessive or foolish fondness for him.
20 Except. 21 Deceitful conduct.
22 There is a black sheep in every flock.
23 Individual, single. 24 Counsel.
25 Employed in singing "annuals" or anniversary masses for the dead, without any cure of souls; the office was such as, in the Prologue to the Tales, Chaucer praises the Parson for not seeking: Nor "ran unto London, unto Saint Poul's, to seekë him a chantery for souls." See page 22. 26 No matter.
27 Neck. 28 Quickly. 29 Times.
30 Pleased. 31 I am not at all unwilling.

To such a man I never can say nay."
"What," quoth this canon, "should I be untrue?
Nay, that were thing y-fallen all of new.[1]
Truth is a thing that I will ever keep,
Unto the day in which that I shall creep
Into my grave; and ellës God forbid;
Believë this as sicker[2] as your creed.
God thank I, and in good time be it said,
That there was never man yet evil apaid[3]
For gold nor silver that he to me lent,
Nor ever falsehood in mine heart I meant.
And Sir," quoth he, "now of my privity,
Since ye so goodly have been unto me,
And kithed[4] to me so great gentleness,
Somewhat, to quitë with your kindëness,
I will you shew, and if you list to lear,[5]
I will you teachë plainly the mannére
How I can worken in philosophý.
Takë good heed, ye shall well see at eye[6]
That I will do a mas'try ere I go."
"Yea," quoth the priest; "yea, Sir, and will ye so?
Mary! thereof I pray you heartily."
"At your commandëment, Sir, truëly,"
Quoth the canón, "and ellës God forbid."
Lo, how this thiefë could his service bede![7]
Full sooth it is that such proffér'd servíce
Stinketh, as witnessë these oldë wise;[8]
And that full soon I will it verify
In this canón, root of all treacherý,
That evermore delight had and gladnéss
(Such fiendly thoughtës in his heart impress[9])
How Christë's people he may to mischief bring.
God keep us from his false dissimulíng!
What wistë this priest with whom that he dealt?
Nor of his harm comíng he nothing felt.
O sely[10] priest, O sely innocent!
With covetíse anon thou shalt be blent;[11]
O gracëless, full blind is thy conceit!
For nothing art thou ware of the deceit
Which that this fox y-shapen[12] hath to thee;
His wily wrenches[13] thou not mayest flee.
Wherefore, to go to the conclusión
That referreth to thy confusión,
Unhappy man, anon I will me hie[14]
To tellë thine unwit[15] and thy follý,
And eke the falseness of that other wretch,
As farforth as that my conníng[16] will stretch.
This canon was my lord, ye wouldë ween;[17]
Sir Host, in faith, and by the heaven's queen,
It was another canon, and not he,
That can[18] an hundred fold more subtletý.
He hath betrayed folkës many a time;
Of his falsenéss it doleth[19] me to rhyme.
And ever, when I speak of his falsehéad,
For shame of him my cheekës waxë red;
Algatës[20] they beginnë for to glow,
For redness have I none, right well I know,
In my visagë; for fumës divérse
Of metals, which ye have me heard rehearse,
Consumed have and wasted my rednéss.
Now take heed of this canon's cursedness.[21]
"Sir," quoth he to the priest, "let your man gon
For quicksilver, that we it had anon;
And let him bringen ounces two or three;
And when he comes, as fastë shall ye see
A wondrous thing, which ye saw ne'er ere this."
"Sir," quoth the priest, "it shall be done, y-wis."[22]
He bade his servant fetchë him this thing,
And he all ready was at his bidding,
And went him forth, and came anon again
With this quicksilver, shortly for to sayn;
And took these ounces three to the canoún;
And he them laidë well and fair adown,
And bade the servant coalës for to bring,
That he anon might go to his working.
The coalës right anon weren y-fet,[23]
And this canón y-took a crossëlet[24]
Out of his bosom, and shew'd to the priest.
"This instrument," quoth he, "which that thou seest,
Take in thine hand, and put thyself therein
Of this quicksilver an ounce, and here begin,
In the name of Christ, to wax a philosópher.
There be full few, which that I wouldë proffer
To shewë them thus much of my sciénce;
For here shall ye see by experiénce
That this quicksilver I will mortify,[25]
Right in your sight anon withoutë lie,
And make it as good silver, and as fine,
As there is any in your purse, or mine,
Or ellëswhere; and make it malleáble;
And ellës holdë me false and unable
Amongë folk for ever to appear.
I have a powder here that cost me dear,
Shall make all good, for it is cause of all
My conning,[26] which that I you shewë shall.
Voidë[27] your man, and let him be thereout;
And shut the doorë, while we be about
Our privity, that no man us espy,
While that we work in this philosophý."
All, as he bade, fulfilled was in deed.
This ilkë servant right anon out yede,[28]
And his master y-shut the door anon,
And to their labour speedily they gon.
This priest, at this cursed canón's biddíng,
Upon the fire anon he set this thing,
And blew the fire, and busied him full fast.
And this canón into the croslet cast
A powder, I know not whereof it was
Y-made, either of chalk, either of glass,
Or somewhat ellës, was not worth a fly,
To blinden with[29] this priest; and bade him hie[30]
The coalës for to couchen[31] all above
The croslet; "for, in token I thee love,"

1 A new thing to happen. 2 Sure.
3 Displeased, dissatisfied. 4 Shown.
5 Learn. 6 With your own eye.
7 Offer. 8 Those wise folk of old.
9 Press their way into his heart. 10 Simple.
11 Blinded; beguiled. 12 Contrived.
13 Stratagems, snares. 14 Hasten.
15 Stupidity. 16 Knowledge. 17 Imagine.
18 Knows. 19 Grieveth. 20 At least.
21 Villainy. 22 Certainly. 23 Fetched.
24 Crucible.
25 A chemical phrase, signifying the dissolution of quicksilver in acid. 26 Knowledge.
27 Send out of the way. 28 Went.
29 With which to deceive.
30 Make haste. 31 Lay in order.

Quoth this canón, "thine owen handës two
Shall work all thing that herë shall be do'."[1]
"*Grand mercy,*"[2] quoth the priest, and was full glad,
And couch'd the coalës as the canon bade.
And while he busy was, this fiendly wretch,
This false canón (the foulë fiend him fetch),
Out of his bosom took a beechen coal,
In which full subtilly was made a hole,
And therein put was of silver limáile[3]
An ounce, and stopped was withoutë fail
The hole with wax, to keep the limaile in.
And understandë, that this falsë gin[4]
Was not made there, but it was made before;
And other thingës I shall tell you more,
Hereafterward, which that he with him brought;
Ere he came there, him to beguile he thought,
And so he did, ere that they went atwin;[5]
Till he had turned him, could he not blin.[6]
It doleth[7] me, when that I of him speak;
On his falsehóod fain would I me awreak,[8]
If I wist how, but he is here and there;
He is so variant,[9] he abides nowhere.
But takë heed, Sirs, now for Goddë's love.
He took his coal, of which I spake above,
And in his hand he bare it privily,
And while the priestë couched busily
The coalës, as I toldä you ere this,
This canon saidë, "Friend, ye do amiss;
This is not couched as it ought to be,
But soon I shall amenden it," quoth he.
"Now let me meddle therewith but a while,
For of you have I pity, by Saint Gile.
Ye be right hot, I see well how ye sweat;
Have here a cloth, and wipe away the wet."
And whilë that the priestë wip'd his face,
This canon took his coal,—with sorry grace,[10]—
And layed it above on the midwárd
Of the croslet, and blew well afterward,
Till that the coals beganně fast to brenn.[11]
"Now give us drinkë," quoth this canon then,
"And swithe[12] all shall be well, I undertake.
Sittë we down, and let us merry make."
And whennë that this canon's beechen coal
Was burnt, all the limáile out of the hole
Into the crossëlet anon fell down;
And so it mustë needës, by reasoún,
Since it above so even couched[13] was;
But thereof wist the priest no thing, alas!
He deemed all the coals alikë good,
For of the sleight he nothing understood.
And when this alchemister saw his time,
"Rise up, Sir Priest," quoth he, "and stand by me;
And, for I wot well ingot[14] have ye none,
Go, walkë forth, and bring me a chalk stone;
For I will make it of the samë shape
That is an ingot, if I may have hap.
Bring eke with you a bowl, or else a pan,
Full of watér, and ye shall well see than[15]
How that our business shall hap and preve.[16]
And yet, for ye shall have no misbelieve[17]
Nor wrong conceit of me, in your absénce,
I willë not be out of your presénce,
But go with you, and come with you again."
The chamber-doorë, shortly for to sayn,
They opened and shut, and went their way,
And forth with them they carried the key;
And came again without any delay.
Why should I tarry all the longë day?
He took the chalk, and shap'd it in the wise
Of an ingot, as I shall you devise;[18]
I say, he took out of his owen sleeve
A teine[19] of silver (evil may he cheve![20])
Which that ne was but a just ounce of weight.
And takë heed now of his cursed sleight;
He shap'd his ingot, in length and in brede[21]
Of this teinë, withouten any drede,[22]
So slily, that the priest it not espied;
And in his sleeve again he gan it hide;
And from the fire he took up his mattére,
And in th' ingot put it with merry cheer;[23]
And in the water-vessel he it cast,
When that him list, and bade the priest as fast
Look what there is; "Put in thine hand and grope;[24]
There shalt thou findë silver, as I hope."
What, devil of hellë! should it ellës be?
Shaving of silver, silver is, pardie.
He put his hand in, and took up a teine[19]
Of silver fine; and glad in every vein
Was this priest, when he saw that it was so.
"Goddë's blessing, and his mother's also,
And allë hallows',[25] have ye, Sir Canón!"
Saidë this priest, "and I their malison[26]
But, an'[27] ye vouchësafe to teachë me
This noble craft and this subtility,
I will be yours in all that ever I may."
Quoth the canón, "Yet will I make assay[28]
The second time, that ye may takë heed,
And be expert of this, and, in your need,
Another day assay in mine absénce
This discipline, and this crafty sciénce.
Let take another ouncë," quoth he tho,[29]
"Of quicksilver, withoutë wordës mo',
And do therewith as ye have done ere this
With that other, which that now silver is."
The priest him busied, all that e'er he can,
To do as this canón, this cursed man,
Commanded him, and fast he blew the fire
For to come to th' effect of his desire.
And this canón right in the meanëwhile
All ready was this priest eft[30] to beguile,
And, for a countenance,[31] in his handë bare
An hollow stickë (take keep[32] and beware),
In th' end of which an ouncë and no more

1 Done. 2 Great thanks.
3 Filings or dust of silver.
4 Contrivance, stratagem.
5 Before they separated.
6 Cease; from Anglo-Saxon, "blinnan," to desist.
7 Grieveth. 8 Revenge myself.
9 Changeable, unsettled.
10 Evil fortune attend him! 11 Burn.
12 Quickly. 13 Evenly or exactly laid.
14 Mould. See note 34, page 179. 15 Then.
16 Turn out, succeed. 17 Mistrust.
18 Describe.
19 Little piece; the adjective "tiny" is connected with the word.
20 Prosper; achieve, end; French, "achever."
21 Breadth. 22 Doubt. 23 Countenance.
24 Search. 25 That of all the saints.
26 Curse. 27 Unless, if.
28 Trial, experiment. 29 Then.
30 Again. 31 Stratagem. 32 Heed.

Of silver limaile put was, as before
Was in his coal, and stopped with wax well
For to keep in his limaile every deal.[1]
And while this priest was in his business,
This canon with his sticke gan him dress[2]
To him anon, and his powder cast in,
As he did erst[3] (the devil out of his skin
Him turn, I pray to God, for his falsehéad,
For he was ever false in thought and deed),
And with his stick, above the crossëlet,
That was ordained with that falsë get,[4]
He stirr'd the coalës, till relentë gan
The wax against the fire, as every man,
But he a fool be, knows well it must need.
And all that in the stickë was out yede,[5]
And in the croslet hastily[6] it fell.
Now, goodë Sirs, what will ye bet[7] than well?
When that this priest was thus beguil'd again,
Supposing naught but truthë, sooth to sayn,
He was so glad, that I can not express
In no mannére his mirth and his gladnéss;
And to the canon he proffér'd eftsoon[8]
Body and good. "Yea," quoth the canon soon,
"Though poor I be, crafty[9] thou shalt me find;
I warn thee well, yet is there more behind.
Is any copper here within?" said he.
"Yea, Sir," the priestë said, "I trow there be."
"Ellës go buy us some, and that as swithë.[10]
Now, goodë Sir, go forth thy way and hie[11] thee."
He went his way, and with the copper came,
And this canón it in his handës name,[12]
And of that copper weighed out an ounce.
Too simple is my tonguë to pronounce,
As minister of my wit, the doubleness
Of this canon, root of all cursedness.
He friendly seem'd to them that knew him not;
But he was fiendly, both in work and thought.
It wearieth me to tell of his falsenéss;
And natheless yet will I it express,
To that intent men may beware thereby,
And for none other causë truëly.
He put this copper in the crossëlet,
And on the fire as swithe[10] he hath it set,
And cast in powder, and made the priest to blow,
And in his working for to stoopë low,
As he did erst,[13] and all was but a jape;[14]
Right as him list the priest he made his ape.[15]
And afterward in the ingot he it cast,
And in the pan he put it at the last
Of water, and in he put his own hand;
And in his sleeve, as ye beforëhand
Heardë me tell, he had a silver teine;[16]
He slily took it out, this cursed heine[17]
(Unweeting[18] this priest of his falsë craft),
And in the pannë's bottom he it laft.[19]
And in the water rumbleth to and fro,
And wondrous privily took up alsó
The copper teine (not knowing thilkë priest),
And hid it, and him hentë[20] by the breast,
And to him spake, and thus said in his game;
"Stoop now adown; by God, ye be to blame;
Helpë me now, as I did you whilére;[21]
Put in your hand, and lookë what is there."
This priest took up this silver teine anon;
And thennë said the canon, "Let us gon,
With these three teinës which that we have wrought,
To some goldsmith, and weet if they be aught:[22]
For, by my faith, I would not for my hood
But if[23] they werë silver fine and good,
And that as swithe[24] well proved shall it be."
Unto the goldsmith with these teinës three
They went anon, and put them in assay[25]
To fire and hammer; might no man say nay,
But that they weren as they ought to be.
This sotted[26] priest, who gladder was than he?
Was never bird gladder against the day;
Nor nightingale in the season of May
Was never none, that better list to sing;
Nor lady lustier in carolling,
Or for to speak of love and womanhead;
Nor knight in arms to do a hardy deed,
To standen in grace of his lady dear,
Than had this priest this craftë for to lear;
And to the canon thus he spake and said;
"For love of God, that for us allë died,
And as I may deserve it unto you,
What shall this réceipt costë? tell me now."
"By our Lady," quoth this canon, "it is dear.
I warn you well, that, save I and a frere,
In Engleland there can no man it make."
"No force,"[27] quoth he; "now, Sir, for Goddë's sake,
What shall I pay? tellë me, I you pray."
"Y-wis,"[28] quoth he, "it is full dear, I say.
Sir, at one word, if that you list it have,
Ye shall pay forty pound, so God me save;
And n'ere[29] the friendship that ye did ere this
To me, ye shouldë payë more, y-wis."
This priest the sum of forty pound anon
Of nobles fet,[30] and took them every one
To this canón, for this ilkë receipt.
All his workíng was but fraud and deceit.
"Sir Priest," he said, "I keep[31] to have no los[32]
Of my craft, for I would it were kept close;
And as ye lovë me, keep it secré:
For if men knewen all my subtletý,
By God, they wouldë have so great envý
To me, because of my philosophý,
I should be dead, there were no other way."
"God it forbid," quoth the priest, "what ye say.
Yet had I lever[33] spenden all the good
Which that I have (and ellës were I wood[34]),

1 Particle. 2 Apply. 3 Before.
4 Provided with that false contrivance.
5 Went. 6 Quickly.
7 Better. 8 Forthwith; again.
9 Skilful. 10 Swiftly. 11 Haste.
12 Took; from Anglo-Saxon, "niman," to take. Compare German, "nehmen," "nahm."
13 Before. 14 Trick. 15 Befooled him.
16 Small piece of silver. 17 Hind; slave, wretch.
18 Unsuspecting. 19 Left.
20 Took. 21 Before, erewhile.
22 Of any value. 23 Unless.
24 Quickly. 25 Proof.
26 Besotted, stupid. 27 No matter.
28 Certainly. 29 Were it not for.
30 Fetched. 31 Care.
32 Praise, renown. See note 10, page 155.
33 Rather. 34 Mad.

Than that ye shouldë fall in such mischfef."
"For your good will, Sir, have ye right good prefe,"[1]
Quoth the canón; "and farewell, *grand mercý*."[2]
He went his way, and never the priest him sey[3]
After that day; and when that this priest should
Maken assay, at such time as he would,
Of this receipt, farewell! it would not be.
Lo, thus bejaped[4] and beguil'd was he;
Thus madë he[5] his introductión
To bringë folk to their destructión.
Consider, Sirs, how that in each estate
Betwixtë men and gold there is debate,
So farforth that unnethës is there none.[6]
This multiplying blint[7] so many a one,
That in good faith I trowë that it be
The causë greatest of such scarcity.
These philosóphers speak so mistily
In this craft, that men cannot come thereby,
For any wit that men have now-a-days.
They may well chatter, as do thesë jays,
And in their termës set their lust and pain,[8]
But to their purpose shall they ne'er attain.
A man may lightly[9] learn, if he have aught,
To multiply, and bring his good to naught.
Lo, such a lucre[10] is in this lusty[11] game;
A mannë's mirth it will turn all to grame,[12]
And empty also great and heavy purses,
And makë folkë for to purchase curses
Of them that have thereto their good y-lent.
Oh, fy for shamë! they that have been brent,[13]
Alas! can they not flee the firë's heat?
Ye that it use, I rede[14] that ye it lete,[15]
Lest ye lose all; for better than never is late;
Never to thrivë, were too long a date.
Though ye prowl aye, ye shall it never find;
Ye be as bold as is Bayard the blind,
That blunders forth, and peril casteth none;[16]
He is as bold to run against a stone,
As for to go beside it in the way:
So farë ye that multiply, I say.
If that your eyen cannot see aright,
Look that your mindë lackë not his sight.
For though you look never so broad, and stare,
Ye shall not win a mite on that chaffare,[17]
But wasten all that ye may rape and renn.[18]
Withdraw the fire, lest it too fastë brenn;[19]
Meddle no morë with that art, I mean;
For if ye do, your thrift[19] is gone full clean.
And right as swithe[20] I will you tellë here
What philosóphers say in this mattére.
Lo, thus saith Arnold of the newë town,[21]
As his Rosáry maketh mentioún,
He saith right thus, withouten any lie;
"There may no man mercúry mortify,
But[22] it be with his brother's knowledging."
Lo, how that he, which firstë said this thing,
Of philosóphers father was, Hermés;[23]
He saith, how that the dragon doubtëless
He dieth not, but if that he be slain
With his brother. And this is for to sayn,
By the dragón, Mercúry, and none other,
He understood, and Brimstone by his brother,
That out of Sol and Luna were y-draw.[24]
"And therefore," said he, "take heed to my saw.[25]
Let no man busy him this art to seech,[26]
But if[22] that he th' intentión and speech
Of philosóphers understandë can;
And if he do, he is a lewëd[27] man.
For this sciénce and this conning,"[28] quoth he,
"Is of the secret of secrets[29] pardie."
Also there was a disciple of Plató,
That on a timë said his master to,
As his book, Senior,[30] will bear witnéss,
And this was his demand in soothfastness:
"Tell me the name of thilkë[31] privy stone."
And Plato answer'd unto him anon;
"Takë the stone that Titanos men name."
"Which is that?" quoth he. "Magnesia is the same,"
Saidë Plató. "Yea, Sir, and is it thus?
This is *ignotum per ignotius*.[32]
What is Magnesia, good Sir, I pray?"
"It is a water that is made, I say,
Of th' elementës fourë," quoth Plató.
"Tell me the rootë, good Sir," quoth he tho,[33]
"Of that watér, if that it be your will."
"Nay, nay," quoth Plato, "certain that I n'ill.[34]
The philosóphers sworn were every one,
That they should not discover it to none,
Nor in no book it write in no mannére;
For unto God it is so lefe[35] and dear,
That he will not that it discover'd be,
But where it liketh to his deity

1 Good result of your experiments.
2 Great thanks. 3 Saw.
4 Befooled. 5 The false Canon.
6 Scarcely is there any (gold). 7 Blinds, deceives.
8 Pleasure and exertion. 9 Easily.
10 Gain, profit. 11 Pleasant.
12 Sorrow; Anglo-Saxon, "gram;" German, "Gram."
13 Burnt. 14 Advise.
15 Leave it—that is, the alchemist's art.
16 Perceives no danger. 17 Traffic, commerce.
18 Seize and plunder; acquire by hook or by crook.
19 Prosperity. 20 Quickly.
21 Arnaldus Villanovanus, or Arnold de Villeneuve, was a distinguished French chemist and physician of the fourteenth century; his "Rosarium Philosophorum" was a favourite text-book with the alchemists of the generations that succeeded. 22 Except.
23 Hermes Trismegistus, counsellor of Osiris, King of Egypt, was credited with the invention of writing and hieroglyphics, the drawing up of the laws of the Egyptians, and the origination of many sciences and arts. The Alexandrian school ascribed to him the mystic learning which it amplified; and the scholars of the Middle Ages regarded with enthusiasm and reverence the works attributed to him—notably a treatise on the philosopher's stone.
24 Drawn, derived. 25 Saying.
26 Study, explore. 27 Ignorant, foolish.
28 Knowledge.
29 "Secreta Secretorum;" a treatise, very popular in the Middle Ages, supposed to contain the sum of Aristotle's instructions to Alexander. Lydgate translated about half of the work, when his labour was interrupted by his death about 1460; and from the same treatise had been taken most of the seventh book of Gower's "Confessio Amantis."
30 Tyrwhitt says that this book was printed in the "Theatrum Chemicum," under the title, "Senioris Zadith fil. Hamuelis tabula chymica;" and the story here told of Plato and his disciple was there related of Solomon, but with some variations. 31 That.
32 To explain the unknown by the more unknown.
33 Then. 34 Will not.
35 Precious.

Man for to inspire, and eke for to defend[1]
Whom that he liketh; lo, this is the end."
Then thus conclude I, since that God of heaven
Will not that thesë philosóphers neven[2]
How that a man shall come unto this stone,
I rede[3] as for the best to let it gon.
For whoso maketh God his adversáry,
As for to work any thing in contráry
Of his will, certes never shall he thrive,
Though that he multiply term of his live.[4]
And there a point;[5] for ended is my tale.
God send ev'ry good man boot of his bale.[6]

THE MANCIPLE'S TALE.

THE PROLOGUE.

WEET[7] ye not where there stands a little town,
Which that y-called is Bob-up-and-down,[8]
Under the Blee, in Canterbury way?
There gan our Hostë for to jape and play,
And saidë, "Sirs, what? Dun is in the mire.[9]
Is there no man, for prayer nor for hire,
That will awaken our fellów behind?
A thief him might full lightly[10] rob and bind.
See how he nappeth, see, for cockë's bones,
As he would fallë from his horse at ones.
Is that a Cook of London,[11] with mischance?
Do[12] him come forth, he knoweth his penánce;
For he shall tell a talë, by my fay,[13]
Although it be not worth a bottle hay.
Awake, thou Cook," quoth he; "God give thee sorrow!
What aileth thee to sleepë by the morrow?[14]
Hast thou had fleas all night, or art thou drunk?
Or hast thou with some quean all night y-swunk,[15]
So that thou mayest not hold up thine head?"
The Cook, that was full pale and nothing red,
Said to our Host, "So God my soulë bless,
As there is fall'n on me such heaviness,
I know not why, that me were lever[16] sleep,
Than the best gallon wine that is in Cheap."
"Well," quoth the Manciple, "if it may do ease
To thee, Sir Cook, and to no wight displease
Which that here rideth in this company,
And that our Host will of his courtesy,
I will as now excuse thee of thy tale;
For in good faith thy visage is full pale:
Thine eyen dazë,[17] soothly as me thinketh,
And well I wot, thy breath full sourë stinketh,
That sheweth well thou art not well disposed;
Of me certáin thou shalt not be y-glosed.[18]
See how he yawneth, lo, this drunken wight,
As though he would us swallow anon right.
Hold close thy mouth, man, by thy father's kin;
The devil of hellë set his foot therein!
Thy cursed breath infectë will us all:
Fy! stinking swine, fy! foul may thee befall.
Ah! takë heed, Sirs, of this lusty man.
Now, sweetë Sir, will ye joust at the fan?[19]
Thereto, me thinketh, ye be well y-shape.
I trow that ye have drunken wine of ape,[20]
And that is when men playë with a straw."
And with this speech the Cook waxed all wraw,[21]
And on the Manciple he gan nod fast
For lack of speech; and down his horse him cast,
Where as he lay, till that men him up took.
This was a fair chevachie[22] of a cook:
Alas! that he had held him by his ladle!
And ere that he again were in the saddle
There was great shoving bothë to and fro
To lift him up, and muchë care and woe,
So unwieldy was this silly paled ghost.
And to the Manciple then spake our Host:
"Because that drink hath dominatión
Upon this man, by my salvatión
I trow he lewëdly[23] will tell his tale.
For were it wine, or old or moisty[24] ale,
That he hath drunk, he speaketh in his nose,
And sneezeth fast, and eke he hath the pose.[25]
He also hath to do more than enough
To keep him on his capel[26] out of the slough;
And if he fall from off his capel eftsoon,[27]
Then shall we allë have enough to do'n
In lifting up his heavy drunken corse.
Tell on thy tale, of him make I no force.[28]
But yet, Manciple, in faith thou art too nice[29]
Thus openly to reprove him of his vice;
Another day he will paráventúre
Reclaimë thee, and bring thee to the lure;[30]

1 Protect. 2 Name. 3 Counsel.
4 Though he pursue the alchemist's art all his days.
5 An end.
6 Remedy for his sorrow or trouble.
7 Know.
8 Mr Wright supposes this to be the village of Harbledown, near Canterbury, which is situated on a hill, and near which there are many ups and downs in the road. Like Boughton, where the Canon and his Yeoman overtook the pilgrims, it stood on the skirts of the Kentish forest of Blean or Blee.
9 A proverbial saying. "Dun" is a name for an ass, derived from his colour. 10 Easily.
11 The mention of the Cook here, with no hint that he had already told a story, confirms the indication given by the imperfect condition of his Tale (page 60), that Chaucer intended to suppress the Tale altogether, and make him tell a story in some other place.
12 Make. 13 Faith.
14 In the day time.
15 Laboured. 16 Preferable.
17 Are dim. 18 Flattered.
19 The quintain; called "fan" or "vane," because it turned round like a weather-cock.
20 Referring to the classification of wine, according to its effects on a man, given in the old "Calendrier des Bergiers." The man of choleric temperament has "wine of lion;" the sanguine, "wine of ape;" the phlegmatic, "wine of sheep;" the melancholic, "wine of sow." There is a Rabbinical tradition that, when Noah was planting vines, Satan slaughtered beside them the four animals named; hence the effect of wine in making those who drink it display in turn the characteristics of all the four. 21 Wroth.
22 Cavalry expedition.
23 Stupidly. 24 New. See note 9, page 22.
25 A defluxion or rheum which stops the nose and obstructs the voice.
26 Horse. 27 Again.
28 I take no account. 29 Foolish.
30 A phrase in hawking—to recall a hawk to the fist; the meaning here is, that the Cook may one day bring the Manciple to account, or pay him off, for the rebuke of his drunkenness.

I mean, he speakë will of smallë things,
As for to pinchen at[1] thy reckonings,
That were not honest, if it came to prefe."[2]
Quoth the Manciple, "That were a great mischíef;
So might he lightly bring me in the snare.
Yet had I lever[3] payë for the mare
Which he rides on, than he should with me strive.
I will not wrathë[4] him, so may I thrive;
That that I spake, I said it in my bourde.[5]
And weet ye what? I have here in my gourd
A draught of wine, yea, of a ripë grape,
And right anon ye shall see a good jape.[6]
This Cook shall drink thereof, if that I may;
On pain of my life he will not say nay."
And certainly, to tellen as it was,
Of this vessél the cook drank fast (alas!
What needed it? he drank enough beforn),
And when he haddë pouped in his horn,[7]
To the Manciple he took the gourd again.
And of that drink the Cook was wondrous fain,
And thanked him in such wise as he could.
Then gan our Host to laughë wondrous loud,
And said, "I see well it is necessary
Where that we go good drink with us to carry;
For that will turnë rancour and disease[8]
T' accord and love, and many a wrong appease.
O Bacchus, Bacchus, blessed be thy name,
That so canst turnen earnest into game!
Worship and thank be to thy deity.
Of that mattére ye get no more of me.
Tell on thy tale, Manciple, I thee pray."
"Well, Sir," quoth he, "now hearken what I say."

THE TALE.[9]

When Phœbus dwelled here in earth adown,
As oldë bookës makë mentioún,
He was the mostë lusty[10] bachelér
Of all this world, and eke the best archér.
He slew Python the serpent, as he lay
Sleeping against the sun upon a day;
And many another noble worthy deed
He with his bow wrought, as men mayë read.
Playen he could on every minstrelsy,
And singë, that it was a melody
To hearen of his clearë voice the soun'.
Certes the king of Thebes, Amphioún,
That with his singing walled the city,
Could never singë half so well as he.
Thereto he was the seemliestë man
That is, or was since that the world began;
What needeth it his features to descrive?
For in this world is none so fair alive.
He was therewith full fill'd of gentleness,
Of honour, and of perfect worthiness.

This Phœbus, that was flower of bach'lery,
As well in freedom[11] as in chivalry,
For his disport, in sign eke of victóry
Of Python, so as telleth us the story,
Was wont to bearen in his hand a bow.
Now had this Phœbus in his house a crow,
Which in a cage he foster'd many a day,
And taught it speaken, as men teach a jay.
White was this crow, as is a snow-white swan,
And counterfeit the speech of every man
He couldë, when he shouldë tell a tale.
Therewith in all this world no nightingale
Ne couldë by an hundred thousand deal[12]
Singë so wondrous merrily and well.
Now had this Phœbus in his house a wife,
Which that he loved morë than his life,
And night and day did ever his diligence
Her for to please, and do her reverence:
Save only, if that I the sooth shall sayn,
Jealous he was, and would have kept her fain.
For him were loth y-japed[13] for to be;
And so is every wight in such degree;
But all for nought, for it availeth nought.
A good wife, that is clean of work and thought,
Should not be kept in none await[14] certáin:
And truëly the labour is in vain
To keep a shrewë,[15] for it will not be.
This hold I for a very nicety,[16]
To spillë[17] labour for to keepë wives;
Thus writen oldë clerkës in their lives.
But now to purpose, as I first began.
This worthy Phœbus did all that he can
To pleasë her, weening, through such pleasánce,
And for his manhood and his governánce,
That no man should have put him from her grace;
But, God it wot, there may no man embrace
As to distrain[18] a thing, which that natúre
Hath naturally set in a creatúre.
Take any bird, and put it in a cage,
And do all thine intent, and thy coráge,[19]
To foster it tenderly with meat and drink
Of allë dainties that thou canst bethink,
And keep it all so cleanly as thou may;
Although the cage of gold be never so gay,
Yet had this bird, by twenty thousand fold,
Lever[3] in a forést, both wild and cold,
Go eatë wormës, and such wretchedness.
For ever this bird will do his business
T' escape out of his cage when that he may:
His liberty the bird desireth aye.[20]
Let take a cat, and foster her with milk
And tender flesh, and make her couch of silk,
And let her see a mouse go by the wall,
Anon she weiveth[21] milk, and flesh, and all,
And every dainty that is in that house,
Such appetite hath she to eat the mouse.

1 Take exception to, pick flaws in.
2 Proof, test.
3 Rather.
4 Provoke.
5 Jest.
6 Trick.
7 Blown into his horn; a metaphor for belching.
8 Trouble, annoyance.
9 "The fable of 'The Crow,'" says Tyrwhitt, "which is the subject of the Manciple's Tale, has been related by so many authors, from Ovid down to Gower, that it is impossible to say whom Chaucer principally followed. His skill in new dressing an old story was never, perhaps, more successfully exerted."
10 Pleasant.
11 Generosity.
12 Part.
13 Tricked, deceived.
14 Observation, espionage.
15 A contrarious or ill-disposed woman.
16 Sheer folly.
17 Lose.
18 Succeed in constraining.
19 All that thy heart prompts.
20 See the parallel to this passage in the Squire's Tale, and note 6, page 121.
21 Forsaketh.

Lo, here hath kind[1] her dominatión,
And appetite flemeth[2] discretión.
A she-wolf hath also a villain's kind;[1]
The lewedestë wolf that she may find,
Or least of reputation, will she take
In timë when her lust[3] to have a make.[4]
All these examples speak I by[5] these men
That be untrue, and nothing by womén.
For men have ever a lik'rous appetite
On lower things to pérform their delight
Than on their wivës, be they never so fair,
Never so truë, nor so debonair.[6]
Flesh is so newëfangled, with mischance,[7]
That we can in no thingë have pleasánce
That souneth[8] unto virtue any while.
This Phœbus, which that thought upon no guile,
Deceived was for all his jollitý;
For under him another haddë she,
A man of little reputatión,
Nought worth to Phœbus in comparison.
The more harm is; it happens often so,
Of which there cometh muchë harm and woe.
And so befell, when Phœbus was absént,
His wife anon hath for her leman[9] sent.
Her leman! certes that is a knavish speech.
Forgive it me, and that I you beseech.
The wisë Plato saith, as ye may read,
The word must needs accordë with the deed;
If men shall tellë properly a thing,
The word must cousin be to the workíng.
I am a boistous[10] man, right thus I say.
There is no differencë truëly
Betwixt a wife that is of high degree
(If of her body dishonést she be),
And any poorë wench, other than this
(If it so be they workë both amiss),
But, for[11] the gentle is in estate above,
She shall be call'd his lady and his love;
And, for that other is a poor womán,
She shall be call'd his wench and his lemán:
And God it wot, mine owen dearë brother,
Men lay the one as low as lies the other.
Right so betwixt a titleless tyránt[12]
And an outlaw, or else a thief erránt,[13]
The same I say, there is no differénce
(To Alexander told was this senténce),
But, for the tyrant is of greater might
By force of meinie[14] for to slay downright,
And burn both house and home, and make all plain,[15]
Lo, therefore is he call'd a capitáin;
And, for the outlaw hath but small meinie,
And may not do so great an harm as he,
Nor bring a country to so great mischíef,
Men callë him an outlaw or a thief.
But, for I am a man not textuel,[16]

1 Nature. 2 Drives out.
3 She desires. 4 Mate.
5 With reference to. 6 Gentle, mild.
7 Ill luck to it. 8 Is consonant to, accords with.
9 Unlawful lover. 10 Rough-spoken, downright.
11 Because. 12 Usurper. 13 Wandering.
14 Followers, people. 15 Level.
16 Well stored with texts or citations. 17 Whit.
18 Light or rash pleasure. 19 Watching.
20 Thou art befooled or betrayed.

I will not tell of texts never a deal;[17]
I will go to my tale, as I began.
When Phœbus' wife had sent for her lemán,
Anon they wroughten all their lust volage.[18]
This whitë crow, that hung aye in the cage,
Beheld their work, and said never a word;
And when that home was come Phœbus the lord,
This crowë sung, "Cuckoo, cuckoo, cuckoo!"
"What? bird," quoth Phœbus, "what song sing'st thou now?
Wert thou not wont so merrily to sing,
That to my heart it was a réjoicíng
To hear thy voice? alas! what song is this?"
"By God," quoth he, "I singë not amiss.
Phœbus," quoth he, "for all thy worthiness,
For all thy beauty, and all thy gentleness,
For all thy song, and all thy minstrelsý,
For all thy waiting,[19] bleared is thine eye[20]
With one of little reputatión,
Not worth to thee, as in comparison,
The mountance[21] of a gnat, so may I thrive;
For on thy bed thy wife I saw him swive."
What will ye more? the crow anon him told,
By sadë[22] tokens, and by wordës bold,
How that his wife had done her lechery,
To his great shame and his great villainy;
And told him oft, he saw it with his eyen.
This Phœbus gan awayward for to wrien;[23]
Him thought his woeful heartë burst in two.
His bow he bent, and set therein a flo,[24]
And in his ire he hath his wifë slain;
This is th' effect, there is no more to sayn.
For sorrow of which he brake his minstrelsy,
Both harp and lute, gitérn[25] and psaltery;
And eke he brake his arrows and his bow;
And after that thus spake he to the crow.
"Traitor," quoth he, "with tongue of scorpión,
Thou hast me brought to my confusión;
Alas that I was wrought![26] why n'ere[27] I dead?
O dearë wife, O gem of lustihead,[28]
That wert to me so sad,[29] and eke so true,
Now liest thou dead, with facë pale of hue,
Full guiltëless, that durst I swear y-wis![30]
O rakel[31] hand, to do so foul amiss![32]
O troubled wit, O irë reckëless,
That unadvised smit'st the guiltëless!
O wantrust,[33] full of false suspición!
Where was thy wit and thy discretión?
O! every man beware of rakelness,[34]
Nor trow[35] no thing withoutë strong witnéss.
Smite not too soon, ere that ye weetë[36] why,
And be advised[37] well and sickerly[38]
Ere ye do any executión
Upon your irë[39] for suspición.
Alas! a thousand folk hath rakel ire
Foully fordone, and brought them in the mire.

21 Value.
22 Grave, trustworthy. 23 To turn aside.
24 Arrow; Anglo-Saxon, "fla." 25 Guitar.
26 Created. 27 Was not. 28 Pleasantness.
29 Steadfast. 30 Certainly. 31 Rash, hasty.
32 So foully wrong.
33 Distrust—want of trust; so "wanhope," despair—want of hope. 34 Rashness. 35 Believe.
36 Know. 37 Consider. 38 Surely.
39 Take any action upon your anger.

Alas! for sorrow I will myselfë slé."[1]
And to the crow, "O falsë thief," said he,
"I will thee quite anon thy falsë tale.
Thou sung whilom[2] like any nightingale,
Now shalt thou, falsë thief, thy song foregon,[3]
And eke thy whitë feathers every one,
Nor ever in all thy lifë shalt thou speak;
Thus shall men on a traitor be awreak.[4]
Thou and thine offspring ever shall be blake,[5]
Nor ever sweetë noisë shall ye make,
But ever cry against[6] tempést and rain,
In token that through thee my wife is slain."
And to the crow he start,[7] and that anon,
And pull'd his whitë feathers every one,
And made him black, and reft him all his song,
And eke his speech, and out at door him flung
Unto the devil, which I him betake;[8]
And for this causë be all crowës blake.
Lordings, by this ensample, I you pray,
Beware, and takë keep[9] what that ye say;
Nor tellë never man in all your life
How that another man hath dight his wife;
He will you hatë mortally certáin.
Dan Solomon, as wisë clerkës sayn,
Teacheth a man to keep his tonguë well;
But, as I said, I am not textuel.
But natheless thus taughtë me my dame;
"My son, think on the crow, in Goddë's name.
My son, keep well thy tongue, and keep thy friend;
A wicked tongue is worse than is a fiend:
My sonë, from a fiend men may them bless.[10]
My son, God of his endëless goodnéss
Walled a tongue with teeth, and lippës eke,
For[11] man should him advisë,[12] what he speak.
My son, full often for too muchë speech
Hath many a man been spilt,[13] as clerkës teach;
But for a little speech advisedly
Is no man shent,[14] to speak generally.
My son, thy tonguë shouldest thou restrain
At allë time, but[15] when thou dost thy pain[16]
To speak of God in honour and prayére.
The firstë virtue, son, if thou wilt lear,[17]
Is to restrain and keepë well thy tongue;[18]
Thus learnë children, when that they be young.
My son, of muchë speaking evil advis'd,
Where lessë speaking had enough suffic'd,
Cometh much harm; thus was me told and taught;
In muchë speechë sinnë wanteth nót.
Wost[19] thou whereof a rakel[20] tonguë serveth?
Right as a sword forcutteth and forcarveth
An arm in two, my dearë son, right so
A tonguë cutteth friendship all in two.
A jangler[21] is to God abominàble.
Read Solomon, so wise and honouràble;

1 Slay. 2 Once on a time. 3 Lose. 4 Revenged. 5 Black. 6 Before, in warning of. 7 Sprang. 8 To whom I commend him. 9 Heed. 10 Defend by crossing themselves. 11 Because. 12 Consider. 13 Destroyed. 14 Ruined. 15 Except. 16 Makest thy best effort. 17 Learn.

18 This is quoted in the French "Romance of the Rose," from Cato "De Moribus," l. i., dist. 3: "Virtutem primam esse puta compescere linguam."

19 Knowest. 20 Hasty. 21 Prating man.

Read David in his Psalms, and read Senec'.
My son, speak not, but with thine head thou beck,[22]
Dissimule as thou wert[23] deaf, if that thou hear
A jangler speak of perilous mattére.
The Fleming saith, and learn if that thee lest,[24]
That little jangling causeth muchë rest.
My son, if thou no wicked word hast said,
Thee thar not dreadë[25] for to be bewray'd;
But he that hath missaid, I dare well sayn,
He may by no way call his word again.
Thing that is said is said, and forth it go'th,[26]
Though him repent, or be he ne'er so loth;
He is his thrall,[27] to whom that he hath said
A tale, of which he is now evil apaid.[28]
My son, beware, and be no author new
Of tidings, whether they be false or true;[29]
Whereso thou come, amongës high or low,
Keep well thy tongue, and think upon the crow."

THE PARSON'S TALE.

THE PROLOGUE.

By that the Manciple his tale had ended,
The sunnë from the south line was descended
So lowë, that it was not to my sight
Degreës nine-and-twenty as in height.
Four of the clock it was then, as I guess,
For eleven foot, a little more or less,
My shadow was at thilkë time, as there,
Of such feet as my lengthë parted were
In six feet equal of proportión.
Therewith the moonë's exaltatión,[30]
In meanë[31] Libra, gan alway ascend,
As we were ent'ring at a thorpë's[32] end.
For which our Host, as he was wont to gie,[33]
As in this case, our jolly company,
Said in this wisë; "Lordings every one,
Now lacketh us no morë tales than one.
Fulfill'd is my senténce and my decree;
I trow that we have heard of each degree.[34]
Almost fulfilled is mine ordinance;
I pray to God so give him right good chance
That telleth us this talë lustily.
Sir Priest," quoth he, "art thou a vicary?[35]
Or art thou a Parson? say sooth by thy fay.[36]
Be what thou be, breakë thou not our play;[37]
For every man, save thou, hath told his tale.
Unbuckle, and shew us what is in thy mail.[38]
For truëly me thinketh by thy cheer

22 Beckon, make gestures. 23 Feign to be. 24 It please thee. 25 Thou hast no need to fear.

26 —"Semel emissum volat irrevocabile verbum." —Horace, Epist. i., 18, 71.

27 Slave. 28 Which he now regrets.

29 This caution is also from Cato "De Moribus," l. i., dist. 12: "Rumoris fuge ne incipias novus auctor haberi."

30 Rising. 31 In the middle of. 32 Village's. 33 Govern. 34 From each class or rank in the company. 35 Vicar. 36 Faith. 37 Interrupt not our diversion. 38 Wallet.

Thou shouldest knit up well a great mattére.
Tell us a fable anon, for cockë's bones."
This Parson him answered all at ones;
"Thou gettest fable none y-told for me,
For Paul, that writeth unto Timothy,
Reproveth them that weivë soothfastness,[1]
And tellë fables, and such wretchedness.
Why should I sowë draff[2] out of my fist,
When I may sowë wheat, if that me list?
For which I say, if that you list to hear
Morality and virtuous mattére,
And then that ye will give me audiénce,
I would full fain at Christë's reverénce
Do you pleasáncë lawful, as I can.
But, trustë well, I am a southern man,
I cannot gest,[3] rom, ram, ruf,[4] by my letter;
And, God wot, rhyme hold I but little better.
And therefore if you list, I will not glose,[5]
I will you tell a little tale in prose,
To knit up all this feast, and make an end.
And Jesus for his gracë wit me send
To shewë you the way, in this voyáge,
Of thilkë perfect glorious pilgrimage,[6]
That hight Jerusalem celestiál.
And if ye vouchësafe, anon I shall
Begin upon my tale, for which I pray
Tell your advice,[7] I can no better say.
But natheless this meditatión
I put it aye under correctión
Of clerkës,[8] for I am not textuel;
I take but the senténcë,[9] trust me well.
Therefore I make a protestatión,
That I will standë to correctión."
Upon this word we have assented soon;
For, as us seemed, it was for to do'n,[10]
To enden in some virtuous senténce,[11]
And for to give him space and audiénce;
And bade our Host he shouldë to him say,
That allë we to tell his tale him pray.
Our Hostë had the wordës for us all:
"Sir Priest," quoth he, "now fairë you befall;
Say what you list, and we shall gladly hear."
And with that word he said in this mannére;
"Tellë," quoth he, "your meditatioún,
But hasten you, the sunnë will adown.
Be fructuous,[12] and that in little space;
And to do well God sendë you his grace."

THE TALE.[13]

[The Parson begins his "little treatise" (which, if given at length, would extend to about thirty of these pages, and which cannot by any stretch of courtesy or fancy be said to merit the title of a "Tale") in these words:—]

Our sweet Lord God of Heaven, that no man will perish, but will that we come all to the knowledge of him, and to the blissful life that is perdurable,[14] admonishes us by the prophet Jeremiah, that saith in this wise: "Stand upon the ways, and see and ask of old paths, that is to say, of old sentences, which is the good way, and walk in that way, and ye shall find refreshing for your souls,"[15] &c. Many be the spiritual ways that lead folk to our Lord Jesus Christ, and to the reign of glory; of which ways there is a full noble way, and full convenable, which may not fail to man nor to woman, that through sin hath misgone from the right way of Jerusalem celestial; and this way is called penitence. Of which men should gladly hearken and inquire with all their hearts, to wit what is penitence, and whence it is called penitence, and in what manner, and in how many manners, be the actions or workings of penitence, and how many species there be of penitences, and what things appertain and behove to penitence, and what things disturb penitence.

[Penitence is described, on the authority of Saints Ambrose, Isidore, and Gregory, as the bewailing of sin that has been wrought, with the purpose never again to do that thing, or any other thing which a man should bewail; for weeping and not ceasing to do the sin will not avail—though it is to be hoped that after every time that a man falls, be it ever so often, he may find grace to arise through penitence. And repentant folk that leave their sin ere sin leave them, are accounted by Holy Church sure of their salvation, even though the repentance be at the last hour. There are three actions of penitence: that a man be baptized after he has sinned; that he do no deadly sin after receiving baptism; and that he fall into no venial sins from day to day. "Thereof saith St Augustine, that penitence of good and humble folk is the penitence of every day." The species of peni-

1 Forsake truth. 2 Chaff, refuse.
3 Relate stories.
4 A contemptuous reference to the alliterative poetry which was at that time very popular, in preference even, it would seem, to rhyme, in the northern parts of the country, where the language was much more barbarous and unpolished than in the south.
5 Mince matters, make false pretensions or promises.
6 The word is used here to signify the shrine, or destination, to which pilgrimage is made.
7 Opinion. 8 Scholars. 9 Meaning, sense.
10 A thing worth doing, that ought to be done.
11 Discourse. 12 Fruitful; profitable.
13 The Parson's Tale is believed to be a translation, more or less free, from some treatise on penitence that was in favour about Chaucer's time. Tyrwhitt says: "I cannot recommend it as a very entertaining or edifying performance at this day; but the reader will please to remember, in excuse both of Chaucer and of his editor, that, considering The Canterbury Tales as a great picture of life and manners, the piece would not have been complete if it had not included the religion of the time." The Editor of the present volume has followed the same plan adopted with regard to Chaucer's Tale of Melibœus, and mainly for the same reasons. (See note 20, page 149.) An outline of the Parson's ponderous sermon—for such it is—has been drawn; while those passages have been given in full which more directly illustrate the social and the religious life of the time—such as the picture of hell, the vehement and rather coarse, but, in an antiquarian sense, most curious and valuable attack on the fashionable garb of the day, the catalogue of venial sins, the description of gluttony and its remedy, &c. The brief third or concluding part, which contains the application of the whole, and the "Retractation" or "Prayer" that closes the Tale and the entire "magnum opus" of Chaucer, have been given in full.
14 Everlasting. 15 Jeremiah vi. 16.

tence are three: solemn, when a man is openly expelled from Holy Church in Lent, or is compelled by Holy Church to do open penance for an open sin openly talked of in the country; common penance, enjoined by priests in certain cases, as to go on pilgrimage naked or barefoot; and privy penance, which men do daily for private sins, of which they confess privately and receive private penance. To very perfect penitence are behoveful and necessary three things: contrition of heart, confession of mouth, and satisfaction; which are fruitful penitence against delight in thinking, reckless speech, and wicked sinful works.

Penitence may be likened to a tree, having its root in contrition, hiding itself in the heart as a tree-root does in the earth; out of this root springs a stalk, that bears branches and leaves of confession, and fruit of satisfaction. Of this root also springs a seed of grace, which is mother of all security, and this seed is eager and hot; and the grace of this seed springs of God, through remembrance on the day of judgment and on the pains of hell. The heat of this seed is the love of God, and the desire of everlasting joy; and this heat draws the heart of man to God, and makes him hate his sin. Penance is the tree of life to them that receive it. In penance or contrition man shall understand four things: what is contrition; what are the causes that move a man to contrition; how he should be contrite; and what contrition availeth to the soul. Contrition is the heavy and grievous sorrow that a man receiveth in his heart for his sins, with earnest purpose to confess and do penance, and never more to sin. Six causes ought to move a man to contrition: 1. He should remember him of his sins; 2. He should reflect that sin putteth a man in great thraldom, and all the greater the higher is the estate from which he falls; 3. He should dread the day of doom and the horrible pains of hell; 4. The sorrowful remembrance of the good deeds that a man hath omitted to do here on earth, and also the good that he hath lost, ought to make him have contrition; 5. So also ought the remembrance of the passion that our Lord Jesus Christ suffered for our sins; 6. And so ought the hope of three things, that is to say, forgiveness of sin, the gift of grace to do well, and the glory of heaven with which God shall reward man for his good deeds.—All these points the Parson illustrates and enforces at length; waxing especially eloquent under the third head, and plainly setting forth the sternly realistic notions regarding future punishments that were entertained in the time of Chaucer:[1]—]

Certes, all the sorrow that a man might make from the beginning of the world, is but a little thing, at regard of[2] the sorrow of hell. The cause why that Job calleth hell the land of darkness;[3] understand, that he calleth it land or earth, for it is stable and never shall fail, and dark, for he that is in hell hath default[4] of light natural; for certes the dark light, that shall come out of the fire that ever shall burn, shall turn them all to pain that be in hell, for it sheweth them the horrible devils that them torment. Covered with the darkness of death; that is to say, that he that is in hell shall have default of the sight of God; for certes the sight of God is the life perdurable.[5] The darkness of death, be the sins that the wretched man hath done, which that disturb[6] him to see the face of God, right as a dark cloud doth between us and the sun. Land of misease, because there be three manner of defaults against three things that folk of this world have in this present life; that is to say, honours, delights, and riches. Against honour have they in hell shame and confusion: for well ye wot, that men call honour the reverence that man doth to man; but in hell is no honour nor reverence; for certes no more reverence shall be done there to a king than to a knave.[7] For which God saith by the prophet Jeremiah; "The folk that me despise shall be in despite." Honour is also called great lordship. There shall no wight serve other, but of harm and torment. Honour is also called great dignity and highness; but in hell shall they be all fortrodden[8] of devils. As God saith, "The horrible devils shall go and come upon the heads of damned folk;" and this is, forasmuch as the higher that they were in this present life, the more shall they be abated[9] and defouled in hell. Against the riches of this world shall they have misease[10] of poverty, and this poverty shall be in four things: in default[11] of treasure; of which David saith, "The rich folk that embraced and oned[12] all their heart to treasure of this world, shall sleep in the sleeping of death, and nothing shall they find in their hands of all their treasure." And moreover, the misease of hell shall be in default of meat and drink. For God saith thus by Moses, "They shall be wasted with hunger, and the birds of hell shall devour them with bitter death, and the gall of the dragon shall be their drink, and the venom of the dragon their morsels." And furthermore, their misease shall be in default of clothing, for they shall be naked in body, as of clothing, save the fire in which they burn, and other filths; and naked shall they be in soul, of all manner virtues, which that is the clothing of the soul. Where be then the gay robes, and the soft sheets, and the fine shirts? Lo, what saith of them the prophet Isaiah, that under them shall be strewed moths, and their covertures shall be of worms of hell. And furthermore, their misease shall be in

1 See note 12, page 87. 2 In comparison with.
3 Just before, the Parson had cited the words of Job to God (Job x. 20-22), "Suffer, Lord, that I may a while bewail and weep, ere I go without returning to the dark land, covered with the darkness of death; to the land of misease and of darkness, where as is the shadow of death; where as is no order nor ordinance, but grisly dread that ever shall last."
4 Is devoid. 5 Everlasting.
6 Prevent, interrupt. 7 Servant.
8 Trampled under foot. 9 Abased.
10 Trouble, torment. 11 Want. 12 United.

default of friends, for he is not poor that hath good friends: but there is no friend; for neither God nor any good creature shall be friend to them, and evereach of them shall hate other with deadly hate. The sons and the daughters shall rebel against father and mother, and kindred against kindred, and chide and despise each other, both day and night, as God saith by the prophet Micah. And the loving children, that whilom loved so fleshly each other, would each of them eat the other if they might. For how should they love together in the pains of hell, when they hated each other in the prosperity of this life? For trust well, their fleshly love was deadly hate; as saith the prophet David; "Whoso loveth wickedness, he hateth his own soul:" and whoso hateth his own soul, certes he may love none other wight in no manner: and therefore in hell is no solace nor no friendship, but ever the more kindreds that be in hell, the more cursing, the more chiding, and the more deadly hate there is among them. And furtherover, they shall have default of all manner delights; for certes delights be after the appetites of the five wits;[1] as sight, hearing, smelling, savouring,[2] and touching. But in hell their sight shall be full of darkness and of smoke, and their eyes full of tears; and their hearing full of waimenting[3] and grinting[4] of teeth, as saith Jesus Christ; their nostrils shall be full of stinking; and, as saith Isaiah the prophet, their savouring[2] shall be full of bitter gall; and touching of all their body shall be covered with fire that never shall quench, and with worms that never shall die, as God saith by the mouth of Isaiah. And forasmuch as they shall not ween[5] that they may die for pain, and by death flee from pain, that may they understand in the word of Job, that saith, "There is the shadow of death." Certes a shadow hath the likeness of the thing of which it is shadowed, but the shadow is not the same thing of which it is shadowed: right so fareth the pain of hell; it is like death, for the horrible anguish; and why? for it paineth them ever as though they should die anon; but certes they shall not die. For, as saith Saint Gregory, "To wretched caitiffs shall be given death without death, and end without end, and default without failing; for their death shall always live, and their end shall evermore begin, and their default shall never fail." And therefore saith Saint John the Evangelist, "They shall follow death, and they shall not find him, and they shall desire to die, and death shall flee from them." And eke Job saith, that in hell is no order of rule. And albeit that God hath created all things in right order, and nothing without order, but all things be ordered and numbered, yet nevertheless they that be damned be not in order, nor hold no order. For the earth shall bear them no fruit (for, as the prophet David saith, "God shall destroy the fruit of the earth, as for them"); nor water shall give them no moisture, nor the air no refreshing, nor the fire no light. For as saith Saint Basil, "The burning of the fire of this world shall God give in hell to them that be damned, but the light and the clearness shall be given in heaven to his children; right as the good man giveth flesh to his children, and bones to his hounds." And for they shall have no hope to escape, saith Job at last, that there shall horror and grisly dread dwell without end. Horror is always dread of harm that is to come, and this dread shall ever dwell in the hearts of them that be damned. And therefore have they lost all their hope for seven causes. First, for God that is their judge shall be without mercy to them; nor they may not please him; nor none of his hallows;[6] nor they may give nothing for their ransom; nor they have no voice to speak to him; nor they may not flee from pain; nor they have no goodness in them that they may shew to deliver them from pain.

[Under the fourth head, of good works, the Parson says:—]

The courteous Lord Jesus Christ will that no good work be lost, for in somewhat it shall avail. But forasmuch as the good works that men do while they be in good life be all amortised[7] by sin following, and also since all the good works that men do while they be in deadly sin be utterly dead, as for to have the life perdurable, well may that man that no good works doth, sing that new French song, *J'ai tout perdu —mon temps et mon labour*. For certes, sin bereaveth a man both the goodness of nature, and eke the goodness of grace. For soothly the grace of the Holy Ghost fareth like fire, that may not be idle; for fire faileth anon as it forleteth[8] its working, and right so grace faileth anon as it forleteth its working. Then loseth the sinful man the goodness of glory, that only is behight[9] to good men that labour and work. Well may he be sorry then, that oweth all his life to God, as long as he hath lived, and also as long as he shall live, that no goodness hath to pay with his debt to God, to whom he oweth all his life: for trust well he shall give account, as saith Saint Bernard, of all the goods that have been given him in his present life, and how he hath them dispended, insomuch that there shall not perish an hair of his head, nor a moment of an hour shall not perish of his time, that he shall not give thereof a reckoning.

[Having treated of the causes, the Parson comes to the manner, of contrition—which should be universal and total, not merely of outward deeds of sin, but also of wicked delights and thoughts and words; "for certes Almighty God is all good, and therefore either he forgiveth all, or else right naught." Further, contrition should be "wonder sorrowful and anguishous," and also continual, with steadfast purpose of confession and amendment. Lastly, of what contrition availeth, the Parson says, that sometimes it delivereth man from sin;

1 Senses. 2 Tasting. 3 Wailing. 4 Gnashing, grinding. 5 Expect. 6 Saints. 7 Killed, deadened. 8 Leaveth. 9 Promised.

that without it neither confession nor satisfaction is of any worth; that it "destroyeth the prison of hell, and maketh weak and feeble all the strengths of the devils, and restoreth the gifts of the Holy Ghost and of all good virtues, and cleanseth the soul of sin, and delivereth it from the pain of hell, and from the company of the devil, and from the servage of sin, and restoreth it to all goods spiritual, and to the company and communion of Holy Church." He who should set his intent to these things, would no longer be inclined to sin, but would give his heart and body to the service of Jesus Christ, and thereof do him homage. "For, certes, our Lord Jesus Christ hath spared us so benignly in our follies, that if he had not pity on man's soul, a sorry song might we all sing."

The Second Part of the Parson's Tale or Treatise opens with an explanation of what is confession—which is termed "the second part of penitence, that is, sign of contrition;" whether it ought needs be done or not; and what things be convenable to true confession. Confession is true shewing of sins to the priest, without excusing, hiding, or forwrapping[1] of anything, and without vaunting of good works. "Also, it is necessary to understand whence that sins spring, and how they increase, and which they be." From Adam we took original sin; "from him fleshly descended be we all, and engendered of vile and corrupt matter;" and the penalty of Adam's transgression dwelleth with us as to temptation, which penalty is called concupiscence. "This concupiscence, when it is wrongfully disposed or ordained in a man, it maketh him covet, by covetise of flesh, fleshly sin by sight of his eyes, as to earthly things, and also covetise of highness by pride of heart." The Parson proceeds to shew how man is tempted in his flesh to sin; how, after his natural concupiscence, comes suggestion of the devil, that is to say the devil's bellows, with which he bloweth in man the fire of concupiscence; and how man then bethinketh him whether he will do or no the thing to which he is tempted. If he flame up into pleasure at the thought, and give way, then is he all dead in soul; "and thus is sin accomplished, by temptation, by delight, and by consenting; and then is the sin actual." Sin is either venial, or deadly; deadly, when a man loves any creature more than Jesus Christ our Creator, venial, if he love Jesus Christ less than he ought. Venial sins diminish man's love to God more and more, and may in this wise skip into deadly sin; for many small make a great. "And hearken this example: A great wave of the sea cometh sometimes with so great a violence, that it drencheth[2] the ship: and the same harm do sometimes the small drops of water that enter through a little crevice in the thurrok,[3] and in the bottom of the ship, if men be so negligent that they discharge them not betimes. And therefore, although there be difference betwixt these two causes of drenching, algates[4] the ship is dreint.[5] Right so fareth it sometimes of deadly sin," and of venial sins when they multiply in a man so greatly as to make him love worldly things more than God. The Parson then enumerates specially a number of sins which many a man peradventure deems no sins, and confesses them not, and yet nevertheless they are truly sins:—]

This is to say, at every time that a man eateth and drinketh more than sufficeth to the sustenance of his body, in certain he doth sin; eke when he speaketh more than it needeth, he doth sin; eke when he heareth not benignly the complaint of the poor; eke when he is in health of body, and will not fast when other folk fast, without cause reasonable; eke when he sleepeth more than needeth, or when he cometh by that occasion too late to church, or to other works of charity; eke when he useth his wife without sovereign desire of engendrure, to the honour of God, or for the intent to yield his wife his debt of his body; eke when he will not visit the sick, or the prisoner, if he may; eke if he love wife, or child, or other worldly thing, more than reason requireth; eke if he flatter or blandish more than he ought for any necessity; eke if he minish or withdraw the alms of the poor; eke if he apparail[6] his meat more deliciously than need is, or eat it too hastily by likerousness;[7] eke if he talk vanities in the church, or at God's service, or that he be a talker of idle words of folly or villainy, for he shall yield account of them at the day of doom; eke when he behighteth[8] or assureth to do things that he may not perform; eke when that by lightness of folly he missayeth or scorneth his neighbour; eke when he hath any wicked suspicion of thing, that he wot of it no soothfastness: these things, and more without number, be sins, as saith Saint Augustine.

[No earthly man may eschew all venial sins yet may he refrain him, by the burning love that he hath to our Lord Jesus Christ, and by prayer and confession, and other good works, so that it shall but little grieve. "Furthermore, men may also refrain and put away venial sin, by receiving worthily the precious body of Jesus Christ; by receiving eke of holy water; by alms-deed; by general confession of *Confiteor* at mass, and at prime, and at compline;[9] and by blessing of bishops and priests, and by other good works." The Parson then proceeds to weightier matters:—]

Now it is behovely[10] to tell which be deadly sins, that is to say, chieftains of sins; forasmuch as all they run in one leash, but in diverse manners. Now be they called chieftains, forasmuch as they be chief, and of them spring all other sins. The root of these sins, then, is pride, the general root of all harms. For of this root spring certain branches: as ire, envy,

1 Disguising. 2 Causes to sink. 3 Hold, bilge. 4 In any case. 5 Sunk.

6 Make ready. 7 Gluttony. 8 Promiseth. 9 Evening service of the Church. 10 Profitable, necessary.

accidie[1] or sloth, avarice or covetousness (to common understanding), gluttony, and lechery: and each of these sins hath his branches and his twigs, as shall be declared in their chapters following. And though so be, that no man can tell utterly the number of the twigs, and of the harms that come of pride, yet will I shew a part of them, as ye shall understand. There is inobedience, vaunting, hypocrisy, despite, arrogance, impudence, swelling of heart, insolence, elation, impatience, strife, contumacy, presumption, irreverence, pertinacity, vain-glory, and many another twig that I cannot tell nor declare. . . .

And yet[2] there is a privy species of pride, that waiteth first to be saluted ere he will salute, all[3] be he less worthy than that other is; and eke he waiteth[4] or desireth to sit or to go above him in the way, or kiss the pax,[5] or be incensed, or go to offering before his neighbour, and such semblable[6] things, against his duty peradventure, but that he hath his heart and his intent in such a proud desire to be magnified and honoured before the people. Now be there two manner of prides; the one of them is within the heart of a man, and the other is without. Of which soothly these foresaid things, and more than I have said, appertain to pride that is within the heart of a man; and there be other species of pride that be without: but nevertheless, the one of these species of pride is sign of the other, right as the gay levesell[7] at the tavern is sign of the wine that is in the cellar. And this is in many things: as in speech and countenance, and outrageous array of clothing; for certes, if there had been no sin in clothing, Christ would not so soon have noted and spoken of the clothing of that rich man in the gospel. And Saint Gregory saith, that precious clothing is culpable for the dearth[8] of it, and for its softness, and for its strangeness and disguising, and for the superfluity or for the inordinate scantness of it; alas! may not a man see in our days the sinful costly array of clothing, and namely[9] in too much superfluity, or else in too disordinate scantness? As to the first sin, in superfluity of clothing, which that maketh it so dear, to the harm of the people, not only the cost of the embroidering, the disguising, indenting or barring, ounding, paling,[10] winding, or banding, and semblable[6] waste of cloth in vanity; but there is also the costly furring[11] in their gowns, so much punching of chisels to make holes, so much dagging[12] of shears, with the superfluity in length of the foresaid gowns, trailing in the dung and in the mire, on horse and eke on foot, as well of man as of woman, that all that trailing is verily (as in effect) wasted, consumed, threadbare, and rotten with dung, rather than it is given to the poor, to great damage of the foresaid poor folk, and that in sundry wise: this is to say, the more that cloth is wasted, the more must it cost to the poor people for the scarceness; and furthermore, if so be that they would give such punched and dagged clothing to the poor people, it is not convenient to wear for their estate, nor sufficient to boot[13] their necessity, to keep them from the distemperance[14] of the firmament. Upon the other side, to speak of the horrible disordinate scantness of clothing, as be these cutted slops or hanselines,[15] that through their shortness cover not the shameful member of man, to wicked intent; alas! some of them shew the boss and the shape of the horrible swollen members, that seem like to the malady of hernia, in the wrapping of their hosen, and eke the buttocks of them, that fare as it were the hinder part of a she-ape in the full of the moon. And moreover the wretched swollen members that they shew through disguising, in departing[16] of their hosen in white and red, seemeth that half their shameful privy members were flain.[17] And if so be that they depart their hosen in other colours, as is white and blue, or white and black, or black and red, and so forth; then seemeth it, by variance of colour, that the half part of their privy members be corrupt by the fire of Saint Anthony, or by canker, or other such mischance. And of the hinder part of their buttocks it is full horrible to see, for certes, in that part of their body where they purge their stinking ordure, that foul part shew they to the people proudly in despite of honesty,[18] which honesty Jesus Christ and his friends observed to shew in his life. Now as of the outrageous array of women, God wot, that though the visages of some of them seem full chaste and debonair,[19] yet notify they, in their array of attire, likerousness and pride. I say not that honesty[20] in clothing of man or woman is unconvenable, but, certes, the superfluity or disordinate scarcity of clothing is reprovable. Also the sin of their ornament, or of apparel, as in things that appertain to riding, as in too many delicate horses, that be holden for delight, that be so fair, fat, and costly; and also in many a vicious knave,[21] that is sustained because of them; in curious harness, as in saddles, cruppers, peytrels,[22] and bridles, covered with precious cloth and rich bars and plates of gold and silver. For which God saith by Zechariah the prophet, "I will confound the riders of such horses." These folk take little regard of the riding of God's Son of heaven, and of his

1 Neglectfulness or indifference; from the Greek, ακηδεια.

2 Moreover. 3 Although. 4 Expecteth.

5 An image which was presented to the people to be kissed, at that part of the mass where the priest said, "Pax Domini sit semper vobiscum." The ceremony took the place, for greater convenience, of the "kiss of peace," which clergy and people, at this passage, used to bestow upon each other.

6 Like. 7 Arbour; bush. 8 Dearness.

9 Especially.

10 Three ways of ornamenting clothes with lace, &c.; in barring it was laid on crossways, in ounding it was waved, in paling it was laid on lengthways.

11 Lining or edging with fur. 12 Slitting, slashing. 13 Help, remedy. 14 Inclemency. 15 Breeches. 16 Dividing. 17 Flayed. 18 Decency. 19 Gentle. 20 Reasonable and appropriate stvle. 21 Servant. 22 Breast-plates.

harness, when he rode upon an ass, and had no other harness but the poor clothes of his disciples; nor we read not that ever he rode on any other beast. I speak this for the sin of superfluity, and not for reasonable honesty,[1] when reason it requireth. And moreover, certes, pride is greatly notified in holding of great meinie,[2] when they be of little profit or of right no profit, and namely[3] when that meinie is felonous and damageous[4] to the people by hardiness[5] of high lordship, or by way of office; for certes, such lords sell then their lordship to the devil of hell, when they sustain the wickedness of their meinie. Or else, when these folk of low degree, as they that hold hostelries, sustain theft of their hostellers, and that is in many manner of deceits: that manner of folk be the flies that follow the honey, or else the hounds that follow the carrion. Such foresaid folk strangle spiritually their lordships; for which thus saith David the prophet, "Wicked death may come unto these lordships, and God give that they may descend into hell adown; for in their houses is iniquity and shrewedness,[6] and not God of heaven." And certes, but if[7] they do amendment, right as God gave his benison to Laban by the service of Jacob, and to Pharaoh by the service of Joseph; right so God will give his malison to such lordships as sustain the wickedness of their servants, but[7] they come to amendment. Pride of the table apaireth[8] eke full oft; for, certes, rich men be called to feasts, and poor folk be put away and rebuked; also in excess of divers meats and drinks, and namely[3] such manner bake-meats and dish-meats burning of wild fire, and painted and castled with paper, and semblable[9] waste, so that it is abuse to think. And eke in too great preciousness of vessel,[10] and curiosity of minstrelsy, by which a man is stirred more to the delights of luxury, if so be that he set his heart the less upon our Lord Jesus Christ, certain it is a sin; and certainly the delights might be so great in this case, that a man might lightly[11] fall by them into deadly sin.

[The sins that arise of pride advisedly and habitually are deadly; those that arise by frailty unadvised suddenly, and suddenly withdraw again, though grievous, are not deadly. Pride itself springs sometimes of the goods of nature, sometimes of the goods of fortune, sometimes of the goods of grace; but the Parson, enumerating and examining all these in turn, points out how little security they possess and how little ground for pride they furnish, and goes on to enforce the remedy against pride—which is humility or meekness, a virtue through which a man hath true knowledge of himself, and holdeth no high esteem of himself in regard of his deserts, considering ever his frailty.]

Now be there three manners[12] of humility; as humility in heart, and another in the mouth, and the third in works. The humility in the heart is in four manners: the one is, when a man holdeth himself as nought worth before God of heaven; the second is, when he despiseth no other man; the third is, when he recketh not though men hold him nought worth; the fourth is, when he is not sorry of his humiliation. Also the humility of mouth is in four things: in temperate speech; in humility of speech; and when he confesseth with his own mouth that he is such as he thinketh that he is in his heart; another is, when he praiseth the bounté[13] of another man and nothing thereof diminisheth. Humility eke in works is in four manners: the first is, when he putteth other men before him; the second is, to choose the lowest place of all; the third is, gladly to assent to good counsel; the fourth is, to stand gladly by the award[14] of his sovereign, or of him that is higher in degree: certain this is a great work of humility.

[The Parson proceeds to treat of the other cardinal sins, and their remedies: (2.) Envy, with its remedy, the love of God principally and of our neighbours as ourselves: (3.) Anger, with all its fruits in revenge, rancour, hate, discord, manslaughter, blasphemy, swearing, falsehood, flattery, chiding and reproving, scorning, treachery, sowing of strife, doubleness of tongue, betraying of counsel to a man's disgrace, menacing, idle words, jangling, japery or buffoonery, &c.—and its remedy in the virtues called mansuetude, debonairté, or gentleness, and patience or sufferance: (4.) Sloth, or "Accidie," which comes after the sin of Anger, because Envy blinds the eyes of a man, and Anger troubleth a man, and Sloth maketh him heavy, thoughtful, and peevish. It is opposed to every estate of man—as unfallen, and held to work in praising and adoring God; as sinful, and held to labour in praying for deliverance from sin; and as in the state of grace, and held to works of penitence. It resembles the heavy and sluggish condition of those in hell; it will suffer no hardness and no penance; it prevents any beginning of good works; it causes despair of God's mercy, which is the sin against the Holy Ghost; it induces somnolency and neglect of communion in prayer with God; and it breeds negligence or recklessness, that cares for nothing, and is the nurse of all mischiefs, if ignorance is their mother. Against Sloth, and these and other branches and fruits of it, the remedy lies in the virtue of fortitude or strength, in its various species of magnanimity or great courage; faith and hope in God and his saints; surety or sickerness, when a man fears nothing that can oppose the good works he has undertaken; magnificence, when he carries out great works of goodness begun; constancy or stableness of heart; and other incentives to energy and laborious service: (5.) Avarice, or Covetousness, which is the root of all harms, since its votaries are idolaters, oppressors and enslavers

1 Seemliness. 2 Retinue of servants. 3 Especially. 4 Violent and harmful. 5 Arrogance. 6 Impiety.

7 Unless. 8 Worketh harm. 9 Like. 10 Plate. 11 Easily. 12 Kinds. 13 Goodness. 14 Judgment.

of men, deceivers of their equals in business, simoniacs, gamblers, liars, thieves, false swearers, blasphemers, murderers, and sacrilegious. Its remedy lies in compassion and pity largely exercised, and in reasonable liberality—for those who spend on "fool-largesse," or ostentation of worldly estate and luxury, shall receive the malison that Christ shall give at the day of doom to them that shall be damned: (6.) Gluttony;—of which the Parson treats so briefly that the chapter may be given in full:—]

After Avarice cometh Gluttony, which is express against the commandment of God. Gluttony is unmeasurable appetite to eat or to drink; or else to do in aught to the unmeasurable appetite and disordered covetousness[1] to eat or drink. This sin corrupted all this world, as is well shewed in the sin of Adam and of Eve. Look also what saith Saint Paul of gluttony: "Many," saith he, "go, of which I have oft said to you, and now I say it weeping, that they be enemies of the cross of Christ, of which the end is death, and of which their womb is their God and their glory;" in confusion of them that so savour[2] earthly things. He that is usant[3] to this sin of gluttony, he may no sin withstand, he must be in servage[4] of all vices, for it is the devil's hoard,[5] where he hideth him in and resteth. This sin hath many species. The first is drunkenness, that is the horrible sepulture of man's reason: and therefore when a man is drunken, he hath lost his reason; and this is deadly sin. But soothly, when that a man is not wont to strong drink, and peradventure knoweth not the strength of the drink, or hath feebleness in his head, or hath travailed,[6] through which he drinketh the more, all[7] be he suddenly caught with drink, it is no deadly sin, but venial. The second species of gluttony is, that the spirit of a man waxeth all troubled for drunkenness, and bereaveth a man the discretion of his wit. The third species of gluttony is, when a man devoureth his meat, and hath no rightful manner of eating. The fourth is, when, through the great abundance of his meat, the humours of his body be distempered. The fifth is, forgetfulness by too much drinking, for which a man sometimes forgetteth by the morrow what he did at eve. In other manner be distinct the species of gluttony, after Saint Gregory. The first is, for to eat or drink before time. The second is, when a man getteth him too delicate meat or drink. The third is, when men take too much over measure.[8] The fourth is, curiosity[9] with great intent[10] to make and apparel[11] his meat. The fifth is, for to eat too greedily. These be the five fingers of the devil's hand, by which he draweth folk to the sin.

Against gluttony the remedy is abstinence, as saith Galen; but that I hold not meritorious, if he do it only for the health of his body. Saint Augustine will that abstinence be done for virtue, and with patience. Abstinence, saith he, is little worth, but[12] if a man have good will thereto, and but it be enforced by patience and by charity, and that men do it for God's sake, and in hope to have the bliss in heaven. The fellows of abstinence be temperance, that holdeth the mean in all things; also shame, that escheweth all dishonesty;[13] sufficiency, that seeketh no rich meats nor drinks, nor doth no force of[14] no outrageous apparelling of meat; measure[15] also, that restraineth by reason the unmeasurable appetite of eating; soberness also, that restraineth the outrage of drink; sparing also, that restraineth the delicate ease to sit long at meat, wherefore some folk stand of their own will to eat, because they will eat at less leisure.

[At great length the Parson then points out the many varieties of the sin of (7.) Lechery, and its remedy in chastity and continence, alike in marriage and in widowhood; also in the abstaining from all such indulgences of eating, drinking, and sleeping as inflame the passions, and from the company of all who may tempt to the sin. Minute guidance is given as to the duty of confessing fully and faithfully the circumstances that attend and may aggravate this sin; and the Treatise then passes to the consideration of the conditions that are essential to a true and profitable confession of sin in general. First, it must be in sorrowful bitterness of spirit; a condition that has five signs—shamefastness, humility in heart and outward sign, weeping with the bodily eyes or in the heart, disregard of the shame that might curtail or garble confession, and obedience to the penance enjoined. Secondly, true confession must be promptly made, for dread of death, of increase of sinfulness, of forgetfulness of what should be confessed, of Christ's refusal to hear if it be put off to the last day of life; and this condition has four terms; that confession be well pondered beforehand, that the man confessing have comprehended in his mind the number and greatness of his sins and how long he has lain in sin, that he be contrite for and eschew his sins, and that he fear and flee the occasions for that sin to which he is inclined.—What follows under this head is of some interest for the light which it throws on the rigorous government wielded by the Romish Church in those days:—]

Also thou shalt shrive thee of all thy sins to one man, and not a parcel[16] to one man, and a parcel to another; that is to understand, in intent to depart[17] thy confession for shame or dread; for it is but strangling of thy soul. For certes Jesus Christ is entirely all good, in him is none imperfection, and therefore either he forgiveth all perfectly, or else never

1 Craving. 2 Take delight in.
3 Accustomed, addicted. 4 Bondage.
5 Lair, lurking-place. 6 Laboured.
7 Although. 8 Immoderately.
9 Nicety. 10 Application, pains.
11 Prepare. 12 Unless.
13 Indecency, impropriety. 14 Sets no value on.
15 Moderation. 16 Portion. 17 Divide.

a deal.[1] I say not that if thou be assigned to thy penitencer [2] for a certain sin, that thou art bound to shew him all the remnant of thy sins, of which thou hast been shriven of thy curate, but if it like thee [3] of thy humility; this is no departing [4] of shrift. And I say not, where I speak of division of confession, that if thou have license to shrive thee to a discreet and an honest priest, and where thee liketh, and by the license of thy curate, that thou mayest not well shrive thee to him of all thy sins: but let no blot be behind, let no sin be untold as far as thou hast remembrance. And when thou shalt be shriven of thy curate, tell him eke all the sins that thou hast done since thou wert last shriven. This is no wicked intent of division of shrift. Also, very shrift [5] asketh certain conditions. First, that thou shrive thee by thy free will, not constrained, nor for shame of folk, nor for malady,[6] or such things: for it is reason, that he that trespasseth by his free will, that by his free will he confess his trespass; and that no other man tell his sin but himself; nor he shall not nay nor deny his sin, nor wrath him against the priest for admonishing him to leave his sin. The second condition is, that thy shrift be lawful, that is to say, that thou that shrivest thee, and eke the priest that heareth thy confession, be verily in the faith of Holy Church, and that a man be not despaired of the mercy of Jesus Christ, as Cain and Judas were. And eke a man must accuse himself of his own trespass, and not another: but he shall blame and wite [7] himself of his own malice and of his sin, and none other: but nevertheless, if that another man be occasion or else enticer of his sin, or the estate of the person be such by which his sin is aggravated, or else that he may not plainly shrive him but [8] he tell the person with which he hath sinned, then may he tell, so that his intent be not to backbite the person, but only to declare his confession. Thou shalt not eke make no leasings [9] in thy confession for humility, peradventure, to say that thou hast committed and done such sins of which that thou wert never guilty. For Saint Augustine saith, "If that thou, because of humility, makest a leasing on thyself, though thou were not in sin before, yet art thou then in sin through thy leasing." Thou must also shew thy sin by thine own proper mouth, but [8] thou be dumb, and not by letter; for thou that hast done the sin, thou shalt have the shame of the confession. Thou shalt not paint thy confession with fair and subtle words, to cover the more thy sin; for then beguilest thou thyself, and not the priest; thou must tell it plainly, be it never so foul nor so horrible. Thou shalt eke shrive thee to a priest that is discreet to counsel thee; and eke thou shalt not shrive thee for vain-glory, nor for hypocrisy, nor for no cause but only for the doubt [10] of Jesus Christ and the health of thy soul. Thou shalt not run to the priest all suddenly, to tell him lightly thy sin, as who telleth a jape [11] or a tale, but advisedly and with good devotion; and generally shrive thee oft; if thou oft fall, oft arise by confession. And though thou shrive thee oftener than once of sin of which thou hast been shriven, it is more merit; and, as saith Saint Augustine, thou shalt have the more lightly [12] release and grace of God, both of sin and of pain. And certes, once a year at the least way, it is lawful to be houseled,[13] for soothly once a year all things in the earth renovelen.[14]

[Here ends the Second Part of the Treatise; the Third Part, which contains the practical application of the whole, follows entire, along with the remarkable "Prayer of Chaucer," as it stands in the Harleian Manuscript:—]

De Tertiâ Parte Pœnitentiæ.

Now have I told you of very [15] confession, that is the second part of penitence: The third part of penitence is satisfaction, and that standeth generally in almsdeed and bodily pain. Now be there three manner of almsdeed: contrition of heart, where a man offereth himself to God; the second is, to have pity of the default of his neighbour; the third is, in giving of good counsel and comfort, ghostly and bodily, where men have need, and namely [16] in sustenance of man's food. And take keep [17] that a man hath need of these things generally; he hath need of food, of clothing, and of herberow,[18] he hath need of charitable counsel and visiting in prison and malady, and sepulture of his dead body. And if thou mayest not visit the needful with thy person, visit them by thy message and by thy gifts. These be generally alms or works of charity of them that have temporal riches or discretion in counselling. Of these works shalt thou hear at the day of doom. This alms shouldest thou do of thine own proper things, and hastily,[19] and privily if thou mayest; but nevertheless, if thou mayest not do it privily, thou shalt not forbear to do alms, though men see it, so that it be not done for thank of the world, but only for thank of Jesus Christ. For, as witnesseth Saint Matthew, chap. v., "A city may not be hid that is set on a mountain, nor men light not a lantern and put it under a bushel, but men set it on a candlestick, to light the men in the house; right so shall your light lighten before men, that they may see your good works, and glorify your Father that is in heaven."

Now as to speak of bodily pain, it is in prayer, in wakings,[20] in fastings, and in virtuous teachings. Of orisons ye shall understand, that ori-

1 Not at all.
2 A priest who enjoined penance in extraordinary cases.
3 Unless thou be pleased.
4 Division.
5 True confession.
6 Sickness.
7 Accuse.
8 Unless.
9 Falsehoods.
10 Fear.
11 Jest.
12 Easily.
13 To receive the holy sacrament; from Anglo-Saxon, "husel;" Latin, "hostia," or "hostiola," the host.
14 Renew themselves.
15 True.
16 Especially.
17 Notice.
18 Lodging.
19 Promptly.
20 Watchings.

sons or prayers is to say a piteous will of heart, that redresseth it in God, and expresseth it by word outward, to remove harms, and to have things spiritual and durable, and sometimes temporal things. Of which orisons, certes in the orison of the *Pater noster* hath our Lord Jesus Christ enclosed most things. Certes, it is privileged of three things in its dignity, for which it is more digne[1] than any other prayer: for Jesus Christ himself made it: and it is short, for[2] it should be coude the more lightly,[3] and to withhold[4] it the more easy in heart, and help himself the oftener with this orison; and for a man should be the less weary to say it; and for a man may not excuse him to learn it, it is so short and so easy: and for it comprehendeth in itself all good prayers. The exposition of this holy prayer, that is so excellent and so digne, I betake[5] to these masters of theology; save thus much will I say, when thou prayest that God should forgive thee thy guilts, as thou forgivest them that they guilt to thee, be full well ware that thou be not out of charity. This holy orison aminisheth[6] eke venial sin, and therefore it appertaineth specially to penitence. This prayer must be truly said, and in very faith, and that men pray to God ordinately, discreetly, and devoutly; and always a man shall put his will to be subject to the will of God. This orison must eke be said with great humbleness and full pure, and honestly, and not to the annoyance of any man or woman. It must eke be continued with the works of charity. It availeth against the vices of the soul; for, as saith Saint Jerome, by fasting be saved the vices of the flesh, and by prayer the vices of the soul.

After this thou shalt understand, that bodily pain stands in waking.[7] For Jesus Christ saith, "Wake and pray, that ye enter not into temptation." Ye shall understand also, that fasting stands in three things: in forbearing of bodily meat and drink, and in forbearing of worldly jollity, and in forbearing of deadly sin; this is to say, that a man shall keep him from deadly sin in all that he may. And thou shalt understand eke, that God ordained fasting, and to fasting appertain four things: largeness[8] to poor folk; gladness of heart spiritual; not to be angry nor annoyed nor grudge[9] for he fasteth; and also reasonable hour for to eat by measure, that is to say, a man should not eat in untime,[10] nor sit the longer at his meal, for[11] he fasteth. Then shalt thou understand, that bodily pain standeth in discipline, or teaching, by word, or by writing, or by ensample. Also in wearing of hairs[12] or of stamin,[13] or of habergeons[14] on their naked flesh for Christ's sake; but ware thee well that such manner penance of thy flesh make not thine heart bitter or angry, nor annoyed of thyself; for better is to cast away thine hair than to cast away the sweetness of our Lord Jesus Christ. And therefore saith Saint Paul, "Clothe you, as they that be chosen of God in heart, of misericorde,[15] debonairté,[16] sufferance,[17] and such manner of clothing," of which Jesus Christ is more apaid[18] than of hairs or of hauberks. Then is discipline eke in knocking of thy breast, in scourging with yards,[19] in kneelings, in tribulations, in suffering patiently wrongs that be done to him, and eke in patient sufferance of maladies, or losing of worldly catel,[20] or of wife, or of child, or of other friends.

Then shalt thou understand which things disturb penance, and this is in four things; that is dread, shame, hope, and wanhope, that is, desperation. And for to speak first of dread, for which he weeneth that he may suffer no penance, thereagainst is remedy for to think that bodily penance is but short and little at the regard of[21] the pain of hell, that is so cruel and so long, that it lasteth without end. Now against the shame that a man hath to shrive him, and namely[22] these hypocrites, that would be holden so perfect, that they have no need to shrive them; against that shame should a man think, that by way of reason he that hath not been ashamed to do foul things, certes he ought not to be ashamed to do fair things, and that is confession. A man should eke think, that God seeth and knoweth all thy thoughts, and all thy works; to him may nothing be hid nor covered. Men should eke remember them of the shame that is to come at the day of doom, to them that be not penitent and shriven in this present life; for all the creatures in heaven, and in earth, and in hell, shall see apertly[23] all that he hideth in this world.

Now for to speak of them that be so negligent and slow to shrive them; that stands in two manners. The one is, that he hopeth to live long, and to purchase[24] much riches for his delight, and then he will shrive him: and, as he sayeth, he may, as him seemeth, timely enough come to shrift: another is, the surquedrie[25] that he hath in Christ's mercy. Against the first vice, he shall think that our life is in no sickerness,[26] and eke that all the riches in this world be in adventure, and pass as a shadow on the wall; and, as saith St Gregory, that it appertaineth to the great righteousness of God, that never shall the pain stint[27] of them, that never would withdraw them from sin, their thanks,[28] but aye continue in sin; for that perpetual will to do sin shall they have perpetual pain. Wanhope[29] is in two manners.[30]

1 Worthy.
2 In order that.
3 The more easily conned or learned.
4 Retain.
5 Commit.
6 Lesseneth.
7 Watching.
8 Liberality.
9 Murmur.
10 Out of time.
11 Because.
12 Haircloth.
13 Coarse hempen cloth.
14 It was a frequent penance among the chivalric orders to wear mail shirts next the skin.
15 With compassion.
16 Gentleness.
17 Patience.
18 Better pleased.
19 Rods.
20 Chattels.
21 In comparison with.
22 Especially.
23 Openly.
24 Acquire.
25 Presumption; from old French, "surcuider," to think arrogantly, be full of conceit.
26 Security.
27 Cease.
28 With their goodwill.
29 Despair.
30 Of two kinds.

The first wanhope is, in the mercy of God: the other is, that they think they might not long persevere in goodness. The first wanhope cometh of that he deemeth that he sinned so highly and so oft, and so long hath lain in sin, that he shall not be saved. Certes against that cursed wanhope should he think, that the passion of Jesus Christ is more strong for to unbind, than sin is strong for to bind. Against the second wanhope he shall think, that as oft as he falleth, he may arise again by penitence; and though he never so long hath lain in sin, the mercy of Christ is always ready to receive him to mercy. Against the wanhope that he thinketh he should not long persevere in goodness, he shall think that the feebleness of the devil may nothing do, but[1] men will suffer him; and eke he shall have strength of the help of God, and of all Holy Church, and of the protection of angels, if him list.

Then shall men understand, what is the fruit of penance; and after the word of Jesus Christ, it is the endless bliss of heaven, where joy hath no contrariety of woe nor of penance nor grievance; there all harms be passed of this present life; there as is the sickerness from the pain of hell; there as is the blissful company, that rejoice them evermore each of the other's joy; there as the body of man, that whilom was foul and dark, is more clear than the sun; there as the body of man, that whilom was sick and frail, feeble and mortal, is immortal, and so strong and so whole, that there may nothing apair[2] it; there is neither hunger, nor thirst, nor cold, but every soul replenished with the sight of the perfect knowing of God. This blissful regne[3] may men purchase by poverty spiritual, and the glory by lowliness, the plenty of joy by hunger and thirst, the rest by travail, and the life by death and mortification of sin; to which life He us bring, that bought us with his precious blood! *Amen.*

Preces de Chauceres.[4]

Now pray I to you all that hear this little treatise or read it, that if there be anything in it that likes them, that thereof they thank our Lord Jesus Christ, of whom proceedeth all wit and all goodness; and if there be anything that displeaseth them, I pray them also that they arette[5] *it to the default of mine unconning,*[6] *and not to my will, that would fain have said better if I had had conning; for the book saith, all that is written for our doctrine is written. Wherefore I beseech you meekly for the mercy of God that ye pray for me, that God have mercy on me and forgive me my guilts, and namely*[7] *my translations and of inditing in worldly vanities, which I revoke in my Retractions, as is the Book of Troilus, the Book also of Fame, the Book of Twenty-five Ladies, the Book of the Duchess, the Book of Saint Valentine's Day and of the Parliament of Birds, the Tales of Canterbury, all those that sounen unto sin,*[8] *the Book of the Lion, and many other books, if they were in my mind or remembrance, and many a song and many a lecherous lay, of the which Christ for his great mercy forgive me the sins. But of the translation of Boece* de Consolatione, *and other books of consolation and of legend of lives of saints, and homilies, and moralities, and devotion, that thank I our Lord Jesus Christ, and his mother, and all the saints in heaven, beseeching them that they from henceforth unto my life's end send me grace to bewail my guilts, and to study to the salvation of my soul, and grant me grace and space of very*[9] *repentance, penitence, confession, and satisfaction, to do in this present life, through the benign grace of Him that is King of kings and Priest of all priests, that bought us with his precious blood of his heart, so that I may be one of them at the day of doom that shall be saved:* Qui cum Patre et Spiritu Sancto vivis et regnas Deus per omnia secula. Amen.

1 Unless. 2 Impair, injure.
3 Kingdom.
4 The genuineness and real significance of this "Prayer of Chaucer," usually called his "Retractation," have been warmly disputed. On the one hand, it has been declared that the monks forged the retractation, and procured its insertion among the works of the man who had done so much to expose their abuses and ignorance, and to weaken their hold on popular credulity; on the other hand, Chaucer himself, at the close of his life, is said to have greatly lamented the "ribaldry" and the attacks on the clergy which marked especially "The Canterbury Tales," and to have drawn up a formal retractation, of which the "Prayer" is either a copy or an abridgment. The beginning and end of the "Prayer," as Tyrwhitt points out, are in tone and terms quite appropriate in the mouth of the Parson, while they carry on the subject of which he has been treating; and, despite the fact that Mr Wright holds the contrary opinion, Tyrwhitt seems to be justified in setting down the "Retractation" as interpolated into the close of the Parson's Tale. Of the circumstances under which the interpolation was made, or the causes by which it was dictated, little or nothing can now be confidently affirmed; but the agreement of the manuscripts and the early editions in giving it, render it impossible to discard it peremptorily as a declaration of prudish or of interested regret, with which Chaucer himself had nothing whatever to do
5 Impute.
6 Unskilfulness. 7 Especially.
8 Are sinful, tend towards sin. 9 True.

THE END OF THE CANTERBURY TALES.

THE COURT OF LOVE.

["THE COURT OF LOVE" was probably Chaucer's first poem of any consequence. It is believed to have been written at the age, and under the circumstances, of which it contains express mention; that is, when the poet was eighteen years old, and resided as a student at Cambridge,—about the year 1346. The composition is marked by an elegance, care, and finish very different from the bold freedom which in so great measure distinguishes the Canterbury Tales; and the fact is easily explained when we remember that, in the earlier poem, Chaucer followed a beaten path, in which he had many predecessors and competitors, all seeking to sound the praises of love with the grace, the ingenuity, and studious devotion, appropriate to the theme. The story of the poem is exceedingly simple. Under the name of Philogenet, a clerk or scholar of Cambridge, the poet relates that, summoned by Mercury to the Court of Love, he journeys to the splendid castle where the King and Queen of Love, Admetus and Alcestis, keep their state. Discovering among the courtiers a friend named Philobone, a chamberwoman to the Queen, Philogenet is led by her into a circular temple, where, in a tabernacle, sits Venus, with Cupid by her side. While he is surveying the motley crowd of suitors to the goddess, Philogenet is summoned back into the King's presence, chidden for his tardiness in coming to Court, and commanded to swear observance to the twenty Statutes of Love—which are recited at length. Philogenet then makes his prayers and vows to Venus, desiring that he may have for his love a lady whom he has seen in a dream; and Philobone introduces him to the lady herself, named Rosial, to whom he does suit and service of love. At first the lady is obdurate to his entreaties; but, Philogenet having proved the sincerity of his passion by a fainting fit, Rosial relents, promises her favour, and orders Philobone to conduct him round the Court. The courtiers are then minutely described; but the description is broken off abruptly, and we are introduced to Rosial in the midst of a confession of her love. Finally she commands Philogenet to abide with her until the First of May, when the King of Love will hold high festival; he obeys; and the poem closes with the May Day festival service, celebrated by a choir of birds, who sing an ingenious, but what must have seemed in those days a more than slightly profane, paraphrase or parody of the matins for Trinity Sunday, to the praise of Cupid. From this outline, it will be seen at once that Chaucer's "Court of Love" is in important particulars different from the institutions which, in the two centuries preceding his own, had so much occupied the attention of poets and gallants, and so powerfully controlled the social life of the noble and refined classes. It is a regal, not a legal, Court which the poet pictures to us; we are not introduced to a regularly constituted and authoritative tribunal in which nice questions of conduct in the relations of lovers are discussed and decided—but to the central and sovereign seat of Love's authority, where the statutes are moulded, and the decrees are issued, upon which the inferior and special tribunals we have mentioned frame their proceedings. The "Courts of Love," in Chaucer's time, had lost none of the prestige and influence which had been conferred upon them by the patronage and participation of Kings, Queens, Emperors, and Popes. But the institution, in its legal or judicial character, was peculiar to France; and although the whole spirit of Chaucer's poem, especially as regards the esteem and reverence in which women were held, is that which animated the French Courts, his treatment of the subject is broader and more general, consequently more fitted to enlist the interest of English readers. The poem consists of 206 stanzas of seven lines each; of which, in this edition, eighty-three are represented by a prose abridgement.]

With timorous heart, and trembling hand of
dread,
Of cunning[1] naked, bare of eloquence,
Unto the flow'r of port in womanhead[2]
I write, as he that none intelligence
Of metres hath,[3] nor flowers of senténce,
Save that me list my writing to convey,
In that I cán, to please her high nobley.[4]

The blossoms fresh of Tullius'[5] garden swoot[6]
Present they not, my matter for to born:[7]
Poems of Virgil takë here no root,
Nor craft of Galfrid[8] may not here sojourn;
Why n' am[9] I cunning? O well may I mourn,
For lack of science, that I cannot write
Unto the princess of my life aright!

No terms are dign[10] unto her excellence,
So is she sprung of noble stirp[11] and high;
A world of honour and of reverence
There is in her, this will I testify.
Calliopé, thou sister wise and sly,[12]
And thou, Minerva, guide me with thy grace,
That language rude my matter not deface!

Thy sugar droppës sweet of Helicon
Distil in me, thou gentle Muse, I pray;
And thee, Melpomené,[13] I call anon
Of ignorance the mist to chase away;
And give me grace so for to write and say,
That she, my lady, of her worthiness,
Accept in gree[14] this little short treatéss,[15]

That is entitled thus, *The Court of Love.*
And ye that be metricians,[16] me excuse,
I you beseech, for Venus' sake above;
For what I mean in this ye need not muse:
And if so be my lady it refuse
For lack of ornate speech, I would be woe
That I presume to her to writë so.

But my intent, and all my busy cure,[17]
Is for to write this treatise, as I can,
Unto my lady, stable, true, and sure,
Faithful and kind, since first that she began
Me to accept in service as her man;[18]
To her be all the pleasure of this book,
That, when her like,[19] she may it read and look.

When [he] was young, at eighteen year of age,
Lusty and light, desirous of pleasánce,
Approaching on[20] full sad and ripe corâge,[21]

Then—says the poet—did Love urge him to do him obeisance, and to go "the Court of Love to see, a lite[22] beside the Mount of Citharee."[23] Mercury bade him, on pain of death, to appear; and he went by strange and far countries in search of the Court. Seeing at last a crowd of people, "as bees," making their way thither, the poet asked whither they went; and "one that answer'd like a maid" said that they were bound to the Court of Love, at Citheron,[23] where "the King of Love, and all his noble rout,[24]

"Dwelleth within a castle royally."
So them apace I journey'd forth among,
And as he said, so found I there trulý;
For I beheld the towers high and strong,
And high pinnácles, large of height and lóng,
With plate of gold bespread on ev'ry side,
And precious stones, the stone work for to hide.

No sapphire of Ind, no ruby rich of price,
There lacked then, nor emerald so green,
Balais,[25] Turkeis,[26] nor thing, to my devise,[27]
That may the castle makë for to sheen;[28]
All was as bright as stars in winter be'n;[29]
And Phœbus shone, to make his peace again,
For trespass[30] done to high estatës twain,—

When he had found Venus in the arms of Mars, and hastened to tell Vulcan of his wife's infidelity.[31] Now he was shining brightly on the castle, "in sign he looked after Lovë's grace;" for there is no god in Heaven or in Hell "but he hath been right subject unto Love." Continuing his description of the castle, Philogenet says that he saw never any so large and high; within and without, it was painted "with many a thousand daisies, red as rose," and white also, in signification of whom, he knew not; unless it was the flower of Alcestis,[32] who, under Venus, was queen of the place, as Admetus was king;

To whom obey'd the ladies good nineteen,[33]
With many a thousand other, bright of face.

1 Skill.
2 One who is the perfection of womanly behaviour.
3 So the Man of Law, in the prologue to his Tale (page 60), is made to say that Chaucer "can but lewëdly (ignorantly or imperfectly) on metres and on rhyming craftily." But the humility of those apologies is not justified by the care and finish of his earlier poems.
4 Nobleness.
5 Cicero's.
6 Sweet.
7 Burnish: the poet means, that his verses do not display the eloquence or brilliancy of Cicero in setting forth his subject-matter.
8 Geoffrey de Vinsauf, to whose treatise on poetical composition a less flattering allusion is made in The Nun's Priest's Tale. See note 12, page 170.
9 Am not.
10 Worthy.
11 Race, stock; Latin, "stirps."
12 Skilful. Calliope is the Epic Muse—"sister" to the other eight.
13 The Tragic Muse.
14 With favour.
15 Treatise.
16 Skilled in versifying.
17 Care.
18 Liegeman, servant.
19 When it so pleases her.
20 Gradually attaining.
21 The same is said of Griselda, in The Clerk's Tale; though she was of tender years, "yet in the breast of her virginity there was inclos'd a sad and ripe coráge" (page 95).
22 Little.
23 The confusion which Chaucer makes between Cithæron and Cythera, has already been remarked. See note 2, page 36.
24 Company.
25 Bastard rubies; said to be so called from Balassa, the Asian country where they were found.
26 Turquoise stones.
27 So far as I can tell; to my judgment.
28 Shine, be beautiful.
29 Are.
30 Offence.
31 Spenser, in his description of the House of Busirane, speaks of the sad distress into which Phœbus was plunged by Cupid, in revenge for the betrayal of "his mother's wantonness, when she with Mars was meint in jöyfulness" (page 439).
32 Alcestis, daughter of Pelias, was won to wife by Admetus, King of Pheræ, who complied with her father's demand that he should come to claim her in a chariot drawn by lions and boars. By the aid of Apollo—who tended the flocks of Admetus during his banishment from heaven—the suitor fulfilled the condition; and Apollo further induced the Moiræ or Fates to grant that Admetus should never die, if his father, mother, or wife would die for him. Alcestis devoted herself in his stead; and, since each had made great efforts or sacrifices for love, the pair are fitly placed as king and queen in the Court of Love.
33 In the prologue to the "Legend of Good Women," Chaucer says that behind the God of Love, upon the

And young men fele[1] came forth with lusty pace,
And aged eke, their homage to dispose;
But what they were, I could not well disclose.

Yet nere and nere[2] forth in I gan me dress,
Into a hall of noble apparail,[3]
With arras[4] spread, and cloth of gold, I guess,
And other silk of easier avail;[5]
Under the cloth of their estate,[6] sans fail,
The King and Queen there sat, as I beheld;
It passed joy of Elysée the feld.[7]

There saintës[8] have their coming and resort,
To see the King so royally beseen,[9]
In purple clad, and eke the Queen in sort;[10]
And on their headës saw I crownës twain,
With stonës frett,[11] so that it was no pain,
Withoutë meat or drink, to stand and see
The Kingë's honour and the royalty.

To treat of state affairs, Danger[12] stood by the King, and Disdain by the Queen; who cast her eyes haughtily about, sending forth beams that seemed "shapen like a dart, sharp and piercing, and small and straight of line;" while her hair shone as gold so fine, "dishevel, crisp, down hanging at her back a yard in length."[13] Amazed and dazzled by her beauty, Philogenet stood perplexed, till he spied a friend, Philobone—a chamberwoman of the Queen's—who asked how and on what errand he came thither. Learning that he had been summoned by Mercury, she told him that he ought to have come of his free will, and that he "will be shent"[14] because he did not.

"For ye that reign in youth and lustiness,
Pamper'd with ease, and jealous in your age,
Your duty is, as far as I can guess,
To Lovë's Court to dressë[15] your voyáge,
As soon as Nature maketh you so sage
That ye may know a woman from a swan,[16]
Or when your foot is growen half a span.

"But since that ye, by wilful negligence,
This eighteen year have kept yourself at large,
The greater is your trespass and offence,
And in your neck you must bear all the charge:
For better were ye be withoutë barge[17]
Amid the sea in tempest and in rain,
Than bidë here, receiving woe and pain

"That órdained is for such as them absent
From Lovë's Court by yearës long and fele.[1]
I lay[18] my life ye shall full soon repent;
For Love will rive your colour, lust, and heal:[19]
Eke ye must bait[20] on many a heavy meal:
No force,[21] y-wis; I stirr'd you long agone
To draw to Court," quoth little Philobone.

"Ye shall well see how rough and angry face
The King of Love will show, when ye him see;
By mine advice kneel down and ask him grace,
Eschewing[22] peril and adversitý;
For well I wot it will none other be;
Comfort is none, nor counsel to your ease;
Why will ye then the King of Love displease?"

Thereupon Philogenet professed humble repentance, and willingness to bear all hardship and chastisement for his past offence.

These wordës said, she caught me by the lap,[23]
And led me forth into a temple round,
Both large and wide; and, as my blessed hap
And good adventure was, right soon I found
A tabernacle[24] raised from the ground,
Where Venus sat, and Cupid by her side;
Yet half for dread I gan my visage hide.

And eft[25] again I looked and beheld,
Seeing full sundry people[26] in the place,
And mister folk,[27] and some that might not weld[28]
Their limbës well,—me thought a wonder case.
The temple shone with windows all of glass,
Bright as the day, with many a fair imáge;
And there I saw the fresh queen of Cartháge,

Dido, that brent her beauty[29] for the love
Of false Æneas; and the waimentíng[30]
Of her, Annélide, true as turtle dove
To Arcite false;[31] and there was in paintíng
Of many a Prince, and many a doughty King,
Whose martyrdom was show'd about the walls;
And how that fele[1] for love had suffer'd falls.[32]

Philogenet was astonished at the crowd of people that he saw, doing sacrifice to the god and goddess. Philobone informed him that they came from other courts; those who knelt in

green, he "saw coming in ladies nineteen;" but the stories of only nine good women are there told. In the prologue to The Man of Law's Tale, sixteen ladies are named as having their stories written in the "Saints' Legend of Cupid"—now known as the "Legend of Good Women"—(see note 1, page 61); and in the "Retractation," at the end of the Parson's Tale (page 199), the "Book of the Twenty-five Ladies" is enumerated among the works of which the poet repents—but there "xxv" is supposed to have been by some copyist written for "xix."

1 Many; German, "viele."
2 Nearer and nearer.
3 Nobly furnished.
4 Tapestry of silk, made at Arras, in France.
5 Of less value, and therefore easier of attainment.
6 State canopy.
7 The Elysian Fields.
8 Sufferers or martyrs for love.
9 So royal to behold; so richly adorned.
10 In keeping, suitably.
11 Fretted; roughened, or adorned, with precious stones.
12 Danger, in the Provençal Courts of Love, was the allegorical personification of the husband; and Disdain suitably represents the lover's corresponding difficulty from the side of the lady.
13 In The Knight's Tale, Emily's yellow hair is braided in a tress, or plait, that hung a yard long behind her back; so that, both as regards colour and fashion, a singular resemblance seems to have existed between the female taste of 1369 and that of 1869.
14 Rebuked, disgraced.
15 Direct, address.
16 In an old monkish story—reproduced by Boccaccio, and from him by La Fontaine in the Tale called "Les Oies de Frère Philippe"—a young man is brought up without sight or knowledge of women, and, when he sees them on a visit to the city, he is told that they are geese.
17 Barque, boat.
18 Wager.
19 Health.
20 Feed.
21 No matter.
22 Avoiding.
23 Skirt or edge of the garment.
24 A shrine or canopy of stone, supported by pillars.
25 Afterwards.
26 People of many sorts.
27 Handicraftsmen, or tradesmen, who have learned "mysteries."
28 Wield, use.
29 Her own beauteous self.
30 Lamenting.
31 The loves "Of Queen Annelida and False Arcite" formed the subject of a short unfinished poem by Chaucer, which was afterwards worked up into The Knight's Tale.
32 Calamities, misfortunes.

blue wore the colour in sign of their changeless truth;[1] those in black, who uttered cries of grief, were the sick and dying of love. The priests, nuns, hermits, and friars, and all that sat in white, in russet and in green, "wailed of their woe;" and for all people, of every degree, the Court was open and free. While he walked about with Philobone, a messenger from the King entered, and summoned all the new-come folk to the royal presence. Trembling and pale, Philogenet approached the throne of Admetus, and was sternly asked why he came so late to Court. He pleaded that a hundred times he had been at the gate, but had been prevented from entering by failure to see any of his acquaintances, and by shamefacedness. The King pardoned him, on condition that thenceforth he should serve Love; and the poet took oath to do so, "though Death therefor me thirlë[2] with his spear." When the King had seen all the new-comers, he commanded an officer to take their oaths of allegiance, and show them the Statutes of the Court, which must be observed till death.

And, for that I was letter'd, there I read
The statutes whole of Lovë's Court and hall:
The first statute that on the book was spread,
Was, To be true in thought and deedës all
Unto the King of Love, the lord royál;
And, to the Queen, as faithful and as kind
As I could think with heartë, will, and mind.

The second statute, Secretly to keep
Counsel[3] of love, not blowing[4] ev'rywhere
All that I know, and let it sink and fleet;[5]
It may not sound in ev'ry wightë's ear:
Exiling slander ay for dread and fear,
And to my lady, which I love and serve,
Be true and kind, her grace for to deserve.

The third statute was clearly writ also,
Withoutë change to live and die the same,
None other love to take, for weal nor woe,
For blind delight, for earnest nor for game:
Without repent, for laughing or for grame,[6]
To bidë still in full persévéránce:
All this was whole the Kingë's ordinance.

The fourth statute, To purchase ever to her,[7]
And stirrë folk to love, and betë[8] fire
On Venus' altar, here about and there,
And preach to them of love and hot desire,
And tell how love will quitë well their hire:[9]
This must be kept; and loth me to displease:
If love be wroth, pass; for thereby is ease.

The fifth statute, Not to be dangerous,[10]
If that a thought would reave[11] me of my sleep:
Nor of a sight to be over squaimous;[12]
And so verily this statute was to keep,
To turn and wallow in my bed and weep,
When that my lady, of her cruelty,
Would from her heart exilen all pitý.

The sixth statute, It was for me to use
Alone to wander, void of companý,
And on my lady's beauty for to muse,
And thinken it no force[13] to live or die;
And eft again to think[14] the remedý,
How to her grace I might anon attain,
And tell my woe unto my sovëreign.

The sev'nth statute was, To be patiént,
Whether my lady joyful were or wroth;
For wordës glad or heavy, diligent,
Whether that she me heldë lefe or loth:[15]
And hereupon I put was to mine oath,
Her, for to serve, and lowly to obey,
And show my cheer,[16] yea, twenty times a day.

The eighth statute, to my rememberance,
Was, For to speak and pray my lady dear,
With hourly labour and great entendánce,[17]
Me for to love with all her heart entere,[18]
And me desire and make me joyful cheer,
Right as she is, surmounting every fair;
Of beauty well,[19] and gentle debonair.

The ninth statute, with letters writ of gold,
This was the sentence, How that I and all
Should ever dread to be too overbold
Her to displease; and truly so I shall;
But be content for all thing that may fall,
And meekly take her chastisement and yerd,[20]
And to offend her ever be afear'd.

The tenth statute was, Equally[21] to discern
Between the lady and thine ability,
And think thyself art never like to earn,
By right, her mercy nor her equity,
But of her grace and womanly pitý:
For, though thyself be noble in thy strene,[22]
A thousand fold more noble is thy Queen.

Thy lifë's lady and thy sovëreign,
That hath thine heart all whole in governance,
Thou may'st no wise it takë to disdain,
To put thee humbly at her ordinance,
And give her free the rein of her pleasánce;
For liberty is thing that women look,[23]
And truly else the matter is a crook.[24]

Th' eleventh statute, Thy signës for to know
With eye and finger, and with smilës soft,
And low to couch, and alway for to show,
For dread of spiës, for to winken oft:
And secretly to bring a sigh aloft,
But still beware of over much resort;
For that peradventure spoileth all thy sport.

The twelfth statute remember to observe:
For all the pain thou hast for love and woe,
All is too lite[25] her mercy to deserve,
Thou mustë think, where'er thou ride or go;
And mortal woundës suffer thou also,
All for her sake, and think it well beset[26]
Upon thy love, for it may not be bet.[27]

The thirteenth statute, Whilom is to think

1 See note 14, page 121. 2 Pierce. 3 Secret. 4 Talking, boasting. 5 Float, swim. 6 Vexation, sorrow. 7 Acquire (new followers) for her, promote her cause. 8 Kindle. 9 Reward their labour. 10 Fastidious, angry. 11 Deprive. 12 Fond, desirous. 13 Matter of indifference.

14 To think upon. 15 In love or in loathing. 16 Countenance. 17 Attention, application. 18 Entire. 19 Fountain. 20 Rod; rule, dictation. 21 Equitably, justly. 22 Strain; stock, descent. 23 Look for, desire to have. 24 Things go wrong. 25 Little. 26 Spent. 27 Better (spent).

What thing may best thy lady like and please,
And in thine heartë's bottom let it sink:
Some thing devise, and take for it thine ease,
And send it her, that may her heart appease:
Some heart, or ring, or letter, or device,
Or precious stone; but spare not for no price.

The fourteenth statute eke thou shalt assay
Firmly to keep, the most part of thy life:
Wish that thy lady in thine armës lay,
And nightly dream, thou hast thy nightë's wife
Sweetly in armës, straining her as blife:[1]
And, when thou seest it is but fantasy,
See that thou sing not over merrily;

For too much joy hath oft a woeful end.
It longeth eke this statute for to hold,[2]
To deem thy lady evermore thy friend,
And think thyself in no wise a cuckóld.
In ev'ry thing she doth but as she sho'ld:
Construe the best, believe no talës new,
For many a lie is told, that seems full true.

But think that she, so bountëous and fair,
Could not be false: imagine this algate;[3]
And think that wicked tongues would her apair,[4]
Sland'ring her name and worshipful estate,[5]
And lovers true to setten at debate:
And though thou seest a fault right at thine eye,
Excuse it blife,[1] and glose[6] it prettily.

The fifteenth statute, Use to swear and stare,
And counterfeit a leasing[7] hardily,[8]
To save thy lady's honour ev'rywhere,
And put thyself for her to fight boldlý:
Say she is good, virtúous, and ghostly,[9]
Clear of intent, and heart, and thought, and will;
And argue not for reason nor for skill

Against thy lady's pleasure nor intent,
For love will not be counterpled[10] indeed:
Say as she saith, then shalt thou not be shent;[11]
"The crow is white;" "Yea truly, so I rede:"[12]
And aye what thing that she will thee forbid,
Eschew all that, and give her sov'reignty,
Her appetite to follow in all degree.

The sixteenth statute, keep it if thou may:[13]
Sev'n times at night thy lady for to please,
And sev'n at midnight, sev'n at morrow day,
And drink a caudle early for thine ease.
Do this, and keep thine head from all disease,
And win the garland here of lovers all,
That ever came in Court, or ever shall.

Full few, think I, this statute hold and keep;
But truly this my reason gives me feel,[14]
That some lovers should rather fall asleep,
Than take on hand to please so oft and weel.
There lay none oath to this statute adele,[15]
But keep who might as gave him his coráge:[16]
Now get this garland, lusty folk of age![17]

Now win who may, ye lusty folk of youth,
This garland fresh, of flowers red and white,
Purple and blue, and colours full uncouth,[18]
And I shall crown him king of all delight!
In all the Court there was not, to my sight,
A lover true, that he was not adread,
When he express[19] had heard the statute read.

The sev'nteenth statute, When age approacheth on,
And lust is laid, and all the fire is queint,[20]
As freshly then thou shalt begin to fon,[21]
And doat in love, and all her image paint
In thy remembrance, till thou gin to faint,
As in the first seasón thine heart began:
And her desire, though thou nor may nor can

Perform thy living actual and lust;
Register this in thine rememberance:
Eke when thou may'st nót keep thy thing from rust,
Yet speak and talk of pleasant dalliance;
For that shall make thine heart rejoice and dance;
And when thou may'st no more the game assay,
The statute bids thee pray for them that may.

The eighteenth statute, wholly to commend,
To please thy lady, is, That thou eschew
With sluttishness thyself for to offend;
Be jolly, fresh, and feat,[22] with thingës new,
Courtly with manner, this is all thy due,
Gentle of port, and loving cleanliness;
This is the thing that liketh thy mistréss.

And not to wander like a dulled ass,
Ragged and torn, disguised in array,
Ribald in speech, or out of measure pass,
Thy bound exceeding; think on this alway:
For women be of tender heartës ay,
And lightly set their pleasure in a place;
When they misthink,[23] they lightly let it pace.

The nineteenth statute, Meat and drink forget:
Each other day see that thou fast for love,
For in the Court they live withoutë meat,
Save such as comes from Venus all above;
They take no heed, in pain of great reprove,[24]
Of meat and drink, for that is all in vain,
Only they live by sight of their sov'réign.

The twentieth statute, last of ev'ry one,
Enrol it in thy heartë's privity;
To wring and wail, to turn, and sigh, and groan,
When that thy lady absent is from thee;
And eke renew[25] the wordës all that she
Between you twain hath said, and all the cheer
That thee hath made thy lifë's lady dear.

And see thy heart in quiet nor in rest
Sojóurn, till time thou see thy lady eft,[26]
But whe'er[27] she won[28] by south, or east, or west,

1 Quickly, eagerly; for "blive" or "belive."
2 It belongs to the proper observance of this statute.
3 By all ways; at all events.
4 Impair, defame.
5 Honourable fame.
6 Gloss it over.
7 Falsehood.
8 Boldly.
9 Spiritual, pure.
10 Met with counterpleas.
11 Chidden, disgraced.
12 Judge, declare.
13 It will be seen afterwards that Philogenet does not relish it, and pleads for its relaxation.
14 My reason enables me to perceive.
15 Annexed.
16 As his heart inspired him.
17 That is, folk of lusty age.
18 Strange.
19 Plainly.
20 Quenched.
21 Fondle, play the fool.
22 Dainty, neat, handsome; the same as "fetis," oftener used in Chaucer; the adverb "featly" is still used, as applied to dancing, &c.
23 Think wrongly.
24 On pain of great reproach.
25 Recall to mind.
26 Again.
27 Whether.
28 Dwell.

With all thy force now see it be not left:
Be diligent, till time[1] thy life be reft,
In that thou may'st, thy lady for to see;
This statute was of old antiquity.

The officer, called Rigour—who is incorruptible by partiality, favour, prayer, or gold—made them swear to keep the statutes; and, after taking the oath, Philogenet turned over other leaves of the book, containing the statutes of women. But Rigour sternly bade him forbear; for no man might know the statutes that belong to women.

"In secret wise they keptë be full close;
They sound[2] each one to liberty, my friend;
Pleasant they be, and to their own purpóse;
There wot[3] no wight of them, but God and fiend,
Nor aught shall wit, unto the worldë's end.
The queen hath giv'n me charge, in pain to die,
Never to read nor see them with mine eye.

"For men shall not so near of counsel be'n
With womanhead, nor knowen of their guise,
Nor what they think, nor of their wit th' engine;[4]
I me report[5] to Solomon the wise,
And mighty Samson, which beguiled thrice
With Delilah was; he wot that, in a throw,
There may no man statúte of women know.

"For it peradventure may right so befall,
That they be bound by nature to deceive,
And spin, and weep, and sugar strew on gall,[6]
The heart of man to ravish and to reave,
And whet their tongue as sharp as sword or gleve:[7]
It may betide this is their ordinance,
So must they lowly do their óbservánce,

"And keep the statute given them of kind,[8]
Of such as Love hath giv'n them in their life.
Men may not wit why turneth every wind,
Nor waxë wise, nor be inquisitife
To know secrét of maid, widow, or wife;
For they their statutes have to them reserved,
And never man to know them hath deserved."

Rigour then sent them forth to pay court to Venus, and pray her to teach them how they might serve and please their dames, or to provide with ladies those whose hearts were yet vacant. Before Venus knelt a thousand sad petitioners, entreating her to punish "the false untrue," that had broken their vows, "barren of ruth, untrue of what they said, now that their lust and pleasure is allay'd." But the mourners were in a minority;

Yet eft again, a thousand millión,
Rejoicing, love, leading their life in bliss:
They said: "Venus, redress[9] of all división,
Goddess eternal, thy name heried[10] is!
By lovë's bond is knit all thing, y-wis,[11]
Beast unto beast, the earth to water wan,[12]
Bird unto bird, and woman unto man;[13]

"This is the life of joy that we be in,
Resembling life of heav'nly paradise;
Love is exiler ay of vice and sin;
Love maketh heartës lusty to devise;
Honour and grace have they in ev'ry wise,
That be to lovë's law obedient;
Love maketh folk benign and diligent;

"Aye stirring them to dreadë vice and shame:
In their degree it makes them honouráble;
And sweet it is of love to bear the name,
So that his love be faithful, true, and stable:
Love pruneth him to seemen amiáble;
Love hath no fault where it is exercis'd,
But sole[14] with them that have all love despis'd:"

And they conclude with grateful honours to the goddess—rejoicing that they are hers in heart, and all inflamed with her grace and heavenly fear. Philogenet now entreats the goddess to remove his grief; for he also loves, and hotly, only he does not know where—

"Save only this, by God and by my troth;
Troubled I was with slumber, sleep, and sloth
This other night, and in a visioún
I saw a woman roamen up and down,

"Of mean statúre,[15] and seemly to behold,
Lusty and fresh, demure of countenance,
Young and well shap'd, with hairë sheen[16] as gold,
With eyne as crystal, farced[17] with pleasance;
And she gan stir mine heart a lite[18] to dance;
But suddenly she vanish gan right there:
Thus I may say, I love, and wot[19] not where."

If he could only know this lady, he would serve and obey her with all benignity; but if his destiny were otherwise, he would gladly love and serve his lady, whosoever she might be. He called on Venus for help to possess his queen and heart's life, and vowed daily war with Diana: "that goddess chaste I keepen[20] in no wise to serve; a fig for all her chastity!" Then he rose and went his way, passing by a rich and beautiful shrine, which, Philobone informed him, was the sepulchre of Pity. "A tender creature," she said,

"Is shrined there, and Pity is her name.
She saw an eagle wreak[21] him on a fly,
And pluck his wing, and eke him, in his game;[22]
And tender heart of that hath made her die:
Eke she would weep, and mourn right piteously,
To see a lover suffer great distress.
In all the Court was none, as I do guess,

"That could a lover half so well avail,[23]
Nor of his woe the torment or the rage
Aslake;[24] for he was sure, withoutë fail,
That of his grief she could the heat assuage.
Instead of Pity, speedeth hot Couráge

1 Until the time that.
2 Tend, accord.
3 Knows.
4 Craft, scheming skill.
5 I refer for evidence. Solomon was beguiled by his heathenish wives to forsake the worship of the true God; Samson fell a victim to the wiles of Delilah.
6 Compare the speech of Proserpine to Pluto, in The Merchant's Tale, page 113.
7 Glaive, sword.
8 By nature.
9 Redresser, healer.
10 Glorified.
11 Assuredly.
12 Pale.
13 See note 3, page 46, for a parallel.
14 Only.
15 Of middling height.
16 Shining, bright.
17 Literally, stuffed, crammed; laden with pleasure.
18 Little.
19 Know.
20 Care.
21 Avenge.
22 For sport.
23 Help.
24 Assuage.

The matters all of Court, now she is dead;
I me report in this to womanhead.[1]

"For wail, and weep, and cry, and speak, and pray,—
Women would not have pity on thy plaint;
Nor by that means to ease thine heart convey,
But thee receivë for their own talént:[2]
And say that Pity caus'd thee, in consent
Of ruth,[3] to take thy service and thy pain,
In that thou may'st, to please thy sovëreign."

Philobone now promised to lead Philogenet to "the fairest lady under sun that is," the "mirror of joy and bliss," whose name is Rosial, and "whose heart as yet is given to no wight;" suggesting that, as he also was "with love but light advanc'd," he might set this lady in the place of her of whom he had dreamed. Entering a chamber gay, "there was Rosial, womanly to see;" and the subtle-piercing beams of her eyes wounded Philogenet to the heart. When he could speak, he threw himself on his knees, beseeching her to cool his fervent woe:

For there I took full purpose in my mind,
Unto her grace my painful heart to bind.

For, if I shall all fully her descrive,[4]
Her head was round, by compass of natúre;
Her hair as gold, she passed all alive,
And lily forehead had this creatúre,
With lively browës flaw,[5] of colour pure,
Between the which was mean disseverance
From ev'ry brow, to show a due distánce.

Her nose directed straight, even as line,
With form and shape thereto convenient,
In which the goddës' milk-white path[6] doth shine;
And eke her eyne be bright and orient
As is the smaragd,[7] unto my judgmént,
Or yet these starrës heav'nly, small, and bright;
Her visage is of lovely red and white.

Her mouth is short, and shut in little space,
Flaming somedeal,[8] not over red I mean,
With pregnant lips, and thick to kiss, percase[9]
(For lippës thin, not fat, but ever lean,
They serve of naught, they be not worth a bean;
For if the bass[10] be full, there is delight;
Maximian[11] trulý thus doth he write).

But to my purpose: I say, white as snow
Be all her teeth, and in order they stand
Of one statúre; and eke her breath, I trow,
Surmounteth all odoúrs that e'er I fand
In sweetness; and her body, face, and hand
Be sharply slender, so that, from the head
Unto the foot, all is but womanhead.[12]

I hold my peace of other thingës hid:
Here shall my soul, and not my tongue, bewray;
But how she was array'd, if ye me bid,
That shall I well discover you and say:
A bend[13] of gold and silk, full fresh and gay,
With hair in tress,[14] y-broidered full well,
Right smoothly kempt,[15] and shining every deal.

About her neck a flow'r of fresh device
With rubies set, that lusty were to see'n;
And she in gown was, light and summer-wise,
Shapen full well, the colour was of green,
With aureate seint[16] about her sidës clean,
With divers stonës, precious and rich:
Thus was she ray'd,[17] yet saw I ne'er her lich.[18]

If Jove had but seen this lady, Calisto and Alcmena had never lain in his arms, nor had he loved the fair Europa, nor Danaé, nor Antiopé; "for all their beauty stood in Rosial; she seemed like a thing celestial." By and by, Philogenet presented to her his petition for love, which she heard with some haughtiness; she was not, she said, well acquainted with him, she did not know where he dwelt, nor his name and condition. He informed her that "in art of love he writes," and makes songs that may be sung in honour of the King and Queen of Love. As for his name—

"My name? alas, my heart, why mak'st thou strange?[19]
Philogenet I call'd am far and near,
Of Cambridge clerk, that never think to change
From you, that with your heav'nly streamës[20] clear
Ravish my heart, and ghost, and all in fere:[21]
Since at the first I writ my bill[22] for grace,
Me thinks I see some mercy in your face;"

And again he humbly pressed his suit. But the lady disdained the idea that, "for a word of sugar'd eloquence," she should have compassion in so little space; "there come but few who speedë here so soon." If, as he says, the beams of her eyes pierce and fret him, then let him withdraw from her presence:

"Hurt not yourself, through folly, with a look;
I would be sorry so to make you sick!
A woman should beware eke whom she took:
Ye be a clerk: go searchë well my book,
If any women be so light[23] to win:
Nay, bide a while, though ye were all my kin."[24]

He might sue and serve, and wax pale, and green, and dead, without murmuring in any wise; but whereas he desired her hastily to lean to love, he was unwise, and must cease that language. For some had been at Court for twenty years, and might not obtain their mis-

1 For evidence I refer to the behaviour of women themselves.
2 Inclination, pleasure.
3 Compassion.
4 Describe.
5 Yellow eyebrows; Latin, "flavus," French, "fauve."
6 The galaxy.
7 Emerald.
8 Somewhat.
9 As it chanced.
10 Kiss; French, "baiser;" and hence the more vulgar "buss."
11 Cornelius Maximianus Gallus flourished in the time of the Emperor Anastasius; in one of his elegies, he professed a preference for flaming and somewhat swelling lips, which, when he tasted them, would give him full kisses.
12 Womanly perfection.
13 Band.
14 Plaited in tresses.
15 Combed.
16 Golden cincture or girdle.
17 Arrayed.
18 Like, match.
19 Why so cold or distant?
20 Beams, glances.
21 All together.
22 Petition.
23 Easy.
24 My whole kindred.

tresses' favour; therefore she marvelled that he was so bold as to treat of love with her. Philogenet, on this, broke into pitiful lamentation; bewailing the hour in which he was born, and assuring the unyielding lady that the frosty grave and cold must be his bed, unless she relented.

With that I fell in swoon, and dead as stone,
With colour slain,[1] and wan as ashes pale;
And by the hand she caught me up anon:
"Arise," quoth she; "what? have ye drunken dwale?[2]
Why sleepë ye? It is no nightertale."[3]
"Now mercy! sweet," quoth I, y-wis afraid;
"What thing," quoth she, "hath made you so dismay'd?"

She said that by his hue she knew well that he was a lover; and if he were secret, courteous, and kind, he might know how all this could be allayed. She would amend all that she had missaid, and set his heart at ease; but he must faithfully keep the statutes, "and break them not for sloth nor ignorance." The lover requests, however, that the sixteenth may be released or modified, for it "doth him great grievance;" and she complies.

And softly then her colour gan appear,
As rose so red, throughout her visage all;
Wherefore methinks it is according her[4]
That she of right be called Rosial.
Thus have I won, with wordës great and small,
Some goodly word of her that I love best,
And trust she shall yet set mine heart in rest.

Rosial now told Philobone to conduct Philogenet all over the Court, and show him what lovers and what officers dwelt there; for he was yet a stranger.

And, stalking soft with easy pace, I saw
About the king standen all environ,[5]
Attendance, Diligence, and their fellaw
Furtherer, Esperance,[6] and many one;
Dread-to-offend there stood, and not alone;
For there was eke the cruel adversair,
The lover's foe, that called is Despair;

Which unto me spake angrily and fell,[7]
And said, my lady me deceivë shall:
"Trow'st thou," quoth she, "that all that she did tell
Is true? Nay, nay, but under honey gall.
Thy birth and hers they be no thing egál:[8]
Cast off thine heart,[9] for all her wordës white,
For in good faith she loves thee but a lite.[10]

"And eke remember, thine ability
May not compare with her, this well thou wot."
Yea, then came Hope and said, "My friend, let be!
Believe him not: Despair he gins to doat."
"Alas," quoth I, "here is both cold and hot:
The one me biddeth love, the other nay;
Thus wot I not what me is best to say.

"But well wot I, my lady granted me
Truly to be my woundë's remedy;
Her gentleness[11] may not infected be
With doubleness,[12] this trust I till I die."
So cast I t' avoid Déspair's company,
And takë Hope to counsel and to friend.
"Yea, keep that well," quoth Philobone, "in mind."

And there beside, within a bay windów,
Stood one in green, full large of breadth and length,
His beard as black as feathers of the crow;
His name was Lust, of wondrous might and strength;
And with Delight to argue there he think'th,
For this was alway his opinión,
That love was sin: and so he hath begun

To reason fast, and ledge authority:[13]
"Nay," quoth Delight, "love is a virtue clear,
And from the soul his progress holdeth he:
Blind appetite of lust doth often steer,[14]
And that is sin; for reason lacketh there:
For thou dost think thy neighbour's wife to win;
Yet think it well that love may not be sin;

"For God, and saint, they love right verily,
Void of all sin and vice: this know I weel,[15]
Affectión of flesh is sin truly;
But very[16] love is virtue, as I feel;
For very love may frail desire akele:[17]
For very love is love withoutë sin."
"Now stint,"[18] quoth Lust, "thou speak'st not worth a pin."

And there I left them in their arguing,
Roaming farther into the castle wide,
And in a corner Liar stood talking
Of leasings[19] fast, with Flattery there beside;
He said that women ware[20] attire of pride,
And men were found of nature variant,
And could be false and showë beau semblant.[21]

Then Flattery bespake and said, y-wis:
"See, so she goes on pattens fair and feat;[22]
It doth right well: what pretty man is this
That roameth here? now truly drink nor meat
Need I not have, my heart for joy doth beat
Him to behold, so is he goodly fresh:
It seems for love his heart is tender and nesh."[23]

This is the Court of lusty folk and glad,
And well becomes their habit and array:
O why be some so sorry and so sad,
Complaining thus in black and white and gray?
Friars they be, and monkës, in good fay:[24]
Alas, for ruth![25] great dole[26] it is to see,
To see them thus bewail and sorry be.

1 Deathlike.
2 Sleeping potion, narcotic. See note 30, page 57.
3 Night-time.
4 Appropriate to her.
5 Around; French, "à l'environ."
6 Hope.
7 Cruelly, fiercely.
8 Equal.
9 From confidence in her.
10 But little.
11 Noble nature.
12 Duplicity.
13 Allege authorities, or adduce examples.
14 Stir, or guide (the heart).
15 Well.
16 True, perfect.
17 Cool, allay.
18 Cease.
19 Falsehoods.
20 Wore.
21 Put on plausible appearances to deceive.
22 Pretty, neat.
23 Soft, delicate; Anglo-Saxon, "nesc."
24 Faith.
25 Pity.
26 Sorrow.

See how they cry and ring their handës white,
For they so soon went to religión![1]
And eke the nuns with veil and wimple plight,[2]
Their thought is, they be in confusión:
"Alas," they say, "we feign perfectión,[3]
In clothës wide, and lack our liberty;
But all the sin must on our friendës be.[4]

"For, Venus wot, we would as fain[5] as ye,
That be attired here and well beseen,[6]
Desirë man, and love in our degree,
Firm and faithful, right as would the Queen:
Our friendës wick', in tender youth and green,
Against our will made us religioús;
That is the cause we mourn and wailë thus."

Then said the monks and friars in the tide,[7]
"Well may we curse our abbeys and our place,
Our statutes sharp to sing in copës wide,[8]
Chastely to keep us out of lovë's grace,
And never to feel comfort nor solace;[9]
Yet suffer we the heat of lovë's fire,
And after some other haply we desire.

"O Fortune cursed, why now and wherefóre
Hast thou," they said, "bereft us liberty,
Since Nature gave us instrument in store,
And appetite to love and lovers be?
Why must we suffer such adversity,
Dian' to serve, and Venus to refuse?
Full often sithe[10] these matters do us muse.[11]

"We serve and honour, sore against our will,
Of chastity the goddess and the queen;
Us liefer were[12] with Venus bidë still,
And have regard for love, and subject be'n
Unto these women courtly, fresh, and sheen.[13]
Fortune, we curse thy wheel of variance!
Where we were well, thou reavest[14] our pleas-
ánce."

Thus leave I them, with voice of plaint and care,
In raging woe crying full piteously;
And as I went, full naked and full bare
Some I beheld, looking dispiteously,
On Poverty that deadly cast their eye;
And "Well-away!" they cried, and were not fain,
For they might not their glad desire attain.

For lack of riches worldly and of good,
They ban and curse, and weep, and say, "Alas!
That povert' hath us hent,[15] that whilom stood
At heartë's ease, and free and in good case!
But now we dare not show ourselves in place,
Nor us embold[16] to dwell in company,
Where as our heart would love right faithfully."

And yet againward shrieked ev'ry nun,
The pang of love so strained them to cry:
"Now woe the time," quoth they, "that we be
boun'![17]
This hateful order nice[18] will do us die!
We sigh and sob, and bleeden inwardlý,
Fretting ourselves with thought and hard com-
plaint,
That nigh for love we waxë wood[19] and faint."

And as I stood beholding here and there,
I was ware of a sort[20] full languishing,
Savage and wild of looking and of cheer,
Their mantles and their clothës aye tearíng;
And oft they were of Nature complainíng,
For they their members lacked, foot and hand,
With visage wry, and blind, I understand.

They lacked shape and beauty to prefer
Themselves in love: and said that God and
Kind[21]
Had forged[22] them to worshippë the sterre,[23]
Venus the bright, and leften all behind[24]
His other workës clean and out of mind:
"For other have their full shape and beautý,
And we," quoth they, "be in deformity."

And nigh to them there was a company,
That have the Sisters warray'd[25] and missaid,
I mean the three of fatal destiny,[26]
That be our workers: suddenly abraid,[27]
Out gan they cry as they had been afraid;
"We curse," quoth they, "that ever hath Natúre
Y-formed us this woeful life t' endure."

And there eke was Contrite,[28] and gan repent,
Confessing whole the wound that Cytheré[29]
Had with the dart of hot desire him sent,
And how that he to love must subject be:
Then held he all his scornës vanity,
And said that lovers held a blissful life,
Young men and old, and widow, maid, and wife.

"Bereave me, Goddess!" quoth he, "of thy
might,
My scornës all and scoffës, that I have
No power for to mocken any wight
That in thy service dwell': for I did rave;
This know I well right now, so God me save,
And I shall be the chief post[30] of thy faith,
And love uphold, the réverse whoso saith."

Dissemble[31] stood not far from him in truth,
With party[32] mantle, party hood and hose;
And said he had upon his lady ruth,[33]
And thus he wound him in, and gan to glose,

1 Because they took religious vows so young.
2 Plaited, folded.
3 Perfectly holy life, in the performance of vows of poverty, chastity, obedience, and other modes of mortifying the flesh.
4 Who made us take the vows before they knew our own dispositions, or ability, to keep them.
5 Gladly.
6 Gaily and elegantly clothed—in contrast with their own poor and sad-coloured robes.
7 At the same time.
8 The large vestment worn in singing the service in the choir. In Chaucer's time it seems to have been a distinctively clerical piece of dress; so, in the prologue to The Monk's Tale (page 156), the Host, lamenting that so stalwart a man as the Monk should have gone into religion, exclaims, "Alas! why wearest thou so wide a cope?"
9 Delight.
10 Full many a time.
11 Cause us to ponder or wonder.
12 We would rather.
13 Bright, beautiful.
14 Takest away.
15 Seized, overtaken.
16 Make bold, venture.
17 Bound.
18 Foolish (that is, into which we foolishly entered).
19 Mad.
20 A company or class of people.
21 Nature.
22 Fashioned, designed.
23 Star.
24 Had left them inferior to.
25 Reproached, assailed with blame.
26 The three Fates.
27 Aroused.
28 Contrition, who repents that once he spurned the sway of Love.
29 Cytherea—Venus, so called from the name of the island, Cythera, into which her worship was first introduced from Phœnicia.
30 Prop, pillar.
31 Dissimulation.
32 Parti-coloured.
33 Pity.

Of his intent full double, I suppose :
In all the world he said he lov'd her weel ;
But ay me thought he lov'd her ne'er a deal.[1]

Eke Shamefastness was there, as I took heed,
That blushed red, and durst not be y-know
She lover was, for thereof had she dread ;
She stood and hung her visage down alow ;
But such a sight it was to see, I trow,
As of these roses ruddy on their stalk :
There could no wight her spy to speak or talk

In lovë's art, so gan she to abash,
Nor durst not utter all her privity :
Many a stripe and many a grievous lash
She gave to them that wouldë lovers be,
And hinder'd sore the simple commonalty,
That in no wise durst grace and mercy crave,
For were not she,[2] they need but ask and have ;

Where if they now approachë for to speak,
Then Shamefastness returneth them [3] again :
They think, "If we our secret counsel break,
Our ladies will have scorn on us certáin,
And peradventure thinkë great disdain :"
Thus Shamefastness may bringen in Despair ;
When she is dead the other will be heir.

"Come forth Avaunter ![4] now I ring thy bell !"
I spied him soon ; to God I make avow,[5]
He looked black as fiendës do in Hell :
"The first," quoth he, "that ever I did wow,[6]
Within a word she came,[7] I wot not how,
So that in armës was my lady free,
And so have been a thousand more than she.

"In England, Britain,[8] Spain, and Picardy,
Artois, and France, and up in high Hollánd,
In Burgoyne,[9] Naples, and in Italy,
Navarre, and Greece, and up in heathen land,
Was never woman yet that would withstand
To be at my commandment when I wo'ld :
I lacked [10] neither silver coin nor gold.

"And there I met with this estate and that ;
And her I broach'd, and her, and her, I trow :
Lo ! there goes one of mine ; and, wot ye what ?
Yon fresh attired have I laid full low ;
And such one yonder eke right well I know ;
I kept the statute [11] when we lay y-fere :[12]
And yet [13] yon same hath made me right good cheer."

Thus hath Avaunter blowen ev'rywhere
All that he knows, and more a thousand fold ;
His ancestry of kin was to Liér,[14]]
For first he maketh promise for to hold
His lady's counsel, and it not unfold ;
Wherefore, the secret when he doth unshit,[15]
Then lieth he, that all the world may wit.

For falsing so his promise and behest,[16]
I wonder sore he hath such fantasy ;[17]
He lacketh wit, I trow, or is a beast,
That can no bet [18] himself with reason guy.[19]
By mine advice,[20] Love shall be contrarý
To his avail,[21] and him eke dishonoúr,
So that in Court he shall no more sojoúr.[22]

"Take heed," quoth she, this little Philobone,
"Where Envy rocketh in the corner yond,[23]
And sitteth dark ; and ye shall see anon
His lean body, fading both face and hand ;
Himself he fretteth,[24] as I understand
(Witness of Ovid Metamorphoseos [25]) ;
The lover's foe he is, I will not glose.[26]

"For where a lover thinketh him promote,[27]
Envy will grudge, repining at his weal ;
It swelleth sore about his heartë's root,
That in no wise he cannot live in heal ;[28]
And if the faithful to his lady steal,
Envy will noise and ring it round about,
And say much worse than done is, out of doubt."

And Privy Thought, rejoicing of himself,
Stood not far thence in habit marvellous ;
"Yon is," thought I, "some spirit or some elf,
His subtile image is so curious :
How is," quoth I, "that he is shaded thus
With yonder cloth, I n'ot [29] of what colór ?"
And near I went and gan to lear and pore,[30]

And frained [31] him a questión full hard.
"What is," quoth I, "the thing thou lovest best ?
Or what is boot [32] unto thy painës hard ?
Me thinks thou livest here in great unrest,
Thou wand'rest aye from south to east and west,
And east to north ; as far as I can see,
There is no place in Court may holdë thee.

"Whom followest thou ? where is thy heart y-set ?
But my demand assoil,[33] I thee require."
"Me thought," quoth he, "no creatúre may let [34]
Me to be here, and where as I desire ;
For where as absence hath done [35] out the fire,
My merry thought it kindleth yet again,
That bodily, me thinks, with my sov'réign [36]

"I stand, and speak, and laugh, and kiss, and halse ;[37]
So that my thought comfórteth me full oft :
I think, God wot, though all the world be false,
I will be true ; I think also how soft
My lady is in speech, and this on loft
Bringeth my heart with joy and great gladnéss ;
This privy thought allays my heaviness.

"And what I think, or where, to be, no man
In all this Earth can tell, y-wis, but I :

1 Never a jot.
2 But for her.
3 Turns them back.
4 Boaster : Philobone calls him out.
5 Confession.
6 Woo.
7 She was won with a single word.
8 Brittany ; Lesser Britain.
9 Burgundy ; French, "Bourgogne."
10 Needed (for my conquests).
11 The sixteenth.
12 Together.
13 Also.
14 Liar.
15 Unshut, disclose.
16 Promise, trust.
17 Such a fancy or liking.
18 Better.
19 Guide.
20 If my counsel were followed.
21 Advantage.
22 Sojourn, remain.
23 Yonder.
24 Devoureth.
25 Lib. ii. 768 *et seqq.*, where a general description of Envy is given.
26 I will speak plainly.
27 To promote himself.
28 Health, comfort.
29 Know not.
30 To ascertain and gaze curiously.
31 Asked.
32 Remedy.
33 Answer my question.
34 Hinder.
35 Put.
36 My lady.
37 Embrace.

And eke there is no swallow swift, nor swan
So wight[1] of wing, nor half so yern[2] can fly;
For I can be, and that right suddenlý,
In Heav'n, in Hell, in Paradise, and here,
And with my lady, when I will desire.

"I am of counsel far and wide, I wot,
With lord and lady, and their privity
I wot it all; but, be it cold or hot,
They shall not speak without licénce of me.
I mean, in such as seasonable[3] be,
Tho[4] first the thing is thought within the heart,
Ere any word out from the mouth astart."[5]

And with the word Thought bade farewell and yede:[6]
Eke forth went I to see the Courtë's guise,
And at the door came in, so God me speed,
Two courtiers of age and of assise[7]
Like high, and broad, and, as I me advise,
The Golden Love and Leaden Love they hight:[8]
The one was sad, the other glad and light.

. . . .

At this point there is a hiatus in the poem, which abruptly ceases to narrate the tour of Philogenet and Philobone round the Court, and introduces us again to Rosial, who is speaking thus to her lover, apparently in continuation of a confession of love:

"Yes! draw your heart, with all your force and might,
To lustiness, and be as ye have said."

She admits that she would have given him no drop of favour, but that she saw him "wax so dead of countenance;" then Pity "out of her shrine arose from death to life," whisperingly entreating that she would do him some pleasance. Philogenet protests his gratitude to Pity, his faithfulness to Rosial; and the lady, thanking him heartily, bids him abide with her till the season of May, when the King of Love and all his company will hold his feast fully royally and well. "And there I bode till that the season fell."

On May Day, when the lark began to rise,
To matins went the lusty nightingale,
Within a temple shapen hawthorn-wise;
He might not sleep in all the nightertale,[9]
But "*Domine labia*"[10] gan he cry and gale,[11]
"My lippës open, Lord of Love, I cry,
And let my mouth thy praising now bewry."[12]

The eagle sang "*Venite*,[13] bodies all,
And let us joy to love that is our health."
And to the desk anon they gan to fall,
And who came late he pressed in by stealth:
Then said the falcon, "Our own heartës' wealth,
'*Domine Dominus noster*,'[14] I wot,
Ye be the God that do[15] us burn thus hot."

"*Cœli enarrant*,"[16] said the popinjay,[17]
"Your might is told in Heav'n and firmament."
And then came in the goldfinch fresh and gay,
And said this psalm with heartly glad intent,
"*Domini est terra*;"[18] this Latin intent,[19]
The God of Love hath earth in governance:
And then the wren began to skip and dance.

"*Jube Domine*;[20] O Lord of Love, I pray
Command me well this lesson for to read;
This legend is of all that wouldë dey[21]
Martyrs for love; God yet their soulës speed!
And to thee, Venus, sing we, out of dread,[22]
By influence of all thy virtue great,
Beseeching thee to keep us in our heat."

The second lesson robin redbreast sang,
"Hail to the God and Goddess of our lay!"[23]
And to the lectern[24] amorously he sprang:
"Hail now," quoth he, "O fresh seasón of May,
Our moneth glad that singen on the spray![25]
Hail to the flowers, red, and white, and blue,
Which by their virtue maken our lust new!"

The third lessón the turtle-dove took up,
And thereat laugh'd the mavis in a scorn:
He said, "O God, as might I dine or sup,
This foolish dove will give us all a horn!
There be right here a thousand better born,
To read this lesson, which as well as he,
And eke as hot, can love in all degree."

The turtle-dove said, "Welcome, welcome May,
Gladsome and light to lovers that be true!
I thank thee, Lord of Love, that doth purvey
For me to read this lesson all of due;[26]
For, in good sooth, of corage[27] I pursue
To serve my make[28] till death us must depart:"
And then "*Tu autem*"[29] sang he all apart.

"*Te Deum amoris*"[30] sang the throstel-cock:[31]
Tubal[32] himself, the first musicián,

1 Nimble, speedy. 2 Eagerly, swiftly.
3 Prudent. 4 Then; at the time when.
5 Escape. 6 Went away. 7 Size.
8 They represent successful and unsuccessful love; the first kindled by Cupid's golden darts, the second by his leaden arrows. 9 Night-time.
10 "Domine, labia mea aperies—et os meum annuntiabit laudem tuam" (Psalms li. 15), was the verse with which Matins began. The stanzas which follow contain a paraphrase of the matins for Trinity Sunday, allegorically setting forth the doctrine that love is the all-controlling influence in the government of the universe. 11 Call out.
12 Now bewray (show forth) thy praise.
13 "Venite, exultemus," are the first words of Psalm xcv., called the "Invitatory."
14 The opening words of Psalm viii.; "O Lord our Lord." 15 Make.
16 Psalm xix. 1; "The heavens declare (thy glory)."
17 Parrot.
18 Psalm xxiv. 1; "The earth is the Lord's and the fulness thereof." The first "nocturn" is now over, and the lessons from Scripture follow.
19 Means.
20 "Command, O Lord;" from Matthew xiv. 28, where Peter, seeing Christ walking on the water, says "Lord, if it be thou, bid me come to thee on the water."
21 Die. 22 Doubt.
23 Law, religion. 24 The reading-desk.
25 Glad month for us that sing upon the bough.
26 In due form. 27 With all my heart.
28 Mate.
29 The formula recited by the reader at the end of each lesson; "Tu autem, Domine, miserere nobis." "But do thou, O Lord, have pity on us!"
30 "Thee, God of Love (we praise)."
31 Thrush.
32 Not Tubal, who was the worker in metals; but Jubal, his brother, "who was the father of all such as handle the harp and organ" (Genesis iv. 21).

With key of harmony could not unlock
So sweet a tune as that the throstel can:
"The Lord of Love we praisë," quoth he thân,[1]
And so do all the fowlës great and lite;[2]
"Honour we May, in false lovers' despite."

"*Dominus regnavit,*"[3] said the peacock there,
"The Lord of Love, that mighty prince, y-wis,
He is received here and ev'rywhere:
Now *Jubilate*[4] sing:" "What meaneth this?"
Said then the linnet; "welcome, Lord of bliss!"
Out start the owl with "*Benedicite,*"[5]
"What meaneth all this merry fare?"[6] quoth he.

"*Laudate,*"[7] sang the lark with voice full shrill;
And eke the kite "*O admirabile;*[8]
This quire will through mine earës pierce and thrill;
But what? welcóme this May seasón," quoth he;
"And honour to the Lord of Love must be,
That hath this feast so solemn and so high:"
"*Amen,*" said all; and so said eke the pie.

And forth the cuckoo gan proceed anon,
With "*Benedictus*"[9] thanking God in haste,
That in this May would visit them each one,
And gladden them all while the feast shall last:
And therewithal a-laughter[10] out he brast;[11]
"I thankë God that I should end the song,
And all the service which hath been so long."

Thus sang they all the service of the feast,
And that was done right early, to my doom;[12]
And forth went all the Court, both most and least,[13]
To fetch the flowers fresh, and branch and bloom;
And namely[14] hawthorn brought both page and groom,
With freshë garlands party blue and white,[15]
And then rejoiced in their great delight.

Eke each at other threw the flowers bright,
The primërose, the violet, and the gold;
So then, as I beheld the royal sight,
My lady gan me suddenly behold,
And with a true love, plighted many a fold,
She smote me through the very heart as blive;[16]
And Venus yet I thank I am alive.

Explicit.

THE CUCKOO AND THE NIGHTINGALE.

[THE noble vindication of true love, as an exalting, purifying, and honour-conferring power, which Chaucer has made in "The Court of Love," is repeated in "The Cuckoo and the Nightingale." At the same time, the close of the poem leads up to "The Assembly of Fowls;" for, on the appeal of the Nightingale, the dispute between her and the Cuckoo, on the merits and blessings of love, is referred to a parliament of birds, to be held on the morrow after Saint Valentine's Day. True, the assembly of the feathered tribes described by Chaucer, though held on Saint Valentine's Day, and engaged in the discussion of a controversy regarding love, is not occupied with the particular cause which in the present poem the Nightingale appeals to the parliament. But "The Cuckoo and the Nightingale" none the less serves as a link between the two poems; indicating as it does the nature of those controversies, in matters subject to the supreme control of the King and Queen of Love, which in the subsequent poem we find the courtiers, under the guise of birds, debating in

1 Then.
2 Little.
3 Psalm xciii. 1, "The Lord reigneth." With this began the "Laudes," or morning service of praise.
4 Psalm c. 1, "Make a joyful noise unto the Lord."
5 "Bless ye the Lord;" the opening of the Song of the Three Children.
6 Doing, fuss.
7 Psalm cxlvii.; "Praise ye the Lord."
8 Psalm viii. 1; "O Lord our God, how excellent is thy name."
9 The first word of the Song of Zacharias (Luke i. 68); "Blessed be the Lord God of Israel."
10 In laughter.
11 Burst.
12 Judgment.
13 Great and small.
14 Especially.
15 In The Knight's Tale we have exemplifications of the custom of gathering and wearing flowers and branches on May Day; where Emily, "doing observance to May," goes into the garden at sunrise and gathers flowers, "party white and red, to make a sotel garland for her head" (page 27); and again, where Arcita rides to the fields "to makë him a garland of the greves; were it of woodbine, or of hawthorn leaves" (page 32.)
16 Straightway.

full conclave and under legal forms. Exceedingly simple in conception, and written in a metre full of musical irregularity and forcible freedom, "The Cuckoo and the Nightingale" yields in vividness, delicacy, and grace to none of Chaucer's minor poems. We are told that the poet, on the third night of May, is sleepless, and rises early in the morning, to try if he may hear the Nightingale sing. Wandering by a brook-side, he sits down on the flowery lawn, and erelong, lulled by the sweet melody of many birds and the well-according music of the stream, he falls into a kind of dose—"not all asleep, nor fully waking." Then (an evil omen) he hears the Cuckoo sing before the Nightingale; but soon he hears the Nightingale request the Cuckoo to remove far away, and leave the place to birds that *can* sing. The Cuckoo enters into a defence of her song, which becomes a railing accusation against Love and a recital of the miseries which Love's servants endure; the Nightingale vindicates Love in a lofty and tender strain, but is at last overcome with sorrow by the bitter words of the Cuckoo, and calls on the God of Love for help. On this the poet starts up, and, snatching a stone from the brook, throws it at the Cuckoo, who flies away full fast. The grateful Nightingale promises that, for this service, she will be her champion's singer all that May; she warns him against believing the Cuckoo, the foe of Love; and then, having sung him one of her new songs, she flies away to all the other birds that are in that dale, assembles them, and demands that they should do her right upon the Cuckoo. By one assent it is agreed that a parliament shall be held, "the morrow after Saint Valentine's Day," under a maple before the window of Queen Philippa at Woodstock, when judgment shall be passed upon the Cuckoo; then the Nightingale flies into a hawthorn, and sings a lay of love so loud that the poet awakes. The five-line stanza, of which the first, second, and fifth lines agree in one rhyme, the third and fourth in another, is peculiar to this poem; and while the prevailing measure is the decasyllabic line used in the "Canterbury Tales," many of the lines have one or two syllables less. The poem is given here without abridgement.]

THE God of Love, ah! benedicite,
How mighty and how great a lord is he! [1]
For he can make of lowë heartës high,
And of high low, and likë for to die,
And hardë heartës he can makë free.

He can make, within a little stound,[2]
Of sickë folkë whole, and fresh, and sound,
And of the whole he can make sick;
He can bind, and unbinden eke,
What he will havë bounden or unbound.

To tell his might my wit may not suffice;
For he can make of wisë folk full nice,[3]—
For he may do all that he will devise,—
And lither[4] folkë to destroyë vice,
And proudë heartës he can make agrise.[5]

Shortly, all that ever he will he may;
Against him dare no wight say nay;
For he can glad and grievë whom him liketh,[6]
And who that he will, he laugheth or siketh,[7]
And most his might he sheddeth ever in May.

For every true gentle heartë free,
That with him is, or thinketh for to be,
Against May now shall havë some stirríng,[8]
Either to joy, or else to some mourníng,
In no seasón so much, as thinketh me.

For when that they may hear the birdës sing,
And see the flowers and the leavës spring,
That bringeth into heartë's rémembránce
A manner easë, medled[9] with grievánce,[10]
And lusty thoughtës full of great longíng.

And of that longing cometh heaviness,
And thereof groweth greatë sickënéss,
And[11] for the lack of that that they desire:
And thus in May be heartës set on fire,
So that they brennen[12] forth in great distress.

I speakë this of feeling truëlý;[13]
If I be old and unlustý,
Yet I have felt the sickness thorough May
Both hot and cold, an access ev'ry day,[14]
How sore, y-wis, there wot no wight but I.

I am so shaken with the fevers white,
Of all this May sleep I but lite;[15]
And also it is not like[16] unto me
That any heartë shouldë sleepy be,
In whom that Love his fiery dart will smite.

But as I lay this other night wakíng,
I thought how lovers had a tokening,[17]
And among them it was a common tale,
That it were good to hear the nightingale
Rather than the lewd cuckoo sing.

And then I thought, anon as[18] it was day,
I would go somewhere to assay
If that I might a nightingalë hear;
For yet had I none heard of all that year,
And it was then the thirdë night of May.

And anon as I the day espied,
No longer would I in my bed abide;
But to a wood that was fast by,
I went forth alone boldëlý,
And held the way down by a brookë's side,

1 These two lines occur also in The Knight's Tale; they commence the speech of Theseus on the love-follies of Palamon and Arcita, whom the Duke has just found fighting in the forest (page 34).
2 A short time, a moment.
3 Foolish; French, "niais."
4 Idle, vicious.
5 Cause to tremble.
6 Whom he pleases.
7 Sigheth.
8 Movement, impulse.
9 Mingled.
10 Sorrow.
11 A stronger reading is "all."
12 Burn.
13 From experience of my own feeling.
14 Every day a hot and a cold fit.
15 Very little.
16 Pleasing.
17 Significance.
18 Whenever.

Till I came to a laund[1] of white and green,
So fair a one had I never in been;
The ground was green, y-powder'd with daisy,[2]
The flowers and the greves[3] like high,[4]
All green and white; was nothing ellës seen.

There sat I down among the fairë flow'rs,
And saw the birdës trip out of their bow'rs,
There as they rested them allë the night;
They were so joyful of the dayë's light,
They began of May for to do honours.

They coud[5] that service all by rote;
There was many a lovely note!
Some sangë loud as they had plain'd,
And some in other manner voicë feign'd,
And some all out with the full throat.

They proined[6] them, and madë them right gay,
And danc'd and leapt upon the spray;
And evermorë two and two in fere,[7]
Right so as they had chosen them to-year[8]
In Feverere[9] upon Saint Valentine's Day.

And the river that I sat upon,[10]
It made such a noise as it ran,
Accordant[11] with the birdë's harmony,
Me thought it was the bestë melody
That might be heard of any man.

And for delight, I wotë never how,
I fell in such a slumber and a swow,[12]—
Not all asleep, nor fully waking,—
And in that swow me thought I heardë sing
The sorry bird, the lewd cuckow;

And that was on a tree right fastë by.
But who was then evil apaid but I?
"Now God," quoth I, "that diëd on the crois,[13]
Give sorrow on thee, and on thy lewëd voice!
Full little joy have I now of thy cry."

And as I with the cuckoo thus gan chide,
I heard, in the next bush beside,
A nightingale so lustily sing,
That her clear voice she madë ring
Through all the greenwood wide.

"Ah, good Nightingale," quoth I then,
"A little hast thou been too long hen;[14]
For here hath been the lewd cuckow,
And sung songs rather[15] than hast thou:
I pray to God that evil fire her bren!"[16]

But now I will you tell a wondrous thing:
As long as I lay in that swooning,
Me thought I wist what the birds meant,
And what they said, and what was their intent,
And of their speech I haddë good knowing.

There heard I the nightingale say:
"Now, good Cuckoo, go somewhere away,
And let us that can singë dwellë here;
For ev'ry wight escheweth[17] thee to hear,
Thy songës be so elenge,[18] in good fay."[19]

"What," quoth she, "what may thee ail now?
It thinketh me, I sing as well as thou,
For my song is both true and plain,
Although I cannot crakel[20] so in vain,
As thou dost in thy throat, I wot ne'er how.

"And ev'ry wight may understandë me,
But, Nightingale, so may they not do thee,
For thou hast many a nice quaint[21] cry;
I have thee heard say, 'ocy, ocy;'
How might I know what that should be?"

"Ah fool," quoth she, "wost thou not what it is?
When that I say, 'ocy, ocy,' y-wis,
Then mean I that I wouldë wonder fain
That all they were shamefully slain,[22]
That meanen aught againë[23] love amiss.

"And also I would that all those were dead,
That thinkë not in love their life to lead,
For who so will the god of Love not serve,
I dare well say he is worthy to sterve,[24]
And for that skill,[25] 'ocy, ocy,' I grede."[26]

"Ey!" quoth the cuckoo, "this is a quaint[27] law,
That every wight shall love or be to-draw![28]
But I forsake allë such company;
For mine intent is not for to die,
Nor ever, while I live, on Lovë's yoke to draw.[29]

"For lovers be the folk that be alive,
That most diseasë have, and most unthrive,[30]
And most endurë sorrow, woe, and care,
And leastë feelen of welfare:
What needeth it against the truth to strive?"

"What?" quoth she, "thou art all out of thy mind!
How mightest thou in thy churlishness find
To speak of Lovë's servants in this wise?
For in this world is none so good service[31]
To ev'ry wight that gentle is of kind;[32]

"For thereof truly cometh all gladness,
All honour and all gentleness,
Worship, ease, and all heartë's lust,
Perfect joy, and full assured trust,
Jollity, pleasance, and freshness,

"Lowlihead, largess, and courtesy,
Seemëlihead, and true company,
Dread of shame for to do amiss;
For he that truly Lovë's servant is,
Were lother[33] to be shamed than to die.

"And that this is sooth that I say,
In that belief I will live and dey;[34]
And, Cuckoo, so I read[35] that thou do y-wis."

1 Lawn. 2 Thickly strown with the daisy. 3 Groves, bushes. 4 Of the same height. 5 Knew. 6 Pruned, trimmed their feathers. 7 In company. 8 This year. 9 February. 10 Beside. 11 Agreeing, keeping time with. 12 Swoon. 13 Cross. 14 Hence, absent. 15 Sooner. 16 Burn. 17 Shuns. 18 Strange, sorrowful. 19 Faith. 20 Quaver, sing tremulously. 21 Foolish, strange.

22 "Ocy, ocy," is supposed to come from the Latin, "occidere," to kill; or rather the old French, "occire," "occis," denoting the doom which the nightingale imprecates or supplicates on all who do offence to Love. 23 Against. 24 Die. 25 Reason. 26 I cry; Italian, "grido." 27 Strange. 28 Torn to pieces. 29 To put on Love's yoke. 30 Misfortune, disappointment. 31 As Love's. 32 Is of gentle, noble nature. 33 More reluctant. 34 Die. 35 Counsel.

"Then," quoth he, "let me never havë bliss,
If ever I to that counsail obey!

"Nightingale, thou speakest wondrous fair,
But, for all that, is the sooth contrair;
For love is in young folk but rage,
And in old folk a great dotáge;
Who most it useth, mostë shall enpair.[1]

"For thereof come disease and heaviness,
Sorrow and care, and many a great sicknéss,
Despite, debate, anger, envý,
Depraving,[2] shame, untrust, and jealousy,
Pride, mischief, povert', and woodnéss.

"Loving is an office of despair,
And one thing is therein that is not fair;
For who that gets of love a little bliss,
But if he be alway therewith, y-wis,
He may full soon of agë have his hair.[3]

"And, Nightingalë, therefore hold thee nigh;[4]
For, 'lieve me well, for all thy quaintë cry,
If thou be far or longë from thy make,[5]
Thou shalt be as other that be forsake,
And then thou shalt hoten[6] as do I."

"Fie," quoth she, "on thy name and on thee!
The god of Lovë let thee never thé![7]
For thou art worse a thousand fold than wood,[8]
For many one is full worthy and full good,
That had been naught, ne haddë Love y-be.[9]

"For evermore Love his servants amendeth,
And from all evile taches[10] them defendeth,
And maketh them to burn right in a fire,
In truth and in worshipful[11] desire,
And, when him liketh, joy enough them sendeth."

"Thou Nightingale," he said, "be still!
For Love hath no reason but his will;[12]
For ofttime untrue folk he easeth,
And truë folk so bitterly displeaseth,
That for default of grace[13] he lets them spill."[14]

Then took I of the nightingale keep,
How she cast a sigh out of her deep,[15]
And said, "Alas, that ever I was bore!
I can for teen[16] not say one wordë more;"
And right with that word she burst out to weep.

"Alas!" quoth she, "my heartë will to-break
To hearë thus this lewd bird speak
Of Love, and of his worshipful servíce.
Now, God of Love, thou help me in some wise,
That I may on this cuckoo be awreak!"[17]

Methought then I start up anon,
And to the brook I ran and got a stone,
And at the cuckoo heartly cast;
And for dread he flew away full fast,
And glad was I when he was gone.

And evermore the cuckoo, as he flay,[18]
He saidë, "Farewell, farewell, popinjay,"
As though he had scorned, thought me;
But ay I hunted him from the tree,
Until he was far out of sight away.

And then came the nightingale to me,
And said, "Friend, forsooth I thank thee
That thou hast lik'd me to rescow;[19]
And one avow to Lovë make I now,
That all this May I will thy singer be."

I thanked her, and was right well apaid:[20]
"Yea," quoth she, "and be thou not dismay'd,
Though thou have heard the cuckoo erst than[21] me;
For, if I live, it shall amended be
The next May, if I be not afraid.

"And one thing I will redë[22] thee also,
Believe thou not the cuckoo, the love's foe,[23]
For all that he hath said is strong leasíng."[24]
"Nay," quoth I, "thereto shall nothing me bring
For love, and it hath done me much woe."[25]

"Yea? Use," quoth she, "this medicíne,
Every day this May ere thou dine:
Go look upon the fresh daisý,
And, though thou be for woe in point to die,
That shall full greatly less thee of thy pine.[26]

"And look alway that thou be good and true,
And I will sing one of my songës new
For love of thee, as loud as I may cry:"
And then she began this song full high:
"I shrew[27] all them that be of love untrue."

And when she had sung it to the end,
"Now farewell," quoth she, "for I must wend,[28]
And, God of Love, that can right well and may,
As much joy sendë thee this day,
As any lover yet he ever send!"

Thus took the nightingale her leave of me.
I pray to God alway with her be,
And joy of love he send her evermore,
And shield us from the cuckoo and his lore;
For there is not so false a bird as he.

Forth she flew, the gentle nightingale,
To all the birdës that were in that dale,
And got them all into a place in fere,[29]
And besought them that they would hear
Her disease,[30] and thus began her tale.

"Ye wittë well,[31] it is not for to hide,
How the cuckoo and I fast have chide,[32]
Ever since that it was daylight;
I pray you all that ye do me right
On that foul false unkind bride."[33]

1 Suffer harm.
2 Loss of fame or character.
3 Unless he be always fortunate in love pursuits, he may full soon have gray hair, through his anxieties.
4 Near the one thou lovest.
5 Mate.
6 Be called.
7 Thrive.
8 Mad.
9 Who would have been wicked and worthless, if love had not been.
10 Stains, blemishes; French, "tache."
11 Honourable.
12 No guide but his caprice.
13 Favour.
14 Come to ruin or sorrow.
15 Sighed deeply.
16 Vexation, grief.
17 Revenged.
18 Flew.
19 Hast been pleased to rescue me.
20 Satisfied.
21 Before. It was of evil omen to hear the cuckoo before the nightingale or any other bird.
22 Counsel.
23 The foe of love.
24 Sheer falsehood.
25 Nothing will bring me to believe the evil the cuckoo has said of love, and it [what the cuckoo has said] has caused me great pain.
26 Assuage thine anguish.
27 Curse.
28 Go.
29 Together.
30 Distress, grievance.
31 Ye know well.
32 Chidden, quarrelled.
33 Bird.

Then spake one bird for all, by one assent :
"This matter asketh good advisëment ;
For we be fewë birdës here in fere,
And sooth it is, the cuckoo is not here,
And therefore we will have a parlément.

"And thereat shall the eagle be our lord,
And other peers that beën of record,[1]
And the cuckoo shall be after sent ;[2]
There shall be given the judgment,
Or else we shall finally make accord.[3]

"And this shall be, withoutë nay,[4]
The morrow after Saint Valentine's Day,
Under a maple that is fair and green,
Before the chamber window of the Queen,[5]
At Woodstock upon the green lay."[6]

She thanked them, and then her leavë took,
And into a hawthorn by that brook,
And there she sat and sang upon that tree,
"Term of life love hath withhold me ;"[7]
So loudë, that I with that song awoke.

Explicit.

The Author to His Book.

O LEWD book ! with thy foul rudenéss,
Since thou hast neither beauty nor eloquence,
Who hath thee caus'd or giv'n the hardiness
For to appear in my lady's presénce?
I am full sicker thou know'st her benevolence,
Full agreeable to all her abying,[8]
For of all good she is the best living.

Alas ! that thou ne haddest worthiness,
To show to her some pleasant senténce,
Since that she hath, thorough her gentleness,
Accepted thee servánt[9] to her dign reverence !
O ! me repenteth that I n' had science,
And leisure als', t' make thee more flourishíng,
For of all good she is the best living.

Beseech her meekly with all lowliness,
Though I be ferrë[10] from her in absénce,
To think on my truth to her and steadfastness,
And to abridge of my sorrows the violence,
Which caused is whereof knoweth your sapiénce ;[11]
She like[12] among to notify me her likíng,
For of all good she is the best living.

L'Envoy; To the Author's Lady.

Aurore of gladness, day of lustiness,
Lucern[13] at night with heav'nly influence
Illumin'd, root of beauty and goodnéss,
Suspirës which I éffund in silénce ![14]
Of grace I beseech, allege let your writíng
Now of all good,[15] since ye be best living.

Explicit.

THE ASSEMBLY OF FOWLS.

[IN "The Assembly of Fowls"—which Chaucer's "Retractation" (page 199) describes as "The Book of Saint Valentine's Day, or of the Parliament of Birds"—we are presented with a picture of the mediæval "Court of Love" far closer to the reality than we find in Chaucer's poem which bears that express title. We have a regularly constituted conclave or tribunal, under a president whose decisions are final. A difficult question is proposed for the consideration and judgment of the Court—the disputants advancing and vindicating their claims in person. The attendants upon the Court, through specially chosen mouthpieces, deliver their opinions on the cause; and finally a decision is authoritatively pronounced by the president—which, as in many of the cases actually judged before the Courts of Love in France, places the reasonable and modest wish of a sensitive and chaste lady above all the eagerness of her lovers, all the incongruous counsels of representative courtiers. So far, therefore, as the poem reproduces the characteristic features of procedure in those romantic Middle Age halls of amatory justice, Chaucer's "Assembly of Fowls" is his real "Court of Love;" for although, in the castle and among the courtiers of Admetus and Alcestis, we have all the personages and machinery necessary for one of those erotic contentions, in the present poem we see the personages and the machinery actually at work, upon another scene and under other guises. The allegory which makes the contention arise out of the loves, and proceed in the assembly, of the feathered race, is quite in keeping with the fanciful yet nature-

1 Of established, well-known, authority and distinction. 2 Sent after, to be summoned or arrested. 3 Effect a reconciliation. 4 Without contradiction. 5 Philippa of Hainault, wife of Edward III. 6 Lawn, lea, level ground. 7 Held possession of me, retained me in her service, for the whole term of my life. 8 Her merit. 9 As servant. 10 Far. 11 By circumstances whereof your wisdom knows. 12 May it please her. 13 Lamp ; Latin, "lucerna." 14 What sighs (French, "soupirs;" Latin, "suspiria") do I pour forth in silence ! 15 Let your writing now allege or declare all that is good and favourable to me.

loving spirit of the poetry of Chaucer's time, in which the influence of the Troubadours was still largely present. It is quite in keeping, also, with the principles that regulated the Courts, the purpose of which was more to discuss and determine the proper conduct of love affairs, than to secure conviction or acquittal, sanction or reprobation, in particular cases—though the jurisdiction and the judgments of such assemblies often closely concerned individuals. Chaucer introduces us to his main theme through the vestibule of a fancied dream—a method which he repeatedly employs with great relish, as for instance in "The House of Fame." He has spent the whole day over Cicero's account of the Dream of Scipio (Africanus the Younger); and, having gone to bed, he dreams that Africanus the Elder appears to him—just as in the book he appeared to his namesake—and carries him into a beautiful park, in which is a fair garden by a river-side. Here the poet is led into a splendid temple, through a crowd of courtiers allegorically representing the various instruments, pleasures, emotions, and encouragements of Love; and in the temple Venus herself is found, sporting with her porter Richess. Returning into the garden, he sees the Goddess of Nature seated on a hill of flowers; and before her are assembled all the birds—for it is Saint Valentine's Day, when every fowl chooses her mate. Having with a graphic touch enumerated and described the principal birds, the poet sees that on her hand Nature bears a female eagle of surpassing loveliness and virtue, for which three male eagles advance contending claims. The disputation lasts all day; and at evening the assembled birds, eager to be gone with their mates, clamour for a decision. The tercelet, the goose, the cuckoo, and the turtle—for birds of prey, water-fowl, worm-fowl, and seed-fowl respectively—pronounce their verdicts on the dispute, in speeches full of character and humour; but Nature refers the decision between the three claimants to the female eagle herself, who prays that she may have a year's respite. Nature grants the prayer, pronounces judgment accordingly, and dismisses the assembly; and after a chosen choir has sung a roundel in honour of the Goddess, all the birds fly away, and the poet awakes. It is probable that Chaucer derived the idea of the poem from a French source; Mr Bell gives the outline of a *fabliau*, of which three versions existed, and in which a contention between two ladies regarding the merits of their respective lovers, a knight and a clerk, is decided by Cupid in a Court composed of birds, which assume their sides according to their different natures. Whatever the source of the idea, its management, and the whole workmanship of the poem, especially in the more humorous passages, are essentially Chaucer's own.]

THE life so short, the craft so long to learn,
Th' assay so hard, so sharp the conquering,
The dreadful joy, alway that flits so yern;[1]
All this mean I by[2] Love, that my feeling
Astoneth[3] with his wonderful working,
So sore, y-wis, that, when I on him think,
Naught wit I well whether I fleet[4] or sink,

For all be[5] that I know not Love indeed,
Nor wot how that he quiteth folk their hire,[6]
Yet happeth me full oft in books to read
Of his miracles, and of his cruel ire;
There read I well, he will be lord and sire;
I dare not sayë, that his strokes be sore;
But God save such a lord! I can no more.

Of usage, what for lust and what for lore,[7]
On bookës read I oft, as I you told.
But wherefore speak I allë this? Not yore
Agone, it happed me for to behold
Upon a book written with letters old;
And thereupon, a certain thing to learn,
The longë day full fast I read and yern.[8]

For out of the old fieldës, as men saith,
Cometh all this new corn, from year to year;
And out of oldë bookës, in good faith,
Cometh all this new science that men lear.[9]
But now to purpose as of this mattére:
To readë forth it gan me so delight,
That all the day me thought it but a lite.[10]

This book, of which I makë mentión,
Entitled was right thus, as I shall tell;
"Tullius, of the Dream of Scipión:"[11]
Chapters seven it had, of heav'n, and hell,
And earth, and soulës that therein do dwell;
Of which, as shortly as I can it treat,
Of his senténce I will you say the great.[12]

First telleth it, when Scipio was come
To Africa, how he met Massinisse,
That him for joy in armës hath y-nome.[13]

1 That fleets so fast.
2 Of, with reference to.
3 Astounds, amazes.
4 Float, swim.
5 Albeit, although.
6 Rewards folk for their service.
7 What for liking and what for learning.
8 Eagerly.
9 Learn.
10 A little while.
11 "The Dream of Scipio"—"Somnium Scipionis"—occupies most of the sixth book of Cicero's "Republic;" which, indeed, as it has come down to us, is otherwise imperfect. Scipio Africanus Minor is represented as relating a dream which he had when, in B.C. 149, he went to Africa as military tribune to the fourth legion. He had talked long and earnestly of his adoptive grandfather with Massinissa, King of Numidia, the intimate friend of the great Scipio; and at night his illustrious ancestor appeared to him in a vision, foretold the overthrow of Carthage and all his other triumphs, exhorted him to virtue and patriotism by the assurance of rewards in the next world, and discoursed to him concerning the future state and the immortality of the soul. Macrobius, about A.D. 500, wrote a Commentary upon the "Somnium Scipionis," which was a favourite book in the Middle Ages. See note 7, page 168.
12 The important part, the substance.
13 Taken; past participle of "nime," from Anglo-Saxon, "niman," to take.

Then telleth he their speech, and all the bliss
That was between them till the day gan miss.[1]
And how his ancéstor Africane so dear
Gan in his sleep that night to him appear.

Then telleth it, that from a starry place
How Africane hath him Cartháge y-shew'd,
And warned him before of all his grace,[2]
And said him, what man, learned either lewd,[3]
That loveth common profit,[4] well y-thew'd,[5]
He should unto a blissful placë wend,[6]
Where as the joy is without any end.

Then asked he,[7] if folk that here be dead
Have life, and dwelling, in another place?
And Africane said, "Yea, withoutë dread;"[8]
And how our present worldly livës' space
Meant but a manner death,[9] what way we trace;
And rightful folk should go, after they die,
To Heav'n; and showed him the galaxy.

Then show'd he him the little earth that here is,
To regard of[10] the heaven's quantity;
And after show'd he him the ninë spherës;[11]
And after that the melody heard he,
That cometh of those spherës thricë three,
That wells of music be and melody
In this world here, and cause of harmony.

Then said he him, since earthë was so lite,[12]
And full of torment and of hardë grace,[13]
That he should not him in this world delight.
Then told he him, in certain yearës' space,
That ev'ry star should come into his place,
Where it was first; and all should out of mind,[14]
That in this world is done of all mankind.

Then pray'd him Scipio, to tell him all
The way to come into that Heaven's bliss;
And he said: "First know thyself immortál,
And look aye busily that thou work and wiss[15]
To common profit, and thou shalt not miss
To come swiftly unto that placë dear,
That full of bliss is, and of soulës clear.[16]

"And breakers of the law, the sooth to sayn,
And likerous folk, after that they be dead,
Shall whirl about the world always in pain,
Till many a world be passed, out of dread;
And then, forgiven all their wicked deed,
They shallë come unto that blissful place,
To which to comë God thee sendë grace!"

The day gan failen, and the darkë night,
That reaveth[17] beastës from their business,
Bereftë me my book for lack of light,
And to my bed I gan me for to dress,[18]
Full fill'd of thought and busy heaviness;
For both I haddë thing which that I n'old,[19]
And eke I had not that thing that I wo'ld.

But, finally, my spirit at the last,
Forweary[20] of my labour all that day,
Took rest, that madë me to sleepë fast;
And in my sleep I mette,[21] as that I say,
How Africane, right in the self array[22]
That Scipio him saw before that tide,[23]
Was come, and stood right at my beddë's side.

The weary hunter, sleeping in his bed,
To wood against his mind goeth anon;
The judgë dreameth how his pleas be sped;
The carter[24] dreameth how his cartës[25] go'n;
The rich of gold, the knight fights with his fone;[26]
The sickë mette he drinketh of the tun;[27]
The lover mette he hath his lady won.

I cannot say, if that the causë were,
For[28] I had read of Africane beforn,
That madë me to mette that he stood there;
But thus said he; "Thou hast thee so well borne
In looking of mine old book all to-torn,
Of which Macrobius raught not a lite,[29]
That somedeal[30] of thy labour would I quite."[31]

Cytherea, thou blissful Lady sweet!
That with thy firebrand dauntest when thee lest,[32]
That madest me this sweven[33] for to mette,
Be thou my help in this, for thou may'st best!
As wisly[34] as I saw the north-north-west,
When I began my sweven for to write,
So give me might to rhyme it and endite.

This foresaid Africane me hent[35] anon,
And forth with him unto a gatë brought
Right of a park, walled with greenë stone;
And o'er the gate, with letters large y-wrought,
There werë verses written, as me thought,
On either half, of full great difference,
Of which I shall you say the plain senténce.[36]

"Through me men go into the blissful place[37]
Of heartë's heal and deadly woundës' cure;
Through me men go unto the well of grace;
Where green and lusty May shall ever dure;

1 Began to fail.
2 Of the favour which the gods would show him, in delivering Carthage into his hands.
3 Ignorant, uncultured.
4 The public advantage.
5 Possessed of noble qualities, morally excellent.
6 Go.
7 The younger Scipio.
8 Doubt.
9 "Vestra vero, quæ dicitur, vita mors est."
10 By comparison with.
11 The nine spheres are God, or the highest heaven, constraining and containing all the others; the Earth, around which the planets and the highest heaven revolve; and the seven planets: the revolution of all producing the "music of the spheres."
12 Small.
13 Evil fortune.
14 Perish from memory.
15 Counsel, guide affairs.
16 Illustrious, noble; Latin, "clarus."
17 Taketh away.
18 Prepare myself.
19 Would not.
20 Utterly wearied.
21 Dreamed.
22 Same garb or aspect.
23 Time.
24 Charioteer.
25 Chariots.
26 Foes.
27 That he drinks wine, as one in health.
28 Because.
29 Recked not a little; which he held in high esteem.
30 Some part.
31 Recompense.
32 Conquerest at thine own pleasure.
33 Dream.
34 As surely; the significance of the poet's looking to the NNW. is not plain; his window may have faced that way.
35 Took, caught.
36 Meaning, sense.
37 The idea of the twin gates, leading to the Paradise and the Hell of lovers, *may* have been taken from the description of the gates of dreams in the Odyssey and the Æneid; but the iteration of "Through me men go" far more directly suggests the legend on Dante's gate of Hell:—

"Per me si va nella città dolente,
Per me si va nell' eterno dolore;
Per me si va tra la perduta gente."

The famous line, "Lasciate ogni speranza, voi che entrate"—"All hope abandon, ye who enter here"—is evidently paraphrased in Chaucer's words "Th' eschewing is the only remedy;" that is, the sole hope consists in the avoidance of that dismal gate.

This is the way to all good adventúre ;
Be glad, thou reader, and thy sorrow off cast ;
All open am I ; pass in and speed thee fast."

"Through me men go," thus spake the other side,
"Unto the mortal strokës of the spear,
Of which disdain and danger is the guide ;
There never tree shall fruit nor leavës bear ;
This stream you leadeth to the sorrowful weir,
Where as the fish in prison is all dry ;[1]
Th' eschewing is the only remedy."

These verses of gold and azure written were,
On which I gan astonish'd to behold ;
For with that one increased all my fear,
And with that other gan my heart to bold ;[2]
That one me het,[3] that other did me cold ;
No wit had I, for error,[4] for to choose
To enter or fly, or me to save or lose.

Right as betwixten adamantës[5] two
Of even weight, a piece of iron set,
Ne hath no might to movë to nor fro ;
For what the one may hale, the other let ;[6]
So far'd I, that n'ist whether me was bet[7]
T' enter or leave, till Africane, my guide,
Me hent[8] and shov'd in at the gatës wide.

And said, "It standeth written in thy face,
Thine error,[4] though thou tell it not to me ;
But dread thou not to come into this place ;
For this writing is nothing meant by[9] thee,
Nor by none, but[10] he Lovë's servant be ;
For thou of Love hast lost thy taste, I guess,
As sick man hath of sweet and bitterness.

"But natheless, although that thou be dull,
That thou canst not do, yet thou mayest see ;
For many a man that may not stand a pull,
Yet likes it him at wrestling for to be,
And deemë[11] whether he doth bet,[12] or he ;
And, if thou haddest cunning[13] to endite,
I shall thee showë matter of to write."[14]

With that my hand in his he took anon,
Of which I comfort caught,[15] and went in fast.
But, Lord! so I was glad and well-begone![16]
For over all,[17] where I mine eyen cast,
Were trees y-clad with leaves that ay shall last,
Each in his kind, with colour fresh and green
As emerald, that joy it was to see'n.

The builder oak ;[18] and eke the hardy ash ;
The pillar elm,[19] the coffer unto carrain ;
The box, pipe tree ;[20] the holm to whippë's lash ;[21]
The sailing fir ;[22] the cypress death to plain ;[23]
The shooter yew ;[24] the aspe for shaftës plain ;[25]
Th' olive of peace, and eke the drunken vine ;
The victor palm ; the laurel, too, divine.[26]

A garden saw I, full of blossom'd boughës,
Upon a river, in a greenë mead,
Where as sweetness evermore enow is,
With flowers whitë, blue, yellow, and red,
And coldë wellë[27] streamës, nothing dead,
That swammë full of smallë fishes light,
With finnës red, and scalës silver bright.

On ev'ry bough the birdës heard I sing,
With voice of angels in their harmony,
That busied them their birdës forth to bring ;
The pretty conies to their play gan hie ;[28]
And further all about I gan espy
The dreadful[29] roe, the buck, the hart, and hind,
Squirrels, and beastës small, of gentle kind.[30]

Of instruments of stringës in accord
Heard I so play a ravishing sweetnéss,
That God, that Maker is of all and Lord,
Ne heardë never better, as I guess:
Therewith a wind, unneth[31] it might be less,
Made in the leavës green a noisë soft,
Accordant to[32] the fowlës' song on loft.

Th' air of the placë so attemper[33] was,
That ne'er was there grievánce[34] of hot nor cold ;
There was eke ev'ry wholesome spice and grass,
Nor no man may there waxë sick nor old :
Yet[35] was there morë joy a thousand fold
Than I can tell, or ever could or might ;
There ever is clear day, and never night.

Under a tree, beside a well, I sey[36]
Cupid our lord his arrows forge and file ;[37]
And at his feet his bow all ready lay ;
And well his daughter temper'd, all the while,
The headës in the well ; and with her wile
She couch'd[38] them after, as they shouldë serve
Some for to slay, and some to wound and kerve.[39]

Then was I ware of Pleasance anon right,

1 A powerful though homely description of torment ; the sufferers being represented as fish enclosed in a weir from which all the water has been withdrawn.
2 Grow bold, take courage.
3 Heated.
4 Perplexity, confusion.
5 Magnets.
6 Whatever force the one exerts to draw, the other puts forth an equal force to restrain.
7 Wist not, knew not, whether it was better for me.
8 Took, caught.
9 Has no reference to.
10 Unless.
11 Judge.
12 Better.
13 Skill.
14 Of which to write.
15 Conceived, took.
16 Fortunate, glad.
17 Everywhere.
18 Compare with this catalogue raisonné of trees the ampler list given by Spenser in "The Faerie Queen," book i. canto i. (page 311). In several instances, as in "the builder oak" and "the sailing pine," the later poet has exactly copied the words of the earlier. In the Middle Ages the oak was as distinctively the building timber on land, as it subsequently became for the sea.
19 Spenser explains this in paraphrasing it into "the vineprop elm"—because it was planted as a pillar or prop to the vine ; it is called "the coffer unto carrain," or "carrion," because coffins for the dead were made from it.
20 The box, tree used for making pipes or horns.
21 The holly, used for whip-handles.
22 Because ships' masts and spars were made of its wood.
23 In Spenser's imitation, "the cypress funeral."
24 Used for bows.
25 Of the aspen, or black poplar, arrows were made.
26 So called, either because it was Apollo's tree—Horace says that Pindar is "laureâ donandus Apollinari"—or because the honour which it signified, when placed on the head of a poet or conqueror, lifted a man as it were into the rank of the gods.
27 Fountain.
28 Haste.
29 Timid.
30 Nature.
31 Scarcely.
32 In keeping with.
33 Temperate, mild.
34 Annoyance, hurt.
35 Moreover.
36 Saw.
37 Polish.
38 She cunningly arranged them in order.
39 Carve, cut.

And of Array, Lust, Beauty,[1] and Courtesy,
And of the Craft, that can and hath the might
To do[2] by force a wight to do folly;
Disfigured[3] was she, I will not lie;
And by himself, under an oak, I guess,
Saw I Delight, that stood with Gentleness.

Then saw I Beauty,[1] with a nice attire,
And Youthë, full of game and jollity,
Foolhardiness, Flattery, and Desire,
Messagerie, and Meed, and other three;[1]
Their namës shall not here be told for me:
And upon pillars great of jasper long
I saw a temple of brass y-founded strong.

And [all] about the temple danc'd alway
Women enough, of whichë some there were
Fair of themselves, and some of them were gay;
In kirtles all dishevell'd[4] went they there;
That was their office[5] ever, from year to year;
And on the temple saw I, white and fair,
Of dovës sitting many a thousand pair.[6]

Before the temple door, full soberly,
Dame Peacë sat, a curtain in her hand;
And her beside, wonder discreetëly,
Dame Patiéncë sitting there I fand,
With facë pale, upon a hill of sand;
And althernext, within and eke without,
Behest,[7] and Art, and of their folk a rout.[8]

Within the temple, of sighës hot as fire
I heard a swough,[9] that gan aboutë ren,[10]
Which sighës were engender'd with desire,
That made every heartë for to bren[11]
Of newë flame; and well espied I then,
That all the cause of sorrows that they dree[12]
Came of the bitter goddess Jealousy.

The God Priápus[13] saw I, as I went
Within the temple, in sov'reign placë stand,
In such array, as when the ass him shent[14]
With cry by night, and with sceptre in hand:
Full busily men gan assay and fand[15]
Upon his head to set, of sundry hue,
Garlandës full of freshë flowers new.

And in a privy corner, in disport,
Found I Venus and her porter Richéss,
That was full noble and hautain[16] of her port;
Dark was that place, but afterward lightnéss
I saw a little, unneth[17] it might be less;
And on a bed of gold she lay to rest,
Till that the hotë sun began to west.[18]

Her gilded hairës with a golden thread
Y-bounden were, untressed,[19] as she lay;
And naked from the breast unto the head
Men might her see; and, soothly for to say,
The remnant cover'd, wellë to my pay,[20]
Right with a little kerchief of Valence;[21]
There was no thicker clothë of defence.

The placë gave a thousand savours swoot;[22]
And Bacchus, god of wine, sat her beside;
And Ceres next, that doth of hunger boot;[23]
And, as I said, amiddës[24] lay Cypride,[25]
To whom on knees the youngë folkë cried
To be their help: but thus I let her lie,[26]
And farther in the temple gan espy,

That, in despite of Dianá the chaste,
Full many a bowë broke hung on the wall,
Of maidens, such as go their time to waste
In her servíce: and painted over all
Of many a story, of which I touchë shall
A few, as of Calist', and Atalant',[27]
And many a maid, of which the name I want.

Semiramis,[28] Canace,[29] and Hercules,[30]
Biblis,[31] Didó, Thisbe and Pyramus,[32]
Tristram, Isoude,[33] Paris, and Achillés,[34]

[1] Beauty is twice included in this list of Love's courtiers; in a similar list given in the description of Venus' temple (The Knight's Tale, page 35), Beauty is mentioned in the same line with Youth; and, if we retain the same association in the present passage, "Hope" may be read for the first "Beauty," with advantage to the metre and to the completeness of the list. If Chaucer had any special trio of courtiers in his mind when he excluded so many names, we may suppose them to be Charms, Sorcery, and Leasings, who, in The Knight's Tale, come after Bawdry and Riches—to whom Messagerie (the carrying of messages) and Meed (reward, bribe) may correspond.

[2] Make, cause. [3] Deformed, or disguised.

[4] In tunics, robes, all disordered.

[5] (To dance there) was their duty or occupation.

[6] The dove was the bird sacred to Venus; hence Ovid enumerates the peacock of Juno, Jove's armour-bearing bird, "Cythereiadasque columbas" ("Metam." xv. 386). [7] Promise. [8] Crowd.

[9] Confused murmuring noise. [10] Run.

[11] Burn. [12] Endure, suffer.

[13] Fitly endowed with a place in the Temple of Love, as being the embodiment of the principle of fertility in flocks and the fruits of the earth. See note 18, page 111.

[14] Ovid, in the "Fasti" (i. 433), describes the confusion of Priapus when, in the night following a feast of sylvan and Bacchic deities, the braying of the ass of Silenus wakened the company to detect the god in a furtive amatory expedition. [15] Endeavour.

[16] Haughty, lofty; French, "hautain."

[17] Scarcely.

[18] To set, decline towards the west.

[19] Not tied in a knot, loose.

[20] Well to my content; from French, "payer," to pay, satisfy; the same word often occurs, in the phrases "well apaid," and "evil apaid."

[21] Valentia, in Spain, was famed for the fabrication of fine and transparent stuffs. [22] Sweet.

[23] Affords the remedy for, relieves, hunger; the obvious reference is to the proverbial "Sine Cerere et Libero friget Venus," quoted in Terence, "Eunuchus," act iv. scene v. [24] In the midst.

[25] Venus; called "Cypria," or "Cypris," from the island of Cyprus, in which her worship was especially celebrated. [26] Left her lying.

[27] For their stories, see note 9, page 37; and note 1, page 387.

[28] Queen of Ninus, the mythical founder of Babylon; Ovid mentions her, along with Laïs, as a type of voluptuousness, in his "Amores," i. 5, 11.

[29] Canace, daughter of Æolus, is named in the prologue to The Man of Law's Tale (page 61) as one of the ladies whose "cursed stories" Chaucer refrained from writing. She loved her brother Macareus, and was slain by her father.

[30] Who was conquered by his love for Omphale, and spun wool for her in a woman's dress, while she wore his lion's skin.

[31] Who vainly pursued her brother Caunus with her love, till she was changed to a fountain; Ovid, "Metam." lib. ix.

[32] The Babylonian lovers, whose death, through the error of Pyramus in fancying that a lion had slain his mistress, forms the theme of the interlude in the "Midsummer Night's Dream."

[33] Sir Tristram was one of the most famous among the knights of King Arthur, and La Belle Isoude was his mistress. Their story is mixed up with the Arthurian romance; but it was also the subject of separate treatment, being among the most popular of the Middle Age legends.

[34] Achilles is reckoned among Love's conquests, because, according to some traditions, he loved Polyxena, the daughter of Priam, who was promised to him if he

Heléna, Cleopatra, Troilus,
Scylla,[1] and eke the mother of Romulus ;[2]
All these were painted on the other side,
And all their love, and in what plight they died.

When I was come again into the place
That I of spake, that was so sweet and green,
Forth walk'd I then, myselfë to solace :
Then was I warë where there sat a queen,
That, as of light the summer Sunnë sheen
Passeth the star, right so over measúre[3]
She fairer was than any creatúre.

And in a lawn, upon a hill of flowers,
Was set this noble goddess of Natúre ;
Of branches were her hallës and her bowers
Y-wrought, after her craft and her measúre ;
Nor was there fowl that comes of engendrúre
That there ne werë prest,[4] in her presénce,
To take her doom,[5] and give her audience.

For this was on Saint Valentinë's Day,
When ev'ry fowl cometh to choose her make,[6]
Of every kind that men thinken may ;
And then so huge a noisë gan they make,
That earth, and sea, and tree, and ev'ry lake,
So full was, that unnethës[7] there was space
For me to stand, so full was all the place.

And right as Alain, in his Plaint of Kind,[8]
Deviseth[9] Natúre of such array and face ;
In such array men mightë her there find.
This noble Emperess, full of all grace,
Bade ev'ry fowlë take her owen place,
As they were wont alway, from year to year,
On Saint Valéntine's Day to standë there.

That is to say, the fowlës of ravíne[10]
Were highest set, and then the fowlës smale,
That eaten as them Nature would incline ;
As wormë-fowl, of which I tell no tale ;
But waterfowl sat lowest in the dale,
And fowls that live by seed sat on the green,
And that so many, that wonder was to see'n.

There mightë men the royal eagle find,
That with his sharpë look pierceth the Sun ;
And other eagles of a lower kind,
Of which that clerkës well devisë con ;[11]
There was the tyrant with his feathers dun
And green, I mean the goshawk, that doth pine[12]
To birds, for his outragëous ravíne.

The gentle falcon, that with his feet distraineth[13]
The kingë's hand ; the hardy sperhawk[14] eke,
The quailë's foe ; the merlion[15] that paineth
Himself full oft the larkë for to seek ;
There was the dovë, with her eyen meek ;
The jealous swan, against[16] his death that singeth;
The owl eke, that of death the bodë[17] bringeth.

The crane, the giant, with his trumpet soun' ;
The thief the chough ; and eke the chatt'ring pie ;
The scorning jay ;[18] the eel's foe the heroún ;
The falsë lapwing, full of treachery ;[19]
The starling, that the counsel can betray ;
The tamë ruddock,[20] and the coward kite ;
The cock, that hórologe is of thorpës lite.[21]

The sparrow, Venus' son ;[22] the nightingale,
That calleth forth the freshë leavës new ;[23]
The swallow, murd'rer of the beës smale,
That honey make of flowers fresh of hue ;
The wedded turtle, with his heartë true ;
The peacock, with his angel feathers bright ;[24]
The pheasant, scorner of the cock by night ;[25]

The waker goose ;[26] the cuckoo ever unkind ;[27]
The popinjay, full of delícacy ;[28]

consented to join the Trojans ; and, going without arms into Apollo's temple at Thymbra, he was there slain by Paris.

1 Love-stories are told of two maidens of this name ; one the daughter of Nisus, King of Megara, who, falling in love with Minos when he besieged the city, slew her father by pulling out the golden hair which grew on the top of his head, and on which his life and kingdom depended. Minos won the city, but rejected her love in horror. The other Scylla, from whom the rock opposite to Charybdis was named, was a beautiful maiden, beloved by the sea-god Glaucus, but changed into a monster through the jealousy and enchantments of Circe.

2 Silvia, daughter and only living child of Numitor, whom her uncle Amulius made a vestal virgin, to preclude the possibility that his brother's descendants could wrest from him the kingdom of Alba Longa. But the maiden was violated by Mars as she went to bring water from a fountain ; she bore Romulus and Remus ; and she was drowned in the Anio, while the cradle with the children was carried down the stream in safety to the Palatine Hill, where the she-wolf adopted them.

3 Out of all proportion.

4 Were not ready; French, "prêt."

5 To receive her judgment or decision.

6 Mate, companion.

7 Scarcely.

8 Alanus de Insulis, a Sicilian poet and orator of the twelfth century, who wrote a book "De Planctu Naturæ"—"The Complaint of Nature."

9 Describeth.

10 The birds of prey.

11 Which scholars well can describe.

12 Causeth pain or woe.

13 Grasps, compresses ; the falcon was borne on the hand by the highest personages, not merely in actual sport, but to be caressed and petted, even on occasions of ceremony. Hence also it is called the "gentle" falcon—as if its high birth and breeding gave it a right to august society.

14 The bold, pert, sparrow-hawk.

15 Elsewhere in the same poem called "emerlon;" French, "emerillon;" the merlin, a small hawk carried by ladies.

16 Before, in anticipation of.

17 Message, omen.

18 Scorning humbler birds, out of pride of his fine plumage.

19 Full of stratagems and pretences to divert approaching danger from the nest where her young ones are.

20 Robin-redbreast.

21 That is the clock of the little hamlets or villages.

22 Because sacred to Venus.

23 Coming with the spring, the nightingale is charmingly said to call forth the new leaves.

24 Many-coloured wings, like those of peacocks, were often given to angels in paintings of the Middle Ages ; and in accordance with this fashion Spenser represents the Angel that guarded Sir Guyon ("Faerie Queen." book ii. canto vii. page 388) as having wings "decked with diverse plumes, like painted jay's."

25 The meaning of this passage is not very plain ; it has been supposed, however, to refer to the frequent breeding of pheasants at night with domestic poultry in the farmyard—thus scorning the sway of the cock, its rightful monarch.

26 Chaucer evidently alludes to the passage in Ovid describing the crow of Apollo, which rivalled the spotless doves, "Nec servaturis vigili Capitolia voce Cederet anseribus"—"nor would it yield (in whiteness) to the geese destined with wakeful or vigilant voice to save the Capitol" ("Metam.," ii. 538) when about to be surprised by the Gauls in a night attack.

27 The significance of this epithet is amply explained by the poem of "The Cuckoo and the Nightingale."

28 The parrot full of pleasingness.

The drake, destroyer of his owen kind;[1]
The stork, the wreaker of adultery;[2]
The hot cormórant, full of gluttony;[3]
The raven and the crow, with voice of care;[4]
The throstle old;[5] and the frosty fieldfare.[6]

What should I say? Of fowls of ev'ry kind
That in this world have feathers and statúre,
Men mighten in that place assembled find,
Before that noble goddess of Natúre;
And each of them did all his busy cure[7]
Benignëly to choose, or for to take,
By her accord,[8] his formel or his make.[9]

But to the point. Nature held on her hand
A formel eagle, of shape the gentilest
That ever she among her workës fand,
The most benign, and eke the goodliest;
In her was ev'ry virtue at its rest,[10]
So farforth that Natúre herself had bliss
To look on her, and oft her beak to kiss.

Nature, the vicar of th' Almighty Lord,—
That hot, cold, heavy, light, and moist, and dry,
Hath knit, by even number of accord,—
In easy voice began to speak, and say:
"Fowlës, take heed of my senténce,[11] I pray;
And for your ease, in furth'ring of your need,
As far as I may speak, I will me speed.

"Ye know well how, on Saint Valéntine's Day,
By my statúte, and through my governance,
Ye choose your mates, and after fly away
With them, as I you prickë with pleasánce;[12]
But nathless, as by rightful ordinance,
May I not let,[13] for all this world to win,
But he that most is worthy shall begin.

"The tercel eagle, as ye know full weel,[14]
The fowl royál, above you all in degree,
The wise and worthy, secret, true as steel,
The which I formed have, as ye may see,
In ev'ry part, as it best liketh me,—
It needeth not his shape you to devise,[15]—
He shall first choose, and speaken in his guise.[16]

"And, after him, by order shall ye choose,
After your kind, evereach as you liketh;
And as your hap[17] is, shall ye win or lose;
But which of you that lovë most entriketh,[18]
God send him her that sorest for him siketh."[19]
And therewithal the tercel gan she call,
And said, "My son, the choice is to thee fall.

"But natheless, in this conditión
Must be the choice of ev'reach that is here,
That she agree to his electión,
Whoso he be, that shouldë be her fere;[20]
This is our usage ay, from year to year;
And whoso may at this time have this grace,
In blissful time[21] he came into this place."

With head inclin'd, and with full humble cheer,[22]
This royal tercel spake, and tarried not:
"Unto my sov'reign lady, and not my fere,[23]
I chose and choose, with will, and heart, and thought,
The formel on your hand, so well y-wrought,
Whose I am all, and ever will her serve,
Do what her list, to do me live or sterve.[24]

"Beseeching her of mercy and of grace,
As she that is my lady sovereign,
Or let me die here present in this place,
For certes long may I not live in pain;
For in my heart is carven ev'ry vein:[25]
Having regard only unto my truth,
My dearë heart, have on my woe some ruth.[26]

"And if that I be found to her untrue,
Disobeisánt,[27] or wilful negligent,
Avaunter, or in process love a new,[28]
I pray to you, this be my judgëment,
That with these fowlës I be all to-rent,[29]
That ilkë[30] day that she me ever find
To her untrue, or in my guilt unkind.

"And since none loveth her so well as I,
Although she never of love me behet,[31]
Then ought she to be mine, through her mercý;
For other bond can I none on her knit;[32]
For weal or for woe, never shall I let[33]
To servë her, how far so that she wend;[34]
Say what you list, my tale is at an end."

1 Of the ducklings—which, if not prevented, he will kill wholesale.

2 The stork is conspicuous for faithfulness to all family obligations, devotion to its young, and care of its parent birds in their old age. Mr Bell quotes from Bishop Stanley's "History of Birds" a little story which peculiarly justifies the special character Chaucer has given:—"A French surgeon, at Smyrna, wishing to procure a stork, and finding great difficulty, on account of the extreme veneration in which they are held by the Turks, stole all the eggs out of a nest, and replaced them with those of a hen: in process of time the young chickens came forth, much to the astonishment of Mr and Mrs Stork. In a short time Mr S. went off, and was not seen for two or three days, when he returned with an immense crowd of his companions, who all assembled in the place, and formed a circle, taking no notice of the numerous spectators whom so unusual an occurrence had collected. Mrs Stork was brought forward into the midst of the circle, and, after some consultation, the whole flock fell upon her and tore her to pieces; after which they immediately dispersed, and the nest was entirely abandoned."

3 The cormorant feeds upon fish, so voraciously, that when the stomach is crammed it will often have the gullet and bill likewise full, awaiting the digestion of the rest.

4 So called from the evil omens supposed to be afforded by their harsh cries.

5 Long-lived.

6 Which visits this country only in hard wintry weather.

7 Care, pains.

8 Consent.

9 Female or mate; "formel," strictly or originally applied to the female of the eagle and hawk, is here used generally of the female of all birds; "tercel" is the corresponding word applied to the male.

10 At its highest point of excellence—so that it rested, unable to proceed farther.

11 Opinion, discourse.

12 Inspire you with pleasure.

13 Hinder.

14 Well.

15 Describe.

16 In his own way.

17 Fortune.

18 Entangles, ensnares; French, "intriguer," to perplex; hence "intricate."

19 Sigheth.

20 Companion, mate.

21 In a happy hour.

22 Demeanour.

23 Not my mate merely, but my queen.

24 Let her do what she will, to make me live or die.

25 Every vein in my heart is wounded with love.

26 Compassion.

27 Disobedient.

28 (If I should be found) a bragger (of her favours) or in process (of time) should love a new (lady).

29 Rent in pieces.

30 Very, self-same.

31 Made me promise of love.

32 For I can bind her by no other obligation.

33 Cease, fail.

34 Go.

Right as the freshë reddë rosë new
Against the summer Sunnë colour'd is,
Right so, for shame, all waxen gan the hue
Of this formél, when she had heard all this;
Neither she answer'd well, nor said amiss,[1]
So sore abashed was she, till Natúre
Said, "Daughter, dread you not, I you assure."[2]

Another tercel eagle spake anon,
Of lower kind, and said that should not be;
"I love her better than ye do, by Saint John!
Or at the least I love her as well as ye,
And longer have her serv'd in my degree;
And if she should have lov'd for long lovíng,
To me alone had been the guerdoning.[3]

"I dare eke say, if she me findë false,
Unkind, janglére,[4] rebel in any wise,
Or jealous, do me hangë by the halse;[5]
And but[6] I bearë me in her servíce
As well ay as my wit can me suffice,
From point to point, her honour for to save,
Take she my life and all the good I have."

A thirdë tercel eagle answer'd tho:[7]
"Now, Sirs, ye see the little leisure here;
For ev'ry fowl cries out to be ago
Forth with his mate, or with his lady dear;
And eke Natúre herselfë will not hear,
For tarrying her, not half that I would say;
And but[6] I speak, I must for sorrow dey.[8]

"Of long servíce avaunt I me no thing,
But as possíble is me to die to-day,
For woe, as he that hath been languishing
This twenty winter; and well happen may
A man may serve better, and more to pay,[9]
In half a year, although it were no more,
Than some man doth that served hath full yore.[10]

"I say not this by me, for that I can
Do no servíce that may my lady please;
But I dare say, I am her truest man,[11]
As to my doom,[12] and fainest[13] would her please;
At shortë words,[14] until that death me seize,
I will be hers, whether I wake or wink,
And true in all that heartë may bethink."

Of all my life, since that day I was born,
So gentle plea,[15] in love or other thing,
Ne heardë never no man me beforn;
Whoso that haddë leisure and cunníng[16]
For to rehearse their cheer and their speakíng:
And from the morrow gan these speeches last,
Till downward went the Sunnë wonder fast.

The noise of fowlës for to be deliver'd[17]
So loudë rang, "Have done and let us wend,"[18]
That well ween'd I the wood had all to-shiver'd:
"Come off!" they cried; "alas! ye will us shend![19]
When will your cursed pleading have an end?
How should a judge either party believe,
For yea or nay, withouten any preve?"[20]

The goose, the duck, and the cuckoo alsó,
So criëd "keke, keke," "cuckoo," "queke queke," high,
That through mine ears the noisë wentë tho.[7]
The goose said then, "All this n'is worth a fly![21]
But I can shape[22] hereof a remedý;
And I will say my verdict, fair and swith,[23]
For water-fowl, whoso be wroth or blith."[24]

"And I for worm-fowl," said the fool cuckow;
"For I will, of mine own authority,
For common speed,[25] take on me the charge now;
For to deliver us is great charity."
"Ye may abide a whilë yet, pardie,"[26]
Quoth then the turtle; "if it be your will
A wight may speak, it were as good be still.

"I am a seed-fowl, one th' unworthiest,
That know I well, and the least of cunníng;
But better is, that a wight's tonguë rest,
Than entremettë him of[27] such doíng
Of which he neither redë[28] can nor sing;
And who it doth, full foul himself accloyeth,[29]
For office uncommanded[30] oft annoyeth."

Natúrë, which that alway had an ear
To murmur of the lewëdness behind,
With facond[31] voice said, "Hold your tonguës there,
And I shall soon, I hope, a counsel find,
You to deliver, and from this noise unbind;
I charge of ev'ry flock[32] ye shall one call,
To say the verdict of you fowlës all."

The tercëlet[33] said then in this mannére:
"Full hard it were to prove it by reasón,
Who loveth best this gentle formel here;
For ev'reach hath such replicatión,[34]
That by skillës may none be brought adown;[35]
I cannot see that arguments avail;
Then seemeth it that there must be battáile."[36]

"All ready!" quoth those eagle tercels tho;[7]
"Nay, Sirs!" quoth he; "if that I durst it say,
Ye do me wrong, my tale is not y-do,[37]
For, Sirs,—and take it not agrief,[38] I pray,—
It may not be as ye would, in this way:
Ours is the voice that have the charge in hand,
And to the judges' doom ye mustë stand.[39]

"And therefore 'Peace!' I say; as to my wit,
Me wouldë think, how that the worthiest
Of knighthood, and had[40] longest used it,
Most of estate, of blood the gentilest,

1 She answered nothing, either well or ill.
2 Confirm, support. 3 Reward.
4 A vain or boastful talker.
5 Make me be hanged by the neck.
6 Unless. 7 Then. 8 Die.
9 Satisfaction. See note 20, page 219.
10 For a long time.
11 Liegeman, servant, to do her homage.
12 Judgment. 13 Most gladly of all.
14 In one word. 15 Excellent, noble pleading.
16 Skill, ability. 17 Set free to depart.
18 Go. 19 Ruin. 20 Proof.
21 All this is worthless, useless.
22 Devise. 23 Speedily.
24 Content, glad. 25 Despatch; advantage.
26 Truly; by God.
27 Meddle with; French, "entremettre," to interfere.
28 Counsel. 29 Embarrasseth.
30 Officious performance of uncommanded service.
31 Eloquent, fluent. 32 Class of fowl.
33 Male hawk. 34 Reply.
35 By arguments may none be overcome.
36 That the tercels must fight for the formel.
37 Done. 38 Be not offended.
39 Ye must abide by the judges' decision.
40 (The one that) had.

Were fitting most for her, if that her lest;[1]
And of these three she knows herself, I trow,[2]
Which that he be; for it is light[3] to know."

The water-fowlës have their headës laid
Together, and of short advisëment,[4]
When evereach his verdict had y-said
They saidë soothly all by one assent,
How that "The goosë with the facond gent,[5]
That so desired to pronounce our need,[6]
Shall tell our tale;" and prayed God her speed.

And for those water-fowlës then began
The goose to speak, and in her cackëling
She saidë, "Peace, now! take keep ev'ry man,
And hearken what reasón I shall forth bring;
My wit is sharp, I love no tarrying;
I say I rede him, though he were my brother,
But[7] she will love him, let him love another!"

"Lo! here a perfect reason of a goose!"
Quoth the sperhawkë.[8] "Never may she thé![9]
Lo! such a thing 'tis t' have a tonguë loose!
Now, pardie! fool, yet were it bet[10] for thee
Have held thy peace, than show'd thy nicetý;[11]
It lies not in his wit, nor in his will,
But sooth is said, a fool cannot be still."

The laughter rose of gentle fowlës all;
And right anon the seed-fowls chosen had
The turtle true, and gan her to them call,
And prayed her to say the soothë sad[12]
Of this mattére, and asked what she rad;[13]
And she answér'd, that plainly her intent
She wouldë show, and soothly what she meant.

"Nay! God forbid a lover shouldë change!"
The turtle said, and wax'd for shame all red:
"Though that his lady evermore be strange,[14]
Yet let him serve her ay, till he be dead;
For, sooth, I praisë not the goose's rede;[15]
For, though she died, I would none other make;[16]
I will be hers till that the death me take."

"Well bourded!"[17] quoth the duckë, "by my hat!
That men should loven alway causëless,
Who can a reason find, or wit, in that?
Danceth he merry, that is mirthëless?
Who shouldë reck of that is reckëless?[18]
Yea! queke yet," quoth the duck, "full well and fair!
There be more starrës, God wot, than a pair!"[19]

"Now fy, churl!" quoth the gentle tercëlet,
"Out of the dunghill came that word aright;
Thou canst not see which thing is well beset;
Thou far'st by love, as owlës do by light,—
The day them blinds, full well they see by night;
Thy kind is of so low a wretchedness,
That what love is, thou canst not see nor guess."

Then gan the cuckoo put him forth in press,[20]
For fowl that eateth worm, and said belive:[21]
"So I," quoth he, "may have my mate in peace,
I reckë not how longë that they strive.
Let each of them be solain[22] all their life;
This is my rede,[15] since they may not accord;
This shortë lesson needeth not recórd."

"Yea, have the glutton fill'd enough his paunch,
Then are we well!" saidë the emerlon;[23]
"Thou murd'rer of the heggsugg,[24] on the branch
That brought thee forth, thou most rueful gluttón,
Live thou solain,[22] wormë's corruptión!
For no force is to lack of thy natúre;[25]
Go! lewëd be thou, while the world may dure!"

"Now peace," quoth Nature, "I commandë here;
For I have heard all your opinión,
And in effect yet be we ne'er the nere.[26]
But, finally, this is my conclusión,—
That she herself shall have her electión
Of whom her list,[27] whoso be wroth or blith;[28]
Him that she chooseth, he shall her have as swith.[29]

"For since it máy not here discussed be
Who loves her best, as said the tercëlet,
Then will I do this favour t' her, that she
Shall have right him on whom her heart is set,
And he her, that his heart hath on her knit:
This judge I, Nature, for[30] I may not lie
To none estate; I have none other eye.[31]

"But as for counsel for to choose a make,
If I were Reason, [certes] then would I
Counsailë you the royal tercel take,
As saith the tercëlet full skilfullý,[32]
As for the gentilest, and most worthý,
Which I have wrought so well to my pleasánce,
That to you it ought be a suffisance."[33]

With dreadful[34] voice the formel her answér'd:

1 If she pleased.
2 Believe, am sure.
3 Easy.
4 After brief deliberation.
5 Refined, flowing eloquence; Latin, "facundia."
6 Pronounce upon our business.
7 Unless.
8 Sparrowhawk.
9 Thrive.
10 Better.
11 Foolishness.
12 The serious truth.
13 From "rede;" counselled.
14 Disdainful, uncomplying.
15 Counsel, opinion.
16 Mate.
17 A pretty joke!
18 Who should care for one that has no care for him.
19 The duck exhorts the contending lovers to be of light heart and sing, for abundance of other ladies were at their command.
20 In the crowd.
21 Quickly.
22 Single, alone; the same word originally as "sullen."
23 See note 15, page 220.
24 The cuckoo is distinguished by its habit of laying its eggs in the nests of other and smaller birds, such as the hedge-sparrow ("heggsugg"); and its young, when hatched, throw the eggs or nestlings of the true parent bird out of the nest, thus engrossing the mother's entire care. The crime on which the emerlon comments so sharply, is explained by the migratory habits of the cuckoo, which prevent its bringing up its own young; and nature has provided facilities for the crime, by furnishing the young bird with a peculiarly strong and broad back, indented by a hollow in which the sparrow's egg is lifted till it is thrown out of the nest.
25 The loss of a bird of your depraved nature is no matter of regret.
26 Nearer.
27 She pleases.
28 Adverse or willing; angry or glad.
29 Immediately.
30 Because.
31 I can see the matter in no other light.
32 Reasonably.
33 It should satisfy you (to have him for your mate.)
34 Full of dread, timid.

"My rightful lady, goddess of Natúre,
Sooth is, that I am ever under your yerd,[1]
As is every other creatúre,
And must be yours, while that my life may dure;
And therefore grantë me my firstë boon,[2]
And mine intent you will I say right soon."

"I grant it you," said she; and right anon
This formel eagle spake in this degree: [3]
"Almighty queen, until this year be done
I askë respite to advisë me;
And after that to have my choice all free;
This is all and some that I would speak and say;
Ye get no more, although ye do me dey.[4]

"I will not servë Venus, nor Cupíde,
For sooth as yet, by no manner [of] way."
"Now since it may none other ways betide," [5]
Quoth Dame Natúre, "there is no more to say;
Then would I that these fowlës were away,
Each with his mate, for longer tarrying here."
And said them thus, as ye shall after hear.

"To you speak I, ye tercels," quoth Natúre;
"Be of good heart, and serve her allë three;
A year is not so longë to endure;
And each of you pain him [6] in his degree
For to do well, for, God wot, quit is she
From you this year, what after so befall;[7]
This entremess is dressed [8] for you all."

And when this work y-brought was to an end,
To ev'ry fowlë Nature gave his make,
By even accord,[9] and on their way they wend: [10]
And, Lord! the bliss and joyë that they make!
For each of them gan other in his wings take,
And with their neckës each gan other wind,[11]
Thanking alway the noble goddéss of Kind.

But first were chosen fowlës for to sing,—
As year by year was alway their usánce,[12]—
To sing a roundel at their departing,
To do to Nature honour and pleasánce;
The note, I trowë, maked was in France;
The wordës were such as ye may here find
The nextë verse, as I have now in mind:

Qui bien aime, tard oublie.[13]

"Now welcome summer, with thy sunnës soft,
That hast these winter weathers overshake;[14]
Saint Valentine, thou art full high on loft,
Which driv'st away the longë nightës blake;[15]
Thus singë smallë fowlës for thy sake:
Well have they causë for to gladden [16] oft,
Since each of them recover'd hath his make;[17]
Full blissful may they sing when they awake."

And with the shouting, when their song was do,[18]
That the fowls maden at their flight away,
I woke, and other bookës took me to,
To read upon; and yet I read alway.
I hope, y-wis, to readë so some day,
That I shall meetë something for to fare
The bet;[19] and thus to read I will not spare.

Explicit.

THE FLOWER AND THE LEAF.

["THE Flower and the Leaf" is pre-eminently one of those poems by which Chaucer may be triumphantly defended against the charge of licentious coarseness, that, founded upon his faithful representation of the manners, customs, and daily life and speech of his own time, in "The Canterbury Tales," are sweepingly advanced against his works at large. In an allegory—rendered perhaps somewhat cumbrous by the detail of chivalric ceremonial, and the heraldic minuteness, which entered so liberally into poetry, as into the daily life of the classes for whom poetry was then written—Chaucer beautifully enforces the lasting advantages of purity, valour, and faithful love, and the fleeting and disappointing character of mere idle pleasure, of sloth and listless retirement from the battle of life. In the "season sweet" of spring, which the great singer of Middle Age England loved so well, a gentlewoman is supposed to seek sleep in vain, to rise "about the springing of the gladsome day," and, by an unfrequented path in a pleasant grove, to arrive at an arbour. Beside the arbour stands a medlar-tree, in which a Goldfinch sings passing sweetly; and the Nightin-

1 Under your rod, or government.
2 Request, favour. 3 Manner.
4 Though ye slay me. 5 Happen.
6 Strive.
7 Whatsoever may afterwards happen.
8 This dainty dish (entremet) is prepared for you all alike. 9 By equal, fair, agreement.
10 Wended, went. 11 Enfold, caress.
12 Custom, usage.
13 "Who well loves, late forgets;" the refrain of the roundel inculcates the duty of constancy, which has been imposed on the three tercels by the decision of the Court.
14 Dispersed, overcome.
15 Black. 16 Be glad, make mirth.
17 Mate. 18 Done.
19 Meet something (in my reading) by which I shall receive advantage; "bet" contracted for "better."

gale answers from a green laurel tree, with so merry and ravishing a note, that the lady resolves to proceed no farther, but sit down on the grass to listen. Suddenly the sound of many voices singing surprises her; and she sees "a world of ladies" emerge from a grove, clad in white, and wearing garlands of laurel, of *agnus castus*, and woodbind. One, who wears a crown and bears a branch of *agnus castus* in her hand, begins a roundel, in honour of the Leaf, which all the others take up, dancing and singing in the meadow before the arbour. Soon, to the sound of thundering trumps, and attended by a splendid and warlike retinue, enter nine knights, in white, crowned like the ladies; and after they have jousted an hour and more, they alight and advance to the ladies. Each dame takes a knight by the hand; and all incline reverently to the laurel tree, which they encompass, singing of love, and dancing. Soon, preceded by a band of minstrels, out of the open field comes a lusty company of knights and ladies in green, crowned with chaplets of flowers; and they do reverence to a tuft of flowers in the middle of the meadow, while one of their number sings a bergerette in praise of the daisy. But now it is high noon; the sun waxes fervently hot; the flowers lose their beauty, and wither with the heat; the ladies in green are scorched, the knights faint for lack of shade. Then a strong wind beats down all the flowers, save such as are protected by the leaves of hedges and groves; and a mighty storm of rain and hail drenches the ladies and knights, shelterless in the now flowerless meadow. The storm overpast, the company in white, whom the laurel-tree has safely shielded from heat and storm, advance to the relief of the others; and when their clothes have been dried, and their wounds from sun and storm healed, all go together to sup with the Queen in white—on whose hand, as they pass by the arbour, the Nightingale perches, while the Goldfinch flies to the Lady of the Flower. The pageant gone, the gentlewoman quits the arbour, and meets a lady in white, who, at her request, unfolds the hidden meaning of all that she has seen; "which," says Speght quaintly, "is this: They which honour the Flower, a thing fading with every blast, are such as look after beauty and worldly pleasure. But they that honour the Leaf, which abideth with the root, notwithstanding the frosts and winter storms, are they which follow Virtue and during qualities, without regard of worldly respects." Mr Bell, in his edition, has properly noticed that there is no explanation of the emblematical import of the medlar-tree, the goldfinch, and the nightingale. "But," he says, "as the fruit of the medlar, to use Chaucer's own expression (see Prologue to Reeve's Tale), is rotten before it is ripe, it may be the emblem of sensual pleasure, which palls before it confers real enjoyment. The goldfinch is remarkable for the beauty of its plumage, the sprightliness of its movements, and its gay, tinkling song, and may be supposed to represent the showy and unsubstantial character of frivolous pleasures. The nightingale's sober outward appearance and impassioned song denote greater depth of feeling." The poem throughout is marked by the purest and loftiest moral tone; and it amply deserved Dryden's special recommendation, "both for the invention and the moral." It is given without abridgement.]

WHEN that Phœbus his car of gold so high
Had whirled up the starry sky aloft,
And in the Bull[1] was enter'd certainly;
When showers sweet of rain descended soft,
Causing the groundë, felë[2] times and oft,
Up for to give many a wholesome air,
And every plain was y-clothed fair

With newë green, and maketh smallë flow'rs
To springë here and there in field and mead;
So very good and wholesome be the show'rs,
That they renewë what was old and dead
In winter time; and out of ev'ry seed
Springeth the herbë, so that ev'ry wight
Of thilkë[3] season waxeth glad and light.

And I, so glad of thilkë season sweet,
Was happed thus[4] upon a certain night,
As I lay in my bed, sleep full unmeet[5]
Was unto me; but why that I not might
Rest, I not wist; for there n'as[6] earthly wight,
As I suppose, had morë heartë's ease
Than I, for I n' had[7] sickness nor disease.[8]

Wherefore I marvel greatly of myself,
That I so long withoutë sleepë lay;
And up I rose three hourës after twelf,
About the springing of the [gladsome] day;
And on I put my gear[9] and mine array,
And to a pleasant grove I gan to pass,
Long ere the brightë sun uprisen was;

In which were oakës great, straight as a line,
Under the which the grass, so fresh of hue,
Was newly sprung; and an eight foot or nine
Every tree well from his fellow grew,
With branches broad, laden with leavës new,
That sprangen out against the sunnë sheen;
Some very red;[10] and some a glad light green;

1 The sign of Taurus, which the sun enters in May.
2 Many.
3 This.
4 Was thus circumstanced.
5 Unfit, uncompliant.
6 Was not.
7 Had not.
8 Distress, uneasiness.
9 Garments.
10 The young oak leaves are red or ashen coloured.

Which, as me thought, was right a pleasant sight.
And eke the birdës' songës for to hear
Would have rejoiced any earthly wight;
And I, that could not yet, in no mannére,
Hearë the nightingale of[1] all the year,
Full busy hearkened with heart and ear,
If I her voice perceive could anywhere.

And at the last a path of little brede[2]
I found, that greatly had not used be;[3]
For it forgrowen[4] was with grass and weed,
That well unneth[5] a wight it mightë see:
Thought I, "This path some whither goes, pardie!"[6]
And so I follow'd [it], till it me brought
To a right pleasant arbour, well y-wrought,

That benched[7] was, and [all] with turfës new
Freshly y-turf'd, whereof the greenë grass,
So small, so thick, so short, so fresh of hue,
That most like to green wool, I wot, it was;
The hedge alsó, that yeden in compáss,[8]
And closed in all the greenë herbére,[9]
With sycamore was set and eglatére,[10]

Wreathed in fere[11] so well and cunninglý,
That ev'ry branch and leaf grew by measúre,[12]
Plain as a board, of a height by and by:[13]
I saw never a thing, I you ensure,
So well y-done; for he that took the cure[14]
To maken it, I trow did all his pain
To make it pass all those that men have seen.

And shapen was this arbour, roof and all,
As is a pretty parlour; and alsó
The hedge as thick was as a castle wall,
That whoso list without to stand or go,
Though he would all day pryen to and fro,
He should not see if there were any wight
Within or no; but one within well might

Perceive all those that wentë there without
Into the field, that was on ev'ry side
Cover'd with corn and grass; that out of doubt,
Though one would seeken all the worldë wide,
So rich a fieldë could not be espied
Upon no coast, as of the quantity;[15]
For of all goodë thing there was plentý.

And I, that all this pleasant sight [did] see,
Thought suddenly I felt so sweet an air
Of the eglénterë, that certainly
There is no heart, I deem, in such despair,
Nor yet with thoughtës froward and contrair
So overlaid, but it should soon have boot,[16]
If it had onës felt this savour swoot.[17]

And as I stood, and cast aside mine eye,
I was ware of the fairest medlar tree
That ever yet in all my life I seye,[18]
As full of blossoms as it mightë be;
Therein a goldfinch leaping prettily
From bough to bough; and as him list he eat
Here and there of the buds and flowers sweet.

And to the arbour side was ádjoining
This fairest tree, of which I have you told;
And at the last the bird began to sing
(When he had eaten what he eatë wo'ld)
So passing sweetly, that by many fold
It was more pleasant than I could devise;[19]
And, when his song was ended in this wise,

The nightingale with so merry a note
Answered him, that all the woodë rung,
So suddenly, that, as it were a sote,
I stood astound';[20] so was I with the song
Thorough ravished, that, till late and long,[21]
I wist not in what place I was, nor where;
Again, me thought, she sung e'en by mine ear.

Wherefore I waited[22] about busilý
On ev'ry side, if that I might her see;
And at the last I gan full well espy
Where she sat in a fresh green laurel tree,
On the further side, even right by me,
That gave so passing a delicious smell,
According to the eglantére full well.[23]

Whereof I had so inly great pleasúre,
That, as me thought, I surely ravish'd was
Into Paradise, where [as] my desire
Was for to be, and no farther to pass,
As for that day; and on the sweetë grass
I sat me down; for, as for mine intent,[24]
The birdë's song was more convenient,[25]

And more pleasánt to me, by many fold,
Than meat, or drink, or any other thing;
Thereto the arbour was so fresh and cold,
The wholesome savours eke so comforting,
That, as I deemed, since the beginning
Of the world was [there] never seen ere than[26]
So pleasant a ground of none earthly man.

And as I sat, the birdës heark'ning thus,
Me thought that I heard voices suddenly,
The most sweetest and most delicious
That ever any wight, I trow truelý,[27]
Heard in their lifë; for the harmony
And sweet accord was in so good musike,
That the voices to angels' most were like.

At the last, out of a grove even by,
That was right goodly, and pleasánt to sight,
I saw where there came, singing lustilý,
A world of ladies; but to tell aright
Their greatë beauty, lies not in my might,
Nor their array; nevertheless I shall
Tell you a part, though I speak not of all.

In surcoats[28] white, of velvet well fitting,

1 During. Chaucer here again refers to the superstition, noticed in "The Cuckoo and the Nightingale," that it was of good omen to hear the nightingale before the cuckoo upon the advent of both with spring.
2 Breadth. 3 Been.
4 Overgrown. 5 Scarcely, with difficulty.
6 Of a surety.
7 Furnished with seats, which had been newly covered with turf.
8 Went all around; "yede" or "yead," is the old form of go.
9 Arbour; akin to "herberow," lodging, shelter.
10 Eglantine, sweet-briar.
11 Together. 12 Regularly.
13 Of the same height side by side.
14 Pains, care. 15 For its abundance or fertility.
16 Remedy, relief. 17 Sweet smell.
18 Saw. 19 Tell, describe.
20 I stood astounded or stupefied, like a fool—French "sot."
21 For a long time. 22 Watched, looked.
23 Agreeing or blending pleasantly with the smell of the sweet-briar. 24 To my mind.
25 Befitting my taste or humour. 26 Then.
27 I verily believe.
28 Upper robes.

They werë clad, and the seamës each one,
As it were a mannére [of] garnishíng,
Was set with emeraldës, one and one,
By and by;[1] but many a richë stone
Was set upon the purfles,[2] out of doubt,
Of collars, sleeves, and trainës round about;

As greatë pearlës, round and orient,[3]
And diamondës fine, and rubies red,
And many another stone, of which I went[4]
The namës now; and ev'reach on her head
[Had] a rich fret[5] of gold, which, without dread,[6]
Was full of stately[7] richë stonës set;
And ev'ry lady had a chapëlet

Upon her head of branches fresh and green,[8]
So well y-wrought, and so marvéllously,
That it was a right noble sight to see'n;
Some of laurel, and some full pleasantly
Had chapëlets of woodbine; and sadly,[9]
Some of *agnus castus*[10] waren also
Chapëlets fresh; but there were many of tho'[11]

That danced and eke sung full soberly;
And all they went in manner of compáss;[12]
But one there went, in mid the company,
Sole by herself; but all follow'd the pace
That she kept, whose heavenly figur'd face
So pleasant was, and her well shap'd persón,
That in beauty she pass'd them ev'ry one.

And more richly beseen, by many fold,
She was alsó in ev'ry manner thing:
Upon her head, full pleasant to behold,
A crown of goldë, rich for any king;
A branch of *agnus castus* eke bearíng
In her hand, and to my sight truëly
She Lady was of all that company.

And she began a roundel[13] lustily,
That "*Suse le foylë, devers moi,*" men call,
"*Siene et mon joly cœur est endormy;*"[14]
And then the company answered all,
With voices sweet entuned, and so small,[15]
That me thought it the sweetest melody
That ever I heard in my life, soothlý.[16]

And thus they camë, dancing and singíng,
Into the middest of the mead each one,
Before the arbour where I was sittíng;
And, God wot, me thought I was well-begone,[17]
For then I might advise[18] them one by one,
Who fairest was, who best could dance or sing,
Or who most womanly was in all thing.

They had not danced but a little throw,[19]
When that I heardë far off, suddenlý,
So great a noise of thund'ring trumpets blow,
As though it should departed[20] have the sky;
And after that, within a while, I sigh,[21]
From the same grove, where the ladies came out,
Of men of armës coming such a rout,[22]

As[23] all the men on earth had been assembled
Unto that place, well horsed for the nonce;[24]
Stirring so fast, that all the earthë trembled;
But for to speak of riches, and of stones,
And men and horse, I trow the largë ones[25]
Of Prester John,[26] nor all his treasury,
Might not unneth[27] have bought the tenth partý[28]

Of their array: whoso list hearë more,
I shall rehearse so as I can a lite.[29]
Out of the grove, that I spake of before,
I saw come first, all in their cloakës white,
A company, that wore, for their delight,
Chapëlets fresh of oakë cerrial,[30]
Newly y-sprung; and trumpets[31] were they all.

On ev'ry trump hanging a broad bannére
Of fine tartarium[32] was, full richly beat;[33]
Every trumpet his lord's armës bare;
About their necks, with greatë pearlës set,
[Were] collars broad; for cost they would not let,[34]
As it would seem, for their scutcheons each one
Were set about with many a precious stone.

Their horses' harness was all white alsó.
And after them next, in one company,
Camë kingës at armës and no mo',
In cloakës of white cloth with gold richly;
Chaplets of green upon their heads on high;
The crownës that they on their scutcheons bare
Were set with pearl, and ruby, and sapphire,

And eke great diamondës many one:
But all their horse harness, and other gear,
Was in a suit according, ev'ry one,
As ye have heard the foresaid trumpets were;
And, by seemíng, they were nothing to lear,[35]
And their guiding they did all mannerly.[36]
And after them came a great company

Of heraldës and pursuivantës eke,
Arrayed in clothës of white velvét;
And, hardily,[37] they were no thing to seek,[38]
How they on them shouldë the harness set:
And ev'ry man had on a chapëlet;
Scutcheonës and ekë harnéss, indeed,
They had in suit of[39] them that 'fore them yede.[40]

1 Side by side, in a row.
2 The embroidered edges.
3 Brilliant.
4 Want; cannot recall.
5 Band.
6 Doubt.
7 Valuable, noble.
8 See note 15, page 211.
9 Sedately.
10 The chaste-tree; a kind of willow.
11 Those.
12 In a circle.
13 French, "rondeau;" a song that comes round again to the verse with which it opened, or that is taken up in turn by each of the singers.
14 In modern French form, "Sous la feuille, devers moi, son et mon joli cœur est endormi"—"Under the foliage, towards me, his and my jolly heart is gone to sleep."
15 Fine.
16 Truly.
17 Fortunate.
18 Consider.
19 A short time.
20 Rent, divided.
21 Saw.
22 Company.
23 As if.
24 For the occasion.
25 The great gems.
26 The half-mythical Eastern potentate, who is now supposed to have been, not a Christian monarch of Abyssinia, but the head of the Indian empire before Zenghis Khan's conquest.
27 Hardly.
28 Part.
29 A little.
30 See note 18, page 39.
31 Trumpeters.
32 Cloth of Tars, or of Tortona.
33 Stamped, embroidered with gold.
34 They would not be restrained by cost.
35 They had nothing to learn—were perfectly instructed in their duties.
36 They performed their office in a perfect manner.
37 Assuredly.
38 In no wise at fault.
39 Corresponding with.
40 Went.

Next after them in came, in armour bright,
All save their headës, seemly knightës nine,
And ev'ry clasp and nail, as to my sight,
Of their harnéss was of red goldë fine;
With cloth of gold, and furred with ermine,
Werë the trappures[1] of their steedes strong,
Both wide and large, that to the groundë hung.

And ev'ry boss of bridle and paytrél[2]
That they had on, was worth, as I would ween,
A thousand pound; and on their headës, well
Dressed, were crownës of the laurel green,
The bestë made that ever I had seen;
And ev'ry knight had after him riding
Three henchëmen[3] upon him awaiting.

Of which ev'ry [first], on a short truncheón,[4]
His lordë's helmet bare, so richly dight,[5]
That the worst of them was worthy the ransón[6]
Of any king; the second a shieldë bright
Bare at his back; the thirdë bare upright
A mighty spear, full sharp y-ground and keen;
And ev'ry childë[7] ware of leavës green

A freshë chaplet on his hairës bright;
And cloakës white of fine velvét they ware;
Their steedës trapped and arrayed right,
Without difference, as their lordës' were;
And after them, on many a fresh coursér,
There came of armed knightës such a rout,[8]
That they bespread the largë field about.

And all they waren, after their degrees,
Chapëlets newë made of laurel green,
Some of the oak, and some of other trees;
Some in their handës barë boughës sheen,
Some of laurél, and some of oakës keen,
Some of hawthórn, and some of the woodbind,
And many more which I had not in mind.

And so they came, their horses fresh stirring
With bloody soundës of their trumpets loud;
There saw I many an uncouth disguising[9]
In the array of thesë knightës proud;
And at the last, as evenly as they could,
They took their place in middest of the mead,
And ev'ry knight turned his horse's head

To his fellów, and lightly laid a spear
Into the rest; and so the jousts began
On ev'ry part aboutë, here and there;
Some brake his spear, some threw down horse and man;
About the field astray the steedës ran;
And, to behold their rule and governance,[10]
I you ensure, it was a great pleasánce.

And so the joustës last[11] an hour and more;
But those that crowned were in laurel green
Wonnë the prize; their dintës[12] were so sore,
That there was none against them might sustene:[13]
And the jousting was allë left off clean,
And from their horse the nine alight' anon,
And so did all the remnant ev'ry one.

And forth they went together, twain and twain,
That to behold it was a worthy sight,
Towárd the ladies on the greenë plain,
That sang and danced, as I said now right;
The ladies, as soon as they goodly might,
They brake off both the song and eke the dance,
And went to meet them with full glad semblánce.[14]

And ev'ry lady took, full womanlý,
By th' hand a knight, and so forth right they yede[15]
Unto a fair laurél that stood fast by,
With leavës lade the boughs of greatë brede;[16]
And, to my doom,[17] there never was, indeed,
Man that had seenë half so fair a tree;
For underneath it there might well have be[18]

A hundred persons, at their own pleasánce,[19]
Shadowed from the heat of Phœbus bright,
So that they shouldë have felt no grievánce[20]
Of rain nor hailë that them hurtë might.
The savour eke rejoice would any wight
That had been sick or melancholious,
It was so very good and virtuous.[21]

And with great rev'rence they inclined low
Unto the tree so sweet and fair of hue;[22]
And after that, within a little throw,[23]
They all began to sing and dance of new,
Some song of love, some plaining of untrue,[24]
Environing[25] the tree that stood upright;
And ever went a lady and a knight.

And at the last I cast mine eye aside,
And was ware of a lusty company
That came roaming out of the fieldë wide;
[And] hand in hand a knight and a ladý;
The ladies all in surcoats, that richlý
Purfiled[26] were with many a richë stone;
And ev'ry knight of green ware mantles on,

Embroider'd well, so as the surcoats were;
And ev'reach had a chaplet on her head
(Which did right well upon the shining hair),
Maked of goodly flowers, white and red.
The knightës eke, that they in handë led,
In suit of them ware chaplets ev'ry one,
And them before went minstrels many one,

As harpës, pipës, lutës, and psaltrý,
All [clad] in green; and, on their headës bare,
Of divers flowers, made full craftily
All in a suit, goodly chaplets they ware;
And so dancing into the mead they fare.
In mid the which they found a tuft that was
All overspread with flowers in compáss,[27]

Whereunto they inclined ev'ry one,
With great reverence, and that full humblý;

1 Trappings.
2 Breast-plate (of a horse's harness).
3 Pages, attendants.
4 Staff.
5 Adorned.
6 Ransom.
7 Youth (among the pages).
8 Company, crowd.
9 Strange, rare, manœuvring.
10 Conduct of the fight.
11 Lasted.
12 Strokes.
13 Bear up, endure.
14 Air, aspect.
15 Went.
16 Whose broad boughs were laden with leaves.
17 Judgment.
18 Been.
19 In perfect comfort.
20 Annoyance.
21 Full of healing virtues.
22 Appearance.
23 Short time.
24 Plaint of lover's untruth.
25 Encompassing.
26 Trimmed at the borders.
27 Around, in a circle.

And at the last there then began anon
A lady for to sing right womanlý,
A bargaret,[1] in praising the daisý.
For, as me thought, among her notës sweet,
She saidë: "*Si douce est la margarete.*"[2]

Then allë they answered her in fere[3]
So passingly well, and so pleasantly,
That it was a [most] blissful noise to hear.
But, I n'ot[4] how, it happen'd suddenly
As about noon the sun so fervently
Wax'd hotë, that the pretty tender flow'rs
Had lost the beauty of their fresh coloúrs,

Forshrunk[5] with heat; the ladies eke to-brent,[6]
That they knew not where they might them bestow;
The knightës swelt,[7] for lack of shade nigh shent;[8]
And after that, within a little throw,
The wind began so sturdily to blow,
That down went all the flowers ev'ry one,
So that in all the mead there left[9] not one;

Save such as succour'd were among the leaves
From ev'ry storm that mightë them assail,
Growing under the hedges and thick greves;[10]
And after that there came a storm of hail
And rain in fere,[3] so that withoutë fail
The ladies nor the knights had not one thread
Dry on them, so dropping was [all] their weed.[11]

And when the storm was passed clean away,
Those in the white, that stood under the tree,
They felt no thing of all the great affray
That they in green without had in y-be:[12]
To them they went for ruth, and for pitý,
Them to comfórt after their great disease;[13]
So fain[14] they were the helpless for to ease.

Then I was ware how one of them in green
Had on a crownë, rich and well sittíng;[15]
Wherefore I deemed well she was a queen,
And those in green on her were awaitíng.[16]
The ladies then in white that were comíng
Towárd them, and the knightës eke in fere,
Began to comfort them, and make them cheer.

The queen in white, that was of great beautý,
Took by the hand the queen that was in green,
And saidë: "Sister, I have great pitý
Of your annoy, and of your troublous teen,[17]
Wherein you and your company have been
So long, alas! and if that it you please
To go with me, I shall you do the ease,

"In all the pleasure that I can or may;"
Whereof the other, humbly as she might,
Thanked her; for in right evil array
She was, with storm and heat, I you behight;[18]
And ev'ry lady then anon aright,
That were in white, one of them took in green
By the hand; which when that the knights had seen,

In like mannére each of them took a knight
Y-clad in green, and forth with them they fare
Unto a hedge, where that they anon right,
To makë their joustës,[19] they would not spare
Boughës to hewë down, and eke trees square,
Wherewith they made them stately firës great,
To dry their clothës, that were wringing wet.

And after that, of herbës that there grew,
They made, for blisters of[20] the sun's burníng,
Ointmentës very good, wholesome, and new,
Wherewith they went the sick fast anointíng;
And after that they went about gath'ríng
Pleasant salädës, which they made them eat,
For to refresh their great unkindly heat.

The Lady of the Leaf then gan to pray
Her of the Flower (for so, to my seemíng,
They should be called, as by their array),
To sup with her; and eke, for anything,
That she should with her all her people bring;
And she again in right goodly mannére
Thanked her fast of her most friendly cheer;

Saying plainëly, that she would obey,
With all her heart, all her commandëment:
And then anon, without longer delay,
The Lady of the Leaf hath one y-sent
To bring a palfrey, after her intent,[21]
Arrayed well in fair harnéss of gold;
For nothing lack'd, that to him longë sho'ld.[22]

And, after that, to all her company
She made to purvey[23] horse and ev'rything
That they needed; and then full lustily,
Ev'n by the arbour where I was sittíng,
They passed all, so merrily singíng,
That it would have comfórted any wight.
But then I saw a passing wondrous sight;

For then the nightingale, that all the day
Had in the laurel sat, and did her might
The whole servíce to sing longing to May,
All suddenly began to take her flight;
And to the Lady of the Leaf forthright
She flew, and set her on her hand softlý;
Which was a thing I marvell'd at greatlý.

The goldfinch eke, that from the medlar tree
Was fled for heat into the bushes cold,
Unto the Lady of the Flower gan flee,
And on her hand he set him as he wo'ld,
And pleasantly his wingës gan to fold;
And for to sing they pain'd them[24] both, as sore
As they had done of all[25] the day before.

And so these ladies rode forth a great pace,[26]
And all the rout of knightës eke in fere;

1 Bergerette, or pastoral song.
2 "So sweet is the daisy" ("la marguérite").
3 Together.
4 Know not.
5 Shrivelled up.
6 Thoroughly scorched.
7 Fainted.
8 Destroyed.
9 Remained.
10 Groves, boughs.
11 Clothing.
12 Had been in.
13 Trouble.
14 Glad, eager.
15 Becoming.
16 In attendance.
17 Injury, grief.
18 I promise you, I assure you.
19 The meaning is not very obvious; but in The Knight's Tale "jousts and array" are in some editions made part of the adornment of the Temple of Venus; and as the word "jousts" would there carry the general meaning of "preparations" to entertain or please a lover, in the present case it may have a similar force.
20 Of the wounds made by.
21 According to her wish.
22 That should belong to him.
23 Provide.
24 Made their utmost exertions.
25 During.
26 Rapidly.

And I, that had seen all this wonder case,[1]
Thought that I would assay in some mannére
To know fully the truth of this mattére,
And what they were that rode so pleasantlý;
And when they were the arbour passed by,

I dress'd me forth,[2] and happ'd to meet anon
A right fair lady, I do you ensure;[3]
And she came riding by herself alone,
All in white; [then] with semblance full demure
I her salued, and bade[4] good adventúre[5]
Might her befall, as I could most humblý;
And she answer'd: "My daughter, gramercy!"[6]

"Madame," quoth I, "if that I durst enquére
Of you, I would fain, of that company,
Wit what they be that pass'd by this herbére?"
And she again answered right friendlý:
"My fairë daughter, all that pass'd hereby
In white clothing, be servants ev'ry one
Unto the Leaf; and I myself am one.

"See ye not her that crowned is," quoth she,
"[Clad] all in white?"—"Madame," then
quoth I, "yes:"
"That is Dian', goddess of chastity;
And for because that she a maiden is,
In her handë the branch she beareth this,
That *agnus castus* men call properly;
And all the ladies in her company,

"Which ye see of that herbë chaplets wear,
Be such as have kept alway maidenhead:
And all they that of laurel chaplets bear,
Be such as hardy[7] were in manly deed,—
Victorious name which never may be dead!
And all they were so worthy of their hand[8]
In their time, that no one might them withstand.

"And those that wearë chaplets on their head
Of fresh woodbind, be such as never were
To love untrue in word, in thought, nor deed,
But ay steadfást; nor for pleasánce, nor fear,
Though that they should their heartës all to-tear,[9]
Would never flit,[10] but ever were steadfást,
Till that their livës there asunder brast."[11]

"Now fair Madáme," quoth I, "yet would I
pray
Your ladyship, if that it mightë be,
That I might knowë, by some manner way
(Sincë that it hath liked your beautý,
The truth of these ladies for to tell me),
What that these knightës be in rich armoúr,
And what those be in green and wear the flow'r?

"And why that some did rev'rence to that tree,
And some unto the plot of flowers fair?"

"With right good will, my daughter fair,"
quoth she,
"Since your desire is good and debonair;[12]
The nine crowned be very exemplair[13]
Of all honoúr longing to chivalrý;
And those certáin be call'd The Nine Worthý,[14]

"Which ye may see now riding all before,
That in their time did many a noble deed,
And for their worthiness full oft have bore
The crown of laurel leaves upon their head,
As ye may in your oldë bookës read;
And how that he that was a conqueroúr
Had by laurél alway his most honoúr.

"And those that bearë boughës in their hand
Of the precíous laurel so notáble,
Be such as were, I will ye understand,
Most noble Knightës of the Roundë Table,[15]
And eke the Doucëperës honouráble;[16]
Whichë they bear in sign of victory,
As witness of their deedës mightily.

"Eke there be knightës old[17] of the Gartér,
That in their timë did right worthily;
And the honoúr they did to the laurér[18]
Is for[19] by it they have their laud whollý,
Their triumph eke, and martial glorý;
Which unto them is more perféct richéss
Than any wight imagine can, or guess.

"For one leaf given of that noble tree
To any wight that hath done worthily,
An'[20] it be done so as it ought to be,
Is more honoúr than any thing earthlý;
Witness of Rome, that founder was trulý
Of allë knighthood and deeds marvellous;
Recórd I take of Titus Livius.[21]

"And as for her that crowned is in green,
It is Flora, of these flowers goddéss;
And all that here on her awaiting be'n,
It are such folk that loved idleness,
And not delighted in no business,
But for to hunt and hawk, and play in meads,
And many other such-like idle deeds.

"And for the great delight and the pleasánce
They have to the flow'r, and so rev'rentlý
They unto it do such obéisánce
As ye may see." "Now, fair Madáme," quoth I,
"If I durst ask, what is the cause, and why,
That knightës have the ensign[22] of honoúr
Rather by the leaf than by the flow'r?"

"Soothly, daughter," quoth she, "this is the
troth:

1 This wondrous incident. 2 Issued forth.
3 I warrant you. 4 Prayed, wished. 5 Fortune.
6 "Grand merci," French; great thanks.
7 Courageous. 8 So valiant in fight.
9 Rend in pieces. 10 Change, swerve.
11 Burst, broke; till they died.
12 Gentle, courteous. 13 The true examples.
14 The Nine Worthies, who at our day survive in the Seven Champions of Christendom. The Worthies were favourite subjects for representation at popular festivals or in masquerades.
15 The famous Knights of King Arthur, who, being all esteemed equal in valour and noble qualities, sat at a round table, so that none should seem to have precedence over the rest.
16 The twelve peers of Charlemagne (*les douze pairs*), chief among whom were Roland and Oliver.
17 Chaucer speaks as if, at least for the purposes of his poetry, he believed that Edward III. did not establish a new, but only revived an old, chivalric institution, when he founded the Order of the Garter.
18 Laurel-tree; French, "laurier."
19 Because. 20 If.
21 The meaning is: "Witness the practice of Rome, that was the founder of all knighthood and marvellous deeds; and I refer for corroboration to Titus Livius"—who, in several passages, has mentioned the laurel crown as the highest military honour. For instance, in l. vii. c. 13, Sextus Tullius, remonstrating for the army against the inaction in which it is kept, tells the Dictator Sulpicius, "Duce te vincere cupimus; tibi *lauream insignem* deferre; tecum triumphantes urbem inire."
22 Insignia, badge.

For knights should ever be persévering,
To seek honoúr, without feintise[1] or sloth,
From well to better in all manner thing:
In sign of which, with leavës aye lastíng
They be rewarded after their degree,
Whose lusty green may not appaired[2] be,

"But ay keeping their beauty fresh and green;
For there is no storm that may them deface,
Nor hail nor snow, nor wind nor frostës keen;
Wherefore they have this property and grace:
And for the flow'r, within a little space,
Wollë[3] be lost, so simple of natúre
They be, that they no grievance[4] may endure;

"And ev'ry storm will blow them soon away,
Nor they lastë not but for a seasón;
That is the cause, the very truth to say,
That they may not, by no way of reasón,
Be put to no such occupatión."
"Madáme," quoth I, "with all my whole servíce
I thank you now, in my most humble wise;

"For now I am ascértain'd thoroughly
Of ev'ry thing that I desir'd to know."
"I am right glad that I have said, soothly,
Aught to your pleasure, if ye will me trow,"[5]
Quoth she again; "but to whom do ye owe
Your service? and which wollë[3] ye honoúr,
Tell me, I pray, this year, the Leaf or the Flow'r?"

"Madame," quoth I, "though I be least worthý,
Unto the Leaf I owe mine óbservánce:"
"That is," quoth she, "right well done, certainlý;
And I pray God, to honour you advance,
And keep you from the wicked remembránce
Of Malebouche,[6] and all his cruelty;
And all that good and well-condition'd be.

"For here may I no longer now abide;
I must follów the greatë companý,
That ye may see yonder before you ride."
And forthwith, as I couldë, most humblý
I took my leave of her, and she gan hie[7]
After them as fast as she ever might;
And I drew homeward, for it was nigh night,

And put all that I had seen in writíng,
Under support[8] of them that list it read.
O little book! thou art so uncunníng,
How dar'st thou put thyself in press,[9] for dread?
It is wonder that thou waxest not red!
Since that thou know'st full lite[10] who shall behold
Thy rude languáge, full boistously unfold.[11]

Explicit.

THE HOUSE OF FAME.

[THANKS partly to Pope's brief and elegant paraphrase, in his "Temple of Fame," and partly to the familiar force of the style and the satirical significance of the allegory, "The House of Fame" is among the best known and relished of Chaucer's minor poems. The octosyllabic measure in which it is written—the same which the author of "Hudibras" used with such admirable effect—is excellently adapted for the vivid descriptions, the lively sallies of humour and sarcasm, with which the poem abounds; and when the poet actually does get to his subject, he treats it with a zest, and a corresponding interest on the part of the reader, which are scarcely surpassed by the best of The Canterbury Tales. The poet, however, tarries long on the way to the House of Fame; as Pope says in his advertisement, the reader who would compare his with Chaucer's poem, "may begin with [Chaucer's] third Book of Fame, there being nothing in the two first books that answers to their title." The first book opens with a kind of prologue (actually so marked and called in earlier editions) in which the author speculates on the causes of dreams; avers that never any man had such a dream as he had on the tenth of December; and prays the God of Sleep to help him to interpret the dream, and the Mover of all things to reward or afflict those readers who take the dream well or ill. Then he relates that, having fallen asleep, he fancied himself within a temple of glass—the abode of Venus—the walls of which were painted with the story of Æneas. The paintings are described at length; and then the poet tells us that, coming out of the temple, he found himself on a vast sandy plain, and saw high in heaven an eagle, that began to descend towards him. With the prologue, the first book numbers

1 Dissimulation. 2 Impaired, decayed. 3 Will.
4 Injury, hardship. 5 Believe.
6 Slander, personified under the title of Evil-mouth —Italian, "Malbocca;" French, "Malebouche."
7 Haste.
8 Encouragement or patience; the phrase means—trusting to the goodwill of my reader.
9 Into a crowd, into the press of competitors for favour; not, it need hardly be said, "into the press" in the modern sense—printing was not invented for a century after this was written.
10 Little.
11 Unfolded, set forth, in homely and unpolished fashion.

508 lines; of which 192 only—more than are actually concerned with or directly lead towards the real subject of the poem—are given here. The second book, containing 582 lines, of which 176 will be found in this edition, is wholly devoted to the voyage from the Temple of Venus to the House of Fame, which the dreamer accomplishes in the eagle's claws. The bird has been sent by Jove to do the poet some "solace" in reward of his labours for the cause of Love; and during the transit through the air the messenger discourses obligingly and learnedly with his human burden on the theory of sound, by which all that is spoken must needs reach the House of Fame; and on other matters suggested by their errand and their observations by the way. The third book (of 1080 lines, only a score of which, just at the outset, have been omitted) brings us to the real pith of the poem. It finds the poet close to the House of Fame, built on a rock of ice engraved with names, many of which are half-melted away. Entering the gorgeous palace, he finds all manner of minstrels and historians; harpers, pipers, and trumpeters of fame; magicians, jugglers, sorcerers, and many others. On a throne of ruby sits the goddess, seeming at one moment of but a cubit's stature, at the next touching heaven; and at either hand, on pillars, stand the great authors who "bear up the name" of ancient nations. Crowds of people enter the hall from all regions of earth, praying the goddess to give them good or evil fame, with and without their own deserts; and they receive answers favourable, negative, or contrary, according to the caprice of Fame. Pursuing his researches further, out of the region of reputation or fame proper into that of tidings or rumours, the poet is led, by a man who has entered into conversation with him, to a vast whirling house of twigs, ever open to the arrival of tidings, ever full of murmurings, whisperings, and clatterings, coming from the vast crowds that fill it—for every rumour, every piece of news, every false report, appears there in the shape of the person who utters it, or passes it on, down in earth. Out at the windows innumerable, the tidings pass to Fame, who gives to each report its name and duration; and in the house travellers, pilgrims, pardoners, couriers, lovers, &c., make a huge clamour. But here the poet meets with a man "of great authority," and, half afraid, awakes; skilfully —whether by intention, fatigue, or accident—leaving the reader disappointed by the non-fulfilment of what seemed to be promises of further disclosures. The poem, not least in the passages the omission of which has been dictated by the exigencies of the present volume, is full of testimony to the vast acquaintance of Chaucer with learning ancient and modern; Ovid, Virgil, Statius, are equally at his command to illustrate his narrative or to furnish the ground-work of his descriptions; while architecture, the Arabic numeration, the theory of sound, and the effects of gunpowder, are only a few among the topics of his own time of which the poet treats with the ease of proficient knowledge. Not least interesting are the vivid touches in which (page 235) Chaucer sketches the routine of his laborious and almost recluse daily life; while the strength, individuality, and humour that mark the didactic portion of the poem prove that "The House of Fame" was one of the poet's riper productions.]

GOD turn us ev'ry dream to good!
For it is wonder thing, by the Rood,[1]
To my wittë, what causeth swevens,[2]
Either on morrows or on evens;
And why th' effect followeth of some,
And of some it shall never come;
Why this is an avisión
And this a revelatión;
Why this a dream, why that a sweven,
And not to ev'ry man like even;[3]
Why this a phantom,[4] why these orácles,[5]
I n'ot; but whoso of these mirácles
The causes knoweth bet than I,
Divine[6] he; for I certainlý
Ne can[7] them not, nor ever think
To busy my wit for to swink[8]
To know of their significánce
The genders, neither the distánce
Of times of them, nor the causes
For why that this more than that cause is;

1 The cross; Anglo-Saxon, "rode."
2 Dreams.
3 Alike.
4 False or fantistic imagination.
5 Truthful foreshadowings of the future.

Or if folkë's complexións
Make them dream of reflectións;
Or ellës thus, as others sayn,
For too great feebleness of the brain
By abstinence, or by sicknéss,
By prison, strife, or great distress,
Or ellës by disordinance
Of natural accustomance;[9]
That some men be too curious
In study, or melancholious,
Or thus, so inly full of dread,
That no man may them bootë bede;[10]
Or ellës that devotión
Of some, and contemplatión,
Causeth to them such dreamës oft;
Or that the cruel life unsoft
Of them that unkind lovës lead,
That often hopë much or dread,
That purely their impressións
Cause them to havë visións;

6 Or "define."
7 Do not know, understand.
8 Labour.
9 By derangement of natural habit or mode of life.
10 Afford them relief.

Or if that spirits have the might
To makë folk to dream a-night;
Or if the soul, of proper kind,[1]
Be so perfect as men find,
That it forewot[2] what is to come,
And that it warneth all and some
Of ev'reach of their adventúres,
By visións, or by figúres,
But that our fleshë hath no might
To understanden it aright,
For it is warnëd too darklý;
But why the cause is, not wot I.
Well worth of this thing greatë clerks,[3]
That treat of this and other works;
For I of none opinión
Will as now makë mentión;
But only that the holy Rood
Turn us every dream to good.
For never since that I was born,
Nor no man ellës me beforn,
Mette,[4] as I trowë steadfastlý,
So wonderful a dream as I,
The tenthë day now of December;
The which, as I can it remember,
I will you tellen ev'ry deal.[5]
But at my beginning, trustë weel,[6]
I will make invocatión,
With speciál devotión,
Unto the god of Sleep anon,
That dwelleth in a cave of stone,[7]
Upon a stream that comes from Lete,
That is a flood of hell unsweet,
Beside a folk men call Cimmerie;
There sleepeth ay this god unmerry,
With his sleepy thousand sonës,
That alway for to sleep their won[8] is;
And to this god, that I of read,[9]
Pray I, that he will me speed
My sweven for to tell aright,
If ev'ry dream stands in his might.
And he that Mover is of all
That is, and was, and ever shall,
So give them joyë that it hear,
Of allë that they dream to-year;[10]
And for to standen all in grace[11]
Of their lovës, or in what place
That them were liefest[12] for to stand,
And shield them from povért' and shand,[13]
And from ev'ry unhap and disease,
And send them all that may them please,
That take it well, and scorn it not,
Nor it misdeemen[14] in their thought,
Through malicious intentión;
And whoso, through presumptión,
Or hate, or scorn, or through envý,
Despite, or jape,[15] or villainý,[16]
Misdeem it, pray I Jesus God,
That dream he barefoot, dream he shod,
That ev'ry harm that any man
Hath had since that the world began,
Befall him thereof, ere he sterve,[17]
And grant that he may it deserve,[18]
Lo! with such a conclusión
As had of his avisión
Crœsus, that was the king of Lyde,[19]
That high upon a gibbet died;
This prayer shall he have of me;
I am no bet in charity.[20]

Now hearken, as I have you said,
What that I mette ere I abraid,[21]
Of December the tenthë day;
When it was night to sleep I lay,
Right as I was wont for to do'n,
And fell asleepë wonder soon,
As he that weary was for go[22]
On pilgrimagë milës two
To the corsaint[23] Leonárd,
To makë lithe that erst was hard.
But, as I slept, me mette I was
Within a temple made of glass;
In which there werë more imáges
Of gold, standing in sundry stages,
And morë richë tabernácles,
And with pierrie[24] more pinnácles,
And more curíous portraitures,
And quaintë manner[25] of figúres
Of goldë work, than I saw ever.
But, certainly, I wistë[26] never
Where that it was, but well wist I
It was of Venus readilý,
This temple; for in portraiture
I saw anon right her figúre
Naked floating in a sea,[27]
And also on her head, pardie,
Her rosë garland white and red,
And her comb to comb her head,
Her dovës, and Dan Cupido,
Her blindë son, and Vulcano,[28]
That in his facë was full brown.

As he "roamed up and down," the dreamer saw on the wall a tablet of brass inscribed with the opening lines of the Æneid; while the whole story of Æneas was told in the "portraitures"

1 Of its own nature. 2 Foreknows.
3 Great scholars set much worth upon this thing—that is, devote much labour, attach much importance, to the subject of dreams. 4 Dreamed.
5 Every part or whit. 6 Well.
7 The poet briefly refers to the description of the House of Somnus, in Ovid's "Metamorphoses," l. xi. 592, *et seqq.*; where the cave of Somnus is said to be "prope Cimmerios," and to have a stream of Lethe's water issuing from the base of the rock:

——"Saxo tamen exit ab imo
Rivus aquæ Lethes."

8 Wont, custom. 9 Of whom I tell you.
10 This year. 11 In favour.
12 Most desired or agreeable.
13 Poverty and shame. 14 Misjudge.
15 Jesting, buffoonery. 16 Baseness of nature.

17 Die. 18 Earn, obtain.
19 See the account of his vision in The Monk's Tale, page 163.
20 No better in charity—no more charitable.
21 Awoke.
22 Was weary through having gone. The meaning of the allusion is not clear; but the story of the pilgrims and the peas is perhaps suggested by the third line following—"to makë lithe [soft] what erst was hard." St Leonard was the patron of captives.
23 The "corpus sanctum,"—the holy body, or relics, preserved in the shrine.
24 Gems, precious stones.
25 Strange kinds. 26 Knew.
27 So, in the Temple of Venus described in The Knight's Tale, the Goddess is represented as "naked floating in the largë sea" (page 36).
28 Vulcan, the husband of Venus.

and gold work. About three hundred and fifty lines are devoted to the description; but they merely embody Virgil's account of Æneas' adventures from the destruction of Troy to his arrival in Italy; and the only characteristic passage is the following reflection, suggested by the death of Dido for her perfidious but fate-compelled guest:

Lo! how a woman doth amiss,
To love him that unknowen is!
For, by Christ, lo! thus it fareth,
It is not all gold that glareth.[1]
For, all so brook I well my head,
There may be under goodlihead
Cover'd many a shrewëd vice;[2]
Therefore let no wight be so nice
To take a love only for cheer,[3]
Or speech, or for friendly mannére;
For this shall ev'ry woman find,
That some man, of his purë kind,[4]
Will showen outward the fairést,
Till he have caught that which him lest;[5]
And then anon will causes find,
And swearë how she is unkind,
Or false, or privy[6] double was.
All this say I by[7] Æneás
And Dido, and her nicë lest,[8]
That loved all too soon a guest;
Therefore I will say a provérb,
That he that fully knows the herb
May safely lay it to his eye;[9]
Withoutë dread,[10] this is no lie.

When the dreamer had seen all the sight in the temple, he became desirous to know who had worked all those wonders, and in what country he was; so he resolved to go out at the wicket, in search of somebody who might tell him.

When I out at the doorës came,
I fast aboutë me beheld;
Then saw I but a largë feld,[11]
As far as that I mightë see,
Withoutë town, or house, or tree,
Or bush, or grass, or ered[12] land,
For all the field was but of sand,
As small as men may see it lie
In the desert of Libýe;
Nor no manner creatúre
That is formed by Natúre,
There saw I, me to rede or wiss.[13]
"O Christ!" thought I, "that art in bliss,
From phantom and illusión[14]
Me save!" and with devotión
Mine eyen to the heav'n I cast.
Then was I ware at the last
That, fastë by the sun on high,
As kennen might I[15] with mine eye,
Me thought I saw an eagle soar,
But that it seemed muchë more[16]
Than I had any eagle seen;
This is as sooth as death, certáin,
It was of gold, and shone so bright,
That never saw men such a sight,
But if[17] the heaven had y-won,
All new from God, another sun;
So shone the eagle's feathers bright:
And somewhat downward gan it light.[18]

The Second Book opens with a brief invocation of Venus and of Thought; then it proceeds:

This eagle, of which I have you told,
That shone with feathers as of gold,
Which that so high began to soar,
I gan beholdë more and more,
To see her beauty and the wonder;
But never was there dint of thunder,
Nor that thing that men callë foudre,[19]
That smote sometimes a town to powder,
And in his swiftë coming brenn'd,[20]
That so swithë[21] gan descend,
As this fowl, when that it beheld
That I a-roam was in the feld;[22]
And with his grim pawës strong,
Within his sharpë nailës long,
Me, flying, at a swap he hent,[23]
And with his sours[24] again up went,
Me carrying in his clawës stark[25]
As light as I had been a lark,
How high, I cannot tellë you,
For I came up, I wist not how.

The poet faints through bewilderment and fear; but the eagle, speaking with the voice of a man, recalls him to himself, and comforts him by the assurance that what now befalls him is for his instruction and profit. Answering the poet's unspoken inquiry whether he is not to die otherwise, or whether Jove will him stellify, the eagle says that he has been sent by Jupiter out of his "great ruth,"

"For that thou hast so truëly
So long served ententively[26]
His blindë nephew[27] Cupido,
And fairë Venus alsó,
Withoutë guerdon[28] ever yet,
And natheless hast set thy wit
(Although that in thy head full lite[29] is)
To makë bookës, songs, and ditties,
In rhyme or ellës in cadénce,
As thou best canst, in reverence
Of Love, and of his servants eke,

1 Glitters.
2 May I possess, or use, my head well, as surely as many a cursed vice may be cloaked by fair show.
3 On account of looks and demeanour.
4 By simple force of his nature.
5 Pleases.
6 Secretly.
7 With reference to.
8 Foolish pleasure, caprice.
9 Only he who fully knows the virtues of the herb, may apply it without danger.
10 Doubt.
11 Field, open country.
12 Ploughed; Latin, "arare," Anglo-Saxon, "erean," to plough.
13 To advise or direct.
14 Vain fancy and deception.
15 As well as I might discern.
16 Larger.
17 Unless.
18 Alight, descend.
19 Thunderbolt; French, "foudre."
20 Burned.
21 Rapidly.
22 Was roaming (on the roam) in the field.
23 At a swoop he seized.
24 Soaring ascent; a hawk was said to be "on the soar" when he mounted, "on the sours" or "souse" when he descended on the prey, and took it in flight.
25 Strong.
26 With attentive zeal.
27 Grandson.
28 Reward.
29 Little.

That have his service sought, and seek,
And pained thee to praise his art,
Although thou haddest never part;[1]
Wherefore, all so God me bless,
Jovis holds it great humbless,
And virtue eke, that thou wilt make
A-night full oft thy head to ache,
In thy study so thou writest,
And evermore of love enditest,
In honour of him and praisíngs,
And in his folkë's furtherings,[2]
And in their matter all devisest,[3]
And not him nor his folk despisest,
Although thou may'st go in the dance
Of them that him list not advance.
Wherefore, as I said now, y-wis,
Jupiter well considers this;
And also, beausire,[4] other things;
That is, that thou hast no tidíngs
Of Lovë's folk, if they be glad,
Nor of naught ellës that God made;
And not only from far countrý
That no tidings come to thee,
But of thy very neighëbours,
That dwellen almost at thy doors,
Thou hearest neither that nor this.
For when thy labour all done is,
And hast y-made thy reckonings,[5]
Instead of rest and newë things,
Thou go'st home to thy house anon,
And, all so dumb as any stone,
Thou sittest at another book,
Till fully dazed[6] is thy look;
And livest thus as a hermíte
Although thine abstinence is lite."[7]

Therefore has Jove appointed the eagle to take the poet to the House of Fame, to do him some pleasure in recompense for his devotion to Cupid; and he will hear, says the bird,

"When we be come there as I say,
More wondrous thingës, dare I lay,[8]
Of Lovë's folkë more tidíngs,
Both soothë sawës and leasíngs;[9]
And morë lovës new begun,
And long y-served lovës won,
And of more lovës casuallý
That be betid,[10] no man knows why,
But as a blind man starts a hare;
And more jollity and welfáre,
While that they findë love of steel,[11]
As thinketh them, and over all weel;
More discords, and more jealousies,
More murmurs, and more novelties,
And more dissimulatións,
And feigned reparatións;
And morë beardës, in two hours,
Withoutë razor or scissoúrs
Y-made,[12] than grainës be of sands;
And ekë more holding in hands,[13]
And also more renovelánces[14]
Of old forleten acquaintánces;[15]
More lovë-days,[16] and more accords,[17]
Than on instruments be chords;
And eke of lovë more exchanges
Than ever cornës were in granges."[18]

The poet can scarcely believe that, though Fame had all the pies and all the spies in a kingdom, she should hear so much; but the eagle proceeds to prove that she can.

First shalt thou hearë where she dwelleth;
And, so as thine own bookë telleth,[19]
Her palace stands, as I shall say,
Right ev'n in middës of the way
Betweenë heav'n, and earth, and sea,
That whatsoe'er in all these three
Is spoken, privy or apert,[20]
The air thereto is so ovért,[21]
And stands eke in so just[22] a place,
That ev'ry sound must to it pace,
Or whatso comes from any tongue,
Be it rowned,[23] read, or sung,
Or spoken in suretý or dread,[24]
Certain it must thither need."[25]

The eagle, in a long discourse, demonstrates that, as all natural things have a natural place towards which they move by natural inclination, and as sound is only broken air, so every sound must come to Fame's House, "though it were piped of a mouse"—on the same principle by which every part of a mass of water is affected by the casting in of a stone. The poet is all the while borne upward, entertained with various information by the bird; which at last cries out—

"Hold up thy head, for all is well!

1 This is only one among many instances in which Chaucer disclaims the pursuits of love; and the description of his manner of life which follows is sufficient to show that the disclaimer was no mere mock-humble affectation of a gallant.
2 In honour and praise of Love, and to advance the cause of Love's servants.
3 Relatest. 4 Fair sir, good sir.
5 This reference, approximately fixing the date at which the poem was composed, points clearly to Chaucer's daily work as Comptroller of the Customs—a post which he held from 1374 to 1386.
6 Blinded, dimmed.
7 Little. This is a frank enough admission that the poet was fond of good cheer; and the effect of his "little abstinence" on his corporeal appearance is humorously described in the Prologue to the Tale of Sir Thopas (page 146), where the Host compliments Chaucer on being as well shapen in the waist as himself. 8 Wager, bet. 9 True sayings and lies.
10 Happened, arisen by chance or accident.
11 Love true as steel.
12 "To make the beard" means to befool or deceive. See note 8, page 57. Precisely the same idea is conveyed in the modern slang word "shave"—meaning a trick or fraud. 13 Salutations, embracings.
14 Renewings. 15 Broken-off acquaintanceships.
16 See note 7, page 20.
17 Reconciliations, agreements.
18 Barns, granaries.
19 If this reference is to any book of Chaucer's in which the House of Fame was mentioned, the book has not come down to us. It has been reasonably supposed, however, that Chaucer means by "his own book" Ovid's "Metamorphoses," of which he was evidently very fond; and in the twelfth book of that poem the Temple of Fame is described.
20 Secretly or openly.
21 The air (between the place where anything is spoken, and the House of Fame) is so open, so free from obstruction.
22 Exactly calculated or suitable.
23 Whispered. 24 In confidence or in doubt.
25 It must needs go thither.

Saint Julian, lo! bon hostél![1]
See here the House of Famë, lo!
May'st thou not hearë that I do?"
"What?" quoth I. "The greatë soun',"
Quoth he, "that rumbleth up and down
In Famë's Housë, full of tidings,
Both of fair speech and of chidings,
And of false and sooth compounded;[2]
Hearken well; it is not rowned.[3]
Hearest thou not the greatë swough?"[4]
"Yes, pardie!" quoth I, "well enough."
"And what sound is it like?" quoth he;
"Peter! the beating of the sea,"
Quoth I, "against the rockës hollow,
When tempests do the shippës swallow.
And let a man stand, out of doubt,
A milë thence, and hear it rout.[5]
Or ellës like the last humbling[6]
After the clap of a thund'ring,
When Jovis hath the air y-beat;
But it doth me for fearë sweat."[7]
"Nay, dread thee not thereof," quoth he;
"It is nothing will bitë thee,
Thou shalt no harmë have, truly."
And with that word both he and I
As nigh the place arrived were,
As men might castë with a spear.
I wist not how, but in a street
He set me fair upon my feet,
And saidë: "Walkë forth apace,
And take thine adventúre or case,[8]
That thou shalt find in Famë's place."
"Now," quoth I, "while we have space
To speak, ere that I go from thee,
For the love of God, as tellë me,
In sooth, that I will of thee lear,[9]
If this noisë that I hear
Be, as I have heard thee tell,
Of folk that down in earthë dwell,
And cometh here in the same wise
As I thee heard, ere this, devise?
And that there living body n' is[10]
In all that house that yonder is,
That maketh all this loudë fare?"[11]
"No," answered he, "by Saint Clare,
And all so wisly God rede me;[12]
But one thing I will warnë thee,
Of the which thou wilt have wonder.
Lo! to the House of Famë yonder,
Thou know'st how cometh ev'ry speech;
It needeth not thee eft[13] to teach.
But understand now right well this;
When any speech y-comen is
Up to the palace, anon right
It waxeth like the samë wight[14]
Which that the word in earthë spake,
Be he cloth'd in red or black;
And so weareth his likenéss,
And speaks the word, that thou wilt guess[15]
That it the samë body be,
Whether man or woman, he or she.
And is not this a wondrous thing?"
"Yes," quoth I then, "by Heaven's king!"
And with this word, "Farewell," quoth he,
And here I will abidë[16] thee,
And God of Heaven send thee grace
Some good to learen[9] in this place."
And I of him took leave anon,
And gan forth to the palace go'n.

At the opening of the Third Book, Chaucer briefly invokes Apollo's guidance, and entreats him, because "the rhyme is light and lewd," to "make it somewhat agreeable, though some verse fail in a syllable." If the god answers the prayer, the poet promises to kiss the next laurel-tree[17] he sees; and he proceeds:

When I was from this eagle gone,
I gan behold upon this place;
And certain, ere I farther pace,
I will you all the shape devise[18]
Of house and city; and all the wise
How I gan to this place approach,
That stood upon so high a roche,[19]
Higher standeth none in Spain;
But up I climb'd with muchë pain,
And though to climbë grieved me,[20]
Yet I ententive[21] was to see,
And for to porë[22] wondrous low,
If I could any wisë know
What manner stone this rockë was,
For it was like a thing of glass,
But that it shonë full more clear;
But of what congealed mattére
It was, I wist not readily,
But at the last espiëd I,
And found that it was ev'ry deal[23]
A rock of ice, and not of steel.
Thought I, "By Saint Thomas of Kent,[24]
This were a feeble fundament[25]
To builden on[26] a place so high;
He ought him lite[27] to glorify
That hereon built, God so me save!"
Then saw I all the half y-grave[28]
With famous folkë's namës fele,[29]
That haddë been in muchë weal,[30]
And their famës wide y-blow.
But well unnethës[31] might I know
Any letters for to read
Their namës by; for out of dread[32]

1 Saint Julian was the patron of hospitality; so the Franklin, in the Prologue to The Canterbury Tales, is said to be "Saint Julian in his country," for his open house and liberal cheer. The eagle, at sight of the House of Fame, cries out "bon hostel!"—"a fair lodging, a glorious house, by St Julian!"
2 Compounded, mingled. 3 Whispered.
4 Rushing, confused sound. 5 Roar.
6 Humming; dull low distant noise.
7 It makes me sweat for fear.
8 Take thy chance of what may befall.
9 Learn. 10 Is not.
11 Hubbub, ado. 12 So surely God guide me.
13 Again.
14 It takes the semblance of the same person.
15 Fancy. 16 Wait for.
17 The tree sacred to Apollo. See note 26, page 218.
18 Describe. 19 French, "roche," a rock.
20 Annoyed me, cost me a painful effort.
21 Attentive. 22 Gaze closely.
23 Entirely, in every part.
24 Thomas à Beckett, whose shrine was at Canterbury. 25 Foundation.
26 On which to build. 27 Little.
28 The half or side of the rock which was towards the poet, was inscribed with, &c.
29 Many. 30 Happiness, good fortune.
31 Scarcely. 32 Doubt.

They were almost off thawed so,
That of the letters one or two
Were molt[1] away of ev'ry name,
So únfamous was wox their fame;[2]
But men say, "What may ever last?"
Then gan I in my heart to cast[3]
That they were molt away for heat,
And not away with stormës beat;
For on the other side I sey[4]
Of this hill, that northward lay,
How it was written full of names
Of folkë that had greatë fames
Of oldë times, and yet they were
As fresh as men had writ them there
The selfë[5] day, right ere that hour
That I upon them gan to pore.
But well I wistë what it made;[6]
It was conserved with the shade,
All the writing which I sigh,[4]
Of a castle that stood on high;
And stood eke on so cold a place,
That heat might it not deface.[7]
  Then gan I on this hill to go'n,
And found upon the cop a won,[8]
That all the men that be alive
Have not the cunning to descrive[9]
The beauty of that ilkë place,
Nor couldë castë no compass[10]
Such another for to make,
That might of beauty be its make,[11]
Nor one so wondrously y-wrought,
That it astonieth yet my thought,
And maketh all my wit to swink,[12]
Upon this castle for to think;
So that the greatë beautý,
Cast,[13] craft, and curiosity,
Ne can I not to you devise;[14]
My wittë may me not suffice.
But natheless all the substánce
I have yet in my remembránce;
For why, me thoughtë, by Saint Gile,
Allë was of stone of beryle,
Bothë the castle and the tow'r,
And eke the hall, and ev'ry bow'r,[15]
Withoutë pieces or joinings,
But many subtile compassings,[16]
As barbicans[17] and pinnacles,
Imageries and tabernacles,
I saw; and eke full of windóws,
As flakës fall in greatë snows.
And eke in each of the pinnácles
Werë sundry habitacles,[18]
In which stooden, all without,
Full the castle all about,
Of all manner of minstrales
And gestiours,[19] that tellë tales
Both of weeping and of game,[20]
Of all that longeth unto Fame.
  There heard I play upon a harp,
That sounded bothë well and sharp,
Him, Orphëus, full craftilý;
And on this sidë fastë by
Sattë the harper Arión,[21]
And eke Æacides Chirón;[22]
And other harpers many a one,
And the great Glasgerion;[23]
And smallë harpers, with their glees,[24]
Satten under them in sees,[25]
And gan on them upwárd to gape,
And counterfeit them as an ape,
Or as craft counterfeiteth kind.[26]
Then saw I standing them behind,
Afar from them, all by themselve,
Many thousand timës twelve,
That madë loudë minstrelsies
In cornmuse[27] and eke in shawmies,[28]
And in many another pipe,
That craftily began to pipe,
Both in dulcet[29] and in reed,
That be at feastës with the bride.
And many a flute and lilting horn,
And pipës made of greenë corn,
As have these little herdë-grooms,[30]
That keepë beastës in the brooms.
There saw I then Dan Citherus,
And of Athéns Dan Pronomus,[31]
And Marsyas[32] that lost his skin,
Both in the face, body, and chin,

1 Molten, melted.
2 So obscure had they become.
3 Consider, conjecture.
4 Saw.
5 Self-same.
6 Meant.
7 Injure, destroy.
8 Upon the summit (German, "Kopf," the head) a dwelling or house.
9 The skill, or ability, to describe.
10 Hit upon no contrivance.
11 Equal, match.
12 Labour.
13 Ingenuity.
14 Tell.
15 Chamber.
16 Contrivances.
17 Turrets, watch-towers.
18 Habitations, apartments; or niches.
19 Tellers of stories; reciters of brave feats or "gests."
20 Mirth.
21 The celebrated Greek bard and citharist, who, in the seventh century before Christ, lived at the court of Periander, tyrant of Corinth. The story of his preservation by the dolphin, when the covetous sailors forced him to leap into the sea, is well known.
22 Chiron the Centaur, renowned for skill in music and the arts, which he owed to the teaching of Apollo and Artemis. He became in turn the instructor of Peleus, Achilles, and other descendants of Æacus; hence he is called "Æacides"—because tutor to the Æacides, and thus, so to speak, of that "family."
23 He is the subject of a ballad given in "Percy's Reliques," where we are told that

"Glasgerion was a king's own son,
And a harper he was good;
He harped in the king's chamber,
Where cup and candle stood."

24 Musical instruments.
25 Seats.
26 As art counterfeits nature.
27 Bagpipe; French, "cornemuse."
28 Shalms or psalteries; an instrument resembling a harp.
29 A kind of pipe, probably corresponding with the "dulcimer;" the idea of sweet—French, "doux;" Latin, "dulcis"—is at the root of both words.
30 Shepherd-boys, herd-lads.
31 In the early printed editions of Chaucer, the two names are "Citherus" and "Proserus;" in the manuscript which Mr Bell followed (No. 16 in the Fairfax collection) they are "Atileris" and "Pseustis." But neither alternative gives more than the slightest clue to identification. "Citherus" has been retained in the text; it may have been employed as an appellative of Apollo, derived from "cithara," the instrument on which he played; and it is not easy to suggest a better substitute for it than "Clonas"—an early Greek poet and musician who flourished six hundred years before Christ. For "Proserus," however, has been substituted "Pronomus," the name of a celebrated Grecian player on the pipe, who taught Alcibiades the flute, and who therefore, although Theban by birth, might naturally be said by the poet to be "of Athens."
32 The Phrygian, who, having found the flute of Athena, which played of itself most exquisite music,

For that he would envyen, lo !
To pipe better than Apolló.
There saw I famous, old and young,
Pipers of allë Dutchë tongue,[1]
To learnë love-dances and springs,
Reyës,[2] and these strangë things.
Then saw I in another place,
Standing in a largë space,
Of them that makë bloody soun',[3]
In trumpet, beam,[4] and clarioún ;
For in fight and blood-sheddíngs
Is usëd gladly clarionings.
There heard I trumpë Messenús,[5]
Of whom speaketh Virgiliús.[6]
There heard I Joab trump also,[7]
Theodamas,[8] and other mo',
And all that used clarion
In Catalogne and Aragon,
That in their timës famous were
To learnë, saw I trumpë there.
There saw I sit in other sees,
Playing upon sundry glees,
Whichë that I cannot neven,[9]
More than starrës be in heaven;
Of which I will not now rhyme,
For ease of you, and loss of time :
For timë lost, this knowë ye,
By no way may recover'd be.
  There saw I play jongelours,[10]
Magiciáns, and tregetours,[11]
And Pythonesses,[12] charmeresses,
And old witches, and sorceresses,
That use exorcisatións,[13]
And eke subfumigatións ;
And clerkës[14] eke, which knowë well
All this magic naturel,
That craftily do their intents
To make, in certain ascendénts,[15]
Images, lo ! through which magíc
To make a man be whole or sick.
There saw I the queen Medeá,[16]
And Circes[17] eke, and Calypsá.[18]
There saw I Hermes Bállenus,[19]
Limote,[20] and eke Simon Magús.[21]
There saw I, and knew by name,
That by such art do men have fame.
There saw I Collë Tregetour[20]
Upon a table of sycamore
Play an uncouth[22] thing to tell ;
I saw him carry a windmell
Under a walnut shell.
Why should I makë longer tale
Of all the people I there say,[23]
From hence even to doomësday?
  When I had all this folk behold,
And found me loose, and not y-hold,[24]
And I had mused longë while
Upon these wallës of beryle,
That shone lighter than any glass,
And madë well more[25] than it was
To seemen ev'rything, y-wis,
As kindly[26] thing of Fame it is ;
I gan forth roam until I fand[27]
The castle-gate on my right hand,
Which all so well y-carven was,
That never such another n' as ;[28]
And yet it was by Adventúre
Y-wrought, and not by subtile cure.[29]
It needeth not you more to tell,
To makë you too longë dwell,
Of these gatës' flourishings,
Nor of compasses,[30] nor carvíngs,
Nor how they had in masonries,
As corbets,[31] full of imageries.

challenged Apollo to a contest, the victor in which was to do with the vanquished as he pleased. Marsyas was beaten, and Apollo flayed him alive.

1 The German (Deutsche) language, in Chaucer's time, had not undergone that marked literary division which was largely accomplished through the influence of the works of Luther and the other Reformers. Even now, the flute is the favourite musical instrument of the Fatherland; and the devotion of the Germans to poetry and music has been celebrated since the days of Tacitus.

2 A kind of dance, or song to be accompanied with dancing.

3 Martial sound, accompanying sanguinary strife.

4 Horn, trumpet; Anglo-Saxon, "bema."

5 Misenus, son of Æolus, the companion and trumpeter of Æneas, was drowned near the Campanian headland called Misenum after his name.

6 Æneid, vi. 162 *et seqq.*

7 Joab's fame as a trumpeter is founded on two verses in 2 Samuel (ii. 28, xx. 22), where we are told that he "blew a trumpet," which all the people of Israel obeyed, in the one case desisting from a pursuit, in the other raising a siege.

8 Theodamas or Thiodamas, king of the Dryopes, who plays a prominent part in the tenth book of Statius' "Thebaid." Both he and Joab are also mentioned as great trumpeters in The Merchant's Tale, page 109.

9 Name. 10 Jugglers; French, "jongleur."

11 For explanation of this word, see note 11, page 126.

12 Women who, like the Pythia in Apollo's temple at Delphi, were possessed with a spirit of divination or prophecy. The barbarous Latin form of the word was "Pythonissa" or "Phitonissa." See note 10, page 85.

13 A ceremony employed to drive away evil spirits by burning incense; the practice of smoking cattle, corn, &c., has not died out in some country districts.

14 Scholars.

15 Under certain planetary influences. The next lines recall the alleged malpractices of witches, who tortured little images of wax, in the design of causing the same torments to the person represented—or, *vice versâ*, treated these images for the cure of hurts or sickness.

16 Celebrated for her magical power, through which she restore to youth Æson, the father of Jason; and caused the death of Jason's wife, Creusa, by sending her a poisoned garment which consumed her to ashes.

17 The sorceress Circe, who changed the companions of Ulysses into swine.

18 Calypso, on whose island of Ogygia Ulysses was wrecked. The goddess promised the hero immortality if he remained with her; but he refused, and, after a detention of seven years, she had to let him go.

19 This is supposed to mean Hermes Trismegistus (of whom see note 23, page 185); but the explanation of the word "Ballenus" is not quite obvious. The god Hermes of the Greeks (Mercurius of the Romans) had the surname "Cyllenius," from the mountain where he was born—Mount Cyllene, in Arcadia; and the alteration into "Ballenus" would be quite within the range of a copyist's capabilities, while we find in the mythological character of Hermes enough to warrant his being classed with jugglers and magicians.

20 Limote and Collë Tregetour seem to have been famous sorcerers or jugglers, but nothing is now known of either.

21 Of whom we read in Acts viii. 9, *et seqq.*

22 Strange, rare. 23 Saw.

24 At liberty and unrestrained. 25 Much greater.

26 Natural; it is in the nature of Fame to exaggerate everything. 27 Found.

28 Was (with negative particle prefixed).

29 And yet it was fashioned by Chance, not by care.

30 Devices.

31 The corbels, or capitals whence the arches spring

But, Lord! so fair it was to shew,
For it was all with gold behew.[1]
But in I went, and that anon;
There met I crying many a one
"A largess! largess![2] hold up well!
God save the Lady of this pell,[3]
Our owen gentle Lady Fame,
And them that will to havë name
Of us!" Thus heard I cryen all,
And fast they came out of the hall,
And shookë nobles and sterlíngs,[4]
And some y-crowned were as kings,
With crownës wrought full of lozénges;
And many ribands, and many fringes,
Were on their clothës truelý.
Then at the last espiëd I
That pursuivantës and herauds,[5]
That cry richë folkë's lauds,[6]
They weren all; and ev'ry man
Of them, as I you tellë can,
Had on him throwen a vestúre
Which that men call a coat-armúre,[7]
Embroidered wondrously rich,
As though there werë naught y-lich;[8]
But naught will I, so may I thrive,
Be aboutë to descrive[9]
All these armës that there were,
That they thus on their coatës bare,
For it to me were impossíble;
Men might make of them a bible
Twenty footë thick, I trow.
For, certain, whoso couldë know
Might there all the armës see'n
Of famous folk that havë been
In Afric', Europe, and Asíe,
Since first began the chivalry.
Lo! how should I now tell all this?
Nor of the hall eke what need is
To tellë you that ev'ry wall
Of it, and floor, and roof, and all,
Was plated half a footë thick
Of gold, and that was nothing wick',[10]
But for to prove in allë wise
As fine as ducat of Venise,[11]
Of which too little in my pouch is?
And they were set as thick of nouches[12]
Fine, of the finest stonës fair,
That men read in the Lapidaire,[13]
As grasses growen in a mead.
But it were all too long to read[14]
The namës; and therefóre I pass.
But in this rich and lusty place,
That Famë's Hall y-called was,
Full muchë press of folk there n' as,[15]
Nor crowding for too muchë press.
But all on high, above a dais,
Set on a see[16] imperial,
That madë was of ruby all,
Which that carbuncle is y-call'd,
I saw perpetually install'd
A femininë creatúre;
That never formed by Natúre
Was such another thing y-sey.[17]
For altherfirstë,[18] sooth to say,
Me thoughtë that she was so lite,[19]
That the length of a cubíte
Was longer than she seem'd to be;
But thus soon in a whilë she
Herself then wonderfully stretch'd,
That with her feet the earth she reach'd,
And with her head she touched heaven,
Where as shine the starrës seven.[20]
And thereto[21] eke, as to my wit,
I saw a greater wonder yet,
Upon her eyen to behold;
But certes I them never told.
For as fele eyen[22] haddë she,
As feathers upon fowlës be,
Or were on the beastës four
That Goddë's thronë gan honoúr,
As John writ in th' Apocalypse.[23]
Her hair, that oundy was and crips,[24]
As burnish'd gold it shone to see;
And, sooth to tellen, also she
Had all so fele upstanding ears,
And tonguës, as on beasts be hairs;
And on her feet waxen saw I
Partridges' wingës readilý.[25]
But, Lord! the pierrie[26] and richésse
I saw sitting on this goddéss,
And the heavenly melody
Of songës full of harmony,
I heard about her throne y-sung,
That all the palace wallës rung!
(So sung the mighty Musë, she
That called is Calliopé,
And her eight sisteren[27] eke,
That in their faces seemë meek);
And evermore eternallý
They sang of Fame as then heard I:
"Heried[28] be thou and thy name,
Goddess of Renown and Fame!"
Then was I ware, lo! at the last,
As I mine eyen gan upcast,
That this ilkë noble queen
On her shoulders gan sustene[29]
Both the armës, and the name
Of those that haddë largë fame;

in a Gothic building; they were often carved with fantastic figures and devices.

1 Behued, coloured.

2 The cry with which heralds and pursuivants at a tournament acknowledged the gifts or largesses of the knights whose achievements they celebrated.

3 Palace, house.

4 Sterling coins; not "luxemburgs" (see note 27, page 156), but stamped and authorised money.

5 Heralds.

6 Praises.

7 The sleeveless coat or "tabard," on which the arms of the wearer or his lord were emblazoned.

8 Nothing like it.

9 Concern myself with describing.

10 For "wicked;" counterfeit.

11 In whatever way it might be proved or tested, it would be found as fine as a Venetian ducat.

12 Bosses, ornaments.

13 A treatise on precious stones.

14 Declare.

15 Was not.

16 Seat. See note 1, page 386.

17 Seen.

18 First of all.

19 Little.

20 Septentrion; the Great Bear or Northern Wain, which in this country appears to be at the top of heaven.

21 Moreover.

22 As many eyes.

23 Revelations iv. 6.

24 Wavy and crisp; "oundy" is the French "ondoyé," from "ondoyer," to undulate or wave.

25 Denoting swiftness.

26 Gems, jewellery.

27 Sisters.

28 Praised.

29 Sustain.

Alexander, and Herculés,
That with a shirt his lifë lese.[1]
Thus found I sitting this goddéss,
In noble honour and richéss;
Of which I stint[2] a whilë now,
Of other things to tellë you.
Then saw I stand on either side,
Straight down unto the doorës wide,
From the dais, many a pillére
Of metal, that shone not full clear;
But though they were of no richess,
Yet were they made for great nobless,
And in them greatë senténce.[3]
And folk of dignë[4] reverence,
Of which I will you tellë fand,[5]
Upon the pillars saw I stand.
Altherfirst, lo! there I sigh[6]
Upon a pillar stand on high,
That was of lead and iron fine,
Him of the sectë Saturnine,[7]
The Hebrew Jósephus the old,
That of Jewes' gestës[8] told;
And he bare on his shoulders high
All the fame up of Jewrý.
And by him stooden other seven,
Full wise and worthy for to neven,[9]
To help him bearen up the charge,[10]
It was so heavy and so large.
And, for they writen of battailes,
As well as other old marváiles,
Therefore was, lo! this pillére,
Of which that I you tellë here,
Of lead and iron both, y-wis;
For iron Martë's metal is,[11]
Which that god is of battaile;
And eke the lead, withoutë fail,
Is, lo! the metal of Satúrn,
That hath full largë wheel[12] to turn.
Then stoodë forth, on either row,
Of them which I couldë know,
Though I them not by order tell,
To makë you too longë dwell.
These, of the which I gin you read,
There saw I standen, out of dread,
Upon an iron pillar strong,
That painted was all endëlong[13]
With tiger's blood in ev'ry place,
The Tholosan that hightë Stace,[14]
That bare of Thebes up the name
Upon his shoulders, and the fame
Also of cruel Achillés.
And by him stood, withoutë lease,[15]
Full wondrous high on a pillére
Of iron, he, the great Homére;
And with him Dares and Dytus,[16]
Before, and eke he, Lollius,[17]
And Guido eke de Colempnis,[18]
And English Gaufrid[19] eke, y-wis.
And each of these, as I have joy,
Was busy for to bear up Troy;
So heavy thereof was the fame,
That for to bear it was no game.
But yet I gan full well espy,
Betwixt them was a little envý.
One said that Homer madë lies,
Feigning in his poetries,
And was to the Greeks favouráble;
Therefore held he it but a fable.
Then saw I stand on a pillére
That was of tinned iron clear,
Him, the Latin poet, Virgile,
That borne hath up a longë while
The fame of pious Æneas.
And next him on a pillar was
Of copper, Venus' clerk Ovide,
That hath y-sowen wondrous wide
The greatë god of Lovë's fame.
And there he bare up well his name
Upon this pillar all so high,
As I might see it with mine eye;
For why? this hall whereof I read
Was waxen in height, and length, and bread,[20]
Well morë by a thousand deal[21]
Than it was erst, that saw I weel.
Then saw I on a pillar by,
Of iron wrought full sternëlý,
The greatë poet, Dan Lucan,
That on his shoulders bare up than,
As high as that I might it see,
The fame of Julius and Pompéy;[22]
And by him stood all those clerks
That write of Romë's mighty works,
That if I would their namës tell,
All too longë must I dwell.
And next him on a pillar stood
Of sulphur, like as he were wood,[23]

1 Lost his life; with the poisoned shirt of Nessus, sent to him by the jealous Dejanira.
2 Refrain (from speaking).
3 Significance; that is, in the appropriateness of the metal of which they are composed to the character of the author represented.
4 Worthy, lofty.
5 I will try to tell you.
6 Saw.
7 Of the Saturnine school; so called because his history of the Jewish wars narrated many horrors, cruelties, and sufferings, over which Saturn was the presiding deity. See note 5, page 41.
8 Feats, deeds of bravery.
9 Name.
10 Burden.
11 Compare the account of the "bodies seven" given by the Canon's Yeoman (p. 180):

"Sol gold is, and Luna silver we threpe;
Mars iron, Mercury quicksilver we clepe;
Saturnus lead, and Jupiter is tin,
And Venus copper, by my father's kin."

12 Orbit.
13 From top to bottom; throughout.
14 Statius is called a "Tholosan," because by some, among them Dante, he was believed to have been a native of Tolosa, now Toulouse. He wrote the "Thebais," in twelve books, and the "Achilleis," of which only two were finished.
15 Without leasing or falsehood; truly.
16 Dares Phrygius and Dictys Cretensis were the names attached to histories of the Trojan War pretended to have been written immediately after the fall of Troy.
17 The unrecognisable author whom Chaucer professes to follow in his "Troilus and Cressida," and who has been thought to mean Boccaccio. See page 248.
18 Guido de Colonna, or de Colempnis, a native of Messina, who lived about the end of the thirteenth century, and wrote in Latin prose a history including the war of Troy.
19 Geoffrey of Monmouth, who drew from Troy the original of the British race. See Spenser's "Faerie Queen," book ii. canto x. pages 395–6.
20 Breadth.
21 Times.
22 In his "Pharsalia," a poem in ten books, recounting the incidents of the war between Cæsar and Pompey.
23 Mad.

Dan Claudian,[1] the sooth to tell,
That bare up all the fame of hell,
Of Pluto, and of Proserpine,
That queen is of the darkë pine.[2]
Why should I tellë more of this?
The hall was allë full, y-wis,
Of them that writen oldë gests,[3]
As be on treës rookës' nests;
But it a full confus'd mattére
Were all these gestës for to hear,
That they of write,[4] and how they hight.
But while that I beheld this sight,
I heard a noise approachë blive,[5]
That far'd[6] as bees do in a hive,
Against their time of outflying;
Right such a manner murmuríng,
For all the world, it seem'd to me.
Then gan I look about, and see
That there came entering the hall
A right great company withal,
And that of sundry regións,
Of all kinds and conditións
That dwell in earth under the moon,
Both poor and rich; and all so soon
As they were come into the hall,
They gan adown on knees to fall,
Before this ilkë[7] noble queen,
And saidë, "Grant us, Lady sheen,[8]
Each of us of thy grace a boon."[9]
And some of them she granted soon,
And some she warned[10] well and fair,
And some she granted the contrair[11]
Of their asking utterly;
But this I say you truëly,
What that her causë was, I n' ist;[12]
For of these folk full well I wist,
They haddë good fame each deserved,
Although they were divérsely served.
Right as her sister, Dame Fortúne,
Is wont to serven in commúne.[13]
Now hearken how she gan to pay
Them that gan of her grace to pray;
And right, lo! all this companý
Saidë sooth,[14] and not a lie.
"Madámë," thus quoth they, "we be
Folk that here beseechë thee
That thou grant us now good fame,
And let our workës have good name.
In full recompensatioún
Of good work, give us good renown!"
"I warn[15] it you," quoth she anon;
"Ye get of me good famë none,
By God! and therefore go your way."
"Alas," quoth they, "and well-away!
Tell us what may your causë be."
"For that it list[16] me not," quoth she,
"No wight shall speak of you, y-wis,
Good nor harm, nor that nor this."
And with that word she gan to call
Her messenger, that was in hall,
And bade that he should fastë go'n,
Upon pain to be blind anon,
For Æolus, the god of wind;
"In Thracë there ye shall him find,
And bid him bring his clarioún,
That is full díverse of his soun',
And it is called Clearë Laud,
With which he wont is to heraud[17]
Them that me list y-praised be,
And also bid him how that he
Bring eke his other clarioún,
That hight Slander in ev'ry town,
With which he wont is to diffame[18]
Them that me list, and do them shame."
This messenger gan fastë go'n,
And found where, in a cave of stone,
In a country that hightë Thrace,
This Æolus, with hardë grace,[19]
Heldë the windës in distress,[20]
And gan them under him to press,
That they began as bears to roar,
He bound and pressed them so sore.
This messenger gan fast to cry,
"Rise up," quoth he, "and fast thee hie,
Until thou at my Lady be,
And take thy clarions eke with thee,
And speed thee forth." And he anon
Took to him one that hight Tritón,[21]
His clarions to bearë tho,[22]
And let a certain windë go,
That blew so hideously and high,
That it leftë not a sky[23]
In all the welkin[24] long and broad.
This Æolus nowhere abode[25]
Till he was come to Famë's feet,
And eke the man that Triton hete,[26]
And there he stood as still as stone.
And therewithal there came anon
Another hugë companý
Of goodë folk, and gan to cry,
"Lady, grant us goodë fame,
And let our workës have that name,
Now in honoúr of gentleness;
And all so God your soulë bless;
For we have well deserved it,
Therefore is right we be well quit."[27]
"As thrive I," quoth she, "ye shall fail;
Good workës shall you not avail
To have of me good fame as now;
But, wot ye what, I grantë you
That ye shall have a shrewdë[28] fame,
And wicked los, and worsë name,

1 Claudian of Alexandria, "the most modern of the ancient poets," who lived some three centuries after Christ, and among other works wrote three books on "The Rape of Proserpine."
2 The dark (realm of) punishment or pain.
3 Histories, tales of great deeds.
4 Of which they write.
5 Quickly.
6 Went.
7 Same.
8 Bright, lovely.
9 A favour.
10 Refused.
11 Contrary.
12 Wist not, know not.
13 Commonly, usually.
14 Truth.
15 Refuse.
16 Pleases.
17 Proclaim or herald the praises of.
18 Disgrace, disparage.
19 Evil favour attend him!
20 Constraint.
21 Triton was a son of Poseidon or Neptune, and represented usually as blowing a trumpet made of a conch or shell; he is therefore introduced by Chaucer as the squire of Æolus.
22 Then.
23 Cloud; Anglo-Saxon, "scua;" Greek, σκια.
24 Sky, heaven.
25 Tarried, delayed.
26 Is called.
27 Requited.
28 Evil, cursed.

Though ye good los[1] have well deserv'd;
Now go your way, for ye be serv'd.
And now, Dan Æolus," quoth she,
"Take forth thy trump anon, let see,
That is y-called Slander light,
And blow their los, that ev'ry wight
Speak of them harm and shrewëdness,[2]
Instead of good and worthiness;
For thou shalt trump all the contrair
Of that they have done, well and fair."
Alas! thought I, what adventúres[3]
Have these sorry creatúres,
That they, amongës all the press,
Should thus be shamed guiltëless?
But what! it mustë needës be.
What did this Æolus, but he
Took out his blackë trump of brass,
That fouler than the Devil was,
And gan this trumpet for to blow,
As all the world 't would overthrow.
Throughout every regioún
Went this foulë trumpet's soun',
As swift as pellet out of gun
When fire is in the powder run.[4]
And such a smokë gan out wend,[5]
Out of this foulë trumpet's end,
Black, blue, greenish, swart,[6] and red,
As doth when that men melt lead,
Lo! all on high from the tewell;[7]
And thereto[8] one thing saw I well,
That the farther that it ran,
The greater waxen it began,
As doth the river from a well,[9]
And it stank as the pit of hell.
Alas! thus was their shame y-rung,
And guiltëless, on ev'ry tongue.
  Then came the thirdë companý,
And gan up to the dais to hie,[10]
And down on knees they fell anon,
And saidë, "We be ev'ry one
Folk that have full truëly
Deserved famë right fully,
And pray you that it may be know
Right as it is, and forth y-blow."
"I grantë," quoth she, "for me list
That now your goodë works be wist;
And yet ye shall have better los,
In despite of all your foes,
Than worthy[11] is, and that anon.
Let now," quoth she, "thy trumpet go'n,
Thou Æolus, that is so black,
And out thine other trumpet take,
That hightë Laud, and blow it so
That through the world their fame may go,
Easily and not too fast,
That it be knowen at the last."
"Full gladly, Lady mine," he said;
And out his trump of gold he braid[12]
Anon, and set it to his mouth,
And blew it east, and west, and south,
And north, as loud as any thunder,
That ev'ry wight had of it wonder,
So broad it ran ere that it stent.[13]
And certes all the breath that went
Out of his trumpet's mouthë smell'd
As[14] men a pot of balmë held
Among a basket full of roses;
This favour did he to their loses.[15]
  And right with this I gan espy
Where came the fourthë companý.
But certain they were wondrous few;
And gan to standen in a rew,[16]
And saidë, "Certes, Lady bright,
We have done well with all our might,
But we not keep[17] to havë fame;
Hide our workës and our name,
For Goddë's love! for certes we
Have surely done it for bountý,[18]
And for no manner other thing."
"I grantë you all your asking,"
Quoth she; "let your workës be dead."
  With that I turn'd about my head,
And saw anon the fifthë rout,[19]
That to this Lady gan to lout,[20]
And down on knees anon to fall;
And to her then besoughten all
To hidë their good workës eke,
And said, they gavë not a leek[21]
For no fame, nor such renown;
For they for contemplatioún
And Goddë's lovë had y-wrought,
Nor of fame would they have aught.
"What!" quoth she, "and be ye wood?
And weenë ye[22] for to do good,
And for to have of that no fame?
Have ye despite[23] to have my name?
Nay, ye shall lie every one!
Blow thy trump, and that anon,"
Quoth she, "thou Æolus, I hote,[24]
And ring these folkës works by note,
That all the world may of it hear."
And he gan blow their los so clear
Within his golden clarioún,
That through the worldë went the soun',
All so kindly, and so soft,
That their fame was blown aloft.
  And then came the sixth companý,
And gunnen fast on Fame to cry;
Right verily in this mannére
They saidë; "Mercy, Lady dear!
To tellë certain as it is,
We have done neither that nor this,
But idle all our life hath be;[25]
But natheless yet prayë we
That we may have as good a fame,
And great renown, and knowen[26] name,

1 Reputation. See note 10, page 155.
2 Wickedness, malice.
3 What (evil) fortunes.
4 As swift as ball out of gun or cannon, when fire is communicated to the powder.
5 Proceed.
6 Black; German, "schwarz."
7 The pipe, chimney, of the furnace; French "tuyau." In the Prologue to The Canterbury Tales, the Monk's head is described as steaming like a lead furnace.
8 Also.
9 Fountain.
10 Hasten.
11 Merited.
12 Pulled forth.
13 Ere the sound ceased.
14 As if.
15 Reputations.
16 Row.
17 Care not.
18 Goodness, virtue.
19 Company.
20 Bow down.
21 Cared not a leek.
22 Do ye imagine.
23 Do ye despise.
24 I command.
25 Been.
26 Well-known.

As they that have done noble gests,[1]
And have achieved all their quests,[2]
As well of Love, as other thing;
All[3] was us never brooch, nor ring,
Nor ellës aught from women sent,
Nor onës in their heartë meant
To make us only friendly cheer,
But mightë teem us upon bier;[4]
Yet let us to the people seem
Such as the world may of us deem,[5]
That women loven us for wood.[6]
It shall us do as muchë good,
And to our heart as much avail,
The counterpoise,[7] ease, and traváil,
As we had won it with laboúr;
For that is dearë bought honoúr,
At the regard of[8] our great ease.
And yet[9] ye must us morë please;
Let us be holden eke thereto
Worthy, and wise, and good also,
And rich, and happy unto love,
For Goddë's love, that sits above;
Though we may not the body have
Of women, yet, so God you save,
Let men glue[10] on us the name;
Sufficeth that we have the fame."
"I grantë," quoth she, "by my troth;
Now Æolus, withoutë sloth,
Take out thy trump of gold," quoth she,
"And blow as they have asked me,
That ev'ry man ween[11] them at ease,
Although they go in full bad leas."[12]
This Æolus gan it so blow,
That through the world it was y-know.
Then came the seventh rout anon,
And fell on kneës ev'ry one,
And saidë, "Lady, grant us soon
The samë thing, the samë boon,
Which this next folk[13] you have done."
"Fy on you," quoth she, "ev'ry one!
Ye nasty swine, ye idle wretches,
Full fill'd of rotten slowë tetches![14]
What? falsë thievës! ere ye would
Be famous good,[15] and nothing n'ould
Deservë why, nor never raught,[16]
Men rather you to hangen ought.
For ye be like the sleepy cat,
That would have fish; but, know'st thou what?
He wouldë no thing wet his claws.
Evil thrift come to your jaws,
And eke to mine, if I it grant,
Or do favour you to avaunt.[17]
Thou Æolus, thou King of Thrace,
Go, blow this folk a sorry grace,"[18]
Quoth she, "anon; and know'st thóu how?
As I shall tellë thee right now,
Say, these be they that would honoúr
Have, and do no kind of laboúr,
Nor do no good, and yet have laud,
And that men ween'd that Belle Isaude[19]
Could them not of lovë wern;[20]
And yet she that grinds at the quern[21]
Is all too good to ease their heart."
This Æolus anon upstart,
And with his blackë clarioún
He gan to blazen out a soun'
As loud as bellows wind in hell;
And eke therewith, the sooth to tell,
This soundë was so full of japes,[22]
As ever werë mows[23] in apes;
And that went all the world about,
That ev'ry wight gan on them shout,
And for to laugh as they were wood;[24]
Such gamë found they in their hood.[25]
Then came another company,
That haddë done the treachery,
The harm, and the great wickedness,
That any heartë couldë guess;
And prayed her to have good fame,
And that she would do them no shame,
But give them los and good renown,
And do it blow[26] in clarioún.
"Nay, wis!" quoth she, "it were a vice;
All be there in me no justíce,
Me listë not[27] to do it now,
Nor this will I grant to you."
Then came there leaping in a rout,[28]
And gan to clappen[29] all about
Every man upon the crown,
That all the hall began to soun';
And saidë; "Lady lefe[30] and dear,
We be such folk as ye may hear.
To tellen all the tale aright,
We be shrewës[31] every wight,
And have delight in wickedness,
As goodë folk have in goodnéss,
And joy to be y-knowen shrews,
And full of vice and wicked thews;[32]
Wherefore we pray you on a row,[33]
That our fame be such y-know
In all things right as it is."
"I grant it you," quoth she, "y-wis.
But what art thou that say'st this tale,
That wearest on thy hose a pale,[34]
And on thy tippet such a bell?"
"Madámë," quoth he, "sooth to tell,
I am that ilkë shrew,[35] y-wis,
That burnt the temple of Isidis,
In Athenës, lo! that city."[36]
"And wherefore didst thou so?" quoth she.

1 Feats. 2 Enterprises; desires.
3 Although.
4 Might lay us on our bier (by their adverse demeanour). 5 Judge. 6 Madly.
7 Compensation. 8 In comparison with.
9 Further, in addition. 10 Fasten. 11 Believe.
12 In evil leash; in sorry plight.
13 The people just before us.
14 Blemishes, spots; French, "tache."
15 Have good fame. 16 Recked, cared (to do so).
17 To boast your deeds, advance vauntingly your fame. 18 Mischance, disgrace.
19 See note 33, page 219.
20 Could not refuse them her love.
21 Mill. See note 20, page 157.
22 Jests, scornful sayings. 23 Grimaces. 24 Mad.
25 So were they turned to ridicule. See note 6, page 433. 26 Cause it to be blown.
27 It is not my pleasure. 28 Crowd.
29 Strike, knock.
30 Loved. 31 Wicked, impious.
32 Evil qualities. 33 All together.
34 Perpendicular stripe; a heraldic term.
35 That same wicked wretch.
36 Obviously Chaucer should have said the temple of Diana, or Artemis (to whom, as Goddess of the Moon, the Egyptian Isis corresponded), at Ephesus. The building, famous for its splendour, was set on fire, in

"By my thrift!" quoth he, "Madáme,
I wouldë fain have had a name
As other folk had in the town;
Although they were of great renown
For their virtue and their thews,[1]
Thought I, as great fame have shrews
(Though it be naught) for shrewdëness,
As good folk have for goodëness;
And since I may not have the one,
The other will I not forgo'n.[2]
So for to gettë famë's hire,[3]
The temple set I all afire.
Now do our los be blowen swithe,
As wisly be thou ever blithe." [5]
"Gladly," quoth she; "thou Æolus,
Hear'st thou what these folk prayen us?"
"Madame, I hear full well," quoth he,
"And I will trumpen it, pardie!"
And took his blackë trumpet fast,
And gan to puffen and to blast,
Till it was at the worldë's end.
With that I gan aboutë wend,[6]
For one that stood right at my back
Me thought full goodly[7] to me spake,
And saidë, "Friend, what is thy name?
Art thou come hither to have fame?"
"Nay, for soothë,[8] friend!" quoth I;
"I came not hither, grand mercy,[9]
For no such causë, by my head!
Sufficeth me, as I were dead,
That no wight have my name in hand.
I wot myself best how I stand,
For what I dree,[10] or what I think,
I will myself it allë drink,
Certain, for the morë part,
As far forth as I know mine art."
"What doest thou here, then," quoth he.
Quoth I, "That will I tellë thee;
The causë why I standë here,
Is some new tidings for to lear,[11]
Some newë thing, I know not what,
Tidings either this or that,
Of love, or suchë thingës glad.
For, certainly, he that me made
To comë hither, said to me
I shouldë bothë hear and see
In this placë wondrous things;
But these be not such tidings
As I meant of." "No?" quoth he.
And I answered, "No, pardie!
For well I wot ever yet,
Since that first I haddë wit,
That some folk have desired fame
Diversëly, and los, and name;
But certainly I knew not how
Nor where that Fame dwelled, ere now;
Nor eke of her descriptión,
Nor also her conditión,
Nor the order of her doom,[12]
Knew I not till I hither come."
"Why, then, lo! be these tidings,
That thou nowë hither brings,
That thou hast heard?" quoth he to me.
"But now no force;[13] for well I see
What thou desirest for to lear.[11]
Come forth, and stand no longer here,
And I will thee, withoutë dread,[14]
Into another placë lead,
Where thou shalt hear many a one."
Then gan I forth with him to go'n
Out of the castle, sooth to say.
Then saw I stand in a valléy,
Under the castle fastë by,
A house, that *domus Dædali*,
That *Labyrinthus*[15] callëd is,
N' as[16] made so wondrously, y-wis,
Nor half so quaintly[17] was y-wrought.
And evermore, as swift as thought,
This quaintë[17] house aboutë went,
That nevermore it stillë stent;[18]
And thereout came so great a noise,
That had it stooden upon Oise,[19]
Men might have heard it easily
To Rome, I trowë sickerly.[20]
And the noisë which I heard,
For all the world right so it far'd
As doth the routing[21] of the stone
That from the engine[22] is let go'n.
And all this house of which I read[23]
Was made of twiggës sallow,[24] red,
And green eke, and some werë white,
Such as men to the cages twight,[25]
Or maken of[26] these panniers,
Or ellës hutches or dossers;[27]
That, for the swough[28] and for the twigs,
This house was all so full of gigs,[29]
And all so full eke of chirkings,[30]
And of many other workings;
And eke this house had of entries
As many as leavës be on trees,
In summer when that they be green,
And on the roof men may yet see'n
A thousand holës, and well mo',
To let the soundës outë go.
And by day in ev'ry tide[31]
Be all the doorës open wide,

B.C. 356, by Erostatus, merely that he might perpetuate his name.
1 Good qualities.
2 Forego.
3 The reward of fame.
4 Cause our renown to be blown abroad quickly.
5 As sure as thou mayest ever be glad.
6 Go, turn.
7 Courteously, fairly.
8 Of a surety.
9 Great thanks! gramercy!
10 Suffer.
11 Learn.
12 The rule, principle, of her judgments.
13 No matter.
14 Doubt.
15 The Labyrinth at Cnossus in Crete, constructed by Dædalus for the safe keeping of the Minotaur, the fruit of Pasiphae's unnatural love.
16 Was not.
17 Strangely: strange.
18 It never ceased to move.
19 The river Oise, an affluent of the Seine, in France.
20 I confidently believe.
21 Roaring, rushing noise.
22 The machines for casting stones, which in Chaucer's time served the purpose of great artillery; they were called "mangonells," "springolds," &c.; and resembled in construction the "ballistæ" and "catapultæ" of the ancients.
23 Of which I tell you.
24 Willow.
25 Plucked or pulled to make cages; "twight" is the past tense of "twitch."
26 Or of which they make.
27 Baskets to be carried on the back.
28 Rushing inarticulate sound.
29 Jigging or irregular sounds produced by the wind.
30 Chirpings, creakings.
31 In every time; continually.

And by night each one unshet;[1]
Nor porter there is none to let[2]
No manner tidings in to pace;
Nor ever rest is in that place,
That it n' is[3] fill'd full of tidíngs,
Either loud, or of whisperings;
And ever all the house's angles
Are full of rownings and of jangles,[4]
Of wars, of peace, of marriáges,
Of rests, of labour, of voyáges,
Of abode, of death, of life,
Of love, of hate, accord, of strife,
Of loss, of lore, and of winníngs,
Of health, of sickness, of buildíngs,
Of fairë weather and tempésts,
Of qualm[5] of folkës and of beasts;
Of divers transmutatións
Of estates and of regións;
Of trust, of dread,[6] of jealousy,
Of wit, of cunning, of follý,
Of plenty, and of great famíne,
Of cheap, of dearth,[7] and of ruín;
Of good or of mis-góvernment,
Of fire, and diverse accident.
And lo! this house of which I write,
Sicker be ye,[8] it was not lite;[9]
For it was sixty mile of length,
All[10] was the timber of no strength;
Yet it is founded to endure,
While that it list to Adventúre,[11]
That is the mother of tidíngs,
As is the sea of wells and springs;
And it was shapen like a cage.
"Certes," quoth I, "in all mine age,[12]
Ne'er saw I such a house as this."
And as I wonder'd me, y-wis,
Upon this house, then ware was I
How that mine eagle, fastë by,
Was perched high upon a stone;
And I gan straightë to him go'n,
And saidë thus; "I prayë thee
That thou a while abidë me,[13]
For Goddë's love, and let me see
What wonders in this placë be;
For yet parauntre[14] I may lear[15]
Some good thereon, or somewhat hear,
That lefe me were,[16] ere that I went."
"Peter! that is mine intent,"
Quoth he to me; "therefore I dwell;[17]
But, certain, one thing I thee tell,
That, but[18] I bringë thee therein,
Thou shalt never can begin[19]
To come into it, out of doubt,
So fast it whirleth, lo! about.
But since that Jovis, of his grace,
As I have said, will thee solace
Finally with these ilkë[20] things,
These úncouth sightës and tidíngs,
To pass away thy heaviness,
Such ruth[21] hath he of thy distress
That thou suff'rest debonairly,[22]
And know'st thyselven utterly
Desperate of allë bliss,
Since that Fortúne hath made amiss
The fruit of all thy heartë's rest
Languish, and eke in point to brest;[23]
But he, through his mighty meríte,
Will do thee ease, all be it lite,[24]
And gave express commandëment,
To which I am obedïént,
To further thee with all my might,
And wiss[25] and teachë thee aright,
Where thou may'st mostë tidings hear,
Shalt thou anon many one lear."
And with this word he right anon
Hent[26] me up betwixt his tone,[27]
And at a window in me brought,
That in this house was, as me thought;
And therewithal me thought it stent,[28]
And nothing it aboutë went;
And set me in the floorë down.
But such a congregatioún
Of folk, as I saw roam about,
Some within and some without,
Was never seen, nor shall be eft,[29]
That, certes, in the world n' is[30] left
So many formed by Natúre,
Nor dead so many a creatúre,
That well unnethës[31] in that place
Had I a footë breadth of space;
And ev'ry wight that I saw there
Rown'd[32] evereach in other's ear
A newë tiding privily,
Or ellës told all openly
Right thus, and saidë, "Know'st not thou
What is betid,[33] lo! rightë now?"
"No," quoth he; "tellë me what."
And then he told him this and that,
And swore thereto, that it was sooth;[34]
"Thus hath he said," and "Thus he do'th,"
And "Thus shall 't be," and "Thus heard I say,"
"That shall be found, that dare I lay;"[35]
That all the folk that is alive
Have not the cunning to descrive[36]
The thingës that I heardë there,
What aloud, and what in th' ear.
But all the wonder most was this;
When one had heard a thing, y-wis,
He came straight to another wight,
And gan him tellen anon right
The same tale that to him was told,
Or it a furlong way was old,[37]

1 Unshut, open. 2 Hinder.
3 Is not. 4 Whisperings and chatterings.
5 Sickness. 6 Doubt.
7 Cheapness and dearness (of provisions).
8 Be assured. 9 Small.
10 Although.
11 While Chance or Fortune pleases.
12 In all my life. 13 Wait for me.
14 Peradventure. 15 Learn.
16 That were pleasing to me. 17 Tarry, remain.
18 Except. 19 Thou shalt never be able.
20 Same. 21 Compassion.
22 Gently.
23 On the point of breaking.
24 Little. 25 Direct.
26 Caught. 27 Toes.
28 Stopped. 29 Again, hereafter.
30 Is not. 31 Scarcely.
32 Whispered. 33 Happened.
34 Truth. 35 Wager.
36 Describe.
37 Before it was older than the space of time during which one might walk a furlong; a measure of time often employed by Chaucer.

And gan somewhat for to eche[1]
To this tiding in his speech,
More than it ever spoken was,
And not so soon departed n' as[2]
He from him, than that he met
With the third; and ere he let
Any stound,[3] he told him als';[4]
Were the tidings true or false,
Yet would he tell it natheless,
And evermore with more increase
Than it was erst.[5] Thus north and south
Went ev'ry tiding from mouth to mouth,
And that increasing evermo',
As fire is wont to quick and go[6]
From a spark y-sprung amiss,[7]
Till all a city burnt up is.
And when that it was full up-sprung,
And waxen[8] more on ev'ry tongue
Than e'er it was, it went anon
Up to a window out to go'n;
Or, but it mightë[9] thereout pass,
It gan creep out at some crevass,[10]
And fly forth fastë for the nonce.
And sometimes saw I there at once
A leasing, and a sad sooth saw,[11]
That gan of adventúrë[12] draw
Out at a window for to pace;
And when they metten in that place,
They werë checked both the two,
And neither of them might out go;
For other so they gan to crowd,[13]
Till each of them gan cryen loud,
"Let me go first!"—"Nay, but let me!
And here I will ensurë thee,
With vowës, if thou wilt do so,
That I shall never from thee go,
But be thine owen sworen brother!
We will us medle[14] each with other,
That no man, be he ne'er so wroth,
Shall have one of us two, but both
At onës, as beside his leave,[15]
Come we at morning or at eve,
Be we criëd or still y-rowned."[16]
Thus saw I false and sooth, compounded,[17]
Together fly for one tidíng.
Then out at holës gan to wring[18]
Every tiding straight to Fame;
And she gan give to each his name
After her dispositión,
And gave them eke duratión,
Some to wax and wanë soon,
As doth the fairë whitë moon;
And let them go. There might I see
Winged wonders full fast flee,
Twenty thousand in a rout,[19]
As Æolus them blew about.
And, Lord! this House in allë times
Was full of shipmen and pilgrímes,[20]
With scrippës bretfull of leasíngs,[21]
Entremedled[22] with tidíngs[23]
And eke alonë by themselve.
And many thousand times twelve
Saw I eke of these pardoners,[24]
Couriers, and eke messengers,
With boistës[25] crammed full of lies
As ever vessel was with lyes.[26]
And as I altherfastë[27] went
About, and did all mine intent
Me for to play and for to lear,[28]
And eke a tiding for to hear
That I had heard of some countrý,
That shall not now be told for me;—
For it no need is, readilý;
Folk can sing it better than I.
For all must out, or late or rath,[29]
All the sheavës in the lath;—[30]
I heard a greatë noise withal
In a corner of the hall,
Where men of lovë tidings told;
And I gan thitherward behold,
For I saw running ev'ry wight
As fast as that they haddë might,
And ev'reach cried, "What thing is that?"
And some said, "I know never what."
And when they were all on a heap,
Those behindë gan up leap,
And clomb upon each other fast,[31]
And up the noise on high they cast,
And trodden fast on others' heels,
And stamp'd, as men do after eels.
But at the last I saw a man,
Which that I not describë can;
But that he seemed for to be
A man of great authority.
And therewith I anon abraid[32]
Out of my sleepë, half afraid;
Rememb'ring well what I had seen,
And how high and far I had been
In my ghost;[33] and had great wonder
Of what the mighty god of thunder

1 Eke, add. 2 Was.
3 Without delaying a moment.
4 Also. 5 At first.
6 Quicken, become alive, and spread.
7 Which has leapt into the wrong place.
8 Increased. 9 If it might not.
10 Crevice, chink; French, "crevasse."
11 A falsehood and an earnest true saying.
12 By chance. 13 Push, squeeze, each other.
14 Mingle.
15 In spite of his desire.
16 Quietly whispered. 17 Compounded.
18 To squeeze, struggle. 19 Company.
20 Sailors and pilgrims, who seem to have in Chaucer's time amply warranted the proverbial imputation against "travellers' tales."
21 With scrips or wallets brimful of falsehoods.
22 Intermingled.
23 "Tidings" are evidently news or stories containing simple reflections of facts.
24 Of whom Chaucer, in the Prologue to The Canterbury Tales, has given us no flattering typical portrait (page 24). 25 Boxes.
26 Lees (of wine, &c.) 27 With all speed.
28 To amuse and instruct myself.
29 Late or soon.
30 Barn; still used in Lincolnshire and some parts of the north. The meaning is, that the poet need not tell what tidings he wanted to hear, since everything of the kind must some day come out—as sooner or later every sheaf in the barn must be brought forth (to be threshed).
31 A somewhat similar heaping-up of people is described in Spenser's account of the procession of Lucifera ("The Faerie Queen," book i. canto iv.), where, as the royal dame passes to her coach,

"The heaps of people, thronging in the hall,
Do ride each other, upon her to gaze."

32 Awoke. 33 Spirit.

Had let me know; and gan to write
Like as ye have me heard endite.
Wherefore to study and read alway
I purpose to do day by day.

And thus, in dreaming and in game,
Endeth this little book of Fame.

Here endeth the Book of Fame.

TROILUS AND CRESSIDA.

[In several respects, the story of "Troilus and Cressida" may be regarded as Chaucer's noblest poem. Larger in scale than any other of his individual works—numbering nearly half as many lines as The Canterbury Tales contain, without reckoning the two in prose—the conception of the poem is yet so closely and harmoniously worked out, that all the parts are perfectly balanced, and from first to last scarcely a single line is superfluous or misplaced. The finish and beauty of the poem as a work of art, are not more conspicuous than the knowledge of human nature displayed in the portraits of the principal characters. The result is, that the poem is more modern, in form and in spirit, than almost any other work of its author; the chaste style and sedulous polish of the stanzas admit of easy change into the forms of speech now current in England; while the analytical and subjective character of the work gives it, for the nineteenth century reader, an interest of the same kind as that inspired, say, by George Eliot's wonderful study of character in "Romola." Then, above all, "Troilus and Cressida" is distinguished by a purity and elevation of moral tone, that may surprise those who judge of Chaucer only by the coarse traits of his time preserved in The Canterbury Tales, or who may expect to find here the Troilus, the Cressida, and the Pandarus of Shakspeare's play. It is to no trivial gallant, no woman of coarse mind and easy virtue, no malignantly subservient and utterly debased procurer, that Chaucer introduces us. His Troilus is a noble, sensitive, generous, pure-souled, manly, magnanimous hero, who is only confirmed and stimulated in all virtue by his love, who lives for his lady, and dies for her falsehood, in a lofty and chivalrous fashion. His Cressida is a stately, self-contained, virtuous, tender-hearted woman, who loves with all the pure strength and trustful abandonment of a generous and exalted nature, and who is driven to infidelity perhaps even less by pressure of circumstances, than by the sheer force of her love, which will go on loving—loving what it can have, when that which it would rather have is for the time unattainable. His Pandarus is a gentleman, though a gentleman with a flaw in him; a man who, in his courtier-like good-nature, places the claims of comradeship above those of honour, and plots away the virtue of his niece, that he may appease the love-sorrow of his friend; all the time conscious that he is not acting as a gentleman should, and desirous that others should give him that justification which he can get but feebly and diffidently in himself. In fact, the "Troilus and Cressida" of Chaucer is the "Troilus and Cressida" of Shakespeare transfigured; the atmosphere, the colour, the spirit, are wholly different; the older poet presents us in the chief characters to noble natures, the younger to ignoble natures in all the characters; and the poem with which we have now to do stands at this day among the noblest expositions of love's workings in the human heart and life. It is divided into five books, containing altogether 8246 lines. The First Book (1092 lines) tells how Calchas, priest of Apollo, quitting beleaguered Troy, left there his only daughter Cressida; how Troilus, the youngest brother of Hector and son of King Priam, fell in love with her at first sight, at a festival in the temple of Pallas, and sorrowed bitterly for her love; and how his friend, Cressida's uncle, Pandarus, comforted him by the promise of aid in his suit. The Second Book (1757 lines) relates the subtle manœuvres of Pandarus to induce Cressida to return the love of Troilus; which he accomplishes mainly by touching at once the lady's admiration for his heroism, and her pity for his love-sorrow on her account. The Third Book (1827 lines) opens with an account of the first interview between the lovers; ere it closes, the skilful stratagems of Pandarus have placed the pair in each other's arms under his roof, and the lovers are happy in perfect enjoyment of each other's love and trust. In the Fourth Book (1701 lines) the course of true love ceases to run smooth; Cressida is compelled to quit the city, in ransom for Antenor, captured in a skirmish; and she sadly departs to the camp of the Greeks, vowing that she will make her escape, and return to Troy and Troilus within ten days. The Fifth Book (1869 lines) sets out by describing the court which Diomedes, appointed to escort her, pays to Cressida on the way to the camp; it traces her gradual progress from indifference to her new suitor, to incontinence with him; and it leaves the deserted Troilus dead on the field of battle, where he has sought an eternal refuge from the new grief provoked by clear proof of his mistress's infidelity. The polish, elegance, and power of the style, and the acuteness of insight into character, which mark the poem, seem to claim for it a date considerably later than that adopted by those who assign its composition to Chaucer's youth: and the literary allusions and proverbial expressions with which it abounds, give ample evidence that, if Chaucer really wrote it at an early age, his youth must have been precocious beyond all actual record. Throughout the poem there are repeated references to the old authors of Trojan histories who are named in "The House of Fame" (page 240); but Chaucer especially mentions one Lollius as the author from whom he takes the groundwork of the poem. Lydgate is responsible for the assertion that Lollius meant Boccaccio; and though there is no authority for supposing that the English really meant to designate the Italian poet under that name, there is abundant internal proof that the poem was really founded on the "Filostrato" of Boccaccio. But the tone of Chaucer's work is much higher than that of his Italian "auctour;" and while in some passages the imitation is very close, in all that is characteristic in "Troilus and Cressida," Chaucer has fairly thrust his models out of sight. In the present edition, it has been possible to give no more than about one-fourth of the poem—274 out of the 1178 seven-line stanzas that compose it; but pains have been taken to convey, in the connecting prose passages, a faithful idea of what is perforce omitted.]

The First Book.

The double sorrow of Troilus[1] to tell,
That was the King Priámus' son of Troy,
In loving how his adventúrës[2] fell
From woe to weal, and after[3] out of joy,
My purpose is, ere I you partë froy.[4]
Tisiphoné,[5] thou help me to endite
These woeful words, that weep as I do write.

To thee I call, thou goddess of tormént!
Thou cruel wight, that sorrowest ever in pain;
Help me, that am the sorry instrument
That helpeth lovers, as I can, to plain.[6]
For well it sits,[7] the soothë for to sayn,
Unto a woeful wight a dreary fere,[8]
And to a sorry tale a sorry cheer.[9]

For I, that God of Lovë's sérvants serve,
Nor dare to love for mine unlikeliness,[10]
Prayë for speed,[11] although I shouldë sterve,[12]
So far I am from his help in darknéss;
But natheless, might I do yet gladnéss
To any lover, or any love avail,[13]
Have thou the thank, and mine be the traváil.

But ye lovers that bathen in gladnéss,
If any drop of pity in you be,
Remember you for old past heaviness,
For Goddë's love, and on adversitý
That others suffer; think how sometime ye
Foundë how Lovë durstë you displease;[14]
Or ellës ye have won it with great ease.

And pray for them that beën in the case
Of Troilus, as ye may after hear,
That Love them bring in heaven to solace;[15]
And for me pray alsó, that God so dear
May give me might to show, in some mannére,
Such pain or woe as Lovë's folk endure,
In Troilus' unseely adventúre.[16]

And pray for them that ekë be despair'd
In love, that never will recover'd be;
And eke for them that falsely be appair'd[17]
Through wicked tonguës, be it he or she:
Or thus bid[18] God, for his benignity,
To grant them soon out of this world to pace,[19]
That be despaired of their lovë's grace.

And bid also for them that be at ease
In love, that God them grant perséverance,
And send them might their lovës so to please,
That it to them be worship and pleasánce;[20]
For so hope I my soul best to advance,
To pray for them that Lovë's servants be,
And write their woe, and live in charity;

And for to have of them compassión,
As though I were their owen brother dear.
Now listen all with good entention,[21]
For I will now go straight to my mattére,
In which ye shall the double sorrow hear
Of Troilus, in loving of Cresside,
And how that she forsook him ere she died.

1 First his suffering before his love was successful; and then his grief after his lady had been separated from him, and had proved unfaithful.
2 Fortunes. 3 Afterwards. 4 From.
5 One of the Eumenides, or Furies, who avenged on men in the next world the crimes committed on earth. Chaucer makes this grim invocation most fitly, since the Trojans were under the curse of the Eumenides, for their part in the offence of Paris in carrying off Helen, the wife of his host Menelaus, and thus impiously sinning against the laws of hospitality.
6 Complain. 7 Befits.
8 Companion. 9 Countenance.
10 Unsuitableness. See Chaucer's description of himself in "The House of Fame," page 235, and note 1.
11 Success. 12 Die.
13 Advantage, advance.
14 Prove adverse to you. 15 Delight, comfort.
16 Unhappy fortuné. 17 Injured, slandered.
18 Pray. 19 Pass, go.
20 Honour and pleasure.
21 Attention.

In Troy, during the siege, dwelt "a lord of great authority, a great divine," named Calchas; who, through the oracle of Apollo, knew that Troy should be destroyed. He stole away secretly to the Greek camp, where he was gladly received, and honoured for his skill in divining, of which the besiegers hoped to make use. Within the city there was great anger at the treason of Calchas; and the people declared that he and all his kin were worthy to be burnt. His daughter, whom he had left in the city, a widow and alone, was in great fear for her life.

Cressída was this lady's name aright;
As to my doom,[1] in allë Troy citý
So fair was none, for over ev'ry wight
So ángelic was her native beautý,
That like a thing immortal seemed she,
As sooth a perfect heav'nly creatúre,
That down seem'd sent in scorning of Natúre.[2]

In her distress, "well nigh out of her wit for purë fear," she appealed for protection to Hector; who, "piteous of nature," and touched by her sorrow and her beauty, assured her of safety, so long as she pleased to dwell in Troy. The siege went on; but they of Troy did not neglect the honour and worship of their deities; most of all of "the relic hight Palladion,[3] that was their trust aboven ev'ry one." In April, "when clothed is the mead with newë green, of jolly Ver the prime," the Trojans went to hold the festival of Palladion—crowding to the temple, "in all their bestë guise," lusty knights, fresh ladies, and maidens bright.

Among the which was this Cresséïda,
In widow's habit black; but natheless,
Right as our firstë letter is now A,
In beauty first so stood she makëless;[4]
Her goodlý looking gladded all the press;[5]
Was never seen thing to be praised derre,[6]
Nor under blackë cloud so bright a sterre;[7]

As she was, as they saiden, ev'ry one
That her behelden in her blackë weed;[8]
And yet she stood, full low and still, alone,
Behind all other folk, in little brede,[9]
And nigh the door, ay under shamë's drede;[10]
Simple of bearing, debonair[11] of cheer,
With a full surë[12] looking and mannére.

Dan Troilus, as he was wont to guide
His youngë knightës, led them up and down
In that large temple upon ev'ry side,
Beholding ay the ladies of the town;
Now here, now there, for no devotioún
Had he to none, to reavë him[13] his rest,
But gan to praise and lackë whom him lest;[14]

And in his walk full fast he gan to wait[15]
If knight or squiër of his companý
Gan for to sigh, or let his eyen bait[16]
On any woman that he could espy;
Then he would smile, and hold it a follý,
And say him thus: "Ah, Lord, she sleepeth soft
For love of thee, when as thou turnest oft.[17]

"I have heard told, pardie, of your livíng,
Ye lovers, and your lewed[18] observánce,
And what a labour folk have in winníng
Of love, and in it keeping with doubtánce;[19]
And when your prey is lost, woe and penánce;[20]
Oh, very foolës! may ye no thing see?
Can none of you aware by other be?"[21]

But the God of Love vowed vengeance on Troilus for that despite, and, showing that his bow was not broken, "hit him at the full."

Within the temple went he forth playíng,
This Troilus, with ev'ry wight about,
On this ladý and now on that lookíng,
Whether she were of town, or of without;[22]
And upon cas[23] befell, that through the rout[24]
His eyë pierced, and so deep it went,
Till on Cresside it smote, and there it stent;[25]

And suddenly wax'd wonder sore astoned,[26]
And gan her bet[27] behold in busy wise:
"Oh, very god!"[28] thought he; "where hast thou woned[29]
That art so fair and goodly to devise?"[30]
Therewith his heart began to spread and rise;
And soft he sighed, lest men might him hear,
And caught again his former playing cheer.[31]

She was not with the least of her statúre,[32]
But all her limbës so well answeríng
Were to womanhood, that creatúre
Was never lessë mannish in seemíng.
And eke the purë wise of her movíng[33]
She showed well, that men might in her guess
Honour, estate,[34] and womanly nobless.

Then Troilus right wonder well withal
Began to like her moving and her cheer,
Which somedeal dainous[35] was, for she let fall
Her look a little aside, in such mannére
Ascauncë[36] "What! may I not standë here?"

[1] In my judgment.
[2] Truly she seemed some angel, sent on earth to put to scorn the works of Nature.
[3] The Palladium, or image of Pallas (daughter of Triton and foster-sister of Athena), was said to have fallen from heaven at Troy, where Ilus was just beginning to found the city; and Ilus erected a sanctuary, in which it was preserved with great honour and care, since on its safety was supposed to depend the safety of the city. In later times a Palladium was any statue of the goddess Athena kept for the safeguard of the city that possessed it.
[4] Matchless.
[5] Crowd.
[6] Dearer, more worthy.
[7] Star.
[8] Garment.
[9] In little breadth; not conspicuously.
[10] Under the doubt or fear of shame (for her father's treason).
[11] Courteous, gracious.
[12] Assured.
[13] Deprive him of.
[14] Point out the deficiencies, speak disparagingly, of whom he pleased.
[15] Watch, observe.
[16] Feed.
[17] Art awake and tossing in bed for thought of her.
[18] Foolish.
[19] Doubt.
[20] Suffering.
[21] Take warning from others.
[22] Or from the region of Troy beyond the walls.
[23] By chance.
[24] Crowd.
[25] Stayed.
[26] Amazed.
[27] Better.
[28] Oh true divinity!—addressing Cressida.
[29] Dwelt.
[30] Tell, describe.
[31] Jesting demeanour.
[32] She was tall.
[33] By her simplest gestures, by the very way in which she moved.
[34] Dignity.
[35] Her demeanour was somewhat disdainful.
[36] As if to say—as much as to say. The word represents "Quasi dicesse" in Boccaccio. See note 20, page 87.

And after that her looking gan she light,[1]
That never thought him see so good a sight.

And of her look in him there gan to quicken
So great desire, and strong affectión,
That in his heartë's bottom gan to sticken
Of her the fix'd and deep impressión;
And though he erst had pored up and down,[2]
Then was he glad his hornës in to shrink;
Unnethës[3] wist he how to look or wink.

Lo! he that held himselfë so cunníng,
And scorned them that Lovë's painës drien,[4]
Was full unware that love had his dwellíng
Within the subtile streamës[5] of her eyen;
That suddenly he thought he feltë dien,
Right with her look, the spirit in his heart;
Blessed be Love, that thus can folk convert!

She thus, in black, looking to Troilus,
Over all things he stoodë to behold;
But his desire, nor wherefore he stood thus,
He neither cheerë made,[6] nor wordë told;
But from afar, his manner for to hold,[7]
On other things sometimes his look he cast,
And eft[8] on her, while that the service last.[9]

And after this, not fully all awhaped,[10]
Out of the temple all easily he went,
Repenting him that ever he had japed[11]
Of Lovë's folk, lest fully the descent
Of scorn fell on himself; but what he meant,
Lest it were wist on any manner side,
His woe he gan dissemble and eke hide.

Returning to his palace, he begins hypocritically to smile and jest at Love's servants and their pains; but by and by he has to dismiss his attendants, feigning "other busy needs." Then, alone in his chamber, he begins to groan and sigh, and call up again Cressida's form as he saw her in the temple—"making a mirror of his mind, in which he saw all wholly her figúre." He thinks no travail or sorrow too high a price for the love of such a goodly woman; and, "full unadvised of his woe coming,"

Thus took he purpose Lovë's craft to sue,[12]
And thought that he would work all privilý,
First for to hide his desire all in mew[13]
From every wight y-born, all utterlý,
But he might aught recover'd be thereby;[14]
Rememb'ring him, that love too wide y-blow[15]
Yields bitter fruit, although sweet seed be sow.

And, over all this, muchë more he thought
What thing to speak, and what to holden in;
And what to arten[16] her to love, he sought;
And on a song anon right to begin,
And gan loud on his sorrow for to win:[17]
For with good hope he gan thus to assent[18]
Cressída for to love, and not repent.

The Song of Troilus.[19]

"If no love is, O God! why feel I so?
And if love is, what thing and which is he?
If love be good, from whence cometh my woe?
If it be wick', a wonder thinketh me[20]
Whence ev'ry torment and adversitý
That comes of love may to me savoury think:[21]
For more I thirst the morë that I drink.

"And if I at mine owen lustë bren[22]
From whence cometh my wailing and my plaint?
If maugré me,[23] whereto[24] then do I plain?
I wot ner[25] why, unweary, that I faint.
O quickë death! O sweetë harm so quaint![26]
How may I see in me such quantity,[27]
But if that I consent that so it be?

"And if that I consent, I wrongfullý
Complain y-wis: thus pushed to and fro,
All starrëless within a boat am I,
Middës the sea, betwixtë windës two,
That in contráry standen evermo'.
Alas! what wonder is this maladý!
For heat of cold, for cold of heat, I die!"

Devoting himself wholly to the thought of Cressida—though he yet knew not whether she was woman or goddess—Troilus, in spite of his royal blood, became the very slave of love. He set at nought every other charge, but to gaze on her as often as he could; thinking so to appease his hot fire, which thereby only burned the hotter. He wrought marvellous feats of arms against the Greeks, that she might like him the better for his renown; then love deprived him of sleep, and made his food his foe; till he had to "borrow a title of other sickness," that men might not know he was consumed with love. Meantime, Cressida gave no sign that she heeded his devotion, or even knew of it; and he was now consumed with a new fear—lest she loved some other man. Bewailing his sad lot—ensnared, exposed to the scorn of those whose love he had ridiculed, wishing himself arrived at the port of death, and praying ever that his lady might glad him with some kind look—Troilus is surprised in his

1 Her countenance assumed a pleasanter, less severe, expression.
2 Though before he had freely cast his eyes about.
3 Hardly.
4 Dree, suffer.
5 Rays, glances.
6 Showed by his countenance.
7 To observe due courtesy or manners.
8 Again; another reading is "oft."
9 Lasted.
10 Confounded, daunted.
11 Jested.
12 Pursue.
13 Closely; in the cage or den of secrecy.
14 Unless he might gain any advantage by revealing his love.
15 Too much spoken of, bruited abroad.
16 Constrain—Latin, "arceo."
17 To gain on, overcome.
18 Consent, resolve.
19 The song is a translation of Petrarch's 88th Sonnet, which opens thus:

"S' amor non è, che dunque è quel ch' i' sento."

20 I must hold it a wonder.
21 Seem sweet and acceptable.
22 If I burn by my own will; "s' a mia voglia ardo."
23 If (I burn) in spite of myself. The usual reading is, "If harm agree me"=if my hurt contents me: but evidently the antithesis is lost which Petrarch intended when, after "s' a mia voglia ardo," he wrote "s' a mal mio grado"—if against my will; and Urry's Glossary points out the probability that in transcription the words "If that maugre me" may have gradually changed into "If harm agre me."
24 To what avail?
25 Neither do I know.
26 Strange.
27 How may so much be in me, unless I consent that it should be so.

chamber by his friend Pandarus, the uncle of Cressida. Pandarus, seeking to divert his sorrow by making him angry, jeeringly asks whether remorse of conscience, or devotion, or fear of the Greeks, has caused all this ado. Troilus pitifully beseeches his friend to leave him to die alone, for die he must, from a cause which he must keep hidden; but Pandarus argues against Troilus' cruelty in hiding from a friend such a sorrow, and Troilus at last confesses that his malady is love. Pandarus suggests that the beloved object may be such that his counsel might advance his friend's desires; but Troilus scouts the suggestion, saying that Pandarus could never govern himself in love.

"Yea, Troilus, hearken to me," quoth Pandare,
"Though I be nice;[1] it happens often so,
That one that access[2] doth full evil fare,
By good counsél can keep his friend therefro'.
I have my selfë seen a blind man go
Where as he fell that lookë could full wide;
A fool may eke a wise man often guide.

"A whetstone is no carving instrument,
But yet it maketh sharpë carving toolës;
And, if thou know'st that I have aught miswent,[3]
Eschew thou that, for such thing to thee school[4] is.
Thus oughtë wise men to beware by foolës;
If so thou do, thy wit is well bewared;
By its contrary is everything declared.

"For how might ever sweetness have been know
To him that never tasted bitterness?
And no man knows what gladness is, I trow,
That never was in sorrow or distress:
Eke white by black, by shame eke worthiness,
Each set by other, more for other seemeth,[5]
As men may see; and so the wise man deemeth."

Troilus, however, still begs his friend to leave him to mourn in peace, for all his proverbs can avail nothing. But Pandarus insists on plying the lover with wise saws, arguments, reproaches; hints that, if he should die of love, his lady may impute his death to fear of the Greeks; and finally induces Troilus to admit that the well of all his woe, his sweetest foe, is called Cressida. Pandarus breaks into praises of the lady, and congratulations of his friend for so well fixing his heart; he makes Troilus utter a formal confession of his sin in jesting at lovers, and bids him think well that she of whom rises all his woe, hereafter may his comfort be also.

"For thilkë[6] ground, that bears the weedës wick',
Bears eke the wholesome herbës, and full oft
Next to the foulë nettle, rough and thick,
The lily waxeth,[7] white, and smooth, and soft;
And next the valley is the hill aloft,
And next the darkë night is the glad morrow,
And also joy is next the fine[8] of sorrow."

Pandarus holds out to Troilus good hope of achieving his desire; and tells him that, since he has been converted from his wicked rebellion against Love, he shall be made the best post of all Love's law, and most grieve Love's enemies. Troilus gives utterance to a hint of fear; but he is silenced by Pandarus with another proverb—"Thou hast full great care, lest that the carl should fall out of the moon." Then the lovesick youth breaks into a joyous boast that some of the Greeks shall smart; he mounts his horse, and plays the lion in the field; while Pandarus retires to consider how he may best recommend to his niece the suit of Troilus.

THE SECOND BOOK.

In the Proem to the Second Book, the poet hails the clear weather that enables him to sail out of those black waves in which his boat so laboured that he could scarcely steer—that is, "the tempestuous matter of despair, that Troilus was in; but now of hope the kalendës begin." He invokes the aid of Clio; excuses himself to every lover for what may be found amiss in a book which he only translates; and, obviating any lover's objection to the way in which Troilus obtained his lady's grace—through Pandarus' mediation—says it seems to him no wonderful thing:

"For ev'ry wightë that to Romë went
Held not one path, nor alway one mannére;
Eke in some lands were all the game y-shent[9]
If that men far'd in love as men do here,
As thus, in open dealing and in cheer,
In visiting, in form, or saying their saws;[10]
For thus men say: Each country hath its laws.

"Eke scarcely be there in this placë three
That have in love done or said like in all;"[11]

And so that which the poem relates may not please the reader—but it actually was done, or it shall yet be done. The Book sets out with the visit of Pandarus to Cressida:—

In May, that mother is of monthës glade,[12]
When all the freshë flowers, green and red,
Be quick[13] again, that winter deadë made,
And full of balm is floating ev'ry mead;
When Phœbus doth his brightë beamës spread
Right in the whitë Bull, so it betid[14]
As I shall sing, on Mayë's day the thrid,[15]

1 Foolish.
2 In an access of fever.
3 Erred, failed.
4 Schooling, lesson.
5 That is, its quality is made more obvious by the contrast.
6 That same.
7 Groweth.
8 The border, the end.
9 All the sport spoilt.
10 Sayings, speeches.
11 Alike in all respects.
12 Glad.
13 Alive.
14 Happened.
15 The Third of May seems either to have possessed peculiar favour or significance with Chaucer personally, or to have had a special importance in connection with those May observances of which the poet so often speaks. It is on the third night of May that Palamon, in The Knight's Tale, breaks out of prison, and at early morn encounters in the forest Arcita, who has gone forth to pluck a garland in honour of May (pages 31, 32); it is on the third night of May that the poet hears the debate of "The Cuckoo and the Nightingale" (page 212); and again in the present passage the favoured date recurs.

That Pandarus, for all his wisë speech,
Felt eke his part of Lovë's shottës keen,
That, could he ne'er so well of Lovë preach,
It madë yet his hue all day full green ;[1]
So shope it,[2] that him fell that day a teen[3]
In love, for which full woe to bed he went,
And made ere it were day full many a went.[4]

The swallow Prognë,[5] with a sorrowful lay,
When morrow came, gan make her waimenting,[6]
Why she forshapen[7] was ; and ever lay
Pandare a-bed, half in a slumbering,
Till she so nigh him made her chittering,
How Tereus gan forth her sister take,
That with the noise of her he did awake,

And gan to call, and dress[8] him to arise,
Rememb'ring him his errand was to do'n
From Tróilus, and eke his great emprise ;
And cast, and knew in good plight[9] was the Moon
To do voyáge, and took his way full soon
Unto his niece's palace there beside :
Now Janus, god of entry, thou him guide !

Pandarus finds his niece, with two other ladies, in a paved parlour, listening to a maiden who reads aloud the story of the Siege of Thebes. Greeting the company, he is welcomed by Cressida, who tells him that for three nights she has dreamed of him. After some lively talk about the book they had been reading, Pandarus asks his niece to do away her hood, to show her face bare, to lay aside the book, to rise up and dance, "and let us do to May some observánce." Cressida cries out, "God forbid!" and asks if he is mad—if that is a widow's life, whom it better becomes to sit in a cave and read of holy saints' lives. Pandarus intimates that he could tell her something which could make her merry ; but he refuses to gratify her curiosity ; and, by way of the siege and of Hector, "that was the townë's wall, and Greekës' yerd" or scourging-rod, the conversation is brought round to Troilus, whom Pandarus highly extols as "the wise worthy Hector the second." She has, she says, already heard Troilus praised for his bravery "of them that her were liefest praised be."[10]

"Ye say right sooth, y-wis," quoth Pandarus ;
"For yesterday, who so had with him been,
Might havë wonder'd upon Troilus ;
For never yet so thick a swarm of been[11]
Ne flew, as did of Greekës from him flee'n ;
And through the field, in ev'ry wightë's ear,
There was no cry but 'Troilus is here.'

"Now here, now there, he hunted them so
fast,
There was but Greekës' blood ; and Troilus
Now him he hurt, now him adown he cast ;
Ay where he went it was arrayed thus :
He was their death, and shield of life for us,
That as that day there durst him none with-
stand,
While that he held his bloody sword in hand."

Pandarus makes now a show of taking leave, but Cressida detains him, to speak of her affairs ; then, the business talked over, he would again go, but first again asks his niece to arise and dance, and cast her widow's garments to mischance, because of the glad fortune that has befallen her. More curious than ever, she seeks to find out Pandarus' secret ; but he still parries her curiosity, skilfully hinting all the time at her good fortune, and the wisdom of seizing on it when offered. In the end he tells her that the noble Troilus so loves her, that with her it lies to make him live or die—but if Troilus dies, Pandarus shall die with him ; and then she will have "fished fair."[12] He beseeches mercy for his friend :

"Woe worth[13] the fairë gemmë virtueless ![14]
Woe worth the herb alsó that doth no boot ![15]
Woe worth the beauty that is ruthëless ![16]
Woe worth that wight that treads each under
foot !
And ye that be of beauty crop and root,[17]
If therewithal in you there be no ruth,
Then is it harm ye livë, by my truth !"

Pandarus makes only the slight request that she will show Troilus somewhat better cheer, and receive visits from him, that his life may be saved ; urging that, although a man be seen going to the temple, nobody will think that he eats the images ; and that "such love of friends reigneth in all this town."

Cressída, which that heard him in this wise,
Thought : "I shall feelë[18] what he means,
y-wis ;"
"Now, eme,"[19] quoth she, "what would ye me
devise ?
What is your rede[20] that I should do of this ?"
"That is well said," quoth he ; "certain best
it is
That ye him love again for his lovíng,
As love for love is skilful guerdoning.[21]

"Think eke how eldë[22] wasteth ev'ry hour
In each of you a part of your beautý ;

1 Pale. 2 So decreed it ; such was its effect.
3 An access or sickness of love.
4 Turning ; from Anglo-Saxon, "wendan ;" German, "wenden." The turning and tossing of uneasy lovers in bed is, with Chaucer, a favourite symptom of their passion. See the fifth "statute," page 203.
5 Procne, daughter of Pandion, king of Attica, was given to wife to Tereus in reward for his aid against an enemy ; but Tereus dishonoured Philomela, Procne's sister ; and his wife, in revenge, served up to him the body of his own child by her. Tereus, infuriated, pursued the two sisters, who prayed the gods to change them into birds. The prayer was granted ; Philomela became a nightingale, Procne a swallow, and Tereus a hawk. 6 Lamentation.
7 Transformed. 8 Prepare.
9 In a favourable position or aspect.
10 By whom it would be most welcome to her to be praised. 11 Bees.
12 A proverbial phrase which probably may be best represented by the phrase "done great execution."
13 Evil befall !
14 Possessing none of the virtues which in the Middle Ages were universally believed to be inherent in precious stones.
15 Has no remedial power. 16 Merciless.
17 Perfection. See note 13, page 32.
18 I shall try, test.
19 Uncle ; the mother's brother ; still used in Lancashire. Anglo-Saxon, "eame ;" German, "Oheim."
20 Counsel, opinion. 21 Reasonable recompense.
22 Age.

And therefore, ere that age do you devour,
Go love, for, old,[1] there will no wight love thee:
Let this provérb a lore[2] unto you be:
'"Too late I was ware," quoth beauty when it past;
And eldë daunteth danger[3] at the last.'

"The kingë's fool is wont to cry aloud,
When that he thinks a woman bears her high,
'So longë may ye liven, and all proud,
Till crowës' feet be wox[4] under your eye!
And send you then a mirror in to pry[5]
In which ye may your facë see a-morrow![6]
I keep then wishë you no morë sorrow.'"[7]

Weeping, Cressida reproaches her uncle for giving her such counsel; whereupon Pandarus, starting up, threatens to kill himself, and would fain depart, but that his niece detains him, and, with much reluctance, promises to "make Troilus good cheer in honour." Invited by Cressida to tell how first he knew her lover's woe, Pandarus then relates two soliloquies which he had accidentally overheard, and in which Troilus had poured out all the sorrow of his passion.

With this he took his leave, and home he went;
Ah! Lord, so was he glad and well-begone![8]
Cresside arose, no longer would she stent,[9]
But straight into her chamber went anon,
And sat her down, as still as any stone,
And ev'ry word gan up and down to wind
That he had said, as it came to her mind.

And wax'd somedeal[10] astonish'd in her thought,
Right for the newë case; but when that she
Was full advised,[11] then she found right naught
Of peril, why she should afeared be:
For a man may love, of possibility,
A woman so, that his heart may to-brest,[12]
And she not love again, but if her lest.[13]

But as she sat alone, and thoughtë thus,
In field arose a skirmish all without;
And men cried in the street then: "Troilus
Hath right now put to flight the Greekës' rout."[14]
With that gan all the meinie[15] for to shout:
"Ah! go we see, cast up the lattice wide,
For through this street he must to palace ride;

"For other way is from the gatës none,
Of Dardanus,[16] where open is the chain."[17]
With that came he, and all his folk anon,
An easy pace riding, in routës twain,[18]
Right as his happy day[19] was, sooth to sayn:
For which men say may not disturbed be
What shall betiden[20] of necessity.

This Troilus sat upon his bay steed
All armed, save his head, full richëly,
And wounded was his horse, and gan to bleed,
For which he rode a pace full softëly:
But such a knightly sightë[21] truëly
As was on him, was not, withoutë fail,
To look on Mars, that god is of Battaile.

So like a man of armës, and a knight,
He was to see, full fill'd of high prowéss;
For both he had a body, and a might
To do that thing, as well as hardiness;[22]
And eke to see him in his gear[23] him dress,
So fresh, so young, so wieldy[24] seemed he,
It was a heaven on him for to see.[25]

His helmet was to-hewn in twenty places,
That by a tissue[26] hung his back behind;
His shield to-dashed was with swords and maces,
In which men might many an arrow find,
That thirled[27] had both horn, and nerve, and rind;[28]
And ay the people cried, "Here comes our joy,
And, next his brother,[29] holder up of Troy."

For which he wax'd a little red for shame,
When he so heard the people on him cryen,
That to behold it was a noble game,
How soberly he cast adown his eyen:
Cresside anon gan all his cheer espien,
And let it in her heart so softly sink,
That to herself she said, "Who gives me drink?"[30]

For of her owen thought she wax'd all red,
Rememb'ring her right thus: "Lo! this is he
Which that mine uncle swears he might be dead,
But[31] I on him have mercy and pity:"
And with that thought for purë shamë she
Gan in her head to pull, and that full fast,
While he and all the people forthby pass'd.

And gan to cast,[32] and rollen up and down
Within her thought his excellent prowéss,
And his estate, and also his renown,
His wit, his shape, and eke his gentleness;
But most her favour was, for[33] his distress
Was all for her, and thought it werë ruth[34]
To slay such one, if that he meant but truth.

. . . .

And, Lord! so gan she in her heart argúe
Of this mattére, of which I have you told;
And what to do best were, and what t' eschew,
That plaited she full oft in many a fold.[35]
Now was her heartë warm, now was it cold.

1 When you are old. 2 Lesson.
3 Old age overcomes fastidiousness or disdain at last, makes a woman more easy to woo. 4 Grown.
5 In which to pry or look. 6 Of a morning.
7 I care to wish you nothing worse.
8 Happy. 9 Refrain, stay. 10 Somewhat.
11 Had fully considered. 12 Break utterly.
13 Unless it so please her. 14 Host.
15 Cressida's household.
16 The mythical ancestor of the Trojans, after whom the gate is supposed to be called.
17 All the other gates being secured with chains, for better defence against the besiegers.
18 Two troops or companies.
19 Good fortune; French, "bonheur;" both "happy day" and "happy hour" are borrowed from the astrological fiction about the influence of the time of birth.
20 Happen. 21 Aspect.
22 Courage. 23 Armour.
24 Active; opposite of "unwieldy."
25 Look. 26 Riband. 27 Pierced.
28 The various layers or materials of the shield—called βοαγριον in the Iliad—which was made from the hide of the wild bull.
29 Hector.
30 Who has given me a love-potion, to charm my heart thus away? 31 Unless.
32 Ponder. 33 Because. 34 Pity.
35 Deliberated carefully, with many arguments this way and that.

And what she thought of, somewhat shall I write,
As to mine author listeth to endite.

She thoughtë first, that Troilus' persón
She knew by sight, and eke his gentleness;
And saidë thus: "All were it not to do'n,[1]
To grant him love, yet for the worthiness
It were honoúr, with play[2] and with gladnéss,
In honesty with such a lord to deal,
For mine estate,[3] and also for his heal.[4]

"Eke well I wot[5] my kingë's son is he;
And, since he hath to see me such delight,
If I would utterly his sightë flee,
Parauntre[6] he might have me in despite,
Through which I mightë stand in worsë plight.[7]
Now were I fool, me hatë to purchåse[8]
Withoutë need, where I may stand in grace.[9]

"In ev'rything, I wot, there lies measúre;[10]
For though a man forbiddë drunkenness,
He not forbids that ev'ry creatúre
Be drinkëless for alway, as I guess;
Eke, since I know for me is his distress,
I oughtë not for that thing him despise,
Since it is so he meaneth in good wise.

. . . .

"Now set a case, that hardest is, y-wis,
Men mightë deemë[11] that he loveth me;
What dishonoúr were it unto me, this?
May I him let of[12] that? Why, nay, pardie!
I know also, and alway hear and see,
Men lovë women all this town about;
Be they the worse? Why, nay, withoutë doubt!

"Nor me to love a wonder is it not;[13]
For well wot I myself, so God me speed!—
All would I[14] that no man wist of this thought—
I am one of the fairest, without drede,[15]
And goodliestë, who so taketh heed;
And so men say in all the town of Troy;
What wonder is, though he on me have joy?

"I am mine owen woman,[16] well at ease,
I thank it God, as after mine estate,[17]
Right young, and stand untied in lusty leas,[18]
Withoutë jealousy, or such debate:
Shall nonë husband say to me 'checkmate;'
For either they be full of jealousy,
Or masterful, or lovë novelty.

"What shall I do? to what fine[19] live I thus?
Shall I not love, in case if that me lest?[20]
What? pardie! I am not religious;[21]
And though that I mine heartë set at rest
Upon this knight that is the worthiest,
And keep alway mine honour and my name,
By all right I may do to me no shame."

But right as when the sunnë shineth bright
In March, that changeth oftentime his face,
And that a cloud is put with wind to flight,
Which overspreads the sun as for a space;
A cloudy thought gan through her heartë pace,[22]
That overspread her brightë thoughtës all,
So that for fear almost she gan to fall.

The cloudy thought is of the loss of liberty and security, the stormy life, and the malice of wicked tongues, that love entails:

[But] after that her thought began to clear,
And saidë, "He that nothing undertakes
Nothing achieveth, be him loth or dear."[23]
And with another thought her heartë quakes;
Then sleepeth hope, and after dread[24] awakes,
Now hot, now cold; but thus betwixt the tway[25]
She rist her up, and wentë forth to play.[26]

Adown the stair anon right then she went
Into a garden, with her nieces three,
And up and down they madë many a went,[27]
Flexippe and she, Tarké, Antigoné,
To playë, that it joy was for to see;
And other of her women, a great rout,[28]
Her follow'd in the garden all about.

This yard was large, and railed the alléys,
And shadow'd well with blossomy boughës green,
And benched new, and sanded all the ways,
In which she walked arm and arm between;
Till at the last Antigoné the sheen[29]
Gan on a Trojan lay to singë clear,
That it a heaven was her voice to hear.

Antigoné's song is of virtuous love for a noble object; and it is singularly fitted to deepen the impression made on the mind of Cressida by the brave aspect of Troilus, and by her own cogitations. The singer, having praised the lover and rebuked the revilers of love, proceeds:

"What is the Sunnë worse of his kind right,[30]
Though that a man, for feebleness of eyen,
May not endure to see on it for bright?[31]
Or Love the worse, tho' wretches on it cryen?
No weal[32] is worth, that may no sorrow drien;[33]
And forthy,[34] who that hath a head of verre,[35]
From cast of stonës ware him in the werre.[36]

"But I, with all my heart and all my might,
As I have lov'd, will love unto my last
My dearë heart, and all my owen knight,
In which my heart y-growen is so fast,
And his in me, that it shall ever last:

1 Although it were impossible, out of the question.
2 Pleasing entertainment.
3 Dignity, reputation.
4 Health; cure (of his love-sickness).
5 Know.
6 Peradventure.
7 In a worse position in the city; since she might through his anger lose the protection of his brother Hector.
8 Obtain for myself.
9 Favour.
10 A good medium, a moderate course.
11 Believe.
12 Prevent him from.
13 Nor is it a wonderful thing that I should love.
14 Although I would.
15 Doubt.
16 My own mistress.
17 Well to do, in accordance with my condition or rank.
18 Not tied in the pleasant leash or snare (of love).
19 End, aim.
20 If it please me.
21 I am not in holy vows. See the complaint of the nuns in "The Court of Love," page 208.
22 Pass.
23 Be he unwilling or desirous.
24 Doubt.
25 Two.
26 To take recreation.
27 Winding, turn.
28 Troop.
29 Bright, lovely.
30 Of his true nature.
31 For brightness; the line recalls Milton's "dark with excessive bright."
32 Happiness, welfare.
33 Endure; the meaning is, that whosoever cannot endure sorrow deserves not happiness.
34 Therefore.
35 French, "verre;" glass.
36 Let him beware of casting stones in battle. The proverb in its modern form warns those who live in glass houses of the folly of throwing stones.

All dread I[1] first to lovë him begin,
Now wot I well there is no pain therein."

Cressida sighs, and asks Antigoné whether there is such bliss among these lovers, as they can fair endite; Antigoné replies confidently in the affirmative; and Cressida answers nothing, "but every wordë which she heard she gan to printen in her heartë fast." Night draws on:

The dayë's honour, and the heaven's eye,
The nightë's foe,—all this call I the Sun,—
Gan west'ren[2] fast, and downward for to wry,[3]
As he that had his dayë's course y-run;
And whitë thingës gan to waxë dun
For lack of light, and starrës to appear;
Then she and all her folk went home in fere.[4]

So, when it liked her to go to rest,
And voided[5] werë those that voiden ought,
She saidë, that to sleepë well her lest.[6]
Her women soon unto her bed her brought;
When all was shut, then lay she still and
thought
Of all these things the manner and the wise;
Rehearse it needeth not, for ye be wise.

A nightingale upon a cedar green,
Under the chamber wall where as she lay,
Full loudë sang against the moonë sheen,
Paraunt re,[7] in his birdë's wise, a lay
Of love, that made her heartë fresh and gay;
Hereat hark'd[8] she so long in good intent,
Till at the last the deadë sleep her hent.[9]

And as she slept, anon right then her mette[10]
How that an eagle, feather'd white as bone,
Under her breast his longë clawës set,
And out her heart he rent, and that anon,
And did[11] his heart into her breast to go'n,
Of which no thing she was abash'd nor smert;[12]
And forth he flew, with heartë left for heart.

Leaving Cressida to sleep, the poet returns to Troilus and his zealous friend—with whose stratagems to bring the two lovers together the remainder of the Second Book is occupied. Pandarus counsels Troilus to write a letter to his mistress, telling her how he "fares amiss," and "beseeching her of ruth;" he will bear the letter to his niece; and, if Troilus will ride past Cressida's house, he will find his mistress and his friend sitting at a window. Saluting Pandarus, and not tarrying, his passage will give occasion for some talk of him, which may make his ears glow. With respect to the letter, Pandarus gives some shrewd hints:

"Touching thy letter, thou art wise enough,
I wot thou n' ilt it dignëly endite[13]
Or make it with these argumentës tough,
Nor scrivener-like, nor craftily it write;
Beblot it with thy tears also a lite;[14]
And if thou write a goodly word all soft,
Though it be good, rehearse it not too oft.

"For though the bestë harper upon live[15]
Would on the best y-sounded jolly harp
That ever was, with all his fingers five
Touch ay one string, or ay one warble harp,[16]
Werë his nailës pointed ne'er so sharp,
He shouldë maken ev'ry wight to dull[17]
To hear his glee, and of his strokës full.

"Nor jompre[18] eke no discordant thing y-fere,[19]
As thus, to usë termës of physic;
In lovë's termës hold of thy mattére
The form alway, and do that it be like;[20]
For if a painter wouldë paint a pike
With ass's feet, and head it as an ape,[21]
It 'cordeth not,[22] so were it but a jape."[23]

Troilus writes the letter, and next morning Pandarus bears it to Cressida. She refuses to receive "scrip or bill that toucheth such mattére;" but he thrusts it into her bosom, challenging her to throw it away. She retains it, takes the first opportunity of escaping to her chamber to read it, finds it wholly good, and, under her uncle's dictation, endites a reply telling her lover that she will not make herself bound in love; "but as his sister, him to please, she would aye fain[24] to do his heart an ease." Pandarus, under pretext of inquiring who is the owner of the house opposite, has gone to the window; Cressida takes her letter to him there, and tells him that she never did a thing with more pain than write the words to which he had constrained her. As they sit side by side, on a stone of jasper, on a cushion of beaten gold, Troilus rides by, in all his goodliness. Cressida waxes "as red as rose," as she sees him salute humbly, "with dreadful cheer, and oft his huës mue;"[25] she likes "all y-fere, his person, his array, his look, his cheer, his goodly manner, and his gentleness;" so that, however she may have been before, "to goodë hope now hath she caught a thorn, she shall not pull it out this nextë week." Pandarus, striking the iron when it is hot, asks his niece to grant Troilus an interview; but she strenuously declines, for fear of scandal, and because it is all too soon to allow him so great a liberty—her purpose being to love him unknown of all, "and guerdon[26] him with nothing but with sight." Pandarus has other intentions; and, while Troilus writes daily letters with increasing love, he contrives the means of an interview. Seeking out Deiphobus, the brother of Troilus, he tells him that Cressida is in danger of violence from Polyphete,

1 Although I feared or hesitated.
2 Began to west or wester—to decline towards the west; so Milton speaks of the morning star as sloping towards heaven's descent "his westering wheel."
3 Turn, incline.
4 In company.
5 Gone out (of the house).
6 Pleased.
7 Perchance.
8 Listened.
9 Seized, came upon.
10 Dreamed.
11 Caused.
12 Amazed nor hurt.
13 Wilt not write it proudly, haughtily (but in respectful terms).
14 Little.
15 Alive.
16 Always harp one strain.
17 To grow dull.
18 Jumble.
19 Together.
20 Make it consistent, congruous, throughout.
21 This is merely another version of the well-known example of incongruity that opens the "Ars Poetica" of Horace.
22 Is not harmonious.
23 An idle jest.
24 Be glad.
25 Change.
26 Reward.

and asks protection for her. Deiphobus gladly complies, promises the protection of Hector and Helen, and goes to invite Cressida to dinner on the morrow. Meantime Pandarus instructs Troilus to go to the house of Deiphobus, plead an access of his fever for remaining all night, and keep his chamber next day. "Lo," says the crafty promoter of love, borrowing a phrase from the hunting-field; "Lo, hold thee at thy tristre[1] close, and I shall well the deer unto thy bowë drive." Unsuspicious of stratagem, Cressida comes to dinner; and at table, Helen, Pandarus, and others, praise the absent Troilus, until "her heart laughs" for very pride that she has the love of such a knight. After dinner they speak of Cressida's business; all confirm Deiphobus' assurances of protection and aid; and Pandarus suggests that, since Troilus is there, Cressida shall herself tell him her case. Helen and Deiphobus alone accompany Pandarus to Troilus' chamber; there Troilus produces some documents relating to the public weal, which Hector has sent for his opinion; Helen and Deiphobus, engrossed in perusal and discussion, roam out of the chamber, by a stair, into the garden; while Pandarus goes down to the hall, and, pretending that his brother and Helen are still with Troilus, brings Cressida to her lover. The Second Book leaves Pandarus whispering in his niece's ear counsel to be merciful and kind to her lover, that hath for her such pain; while Troilus lies "in a kankerdort,"[2] hearing the whispering without, and wondering what he shall say—for this "was the first time that he should her pray of love; O! mighty God! what shall he say?"

The Third Book.

To the Third Book is prefixed a beautiful invocation of Venus, under the character of light:

O blissful light, of which the beamës clear
Adornen all the thirdë heaven fair!
O Sunnë's love, O Jovë's daughter dear!
Pleasance of love, O goodly debonair,[3]
In gentle hearts ay ready to repair![4]
O very[5] cause of heal[6] and of gladnéss,
Y-heried[7] be thy might and thy goodnéss!

In heav'n and hell, in earth and saltë sea,
Is felt thy might, if that I well discern;
As man, bird, beast, fish, herb, and greenë tree,
They feel in timës, with vapour etern,[8]
God loveth, and to love he will not wern;[9]
And in this world no living creatúre
Withoutë love is worth, or may endure.[10]

Ye Jovë first to those effectës glad,
Through which that thingës allë live and be,
Commended; and him amorous y-made
Of mortal thing; and as ye list, ay ye
Gave him, in love, ease[11] or adversity,
And in a thousand formës down him sent
For love in earth; and whom ye list ye hent.[12]

Ye fiercë Mars appeasen of his ire,
And as you list ye makë heartës dign;[13]
Algatës[14] them that ye will set afire,
They dreadë shame, and vices they resign;
Ye do[15] him courteous to be, and benign;
And high or low, after[16] a wight intendeth,
The joyës that he hath your might him sendeth.

Ye holdë realm and house in unity;
Ye soothfast[17] cause of friendship be alsó;
Ye know all thilkë cover'd quality[18]
Of thingës which that folk on wonder so,
When they may not construe how it may go
She loveth him, or why he loveth her,
As why this fish, not that, comes to the weir.[19]

Knowing that Venus has set a law in the universe, that whoso strives with her shall have the worse, the poet prays to be taught to describe some of the joy that is felt in her service; and the Third Book opens with an account of the scene between Troilus and Cressida:

Lay all this meanë whilë Troilus
Recording[20] his lessón in this mannére;
"My fay!"[21] thought he, "thus will I say, and thus;
Thus will I plain[22] unto my lady dear;
That word is good; and this shall be my cheer;
This will I not forgetten in no wise;"
God let him worken as he can devise.

And, Lord! so as his heart began to quap,[23]
Hearing her coming, and short for to sike;[24]
And Pandarus, that led her by the lap,[25]
Came near, and gan in at the curtain pick,[26]
And saidë: "God do boot on[27] allë sick!
See who is here you coming to visíte;
Lo! here is she that is your death to wite!"[28]

Therewith it seemed as he wept almóst.
"Ah! ah! God help!" quoth Troilus ruefully;
"Whe'er[29] me be woe, O mighty God, thou know'st!
Who is there? for I see not truëly."

1 Tryst; a preconcerted spot to which the beaters drove the game, and at which the sportsmen waited with their bows.

2 A condition or fit of perplexed anxiety; probably connected with the word "kink," meaning in sea phrase a twist in a rope—and, as a verb, to twist or entangle.

3 Lovely and gracious.

4 Ever ready to enter and abide in gentle hearts.

5 True.

6 Welfare.

7 Praised.

8 They feel in their seasons, by the emission of an eternal breath or inspiration (that God loves, &c.)

9 Forbid.

10 The idea of this stanza is the same with that developed in the speech of Theseus at the close of The Knight's Tale; and it is probably derived from the lines of Boethius, quoted in note 3, page 46.

11 Pleasure.

12 Seize.

13 Worthy. In this and the following lines reappears the noble doctrine of the exalting and purifying influence of true love, advanced in "The Court of Love," "The Cuckoo and the Nightingale," &c.

14 At all events.

15 Make, cause.

16 According as.

17 True.

18 That secret power or quality.

19 A trap or enclosed place in a stream, for catching fish. See note 1, page 218.

20 Conning, committing to memory.

21 By my faith!

22 Make my plaint.

23 Quake, pant.

24 To heave short, interrupted sighs.

25 Skirt of the garment.

26 Or "pike;" peep.

27 Afford a remedy to.

28 That is to blame for your death.

29 Whether.

"Sir," quoth Cressíde, "it is Pandáre and I;"
"Yea, sweetë heart? alas, I may not rise
To kneel and do you honour in some wise."

And dressed him upwárd, and she right tho[1]
Gan both her handës soft upon him lay.
"O! for the love of God, do ye not so
To me," quoth she; "ey! what is this to say?
For come I am to you for causes tway;[2]
First you to thank, and of your lordship[3] eke
Continuance I wouldë you beseek."[4]

This Troilus, that heard his lady pray
Him of lordshíp, wax'd neither quick nor dead;
Nor might one word for shamë to it say,[5]
Although men shouldë smiten off his head.
But, Lord! how he wax'd suddenly all red!
And, Sir, his lesson, that he ween'd have con,[6]
To prayë her, was through his wit y-run.

Cressíde all this espied well enow,—
For she was wise,—and lov'd him ne'er the less,
All n'ere he malapert,[7] nor made avow,[8]
Nor was so bold to sing a foolë's mass;[9]
But, when his shame began somewhat to pass,
His wordës, as I may my rhymës hold,
I will you tell, as teachë bookës old.

In changed voice, right for his very dread,
Which voice eke quak'd, and also his mannére
Goodly[10] abash'd, and now his hue is red,
Now pale, unto Cressíde, his lady dear,
With look downcást, and humble yielden[11] cheer,
Lo! altherfirstë word that him astert,[12]
Was twicë: "Mercy, mercy, my dear heart!"

And stent[13] a while; and when he might out bring,[14]
The nextë was: "God wotë, for I have,
As farforthly as I havë conníng,[15]
Been yourës all, God so my soulë save,
And shall, till that I, woeful wight, be grave;[16]
And though I dare not, cannot, to you plain,
Y-wis, I suffer not the lessë pain.

"This much as now, O womanlikë wife!
I may out bring,[14] and if it you displease,
That shall I wreak[17] upon mine ownë life,
Right soon, I trow, and do your heart an ease,
If with my death your heart I may appease:
But, since that ye have heard me somewhat say,
Now reck I never how soon that I dey."[18]

Therewith his manly sorrow to behold
It might have made a heart of stone to rue;
And Pandare wept as he to water wo'ld,[19]
And saidë, "Woe-begone[20] be heartës true,"
And procur'd[21] his niece ever new and new,
"For love of Goddë, make of him an end,[22]
Or slay us both at onës, ere we wend."[23]

"Ey! what?" quoth she; "by God and by my truth,
I know not what ye wouldë that I say;"
"Ey! what?" quoth he; "that ye have on him ruth,[24]
For Goddë's love, and do him not to dey."[18]
"Now thennë thus," quoth she, "I would him pray
To tellë me the fine of his intent;[25]
Yet wist I never[26] well what that he meant."

"What that I meanë, sweetë heartë dear?"
Quoth Troilus, "O goodly, fresh, and free!
That, with the streamës[27] of your eyne so clear,
Ye wouldë sometimes on me rue and see,[28]
And then agreën[29] that I may be he,
Withoutë branch of vice, in any wise,
In truth alway to do you my servíce,

"As to my lady chief, and right resort,
With all my wit and all my diligence;
And for to have, right as you list, comfórt;
Under your yerd,[30] equal to mine offence,
As death,[31] if that I breakë your defence;[32]
And that ye deignë me so much honoúr,
Me to commanden aught in any hour.

"And I to be your very humble, true,
Secret, and in my painës[33] patiént,
And evermore desirë, freshly new,
To serven, and be alike diligent,
And, with good heart, all wholly your talént[34]
Receive in gree,[35] how sorë that me smart;
Lo, this mean I, mine owen sweetë heart."

. . . .

With that she gan her eyen on him cast,
Full easily and full debonairly,[36]
Advising her, and hied not too fast,[37]
With ne'er a word, but said him softëly,
"Mine honour safe, I will well truëly,
And in such form as ye can now devise,
Receivë him[38] fully to my servíce;

"Beseeching him, for Goddë's love, that he
Would, in honoúr of truth and gentleness,
As I well mean, eke meanë well to me;
And mine honoúr, with wit and business,[39]
Aye keep; and if I may do him gladnéss,
From hencëforth, y-wis I will not feign:
Now be all whole, no longer do ye plain.

1 Then. 2 Two.
3 Protection. 4 Beseech from you.
5 Nor could he answer one word for shame (at the stratagem that brought Cressida to implore his protection). 6 Known by heart.
7 Though he was not over-forward.
8 Confession (of his love).
9 That is, to be rash and ill-advised in his declarations of love and worship.
10 Becomingly. 11 Yielded, submissive.
12 The first word of all that escaped him.
13 Stopped. 14 Express.
15 As far as I am able. 16 Buried.
17 Avenge. 18 Die.
19 As if he would turn to water; so, in The Squire's Tale, did Canace weep for the woes of the falcon (note 10, page 120).
20 In woeful plight. 21 Urged, prompted.
22 Put him out of pain, by granting his desire.
23 Go. 24 Pity.
25 Sum, end, of his desire.
26 Never hitherto knew I.
27 Beams, glances. 28 Have pity and look.
29 Take it in good part, vouchsafe.
30 Correction, chastisement.
31 Even were it death.
32 If I transgress in whatever you may forbid; French, "defendre," to prohibit.
33 Sufferings. 34 Inclination, will.
35 With gladness, in good part.
36 Full softly and full graciously.
37 Bethinking her, and not making too great haste.
38 Troilus. These lines and the succeeding stanza are addressed to Pandarus, who had interposed some words of incitement to Cressida.
39 Wisdom and zeal.

"But, natheless, this warn I you," quoth she,
"A kingë's son although ye be, y-wis,
Ye shall no more have sovereignëty
Of me in love, than right in this case is;
Nor will I forbear, if ye do amiss,
To wrathë you,[1] and, while that ye me serve,
To cherish you, right after ye deserve.[2]

"And shortly, dearë heart, and all my knight,
Be glad, and drawë you to lustiness,[3]
And I shall truëly, with all my might,
Your bitter turnen all to sweetëness;
If I be she that may do you gladnéss,
For ev'ry woe ye shall recover a bliss:"
And him in armës took, and gan him kiss.

Pandarus, almost beside himself for joy, falls on his knees to thank Venus and Cupid, declaring that for this miracle he hears all the bells ring; then, with a warning to be ready at his call to meet at his house, he parts the lovers, and attends Cressida while she takes leave of the household—Troilus all the time groaning at the deceit practised on his brother and Helen. When he has got rid of them by feigning weariness, Pandarus returns to the chamber, and spends the night with him in converse. The zealous friend begins to speak "in a sober wise" to Troilus, reminding him of his love-pains now all at an end.

"So that through me thou standest now in way
To farë well;[4] I say it for no boast;
And know'st thou why? For, shame it is to say,
For thee have I begun a game to play,
Which that I never shall do eft[5] for other,[6]
Although he were a thousand fold my brother.

"That is to say, for thee I am become,
Betwixtë game and earnest, such a mean[7]
As makë women unto men to come;
Thou know'st thyselfë what that wouldë mean;
For thee have I my niece, of vices clean,[8]
So fully made thy gentleness[9] to trust,
That all shall be right as thyselfë lust.[10]

"But God, that all wot, take I to witnéss,
That never this for covetise[11] I wrought,
But only to abridgë[12] thy distress,
For which well nigh thou diedst, as me thought;
But, goodë brother, do now as thee ought,
For Goddë's love, and keep her out of blame;
Since thou art wise, so savë thou her name.

"For, well thou know'st, the namë yet of her,
Among the people, as who saith[13] hallow'd is;
For that man is unborn, I dare well swear,
That ever yet wist that she did amiss;
But woe is me, that I, that cause all this,
May thinkë that she is my niecë dear,
And I her eme, and traitor eke y-fere.[14]

"And were it wist that I, through mine engíne,[15]
Had in my niecë put this fantasý[16]
To do thy lust,[17] and wholly to be thine,
Why, all the people would upon it cry,
And say, that I the worstë treacherý
Did in this case, that ever was begun,
And she fordone, and thou right naught y-won."[18]

Therefore, ere going a step further, Pandarus prays Troilus to give him pledges of secrecy, and impresses on his mind the mischiefs that flow from vaunting in affairs of love. "Of kind,"[19] he says, no vaunter is to be believed:

"For a vaunter and a liar all is one;
As thus: I pose[20] a woman granteth me
Her love, and saith that other will she none,
And I am sworn to holden it secré,
And, after, I go tell it two or three;
Y-wis, I am a vaunter, at the least,
And eke a liar, for I break my hest.[21]

"Now lookë then, if they be not to blame,
Such manner folk; what shall I call them, what?
That them avaunt of women, and by name,
That never yet behight[22] them this nor that,
Nor knowë them no more than mine old hat?
No wonder is, so God me sendë heal,[23]
Though women dreadë with us men to deal!

"I say not this for no mistrust of you,
Nor for no wise men, but for foolës nice;[24]
And for the harm that in the world is now,
As well for folly oft as for malíce;
For well wot I, that in wise folk that vice
No woman dreads, if she be well advised;
For wise men be by foolës' harm chastised."[25]

So Pandarus begs Troilus to keep silent, promises to be true all his days, and assures him that he shall have all that he will in the love of Cressida: "thou knowest what thy lady granted thee; and day is set the charters up to make."

Who mightë tellë half the joy and feast
Which that the soul of Troilus then felt,
Hearing th' effect of Pandarus' behest?
His oldë woe, that made his heartë swelt,[26]
Gan then for joy to wasten and to melt,
And all the reheating[27] of his sighës sore
At onës fled, he felt of them no more.

1 Be angry with you, chide you.
2 According to your desert.
3 Pleasantness.
4 In a fair way to be prosperous (in love).
5 Again.
6 Another.
7 An instrument; a procurer.
8 Pure, devoid.
9 Nobleness of nature.
10 As thou wilt.
11 Greed of gain.
12 Cut short, abate.
13 As who should say; as it were.
14 Her uncle and betrayer both in one.
15 Arts, contrivance.
16 Fancy.
17 Pleasure.
18 She would be ruined, and thou wouldst have won nothing.
19 By his very nature.
20 Suppose, assume.
21 Promise. In "The Court of Love," the poet says of Avaunter, that "his ancestry of kin was to Liér; and the stanza in which that line occurs (page 209) expresses precisely the same idea as in the text. Vain boasters of ladies' favours are also satirised in "The House of Fame;" page 243.
23 Prosperity.
22 Promised (—much less granted).
24 Silly, stupid; French, "niais."
25 Corrected, instructed.
26 Faint, die.
27 The hotness: "reheating" is read by preference for "richesse," which stands in the older printed

But right so as these holtës and these hayës,[1]
That have in winter deadë been and dry,
Revestë them in greenë, when that May is,
When ev'ry lusty listeth best to play;[2]
Right in that selfë wisë, sooth to say,
Wax'd suddenly his heartë full of joy,
That gladder was there never man in Troy.

Troilus solemnly swears that never, "for all the good that God made under sun," will he reveal what Pandarus asks him to keep secret; offering to die a thousand times, if need were, and to follow his friend as a slave all his life, in proof of his gratitude.

"But here, with all my heart, I thee beseech,
That never in me thou deemë such folly[3]
As I shall say; me thoughtë, by thy speech,
That this which thou me dost for company,[4]
I shouldë ween it were a bawdery;
I am not wood, all if I lewëd be;[5]
It is not one,[6] that wot I well, pardie!

"But he that goes for gold, or for richéss,
On such messáges, call him as thee lust;
And this that thou dost, call it gentleness,
Compassión, and fellowship, and trust;
Depart[7] it so, for widëwhere is wist[8]
How that there is diversity requer'd
Betwixtë thingës like, as I have lear'd.[9]

"And that thou know I think it not nor ween,[10]
That this service a shame be or a jape,[11]
I have my fairë sister Polyxene,
Cassandr', Heléne, or any of the frape;[12]
Be she never so fair, or well y-shape,
Tellë me which thou wilt of ev'ry one,
To have for thine, and let me then alone."[13]

Then, beseeching Pandarus soon to perform out the great emprise of crowning his love for Cressida, Troilus bade his friend good night. On the morrow Troilus burned as the fire, for hope and pleasure; yet "he not forgot his wisë governance;"[14]

But in himself with manhood gan restrain
Each rakel[15] deed, and each unbridled cheer,[16]
That allë those that livë, sooth to sayn,
Should not have wist, by word or by mannére,
What that he meant, as touching this mattére;
From ev'ry wight as far as is the cloud
He was, so well dissimulate he could.

And all the whilë that I now devise,[17]
This was his life: with all his fullë might,
By day he was in Martë's high service,
That is to say, in armës as a knight;
And, for the mostë part, the longë night
He lay, and thought how that he mightë serve
His lady best, her thank[18] for to deserve.

I will not swear, although he layë soft,
That in his thought he n' as somewhat diseas'd;[19]
Nor that he turned on his pillows oft,
And would of that him missed have been seis'd;[20]
But in such case men be not alway pleas'd,
For aught I wot, no morë than was he;
That can I deem[21] of possibility.

But certain is, to purpose for to go,
That in this while, as written is in gest,[22]
He saw his lady sometimes, and alsó
She with him spake, when that she durst and lest;[23]
And, by their both advice,[24] as was the best,
Appointed full warily[25] in this need,
So as they durst, how far they would proceed.

But it was spoken in so short a wise,
In such await alway, and in such fear,[26]
Lest any wight divinen or devise[27]
Would of their speech, or to it lay an ear,
That all this world them not so lefë[28] were,
As that Cupído would them gracë send
To maken of their speeches right an end.

But thilkë[29] little that they spake or wrought,
His wisë ghost[30] took ay of all such heed,
It seemed her he wistë what she thought
Withoutë word, so that it was no need
To bid him aught to do, nor aught forbid;
For which she thought that love, all came it late,
Of allë joy had open'd her the gate.[31]

Troilus, by his discretion, his secrecy, and his devotion, made ever a deeper lodgment in Cressida's heart; so that she thanked God twenty thousand times that she had met with a man who, as she felt, "was to her a wall of steel, and shield from ev'ry displeasánce;" while Pandarus ever actively fanned the fire. So passed a "timë sweet" of tranquil and harmonious love; the only drawback being, that the lovers might not often meet, "nor leisure have, their speeches to fulfil." At last Pandarus found an occasion for bringing them together at his house unknown to anybody, and put his plan in execution.

For he, with great deliberatión,
Had ev'ry thing that hereto might avail[32]
Forecast, and put in executión,
And neither left[33] for cost nor for traváil;[34]
Come if them list, them shouldë nothing fail,

editions; though "richesse" certainly better represents the word used in the original of Boccaccio—"dovizia," meaning abundance or wealth.

1 Woods or groves, and hedges.
2 When it best pleases every pleasant (wight, thing) to sport.
3 Judge such folly (to exist).
4 Comradeship, friendship.
5 I am not mad, although I may be unlearned.
6 It is not a bawd's act.
7 Make this distinction.
8 It is universally known. 9 Learned.
10 Suppose. 11 A subject for jeering.
12 The set, or company; French, "frappe," a stamp (on coins), a set (of moulds).
13 To accomplish thy desire.
14 Control (of himself). 15 Rash, ill-advised.
16 Gesture, demeanour. 17 Of which I now tell.
18 Grateful favour. 19 Was not somewhat troubled.
20 Would fain have possessed that which he missed—that is, his lady. 21 Judge.
22 In the history of the events. 23 Pleased.
24 Consultation, opinion.
25 Made very careful preparations or resolves.
26 So briefly, with so much vigilance, and in such fear (of observation).
27 Conjecture or divine. 28 Dear.
29 That. 30 Spirit.
31 Love, though late come, had opened to her the gate of all joy.
32 Be of service, aid.
33 Left anything undone. 34 Labour.

Nor for to be in aught espied there,
That wistë he an impossible were.[1]

And dreadëless[2] it clear was in the wind
Of ev'ry pie, and every let-game;[3]
Now all is well, for all this world is blind,
In this mattérë, bothë fremd and tame;[4]
This timber is all ready for to frame;
Us lacketh naught, but that we weetë wo'ld[5]
A certain hour in which we comë sho'ld.

Troilus had informed his household, that if at any time he was missing, he had gone to worship at a certain temple of Apollo, "and first to see the holy laurel quake, or that the goddë spake out of the tree." So, at the changing of the moon, when "the welkin shope him for to rain,"[6] Pandarus went to invite his niece to supper; solemnly assuring her that Troilus was out of the town—though all the time he was safely shut up, till midnight, in "a little stew," whence through a hole he joyously watched the arrival of his mistress and her fair niece Antigoné, with half a score of her women. After supper Pandarus did everything to amuse his niece; "he sung, he play'd, he told a tale of Wade;"[7] at last she would take her leave; but

The bentë Moonë with her hornës pale,
Satúrn, and Jòve, in Cancer joined were,[8]
That madë such a rain from heav'n avail,[9]
That ev'ry manner woman that was there
Had of this smoky[10] rain a very fear;
At which Pandarus laugh'd, and saidë then,
"Now were it time a lady to go hen!"[11]

He therefore presses Cressida to remain all night; she complies with a good grace; and after the sleeping cup has gone round, all retire to their chambers—Cressida, that she may not be disturbed by the rain and thunder, being lodged in the "inner closet" of Pandarus, who, to lull suspicion, occupies the outer chamber, his niece's women sleeping in the intermediate apartment. When all is quiet, Pandarus liberates Troilus, and by a secret passage brings him to the chamber of Cressida; then, going forward alone to his niece, after calming her fears of discovery, he tells her that her lover has "through a gutter, by a privy went,"[12] come to his house in all this rain, mad with grief because a friend has told him that she loves Horastes. Suddenly cold about her heart, Cressida promises that on the morrow she will reassure her lover; but Pandarus scouts the notion of delay, laughs to scorn her proposal to send her ring in pledge of her truth, and finally, by pitiable accounts of Troilus' grief, induces her to receive him and reassure him at once with her own lips.

This Troilus full soon on knees him set,
Full soberly, right by her beddë's head,
And in his bestë wise his lady gret;[13]
But Lord! how she wax'd suddenly all red,
And thought anon how that she would be dead;
She couldë not one word aright out bring,
So suddenly for his sudden coming.

Cressida, though thinking that her servant and her knight should not have doubted her truth, yet sought to remove his jealousy, and offered to submit to any ordeal or oath he might impose; then, weeping, she covered her face, and lay silent. "But now," exclaims the poet—

But now help, God, to quenchen all this
    sorrow!
So hope I that he shall, for he best may;
For I have seen, of a full misty morrow,[14]
Followen oft a merry summer's day,
And after winter cometh greenë May;
Folk see all day, and eke men read in stories,
That after sharpë stourës[15] be victóries.

Believing his mistress to be angry, Troilus felt the cramp of death seize on his heart, "and down he fell all suddenly in swoon." Pandarus "into bed him cast," and called on his niece to pull out the thorn that stuck in his heart, by promising that she would "all forgive." She whispered in his ear the assurance that she was not wroth; and at last, under her caresses, he recovered consciousness, to find her arm laid over him, to hear the assurance of her forgiveness, and receive her frequent kisses. Fresh vows and explanations passed; and Cressida implored forgiveness of "her own sweet heart," for the pain she had caused him. Surprised with sudden bliss, Troilus put all in God's hand, and strained his lady fast in his arms. "What might or may the seely[16] larkë say, when that the sperhawk[17] hath him in his foot?"

Cressída, which that felt her thus y-take,
As writë clerkës in their bookës old,
Right as an aspen leaf began to quake,
When she him felt her in his armës fold;
But Troilus, all whole of carës cold,[18]
Gan thankë then the blissful goddës seven.[19]
Thus sundry painës bringë folk to heaven.

1 And he knew that it was impossible that they could be discovered there.
2 Without doubt.
3 To be "in the wind" of noisy magpies, or other birds that might spoil sport by alarming the game, was not less desirable than to be on the "lee-side" of the game itself, that the hunter's presence might not be betrayed by the scent. "In the wind of," thus signifies *not* to windward of, but to leeward of—that is, in the wind that comes *from* the object of pursuit.
4 Both foes and friends—literally, both wild and tame, the sporting metaphor being sustained.
5 The lovers are supposed to say, that nothing is wanting but to know the time at which they should meet.
6 When the sky was preparing to rain.
7 See note 16, page 106.
8 A conjunction that imported rain.
9 Descend.
10 An admirably graphic description of dense rain.
11 Hence.
12 Secret way or passage.
13 Greeted.
14 Morn.
15 Conflicts, struggles.
16 Innocent, harmless.
17 Sparrowhawk.
18 Entirely healed from his painful sorrows. For the force of "cold," see note 2, page 169.
19 The divinities who gave their names to the seven planets, which, in association with the seven metals, are mentioned in The Canon's Yeoman's Tale, page 180.

This Troilus her gan in armës strain,
And said, "O sweet, as ever may I go'n,[1]
Now be ye caught, now here is but we twain,
Now yieldë you, for other boot[2] is none."
To that Cresside answered thus anon,
"N' had I ere now, my sweetë heartë dear,
Been yolden,[3] y-wis, I werë now not here!"

O sooth is said, that healed for to be
Of a fever, or other great sicknéss,
Men mustë drink, as we may often see,
Full bitter drink; and for to have gladnéss
Men drinken often pain and great distress!
I mean it here, as for this adventúre,
That thorough pain hath founden all his cure.

And now sweetnessë seemeth far more sweet,
That bitterness assayed[4] was beforn;
For out of woe in blissë now they fleet,[5]
None such they feltë since that they were born;
Now is it better than both two were lorn![6]
For love of God, take ev'ry woman heed
To workë thus, if it come to the need!

Cresside, all quit from ev'ry dread and teen,[7]
As she that justë cause had him to trust,
Made him such feast,[8] it joy was for to see'n,
When she his truth and intent cleanë wist;[9]
And as about a tree, with many a twist,
Bitrent and writhen[10] is the sweet woodbind,
Gan each of them in armës other wind.[11]

And as the new abashed nightingale,[12]
That stinteth,[13] first when she beginneth sing,
When that she heareth any herdë's tale,[14]
Or in the hedges any wight stirring;
And, after, sicker[15] out her voice doth ring;
Right so Cressida, when her dreadë stent,[16]
Open'd her heart, and told him her intent.[17]

And right as he that sees his death y-shapen,[18]
And dien must, in aught that he may guess,[19]
And suddenly rescousë doth him escapen,[20]
And from his death is brought in sickerness;[21]
For all the world, in such presént gladness
Was Troilus, and had his lady sweet;
With worsë hap God let us never meet!

Her armës small, her straightë back and soft,
Her sidës longë, fleshly, smooth, and white,
He gan to stroke; and good thrift[22] bade full oft
On her snow-white throat, her breastës round and lite;[23]
Thus in this heaven he gan him delight,
And therewithal a thousand times her kist,
That what to do for joy unneth he wist.[24]

The lovers exchanged vows, and kisses, and embraces, and speeches of exalted love, and rings; Cressida gave to Troilus a brooch of gold and azure, "in which a ruby set was like a heart;" and the too short night passed.

"When that the cock, commúne astrologer,[25]
Gan on his breast to beat, and after crow,
And Lucifer, the dayë's messenger,
Gan for to rise, and out his beamës throw;
And eastward rose, to him that could it know,
Fortuna Major,[26] then anon Cresseide,
With heartë sore, to Troilus thus said:

"My heartë's life, my trust, and my pleasánce!
That I was born, alas! that me is woe,
That day of us must make disseverance!
For time it is to rise, and hence to go,
Or else I am but lost for evermo'.
O Night! alas! why n' ilt thou o'er us hove,[27]
As long as when Alcmena lay by Jove?[28]

"O blackë Night! as folk in bookës read,
That shapen[29] art by God, this world to hide,
At certain timës, with thy darkë weed,[30]
That under it men might in rest abide,
Well oughtë beastës plain, and folkë chide,
That where as Day with labour would us brest,[31]
There thou right flee'st, and deignest[32] not us rest.

"Thou dost, alas! so shortly thine office,[33]
Thou rakel[34] Night! that God,[35] maker of kind,
Thee for thy haste and thine unkindë vice,
So fast ay to our hemispherë bind,
That never more under the ground thou wind;[36]
For through thy rakel hieing[37] out of Troy
Have I forgone[38] thus hastily my joy!"

This Troilus, that with these wordës felt,
As thought him then, for piteous distress,
The bloody tearës from his heartë melt,
As he that never yet such heaviness
Assayed had out of so great gladnéss,
Gan therewithal Cresside, his lady dear,
In armës strain, and said in this mannére:

"O cruel Day! accuser of the joy
That Night and Love have stol'n, and fast y-wrien![39]
Accursed be thy coming into Troy!

1 Prosper. 2 Remedy, resource.
3 If I had not yielded myself ere now.
4 Experienced, tasted. See note 8, page 116.
5 Float, swim.
6 Better this happy issue, than that both two should be lost (through the sorrow of fruitless love).
7 Freed from every doubt and pain.
8 "Lui fit fête"—made holiday for him.
9 Knew his truth and the purity of his purpose.
10 Plaited and wreathed. 11 Embrace, encircle.
12 The newly-arrived and timid nightingale.
13 Stops. 14 The talking of any shepherd.
15 With confidence; clearly and surely.
16 When her doubt had ceased to affect her.
17 Mind. 18 Prepared.
19 For all that he can tell.
20 Rescue causeth him to escape. 21 Safety.
22 Blessing, prosperity. 23 Small.
24 He hardly knew.
25 The cock is called, in "The Assembly of Fowls," "the horologe of thorpës lite;" and in The Nun's Priest's Tale Chanticleer knew by nature each ascension of the equinoctial, and, when the sun had ascended fifteen degrees, "then crew he, that it might not be amended." Here he is termed the "common astrologer," as employing for the public advantage his knowledge of astronomy.
26 The planet Jupiter.
27 Why wilt not thou hover over us?
28 When Jupiter visited Alcmena in the form of her husband Amphitryon, he is said to have prolonged the night to the length of three natural nights. Hercules was the fruit of the union.
29 Appointed. 30 Robe.
31 Burst, overcome. 32 Grantest.
33 Performest thy duty in so short a time.
34 Rash, hasty. 35 Would that God would, &c.
36 Turn, revolve. 37 Hasting.
38 Lost.
39 Closely concealed.

For ev'ry bow'r[1] hath one of thy bright eyen:
Envious Day! Why list thee to espyen?
What hast thou lost? Why seekest thou this place?
There God thy light so quenchë, for his grace!

"Alas! what have these lovers thee aguilt?[2]
Dispiteous[3] Day, thine be the pains of hell!
For many a lover hast thou slain, and wilt;
Thy peering in will nowhere let them dwell:
What! proff'rest thou thy light here for to sell?
Go sell it them that smallë sealës grave![4]
We will thee not, us needs no day to have."

And eke the Sunnë, Titan, gan he chide,
And said, "O fool! well may men thee despise!
That hast the Dawning[5] all night thee beside,
And suff'rest her so soon up from thee rise,
For to disease[6] us lovers in this wise!
What! hold[7] thy bed, both thou, and eke thy Morrow!
I biddë[8] God so give you bothë sorrow!"

The lovers part with many sighs and protestations of unswerving and undying love; Cressida responding to the vows of Troilus with the assurance—

"That first shall Phœbus[9] fallë from his sphere,
And heaven's eagle be the dovë's fere,
And ev'ry rock out of his placë start,
Ere Troilus out of Cressída's heart."

When Pandarus visits Troilus in his palace later in the day, he warns him not to mar his bliss by any fault of his own:

"For, of Fortúnë's sharp adversity,
The worstë kind of infortúne is this,
A man to have been in prosperity,
And it remember when it passed is.[10]
Thou art wise enough; forthy,[11] do not amiss;
Be not too rakel,[12] though thou sittë warm;
For if thou be, certain it will thee harm.

"Thou art at ease, and hold thee well therein;
For, all so sure as red is ev'ry fire,
As great a craft is to keep weal as win;[13]
Bridle alway thy speech and thy desire,
For worldly joy holds not but by a wire;
That proveth well, it breaks all day so oft,
Forthy need is to workë with it soft."

Troilus sedulously observes the counsel; and the lovers have many renewals of their pleasure, and of their bitter chidings of the Day. The effects of love on Troilus are altogether refining and ennobling; as may be inferred from the song which he sung often to Pandarus:

The Second Song of Troilus.

"Love, that of Earth and Sea hath governance!
Love, that his hestës[14] hath in Heaven high!
Love, that with a right wholesome álliánce
Holds people joined, as him list them guy![15]
Lovë, that knitteth law and companý,
And couples doth in virtue for to dwell,
Bind this accord, that I have told, and tell!

"That the worldë, with faith which that is stable,
Diverseth so, his stoundës accordíng;[16]
That elementës, that be discordáble,[17]
Holden a bond perpetually duríng;
That Phœbus may his rosy day forth bring;
And that the Moon hath lordship o'er the night;—
All this doth Love, ay heried[18] be his might!

"That the sea, which that greedy is to flowen,
Constraineth to a certain endë[19] so
His floodës, that so fiercely they not growen
To drenchen[20] earth and all for evermo';
And if that Love aught let his bridle go,
All that now loves asunder shouldë leap,
And lost were all that Love holds now to heap.[21]

"So wouldë God, that author is of kind,
That with his bond Love of his virtue list
To cherish heartës, and all fast to bind,
That from his bond no wight the way out wist!
And heartës cold, them would I that he twist,[22]
To make them love; and that him list ay rue[23]
On heartës sore, and keep them that be true."

But Troilus' love had higher fruits than singing:

In allë needës for the townë's werre[24]
He was, and ay the first in armës dight,[25]
And certainly, but if that bookës err,
Save Hector, most y-dread[26] of any wight;
And this increase of hardiness[27] and might
Came him of love, his lady's grace to win,
That altered his spirit so within.

In time of truce, a-hawking would he ride,
Or ellës hunt the boarë, bear, lioún;
The smallë beastës let he go beside;[28]
And when he came riding into the town,
Full oft his lady, from her window down,
As fresh as falcon coming out of mew,[29]
Full ready was him goodly to salue.[30]

And most of love and virtue was his speech,
And in despite he had all wretchedness;[31]

1 Chamber. 2 Offended, sinned against.
3 Cruel, spiteful. 4 That cut devices on small seals.
5 Chaucer seems to confound Titan, the title of the sun, with Tithonus (or Tithon, as contracted in poetry), whose couch Aurora was wont to share. 6 Annoy.
7 Keep. 8 Pray. 9 The Sun.
10 So, in "Locksley Hall," Tennyson says that "a sorrow's crown of sorrow is rememb'ring better things." The original is in Dante's words:

—"Nessun maggior dolore
Che ricordarsi del tempo felice
Nella miseria."—"Inferno," v. 121.

11 Therefore. 12 Rash, over-hasty.
13 It needs as much skill to keep prosperity as to attain it.
14 Commandments. 15 Guide.
16 Diversifieth so, according to its seasons.
17 That are in themselves discordant.
18 Praised. 19 Limit.
20 Drown, submerge.
21 Together. See the reference to Boethius in note 3, page 46. 22 Turned. 23 Have pity.
24 War. 25 Equipped, prepared.
26 Dreaded. 27 Courage.
28 A charming touch, indicative of the noble and generous inspiration of his love.
29 The cage or chamber in which hawks were kept and carefully tended during the moulting season.
30 Salute.
31 He held in scorn all despicable actions.

And doubtless no need was him to beseech
To honour them that haddë worthiness,
And easë them that weren in distress;
And glad was he, if any wight well far'd,
That lover was, when he it wist or heard.

For he held every man lost unless he were in Love's service; and, so did the power of Love work within him, that he was ay humble and benign, and "pride, envy, ire, and avarice, he gan to flee, and ev'ry other vice."

The Fourth Book.

A brief Proem to the Fourth Book prepares us for the treachery of Fortune to Troilus; from whom she turned away her bright face, and took of him no heed, "and cast him clean out of his lady's grace, and on her wheel she set up Diomede." Then the narrative describes a skirmish in which the Trojans were worsted, and Antenor, with many of less note, remained in the hands of the Greeks. A truce was proclaimed for the exchange of prisoners; and as soon as Calchas heard the news, he came to the assembly of the Greeks, to "bid a boon." Having gained audience, he reminded the besiegers how he had come from Troy to aid and encourage them in their enterprise; willing to lose all that he had in the city, except his daughter Cressida, whom he bitterly reproached himself for leaving behind. And now, with streaming tears and pitiful prayer, he besought them to exchange Antenor for Cressida; assuring them that the day was at hand when they should have both town and people. The soothsayer's petition was granted; and the ambassadors charged to negotiate the exchange, entering the city, told their errand to King Priam and his parliament.

This Troilus was present in the place
When asked was for Antenor Cresside;
For which to changë soon began his face,
As he that with the wordës well nigh died;
But natheless he no word to it seid;[1]
Lest men should his affectión espy,
With mannë's heart he gan his sorrows drie;[2]

And, full of anguish and of grisly dread,
Abode what other lords would to it say,
And if they wouldë grant,—as God forbid!—
Th' exchange of her, then thought he thingës
 tway:[3]
First, for to save her honour; and what way
He mightë best th' exchange of her withstand;
This cast he then how all this mightë stand.

Love made him allë prest to do her bide,[4]
And rather die than that she shouldë go;
But Reason said him, on the other side,
"Without th' assent of her, do thou not so,
Lest for thy workë she would be thy foe;
And say, that through thy meddling is y-blow[5]
Your bothë love,[6] where it was erst unknow."[7]

For which he gan deliberate for the best,
That though the lordës wouldë that she went,
He wouldë suffer them grant what them lest,[8]
And tell his lady first what that they meant;
And, when that she had told him her intent,
Thereafter[9] would he worken all so blive,[10]
Though all the world against it wouldë strive.

Hector, which that full well the Greekës heard,
For Antenor how they would have Cresseide,
Gan it withstand, and soberly answér'd;
"Sirs, she is no prisoner," [thus] he said;
"I know not on you who this chargë laid;
But, for my part, ye may well soon him tell,
We usë[11] here no women for to sell."

The noise of the people then upstart at once,
As breme[12] as blaze of straw y-set on fire;
For Infortunë[13] wouldë for the nonce
They shouldë their confusión desire:
"Hector," quoth they, "what ghost[14] may you
 inspire
This woman thus to shield, and do[15] us lose
Dan Antenor?—a wrong way now ye choose,—

"That is so wise, and eke so bold baroún;
And we have need of folk, as men may see;
He eke is one the greatest of this town;
O Hector! lettë such fantásies be!
O King Priám!" quoth they, "lo! thus say we,
That all our will is to forego Cresseide;"
And to deliver Antenor they pray'd.

Though Hector often prayed them "nay," it was resolved that Cressida should be given up for Antenor; then the parliament dispersed. Troilus hastened home to his chamber, shut himself up alone, and threw himself on his bed.

And as in winter leavës be bereft,
Each after other, till the tree be bare,
So that there is but bark and branch y-left,
Lay Troilus, bereft of each welfáre,
Y-bounden in the blackë bark of care,
Disposed wood out of his wit to braid,[16]
So sore him sat[17] the changing of Cresseide.

He rose him up, and ev'ry door he shet,[18]
And window eke; and then this sorrowful man
Upon his beddë's side adown him set,
Full like a dead imágë, pale and wan,
And in his breast the heaped woe began
Out burst, and he to worken in this wise,
In his woodnéss,[19] as I shall you devise.[20]

Right as the wildë bull begins to spring,
Now here, now there, y-darted[21] to the heart,
And of his death roareth in complaining;
Right so gan he about the chamber start,
Smiting his breast aye with his fistës smart;[22]
His head to the wall, his body to the ground,
Full oft he swapt,[23] himselfë to confound.

1 Said. 2 Dree, endure. 3 Two.
4 All eager to make her remain (in the city).
5 Divulged, blown abroad.
6 The love of you both. 7 Formerly unknown.
8 What they pleased.
9 That is, according to her wish.
10 Speedily, with alacrity.

11 Are used, accustomed. 12 Violent, furious.
13 Misfortune. 14 Spirit.
15 Make. 16 To go out of his senses.
17 So ill did he bear. 18 Shut.
19 Madness. 20 Relate.
21 Pierced with a dart. 22 Painfully, cruelly.
23 Struck, dashed.

His eyen then, for pity of his heart,
Out streameden as swiftë wellës[1] tway;
The highë sobbës of his sorrow's smart
His speech him reft; unnethës[2] might he say,
"O Death, alas! why n' ilt thou do me dey?[3]
Accursed be that day which that Natúre
Shope[4] me to be a living creatúre!"

Bitterly reviling Fortune, and calling on Love to explain why his happiness with Cressida should be thus repealed, Troilus declares that, while he lives, he will bewail his misfortune in solitude, and will never see it shine or rain, but will end his sorrowful life in darkness, and die in distress.

"O weary ghost, that errest to and fro!
Why n' ilt[5] thou fly out of the woefulest
Body that ever might on groundë go?
O soulë, lurking in this woeful nest!
Flee forth out of my heart, and let it brest,[6]
And follow alway Cressíde, thy lady dear!
Thy rightë place is now no longer here.

"O woeful eyen two! since your disport[7]
Was all to see Cressída's eyen bright,
What shall ye do, but, for my discomfórt,
Standë for naught, and weepen out your sight,
Since she is quench'd, that wont was you to light?
In vain, from this forth, have I eyen tway
Y-formed, since your virtue is away!

"O my Cressíde! O lady sovereign
Of thilkë[8] woeful soulë that now cryeth!
Who shall now givë comfort to thy pain?
Alas! no wight; but, when my heartë dieth,
My spirit, which that so unto you hieth,[9]
Receive in gree,[10] for that shall ay you serve;
Forthy no force is[11] though the bódy sterve.[12]

"O ye lovers, that high upon the wheel
Be set of Fortune, in good adventúre,
God lenë[13] that ye find ay love of steel,[14]
And longë may your life in joy endure!
But when ye comë by my sepulture,[15]
Remember that your fellow resteth there;
For I lov'd eke, though I unworthy were.

"O old, unwholesome, and mislived man,
Calchas I mean, alas! what ailed thee
To be a Greek, since thou wert born Troján?
O Calchas! which that will my banë[16] be,
In cursëd timë wert thou born for me!
As wouldë blissful Jovë, for his joy,
That I thee haddë where I would in Troy!"

Soon Troilus, through excess of grief, fell into a trance; in which he was found by Pandarus, who had gone almost distracted at the news that Cressida was to be exchanged for Antenor. At his friend's arrival, Troilus "gan as the snow against the sun to melt;" the two mingled their tears a while; then Pandarus strove to comfort the woeful lover. He admitted that never had a stranger ruin than this been wrought by Fortune:

"But tell me this, why thou art now so mad
To sorrow thus? Why li'st thou in this wise,
Since thy desire all wholly hast thou had,
So that by right it ought enough suffice?
But I, that never felt in my servíce[17]
A friendly cheer or looking of an eye,
Let me thus weep and wail until I die.

"And over all this, as thou well wost[18] thyselve,
This town is full of ladies all about,
And, to my doom,[19] fairer than suchë twelve
As ever she was, shall I find in some rout,[20]
Yea! one or two, withouten any doubt:
Forthy[21] be glad, mine owen dearë brother!
If she be lost, we shall recover another.

"What! God forbid alway that each pleasánce
In one thing were, and in none other wight;
If one can sing, another can well dance;
If this be goodly, she is glad and light;
And this is fair, and that can good[22] aright;
Each for his virtue holden is full dear,
Both heroner, and falcon for rivére.[23]

"And eke as writ Zausis,[24] that was full wise,
The newë love out chaseth oft the old,
And upon new case lieth new advice;[25]
Think eke thy life to savë thou art hold;[26]
Such fire by process shall of kindë cold;[27]
For, since it is but casual pleasánce,
Some case[28] shall put it out of remembránce.

"For, all so sure as day comes after night,
The newë love, labour, or other woe,
Or ellës seldom seeing of a wight,
Do old affectións all over go;[29]
And for thy part, thou shalt have one of tho[30]
T' abridgë with thy bitter painë's smart;
Absence of her shall drive her out of heart."

These wordës said he for the nonës all,[31]
To help his friend, lest he for sorrow died;
For, doubtëless, to do his woe to fall,[32]
He raughtë[33] not what unthrift[34] that he said;
But Troilus, that nigh for sorrow died,
Took little heed of all that ever he meant;
One ear it heard, at th' other out it went.

But, at the last, he answer'd and said, "Friend,
This leachcraft, or y-healed thus to be,
Were well sitting[35] if that I were a fiend,
To traisen[36] her that true is unto me;

1 Fountains. 2 Scarcely.
3 Why wilt thou not make me die?
4 Shaped, appointed. 5 Wilt not.
6 Burst, break. 7 Delight.
8 This. 9 Hasteneth.
10 With favour. 11 Therefore no matter.
12 Die. 13 Lend, grant.
14 Love as true as steel. 15 Sepulchre.
16 Destruction.
17 Pandarus, as it repeatedly appears, was an unsuccessful lover. 18 Knowest.
19 In my judgment. 20 Company.
21 Therefore. 22 Knows what is virtuous.

23 That is, each is esteemed for a special virtue or faculty, as the large gerfalcon for the chase of heron, the smaller goshawk for the chase of river fowl.
24 An author of whom no record survives.
25 New counsels must be adopted as new circumstances arise. 26 Bound.
27 Shall grow cold by process of nature.
28 Chance. 29 Overcome.
30 One of those (means of alleviation).
31 Only for the nonce.
32 To cause his woe to subside.
33 Recked. 34 Folly.
35 Becoming. 36 Betray.

I pray God, let this counsel never thé,[1]
But do me rather sterve[2] anon right here,
Ere I thus do, as thou me wouldest lear!"[3]

Troilus protests that his lady shall have him wholly hers till death; and, debating the counsels of his friend, declares that even if he would, he could not love another. Then he points out the folly of not lamenting the loss of Cressida because she had been his in ease and felicity—while Pandarus himself, though he thought it so light to change to and fro in love, had not done busily his might to change her that wrought him all the woe of his unprosperous suit.

"If thou hast had in love ay yet mischance,
And canst it not out of thine heartë drive,
I that lived in lust[4] and in pleasánce
With her, as much as creatúre alive,
How should I that forget, and that so blive?[5]
O where hast thou been so long hid in mew,[6]
That canst so well and formally argúe!"

The lover condemns the whole discourse of his friend as unworthy, and calls on Death, the ender of all sorrows, to come to him and quench his heart with his cold stroke. Then he distils anew in tears, "as liquor out of alembic;" and Pandarus is silent for a while, till he bethinks him to recommend to Troilus the carrying off of Cressida. "Art thou in Troy, and hast no hardiment[7] to take a woman which that loveth thee?" But Troilus reminds his counsellor that all the war had come from the ravishing of a woman by might (the abduction of Helen by Paris); and that it would not beseem him to withstand his father's grant, since the lady was to be changed for the town's good. He has dismissed the thought of asking Cressida from his father, because that would be to injure her fair fame, to no purpose, for Priam could not overthrow the decision of "so high a place as parliament;" while most of all he fears to perturb her heart with violence, to the slander of her name—for he must hold her honour dearer than himself in every case, as lovers ought of right:

"Thus am I in desire and reason twight:[8]
Desire, for to disturbë her, me redeth;[9]
And Reason will not, so my heartë dreadeth."[10]

Thus weeping, that he couldë never cease,
He said, "Alas! how shall I, wretchë, fare?
For well feel I alway my love increase,
And hope is less and less alway, Pandare!
Increasen eke the causes of my care;
So well-away! why n'ill my heartë brest?[11]
For us in love there is but little rest."

Pandare answered, "Friend, thou may'st for me
Do as thee list;[12] but had I it so hot,
And thine estate,[13] she shouldë go with me!
Though all this town cried on this thing by note,
I would not set at[14] all that noise a groat;
For when men have well cried, then will they rown,[15]
Eke wonder lasts but nine nights ne'er in town.

"Divinë not in reason ay so deep,
Nor courteously, but help thyself anon;
Bet is that others than thyselfë weep;
And namëly, since ye two be all one,
Rise up, for, by my head, she shall not go'n!
And rather be in blame a little found,
Than sterve here as a gnat,[16] withoutë wound!

"It is no shame unto you, nor no vice,
Her to withholdë, that ye loveth most;
Paráuntre[17] she might holdë thee for nice,[18]
To let her go thus unto the Greeks' host;
Think eke, Fortúne, as well thyselfë wost,
Helpeth the hardy man to his emprise,
And weiveth[19] wretches for their cowardice.

"And though thy lady would a lite her grieve,
Thou shalt thyself thy peace thereafter make;
But, as to me, certain I cannot 'lieve
That she would it as now for evil take:
Why shouldë then for fear thine heartë quake?
Think eke how Paris hath, that is thy brother,
A love; and why shalt thou not have another?

"And, Troilus, one thing I dare thee swear,
That if Cressída, which that is thy lief,[20]
Now loveth thee as well as thou dost her,
God help me so, she will not take agrief[21]
Though thou anon do boot[22] in this mischíef;
And if she willeth from thee for to pass,
Then is she false, so love her well the lass.[23]

"Forthy,[24] take heart, and think, right as a knight,
Through love is broken all day ev'ry law;
Kithe[25] now somewhat thy courage and thy might;
Have mercy on thyself, for any awe;[26]
Let not this wretched woe thine heartë gnaw;
But, manly, set the world on six and seven,[27]
And, if thou die a martyr, go to heaven."

Pandarus promises his friend all aid in the enterprise; it is agreed that Cressida shall be carried off, but only with her own consent; and Pandarus sets out for his niece's house, to arrange an interview. Meantime Cressida has heard the news; and, caring nothing for her father, but everything for Troilus, she burns in love and fear, unable to tell what she shall do.

But, as men see in town, and all about,
That women usë[28] friendës to visíte,
So to Cressíde of women came a rout,[29]

1 Thrive. 2 Die. 3 Teach.
4 Delight. 5 Quickly.
6 Den, place remote from the world—of which thou thus betrayest ignorance. 7 Daring, boldness.
8 Twisted, pulled contrary ways.
9 Counseleth. 10 Is in doubt.
11 Why will not my heart break?
12 As thou pleasest.
13 If I loved so hotly, and were of the same rank as thou.
14 Value. 15 Whisper.

16 Perish like a gnat or fly, by simply pining away.
17 Peradventure. 18 Foolish.
19 Forsaketh. 20 Love.
21 Amiss. 22 Provide a remedy immediately.
23 Less. 24 Therefore. 25 Show.
26 In spite of any fear (of consequences).
27 The modern phrase "sixes and sevens," means "in confusion:" but here the idea of gaming perhaps suits the sense better—"set the world upon a cast of the dice."
28 Are accustomed. 29 Troop.

For piteous joy, and weened her delight,[1]
And with their talës, dear enough a mite,[2]
These women, which that in the city dwell,
They set them down, and said as I shall tell.

Quoth first that one, "I am glad, truëly,
Because of you, that shall your father see;"
Another said, "Y-wis, so am not I,
For all too little hath she with us be."[3]
Quoth then the third, "I hope, y-wis, that she
Shall bringen us the peace on ev'ry side;
Then, when she goes, Almighty God her guide!"

Those wordës, and those womanishë thingës,
She heard them right as though she thennës[4] were,
For, God it wot, her heart on other thing is;
Although the body sat among them there,
Her adverténce[5] is always ellëswhere;
For Troilus full fast her soulë sought;
Withoutë word, on him alway she thought.

These women that thus weened her to please,
Aboutë naught gan all their talës spend;
Such vanity ne can do her no ease,
As she that all this meanë whilë brenn'd[6]
Of other passión than that they wend;[7]
So that she felt almost her heartë die
For woe, and weary[8] of that companý.

For whichë she no longer might restrain
Her tearës, they began so up to well,
That gavë signës of her bitter pain,
In which her spirit was, and mustë dwell,
Rememb'ring her from heav'n into which hell
She fallen was, since she forwent[9] the sight
Of Troilus; and sorrowfully she sight.[10]

And thilkë foolës, sitting her about,
Weened that she had wept and siked[10] sore,
Becausë that she should out of that rout[11]
Depart, and never playë with them more;
And they that haddë knowen her of yore
Saw her so weep, and thought it kindëness,
And each of them wept eke for her distress.

And busily they gonnen[12] her comfórt
Of thing, God wot, on which she little thought;
And with their talës weened her disport,
And to be glad they often her besought;
But such an ease therewith they in her wrought,
Right as a man is eased for to feel,
For ache of head, to claw him on his heel.

But, after all this nicë[13] vanity,
They took their leave, and home they wenten all;
Cressída, full of sorrowful pitý,
Into her chamber up went out of the hall,
And on her bed she gan for dead to fall,
In purpose never thennës for to rise;
And thus she wrought, as I shall you devise.

She rent her sunny hair, wrung her hands, wept, and bewailed her fate; vowing that, since, "for the cruelty," she could handle neither sword nor dart, she would abstain from meat and drink until she died. As she lamented, Pandarus entered, making her complain a thousand times more at the thought of all the joy which he had given her with her lover; but he somewhat soothed her by the prospect of Troilus's visit, and by the counsel to contain her grief when he should come. Then Pandarus went in search of Troilus, whom he found solitary in a temple, as one that had ceased to care for life:

For right thus was his argument alway:
He said he was but lornë,[14] well-away!
"For all that comes, comes by necessity;
Thus, to be lorn,[14] it is my destiny.

"For certainly this wot I well," he said,
"That foresight of the divine purveyánce[15]
Hath seen alway me to forgo[16] Cresseide,
Since God sees ev'ry thing, out of doubtánce,[17]
And them disposeth, through his ordinance,
In their merítës soothly for to be,
As they should comë by predestiny.

"But natheless, alas! whom shall I 'lieve?
For there be greatë clerkës[18] many one
That destiny through argumentës preve,[19]
And somë say that needly[20] there is none,
But that free choice is giv'n us ev'ry one;
O well-away! so sly are clerkës old,
That I n'ot[21] whose opinion I may hold.

"For some men say, if God sees all beforn,
Goddë may not deceived be, pardie!
Then must it fallen,[22] though men had it sworn,
That purveyance hath seen before to be;
Wherefore I say, that from etern[23] if he
Hath wist before our thought eke as our deed,
We have no free choice, as these clerkës read.[24]

"For other thought, nor other deed alsó,
Might never be, but such as purveyánce,
Which may not be deceived never mo',
Hath feeled[25] before, without ignorance;
For if there mightë be a variance,
To writhen out from Goddë's purveyíng,
There were no prescience of thing comíng,

"But it were rather an opinión
Uncertain, and no steadfast foreseeíng;
And, certes, that were an abusión,[26]
That God should have no perfect clear weetíng,[27]
More than we men, that have doubtous weeníng;[28]
But such an error upon God to guess,[29]
Were false, and foul, and wicked cursedness.[30]

1 Thought to please her.
2 Not worth a mite—the smallest coin.
3 Been.
4 Thence; in some other place.
5 Attention, mind.
6 Burned.
7 For "weened;" supposed.
8 Weariness.
9 Lost.
10 Sighed.
11 Company.
12 Began.
13 Silly, foolish.
14 Lost, ruined.
15 Providence.
16 That I should lose.
17 Without doubt.
18 Scholars, divines. The controversy between those who maintained the doctrine of predestination and those who held that of free-will raged with no less animation at Chaucer's day, and before it, than it has done in the subsequent five centuries; the Dominicans upholding the sterner creed, the Franciscans taking the other side. Chaucer has more briefly, and with the same care not to commit himself, referred to the discussion in The Nun's Priest's Tale, page 169.
19 Prove.
20 Necessarily.
21 Know not.
22 Befall, happen.
23 Eternity.
24 Maintain.
25 Perceived.
26 An illusion (to believe).
27 Knowledge.
28 Dubious belief or opinion.
29 To impute to God such an error.
30 Impiety.

"Eke this is an opinión of some
That have their top full high and smooth y-shore,[1]
They say right thus, that thing is not to come,
For[2] that the prescience hath seen before
That it shall come; but they say, that therefóre
That it shall come, therefore the purveyánce
Wot it before, withouten ignorance.

"And, in this manner, this necessity
Returneth in his part contrary again;[3]
For needfully behoves it not to be,
That thilkë thingës fallen in certáin,[4]
That be purvey'd; but needly, as they sayn,
Behoveth it that thingës, which that fall,
That they in certain be purveyed all.

"I mean as though I labour'd me in this
To ínquire which thing cause of which thing be;
As, whether that the prescience of God is
The certain cause of the necessity
Of thingës that to comë be, pardie!
Or if necessity of thing comíng
Be causë certain of the purveyíng.

"But now enforce I me not[5] in shewíng
How th' order of causes stands; but well wot I,
That it behoveth, that the befallíng
Of thingës wistë[6] before certainlý,
Be necessary, all seem it not[7] thereby,
That prescience put falling necessair
To thing to come, all fall it foul or fair.

"For, if there sit a man yond on a see,[8]
Then by necessity behoveth it
That certes thine opinión sooth be,
That weenest, or conjectest,[9] that he sit;[10]
And, furtherover, now againward yet,
Lo! right so is it on the part contráry;
As thus,—now hearken, for I will not tarry;—

"I say that if th' opinion of thee
Be sooth, for that he sits, then say I this,
That he must sittë by necessity;
And thus necessity in either is,
For in him need of sitting is, y-wis,
And, in thee, need of sooth; and thus forsooth
There must necessity be in you both.

"But thou may'st say, the man sits not therefóre
That thine opinion of his sitting sóoth is;
But rather, for the man sat there before,
Therefore is thine opinion sooth, y-wis;
And I say, though the cause of sooth of this
Comes of his sitting, yet necessity
Is interchanged both in him and thee.

"Thus in the samë wise, out of doubtánce,
I may well maken, as it seemeth me,
My reasoning of Goddë's purveyánce,
And of the thingës that to comë be;
By whichë reason men may well y-see
That thilkë[11] thingës that in earthë fall,[12]
That by necessity they comen all.

"For although that a thing should come, y-wis,
Therefore it is purveyed certainly,
Not that it comes for it purveyed is;
Yet, natheless, behoveth needfully
That thing to come be purvey'd truëly;
Or ellës thingës that purveyed be,
That they betidë[12] by necessity.

"And this sufficeth right enough, certáin,
For to destroy our free choice ev'ry deal;
But now is this abusión,[13] to sayn
That falling of the thingës temporel
Is cause of Goddë's prescience eternél;
Now truëly that is a false senténce,[14]
That thing to come should cause his prescience.

"What might I ween, an'[15] I had such a thought,
But that God purveys thing that is to come,
For that it is to come, and ellës nought?
So might I ween that thingës, all and some,
That whilom be befall and overcome,[16]
Be cause of thilkë sov'reign purveyánce,
That foreknows all, withouten ignorance.

"And over all this, yet say I more thereto,—
That right as when I wot there is a thing,
Y-wis, that thing must needfully be so;
Eke right so, when I wot a thing comíng,
So must it come; and thus the befallíng
Of thingës that be wist before the tide,[17]
They may not be eschew'd[18] on any side."

While Troilus was in all this heaviness, disputing with himself in this matter, Pandarus joined him, and told him the result of the interview with Cressida; and at night the lovers met, with what sighs and tears may be imagined. Cressida swooned away, so that Troilus took her for dead; and, having tenderly laid out her limbs, as one preparing a corpse for the bier, he drew his sword to slay himself upon her body. But, as God would, just at that moment she awoke out of her swoon; and by and by the pair began to talk of their prospects. Cressida declared the opinion, supporting it at great length and with many reasons, that there was no cause for half so much woe on either part. Her surrender, decreed by the parliament, could not be resisted; it was quite easy for them soon to meet again; she would so bring things about that she should be back in Troy within a week or two; she would take advantage of the constant coming and going while the truce lasted; and the issue would be, that the Trojans would have both her and Antenor; while, to facilitate her return, she had devised a stratagem by which, working on her father's avarice, she might tempt him to desert from the Greek camp back to the city. "And truly," says the poet, having fully reported her plausible speech,

And truëly, as written well I find,

1 That are eminent among the clergy, who wear the tonsure.
2 Because.
3 Reacts in the opposite direction.
4 Certainly happen.
5 I do not make an effort, lay stress.
6 Known.
7 Although it does not appear.
8 Seat.
9 Conjecturest.
10 Sits.
11 Those.
12 Happen.
13 Illusion, self-deception.
14 Opinion, judgment.
15 If.
16 That have happened and passed in times gone by.
17 Time.
18 Avoided.

That all this thing was said of good intent,[1]
And that her heartë truë was and kind
Towardës him, and spake right as she meant,
And that she starf[2] for woe nigh when she went,
And was in purpose ever to be true;
Thus writë they that of her workës knew.

This Troilus, with heart and ears y-sprad,[3]
Heard all this thing devised to and fro,
And verily it seemed that he had
The selfë wit;[4] but yet to let her go
His heartë misforgave[5] him evermo';
But, finally, he gan his heartë wrest[6]
To trustë her, and took it for the best.

For which the great fury of his penánce[7]
Was quench'd with hope, and therewith them between
Began for joy the amorousë dance;
And as the birdës, when the sun is sheen,[8]
Delighten in their song, in leavës green,
Right so the wordës that they spake y-fere[9]
Delighten them, and make their heartës cheer.[10]

Yet Troilus was not so well at ease, that he did not earnestly entreat Cressida to observe her promise; for, if she came not into Troy at the set day, he should never have heal, honour, or joy; and he feared that the stratagem by which she would try to lure her father back would fail, so that she might be compelled to remain among the Greeks. He would rather have them steal away together, with sufficient treasure to maintain them all their lives; and even if they went in their bare shirt, he had kin and friends elsewhere, who would welcome and honour them.

Cressida, with a sigh, right in this wise
Answer'd; "Y-wis, my dearë heartë true,
We may well steal away, as ye devise,
And findë such unthrifty wayës new;
But afterward full sore it will us rue;[11]
And help me God so at my mostë need
As causëless ye suffer all this dread!

"For thilkë[12] day that I for cherishing
Or dread of father, or of other wight,
Or for estate, delight, or for wedding,
Be false to you, my Troilus, my knight,
Saturnë's daughter Juno, through her might,
As wood as Athamantë[13] do me dwell
Eternally in Styx the pit of hell!

"And this, on ev'ry god celestial
I swear it you, and eke on each goddéss,
On ev'ry nymph, and deity infernál,
On Satyrs and on Faunës more or less,
That halfë goddës[14] be of wilderness;
And Atropos my thread of life to-brest,[15]
If I be false! now trow[16] me if you lest.[17]

"And thou Simoïs,[18] that as an arrow clear
Through Troy ay runnest downward to the sea,
Bear witness of this word that said is here!
That thilkë day that I untruë be
To Troilus, mine owen heartë free,
That thou returnë backward to thy well,
And I with body and soul sink in hell!"

Even yet Troilus was not wholly content, and urged anew his plan of secret flight; but Cressida turned upon him with the charge that he mistrusted her causelessly, and demanded of him that he should be faithful in her absence, else she must die at her return. Troilus promised faithfulness in far simpler and briefer words than Cressida had used.

"Grand mercy, good heart mine, y-wis," quoth she;
"And blissful Venus let me never sterve,[19]
Ere I may stand of pleasance in degree
To quite him well[20] that so well can deserve;
And while that God my wit will me conserve,
I shall so do; so true I have you found,
That ay honour to meward shall rebound.

"For trustë well that your estate[21] royál,
Nor vain delight, nor only worthiness
Of you in war or tourney martiál,
Nor pomp, array, nobley, nor eke richéss,
Ne madë me to rue[22] on your distress;
But moral virtue, grounded upon truth,
That was the cause I first had on you ruth.

"Eke gentle heart, and manhood that ye had,
And that ye had,—as me thought,—in despite
Every thing that sounded unto[23] bad,
As rudëness, and peoplish[24] appetite,
And that your reason bridled your delight;
This made, aboven ev'ry creatúre,
That I was yours, and shall while I may dure.

"And this may length of yearës not fordo,[25]
Nor remuable[26] Fortunë deface;
But Jupiter, that of his might may do[27]
The sorrowful to be glad, so give us grace,
Ere nightës ten to meeten in this place,
So that it may your heart and mine suffice!
And fare now well, for time is that ye rise."

The lovers took a heart-rending adieu; and Troilus, suffering unimaginable anguish, "withoutë more, out of the chamber went."

The Fifth Book.

Approachë gan the fatal destiny
That Jovis hath in dispositión,
And to you angry Parcæ, Sisters three,
Committeth to do executión;
For which Cressída must out of the town,

1 Of sincere purpose. 2 Died.
3 All open. 4 The same opinion.
5 Misgave.
6 Compel: wrest away from doubt and misgiving.
7 Anguish. 8 Bright.
9 Together. 10 Give gladness to their hearts.
11 We will regret it. 12 That same.
13 Athamas, son of Æolus; who, seized with madness, under the wrath of Juno for his neglect of his wife Nephele, slew his son Learchus.
14 Demigods. 15 Break utterly.
16 Believe. 17 If it please you.
18 One of the rivers of the Troad, flowing into the Xanthus. 19 Die.
20 In a position to reward him well with pleasure.
21 Rank. 22 Take pity.
23 Tended unto, accorded with.
24 Vulgar. 25 Destroy, do away.
26 Unstable. 27 Cause.
28 The Fates.

And Troilus shall dwellë forth in pine,[1]
Till Lachesis his thread no longer twine.[2]

The golden-tressed Phœbus, high aloft,
Thriës[3] had allë, with his beamës clear,
The snowës molt,[4] and Zephyrus as oft
Y-brought again the tender leavës green,
Since that the son of Hecuba the queen[5]
Began to love her[6] first, for whom his sorrow
Was all, that she depart should on the morrow.

In the morning, Diomede was ready to escort Cressida to the Greek host; and Troilus, seeing him mount his horse, could with difficulty resist an impulse to slay him—but restrained himself, lest his lady should be also slain in the tumult. When Cressida was ready to go,

This Troilus, in guise of courtesy,
With hawk on hand, and with a hugë rout[7]
Of knightës, rode, and did her 'company,
Passing allë the valley far without;
And farther would have ridden, out of doubt,
Full fain,[8] and woe was him to go so soon,
But turn he must, and it was eke to do'n.

And right with that was Antenor y-come
Out of the Greekës' host, and ev'ry wight
Was of it glad, and said he was welcóme;
And Troilus, all n'ere his heartë light,[9]
He pained him,[10] with all his fullë might,
Him to withhold from weeping at the least;
And Antenor he kiss'd, and madë feast.

And therewithal he must his leavë take,
And cast his eye upon her piteously,
And near he rode, his causë[11] for to make
To take her by the hand all soberly;
And, Lord! so she gan weepë tenderly!
And he full soft and slily gan her say,
"Now hold your day, and do me not to dey."[12]

With that his courser turned he about,
With facë pale, and unto Diomede
No word he spake, nor none of all his rout;
Of which the son of Tydeus[13] tookë heed,
As he that couthë[14] morë than the creed[15]
In such a craft, and by the rein her hent;[16]
And Troilus to Troyë homeward went.

This Diomede, that led her by the bridle,
When that he saw the folk of Troy away,
Thought, "All my labour shall nót be on idle,[17]
If that I may, for somewhat shall I say;
For, at the worst, it may yet short our way;
I have heard say eke, times twicë twelve,
He is a fool that will forget himselve."

But natheless, this thought he well enough,
That "Certainly I am aboutë naught,
If that I speak of love, or make it tough;[18]
For, doubtëless, if she have in her thought
Him that I guess, he may not be y-brought
So soon away; but I shall find a mean,
That she not wit as yet shall[19] what I mean."

So he began a general conversation, assured her of not less friendship and honour among the Greeks than she had enjoyed in Troy, and requested of her earnestly to treat him as a brother and accept his service—for, at last he said, "I am and shall be ay, while that my life may dure, your own, aboven ev'ry creature.

"Thus said I never e'er now to woman born;
For, God mine heart as wisly[20] gladden so!
I loved never woman herebeforn,
As paramours, nor ever shall no mo';
And for the love of God be not my foe,
All[21] can I not to you, my lady dear,
Complain aright, for I am yet to lear.[22]

"And wonder not, mine owen lady bright,
Though that I speak of love to you thus blive;[23]
For I have heard ere this of many a wight
That loved thing he ne'er saw in his live;
Eke I am not of power for to strive
Against the god of Love, but him obey
I will alway, and mercy I you pray."

Cressida answered his discourses as though she scarcely heard them; yet she thanked him for his trouble and courtesy, and accepted his offered friendship—promising to trust him, as well she might. Then she alighted from her steed, and, with her heart nigh breaking, was welcomed to the embrace of her father. Meanwhile Troilus, back in Troy, was lamenting with tears the loss of his love, despairing of his or her ability to survive the ten days, and spending the night in wailing, sleepless tossing, and troublous dreams. In the morning, he was visited by Pandarus, to whom he gave directions for his funeral; desiring that the powder into which his heart was burned should be kept in a golden urn, and given to Cressida. Pandarus renewed his old counsels and consolations, reminded his friend that ten days were a short time to wait, argued against his faith in evil dreams, and urged him to take advantage of the truce, and beguile the time by a visit to King Sarpedon (a Lycian Prince who had come to aid the Trojans). Sarpedon entertained them splendidly; but no feasting, no pomp, no music of instruments, no singing of fair ladies, could make up for the absence of Cressida to the desolate Troilus, who was for ever poring upon her old letters, and recalling her loved form. Thus he "drove to an end" the fourth day, and would have then returned to Troy, but for the remonstrances of Pandarus, who asked if they had visited Sarpedon only to fetch fire? At last, at the end of a week, they returned to Troy;

1 Pain.
2 No longer twist the thread of his life.
3 Thrice.
4 Melted.
5 Troilus, who was son of Priam and Hecuba.
6 Cressida.
7 Retinue, crowd.
8 Gladly.
9 Although his heart was not light.
10 Strove.
11 Excuse, occasion.
12 Make me not die.
13 Diomedes; far oftener called Tydides, after his father Tydeus, king of Argos.
14 Knew.
15 More than the mere elements (of the science of Love).
16 Took.
17 In vain.
18 Make any violent immediate effort.
19 Shall not know as yet.
20 Surely.
21 Although.
22 Teach.
23 Soon.

Troilus hoping to find Cressida again in the city, Pandarus entertaining a scepticism which he concealed from his friend. The morning after their return, Troilus was impatient till he had gone to the palace of Cressida; but when he found her doors all closed, "well nigh for sorrow adown he gan to fall."

Therewith, when he was ware, and gan behold
How shut was ev'ry window of the place,
As frost him thought his heartë gan to cold;[1]
For which, with changed deadly palë face,
Withoutë word, he forth began to pace;
And, as God would, he gan so fastë ride,
That no wight of his countenance espied.

Then said he thus: "O palace desolate!
O house of houses, whilom bestë hight!
O palace empty and disconsolate!
O thou lantérn, of which quench'd is the light!
O palace, whilom day, that now art night!
Well oughtest thou to fall, and I to die,
Since she is gone that wont was us to guy![2]

"O palace, whilom crown of houses all,
Illumined with sun of allë bliss!
O ring, from which the ruby is out fall!
O cause of woe, that cause hast been of bliss!
Yet, since I may no bet, fain would I kiss
Thy coldë doorës, durst I for this rout;[3]
And farewell shrine, of which the saint is out!"

. . . .

From thencë forth he rideth up and down,
And ev'ry thing came him to rémembránce,
As he rode by the places of the town,
In which he whilom had all his pleasánce;
"Lo! yonder saw I mine own lady dance;
And in that temple, with her eyen clear,
Me caughtë first my rightë lady dear.

"And yonder have I heard full lustily
My dearë heartë laugh; and yonder play
Saw I her onës eke full blissfully;
And yonder onës to me gan she say,
'Now, goodë sweetë! love me well, I pray;'
And yond so gladly gan she me behold,
That to the death my heart is to her hold.[4]

"And at that corner, in the yonder house,
Heard I mine allerlevest[5] lady dear,
So womanly, with voice melodioús,
Singë so well, so goodly and so clear,
That in my soulë yet me thinks I hear
The blissful sound; and in that yonder place
My lady first me took unto her grace."

Then he went to the gates, and gazed along the way by which he had attended Cressida at her departure; then he fancied that all the passers-by pitied him; and thus he drove forth a day or two more, singing a song, of few words, which he had made to lighten his heart:

"O star, of which I lost have all the light,
With heartë sore well ought I to bewail,
That ever dark in torment, night by night,
Towárd my death, with wind I steer and sail;
For which, the tenthë night, if that I fail[6]
The guiding of thy beamës bright an hour,
My ship and me Charybdis will devour."

By night he prayed the moon to run fast about her sphere; by day he reproached the tardy sun—dreading that Phaethon had come to life again, and was driving the chariot of Apollo out of its straight course. Meanwhile Cressida, among the Greeks, was bewailing the refusal of her father to let her return, the certainty that her lover would think her false, and the hopelessness of any attempt to steal away by night. Her bright face waxed pale, her limbs lean, as she stood all day looking toward Troy; thinking on her love and all her past delights, regretting that she had not followed the counsel of Troilus to steal away with him, and finally vowing that she would at all hazards return to the city. But she was fated, ere two months, to be full far from any such intention; for Diomede now brought all his skill into play, to entice Cressida into his net. On the tenth day, Diomede, "as fresh as branch in May," came to the tent of Cressida, feigning business with Calchas.

Cressíde, at shortë wordës[7] for to tell,
Welcomed him, and down by her him set,
And he was eath enough to makë dwell;[8]
And after this, withoutë longë let,[9]
The spices and the wine men forth him fet,[10]
And forth they speak of this and that y-fere,[11]
As friendës do, of which some shall ye hear.

He gan first fallen of the war in speech
Between them and the folk of Troyë town,
And of the siege he gan eke her beseech
To tell him what was her opinioún;
From that demand he so descended down
To askë her, if that her strangë thought
The Greekës' guise,[12] and workës that they wrought.

And why her father tarriëd[13] so long
To weddë her unto some worthy wight.
Cressída, that was in her painës strong
For love of Troilus, her owen knight,
So farforth as she cunning[14] had or might,
Answer'd him then; but, as for his intent,[15]
It seemed not she wistë[16] what he meant.

But natheless this ilkë[17] Diomede
Gan in himself assure,[18] and thus he said:
"If I aright have taken on you heed,[19]
Me thinketh thus, O lady mine Cressíde,
That since I first hand on your bridle laid,
When ye out came of Troyë by the morrow,
Ne might I never see you but in sorrow.

"I cannot say what may the causë be,
But if for love of some Troján it were;
The which right sorë would a-thinkë me,[20]
That ye for any wight that dwelleth there

1 To grow cold.
2 Guide, rule.
3 Company.
4 Holden, bound.
5 Dearest of all.
6 Miss; be left without.
7 Briefly.
8 Easy enough to persuade to stay.
9 Delay.
10 Fetched.
11 Together.
12 Fashion.
13 Delayed.
14 Ability.
15 Purpose.
16 Knew.
17 Same.
18 Grow confident.
19 If I have observed you aright.
20 Which it would much pain me to think.

Should [ever] spill[1] a quarter of a tear,
Or piteously yourselfë so beguile;[2]
For dreadëless[3] it is not worth the while.

"The folk of Troy, as who saith, all and some
In prison be, as ye yourselfë see;
From thencë shall not one alivë come
For all the gold betwixtë sun and sea;
Trustë this well, and understandë me;
There shall not one to mercy go alive,
All[4] were he lord of worldës twicë five

. . . .

"What will ye morë, lovesome lady dear?
Let Troy and Trojan from your heartë pace;
Drive out that bitter hope, and make good cheer,
And call again the beauty of your face,
That ye with saltë tearës so deface;
For Troy is brought into such jeopardy,
That it to save is now no remedy.

"And thinkë well, ye shall in Greekës find
A love more perfect, ere that it be night,
Than any Trojan is, and morë kind,
And better you to serve will do his might;
And, if ye vouchësafe, my lady bright,
I will be he, to servë you, myselve,—
Yea, lever[5] than be a lord of Greekës twelve!"

And with that word he gan to waxë red,
And in his speech a little while he quoke,[6]
And cast aside a little with his head,
And stint a while; and afterward he woke,
And soberly on her he threw his look,
And said, "I am, albeit to you no joy,
As gentle[7] man as any wight in Troy.

. . . .

"But, heartë mine! since that I am your man,[8]
And be[9] the first of whom I seekë grace,
To serve you as heartily as I can,
And ever shall, while I to live have space,
So, ere that I depart out of this place,
Ye will me grantë that I may, to-morrow,
At better leisure, tellë you my sorrow."

Why should I tell his wordës that he said?
He spake enough for one day at the mest;[10]
It proveth well he spake so, that Cresseide
Granted upon the morrow, at his request,
Farther to speakë with him, at the least,
So that he would not speak of such mattére;
And thus she said to him, as ye may hear:

As she that had her heart on Troilus
So fastë set, that none might it arace;[11]
And strangëly[12] she spake, and saidë thus;
"O Diomede! I love that ilkë place
Where I was born; and Jovis, for his grace,
Deliver it soon of all that doth it care![13]
God, for thy might, so leave it[14] well to fare!"

1 Shed.
2 Deceive.
3 Undoubtedly.
4 Although.
5 Rather.
6 Quaked; trembled.
7 High-born.
8 Liegeman, subject (in love).
9 That is, "and since you are."
10 Most.
11 Wrench away, unroot (French, "arracher"); the opposite of "enrace," to root in, implant.
12 As not entertaining his suit willingly.
13 Of all that afflicts it, that causes it care or sorrow.
14 Grant it, give it leave.

She knows that the Greeks would fain wreak their wrath on Troy, if they might; but that shall never befall: she knows that there are Greeks of high condition—though as worthy men would be found in Troy: and she knows that Diomede could serve his lady well.

"But, as to speak of love, y-wis," she said,
"I had a lord, to whom I wedded was,[15]
He whose mine heart was all, until he died;
And other love, as help me now Pallás,
There in my heart nor is, nor ever was;
And that ye be of noble and high kindréd,
I have well heard it tellen, out of dread.[16]

"And that doth[17] me to have so great a wonder
That ye will scornen any woman so;
Eke, God wot, love and I be far asunder;
I am disposed bet, so may I go,[18]
Unto my death to plain and makë woe;
What I shall after do I cannot say,
But truëly as yet me list not play.[19]

"Mine heart is now in tribulatioún;
And ye in armës busy be by day;
Hereafter, when ye wonnen have the town,
Parauntre[20] then, so as it happen may,
That when I see that I never ere sey,[21]
Then will I work that I never ere wrought;
This word to you enough sufficen ought.

"To-morrow eke will I speak with you fain,[22]
So that ye touchë naught of this mattére;
And when you list, ye may come here again,
And ere ye go, thus much I say you here:
As help me Pallas, with her hairës clear,
If that I should of any Greek have ruth,
It shouldë be yourselfë, by my truth!

"I say not therefore that I will you love;
Nor say not nay;[23] but, in conclusioún,
I meanë well, by God that sits above!"
And therewithal she cast her eyen down,
And gan to sigh, and said; "O Troyë town!
Yet bid[24] I God, in quiet and in rest
I may you see, or do my heartë brest!"[25]

But in effect, and shortly for to say,
This Diomede all freshly new again
Gan pressen on, and fast her mercy pray;
And after this, the soothë for to sayn,
Her glove he took, of which he was full fain,
And finally, when it was waxen eve,
And all was well, he rose and took his leave.

Cressida retired to rest

Returning in her soul ay up and down
The wordës of this sudden Diomede,[26]
His great estate,[27] the peril of the town,
And that she was alone, and haddë need
Of friendës' help; and thus began to dread

15 It will be remembered that, at the beginning of the first book, Cressida is introduced to us as a widow.
16 Doubt.
17 Causeth.
18 So may I fare or prosper.
19 I am not disposed for sport.
20 Peradventure.
21 Saw before.
22 Willingly.
23 Nor say I that I will not.
24 Pray.
25 Cause my heart to break.
26 Diomede is called "sudden," for the unexpectedness of his assault on Cressida's heart—or, perhaps, for the abrupt abandonment of his indifference to love.
27 Rank.

The causes why, the soothë for to tell,
That she took fully the purpose for to dwell.[1]

The morrow came, and, ghostly[2] for to speak,
This Diomede is come unto Cresseide;
And shortly, lest that ye my talë break,
So well he for himselfë spake and said,
That all her sighës sore adown he laid;
And finally, the soothë for to sayn,
He reftë her the great[3] of all her pain.

And after this, the story telleth us
That she him gave the fairë bayë steed
The which she onës won of Troilus;
And eke a brooch (and that was little need)
That Troilus' was, she gave this Diomede;
And eke, the bet from sorrow him to relieve,
She made him wear a pensel[4] of her sleeve.

I find eke in the story ellëswhere,
When through the body hurt was Diomede
By Troilus, she wept many a tear,
When that she saw his wide woundës bleed,
And that she took to keepë[5] him good heed,
And, for to heal him of his sorrow's smart,
Men say, I n'ot,[6] that she gave him her heart.

And yet, when pity had thus completed the triumph of inconstancy, she made bitter moan over her falseness to one of the noblest and worthiest men that ever was; but it was now too late to repent, and at all events she resolved that she would be true to Diomede—all the while weeping for pity of the absent Troilus, to whom she wished every happiness. The tenth day, meantime, had barely dawned, when Troilus, accompanied by Pandarus, took his stand on the walls, to watch for the return of Cressida. Till noon they stood, thinking that every comer from afar was she; then Troilus said that doubtless her old father bore the parting ill, and had detained her till after dinner; so they went to dine, and returned to their vain observation on the walls. Troilus invented all kinds of explanations for his mistress's delay; now, her father would not let her go till eve; now, she would ride quietly into the town after nightfall, not to be observed; now, he must have mistaken the day. For five or six days he watched, still in vain, and with decreasing hope. Gradually his strength decayed, until he could walk only with a staff; answering the wondering inquiries of his friends, by saying that he had a grievous malady about his heart. One day he dreamed that in a forest he saw Cressida in the embrace of a boar; and he had no longer doubt of her falsehood. Pandarus, however, explained away the dream to mean merely that Cressida was detained by her father, who might be at the point of death; and he counselled the disconsolate lover to write a letter, by which he might perhaps get at the truth. Troilus complied, entreating from his mistress, at the least, a "letter of hope;" and the lady answered, that she could not come now, but would so soon as she might; at the same time "making him great feast," and swearing that she loved him best—"of which he found but bottomless behest."[7] Day by day increased the woe of Troilus; he laid himself in bed, neither eating, nor drinking, nor sleeping, nor speaking, almost distracted by the thought of Cressida's unkindness. He related his dream to his sister Cassandra, who told him that the boar betokened Diomede, and that, wheresoever his lady was, Diomede certainly had her heart, and she was his: "weep if thou wilt, or leave, for, out of doubt, this Diomede is in, and thou art out." Troilus, enraged, refused to believe Cassandra's interpretation; as well, he cried, might such a story be credited of Alcestis, who devoted her life for her husband; and in his wrath he started from bed, "as though all whole had him y-made a leach,"[8] resolving to find out the truth at all hazards. The death of Hector meanwhile enhanced the sorrow which he endured; but he found time to write often to Cressida, beseeching her to come again and hold her truth; till one day his false mistress, out of pity, wrote him again, in these terms:

"Cupidë's son, ensample of goodlihead,[9]
O sword of knighthood, source of gentleness!
How might a wight in torment and in dread,
And healëless,[10] you send as yet gladness?
I heartëless, I sick, I in distress?
Since ye with me, nor I with you, may deal,
You neither send I may nor heart nor heal.

"Your letters full, the paper all y-plainted,[11]
Commoved havë minë heart's pity;
I have eke seen with tearës all depainted
Your letter, and how ye requirë me
To come again; the which yet may not be;
But why, lest that this letter founden were,
No mentión I makë now for fear.

"Grievous to me, God wot, is your unrest,
Your haste,[12] and that the goddës' ordinance
It seemeth not ye take as for the best;
Nor other thing is in your rémembránce,
As thinketh me, but only your pleasánce;
But be not wroth, and that I you beseech,
For that I tarry is all for wicked speech.[13]

"For I have heard well morë than I wend[14]
Touching us two, how thingës havë stood,
Which I shall with dissimuling amend;
And, be not wroth, I have eke understood
How ye ne do but holdë me on hand;[15]
But now no force,[16] I cannot in you guess
But allë truth and allë gentleness.

1 To remain among the Greeks.
2 Plainly.
3 Took away from her great part: relieved her.
4 A pennon or pendant; French, "penoncel." It was the custom in chivalric times for a knight to wear, on days of tournament or in battle, some such token of his lady's favour, or badge of his service to her.
5 Tend, care for.
6 I know not (whether truly or not).
7 Which he found but groundless promises.
8 Physician.
9 Beauty, excellence.
10 Devoid of health.
11 Covered with complainings.
12 Impatience.
13 She excuses herself by saying that she stays to avoid or silence malicious gossip about their love.
14 Weened, thought.
15 She has been told that Troilus is deceiving her.
16 No matter (for such tales).

"Comen I will, but yet in such disjoint[1]
I standë now, that what year or what day
That this shall be, that can I not appoint;
But in effect I pray you, as I may,
For your good word and for your friendship ay;
For truëly, while that my life may dure,
As for a friend, ye may in me assure.[2]

"Yet[3] pray I you, on evil ye not take[4]
That it is short, which that I to you write;
I dare not, where I am, well letters make;
Nor never yet ne could I well endite;
Eke great effect men write in placë lite;[5]
Th' intent[6] is all, and not the letter's space;
And fare now well, God have you in his grace!
"La Vostre C."

Though he found this letter "all strange," and thought it like "a kalendës of change,"[7] Troilus could not believe his lady so cruel as to forsake him; but he was put out of all doubt, one day that, as he stood in suspicion and melancholy, he saw a "coat-armour" borne along the street, in token of victory, before Deiphobus his brother. Deiphobus had won it from Diomede in battle that day; and Troilus, examining it out of curiosity, found within the collar a brooch which he had given to Cressida on the morning she left Troy, and which she had pledged her faith to keep for ever in remembrance of his sorrow and of him. At this fatal discovery of his lady's untruth,

Great was the sorrow and plaint of Troilus;
But forth her course Fortúne ay gan to hold;
Cressida lov'd the son of Tydeus,
And Troilus must weep in carës cold.
Such is the world, whoso it can behold!
In each estate is little heartë's rest;
God lend[8] us each to take it for the best!

In many a cruel battle Troilus wrought havoc among the Greeks, and often he exchanged blows and bitter words with Diomede, whom he always specially sought; but it was not their lot that either should fall by the other's hand. The poet's purpose, however, he tells us, is to relate, not the warlike deeds of Troilus, which Dares has fully told, but his love-fortunes:

Beseeching ev'ry lady bright of hue,
And ev'ry gentle woman, what she be,[9]
Albeit that Cressída was untrue,
That for that guilt ye be not wroth with me;
Ye may her guilt in other bookës see;
And gladder I would writen, if you lest,
Of Penelópé's truth, and good Alceste.

Nor say I not this only all for men,
But most for women that betrayed be
Through falsë folk (God give them sorrow, Amen!)
That with their greatë wit and subtilty
Betrayë you; and this commoveth me
To speak; and in effect you all I pray,
Beware of men, and hearken what I say.

Go, little book, go, little tragedy!
There God my maker, yet ere that I die,
So send me might to make some comedy!
But, little book, no making thou envý,[10]
But subject be unto all poesý;
And kiss the steps, where as thou seëst space,
Of Virgil, Ovid, Homer, Lucan, Stace.

And, for there is so great diversity
In English, and in writing of our tongue,
So pray I God, that none miswritë thee,
Nor thee mismetre, for default of tongue!
And read whereso thou be, or ellës sung,
That thou be understanden, God I 'seech![11]
But yet to purpose of my rather speech.[12]

The wrath, as I began you for to say,
Of Troilus the Greekës boughtë dear;
For thousandës his handës madë dey,[13]
As he that was withouten any peer,
Save in his time Hector, as I can hear;
But, well-away! save only Goddë's will,
Dispiteously him slew the fierce Achill'.

And when that he was slain in this mannére,
His lightë ghost[14] full blissfully is went[15]
Up to the hollowness of the seventh sphere,
In converse[16] leaving ev'ry element;
And there he saw, with full advisëment,[17]
Th' erratic starrës heark'ning harmony,
With soundës full of heav'nly melody.

And down from thennës fast he gan advise[18]
This little spot of earth, that with the sea
Embraced is; and fully gan despise
This wretched world, and held all vanity,
To réspect of the plein felicity[19]
That is in heav'n above; and, at the last,
Where he was slain his looking down he cast.

And in himself he laugh'd right at the woe
Of them that weptë for his death so fast;
And damned[20] all our works, that follow so
The blindë lust, the which that may not last,
And shoulden[21] all our heart on heaven cast;
And forth he wentë, shortly for to tell,
Where as Mercury sorted[22] him to dwell.

Such fine[23] hath, lo! this Troilus for love!
Such fine hath all his greatë worthiness!
Such fine hath his estate royal above![24]

1 Jeopardy, critical position.
2 Depend on me.
3 Moreover.
4 Do not take it ill.
5 Men write great matter in little space.
6 Meaning.
7 The Roman kalends were the first day of the month, when a change of weather was usually expected.
8 Grant.
9 Whatsoever she be.
10 Be envious of no poetry (of others). Maker, and making, words used in the Middle Ages to signify the composer and the composition of poetry, correspond exactly with the Greek ποιητης and ποιημα, from ποιεω, I make.
11 Beseech.
12 My earlier, former subject; "rather" is the comparative of the old adjective "rath," early.
13 Made to die.
14 Spirit.
15 Gone.
16 Passing up through the hollowness or concavity of the spheres, which all revolve round each other and are all contained by God (see note 11, page 217), the soul of Troilus, looking downward, beholds the converse or convex side of the spheres which it has traversed.
17 Clear observation or understanding.
18 Consider, look upon.
19 In comparison with the full felicity.
20 Condemned.
21 While we should.
22 Allotted; from Latin, "sors," lot, fortune.
23 End.
24 His exalted royal rank.

Such fine his lust,[1] such fine hath his nobless!
Such fine hath falsë worldë's brittleness![2]
And thus began his loving of Cresside,
As I have told; and in this wise he died.

O young and freshë folkë, he or she,[3]
In which that love upgroweth with your age,
Repairë home from worldly vanity,
And of your heart upcastë the viságe[4]
To thilkë[5] God, that after his imáge
You made, and think that all is but a fair,
This world that passeth soon, as flowers fair!

And lovë Him, the which that, right for love,
Upon a cross, our soulës for to bey,[6]
First starf,[7] and rose, and sits in heav'n above;
For he will falsë[8] no wight, dare I say,
That will his heart all wholly on him lay;
And since he best to love is, and most meek,
What needeth feigned lovës for to seek?

Lo! here of paynims[9] cursed oldë rites!
Lo! here what all their goddës may avail!
Lo! here this wretched worldë's appetites!
Lo! here the fine and guerdon for traváil,[10]
Of Jove, Apollo, Mars, and such rascaille![11]
Lo! here the form of oldë clerkës' speech,
In poetry, if ye their bookës seech![12]

L'Envoy of Chaucer.

O moral Gower![13] this book I direct
To thee, and to the philosophical Strode,[14]
To vouchësafe, where need is, to correct,
Of your benignities and zealës good.
And to that soothfast Christ that starf on rood,[15]
With all my heart, of mercy ever I pray,
And to the Lord right thus I speak and say:

"Thou One, and Two, and Three, etern on live,[16]
That reignest ay in Three, and Two, and One,
Uncircumscrib'd, and all may'st circumscrive,[17]
From visible and invisible fone[18]
Defend us in thy mercy ev'ry one;
So make us, Jesus, for thy mercy dign,[19]
For love of Maid and Mother thine benign!"

Explicit Liber Troili et Cresseidis.

CHAUCER'S DREAM.

[THIS pretty allegory, or rather conceit, containing one or two passages that for vividness and for delicacy yield to nothing in the whole range of Chaucer's poetry, had never been printed before the year 1597, when it was included in the edition of Speght. Before that date, indeed, a Dream of Chaucer had been printed; but the poem so described was in reality "The Book of the Duchess; or the Death of Blanche, Duchess of Lancaster"—which is not included in the present edition. Speght says that "This Dream, devised by Chaucer, seemeth to be a covert report of the marriage of John of Gaunt, the King's son, with Blanche, the daughter of Henry, Duke of Lancaster; who after long love (during the time whereof the poet feigneth them to be dead) were in the end, by consent of friends, happily married; figured by a bird bringing in his bill an herb, which restored them to life again. Here also is showed Chaucer's match with a certain gentlewoman, who, although she was a stranger, was, notwithstanding, so well liked and loved of the Lady Blanche and her Lord, as Chaucer himself also was, that gladly they concluded a marriage between them." John of Gaunt, at the age of nineteen, and while yet Earl of Richmond, was married to the Lady Blanche at Reading in May 1359; Chaucer, then a prisoner in France, probably did not return to England till peace was concluded in the following year; so that his marriage to Philippa Roet, the sister of the Duchess Blanche's favourite attendant Katharine Roet, could not have taken place till some time after that of the Duke. In the poem, it is represented to have immediately followed; but no consequence need be attached to that statement. Enough that it followed at no great interval of time; and that the intimate relations which Chaucer had already begun to form with John of Gaunt, might well warrant him in writing this poem on the occasion of the Duke's marriage, and in weaving his own love-fortunes with those of the principal figures. In the necessary abridgement of the poem for the present edition, the

1 Pleasure. 2 Fickleness, instability.
3 Of either sex.
4 "Lift up the countenance of your heart."
5 That. 6 Buy, redeem.
7 Died. 8 Deceive, fail.
9 Pagans. 10 The end and reward for labour.
11 "And all that rabble;" French, "racaille"—a mob or multitude, the riff-raff; so Spencer speaks of the "rascal routs" of inferior combatants.
12 Seek, search.
13 John Gower, the poet, a contemporary and friend of Chaucer's; author, among other works, of the "Confessio Amantis." See note 9, page 61.
14 Strode was an eminent scholar of Merton College, Oxford, and tutor to Chaucer's son Lewis.
15 Died on cross. 16 Eternally living.
17 Yet able to circumscribe or comprehend all.
18 Foes. 19 Worthy of thy mercy.

subsidiary branch of the allegory, relating to the poet's own love affair, has been so far as possible separated from the main branch, which shadows forth the fortunes of John and Blanche. The poem, in full, contains, with an "Envoy" arbitrarily appended, 2233 lines; of which 510 are given here.]

WHEN Flora, the queen of pleasánce,
Had wholly achiev'd the obéisánce[1]
Of the fresh and the new seasón,
Thorough ev'ry región;
And with her mantle whole covért
What winter had made discovért,[2]—

On a May night, the poet lay alone, thinking of his lady, and all her beauty; and, falling asleep, he dreamed that he was in an island

Where wall, and gate, was all of glass,
And so was closed round about,
That leaveless[3] none came in nor out;
Uncouth and strangë to behold;
For ev'ry gate, of finë gold,
A thousand fanës,[4] ay turníng,
Entuned[5] had, and birds singíng
Divérsely, on each fane a pair,
With open mouth, against the air;[6]
And of a suit[7] were all the tow'rs,
Subtilly carven after[8] flow'rs
Of úncouth colours, during ay,
That never be none seen in May,
With many a small turret high;
But man alive I could not sigh,[9]
Nor creatúres, save ladies play,[10]
Which werë such of their array,
That, as me thought, of goodlihead[11]
They passed all, and womanhead.
For to behold them dance and sing,
It seemed like none earthly thing;

And all were of the same age, save one; who was advanced in years, though no less gay in demeanour than the rest. While he stood admiring the richness and beauty of the place, and the fairness of the ladies, which had the notable gift of enduring unimpaired till death, the poet was accosted by the old lady, to whom he had to yield himself prisoner; because the ordinance of the isle was, that no man should dwell there; and the ladies' fear of breaking the law was enhanced by the temporary absence of their queen from the realm. Just at this moment the cry was raised that the queen came; all the ladies hastened to meet her; and soon the poet saw her approach—but in her company his mistress, wearing the same garb, and a seemly knight. All the ladies wondered greatly at this; and the queen explained:

"My sisters, how it hath befall,[12]
I trow ye know it one and all,
That of long time here have I been
Within this isle biding as queen,
Living at ease, that never wight
More perfect joyë have not might;
And to you been of governance
Such as you found in whole pleasánce,[13]
In every thing as ye know,
After our custom and our law;
Which how they firstë founded were,
I trow ye wot all the mannére.
And who the queen is of this isle,—
As I have been this longë while,—
Each seven years must, of uságe,
Visit the heav'nly hermitage,
Which on a rock so highë stands,
In a strange sea, out from all lands,
That for to make the pilgrimage
Is call'd a perilous voyáge;
For if the wind be not good friend,
The journey dureth to the end
Of him which that it undertakes;
Of twenty thousand not one scapes.
Upon which rock groweth a tree,
That certain years bears apples three;
Which three apples whoso may have,
Is from all displeasánce[14] y-save[15]
That in the seven years may fall;
This wot you well, both one and all.
For the first apple and the hext,[16]
Which groweth unto you the next,
Hath three virtues notable,
And keepeth youth ay durable,
Beauty, and looks, ever-in-one,[17]
And is the best of ev'ry one.
The second apple, red and green,
Only with lookës of your eyne,
You nourishes in great pleasánce,
Better than partridge or fesaunce,[18]
And feedeth ev'ry living wight
Pleasantly, only with the sight.
And the third apple of the three,
Which groweth lowest on the tree,
Whoso it beareth may not fail[19]
That[20] to his pleasance may avail.
So your pleasure and beauty rich,
Your during youth ever y-lich,[21]
Your truth, your cunning,[22] and your weal,
Hath flower'd ay, and your good heal,
Without sickness or displeasánce,
Or thing that to you was noyánce.[23]
So that you have as goddesses

1 Won the obedience, made subject to her.
2 Wholly covered that which winter had stripped—that is, the earth.
3 Without permission.
4 Vanes, weathercocks.
5 Contrived so as to emit a musical sound; attuned.
6 Meeting the wind, so that it entered their open mouths, and by some mechanism produced the musical sound.
7 Of the same plan.
8 Carved to represent.
9 See.
10 Sporting themselves.
11 For comeliness.
12 Befallen.
13 That is, "and have governed you in a manner which you have found wholly pleasant."
14 Pain, unpleasantness.
15 Safe.
16 Highest; from "high," as "next" from "nigh." Compare the sounds of the German, "höchst," highest, and "nächst," next.
17 Continually.
18 Pheasant.
19 Miss, fail to obtain.
20 That which.
21 Alike.
22 Knowledge.
23 Offence, injury.

Lived above all princesses.
Now is befall'n, as ye may see;
To gather these said apples three,
I have not fail'd, against the day,
Thitherward to take the way,
Weening to speed[1] as I had oft.
But when I came, I found aloft
My sister, which that herë stands,
Having those apples in her hands,
Advising[2] them, and nothing said,
But look'd as she were well apaid:[3]
And as I stood her to behold,
Thinking how my joys were cold,
Since I these apples have not might,[4]
Even with that so came this knight,
And in his arms, of me unware,
Me took, and to his ship me bare,
And said, though him I ne'er had seen,
Yet had I long his lady been;
Wherefore I shouldë with him wend,
And he would, to his lifë's end,
My servant be; and gan to sing,
As one that had won a rich thing.
Then were my spirits from me gone,
So suddenly every one,
That in me appear'd but death,
For I felt neither life nor breath,
Nor good nor harmë none I knew,
The sudden pain me was so new,
That had not the hasty grace be[5]
Of this lady, that from the tree
Of her gentleness so hied,[6]
Me to comfórten, I had died;
And of her three apples she one
Into mine hand there put anon,
Which brought again my mind and breath,
And me recover'd from the death.
Wherefore to her so am I hold,[7]
That for her all things do I wo'ld,
For she was leach[8] of all my smart,
And from great pain so quit[9] my heart.
And as God wot, right as ye hear,
Me to comfórt with friendly cheer,
She did her prowess and her might.
And truly eke so did this knight,
In that he could; and often said,
That of my woe he was ill paid,[10]
And curs'd the ship that him there brought,
The mast, the master that it wrought.
And, as each thing must have an end,
My sister here, our bother friend,[11]
Gan with her words so womanly
This knight entreat, and cunningly,
For mine honoúr and hers alsó,
And said that with her we should go
Both in her ship, where she was brought,
Which was so wonderfully wrought,
So clean, so rich, and so array'd,
That we were both content and paid;[12]
And me to comfort and to please,
And my heart for to put at ease,
She took great pain in little while,
And thus hath brought us to this isle,
As ye may see; wherefore each one
I pray you thank her one and one,
As heartily as ye can devise,
Or imagine in any wise."
At once there then men mightë see'n,
A world of ladies fall on kneen
Before my lady,—

Thanking her, and placing themselves at her commandment. Then the queen sent the aged lady to the knight, to learn of him why he had done her all this woe; and when the messenger had discharged her mission, telling the knight that in the general opinion he had done amiss, he fell down suddenly as if dead for sorrow and repentance. Only with great difficulty, by the queen herself, was he restored to consciousness and comfort; but though she spoke kind and hope-inspiring words, her heart was not in her speech,

For her intent was, to his barge
Him for to bring against the eve,
With certain ladies, and take leave,
And pray him, of his gentleness,
To suffer her[13] thenceforth in peace,
As other princes had before;
And from thenceforth, for evermore,
She would him worship in all wise
That gentlenessë might devise;
And pain her[14] wholly to fulfil,
In honour, his pleasúre and will.
And during thus this knightë's woe,—
Present[15] the queen and other mo',
My lady and many another wight,—
Ten thousand shippës at a sight
I saw come o'er the wavy flood,
With sail and oar; that, as I stood
Them to behold, I gan marváil
From whom might come so many a sail;
For, since the time that I was born,
Such a navy therebeforn
Had I not seen, nor so array'd,
That for the sight my heartë play'd
Ay to and fro within my breast;
For joy long was ere it would rest.
For there were sailës full of flow'rs;[16]
After, castles with huge tow'rs,[17]
Seeming full of armës bright,
That wond'rous lusty[18] was the sight;
With largë tops, and mastës long,
Richly depaint' and rear'd among.[19]
At certain timës gan repair
Smallë birdës down from the air,

1 Expecting to succeed. 2 Regarding, gazing on.
3 Well satisfied. 4 Might not have.
5 Had it not been for the prompt kindness.
6 Hastened. 7 Holden, obliged.
8 Physician. 9 Delivered.
10 Distressed, ill-pleased with himself.
11 "Your brother friend," is the common reading; but the phrase has no apparent applicability; and perhaps the better reading is "our bother friend"—that is, the lady who has proved herself a friend both to me and to you. In the same way, Reason, in Troilus' soliloquy on the impending loss of his mistress, is made, addressing Troilus and Cressida, to speaks of "your bother," or "bothë," love. 12 Satisfied.
13 That is, to let her dwell. 14 Make her utmost efforts.
15 (There being) present.
16 Embroidered with flowers.
17 High embattled poops and forecastles, as in mediæval ships of war. 18 Pleasant.
19 Raised among them.

And on the shippës' bounds[1] about
Sat and sang, with voice full out,
Ballads and lays right joyously,
As they could in their harmony.

The ladies were alarmed and sorrow-stricken at sight of the ships, thinking that the knight's companions were on board; and they went towards the walls of the isle, to shut the gates. But it was Cupid who came; and he had already landed, and marched straight to the place where the knight lay. Then he chid the queen for her unkindness to his servant; shot an arrow into her heart; and passed through the crowd, until he found the poet's lady, whom he saluted and complimented, urging her to have pity on him that loved her. While the poet, standing apart, was revolving all this in his mind, and resolving truly to serve his lady, he saw the queen advance to Cupid, with a petition in which she besought forgiveness of past offences, and promised continual and zealous service till her death. Cupid smiled, and said that he would be king within that island, his new conquest; then, after long conference with the queen, he called a council for the morrow, of all who chose to wear his colours. In the morning, such was the press of ladies, that scarcely could standing-room be found in all the plain. Cupid presided; and one of his counsellors addressed the mighty crowd, promising that ere his departure his lord should bring to an agreement all the parties there present. Then Cupid gave to the knight and the dreamer each his lady; promised his favour to all the others in that place who would truly and busily serve in love; and at evening took his departure. Next morning, having declined the proffered sovereignty of the island, the poet's mistress also embarked, leaving him behind; but he dashed through the waves, was drawn on board her ship from peril of death, and graciously received into his lady's lasting favour. Here the poet awakes, finding his cheeks and body all wet with tears; and, removing into another chamber, to rest more in peace, he falls asleep anew, and continues the dream. Again he is within the island, where the knight and all the ladies are assembled on a green, and it is resolved by the assembly, not only that the knight shall be their king, but that every lady there shall be wedded also. It is determined that the knight shall depart that very day, and return, within ten days, with such a host of Benedicts, that none in the isle need lack husbands. The knight

Anon into a little barge
Brought was, late against an eve,
Where of all he took his leave.
Which bargë was, as a man thought,
After[2] his pleasure to him brought;
The queen herself accustom'd ay
In the samë barge to play.[3]
It needed neither mast nor rother[4]
(I have not heard of such another),
Nor master for the governance;[5]
It sailed by thought and pleasánce,
Withoutë labour, east and west;
All was one, calm or tempést.[6]
And I went with, at his request,
And was the first pray'd to the feast.[7]
When he came unto his countrý,
And passed had the wavy sea,
In a haven deep and large
He left his rich and noble barge,
And to the court, shortly to tell,
He went, where he was wont to dwell,—

And was gladly received as king by the estates of the land; for during his absence his father, "old, and wise, and hoar," had died, commending to their fidelity his absent son. The prince related to the estates his journey, and his success in finding the princess in quest of whom he had gone seven years before; and said that he must have sixty thousand guests at his marriage feast. The lords gladly guaranteed the number within the set time; but afterwards they found that fifteen days must be spent in the necessary preparations. Between shame and sorrow, the prince, thus compelled to break his faith, took to his bed, and, in wailing and self-reproach,

—Endur'd the days fifteen,
Till that the lords, on an evéne,[8]
Him came and told they ready were,
And showed in few wordës there,
How and what wise they had purvey'd
For his estate,[9] and to him said,
That twenty thousand knights of name,
And forty thousand without blame,
Allë come of noble lignë[10]
Together in a company
Were lodged on a river's side,
Him and his pleasure there t' abide.
The princë then for joy uprose,
And, where they lodged were, he goes,
Withoutë more, that samë night,
And there his supper made to dight;[11]
And with them bode[12] till it was day.
And forthwith to take his journéy,
Leaving the strait, holding the large,
Till he came to his noble barge:
And when the prince, this lusty knight,
With his people in armës bright,
Was comë where he thought to pass,[13]
And knew well none abiding was
Behind, but all were there presént,
Forthwith anon all his intent
He told them there, and made his cries[14]
Thorough his hostë that day twice,
Commanding ev'ry living wight
There being present in his sight,

1 Bulwarks. 2 According to. 3 Take her sport. 4 Rudder. 5 Steerage.
13 Compare Spenser's account of Phædria's barque, in "The Faerie Queen," canto vi. book ii., page 380; and, *mutatis mutandis*, Chaucer's description of the wondrous horse, in The Squire's Tale, pages 116, 118.

7 The bridal feast. 8 Evening.
9 Provided suitably to his rank.
10 Line, lineage. 11 Prepare.
12 Abode, waited.
13 From his own land to the ladies' isle.
14 Proclamation.

To be the morrow on the rivâge,[1]
Where he begin would his voyâge.
The morrow come, the cry was kept;[2]
But few were there that night that slept,
But truss'd and purvey'd[3] for the morrow;
For fault of ships was all their sorrow;
For, save the barge, and other two,
Of shippës there I saw no mo'.
Thus in their doubtës as they stood,
Waxing the sea, coming the flood,
Was cried "To ship go ev'ry wight!"
Then was but hie that hie him might,[4]
And to the barge, me thought, each one
They went, without was left not one,
Horsë, nor male,[5] truss, nor baggâge,
Salad,[6] spear, gardëbrace,[7] nor page,
But was lodged and room enough;
At which shipping me thought I lough,[8]
And gan to marvel in my thought,
How ever such a ship was wrought.[9]
For what people that can increase,[10]
Nor ne'er so thick might be the prease,[11]
But allë haddë room at will;
There was not one was lodged ill.
For, as I trow, myself the last
Was one, and lodged by the mast;
And where I look'd I saw such room
As all were lodged in a town.
Forth went the ship, said was the creed;[12]
And on their knees, for their good speed,[13]
Down kneeled ev'ry wight a while,
And prayed fast that to the isle
They mightë come in safëty,
The prince and all the company,
With worship and withoutë blame,
Or disclander[14] of his name,
Of the promise he should return
Within the time he did sojourn
In his landë biding[15] his host;
This was their prayer least and most:
To keep the day it might not be'n,
That he appointed with the queen.

Wherefore the prince slept neither day nor night, till he and his people landed on the glass-walled isle, "weening to be in heav'n that night." But ere they had gone a little way, they met a lady all in black, with piteous countenance, who reproached the prince for his untenance, and informed him that, unable to bear the reproach to their name, caused by the lightness of their trust in strangers, the queen and all the ladies of the isle had vowed neither to eat, nor drink, nor sleep, nor speak, nor cease weeping till all were dead. The queen had died the first; and half of the other ladies had already "under the earth ta'en lodging new." The woeful recorder of all these woes invites the prince to behold the queen's hearse:

"Come within, come see her hearse;
Where ye shall see the piteous[16] sight
That ever yet was shown to knight;
For ye shall see ladies stand,
Each with a greatë rod in hand,
Clad in black, with visage white,
Ready each other for to smite,
If any be that will not weep;
Or who makes countenance to sleep.
They be so beat, that all so blue
They be as cloth that dy'd is new."

Scarcely has the lady ceased to speak, when the prince plucks forth a dagger, plunges it into his heart, and, drawing but one breath, expires.

For whichë cause the lusty host,
Which [stood] in battle on the coast,
At once for sorrow such a cry
Gan rear, thorough the companý,
That to the heav'n heard was the soun',
And under th' earth as far adown,
And wildë beastës for the fear
So suddenly affrayed were,
That for the doubt, while they might dure,[17]
They ran as of their lives unsure,
From the woodës into the plain,
And from valleys the high mountâin
They sought, and ran as beastës blind,
That clean forgotten had their kind.[18]

The lords of the laggard host ask the woe-begone lady what should be done; she answers that nothing can now avail, but that for remembrance they should build in their land, open to public view, "in some notable old city," a chapel engraved with some memorial of the queen. And straightway, with a sigh, she also "pass'd her breath."

Then said the lordës of the host,
And so concluded least and most,
That they would ay in houses of thack[19]
Their livës lead, and wear but black,
And forsake all their pleasances,
And turn all joy to penances;
And bare the dead prince to the barge,
And named them should[20] have the charge;
And to the hearse where lay the queen
The remnant went, and down on kneen,
Holding their hands on high, gan cry,
"Mercy! mercy!" evereach thry;[21]
And curs'd the time that ever sloth
Should have such masterdom of troth.
And to the barge, a longë mile,
They bare her forth; and, in a while,
All the ladies, one and one,

1 Shore.
2 The command of the proclamation was obeyed.
3 Packed up and provided.
4 Then it was all haste who haste might.
5 Trunk, wallet.
6 A small helmet; French, "salade."
7 French, "garde-bras," an arm-shield; probably resembling the "gay bracer" which the Yeoman, in the Prologue to The Canterbury Tales, wears on his arm; see page 18.
8 Laughed.
9 Constructed.
10 No matter how much the people might increase.
11 Press, crowd.
12 Confession and prayer were the usual preliminaries of any enterprise in those superstitious days; and in these days of enlightenment the fashion yet lingers among the most superstitious class—the fisher-folk.
13 To pray for success.
14 Reproach, slander.
15 Waiting for.
16 The most piteous.
17 While they had yet a chance of safety.
18 Nature.
19 Thatch; they would quit their castles and houses of stone for humble huts.
20 Those who should.
21 Each one thrice.

By companies were brought each one.
And pass'd the sea, and took the land,
And in new hearses, on a sand,
Put and brought were all anon,
Unto a city clos'd with stone,
Where it had been used ay
The kingës of the land to lay,
After they reigned in honoúrs;
And writ was which were conqueroúrs;
In an abbéy of nunnës black,
Which accustom'd were to wake,
And of uságe rise each a-night,
To pray for ev'ry living wight.
And so befell, as is the guise,
Ordain'd and said was the servíce
Of the prince and eke of the queen,
So devoutly as mightë be'n;
And, after that, about the hearses,
Many orisons and verses,
Withoutë note[1] full softëly
Said were, and that full heartily;
That all the night, till it was day,
The people in the church gan pray
Unto the Holy Trinitý,
Of those soulës to have pitý.
And when the nightë past and run
Was, and the newë day begun,—
The young morrow with rayës red,
Which from the sun all o'er gan spread,
Attemper'd[2] clearë was and fair,
And made a time of wholesome air,—
Befell a wondrous case[3] and strange
Among the people, and gan change
Soon the word, and ev'ry woe
Unto a joy, and some to two.
A bird, all feather'd blue and green,
With brightë rays like gold between,
As small thread over ev'ry joint,
All full of colour strange and coint,[4]
Uncouth[5] and wonderful to sight,
Upon the queenë's hearse gan light,
And sung full low and softëly
Three songës in their harmony,
Unletted of[6] every wight;
Till at the last an aged knight,
Which seem'd a man in greatë thought,
Like as he set all thing at nought,
With visage and eyes all forwept,[7]
And pale, as a man long unslept,
By the hearses as he stood,
With hasty handling of his hood
Unto a prince that by him past,
Made the bird somewhat aghast.[8]
Wherefore he rose and left his song,
And departed from us among,
And spread his wingës for to pass
By the place where he enter'd was.
And in his haste, shortly to tell,
Him hurt, that backward down he fell,
From a window richly paint,
With lives of many a divers saint,
And beat his wingës and bled fast,
And of the hurt thus died and past;
And lay there well an hour and more.
Till, at the last, of birds a score
Came and assembled at the place
Where the window broken was,
And made such waimentatioún,[9]
That pity was to hear the soun',
And the warbles of their throats,
And the cómplaint of their notes,
Which from joy clean was reversed.
And of them one the glass soon pierced,
And in his beak, of colours nine,
An herb he brought, flow'rless, all green,
Full of smallë leaves, and plain,[10]
Swart,[11] and long, with many a vein.
And where his fellow lay thus dead,
This herb he down laid by his head,
And dressed[12] it full softëlý,
And hung his head, and stood thereby.
Which herb, in less than half an hour,
Gan over all knit,[13] and after flow'r
Full out; and waxed ripe the seed;
And, right as one another feed
Would, in his beak he took the grain,
And in his fellow's beak certáin
It put, and thus within the third[14]
Upstood and pruned him the bird,
Which dead had been in all our sight;
And both together forth their flight
Took, singing, from us, and their leave;
Was none disturb them would nor grieve.
And, when they parted were and gone,
Th' abbess the seedës soon each one
Gathered had, and in her hand
The herb she took, well ávisand[15]
The leaf, the seed, the stalk, the flow'r,
And said it had a good savoúr,
And was no common herb to find,
And well approv'd of úncouth kind,[16]
And more than other virtuous;
Whoso might it have for to use
In his need, flower, leaf, or grain,
Of his heal might be certáin.
[She] laid it down upon the hearse
Where lay the queen; and gan rehearse
Each one to other what they had seen.
And, taling thus,[17] the seed wax'd green,
And on the dry hearse gan to spring,—
Which me thought was a wondrous thing,—
And, after that, flow'r and new seed;[18]
Of which the people all took heed,
And said it was some great mirácle,
Or medicine fine more than triácle;[19]
And were well done there to assay
If it might ease, in any way,
The corpses, which with torchëlight

1 Without music—although the office for the dead was generally sung.
2 Clement, calm.
3 Chance, event.
4 Quaint, strange.
5 Unfamiliar.
6 Unhindered by.
7 All steeped in tears.
8 Frightened.
9 Lamentation.
10 Smooth.
11 Black.
12 Arranged.
13 Bud.
14 Within the third hour after the bird had fallen dead.
15 Considering; present participle from "avise" or "advise."
16 Strange nature.
17 As they gossiped thus.
18 To flower and seed anew.
19 Or "treacle;" corrupted from Latin, "theriaca," an antidote. The word is used for medicine in general.

They waked had there all that night.
Soon did the lordës there consent,
And all the people thereto content,
With easy words and little fare;[1]
And made the queenë's visage bare,
Which showed was to all about,
Wherefore in swoon fell all the rout,[2]
And were so sorry, most and least,
That long of weeping they not ceas'd;
For of their lord the rémembránce
Unto them was such displeasánce,[3]
That for to live they called pain,
So were they very true and plain.
And after this the good abbéss
Of the grains gan choose and dress[4]
Three, with her fingers clean and smale,
And in the queenë's mouth, by tale,
One after other, full easily
She put, and eke full cunningly.[5]
Which showed somë such virtúe,
That proved was the medicine true.
For with a smiling countenance
The queen uprose, and of usánce[6]
As she was wont, to ev'ry wight
She made good cheer;[7] for whichë sight
The people, kneeling on the stones,
Thought they in heav'n were, soul and bones;
And to the prince, where that he lay,
They went to make the same assay.[8]
And when the queen it understood,
And how the medicine was good,
She pray'd that she might have the grains,
To relieve him from the pains
Which she and he had both endur'd.
And to him went, and so him cur'd,
That, within a little space,
Lusty and fresh alive he was,
And in good heal, and whole of speech,
And laugh'd, and said, "Gramercy, leach!"[9]
For which the joy throughout the town
So great was, that the bellës' soun'
Affray'd the people a journéy[10]
About the city ev'ry way;
And came and ask'd the cause, and why
They rungen were so statëlý.[11]
And after that the queen, th' abbéss,
Made diligence,[12] ere they would cease,
Such, that of ladies soon a rout[2]
Suing[13] the queen was all about;
And, call'd by name each one and told,[14]
Was none forgotten, young nor old.
There mightë men see joyës new,
When the medicine, fine and true,
Thus restor'd had ev'ry wight,
So well the queen as the knight,
Unto perfect joy and heal,
That floating they were in such weal[15]
As folk that woulden in no wise
Desire more perfect paradise.

On the morrow a general assembly was convoked, and it was resolved that the wedding-feast should be celebrated within the island. Messengers were sent to strange realms, to invite kings, queens, duchesses, and princesses; and a special embassy was despatched, in the magic barge, to seek the poet's mistress—who was brought back after fourteen days, to the great joy of the queen. Next day took place the wedding of the prince and all the knights to the queen and all the ladies; and a three months' feast followed, on a large plain "under a wood, in a champaign, betwixt a river and a well, where never had abbéy nor cell been, nor church, house, nor villáge, in time of any mannë's age." On the day after the general wedding, all entreated the poet's lady to consent to crown his love with marriage; she yielded; the bridal was splendidly celebrated; and to the sound of marvellous music the poet awoke, to find neither lady nor creature—but only old portraitures on the tapestry, of horsemen, hawks, and hounds, and hurt deer full of wounds. Great was his grief that he had lost all the bliss of his dream; and he concludes by praying his lady so to accept his love-service, that the dream may turn to reality.

Or ellës, without more I pray,
That this night, ere it be day,
I may unto my dream return,
And sleeping so forth ay sojourn
Aboutë the Isle of Pleasánce,
Under my lady's óbeisánce,[16]
In her servíce, and in such wise,
As it may please her to devise;
And gracë once to be accept',
Like as I dreamed when I slept,
And dure a thousand year and ten
In her good will: Amen, amen!

1 Ado, trouble.
2 Company, crowd.
3 Cause of grief.
4 Prepare.
5 Skilfully.
6 Custom.
7 Showed a gracious countenance.
8 Trial, experiment.
9 "Great thanks, my physician!"
10 To the distance of a day's journey.
11 Proudly, solemnly.
12 To administer the grain to the dead ladies.
13 Following.
14 Numbered.
15 Swimming in such happiness.
16 Subject to my lady.

THE PROLOGUE TO

THE LEGEND OF GOOD WOMEN.

[SOME difference of opinion exists as to the date at which Chaucer wrote "The Legend of Good Women." Those who would fix that date at a period not long before the poet's death—who would place the poem, indeed, among his closing labours—support their opinion by the fact that the Prologue recites most of Chaucer's principal works, and glances, besides, at a long array of other productions, too many to be fully catalogued. But, on the other hand, it is objected that the "Legend" makes no mention of "The Canterbury Tales" as such; while two of those Tales—the Knight's and the Second Nun's—are enumerated by the titles which they bore as separate compositions, before they were incorporated in the great collection: "The Love of Palamon and Arcite," and "The Life of Saint Cecile."[1] Tyrwhitt seems perfectly justified in placing the composition of the poem immediately before that of Chaucer's *magnum opus*, and after the marriage of Richard II. to his first queen, Anne of Bohemia. That event took place in 1382; and since it is to Anne that the poet refers when he makes Alcestis bid him give his poem to the queen "at Eltham or at Sheen," the "Legend" could not have been written earlier. The old editions tell us that "several ladies in the Court took offence at Chaucer's large speeches against the untruth of women; therefore the queen enjoin'd him to compile this book in the commendation of sundry maidens and wives, who show'd themselves faithful to faithless men. This seems to have been written after *The Flower and the Leaf*." Evidently it was, for distinct references to that poem are to be found in the Prologue; but more interesting is the indication which it furnishes, that "Troilus and Cressida" was the work, not of the poet's youth, but of his maturer age. We could hardly expect the queen—whether of Love or of England—to demand seriously from Chaucer a retractation of sentiments which he had expressed a full generation before, and for which he had made atonement by the splendid praises of true love sung in "The Court of Love," "The Cuckoo and the Nightingale," and other poems of youth and middle life. But "Troilus and Cressida" is coupled with "The Romance of the Rose," as one of the poems which had given offence to the servants and the God of Love; therefore we may suppose it to have more prominently engaged courtly notice at a late period of the poet's life, than even its undoubted popularity could explain. At whatever date, or in whatever circumstances, undertaken, "The Legend of Good Women" is a fragment. There are several signs that it was designed to contain the stories of twenty-five ladies, although the number of the good women is in the poem itself set down at nineteen; but nine legends only were actually composed, or have come down to us. They are, those of Cleopatra Queen of Egypt (126 lines), Thisbe of Babylon (218), Dido Queen of Carthage (442), Hypsipyle and Medea (312), Lucrece of Rome (206), Ariadne of Athens (340), Philomela (167), Phyllis (168), and Hypermnestra (162). Prefixed to these stories, which are translated or imitated from Ovid, is a Prologue containing 579 lines—the only part of the "Legend" given in the present edition. It is by far the most original, the strongest, and most pleasing part of the poem; the description of spring, and of his enjoyment of that season, are in Chaucer's best manner; and the political philosophy by which Alcestis mitigates the wrath of Cupid, adds another to the abounding proofs that, for his knowledge of the world, Chaucer fairly merits the epithet of "many-sided" which Shakespeare has won by his knowledge of man.]

A THOUSAND timës I have heardë tell,
That there is joy in heav'n, and pain in hell;
And I accord[2] it well that it is so;
But, natheless, yet wot[3] I well alsó,
That there is none dwelling in this countrý
That either hath in heav'n or hell y-be;[4]
Nor may of it no other wayës witten[3]

1 See note 19, page 171. 2 Grant agree.
3 Know. 4 Been.

But as he hath heard said, or found it written;
For by assay[5] there may no man it preve.[6]
But God forbid but that men should believe
Well morë thing than men have seen with eye!
Men shall not weenen ev'ry thing a lie
But if[7] himself it seëth, or else do'th;
For, God wot, thing is never the less sooth,[8]

5 Practical trial. 6 Prove, test.
7 Unless. 8 True.

Though ev'ry wightë may it not y-see.
Bernard, the Monkë, saw not all, pardie![1]
Then mustë we to bookës that we find
(Through which that oldë thingës be in mind),
And to the doctrine of these oldë wise,
Givë credénce, in ev'ry skilful[2] wise,
That tellen of these old approved stories,
Of holiness, of regnës,[3] of victóries,
Of love, of hate, and other sundry things
Of which I may not makë réhearsíngs;
And if that oldë bookës were away,
Y-lorn were of all rémembránce the key.
Well ought we, then, to honour and believe
These bookës, where we have none other preve.[4]
And as for me, though that I know but lite,
On bookës for to read I me delight,
And to them give I faith and good credénce,
And in my heart have them in reverence,
So heartily, that there is gamë none[5]
That from my bookës maketh me to go'n,
But it be seldom on the holyday;
Save, certainly, when that the month of May
Is comen, and I hear the fowlës sing,
And that the flowers ginnen for to spring,
Farewell my book and my devotión!
Now have I then such a condition,
That, above all the flowers in the mead,
Then love I most these flowers white and red,
Such that men callë Day's-eyes in our town;
To them have I so great affectioún,
As I said erst, when comen is the May,
That in my bed there dawneth me no day
That I n' am[6] up, and walking in the mead,
To see this flow'r against the sunnë spread,
When it upriseth early by the morrow;
That blissful sight softeneth all my sorrow,
So glad am I, when that I have presénce
Of it, to do it allë reverence,
As she that is of allë flowers flow'r,
Fulfilled of all virtue and honoúr,
And ever alike fair, and fresh of hue;
As well in winter, as in summer new,
This love I ever, and shall until I die;
All[7] swear I not, of this I will not lie,
There loved no wight hotter in his life.
And when that it is eve, I runnë blife,[8]
As soon as ever the sun begins to west,[9]
To see this flow'r, how it will go to rest,
For fear of night, so hateth she darknéss!
Her cheer[10] is plainly spread in the brightnéss
Of the sunnë, for there it will unclose.
Alas! that I had English, rhyme or prose,
Sufficiént this flow'r to praise aright!
But help me, ye that have cunning or might;[11]
Ye lovers, that can make of sentiment,
In this case ought ye to be diligent
To further me somewhat in my laboúr,
Whether ye be with the Leaf or the Flow'r;[12]
For well I wot, that ye have herebeforn
Of making ropen,[13] and led away the corn;
And I come after, gleaning here and there,
And am full glad if I may find an ear
Of any goodly word that you have left.
And though it hap me to rehearsen eft[14]
What ye have in your freshë songës said,
Forbearë me, and be not evil apaid,[15]
Since that ye see I do it in th' honoúr
Of love, and eke in service of the flow'r
Whom that I serve as I have wit or might.[16]
She is the clearness, and the very[17] light,
That in this darkë world me winds[18] and leads;
The heart within my sorrowful breast you dreads,
And loves so sore, that ye be, verilý,
The mistress of my wit, and nothing I.
My word, my works, are knit so in your bond,
That, as a harp obeyeth to the hand,
That makes it sound after his fingeríng,
Right so may ye out of my heartë bring
Such voice, right as you list, to laugh or plain;[19]
Be ye my guide, and lady sovëreign.
As to mine earthly god, to you I call,
Both in this work, and in my sorrows all.
But wherefore that I spake to give credénce
To old stories, and do them reverence,
And that men mustë morë things believe
Than they may see at eye, or ellës preve,[4]
That shall I say, when that I see my time;
I may not all at onës speak in rhyme.
My busy ghost,[20] that thirsteth always new
To see this flow'r so young, so fresh of hue,
Constrained me with so greedy desire,
That in my heart I feelë yet the fire,
That madë me to rise ere it were day,—
And this was now the first morrow of May,—
With dreadful heart, and glad devotión,
For to be at the resurrectión
Of this flower, when that it should unclose
Against the sun, that rose as red as rose,
That in the breast was of the beast[21] that day,
That Agenorë's daughter[22] led away.
And down on knees anon right I me set,
And as I could this freshë flow'r I gret,[23]
Kneeling alway, till it unclosed was,
Upon the smallë, softë, sweetë grass,
That was with flowers sweet embroider'd all,
Of such sweetness and such odoúr o'er all,[24]
That, for to speak of gum, or herb, or tree,
Comparison may none y-maked be;
For it surmounteth plainly all odoúrs,
And for rich beauty the most gay of flow'rs.
Forgotten had the earth his poor estate

1 A proverbial saying, signifying that even the wisest, or those who claim to be the wisest, cannot know everything. Saint Bernard, who was the last, or among the last, of the Fathers, lived in the first half of the twelfth century.
2 Reasonable.
3 Reigns, kingdoms.
4 Proof; prove.
5 No amusement. Compare Chaucer's account of his habits, in "The House of Fame," page 235.
6 Am not.
7 Although.
8 Quickly, eagerly.
9 To decline westward.
10 Countenance.
11 Skill or power.
12 See introductory note to "The Flower and the Leaf," pages 224–25.
13 Reaped. The meaning is, that the "lovers" have long ago said all that can be said, by way of poetry, or "making," on the subject. See note 10, page 273.
14 Again.
15 Displeased.
16 The poet glides here into an address to his lady.
17 True.
18 Turns, guides.
19 Complain, mourn.
20 Spirit.
21 The (constellation of the) Bull.
22 Europa. See note 6, page 438.
23 Greeted.
24 Everywhere.

Of winter, that him naked made and mate,[1]
And with his sword of cold so sorë grieved;
Now hath th' attemper[2] sun all that releaved[3]
That naked was, and clad it new again.
The smallë fowlës, of the season fain,[4]
That of the panter[5] and the net be scap'd,
Upon the fowler, that them made awhap'd[6]
In winter, and destroyed had their brood,
In his despite them thought it did them good
To sing of him, and in their song despise
The foulë churl, that, for his covetise,[7]
Had them betrayed with his sophistrý.[8]
This was their song: "The fowler we defy,
And all his craft:" and somë sungë clear
Layës of love, that joy it was to hear,
In worshipping[9] and praising of their make;[10]
And for the blissful newë summer's sake,
Upon the branches full of blossoms soft,
In their delight they turned them full oft,
And sungë, "Blessed be Saint Valentine![11]
For on his day I chose you to be mine,
Withoutë répentíng, my heartë sweet."
And therewithal their beaks began to meet,
Yielding honoúr, and humble obeisánces,
To love, and did their other observánces
That longen unto Love and to Natúre;
Construe that as you list, I do no cure.[12]
And those that haddë done unkindëness,[13]
As doth the tidife, for newfangleness,[14]
Besoughtë mercy for their trespassing,
And humblely sangë their repentíng,
And swore upon the blossoms to be true,
So that their matës would upon them rue,[15]
And at the lastë madë their accord.[16]
All[17] found they Danger[18] for a time a lord,
Yet Pity, through her strongë gentle might,
Forgave, and madë mercy pass aright
Through Innocence, and ruled Courtesy.
But I ne call not innocence follý
Nor false pity, for virtue is the mean,
As Ethic[19] saith, in such manner I mean.
And thus these fowlës, void of all malíce,
Accorded unto Love, and leftë vice
Of hate, and sangen all of one accord,
"Welcome, Summer, our governor and lord!"
And Zephyrus and Flora gentilly
Gave to the flowers, soft and tenderly,
Their sweetë breath, and made them for to spread,
As god and goddess of the flow'ry mead;
In which me thought I mightë, day by day,
Dwellen alway, the jolly month of May,
Withoutë sleep, withoutë meat or drink.
Adown full softly I began to sink,
And, leaning on mine elbow and my side
The longë day I shope me[20] to abide,
For nothing ellës, and I shall not lie,
But for to look upon the daïsý;
That men by reason well it callë may
The Dayë's-eye, or else the Eye of Day,
The empress and the flow'r of flowers all.
I pray to God that fairë may she fall!
And all that lovë flowers, for her sake:
But, nathelessë, ween not[21] that I make[22]
In praising of the Flow'r against the Leaf,
No more than of the corn against the sheaf;
For as to me is lever none nor lother,[23]
I n'am withholden yet with neither n' other.[24]
Nor I n'ot[25] who serves Leaf, nor who the Flow'r;
Well brookë they[26] their service or laboúr!
For this thing is all of another tun,[27]
Of old story, ere such thing was begun.
When that the sun out of the south gan west,
And that this flow'r gan close, and go to rest,
For darkness of the night, the which she dread;[28]
Home to my house full swiftly I me sped,
To go to rest, and early for to rise,
To see this flower spread, as I devise.[29]
And in a little arbour that I have,
That benched was of turfës fresh y-grave,[30]
I bade men shouldë me my couchë make;
For dainty[31] of the newë summer's sake,
I bade them strowë flowers on my bed.
When I was laid, and had mine eyen hid,
I fell asleep; within an hour or two,
Me mette[32] how I lay in the meadow tho,[33]
To see this flow'r that I love so and dread.
And from afar came walking in the mead
The God of Love, and in his hand a queen;
And she was clad in royal habit green;
A fret[34] of gold she haddë next her hair,
And upon that a white corown she bare,
With flowrons[35] small, and, as I shall not lie,
For all the world right as a daïsý
Y-crowned is, with whitë leavës lite,[36]
So were the flowrons of her crownë white.
For of one pearlë, fine, orientiál,
Her whitë crownë was y-maked all,
For which the whitë crown above the green
Madë her like a daisy for to see'n,[37]
Consider'd eke her fret of gold above.
Y-clothed was this mighty God of Love
In silk embroider'd, full of greenë greves,[38]
In which there was a fret of red rose leaves,
The freshest since the world was first begun.
His gilt hair was y-crowned with a sun,
Instead of gold, for[39] heaviness and weight;

1 Dejected, lifeless. 2 Temperate.
3 Furnished anew with leaves.
4 Glad. 5 Draw-net, bag-net.
6 Terrified, confounded.
7 Greed. 8 Stratagems, deceptions.
9 Honouring. 10 Mate.
11 See "The Assembly of Fowls," pages 220-221.
12 I care nothing.
13 Committed offence against natural laws.
14 The titmouse, or any other small bird, which sometimes brings up the cuckoo's young when its own have been destroyed. See note 24, page 223.
15 Take pity. 16 Reconciliation.
17 Although. 18 Anger, disdain.
19 The Ethics of Aristotle.
20 Resolved, prepared. 21 Do not fancy.
22 Rhyme, make (this poem).
23 Neither is more nor less liked.
24 I am not bound by, holden to, either the one or the other. 25 Nor do I know.
26 Much may they profit by—well may they enjoy.
27 Wine of another tun—a quite different matter.
28 Dreaded. 29 Describe.
30 With turfs freshly dug or cut. Compare the description of the arbour in "The Flower and the Leaf," page 226.
31 Pleasure. 32 I dreamed.
33 Then. 34 Band.
35 Florets; little flowers on the disk of the main flower; French, "fleuron."
36 Small. 37 To look upon.
38 Boughs. 39 In order to avoid.

Therewith me thought his facë shone so bright,
That well unnethës might I him behold;
And in his hand me thought I saw him hold
Two fiery dartës, as the gledës[1] red;
And angel-like his wingës saw I spread.
And all be[2] that men say that blind is he,
Algate[3] me thoughtë that he might well see;
For sternly upon me he gan behold,
So that his looking did my heartë cold.[4]
And by the hand he held this noble queen,
Crowned with white, and clothed all in green,
So womanly, so benign, and so meek,
That in this worldë, though that men would seek,
Half of her beauty shouldë they not find
In creatúre that formed is by Kind;[5]
And therefore may I say, as thinketh me,
This song in praising of this lady free:

"Hide, Absolon, thy giltë[6] tresses clear;
Esther, lay thou thy meekness all adown;
Hide, Jonathan, all thy friendly mannére,
Penelopé, and Marcia Catoún,[7]
Make of your wifehood no comparisoún;
Hide ye your beauties, Isoude[8] and Heléne;
My lady comes, that all this may distain.[9]

"Thy fairë body let it not appear,
Lavine;[10] and thou, Lucrece of Romë town;
And Polyxene,[11] that boughtë love so dear,
And Cleopatra, with all thy passioún,
Hide ye your truth of love, and your renown;
And thou, Thisbe, that hadst of love such pain;
My lady comes, that all this may distain.

"Hero, Didó, Laodamia, y-fere,
And Phyllis, hanging for Demophoön,
And Canacé, espiëd by thy cheer,
Hypsipylé, betrayed by Jasoún,
Make of your truthë neither boast nor soun';
Nor Hypermnestr' nor Ariadne, ye twain;
My lady comes, that all this may distain."

This ballad may full well y-sungen be,
As I have said erst, by my lady free;
For, certainly, all these may not suffice
T' appairë[12] with my lady in no wise;
For, as the sunnë will the fire distain,
So passeth all my lady sovëreign,
That is so good, so fair, so debonair,
I pray to God that ever fall her fair!
For n' haddë comfort been of her presénce,[13]
I had been dead, without any defence,
For dread of Lovë's wordës, and his cheer;
As, when time is, hereafter ye shall hear.
Behind this God of Love, upon the green,
I saw coming of Ladies ninëteen,
In royal habit, a full easy pace;
And after them of women such a trace,[14]
That, since that God Adam had made of earth,
The thirdë part of mankind, or the ferth,[15]
Ne ween'd I not[16] by possibility,
Had ever in this widë world y-be;[17]
And true of love these women were each one.
Now whether was that a wonder thing, or non,[18]
That, right anon as that they gan espy
This flow'r, which that I call the daïsý,
Full suddenly they stenten[19] all at once,
And kneeled down, as it were for the nonce,
And sangë with one voice, "Heal and honoúr
To truth of womanhead, and to this flow'r,
That bears our aller prize in figuring;[20]
Her whitë crownë bears the witnessing!"
And with that word, a-compass enviroun[21]
They settë them full softëly adown.
First sat the God of Love, and since[22] his queen,
With the whitë corownë, clad in green;
And sithen[23] all the remnant by and by,
As they were of estate, full courteouslý;
And not a word was spoken in the place,
The mountance[24] of a furlong way of space.
I, kneeling by this flow'r, in good intent
Abode, to knowë what this people meant,
As still as any stone, till, at the last,
The God of Love on me his eyen cast,
And said, "Who kneeleth there?" and I answér'd
Unto his asking, when that I it heard,
And said, "It am I," and came to him near,
And salued[25] him. Quoth he, "What dost thou here,
So nigh mine owen flow'r, so boldëly?
It werë better worthy, truëly,
A worm to nighë[26] near my flow'r than thou."
"And why, Sir," quoth I, "an'[27] it liketh you?"
"For thou," quoth he, "art thereto nothing able,
It is my relic,[28] dign[29] and delectáble,
And thou my foe, and all my folk warrayest,[30]
And of mine oldë servants thou missayest,
And hind'rest them, with thy translatión,
And lettest[31] folk from their devotión
To servë me, and holdest it follý
To servë Love; thou may'st it not deny;
For in plain text, withoutë need of glose,[32]
Thou hast translated the Romance of the Rose,
That is a heresy against my law,
And maketh wisë folk from me withdraw;
And of Cressíde thou hast said as thee list,
That maketh men to women less to trust,
That be as true as e'er was any steel.

1 Glowing coals. 2 Although.
3 At all events.
4 Made my heart grow cold.
5 Nature. 6 Golden.
7 Mr Bell thinks that Chaucer here praises the complaisance of Marcia, the wife of Cato, in complying with his will when he made her over to his friend Hortensius. It would be in better keeping with the spirit of the poet's praise, to believe that we should read "Porcia Catoun"—Porcia the daughter of Cato, who was married to Brutus, and whose perfect wifehood has been celebrated in The Franklin's Tale. See note 3, page 129.
8 See note 33, page 219. 9 Outdo, obscure.
10 Lavinia, the heroine of the Æneid, who became the wife of Æneas.
11 Polyxena, daughter of Priam, king of Troy, fell in love with Achilles, and, when he was killed (note 34, page 219), she fled to the Greek camp, and slew herself on the tomb of her hero-lover.
12 With which to impair, surpass in beauty or honour.
13 If it had not been for the comfort afforded by her presence. 14 Train.
15 Fourth. 16 I never fancied.
17 Been. 18 Not. 19 Stopped.
20 That in its figure bears the prize from us all.
21 All around in a ring.
22 Afterwards. 23 Then.
24 Extent, duration. See note 37, page 245.
25 Saluted. 26 Approach, draw nigh. 27 If.
28 Emblem; or cherished treasure; like the relics at the shrines of saints. 29 Worthy.
30 Molestest, censurest. 31 Preventest.
32 Comment, gloss.

Of thine answér advisë thee right weel;[1]
For though that thou reniëd hast my lay,[2]
As other wretches have done many a day,
By Saintë Venus, that my mother is,
If that thou live, thou shalt repentë this,
So cruelly, that it shall well be seen."
Then spake this Lady, clothed all in green,
And saidë, "God, right of your courtesý,
Ye mightë hearken if he can reply
Against all this, that ye have to him meved;[3]
A goddë shouldë not be thus aggrieved,
But of his deity he shall be stable,
And thereto gracious and merciáble.[4]
And if ye n'ere[5] a god, that knoweth all,
Then might it be, as I you tellë shall,
This man to you may falsely be accused,
Whereas by right him ought to be excused;
For in your court is many a losengeour,[6]
And many a quaint toteler accusour,[7]
That tabour[8] in your earës many a soun',
Right after their imaginatioún,
To have your dalliance,[9] and for envý;
These be the causes, and I shall not lie,
Envy is lavender[10] of the Court alway,
For she departeth neither night nor day
Out of the house of Cæsar, thus saith Dant';
Whoso that go'th, algate she shall not want.[11]
And eke, parauntre,[12] for this man is nice,[13]
He mightë do it guessing[14] no malice;
For he useth thingës for to make;[15]
Him recketh naught of[16] what mattére he take;
Or he was bidden makë thilkë tway[17]
Of[18] some persón, and durst it not withsay;[19]
Or him repenteth utterly of this.
He hath not done so grievously amiss,
To translatë what oldë clerkës write,
As though that he of malice would endite,[20]
Despite of Love, and had himself it wrought.
This should a righteous lord have in his thought,
And not be like tyrants of Lombardy,
That have no regard but at tyranny.[21]
For he that king or lord is naturel,
Him oughtë not be tyrant or cruél,
As is a farmer,[22] to do the harm he can;
He mustë think, it is his liegëman,
And is his treasure, and his gold in coffer;
This is the sentence[23] of the philosópher:
A king to keep his lieges in justíce,
Withoutë doubtë that is his office.
All[24] will he keep his lords in their degree,—
As it is right and skilful[25] that they be,
Enhanced and honoúred, and most dear,
For they be halfë gods[26] in this world here,—
Yet must he do both right to poor and rich,
All be[24] that their estate be not y-lich;[27]
And have of poorë folk compassión.
For lo! the gentle kind[28] of the lión;
For when a fly offendeth him, or biteth,
He with his tail away the flyë smiteth,
All easily; for of his genterý[29]
Him deigneth not to wreak him on a fly,
As doth a cur, or else another beast.
In noble corage ought to be arrest,[30]
And weighen ev'rything by equity,
And ever have regard to his degree.
For, Sir, it is no mastery for a lord
To damn[31] a man, without answer of word;
And for a lord, that is full foul to use.[32]
And it be so he may him not excuse,[33]
But asketh mercy with a dreadful[34] heart,
And proffereth him, right in his bare shirt,
To be right at your owen judgëment,
Then ought a god, by short advisëment,[35]
Consider his own honoúr, and his trespass;
For since no pow'r of death lies in this case,
You ought to be the lighter merciáble;[36]
Lettë[37] your ire, and be somewhat tractáble!
This man hath served you of his cunníng,[38]
And further'd well your law in his makíng.[39]
Albeit that he cannot well endite,
Yet hath he madë lewëd[40] folk delight
To servë you, in praising of your name.
He made the book that hight the House of Fame,
And eke the Death of Blanchë the Duchess,
And the Parliament of Fowlës, as I guess,
And all the Love of Palamon and Arcite,[41]
Of Thebes, though the story is known lite;[42]
And many a hymnë for your holydays,
That hightë ballads, roundels, virëlays.
And, for to speak of other holiness,
He hath in prosë tránslatéd Boece,[43]
And made the Life also of Saint Cecile;[41]

1 Consider right well.
2 Abjured my law or religion.
3 All this accusation that you have moved, advanced, against him.
4 Merciful.
5 Were not.
6 Deceiver. See note 5, page 170, on a parallel passage in The Nun's Priest's Tale.
7 Many a strange prating accuser. "Toteler" is an old form of the word "tatler," from the Anglo-Saxon, "totælan," to talk much, to tattle.
8 Drum.
9 Pleasant conversation, company.
10 Washerwoman, laundress; the word represents "meretrice" in Dante's original—meaning a courtezan; but we can well understand that Chaucer thought it prudent, and at the same time more true to the moral state of the English Court, to change the character assigned to Envy. He means that Envy is perpetually at Court, like some garrulous, bitter old woman employed there in the most servile offices, who remains at her post through all the changes among the courtiers. The passage cited from Dante will be found in the "Inferno," canto xiii. 64-69.
11 At all events *she* will not be wanting.
12 Peradventure.
13 Foolish.
14 Thinking.
15 To compose poetry.
16 He cares nothing.
17 Compose those two.
18 By.
19 Refuse, deny.
20 Would himself endite, out of malice.
21 Chaucer says that the usurping lords who seized on the government of the free Lombard cities, had no regard for any rule of government save sheer tyranny—but a natural lord, and no usurper, ought not to be a tyrant.
22 One who merely farms power or revenue for his own purposes and his own gain.
23 Opinion, sentiment.
24 Although.
25 Reasonable.
26 Demigods.
27 Alike.
28 Nature.
29 Nobleness.
30 In a noble nature ought to be self-restraint.
31 Condemn.
32 Such a practice is most infamous.
33 And if he (the offender) cannot excuse himself.
34 Fearing, timid.
35 Deliberation.
36 The more easily merciful.
37 Restrain, or dismiss.
38 Ability.
39 Poetising.
40 Ignorant.
41 See the introductory note, page 281.
42 Little.
43 "De Consolatione Philosophiæ;" to which frequent reference is made in The Canterbury Tales. See, for instances, note 3, page 46; and note 6, page 121.

He made also, gone is a greatë while,
Origenes upon the Magdalene.[1]
Him oughtë now to have the lessë pain ;[2]
He hath made many a lay, and many a thing.
Now as ye be a god, and eke a king,
I your Alcestis,[3] whilom queen of Thrace,
I askë you this man, right of your grace,
That ye him never hurt in all his life ;
And he shall swearë to you, and that blife,[4]
He shall no more aguilten[5] in this wise,
But shall maken, as ye will him devise,
Of women true in loving all their life,
Whereso ye will, of maiden or of wife,
And further you as much as he missaid
Or[6] in the Rose, or ellës in Cresseide."
The God of Love answered her anon :
"Madame," quoth he, "it is so long agone
That I you knew, so charitable and true,
That never yet, since that the world was new,
To me ne found I better none than ye ;
If that I wouldë savë my degree,
I may nor will not warnë[7] your request ;
All lies in you, do with him as you lest.
I all forgive withoutë longer space ;[8]
For he who gives a gift, or doth a grace,
Do it betimes, his thank is well the more ;[9]
And deemë[10] ye what he shall do therefor.
Go thankë now my Lady here," quoth he.
I rose, and down I set me on my knee,
And saidë thus ; "Madame, the God above
Foryieldë[11] you that ye the God of Love
Have madë me his wrathë to forgive ;
And gracë me[12] so longë for to live,
That I may knowë soothly what ye be,
That have me help'd, and put in this degree!
But truëly I ween'd, as in this case,
Naught t' have aguilt,[13] nor done to Love trespáss ;[14]
For why ? a truë man, withoutë dread,
Hath not to partë[15] with a thievë's deed.
Nor a true lover oughtë me to blame,
Though that I spoke a false lover some shame.
They oughtë rather with me for to hold,
For that I of Cressída wrote or told,
Or of the Rose, what so mine author meant ;[16]
Algatë,[17] God wot, it was mine intent
To further truth in love, and it cherice,[18]
And to beware from falseness and from vice,
By such example ; this was my meaníng."
And she answér'd ; "Let be thine arguing,
For Lovë will not counterpleaded be[19]
In right nor wrong, and learnë that of me ;
Thou hast thy grace, and hold thee right thereto.
Now will I say what penance thou shalt do
For thy trespáss ;[14] and understand it here :
Thou shalt, while that thou livest, year by year,
The mostë partie of thy timë spend
In making of a glorious Legénd
Of Goodë Women, maidenës and wives,
That werë true in loving all their lives ;
And tell of falsë men that them betray,
That all their lifë do naught but assay
How many women they may do a shame ;
For in your world that is now held a game.[20]
And though thou likë not a lover be,[21]
Speak well of love ; this penance give I thee.
And to the God of Love I shall so pray,
That he shall charge his servants, by any way,
To further thee, and well thy labour quite :[22]
Go now thy way, thy penance is but lite.
And, when this book ye make, give it the queen
On my behalf, at Eltham, or at Sheen."
The God of Love gan smile, and then he said :
"Know'st thou," quoth he, "whether this be wife or maid,
Or queen, or countess, or of what degree,
That hath so little penance given thee,
That hath deserved sorely for to smart ?
But pity runneth soon in gentle heart ;[23]
That may'st thou see, she kitheth[24] what she is.'
And I answér'd : "Nay, Sir, so have I bliss,
No more but that I see well she is good."
"That is a truë talë, by my hood,"
Quoth Love ; "and that thou knowest well, pardie !
If it be so that thou advisë[25] thee.
Hast thou not in a book, li'th[26] in thy chest,
The greatë goodness of the queen Alceste,
That turned was into a daïsý ?
She that for her husbandë chose to die,
And eke to go to hell rather than he ;
And Hercules rescúëd her, pardie !
And brought her out of hell again to bliss ?"
And I answér'd again, and saidë ; "Yes,
Now know I her ; and is this good Alceste,
The daïsý, and mine own heartë's rest ?
Now feel I well the goodness of this wife,
That both after her death, and in her life,
Her greatë bounty[27] doubleth her renown.
Well hath she quit[28] me mine affectioún
That I have to her flow'r the daïsý ;
No wonder is though Jove her stellify,[29]
As telleth Agathon,[30] for her goodnéss ;
Her whitë crownë bears of it witnéss ;
For all so many virtues haddë she
As smallë flowrons in her crownë be.

1 A poem entitled "The Lamentation of Mary Magdalene," said to have been "taken out of St Origen," is included in the editions of Chaucer; but its authenticity, and consequently its identity with the poem here mentioned, are doubted.
2 Penalty.
3 See note 32, page 201.
4 Quickly.
5 Offend.
6 Either.
7 Refuse.
8 Delay.
9 A paraphrase of the well-known proverb, "Bis dat qui cito dat."
10 Adjudge.
11 Reward.
12 Give me grace.
13 Offended.
14 Offence.
15 Hath no share in.
16 That is, they ought rather to thank me for giving a faithful translation.
17 By all ways.
18 Cherish.
19 The same prohibition occurs in the Fifteenth Statute of "The Court of Love," page 204.
20 Considered a sport.
21 Chaucer is always careful to allege his abstinence from the pursuits of gallantry ; he does so prominently in "The Court of Love," "The Assembly of Fowls," and "The House of Fame."
22 Requite.
23 Into the heart of one nobly born. The same is said of Theseus, in The Knight's Tale, page 34 ; and of Canacé, by the falcon, in The Squire's Tale, page 120.
24 Showeth.
25 Bethink.
26 (That) lies.
27 Virtue.
28 Recompensed.
29 Assign to her a place among the stars ; as he did to Andromeda and Cassiopeia.
30 There was an Athenian dramatist of this name, who might have made the virtues and fortunes of Alcestis his theme ; but the reference is too vague for the author to be identified with any confidence.

In rémembránce of her, and in honoúr,
Cybelé made the daisy, and the flow'r,
Y-crowned all with white, as men may see,
And Mars gave her a crownë red, pardie!
In stead of rubies set among the white."
Therewith this queen wax'd red for shame a lite
When she was praised so in her presénce.
Then saidë Love: "A full great negligence
Was it to thee, that ilkë [1] time thou made
'Hide Absolon thy tresses,' in balláde,
That thou forgot her in thy song to set,
Since that thou art so greatly in her debt,
And knowest well that calendar [2] is she
To any woman that will lover be:
For she taught all the craft of true lovíng,
And namëly [3] of wifehood the livíng,
And all the boundës that she ought to keep:
Thy little wit was thilkë time asleep.
But now I chargë thee, upon thy life,
That in thy Legend thou make [4] of this wife,
When thou hast other small y-made before;
And fare now well, I chargë thee no more.
But ere I go, thus much I will thee tell,—
Never shall no true lover come in hell.
These other ladies, sitting here a-row,
Be in my ballad, if thou canst them know,
And in thy bookës all thou shalt them find;
Have them in thy Legénd now all in mind;
I mean of th em that be in thy knowíng.
For here be twenty thousand more sittíng
Than that thou knowest, goodë women all,
And true of love, for aught that may befall;
Makë the metres of them as thee lest;
I must go home,—the sunnë draweth west,—
To Paradise, with all this companý:
And serve alway the freshë daïsý.
At Cleopatra I will that thou begin,
And so forth, and my love so shalt thou win;
For let see now what man, that lover be,
Will do so strong a pain for love as she.
I wot well that thou may'st not all it rhyme,
That suchë lovers didden in their time;
It were too long to readen and to hear;
Sufficë me thou make in this mannére,
That thou rehearse of all their life the great, [5]
After [6] these old authórs list for to treat;
For whoso shall so many a story tell,
Say shortly, or he shall too longë dwell."
And with that word my bookës gan I take,
And right thus on my Legend gan I make.

Thus endeth the Prologue.

CHAUCER'S A. B. C.

CALLED

LA PRIERE DE NOSTRE DAME.[7]

A.

ALMIGHTY and all-merciable [8] Queen,
To whom all this world fleëth for succoúr,
To have release of sin, of sorrow, of teen! [9]
Glorious Virgin! of all flowers flow'r,
To thee I flee, confounded in erroúr!
Help and relieve, almighty debonair, [10]
Have mercy of my perilous languoúr!
Vanquish'd me hath my cruel adversair.

B.

Bounty [11] so fix'd hath in thy heart his tent,
That well I wot thou wilt my succour be;
Thou canst not warnë that [12] with good intent
Asketh thy help, thy heart is ay so free!
Thou art largess [13] of plein [14] felicity,
Haven and refuge of quiét and rest!
Lo! how that thievës seven [15] chasë me!
Help, Lady bright, ere that my ship to-brest! [16]

C.

Comfort is none, but in you, Lady dear!
For lo! my sin and my confusión,
Which ought not in thy presence to appear,
Have ta'en on me a grievous actión, [17]
Of very right and desperatión!
And, as by right, they mightë well sustene
That I were worthy my damnatión,
Ne were it mercy of you, blissful Queen!

D.

Doubt is there none, Queen of misericorde, [18]
That thou art cause of grace and mercy here;
God vouchësaf'd, through thee, with us t' accord; [19]
For, certes, Christë's blissful mother dear!
Were now the bow y-bent, in such mannére
As it was first, of justice and of ire,
The rightful God would of no mercy hear;
But through thee have we grace as we desire.

1 That same.
2 Guide, example.
3 Especially.
4 Poetise, compose.
5 The substance.
6 According as.
7 Chaucer's A. B. C.—a prayer to the Virgin, in twenty-three verses, beginning with the letters of the alphabet in their order—is said to have been written "at the request of Blanche, Duchess of Lancaster, as a prayer for her private use, being a woman in her religion very devout." It was first printed in Speght's edition of 1597.
8 All-merciful.
9 Affliction.
10 Gracious, gentle.
11 Goodness, charity.
12 Thou canst not refuse (the prayer of him) that.
13 Thou art the liberal bestower.
14 Full.
15 The seven deadly sins.
16 Be broken to pieces.
17 Control.
18 Compassion.
19 To be reconciled.

E.

Ever hath my hope of refuge in thee be';
For herebefore full oft in many a wise
Unto mercý hast thou received me.
But mercy, Lady! at the great assize,
When we shall come before the high Justíce!
So little fruit shall then in me be found,
That, but[1] thou ere that day correctë me,
Of very right my work will me confound.

F.

Flying, I flee for succour to thy tent,
Me for to hide from tempest full of dread;
Beseeching you, that ye you not absent,
Though I be wick'. O help yet at this need!
All[2] have I been a beast in wit and deed,
Yet, Lady! thou me close in with thy grace;
Thine enemy and mine,[3]—Lady, take heed!—
Unto my death in point is me to chase.

G.

Gracïous Maid and Mother! which that never
Wert bitter[4] nor in earthë nor in sea,
But full of sweetness and of mercy ever,
Help, that my Father be not wroth with me!
Speak thou, for I ne darë Him not see;
So have I done in earth, alas the while!
That, certes, but if thou my succour be,
To sink etern He will my ghost exile.

H.

He vouchësaf'd, tell Him, as was His will,
Become a man, as for our álliánce,[5]
And with His blood He wrote that blissful bill
Upon the cross, as general ácquittánce
To ev'ry penitent in full creance;
And therefore, Lady bright! thou for us pray;
Then shalt thou stenten[6] allë His grievánce,
And make our foe to failen of his prey.

I.

I wotë well thou wilt be our succoúr,
Thou art so full of bounty in certáin;
For, when a soulë falleth in erroúr,
Thy pity go'th, and haleth[7] him again;
Then makest thou his peace with his Sov'réign,
And bringest him out of the crooked street:
Whoso thee loveth shall not love in vain,
That shall he find as he the life shall lete.[8]

K.

Kalendarës illumined[9] be they
That in this world be lighted with thy name;
And whoso goeth with thee the right way,
Him shall not dread in soulë to be lame;
Now, Queen of comfort! since thou art the
same
To whom I seekë for my medicine,
Let not my foe no more my wound entame;[10]
My heal into thy hand all I resign.

L.

Lady, thy sorrow can I not portray
Under that cross, nor his grievous penánce;
But, for your bothë's pain, I you do pray,
Let not our aller foe[11] make his boastance,
That he hath in his listës, with mischance,
Convictë that ye both have bought so dear;[12]
As I said erst, thou ground of all substánce!
Continue on us thy piteous eyen clear.

M.

Moses, that saw the bush of flamës red
Burning, of which then never a stick brenn'd,[13]
Was sign of thine unwemmed[14] maidenhead.
Thou art the bush, on which there gan descend
The Holy Ghost, the which that Moses wend[15]
Had been on fire; and this was in figúre.[16]
Now, Lady! from the fire us do defend,
Which that in hell eternally shall dure.

N.

Noble Princéss! that never haddest peer;
Certes if any comfort in us be,
That cometh of thee, Christë's mother dear!
We have none other melody nor glee,[17]
Us to rejoice in our adversity;
Nor advocate, that will and dare so pray
For us, and for as little hire as ye,
That helpë for an Ave-Marý or tway.

O.

O very light of eyen that be blind!
O very lust of labour and distress!
O treasurer of bounty to mankind!
The whom God chose to mother for humbless!
From his ancill[18] he madë thee mistréss
Of heav'n and earth, our billës up to bede;[19]
This world awaiteth ever on thy goodnéss;
For thou ne failedst never wight at need.

P.

Purpose I have sometime for to enquére
Wherefore and why the Holy Ghost thee sought,
When Gabrielis voice came to thine ear;
He not to war[20] us such a wonder wrought,
But for to save us, that sithens us bought:
Then needeth us no weapon us to save,
But only, where we did not as we ought,
Do penitence, and mercy ask and have.

Q.

Queen of comfórt, right when I me bethink
That I aguilt[21] have bothë Him and thee,
And that my soul is worthy for to sink,
Alas! I, caitiff, whither shall I flee?
Who shall unto thy Son my meanë[22] be?

[1] Unless. [2] Although. [3] The Devil.

[4] Mary's name recals the waters of "Marah" or bitterness (Exod. xv. 23), or the prayer of Naomi in her grief that she might be called not Naomi, but "Mara" (Ruth i. 20). Mary, however, is understood to mean "exalted."

[5] To ally us with God. [6] Put an end to.

[7] Draweth. [8] When he leaves life.

[9] That is, brilliant exemplars by which others may shape their daily life. [10] Injure, molest.

[11] The foe of us all—Satan.

[12] That he hath entangled in his wiles that (soul) which ye both redeemed at such a cost. [13] Burned.

[14] Unblemished. [15] Weened, supposed.

[16] A typical representation. See The Prioress's Tale, page 144. [17] Pleasure.

[18] Handmaid. The reference evidently is to Luke i. 38—"Ecce ancilla Domini," the Virgin's humble answer to Gabriel at the Annunciation.

[19] To offer up our petitions or prayers.

[20] To "warray" or afflict. [21] Offended.

[22] Medium of approach, intercessor.

Who, but thyself, that art of pity well?[1]
Thou hast more ruth on our adversity
Than in this world might any tonguë tell!

R.

Redress me, Mother, and eke me chastise!
For certainly my Father's chástising
I darë not abiden in no wise,
So hidëous is his full reckoning.
Mother! of whom our joy began to spring,
Be ye my judge, and eke my soulë's leach;[2]
For ay in you is pity aboundíng
To each that will of pity you beseech.

S.

Sooth is it that He granteth no pitý
Withoutë thee; for God of his goodnéss
Forgiveth none, but it like unto thee;[3]
He hath thee madë vicar and mistréss
Of all this world, and ekë governess
Of heaven; and represseth his justíce
After[4] thy will; and therefore in witnéss
He hath thee crowned in so royal wise.

T.

Temple devout! where God chose his wonníng,[5]
From which these misbeliev'd deprived be,
To you my soulë penitent I bring;
Receive me, for I can no farther flee.
With thornës venomous, O Heaven's Queen!
For which the earth accursëd was full yore,
I am so wounded, as ye may well see,
That I am lost almóst, it smart so sore!

V.

Virgin! that art so noble of apparail,[6]
That leadest us into the highë tow'r
Of Paradise, thou me wiss and counsail[7]
How I may have thy grace and thy succoúr:
All have I been in filth and in erroúr,
Lady! on that country thou me adjourn,[8]
That called is thy bench of freshë flow'r,
There as that mercy ever shall sojourn.

X.

Xpe[9] thy Son, that in this world alight,
Upon a cross to suffer his passioún,
And suffer'd eke that Longeus his heart pight,[10]
And made his heartë-blood to run adown;
And all this was for my salvatioún:
And I to him am false and eke unkind,
And yet he wills not my damnatioún;
This thank I you,[11] succoúr of all mankind!

Y.

Ysaac was figure of His death certáin,
That so farforth his father would obey,
That him ne raughtë[12] nothing to be slain;
Right so thy Son list as a lamb to dey:[13]
Now, Lady full of mercy! I you pray,
Since he his mercy 'sured me so large,
Be ye not scant, for all we sing and say,
That ye be from vengeánce alway our targe.[14]

Z.

Zachary you calleth the open well[15]
That washëd sinful soul out of his guilt;
Therefore this lesson out I will to tell,
That, n'ere[16] thy tender heartë, we were spilt.[17]
Now, Lady brightë! since thou canst and wilt,
Be to the seed of Adam merciáble;
Bring us unto that palace that is built
To penitents that be to mercy able![18]

Explicit.

A GOODLY BALLAD OF CHAUCER.[19]

MOTHER of nurture, best belov'd of all,
And freshë flow'r, to whom good thrift God send!
Your child, if it lust[20] you me so to call,
All be I[21] unable myself so to pretend,
To your discretïon I recommend
My heart and all, with ev'ry circumstance,
All wholly to be under your governance.

Most desire I, and have and ever shall,
Thingë which might your heartë's ease amend;
Have me excus'd, my power is but small;
Nathless, of right, ye oughtë to commend
My goodë will, which fainë would entend[22]
To do you service; for my suffisance[23]
Is wholly to be under your governance.

Mieux un in heart which never shall apall,[24]
Ay fresh and new, and right glad to dispend
My time in your servíce, what so befall,
Beseeching your excéllence to defend
My simpleness, if ignorance offend
In any wise; since that mine áffiánce
Is wholly to be under your governance.

Daisy of light, very ground of comfórt,
The sunnë's daughter ye hight, as I read;
For when he west'reth, farewell your disport!
By your natúre alone, right for pure dread

1 Fountain. 2 Physician.
3 Unless it please thee. 4 According to.
5 Abode. 6 Aspect.
7 Direct and counsel. 8 Take me to that place.
9 "Xpe" represents the Greek Χρε, and is a contraction for "Christe."
10 According to tradition, the soldier who struck the Saviour to the heart with his spear was named Longeus, and was blind; but, touching his eyes by chance with the mingled blood and water that flowed down the shaft upon his hands, he was instantly restored to sight.
11 For this I am indebted to you. 12 He cared not.
13 Die. 14 Our buckler, defence.
15 "In that day there shall be a fountain opened to the house of David and to the inhabitants of Jerusalem for sin and for uncleanness" (Zech. xiii. 1).
16 Were it not for. 17 Destroyed, undone.
18 Fit to receive mercy.
19 This elegant little poem is believed to have been addressed to Margaret, Countess of Pembroke, in whose name Chaucer found one of those opportunities of praising the daisy he never lost.
20 Please. 21 Although I be.
22 Attend, strive. 23 Contentment.
24 Better one who in heart shall never pall—whose love will never weary.

Of the rude night, that with his boistous weed[1]
Of darkness shadoweth our hemisphere,
Then closë ye, my lifë's lady dear!

Dawneth the day unto his kind resort,
And Phœbus your father, with his streamës red,
Adorns the morrow, cónsuming the sort[2]
Of misty cloudës, that would overlade
True humble heartës with their mistihead.[3]
New comfort adaws,[4] when your eyen clear
Disclose and spread, my lifë's lady dear.

Je voudrais—but the greatë God disposeth,
And maketh casual, by his Providence,
Such thing as mannë's frailë wit purpóseth,
All for the best, if that your consciénce
Not grudge it, but in humble patiénce
It receive; for God saith, withoutë fable,
A faithful heart ever is acceptáble.

Cautelës[5] whoso useth gladly, gloseth;[6]
To eschew such it is right high prudénce;
What ye said onës minë heart opposeth,
That my writing japës[7] in your absénce
Pleased you much better than my presénce:
Yet can I more; ye be not excusáble;
A faithful heart is ever acceptáble.

Quaketh my pen; my spirit supposeth
That in my writing ye will find offence;
Mine heartë welketh[8] thus; anon it riseth;
Now hot, now cold, and after in fervénce;
That is amiss, is caus'd of negligence,
And not of malice; therefore be merciáble;
A faithful heart is ever acceptáble.

L'Envoy.

Forthë, complaint! forth, lacking eloquence;
Forth little letter, of enditing lame!
I have besought my lady's sapiénce
On thy behalfë, to accept in game
Thine inability; do thou the same.
Abide! have morë yet! *Je serve Joyesse!*[9]
Now forth, I close thee in holy Venus' name!
Thee shall unclose my heartë's governess.

A BALLAD SENT TO KING RICHARD.

Sometime this world was so steadfást and stable,
That man's word was held obligatión;
And now it is so false and deceiváble,[10]
That word and work, as in conclusión,
Be nothing one; for turned up so down
Is all this world, through meed[11] and wilfulness,
That all is lost for lack of steadfastness.

What makes this world to be so variáble,
But lust[12] that folk have in dissensión?
For now-a-days a man is held unable[13]
But if[14] he can, by some collusión,[15]
Do his neighbour wrong or oppressión.
What causeth this but wilful wretchedness,
That all is lost for lack of steadfastness?

Truth is put down, reason is holden fable;
Virtue hath now no dominatión;
Pity exil'd, no wight is merciáble;
Through covetise is blent[16] discretión;
The worldë hath made permutatión
From right to wrong, from truth to fickleness,
That all is lost for lack of steadfastness.

L'Envoy.

O Prince! desirë to be honourable;
Cherish thy folk, and hate extortión;
Suffer nothing that may be reprovable[17]
To thine estate, done[18] in thy región;[19]
Show forth the sword of castigatión;
Dread God, do law, love thorough worthiness,
And wed thy folk again to steadfastness!

L'ENVOY OF CHAUCER TO BUKTON.[20]

My Master Bukton, when of Christ our King
Was asked, What is truth or soothfastness?
He not a word answér'd to that asking,
As who saith, no man is all true, I guess;
And therefore, though I hightë[21] to express
The sorrow and woe that is in marriáge,
I dare not write of it no wickedness,
Lest I myself fall eft in such dotage.[22]

I will not say how that it is the chain
Of Satanas, on which he gnaweth ever;
But I dare say, were he out of his pain,
As by his will he would be bounden never.
But thilkë[23] doited fool that eft had lever
Y-chained be, than out of prison creep,
God let him never from his woe dissever,
Nor no man him bewailë though he weep!

But yet, lest thou do worsë, take a wife;
Bet is to wed than burn in worsë wise;[24]
But thou shalt have sorrow on thy flesh thy life,[25]
And be thy wifë's thrall, as say these wise.
And if that Holy Writ may not suffice,
Experience shall thee teachë, so may hap,
That thee were lever to be taken in Frise,[26]
Than eft[27] to fall of wedding in the trap.

This little writ, proverbës, or figúre,
I sendë you; take keep[28] of it, I read!
"Unwise is he that can no weal endure;
If thou be sicker,[29] put thee not in dread."[30]
The Wife of Bath I pray you that you read,

1 Rude, rough, garment.
2 Crowd.
3 Dimness, mistiness.
4 New comfort dawns or awakens (in my breast).
5 Cautious or wary speeches.
6 Deceiveth.
7 Jests, coarse stories.
8 Withers, faints.
9 I serve Joy.
10 Deceitful.
11 Bribery.
12 Pleasure.
13 Fit for nothing.
14 Unless.
15 Fraud, trick.
16 Blinded.
17 A subject of reproach.
18 That is, to be done.
19 Kingdom.
20 Tyrwbitt, founding on the reference to the Wife of Bath, places this among Chaucer's latest compositions; and states that one Peter de Bukton held the office of king's escheator for Yorkshire in 1397. In some of the old editions, the verses were made the Envoy to the Book of the Duchess Blanche—in very bad taste, when we consider that the object of that poem was to console John of Gaunt under the loss of his wife.
21 Promised.
22 Fall again into such folly.
23 That.
24 See 1 Cor. vii. 9.
25 All thy life.
26 Better to be taken prisoner in Friesland—where probably some conflict was raging at the time.
27 Again.
28 Heed.
29 In security.
30 Doubt, danger.

Of this mattére which that we have on hand.
God grantë you your life freely to lead
In freedom, for full hard is to be bond.

A BALLAD OF GENTLENESS.

The firstë stock-father of gentleness,[1]
What man desireth gentle for to be,
Must follow his trace, and all his wittës dress,[2]
Virtue to love, and vices for to flee;
For unto virtue longeth dignity,
And not the réverse, safely dare I deem,
All wear he mitre, crown, or diademe.

This firstë stock was full of righteousness,
True of his word, sober, pious, and free,
Clean of his ghost,[3] and loved business,
Against the vice of sloth, in honesty;
And, but his heir love virtue as did he,
He is not gentle, though he richë seem,
All wear he mitre, crown, or diademe.

Vicë may well be heir to old richess,
But there may no man, as men may well see,
Bequeath his heir his virtuous nobless;
That is appropriëd[4] to no degree,
But to the first Father in majesty,
Which makes his heirë him that doth him queme,[5]
All wear he mitre, crown, or diademe.

THE COMPLAINT OF CHAUCER TO HIS PURSE.

To you, my purse, and to none other wight,
Complain I, for ye be my lady dear!
I am sorry now that ye be so light,
For certes ye now make me heavy cheer;
Me were as lief be laid upon my bier.
For which unto your mercy thus I cry,
Be heavy again, or ellës must I die!

Now vouchësafe this day, ere it be night,
That I of you the blissful sound may hear,
Or see your colour like the sunnë bright,
That of yellówness haddë never peer.
Ye be my life! Ye be my heartë's steer![6]
Queen of comfórt and of good company!
Be heavy again, or ellës must I die!

Now, purse! that art to me my lifë's light
And savour, as down in this worldë here,
Out of this townë help me through your might,
Since that you will not be my treasurére;
For I am shave as nigh as any frere.[7]
But now I pray unto your courtesy̆,
Be heavy again, or ellës must I die!

Chaucer's Envoy to the King.

O conqueror of Brutë's Albion,[8]
Which by lineage and free electión
Be very king, this song to you I send;
And ye which may all minë harm amend,
Have mind upon my supplicatión!

GOOD COUNSEL OF CHAUCER.[9]

Flee from the press, and dwell with soothfastness;
Sufficë thee thy good, though it be small;
For hoard[10] hath hate, and climbing tickleness,[11]
Press hath envy̆, and weal is blent[12] o'er all,
Savour[13] no more than thee behovë shall;
Read[14] well thyself, that other folk canst read;
And truth thee shall deliver, it is no dread.[15]

Painë thee not each crooked to redress,
In trust of her that turneth as a ball;[16]
Great rest standeth in little business:
Beware also to spurn against a nall;[17]
Strive not as doth a crockë[18] with a wall;
Deemë[19] thyself that deemest others' deed,
And truth thee shall deliver, it is no dread.

What thee is sent, receive in buxomness;[20]
The wrestling of this world asketh a fall;
Here is no home, here is but wilderness.
Forth, pilgrim! forthë, beast, out of thy stall!
Look up on high, and thank thy God of all!
Weivë thy lust,[21] and let thy ghost[22] thee lead,
And truth thee shall deliver, it is no dread.

PROVERBS OF CHAUCER.

What should these clothes thus manifold,
Lo!, this hot summer's day?
After great heatë cometh cold;
No man cast his pilche[23] away.
Of all this world the large compáss
Will not in mine arms twain;
Who so muchë will embrace,
Little thereof he shall distrain.[24]

The world so wide, the air so remuable,[25]
The silly man so little of statúre;
The green of ground and clothing so mutáble,
The fire so hot and subtile of natúre;
The water never in one[26]—what creatúre
That made is of these fourë[27] thus flittíng,
May steadfast be, as here, in his living?

The more I go, the farther I am behind;
The farther behind, the nearer my war's end;

1 Christ. 2 Apply.
3 Pure of spirit. 4 Specially reserved.
5 Please. 6 Rudder.
7 "I am as bare of coin as a friar's tonsure of hair."
8 See page 396.
9 Said to have been composed by Chaucer "upon his deathbed, lying in anguish."
10 Treasure. 11 Instability.
12 Prosperity is blinded or deceived as to the truth.
13 Have a taste or desire for. 14 Counsel.
15 Doubt. 16 Fortune.
17 To kick against a nail, "against the pricks."
18 An earthen pot.
19 Judge. 20 Submission.
21 Forsake thy inclinations.
22 Spirit. 23 Pelisse, furred cloak.
24 Grasp. 25 Unstable.
26 Never the same.
27 That is, the four elements, of which man was believed to be composed.

The more I seek, the worsë can I find;
The lighter leave, the lother for to wend;[1]
The better I live, the more out of mind;
Is this fortúne, n' ot I, or infortúne;[2]
Though I go loose, tied am I with a loigne.[3]

VIRELAY.

ALONE walking,
In thought plaining,
And sore sighing,
All desolate,
Me rememb'ring
Of my living;
My death wishing
Both early and late.

Infortunate
Is so my fate,
That, wot ye what?
Out of measúre
My life I hate;
Thus desperate,
In such poor estate,
Do I endure.

Of other cure
Am I not sure;
Thus to endure
Is hard, certáin;
Such is my ure,[4]
I you ensure;
What creatúre
May have more pain?

My truth so plain
Is taken in vain,
And great disdain
In rémembránce;
Yet I full fain
Would me complain,
Me to abstain
From this penánce.

But, in substánce,
None alleggeánce[5]
Of my grievánce
Can I not find;
Right so my chance,
With displeasánce,
Doth me advance;
And thus an end.

"SINCE I FROM LOVE."

SINCE I from Love escaped am so fat,
I ne'er think to be in his prison ta'en;
Since I am free, I count him not a bean.[6]

He may answer, and sayë this and that;
I do no force,[7] I speak right as I mean;
Since I from Love escaped am so fat.

Love hath my namë struck out of his slat,[8]
And he is struck out of my bookës clean,
For ever more; there is none other mean;
Since I from Love escaped am so fat.

CHAUCER'S WORDS TO HIS SCRIVENER.

ADAM Scrivener, if ever it thee befall
Boece or Troilus[9] for to write anew,
Under thy long locks thou may'st have the scall[10]
But after my making[11] thou write more true!
So oft a day I must thy work renew,
It to correct, and eke to rub and scrape;
And all is through thy negligence and rape.[12]

CHAUCER'S PROPHECY.

WHEN priestës failen in their saws,[13]
And lordës turnë Goddë's laws
Against the right;
And lechery is holden as privy solace,[14]
And robbery as free purcháse,[15]
Beware then of ill!
Then shall the Land of Albion
Turnë to confusión,
As sometime it befell.

Ora pro Anglia Sancta Maria, quod Thomas Cantuaria.

Sweet Jesus, heaven's King,
Fair and best of all thing,
You bring us out of this mourning,
To come to thee at our ending!

1 The more easy (through age) for me to depart, the less willing I am to go.
2 I know not whether this is fortune or misfortune.
3 With a line or tether—by marriage.
4 My "heur," or destiny; the same word that enters into "bonheur" and "malheur."
5 Alleviation.
6 I care not a bean for him.
7 Make no matter.
8 Slate, list.
9 That is, Chaucer's translation of Boethius, or his "Troilus and Cressida."
10 Scab.
11 According to my composing.
12 Haste.
13 Come short of their professions.
14 Secret delight.
15 Legitimate gain.

THE END.

Drawn by T. Uwins. Engraved by C. Warren.

EDMUND SPENSER.

From an original Picture, in the Collection of the Right Honorable the Earl of Kinnoul.

THE FAERIE QUEEN;

AND OTHER POEMS

OF

EDMUND SPENSER.

LIFE OF EDMUND SPENSER.

THOSE familiar with London and London life in the second half of the nineteenth century, will more or less consciously take a Carlylean view of its intellectually productive capability, and affirm that no poet could be born there. Yet it may be questioned whether, in times past, London did not hold to the rest of these Islands, not numerically alone, but in activity and intensity of material life, a much more important relation than it does at present. In many senses, London was far more conspicuously the centre of the kingdom at a time when everything circulated to it, and little or nothing from it, than in these days, when the inward and the outward currents fairly compete with each other, and the facilities of intercommunication, the growth of independent political life, have destroyed the commercial and intellectual monopoly which in the older days the metropolis enjoyed. Certain it is, nevertheless, that London produced three of England's greatest Poets; and if the fourth, Shakespeare, did not draw his first or his last breath in the capital, at least he spent there the most important part of his life, and made the little fortune on which he quietly waited for death at Stratford-on-Avon. Chaucer, Spenser, and Milton, however, indubitably were born in London; the first and the last of that splendid trio were Londoners most of their days—men of the Court, men of the council, men at head-quarters. Spenser's future fate led him afield into lonely and rough places; but London claims the honour of giving him birth. We have his own word for the fact; for in a poem entitled "Prothalamion," written to celebrate "the double marriage of the two honourable and virtuous Ladies, the Lady Elizabeth and the Lady Katherine Somerset, daughters to the right honourable the Earl of Worcester," Spenser says—describing the progress of the two Swans who represent the brides, with their attendant train of nymphs—

"At length they all to merry London came,
To merry London, my most kindly nurse,
That to me gave this life's first native source,
Though from another place I take my name,
A house of ancient fame:"

Some now wholly unrecognisable or demolished house "in East Smithfield, by the Tower," saw the poet ushered into this world, towards the close of the year 1552. (See note 1, page 618.) The general belief is, that his parents were in indifferent circumstances; but little doubt is entertained regarding the "respectability," if not even the nobility, of their original condition. Repeatedly, in dedications prefixed to his minor poems, Spenser claims kindred with the Spencers of Althorpe, in Northamptonshire—from whom the noble houses of Spencer and Marlborough took their rise. In 1590, he dedicates "Muiopotmos" to Lady Carey, the second daughter of Sir John Spencer; next year, he dedicates "The Tears of the Muses" to Lady Strange, Sir John's sixth daughter, afterwards Countess of Derby; and, in both cases, the poet makes carefully distinct reference to his relationship—a claim which does not seem to have been repudiated, and which, in the brilliant but too brief days of his stay in London as the friend of Sidney and Leicester, we may reasonably suppose to have been acknowledged with satisfaction and even pride.

From whatever parentage he sprang, then, or whatever were the worldly circumstances of his immediate ancestors about the time of his birth, Spenser appears to have come of gentle lineage. Even in absence of any direct or collateral testimonies to that effect, we might almost be disposed to believe it on the strength of a single stanza in "The Faerie Queen"—the first in the fourth canto of the second book (page 375)—where the poet asserts for "gentle blood" a peculiar possession of the "skill to ride." But the branch of the Spenser family with which Edmund was immediately connected, was not that to whose daughters he inscribed his dedications, but that of the Spensers, or Le Spensers, of Hurstwood, near Burnley, in eastern Lancashire. A small domain, called "the Spensers," exists to this day, in the Forest of Pendle, about three miles north of Hurstwood; and it has been noticed that, in the churchyards and parish registers of the district around "the Spensers," the not very usual Christian names of Edmund and Laurence abound—those being familiar names in the pedigree of the poet's descendants. Another evidence that the Spensers of Spensers were the poet's relations—though the circumstances of his birth show that he came of a distinct and perhaps less prosperous offshoot of the family—is furnished by what we may infer to have been his prolonged residence in the north country during his youth. Spenser speaks of London rather as one who had chanced to be born there, than as one whose youthful memory and cast of thought had been wholly moulded by the life of the city: while the form and the topics of his earlier poems attest a long experience of rural affairs, and intimate enjoyment of rural existence. But we can merely infer that the poet's youth was thus spent; for we have no authentic trace of him between the date of his birth and the 20th of May, 1569, when he was entered a sizar of Pembroke Hall, in Cambridge University—the position which he took as a student indicating that affluence had not yet come to his immediate relatives. His college career was not so eminently distinguished that tradition has preserved his memory as among the brilliant *alumni* of his college; and his works, while they display a general acquaintance with the philosophies of Lucretius and Plato, do not show remarkable traces of extended or rigidly accurate scholarship. Whether or not we should connect any shortcomings in the mere routine of his studies with the evidence that there was a good deal of "friction" between Spenser and the authorities of his own college, it is tolerably plain that the poet quitted his Alma Mater with something like the same grudge which Swift bore against Dublin University. But although, in correspondence with his intimates, Spenser seems to have freely expressed himself regarding his "old controller," or tutor, Dr. Perne, and to have relished the sarcasms of his friends on the same theme, no trace of such small animosities appears in his poems. True it is that he makes no grateful or celebrative mention of Pembroke Hall; but in "The Faerie Queen" (canto xi., book iv., page 477), when enumerating the Ouse among the rivers that attend the wedding of the Thames and the Medway, he says that the stream—

> "Doth by Huntingdon and Cambridge flit;
> My mother Cambridge, whom as with a crown
> He doth adorn, and is adorn'd of it
> With many a gentle Muse and many a learned wit."

Whatever may have been the cause of his disagreement with the Dons—whether his own remissness, his independence, or their exacting and unfair behaviour—Spenser passed honourably through the academic grades. On January 16th, 1572-3, he took the degree of Bachelor of Arts; on June 26th, 1576, that of Master of Arts; and he quitted Cambridge immediately, to go to the north country—whither, if, as we suppose, he was merely returning to the scenes of his boyhood, the memory of "Rosalind" may have powerfully attracted him.

Between 1576 and 1578, we know little more of Spenser's life than what can be gathered by inference from "The Shepherd's Calendar." We learn there, that he resided for a season in the North; that his University friend, Gabriel Harvey, subsequently a Fellow of Trinity Hall, Cambridge (who is the "Hobbinol" of the "Calendar" and of "Colin Clout"), besought him to quit the bleak and shelterless hills, and come down to the warmer and softer South; and that Spenser lingered for a while in the North, through his passion for "Rosalind"—hoping against hope, perchance, that after all the fickle fair would relent, and prefer his suit to that of the favoured "Menalcas." Many and ingenious have been the endeavours made to raise the veil that hides the identity of Spenser's early love. Edmund Kirke, another Cambridge friend of the poet's—who, under his initials E. K., introduced and annotated "The Shepherd's Calendar"—set wits hopefully to work by his remark that perhaps the feigned name of "Rosalind," "being well ordered, will bewray the very name of his love and mistress, whom by that name he coloureth." Though the parallel cases of such pedantic counterfeiting which E. K. enumerates do not exactly point to an anagrammatic solution, that is the favourite mode in which biographers of Spenser have sought to "well order" the name of "Rosalind." Hence we have her made a lady of Kent, Rose Lynde; again a lady of Kent, Eliza Horden, the aspirate being omitted: but unfortunately those conjectures are based merely on documentary evidence that in the time of Henry VI. there lived gentlemen of Kent named Horden and Linde. Better authenticated and more consistent with probability is the theory that "Rosalinde" was Rose Daniel, sister of Samuel Daniel the poet, a contemporary and friend of Spenser: and the theory, so plausible from the anagrammatic point of view which E. K. seems to favour, is buttressed by the fact that Rose Daniel actually married a man who might be most significantly described as "Menalcas"—the poet's fictitious name for the triumphant swain. Her husband, John Florio, a poet and litterateur of some pretensions, was of eccentric and bombastic humour; he would fairly have stood for the double picture of the carl and fool that, in the seventh canto of the sixth book of "The Faerie Queen," lead along the once proud but now humiliated "Mirabella"—who there represents Spenser's first love; and he was in the constant habit of signing himself "Resolute John Florio"—"Menalcas," compounded from two Greek words, signifying "resolute." It is sufficient to state in outline these various theories; and to remark, that however well they may harmonise within themselves, or with other passages in Spenser's poetry, they do not agree with the obvious fact that "The Widow's Daughter of the Glen" was a northern lady—probably a near neighbour of the Spensers of Spensers. Of Rosalind's person and character extremely little is known. It would be idle to doubt her beauty; the scanty descriptions which are on record represent her as accomplished and witty—familiar with Petrarch in his own tongue, and not afraid to bandy classical jests with the young scholar and poet; while the supposition that she was merely some peasant's daughter is discountenanced by the facts which have just been stated, and also by the consideration that not only was the attribution of lowly estate a *façon de parler* in pastoral poetry not peculiar to Spenser, but the poet was obviously proud of his own high connections, and may have taken a more moderate view of good birth than his own actual worldly circumstances seem to have warranted.

In 1578—solicited by his friend Harvey to come to the South, and also, as E. K. hints, desirous to obtain, by solicitation at Court, some preferment or office that might help his slender resources—Spenser quitted Lancashire for London. There can be no doubt that he did not come up quite weaponless to the battle of fortune in the capital. Long before, he had made some slight poetical essays. John Van der Noodt, a Dutch Protestant who had taken refuge in England for hatred of Popery not less than love of life, published in 1569—the year in which Spenser entered at Pembroke Hall—a volume entitled "A Theatre wherein be represented as well the Miseries and Calamities that follow the Voluptuous Worldlings, as also the great Joys and Pleasures which the Faithful do enjoy." Prefixed to this volume were twenty-one "Epigrams" and Sonnets, by an anonymous hand; and these pieces are, either in substance or in form, identical with a number of the Sonnets, illustrating the vanity of human things, that were published with Spenser's name more than a score of years afterwards, under the titles of "Visions of the World's Vanity," "The Visions of Petrarch," and "The Visions of Bellay." It is probable also, that "Prosopopoia"—perhaps Spenser's most spirited poem, certainly that in which he best caught the spirit of his great model, Chaucer—was written, at least in part, during his residence at Cambridge. But it is beyond question that he brought "The Shepherd's Calendar" to London with him, ready or nearly ready for the press; and at the end of 1579 it was published, in small quarto, with an inscription "To the noble and virtuous gentleman, most worthy of all titles, both of learning and chivalry, Master Philip Sidney." To "him that is the President of Nobless and of Chivalry"—as Spenser, writing under the pseudonym of "Immerito," styles Sidney in the lines prefixed to the "Calendar" —the author had been introduced by Gabriel Harvey. A close friendship appears to have sprung up between the two young poets—as was, in truth, a most natural consequence of their introduction; Sidney made the newcomer acquainted with his uncle, the famous Earl of Leicester; and for two years Spenser moved amid the witty and splendid courtier-throng that surrounded the throne of the Maiden Queen. The friend of Sidney and the protégé of Leicester, whatever his private fortunes, might well lay claim to kinship with the proud Spencers of Althorpe; and it is probable that the poet made the most of every such opportunity to advance his interests and better his revenues. Meantime, while he paid unadulating court to the great, he did not neglect the Muses. The impression made upon his imaginative and generous mind by the brilliancy, the elegance, the high spirit, and chivalrous daring, which marked the principal figures at the Court of Elizabeth, impelled him to a loftier effort than the pathetic love-plaints of the "Calendar," or the homely satire of "Mother Hubberd." The aspirations after a nobler theme and a bolder song may be traced in the later portions of the "Calendar"—especially in the October Eclogue; and during Spenser's two years in town, the scheme of "The Faerie Queen" was doubtless drawn up, and part of the poem composed. It does not say much for the penetration of Gabriel Harvey, or the influence which his veneration for the antique might have exerted if Spenser had been a poet of weaker will, to find that "The Faerie Queen" positively horrified him. "Nine comedies, whereunto, in imitation of Herodotus," Spenser had given the names of the nine Muses, pleased the intellectually superstitious pedant better than the "Elvish Queen"—in which, with characteristic faith in his own powers and merits, Spenser had expressed a purpose to emulate and a hope to surpass Ariosto in his Orlando Furioso. "If so be," says Harvey, writing in April 1580; "if so be the Faery Queen be fairer in your eye than the Nine Muses, and Hobgoblin run away with the garland from Apollo; mark what I say—and yet I will not say that [what] I thought; but there is an end for this once, and fare you well, till God or some good angel put you in a better mind." Providence did not interfere with the impulse of the poet; the nine Comedies christened after the Muses are now preserved from oblivion only in the futile praise of Harvey; and the scholar's attempts to induce Spenser to adopt a metrical system founded on that of the ancients, met with no more attention than a half-amused and half-courteous experimentation, in letters between the two friends, which reminds us of similar exercises not long ago put forth by Mr Tennyson. Besides the nine comedies, other poems are mentioned in correspondence about this time, of which no memorial remains, at least in their original form. Such are "Dreams," "Legends," the "Court of Cupid," "The English Poet," "The Dying Pelican," "Stemmata Dudleiana," "Slumber," and "Epithalamium Thamesis." "Stemmata Dudleiana" probably survives in "The Ruins of Time;" "Slumber" and "Dreams" in the "Visions" formerly mentioned; the "Court of Cupid" and "Epithalamium Thamesis" in "The Faerie Queen" (cantos x. and xi. of book iv.) "The English Poet" and "The Dying Pelican" are lost.

In August 1580 Spenser—who seems to have for some time acted as secretary to the Earl of Leicester—attended Arthur Lord Grey of Wilton, who had been appointed Lord Deputy of Ireland, in the capacity of private secretary. Raleigh, who had not long returned from his voyage to Newfoundland with Sir Humphrey Gilbert, his half-brother, was serving in the English forces; and in all probability the friendship now began which was destined to bear fruit in the poet's introduction to Queen Elizabeth. Of this, however, we have no evidence: what we do know is, that in March 1581 Spenser was appointed to the office of Clerk of Degrees and Recognizances in the Irish Court of Chancery—an office which he held until, in 1588, he was made Clerk to the Council of Munster. Before the end of 1581, also, he received a Crown grant of a lease of the manor, castle, and abbey of Enniscorthy, in Wexford, at a rent of £300, on the condition of his keeping the buildings in repair. Though Enniscorthy was a pleasant and lovely place, Spenser did not hold it long; in December 1581, he sold his interest to one Richard Synot, from whom it passed into the hands of Sir H. Wallop, the ancestor of the present Portsmouth family We have sufficient proof of the high esteem in which the poet held the chivalrous and high-minded but somewhat absolute Deputy whom he served, in the character of Grey drawn under the name of Sir Artegall in the fifth book of "The Faerie Queen;" and in the recommendatory Sonnet prefixed to that Poem, where Spenser addresses Grey as the pillar of his life and patron of his Muse's pupilage. When Grey was recalled, in 1582, Spenser is generally stated to have returned with him; but there are reasons for believing that the poet remained at his post in Dublin, and devoted his labour to "The Faerie Queen." He distinctly describes that poem, in his introductory Sonnet addressed to the Earl of Ormond (page 308), as "the wild fruit which salvage soil hath bred," and in the Sonnet to Grey as "rude rhymes, the which a rustic Muse did weave in salvage soil, far from Parnassus Mount." Moreover, the duties of his Chancery office required him to reside in Ireland; there are no well-authenticated notices of his presence in England between 1582 and 1590—a thing incomprehensible if he had been within easy reach of Harvey's letters, Sidney's friendship, or Leicester's good offices; there is evidence, in a work by his friend Lodowick Briskett, that Spenser lived at or near Dublin, in high repute for literary judgment, for scholarship, and genius, during those years in which direct authentic record loses sight of him; while his intimate knowledge of the condition of Ireland, displayed in his sole prose work, testifies to far more than that cursory observation which the leisure of two years' official life could afford. Another token that his Chancery duties detained him in Dublin, is furnished by a Sonnet addressed to Gabriel Harvey, dated at that city on the 18th of July 1586; while it is not easy to understand why, on the 27th of June in the same year, the Queen should have made him a grant of 3028 acres of land in the county of Cork, unless it was in reward of services in Ireland. We may therefore conceive Spenser going through the daily routine of Chancery work at Dublin—as Chaucer performed the dull duties of his post as Controller of Customs at London—until, in 1586, he was banished from such society as the Irish chief city afforded, to the lovely but lonely vicinity of Kilcolman.

The estate consisted of lands forfeit by the Earl of Desmond. The ancient castle that stood upon it—now a mere mound of ruins—had been a residence of the old Earls. It was romantically situated, two miles from Doneraile, on the northern side of a lake fed by the waters of the Awbeg, which the poet fancifully named the Mulla; and all around rose mountain ranges, at a distance sufficient to permit the boast, that from the battlements half the breadth of Ireland could be seen. The extensive plain in which Spenser's mansion stood is bounded on the north by what the poet styled the Mountains of Mole,—the Ballyhoura Hills, or, more properly, the range of Galty More, in which sprang the Mulla, the Bregog, the Molanna (or Brackbawn), and the Funcheon, all named in his "Faerie Queen" or "Colin Clout:" the eastern horizon was shut in by the distant mountains of Waterford; the western by the mountains of Kerry; the southern by the mountains of Nagle—all covered, in those days, with dense natural timber, for which the pilgrim to Spenser's ruined shrine now looks around in vain. It is supposed that the grant of this picturesque domain was procured for the poet through the good offices of Sidney—whose enforced retirement from the gay and brave Court, beyond the atmosphere of which men of Raleigh's stamp could scarcely breathe, had been solaced by those imaginations of pastoral simplicity and happiness, far from the whirling city and the intriguing palace, which the young warrior-poet indulged in his romance of "Arcadia." Perhaps Spenser coveted the retirement of Kilcolman; the place, if it came to him through the influence of Sidney, must have been rendered peculiarly dear when the hero's death in Holland, towards the close of 1586, made it seem, as it were, the last bequest of his friendship and admiration. The condition of the grant is said to have made residence on the estate obligatory; but it may be questioned whether Spenser hastened to take possession—for it was not until 1588 that, quitting his Chancery post at Dublin, he became Clerk to the Council of Munster; and it may be supposed, that, if he had taken earlier possession of his castle, he must have resigned his Chancery appointment sooner. We know, however, that in the later half of 1589 Sir Walter Raleigh, driven from Court to his Irish estates and duties by the prevalence of the Essex influence, found Spenser at Kilcolman, with three books of his "Faerie Queen" ready for the press. Spenser himself, in "Colin Clout 's Come Home Again," describes the arrival of the "Shepherd of the Ocean"—so he terms Raleigh—and his voyage to England at the request and in the company of his illustrious visitor. It is easy to fancy the pleasures which these two high-souled and accomplished men—alike instinct with the tender magnanimity, the chivalrous ardour, of the period—found in each other's society; and the hope of favour and fame with which Spenser set out anew for Court—invited by the foremost soldier and most brilliant courtier of the time, and bearing with him a work of which the author measured the worth and the renown not less liberally than any of this generation.

Raleigh was as good as his word to Spenser; he introduced the poet to the Queen, who was to find in him her most brilliant and enduring eulogist; and—rather tardily, it must be admitted—in the year after the poem was printed, her Majesty bestowed on Spenser a pension of £50 per annum. On the 1st of December 1589, "The Faerie Queen" first made her mark on the books of the Stationers'

Company; early in 1590, the First, Second, and Third Books were published, in a small quarto, by Ponsonby. They were dedicated "To the most (high) mighty, and magnificent Empress (renowned for piety, virtue, and all gracious Government), ELIZABETH, by the grace of God, Queen of England, France, and Ireland (and of Virginia), Defender of the Faith, &c., her most humble servant, Edmund Spenser (doth, in all humility, dedicate, present, and consecrate these his labours, to live with the eternity of her fame)." The dedication of 1590—amplified, when the three books were reprinted six years afterwards, by the words here placed within brackets—was accompanied by a letter to Raleigh, serving as introduction and preliminary explanation to the whole poem; and, besides some commendatory sonnets by friends, there were also seventeen sonnets addressed by the author to as many illustrious persons of the Court, &c. Great was the marvel and delight of all who read the new poet; his performance had so far transcended even the promise of "The Shepherd's Calendar," that "The Faerie Queen" was hailed as a new revelation—"as if," says one, "another moon, as quiet and as lustrous as Cynthia, had come up the sky." Neither space nor the scope of this brief notice permits anything like a critical consideration of Spenser's great allegorical poem. It has many faults, of unreality, of redundancy, confusion, and inequality; but its faults, where they do not actually create, are nobly redeemed by its beauties. In the main, the allegory, never very rigidly maintained as a whole, is easy to be penetrated; the House of Holiness in the first book, for example, and the House of Alma in the second, are as charming and simple as the Interpreter's House in Bunyan's "Pilgrim's Progress," or the City of Mansoul in his "Holy War;" while, even where the reader may be at any loss to discover the poet's meaning, or where the poet means nothing in particular save to carry forward the story that lies on the surface, the flow, the roll, the melody of the verse reconcile him to everything. Reading "The Faerie Queen," indeed, is like drifting at the will of that ocean to a voyage on which the author repeatedly compares the course of his work. We are at the mercy of a magnificent caprice. Now all is sunlit calm, like the life of Calidore among the shepherds, or of the Squire in the favour of Belphœbe. Now night falls, and the waters leap, and clash, and moan in sorrow, with Una's woe for her captive knight, or Timias' lamentation over Belphœbe's sudden wrath, or Britomart's anguish for her degraded if not faithless Artegall. Now the waves move in cadence under the returning sun, and the golden clouds attend their march in silent but gorgeous procession, as when we follow the Masque of Cupid, or trace the steps of Scudamour in the Temple of Love, or watch the trooping river-gods that come to the wedding of Thames and Medway, or the stately advance of the Seasons and the Months to the audience of Nature upon Arlo Hill. We have tempests and glassy tranquillity, gloom and glancing brightness, the majesty, the cruelty, the gentleness of the sea, all by turns, gliding from one to the opposite phase with the natural ease and swiftness of relentless purpose and resistless might; while over all, and through all, we recognise that we are in the grasp of a superhuman spirit, to which the whole material world, and all the elements of man's nature, are but playthings at the will of its fancy. Power, Nobility, and Beauty, inseparably wedded like the Graces—such is "The Faerie Queen," imperfect as it is: for is not every part of a matchless statue instinct with the loveliness and majesty of the whole?

Such was the fame which the publication of his *magnum opus* won for Spenser, that his printer made haste to collect what works of the poet were accessible in the hands of his friends, or otherwise "loosely scattered abroad;" and in 1591, when Spenser, having been endowed with his pension, was back at Kilcolman, Ponsonby put forth a volume of "Complaints; containing sundry small Poems of the World's Vanity." These were, in their order, "The Ruins of Time," "The Tears of the

Muses," "Virgil's Gnat," "Prosopopoia, or Mother Hubberd's Tale," "The Ruins of Rome, by Bellay," "Muiopotmos, or the Fate of the Butterfly" (which seems to have appeared under some shape in 1590); "Visions of the World's Vanity;" "Bellay's Visions;" and "Petrarch's Visions." In his notice "to the gentle reader," the printer gives the titles of a number of other poems, on which he could not lay his hands, and which are now lost to us for ever—for Spenser either was content with the renown gained by "The Faerie Queen," or was prevented by his premature death from rendering justice to the labours of his youth. "The Ruins of Time," an elegy on the recent deaths of Sidney (1586), Leicester (1588), and Leicester's brother, the Earl of Warwick (1589), was written during the poet's stay in England; and so was his "Daphnaïda," an elegy on the death of the daughter of Henry Lord Howard Viscount Byndon, and wife of Arthur Gorges, Esq. Immediately after his return to Kilcolman, Spenser recounted the visit of Raleigh, and his voyage to England, in "Colin Clout 's Come Home Again;" a poem which he kept by him for some years, and published in 1595, to refute—as the dedication to Raleigh shows—a reproach of his friend that he was "idle." In this, as in Spenser's greater pastoral, "Rosalind" holds a conspicuous place; but merely as a fondly-remembered and still reverenced idol of the past—not, as twelve years before, an object of fruitless desire embittering the poet's whole life. But "Rosalind" was soon to be dismissed from the place she yet held in Spenser's heart. About the end of 1592, it would seem, he fell in love with a fair Irishwoman, of whom we know little more than the fact that she had golden hair; bore—like Spenser's mother, and his Sovereign—the name of Elizabeth; and was, by birth and personal qualities, fully worthy to occupy the throne where Rosalind had reigned so long. The woman whom Spenser wooed as his "Sonnets" show, and, when he had won her, celebrated in his magnificent "Epithalamion," must surely have been of no ordinary attractions and character; but, save the particulars already stated, and the record that the poet married her on St Barnabas' Day, June the 11th, 1594, we know nothing about one whom her husband has rendered immortal in her obscurity.

Before his marriage, Spenser had completed the Fourth, Fifth, and Sixth Books of "The Faerie Queen;" but they were not at once given to the press. In 1595, the "Sonnets" and "Epithalamion" were published; and towards the end of that year Spenser came to England, bearing the second portion of his great poem, which was issued from Ponsonby's press in 1596, along with a reprint of the first three books. The publication raised Spenser, if possible, still higher in the regard of his contemporaries than before. But he was not destined long to enjoy his fame, which was all the greater for the rare rivalry of genius that distinguished the closing years of the sixteenth century. He found his friend Essex the reigning favourite; and although Burleigh was yet powerful in the Queen's councils, and, never having been friendly, could not be expected to further the poet's desire for preferment while he remained an intimate and protégé of Essex—still Spenser laid the foundation of what might have been a prosperous career, but for the blow of unforeseen misfortune. Dating from Greenwich, 1st September, 1596, Spenser dedicated to the Countess of Cumberland and the Countess of Warwick his four "Hymns"—in honour of Love, of Beauty, of Heavenly Love, and of Heavenly Beauty; and later in the year he published the "Prothalamion." Next year, he returned to Ireland; and we have no knowledge of his life there, until it was overtaken by fatal calamity. Lord Grey's stern suppression of the revolt of 1580 had but confined the flames of disaffection, which broke forth in 1598 with proportionately increased violence. Spenser was among the first marks for the vengeance of the wild Irishry. From whatever cause—it is said, through over-keen attention to his worldly interests—the poet was not popular in his own region. His "View of the Present State of

Ireland," recommending drastic remedies for the disorders and discontent of the country, had not been published; but it had circulated freely in manuscript, and the sentiments of its author were well known. He held the seat of the banned and impoverished Desmonds. To crown all, the great obstacle to Court advancement having been removed by Burleigh's death, Spenser had just been nominated Sheriff of Cork. It was not surprising that, at the signal of rebellion, the owner of Kilcolman, the authoritative embodiment of armed aggression, should be the first to experience the wrath of the down-trodden race. The furious Munster hillsmen swooped on the doomed household. Spenser, his wife, and all his children but one, narrowly escaped with life—one child, an infant, was left behind in the haste and confusion, and perished amid the ruins of the sacked and burning mansion. It is not probable that this catastrophe lost to the world much of "The Faerie Queen;" considering the time over which the production of the first six books had extended, and the recent long absence of the poet in England, much progress could not have been made with the contemplated second six—far less could they have been lost in the fire or the flight. But none the less did they perish on that cruel October day of 1598. The poet never wrote more. Arriving in London, destitute and sorrow-stricken, his heart broken by the common ruin of his home and his hopes, he died, apparently of sheer grief, in a tavern in King Street, Westminster, on the 16th of January 1599.

There is no ground for supposing that he died in actual distress; he had many friends, he had great patrons, he still held a small but sufficient pension. But the end was sad enough, for all that. He died at the very height of his fame and his powers; he had barely completed his forty-sixth year; and the bitterness of that despairing death-bed must have been intensified by the poet's own consciousness of all that was passing away with him into the voiceless realm. His friend Essex buried him honourably in the great Abbey, near the resting-place of Chaucer; poets attended his hearse, bearing elegies and mournful poems, and threw into the too early tomb the pens that wrote them. "A little man, who wore short hair;" his contemporaries tell us no more of his personal presence: posterity has it that he was among the giants of the olden time, and that around his head will play for ever the glory of intellectual power, tempered by the chaste light of spiritual purity.

NOTE ON THE FAERIE QUEEN.

In abridging The Faerie Queen for the present volume, the endeavour has been to retain every stanza that either possessed some peculiar beauty, or was essential for the carrying on of the story. But it has been above all sought to present the finer *passages* of the poem; and in seeking that end stanzas and lines may have been omitted whose absence some readers will regret. The Editor would fain believe that such will rarely be found the case; for, as in the prose outline representing the omitted passages every line of especial beauty or force has been embodied, so isolated stanzas, containing brilliant images, have almost invariably been preserved. To show to what extent the abridgment represents the original, the following table has been prepared, showing the entire number of stanzas in each canto, and the number of those stanzas which are retained in this volume:

	Book I.	Book II.		Book III.		Book IV.		Book V.		Book VI.		Book VII.
	Full.	Full.	Abdgd.	Full.	Abdgd.	Full.	Abdgd.	Full.	Abdgd.	Full.	Abdgd.	Full.
Proem .	4	5	5	5	5	5	5	11	11	7	7	—
Canto I.	55	61	21	67	28	54	17	30	9	47	17	—
,, II.	45	46	20	52	17	54	28	54	31	48	17	—
,, III.	44	46	23	62	19	52	24	40	14	51	13	—
,, IV.	51	46	23	61	21	48	17	51	15	40	16	—
,, V.	53	38	13	55	23	46	21	57	26	41	14	—
,, VI.	48	51	23	54	37	47	21	40	11	44	18	55
,, VII.	52	66	52	61	20	47	26	45	27	50	22	59
,, VIII.	50	56	17	52	18	64	32	51	18	51	28	2
,, IX.	54	60	46	53	19	41	16	50	36	46	34	—
,, X.	68	77	24	60	25	58	58	39	12	44	28	—
,, XI.	55	49	24	55	29	53	53	65	24	51	16	—
,, XII.	42	87	66	45	31	35	22	43	24	41	24	—
Total,	621	688	357	682	292	604	340	576	258	561	254	116

Thus it appears, that, out of the 3848 stanzas of which the Faerie Queen consists, 2238, or nearly two-thirds, are retained; the remaining 1610 being condensed into a prose outline occupying one-fourth of their space, and thus making the bulk of the poem, as here given, about one-third less than that of the full text. The First Book, containing the Legend of the Red Cross Knight, or of Holiness, has been presented without curtailment, both because it is the best known and perhaps the best sustained of the six, and because it seemed desirable to give an idea of the manner in which Spenser worked out his conceptions. The marks employed in the text are the same as those used in Chaucer; the note of diæresis, to show where a usually silent "e" should be sounded, or to indicate where the termination "ed" of the past tense should have the value of a distinct syllable; and the acute accent, to show where the termination "tion" is dissyllabic, or where the accent differs from the modern usage. When several verses are quoted together in the prose outline, a wider space has been employed to mark the commencement of a new line.

THE

POEMS OF EDMUND SPENSER.

THE FAERIE QUEEN:

DISPOSED INTO TWELVE BOOKS, FASHIONING TWELVE MORAL VIRTUES.

A LETTER OF THE AUTHOR'S,

EXPOUNDING HIS WHOLE INTENTION IN THE COURSE OF THIS WORK; WHICH, FOR THAT IT GIVETH GREAT LIGHT TO THE READER, FOR THE BETTER UNDERSTANDING IS HEREUNTO ANNEXED.

TO THE RIGHT NOBLE AND VALOROUS

SIR WALTER RALEIGH, Knight,

LORD WARDEN OF THE STANNARIES, AND HER MAJESTY'S LIEUTENANT OF THE COUNTY OF CORNWALL.

SIR,—Knowing how doubtfully all allegories may be construed, and this book of mine, which I have entituled "The Faerie Queen," being a continued Allegory, or dark Conceit, I have thought good, as well for avoiding of jealous opinions and misconstructions, as also for your better light in reading thereof (being so by you commanded), to discover unto you the general intention and meaning, which in the whole course thereof I have fashioned, without expressing of any particular purposes, or by-accidents,[1] therein occasioned. The general end, therefore, of all the book, is to fashion a gentleman or noble person in virtuous and gentle discipline: which for that I conceived should be most plausible and pleasing, being coloured with an historical fiction, the which the most part of men delight to read, rather for variety of matter than for profit of the ensample, I chose the History of King Arthur, as most fit for the excellency of his person, being made famous by many men's former works, and also farthest from the danger of envy and suspicion of present time. In which I have followed all the antique poets historical: first Homer, who in the persons of Agamemnon and Ulysses hath ensampled a good governor and a virtuous man, the one in his Ilias, the other in his Odysseis; then Virgil, whose like intention was to do in the person of Æneas; after him Ariosto comprised them both in his Orlando; and lately Tasso dissevered them again, and formed both parts in two persons, namely that part which they in philosophy call *Ethicé*, or virtues of a private man, coloured in his Rinaldo; the other, named *Politicé*, in his Godfredo. By ensample of which excellent poets, I labour to pourtray in Arthur, before he was king, the image of a brave knight, perfected in the twelve private Moral Virtues, as Aristotle hath devised;[2] the which is the purpose of these first twelve books: which if I find to be well accepted, I may be perhaps encouraged to frame the other part of Political Virtues in his person, after that he came to be king. To some I know this method will seem displeasant, which had rather have good discipline delivered plainly in way of precepts, or sermoned at large, as they use, than thus cloudily enwrapped in allegorical devices. But such, me seems, should be satisfied with the use of these days, seeing all things accounted by their shows, and nothing esteemed of, that is not delightful and pleasing to common sense. For this cause is Xenophon preferred before Plato, for that the one, in the exquisite depth of his judgment, formed a commonwealth, such as it should be; but the other, in the person of Cyrus, and the Persians, fashioned a government, such as might best be; so much more profitable and gracious is doctrine by ensample,

1 Episodes, incidents.

2 Described.

than by rule. So have I laboured to do in the person of Arthur: whom I conceive, after his long education by Timon, to whom he was by Merlin delivered to be brought up, so soon as he was born of the Lady Igrayne, to have seen in a dream or vision the Faerie Queen, with whose excellent beauty ravished, he awaking resolved to seek her out; and so being by Merlin armed, and by Timon throughly instructed, he went to seek her forth in Faerie Land. In that Faerie Queen I mean *Glory* in my general intention, but in my particular I conceive the most excellent and glorious person of our Sovereign *the Queen*, and her kingdom in *Faerie Land.* And yet, in some places else, I do otherwise shadow her. For considering she beareth two persons, the one of a most royal Queen or Empress, the other of a most virtuous and beautiful lady, this latter part in some places I do express in Belphœbe, fashioning her name according to your own excellent conceit of Cynthia: Phœbe and Cynthia being both names of Diana. So in the person of Prince Arthur I set forth *Magnificence* in particular; which Virtue, for that (according to Aristotle and the rest) it is the perfection of all the rest, and containeth in it them all, therefore in the whole I mention the deeds of Arthur applyable to that Virtue, which I write of in that book. But of the twelve other Virtues, I make twelve other knights the patterns, for the more variety of the history: of which these three books contain three.[1] The first, of the Knight of the Redcross, in whom I express *Holiness:* The second, of Sir Guyon, in whom I set forth *Temperance:* The third, of Britomartis, a lady knight, in whom I picture *Chastity.* But, because the beginning of the whole work seemeth abrupt and as depending upon other antecedents, it needs that ye know the occasion of these three knights' several adventures; for the method of a poet historical is not such, as of an historiographer. For an historiographer discourseth of affairs orderly as they were done, accounting as well the times as the actions; but a poet thrusteth into the midst, even where it most concerneth him, and there recoursing[2] to the things forepast, and divining of things to come, maketh a pleasing analysis of all. The beginning therefore of my history, if it were to be told by an historiographer, should be the twelfth book, which is the last; where I devise that the Faerie Queen kept her annual feast twelve days; upon which twelve several days, the occasions of the twelve several adventures happened, which, being undertaken by twelve several knights, are in these twelve books severally handled and discoursed. The first was this. In the beginning of the feast, there presented himself a tall clownish young man, who, falling before the Queen of Faeries, desired a boon (as the manner then was) which during that feast she might not refuse; which was that he might have the achievement of any adventure, which during that feast should happen. That being granted, he rested him on the floor, as unfit, through his rusticity, for a better place. Soon after entered a fair lady in mourning weeds, riding on a white ass, with a dwarf behind her leading a warlike steed, that bore the arms of a knight, and his spear in the dwarf's hand. She, falling before the Queen of Faeries, complained that her father and mother, an ancient king and queen, had been by an huge dragon many years shut up in a brazen castle, who thence suffered them not to issue: and therefore besought the Faerie Queen to assign her some one of her knights, to take on him that exploit. Presently that clownish person upstarting, desired that adventure; whereat the Queen much wondering, and the lady much gainsaying, yet he earnestly importuned his desire. In the end the lady told him, that unless that armour, which she brought, would serve him (that is, the armour of a Christian man, specified by St Paul, vi. Ephes.) he could not succeed in that enterprise; which being forthwith put upon him with due furnitures thereunto, he seemed the goodliest man in all that company, and was well liked of the lady. And eftsoons[3] taking on him knighthood, and mounting on that strange courser, he went forth with her on that adventure; where beginneth the first book, viz.

A gentle Knight was pricking on the plain, &c.[4]

The second day there came in a palmer, bearing an infant with bloody hands, whose parents he complained to have been slain by an enchantress called Acrasia; and therefore craved of the Faery Queen, to appoint him some knight, to perform that adventure; which being assigned to Sir Guyon, he presently went forth with that same palmer: which is the beginning of the second book and the whole subject thereof. The third day there came in a groom, who complained before the Faery Queen, that a vile enchanter, called Busirane, had in hand a most fair lady, called Amoretta, whom he kept in most grievous torment, because she would not yield him the pleasure of her body. Whereupon Sir Scudamour, the lover of that lady, presently took on him that adventure. But being unable to perform it by reason of the hard enchantments, after long sorrow, in the end he met with Britomartis, who succoured him, and rescued his love. But, by occasion hereof, many other adventures are intermedled,[5] but rather as accidents, than intendments:[6] As the love of Britomart, the overthrow of Marinell, the misery of Florimell, the virtuousness of Belphœbe, the lasciviousness of Hellenora, and many the like. This much, Sir, I have

1 The letter was sent to Raleigh with the first three books only; the second three were not published till several years afterwards.

2 Recurring.

3 Immediately.

4 What is said here explains the fifth line of the First Book—"Yet arms till that time did he never wield."

5 Intermingled.

6 Deliberate parts of the plan.

briefly overrun to direct your understanding to the well-head of the history, that, from thence gathering the whole intention of the conceit, ye may as in a handful gripe[1] all the discourse, which otherwise may haply seem tedious and confused. So, humbly craving the continuance of your honourable favour toward me, and the eternal establishment of your happiness, I humbly take leave.

Yours most humbly affectionate,

ED. SPENSER.

Jan. 23, 1589.

VERSES

ADDRESSED BY

THE AUTHOR OF THE FAERIE QUEEN

TO SEVERAL NOBLEMEN, ETC.

To the Right Honourable Sir Christopher Hatton,[2] *Lord High Chancellor of England, &c.*

THOSE prudent heads, that with their counsels wise
Whilóm[3] the pillars of th' earth did sustain,
And taught ambitious Rome to tyrannise
And on the neck of all the world to reign,
Oft from those grave affairs were wont abstain,
With the sweet lady Muses for to play:
So Ennius the elder Africain,[4]
So Maro[5] oft did Cæsar's cares allay.
So you, great Lord, that with your counsel sway
The burden of this kingdom mightily,
With like delights sometimes may eke delay[6]
The rugged brow of careful Policy;
And to these idle rhymes lend little space,
Which for their title's sake may find more grace.

E. S.

To the Right Honourable the Lord Burleigh,[7] *Lord High Treasurer of England.*

To you, right noble Lord, whose careful breast
To menage[8] of most grave affairs is bent,
And on whose mighty shoulders most doth rest
The burden of this kingdom's government
(As the wide compass of the firmament
On Atlas' mighty shoulders is upstay'd),
Unfitly I these idle rhymes present,
The labour of lost time, and wit unstay'd:
Yet if their deeper sense be inly weigh'd,
And the dim veil, with which from common view
Their fairer parts are hid, aside be laid,
Perhaps not vain they may appear to you.
Such as they be, vouchsafe them to receive,
And wipe their faults out of your censure grave.

E. S.

To the Right Honourable the Earl of Oxford,[9] *Lord High Chamberlain of England, &c.*

RECEIVE, most noble Lord, in gentle gree,[10]
The unripe fruit of an unready wit;
Which, by thy countenance, doth crave to be
Defended from foul envy's pois'nous bit.[11]
Which so to do may thee right well befit,
Since th' antique glory of thine ancestry
Under a shady veil is therein writ,
And eke thine own long-living memory,
Succeeding them in true nobility:
And also for the love which thou dost bear
To th' Heliconian imps,[12] and they to thee;
They unto thee, and thou to them, most dear:
Dear as thou art unto thyself, so love,—
That loves and honours thee, as doth behove,—

E. S.

To the Right Honourable the Earl of Northumberland.[13]

THE sacred Muses have made always claim
To be the nurses of nobility,
And registers of everlasting fame
To all that arms profess and chivalry.
Then, by like right, the noble progeny,
Which them succeed in fame and worth, are tied
T' embrace the service of sweet Poetry,
By whose endeavours they are glorified;
And eke from all, of whom it is envíed,[14]
To patronize the author of their praise,
Which gives them life that else would soon have died,
And crowns their ashes with immortal bays.
To thee therefóre, right noble Lord, I send
This present of my pains, it to defend.

E. S.

To the Right Honourable the Earl of Cumberland.[15]

REDOUBTED Lord, in whose courageous mind
The flower of chivalry, now bloss'ming fair,
Doth promise fruit worthy the noble kind[16]
Which of their praises have you left the heir;

1 Grasp.
2 Made Lord Chancellor in 1587; he died in 1591.
3 Of old time.
4 Publius Cornelius Scipio, surnamed "Africanus" from his exploits in Africa. His adoptive son, Publius Æmilianus Scipio—son of Paulus Æmilius—also distinguished himself in Africa, and was termed "Africanus Junior."
5 Virgil; whose full name was Publius Virgilius Maro.
6 Allay; soften.
7 William Cecil, created Baron of Burghley 1571; he was Elizabeth's most famous Minister, and died in 1598.
8 Management; French, "ménage."
9 Edward de Vere, seventeenth Earl, who died in 1604; all his ancestors, except the tenth and eleventh Earls, had held the office of chamberlain, as did himself and his son, Henry. He wrote verses, among them a "Dialogue between Fancy and Desire."
10 Favour.
11 Bite.
12 The Muses, the children of Helicon.
13 Henry Percy, nephew of Thomas Percy, who was beheaded at York in 1572; the nephew succéeded his father Henry in 1585, and he died in 1632.
14 Regarded with jealousy or dislike.
15 George Clifford, third Earl; he had in 1587 done good service against the Spaniards in the West Indies; he died in 1605.
16 Race, ancestry.

To you this humble present I prepare,
For love of virtue and of martial praise;
To which though nobly ye inclinëd are
(As goodly well ye show'd in late assays),[1]
Yet brave ensample of long passëd days,
In which true honour ye may fashion'd see,
To like desire of honour may ye raise,
And fill your mind with magnanimity.
Receive it, Lord, therefóre, as it was meant,
For honour of your name and high descent.
E. S.

To the most Honourable and excellent Lord the Earl of Essex,[2] Great Master of the Horse to her Highness, and Knight of the Noble Order of the Garter, &c.

MAGNIFIC Lord, whose virtues excellent
Do merit a most famous poet's wit
To be thy living praise's instrument;
Yet do not sdeign[3] to let thy name be writ
In this base poem, for thee far unfit;
Naught is thy worth disparagëd thereby.
But when my Muse,—whose feathers, nothing flit,[4]
Do yet but flag and lowly learn to fly,—
With bolder wing shall dare aloft to sty[5]
To the last praises of this Faery Queen;
Then shall it make most famous memory
Of thine heroic parts, such as they been:[6]
Till then, vouchsafe thy noble countenance
To their first labour's needed furtherance.
E. S.

To the Right Honourable the Earl of Ormond and Ossory.[7]

RECEIVE, most noble Lord, a simple taste
Of the wild fruit which salvage[8] soil hath bred;
Which, being through long wars left almost waste,
With brutish barbarism is overspread:
And, in so fair a land as may be read,[9]
Not one Parnassus, nor one Helicon
Left for sweet Muses to be harbourëd,
But where thyself hast thy brave mansión:
There indeed dwell fair Graces many one,
And gentle Nymphs, delights of learned wits;
And in thy person, without paragon,[10]
All goodly bounty and true honour sits.
Such therefore, as that wasted soil doth yield,
Receive, dear Lord, in worth,[11] the fruit of barren field.
E. S.

To the Right Honourable the Lord Charles Howard, Lord high Admiral of England,[12] Knight of the Noble Order of the Garter, and one of her Majesty's Privy Council, &c.

AND ye, brave Lord,—whose goodly personage
And noble deeds, each other garnishing,
Make you example, to the present age,
Of the old heroes, whose famoús offspríng
The antique poets wont so much to sing,—
In this same pageant have a worthy place,
Since those huge castles of Castilian King,
That vainly threaten'd kingdoms to displace,
Like flying doves ye did before you chase;
And that proud people, waxen[13] insolent
Through many victories, didst first deface:
Thy praise's everlasting monument
Is in this verse engraven semblably,[14]
That it may live to all posterity. E. S.

To the Right Honourable the Lord of Hunsdon,[15] High Chamberlain to her Majesty.

RENOWNËD Lord, that, for your worthiness
And noble deeds, have your deservëd place
High in the favour of that Emperess,
The world's sole glory and her sex's grace;
Here eke of right have you a worthy place,
Both for your nearness to that Faery Queen,
And for your own high merit in like case:
Of which apparent proof was to be seen
When that tumultuous rage and fearful deen[16]
Of Northern rebels ye did pacify,[17]
And their disloyal power defacëd clean,
The record of enduring memory.
Live, Lord, for ever in this lasting verse,
That all posterity thy honour may rehearse.
E. S.

To the most renowned and valiant Lord, the Lord Grey of Wilton, Knight of the Noble Order of the Garter, &c.

MOST noble Lord, the pillar of my life,
And patron of my Muse's pupilage;
Through whose large bounty, pourëd on me rife
In the first season of my feeble age,
I now do live bound yours by vassalage
(Since nothing ever may redeem, nor reave[18]
Out of your endless debt, so sure a gage[19]);
Vouchsafe in worth this small gift to receive,
Which in your noble hands for pledge I leave
Of all the rest that I am tied t' account:[20]
Rude rhymes, the which a rustic Muse did weave
In salvage[8] soil, far from Parnassus Mount,
And roughly wrought in an unlearnëd loom:
The which vouchsafe, dear Lord, your favourable doom.[21]
E. S.

1 Essays, trials.
2 Robert Devereux, who succeeded his father Walter in the Earldom in 1576; he was Queen Elizabeth's favourite, made Lord-Lieutenant of Ireland 1599, and beheaded 1601.
3 Disdain; from Italian, "sdegnare."
4 Fleet, swift.
5 Ascend; German, "steigen," to climb, mount.
6 Are.
7 Lieutenant-General of the Army in Ireland when Spenser sent to him his first three books; he lived in Ireland.
8 Savage, uncultured.
9 Read of, found.
10 Equal; rival.
11 As worthy of your esteem.
12 Who commanded at sea against the Spanish Armada in 1588.
13 Grown.
14 With faithful resemblance.
15 Henry Carey, first Baron Hunsdon; he died in 1596. His mother was sister to Anne Boleyn; so that Queen Elizabeth was his cousin.
16 Din
17 In the Rebellion of the North in 1569.
18 Pluck away.
19 Pledge.
20 For which I am bound to account.
21 Judgment.

To the Right Honourable the Lord of Buckhurst,[1] *one of her Majesty's Privy Council.*

In vain I think, right honourable Lord,
By this rude rhyme to memorize thy name,
Whose learned Muse hath writ her own recórd
In golden verse, worthy immortal fame:
Thou much more fit (were leisure to the same)
Thy gracious Sov'reign's praises to compile,
And her imperial Majesty to frame
In lofty numbers and heroic style.
But, since thou may'st not so, give leave a while
To baser wit his power therein to spend,
Whose gross defaults thy dainty pen may file,[2]
And unadvisëd oversights amend.
But evermore vouchsafe it to maintain
Against vile Zoilus'[3] backbitings vain. E. S.

To the Right Honourable Sir Francis Walsingham, Knight, principal Secretary to her Majesty, and one of her honourable Privy Council.

That Mantuan poet's[4] incomparëd[5] spirit,
Whose garland now is set in highest place,—
Had not Mæcenas, for his worthy merit,
It first advanc'd to great Augustus' grace,—
Might long perhaps have lain in silence base,
Nor been so much admir'd of later age.
This lowly Muse, that learns like steps to trace,
Flies for like aid unto your patronage
(That are the great Mæcenas of this age,
As well to all that civil arts profess,
As those that are inspir'd with martial rage),
And craves protection of her feebleness:
Which if ye yield, perhaps ye may her raise
In bigger tunes to sound your living praise.
E. S.

To the Right Noble Lord and most valiant Captain, Sir John Norris, Knight, Lord President of Munster.

Who ever gave more honourable prize[6]
To the sweet Muse, than did the martial crew,
That their brave deeds she might immortalize
In her shrill trump, and sound their praises due?
Who then ought more to favour her than you,
Most noble Lord, the honour of this age,
And precedent of all that arms ensue?[7]
Whose warlike prowess and manly courage,
Temper'd with reason and advisement[8] sage,
Hath fill'd sad Belgic with victorious spoil;
In France and Ireland left a famous gage;[9]
And lately shak'n the Lusitanian soil.
Since, then, each where thou hast dispread thy fame,
Love him that hath eternizëd your name. E. S.

To the Right Noble and Valorous Knight, Sir Walter Raleigh,[10] *Lord Warden of the Stannaries, and Lieutenant of Cornwall.*

To thee, that art the summer's nightingale,
Thy sov'reign Goddess's[11] most dear delight,
Why do I send this rustic madrigale,
That may thy tuneful ear unseason[12] quite?
Thou only fit this argument to write,
In whose high thoughts Pleasure hath built her bow'r,
And dainty Love learn'd sweetly to indite.
My rhymes I know unsavoury and sour,
To taste the streams that, like a golden show'r,
Flow from thy fruitful head of thy love's praise;
Fitter perhaps to thunder martial stowre,[13]
When so thee list thy lofty Muse to raise:
Yet, till that thou thy poem wilt make known,
Let thy fair Cynthia's[14] praises be thus rudely shown. E. S.

To the Right Honourable and most virtuous Lady, the Countess of Pembroke.

Remembrance of that most heroic spirit,[15]—
The Heaven's pride, the glory of our days,
Which now triúmpheth (through immortal merit
Of his brave virtues) crown'd with lasting bays
Of heavenly bliss and everlasting praise;
Who first my Muse did lift out of the floor,
To sing his sweet delights in lowly lays,—
Bids me, most noble Lady, to adore
His goodly image living evermore
In the divine resemblance of your face;
Which with your virtues ye embellish more,
And native beauty deck with heav'nly grace:
For his, and for your own especial sake,
Vouchsafe from him this token in good worth to take. E. S.

---

1 Thomas Sackville, who was created Earl of Dorset in 1603. He was in his youth a poet, but, betaking himself to politics, became Lord Treasurer and Privy Councillor to the Queen.

2 Polish.

3 A rhetorician of Thrace, whose name became a proverb for a carping and envious critic, through his abusive and bitter strictures on the works of Homer, Hesiod, Demosthenes, Aristotle, Plato, and others. His great delight was to be known as "Homero-mastyx," the Homer-scourger.

4 Virgil.

5 Matchless, unrivalled.

6 Praise, esteem.

7 Follow.

8 Counsel, prudence.

9 Pledge.

10 Raleigh was at this time at the height of royal favour and of activity; incessantly planning expeditions abroad, and busied in affairs of State at home.

11 Queen Elizabeth's.

12 Jar on; be ill-timed to.

13 Conflict, strife.

14 In Raleigh's poem of "Cynthia," as in Spenser's Faerie Queen, the praises of his royal mistress were sung under an allegory. See the introductory letter to Raleigh. Cynthia is one of the names of Diana.

15 The Countess was the sister of the chivalrous and accomplished Sir Philip Sidney, the author of "Arcadia" and of the "Defence of Poetry." He was mortally wounded at the battle of Zutphen, in the Netherlands, in 1586.

To the most virtuous and beautiful Lady, the Lady Carew.[1]

Ne[2] may I, without blot of endless blame,
You, fairest Lady, leave out of this place;
But with remembrance of your gracious name
(Wherewith that courtly garland most ye grace
And deck the world), adorn these verses base:
Not that these few lines can in them comprise
Those glorious ornaments of heav'nly grace
Wherewith ye triumph over feeble eyes,
And in subduëd hearts do tyrannise
(For thereunto doth need a golden quill,
And silver leaves, them rightly to devise[3]);
But to make humble present of good will:
Which, when as timely means it purchase may,
In ampler wise itself will forth display. E. S.

To all the gracious and beautiful Ladies in the Court.

The Chian painter, when he was requir'd
To pourtray Venus in her perfect hue,
To make his work more absolute,[4] desir'd
Of all the fairest maids to have the view.
Much more me needs (to draw the semblance[5] true
Of Beauty's Queen, the world's sole wonderment),
To sharp my sense with sundry beauties' view,
And steal from each some part of ornament.
If all the world to seek I over went,
A fairer crew yet nowhere could I see
Than that brave Court doth to mine eye present;
That the world's pride seems gather'd there to be.
Of each a part I stole by cunning theft:
Forgive it me, fair Dames, since less ye have not left. E. S.

THE FIRST BOOK

OF

THE FAERIE QUEEN:

CONTAINING

THE LEGEND OF THE KNIGHT OF THE REDCROSS, OR OF HOLINESS.

Lo! I, the man whose Muse whilóm[6] did mask,
As time her taught, in lowly shepherds' weeds,[7]
Am now enforc'd, a far unfitter task,
For trumpets stern to change mine oaten reeds,
And sing of Knights' and Ladies' gentle deeds;
Whose praises having slept in silence long,
Me, all too mean, the sacred Muse areads[8]
To blazon broad amongst her learned throng:
Fierce wars and faithful loves shall moralize my song.

Help then, O holy Virgin,[9] chief of Nine,
Thy weaker novice to perform thy will;
Lay forth out of thine everlasting scrine[10]
The ántique rolls, which there lie hidden still,
Of Faery Knights, and fairest Tanaquill,[11]
Whom that most noble Briton Prince so long
Sought through the world, and suffer'd so much ill,
That I must rue[12] his undeservëd wrong:
O, help thou my weak wit, and sharpen my dull tongue!

And thou, most dreaded imp[13] of highest Jove,
Fair Venus' son, that with thy cruel dart
At that good Knight so cunningly didst rove,[14]
That glorious fire it kindled in his heart;
Lay now thy deadly ebon bow apart,
And, with thy mother mild, come to mine aid;
Come, both; and with you bring triumphant Mart,[15]
In loves and gentle jollities array'd,
After his murderous spoils and bloody rage allay'd.

And with them eke, O Goddess heav'nly bright,[16]
Mirror of grace and majesty divine,
Great Lady of the greatest Isle, whose light
Like Phœbus' lamp throughout the world doth shine,
Shed thy fair beams into my feeble eyne,[17]
And raise my thoughts, too humble and too vile,
To think of that true glorious type of thine,
The argument of mine afflicted[18] style:
The which to hear vouchsafe, O dearest Dread,[19] a while.

CANTO I.

The Patron of true Holiness
Foul Error doth defeat;
Hypocrisy, him to entrap,
Doth to his home entreat.

A gentle Knight was pricking[20] on the plain,
Y-clad in mighty arms and silver shield,

1 Supposed to be the same as Lady Carey, whose maiden name was Spenser, and who was related to the poet.
2 Not.
3 Tell, set forth.
4 Perfect. Zeuxis, when he painted Helen for the temple of Juno at Crotona, in Italy, took as his models five of the most beautiful girls in the city.
5 Likeness.
6 Formerly.
7 Referring to the "Shepherd's Calendar," which had been published ten years before, in 1579.
8 Counsels, commands.
9 Clio, the Muse of history.
10 The same word as "shrine;" from Latin, "scrinium," a chest or casket in which books, manuscripts, &c., were deposited. Clio, in ancient works of art, was usually represented with an open chest of books by her side.
11 Gloriana; the Faerie Queen.
12 Pity.
13 Descendant. See note 26, page 156.
14 Shoot.
15 Mars.
16 Queen Elizabeth.
17 Eyes.
18 Humble.
19 Object of reverence; so Milton speaks of "our Living Dread."
20 Spurring, riding.

Wherein old dints of deep wounds did remain,
The cruel marks of many a bloody field;
Yet arms till that time did he never wield:
His angry steed did chide his foaming bit,
As much disdaining to the curb to yield:
Full jolly[1] knight he seem'd, and fair did sit,
As one for knightly jousts and fierce encounters fit.

And on his breast a bloody cross he bore,
The dear remembrance of his dying Lord,
For whose sweet sake that glorious badge he wore,
And dead, as living ever, him ador'd:
Upon his shield the like was also scor'd,
For sov'reign hope which in his help he had.
Right faithful true he was in deed and word;
But of his cheer[2] did seem too solemn sad;
Yet nothing did he dread, but ever was y-drad.[3]

Upon a great adventure he was bond,[4]
That greatest Gloriana to him gave
(That greatest glorious Queen of Faery Lond[5]),
To win him worship,[6] and her grace to have,
Which of all earthly things he most did crave:
And ever, as he rode, his heart did yearn
To prove his puissánce[7] in battle brave
Upon his foe, and his new force to learn;
Upon his foe, a Dragon horrible and stern.

A lovely Lady rode him fair beside,
Upon a lowly ass more white than snow;
Yet she much whiter; but the same did hide
Under a veil, that wimpled was full low;
And over all a black stole[8] she did throw:
As one that inly mourn'd, so was she sad,
And heavy sate upon her palfrey slow;
Seemëd in heart some hidden care she had;
And by her in a line a milk-white lamb she lad.[9]

So pure and innocent as that same lamb
She was, in life and ev'ry virtuous lore;
And by descent from royal lineage came
Of ancient kings and queens, that had of yore
Their sceptres stretch'd from east to western shore,
And all the world in their subjection held;
Till that infernal Fiend with foul uproar
Forwasted[10] all their land, and them expell'd;
Whom to avenge she had this Knight from far compell'd.

Behind her far away a Dwarf did lag,
That lazy seem'd, in being ever last,
Or wearïed with bearing of her bag
Of needments[11] at his back. Thus as they past,
The day with clouds was sudden overcast,
And angry Jove a hideous storm of rain
Did pour into his leman's[12] lap so fast,
That every wight to shroud[13] it did constrain;
And this fair couple eke to shroud themselves were fain.

Enforc'd to seek some covert nigh at hand,
A shady grove not far away they spied,
That promis'd aid the tempest to withstand;
Whose lofty trees, y-clad with summer's pride,
Did spread so broad, that heaven's light did hide,
Not pierceable with power of any star;
And all within were paths and alleys wide,
With footing worn, and leading inward far:
Fair harbour[14] that them seems; so in they enter'd are.

And forth they pass, with pleasure forward led,
Joying to hear the birds' sweet harmony,
Which, therein shrouded from the tempest dread,
Seem'd in their song to scorn the cruel sky.
Much gan[15] they praise the trees so straight and high:
The sailing pine;[16] the cedar proud and tall;
The vine-prop elm; the poplar never dry;
The builder oak, sole king of forests all;
The aspen good for staves; the cypress funeral;
The laurel, meed of mighty conquerours
And poets sage; the fir that weepeth still;
The willow, worn of fórlorn paramours;[17]
The yew, obedient to the bender's will;[18]
The birch for shafts;[19] the sallow for the mill;[20]
The myrrh sweet-bleeding in the bitter wound;[21]
The warlike beech;[22] the ash for nothing ill;
The fruitful olive; and the platane[23] round;
The carver holm;[24] the maple seldom inward sound.

Led with delight, they thus beguile the way,
Until the blust'ring storm is overblown;
When, weening[25] to return whence they did stray,
They cannot find that path which first was shown,
But wander to and fro in ways unknown,
Farthest from end then, when they nearest ween;
That makes them doubt their wits be not their own:
So many paths, so many turnings seen,
That, which of them to take, in diverse doubt they been.[26]

At last, resolving forward still to fare,[27]
Till that some end they find, or[28] in or out,
That path they take that beaten seem'd most bare,
And like to lead the labyrinth about;
Which when by tract they hunted had throughout,
At length it brought them to a hollow cave,
Amid the thickest woods. The Champion stout
Eftsoons[29] dismounted from his courser brave,
And to the Dwarf a while his needless[30] spear he gave.

"Be well aware," quoth then that Lady mild,
"Lest sudden mischief ye too rash provoke:
The danger hid, the place unknown and wild,
Breeds dreadful doubts: oft fire is without smoke,

1 Joyous; handsome. 2 Countenance, air.
3 Dreaded. 4 Bound.
5 Land. 6 Honour.
7 Power. 8 Robe. 9 Led.
10 Utterly devastated. 11 Necessaries.
12 His mistress—Tellus, or the Earth.
13 Seek cover or protection.
14 Shelter. 15 Began.
16 So called because it is used for the masts of ships. The enumeration of the trees in this and the succeeding stanza is imitated from Chaucer's description of the park in the "Assembly of Fowls;" but Spenser has amplified the list and improved upon the original.
17 Lovers. 18 When fashioned into bows.
19 Arrows.
20 For the sails of windmills, into which it was plaited.
21 The incision made to extract its odorous gum.
22 Used for the shafts of spears. 23 Plane-tree.
24 The cutting holly; so called from its prickles.
25 Thinking. 26 Are. 27 Go.
28 Either. 29 Immediately.
30 Unneeded now, because used only on horseback.

And peril without show: therefore your stroke,
Sir Knight, withhold, till farther trial made."
"Ah, Lady," said he, "shame were to revoke [1]
The forward footing for a hidden shade:
Virtue gives herself light through darkness for to wade."

"Yea, but," quoth she, "the peril of this place
I better wot than you: though now too late
To wish you back return with foul disgrace,
Yet wisdom warns, whilst foot is in the gate,
To stay the step, ere forcëd to retrate.[2]
This is the wand'ring wood, this Error's den,
A monster vile, whom God and man does hate:
Therefore I read [3] beware." "Fly, fly," quoth then
The fearful Dwarf; "this is no place for living men."

But, full of fire and greedy hardiment,[4]
The youthful Knight could not for aught be stay'd;
But forth into the darksome hole he went,
And lookëd in: his glist'ning armour made
A little glooming light, much like a shade;
By which he saw the ugly monster plain,
Half like a serpent horribly display'd,
But th' other half did woman's shape retain,
Most loathsome, filthy, foul, and full of vile disdain.

And, as she lay upon the dirty ground,
Her huge long tail her den all overspread;
Yet was in knots and many boughts [5] upwound,
Pointed with mortal sting; of her there bred
A thousand young ones, which she daily fed,
Sucking upon her pois'nous dugs; each one
Of sundry shapes, yet all ill-favourëd:
Soon as that uncouth [6] light upon them shone,
Into her mouth they crept, and sudden all were gone.

Their dam upstart out of her den afraid,
And rushëd forth, hurling her hideous tail
About her cursëd head; whose folds display'd
Were stretch'd now forth at length without entrail.[7]
She look'd about, and seeing one in mail,
Armëd to point, sought back to turn again;
For light she hated as the deadly bale,[8]
Aye wont in desert darkness to remain,
Where plain none might her see, nor she see any plain.

Which when the valiant Elf [9] perceiv'd, he leapt
As lion fierce upon the flying prey;
And with his trenchant blade her boldly kept
From turning back, and forcëd her to stay:
Therewith enrag'd she loudly gan to bray,
And turning fierce her speckled tail advanc'd,
Threat'ning her angry sting, him to dismay;
Who, naught aghast, his mighty hand enhanc'd;[10]
The stroke down from her head unto her shoulder glanc'd.

Much daunted with that dint [11] her sense was daz'd;[12]
Yet, kindling rage, herself she gather'd round,
And all at once her beastly body rais'd
With doubled forces high above the ground:
Tho,[13] wrapping up her wreathëd stern [14] around,
Leapt fierce upon his shield, and her huge train
All suddenly about his body wound,
That hand or foot to stir he strove in vain.
God help the man so wrapt in Error's endless train!

His Lady, sad to see his sore constraint,
Cried out, "Now, now, Sir Knight, shew what ye be;
Add faith unto your force, and be not faint;
Strangle her, else she sure will strangle thee."
That when he heard, in great perplexity,
His gall did grate [15] for grief and high disdain;
And, knitting all his force, got one hand free,
Wherewith he gript her gorge [16] with so great pain,
That soon to loose her wicked bands did her constrain.

Therewith she spued out of her filthy maw
A flood of poison horrible and black,
Full of great lumps of flesh and gobbets raw,
Which stunk so vilely, that it forc'd him slack
His grasping hold, and from her turn him back:
Her vomit full of books and papers was,
With loathly frogs and toads, which eyes did lack,
And, creeping, sought way in the weedy grass:
Her filthy parbreak [17] all the place defilëd has.

As when old father Nilus gins to swell
With timely pride above th' Egyptian vale,
His fatty waves do fertile slime outwell,[18]
And overflow each plain and lowly dale:
But, when his later ebb gins to avale,[19]
Huge heaps of mud he leaves, wherein there breed
Ten thousand kinds of creatures, partly male
And partly female, of his fruitful seed;
Such ugly monstrous shapes elsewhere may no man read.[20]

The same so sore annoyëd [21] has the Knight,
That, well-nigh chokëd with the deadly stink,
His forces fail, nor can no longer fight.
Whose courage when the fiend perceiv'd to shrink,
She pourëd forth out of her hellish sink
Her fruitful cursëd spawn of serpents small
(Deformëd monsters, foul, and black as ink),
Which swarming all about his legs did crawl,
And him encumber'd sore, but could not hurt at all.

As gentle shepherd in sweet eventide,
When ruddy Phœbus gins to welk [22] in west,
High on a hill, his flock to viewen wide,
Marks which do bite their hasty supper best;
A cloud of cumbrous gnats do him molest,
All striving to infix their feeble stings,

1 Take back. 2 Retreat. 3 Advise.
4 Boldness. 5 Coils.
6 Strange, unknown.
7 Twisting or intertwining.
8 Misery, destruction. 9 The Faery Knight.
10 Lifted up. 11 Blow.
12 Confused. 13 Then.
14 Her twisted tail.
15 His bile was harshly stirred—his anger was aroused.
16 Throat. 17 Vomit.
18 Make fertile slime flow forth. 19 Abate.
20 Discover, imagine. 21 Tormented. 22 Decline.

That from their noyance[1] he nowhere can rest;
But with his clownish hands their tender wings
He brusheth oft, and oft doth mar their murmurings;

Thus ill bested, and fearful more of shame
Than of the certain peril he stood in,
Half furious unto his foe he came,
Resolv'd in mind all suddenly to win,
Or soon to lose, before he once would lin;[2]
And struck at her with more than manly force,
That from her body, full of filthy sin,
He reft her hateful head without remorse:
A stream of coal-black blood forth gushëd from her corse.

Her scatter'd brood, soon as their parent dear
They saw so rudely falling to the ground,
Groaning full deadly all with troublous fear,
Gather'd themselves about her body round,
Weening[3] their wonted entrance to have found
At her wide mouth; but, being there withstood,
They flockëd all about her bleeding wound,
And suckëd up their dying mother's blood;
Making her death their life, and eke her hurt their good.

That détestáble sight him much amaz'd,
To see th' unkindly imps, of heav'n accurst,
Devour their dam; on whom while so he gaz'd,
Having all satisfied their bloody thirst,
Their bellies swoll'n he saw with fulness burst,
And bowels gushing forth: well worthy end
Of such as drunk her life, the which them nurst!
Now needeth him no longer labour spend,
His foes have slain themselves, with whom he should contend.

His Lady, seeing all that chanc'd from far,
Approach'd in haste to greet his victory;
And said, "Fair Knight, born under happy star,
Who see your vanquish'd foes before you lie;
Well worthy be you of that armoury
Wherein ye have great glory won this day,
And prov'd your strength on a strong enemy;
Your first adventure: many such I pray,
And henceforth ever wish that like succeed it may!"

Then mounted he upon his steed again,
And with the Lady backward sought to wend:
That path he kept, which beaten was most plain,
Nor ever would to any by-way bend;
But still did follow one unto the end,
The which at last out of the wood them brought.
So forward on his way (with God to friend)
He passëd forth, and new adventure sought:
Long way he travellëd, before he heard of aught.

At length they chanc'd to meet upon the way
An aged Sire, in long black weeds y-clad,
His feet all bare, his beard all hoary gray,
And by his belt his book he hanging had;
Sober he seem'd, and very sagely sad;[4]
And to the ground his eyes were lowly bent,
Simple in show, and void of malice bad;
And all the way he prayëd, as he went,
And often knock'd his breast, as one that did repent.

He fair the Knight saluted, louting[5] low,
Who fair him quited,[6] as that courteous was;
And after askëd him, if he did know
Of strange adventures, which abroad did pass.
"Ah! my dear son," quoth he, "how should, alas!
Silly old man, that lives in hidden cell,
Bidding his beads all day for his trespáss,[7]
Tidings of war and worldly trouble tell?
With holy father sits not[8] with such things to mell.[9]

"But if of danger, which hereby doth dwell,
And homebred evil ye desire to hear,
Of a strange man I can you tidings tell,
That wasteth all this country far and near."
"Of such," said he, "I chiefly do inquére;
And shall thee well reward to show the place,
In which that wicked wight his days doth wear:
For to all knighthood it is foul disgrace,
That such a cursëd creature lives so long a space."

"Far hence," quoth he, "in wasteful wilderness
His dwelling is, by which no living wight
May ever pass, but thorough great distress."
"Now," said the Lady, "draweth toward night;
And well I wot, that of your later fight
Ye all forwearied[10] be; for what so strong,
But, wanting rest, will also want of might?
The sun, that measures heaven all day long,
At night doth bait his steeds the ocean waves among.

"Then with the sun take, Sir, your timely rest,
And with new day new work at once begin:
Untroubled night, they say, gives counsel best."
"Right well, Sir Knight, ye have advisëd been,"
Quoth then that aged man; "the way to win
Is wisely to advise:[11] now day is spent;
Therefore with me ye may take up your inn[12]
For this same night." The Knight was well content:
So with that godly Father to his home they went.

A little lowly hermitage it was,
Down in a dale, hard by a forest's side,
Far from resort of people that did pass
In travel to and fro: a little wide[13]
There was a holy chapel edified,[14]
Wherein the Hermit duly wont to say
His holy things each morn and eventide;
Thereby a crystal stream did gently play,
Which from a sacred fountain wellëd forth alway.

Arrivëd there, the little house they fill,
Nor look for entertainment, where none was;
Rest is their feast, and all things at their will:
The noblest mind the best contentment has.
With fair discourse the ev'ning so they pass;
For that old man of pleasing words had store,
And well could file[15] his tongue, as smooth as glass:

1 Torment. 2 Desist. 3 Thinking. 4 Grave. 5 Bowing. 6 Returned his greeting. 7 Sins.

8 It is not fitting. 9 Meddle. 10 Utterly wearied. 11 Consider. 12 Lodging. 13 Apart. 14 Built. 15 Polish.

He told of saints and popes, and evermore
He strow'd an Ave-Mary after and before.

The drooping night thus creepeth on them fast;
And the sad humour loading their eye-lids,
As messenger of Morpheus, on them cast
Sweet slumb'ring dew, the which to sleep them bids.
Unto their lodgings then his guest he rids:[1]
Where when all drown'd in deadly sleep he finds,
He to his study goes; and there amids
His magic books, and arts of sundry kinds,
He seeks out mighty charms to trouble sleepy minds.

Then choosing out few words most horrible
(Let none them read!) thereof did verses frame;
With which, and other spells like terrible,
He bade awake black Pluto's grisly dame;[2]
And cursëd Heaven; and spake reproachful shame
Of highest God, the Lord of life and light.
A bold bad man! that dar'd to call by name
Great Gorgon,[3] prince of darkness and dead night;
At which Cocytus[4] quakes, and Styx[4] is put to flight.

And forth he call'd out of deep darkness dread
Legions of sprites, the which, like little flies,
Flutt'ring about his ever-damnëd head,
Await whereto their service he applies,
To aid his friends, or fray[5] his enemies:
Of those he chose out two, the falsest two,
And fittest for to forge true-seeming lies;
The one of them he gave a message to,
The other by himself stay'd other work to do.

He, making speedy way through spersëd[6] air,
And through the world of waters wide and deep,
To Morpheus'[7] house doth hastily repair.
Amid the bowels of the earth, full steep
And low, where dawning day doth never peep,
His dwelling is; there Tethys[8] his wet bed
Doth ever wash, and Cynthia[9] still doth steep
In silver dew his ever-drooping head,
While sad Night over him her mantle black doth spread.

Whose double gates he findeth lockëd fast;
The one fair fram'd of burnish'd ivory,
The other all with silver overcast;
And wakeful dogs before them far do lie,
Watching to banish Care their enemy,
Who oft is wont to trouble gentle Sleep.
By them the sprite doth pass in quietly,
And unto Morpheus comes, whom drownëd deep
In drowsy fit he finds; of nothing he takes keep.[10]

And, more to lull him in his slumber soft,
A trickling stream from high rock tumbling down,
And ever-drizzling rain upon the loft,[11]
Mix'd with a murmuring wind, much like the soun'[12]
Of swarming bees, did cast him in a swown.[13]
No other noise, nor people's troublous cries,
As still are wont t' annoy the wallëd town,
Might there be heard: but careless Quiet lies,
Wrapt in eternal silence, far from enemies.

The messenger approaching to him spake;
But his waste words return'd to him in vain:
So sound he slept, that naught might him awake.
Then rudely he him thrust, and push'd with pain,
Whereat he gan to stretch: but he again
Shook him so hard, that forcëd him to speak.
As one then in a dream, whose drier brain
Is toss'd with troubled sights and fancies weak,
He mumbled soft, but would not all his silence break.

The Sprite then gan more boldly him to wake,
And threaten'd unto him the dreaded name
Of Hecate: whereat he gan to quake,
And, lifting up his lumpish[14] head, with blame
Half angry askëd him, for what he came.
"Hither," quoth he, "me Archimago sent,
He that the stubborn sprites can wisely tame;
He bids thee to him send, for his intent,[15]
A fit false dream, that can delude the sleeper's scent."[16]

The god obey'd; and, calling forth straightway
A diverse[17] dream out of his prison dark,
Deliver'd it to him, and down did lay
His heavy head, devoid of careful cark;[18]
Whose senses all were straight benumb'd and stark.
He,[19] back returning by the ivory door,
Remounted up as light as cheerful lark;
And on his little wings the dream he bore
In haste unto his lord, where he him left before.

Who all this while, with charms and hidden arts,
Had made a lady of that other sprite,
And fram'd of liquid air her tender parts,
So lively,[20] and so like in all men's sight,
That weaker sense it could have ravish'd quite:
The maker's self, for all his wondrous wit,
Was nigh beguilëd with so goodly sight.
Her all in white he clad, and over it
Cast a black stole,[21] most like to seem for Una fit.

Now when that idle dream was to him brought,
Unto that Elfin Knight he bade him fly,—
Where he slept soundly, void of evil thought,—
And with false shows abuse his fantasy,[22]
In sort[23] as he him schoolëd privily.

1 Conducts, and thus rids himself of their company.
2 Hecate; the mysterious divinity identified with Luna in heaven, Diana on earth, Proserpine in hell.
3 A mysterious and dreaded deity, whose name the ancients feared to utter. Hence Milton speaks of "the dreaded name of Demogorgon." The derivation of the word is from the Greek, γοργος, dreadful; and the idea no doubt arose from the fable of the Gorgons—the three malign goddesses whose hairs were twisted snakes, and whose glance turned their victim to stone.
4 Rivers in hell.
5 Affright.
6 Dispersed, thin.
7 Son of Somnus, the god of sleep; usually represented as a fat child, though here he is placed in the supreme position of his father.
8 The principal goddess of the sea; wife of Oceanus, and daughter of Uranus and Terra.
9 Diana; the Moon.
10 Heed.
11 On high.
12 Noise, sound.
13 Deep sleep, like that of one who has swooned.
14 Heavy.
15 Purpose.
16 Perception, sense.
17 Erroneous, misleading.
18 Anxiety.
19 The messenger.
20 Lifelike.
21 Robe.
22 Fancy.
23 Such manner.

And that new creature, born without her due,[1]
Full of the maker's guile, with usage sly
He taught to imitate that Lady true,
Whose semblance she did carry under feignëd hue.

Thus well instructed, to their work they haste;
And, coming where the Knight in slumber lay,
The one upon his hardy[2] head him plac'd,
And made him dream of loves and lustful play;
That nigh his manly heart did melt away,
Bathëd in wanton bliss and wicked joy.
Then seemëd him his Lady by him lay,
And to him plain'd, how that false wingëd boy
Her chaste heart had subdu'd to learn dame Pleasure's toy;

And she herself, of beauty sov'reign queen,
Fair Venus, seem'd unto his bed to bring
Her whom he, waking, evermore did ween[3]
To be the chastest flower that aye did spring
On earthly branch, the daughter of a king,
Now a loose leman[4] to vile service bound:
And eke the Graces seemëd all to sing
Hymen Io Hymen, dancing all around;
Whilst freshest Flora her with ivy garland crown'd.

In this great passion of unwonted lust,
Or wonted fear of doing aught amiss,
He starteth up, as seeming to mistrust
Some secret ill, or hidden foe of his:
Lo, there before his face his Lady is,
Under black stole hiding her baited hook;
And, as half blushing, offer'd him to kiss,
With gentle blandishment and lovely look,
Most like that Virgin true, which for her Knight him took.

All clean dismay'd to see so uncouth[5] sight,
And half enragëd at her shameless guise,
He thought have slain her in his fierce despite;[6]
But, hasty heat temp'ring with suff'rance[7] wise,
He stay'd his hand; and gan himself advise[8]
To prove his sense,[9] and tempt her feignëd truth.
Wringing her hands, in women's piteous wise,
Then gan she weep, to stir up gentle ruth,[10]
Both for her noble blood, and for her tender youth.

And said, "Ah Sir, my liege lord, and my love,
Shall I accuse the hidden cruel fate,
And mighty causes wrought in heaven above,
Or the blind god, that doth me thus amate,[11]
For hopëd love, to win me certain hate?
Yet thus perforce he bids me do, or die.
Die is my due;[12] yet rue[10] my wretched state,
You, whom my hard avenging destiny
Hath made judge of my life or death indif-f'rently:

"Your own dear sake forc'd me at first to leave
My father's kingdom"—There she stopt with tears;
Her swollen heart her speech seem'd to bereave;
And then again begun; "My weaker years,
Captiv'd to fortune and frail worldly fears,
Fly to your faith for succour and sure aid:
Let me not die in languor and long tears."
"Why, dame," quoth he, "what hath ye thus dismay'd?
What frays[13] ye, that were wont to comfort me affray'd?"

"Love of yourself," she said, "and dear con-straint,
Lets me not sleep, but waste the weary night
In secret anguish and unpitied plaint,
While you in careless sleep are drownëd quite."
Her doubtful words made that redoubted Knight
Suspect her truth; yet since n' untruth he knew,
Her fawning love with foul disdainful spite
He would not shend;[14] but said, "Dear Dame, I rue
That for my sake unknown such grief unto you grew:

"Assure yourself, it fell not all to ground;
For all so dear, as life is to my heart,
I deem your love, and hold me to you bound:
Nor let vain fears procure your needless smart,
Where cause is none; but to your rest depart."
Not all content, yet seem'd she to appease
Her mournful plaints, beguilëd of her art,
And fed with words that could not choose but please:
So, sliding softly forth, she turn'd as to her ease.

Long after lay he musing at her mood,
Much griev'd to think that gentle Dame so light,
For whose defence he was to shed his blood.
At last dull weariness of former fight
Having y-rock'd asleep his irksome sprite,[15]
That troublous dream gan freshly toss his brain
With bowers, and beds, and ladies' dear delight:
But, when he saw his labour all was vain,
With that misformëd Sprite he back return'd again.

CANTO II.

The guileful great Enchanter parts
The Redcross Knight from Truth:
Into whose stead fair Falsehood steps,
And works him woeful ruth.

By this the Northern Waggoner[16] had set
His sev'nfold team behind the steadfast star[17]
That was in ocean waves yet never wet,
But firm is fix'd, and sendeth light from far
To all that in the wide deep wand'ring are;
And cheerful chanticleer, with his note shrill,
Had warnëd once, that Phœbus' fiery car
In haste was climbing up the eastern hill,
Full envious that Night so long his room did fill:

When those accursëd messengers of hell,
That feigning Dream, and that fair-forgëd Sprite,

1 Produced without the due qualities of a real woman—or not according to the due process of nature.
2 Bold. 3 Suppose. 4 Wanton. 5 Unfamiliar.
6 Anger. 7 Patience. 8 Counsel.
9 Whether his senses did not deceive him.
10 Pity. 11 Bewilder, subdue.
12 I deserve to die.
13 Affrights. 14 Disgrace, chide.
15 Wearied, distressed spirit.
16 Boötes; the Great Bear; popularly called "Charles's Wain" in some parts of the country.
17 The Pole-star.

Came to their wicked master, and gan tell
Their bootless pains and ill-succeeding night:
Who, all in rage to see his skilful might
Deluded so, gan threaten hellish pain
And sad Proserpine's wrath, them to affright.
But, when he saw his threat'ning was but vain,
He cast about, and search'd his baleful books
again.

Eftsoons[1] he took that miscreated Fair,
And that false other Sprite, on whom he spread
A seeming body of the subtile air,
Like a young squire, in loves and lustihead[2]
His wanton days that ever loosely led,
Without regard of arms and dreaded fight:
Those two he took, and in a secret bed,
Cover'd with darkness and misdeeming[3] night,
Them both together laid, to joy in vain delight.

Forthwith he runs, with feignëd-faithful haste,
Unto his guest, who, after troublous sights
And dreams, gan now to take more sound repast;[4]
Whom suddenly he wakes with fearful frights,
As one aghast[5] with fiends or damnëd sprites,
And to him calls; "Rise, rise, unhappy swain,
That here wax old in sleep,[6] while wicked wights
Have knit themselves in Venus' shameful chain:
Come, see where your false Lady doth her
honour stain."

All in a maze he suddenly upstart,
With sword in hand, and with the old man went;
Who soon him brought into a secret part,
Where that false couple were full closely ment[7]
In wanton lust and lewd embracëment:
Which when he saw, he burn'd with jealous fire;
The eye of reason was with rage y-blent;[8]
And would have slain them in his furious ire,
But hardly was restrainëd of that aged sire.

Returning to his bed, in torment great
And bitter anguish of this guilty sight,
He could not rest: but did his stout heart eat,
And waste his inward gall with deep despite,
Irksome[9] of life, and too long ling'ring night.
At last fair Hesperus in highest sky
Had spent his lamp, and brought forth dawn-
ing light;
Then up he rose, and clad him hastilý;
The Dwarf him brought his steed: so both
away do fly.

Now when the rosy-finger'd Morning fair,
Weary of aged Tithon's[10] saffron bed,
Had spread her purple robe through dewy air,
And the high hills Titan[11] discoverëd;
The royal Virgin shook off drowsihead:[12]
And, rising forth out of her baser bow'r,[13]
Look'd for her Knight, who far away was fled,
And for her Dwarf, that wont to wait each hour.
Then gan she wail and weep to see that woeful
stowre.[14]

And after him she rode, with so much speed
As her slow beast could make; but all in vain:
For him so far had borne his light-foot steed,
Prickëd[15] with wrath and fiery fierce disdain.
That him to follow was but fruitless pain:
Yet she her weary limbs would never rest;
But ev'ry hill and dale, each wood and plain,,
Did search, sore grievëd in her gentle breast,
He so ungently left her, whom she lovëd best

But subtile Archimago, when his guests
He saw divided into double parts,[16]
And Una wand'ring in woods and forësts
(Th' end of his drift), he prais'd his devilish arts,
That had such might over true-meaning hearts:
Yet rests not so, but other means doth make
How he may work unto her further smarts:
For her he hated as the hissing snake,
And in her many troubles did most pleasure
take.

He then devis'd himself how to disguise;
For by his mighty science he could take
As many forms and shapes, in seeming wise,
As ever Proteus to himself could make:
Sometimes a fowl, sometimes a fish in lake,
Now like a fox, now like a dragon fell;
That of himself he oft for fear would quake,
And oft would fly away. O who can tell
The hidden power of herbs, and might of magic
spell!

But now seem'd best the person[17] to put on
Of that good Knight, his late beguilëd guest:—
In mighty arms he was y-clad anon,
And silver shield; upon his coward breast
A bloody cross, and on his craven crest
A bunch of hairs discolour'd diversely.
Full jolly Knight he seem'd, and well addrest;[18]
And, when he sat upon his courser free,
Saint George himself ye would have deemëd
him to be.

But he, the Knight, whose semblance he did bear,
The true Saint George, was wander'd far away,
Still flying from his thoughts and jealous fear:
Will was his guide, and grief led him astray.
At last him chanc'd to meet upon the way
A faithless Saracen, all arm'd to point,[19]
In whose great shield was writ with letters gay
Sans foy;[20] full large of limb and every joint
He was, and carëd not for God or man a point.

He had a fair companion of his way,
A goodly lady clad in scarlet red,
Purfled[21] with gold and pearl of rich assay;[22]
And like a Persian mitre on her head
She wore, with crowns and ouches[23] garnishëd,
The which her lavish lovers to her gave:
Her wanton palfrey all was overspread
With tinsel trappings, woven like a wave,
Whose bridle rang with golden bells and bosses
brave.

With fair disport, and courting dalliance,

1 Immediately. 2 Pleasure. 3 Misleading.
4 Repose. 5 Terrified. 6 Linger too long in sleep.
7 Mingled. 8 Blinded, deceived. 9 Weary.
10 Tithonus, the brother of Priam, was beloved of Aurora, goddess of the Morn, whose prayers won for him immortality, but not everlasting youth; he shrank into a wretched figure in his old age, and Aurora changed him to a cicada. 11 The Sun. 12 Drowsiness.
13 Her lower, humbler, chamber—in comparison with Aurora's.
14 Trouble, mischance.
15 Spurred. 16 Into two parties.
17 Appearance. 18 Equipped.
19 Armed at all points. 20 Without Faith.
21 Embroidered, bordered. 22 Of great value.
23 Bosses or buttons of gold.

She entertain'd her lover all the way:
But, when she saw the Knight his spear advance,
She soon left off her mirth and wanton play,
And bade her knight address him to the fray:
His foe was nigh at hand. He, prick'd with pride,
And hope to win his lady's heart that day,
Forth spurrëd fast; adown his courser's side
The red blood trickling, stain'd the way as he did ride.

The Knight of the Redcross, when him he spied
Spurring so hot with rage dispiteous,[1]
Gan fairly couch his spear, and toward ride:
Soon meet they both, both fell and furious,
That, daunted with their forces hideous,
Their steeds do stagger, and amazëd stand;
And eke themselves, too rudely rigorous,
Astonish'd with the stroke of their own hand,
Do back rebut,[2] and each to other yieldeth land.[3]

As when two rams, stirr'd with ambitious pride,
Fight for the rule of the rich-fleecëd flock,
Their hornëd fronts so fierce on either side
Do meet, that, with the terror of the shock
Astonish'd, both stand senseless as a block,
Forgetful of the hanging [4] victory:
So stood these twain, unmovëd as a rock,
Both staring fierce, and holding idlely
The broken reliques of their former cruelty.[5]

The Saracen, sore daunted with the buff,[6]
Snatcheth his sword, and fiercely to him flies;
Who well it wards, and quiteth cuff with cuff;[7]
Each th' other's equal puissánce envíes,[8]
And through their iron sides with cruel spies [9]
Does seek to pierce; repining courage yields
No foot to foe: the flashing fiër flies,
As from a forge, out of their burning shields;
And streams of purple blood new dye the verdant fields.

"Curse on that Cross," quoth then the Saracen,
"That keeps thy body from the bitter fit;[10]
Dead long ago, I wot, thou haddest been,
Had not that charm from thee forwarnëd it:[11]
But yet I warn thee now, assurëd sit,
And hide thy head." Therewith upon his crest
With rigour so outrageoús he smit,
That a large share it hew'd out of the rest,
And, glancing down, his shield from blame him fairly blest.[12]

Who, thereat wondrous wroth, the sleeping spark
Of native virtue gan eftsoons [13] revive;
And, at his haughty helmet making mark,
So hugely struck, that it the steel did rive,
And cleft his head: he, tumbling down alive,
With bloody mouth his mother earth did kiss,
Greeting his grave: his grudging[14] ghost did strive
With the frail flesh; at last it flitted is,
Whither the souls do fly of men that live amiss.

The lady, when she saw her champion fall,
Like the old ruins of a broken tow'r,
Stay'd not to wail his woeful funeral;
But from him fled away with all her pow'r:
Who after her as hastily gan scour,
Bidding the Dwarf with him to bring away
The Saracen's shield, sign of the conqueroúr;
Her soon he overtook, and bade to stay;
For present cause was none of dread her to dismay.

She, turning back, with rueful countenance
Cried, "Mercy, mercy, Sir, vouchsafe to show
On silly [15] dame, subject to hard mischance,
And to your mighty will." Her humbless[16] low
In so rich weeds,[17] and seeming glorious show,
Did much enmove [18] his stout heroic heart;
And said, "Dear Dame, your sudden overthrow[19]
Much rueth [20] me; but now put fear apart,
And tell, both who ye be, and who that took your part."

Melting in tears, then gan she thus lament:
"The wretched woman, whom unhappy hour
Hath now made thrall to your commandëment,
Before that angry heavens list [21] to low'r,
And fortune false betray'd me to your pow'r,
Was (O what now availeth that I was!)
Born the sole daughter of an emperoúr;
He that the wide West under his rule has,
And high hath set his throne where Tiberis doth pass.

"He, in the first flow'r of my freshest age,
Betrothëd me unto the only heir
Of a most mighty king, most rich and sage;
Was never prince so faithful and so fair,
Was never prince so meek and debonair![22]
But, ere my hopëd day of spousal shone,
My dearest lord fell from high honour's stair
Into the hands of his accursed fone,[23]
And cruelly was slain; that shall I ever moan!

"His blessëd body, spoil'd of lively breath,
Was afterward, I know not how, convey'd,
And from me hid; of whose most innocent death
When tidings came to me, unhappy maid,
O, how great sorrow my sad soul assay'd![24]
Then forth I went his woeful corse to find,
And many years throughout the world I stray'd,
A virgin widow; whose deep-wounded mind
With love long time did languish, as the stricken hind.

"At last it chancëd this proud Saracen
To meet me wand'ring; who perforce me led
With him away; but yet could never win
The fort that ladies hold in sov'reign dread.
There lies he now, with foul dishonour dead,
Who, while he liv'd, was callëd proud Sansfoy,
The eldest of three brethren; all three bred
Of one bad sire, whose youngest is Sansjoy;[25]
And 'twixt them both was born the bloody bold Sansloy.[26]

1 Despiteful. 2 Recoil. 3 Gives ground. 4 Dubious. 5 Their broken spears. 6 Buffet, stroke 7 Repays blow with blow. 8 Begrudges the other's equal strength—would fain weaken his foe. 9 Their weapons. 10 Stroke. 11 Warded it off. 12 Protected from harm. 13 Straightway.

14 Reluctant. 15 Innocent. 16 Humility. 17 Garments. 18 Stir, disturb. 19 Misfortune. 20 Grieveth. 21 Pleased. 22 Gentle. 23 Foes. 24 Tried, assailed. 25 Without Joy. 26 Without Law.

"In this sad plight, friendless, unfortunate,
Now miserable I Fidessa[1] dwell,
Craving of you, in pity of my state,
To do none ill, if please ye not do well."
He in great passion[2] all this while did dwell,
More busying his quick eyes her face to view,
Than his dull ears to hear what she did tell;
And said, "Fair Lady, heart of flint would rue[3]
The undeservëd woes and sorrows which ye shew.

"Henceforth in safe assurance may ye rest,
Having both found a new friend you to aid,
And lost an old foe that did you molest:
Better new friend than an old foe, is said."
With change of cheer[4] the seeming-simple maid
Let fall her eyne, as shamefast, to the earth,
And, yielding soft, in that she naught gainsay'd.
So forth they rode, he feigning seemly mirth,
And she coy looks: so dainty, they say, maketh dearth.[5]

Long time they thus together travellëd;
Till, weary of their way, they came at last
Where grew two goodly trees, that fair did spread
Their arms abroad, with gray moss overcast;
And their green leaves, trembling with every blast,
Made a calm shadow far in compass round:
The fearful shepherd, often there aghast,[6]
Under them never sat, nor wont there sound
His merry oaten pipe; but shunn'd th' unlucky ground.

But this good Knight, soon as he them gan spy,
For the cool shade him thither hast'ly got;
For golden Phœbus, now y-mounted high,
From fiery wheels of his fair chariot
Hurlëd his beam so scorching cruel hot,
That living creature might it not abide;
And his new lady it endurëd not.
There they alight, in hope themselves to hide
From the fierce heat, and rest their weary limbs a tide.[7]

Fair-seemly pleasance[8] each to other makes,
With goodly purposes,[9] there as they sit;
And in his falsëd[10] fancy he her takes
To be the fairest wight that livëd yet;
Which to express, he bends his gentle wit;
And, thinking of those branches green to frame
A garland for her dainty forehead fit,
He pluck'd a bough; out of whose rift[11] there came
Small drops of gory blood, that trickled down the same.

Therewith a piteous yelling voice was heard,
Crying, "O spare with guilty hands to tear
My tender sides in this rough rind embarr'd;[12]
But fly, ah! fly far hence away, for fear
Lest to you hap what happen'd to me here,
And to this wretched lady, my dear love;
O too dear love, love bought with death too dear!"
Aston'd[13] he stood, and up his hair did hove;[14]
And with that sudden horror could no member move.

At last, when as the dreadful passión[15]
Was overpast, and manhood well awake,
Yet musing at the strange occasión,[16]
And doubting much his sense, he thus bespake;
"What voice of damnëd ghost from Limbo Lake,
Or guileful sprite wand'ring in empty air
(Both which frail men do oftentimes mistake),
Sends to my doubtful ears these speeches rare,[17]
And rueful[18] plaints, me bidding guiltless blood to spare?"

Then groaning deep; "Nor damnëd ghost," quoth he,
"Nor guileful sprite, to thee these words doth speak;
But once a man, Fradubio,[19] now a tree;
Wretched man, wretched tree! whose nature weak
A cruel witch, her cursëd will to wreak,
Hath thus transform'd, and plac'd in open plains,
Where Boreas doth blow full bitter bleak,
And scorching sun does dry my secret veins;
For though a tree I seem, yet cold and heat me pains."

"Say on, Fradubio, then, or man or tree,"
Quoth then the Knight; "by whose mischievous arts
Art thou misshapëd thus, as now I see?
He oft finds med'cine who his grief imparts;
But double griefs afflict concealing hearts,
As raging flames who striveth to suppress."
"The author then," said he, "of all my smarts,
Is one Duessa,[20] a false sorceress,
That many errant knights hath brought to wretchedness.

"In prime of youthly years, when courage hot
The fire of love and joy of chivalry
First kindled in my breast, it was my lot
To love this gentle lady, whom ye see
Now not a lady, but a seeming tree;
With whom as once I rode accompanied,
Me chancëd of a knight encounter'd be,
That had a like fair lady by his side;
Like a fair lady, but did foul Duessa hide;

"Whose forgëd[21] beauty he did take in hand
All other dames to have exceeded far;
I in defence of mine did likewise stand,
Mine, that did then shine as the morning star.
So both to battle fierce arrangëd are:
In which his harder fortune was to fall
Under my spear; such is the die[22] of war.
His lady, left as a prize martiál,[23]
Did yield her comely person to be at my call.[24]

"So doubly lov'd of ladies unlike fair,
Th' one seeming such, the other such indeed,
One day in doubt I cast for to compare

1 Faithful.
2 Emotion.
3 Pity.
4 Countenance.
5 Rareness maketh dearness.
6 Afraid.
7 While.
8 Pleasure.
9 Discourses; French, "propos."
10 Deceived.
11 Cleft.
12 Imprisoned.
13 Amazed, astounded.
14 Heave, stand on end, with dread.
15 Emotion.
16 Incident.
17 Strange.
18 Pitiful.
19 Doubtful.
20 Duplex, Double-minded. Some commentators have supposed that Spenser here refers to Mary Queen of Scots.
21 False, assumed.
22 Lot, decision.
23 Prize of war.
24 Will.

Whether in beauty's glory did exceed;
A rosy garland was the victor's meed.
Both seem'd to win, and both seem'd won to be;
So hard the discord was to be agreed.
Frælissa [1] was as fair as fair might be,
And ever false Duessa seem'd as fair as she.

"The wicked witch, now seeing all this while
The doubtful balance equally to sway,
What not by right she cast [2] to win by guile;
And, by her hellish science, rais'd straightway
A foggy mist that overcast the day,
And a dull blast that, breathing on her face,
Dimmëd her former beauty's shining ray,
And with foul ugly form did her disgrace:
Then was she fair alone, when none was fair in place.[3]

"Then cried she out, 'Fy, fy, deformëd wight,
Whose borrow'd beauty now appeareth plain
To have before bewitchëd all men's sight:
O leave her soon, or let her soon be slain!'
Her loathly visage viewing with disdain,
Eftsoons [4] I thought her such as she me told,
And would have kill'd her; but with feignëd pain
The false witch did my wrathful hand withhold:
So left her, where she now is turn'd to treën mould.[5]

"Thenceforth I took Duessa for my dame,
And in the witch, unweeting,[6] joy'd long time;
Nor ever wist but that she was the same:
Till on a day (that day is ev'ry prime,[7]
When witches wont do penance for their crime),
I chanc'd to see her in her proper hue,
Bathing herself in origan [8] and thyme:
A filthy foul old woman I did view,
That ever to have touch'd her I did deadly rue.

"Her nether parts, misshapen, monstruous,
Were hid in water, that I could not see;
But they did seem more foul and hideous
Than woman's shape man would believe to be.
Thenceforth from her most beastly company
I gan refrain, in mind to slip away,
Soon as appear'd safe opportunity;
For danger great, if not assur'd decay,[9]
I saw before mine eyes, if I were known to stray.

"The devilish hag, by changes of my cheer,[10]
Perceiv'd my thought; and, drown'd in sleepy night,
With wicked herbs and ointments did besmear
My body, all through charms and magic might,
That all my senses were bereavëd quite:
Then brought she me into this desert waste,
And by my wretched lover's side me pight;[11]
Where now enclos'd in wooden walls full fast,
Banish'd from living wights, our weary days we waste."

"But how long time," said then the Elfin Knight,
"Are you in this misformëd house to dwell?"
"We may not change," quoth he, "this evil plight,
Till we be bathëd in a living well:
That is the term prescribëd by the spell."
"O how," said he, "might I that well out find,
That may restore you to your wonted well?"[12]
"Time and sufficëd [13] fates to former kind [14]
Shall us restore; none else from hence may us unbind."

The false Duessa, now Fidessa hight,[15]
Heard how in vain Fradubio did lament,
And knew well all was true. But the good Knight,
Full of sad fear and ghastly dreariment,[16]
When all this speech the living tree had spent,
The bleeding bough did thrust into the ground,
That from the blood he might be innocent,
And with fresh clay did close the wooden wound:
Then, turning to his lady, dead with fear her found.

Her seeming dead he found with feignëd fear,
As all unweeting [17] of that [18] well she knew;
And pain'd himself with busy care to rear
Her out of careless swoon. Her eyelids blue,
And dimmëd sight with pale and deadly hue,
At last she up gan lift; with trembling cheer
Her up he took (too simple and too true),
And oft her kiss'd. At length, all passëd fear,
He set her on her steed, and forward forth did bear.

CANTO III.

Forsaken Truth long seeks her Love,
And makes the lion mild;
Mars blind Devotion's mart, and falls
In hand of lechour vild.[19]

NAUGHT is there under heav'n's wide hollowness
That moves more dear compassión of mind,
Than beauty brought t' unworthy wretchedness
Through envy's snares, or fortune's freaks unkind.
I, whether lately through her brightness blind,
Or through allegiance, and fast fealty,
Which I do owe unto all womankind,
Feel my heart piercëd with so great agony,
When such I see, that all for pity I could die.

And now it is empassionëd [20] so deep
For fairest Una's sake, of whom I sing,
That my frail eyes these lines with tears do steep,
To think how she, through guileful handeling,
Though true as touch,[21] though daughter of a king,
Though fair as ever living wight was fair,
Though nor in word nor deed ill meriting,
Is from her Knight divorcëd in despair,
And her due loves deriv'd [22] to that vile witch's share.

1 Frail.
2 Planned, sought.
3 In the place, beside her.
4 Immediately.
5 Shape of a tree.
6 Unsuspecting.
7 Spring.
8 Wild or bastard marjoram.
9 Certain ruin.
10 Demeanour
11 Fixed, pitched.
12 Welfare, weal.
13 Fulfilled, satisfied.
14 Nature.
15 Called.
16 Sorrow, terror.
17 Ignorant.
18 That which.
19 Vile.
20 Moved.
21 The touchstone.
22 Drawn away.

Yet she, most faithful Lady, all this while,
Forsaken, woeful, solitary maid,
Far from all people's press, as in exile,
In wilderness and wasteful deserts stray'd,
To seek her Knight; who, subtilly betray'd
Through that late vision which th' Enchanter wrought,
Had her abandon'd: she, of naught affray'd,
Through woods and wasteness wide him daily sought;
Yet wishëd tidings none of him unto her brought.

One day, nigh weary of the irksome [1] way,
From her unhasty [2] beast she did alight;
And on the grass her dainty limbs did lay
In secret shadow, far from all men's sight;
From her fair head her fillet she undight,[3]
And laid her stole [4] aside: Her angel's face
As the great eye of heaven shinëd bright,
And made a sunshine in the shady place;
Did never mortal eye behold such heav'nly grace.

It fortunëd,[5] out of the thickest wood
A ramping [6] lion rushëd suddenly,
Hunting full greedy after salvage blood: [7]
Soon as the royal Virgin he did spy,
With gaping mouth at her ran greedily,
To have at once devour'd her tender corse:
But to the prey when as he drew more nigh,
His bloody rage assuagëd with remorse,[8]
And, with the sight amaz'd, forgot his furious force.

Instead thereof he kiss'd her weary feet,
And lick'd her lily hands with fawning tongue,
As [9] he her wrongëd innocence did weet.[10]
O how can beauty master the most strong,
And simple truth subdue avenging wrong!
Whose yielded pride and proud submissión,
Still dreading death, when she had markëd long,
Her heart gan melt in great compassión;
And drizzling tears did shed for pure affectión.

"The lion, lord of every beast in field,"
Quoth she, "his princely puíssance doth abate,
And mighty proud to humble weak does yield,
Forgetful of the hungry rage, which late
Him prick'd, in pity of my sad estate:
But he, my lion, and my noble lord,
How does he find in cruel heart to hate
Her that him lov'd, and ever most ador'd
As the god of my life? why hath he me abhorr'd?"

Redounding tears did choke th' end of her plaint,
Which softly echo'd from the neighbour wood;
And, sad to see her sorrowful constraint,
The kingly beast upon her gazing stood;
With pity calm'd, down fell his angry mood.
At last, in close heart shutting up her pain,
Arose the Virgin born of heav'nly brood,[11]
And to her snowy palfrey got again,
To seek her strayëd champion if she might attain.

The lion would not leave her desolate,
But with her went along, as a strong guard
Of her chaste person, and a faithful mate
Of her sad troubles and misfortunes hard:
Still, when she slept, he kept both watch and ward;
And, when she wak'd, he waited diligent,
With humble service to her will prepar'd:
From her fair eyes he took commandëment,
And ever by her looks conceivëd her intent.

Long she thus travellëd through deserts wide,
By which she thought her wand'ring Knight should pass,
Yet never show of living wight espied;
Till that at length she found the trodden grass,
In which the track of people's footing was,
Under the steep foot of a mountain hoar:
The same she follows, till at last she has
A damsel spied slow-footing [12] her before,
That on her shoulders sad [13] a pot of water bore.

To whom approaching she to her gan call,
To weet [10] if dwelling place were nigh at hand;
But the rude wench her answer'd not at all;
She could not hear, nor speak, nor understand:
Till, seeing by her side the lion stand,
With sudden fear her pitcher down she threw,
And fled away: for never in that land
Face of fair lady she before did view,
And that dread lion's look her cast in deadly hue.

Full fast she fled, nor ever look'd behind,
As if her life upon the wager lay;
And home she came, where as her mother blind
Sat in eternal night; naught could she say;
But, sudden catching hold, did her dismay
With quaking hands, and other signs of fear;
Who, full of ghastly fright and cold affray,[14]
Gan shut the door. By this arrivëd there
Dame Una, weary dame, and entrance did requére:

Which when none yielded, her unruly page
With his rude claws the wicket open rent,
And let her in; where, of his cruel rage
Nigh dead with fear and faint astonishment,
She found them both in darksome corner pent;
Where that old woman day and night did pray
Upon her beads, devoutly penitent:
Nine hundred *Pater nosters* every day,
And thrice nine hundred *Aves*, she was wont to say.

And, to augment her painful penance more,
Thrice every week in ashes she did sit,
And next her wrinkled skin rough sackcloth wore,
And thrice three times did fast from any bit:
But now for fear her beads she did forget.
Whose needless dread for to remove away,
Fair Una framëd words and countenance fit:
Which hardly [15] done, at length she gan them pray,
That in their cottage small that night she rest her may.

1 Fatiguing.
2 Tardy.
3 Undid, unbound.
4 Robe.
5 Chanced.
6 Springing.
7 Blood of wild animals.
8 Pity.
9 As if.
10 Know.
11 Race.
12 Walking slowly.
13 Steady.
14 Affright.
15 With difficulty.

The day is spent; and cometh drowsy night,
When every creature shrouded is in sleep:
Sad Una down her lays in weary plight,
And at her feet the lion watch doth keep:
Instead of rest she does lament and weep
For the late loss of her dear-lovëd Knight,
And sighs, and groans, and evermore does steep
Her tender breast in bitter tears all night;
All night she thinks too long, and often looks
for light.

Now when Aldeboran was mounted high
Above the shiny Cassiopeia's chair,
And all in deadly sleep did drownëd lie,
One knockëd at the door, and in would fare;[1]
He knockëd fast, and often curs'd and sware,
That ready entrance was not at his call;
For on his back a heavy load he bare
Of nightly stealths, and pillage several,[2]
Which he had got abroad by purchase criminal.[3]

He was, to wit,[4] a stout and sturdy thief,
Wont to rob churches of their ornaments,
And poor men's boxes of their due relief,
Which given was to them for good intents:
The holy saints of their rich vestiments
He did disrobe, when all men careless slept;
And spoil'd the priests of their habiliments;
While none the holy things in safety kept,
Then he by cunning sleights in at the window
crept.

And all that he by right or wrong could find,
Unto this house he brought, and did bestow
Upon the daughter of this woman blind,
Abessa,[5] daughter of Corceca[6] slow,
With whom he whoredom us'd that few did know,
And fed her fat with feast of offerings,
And plenty, which in all the land did grow;
Nor sparëd he to give her gold and rings:
And now he to her brought part of his stolen
things.

Thus long the door with rage and threats he bet;[7]
Yet of those fearful women none durst rise
(The lion frayëd[8] them), him in to let;
He would no longer stay him to advise,[9]
But open breaks the door in furious wise,
And ent'ring is; when that disdainful beast,
Encount'ring fierce, him sudden doth surprise;
And, seizing cruel claws on trembling breast,
Under his lordly foot him proudly hath supprest.

Him booteth[10] not resist, nor succour call;
His bleeding heart is in the venger's hand;
Who straight him rent in thousand pieces small,
And quite dismember'd hath: the thirsty land
Drank up his life; his corse left on the strand.
His fearful friends wear out the woeful night,
Nor dare to weep, nor seem to understand
The heavy hap, which on them is alight;
Afraid, lest to themselves the like mishappen
might.[11]

Now when broad day the world discover'd has,
Up Una rose, up rose the lion eke;
And on their former journey forward pass,
In ways unknown, her wand'ring Knight to seek,
With pains forpassing[12] that long-wand'ring
Greek,[13]
That for his love refusëd deity:[14]
Such were the labours of this Lady meek,
Still seeking him that from her still did fly;
Then farthest from her hope, when most she
weenëd[15] nigh.

Soon as she parted thence, the fearful twain,
That blind old woman and her daughter dear,
Came forth; and, finding Kirkrapine[16] there slain,
For anguish great they gan to rend their hair,
And beat their breasts, and naked flesh to tear:
And when they both had wept and wail'd their fill,
Then forth they ran, like two amazëd[17] deer,
Half mad through malice and revenging will,
To follow her that was the causer of their ill:

Whom overtaking, they gan loudly bray,
With hollow howling and lamenting cry;
Shamefully at her railing all the way,
And her accusing of dishonesty,
That was the flow'r of faith and chastity:
And still amidst her railing she did pray
That plagues, and mischiefs, and long misery,
Might fall on her, and follow all the way;
And that in endless error she might ever stray.

But when she saw her prayers naught prevail,
She back returnëd with some labour lost;
And in the way, as she did weep and wail,
A knight her met in mighty arms embost,[18]
Yet knight was not, for all his bragging boast;
But subtle Archimage, that Una sought
By trains[19] into new troubles to have tost:
Of that old woman tidings he besought,
If that of such a lady she could tellen aught.

Therewith she gan her passion to renew,
And cry, and curse, and rail, and rend her hair,
Saying, that harlot she too lately knew,
That caus'd her shed so many a bitter tear;
And so forth told the story of her fear.
Much seemëd he to moan her hapless chance,
And after for that Lady did inquére;
Which being taught, he forward gan advance
His fair enchanted steed, and eke his charmëd
lance.

Ere long he came where Una travell'd slow,
And that wild champion waiting her beside;
Whom seeing such, for dread he durst not show
Himself too nigh at hand, but turnëd wide
Unto a hill; from whence when she him spied,
By his like-seeming shield, her Knight by name
She ween'd[20] it was, and toward him gan ride:
Approaching nigh she wist[21] it was the same;
And with fair fearful humbless toward him she
came:

1 Come.
2 Various plunder. 3 By robbery.
4 Indeed, in truth. 5 Ignorance.
6 Superstition, or Blind Devotion; she represents the Romish religion. 7 Beat.
8 Terrified. 9 Consider. 10 Availeth.
11 The like misfortune might happen.
12 Exceeding. 13 Ulysses.
14 Offered to him by the goddess Calypso, if he would stay with her in her isle, and think no more of Penelope.
15 Thought.
16 The Robber of the Church, Sacrilege.
17 Startled, bewildered. 18 Clad, enclosed.
19 Stratagems. 20 Fancied.
21 Believed; was certain.

And weeping said, "Ah! my long-lackëd Lord,
Where have ye been thus long out of my sight?
Much fearëd I to have been quite abhorr'd,
Or aught have done that ye displeasen might;
That should as death unto my dear heart light:[1]
For since mine eye your joyous sight did miss,
My cheerful day is turn'd to cheerless night,
And eke my night of death the shadow is:
But welcome now, my light, and shining lamp of bliss!"

He thereto meeting said, "My dearest Dame,
Far be it from your thought, and from my will,
To think that knighthood I so much should shame,
As you to leave that have me lovëd still,
And chose in Faery Court, of mere goodwill,
Where noblest knights were to be found on earth.
The earth shall sooner leave her kindly[2] skill
To bring forth fruit, and make eternal dearth,
Than I leave you, my lefe,[3] y-born of heavenly birth.

"And sooth to say, why I left you so long,
Was for to seek adventure in strange place;
Where," Archimago said, "a felon strong
To many knights did daily work disgrace;
But knight he now shall never more deface:[4]
Good cause of mine excuse that must ye please
Well to accept, and evermore embrace
My faithful service, that by land and seas
Have vow'd you to defend: now then your plaint appease."

His lovely[5] words her seem'd due recompense
Of all her passëd pains: one loving hour
For many years of sorrow can dispense;[6]
A dram of sweet is worth a pound of sour.
She has forgot how many a woeful stowre[7]
For him she late endur'd; she speaks no more
Of past: true is, that true love hath no pow'r
To looken back; his eyes be fix'd before.
Before her stands her Knight, for whom she toil'd so sore.

Much like as when the beaten marinére,
That long hath wander'd in the ocean wide,
Oft sous'd[8] in swelling Tethys' saltish tear;
And long time having tann'd his tawny hide
With blustering breath of heav'n, that none can bide,
And scorching flames of fierce Orion's hound;[9]
Soon as the port from far he has espied,
His cheerful whistle merrily doth sound,
And Nereus crowns with cups; his mates him pledge around:

Such joy made Una when her Knight she found;
And eke th' Enchanter joyous seem'd no less
Than the glad merchant, that does view from ground
His ship far come from watery wilderness;
He hurls out vows, and Neptune oft doth bless.
So forth they pass'd; and all the way they spent
Discoursing of her dreadful late distress,
In which he ask'd her, what the lion meant;
Who told her all that fell,[10] in journey as she went.

They had not ridden far, when they might see
One pricking toward them with hasty heat,
Full strongly arm'd, and on a courser free,
That through his fierceness foamëd all with sweat,
And the sharp iron did for anger eat,
When his hot rider spurr'd his chafëd side;
His look was stern, and seemëd still to threat
Cruel revenge, which he in heart did hide;
And on his shield *Sans loy*[11] in bloody lines was dy'd.

When nigh he drew unto this gentle pair,
And saw the red cross, which the knight did bear,
He burn'd in ire; and gan eftsoons[12] prepare
Himself to battle with his couchëd spear.
Loth was that other, and did faint through fear,
To taste the untried dint of deadly steel:
But yet his Lady did so well him cheer,
That hope of new good hap he gan to feel;
So bent his spear, and spurr'd his horse with iron heel.

But that proud Paynim forward came so fierce
And full of wrath, that, with his sharp-head spear,
Through vainly crossëd[13] shield he quite did pierce;
And, had his stagg'ring steed not shrunk for fear,
Through shield and body eke he should him bear:
Yet so great was the puíssance[14] of his push,
That from his saddle quite he did him bear:
He tumbling rudely down to ground did rush,
And from his gorëd wound a well of blood did gush.

Dismounting lightly from his lofty steed,
He to him leapt, in mind to reave[15] his life,
And proudly said; "Lo, there the worthy meed
Of him that slew Sansfoy with bloody knife:
Henceforth his ghost, freed from repining strife,
In peace may passen over Lethe Lake;
When mourning altars, purg'd with enemy's life,
The black infernal Furies do aslake:[16]
Life from Sansfoy thou took'st, Sansloy shall from thee take."

Therewith in haste his helmet gan unlace,
Till Una cried, "O hold that heavy hand,
Dear Sir, whatever that thou be in place![17]
Enough is, that thy foe doth vanquish'd stand
Now at thy mercy; mercy not withstand;
For he is one the truest knight alive,
Though conquer'd now he lie on lowly land;
And, whilst him fortune favour'd, fair did thrive
In bloody field; therefore of life him not deprive."

Her piteous words might not abate his rage;
But, rudely rending up his helmet, would
Have slain him straight: but when he sees his age,
And hoary head of Archimago old,
His hasty hand he doth amazëd hold,

1 Would fall like death upon my heart, to which you are so dear.
2 Natural.
3 Love.
4 Destroy.
5 Loving.
6 Make amends.
7 Misfortune.
8 Plunged, tossed.
9 The Dog-star.
10 All that befell her.
11 Without Law.
12 Immediately.
13 Marked with the cross.
14 Power.
15 Bereave, take away.
16 Appease.
17 Whoever you may be.

And, half ashamëd, wonder'd at the sight:
For that old man well knew he, though untold,
In charms and magic to have wondrous might;
Nor ever wont in field, nor in round lists, to fight:

And said, "Why, Archimago, luckless Sire!
What do I see? what hard mishap is this
That hath thee hither brought to taste mine ire?
Or thine the fault, or mine the error is,
Instead of foe to wound my friend amiss?"
He answer'd naught, but in a trance still lay,
And on those guileful dazëd[1] eyes of his
The cloud of death did sit; which done away,[2]
He left him lying so, nor would no longer stay:

But to the Virgin comes, who all this while
Amazëd stands, herself so mock'd to see
By him who has the guerdon[3] of his guile,
For so misfeigning her true Knight to be:
Yet is she now in more perplexity,
Left in the hand of that same Paynim[4] bold,
From whom her booteth not[5] at all to fly:
Who, by her cleanly garment catching hold,
Her from her palfrey pluck'd, her visage to behold.

But her fierce servant, full of kingly awe
And high disdain, when as his sov'reign dame
So rudely handled by her foe he saw,
With gaping jaws full greedy at him came,
And, ramping[6] on his shield, did ween[7] the same
Have reft away with his sharp rending claws:
But he was stout, and lust did now inflame
His courage more, that from his griping paws
He hath his shield redeem'd; and forth his sword he draws.

O, then too weak and feeble was the force
Of salvage beast, his puíssance to withstand!
For he was strong, and of so mighty corse,[8]
As ever wielded spear in warlike hand;
And feats of arms did wisely understand.
Eftsoons[9] he piercëd through his chafëd chest
With thrilling point of deadly iron brand,
And lanc'd his lordly heart: with death opprest
He roar'd aloud, while life forsook his stubborn breast.

Who now is left to keep the fórlorn maid
From raging spoil of lawless victor's will?
Her faithful guard remov'd; her hope dismay'd;
Herself a yielded prey to save or spill![10]
He now, lord of the field, his pride to fill,
With foul reproaches and disdainful spite
Her vilely entertains; and, will or nill,[11]
Bears her away upon his courser light:
Her prayers naught prevail; his rage is more of might.

And, all the way, with great lamenting pain
And piteous plaints she filleth his dull ears,
That stony heart could riven have in twain;
And all the way she wets with flowing tears;
But he, enrag'd with rancour, nothing hears.
Her servile beast[12] yet would not leave her so,
But follows her far off, nor aught he fears
To be partaker of her wand'ring woe.
More mild in beastly kind,[13] than that her beastly foe.

CANTO IV.

To sinful House of Pride Duessa guides the faithful Knight;
Where, brother's death to wreak, Sansjoy
Doth challenge him to fight.

Young knight whatever, that dost arms profess,
And through long labours huntest after fame,
Beware of fraud, beware of fickleness,
In choice, and change, of thy dear-lovëd dame;
Lest thou of her believe too lightly blame,
And rash misweening[14] do thy heart remove:
For unto knight there is no greater shame
Than lightness and inconstancy in love:
That doth this Redcross Knight's ensample plainly prove.

Who, after that he had fair Una lorn,[15]
Through light misdeeming of her loyalty;
And false Duessa in her stead had borne,
Callëd Fidessa, and so suppos'd to be;
Long with her travell'd; till at last they see
A goodly building, bravely garnishëd;
The house of mighty prince it seem'd to be;
And toward it a broad highway that led,
All bare through people's feet which thither travellëd.

Great troops of people travell'd thitherward,
Both day and night, of each degree and place;
But few returnëd, having scapëd hard[16]
With baleful beggary or foul disgrace;
Which ever after in most wretched case,
Like loathsome lazars,[17] by the hedges lay.
Thither Duessa bade him bend his pace;
For she is weary of the toilsome way;
And also nigh consumëd is the lingering day.

A stately palace built of squarëd brick,
Which cunningly was without mortar laid,
Whose walls were high, but nothing strong nor thick,
And golden foil[18] all over them display'd,
That purest sky with brightness they dismay'd;
High lifted up were many lofty tow'rs,
And goodly galleries far over laid,
Full of fair windows and delightful bow'rs;[19]
And on the top a dial told the timely hours.

It was a goodly heap for to behold,
And spake the praises of the workman's wit;
But full great pity, that so fair a mould
Did on so weak foundation ever sit:
For on a sandy hill, that still did flit[20]
And fall away, it mounted was full high,
That every breath of heaven shakëd it;

1 Dimmed.
2 Having passed off.
3 Reward.
4 Infidel, Saracen.
5 It availeth her not.
6 Springing.
7 Think.
8 Bodily frame.
9 Immediately.
10 Destroy.
11 Will she or will she not.
12 Her obedient ass.
13 Nature.
14 Misjudgment.
15 Deserted, lost.
16 Escaped with difficulty.
17 Lepers.
18 Gold leaf.
19 Chambers.
20 Shift.

And all the hinder parts, that few could spy,
Were ruinous and old, but painted cunningly.

Arrivëd there, they passëd in forthright;[1]
For still to all the gates stood open wide:
Yet charge of them was to a porter hight,[2]
Call'd Malvenú, who entrance none denied:
Thence to the hall, which was on every side
With rich array and costly arras dight:[3]
Infinite sorts of people did abide
There waiting long, to win the wishëd sight
Of her that was the lady of that palace bright.

By them they pass, all gazing on them round,
And to the presence[4] mount; whose glorious view
Their frail amazëd senses did confound.
In living prince's court none ever knew
Such endless riches, and so sumptuous shew:
Not Persia's self, the nurse of pompous pride,
Like ever saw: and there a noble crew
Of lords and ladies stood on ev'ry side,
Which with their presence fair the place much beautified.

High above all a cloth of state was spread,
And a rich throne, as bright as sunny day;
On which there sat, most brave embellishëd
With royal robes and gorgeous array,
A maiden queen, that shone as Titan's ray[5]
In glist'ring gold and peerless precious stone;
Yet her bright blazing beauty did assay[6]
To dim the brightness of her glorious throne,
As envying herself, that too exceeding shone:

Exceeding shone, like Phœbus' fairest child,[7]
That did presume his father's fiery wain,
And flaming mouths of steeds unwonted wild,
Through highest heav'n with weaker hand to rein;
Proud of such glory and advancement vain,
While flashing beams do daze[8] his feeble eyen,
He leaves the welkin[9] way most beaten plain,
And, wrapp'd with whirling wheels, inflames the skien
With fire not made to burn, but fairly for to shine.

So proud she shinëd in her princely state,
Looking to heav'n; for earth she did disdain:
And sitting high; for lowly she did hate:
Lo, underneath her scornful feet was lain
A dreadful dragon with a hideous train;[10]
And in her hand she held a mirror bright,
Wherein her face she often viewëd fain,[11]
And in her self-lov'd semblance took delight;
For she was wondrous fair, as any living wight.

Of grisly Pluto she the daughter was,
And sad Proserpina, the queen of hell;
Yet did she think her peerless worth to pass
That parentage, with pride so did she swell;
And thund'ring Jove, that high in heaven doth dwell
And wield the world, she claimëd for her sire;
Or if that any else did Jove excel;
For to the highest she did still aspire;
Or, if aught higher were than that, did it desire.

And proud Lucifera men did her call,
That made herself a queen, and crown'd to be;
Yet rightful kingdom she had none at all,
Nor heritage of native sov'reignty;
But did usurp with wrong and tyranny
Upon the sceptre which she now did hold:
Nor rul'd her realm with laws, but policy,
And strong advisement[12] of six wizards old,
That with their counsels bad her kingdom did uphold.

Soon as the Elfin Knight in presence came,
And false Duessa, seeming lady fair,
A gentle usher, Vanity by name,
Made room, and passage for them did prepare:
So goodly brought them to the lowest stair[13]
Of her high throne; where they, on humble knee
Making obeisance, did the cause declare
Why they were come her royal state to see,
To prove the wide report of her great majesty.

With lofty eyes, half loth to look so low,
She thankëd them in her disdainful wise;
Nor other grace vouchsafëd them to show
Of princess worthy; scarce them bade arise.
Her lords and ladies all this while devise
Themselves to setten forth to stranger's sight:
Some frounce[14] their curlëd hair in courtly guise;
Some prank[15] their ruffs; and others trimly dight[16]
Their gay attire: each other's greater pride does spite.

Goodly they all that Knight do entertain,
Right glad with him to have increas'd their crew;
But to Duess' each one himself did pain[17]
All kindness and fair courtesy to show;
For in that court whilóm[18] her well they knew:
Yet the stout Faery mongst the middest crowd
Thought all their glory vain in knightly view,
And that great princess too exceeding proud,
That to strange knight no better countenance allow'd.

Sudden upriseth from her stately place
The royal dame, and for her coach doth call:
All hurtle forth;[19] and she, with princely pace,
As fair Aurora, in her purple pall,
Out of the east the dawning day doth call,
So forth she comes; her brightness broad doth blaze.
The heaps of people, thronging in the hall,
Do ride each other,[20] upon her to gaze:
Her glorious glitt'ring light doth all men's eyes amaze.

So forth she comes, and to her coach does climb,
Adornëd all with gold and garlands gay,
That seem'd as fresh as Flora in her prime,
And strove to match, in royal rich array,
Great Juno's golden chair;[21] the which, they say,
The gods stand gazing on, when she does ride

1 Directly.
2 Entrusted.
3 Decked.
4 Presence-chamber.
5 Like the sun.
6 Attempt.
7 Phaethon.
8 Dazzle, dim.
9 Heavenly.
10 Tail.
11 With pleasure.
12 Counselling.
13 Step.
14 Plait.
15 Adjust ostentatiously.
16 Arrange.
17 Exert.
18 Of former days.
19 Rush forth in a jostling crowd.
20 Crowd and strain to peer over each other's heads.
21 Chariot.

To Jove's high house through heav'n's brass-paved way,
Drawn of fair peacocks, that excel in pride,
And full of Argus' eyes their tails dispreaden wide.

But this[1] was drawn of six unequal beasts,
On which her six sage councillors did ride,
Taught to obey their bestial behests,
With like conditions to their kinds applied:
Of which the first, that all the rest did guide,
Was sluggish Idleness, the nurse of sin;
Upon a slothful ass he chose to ride,
Array'd in habit black, and amice[2] thin;
Like to a holy monk, the service to begin.

And in his hand his portess[3] still he bare,
That much was worn, but therein little read;
For of devotion he had little care,
Still drown'd in sleep, and most of his days dead:
Scarce could he once uphold his heavy head,
To looken whether it were night or day.
May seem the wain[4] was very evil led,
When such an one had guiding of the way,
That knew not whether right he went or else astray.

From worldly cares himself he did esloyne,[5]
And greatly shunnëd manly exercise;
From every work he challengëd essoyne,[6]
For contemplation sake: yet otherwise
His life he led in lawless riotise;[7]
By which he grew to grievous malady:[8]
For in his lustless[9] limbs, through evil guise,
A shaking fever reign'd continually:
Such one was Idleness, first of this company.

And by his side rode loathsome Gluttony,
Deformëd creature, on a filthy swine;
His belly was upblown with luxury,
And eke with fatness swollen were his eyne;
And like a crane his neck was long and fine,
With which he swallow'd up excessive feast,
For want whereof poor people oft did pine:
And all the way, most like a brutish beast,
He spuëd up his gorge,[10] that all did him detest.

In green vine leaves he was right fitly clad;
For other clothes he could not wear for heat:
And on his head an ivy garland had,
From under which fast trickled down the sweat:
Still as he rode, he somewhat still did eat,
And in his hand did bear a boozing can,[11]
Of which he supp'd so oft, that on his seat
His drunken corse he scarce upholden can:
In shape and life more like a monster than a man.

Unfit he was for any worldly thing,
And eke unable once to stir or go;
Not meet to be of counsel to a king,
Whose mind in meat and drink was drownëd so,
That from his friend he seldom knew his foe:
Full of diseases was his carcase blue,
And a dry dropsy through his flesh did flow,
Which by misdiet daily greater grew;
Such one was Gluttony, the second of that crew.

And next to him rode lustful Lechery,
Upon a bearded goat, whose rugged hair,
And whally[12] eyes (the sign of jealousy),
Was like the person's self whom he did bear:
Who rough, and black, and filthy, did appear;
Unseemly man to please fair lady's eye:
Yet he of ladies oft was lovëd dear,
When fairer faces were bid standen by:
O who does know the bent of women's fantasy!

In a green gown he clothëd was full fair,
Which underneath did hide his filthiness;
And in his hand a burning heart he bare,
Full of vain follies and newfangleness;
For he was false, and fraught with fickleness;
And learnëd had to love with secret looks;
And well could dance; and sing with ruefulness;[13]
And fortunes tell; and read in loving books:
And thousand other ways, to bait his fleshly hooks.

Inconstant man, that lovëd all he saw,
And lusted after all that he did love;
Nor would his looser life be tied to law,
But joy'd weak women's hearts to tempt and prove,
If from their loyal loves he might them move:
Which lewdness fill'd him with reproachful pain
Of that foul evil, which all men reprove,
That rots the marrow and consumes the brain:
Such one was Lechery, the third of all this train.

And greedy Avarice by him did ride,
Upon a camel loaded all with gold:
Two iron coffers hung on either side,
With precious metal full as they might hold;
And in his lap a heap of coin he told;
For of his wicked pelf his god he made,
And unto hell himself for money sold;
Accursëd usury was all his trade;
And right and wrong alike in equal balance weigh'd.

His life was nigh unto death's door y-plac'd;
And thread-bare coat and cobbled shoes he ware;
Nor scarce good morsel all his life did taste;
But both from back and belly still did spare
To fill his bags, and riches to compare:[14]
Yet child nor kinsman living had he none
To leave them to; but thorough daily care
To get, and nightly fear to lose, his own,
He led a wretched life, unto himself unknown.

Most wretched wight, whom nothing might suffice;
Whose greedy lust did lack in greatest store;
Whose need had end, but no end covetise;[15]
Whose wealth was want; whose plenty made him poor;
Who had enough, yet wishëd ever more:
A vile disease; and eke in foot and hand

1 Lucifera's car. The Princess and her councillors are the seven cardinal sins, the principal and root of which, as the Parson in the Canterbury Tales has said, is Pride. See page 193. 2 Robe.
3 Breviary. 4 Chariot.
5 Withdraw; French, "éloigner."
6 Excuse, exoneration; French, "essoine" or "exoine." 7 Riot.
8 Sickness. 9 Feeble; opposite of "lusty."
10 That with which he had gorged himself.
11 A drinking can.
12 Streaky or greenish-white eyes, like those of a wall-eyed horse; Shakespeare uses "wall-eyed" as a term of reproach. 13 Touchingly.
14 Latin, "comparare," to procure, obtain.
15 His covetousness.

A grievous gout tormented him full sore;
That well he could not touch, nor go, nor stand:
Such one was Avarice, the fourth of this fair band.

And next to him malicious Envy rode
Upon a ravenous wolf, and still did chaw
Between his canker'd teeth a venomous toad,
That all the poison ran about his jaw;
But inwardly he chawëd his own maw
At neighbour's wealth, that made him ever sad;
For death it was, when any good he saw;
And wept, that cause of weeping none he had;
But when he heard of harm, he waxëd wondrous glad.

All in a kirtle of discolour'd say[1]
He clothëd was, y-painted full of eyes;
And in his bosom secretly there lay
A hateful snake, the which his tail upties[2]
In many folds, and mortal sting implies:[3]
Still as he rode, he gnash'd his teeth to see
Those heaps of gold with griple Covetise;[4]
And grudgëd at the great felicity
Of proud Lucifera, and his own company.

He hated all good works and virtuous deeds,
And him no less that any like did use;
And, who with gracious bread the hungry feeds,
His alms for want of faith he doth accuse;
So ev'ry good to bad he doth abuse:
And eke the verse of famous poets' wit
He does backbite, and spiteful poison spues
From leprous mouth on all that ever writ:
Such one vile Envy was, that fifth in row[5] did sit.

And him beside rides fierce revenging Wrath,
Upon a lion, loth[6] for to be led;
And in his hand a burning brand he hath,
The which he brandisheth about his head:
His eyes did hurl forth sparkles fiery red,
And starëd stern on all that him beheld;
As ashes pale of hue, and seeming dead;
And on his dagger still his hand he held,
Trembling through hasty rage, when choler in him swell'd.

His ruffian raiment all was stain'd with blood
Which he had spilt, and all to rags y-rent;
Through unadvisëd rashness waxen wood;[7]
For of his hands he had no government,
Nor car'd for blood in his avengëment;[8]
But when the furious fit was overpast,
His cruel facts[9] he often would repent;
Yet, wilful man, he never would forecast
How many mischiefs should ensue[10] his heedless haste.

Full many mischiefs follow cruel Wrath;
Abhorrëd Bloodshed, and tumultuous Strife,
Unmanly Murder, and unthrifty Scath,[11]
Bitter Despite, with Rancour's rusty knife;
And fretting Grief, the enemy of life:
All these, and many evils more, haunt Ire,
The swelling Spleen, and Frenzy raging rife,
The shaking Palsy, and Saint Francis' fire:
Such one was Wrath, the last of this ungodly tire.[12]

And after all, upon the waggon beam,
Rode Satan with a smarting whip in hand,
With which he forward lash'd the lazy team,
So oft as Sloth still in the mire did stand.
Huge routs[13] of people did about them band,[14]
Shouting for joy; and still before their way
A foggy mist had cover'd all the land;
And, underneath their feet, all scatter'd lay
Dead skulls and bones of men, whose life had gone astray.

So forth they marchen in this goodly sort,
To take the solace of the open air,
And in fresh flow'ring fields themselves to sport:
Amongst the rest rode that false lady fair,
The foul Duessa, next unto the chair[15]
Of proud Lucifer', as one of the train:
But that good Knight would not so nigh repair,
Himself estranging from their joyance vain,
Whose fellowship seem'd far unfit for warlike swain.

So, having solacëd themselves a space,
With pleasance of the breathing fields y-fed,[16]
They back returnëd to the princely place;
Where as an errant knight in arms y-cled,
And heathenish shield, wherein with letters red
Was writ *Sans joy*, they new arrivëd find:
Inflam'd with fury and fierce hardihead,[17]
He seem'd in heart to harbour thoughts unkind,[18]
And nourish bloody vengeance in his bitter mind.

Who, when the shamëd shield of slain Sansfoy
He spied with that same Faery champion's page,
Betraying him that did of late destroy
His eldest brother; burning all with rage,
He to him leapt, and that same envious[19] gage
Of victor's glory from him snatch'd away:
But th' Elfin Knight, which ought[20] that warlike wage,[21]
Disdain'd to loose the meed he won in fray;
And, him encount'ring fierce, rescued the noble prey.

Therewith they gan to hurtle[22] greedily,
Redoubted battle ready to darrain,[23]
And clash their shields, and shake their swords on high,
That with their stowre[24] they troubled all the train:
Till that great queen, upon eternal pain
Of high displeasure that ensuen might,
Commanded them their fury to refrain;
And, if that either to that shield had right,
In equal lists they should the morrow next it fight.

"Ah, dearest Dame," quoth then the Paynim bold,
"Pardon the error of enragëd wight,
Whom great grief made forget the reins to hold

1 Many-coloured silk; French, "soie."
2 Twists or knots up.
3 Contains in the folds.
4 In the possession of grasping or tenacious Avarice.
5 Order.
6 Unwilling.
7 Grown mad.
8 In revenging himself.
9 Deeds.
10 Result from.
11 Mischief.
12 Procession, row.
13 Crowds.
14 Gather.
15 Chariot.
16 Refreshed, satisfied.
17 Courage.
18 Unnatural.
19 Envy-inspiring.
20 Owned.
21 Prize, reward of combat.
22 Rush together.
23 Wage.
24 Struggle.

Of reason's rule, to see this recreant Knight
(No knight, but traitor full of false despite
And shameful treason), who through guile hath slain
The prowest [1] knight that ever field did fight,
Ev'n stout Sansfoy (O who can then refrain?)
Whose shield he bears revers'd, the more to heap disdain.

"And, to augment the glory of his guile,
His dearest love, the fair Fidessa, lo!
Is there possessëd of the traitor vile;
Who reaps the harvest sowen by his foe,
Sowen in bloody field, and bought with woe:
That, brother's hand shall dearly well requite,
So be, O Queen, you equal favour show."
Him little answer'd th' angry Elfin Knight;
He never meant with words, but swords, to plead his right:

But threw his gauntlet, as a sacred pledge
His cause in combat the next day to try:
So be they parted both, with hearts on edge
To be aveng'd each on his enemy.
That night they pass in joy and jollity,
Feasting and courting both in bower and hall;
For steward was excessive Gluttony,
That of his plenty pourëd forth to all:
Which done, the chamberlain Sloth did to rest them call.

Now when as darksome Night had all display'd
Her coal-black curtain over brightest sky;
The warlike youths, on dainty couches laid,
Did chase away sweet sleep from sluggish eye,
To muse on means of hopëd victory.
But when as Morpheus had with leaden mace
Arrested all that courtly company,
Uprose Duessa from her resting-place,
And to the Paynim's lodging comes with silent pace:

Whom broad awake she finds, in troublous fit,
Forecasting [2] how his foe he might annoy;
And him amoves [3] with speeches seeming fit:
"Ah dear Sansjoy, next dearest to Sansfoy,
Cause of my new grief, cause of my new joy;
Joyous, to see his image in mine eye,
And griev'd, to think how foe did him destroy
That was the flower of grace and chivalry;
Lo, his Fidessa, to thy secret faith I fly."

With gentle words he gan her fairly greet,
And bade say on the secret of her heart:
Then, sighing soft; "I learn that little sweet
Oft temper'd is," quoth she, "with muchel smart:
For, since my breast was lanc'd with lovely dart [4]
Of [5] dear Sansfoy, I never joyëd hour,
But in eternal woes my weaker heart
Have wasted, loving him with all my pow'r,
And for his sake have felt full many a heavy stowre.[6]

"At last, when perils all I weenëd past,
And hop'd to reap the crop [7] of all my care,
Into new woes unweeting [8] I was cast
By this false faitour,[9] who unworthy ware
His worthy shield, whom he with guileful snare
Entrappëd slew, and brought to shameful grave:
Me, silly [10] maid, away with him he bare,
And ever since hath kept in darksome cave,
For that I would not yield what to Sansfoy I gave.

"But since fair sun hath spers'd [11] that low'ring cloud,
And to my loathëd life now shows some light,
Under your beams I will me safely shroud [12]
From dreaded storm of his disdainful spite: [13]
To you th' inheritance belongs by right
Of brother's praise, to you eke 'longs his love.
Let not his love, let not his restless sprite,
Be unreveng'd, that calls to you above
From wand'ring Stygian shores, where it doth endless move."

Thereto said he, "Fair Dame, be not dismay'd
For sorrows past; their grief is with them gone.
Nor yet of present peril be afraid:
For needless fear did never vantage none;
And helpless hap [14] it booteth [15] not to moan.
Dead is Sansfoy, his vital pains are past,
Though grievëd ghost for vengeance deep do groan:
He lives, that shall him pay his duties last,
And guilty Elfin blood shall sacrifice in haste."

"O, but I fear the fickle freaks," quoth she,
"Of Fortune false, and odds of arms in field."
"Why, Dame," quoth he, "what odds can ever be,
Where both do fight alike, to win or yield?"
"Yea, but," quoth she, "he bears a charmëd shield,
And eke enchanted arms, that none can pierce;
Nor none can wound the man that does them wield."
"Charm'd or enchanted," answer'd he then fierce,
"I no whit reck; [16] nor you the like need to rehearse.

"But, fair Fidessa, sithens [17] fortune's guile,
Or enemy's pow'r, hath now captivëd you,
Return from whence ye came, and rest a while,
Till morrow next, that I the Elf subdue,
And with Sansfoy's dead dowry you endue."
"Ay me, that is a double death," she said,
"With proud foe's sight my sorrow to renew:
Wherever yet I be, my secret aid
Shall follow you." So, passing forth, she him obey'd.

1 Bravest. 2 Contriving. 3 Incites.
4 Love's dart. 5 By.
6 Trouble, affliction. 7 Harvest, fruit.
8 Unsuspecting. 9 Impostor, deceiver.
10 Innocent.
11 Dispersed, scattered.
12 Shelter. 13 Wrath.
14 Fortune that cannot be remedied.
15 Availeth. 16 Care not a jot.
17 Since.

CANTO V.

The faithful Knight in equal field
Subdues his faithless foe;
Whom false Duessa saves, and for
His cure to Hell does go.

THE noble heart that harbours virtuous thought,
And is with child of glorious great intent,
Can never rest until it forth have brought
Th' eternal brood of glory excellent.
Such restless passion did all night torment
The flaming courage of that Faery Knight,
Devising how that doughty tournament
With greatest honour he achieven might:
Still did he wake, and still did watch for dawning light.

At last the golden oriental gate
Of greatest heaven gan to open fair;
And Phœbus, fresh as bridegroom to his mate,
Came dancing forth, shaking his dewy hair,
And hurl'd his glist'ring beams through gloomy air.
Which when the wakeful Elf perceiv'd, straightway
He started up, and did himself prepare
In sunbright arms, and battailous[1] array;
For with that Pagan proud he combat will that day.

And forth he comes into the common hall;
Where early wait him many a gazing eye,
To weet[2] what end to stranger knights may fall.
There many minstrels maken melody,
To drive away the dull meláncholy;
And many bards, that to the trembling chord
Can tune their timely voices cunningly;[3]
And many chroniclers, that can record
Old loves, and wars for ladies done by many a lord.

Soon after comes the cruel Saracen,
In woven mail all armëd warily;[4]
And sternly looks at him, who not a pin
Does care for look of living creature's eye.
They bring them wines of Greece and Araby,
And dainty spices fetch'd from farthest Ind,
To kindle heat of courage privily;
And in the wine a solemn oath they bind
T' observe the sacred laws of arms that are assign'd.

At last forth comes that far renownëd queen.
With royal pomp and princely majesty
She is y-brought unto a palëd green,[5]
And placëd under stately canopy,
The warlike feats of both those knights to see.
On th' other side, in all men's open view,
Duessa placëd is, and on a tree
Sansfoy his shield is hang'd, with bloody hue:
Both those the laurel garlands to the victor due.

A shrilling trumpet sounded from on high,
And unto battle bade themselves address:

1 Martial. 2 Know.
3 Skilfully.
4 Carefully. 5 A lawn fenced around.
6 Brandish, move swiftly; the idea is taken from the motion in making the sign of the cross.

Their shining shields about their wrists they tie,
And burning blades about their heads do bless,[6]
The instruments of wrath and heaviness:
With greedy force each other doth assail,
And strike so fiercely, that they do impress[7]
Deep dinted furrows in the batter'd mail:
The iron walls to ward their blows are weak and frail.

The Saracen was stout and wondrous strong,
And heapëd blows like iron hammers great;
For after blood and vengeance he did long.
The Knight was fierce, and full of youthly heat,
And doubled strokes like dreaded thunder's threat:
For all for praise and honour did he fight.
Both, stricken, strike; and beaten, both do beat;
That from their shields forth flieth fiery light,
And helmets, hewen deep, show marks of either's might.

So th' one for wrong, the other strives for right:
As when a griffin, seizëd of[8] his prey,
A dragon fierce encounters in his flight,
Through widest air making his idle way,
That would his rightful ravin[9] rend away:
With hideous horror both together smite,
And souse[10] so sore, that they the heav'ns affray:
The wise soothsayer, seeing so sad sight,
Th' amazëd vulgar tells of wars and mortal fight.

So th' one for wrong, the other strives for right;
And each to deadly shame would drive his foe:
The cruel steel so greedily doth bite
In tender flesh, that streams of blood down flow;
With which the arms, that erst[11] so bright did show,
Into a pure vermilion now are dy'd.
Great ruth[12] in all the gazers' hearts did grow,
Seeing the gorëd wounds to gape so wide,
That victory they dare not wish to either side.

At last the Paynim chanc'd to cast his eye,
His sudden eye, flaming with wrathful fire,
Upon his brother's shield, which hung thereby:
Therewith redoubled was his raging ire,
And said; "Ah! wretched son of woeful sire,
Dost thou sit wailing by black Stygian Lake,
Whilst here thy shield is hang'd for victor's hire?[13]
And, sluggish german,[14] do thy forces slake
To after-send his foe, that him may overtake?

"Go, caitiff Elf, him quickly overtake,
And soon redeem from his long-wand'ring woe:
Go, guilty ghost, to him my message make,
That I his shield have quit[15] from dying foe."
Therewith upon his crest he struck him so,
That twice he reelëd, ready twice to fall:
End of the doubtful battle deemëd tho[16]
The lookers on; and loud to him gan call
The false Duessa, "Thine the shield, and I, and all!"

Soon as the Faery heard his lady speak,
Out of his swowning[17] dream he gan awake;

7 Imprint. 8 Which has seized.
9 Prey. 10 Dash against each other.
11 Before. 12 Pity. 13 Reward.
14 Kinsman, brother. 15 Rescued.
16 Then. 17 Fainting.

And quick'ning faith, that erst was waxen weak,
The creeping deadly cold away did shake:
Then mov'd with wrath, and shame, and lady's sake,
Of all at once he cast[1] aveng'd to be,
And with exceeding fury at him strake,[2]
That forcëd him to stoop upon his knee:
Had he not stoopëd so, he should have cloven be.[3]

And to him said; "Go now, proud miscreant,[4]
Thyself thy message do to german dear;
Alone he, wand'ring, thee too long doth want:
Go, say, his foe thy shield with his doth bear."
Therewith his heavy hand he high gan rear,
Him to have slain; when lo! a darksome cloud
Upon him fell; he nowhere doth appear,
But vanish'd is. The Elf him calls aloud,
But answer none receives; the darkness him does shroud.

In haste Duessa from her place arose,
And to him running said; "O prowest[5] Knight
That ever lady to her love did choose,
Let now abate the terror of your might,
And quench the flame of furious despite
And bloody vengeance: lo! th' infernal Pow'rs,
Cov'ring your foe with cloud of deadly night,
Have borne him hence to Pluto's baleful bow'rs:
The conquest yours; I yours; the shield and glory yours!"

Not all so satisfied, with greedy eye
He sought all round about, his thirsty blade
To bathe in blood of faithless enemy,
Who all that while lay hid in secret shade:
He stands amazëd how he thence should fade.
At last the trumpets triumph sound on high;
And running heralds humble homage made,
Greeting him goodly with new victory;
And to him brought the shield, the cause of enmity.

Wherewith he goeth to that sovereign queen,
And, falling her before on lowly knee,
To her makes present of his service seen:
Which she accepts with thanks and goodly gree,[6]
Greatly advancing[7] his gay chivalry:
So marcheth home, and by her takes the Knight,
Whom all the people follow with great glee,
Shouting, and clapping all their hands on height,[8]
That all the air it fills, and flies to heaven bright.

Home is he brought, and laid in sumptuous bed:
Where many skilful leeches him abide[9]
To salve his hurts, that yet still freshly bled.
In wine and oil they wash his woundës wide,
And softly gan embalm[10] on every side.
And all the while most heav'nly melody
About the bed sweet music did divide,[11]
Him to beguile of grief and agony.
And all the while Duessa wept full bitterly.

As when a weary traveller, that strays
By muddy shore of broad sev'n-mouthëd Nile,
Unweeting[12] of the perilous wand'ring ways,
Doth meet a cruel crafty crocodile,
Which, in false grief hiding his harmful guile,
Doth weep full sore, and sheddeth tender tears;
The foolish man, that pities all the while
His mournful plight, is swallow'd up unwares;
Forgetful of his own, that minds another's cares.

So wept Duessa until eventide,
That shining lamps in Jove's high house were light:
Then forth she rose, nor longer would abide;
But comes unto the place where th' heathen knight
In slumb'ring swoon, nigh void of vital sprite,
Lay cover'd with enchanted cloud all day:
Whom when she found as she him left in plight,[13]
To wail his woeful case she would not stay,
But to the eastern coast of heav'n makes speedy way:

Where grisly Night, with visage deadly sad,
That Phœbus' cheerful face durst never view,
And in a foul black pitchy mantle clad,
She finds forth coming from her darksome mew,[14]
Where she all day did hide her hated hue.
Before the door her iron chariot stood,
Already harnessëd for journey new,
And coal-black steeds y-born of hellish brood,
That on their rusty bits did champ as they were wood.[15]

Who when she saw Duessa, sunny bright,
Adorn'd with gold and jewels shining clear,
She greatly grew amazëd at the sight,
And th' unacquainted[16] light began to fear
(For never did such brightness there appear);
And would have back retirëd to her cave,
Until the witch's speech she gan to hear,
Saying; "Yet, O thou dreaded Dame, I crave
Abide, till I have told the message which I have."

She stay'd; and forth Duessa gan proceed:
"O thou, most ancient grandmother of all,
More old than Jove, whom thou at first didst breed,
Or that great house of gods celestial;
Which wast begot in Dæmogorgon's hall,
And saw'st the secrets of the world unmade;[17]
Why suff'redst thou thy nephews[18] dear to fall
With Elfin sword, most shamefully betray'd?
Lo, where the stout Sansjoy doth sleep in deadly shade!

"And, him before, I saw with bitter eyes
The bold Sansfoy shrink underneath his spear;
And now the prey of fowls in field he lies,
Nor wail'd of friends, nor laid on groaning bier,
That whilom[19] was to me too dearly dear.
O! what of gods then boots it to be born,
If old Aveugle's[20] sons so evil hear?[21]

1 Resolved.
2 Struck. 3 Been.
4 Misbeliever, infidel. 5 Bravest.
6 Favour. 7 Extolling.
8 High. 9 Await, attend.
10 Dress with balm. 11 Distribute, diffuse.
12 Ignorant.
13 In the same condition in which she had left him.

14 Cave or den, in which she immured herself.
15 Mad. 16 Unfamiliar. 17 Ere it was made.
18 Descendants, grandchildren; Latin, "nepos."
19 Once. 20 The Blind One; a name for Night.
21 A literal rendering of the classical phrases, κακως ακουειν, and "male audire," to be contemned or in evil repute, to hear or have evil things spoken of one.

Or who shall not great Nightë's children scorn,
When two of three her nephews are so foul forlorn?

"Up, then; up, dreary Dame, of darkness queen;
Go gather up the reliques of thy race;
Or else go them avenge; and let be seen
That dreaded Night in brightest day hath place,
And can the children of fair Light deface."[1]
Her feeling speeches some compassion mov'd
In heart, and change in that great mother's face;
Yet pity in her heart was never prov'd
Till then; for evermore she hated, never lov'd:

And said, "Dear daughter, rightly may I rue[2]
The fall of famous children born of me,
And good successes which their foes ensue:[3]
But who can turn the stream of destiny,
Or break the chain of strong necessity,
Which fast is tied to Jove's eternal seat?
The sons of Day he favoureth, I see,
And by my ruins thinks to make them great:
To make one great by others' loss is bad escheat.[4]

"Yet shall they not escape so freely all;
For some shall pay the price of others' guilt:
And he, the man that made Sansfoy to fall,
Shall with his own blood price[5] that he hath spilt.
But what art thou, that tell'st of nephews kilt?"[6]
"I, that do seem not I, Duessa am,"
Quoth she, "however now, in garments gilt
And gorgeous gold array'd, I to thee came;
Duessa I, the daughter of Deceit and Shame."

Then, bowing down her aged back, she kist
The wicked witch, saying; "In that fair face
The false resemblance of Deceit, I wist,
Did closely lurk; yet so true-seeming grace
It carried, that I scarce in darksome place
Could it discern; though I the mother be
Of Falsehood, and root of Duessa's race.
O welcome, child, whom I have long'd to see,
And now have seen unwares! Lo, now I go with thee."

Then to her iron waggon she betakes,
And with her bears the foul well-favour'd witch:
Through mirksome[7] air her ready way she makes.
Her twyfold[8] team (of which two black as pitch,
And two were brown, yet each to each unlich[9]),
Did softly swim away, nor ever stamp
Unless she chanc'd their stubborn mouths to twitch;
Then, foaming tar, their bridles they would champ,
And trampling the fine element would fiercely ramp.[10]

So well they sped, that they be come at length
Unto the place where as the Paynim lay,
Devoid of outward sense and native strength,
Cover'd with charmëd cloud from view of day
And sight of men, since his late luckless fray.
His cruel wounds, with cruddy[11] blood congeal'd,
They binden up so wisely as they may,
And handle softly, till they can be heal'd:
So lay him in her chariot, close in night conceal'd.

And, all the while she stood upon the ground,
The wakeful dogs did never cease to bay;
As giving warning of th' unwonted sound
With which her iron wheels did them affray,[12]
And her dark grisly look them much dismay.
The messenger of death, the ghastly owl,
With dreary shrieks did also her bewray;
And hungry wolves continually did howl
At her abhorrëd face, so filthy and so foul.

Thence, turning back in silence, soft they stole,
And brought the heavy corse with easy pace
To yawning gulf of deep Avernus' hole:
By that same hole an entrance, dark and base,[13]
With smoke and sulphur hiding all the place,
Descends to hell: there creature never pass'd
That back returnëd without heavenly grace;
But dreadful Furies, which their chains have brast,[14]
And damnëd sprites sent forth to make ill men aghast.[15]

By that same way the direful dames do drive
Their mournful chariot, fill'd with rusty blood,
And down to Pluto's house are come belive;[16]
Which passing through, on every side them stood
The trembling ghosts with sad amazëd mood,
Chatt'ring their iron teeth, and staring wide
With stony eyes; and all the hellish brood
Of fiends infernal flock'd on ev'ry side,
To gaze on earthly wight that with the Night durst ride.

They pass the bitter waves of Acheron,
Where many souls sit wailing woefully;
And come to fiery flood of Phlegethon,
Where as the damnëd ghosts in torments fry,
And with sharp shrilling shrieks do bootless[17] cry,
Cursing high Jove, the which them thither sent.
The house of endless Pain is built thereby,
In which ten thousand sorts of punishment
The cursëd creatures do eternally torment.

Before the threshold dreadful Cerberus
His three deformëd heads did lay along,
Curlëd with thousand adders venomous;
And lillëd[18] forth his bloody flaming tongue;
At them he gan to rear his bristles strong,
And felly gnarr,[19] until Day's enemy[20]
Did him appease; then down his tail he hung,
And suffer'd them to passen quietly:
For she in hell and heav'n had power equally.

There was Ixion turnëd on a wheel,
For daring tempt the queen of heaven to sin;
And Sisyphus a huge round stone did reel
Against a hill, nor might from labour lin;[21]
There thirsty Tantalus hung by the chin;
And Tityus fed a vulture on his maw;
Typhœus' joints were stretchëd on a gin;[22]

1 Destroy. 2 Lament. 3 Attend. 4 Forfeit. 5 Purchase, atone. 6 Slain. 7 Darksome, murky. 8 Double, twofold. 9 Unlike. 10 Leap. 11 Curdled or clotted.

12 Terrify. 13 Low. 14 Burst. 15 Afraid. 16 Quickly. 17 Uselessly. 18 Lolled. 19 Snarl. 20 Night. 21 Desist, rest. 22 Rack.

Theseus condemn'd to endless sloth by law;
And fifty sisters water in leak[1] vessels draw.

They all, beholding worldly wights in place,[2]
Leave off their work, unmindful of their smart,
To gaze on them; who forth by them do pace,
Till they be come unto the farthest part;
Where was a cave y-wrought by wondrous art,
Deep, dark, uneasy, doleful, comfortless,
In which sad Æsculapius far apart
Imprison'd was in chains remédiless,
For that Hippolytus' rent corse he did redress.[3]

Hippolytus a jolly huntsman was,
That wont in chariot chase the foaming boar:
He all his peers in beauty did surpass;
But ladies' love, as loss of time, forbore:
His wanton stepdame[4] lovëd him the more;
But, when she saw her offer'd sweets refus'd,
Her love she turn'd to hate, and him before
His father fierce of treason false accus'd,
And with her jealous terms his open ears abus'd;

Who, all in rage, his sea-god sire[5] besought
Some cursëd vengeance on his son to cast;
From surging gulf two monsters straight were brought,
With dread whereof his chasing steeds aghast
Both chariot swift and huntsman overcast.
His goodly corse, on ragged cliffs y-rent,[6]
Was quite dismember'd, and his members chaste
Scatter'd on every mountain as he went,
That of Hippolytus was left no moniment.[7]

His cruel stepdame, seeing what was done,
Her wicked days with wretched knife did end,
In death avowing th' innocence of her son.
Which hearing, his rash sire began to rend
His hair, and hasty tongue that did offend:
Then, gath'ring up the reliques of his smart,[8]
By Dian's means who was Hippolyt's friend,
Them brought to Æsculape, that by his art
Did heal them all again, and joinëd every part.

Such wondrous science in man's wit to reign
When Jove advis'd,[9] that could the dead revive,
And fates expirëd could renew again,
Of endless life he might him not deprive;
But unto hell did thrust him down alive,
With flashing thunderbolt y-wounded sore:
Where, long remaining, he did always strive
Himself with salves to health for to restore,
And slake the heav'nly fire that ragëd evermore.

There ancient Night arriving, did alight
From her nigh-weary wain, and in her arms
To Æsculapius brought the wounded knight:
Whom having softly disarray'd of arms,
Then gan to him discover all his harms,
Beseeching him with prayer, and with praise,
If either salves, or oils, or herbs, or charms,
A fordone[10] wight from door of death might raise,
He would at her request prolong her nephew's[11] days.

"Ah Dame," quoth he, "thou temptest me in vain
To dare the thing, which daily yet I rue;
And the old cause of my continued pain
With like attempt to like end to renew.
Is not enough, that, thrust from heaven due,[12]
Here endless penance for one fault I pay;
But that redoubled crime with vengeance new
Thou biddest me to eke?[13] can Night defray[14]
The wrath of thund'ring Jove, that rules both Night and Day?"

"Not so," quoth she; "but, since that heaven's king
From hope of heav'n hath thee excluded quite,
Why fearest thou, that canst not hope for thing?
And fearest not that more thee hurten might,
Now in the power of everlasting Night?
Go to, then, O thou far renownëd son
Of great Apollo! show thy famous might
In medicine, that else[15] hath to thee won
Great pains, and greater praise, both never to be done."

Her words prevail'd: and then the learned leech[16]
His cunning hand gan to his wounds to lay,
And all things else, the which his art did teach:
Which having seen, from thence arose away
The Mother of dread darkness, and let stay
Aveugle's son there in the leech's cure;[17]
And, back returning, took her wonted way
To run her timely race, whilst Phœbus pure
In western waves his weary waggon did recure.[18]

The false Duessa, leaving noyous[19] Night,
Return'd to stately palace of Dame Pride:
Where when she came, she found the Faery Knight
Departed thence; although (his woundës wide
Not throughly heal'd) unready were to ride.
Good cause he had to hasten thence away;
For on a day his wary Dwarf had spied
Where, in a dungeon deep, huge numbers lay
Of caitive[20] wretched thralls, that wailëd night and day;—

A rueful sight as could be seen with eye;—
Of whom he learnëd had in secret wise
The hidden cause of their captivity;
How, mortgaging their lives to Covetise,
Through wasteful pride and wanton riotise,
They were, by law of that proud tyranness,
Provok'd with Wrath and Envy's false surmise,
Condemnëd to that dungeon merciless,
Where they should live in woe, and die in wretchedness.

There was that great proud king of Babylon,
That would compel all nations to adore,
And him as only God to call upon;
Till, through celestial doom[21] thrown out of door,

1 Leaky; the Danaïdes are meant.
2 Present.
3 Restore.
4 Phædra, whom Theseus had married; Hippolytus was his son by Hippolyta, Queen of the Amazons.
5 Ægeus; or Poseidon.
6 Torn; he was dragged along the ground by his own horses till he died.
7 Memorial, trace.
8 The remains of his son—the relics of his anguish.
9 Perceived.
10 Ruined, undone.
11 Grandson's.
12 Where, as the son of Apollo, and an immortal, he had a right to dwell.
13 Augment, add to.
14 Satisfy.
15 Already, in other cases.
16 Surgeon.
17 Care.
18 Recover from fatigue.
19 Baleful, noisome.
20 Captive.
21 Judgment.

Into an ox he was transform'd of yore.
There also was king Crœsus, that enhanc'd[1]
His heart too high, through his great riches' store;
And proud Antiochus, the which advanc'd
His cursëd hand 'gainst God, and on his altars danc'd.[2]

And, them long time before, great Nimrod was,
That first the world with sword and fire warray'd;[3]
And after him old Ninus far did pass
In princely pomp, of all the world obey'd.
There also was that mighty monarch[4] laid
Low under all, yet above all in pride,
That name of native sire did foul upbraid,
And would as Ammon's son be magnified;
Till, scorn'd of God and man, a shameful death he died.

All these together in one heap were thrown,
Like carcases of beasts in butcher's stall.
And in another corner wide were strown
The ántique ruins of the Romans' fall:
Great Romulus, the grandsire of them all;
Proud Tarquin; and too lordly Lentulus;
Stout Scipio; and stubborn Hannibal;
Ambitious Sylla; and stern Marius;
High Cæsar; great Pompéy; and fierce Antonius.

Amongst these mighty men were women mix'd,
Proud women, vain, forgetful of their yoke:[5]
The bold Semiramis, whose sides, transfix'd
With son's own blade, her foul reproaches spoke:
Fair Sthenobœa,[6] that herself did choke
With wilful cord, for wanting of her will;
High-minded Cleopatra, that with stroke
Of aspë's sting herself did stoutly kill:
And thousands more the like, that did that dungeon fill.

Besides the endless routs[7] of wretched thralls[8]
Which thither were assembled, day by day,
From all the world, after their woeful falls
Through wicked pride, and wasted wealth's decay.
But most, of all which in that dungeon lay,
Fell from high princes' courts, or ladies bow'rs;
Where they in idle pomp, or wanton play,
Consumëd had their goods and thriftless hours,
And lastly thrown themselves into these heavy stowres.[9]

Whose case when as the careful Dwarf had told,
And made ensample of their mournful sight
Unto his master, he no longer wo'ld
There dwell in peril of like painful plight,
But early rose; and, ere that dawning light
Discover'd had the world to heaven wide,
He by a privy postern took his flight,
That of no envious eyes he might be spied:
For doubtless death ensued if any him descried.

Scarce could he footing find in that foul way,
For many corses, like a great lay-stall,[10]
Of murder'd men, which therein strowëd lay
Without remorse or decent funeral;
Which, all through that great Princess Pride, did fall,
And came to shameful end: and them beside,
Forth riding underneath the castle wall,
A dunghill of dead carcases he spied:
The dreadful spectacle of that sad House of Pride.

CANTO VI.

From lawless lust by wondrous grace
Fair Una is releast:
Whom salvage nation does adore,
And learns her wise behest.

As when a ship, that flies fair under sail,
A hidden rock escapëd hath unwares,
That lay in wait her wreck for to bewail;
The mariner yet half amazëd stares
At peril past, and yet in doubt not dares
To joy at his foolhappy oversight:[11]
So doubly is distress'd, 'twixt joy and cares,
The dreadless courage of this Elfin Knight,
Having escap'd so sad ensamples in his sight.

Yet sad he was, that his too hasty speed
The fair Duess' had forc'd him leave behind;
And yet more sad, that Una, his dear dread,[12]
Her truth had stain'd with treason so unkind;
Yet crime in her could never creature find;
But for his love, and for her own self sake,
She wander'd had from one to other Ind,
Him for to seek, nor ever would forsake;
Till her unwares the fierce Sansloy did overtake;

Who, after Archimago's foul defeat,
Led her away into a forest wild;
And, turning wrathful fire to lustful heat,
With beastly sin thought her to have defil'd,
And made the vassal of his pleasures vild.[13]
Yet first he cast by treaty, and by trains,[14]
Her to persuade that stubborn fort to yield:
For greater conquest of hard love he gains,
That works it to his will, than he that it constrains.

With fawning words he courted her a while;
And, looking lovely[15] and oft sighing sore,
Her constant heart did tempt with diverse guile:
But words, and looks, and sighs she did abhor—
As rock of diamond steadfast evermore.
Yet, for to feed his fiery lustful eye,

1 Lifted up.

2 See their "Tragedies," as recited by Chaucer in the Monk's Tale, pages 158 *et seqq.*

3 Harassed with war.

4 Alexander the Great.

5 Their natural subjection to men, or to the restraints and honour of their sex.

6 Wife of Prœtus, king of Argos, to whose protection Bellerophon fled after he had slain the Corinthian Bellerus. Sthenobœa, otherwise called Antea, made proffer of her love to the refugee; but Bellerophon rejected her advances, and she accused him to her husband of abusing his hospitality. Thence sprang various futile endeavours to kill Bellerophon, after whose departure the baffled temptress is said to have strangled herself.

7 Crowds.

8 Slaves.

9 Calamities.

10 A rubbish-heap.

11 Fortuitous escape.

12 See note 19, page 310.

13 Vile.

14 Deceits, stratagems.

15 Lovingly.

He snatch'd the veil that hung her face before;
Then gan her beauty shine as brightest sky,
And burn'd his beastly heart t' enforce her chastity.

So, when he saw his flatt'ring arts to fail,
And subtle engines beat from battery,
With greedy force he gan the fort assail,
Whereof he ween'd[1] possessëd soon to be,
And win rich spoil of ransack'd chastity.
Ah heav'ns! that do this hideous act behold,
And heav'nly virgin thus outragëd see,
How can ye vengeance just so long withhold,
And hurl not flashing flames upon that Paynim bold?

The piteous maiden, careful,[2] comfortless,
Does throw out thrilling shrieks, and shrieking cries
(The last vain help of women's great distress);
And with loud plaints impórtuneth the skies,
That molten stars do drop like weeping eyes;
And Phœbus, flying so most shameful sight,
His blushing face in foggy cloud implies,[3]
And hides for shame. What wit of mortal wight
Can now devise to quit a thrall from such a plight?

Eternal Providence, exceeding thought,
Where none appears can make herself a way!
A wondrous way it for this Lady wrought,
From lions' claws to pluck the gripëd prey.
Her shrill outcries and shrieks so loud did bray,[4]
That all the woods and forests did resound:
A troop of Fauns and Satyrs far away
Within the wood were dancing in a round,
While old Sylvanus slept in shady arbour sound:

Who when they heard that piteous strainëd voice,
In haste forsook their rural merriment,
And ran towárd the far rebounded[5] noise,
To weet[6] what wight so loudly did lament.
Unto the place they come incontinent:
Whom when the raging Saracen espied,
A rude, misshapen, monstrous rabblement,
Whose like he never saw, he durst not bide;[7]
But got his ready steed, and fast away gan ride.

The wild wood-gods, arrivëd in the place,
There find the Virgin, doleful, desolate,
With ruffled raiments, and fair blubber'd[8] face,
As her outrageous foe had left her late;
And trembling yet through fear of former hate:
All stand amazëd at so úncouth sight,
And gin to pity her unhappy state;
All stand astonish'd at her beauty bright,
In their rude eyes unworthy of so woeful plight.

She, more amaz'd, in double dread doth dwell,
And every tender part for fear does shake.
As when a greedy wolf, through hunger fell,
A seely[9] lamb far from the flock does take,
Of whom he means his bloody feast to make,
A lion spies fast running toward him,
Th' innocent prey in haste he does forsake;
Which, quit from death, yet quakes in every limb
With change of fear, to see the lion look so grim.

Such fearful fit assay'd[10] her trembling heart;
No word to speak nor joint to move she had;
The salvage nation feel her secret smart,
And read her sorrow in her count'nance sad;
Their frowning foreheads, with rough horns yclad,
And rustic horror, all aside do lay,
And, gently grinning, shew a semblance glad,
To comfort her; and, fear to put away,
Their backward-bent knees[11] teach her humbly to obey.

The doubtful damsel dare not yet commit
Her single person to their barbarous truth;
But still 'twixt fear and hope amaz'd does sit,
Late learn'd what harm to hasty truth ensu'th:
They in compassion of her tender youth,
And wonder of her beauty sovereign,
Are won with pity and unwonted ruth;[12]
And, prostrate all upon the lowly plain,
Do kiss her feet, and fawn on her with count'-nance fain.[13]

Their hearts she guesseth by their humble guise,
And yields her to extremity of time:[14]
So from the ground she fearless doth arise,
And walketh forth without suspéct[15] of crime:
They, all as glad as birds of joyous prime,[16]
Thence lead her forth, about her dancing round,
Shouting, and singing all a shepherd's rhyme;
And, with green branches strowing all the ground,
Do worship her as queen, with olive garland crown'd.

And all the way their merry pipes they sound,
That all the woods with doubled echo ring;
And with their hornëd feet do wear the ground,
Leaping like wanton kids in pleasant spring.
So toward old Sylvanus they her bring;
Who, with the noise awakëd, cometh out
To weet the cause, his weak steps governing,
And aged limbs, on cypress stadle[17] stout;
And with an ivy twine his waist is girt about.

Far off he wonders what them makes so glad;
Or Bacchus' merry fruit they did invent,[18]
Or Cybele's frantic rites have made them mad:
They, drawing nigh, unto their god present
That flower of faith and beauty excellent:
The god himself, viewing that mirror rare,
Stood long amaz'd, and burnt in his intent:
His own fair Dryop' now he thinks not fair,
And Pholoë foul, when her to this he doth compare.

The wood-born people fall before her flat,
And worship her as goddess of the wood;
And old Sylvanus' self bethinks not what
To think of wight so fair; but gazing stood
In doubt to deem her born of earthly brood:
Sometimes dame Venus' self he seems to see;
But Venus never had so sober mood:

1 Thought. 2 Sorrowful.
3 Enwraps, enfolds. 4 Sound, re-echo.
5 Reverberated. 6 Know, learn.
7 Tarry on the spot. 8 Tear-stained.
9 Simple, innocent. 10 Tested, attacked.
11 Like those of fauns and satyrs in antique works of art. 12 Compassion.
13 Glad. 14 The emergency of the moment.
15 Suspicion, apprehension. 16 Spring.
17 Staff, support. 18 Discover grapes.

Sometimes Diana he her takes to be;
But misseth bow and shafts, and buskins to her knee.

By view of her he ginneth[1] to revive
His ancient love, and dearest Cyparisse;[2]
And calls to mind his portraiture alive,
How fair he was, and yet not fair to this;
And how he slew with glancing dart amiss
A gentle hind, the which the lovely boy
Did love as life, above all worldly bliss:
For grief whereof the lad n' ould after joy;[3]
But pin'd away in anguish and self-will'd annoy.[4]

The woody nymphs, fair Hamadryades,
Her to behold do thither run apace;
And all the troop of light-foot Naiades
Flock all about to see her lovely face:
But, when they viewëd have her heav'nly grace,
They envy her in their malicious mind,
And fly away for fear of foul disgrace:[5]
But all the Satyrs scorn their woody kind,
And henceforth nothing fair, but her, on earth they find.

Glad of such luck, the luckless lucky maid
Did her content to please their feeble eyes;
And long time with that salvage people stay'd,
To gather breath in many miseries.
During which time her gentle wit she plies
To teach them truth, which worshipt her in vain,
And made her th' image of idolatries:
But, when their bootless zeal she did restrain
From her own worship, they her ass would worship fain.

It fortunëd, a noble warlike knight
By just occasion to that forest came,
To seek his kindred, and the lineage right
From whence he took his well-deservëd name:
He had in arms abroad won muchel fame,
And fill'd far lands with glory of his might;
Plain, faithful, true, and enemy of shame,
And ever lov'd to fight for ladies' right:
But in vain-glorious frays he little did delight.

A Satyr's son, y-born in forest wild,
By strange adventure as it did betide,[6]
And there begotten of a lady mild,
Fair Thyamis, the daughter of Labryde;
That was in sacred bands of wedlock tied
To Therion, a loose unruly swain,
Who had more joy to range the forest wide,
And chase the salvage beast with busy pain,
Than serve his lady's love, and waste in pleasures vain.

The fórlorn maid did with love's longing burn,
And could not lack her lover's companý;
But to the wood she goes, to serve her turn,
And seek her spouse, that from her still does fly,
And follows other game and venerý:[7]
A Satyr chanc'd her wand'ring for to find;
And, kindling coals of lust in brutish eye,
The loyal links of wedlock did unbind,
And made her person thrall unto his beastly kind.[8]

So long in secret cabin there he held
Her captive to his sensual desire;
Till that with timely fruit her belly swell'd,
And bore a boy unto that salvage sire:
Then home he suffer'd her for to retire,
For ransom leaving him the late-born child:
Whom, till to riper years he gan aspire,
He nousled[9] up in life and manners wild,
Amongst wild beasts and woods, from laws of men exil'd.

For all he taught the tender imp,[10] was but
To banish cowardice and bastard fear:
His trembling hand he would him force to put
Upon the lion and the rugged bear;
And from the she-bear's teats her whelps to tear;
And eke wild roaring bulls he would him make
To tame, and ride their backs not made to bear;
And the roebucks in flight to overtake:
That every beast for fear of him did fly and quake.

Thereby so fearless and so fell he grew,
That his own sire and master of his guise[11]
Did often tremble at his horrid view;
And oft, for dread of hurt, would him advise
The angry beasts not rashly to despise,
Nor too much to provoke; for he would learn[12]
The lion stoop to him in lowly wise
(A lesson hard), and make the libbard[13] stern
Leave roaring, when in rage he for revenge did yearn.

And, for to make his power approvëd more,[14]
Wild beasts in iron yokes he would compel;
The spotted panther, and the tuskëd boar,
The pardale swift, and the tiger cruël,
The antelope and wolf, both fierce and fell;
And them constrain in equal team to draw.
Such joy he had their stubborn hearts to quell,
And sturdy courage tame with dreadful awe,
That his behest they fearëd as a tyrant's law.

His loving mother came upon a day
Unto the woods, to see her little son;
And chanc'd unwares to meet him in the way,
After his sports and cruel pastime done;
When after him a lioness did run,
That, roaring all with rage, did loud requére
Her children dear, whom he away had won:
The lion whelps she saw how he did bear,
And lull in rugged arms withouten childish fear.

The fearful dame all quakëd at the sight,
And, turning back, gan fast to fly away;
Until, with love revok'd from vain affright,
She hardly yet persuaded was to stay,
And then to him these womanish words gan say;
"Ah, Satyrane, my darling and my joy,
For love of me leave off this dreadful play;

1 Begins.
2 Cyparissus, a boy beloved of Sylvanus, killed a favourite stag of Apollo, and pining away in grief, was changed into a cypress.
3 Would afterwards have no joy.
4 Grief.
5 In the comparison with her.
6 Happen.
7 Sport.
8 Nature.
9 Nursed.
10 Child.
11 His own father, who had trained him into his present condition or fashion.
12 Teach.
13 Leopard.
14 More evident by practical proof.

To dally thus with death is no fit toy:[1]
Go, find some other play-fellows, mine own sweet boy."

In these and like delights of bloody game
He trainëd was, till riper years he raught,[2]
And there abode, whilst any beast of name
Walk'd in that forest, whom he had not taught
To fear his force: and then his courage haught[3]
Desir'd of foreign foemen to be known,
And far abroad for strange adventures sought;
In which his might was never overthrown;
But through all Faery Land his famous worth was blown.

Yet evermore it was his manner fair,
After long labours and adventures spent,
Unto those native woods for to repair,
To see his sire and offspring ancient.
And now he thither came for like intent;
Where he unwares the fairest Una found,
Strange lady, in so strange habiliment,
Teaching the Satyrs, which her sat around,
True sacred lore, which from her sweet lips did redound.[4]

He wonder'd at her wisdom heav'nly rare,
Whose like in woman's wit he never knew;
And, when her courteous deeds he did compare,
Gan her admire, and her sad sorrows rue,[5]
Blaming of Fortune, which such troubles threw,
And joy'd to make proof of her cruelty
On gentle dame, so hurtless and so true:
Thenceforth he kept her goodly company,
And learn'd her discipline[6] of faith and verity.

But she, all vow'd unto the Redcross Knight,
His wand'ring peril closely[7] did lament,
Nor in this new acquaintance could delight;
But her dear heart with anguish did torment,
And all her wit in secret counsels spent,
How to escape. At last in privy wise
To Satyrane she showëd her intent;
Who, glad to gain such favour, gan devise
How with that pensive maid he best might thence arise.[8]

So on a day, when Satyrs all were gone
To do their service to Sylvanus old,
The gentle Virgin, left behind alone,
He led away with courage stout and bold.
Too late it was to Satyrs to be told,
Or ever hope recover her again:
In vain he seeks that, having, cannot hold.
So fast he carried her with careful pain,
That they the woods are past, and come now to the plain.

The better part now of the ling'ring day
They travell'd had, when as they far espied
A weary wight forwand'ring by the way;
And toward him they gan in haste to ride,
To weet[9] of news that did abroad betide,
Or tidings of her Knight of the Redcross;
But he, them spying, gan to turn aside
For fear, as seem'd, or for some feignëd loss:
More greedy they of news fast toward him do cross.

A silly[10] man, in simple weeds forworn,
And soil'd with dust of the long driëd way;
His sandals were with toilsome travel torn,
And face all tann'd with scorching sunny ray,
As he had travell'd many a summer's day
Through boiling sands of Araby and Ind;
And in his hand a Jacob's staff,[11] to stay
His weary limbs upon; and eke behind
His scrip did hang, in which his needments he did bind.

The knight, approaching nigh, of him inquér'd
Tidings of war, and of adventures new;
But wars, nor new adventures, none he heard.
Then Una gan to ask, if aught he knew
Or heard abroad of that her champion true,
That in his armour bare a crosslet[12] red.
"Ay me! dear Dame," quoth he, "well may I rue[13]
To tell the sad sight which mine eyes have read;[14]
These eyes did see that Knight both living and eke dead."

That cruel word her tender heart so thrill'd,
That sudden cold did run through every vein,
And stony horror all her senses fill'd
With dying fit, that down she fell for pain.
The knight her lightly rearëd up again,
And comforted with courteous kind relief:
Then, won from death, she bade him tellen plain
The farther process of her hidden grief:
The lesser pangs can bear, who hath endur'd the chief.

Then gan the pilgrim thus; "I chanc'd this day,
This fatal day, that shall I ever rue,[13]
To see two knights, in travel on my way
(A sorry sight), arrang'd in battle new,
Both breathing vengeance, both of wrathful hue:
My fearful flesh did tremble at their strife,
To see their blades so greedily imbrue,
That, drunk with blood, yet thirsted after life:
What more? the Redcross Knight was slain with Paynim knife."

"Ah! dearest Lord," quoth she, "how might that be,
And he the stoutest knight that ever wonne?"[15]
"Ah! dearest Dame," quoth he, "how might I see
The thing, that might not be, and yet was done?"
"Where is," said Satyrane, "that Paynim's son
That him of life, and us of joy, hath reft?"
"Not far away," quoth he, "he hence doth won,[16]
Foreby[17] a fountain, where I late him left
Washing his bloody wounds, that through the steel were cleft."

Therewith the knight then marchëd forth in haste,

1 Amusement. 2 Reached. 3 Lofty; French, "haut." 4 Overflow. 5 Pity. 6 Teaching. 7 Secretly. 8 Depart. 9 Learn, know. 10 Simple.

11 A staff used in pilgrimages to the shrine of St James, or St Iago, of Spain. 12 Small cross. 13 Regret. 14 Perceived. 15 Lived. 16 Dwell, abide. 17 Near.

While Una, with huge heaviness opprest,
Could not for sorrow follow him so fast;
And soon he came, as he the place had guess'd,
Where as that Pagan proud [1] himself did rest
In secret shadow by a fountain side;
Ev'n he it was, that erst [2] would have suppress [3]
Fair Una; whom when Satyrane espied,
With foul reproachful words he boldly him defied;

And said; "Arise, thou cursed miscreant,[4]
That hast with knightless guile, and treach'rous train,[5]
Fair knighthood foully shamëd, and dost vaunt
That good Knight of the Redcross to have slain:
Arise, and with like treason now maintain
Thy guilty wrong, or else thee guilty yield."
The Saracen, this hearing, rose amain,
And, catching up in haste his three-squared shield
And shining helmet, soon him buckled to the field;

And, drawing nigh him, said; "Ah! misborn Elf,
In evil hour thy foes thee hither sent
Another's wrongs to wreak upon thyself:
Yet ill thou blamest me, for having blent [6]
My name with guile and traitorous intent:
That Redcross Knight, pardie,[7] I never slew;
But had he been, where erst his arms were lent,[8]
Th' enchanter vain his error should not rue:
But thou his error shalt, I hope, now proven true."

Therewith they gan, both furious and fell,
To thunder blows, and fiercely to assail
Each other, bent his enemy to quell;
That with their force they pierc'd both plate and mail,
And made wide furrows in their fleshes frail,
That it would pity any living eye:
Large floods of blood adown their sides did rail;[9]
But floods of blood could not them satisfy:
Both hunger'd after death; both chose to win, or die.

So long they fight, and full revenge pursue,
That, fainting, each themselves to breathen let;[10]
And, oft refreshëd, battle oft renew.
As when two boars, with rankling malice met,
Their gory sides fresh bleeding fiercely frett;[11]
Till breathless both themselves aside retire,
Where, foaming wrath, their cruel tusks they whet,
And trample th' earth, the while they may respire;
Then back to fight again, new breathëd and entire.

So fiercely, when these knights had breathëd once,
They gan to fight return; increasing more
Their puissant force and cruel rage at once,
With heapëd strokes more hugely than before;
That with their dreary wounds, and bloody gore,
They both deformëd,[12] scarcely could be known.
By this, sad Una, fraught with anguish sore,
Led with their noise which through the air was thrown,
Arriv'd where they in earth their fruitless blood had sown.

Whom all so soon as that proud Saracen
Espied, he gan revive the memory
Of his lewd lusts, and late attempted sin;
And left the doubtful battle hastily,
To catch her, newly offer'd to his eye:
But Satyrane, with strokes him turning, stay'd,
And sternly bade him other business ply
Than hunt the steps of pure unspotted maid:
Wherewith he, all enrag'd, these bitter speeches said;

"O foolish Faery's son, what fury mad
Hath thee incens'd to haste thy doleful fate?
Were it not better I that Lady had,
Than that thou hadst repented it too late?
Most senseless man he, that himself doth hate
To love another: Lo then, for thine aid,
Here take thy lover's token on thy pate."
So they to fight; the while the royal maid
Fled far away, of that proud Paynim sore afraid.

But that false pilgrim, which that leasing[13] told,
Being indeed old Archimage, did stay
In secret shadow all this to behold;
And much rejoicëd in their bloody fray:
But, when he saw the damsel pass away,
He left his stand,[14] and her pursued apace,
In hope to bring her to her last decay.[15]
But for to tell her lamentable case,
And eke this battle's end, will need another place.

CANTO VII.

The Redcross Knight is captive made,
By Giant proud opprest:
Prince Arthur meets with Una great-
ly with those news distrest.

What man so wise, what earthly wit so ware,[16]
As to descry the crafty cunning train
By which Deceit doth mask in visor fair,
And cast [17] her colours, dyëd deep in grain,
To seem like Truth whose shape she well can fain,
And fitting gestures to her purpose frame,
The guiltless man with guile to entertain?
Great mistress of her art was that false dame,
The false Duessa, cloakëd with Fidessa's name.

Who when, returning from the dreary Night,
She found not in that perilous House of Pride,
Where she had left, the noble Redcross Knight,
Her hopëd prey; she would no longer bide,
But forth she went to seek him far and wide.
Ere long she found, where as he weary sate
To rest himself, foreby [18] a fountain side,
Disarmëd all of iron-coated plate;
And by his side his steed the grassy forage ate.

1 Sansloy. 2 Before. 3 Outraged.
4 Unbeliever. 5 Stratagem.
6 Obscured, disgraced. 7 By the gods.
8 Where formerly he had lent his arms—when Archimago, in the semblance of the Redcross Knight's armour, was overthrown by Sansloy.

9 Flow.
10 Left off to give themselves breath.
11 Tear. 12 Disfigured.
13 Falsehood. 14 Station.
15 Destruction. 16 Cautious.
17 Contrive, arrange. 18 Near.

He feeds upon the cooling shade, and bays[1]
His sweaty forehead in the breathing wind,
Which through the trembling leaves full gently plays,
Wherein the cheerful birds of sundry kind
Do chant sweet music, to delight his mind.
The witch approaching gan him fairly greet,
And, with reproach of carelessness unkind,
Upbraid for leaving her in place unmeet,
With foul words temp'ring fair, sour gall with honey sweet.

Unkindness past, they gan of solace treat,
And bathe in pleasance of the joyous shade,
Which shielded them against the boiling heat,
And, with green boughs decking a gloomy glade,
About the fountain like a garland made;
Whose bubbling wave did ever freshly well,
Nor ever would through fervent summer fade:
The sacred nymph, which therein wont to dwell,
Was out of Dian's favour, as it then befell.

The cause was this: One day, when Phœbe fair
With all her band was following the chase,
This nymph, quite tir'd with heat of scorching air
Sat down to rest in middest of the race:
The goddess, wroth, gan foully her disgrace,[2]
And bade the waters, which from her did flow,
Be such as she herself was then in place.[3]
Thenceforth her waters waxëd dull and slow;
And all that drank thereof did faint and feeble grow.

Hereof this gentle Knight unweeting[4] was;
And, lying down upon the sandy grail,[5]
Drank of the stream, as clear as crystal glass:
Eftsoons[6] his manly forces gan to fail,
And mighty strong was turn'd to feeble frail.
His changëd powers at first themselves not felt;
Till curdled cold his courage gan assail,
And cheerful blood in faintness chill did melt,
Which, like a fever fit, through all his body swelt.[7]

Yet goodly court he made still to his dame,
Pour'd out in looseness on the grassy ground,
Both careless of his health and of his fame:
Till at the last he heard a dreadful sound,
Which through the wood loud bellowing did rebound,
That all the earth for terror seem'd to shake,
And trees did tremble. Th' Elf, therewith astound',[8]
Upstarted lightly from his looser make,[9]
And his unready weapons gan in hand to take.

But ere he could his armour on him dight,
Or get his shield, his monstrous enemy
With sturdy steps came stalking in his sight,
A hideous giant, horrible and high,
That with his tallness seem'd to threat the sky;
The ground eke groanëd under him for dreed:[10]
His living like saw never living eye,
Nor durst behold; his stature did exceed
The height of three the tallest sons of mortal seed.

The greatest Earth his uncouth mother was,
And blust'ring Æolus his boasted sire;
Who with his breath, which through the world doth pass,
Her hollow womb did secretly inspire,
And fill'd her hidden caves with stormy ire,
That she conceiv'd; and, trebling the due time
In which the wombs of women do expire,[11]
Brought forth this monstrous mass of earthly slime,
Puff'd up with empty wind, and fill'd with sinful crime.

So growen great, through arrogant delight
Of th' high descent whereof he was y-born,
And through presumption of his matchless might,
All other pow'rs and knighthood he did scorn.
Such now he marcheth to this man forlorn[12]
And left to loss; his stalking steps are stay'd
Upon a snaggy[13] oak, which he had torn
Out of his mother's bowels, and it made
His mortal mace, wherewith his foemen he dismay'd.

That, when the Knight he spied, he gan advance
With huge force and insupportable main,[14]
And toward him with dreadful fury prance;
Who, hapless and eke hopeless, all in vain
Did to him pace sad battle to darrain,[15]
Disarm'd, disgrac'd, and inwardly dismay'd;
And eke so faint in every joint and vein,
Through that frail fountain, which him feeble made,
That scarcely could he wield his bootless[16] single blade.

The giant struck so mainly[17] merciless,
That could have overthrown a stony tow'r;
And, were not heav'nly grace that did him bless,
He had been powder'd[18] all as thin as flour:
But he was wary of that deadly stowre,[19]
And lightly leapt from underneath the blow:
Yet so exceeding was the villain's pow'r,
That with the wind it did him overthrow,
And all his senses stunn'd, that still he lay full low.

As when that devilish iron engine, wrought
In deepest hell, and fram'd by Furies' skill,
With windy nitre and quick sulphur fraught,
And ramm'd with bullet round, ordain'd to kill,
Conceiveth fire; the heavens it doth fill
With thund'ring noise, and all the air doth choke,
That none can breathe, nor see, nor hear at will,
Through smould'ry[20] cloud of duskish stinking smoke;
That th' only breath[21] him daunts, who hath escap'd the stroke.

So daunted when the giant saw the Knight,
His heavy hand he heavëd up on high,

1 Bathes.
2 Reproach.
3 On the spot where she rested.
4 Ignorant.
5 Gravel.
6 Immediately.
7 Diffused faintness.
8 Astonished.
9 Companion.
10 Dread.
11 Give forth their burden.
12 The Redcross Knight.
13 Knotted.
14 Strength.
15 Offer.
16 Ineffectual.
17 Strongly.
18 Beaten to powder.
19 Peril.
20 Smothering.
21 The very breath, the mere breathing of the smoke.

And him to dust thought to have batter'd quite,
Until Duessa loud to him gan cry;
"O great Orgoglio,[1] greatest under sky,
Oh! hold thy mortal hand for lady's sake;
Hold for my sake, and do him not to die,[2]
But vanquish'd thine eternal bond-slave make,
And me, thy worthy meed,[3] unto thy leman[4] take."

He hearken'd, and did stay from farther harms,
To gain so goodly guerdon[5] as she spake:
So willingly she came into his arms,
Who her as willingly to grace[6] did take,
And was possessëd of his new-found make.[7]
Then up he took the slumb'ring senseless corse;
And, ere he could out of his swoon awake,
Him to his castle brought with hasty force,
And in a dungeon deep him threw without remorse.

From that day forth Duessa was his dear,
And highly honour'd in his haughty eye:
He gave her gold and purple pall to wear,
And triple crown set on her head full high,
And her endow'd with royal majesty:
Then, for to make her dreaded more of men,
And people's hearts with awful terror tie,[8]
A monstrous beast, y-bred in filthy fen,
He chose, which he had kept long time in darksome den.

Such one it was, as that renowned snake[9]
Which great Alcides in Stremona slew,
Long foster'd in the filth of Lerna Lake:
Whose many heads, out-budding ever new,
Did breed him endless labour to subdue.
But this same monster much more ugly was;
For sev'n great heads out of his body grew,
An iron breast, and back of scaly brass,
And all-embrued in blood his eyes did shine as glass.

His tail was stretchëd out in wondrous length,
That to the house of heav'nly gods it raught;[10]
And with extorted power, and borrow'd strength,
The ever-burning lamps from thence it brought,
And proudly threw to ground, as things of naught;
And underneath his filthy feet did tread
The sacred things, and holy hests foretaught.[11]
Upon this dreadful beast, with sev'nfold head,
He set the false Duessa, for more awe and dread.

The woeful Dwarf, which saw his master's fall
(While he had keeping of his grazing steed),
And valiant Knight become a caitive thrall;[12]
When all was past, took up his fórlorn weed;[13]
His mighty armour, missing most at need;
His silver shield, now idle, masterless;
His poignant spear, that many made to bleed;
The rueful monuments of heaviness;
And with them all departs, to tell his great distress.

He had not travell'd long, when on the way
He woeful Lady, woeful Una, met
Fast flying from that Paynim's[14] greedy prey,[15]
Whilst Satyrane him from pursuit did let:[16]
Who when her eyes she on the Dwarf had set,
And saw the signs that deadly tidings spake,
She fell to ground for sorrowful regret,
And lively breath her sad breast did forsake;
Yet might her piteous heart be seen to pant and quake.

The messenger of so unhappy news
Would fain have died; dead was his heart within;
Yet outwardly some little comfort shews:
At last, recov'ring heart, he does begin
To rub her temples, and to chafe her chin,[17]
And every tender part does toss and turn:
So hardly he the flitted life does win
Unto her native prison to return.
Then gins her grievëd ghost[18] thus to lament and mourn:

"Ye dreary instruments of doleful sight,
That do this deadly spectacle behold,
Why do ye longer feed on loathëd light,
Or liking find to gaze on earthly mould,
Since cruel Fates the careful threads unfold,
The which my life and love together tied?
Now let the stony dart of senseless cold
Pierce to my heart, and pass through every side;
And let eternal night so sad sight from me hide.

"O lightsome Day, the lamp of highest Jove,
First made by him men's wand'ring ways to guide,
When darkness he in deepest dungeon drove;
Henceforth thy hated face for ever hide,
And shut up heaven's windows shining wide:
For earthly sight can naught but sorrow breed,
And late repentance, which shall long abide.
Mine eyes no more on vanity shall feed,
But, sealëd up with death, shall have their deadly meed."[19]

Then down again she fell unto the ground;
But he her quickly rearëd up again:
Thrice did she sink adown in deadly swound,
And thrice he her reviv'd with busy pain.
At last, when life recover'd had the rein,
And over-wrestled his strong enemy,
With falt'ring tongue, and trembling every vein,
"Tell on," quoth she, "the woeful tragedy,
The which these reliques sad present unto mine eye:

"Tempestuous Fortune hath spent all her spite,
And thrilling Sorrow thrown his utmost dart:
Thy sad tongue cannot tell more heavy plight
Than that I feel, and harbour in mine heart:
Who hath endur'd the whole, can bear each part.
If death it be, it is not the first wound
That lancëd hath my breast with bleeding smart.
Begin, and end the bitter baleful stound;[20]
If less than that I fear, more favour I have found."

1 Arrogance.
2 Slay him not.
3 Reward, prize.
4 Mistress.
5 Recompense.
6 Favour.
7 Companion, consort.
8 Subdue, bind.
9 The Lernean Hydra, the slaughter of which was among the great feats of Hercules.
10 Reached.
11 Old commandments, taught in former time.
12 Captive slave.
13 Abandoned arms.
14 Sansloy's.
15 Pursuit.
16 Hinder.
17 Face.
18 Spirit.
19 Gift, destiny.
20 Sorrow.

Then gan the Dwarf the whole discourse declare:
The subtle trains[1] of Archimago old;
The wanton loves of false[2] Fidessa fair,
Bought with the blood of vanquish'd Paynim bold;[3]
The wretched pair transform'd to treën mould;
The House of Pride, and perils round about;
The combat which he with Sansjoy did hold;
The luckless conflict with the giant stout,
Wherein captív'd, of life or death he stood in doubt.

She heard with patience all unto the end;
And strove to master sorrowful assay,[4]
Which greater grew the more she did contend,
And almost rent her tender heart in tway;[5]
And love fresh coals unto her fire did lay:
For, greater love, the greater is the loss.
Was never lady lovëd dearer day
Then she did love the Knight of the Redcross;
For whose dear sake so many troubles her did toss.

At last, when fervent sorrow slakëd was,
She up arose, resolving him to find
Alive or dead; and forward forth doth pass,
All as the Dwarf the way to her assign'd:[6]
And evermore, in constant careful mind,
She fed her wound with fresh renewëd bale:[7]
Long tost with storms, and beat with bitter wind,
High over hills, and low adown the dale,
She wander'd many a wood, and measur'd many a vale.

At last she chancëd by good hap to meet
A goodly knight,[8] fair marching by the way,
Together with his squire, arrayëd meet:
His glittering armour shinëd far away,
Like glancing light of Phœbus' brightest ray;
From top to toe no place appearëd bare,
That deadly dint of steel endanger may:
Athwart his breast a baldric[9] brave he ware,
That shin'd, like twinkling stars, with stones most precious rare:

And, in the midst thereof, one precious stone
Of wondrous worth, and eke of wondrous mights,[10]
Shap'd like a lady's head,[11] exceeding shone,
Like Hesperus amongst the lesser lights,
And strove for to amaze the weaker sights:
Thereby his mortal blade full comely hung
In ivory sheath, y-carv'd with curious sleights,[12]
Whose hilts were burnish'd gold, and handle strong
Of mother pearl; and buckled with a golden tongue.

His haughty helmet, horrid[13] all with gold,
Both glorious brightness and great terror bred:
For all the crest a dragon did enfold
With greedy paws, and over all did spread
His golden wings;[14] his dreadful hideous head,
Close couchëd on the beaver, seem'd to throw
From flaming mouth bright sparkles fiery red,
That sudden horror to faint hearts did show;
And scaly tail was stretch'd adown his back full low.

Upon the top of all his lofty crest,
A bunch of hairs discolour'd diversely,
With sprinkled pearl and gold full richly drest,
Did shake, and seem'd to dance for jollity;
Like to an almond tree y-mounted high
On top of green Selinis all alone,
With blossoms brave bedeckëd daintily;
Whose tender locks do tremble ev'ry one
At ev'ry little breath that under heaven is blown.

His warlike shield[15] all closely cover'd was,
Nor might of mortal eye be ever seen;
Not made of steel, nor of enduring brass
(Such earthly metals soon consumëd been[16]),
But all of diamond perfect pure and clean
It framëd was, one massy éntire mould,
Hewn out of adamant rock with engines keen,
That point of spear it never piercen could,
Nor dint of direful sword divide the substance would.

The same to wight he never wont disclose,[17]
But when as monsters huge he would dismay,
Or daunt unequal armies of his foes,
Or when the flying heav'ns he would affray:
For so exceeding shone his glist'ning ray,
That Phœbus' golden face it did attaint,[18]
As when a cloud his beams doth over-lay;
And silver Cynthia[19] waxëd pale and faint,
As when her face is stain'd with magic arts' constraint.

No magic arts hereof had any might,
Nor bloody words of bold enchanters' call;
But all that was not such as seem'd in sight,
Before that shield did fade, and sudden fall:
And, when him list the rascal routs[20] appal,
Men into stones therewith he could transmue,[21]
And stones to dust, and dust to naught at all;
And, when him list the prouder looks subdue,
He would them gazing blind, or turn to other hue.

Nor let it seem that credence this exceeds;
For he that made the same was known right well
To have done much more admirable[22] deeds:
It Merlin was, which whilom did excell
All living wights in might of magic spell:
Both shield, and sword, and armour all he wrought

1 Stratagems.
2 The pretended.
3 Sansfoy. See Canto II.
4 The trial or attack of sorrow.
5 Two.
6 Pointed out.
7 Misery.
8 Prince Arthur, who was to have been the principal hero of the poem, according to Spenser's uncompleted design.
9 Belt.
10 Virtues, powers.
11 In the likeness of the Faery Queen.
12 Devices.
13 Rugged; studded or ornamented.
14 The golden dragon was the cognisance of the royal race among the Britons. Tennyson, in the "Idylls of the King" (page 256), describing Arthur's parting from Guinevere, tells us that she saw,
"Wet with the mists and smitten with the lights,
The Dragon of the great Pendragonship
Blaze, making all the night a steam of fire."
15 The ancient romancers called Arthur's shield "Pridwen," his sword "Caliburn" or "Excalibar," and his spear "Roan."
16 Are.
17 He was never wont to show to mortal.
18 Obscure.
19 The Moon.
20 The base crowds of his enemies.
21 Transform.
22 Wonderful.

For this young Prince, when first to arms he fell,[1]
But, when he died, the Faery Queen it brought
To Faery Land; where yet it may be seen, if sought.

A gentle youth, his dearly lovëd squire,
His spear of ebon wood behind him bare,
Whose harmful head, thrice heated in the fire,
Had riven many a breast with pikehead square;
A goodly person; and could manage fair
His stubborn steed with curbëd canon bit,[2]
Who under him did trample as the air,
And, chaf'd that any on his back should sit,
The iron rowels[3] into frothy foam he bit.

When as this knight nigh to the Lady drew,
With lovely court he gan her entertain;
But, when he heard her answers loth,[4] he knew
Some secret sorrow did her heart distrain:[5]
Which to allay, and calm her storming pain,
Fair feeling words he wisely gan display,
And for her humour fitting purpose feign,[6]
To tempt the cause itself for to bewray;
Wherewith enmov'd, these bleeding words she gan to say;

"What world's delight, or joy of living speech,
Can heart, so plung'd in sea of sorrows deep,
And heapëd with so huge misfortunes, reach?
The careful cold[7] beginneth for to creep,
And in my heart his iron arrow steep,
Soon as I think upon my bitter bale.[8]
Such helpless harms 'tis better hidden keep,
Than rip up grief, where it may naught avail;
My last-left comfort is my woes to weep and wail."

"Ah Lady dear," quoth then the gentle knight,
"Well may I ween your grief is wondrous great;
For wondrous great grief groaneth in my sprite,[9]
While thus I hear you of your sorrows treat.
But, woeful Lady, let me you intreat
For to unfold the anguish of your heart:
Mishaps are master'd by advice discreet,
And counsel mitigates the greatest smart;
Found never help, who never would his hurts impart."

"O! but," quoth she, "great grief will not be told,
And can more easily be thought than said."
"Right so," quoth he; "but he that never wo'ld
Could never: will to might gives greatest aid."
"But grief," quoth she, "does greater grow, display'd,
If then it find not help, and breeds despair."
"Despair breeds not," quoth he, "where faith is stay'd."
"No faith so fast," quoth she, "but flesh does pair."[10]
"Flesh may impair," quoth he, "but reason can repair."

His goodly reason, and well-guided speech,
So deep did settle in her gracious thought,
That her persuaded to disclose the breach
Which love and fortune in her heart had wrought;
And said; "Fair Sir, I hope good hap hath brought
You to inquire the secrets of my grief;
Or that your wisdom will direct my thought;
Or that your prowess can me yield relief;
Then hear the story sad, which I shall tell you brief.

"The fórlorn maiden, whom your eyes have seen
The laughing stock of Fortune's mockeries,
Am th' only daughter of a king and queen,
Whose parents dear (while equal destinies
Did run about, and their felicities
The favourable heav'ns did not envý),
Did spread their rule through all the territories,
Which Pison and Euphrates floweth by,
And Gihon's golden waves do wash continuallý:[11]

"Till that their cruel cursëd enemy,
A huge great dragon, horrible in sight,
Bred in the loathly lakes of Tartary,[12]
With murd'rous ravin and devouring might
Their kingdom spoil'd, and country wasted quite:
Themselves, for fear into his jaws to fall,
He forc'd to castle strong to take their flight;
Where, fast embarr'd[13] in mighty brazen wall,
He has them now four years besieg'd to make them thrall.

"Full many knights, adventurous and stout,
Have enterpris'd that monster to subdue:
From every coast, that heaven walks about,[14]
Have thither come the noble martial crew,
That famous hard achievements still pursue;
Yet never any could that garland win,
But all still shrunk; and still he greater grew:
All they, for want of faith, or guilt of sin,
The piteous prey of his fierce cruelty have been.

"At last, y-led with far-reported praise,
Which flying fame throughout the world had spread,
Of doughty knights, whom Faery Land did raise,
That noble order hight[15] of Maidenhead,
Forthwith to court of Gloriane I sped,
Of Gloriane, great queen of glory bright,
Whose kingdom's seat Cleopolis is read;[15]
There to obtain some such redoubted knight,
That parents dear from tyrant's pow'r deliver might.

"It was my chance (my chance was fair and good)
There for to find a fresh unprovëd[16] Knight;
Whose manly hands embrued in guilty blood
Had never been, nor ever by his might
Had thrown to ground the unregarded right:
Yet of his prowess proof he since hath made
(I witness am) in many a cruel fight;
The groaning ghosts of many a one dismay'd
Have felt the bitter dint of his avenging blade.

"And ye, the fórlorn[17] reliques of his pow'r,
His biting sword, and his devouring spear,
Which have endurëd many a dreadful stowre,[18]

1 Applied himself.
2 That part of the bit which is enclosed in the horse's mouth.
3 Rings of the bit.
4 Reluctant.
5 Oppress.
6 Adapt his discourse to her mood.
7 The chill of pain or grief. See note 2, page 169.
8 Misfortune.
9 Spirit.
10 Impair it.
11 Three of the rivers of Eden. See Gen. ii. 11, 13.
12 Tartarus, hell.
13 Imprisoned.
14 Surrounds.
15 Called.
16 Untried in battle.
17 Lost.
18 Conflict.

Can speak his prowess, that did erst[1] you bear,
And well could rule; now he hath left you here
To be the record of his rueful[2] loss,
And of my doleful disadventurous dere:[3]
O heavy record of the good Redcross,
Where have you left your lord, that could so well you toss?

"Well hopëd I, and fair beginnings had,
That he my captive languor should redeem:[4]
Till all unweeting[5] an enchanter bad
His sense abus'd, and made him to misdeem[6]
My loyalty not such as it did seem,
That rather death desire than such despite.
Be judge, ye heav'ns, that all things right esteem,
How I him lov'd, and love with all my might!
So thought I eke of him, and think I thought aright.

"Thenceforth me desolate he quite forsook,
To wander where wild Fortune would me lead,
And other by-ways he himself betook,
Where never foot of living wight did tread
That brought not back the baleful body dead;
In which him chancëd false Duessa meet,
Mine only foe, mine only deadly dread;
Who with her witchcraft, and misseeming[7] sweet,
Inveigled him to follow her desires unmeet.

"At last, by subtle sleights she him betray'd
Unto his foe, a giant huge and tall;
Who him, disarmëd, dissolute,[8] dismay'd,
Unwares surprisëd, and with mighty mall[9]
The monster merciless him made to fall,
Whose fall did never foe before behold:
And now in darksome dungeon, wretched thrall,
Remédiless, for aye he doth him hold:
This is my cause of grief, more great than may be told."

Ere she had ended all, she gan to faint:
But he her comforted, and fair bespake;
"Certes, Madáme, ye have great cause of plaint,
That stoutest heart, I ween, could cause to quake.
But be of cheer, and comfort to you take;
For till I have acquit[10] your captive Knight,
Assure yourself, I will you not forsake."
His cheerful words reviv'd her cheerless sprite:
So forth they went, the Dwarf them guiding ever right.

CANTO VIII.

Fair Virgin, to redeem her dear,
Brings Arthur to the fight:
Who slays the Giant, wounds the Beast,
And strips Duessa quite.

Ah me, how many perils do enfold
The righteous man, to make him daily fall,
Were not that heav'nly grace doth him uphold,
And steadfast Truth acquit[10] him out of all!
Her love is firm, her care continual,
So oft as he, through his own foolish pride
Or weakness, is to sinful bands made thrall:
Else should this Redcross Knight in bands have died,
For whose deliv'rance she this prince doth thither guide.

They sadly travell'd thus, until they came
Nigh to a castle builded strong and high:
Then cried the Dwarf, "Lo! yonder is the same,
In which my lord, my liege, doth luckless lie
Thrall to that giant's hateful tyranny:
Therefore, dear Sir, your mighty pow'rs assay."
The noble Knight alighted by and by
From lofty steed, and bade the Lady stay,
To see what end of fight should him befall that day.

So with his squire, th' admirer[11] of his might,
He marchëd forth towárd that castle wall;
Whose gates he found fast shut, nor living wight
To ward the same nor answer comer's call.
Then took that squire a horn of bugle small,
Which hung adown his side in twisted gold
And tassels gay; wide wonders over all[12]
Of that same horn's great virtues weren told,
Which had approvëd[13] been in uses manifold.

Was never wight that heard that shrilling sound,
But trembling fear did feel in every vein:
Three miles it might be easy heard around,
And echoes three answer'd itself again:
No false enchantment, nor deceitful train,[14]
Might once abide the terror of that blast,
But presently was void and wholly vain:
No gate so strong, no lock so firm and fast,
But with that piercing noise flew open quite, or brast.[15]

The same before the giant's gate he blew,
That all the castle quakëd from the ground,
And every door of free-will open flew.
The giant's self, dismayëd with that sound,
Where he with his Duessa dalliance found,
In haste came rushing forth from inner bow'r,
With staring count'nance stern, as one astound',[16]
And staggering steps, to weet[17] what sudden stowre[18]
Had wrought that horror strange, and dar'd his dreaded power.

And after him the proud Duessa came,
High mounted on her many-headed beast;
And every head with fiery tongue did flame,
And every head was crownëd on his crest,
And bloody-mouthëd with late cruel feast;
That when the knight beheld, his mighty shield
Upon his manly arm he soon addrest,[19]
And at him fiercely flew, with courage fill'd,
And eager greediness through every member thrill'd.

Therewith the giant buckled him to fight,
Inflam'd with scornful wrath and high disdain,

1 Before. 2 Pitiful.
3 My sad and luckless misfortune.
4 Should deliver me from my grief for the captivity of my parents.
5 Without his suspecting it.
6 Misjudge. 7 Deception.
8 Languid. 9 Club, mace.
10 Set free. 11 Wondering witness.
12 Everywhere. 13 Tested, proved.
14 Stratagem. 15 Burst.
16 Stupefied. 17 Learn.
18 Assault, trouble. 19 Adjusted.

And lifting up his dreadful club on height,[1]
All arm'd with ragged snubs[2] and knotty grain,
Him thought at first encounter to have slain.
But wise and wary was that noble peer;
And, lightly leaping from so monstrous main,[3]
Did fair avoid the violence him near;
It booted not to think such thunderbolts to bear;

Nor shame he thought to shun so hideous might:
The idle stroke, enforcing furious way,
Missing the mark of his misaimèd sight,
Did fall to ground, and with his heavy sway
So deeply dinted in the driven clay,
That three yards deep a furrow up did throw:
The sad[4] earth, wounded with so sore assay,[5]
Did groan full grievous underneath the blow;
And, trembling with strange fear, did like an earthquake show.

As when almighty Jove, in wrathful mood,
To wreak the guilt of mortal sins is bent,
Hurls forth his thund'ring dart with deadly feud,[6]
Enroll'd in flames and smould'ring dreariment,[7]
Through riven clouds and molten firmament;
The fierce three-forkèd engine, making way,
Both lofty tow'rs and highest trees hath rent,
And all that might his angry passage stay;
And, shooting in the earth, casts up a mount of clay.

His boist'rous club, so buried in the ground,
He could not rearen up again so light,[8]
But that the knight him at advantage found;
And, while he strove his cumber'd[9] club to quite[10]
Out of the earth, with blade all burning bright
He smote off his left arm, which like a block
Did fall to ground, depriv'd of native might;
Large streams of blood out of the trunkèd stock[11]
Forth gushèd, like fresh water stream from riven rock.

Dismayèd with so desp'rate deadly wound,
And eke impatient of unwonted pain,
He loudly bray'd with beastly yelling sound,
That all the fields rebellowèd again:
As great a noise, as when in Cimbrian[12] plain
A herd of bulls, whom kindly[13] rage doth sting,
Do for the milky mothers' want complain,
And fill the fields with troublous bellowing:
The neighbour woods around with hollow murmur ring.

That when his dear Duessa heard, and saw
The evil stound[14] that danger'd her estate,
Unto his aid she hastily did draw
Her dreadful beast; who, swoll'n with blood of late,
Came ramping forth with proud presumptuous gait,
And threaten'd all his heads like flaming brands.
But him the squire made quickly to retrate,[15]
Encount'ring fierce with single sword in hand;
And 'twixt him and his lord did like a bulwark stand.

The proud Duessa, full of wrathful spite
And fierce disdain, to be affronted[16] so,
Enforc'd her purple beast with all her might,
That stop[17] out of the way to overthrow,
Scorning the let[18] of so unequal foe:
But nathemore[19] would that courageous swain
To her yield passage, 'gainst his lord to go;
But with outrageous strokes did him restrain,
And with his body barr'd the way atwixt them twain.

Then took the angry witch her golden cup,
Which still she bore, replete with magic arts;
Death and despair did many thereof sup,
And secret poison through their inner parts;
Th' eternal bale[20] of heavy wounded hearts:
Which, after charms and some enchantments said,
She lightly sprinkled on his weaker parts:
Therewith his sturdy courage soon was quay'd,[21]
And all his senses were with sudden dread dismay'd.

So down he fell before the cruel beast,
Who on his neck his bloody claws did seize,
That life nigh crush'd out of his panting breast:
No pow'r he had to stir, nor will to rise.
That when the careful knight gan well advise,[22]
He lightly left the foe with whom he fought,
And to the beast gan turn his enterprise;
For wondrous anguish in his heart it wrought
To see his lovèd squire into such thraldom brought;

And, high advancing his blood-thirsty blade,
Struck one of those deformèd heads so sore,
That of his puissance proud ensample made;
His monstrous scalp down to his teeth it tore,
And that misformèd shape misshapèd more:
A sea of blood gush'd from the gaping wound,
That her gay garments stain'd with filthy gore,
And overflowèd all the field around,
That over shoes in blood he waded on the ground.

Thereat he roarèd for exceeding pain,
That to have heard, great horror would have bred;
And, scourging th' empty air with his long train,[23]
Through great impatience of his grievèd[24] head,
His gorgeous rider from her lofty stead[25]
Would have cast down, and trod in dirty mire,
Had not the giant soon her succourèd;
Who, all enrag'd with smart and frantic ire,
Came hurtling[26] in full fierce, and forc'd the knight retire.

1 High. 2 Knobs.
3 Force. 4 Steadfast.
5 Assault. 6 Wrath, vengeance.
7 Dismalness, terror. 8 Easily.
9 Embarrassed. 10 Disengage.
11 The truncated stump.
12 The Cimbri, of old time, inhabited the north of Europe—principally the portion which is now the kingdom of Denmark, and was called the Cimbric Chersonese. Jutland even at the present day is famous for its herds.
13 Natural.
14 Misfortune. 15 Withdraw.
16 Encountered. 17 Obstacle.
18 Hindrance. 19 None the more.
20 Misery. 21 Quelled.
22 Perceive.
23 Tail. 24 Wounded
25 Station, place. 26 Rushing.

The force, which wont in two to be disperst,
In one alone left hand [1] he now unites,
Which is through rage more strong than both were erst; [2]
With which his hideous club aloft he dights, [3]
And at his foe with furious rigour smites,
That strongest oak might seem to overthrow:
The stroke upon his shield so heavy lights,
That to the ground it doubleth him full low:—
What mortal wight could ever bear so monstrous blow?

And in his fall his shield, that cover'd was,
Did loose his veil by chance, and open flew;
The light whereof, that heaven's light did pass,
Such blazing brightness through the aïr threw,
That eye might not the same endure to view.
Which when the giant spied with staring eye,
He down let fall his arm, and soft withdrew
His weapon huge, that heavëd was on high
For to have slain the man that on the ground did lie.

And eke the fruitful-headed [4] beast, amaz'd
At flashing beams of that sunshiny shield,
Became stark blind, and all his senses daz'd, [5]
That down he tumbled on the dirty field,
And seem'd himself as conquerëd to yield.
Whom when his mistress proud perceiv'd to fall,
While yet his feeble feet for faintness reel'd,
Unto the giant loudly she gan call;
"O! help, Orgoglio; help, or else we perish all!"

At her so piteous cry was much amov'd
Her champion stout; and, for to aid his friend,
Again his wonted angry weapon prov'd: [6]
But all in vain; for he has read his end
In that bright shield, and all his forces spend
Themselves in vain: for, since that glancing sight,
He hath no pow'r to hurt nor to defend.
As, where th' Almighty's lightning brand does light,
It dims the dazëd eyne, and daunts the senses quite.

Whom when the Prince to battle new addrest,
And threat'ning high his dreadful stroke, did see,
His sparkling blade about his head he blest, [7]
And smote off quite his left leg by the knee,
That down he tumbled: as an aged tree,
High growing on the top of rocky clift, [8]
Whose heart-strings with keen steel nigh hewen be;
The mighty trunk, half rent with ragged rift,
Doth roll adown the rocks, and fall with fearful drift.

Or as a castle, rearëd high and round,
By subtle engines [9] and malicious sleight
Is underminëd from the lowest ground,
And, her foundation forc'd and feebled quite,
At last down falls; and with her heapëd height
Her hasty ruin does more heavy make,
And yields itself unto the victor's might:

1 In a single hand left to him.
2 Before.
3 Raises.
4 Many-headed.
5 Confused.
6 Tried.
7 Brandished.
8 Cliff.
9 Contrivances, stratagems.

Such was this giant's fall, that seem'd to shake
The steadfast globe of earth, as [10] it for fear did quake.

The knight then, lightly leaping to the prey,
With mortal steel him smote again so sore,
That headless his unwieldy body lay,
All wallow'd in his own foul bloody gore,
Which flowëd from his wounds in wondrous store.
But, soon as breath out of his breast did pass,
That huge great body which the giant bore
Was vanish'd quite; and of that monstrous mass
Was nothing left, but like an empty bladder was.

Whose grievous fall when false Duessa spied,
Her golden cup she cast unto the ground,
And crownëd mitre rudely threw aside;
Such piercing grief her stubborn heart did wound,
That she could not endure that doleful stound; [11]
But, leaving all behind her, fled away:
The light-foot squire her quickly turn'd around,
And, by hard means enforcing her to stay,
So brought unto his lord, as his deservëd prey.

The royal Virgin, which beheld from far,
In pensive plight and sad perplexity,
The whole achievement of this doubtful war,
Came running fast to greet his victory,
With sober gladness and mild modesty;
And, with sweet joyous cheer, [12] him thus bespake;
"Fair branch of nobless, flower of chivalry,
That with your worth the world amazëd make,
How shall I quite [13] the pains ye suffer for my sake?

"And you, [14] fresh bud of virtue springing fast,
Whom these sad eyes saw nigh unto death's door,
What hath poor virgin for such peril past
Wherewith you to reward? Accept therefore
My simple self, and service evermore.
And He that high does sit, and all things see
With equal eye, their merits to restore,
Behold what ye this day have done for me;
And, what I cannot quite, [13] requite with usury!

"But since the heav'ns, and your fair handëling, [15]
Have made you master of the field this day;
Your fortune master eke with governing, [16]
And, well begun, end all so well, I pray!
Nor let that wicked woman scape away;
For she it is that did my lord bethrall, [17]
My dearest lord, and deep in dungeon lay;
Where he his better days hath wasted all:
O hear, how piteous he to you for aid does call!"

Forthwith he gave in charge unto his squire
That scarlet whore to keepen carefully;
While he himself, with greedy great desire,
Into the castle enter'd forcibly,
Where living creature none he did espy:
Then gan he loudly through the house to call;
But no man car'd to answer to his cry:

10 As if.
11 Calamity.
12 Countenance.
13 Recompense.
14 The squire.
15 Conduct.
16 Master also your fortune by prudent use of your success.
17 Enslave.

There reign'd a solemn silence over all;
Nor voice was heard, nor wight was seen, in bow'r or hall!

At last, with creeping crooked pace, forth came
An old, old man, with beard as white as snow;
That on a staff his feeble steps did frame,
And guide his weary gait both to and fro;
For his eyesight him failëd long ago:
And on his arm a bunch of keys he bore,
The which, unusëd, rust did overgrow:
Those were the keys of every inner door;
But he could not them use, but kept them still in store.

But very úncouth sight was to behold
How he did fashion his untoward[1] pace;
For, as he forward mov'd his footing old,
So backward still was turn'd his wrinkled face:
Unlike to men, who ever, as they trace,[2]
Both feet and face one way are wont to lead.
This was the ancient keeper of that place,
And foster-father of the giant dead;
His name Ignaro[3] did his nature right aread.[4]

His rev'rend hairs and holy gravity
The knight much honour'd, as beseemëd well;
And gently ask'd where all the people be
Which in that stately building wont to dwell:
Who answer'd him full soft, *He could not tell.*
Again he ask'd, where that same knight was laid
Whom great Orgoglio, with his puíssance fell,
Had made his caitive thrall:[5] again he said,
He could not tell; nor ever other answer made.

Then askëd he, which way he in might pass:
He could not tell, again he answerëd.
Thereat the courteous knight displeasëd was,
And said; "Old sire, it seems thou hast not read[6]
How ill it sits with[7] that same silver head
In vain to mock, or mock'd in vain to be:
But if thou be, as thou art pórtrayëd
With Nature's pen, in age's grave degree,
Aread[8] in graver wise what I demand of thee."

His answer likewise was, *He could not tell.*
Whose senseless speech, and doted ignorance,
When as the noble Prince had markëd well,
He guess'd his nature by his countenance;[9]
And calm'd his wrath with goodly temperance.
Then, to him stepping, from his arm did reach
Those keys, and made himself free enterance.
Each door he open'd without any breach:
There was no bar to stop, nor foe him to impeach.[10]

There all within full rich array'd he found,
With royal arras, and resplendent gold,
And did with store of every thing abound,
That greatest prince's presence might behold.
But all the floor (too filthy to be told)
With blood of guiltless babes, and innocents true,
Which there were slain, as sheep out of the fold,
Defilëd was, that dreadful was to view;
And sacred[11] ashes over it were strowëd new.

And there beside of marble stone was built
An altar, carv'd with cunning imag'ry;
On which true Christians' blood was often spilt,
And holy martyrs often done to die,[12]
With cruel malice and strong tyranny:
Whose blessed sprites,[13] from underneath the stone,
To God for vengeance cried continually;
And with great grief were often heard to groan,
That hardest heart would bleed to hear their piteous moan.

Through every room he sought, and every bow'r;
But nowhere could he find that woeful thrall.[14]
At last he came unto an iron door,
That fast was lock'd; but key found not at all
Amongst that bunch to open it withal;
But in the same a little grate was pight,[15]
Through which he sent his voice, and loud did call
With all his pow'r, to weet[16] if living wight
Were housëd therewithin, whom he enlargen[17] might.

Therewith an hollow, dreary, murmuring voice
These piteous plaints and dolours did resound;
"O! who is that which brings me happy choice
Of death, that here lie dying every stound,[18]
Yet live perforce in baleful darkness bound?
For now three moons have changëd thrice their hue,
And have been thrice hid underneath the ground,
Since I the heaven's cheerful face did view:
O, welcome, thou that dost of death bring tidings true!"

Which when that champion heard, with piercing point
Of pity dear his heart was thrillëd sore;
And trembling horror ran through every joint,
For ruth[19] of gentle knight so foul forlore:[20]
Which shaking off, he rent that iron door
With furious force and indignation fell;
Where enter'd in, his foot could find no floor,
But all a deep descent, as dark as hell,
That breathëd forth a filthy baneful smell.

But neither darkness foul, nor filthy bands,
Nor noyous[21] smell, his purpose could withhold
(Entire affection hateth nicer hands[22]),
But that with constant zeal and courage bold,
After long pains and labours manifold,
He found the means that prisoner up to rear;
Whose feeble thighs, unable to uphold
His pinëd corse,[23] him scarce to light could bear;
A rueful spectacle of death and ghastly drear.[24]

His sad dull eyes, deep sunk in hollow pits,
Could not endure th' unwonted sun to view;
His bare thin cheeks, for want of better bits,[25]
And empty sides deceivëd[26] of their due,

1 Awkward, reluctant. 2 Walk.
3 Ignorance. 4 Describe.
5 Captive slave. 6 Learned.
7 Becomes. 8 Declare.
9 Demeanour.
10 From French, "empêcher," to prevent, hinder.
11 Accursed. 12 Slain.
13 Spirits. 14 Captive; the Redcross Knight.
15 Fixed. 16 Know.
17 Liberate. 18 Moment.
19 Pity. 20 Forlorn, undone.
21 Loathsome.
22 Earnest resolution, or all-absorbing love, does not halt for fastidiousness or delicacy.
23 Wasted body. 24 Wretchedness.
25 Food. 26 Defrauded.

Could make a stony heart his hap to rue;[1]
His raw-bone arms, whose mighty brawnëd bow'rs[2]
Were wont to rive steel plates, and helmets hew,
Were clean consum'd; and all his vital pow'rs
Decay'd; and all his flesh shrunk up like wither'd flow'rs.

Whom when his lady saw, to him she ran
With hasty joy: to see him made her glad,
And sad to view his visage pale and wan;
Who erst[3] in flow'rs of freshest youth was clad.
Then, when her well of tears she wasted[4] had,
She said; "Ah, dearest Lord! what evil star
On you hath frown'd, and pour'd his influence bad,
That of yourself ye thus berobbëd[5] are,
And this misseeming hue your manly looks doth mar?

"But welcome now, my lord, in weal or woe,
Whose presence I have lack'd too long a day:
And fie on Fortune, mine avowëd foe,
Whose wrathful wreaks[6] themselves do now allay,
And for these wrongs shall treble penance pay
Of treble good: good grows of evil's prefe."[7]
The cheerless man, whom sorrow did dismay,
Had no delight to treaten of his grief;
His long-endurëd famine needed more relief.

"Fair Lady," then said that victorious knight,
"The things that grievous were to do or bear,
Them to renew, I wot, breeds no delight;
Best music breeds dislike in loathing ear:
But th' only good, that grows of passëd fear,
Is to be wise, and ware of like again.
This day's ensample hath this lesson dear
Deep written in my heart with iron pen,
That bliss may not abide in state of mortal men.

"Henceforth, Sir Knight, take to you wonted strength,
And master these mishaps with patient might:
Lo! where your foe lies stretch'd in monstrous length;
And lo! that wicked woman in your sight,
The root of all your care and wretched plight,
Now in your pow'r, to let[8] her live, or die."
"To do[8] her die," quoth Una, "were despite,
And shame t' avenge so weak an enemy;
But spoil her of her scarlet robe, and let her fly."

So, as she bade, that witch they disarray'd,
And robb'd of royal robes, and purple pall,
And ornaments that richly were display'd;
Nor sparëd they to strip her naked all.
Then, when they had despoil'd her tire and caul,[9]
Such as she was, their eyes might her behold,
That her misshapëd parts did them appal;
A loathly, wrinkled hag, ill-favour'd, old,
Whose secret filth good manners biddeth not be told.

Her crafty head was altogether bald,
And, as in hate of honourable eld,[10]
Was overgrown with scurf and filthy scald;[11]
Her teeth out of her rotten gums were fell'd,[12]
And her sour breath abominably smell'd;
Her driëd dugs, like bladders lacking wind,
Hung down, and filthy matter from them well'd;
Her wrizzled[13] skin, as rough as maple rind,
So scabby was, that would have loath'd all woman kind.

Her nether parts, the shame of all her kind,
My chaster Muse for shame doth blush to write:
But at her rump she growing had behind
A fox's tail, with dung all foully dight:
And eke her feet most monstrous were in sight;[14]
For one of them was like an eagle's claw,
With griping talons arm'd to greedy fight;
The other like a bear's uneven paw:
More ugly shape yet never living creature saw.

Which when the knights beheld, amaz'd they were,
And wonder'd at so foul deformëd wight.
"Such, then," said Una, "as she seemeth here,
Such is the face of Falsehood; such the sight
Of foul Duessa, when her borrow'd light
Is laid away, and counterfeasance[15] known."
Thus when they had the witch disrobëd quite,
And all her filthy feature open shown,
They let her go at will, and wander ways unknown.

She, flying fast from heaven's hated face,
And from the world that her discover'd wide,
Fled to the wasteful wilderness apace,
From living eyes her open shame to hide;
And lurk'd in rocks and caves, long unespied.
But that fair crew[16] of knights, and Una fair,
Did in that castle afterwards abide,
To rest themselves, and weary powers repair:
Where store they found of all that dainty was and rare.

CANTO IX.

His loves and lineage Arthur tells:
The knights knit friendly bands:
Sir Trevisan flies from Despair,
Whom Redcross Knight withstands.

O! GOODLY golden chain, wherewith y-fere[17]
The virtues linkëd are in lovely wise;
And noble minds of yore alliëd were
In brave pursuit of chivalrous emprise,
That none did other's safëty despise,
Nor aid envy[18] to him in need that stands;
But friendly each did other's praise devise

1 To pity his fate.
2 Muscles; so poetically entitled from their rounded or arched appearance.
3 Before.
4 Exhausted, completely shed.
5 Robbed.
6 Revenges.
7 Proof.
8 Make.
9 Tiara and head-dress; perhaps, as both words are used for clothing or covering generally, the phrase has here the force of "utterly."
10 Old age.
11 Scab.
12 Fallen.
13 Wrinkled.
14 To see.
15 Counterfeiting.
16 Company.
17 Together.
18 Begrudge.

How to advance with favourable hands,
As this good Prince redeem'd the Redcross Knight from bands.[1]

Who when their powers, impair'd through labour long,
With due repast they had recurëd[2] well,
And that weak captive wight now waxëd strong,
Them list no longer there at leisure dwell,
But forward fare, as their adventures fell:
But, ere they parted, Una fair besought
That stranger knight his name and nation tell;
Lest so great good, as he for her had wrought,
Should die unknown, and buried be in thankless thought.

"Fair Virgin," said the Prince, "ye me require
A thing without the compass of my wit:
For both the lineage, and the certain sire,
From which I sprung, from me are hidden yet.
For all so soon as life did me admit
Into this world, and shewëd heaven's light,
From mother's pap I taken was unfit,
And straight deliver'd to a Faery knight,
To be upbrought in gentle thews[3] and martial might.

"Unto old Timon[4] he me brought belive;[5]
Old Timon, who in youthly years hath been
In warlike feats th' expertest man alive,
And is the wisest now on earth, I ween:
His dwelling is, low in a valley green,
Under the foot of Rauran[6] mossy hoar,
From whence the river Dee, as silver clean,
His tumbling billows rolls with gentle roar;
There all my days he train'd me up in virtuous lore.

"Thither the great magician Merlin came,
As was his use, oft-times to visit me;
For he had charge my discipline to frame,
And tutor's noriture[7] to oversee.
Him oft and oft I ask'd in privity,
Of what loins and what lineage I did spring.
Whose answer bade me still assurëd be
That I was son and heir unto a king,
As time in her just term the truth to light should bring."

"Well worthy imp,"[8] said then the Lady gent,[9]
"And pupil fit for such a tutor's hand!
But what adventure, or what high intent,
Hath brought you hither into Faery Land,
Aread,[10] Prince Arthur, crown of martial band?"
"Full hard it is," quoth he, "to read aright
The course of heavenly cause, or understand
The secret meaning of th' Eternal Might,
That rules men's ways, and rules the thoughts of living wight.

"For whether He, through fatal deep foresight,
Me hither sent, for cause to me unguess'd;
Or that fresh bleeding wound which day and night
Whilóm[11] doth rankle in my riven breast,
With forcëd fury following his behest,
Me hither brought by ways yet never found;
You to have help'd I hold myself yet blest."
"Ah! courteous Knight," quoth she, "what secret wound
Could ever find to grieve the gentlest heart on ground?"[12]

"Dear Dame," quoth he, "you sleeping sparks awake,
Which, troubled once, into huge flames will grow;
Nor ever will their fervent fury slake,
Till living moisture into smoke do flow,
And wasted life do lie in ashes low.
Yet sithens[13] silence lesseneth not my fire,—
But, told, it flames; and, hidden, it does glow,—
I will reveal what ye so much desire:
Ah! Love, lay down thy bow, the while I may respire.

"It was in freshest flow'r of youthly years,
When courage first does creep in manly chest;
Then first that coal of kindly[14] heat appears
To kindle love in ev'ry living breast:
But me had warn'd old Timon's wise behest,
Those creeping flames by reason to subdue,
Before their rage grew to so great unrest,
As miserable lovers use to rue,
Which still wax old in woe, while woe still waxeth new.

"That idle name of love, and lover's life,
As loss of time, and virtue's enemy,
I ever scorn'd, and joy'd to stir up strife
In middest of their mournful tragedy;
Ay wont to laugh when them I heard to cry,
And blow the fire which them to ashes brent:[15]
Their god himself, griev'd at my liberty,
Shot many a dart at me with fierce intent;
But I them warded all with wary government.[16]

"But all in vain; no fort can be so strong,
Nor fleshly breast can armëd be so sound,
But will at last be won with battery long,
Or unawares at disadvantage found:
Nothing is sure that grows on earthly ground.
And who most trusts in arm of fleshly might,
And boasts in beauty's chain not to be bound,
Doth soonest fall in disadventurous fight,
And yields his caitive[17] neck to victor's most despite.[18]

"Ensample make of him, your hapless joy,
And of myself, now mated[19] as ye see;
Whose prouder vaunt that proud avenging boy
Did soon pluck down, and curb'd my liberty.
For on a day, prick'd[20] forth with jollity
Of looser life and heat of hardiment,[21]

1 Captivity.
2 Restored, recruited.
3 Noble qualities.
4 Honour—from the Greek, τιμαω, I honour.
5 Immediately.
6 "Rauran Vaur" is a hill in Merionethshire.
7 Nurture, training; French, "nourriture."
8 Youth.
9 Noble, courteous.
10 Declare.
11 Now for a long time.
12 On earth.
13 Since.
14 Natural.
15 Burned.
16 Management.
17 Captive.
18 Utmost severity.
19 Overmatched.
20 Spurred.
21 Boldness.

Ranging the forest wide on courser free,
The fields, the floods, the heav'ns, with one consent,
Did seem to laugh on me, and favour mine intent.

"Forwearied with my sports, I did alight
From lofty steed, and down to sleep me laid:
The verdant grass my couch did goodly dight,[1]
And pillow was my helmet fair display'd:
While every sense the humour sweet embay'd,[2]
And slumb'ring soft my heart did steal away,
Me seemëd, by my side a royal maid
Her dainty limbs full softly down did lay;
So fair a creature yet saw never sunny day.

"Most goodly glee[3] and lovely blandishment
She to me made, and bade me love her dear;
For dearly sure her love was to me bent,
As, when just time expirëd, should appear.
But, whether dreams delude, or true it were,
Was never heart so ravish'd with delight,
Nor living man like words did ever hear,
As she to me deliver'd all that night;
And at her parting said, she Queen of Faeries hight.

"When I awoke, and found her place devoid,[4]
And naught but pressëd grass where she had lien,[5]
I sorrow'd all so much as erst[6] I joy'd,
And washëd all her place with wat'ry eyne.
From that day forth I lov'd that face divine;
From that day forth I cast in careful mind
To seek her out with labour and long tine,[7]
And never vow'd to rest till her I find:
Nine months I seek in vain, yet n'ill[8] that vow unbind."

Thus as he spake, his visage waxëd pale,
And change of hue great passion did bewray;
Yet still he strove to cloak his inward bale,[9]
And hide the smoke that did his fire display;
Till gentle Una thus to him gan say;
"O happy Queen of Faeries, that hast found,
Mongst many, one that with his prowess may
Defend thine honour, and thy foes confound!
True loves are often sown, but seldom grow on ground."

"Thine, O! then," said the gentle Redcross Knight,
"Next to that lady's love, shall be the place,
O fairest Virgin, full of heav'nly light,
Whose wondrous faith, exceeding earthly race,
Was firmest fix'd in mine extremest case.
And you, my lord, the patron of my life,
Of that great Queen may well gain worthy grace;
For only worthy you through prowess' prefe,[10]
If living man might worthy be, to be her lefe."[11]

So diversely discoursing of their loves,
The golden sun his glist'ning head gan shew;
And sad remembrance now the Prince amoves
With fresh desire his voyage to pursue:
Als'[12] Una yearn'd her travel to renew.

Then those two knights, fast friendship for to bind,
And love establish each to other true,
Gave goodly gifts, the signs of grateful mind,
And eke, as pledges firm, right hands together join'd.

Prince Arthur gave a box of diamonds sure,
Embow'd[13] with gold and gorgeous ornament,
Wherein were clos'd few drops of liquor pure,
Of wondrous worth, and virtue excellent,
That any wound could heal incontinent.[14]
Which to requite, the Redcross Knight him gave
A book, wherein his Saviour's Testament
Was writ with golden letters rich and brave;
A work of wondrous grace, and able souls to save.

Thus be they parted; Arthur on his way
To seek his love, and th' other for to fight
With Una's foe, that all her realms did prey.[15]
But she, now weighing the decayëd plight
And shrunken sinews of her chosen Knight,
Would not a while her forward course pursue,
Nor bring him forth in face of dreadful fight,
Till he recover'd had his former hue:
For him to be yet weak and weary well she knew.

So as they travell'd, lo! they gan espy
An armëd knight toward them gallop fast,
That seemëd from some fearëd foe to fly,
Or other grisly thing, that him aghast.[16]
Still, as he fled, his eye was backward cast,
As if his fear[17] still follow'd him behind:
Als' flew his steed, as he his bands had brast,[18]
And with his wingëd heels did tread the wind,
As he had been a foal of Pegasus his kind.

Nigh as he drew, they might perceive his head
To be unarm'd, and curl'd uncombëd hairs
Upstaring stiff, dismay'd with uncouth dread:
Nor drop of blood in all his face appears,
Nor life in limb; and, to increase his fears,
In foul reproach of knighthood's fair degree,
About his neck a hempen rope he wears,
That with his glist'ning arms does ill agree:
But he of rope or arms has now no memory.

The Redcross Knight toward him crossëd fast,
To weet[19] what mister wight[20] was so dismay'd:
There him he finds all senseless and aghast,[16]
That of himself he seem'd to be afraid;
Whom hardly he from flying forward stay'd,
Till he these words to him deliver might;
"Sir Knight, aread[21] who hath ye thus array'd,
And eke from whom make ye this hasty flight?
For never knight I saw in such misseeming plight."

He answer'd naught at all; but adding new
Fear to his first amazement, staring wide
With stony eyes and heartless[22] hollow hue,
Astonish'd stood, as one that had espied
Infernal Furies with their chains untied.
Him yet again, and yet again, bespake
The gentle Knight; who naught to him replied;

1 Prepare, deck. 2 Bathed.
3 Delight. 4 Empty.
5 Lain. 6 Before.
7 Otherwise "teen" or "teene;" anxiety.
8 Will not. 9 Anguish.
10 Proof of courage. 11 Love.

12 Also. 13 Arched over, embossed.
14 Immediately. 15 Ravage.
16 Terrified. 17 The cause of his fear.
18 Burst. 19 Learn.
20 Manner of man. 21 Declare.
22 Timid, fearful.

But, trembling every joint, did inly quake,
And falt'ring tongue at last these words seem'd forth to shake;

"For God's dear love, Sir Knight, do me not stay;[1]
For lo! he comes, he comes fast after me!"
Eft,[2] looking back, would fain have run away;
But he him forc'd to stay, and tellen free
The secret cause of his perplexity:
Yet nathemore[3] by his bold hearty speech
Could his blood-frozen heart embolden'd be,
But through his boldness rather fear did reach;
Yet forc'd, at last he made through silence sudden breach:

"And am I now in safety sure," quoth he,
"From him that would have forcĕd me to die?
And is the point of death now turn'd from me,
That I may tell this hapless history?"
"Fear naught," quoth he, "no danger now is nigh."
"Then shall I you recount a rueful case,"
Said he, "the which with this unlucky eye
I late beheld; and, had not greater grace
Me reft from it, had been partaker of the place.[4]

"I lately chanc'd (would I had never chanc'd!)
With a fair knight to keepen company,
Sir Terwin hight, that well himself advanc'd
In all affairs, and was both bold and free;
But not so happy as might happy be:
He lov'd, as was his lot, a lady gent,[5]
That him again lov'd i the least degree;
For she was proud, and of too high intent,[6]
And joy'd to see her lover anguish and lament:

"From whom returning, sad and comfortless,
As on the way together we did fare,
We met that villain (God from him me bless![7])
That cursĕd wight, from whom I scap'd whilére,[8]
A man of hell, that calls himself Despair:
Who first us greets, and after fair areads[9]
Of tidings strange, and of adventures rare:
So creeping close, as snake in hidden weeds,
Inquireth of our states, and of our knightly deeds.

"Which when he knew, and felt our feeble hearts,
Emboss'd with bale[10] and bitter biting grief,
Which love had lancĕd with his deadly darts;
With wounding words, and terms of foul reprefe,[11]
He pluck'd from us all hope of due relief,
That erst[12] us held in love of ling'ring life:
Then hopeless, heartless, gan the cunning thief
Persuade us die, to stint all farther strife;
To me he lent this rope, to him a rusty knife:

"With which sad instrument of hasty death,
That woeful lover, loathing longer light,
A wide way made to let forth living breath.
But I, more fearful or more lucky wight,
Dismay'd with that deformĕd dismal sight,
Fled fast away, half dead with dying fear;
Nor yet assur'd of life by you, Sir Knight,
Whose like infirmity like chance may bear:
But God you never let his charmĕd speeches hear!"

"How may a man," said he, "with idle speech
Be won to spoil the castle of his health?"
"I wot,"[13] quoth he, "whom trial late did teach,
That like would not for all this worldĕ's wealth:
His subtle tongue, like dropping honey, mel'th[14]
Into the heart, and searcheth every vein;
That, ere one be aware, by secret stealth
His pow'r is reft,[15] and weakness doth remain.
O never, Sir, desire to try his guileful train!"

"Certes," said he, "hence shall I never rest,
Till I that traitor's art have heard and tried:
And you, Sir Knight, whose name might I request,
Of grace do me unto his cabin guide."
"I, that hight Trevisan," quoth he, "will ride,
Against my liking, back to do you grace:
But not for gold nor glee will I abide
By you, when ye arrive in that same place;
For lever[16] had I die than see his deadly face."

Ere long they come where that same wicked wight
His dwelling has, low in a hollow cave,
Far underneath a craggy cliff y-pight,[17]
Dark, doleful, dreary, like a greedy grave,
That still for carrion carcases doth crave:
On top whereof ay dwelt the ghastly owl,
Shrieking his baleful note, which ever drave
Far from that haunt all other cheerful fowl;
And all about it wand'ring ghosts did wail and howl:

And, all about, old stocks and stubs of trees,
Whereon nor fruit nor leaf was ever seen,
Did hang upon the ragged rocky knees;[18]
On which had many wretches hangĕd been,
Whose carcases were scatter'd on the green,
And thrown about the cliffs. Arrivĕd there,
That bare-head knight, for dread and doleful teen,[19]
Would fain have fled, nor durst approachen near;
But th' other forc'd him stay, and comforted in fear.

That darksome cave they enter, where they find
That cursĕd man, low sitting on the ground,
Musing full sadly in his sullen mind:
His greasy locks, long growen and unbound,
Disorder'd hung about his shoulders round,
And hid his face; through which his hollow eyne
Look'd deadly dull, and starĕd as astound';[20]
His raw-bone cheeks, through penury and pine,[21]
Were shrunk into his jaws, as[22] he did never dine.

His garment, naught but many ragged clouts,
With thorns together pinn'd and patchĕd was,
The which his naked sides he wrapt abouts:
And him beside there lay upon the grass
A dreary corse, whose life away did pass,

1 Make me not linger.
2 Then.
3 None the more.
4 Had shared the same fate—lain on the same place—as the companion whose suicide he is about to describe.
5 Noble.
6 Mind.
7 Deliver.
8 A short time ago.
9 Informs.
10 Overwhelmed with misery.
11 Reproach.
12 Formerly.
13 Know.
14 Melteth.
15 Taken away.
16 Rather.
17 Placed, fixed.
18 Projections.
19 Trouble.
20 Amazed, stupefied.
21 Decay.
22 As if.

All wallow'd in his own yet lukewarm blood,
That from his wound yet wellëd fresh, alas !
In which a rusty knife fast fixëd stood,
And made an open passage for the gushing flood.

Which piteous spectacle, approving true
The woeful tale that Trevisan had told,
When as the gentle Redcross Knight did view,
With fiery zeal he bürn'd in courage bold
Him to avenge, before his blood were cold ;
And to the villain said ; "Thou damnëd wight,
The author of this fact we here behold,
What justice can but judge against thee right,
With thine own blood to price[1] his blood, here shed in sight ?"

"What frantic fit," quoth he,[2] "hath thus distraught
Thee, foolish man, so rash a doom[3] to give ?
What justice ever other judgment taught,
But he should die, who merits not to live ?
None else to death this man despairing drive
But his own guilty mind, deserving death.
Is then unjust to each his due to give ?
Or let him die, that loatheth living breath ?
Or let him die at ease, that liveth here unneth ?[4]

"Who travels by the weary wand'ring way,
To come unto his wishëd home in haste,
And meets a flood, that doth his passage stay ;
Is not great grace to help him over past,
Or free his feet that in the mire stick fast ?
Most envious man, that grieves at neighbour's good ;
And fond,[5] that joyest in the woe thou hast ;
Why wilt not let him pass, that long hath stood
Upon the bank, yet wilt thyself not pass the flood ?

"He there does now enjoy eternal rest
And happy ease, which thou dost want and crave,
And farther from it daily wanderest :
What if some little pain the passage have,
That makes frail flesh to fear the bitter wave ;
Is not short pain well borne, that brings long ease,
And lays the soul to sleep in quiet grave ?
Sleep after toil, port after stormy seas,
Ease after war, death after life, does greatly please."

The Knight much wonder'd at his sudden wit,
And said ; "The term of life is limited,
Nor may a man prolong nor shorten it :
The soldier may not move from watchful stead,[6]
Nor leave his stand until his captain bid."
"Who life did limit by almighty doom,"[7]
Quoth he, "knows best the terms establishëd ;
And he, that points[8] the sentinel his room,[9]
Doth license him depart at sound of morning drum.

"Is not His deed, whatever thing is done
In heav'n and earth ? Did not He all create
To die again ? All ends, that was begun :
Their times in His eternal book of fate
Are written sure, and have their certain date.

Who then can strive with strong necessity,
That holds the world in his still changing state ;
Or shun the death ordain'd by destiny ?
When hour of death is come, let none ask whence nor why.

"The longer life, I wot,[10] the greater sin ;
The greater sin, the greater punishment :
All those great battles, which thou boasts to win
Through strife, and bloodshed, and avengëment,
Now prais'd, hereafter dear thou shalt repent :
For life must life, and blood must blood, repay.
Is not enough thy evil life forespent ?[11]
For he that once hath missëd the right way,
The farther he doth go, the farther he doth stray;

"Then do no farther go, no farther stray ;
But here lie down, and to thy rest betake,
Th' ill to prevent, that life ensuen[12] may.
For what hath life, that may it lovëd make,
And gives not rather cause it to forsake ?
Fear, sickness, age, loss, labour, sorrow, strife,
Pain, hunger, cold that makes the heart to quake;
And ever fickle Fortune rageth rife ;
All which, and thousands more, do make a loathsome life.

"Thou, wretched man, of death hast greatest need,
If in true balance thou wilt weigh thy state ;
For never knight that darëd warlike deed
More luckless disadventures[13] did amate :[14]
Witness the dungeon deep, wherein of late
Thy life shut up for death so oft did call ;
And though good luck prolongëd hath thy date,
Yet death then would the like mishaps forestall,
Into the which hereafter thou may'st happen fall.

"Why then dost thou, O man of sin, desire
To draw thy days forth to their last degree ?
Is not the measure of thy sinful hire
High heapëd up with huge iniquity,
Against the day of wrath, to burden thee ?
Is not enough, that to this Lady mild
Thou falsëd[15] hast thy faith with perjury,
And sold thyself to serve Duessa vild,[16]
With whom in all abuse thou hast thyself defil'd ?

"Is not he just, that all this doth behold
From highest heav'n, and bears an equal eye ?
Shall He thy sins up in His knowledge fold,
And guilty be of thine impiety ?
Is not His law, 'Let every sinner die,'
'Die shall all flesh ?' What then must needs be done ?
Is it not better to die willingly,
Than linger till the glass be all out run ?
Death is the end of woes : die soon, O Faery's son."

The Knight was much enmovëd with his speech,
That as a sword's point through his heart did pierce,
And in his conscience made a secret breach,
Well knowing true all that he did rehearse,
And to his fresh remembrance did reverse[17]

1 Pay for. 2 Despair. 3 Judgment. 4 With difficulty. 5 Foolish. 6 Station. 7 Decree. 8 Appoints. 9 Place.

10 Deem. 11 Already spent. 12 Follow. 13 Misfortunes. 14 Subdue, abase. 15 Violated. 16 Vile. 17 Recall.

The ugly view of his deformëd crimes;
That all his manly pow'rs it did disperse,
As[1] he were charmëd with enchanted rhymes;
That oftentimes he quak'd, and fainted oftentimes.

In which amazement when the miscreant
Perceivëd him to waver weak and frail,
While trembling horror did his conscience daunt,
And hellish anguish did his soul assail;
To drive him to despair, and quite to quail,
He shew'd him, painted in a table[2] plain,
The damnëd ghosts that do in torments wail,
And thousand fiends, that do[3] them endless pain
With fire and brimstone, which for ever shall remain.

The sight whereof so throughly him dismay'd,
That naught but death before his eyes he saw,
And ever burning wrath before him laid,
By righteous sentence of th' Almighty's law.
Then gan the villain him to overcraw,[4]
And brought unto him swords, ropes, poison, fire,
And all that might him to perdition draw;
And bade him choose, what death he would desire:
For death was due to him, that had provok'd God's ire.

But when as none of them he saw him take,
He to him raught[5] a dagger sharp and keen,
And gave it him in hand: his hand did quake
And tremble like a leaf of aspen green,
And troubled blood through his pale face was seen
To come and go, with tidings from the heart,
As it a running messenger had been.
At last, resolv'd to work his final smart,[6]
He lifted up his hand, that back again did start.

Which when as Una saw, through ev'ry vein
The curdled cold ran to her well of life,[7]
As in a swoon: but, soon reliv'd[8] again,
Out of his hand she snatch'd the cursëd knife,
And threw it to the ground, enragëd rife,[9]
And to him said; "Fy, fy, faint-hearted Knight!
What meanest thou by this reproachful[10] strife?
Is this the battle, which thou vaunt'st to fight
With that fire-mouthëd dragon, horrible and bright?

"Come, come away, frail, feeble, fleshly wight!
Nor let vain words bewitch thy manly heart,
Nor devilish thoughts dismay thy constant sprite:
In heav'nly mercies hast thou not a part?
Why should'st thou then despair, that chosen art?
Where justice grows, there grows eke greater grace,
The which doth quench the brand of hellish smart,
And that accurs'd handwriting doth deface:
Arise, sir Knight; arise, and leave this cursëd place."

So up he rose, and thence amounted[11] straight.
Which when the carl beheld, and saw his guest
Would safe depart, for all his subtle sleight,
He chose a halter from among the rest,
And with it hung himself, unbid, unblest.
But death he could not work himself thereby;
For thousand times he so himself had drest,[12]
Yet natheless it could not do him die,[13]
Till he should die his last, that is, eternally.

CANTO X.

Her faithful Knight fair Una brings
To house of Holiness;
Where he is taught repentance, and
The way to heav'nly bliss.

What man is he, that boasts of fleshly might
And vain assurance of mortality,
Which, all so soon as it doth come to fight
Against spiritual foes, yields by and by,[14]
Or from the field most cowardly doth fly!
Nor let the man ascribe it to his skill,
That thorough grace hath gainëd victory:
If any strength we have, it is to ill;
But all the good is God's, both power and eke will.

By that which lately happen'd, Una saw
That this her Knight was feeble and too faint;
And all his sinews waxen weak and raw,
Through long imprisonment, and hard constraint,
Which he endurëd in his late restraint,
That yet he was unfit for bloody fight.
Therefore, to cherish him with diets daint,[15]
She cast[16] to bring him where he cheeren[17] might,
Till he recover'd had his late decayëd plight.

There was an ancient house not far away,
Renown'd throughout the world for sacred lore
And pure unspotted life: so well, they say,
It govern'd was, and guided evermore,
Through wisdom of a matron grave and hoar;
Whose only joy was to relieve the needs
Of wretched souls, and help the helpless poor:
All night she spent in bidding of her beads,
And all the day in doing good and godly deeds.

Dame Cælia[18] men did her call, as thought
From heav'n to come, or thither to arise;
The mother of three daughters, well upbrought
In goodly thews[19] and godly exercise:
The eldest two, most sober, chaste, and wise,
Fidelia[20] and Speranza,[21] virgins were;
Though spous'd, yet wanting wedlock's solemnise;[22]
But fair Charissa[23] to a lovely fere[24]
Was linkëd, and by him had many pledges dear.

Arrivëd there, the door they find fast lock'd;
For it was warely[25] watchëd night and day,

1 As if. 2 Picture. 3 Cause. 4 Triumph over. 5 Reached. 6 Pain, mischief. 7 Heart. 8 Revived. 9 Greatly. 10 Disgraceful. 11 Departed. 12 He had made the same attempt.

13 Kill him. 14 Speedily. 15 Delicate, dainty. 16 Thought, resolved. 17 Be entertained, nourished. 18 Heavenly. 19 Qualities. 20 Faith. 21 Hope. 22 Solemnization. 23 Charity. 24 Companion, husband. 25 Carefully.

For fear of many foes; but, when they knock'd,
The porter open'd unto them straightway.
He was an aged sire, all hoary gray,
With looks full lowly cast, and gait full slow,
Wont on a staff his feeble steps to stay,
Hight Humiltá.[1] They pass in, stooping low;
For strait and narrow was the way which he did show.

Each goodly thing is hardest to begin;
But, enter'd in, a spacious court they see,
Both plain and pleasant to be walkëd in;
Where them does meet a franklin[2] fair and free,
And entertains with comely courteous glee;
His name was Zeal, that him right well became:
For in his speeches and behaviour he
Did labour lively to express the same,
And gladly did them guide, till to the hall they came.

There fairly them receives a gentle squire,
Of mild demeanour and rare courtesy,
Right cleanly clad in comely sad[3] attire:
In word and deed that show'd great modesty,
And knew his good[4] to all of each degree;
Hight Reverence: He them with speeches meet
Does fair entreat[5]; no courting nicety,[6]
But simple, true, and eke unfeignëd sweet,
As might become a squire so great persóns to greet.

And afterwards them to his Dame he leads,
That aged dame, the Lady of the place,
Who all this while was busy at her beads;
Which done, she up arose with seemly grace,
And toward them full matronly did pace.
Where, when that fairest Una she beheld,
Whom well she knew to spring from heav'nly race,
Her heart with joy unwonted inly swell'd,
As feeling wondrous comfort in her weaker eld:[7]

And, her embracing, said; "O happy earth,
Whereon thy innocent feet do ever tread!
Most virtuous Virgin, born of heav'nly birth,
That, to redeem thy woeful parents' head
From tyrant's rage and ever-dying dread,[8]
Hast wander'd through the world now long a day,
Yet ceasest not thy weary soles to lead;
What grace hath thee now hither brought this way?
Or do thy feeble feet unweeting[9] hither stray?

"Strange thing it is an errant knight to see
Here in this place; or any other wight,
That hither turns his steps: so few there be
That choose the narrow path, or seek the right!
All keep the broad highway, and take delight
With many rather for to go astray,
And be partakers of their evil plight,
Than with a few to walk the rightest way:
O! foolish men, why haste ye to your own decay?"

"Thy self to see, and tirëd limbs to rest,
O Matron sage," quoth she, "I hither came;
And this good Knight his way with me addrest,
Led with thy praises, and broad-blazëd fame,
That up to heav'n is blown." The ancient Dame
Him goodly greeted in her modest guise,
And entertain'd them both, as best became,
With all the court'sies that she could devise,
Nor wanted aught to shew her bounteous or wise.

Thus as they gan of sundry things devise,[10]
Lo! two most goodly virgins came in place,[11]
Y-linkëd arm in arm in lovely[12] wise;
With countenance demure, and modest grace,
They number'd even steps and equal pace:
Of which the eldest, that Fidelia hight,
Like sunny beams threw from her crystal face,
That could have daz'd[13] the rash beholder's sight,
And round about her head did shine like heaven's light.

She was arrayëd all in lily white,
And in her right hand bore a cup of gold,
With wine and water fill'd up to the height,[14]
In which a serpent did himself enfold,
That horror made to all that did behold;
But she no whit did change her constant mood:
And in her other hand she fast did hold
A book, that was both sign'd and seal'd with blood;[15]
Wherein dark things were writ, hard to be understood.

Her younger sister, that Speranza hight,
Was clad in blue, that her beseemëd well;
Not all so cheerful seemëd she of sight
As was her sister; whether dread did dwell,
Or anguish, in her heart, is hard to tell:
Upon her arm a silver anchor lay,
Whereon she leanëd ever, as befell;
And ever up to heav'n, as she did pray,
Her steadfast eyes were bent, nor swervëd other way.

They, seeing Una, toward her gan wend,
Who them encounters with like courtesy;
Many kind speeches they between them spend,
And greatly joy each other for to see:
Then to the Knight with shamefac'd modesty
They turn themselves, at Una's meek request,
And him salute with well beseeming glee;[16]
Who fair them quites,[17] as him beseemëd[18] best,
And goodly gan discourse of many a noble gest.[19]

Then Una thus; "But she, your sister dear,
The dear Charissa, where is she become?

1 Humility.
2 Gentleman. See note 34, page 20, for the precise meaning of the word. 3 Sober.
4 Knew his proper demeanour and conduct.
5 Entertain.
6 No trifling fastidiousness of a courtier.
7 Age. 8 Constant fear of death.
9 Unknowing, by mere chance.
10 Talk, tell. 11 Entered, drew near.
12 Loving. 13 Dazzled.

14 The sacramental cup, filled with wine and water to signify the mingled blood and water which streamed from the pierced side of the Saviour on the cross; the serpent coiled in the cup is probably intended to denote the conquest or destruction of the power of Satan through Christ's suffering.
15 The New Testament; or perhaps more especially the Apocalypse. 16 Pleasure.
17 Salutes in return. 18 Became.
19 Action, history.

Or wants she health, or busy is elsewhere?"
"Ah! no," said they, "but forth she may not come;
For she of late is lighten'd of her womb,
And hath increas'd the world with one son more,
That her to see should be but troublesome."
"Indeed," quoth she, "that should her trouble sore;
But thank'd be God, and her increase so evermore!"

Then said the aged Cælia; "Dear Dame,
And you, good Sir, I wot[1] that of your toil
And labours long, through which ye hither came,
Ye both forwearied be: therefore a while
I read[2] you rest, and to your bow'rs recoil."[3]
Then callëd she a groom, that forth him led
Into a goodly lodge, and gan despoil
Of puissant arms, and laid in easy bed:
His name was Meek Obedience rightfully aread.[4]

Now when their weary limbs with kindly rest,
And bodies were refresh'd with due repast,
Fair Una gan Fidelia fair request
To have her Knight into her schoolhouse plac'd,
That of her heav'nly learning he might taste,
And hear the wisdom of her words divine.
She granted, and that Knight so much agrac'd,[5]
That she him taught celestial discipline,
And open'd his dull eyes, that light might in them shine.

And that her sacred book, with blood y-writ,
That none could read except she did them teach,
She unto him disclosëd every whit;
And heav'nly documents[6] thereout did preach,
That weaker wit of man could never reach;
Of God; of Grace; of Justice; of Free-will;
That wonder was to hear her goodly speech:
For she was able with her words to kill,
And raise again to life the heart that she did thrill.[7]

And, when she list pour out her larger sprite,[8]
She would command the hasty sun to stay,
Or backward turn his course from heaven's height:
Sometimes great hosts of men she could dismay;
Dry-shod to pass she parts the floods in tway;
And eke huge mountains from their native seat
She would command themselves to bear away,[9]
And throw in raging sea with roaring threat:
Almighty God her gave such pow'r and puissance[10] great.

The faithful Knight now grew in little space,
By hearing her, and by her sisters' lore,
To such perfection of all heav'nly grace,
That wretched world he gan for to abhor,
And mortal life gan loathe as thing forlore,[11]
Griev'd with remembrance of his wicked ways,
And prick'd with anguish of his sins so sore,
That he desir'd to end his wretched days:
So much the dart of sinful guilt the soul dismays!

But wise Speranza gave him comfort sweet,
And taught him how to take assurëd hold
Upon her silver anchor, as was meet;
Else had his sins so great and manifold
Made him forget all that Fidelia told.
In this distressëd doubtful agony,
When him his dearest Una did behold
Disdaining life, desiring leave to die,
She found herself assail'd with great perplexitý;

And came to Cælia to declare her smart;
Who, well acquainted with that common plight
Which sinful horror works in wounded heart,
Her wisely comforted all that she might,
With goodly counsel and advisement right;
And straightway sent with careful diligence,
To fetch a leech,[12] the which had great insight
In that disease of grievëd consciénce,
And well could cure the same; his name was Patiénce.

Who, coming to that soul-diseasëd Knight,
Could hardly him entreat to tell his grief:
Which known, and all that noy'd[13] his heavy sprite
Well search'd, eftsoons he gan apply relief
Of salves and med'cines which had passing prefe;[14]
And thereto added words of wondrous might:
By which to ease he him recurëd brief,[15]
And much assuag'd the passion of his plight,[16]
That he his pain endur'd, as seeming now more light.

But yet the cause and root of all his ill,
Inward corruption and infected sin,
Not purg'd nor heal'd, behind remainëd still,
And fest'ring sore did rankle yet within,
Close creeping 'twixt the marrow and the skin:
Which to extirp,[17] he laid him privily
Down in a darksome lowly place far in,
Where as he meant his córrosives t' apply,
And with strait[18] diet tame his stubborn maladý.

In ashes and sackclóth he did array
His dainty corse, proud humours to abate;
And dieted with fasting every day,
The swelling of his wounds to mitigate;
And made him pray both early and eke late:
And ever, as superfluous flesh did rot,
Amendment ready still at hand did wait
To pluck it out with pincers fiery hot,
That soon in him was left no one corrupted jot.

And bitter Penance, with an iron whip,
Was wont him once to disple[19] every day:
And sharp Remorse his heart did prick and nip,
That drops of blood thence like a well did play:
And sad Repentance usëd to embay[20]

1 Know. 2 Counsel.
3 Retire to your chambers.
4 Declared. 5 Favoured.
6 Teachings, doctrines. 7 Pierce.
8 Spirit.
9 Matt. xvii. 20: "If ye have faith as a grain of mustard-seed, ye shall say unto this mountain, Remove hence to yonder place; and it shall remove: and nothing shall be impossible unto you."
10 Might. 11 Undone, lost.
12 Physician. 13 Injured, troubled.
14 Surpassing effect. 15 Quickly restored.
16 The sufferings of his condition. 17 Root out.
18 Strict. 19 Discipline, chastise. 20 Bathe.

His body in salt water smarting sore,
The filthy blots of sin to wash away.
So in short space they did to health restore
The man that would not live, but erst lay at death's door.

In which his torment often was so great,
That like a lion he would cry and roar;
And rend his flesh; and his own sinews eat.
His own dear Una, hearing evermore
His rueful shrieks and groanings, often tore
Her guiltless garments and her golden hair,
For pity of his pain and anguish sore:
Yet all with patience wisely she did bear;
For well she wist his crime could else be never clear.[1]

Whom, thus recover'd by wise Patiénce
And true Repentance, they to Una brought;
Who, joyous of his curëd consciénce,
Him dearly kiss'd, and fairly eke besought
Himself to cherish, and consuming thought
To put away out of his careful breast.
By this[2] Charissa, late in childbed brought,
Was waxen strong, and left her fruitful nest:
To her fair Una brought this unacquainted guest.

She was a woman in her freshest age,
Of wondrous beauty, and of bounty rare,
With goodly grace and comely personage,
That was on earth not easy to compare;
Full of great love; but Cupid's wanton snare
As hell she hated; chaste in work and will;
Her neck and breasts were ever open bare,
That aye thereof her babes might suck their fill;
The rest was all in yellow robes arrayëd still.

A multitude of babes about her hung,
Playing their sports, that joy'd her to behold;
Whom still she fed, while they were weak and young,
But thrust them forth still as they waxëd old:
And on her head she wore a tire[3] of gold,
Adorn'd with gems and ouches[4] wondrous fair,
Whose passing price unneth[5] was to be told:[6]
And by her side there sat a gentle pair
Of turtle doves, she sitting in an ivory chair.

The Knight and Una, ent'ring, fair her greet,
And bid her joy of that her happy brood;
Who them requites with court'sies seeming meet,
And entertains with friendly cheerful mood.
Then Una her besought, to be so good
As in her virtuous rules to school her Knight,
Now after all his torment well withstood
In that sad house of Penance, where his sprite
Had pass'd the pains of hell and long-enduring night.

She was right joyous of her just request;
And, taking by the hand that Faery's son,
Gan him instruct in every good behest,[7]
Of Love; and Righteousness; and Well to don;[8]
And wrath and hatred warily[9] to shun,
That drew on men God's hatred and his wrath,
And many souls in dolours[10] had fordone:[11]
In which when him she well instructed hath,
From thence to heav'n she teacheth him the ready path.

Wherein his weaker wand'ring steps to guide,
An ancient matron she to her does call,
Whose sober looks her wisdom well descried;[12]
Her name was Mercy; well known over all[13]
To be both gracious and eke liberal:
To whom the careful charge of him she gave,
To lead aright, that he should never fall
In all his ways through this wide worldes wave;[14]
That Mercy in the end his righteous soul might save.

The godly matron by the hand him bears
Forth from her presence, by a narrow way,
Scatter'd with bushy thorns and ragged breres,[15]
Which still before him she remov'd away,
That nothing might his ready passage stay:
And ever when his feet encumber'd were,
Or gan to shrink, or from the right to stray,
She held him fast, and firmly did upbear;
As careful nurse her child from falling oft does rear.

Eftsoons unto a holy hospital,
That was foreby[16] the way, she did him bring;
In which seven beadmen,[17] that had vowëd all
Their life to service of high heaven's King,
Did spend their days in doing godly thing:
Their gates to all were open evermore,
That by the weary way were travelling;
And one sat waiting ever them before,
To call in comers-by, that needy were and poor.

The first of them, that eldest was and best,[18]
Of all the house had charge and government,
As guardian and steward of the rest:
His office was to give entértainmént
And lodging unto all that came and went;
Not unto such as could him feast again,
And double quite[19] for that he on them spent;
But such as want of harbour[20] did constrain:
Those for God's sake his duty was to entertain.

The second was as almoner of the place:
His office was the hungry for to feed,
And thirsty give to drink; a work of grace.
He fear'd not once himself to be in need,
Nor car'd to hoard for those whom he did breed:
The grace of God he laid up still in store,
Which as a stock he left unto his seed:
He had enough; what need him care for more?
And had he less, yet some he would give to the poor.

The third had of their wardrobe custody,
In which were not rich tires, nor garments gay,
The plumes of pride, and wings of vanity,

1 Washed away, atoned.
2 By this time; meanwhile.
3 Head-dress, tiara.
4 Ornaments, buttons or bosses.
5 Scarcely.
6 Reckoned.
7 Commandment.
8 Well-doing.
9 Carefully.
10 Griefs.
11 Ruined.
12 Declared.
13 Everywhere.
14 Uneven way.
15 Briars.
16 Near.
17 Men of prayer, the virtue of Charity was divided by the old theologians into seven heads or branches.
18 Highest in order of precedence.
19 Return a double recompense.
20 Refuge, shelter.

But clothës meet to keep keen cold away,
And naked nature seemly to array;
With which bare wretched wights[1] he daily clad,
The images of God in earthly clay;
And, if that no spare clothes to give he had,
His own coat he would cut, and it distribute glad.

The fourth appointed by his office was
Poor prisoners to relieve with gracious aid,
And captives to redeem with price of brass
From Turks and Saracens, which them had stay'd;[2]
And though they faulty were, yet well he weigh'd,[3]
That God to us forgiveth every hour
Much more than that why they in bands were laid;
And He, that harrow'd[4] hell with heavy stowre,[5]
The faulty souls from thence brought to his heav'nly bow'r.

The fifth had charge sick persons to attend,
And comfort those in point of death which lay;
For them most needeth comfort in the end,
When Sin, and Hell, and Death, do most dismay
The feeble soul departing hence away.
All is but lost, that living we bestow,
If not well ended at our dying day.
O man! have mind of that last bitter throe:
For as the tree does fall, so lies it ever low.

The sixth had charge of them now being dead,
In seemly sort their corses to engrave,[6]
And deck with dainty flow'rs their bridal bed,
That to their heav'nly spouse both sweet and brave
They might appear, when He their souls shall save.
The wondrous workmanship of God's own mould,[7]
Whose face He made all beasts to fear, and gave
All in his hand, ev'n dead we honour should.
Ah, dearest God, me grant I dead be not defoul'd![8]

The sev'nth, now after death and burial done,
Had charge the tender orphans of the dead
And widows aid, lest they should be undone:
In face of judgment he their right would plead,
Nor aught the power of mighty men did dread
In their defence; nor would for gold or fee
Be won their rightful causes down to tread:
And, when they stood in most necessity,
He did supply their want, and gave them ever free.[9]

There when the Elfin Knight arrivëd was,
The first and chiefest of the sev'n, whose care
Was guests to welcome, toward him did pass;
Where seeing Mercy, that his steps upbare
And always led, to her with reverence rare
He humbly louted[10] in meek lowliness,
And seemly welcome did for her prepare:
For of their Order she was patroness,
All be[11] Charissa were their chiefest founderess.

Then she a while him stays, himself to rest,
That to the rest[12] more able he might be:
During which time in every good behest,[13]
And godly work of alms and charity,
She him instructed with great industry.
Shortly, therein so perfect he became,
That, from the first unto the last degree,
His mortal life he learnëd had to frame
In holy righteousness, without rebuke or blame.

Thence forward by that painful way they pass
Forth to a hill, that was both steep and high;
On top whereof a sacred chapel was,
And eke a little hermitage thereby,
Wherein an aged holy man did lie,
That day and night said his devotión,
Nor other worldly business did apply:[14]
His name was Heavenly Contemplatión;
Of God and goodness was his meditatión.

Great grace that old man to him given had;
For God he often saw from heaven's height:
All[15] were his earthly eyne both blunt and bad,
And through great age had lost their kindly[16] sight,
Yet wondrous quick and piercing was his sprite,[17]
As eagle's eye, that can behold the sun.
That hill they scale with all their pow'r and might,
That his frail thighs, nigh weary and fordone,[18]
Gan fail; but, by her help, the top at last he won.

There they do find that godly aged sire,
With snowy locks adown his shoulders shed;
As hoary frost with spangles doth attire
The mossy branches of an oak half dead.
Each bone might through his body well be read,[19]
And every sinew seen, through his long fast:
For naught he car'd his carcase long unfed;
His mind was full of spiritual repast,
And pin'd his flesh to keep his body low and chaste.

Who, when these two approaching he espied,
At their first presence grew aggrievëd[20] sore,
That forc'd him lay his heav'nly thoughts aside;
And had he not that Dame respected more,
Whom highly he did reverence and adore,
He would not once have movëd for the Knight.
They him saluted, standing far afore;
Who, well them greeting, humbly did requite,[21]
And askëd, to what end they clomb that tedious height.

"What end," quoth she, "should cause us take such pain,
But that same end, which every living wight
Should make his mark,—high heaven to attain?
Is not from hence the way that leadeth right
To that most glorious house, that glist'neth bright
With burning stars and ever-living fire,
Whereof the keys are to thy hand behight[22]
By wise Fidelia? She doth thee require
To show it to this Knight, according[23] his desire."

1 Mortals.
2 Detained.
3 Considered.
4 Ravaged. See note 11, page 51.
5 Assault.
6 Bury.
7 Image.
8 Outraged, insulted.
9 Bounteously.
10 Bowed, made reverence.
11 Although.
12 The remainder of his task.
13 Commandment.
14 Attend to.
15 Although.
16 Natural.
17 Spirit.
18 Exhausted.
19 Perceived.
20 Distressed, vexed.
21 Respond.
22 Entrusted.
23 Granting.

"Thrice happy man," said then the father grave,
"Whose staggering steps thy steady hand doth lead,
And shows the way his sinful soul to save!
Who better can the way to heav'n aread[1]
Than thou thyself, that wast both born and bred
In heav'nly throne, where thousand angels shine?
Thou dost the prayers of the righteous seed
Present before the Majesty Divine,
And His avenging wrath to clemency incline.

"Yet, since thou bid'st, thy pleasure shall be done.
Then come, thou Man of Earth! and see the way
That never yet was seen of Faery's son;
That never leads the traveller astray,
But, after labours long and sad delay,
Brings them to joyous rest and endless bliss.
But first thou must a season fast and pray,
Till from her bands the sprite assoilëd[2] is,
And have her strength recur'd[3] from frail infirmities."

That done, he leads him to the highest mount;
Such one as that same mighty Man of God,[4]
That blood-red billows like a wallëd front
On either side disparted with his rod,
Till that his army dry-foot through them yode,[5]
Dwelt forty days upon; where, writ in stone
With bloody letters by the hand of God,
The bitter doom of death and baleful moan
He did receive, while flashing fire about him shone:

Or like that sacred hill,[6] whose head full high,
Adorn'd with fruitful olives all around,
Is, as it were for endless memory
Of that dear Lord who oft thereon was found,
For ever with a flowering garland crown'd:
Or like that pleasant mount,[7] that is for aye
Through famous poets' verse each where renown'd,
On which the thrice three learned Ladies[8] play
Their heav'nly notes, and make full many a lovely lay.

From thence, far off he unto him did shew
A little path, that was both steep and long,
Which to a goodly city led his view;
Whose walls and tow'rs were builded high and strong
Of pearl and precious stone, that earthly tongue
Cannot describe, nor wit of man can tell;
Too high a ditty[9] for my simple song!
The City of the Great King hight it well,
Wherein eternal peace and happiness do dwell.

As he thereon stood gazing, he might see
The blessëd angels to and fro descend
From highest heav'n in gladsome company,
And with great joy into that city wend,
As commonly[10] as friend does with his friend.
Whereat he wonder'd much, and gan inquére
What stately building durst so high extend
Her lofty tow'rs unto the starry sphere,
And what unknowen nation there empeopled were.[11]

"Fair Knight," quoth he, "Jerusalem that is,
The New Jerusalem, that God has built
For those to dwell in that are chosen his,
His chosen people purg'd from sinful guilt,
With precious blood, which cruelly was spilt
On cursed tree, of that unspotted Lamb,
That for the sins of all the world was kilt:[12]
Now are they saints all in that city sam',[13]
More dear unto their God than younglings to their dam."

"Till now," said then the Knight, "I weenëd well
That great Cleopolis[14] where I have been,
In which that fairest Faery Queen doth dwell,
The fairest city was that might be seen;
And that bright tow'r, all built of crystal clean,[15]
Panthea, seem'd the brightest thing that was:
But now by proof all otherwise I ween;
For this great city that does far surpass,
And this bright angels' tow'r quite dims that tow'r of glass."

"Most true," then said the holy aged man;
"Yet is Cleopolis, for earthly frame,
The fairest piece[16] that eye beholden can;
And well beseems all knights of noble name,
That covet in th' immortal book of fame
To be etérnisëd, that same to haunt,
And do their service to that sov'reign Dame
That glory does to them for guerdon[17] grant:
For she is heav'nly born, and heav'n may justly vaunt.

"And thou, fair imp,[18] sprung out from English race,
However now accounted Elfin's son,
Well worthy dost thy service for her grace,
To aid a virgin desolate, fordone.[19]
But when thou famous victory hast won,
And high amongst all knights hast hung thy shield,
Thenceforth the suit[20] of earthly conquest shun,
And wash thy hands from guilt of bloody field:
For blood can naught but sin, and wars but sorrows, yield.

"Then seek this path that I to thee preságe,[21]
Which after all to heaven shall thee send;
Then peaceably thy painful pilgrimage
To yonder same Jerusalem do bend,
Where is for thee ordain'd a blessed end:
For thou amongst those saints, whom thou dost see,
Shalt be a saint, and thine own nation's friend
And patron: Thou *Saint George* shalt callëd be,
Saint George of merry England, the sign of victory."

"Unworthy wretch," quoth he, "of so great grace,

1 Declare. 2 Absolved, set free. 3 Recovered.
4 Moses, who commanded the Red Sea to divide for the passage of the Israelite host.
5 Went; past tense of "yede" or "yead," go.
6 The Mount of Olivet. 7 Parnassus.
8 The Nine Muses. 9 Theme.

10 Familiarly. 11 Dwelt there.
12 Killed. 13 Same.
14 "The City of Glory." 15 Pure.
16 Structure. 17 Reward.
18 Youth. 19 Overwhelmed with calamity.
20 Pursuit. 21 Point out.

How dare I think such glory to attain!"
"These, that have it attain'd, were in like case,"
Quoth he, "as wretched, and liv'd in like pain."[1]
"But deeds of arms must I at last be fain,[2]
And ladies' love, to leave, so dearly bought?"
"What need of arms, where peace doth aye remain,"
Said he, "and battles none are to be fought?
As for loose loves, they 're vain, and vanish into naught."

"O let me not," quoth he, "then turn again
Back to the world, whose joys so fruitless are;
But let me here for ay in peace remain,
Or straightway on that last long voyage fare,
That nothing may my present hope impair."[3]
"That may not be," said he, "nor may'st thou yet
Forego that royal Maid's bequeathëd care,
Who did her cause into thy hand commit,
Till from her cursëd foe thou have her freely quit."[4]

"Then shall I soon," quoth he, "so God me grace,[5]
Abet[6] that Virgin's cause disconsolate,
And shortly back return unto this place,
To walk this way in pilgrim's poor estate.
But now aread,[7] old Father, why of late
Didst thou behight[8] me born of English blood,
Whom all a Faery's son do nominate?"[8]
"That word shall I," said he, "avouchen good,[9]
Since to thee is unknown the cradle of thy brood.

"For well I wot thou spring'st from ancient race
Of Saxon kings, that have with mighty hand,
And many bloody battles fought in place,
High rear'd their royal throne in Britons' land,
And vanquish'd them, unable to withstand:
From thence a Faery thee unweeting[10] reft,
There as thou slept in tender swaddling band,
And her base Elfin brood there for thee left:
Such men do changelings call, so chang'd by Faery's theft.

"Thence she thee brought into this Faery Land,
And in a heapëd furrow did thee hide;
Where thee a ploughman all unweeting fand,
As he his toilsome team that way did guide,
And brought thee up in ploughman's state to bide,
Whereof Gëorgos[11] he thee gave to name;
Till, prick'd with courage and thy force's pride,
To Faery Court thou cam'st to seek for fame,
And prove thy puissant arms, as seems thee best became."

"O holy Sire," quoth he, "how shall I quite[12]
The many favours I with thee have found,
That hast my name and nation read[13] aright,
And taught the way that does to heaven bound!"[14]
This said, adown he lookëd to the ground,
To have return'd;[15] but dazëd[16] were his eyne
Through passing brightness, which did quite confound
His feeble sense, and too exceeding shine.
So dark are earthly things compar'd to things divine!

At last, when as himself he gan to find,
To Una back he cast him[17] to retire;
Who him awaited still with pensive mind.
Great thanks, and goodly meed, to that good sire
He thence departing gave for his pain's hire.[18]
So came to Una, who him joy'd to see;
And, after little rest, gan him desire
Of her adventure mindful for to be.
So leave they take of Cælia and her daughters three.

CANTO XI.

The Knight with that old Dragon fights
Two days incessantly:
The third, him overthrows: and gains
Most glorious victory.

High time now gan it wax[19] for Una fair
To think of those her captive parents dear,
And their forwasted kingdom to repair:
Whereto when as they now approachëd near,
With hearty words her Knight she gan to cheer,
And in her modest manner thus bespake;
"Dear Knight, as dear as ever knight was dear,
That all these sorrows suffer for my sake,
High heav'n behold the tedious toil ye for me take!

"Now are we come unto my native soil,
And to the place where all our perils dwell;
Here haunts that fiend, and does his daily spoil;
Therefore henceforth be at your keeping[20] well,
And ever ready for your foeman fell:
The spark of noble courage now awake,
And strive your excellent self to excel:
That shall ye evermore renownëd make
Above all knights on earth that battle undertake."

And pointing forth, "Lo! yonder is," said she,
"The brazen tow'r in which my parents dear
For dread of that huge fiend imprison'd be;
Whom I from far see on the walls appear,
Whose sight my feeble soul doth greatly cheer:
And on the top of all I do espy
The watchman waiting tidings glad to hear;
That, O my parents, might I happily
Unto you bring, to ease you of your misery!"

With that they heard a roaring hideous sound,
That all the air with terror fillëd wide,
And seem'd uneath[21] to shake the steadfast ground.
Eftsoons that dreadful dragon they espied,

1 Rev. vii. 14: "These are they which came out of great tribulation."
2 Constrained.
3 Diminish.
4 Delivered.
5 Favour.
6 Assist.
7 Explain.
8 Call.
9 Vindicate as true.
10 Unconscious.
11 Γεωργος, Greek for a husbandman.
12 Repay.
13 Declared.
14 Ascend.
15 With the purpose of returning.
16 Dazzled.
17 Resolved.
18 To reward his trouble.
19 It became.
20 On your guard.
21 Underneath.

Where stretch'd he lay upon the sunny side
Of a great hill, himself like a great hill:
But, all so soon as he from far descried
Those glist'ring arms that heav'n with light did fill,
He rous'd himself full blithe, and hastened them until.[1]

Then bade the Knight his Lady yede[2] aloof,
And to a hill herself withdraw aside;
From whence she might behold that battle's proof,
And eke be safe from danger far descried:
She him obey'd, and turn'd a little wide.—
Now, O thou sacred Muse, most learnëd Dame,
Fair imp[3] of Phœbus and his aged bride,[4]
The nurse of Time and everlasting Fame,
That warlike hands ennoblest with immortal name;

O gently come into my feeble breast;
Come gently; but not with that mighty rage
Wherewith the martial troops thou dost infest,
And hearts of great herōës dost enrage,
That naught their kindled courage may assuage:
Soon as thy dreadful trump begins to sound,
The god of war with his fierce equipage
Thou dost awake, sleep never he so sound;
And scarëd nations dost with horror stern astound.

Fair Goddess, lay that furious fit aside,
Till I of wars and bloody Mars do sing,[5]
And Briton fields with Saracen blood bedy'd,
'Twixt that great Faery Queen and Paynim king,
That with their horror heav'n and earth did ring;
A work of labour long, and endless praise:
But now awhile let down that haughty string,
And to my tunes thy second tenor raise,
That I this man of God his godly arms may blaze.[6]

By this the dreadful beast drew nigh to hand,
Half flying and half footing in his haste,
That with his largeness measurëd much land,
And made wide shadow under his huge waist,
As mountain doth the valley overcast.
Approaching nigh, he rearëd high afore
His body monstrous, horrible, and vast;
Which, to increase his wondrous greatness more,
Was swoll'n with wrath and poison, and with bloody gore;

And over all with brazen scales was arm'd,
Like plated coat of steel, so couchëd near[7]
That naught might pierce; nor might his corse be harm'd
With dint of sword, nor push of pointed spear:
Which, as an eagle, seeing prey appear,
His airy plumes doth rouse full rudely dight;[8]
So shakëd he, that horror was to hear:
For, as the clashing of an armour bright,
Such noise his rousëd scales did send unto the Knight.

His flaggy[9] wings, when forth he did display,
Were like two sails, in which the hollow wind
Is gather'd full, and worketh speedy way:
And eke the pens,[10] that did his pinions bind,
Were like main-yards with flying canvas lin'd;
With which when as him list the air to beat,
And there by force unwonted passage find,
The clouds before him fled for terror great,
And all the heav'ns stood still, amazëd with his threat.

His huge long tail, wound up in hundred folds,
Does overspread his long brass-scaly[11] back,
Whose wreathëd boughts[12] whenever he unfolds,
And thick-entangled knots adown does slack,
Bespotted as with shields of red and black,
It sweepeth all the land behind him far,
And of three furlongs does but little lack;
And at the point two stings infixëd are,
Both deadly sharp, that sharpest steel exceeden far.

But stings and sharpest steel did far exceed
The sharpness of his cruel rending claws:
Dead was it sure, as sure as death indeed,
Whatever thing does touch his ravenous paws,
Or what within his reach he ever draws.
But his most hideous head my tongue to tell
Does tremble; for his deep devouring jaws
Wide gapëd, like the grisly mouth of hell,
Through which into his dark abyss all ravin[13] fell.

And, what more wondrous was, in either jaw
Three ranks of iron teeth enrangëd were,
In which yet trickling blood, and gobbets raw,
Of late-devourëd bodies did appear;
That sight thereof bred cold congealëd fear:
Which to increase, and all at once to kill,
A cloud of smoth'ring smoke and sulphur sear[14]
Out of his stinking gorge[15] forth steamëd still,
That all the air about with smoke and stench did fill.

His blazing eyes, like two bright shining shields,
Did burn with wrath, and sparkled living fire:
As two broad beacons, set in open fields,
Send forth their flames far off to every shire,
And warning give, that enemies conspire
With fire and sword the region to invade;
So flam'd his eyne with rage and rancorous ire:
But far within, as in a hollow glade,
Those glaring lamps were set, that made a dreadful shade.

So dreadfully he toward him did pass,
Forelifting up aloft his speckled breast,
And often bounding on the bruisëd grass,

1 Towards. 2 Go. 3 Offspring.

4 Mnemosyne, or Memory; who, in most of the traditions about the genealogy of the Muses, is said to have been their mother. Most commonly, however, their paternity is ascribed to Zeus. The tuneful Nine were often called the "Mnemonides." The invocation of the poet is addressed to Clio, the historic Muse, to whom he had appealed at the outset of his work.

5 Spenser is understood here to refer to his purpose of singing, under the guise of the allegory described just below, the war between Queen Elizabeth and Spain, in the later books of the "Faerie Queen."

6 Celebrate. 7 Laid so close together.

8 Doth stir her ruffled or roughly-trimmed feathers.

9 Floating. 10 Feathers.

11 Covered with brazen scales.

12 Folds, coils. 13 Prey.

14 Burning. 15 Throat.

As for great joyance of his new-come guest.
Eftsoons he gan advance his haughty crest,
As chafëd boar his bristles doth uprear;
And shook his scales to battle ready drest.[1]
(That made the Redcross Knight nigh quake for fear),
As bidding bold defiance to his foeman near.

The Knight gan fairly couch his steady spear,
And fiercely ran at him with rigorous might:
The pointed steel, arriving rudely there,
His harder hide would neither pierce nor bite,
But, glancing by, forth passëd forward right:
Yet, sore amovëd with so puissant push,
The wrathful beast about him turnëd light,
And him so rudely, passing by, did brush
With his long tail, that horse and man to ground did rush.

Both horse and man up lightly rose again,
And fresh encounter toward him addrest:
But th' idle stroke yet back recoil'd in vain,
And found no place his deadly point to rest.
Exceeding rage inflam'd the furious beast,
To be avengëd of so great despite;
For never felt his impierceáble breast
So wondrous force from hand of living wight;
Yet had he prov'd the power of many a puissant knight.

Then, with his waving wings displayëd wide,
Himself up high he lifted from the ground,
And with strong flight did forcibly divide
The yielding air, which nigh too feeble found
Her flitting parts, and element unsound,
To bear so great a weight: he, cutting way
With his broad sails, about him soarëd round;
At last, low stooping with unwieldy sway,
Snatch'd up both horse and man, to bear them quite away.

Long he them bore above the subject plain,[2]
So far as yewen bow a shaft may send;
Till struggling strong did him at last constrain
To let them down before his flightë's end:
As haggard [3] hawk, presuming to contend
With hardy fowl above his able might,[4]
His weary pounces [5] all in vain doth spend
To truss [6] the prey too heavy for his flight;
Which, coming down to ground, does free itself by fight.

He so disseizëd [7] of his griping gross,[8]
The Knight his thrillant [9] spear again assay'd
In his brass-plated body to emboss,[10]
And three men's strength unto the stroke he laid;
Wherewith the stiff beam quakëd, as afraid,
And glancing from his scaly neck did glide
Close under his left wing, then broad display'd:
The piercing steel there wrought a wound full wide,
That with the úncouth [11] smart the monster loudly criëd.

He cried, as raging seas are wont to roar,
When wintry storm his wrathful wreck does threat;
The rolling billows beat the ragged shore,
As they the earth would shoulder from her seat;
And greedy gulf does gape, as he would eat
His neighbour element in his revenge:
Then gin the blust'ring brethren boldly threat
To move the world from off his steadfast henge,[12]
And boist'rous battle make, each other to avenge.

The steely head stuck fast still in his flesh,
Till with his cruel claws he snatch'd the wood,
And quite asunder broke: forth flowëd fresh
A gushing river of black gory blood,
That drownëd all the land whereon he stood;
The stream thereof would drive a water-mill:
Trebly augmented was his furious mood
With bitter sense of his deep-rooted ill,[13]
That flames of fire he threw forth from his large nosethrill.[14]

His hideous tail then hurlëd he about,
And therewith all enwrapt the nimble thighs
Of his froth-foamy steed, whose courage stout,
Striving to loose the knot that fast him ties,
Himself in straiter bands too rash implies,[15]
That to the ground he is perforce constrain'd
To throw his rider: who gan quickly rise
From off the earth, with dirty blood distain'd,
For that reproachful fall right foully he disdain'd;

And fiercely took his trenchant blade in hand,
With which he struck so furious and so fell,
That nothing seem'd the puíssance could withstand:
Upon his crest the harden'd iron fell;
But his more harden'd crest was arm'd so well,
That deeper dint therein it would not make;
Yet so extremely did the buff [16] him quell,
That from thenceforth he shunn'd the like to take,
But, when he saw them come, he did them still forsake.[17]

The Knight was wroth to see his stroke beguil'd,
And smote again with more outrageous might;
But back again the sparkling steel recoil'd,
And left not any mark where it did light,
As if in adamant rock it had been pight.[18]
The beast, impatient of his smarting wound,
And of so fierce and forcible despite,
Thought with his wings to sty [19] above the ground;
But his late-wounded wing unserviceable found.

1 Prepared. 2 The plain beneath.
3 Untrained or refractory — which flew at unpermitted game, and would not obey the falconer's recall.
4 More than his strength can match.
5 Talons. 6 Gather up.
7 Dispossessed.
8 The bulky prey which he had grasped.
9 Piercing; akin to the word "drill," in the same signification of boring or piercing; from the Anglo-Saxon, "thirlian." See note 11, page 23; and the closing line of next stanza but one.
10 Lodge. 11 Unwonted.
12 Hinge. 13 Hurt, wound.
14 Nostril; Chaucer used "nose-thirle," for the derivation of which see note 9.
15 Enfolds. 16 Buffet, blow.
17 Avoid. 18 Struck, fixed.
19 Mount; German, "steigen," to ascend.

Then, full of grief and anguish vehement,
He loudly bray'd, that like was never heard;
And from his wide devouring oven sent
A flake of fire, that, flashing in his[1] beard,
Him all amaz'd, and almost made afear'd:
The scorching flame sore singëd all his face,
And through his armour all his body sear'd,[2]
That he could not endure so cruel case,
But thought his arms to leave,[3] and helmet to unlace.

Not that great champion of the ántique world,[4]
Whom famous poets' verse so much doth vaunt,
And hath for twelve huge labours high extoll'd,
So many furies and sharp fits did haunt,
When him the poison'd garment did enchant,
With Centaur's blood and bloody verses charm'd;
As did this Knight twelve thousand dolours daunt,
Whom fiery steel now burn'd, that erst him arm'd;
That erst him goodly arm'd, now most of all him harm'd.

Faint, weary, sore, emboilëd,[5] grievëd, brent,[2]
With heat, toil, wounds, arms, smart, and inward fire,
That never man such mischiefs did torment;
Death better were; death did he oft desire;
But death will never come, when needs require.
Whom so dismay'd when that his foe beheld,
He cast[6] to suffer him no more respire,[7]
But gan his sturdy stern[8] about to weld,[9]
And him so strongly struck, that to the ground him fell'd.

It fortunëd (as fair it then befell),
Behind his back, unweeting[10] where he stood,
Of ancient time there was a springing well,
From which fast trickled forth a silver flood,
Full of great virtues, and for med'cine good:
Whilóm, before that cursed dragon got
That happy land, and all with innocent blood
Defil'd those sacred waves, it rightly hot[11]
The Well of Life; nor yet his virtues had forgot:

For unto life the dead it could restore,
And guilt of sinful crimes clean wash away;
Those that with sickness were infected sore
It could recure;[12] and aged long decay
Renew, as one were born that very day.
Both Silo[13] this, and Jordan did excel,
And th' English Bath, and eke the German Spa;
Nor can Cephise, nor Hebrus,[14] match this Well:
Into the same the Knight back overthrowen fell.

Now gan the golden Phœbus for to steep
His fiery face in billows of the west,
And his faint steeds water'd in ocean deep,
While from their journal[15] labours they did rest;
When that infernal monster, having kest[16]
His weary foe into that living well,
Gan high advance his broad discolour'd breast
Above his wonted pitch, with count'nance fell,
And clapt his iron wings, as victor he did dwell.

Which when his pensive Lady saw from far,
Great woe and sorrow did her soul assay,[17]
As weening that the sad end of the war;
And gan to Highest God entirely[18] pray
That fearëd chance from her to turn away:
With folded hands, and knees full lowly bent,
All night she watch'd; nor once adown would lay
Her dainty limbs in her sad neariment,[19]
But praying still did wake, and waking did lament.

The morrow next gan early to appear,
That Titan rose to run his daily race;
But early, ere the morrow next gan rear
Out of the sea fair Titan's dewy face,
Uprose the gentle Virgin from her place,
And lookëd all about, if she might spy
Her lovëd Knight to move his manly pace:
For she had great doubt of his safëty,
Since late she saw him fall before his enemy.

At last she saw where he upstarted brave
Out of the well wherein he drenchëd lay:
As eagle fresh out of the ocean wave,
Where he hath left his plumes all hoary gray,
And deck'd himself with feathers youthly gay,
Like eyas[20] hawk upmounts unto the skies,
His newly-budded pinions to assay,[21]
And marvels at himself, still as he flies:
So new this new-born Knight to battle new did rise.

Whom when the damnëd fiend so fresh did spy,
No wonder if he wonder'd at the sight,
And doubted whether his late enemy
It were, or other new suppliëd knight.
He now, to prove his late-renewëd might,
High brandishing his bright dew-burning[22] blade,
Upon his crested scalp so sore did smite,
That to the skull a yawning wound it made:
The deadly dint his dullëd senses all dismay'd.

I wot not whether the revenging steel
Were harden'd with that holy water dew
Wherein he fell; or sharper edge did feel;
Or his baptizëd hands now greater grew;
Or other secret virtue did ensue;
Else never could the force of fleshly arm,
Nor molten metal, in his blood embrue:[23]
For, till that stound,[24] could never wight him harm
By subtilty, nor sleight, nor might, nor mighty charm.

1 The Knight's. 2 Burned.
3 Cast off. 4 Hercules.
5 Boiled, intensely heated.
6 Resolved.
7 Breathe. 8 Tail.
9 Wield, swing. 10 Without his knowledge.
11 Was called. 12 Recover.
13 The Pool of Siloam, to which Christ sent the man born blind to wash his eyes and regain his sight (John ix. 7).
14 Cephisus and Hebrus were famous rivers, the one in Bœotia, the other in Thrace.
15 Diurnal, daily; French, "journel."
16 Cast. 17 Beset, assail.
18 Earnestly, sincerely.
19 Distress, terror.
20 Newly-fledged; lately out of the "ey," or egg.
21 Try. 22 Bright with the water of the well.
23 Dip itself in his (the dragon's) blood.
24 Moment.

The cruel wound enragëd him so sore,
That loud he yellëd for exceeding pain;
As hundred ramping lions seem'd to roar,
Whom ravenous hunger did thereto constrain.
Then gan he toss aloft his stretchëd train,[1]
And therewith scourge the buxom[2] air so sore,
That to his force to yielden it was fain;
Nor aught his sturdy strokes might stand afore,
That high trees overthrew, and rocks in pieces tore:

The same advancing high above his head,
With sharp intended[3] sting so rude him smote,
That to the earth him drove, as stricken dead;
Nor living wight would have him life behot:[4]
The mortal sting his angry needle shot
Quite through his shield, and in his shoulder seas'd,[5]
Where fast it stuck, nor would thereout be got:
The grief thereof him wondrous sore diseas'd,
Nor might his rankling pain with patience be appeas'd.

But yet, more mindful of his honour dear
Than of the grievous smart which him did wring,
From loathëd soil he gan him lightly rear,
And strove to loose the far-infixëd sting:
Which when in vain he tried with struggëling,
Inflam'd with wrath, his raging blade he heft,[6]
And struck so strongly, that the knotty string
Of his huge tail he quite asunder cleft;
Five joints thereof he hew'd, and but the stump him left.

Heart cannot think what outrage and what cries,
With foul enfoulder'd[7] smoke and flashing fire,
The hell-bred beast threw forth unto the skies,
That all was coverëd with darkness dire:
Then fraught with rancour, and engorgëd[8] ire,
He cast[9] at once him to avenge for all;
And, gath'ring up himself out of the mire
With his uneven wings, did fiercely fall
Upon his sun-bright shield, and gript it fast withal.

Much was the man encumber'd with his hold,
In fear to lose his weapon in his paw,
Nor wist yet how his talons to unfold;
Nor harder was from Cerberus' greedy jaw
To pluck a bone, than from his cruel claw
To reave[10] by strength the gripëd gage[11] away:
Thrice he essay'd it from his foot to draw,
And thrice in vain to draw it did essay;
It booted[12] naught to think to rob him of his prey.

Then, when he saw no power might prevail,
His trusty sword he call'd to his last aid,
Wherewith he fiercely did his foe assail,
And double blows about him stoutly laid,
That glancing fire out of the iron play'd;
As sparkles from the anvil use to fly,
When heavy hammers on the wedge are sway'd;
Therewith at last he forc'd him to untie
One of his grasping feet, him to defend thereby.

The other foot, fast fixëd on his shield,
When as no strength nor strokes might him constrain
To loose, nor yet the warlike pledge to yield,
He smote thereat with all his might and main,
That naught so wondrous puíssance might sustain:
Upon the joint the lucky steel did light,
And made such way, that hew'd it quite in twain;
The paw yet missëd not his minish'd might,
But hung still on the shield, as it at first was pight.[13]

For grief thereof, and devilish despite,[14]
From his infernal furnace forth he threw
Huge flames, that dimmëd all the heaven's light,
Enroll'd in duskish smoke and brimstone blue:
As burning Etna from his boiling stew
Doth belch out flames, and rocks in pieces broke,
And ragged ribs of mountains molten new,
Enwrapt in coal-black clouds and filthy smoke,
That all the land with stench, and heav'n with horror, choke.

The heat whereof, and harmful pestilence,
So sore him noy'd,[15] that forc'd him to retire
A little backward for his best defence,
To save his body from the scorching fire,
Which he from hellish entrails did expire.[16]
It chanc'd (Eternal God that chance did guide),
As he recoilëd backward, in the mire
His nigh forwearied feeble feet did slide,
And down he fell, with dread of shame sore terrified.

There grew a goodly tree him fair beside,
Loaden with fruit and apples rosy red,
As they in pure vermilion had been dy'd,
Whereof great virtues over all were read:[17]
For happy life to all which thereon fed,
And life eke everlasting, did befall:
Great God it planted in that blessed stead[18]
With his Almighty hand, and did it call
The Tree of Life, the crime[19] of our first father's fall.

In all the world like was not to be found,
Save in that soil, where all good things did grow,
And freely sprung out of the fruitful ground,
As incorrupted Nature did them sow,
Till that dread dragon all did overthrow.
Another like fair tree eke grew thereby,
Whereof whoso did eat, eftsoons did know
Both good and ill: O mournful memory!
That tree through one man's fault hath done[20] us all to die!

From that first tree forth flow'd, as from a well,
A trickling stream of balm, most sovereign
And dainty dear,[21] which on the ground still fell,

1 Outstretched tail.
2 Yielding. See note 24, page 94.
3 Stretched out.
4 Promised, assured of.
5 Stayed, seated itself.
6 Heaved, uplifted.
7 Mixed with lightning; from French "foudroyer," "foudre."
8 Swallowed, suppressed.
9 Resolved, strove.
10 Wrench.
11 Object of combat.
12 Availed.
13 Fastened.
14 Fury.
15 Annoyed.
16 Breathe out.
17 Everywhere were reported.
18 Place.
19 Cause; that is, the Tree was the occasion of the sin which led to the Fall.
20 Caused.
21 Precious.

And overflowëd all the fertile plain,
As it had dewëd been with timely rain:
Life and long health that gracious ointment gave;
And deadly wounds could heal; and rear again
The senseless corse appointed for the grave:
Into that same he fell, which did from death
him save.

For nigh thereto the ever-damnëd beast
Durst not approach, for he was deadly made,[1]
And all that life preservëd did detest;
Yet he it oft adventur'd to invade.
By this the drooping Daylight gan to fade,
And yield his room to sad succeeding Night,
Who with her sable mantle gan to shade
The face of earth and ways of living wight,
And high her burning torch set up in heaven
bright.

When gentle Una saw the second fall
Of her dear Knight, who, weary of long fight,
And faint through loss of blood, mov'd not at all,
But lay, as in a dream of deep delight,
Besmear'd with precious balm, whose virtuous
might
Did heal his wounds, and scorching heat allay;
Again she stricken was with sore affright,
And for his safety gan devoutly pray,
And watch the noyous[2] night, and wait for
joyous day.

The joyous day gan early to appear;
And fair Aurora from the dewy bed
Of aged Tithone gan herself to rear
With rosy cheeks, for shame as blushing red:
Her golden locks, for haste, were loosely shed
About her ears, when Una her did mark
Climb to her chariot, all with flowers spread,
From heaven high to chase the cheerless Dark;
With merry note her loud salutes the mounting
lark.

Then freshly up arose the doughty Knight,
All healëd of his hurts and woundës wide,
And did himself to battle ready dight;[3]
Whose early foe awaiting him beside
To have devour'd, so soon as day he spied,
When now he saw himself so freshly rear,
As if late fight had naught him damnified,[4]
He wox[5] dismay'd, and gan his fate to fear;
Nathless with wonted rage he him advancëd near;

And in his first encounter, gaping wide,
He thought at once him to have swallow'd quite,
And rush'd upon him with outrageous pride;
Who him rencount'ring fierce, as hawk in flight,
Perforce rebutted back:[6] the weapon bright,
Taking advantage of his open jaw,
Ran through his mouth with so impórtune[7]
might,
That deep empierc'd his darksome hollow maw,[8]
And, back retir'd, his life-blood forth withal
did draw.

So down he fell, and forth his life did breathe,
That vanish'd into smoke and cloudës swift;
So down he fell, that th' earth him underneath
Did groan, as feeble so great load to lift;
So down he fell, as a huge rocky clift,[9]
Whose false[10] foundation waves have wash'd
away,
With dreadful poise[11] is from the mainland rift,
And, rolling down, great Neptune doth dismay:
So down he fell, and like a heapëd mountain lay.

The Knight himself ev'n trembled at his fall,
So huge and horrible a mass it seem'd;
And his dear lady, that beheld it all,
Durst not approach for dread which she mis-
deem'd;[12]
But yet at last, when as the direful fiend
She saw not stir, off-shaking vain affright
She nigher drew, and saw that joyous end:
Then God she prais'd, and thank'd her faithful
Knight,
That had achiev'd so great a conquest by his
might.

1 Of a deadly nature.
2 Baleful.
3 Prepare.
4 Injured.
5 Became, waxed.
6 Repelled.
7 Urgent, persistent.
8 Belly.
9 Cliff.

CANTO XII.

Fair Una to the Redcross Knight
Betrothëd is with joy:
Though false Duessa, it to bar,
Her false sleights do employ.

BEHOLD I see the haven nigh at hand,
To which I mean my weary course to bend;
Veer the main sheet,[13] and bear up with the land,
The which afore[14] is fairly to be kenn'd,[15]
And seemeth safe from storms that may offend:
There this fair Virgin, weary of her way,
Must landed be, now at her journey's end:
There eke my feeble bark a while may stay,
Till merry wind and weather call her thence
away.

Scarcely had Phœbus in the glooming east
Yet harnessëd his fiery-footed team,
Nor rear'd above the earth his flaming crest;
When the last deadly smoke aloft did steam,
That sign of last outbreathëd life did seem
Unto the watchman on the castle-wall,
Who thereby dead that baleful beast did deem,
And to his lord and lady loud gan call,
To tell how he had seen the dragon's fatal fall.

Uprose with hasty joy, and feeble speed,
That aged sire, the lord of all that land,
And lookëd forth, to weet[16] if true indeed
Those tidings were as he did understand:
Which when as true by trial he out fand,[17]
He bade to open wide his brazen gate,
Which long time had been shut, and out of
hand[18]
Proclaimëd joy and peace through all his state;
For dead now was their foe, which them fo-
ráyëd[19] late.

10 Treacherous.
11 Force, weight.
12 Groundlessly conceived.
13 Wear or turn the mainsail.
14 Before us.
15 Discerned.
16 Learn.
17 Found.
18 Immediately.
19 Ravaged.

Then gan triumphant trumpets sound on high,
That sent to heav'n the echoëd report
Of their new joy, and happy victory
'Gainst him that had them long oppress'd with tort,[1]
And fast imprisonëd in siegëd fort.
Then all the people, as in solemn feast,
To him assembled with one full consórt,[2]
Rejoicing at the fall of that great beast,
From whose eternal bondage now they were releast.

Forth came that ancient lord and aged queen,
Array'd in ántique robes down to the ground,
And sad[3] habiliments right well beseen:[4]
A noble crew[5] about them waited round,
Of sage and sober peers, all gravely gown'd;
Whom far before did march a goodly band
Of tall young men, all able arms to sound,[6]
But now they laurel branches bore in hand;
Glad sign of victory and peace in all their land.

Unto that doughty conqueror they came,
And, him before themselves prostráting low,
Their lord and patron loud did him proclaim,
And at his feet their laurel boughs did throw.
Soon after them, all dancing on a row,
The comely virgins came, with garlands dight,[7]
As fresh as flow'rs in meadow green do grow,
When morning dew upon their leaves doth light;
And in their hands sweet timbrels all upheld on height.[8]

And, them before, the fry[9] of children young
Their wanton sports and childish mirth did play,
And to the maidens' sounding timbrels sung
In well attunëd notes a joyous lay,
And made delightful music all the way,
Until they came where that fair Virgin stood:
As fair Diana in fresh summer's day
Beholds her nymphs enrang'd in shady wood,
Some wrestle, some do run, some bathe in crystal flood;

So she beheld those maidens' merriment
With cheerful view; who, when to her they came,
Themselves to ground with gracious humbless[10] bent,
And her ador'd by honourable name,
Lifting to heav'n her everlasting fame:
Then on her head they set a garland green,
And crownëd her 'twixt earnest and 'twixt game:
Who, in her self-resemblance well beseen,
Did seem, such as she was, a goodly Maiden Queen.

And after all the rascal many[11] ran,
Heapëd together in rude rabblement,
To see the face of that victorious man,
Whom all admirëd as from heaven sent,
And gaz'd upon with gaping wonderment.
But when they came where that dead dragon lay,
Stretch'd on the ground in monstrous large extent,
The sight with idle fear did them dismay,
Nor durst approach him nigh, to touch, or once assay.[12]

Some fear'd, and fled; some fear'd, and well it feign'd;[13]
One, that would wiser seem than all the rest,
Warn'd him not touch, for yet perhaps remain'd
Some ling'ring life within his hollow breast,
Or in his womb might lurk some hidden nest
Of many dragonets,[14] his fruitful seed;
Another said, that in his eyes did rest
Yet sparkling fire, and bade thereof take heed;
Another said, he saw him move his eyes indeed.

One mother, when as her foolhardy child
Did come too near, and with his talons play,
Half dead through fear, her little babe revil'd,
And to her gossips gan in counsel say;
"How can I tell, but that his talons may
Yet scratch my son, or rend his tender hand?"
So diversely themselves in vain they fray;[15]
While some, more bold, to measure him nigh stand,
To prove how many acres he did spread of land.

Thus flockëd all the folk him round about;
The while that hoary king, with all his train,
Being arrivëd where that champion stout
After his foe's defeasance[16] did remain,
Him goodly greets, and fair does entertain
With princely gifts of ivory and gold,
And thousand thanks him yields for all his pain.[17]
Then, when his daughter dear he does behold,
Her dearly doth embrace, and kisseth manifold.

And after to his palace he them brings,
With shawms, and trumpets, and with clarions sweet;
And all the way the joyous people sings,
And with their garments strows the pavëd street;
Whence mounting up, they find purveyance[18] meet
Of all that royal prince's court became;
And all the floor was underneath their feet
Bespread with costly scarlet of great name,[19]
On which they lowly sit, and fitting purpose[20] frame.

What needs me tell their feast and goodly guise,[21]
In which was nothing riotous nor vain?
What needs of dainty dishes to devise,
Of comely services, or courtly train?
My narrow leaves cannot in them contain
The large discourse of royal princes' state.
Yet was their manner then but bare and plain;
For th' ántique world excess and pride did hate:
Such proud luxurious pomp is swollen up but late.

1 Wrong; French, "tort."
2 In one great concourse.
3 Grave.
4 Rich and appropriate to their state.
5 Crowd, suite.
6 To make use of, cause to resound in fray.
7 Decked.
8 Aloft.
9 Swarm, crowd.
10 Humility.
11 Common multitude.
12 Examine.
13 Disguised.
14 Young dragons.
15 Frighten.
16 Defeat.
17 Labour.
18 Provision.
19 Value, excellence.
20 Discourse; French, "propos."
21 Manner (of entertainment).

Then, when with meats and drinks of every kind
Their fervent appetites they quenchĕd had,
That ancient lord gan fit occasion find
Of strange adventures, and of perils sad,
Which in his travel him befallen had,
For to demand of his renownĕd guest:
Who then with utterance grave, and count'n-ance sad,[1]
From point to point, as is before exprest,
Discours'd his voyage long, according[2] his request.

Great pleasure, mix'd with pitiful regard,
That goodly king and queen did passionate,[3]
While they his pitiful adventures heard;
That oft they did lament his luckless state,
And often blame the too impórtune[4] fate
That heap'd on him so many wrathful wreaks;[5]
(For never gentle knight, as he of late,
So tossĕd was in Fortune's cruel freaks);
And all the while salt tears bedew'd the hearers' cheeks.

Then said that royal peer in sober wise;
"Dear son, great be the evils which ye bore
From first to last in your late enterprise,
That I n'ot[6] whether praise or pity more:
For never living man, I ween, so sore
In sea of deadly dangers was distrest:
But since now safe ye seizĕd have the shore,
And well arrivĕd are (High God be blest!)
Let us devise[7] of ease and everlasting rest."

"Ah, dearest Lord," said then that doughty Knight,
"Of ease or rest I may not yet devise;
For, by the faith which I to arms have plight',
I bounden am, straight after this emprise,
As that your daughter can ye well advise,
Back to return to that great Faery Queen,
And her to serve six years in warlike wise,
'Gainst that proud Paynim king[8] that works her teen:[9]
Therefore I ought crave pardon, till I there have been."

"Unhappy falls that hard necessity,"
Quoth he, "the troubler of my happy peace,
And vowĕd foe of my felicity;
Nor I against the same can justly preace.[10]
But since that band[11] ye cannot now release,
Nor done undo (for vows may not be vain),
Soon as the term of those six years shall cease,
Ye then shall hither back return again,
The marriage to accomplish vow'd betwixt you twain:

"Which, for my part, I covet to perform,
In sort as[12] through the world I did proclaim,
That whoso kill'd that monster most deform,
And him in hardy battle overcame,
Should have mine only daughter to his dame,
And of my kingdom heir apparent be:
Therefore, since now to thee pertains the same
By due desert of noble chivalry,
Both daughter and eke kingdom, lo! I yield to thee."

Then forth he callĕd that his daughter fair,
The fairest Une, his only daughter dear,
His only daughter and his only heir;
Who, forth proceeding with sad sober cheer,
As bright as doth the morning star appear
Out of the east, with flaming locks bedight,[13]
To tell that dawning day is drawing near,
And to the world does bring long-wishĕd light:
So fair and fresh that Lady show'd herself in sight:

So fair and fresh as freshest flower in May;
For she had laid her mournful stole[14] aside,
And widow-like sad wimple[15] thrown away,
Wherewith her heav'nly beauty she did hide
While on her weary journey she did ride;
And on her now a garment she did wear
All lily white, withouten spot or pride,
That seem'd like silk and silver woven near;[16]
But neither silk nor silver therein did appear.

The blazing brightness of her beauty's beam,
And glorious light of her sunshiny face,
To tell, were as to strive against the stream:
My ragged rhymes are all too rude and base
Her heav'nly lineaments for to enchase.[17]
Nor wonder; for her own dear lovĕd Knight,
All[18] were she daily with himself in place,
Did wonder much at her celestial sight:[19]
Oft had he seen her fair, but never so fair dight.[20]

So fairly dight when she in presence came,
She to her sire made humble reverence,
And bowĕd low, that her right well became,
And added grace unto her excellence:
Who, with great wisdom and grave eloquence,
Thus gan to say ——But, ere he thus had said,
With flying speed, and seeming great pretence,[21]
Came running in, much like a man dismay'd,
A messenger with letters which his message said.

All in the open hall amazĕd stood
At suddenness of that unwary[22] sight,
And wonder'd at his breathless hasty mood:
But he for naught would stay his passage right,
Till fast before the king he did alight;
Where, falling flat, great humbless[23] he did make,
And kiss'd the ground whereon his foot was pight;[24]
Then to his hands that writ[25] he did betake,[26]
Which he disclosing,[27] read thus, as the paper spake:

"To thee, most mighty King of Eden fair,
Her greeting sends, in these sad lines addrest,
The woeful daughter and forsaken heir

1 Sedate.
2 Complying with. 3 Powerfully affect.
4 Persistent in persecution. 5 Revenges.
6 Know not. 7 Speak, consider.
8 Philip II. of Spain, and his wars against England, are here again intended.
9 Harm, trouble. 10 Press, urge reasons.
11 Bond, obligation. 12 Inasmuch as.

13 Arrayed, bedecked.
14 The black robe which she had formerly worn.
15 Veil. 16 Together.
17 Enshrine, worthily describe. 18 Although.
19 Aspect. 20 Apparelled, adorned.
21 Assumption of importance. 22 Unexpected.
23 Reverence. 24 Placed.
25 Written paper. 26 Commit. 27 Opening.

Of that great Emperor of all the West;
And bids thee be advisëd for the best,[1]
Ere thou thy daughter link in holy band
Of wedlock to that new unknowen guest:
For he already plighted his right hand
Unto another love, and to another land.

"To me, sad maid, or rather widow sad,
He was affiancëd long time before,
And sacred pledges he both gave and had;
False errant Knight, infámous, and forswore!
Witness the burning altars, which[2] he swore,
And guilty heav'ns, of his bold perjurý;
Which though he hath polluted oft of yore,
Yet I to them for judgment just do fly,
And them conjure t' avenge this shameful injurý!

"Therefore, since mine he is, or free or bond,[3]
Or false or true, or living or else dead,
Withhold, O sov'reign Prince, your hasty hand
From knitting league with him, I you aread,[4]
Nor ween[5] my right with strength adown to tread,
Through weakness of my widowhood or woe:
For Truth is strong her rightful cause to plead,
And shall find friends, if need requireth so.
So bids thee well to fare, thy neither friend nor foe, FIDESSA."

When he these bitter biting words had read,
The tidings strange did him abashëd[6] make,
That still he sat long time astonishëd,
As in great muse, nor word to creature spake.
At last his solemn silence thus he brake,
With doubtful eyes fast fixëd on his guest;
"Redoubted Knight, that for mine only sake
Thy life and honour late adventurest;
Let naught be hid from me, that ought to be exprest.

"What mean these bloody vows and idle threats,
Thrown out from womanish impatient mind?
What heav'ns? what altars? what enragëd heats,
Here heapëd up with terms of love unkind,
My conscience clear with guilty bands would bind?
High God be witness that I guiltless am!
But if yourself, Sir Knight, ye faulty find,
Or wrappëd be in loves of former dame,
With crime do not it cover, but disclose the same."

To whom the Redcross Knight this answer sent;
"My lord, my king, be naught hereat dismay'd,
Till well ye wot[7] by grave intendiment,[8]
What woman, and wherefóre, doth me upbraid
With breach of love and loyalty betray'd.
It was in my mishaps, as hitherward
I lately travell'd, that unwares I stray'd
Out of my way, through perils strange and hard,
That day should fail me ere I had them all declar'd.

"There did I find, or rather I was found
Of this false woman that Fidessa hight;
Fidessa hight the falsest dame on ground,
Most false Duessa, royal richly dight,[9]
That easy was t' inveigle weaker sight:
Who, by her wicked arts and wily skill,
Too false and strong for earthly skill or might,
Unwares me wrought unto her wicked will,
And to my foe betray'd when least I fearëd ill."

Then steppëd forth the goodly royal Maid,[10]
And, on the ground herself prostráting low,
With sober countenance thus to him said;
"O pardon me, my sov'reign lord, to show
The secret treasons, which of late I know
To have been wrought by that false sorceress:
She, only she, it is, that erst did throw
This gentle Knight into so great distress,
That death him did await in daily wretchedness.

"And now it seems, that she subornëd hath
This crafty messenger, with letters vain,[11]
To work new woe and unprovided scath,[12]
By breaking of the band betwixt us twain;
Wherein she usëd hath the practic pain[13]
Of this false footman, cloak'd with simpleness,
Whom if ye please for to discover plain,
Ye shall him Archimago find, I guess,
The falsest man alive; who tries, shall find no less."

The king was greatly movëd at her speech;
And, all with sudden indignation freight,[14]
Bade on that messenger rude hands to reach.
Eftsoons the guard, which on his state did wait,
Attach'd that faitour false[15] and bound him strait:
Who, seeming sorely chafëd at his band,
As chainëd bear whom cruel dogs do bait,
With idle force did feign them to withstand;
And often semblance made to scape out of their hand.

But they him laid full low in dungeon deep,
And bound him hand and foot with iron chains;
And with continual watch did warely keep.
Who then would think, that by his subtle trains[16]
He could escape foul death or deadly pains?
Thus, when that Prince's wrath was pacified,
He gan renew the late forbidden bains,[17]
And to the Knight his daughter dear he tied
With sacred rites and vows for ever to abide.

His own two hands the holy knots did knit,
That none but death for ever can divide;
His own two hands, for such a turn most fit,
The houseling[18] fire did kindle and provide,
And holy water thereon sprinkled wide;
At which the bushy tead[19] a groom did light,
And sacred lamp in secret chamber hide,
Where it should not be quenchëd day nor night
For fear of evil fates, but burnen ever bright.

1 Well consider.
2 By which.
3 Bound.
4 Advise.
5 Think.
6 Confounded.
7 Know.
8 Attention.
9 Attired.
10 Una.
11 Idle, false.
12 Unforeseen mischief.
13 The crafty labour, the trickery.
14 Fraught, filled.
15 Seized that treacherous malefactor.
16 Stratagems.
17 Bans.
18 Sacramental.
19 Torch.

Then gan they sprinkle all the posts with wine,
And made great feast to solemnise that day:
They all perfum'd with frankincénse divine,
And preciòus odours fetch'd from far away,
That all the house did sweat with great array:
And all the while sweet music did apply
Her curious skill the warbling notes to play,
To drive away the dull melánchol ý;
The while one sung a song of love and jollit ý.

During the which there was a heav'nly noise
Heard sound through all the palace pleasantly,
Like as it had been many an angel's voice
Singing before th' Eternal Majesty
In their trinál triplicities[1] on high:
Yet wist no creature whence that heav'nly sweet
Proceeded, yet each one felt secretl ý
Himself thereby reft of his senses meet,
And ravishëd with rare impression in his sprite.

Great joy was made that day of young and old,
And solemn feast proclaim'd throughout the land,
That their exceeding mirth may not be told:
Suffice it here by signs to understand
The usual joys at knitting of love's band.

Thrice happy man the Knight himself did hold,
Possessëd of his Lady's heart and hand;
And ever, when his eye did her behold,
His heart did seem to melt in pleasures manifold.

Her joyous presence and sweet company
In full content he there did long enjoy;
Nor wicked envy, nor vile jealousy,
His dear delights were able to annoy:
Yet, swimming in that sea of blissful joy,
He naught forgot how he whilóm had sworn,
In case he could that monstrous beast destroy,
Unto his Faery Queen back to return;
The which he shortly did, and Una left to mourn.

Now strike your sails, ye jolly mariners,
For we be come unto a quiet road,[2]
Where we must land some of our passengers,
And light this weary vessel of her load;
Here she a while may make her safe abode,
Till she repairëd have her tackles spent,[3]
And wants supplied; and then again abroad
On the long voyage whereto she is bent:
Well may she speed, and fairly finish her intent![4]

THE SECOND BOOK

OF

THE FAERIE QUEEN:

CONTAINING

THE LEGEND OF SIR GUYON, OR OF TEMPERANCE.

RIGHT well I wot, most mighty Sovereign,
That all this famous ántique history
Of[5] some th' abundance of an idle brain
Will judgëd be, and painted forgery,
Rather than matter of just memory;
Since none that breatheth living air doth know
Where is that happy land of Faëry
Which I so much do vaunt, yet nowhere show;
But vouch antiquities, which nobody can know.

But let that man with better sense advise[6]
That of the world least part to us is read;[7]
And daily how, through hardy enterprise,
Many great regions are discoverëd
Which to late age were never mentionëd.
Who ever heard of th' Indian Peru?
Or who in venturous vessel measurëd
The Amazon huge river, now found true?
Or fruitfullest Virginia who did ever view?

Yet all these were, when no man did them know,
Yet have from wisest ages hidden been;
And later times things more unknown shall show.
Why then should witless man so much misween[8]
That nothing is, but that which he hath seen?
What if, within the moon's fair shining sphere,
What if, in every other star unseen,
Of other worlds he happily[9] should hear?
He wonder would much more; yet such to some appear.

Of Faery Land yet if he more inquire,
By certain signs, here set in sundry place,
He may it find; nor let him then admire,[10]
But yield[11] his sense to be too blunt and base,
That n'ot[12] without a hound fine footing trace.
And thou, O fairest Princess[13] under sky,
In this fair mirror may'st behold thy face,
And thine own realms in land of Faër ý,
And in this ántique image thy great ancestr ý.

The which, O! pardon me thus to enfold
In covert veil, and wrap in shadows light,
That feeble eyes your glory may behold,
Which else could not endure those beamës bright,
But would be dazzled with exceeding light.
O! pardon, and vouchsafe with patient ear
The brave adventures of this Faery Knight,
The good Sir Guyon, graciously to hear;
In whom great rule of Temp'rance goodly doth appear.

1 In their three hierarchies, with three ranks in each hierarchy.
2 Roadstead, anchorage.
3 Worn out.
4 Designed voyage.
5 By.
6 Consider.
7 Known, discovered.
8 So wrongly think.
9 Perchance, haply.
10 Wonder.
11 Confess.
12 Knows not, cannot.
12 Queen Elizabeth.

CANTO I.

Guyon, by Archimage abus'd,
The Redcross Knight awaits;
Finds Mordant and Amavia slain
With Pleasure's poison'd baits.

ARCHIMAGO, "that cunning architect of canker'd guile," when he knew that the Redcross Knight had quitted Eden lands, freed himself from prison; "his shackles empty left, himself escapëd clean." He went forth, full of malice, to work the Knight mischief and avenging woe, wherever he might find "his only heart-sore and his only foe;" since the Knight must needs quit Una, who now at last "enjoys sure peace for evermore, as weather-beaten ship arriv'd on happy shore." But all Archimago's craft, espial, and endeavour to catch his foe at vantage in his snares, were fruitless; the Knight "descried, and shunnëd still, his sleight; the fish that once was caught, new bait will hardly bite."

Nathless th' enchanter would not spare his pain,
In hope to win occasion to his will;
Which when he long awaited had in vain,
He chang'd his mind from one to other ill:
For to all good he enemy was still.
Upon the way him fortunëd to meet,
Fair marching underneath a shady hill,
A goodly knight, all arm'd in harness meet,
That from his head no place appearëd to his feet.

His carriage was full comely and upright;
His countenance demure and temperate;
But yet so stern and terrible in sight,
That cheer'd his friends, and did his foes amate:[1]
He was an Elfin born, of noble state
And mickle worship[2] in his native land;
Well could he tourney, and in lists debate,[3]
And knighthood took of good Sir Huon's hand,
When with king Oberon he came to Faery land.

Him als'[4] accompanied upon the way
A comely Palmer,[5] clad in black attire,
Of ripest years, and hairs all hoary gray,
That with a staff his feeble steps did stire,[6]
Lest his long way his aged limbs should tire:
And, if by looks one may the mind aread,[7]
He seem'd to be a sage and sober sire;
And ever with slow pace the Knight did lead,
Who taught his trampling steed with equal steps to tread.

Archimago, seeing them, "weenëd well to work some uncouth wile;" and straightway, "untwisting his deceitful clue, he gan to weave a web of wicked guile." Feigning to quake and tremble with fear, he prayed Sir Guyon to "stay his steed for humble miser's (wretch's) sake," and began to lament the dishonour of his lady by a lewd ribald knight. His piteous tale, "of chastity and honour virginal" shamefully outraged, inflamed Sir Guyon with wrath against the violator; and he asked how he might trace him out, to avenge the wrong. "That shall I show," said the crafty Archimago, "as sure as hound the stricken deer doth challenge by the bleeding wound."

He stay'd not longer talk, but with fierce ire
And zealous haste away is quickly gone
To seek that knight, where him that crafty squire
Suppos'd to be. They do arrive anon
Where sat a gentle lady all alone,
With garments rent, and hair dishevellëd,
Wringing her hands, and making piteous moan:
Her swollen eyes were much disfigurëd,
And her fair face with tears was foully blubberëd.

Approaching nigh, the Knight endeavoured to comfort her, praying her to "tell the cause of her conceivëd pain;" for if he who had wronged her lived, he should her "do due recompense again, or else his wrong with greater puissánce maintain." But her sorrow only redoubled; she tore her hair, scratched and hid her face, and bent down her head, "either for grievous shame, or for great teen" (grief). The soothing speech of her squire somewhat appeased her sorrow; and she at last described the false traitor that reft her honour. She knew not his name, but he rode a gray steed whose sides were marked with dappled circles, "and in his silver shield he bore a bloody cross, that quarter'd all the field." Guyon much wondered "how that same knight should do so foul amiss;" for he at once recognised him as the Redcross Knight, who had won so great glory in "the adventure of the Errant Damosell" (Una). Nevertheless, if he had done such a wrong, he should dear abide it, or make good amends; for "all wrongs have mends, but no amends of shame." He called on her to rise out of her pain, and see "the salving of her blotted name;" and with seeming reluctance, but inward joy, she complied.

Her purpose was not such as she did feign,
Nor yet her person such as it was seen;
But under simple show, and semblant[8] plain,
Lurk'd false Duessa secretly unseen,
As a chaste virgin that had wrongëd been;
So had false Archimago her disguis'd,
To cloak her guile with sorrow and sad teen:[9]
And eke himself had craftily devis'd
To be her squire, and do her service well aguis'd.[10]

Her late, forlorn and naked, he had found
Where she did wander in waste wilderness,
Lurking in rocks and caves far under ground,
And with green moss cov'ring her nakedness,
To hide her shame and loathly filthiness,
Since her Prince Arthur of proud ornaments
And borrow'd beauty spoil'd: her nathëless
Th' enchanter, finding fit for his intents,
Did thus revest,[11] and deck'd with due habiliments.

1 Terrify, confound.
2 Much honour.
3 Do battle, contend.
4 Also.
5 Personifying Reason, the constant attendant and guide of Temperance.
6 Steer.
7 Discern, read.
8 Appearance.
9 Grief.
10 Equipped.
11 Reclothe; French, "revêtir."

For all he did was to deceive good knights,
And draw them from pursuit of praise and fame,
To slug[1] in sloth and sensual delights,
And end their days with unrenownëd shame:
And now exceeding grief him overcame,
To see the Redcross thus advancëd high;
Therefore this crafty engine[2] he did frame,
Against his praise to stir up enmity
Of such as virtues like[3] might unto him ally.

So now he Guyon guides an uncouth way,
Through woods and mountains, till they came
at last
Into a pleasant dale that lowly lay
Betwixt two hills, whose high heads, overplac'd,
The valley did with cool shade overcast;
Through midst thereof a little river roll'd,
By which there sat a knight with helm unlac'd,
Himself refreshing with the liquid cold,
After his travel long and labours manifold.

Archimago cried aloud that yonder was the false knight, shrouding himself in secret to shun due vengeance; and, while the lady and her squire abode far off to view the encounter, Sir Guyon, inflamed with wrathfulness, "straight against that knight his spear he did redress." The Redcross Knight seized his arms, laid lance in rest, and "gan rencounter him in equal race;" but suddenly Sir Guyon lowered his spear, and besought mercy from his opponent and from God, for his offence and heedless boldness in bending cursed steel against that sacred badge of his Redeemer's death, set on the other's shield for ornament. The Redcross Knight, with difficulty staying his steed, met Sir Guyon's apologies with counter-apologies for the hasty hand that had almost done heinous violence on the fair image of that heavenly maid that decked his shield. "So be they both at one;" they raise their beavers bright to greet each other; the falsehood which provoked Sir Guyon to his fierce attack is explained; and the aged Palmer, coming up, recognises and salutes fairly the Redcross Knight, praying for happy chance for him and that dear cross upon his shield.

"Joy may you have, and everlasting fame,
Of late most hard achievement by you done,
For which enrollëd is your glorious name
In heav'nly registers above the sun,
Where you a saint with saints your seat have
won!
But wretched we, where ye have left your mark,
Must now anew begin like race to run.
God guide thee, Guyon, well to end thy wark,[4]
And to the wishëd haven bring thy weary bark!"

"Palmer," him answerëd the Redcross Knight,
"His be the praise, that this achievement
wrought,
Who made my hand the organ of His might!
More than good will to me attribute naught;
For all I did, I did but as I ought.
But you, fair Sir, whose pageant[5] next ensues,
Well may ye thé,[6] as well can wish your thought,
That home ye may report thrice happy news!
For well ye worthy be for worth and gentle
thews."[7]

So courteous congé[8] both did give and take,
With right hands plighted, pledges of good will,
Then Guyon forward gan his voyage make
With his black Palmer, that him guided still:
Still he him guided over dale and hill,
And with his steady staff did point his way;
His race with reason, and with words his will,
From foul intemperance he oft did stay,
And suffer'd not in wrath his hasty steps to stray.

Thus they travelled long, through many hard but glorious adventures; until, as they passed by a forest side, "for succour from the scorching ray," they heard a rueful voice, crying mournfully "with piercing shrieks, and many a doleful lay." It was the voice of a lady, who called on sweetest Death to "take away this long-lent loathed light;" and who wished for her sweet babe—whom frowning froward fate had made sad witness of his father's fall—that he might live long and better thrive than his luckless parents. To his dead mother he is to "attest that clear she died from blemish criminal;" and she added, "thy little hands embrued in bleeding breast, lo, I for pledges leave! so give me leave to rest."

With that a deadly shriek she forth did throw,
That through the wood re-echoëd again;
And after gave a groan so deep and low,
That seem'd her tender heart was rent in twain,
Or thrill'd with point of thorough-piercing pain;
As gentle hind, whose sides with cruel steel
Through lancëd, forth her bleeding life does rain,
While the sad pang approaching she does feel,
Brays out[9] her latest breath, and up her eyes
doth seal.

Which when that warrior heard, dismounting
straight
From his tall steed, he rush'd into the thick,[10]
And soon arrivëd where that sad portrait[11]
Of death and dolour lay, half dead, half quick;
In whose white alabaster breast did stick
A cruel knife that made a grisly wound,
From which forth gush'd a stream of gore-blood
thick,
That all her goodly garments stain'd around,
And into a deep sanguine dy'd the grassy ground.

Pitiful spectacle of deadly smart,
Beside a bubbling fountain low she lay
Which she increasëd with her bleeding heart,
And the clean waves with purple gore did ray:[12]
Als' in her lap a lovely babe did play
His cruel sport, instead of sorrow due;
For in her streaming blood he did embay[13]
His little hands, and tender joints embrue:
Pitiful spectacle as ever eye did view!

1 Lie sluggishly, live idly.
2 Means, contrivance.
3 Similar virtues to his own.
4 Work.
5 Splendid achievement, glory of a completed enterprise.
6 Prosper.
7 Noble qualities.
8 Leave.
9 Breathes out hard or loudly.
10 Thicket.
11 Image.
12 Streak, defile.
13 Bathe.

Beside them both, upon the soilëd grass
The dead corse of an armëd knight was spread,
Whose armour all with blood besprinkled was;
His ruddy lips did smile, and rosy red
Did paint his cheerful cheeks, yet[1] being dead;
Seem'd to have been a goodly personage,
Now in his freshest flow'r of lustihead,[2]
Fit to inflame fair lady with love's rage,
But that fierce fate did crop the blossom of his age.

Beholding this sight, Sir Guyon's "heart gan wax as stark as marble stone, and his fresh blood did freeze with fearful cold;" but, recovering himself, "out of her gorëd wound the cruel steel he lightly snatch'd, and did the floodgate stop with his fair garment." Feeling her pulse move, he hoped "to call back life to her forsaken shop," and at last was rejoiced to find her "breathe out living air." Gently he inquired the cause of her cruel plight: "Speak, O dear lady, speak! help never comes too late." Raising up her dim eyelids, "on which the dreary death did sit as sad as lump of lead, and make dark clouds appear," she saw the Knight all in bright armour clad, and threw herself down again to the ground, as hating life and light. Thrice the gentle Knight reared her up, thrice she sank again; till he folded his arms about her sides, and again entreated her to tell her grief. She prayed to be left in peace to die; but his importunity prevailed at last, and, "with feeble hands then stretched forth on high, as heav'n accusing guilty of her death," she told him that the dead corpse lying near once "the gentlest knight that ever on green grass gay steed with spurs did prick, the good Sir Mordant, was." He was her lord, her love, her dear lord, her dear love; and, riding forth to seek adventure, he left her "enwombëd of this child, this luckless child."

"Him fortunëd (hard fortune ye may guess!)
To come where vile Acrasia[3] does won;[4]
Acrasia, a false enchanteress,
That many errant knights has foul fordone;[5]
Within a wand'ring island, that doth run
And stray in perilous gulf, her dwelling is:
Fair Sir, if ever there ye travel, shun
The cursëd land where many wend[6] amiss,
And know it by the name: it hight the *Bower of Bliss.*

"Her bliss is all in pleasure and delight,
Wherewith she makes her lovers drunken mad;
And then, with words and weeds[7] of wondrous might,
On them she works her will to uses bad:
My liefest[8] lord she thus beguilëd had;
For he was flesh (all flesh doth frailty breed!)
Whom when I heard to be so ill bestad,[9]
(Weak wretch) I wrapt myself in palmer's weed,[10]
And cast[11] to seek him forth through danger and great dread.

"Now had fair Cynthia by even turns
Full measurëd three quarters of her year,
And thrice three times had fill'd her crooked horns,
When as my womb her burden would forbear,[12]
And bade me call Lucina[13] to me near.
Lucina came: a man-child forth I brought:
The woods, the nymphs, my bow'rs,[14] my midwives, were:
Hard help at need! So dear thee, babe, I bought;
Yet naught too dear I deem'd, while so my dear I sought."

She found at last her lord, "in chains of lust and lewd desires y-bound," and so changed, that he knew neither his lady nor his own ill; but she succeeded in restoring him to a better will, and began to devise means for his deliverance. This the enchantress perceiving, gave him at parting to drink from a cup thus charmed:

"Sad verse,[15] give death to him that death does give,
And loss of love to her that loves to live,
So soon as Bacchus with the Nymph does link!"[16]

Stooping to drink at the fountain hard by, the charm worked, and he fell dead——But at this point the poor lady breaks off for want of breath, and sliding soft, lays her down in the sleep of death. Sir Guyon, unable to bear the sight, averts his head;

Then, turning to his Palmer, said; "Old Sire,
Behold the image of mortality,
And feeble nature cloth'd with fleshy tire![17]
When raging Passion with fierce tyranny
Robs Reason of her due regality,
And makes it servant to her basest part;
The strong it weakens with infirmity,
And with bold fury arms the weakest heart:
The strong through pleasure soonest falls, the weak through smart."

"But Temperance," said he, "with golden squire[18]
Betwixt them both can measure out a mean;
Neither to melt in pleasure's hot desire,
Nor fry[19] in heartless grief and doleful teen:[20]
Thrice happy man, who fares them both atween!
But since this wretched woman overcome
Of anguish, rather than of crime, hath been,
Reserve her cause to her eternal doom;
And, in the mean,[21] vouchsafe her honourable tomb."

"Palmer," quoth he, "death is an equal doom

1 Though.
2 Pleasantness, youthful beauty.
3 Excess or Intemperance; from the Greek, ακρασια; "acrasy" is a word employed in medicine in the same sense.
4 Dwell.
5 Ruined.
6 Go.
7 Herbs.
8 Dearest.
9 So ill bestead; in such a grievous plight.
10 Garment.
11 Resolved.
12 Get rid of, cease to bear.
13 Diana. See note 17, page 37.
14 Chambers.
15 Fatal spell.
16 So soon as the wine in the cup shall be mixed with water.
17 Attire.
18 Square, rule.
19 Burn.
20 Sorrow.
21 Meanwhile.

To good and bad, the common inn of rest;
But after death the trial is to come,
When best shall be to them that livëd best:
But both alike, when death hath both suppress,
Religious reverence doth burial teen;[1]
Which whoso wants, wants so much of his rest:
For all so great shame after death I ween,
As self to dien bad, unburied bad to been.[2]

Then "the great earth's womb they open to the sky," and embrave or adorn the grave "with sad cypress seemly;" therein, "cov'ring with a clod their closëd eye," they tenderly lay the bodies; but first Guyon, drawing the dead knight's sword out of its sheath, cuts a lock of all their hair, mingles it with their blood and earth, casts it into their grave, and swears a solemn vow that neither he nor the orphan shall ever forbear due vengeance; "so, shedding many tears, they clos'd the earth again."

CANTO II.

Babe's bloody hands may not be cleans'd.
The face of Golden Mean:
Her sisters, Two Extremities,
Strive her to banish clean.

Sir Guyon, having thus "with due rites and dolorous lament" performed the obsequies of Mordant and Amavia, took up the babe, that smiled on him when it should rather weep; and, "soft himself inclining on his knee down to that well," tried, but in vain, to wash the gore from the little hands. In great amazement, he asked himself whether the "blot of foul offence might not be purg'd with water or with bath"—or whether God had imprinted that token of his wrath to show how sore he hates blood-guiltiness—or whether the charm and venom had infected the blood with secret filth. The Palmer, Reason, seeing him "at gaze," explained his error. Secret virtues, he said, are infused in every fountain and in every lake.

"Of those, some were so from their source indued
By great Dame Nature, from whose fruitful pap
Their well-heads spring, and are with moisture dew'd;
Which feeds each living plant with liquid sap,
And fills with flow'rs fair Flora's painted lap:
But other some, by gift of later grace,
Or by good prayers, or by other hap,
Had virtue pour'd into their waters base,
And thenceforth were renown'd, and sought from place to place.

"Such is this well, wrought by occasion strange
Which to her nymph befell. Upon a day,
As she the woods with bow and shafts did range,
The heartless[3] hind and roebuck to dismay,
Dan Faunus chanc'd to meet her by the way,
And, kindling fire at her fair-burning eye,
Inflamëd was to follow beauty's chase,
And chasëd her, that fast from him did fly;
As hind from her, so she fled from her enemy.

"At last, when failing breath began to faint,
And saw no means to scape; of shame afraid,
She sat her down to weep for sore constraint;[4]
And, to Diana calling loud for aid,
Her dear besought to let her die a maid.
The goddess heard; and sudden, where she sate
Welling out streams of tears, and quite dismay'd
With stony fear of that rude rustic mate,[5]
Transform'd her to a stone from steadfast virgin's state.

"Lo! now she is that stone; from whose two heads,
As from two weeping eyes, fresh streams do flow,
Yet cold through fear and old conceivëd dreads:
And yet the stone her semblance seems to show,
Shap'd like a maid, that such ye may her know;
And yet her virtues in her water bide:
For it is chaste and pure as purest snow,
Nor lets her waves with any filth be dy'd;
But ever, like herself, unstainëd hath been tried.[6]

"From thence it comes, that this babe's bloody hand
May not be cleans'd with water of this well:
Nor certes, Sir, strive you it to withstand,
But let them still be bloody, as befell,
That they his mother's innocence may tell,
As she bequeath'd in her last testament;
That, as a sacred symbol, it may dwell
In her son's flesh, to mind revengëment,[7]
And be for all chaste dames an endless monument."[8]

The Knight "hearkened to his reason," took up the child, and gave him to the Palmer to bear; he himself carried the dead father's bloody armour; and they returned to the place where Guyon's steed had been left, only to find it gone. Subduing his anger, the Knight fared along on foot, though toiling under his double burden; so they travelled long with little ease, till they came to a rock-built castle by the sea: "an ancient work of ántique fame, and wondrous strong by nature and by skilful frame."

Therein three sisters dwelt of sundry sort,
The children of one sire by mothers three;
Who, dying whilom, did divide this fort
To them by equal shares in equal fee:
But strifeful mind and diverse quality
Drew them in parts,[9] and each made other's foe:
Still did they strive and daily disagree;
The eldest did against the youngest go,
And both against the middest meant to worken woe.

Where when the Knight arriv'd, he was right well
Receiv'd, as knight of so much worth became,
Of second sister, who did far excel
The other two; Medina[10] was her name,

[1] Require. [2] To be unburied bad, as to die bad. [3] Timid. [4] Distress. [5] Companion. [6] Proved.

[7] To remind him of his duty of revenge. [8] Lesson, reminder. [9] Apart; into quarrel. [10] Moderation, or Golden Mean.

A sober, sad,[1] and comely courteous dame:
Who rich array'd, and yet in modest guise,
In goodly garments that her well became,
Fair marching forth in honourable wise,
Him at the threshold met and well did enterprise.[2]

She led him up into a goodly bow'r,
And comely courted[3] with meet modesty;
Nor in her speech, nor in her 'haviour,
Was lightness seen or looser vanity,
But gracious womanhood, and gravity
Above the reason[4] of her youthly years:
Her golden locks she roundly did uptie
In braided trammels,[5] that no looser hairs
Did out of order stray about her dainty ears.

News of Guyon's arrival come to her sisters, who "are at their wanton rest, accourting each her friend with lavish feast." The eldest, Elissa or Deficiency, has for her suitor Sir Huddibras, "a hardy man, yet not so good of deeds as great of name," which he had won by many rash adventures; "more huge in strength than wise in works he was," foolhardy, morose, and, for greater terror, "all arm'd in shining brass." The youngest sister, Perissa or Excess, is loved by Sansloy, "he that fair Una late foul outragëd; the most unruly and the boldest boy" that ever wielded arms. The two knights regard each other with deadly hate, and move daily battle against each other, to advance themselves in their ladies' favour. At the news of Guyon's arrival, "both knights and ladies forth right angry fared, and fiercely unto battle stern themselves prepared." But on the way the knights' momentary agreement against the stranger breaks down, and they join cruel combat in middle space, with an uproar that alarms the whole house, as if a thunderstorm were raging. Guyon, binding "his sunbroad shield about his wrist," runs "with shining blade unsheathed" to learn the cause of quarrel, "and, at his first arrival, them began with goodly means to pacify, well as he can."

But they, him spying, both with greedy force
At once upon him ran, and him beset
With strokes of mortal steel without remorse,
And on his shield like iron sledges bet.[6]
As when a bear and tiger, being met
In cruel fight on Libyc ocean[7] wide,
Espy a traveller with feet surbet,[8]
Whom they in equal prey hope to divide,
They stint their strife, and him assail on every side.

But he, not like a weary traveller,
Their sharp assault right boldly did rebut,
And suffer'd not their blows to bite him near,
But with redoubled buffs them back did put;
Whose grievëd minds, which choler did englut,[9]
Against themselves turning their wrathful spite,
Gan with new rage their shields to hew and cut.
But still, when Guyon came to part their fight,
With heavy load on him they freshly gan to smite.

As a tall ship, tossëd in troublous seas,
Whom raging winds, threat'ning to make the prey
Of the rough rocks, do díversely disease,[10]
Meets two contráry billows by the way,
That her on either side do sore assay,
And boast to swallow her in greedy grave;
She, scorning both their spites, does make wide way,
And, with her breast breaking the foamy wave,
Does ride on both their backs, and fair herself doth save:

So boldly he him bears, and rushes forth
Between them both, by conduct of his blade.
Wondrous great prowess and heroic worth
He show'd that day, and rare ensample made,
When two so mighty warriors he dismay'd:
At once he wards and strikes; he takes and pays;
Now forc'd to yield, now forcing to invade;
Before, behind, and round about him lays:
So double was his pains, so double be his praise.

Strange sort of fight, three valiant knights to see
Three combats join in one, and to darrain[11]
A triple war with triple enmity,
All for their ladies' froward love[12] to gain,
Which, gotten, was but hate. So Love does reign
In stoutest minds, and maketh monstrous war:
He maketh war, he maketh peace again,
And yet his peace is but continual jar:
O miserable men, that to him subject are!

Whilst thus they mingled were in furious arms,
The fair Medina, with her tresses torn,
And naked breast, in pity of their harms,
Amongst them ran; and, falling them beforn,
Besought them by the womb which them had borne,
And by the loves which were to them most dear,
And by the knighthood which they sure had sworn,
Their deadly cruel discord to forbear,
And to her just conditions of fair peace to hear.

But her sisters opposed her counsel, and urged their knights to "pursue the end of their strong enmity;" still Medina persisted, until, "suppressing fury mad," the combatants desisted and listened to her "sober speeches." She asked if this was the joy of arms—if these were the parts of noble knighthood? "Vain is the vaunt, and victory unjust, that more to mighty hands than rightful cause doth trust."

"And were there rightful cause of difference,
Yet were not better fair it to accord,
Than with blood-guiltiness to heap offence,
And mortal vengeance join to crime abhorr'd?

1 Grave. 2 Receive.
3 Entertained.
4 Reasonable power or expectation.
5 Nets; Italian, "tramaglio;" French, "tramail."
6 Beat like sledge-hammers.
7 The Libyan desert, or ocean of sand.
8 For "surbated;" sore beaten, bruised, wearied.
9 Gorge. 10 Distress. 11 Wage.
12 The love of their ladies, who, all at variance, demand of each different service.

O! fly from wrath; fly, O my liefest[1] lord!
Sad be the sights and bitter fruits of war,
And thousand furies wait on wrathful sword:
Nor aught the praise of prowess more doth mar
Than foul revenging rage, and base contentious
jar.

"But lovely concord, and most sacred peace,
Doth nourish virtue, and fast friendship breeds;
Weak she makes strong, and strong thing does
increase,
Till it the pitch of highest praise exceeds:
Brave be her wars, and honourable deeds,
By which she triumphs over ire and pride,
And wins an olive garland for her meeds.
Be therefore, O my dear lords! pacified,
And this misseeming[2] discord meekly lay aside."

Her gracious words assuaged their rancour, and, dropping their cruel weapons, they "lowly did abase their lofty crests to her fair presence and discreet behests." She laid the basis of an agreement which should "stablish terms betwixt both their requests;" and, to confirm the treaty of peace, she invited them to her lodging, where they were well received, and prepared "their minds to pleasure and their mouths to dainty fare." The two froward sisters also came, though much against their mind; both grudging and grieving inwardly against their second sister, "as doth a hidden moth the inner garment fret, not th' outer touch: one thought her cheer too little, th' other thought too much."

Elissa (so the eldest hight) did deem
Such entertainment base, nor aught would eat,
Nor aught would speak, but evermore did seem
As discontent[3] for want of mirth or meat:
No solace could her paramour intreat[4]
Her once to show, nor court, nor dalliance;
But with bent louring brows, as she would
threat,
She scowl'd, and frown'd with froward countenance;
Unworthy of fair lady's comely governance.

But young Perissa was of other mind,
Full of disport, still laughing, loosely light,
And quite contráry to her sister's kind;[5]
No measure in her mood, no rule of right,
But pourëd out in pleasure and delight:
In wine and meats she flow'd above the bank,
And in excess exceeded her own might;
In sumptuous tire[6] she joy'd herself to prank,[7]
But of her love too lavish: little have she thank!

By her sat bold Sansloy, "fit mate for such a mincing minion;" while Huddibras, "more like a malcontent," grieving at the other's bold fashion, sat still, "and inly did himself torment."

Betwixt them both the fair Medina sate,
With sober grace and goodly carriáge:
With equal measure she did moderate
The strong extremities of their outráge;
The froward pair[8] she ever would assuage,[9]
When they would strive due reason to exceed;
But that same froward twain[10] would accoráge,[11]
And of her plenty add unto their need:
So kept she them in order, and herself in heed.

Thus fairly attempering her feast, she "pleas'd them all with meet satiety;" and at the end besought Guyon of courtesy to tell "whence he came through jeopardy, and whither now on new adventure bound." The Knight complied. Having loftily lauded the Queen of Faery Land —"most great and most glorious Virgin Queen alive"—to whom he owes homage and service, and who has conferred on him the most renowned Order of Maidenhead, he relates that at the yearly solemn feast which she is wont to hold, on "the day that first doth lead the year around," the old Palmer, now his companion, presented himself with a complaint against a wicked Fay, who had wrought grievous mischiefs, "and many whelmed in deadly pain." The Queen, "whose glory is in gracious deeds," employed him, all unfit, to work redress for such annoys; and "now hath fair Phœbe with her silver face thrice seen the shadows of the nether world" since he quitted Faery Court. Never shall he rest in house or hold till he that false Acrasia has won; and then he tells the story of Mordant and Amavia, whose little son is witness of the enchantress's foul deeds.

Night was far spent; and now in ocean deep
Orion, flying fast from hissing Snake,[12]
His flaming head did hasten for to steep,
When of his piteous tale he end did make:
Whilst with delight of that he wisely spake
Those guests beguilëd, did beguile their eyes
Of kindly sleep, that did them overtake.
At last, when they had mark'd the changëd skies,
They wist their hour was spent; then each to
rest him hies.

CANTO III.

Vain Braggadocio, getting Guy-
on's horse, is made the scorn
Of knighthood true; and is of fair
Belphœbe foul forlorn.

SOON as the morrow fair with purple beams
Dispers'd the shadows of the misty night,
And Titan, playing on the eastern streams,
Gan clear the dewy air with springing light—

Sir Guyon rose from drowsy couch, armed himself, and continued his journey; having first taken leave of that Virgin pure, into whose care he committed the bloody-handed babe, to be trained in virtuous lore, and, when he reached riper years, to be called "Ruddymane"—or

1 Dearest. 2 Unseemly.
3 Discontented. 4 Induce by entreaties.
5 Nature. 6 Attire.
7 Adorn vainly or coquettishly.

8 Sansloy and Perissa. 9 Restrain.
10 Huddibras and Elissa.
11 Encourage, stimulate.
12 Setting when Scorpio rises.

Bloody-hand—that so he might be taught to avenge his parents' death. So forth he fared on foot, for he had lately lost his good steed. He had left the horse outside the wood where he heard the dying lady's groan:

The while a losel[1] wand'ring by the way,
One that to bounty[2] never cast his mind,
Nor thought of honour ever did assay
His baser breast, but in his kestrel kind[3]
A pleasing vein of glory he did find,
To which his flowing tongue and troublous[4] sprite
Gave him great aid, and made him more inclin'd;
He, that brave steed there finding ready dight,
Purloin'd both steed and spear, and ran away full light.

Now gan his heart all swell in jollity,
And of himself great hope and help conceiv'd,
That puffëd up with smoke of vanity,
And with self-lovëd personage deceiv'd,
He gan to hope of men to be receiv'd
For such as he him thought, or fain would be:[5]
But, for[6] in Court gay portance[7] he perceiv'd,
And gallant show, to be in greatest gree,[8]
Eftsoons to Court he cast[9] t' advance his first degree.

And by the way he chancëd to espy
One sitting idle on a sunny bank,
To whom advancing in great bravery,
As peacock that his painted plumes doth prank,[10]
He smote his courser in the trembling flank,
And to him threat'ned his heart-thrilling spear:
The silly man, seeing him ride so rank[11]
And aim at him, fell flat to ground for fear,
And crying, "Mercy!" loud, his piteous hands gan rear.

Thereat the scarecrow waxëd wondrous proud,
Through fortune of his first adventure fair,
And with big thund'ring voice revil'd him loud;
"Vile caitive, vassal of dread and despair,
Unworthy of the common breathëd air,
Why livest thou, dead dog, a longer day,
And dost not unto death thyself prepare?
Die, or thyself my captive yield for ay.
Great favour I thee grant for answer thus to stay."

The wretch, yielding himself Braggadocio's humble thrall, kissed his stirrup, and hailed him as his liege lord. By and by the liegeman began to wax more bold, "and, when he felt the folly of his lord," to display his own true nature. From that day he contrived to uphold his master's idle humour with fine flattery, "and blow the bellows to his swelling vanity."

Trompart,[12] fit man for Braggadocio
To serve at Court in view of vaunting eye;
Vain-glorious man, when flutt'ring wind does blow
In his light wings, is lifted up to sky;
The scorn of knighthood and true chivalry,
To think, without desert of gentle deed
And noble worth, to be advancëd high;
Such praise is shame; but honour, virtue's meed,
Doth bear the fairest flow'r in honourable seed.

"So forth they pass, a well-consorted pair," till they meet Archimago, whom the brave array of Braggadocio deceives into thinking him a meet instrument for his vengeance on Sir Guyon; against whom he has turned the malice formerly cherished against the Redcross Knight. He asks Trompart what mighty warrior that may be that rides in golden saddle, with spear alone, and no sword. Trompart replies, that his master is a great adventurer, who has lost his sword through hard assay, and vowed to wear none till he should be avenged. The enchanter, glad at heart, and louting low, then complains to Braggadocio of wrongs done by Sir Guyon and the Redcross Knight, whom he charges with the murder of Mordant and Amavia. Braggadocio seems all suddenly enraged, and threatens death with dreadful countenance, shaking his spear. He calls on Archimago to tell him where those knights lurk; and the enchanter promises to guide him, while earnestly advising him to give no odds to his valiant foes, but provide himself with a sword. Braggadocio scouts the advice of the "dotard" who measures manhood by the sword or mail, and asks: "Is not enough four quarters of a man, withouten sword or shield, a host to quail?"—for Archimago little suspects the power of that right hand. The enchanter is surprised at his boast, knowing that whoever encountered either of the knights would need all his arms; but Braggadocio caps his own vaunt by the declaration that once he swore, when with one sword seven knights he brought to end, thenceforth never to bear sword in battle, "but it were that which noblest knight on earth doth wear." Reassured, Archimago promises to procure by the morrow the sword of Prince Arthur, "the best and noblest knight alive"—a "sword that flames like burning brand;" "at which bold word that boaster gan to quake, and wonder in his mind what might that portent make" (signify).

He[13] stay'd not for more bidding, but away
Was sudden vanishëd out of his sight:
The northern wind his wings did broad display
At his command, and rearëd him up light
From off the earth, to take his airy flight.
They look'd about, but nowhere could espy
Track of his foot: then dead through great affright

1 Loose fellow. 2 Goodness.
3 Base nature: a kestrel is a species of hawk, which was trained to fly at small game. 4 Restless.
5 Such as he thought himself, or would fain be thought by others.
6 Because 7 Carriage.
8 Favour. 9 Purposed to go.
10 Proudly or conceitedly display.
11 Fiercely. 12 Deceiver; French, "trompeur."
13 Archimago.

They both nigh were, and each bade other fly:
Both fled at once, nor ever back returnëd eye;

Till that they come unto a forest green,
In which they shroud themselves from causeless fear:
Yet fear them follows still, whereso they been:
Each trembling leaf and whistling wind they hear
As ghastly bug[1] does greatly them afear:
Yet both do strive their fearfulness to feign.[2]
At last they heard a horn that shrillëd clear
Throughout the wood that echoëd again,
And made the forest ring, as it would rive in twain.

Eft[3] through the thick[4] they heard one rudely rush;
With noise whereof he from his lofty steed
Down fell to ground, and crept into a bush,
To hide his coward head from dying dread.[5]
But Trompart stoutly stay'd to taken heed
Of what might hap. Eftsoons there steppëd forth
A goodly lady clad in hunter's weed,
That seem'd to be a woman of great worth,
And by her stately portance[6] born of heav'nly birth.

Her face so fair, as flesh it seemëd not,
But heav'nly portrait of bright angel's hue,
Clear as the sky, withouten blame or blot,
Through goodly mixture of complexions due;
And in her cheeks the vermeil red did shew
Like roses in a bed of lilies shed,
The which ambrosial odours from them threw,
And gazers' sense with double pleasure fed,
Able to heal the sick and to revive the dead.

In her fair eyes two living lamps did flame,
Kindled above at th' heav'nly Maker's light,
And darted fiery beams out of the same,
So passing persant,[7] and so wondrous bright,
That quite bereav'd the rash beholder's sight:
In them the blinded god his lustful fire
To kindle oft assay'd, but had no might;
For, with dread majesty and awful ire,
She broke his wanton darts, and quenchëd base desire.[8]

Her ivory forehead, full of bounty brave,
Like a broad table did itself dispread,
For love his lofty triumphs to engrave,
And write the battles of his great godhéad:
All good and honour might therein be read;
For there their dwelling was. And, when she spake,
Sweet words, like dropping honey, she did shed;
And 'twixt the pearls and rubies softly brake
A silver sound, that heav'nly music seem'd to make.

Upon her eyelids many graces sate,
Under the shadow of her even brows,
Working belgardes[9] and amorous retrate;[10]
And ev'ry one her with a grace endows,
And ev'ry one with meekness to her bows:
So glorious mirror of celestial grace,
And sov'reign monument of mortal vows,
How shall frail pen describe her heav'nly face,
For fear, through want of skill, her beauty to disgrace!

So fair, and thousand thousand times more fair,
She seem'd, when she presented was to sight;
And was y-clad, for heat of scorching air,
All in a silken camus[11] lily white,
Purfled[12] upon with many a folded plight,[13]
Which all above besprinkled was throughout
With golden aigulettes, that glister'd bright
Like twinkling stars; and all the skirt about
Was hemm'd with golden fringe [most gorgeously set out[14]].

Below her ham her weed[15] did somewhat train,[16]
And her straight legs most bravely were embail'd[17]
In gilden buskins of costly cordwáin,[18]
And barr'd with golden bands, which were entail'd[19]
With curious antics,[20] and full fair email'd:[21]
Before, they fasten'd were under her knee
In a rich jewel, and therein entrail'd[22]
The ends of all the knots, that none might see
How they within their foldings close enwrappëd be:

Like two fair marble pillars they were seen,
Which do the temple of the gods support,
Whom all the people deck with garlands green,
And honour in their festival resort;
Those same with stately grace and princely port
She taught to tread, when she herself would grace;
But with the woody nymphs when she did sport,
Or when the flying libbard[23] she did chase,
She could them nimbly move, and after fly apace.

And in her hand a sharp boar-spear she held,
And at her back a bow and quiver gay,
Stuff'd with steel-headed darts, wherewith she quell'd
The salvage beasts in her victorious play;
Knit with a golden baldric[24] which forelay
Athwart her snowy breast, and did divide
Her dainty paps; which, like young fruit in May,
Now little gan to swell, and, being tied,
Through her thin weed their places only signified.

Her yellow locks, crispëd like golden wire,
About her shoulders weren loosely shed,

1 Bugbear.
2 Dissemble, conceal.
3 Soon after.
4 Thicket.
5 Fear of death, or deadly fear.
6 Carriage.
7 Piercing.
8 The portrait of Belphœbe, like that of the Faery Queen herself, and of most of Spenser's fair and virtuous ladies, is designed to show forth the praises of the Virgin Queen Elizabeth. See the Introductory Letter to Raleigh, page 306.
9 Lovely looks.
10 Aspect.
11 A tunic, or short robe; the word has an analogy with "chemise," it is found in the French word "camisade," and in the same language "camisole" means a short night-robe.
12 Embroidered.
13 Plait.
14 This is the first instance in the "Faerie Queen" of a hemistich, or broken line; the words in brackets were suggested by a contemporary of Spenser's, to complete the line.
15 Dress.
16 Hang.
17 Enclosed.
18 Cordovan leather.
19 Engraved, ornamented in intaglio.
20 Devices.
21 Enamelled; French, "émailler," to enamel.
22 Twisted, interwoven.
23 Leopard.
24 Belt.

And, when the wind amongst them did inspire,[1]
They wavëd like a pennon wide dispread,
And low behind her back were scatterëd:
And, whether art it were or heedless hap,
As through the flow'ring forest rash she fled,
In her rude hairs sweet flow'rs themselves did lap,[2]
And flourishing fresh leaves and blossoms did enwrap.

Such as Diana by the sandy shore
Of swift Eurotas, or on Cynthus green,
Where all the nymphs have her unwares forlore,[3]
Wanders alone with bow and arrows keen,
To seek her game: or as that famous queen[4]
Of Amazons, whom Pyrrhus did destroy,
The day that first of Priam she was seen,
Did show herself in great triumphant joy,
To succour the weak state of sad afflicted Troy.

Heartless Trompart, all dismayed, knew not whether to fly or hide, until the forest-queen asked him if he had seen a bleeding hind in whose haunch she had fixed an arrow. Reassured, Trompart, addressing her as "goddess," said that he had seen no such beast, and inquired which of the gods he might her name, that he might do her worship aright. Ere she could reply, her eye detected a movement in the bush where Braggadocio lay; and she was about to launch a deadly shaft, when Trompart interposed to save his liege lord, who was of warlike name and wide renowned. Braggadocio crawled out of his nest on "caitiff hands and thighs, and standing stoutly up, his lofty crest did fiercely shake, and rouse as coming late from rest."

As fearful fowl, that long in secret cave
For dread of soaring hawk herself hath hid,
Not caring how, her silly life to save,
She her gay painted plumes disorderëd;
Seeing at last herself from danger rid,
Peeps forth, and soon renews her native pride;
She gins her feathers foul disfigurëd
Proudly to prune, and set on every side;
She shakes off shame, nor thinks how erst[5] she did her hide.

So Braggadocio, when her goodly visage he beheld, began to vaunt himself, but was daunted by the sight of her arms. She saluted him graciously as a knight in pursuit of honour; he declared that in that pursuit he had spent all his youthly days, "endeavouring his dreaded name to raise above the moon;" then he asked why she ranged the wild forest, where no pleasure is, instead of frequenting the Court; for "the wood is fit for beasts, the Court is fit for thee."

"Whoso in pomp of proud estate," quoth she,
"Does swim, and bathes himself in courtly bliss,
Does waste his days in dark obscurity,
And in oblivion ever buried is:
Where ease abounds, 'tis eath[6] to do amiss:
But who his limbs with labours, and his mind
Behaves[7] with cares, cannot so easy miss.[8]
Abroad in arms, at home in studious kind,
Who seeks with painful toil, shall Honour soonest find:

"In woods, in waves, in wars, she wonts to dwell,
And will be found with peril and with pain;
Nor can the man that moulds in idle cell
Unto her happy mansiön attain:
Before her gate High God did Sweat ordain,
And wakeful Watches, ever to abide:
But easy is the way and passage plain
To Pleasure's palace: it may soon be spied,
And day and night her doors to all stand open wide."

But ere she could proceed, Braggadocio, carried away by her sweet words and her beauty, "gan burn in filthy lust," and leaped forward to embrace her; she started back, bent against him her bright javelin, and, turning, fled apace. "The peasant" was amazed and grieved at her flight; but he feared the unknown wood, and the lady's wrath. Trompart advised that she should be let pass at will, for who could tell but that she was some power celestial. Braggadocio admits that he thought no less "when first he heard her horn sound with such ghastliness."

"For from my mother's womb this grace I have
Me given by eternal destiny,
That earthly thing may not my courage brave
Dismay with fear, or cause one foot to fly,
But either hellish fiends, or pow'rs on high:
Which was the cause, when erst[5] that horn I heard,
Weening it had been thunder in the sky,
I hid myself from it, as one afear'd;
But, when I other knew, myself I boldly rear'd.

"But now, for fear of worse that may betide,
Let us soon hence depart." They soon agree:
So to his steed he got, and gan to ride
As one unfit therefor, that all might see
He had not trainëd been in chivalry.
Which well that valiant courser did discern;
For he despis'd to tread in due degree,
But chaf'd and foam'd with courage fierce and stern,
And to be eas'd of that base burden still did yearn.

CANTO IV.

Guyon does Furor bind in chains,
And stops Occasiön:
Delivers Phaon, and therefore
By Strife is rail'd upon.

In brave pursuit of honourable deed
There is I know not what great difference

1 Breathe. 2 Entwine.
3 Abandoned.
4 Penthesilea; who came to succour King Priam, towards the close of the siege of Troy, and was slain—not by Pyrrhus, however, as Spenser says, but—by Achilles.
5 Lately. 6 It is easy.
7 Occupies. 8 Err.

Between the vulgar and the noble seed,
Which unto things of valorous pretence
Seems to be borne by native influence;
As feats of arms; and love to entertain:
But chiefly skill to ride seems a sciénce
Proper to gentle blood: some others feign
To manage steeds, as did this vaunter; but in vain.

Meantime the steed's rightful owner fared on foot with the Palmer—"his most trusty guide, who suffer'd not his wandering feet to slide"—till he beheld from far "some troublous uproar or contentious fray," and drawing near saw a madman, or one that feigned to be mad, dragging by the hair along the ground a handsome stripling, whom he beat savagely and gored with many a wound.

And him behind a wicked hag did stalk,
In ragged robes and filthy disarray;
Her other leg [1] was lame, that she n'ot [2] walk,
But on a staff her feeble steps did stay:
Her locks, that loathly were and hoary gray,
Grew all afore, and loosely hung unroll'd;
But all behind was bald, and worn away,
That none thereof could ever taken hold;
And eke her face ill-favour'd, full of wrinkles old.

And, ever as she went, her tongue did walk
In foul reproach and terms of vile despite,
Provoking him, by her outrageous talk,
To heap more vengeance on that wretched wight:
Sometimes she raught [3] him stones, wherewith to smite;
Sometimes her staff, though it her one leg were,
Withouten which she could not go upright;
Nor any evil means she did forbear,
That might him move to wrath, and indignation rear.[4]

Guyon drew near, thrust away the hag, and laid his mighty hands on the madman; who at once turned his beastly brutal rage against the Knight, "and smote, and bit, and kicked, and scratched, and rent," unknowing in his fury what he did. He was a man of great strength, if he could have guided it aright; but in his passion he was wont to strike wide, and often hurt himself unawares; he "as a blindfold bull, at random fares, and where he hits naught knows, and whom he hurts naught cares." Guyon, trying to overthrow him, overthrew himself unawares, and lay low on the ground; on which the villain and the hag united their forces to kill him. But, with a great effort, the Knight regained his feet, and drew his sword.

Which when the Palmer saw, he loudly cried,
"Not so, O Guyon, never think that so
That monster can be master'd or destroy'd:
He is not, ah! he is not such a foe
As steel can wound, or strength can overthrow.
That same is Furor, cursëd cruel wight,
That unto knighthood works much shame and woe;
And that same hag, his aged mother, hight
Occasión; the root of all wrath and despite.

"With her, whoso will raging Furor tame,
Must first begin, and well her ámenáge:[5]
First her restrain from her reproachful blame
And evil means, with which she doth enrage
Her frantic son, and kindles his couráge;
Then, when she is withdrawn or strong withstood,
'Tis eath [6] his idle fury to assuage,
And calm the tempest of his passion wood:[7]
The banks are overflown when stoppëd is the flood."

Guyon, seizing Occasion "by the hoar locks that hung before her eyes," threw her to the ground; but she continued her railings and incitements to her son, till an iron lock was fastened firm and strong on her ungracious tongue. Even then she made signs to him with her crooked hands, and only when she had been tied hand and foot to a stake did Furor fly. Guyon soon overtook him, and, after a stout wrestle, in which Furor showed sadly impaired power, he was overcome and bound.

With hundred iron chains he did him bind,
And hundred knots, that did him sore constrain:
Yet his great iron teeth he still did grind
And grimly gnash, threat'ning revenge in vain:
His burning eyne, which bloody streaks did stain,
Starëd full wide, and threw forth sparks of fire;
And, more for rank despite than for great pain,
Shak'd his long locks, colour'd like copper wire,
And bit his tawny beard to show his raging ire.

Guyon now raised and restored the wretched squire, inquiring how he fell into such a sorry plight. He told the following doleful tale:

"It was a faithless squire, that was the source
Of all my sorrow and of these sad tears,
With whom from tender dug of common nurse
At once I was upbrought; and eft,[8] when years
More ripe us reason lent to choose our peers,
Ourselves in league of vowëd love we knit;
In which we long time, without jealous fears
Or faulty thoughts, continu'd as was fit;
And, for my part I vow, dissembled not a whit.

"It was my fortune, common to that age,
To love a lady fair of great degree,
The which was born of noble parentage,
And set in highest seat of dignity,
Yet seem'd no less to love than lov'd to be;
Long I her serv'd, and found her faithful still,
Nor ever thing could cause us disagree;
Love, that two hearts makes one, makes eke one will:
Each strove to please, and other's pleasure to fulfil.

"My friend, hight Philemon, I did partake [9]
Of all my love and all my privity;[10]
Who greatly joyous seemëd for my sake,
And gracious to that lady, as to me;
Nor ever wight, that might so welcome be

1 Left leg. 2 Could not.
3 Reached. 4 Raise, excite.
5 Manage.

6 Easy. 7 Mad.
8 Afterwards. 9 Make the confidant.
10 Secret.

As he to her, withouten blot or blame;
Nor ever thing that she could think or see,
But unto him she would impart the same:
O wretched man, that would abuse so gentle dame!

"At last such grace I found, and means I wrought,
That I that lady to my spouse had won;
Accord of friends, consent of parents sought,
Affiance made, my happiness begun,
There wanted naught but few rites to be done,
Which marriage make: that day too far did seem!
Most joyous man, on whom the shining sun
Did show his face, myself I did esteem,
And that my falser friend did no less joyous deem.

"But, ere that wishëd day his beam disclos'd,
He, either envying my toward good,[1]
Or of himself to treason ill dispos'd,
One day unto me came in friendly mood,
And told, for secret, how he understood
That lady, whom I had to me assign'd,
Had both distain'd her honourable blood,
And eke the faith which she to me did bind;
And therefore wish'd me stay, till I more truth should find.

"The gnawing anguish, and sharp jealousy,
Which his sad speech infixëd in my breast,
Rankled so sore, and fester'd inwardly,
That my engrievëd mind could find no rest,
Till that the truth thereof I did out wrest;
And him besought, by that same sacred band
Betwixt us both, to counsel me the best:
He then, with solemn oath and plighted hand,
Assur'd ere long the truth to let me understand.

"Ere long with like again he borded[2] me,
Saying, he now had boulted[3] all the flour,
And that it was a groom of base degree
Which of my love was partner paramour:
Who usëd in a darksome inner bow'r
Her oft to meet: which better to approve,
He promisëd to bring me at that hour,
When I should see that would me nearer move,[4]
And drive me to withdraw my blind abusëd love.

"This graceless man, for furtherance of his guile,
Did court the handmaid of my lady dear,
Who, glad t' embosom[5] his affection vile,
Did all she might more pleasing to appear.
One day, to work her to his will more near,
He woo'd her thus; 'Pryené (so she hight),
What great despite doth fortune to thee bear,
Thus lowly to abase thy beauty bright,
That it should not deface all others' lesser light?

"'But if she had her least help to thee lent,
T' adorn thy form according thy desart,[6]
Their blazing pride thou wouldest soon have blent,[7]
And stain'd their praises with thy least good part;
Nor should fair Claribell' with all her art,
Though she thy lady be, approach thee near:
For proof thereof, this ev'ning, as thou art,
Array thyself in her most gorgeous gear,
That I may more delight in thy embracement dear.'

"The maiden, proud through praise, and mad through love,
Him hearken'd to, and soon herself array'd;
The while to me the traitor did remove
His crafty engine; and, as he had said,
Me leading, in a secret corner laid,
The sad spectator of my tragedy:
Where left, he went, and his own false part play'd,
Disguisëd like that groom of base degree,
Whom he had feign'd th' abuser of my love to be.

"Eftsoons he came unto th' appointed place,
And with him brought Pryené, rich array'd
In Claribella's clothes: her proper face
I not discernëd in that darksome shade,
But ween'd[8] it was my love with whom he play'd.
Ah God! what horror and tormenting grief
My heart, my hands, mine eyes, and all assay'd!
Me liefer[9] were ten thousand deathës' prefe[10]
Than wound of jealous worm, and shame of such reprefe.[11]

"I home returning, fraught with foul despite,
And chawing[12] vengeance all the way I went,
Soon as my loathëd love appear'd in sight,
With wrathful hand I slew her innocent;
That after soon I dearly did lament:
For when the cause of that outrageous deed,
Demanded, I made plain and evident,
Her faulty handmaid, which that bale[13] did breed,
Confess'd how Phïlemon her wrought to change her weed.

"Which when I heard, with horrible affright
And hellish fury all enrag'd, I sought
Upon myself that vengeable despite
To punish: yet it better first I thought
To wreak my wrath on him, that first it wrought:
To Phïlemon, false faitour[14] Phïlemon,
I cast[15] to pay that I so dearly bought:
Of deadly drugs I gave him drink anon,
And wash'd away his guilt with guilty potión.

"Thus heaping crime on crime, and grief on grief, to loss of love adjoining loss of friend," he then tried to kill Pryené; she fled, and he pursued. "Fear gave her wings, and rage enforced my flight;" but Furor pursued and seized him, and, with his mother, "betwixt them both they have me done to die." Guyon assured the squire that all his hurts might soon through temperance be eased; but

Then gan the Palmer thus; "Most wretched man,
That to Affections[16] does the bridle lend!

1 My happiness near at hand.
2 Addressed; French, "aborder," to accost.
3 Sifted. See note 12, page 169.
4 Affect more deeply.
5 Admit to her heart.
6 According to thy desert.
7 Obscured.
8 Supposed.
9 Preferable.
10 The test or suffering of ten thousand deaths.
11 Disgrace.
12 Brooding.
13 Misery.
14 Deceiver.
15 Resolved, sought means.
16 The passions.

In their beginning they are weak and wan,
But soon through sufferance grow to fearful end:
While they are weak, betimes with them contend;
For, when they once to perfect strength do grow,
Strong wars they make, and cruel battery bend
'Gainst fort of Reason, it to overthrow:
Wrath, Jealousy, Grief, Love, this squire have laid thus low.

"Wrath, Jealousy, Grief, Love, do thus expel:
Wrath is a fire; and Jealousy a weed;
Grief is a flood; and Love a monster fell;
The fire of sparks, the weed of little seed,
The flood of drops, the monster filth did breed:
But sparks, seed, drops, and filth, do thus delay;[1]
The sparks soon quench, the springing seed outweed,
The drops dry up, and filth wipe clean away:
So shall Wrath, Jealousy, Grief, Love, die and decay."

Just as the squire has informed Guyon that his name is Phaon, and that he is sprung from "famous Coradin," they spy far off a varlet running towards them hastily, covered with dust and sweat, panting, breathless, and hot. Behind his back he bears a brazen shield, on which is painted "a flaming fire in midst of bloody field," with the motto writ round about the wreath, "Burnt I do burn;" and in his hand are two swift darts, deadly sharp and dipped "in poison and in blood of malice and despite." He boldly warns Guyon to "abandon this forestallëd place" at once, or bide the chance at his own jeopardy. Scornfully but mildly the Knight declares that the place is his by right, and inquires whom he has to fear. The "varlet" then vaunts the might of his lord, whose name is Pyrochles,[2] the brother of Cymochles;[3]

——"Both which are
The sons of old Acrates and Despite;
Acrates, son of Phlegethon and Jar;
Phlegethon, son of Erebus and Night;
But Erebus son of Eternity is hight."

Proceeding from immortal race, mortal hands may not withstand his might; and "all in blood and spoil is his delight." The speaker, Atin,[4] "his in wrong and right," is the maker of matter for him to work upon, and his instigator to strife and cruel fight. His lord has sent him in haste

"To seek Occasión, whereso she be:
For he is all dispos'd to bloody fight,
And breathes out wrath and heinous cruelty;
Hard is his hap, that first falls in his jeopardy."

"Mad man," said then the Palmer, "that does seek
Occasión to wrath, and cause of strife;
She comes unsought, and shunnëd follows eke.
Happy! who can abstain, when Rancour rife
Kindles Revenge, and threats his rusty knife:
Woe never wants, where every cause is caught;
And rash Occasion makes unquiet life!"
"Then lo! where bound she sits, whom thou hast sought,"
Said Guyon; "let that message to thy lord be brought."

The squire of Pyrochles, waxing wondrous wroth, sarcastically complimented Guyon on the great glory and gay spoil won by his combat with "silly weak old woman," and threatened that Pyrochles should with his blood abolish so reproachful blot. Then, having fruitlessly aimed one of his darts at the Knight, "he fled away, and might nowhere be seen."

CANTO V.

Pyrochles does with Guyon fight,
And Furor's chain unties,
Who him sore wounds; while Atin to
Cymochles for aid flies.

WHOEVER doth to Temperance apply
His steadfast life, and all his actions frame,
Trust me, shall find no greater enemy,
Than stubborn Perturbation, to the same;
To which right well the wise do give that name;
For it the goodly peace of stayëd[5] minds
Does overthrow, and troublous war proclaim:
His own woe's author, whoso bound it finds,
As did Pyrochles, and it wilfully unbinds.

Soon Guyon saw pricking fast over the plain a knight in bright armour, that shone like the sun on the trembling wave; his steed was bloody red, and foamed angrily under the spur. Without greeting or exchange of words, Pyrochles—for it was he—rushed upon Guyon in a cloud of dust, with his spear in rest. The Knight, being on foot, lightly shunned the stroke, and, passing by, smote at his assailant so fiercely, that the sword, glancing from Pyrochles' shield, severed the horse's head from the body, and thus reduced the contest to equal terms. Sore bruised, Pyrochles rose from the ground, overwhelming Guyon with loud abuse, and struck at him with his flaming sword so fiercely, that the stroke shore away "the upper marge of his sev'nfolded shield," and laid open his helmet. A bitter combat ensued, in which Guyon was wary wise and cool, waiting the advantage which his furious foe was sure to give; and often he made feints, to provoke Pyrochles to new rashness in his conduct of the battle.

1 Hinder of their effect.

2 One who rages as a flame; From Greek πυρ, fire, and οχλεω, I am troubled or turbulent—the idea being taken from the riot and uproar caused by a crowd of people, οχλος.

3 One who rages as a billow; from Greek κυμα, a billow, and οχλεω.

4 From Ατη, Destiny, Necessity; personified as a female goddess by the Greeks, though Spenser has changed the sex, and altered the word to a more masculine form.

5 Steadfast.

Like as a lion, whose imperial pow'r
A proud rebellious unicorn defies,
T' avoid the rash assault and wrathful stowre[1]
Of his fierce foe, him to a tree applies,
And when him running in full course he spies,
He slips aside; the while that furious beast
His precious horn, sought of his enemies,
Strikes in the stock,[2] nor thence can be releast,
But to the mighty victor yields a bounteous feast.

Thus did the Knight often foil his opponent, till at last, assailing him with fresh onset, he made him stoop perforce unto his knee, and soon, following up his victory, struck him to the ground, and obliged him to call for mercy. Sir Guyon, "tempering his passion with advisement slow," stayed his hand; "for the equal die of war he well did know;" and bade Pyrochles live to repent his "hasty wrath and heedless hazardry." The vanquished warrior rose with grim look, grinding his grated teeth for great disdain, and shook for grief his long sandy locks; yet finding in himself some comfort that he had been mastered by such a noble knight, at whose generosity he marvelled even more than at his might. Guyon consoled him by the reflection that the greatest conqueror sometimes has the worse; that "loss is no shame, nor to be less than foe; but to be lesser than himself doth mar both loser's lot, and victor's praise also; vain others overthrows who self doth overthrow."

"Fly, O Pyrochles, fly the dreadful war
That in thyself thy lesser parts[3] do move:
Outrageous Anger, and woe-working Jar,
Direful Impatience, and heart-murd'ring Love:
Those, those thy foes, those warriors, far remove,
Which thee to endless bale[4] captivëd lead.
But, since in might thou didst my mercy prove,
Of courtesy to me the cause aread[5]
That thee against me drew with so impetuous
dread."

Pyrochles replied that it had been complained to him that Guyon had done great wrong to an aged woman, poor and bare; and exhorted him to set Occasion and her son at liberty. Guyon warned him that their freedom should turn to his greatest scath; but granted his request. "Soon as Occasion felt herself untied," she began to defy both the knights—the one because he won, the other because he was won; and, whenever "Furor was enlarged, she sought to kindle his quench'd fire, and thousand causes wrought." She so inflamed Furor, that he would fight with Pyrochles, his deliverer, "because he had not well maintain'd his right," but had yielded to Sir Guyon. Guyon, standing by to watch their uncouth strife, saw them "both together fierce engrasped;" while Occasion attempted, but in vain, to provoke him to a new conflict with Pyrochles. The longer the battle lasted, the more Furor's rage increased, till he had sore wounded and disfigured his adversary; while Occasion armed her son with a firebrand, "which she in Stygian Lake, ay burning bright, had kindled." Then Furor waxed irresistibly fierce and strong; he threw Pyrochles to the ground, dragging his comely corse through dirt and mire, till he had to cry to Sir Guyon for help. The Knight would fain have interposed; but the Palmer, by his grave restraint, stayed him from vainly pitying a man who sought his sorrow through wilfulness, by releasing again his fettered foe. Guyon obeyed the counsel, and pursued his journey; but Atin, Pyrochles' varlet, had fled, after seeing his master under Guyon's foot, to bear tidings of his brother's death to Cymochles.

He was a man of rare redoubted might,
Famous throughout the world for warlike praise,
And glorious spoils, purchas'd in perilous fight:
Full many doughty knights he in his days
Had done to death, subdued in equal frays;
Whose carcases, for terror of his name,
Of fowls and beasts he made the piteous preys,
And hung their conquer'd arms for more defame[6]
On gallows-trees, in honour of his dearest dame.

His dearest dame is that enchanteress,
The vile Acrasia, that with vain delights,
And idle pleasures, in her Bower of Bliss
Does charm her lovers, and the feeble sprites
Can call out of the bodies of frail wights;
Whom then she does transform to monstrous
hues,[7]
And horribly misshapes with ugly sights,
Captiv'd eternally in iron mews.[8]
And darksome dens, where Titan[9] his face never
shews.

There Atin found Cymochles sojourning,
To serve his leman's[10] love: for he by kind[11]
Was given all to lust and loose living,
Whenever his fierce hands he free might find:
And now he has pour'd out his idle mind
In dainty délicés[12] and lavish joys,
Having his warlike weapons cast behind,
And flows in pleasures and vain pleasing toys,
Mingled amongst loose ladies and lascivious boys.

And over him Art, striving to compare
With Nature, did an arbour green dispread,
Framëd of wanton ivy, flowering fair,
Through which the fragrant eglantine did spread
His prickling arms, entrail'd[13] with roses red,
Which dainty odours round about him threw:
And all within with flowers was garnishëd,
That, when mild Zephyrus amongst them blew,
Did breathe out bounteous smells, and painted
colours shew.

And fast beside there trickled softly down
A gentle stream, whose murmuring wave did play
Amongst the pumy[14] stones, and made a soun'
To lull him soft asleep that by it lay:
The weary traveller, wandering that way,

1 Shock. 2 Trunk.
3 Lower parts or qualities of the nature.
4 Misery. 5 Declare.
6 Disgrace. 7 Shapes, appearances.
8 Prisons, cages. 9 The Sun.
10 Mistress's. 11 Nature.
12 Delights. 13 Intertwined.
14 Porous.

Therein did often quench his thirsty heat,
And then by it his weary limbs display
(While creeping slumber made him to forget
His former pain), and wip'd away his toilsome
sweat.

And on the other side a pleasant grove
Was shot up high, full of the stately tree[1]
That dedicated is t' Olympic Jove,
And to his son Alcides, when as he
In Nemea gain'd goodly victory:
Therein the merry birds of ev'ry sort
Chanted aloud their cheerful harmony,
And made amongst themselves a sweet consórt,
That quicken'd the dull sprite with musical
comfórt.

There he him found[2] all carelessly display'd
In secret shadow from the sunny ray,
On a sweet bed of lilies softly laid,
Amidst a flock of damsels fresh and gay,
That round about him dissolute did play
Their wanton follies and light merriments;
Ev'ry of which did loosely disarray
Her upper parts of meet habiliments,
And show'd them naked, deck'd with many ornaments.

And ev'ry of them strove with most delights
Him to aggrate,[3] and greatest pleasures shew:
Some fram'd fair looks, glancing like ev'ning
lights;
Others sweet words, dropping like honey-dew;
Some bathëd kisses, and did soft embrue
The sugar'd liquor through his melting lips:
One boasts her beauty, and does yield to view
Her dainty limbs above her tender hips;
Another her outboasts, and all for trial strips.

He, like an adder lurking in the weeds,
His wand'ring thought in deep desire does steep,
And his frail eye with spoil of beauty feeds:
Sometimes he falsely feigns himself to sleep,
While through their lids his wanton eyes do
peep
To steal a snatch of amorous conceit,
Whereby close[4] fire into his heart does creep:
So he them deceives, deceiv'd in his deceit,
Made drunk with drugs of dear voluptuous
receipt.

Atin, when he spied Cymochles "thus in still waves of deep delight to wade," fiercely approached, and reviled him for his sloth and neglect of arms. "Up, up, thou womanish weak wight," he cried, and bade him fly to the help of Pyrochles; pricking him at the same time with his sharp-pointed dart. Suddenly Cymochles awoke out of his delightful dream, and, uprising "as one affright with hellish fiends, or Furies' mad uproar," inflamed with fell despite, he calls for his arms.

They be y-brought; he quickly does him dight,[5]
And, lightly mounted, passeth on his way;
Nor ladies' loves, nor sweet entreaties, might
Appease his heat, or hasty passage stay;
For he has vow'd to be aveng'd that day
(That day itself him seemëd all too long)
On him, that did Pyrochles dear dismay:[6]
So proudly pricketh on his courser strong,
And Atin ay him pricks with spurs of shame
and wrong.

CANTO VI.

Guyon is of immodest Mirth
Led into loose desire;
Fights with Cymochles, while his brother burns in furious fire.

A HARDER lesson to learn continence
In joyous pleasure than in grievous pain:
For sweetness doth allure the weaker sense
So strongly, that unneth[7] it can refrain
From that which feeble nature covets fain:
But grief and wrath, that be her enemies
And foes of life, she better can restrain:
Yet Virtue vaunts in both her victories;
And Guyon in them all shows goodly masteries.[8]

Whom bold Cymochles travelling to find,
With cruel purpose bent to wreak on him
The wrath which Atin kindled in his mind,
Came to a river, by whose utmost brim
Waiting to pass, he saw where as did swim
Along the shore, as swift as glance of eye,
A little gondelay,[9] bedeckëd trim
With boughs and arbours woven cunninglý,
That like a little forest seemëd outwardlý.

And therein sat a lady fresh and fair,
Making sweet solace to herself alone:
Sometimes she sung as loud as lark in air,
Sometimes she laugh'd, that nigh her breath
was gone;
Yet was there not with her else any one,
That to her might move cause of merriment:
Matter of mirth enough, though there were
none,
She could devise; and thousand ways invent
To feed her foolish humour and vain jolliment.[10]

Which when, far off, Cymochles heard and saw,
He loudly call'd to such as were aboard,
The little bark unto the shore to draw,
And him to ferry over that deep ford.
The merry mariner unto his word
Soon hearken'd, and her painted boat straightway
Turn'd to the shore, where that same warlike
lord
She in receiv'd; but Atin by no way
She would admit, although the Knight her
much did pray.

Eftsoons her shallow ship away did slide,
More swift than swallow shears the liquid sky,
Withouten oar or pilot it to guide,

1 The oak, sacred to Jove; and the poplar, to Hercules. 2 Atin found Cymochles. 3 Gratify. 4 Secret.

5 Array himself. 6 Subdue. 7 Scarcely. 8 Superiority. 9 Gondola; light swift boat. 10 Jollity.

Or wingëd canvas with the wind to fly:
Only she turn'd a pin, and by and by
It cut away upon the yielding wave
(Nor carëd she her course for to apply [1]),
For it was taught the way which she would have,
And both from rocks and flats itself could wisely save.

And all the way the wanton damsel found
New mirth her passenger to entertain;
For she in pleasant purpose [2] did abound,
And greatly joyëd merry tales to feign, [3]
Of which a store-house did with her remain;
Yet seemëd, nothing well they her became:
For all her words she drown'd with laughter vain,
And wanted grace in uttering of the same,
That turnëd all her pleasance to a scoffing game.

And other whiles vain toys she would devise,
As her fantastic wit did most delight:
Sometimes her head she fondly would aguise [4]
With gaudy garlands, or fresh flow'rets dight
About her neck, or rings of rushes plight: [5]
Sometimes, to do [6] him laugh, she would assay
To laugh at shaking of the leavës light,
Or to behold the water work and play
About her little frigate, therein making way.

Wondrously well pleased with "her light behaviour and loose dalliance," the knight forgot all about his revenge in the pleasure of the moment: "so easy is t' appease the stormy wind of malice in the calm of pleasant womankind." In answer to his inquiry, she told him that her name was Phædria, [7] and that she was, as well as he, a servant of Acrasia.

"In this wide inland sea, that hight by name
The Idle Lake, my wand'ring ship I row,
That knows her port, and thither sails by aim,
Nor care nor fear I how the wind do blow,
Or whether swift I wend or whether slow:
Both slow and swift alike do serve my turn:
Nor swelling Neptune nor loud-thund'ring Jove
Can change my cheer, [8] or make me ever mourn:
My little boat can safely pass this perilous bourn." [9]

While thus she talkëd, and while thus she toy'd,
They were far past the passage which he spake, [10]
And come unto an island waste and void, [11]
That floated in the midst of that great lake;
There her small gondelay her port did make,
And that gay pair, issuing on the shore,
Disburden'd her: their way they forward take
Into the land that lay them fair before,
Whose pleasance she him show'd, and plentiful great store.

It was a chosen plot of fertile land,
Amongst wide waves set, like a little nest,
As if it had by Nature's cunning hand
Been choicely pickëd out from all the rest,
And laid forth for ensample of the best:
No dainty flow'r or herb that grows on ground,
No arboret [12] with painted blossoms drest
And smelling sweet, but there it might be found
To bud out fair, and her sweet smells throw all around.

No tree, whose branches did not bravely spring;
No branch, whereon a fine bird did not sit;
No bird, but did her shrill notes sweetly sing;
No song, but did contain a lovely ditt. [13]
Trees, branches, birds, and songs, were framëd fit
For to allure frail mind to careless ease.
Careless the man soon wax'd, and his weak wit
Was overcome of thing that did him please:
So pleasëd did his wrathful purpose fair appease.

Thus when she had his eyes and senses fed
With false delights, and fill'd with pleasures vain,
Into a shady dale she soft him led,
And laid him down upon a grassy plain;
And her sweet self without dread or disdain
She set beside, laying his head disarm'd
In her loose lap, it softly to sustain,
Where soon he slumber'd fearing not be harm'd:
The while with a love lay she thus him sweetly charm'd:

"Behold, O man! that toilsome pains dost take,
The flowers, the fields, and all that pleasant grows,
How they themselves do thine ensample make,
While nothing envious Nature them forth throws
Out of her fruitful lap; how, no man knows,
They spring, they bud, they blossom fresh and fair,
And deck the world with their rich pompous shows;
Yet no man for them taketh pains or care,
Yet no man to them can his careful pains compare.

"The lily, lady of the flow'ring field,
The flow'r-de-luce, [14] her lovely paramoúr,
Bid thee to them thy fruitless labours yield,
And soon leave off this toilsome weary stowre: [15]
Lo! lo! how brave she decks her bounteous bow'r,
With silken curtains and gold coverlets,
Therein to shroud her sumptuous belamour! [16]
Yet neither spins nor cards, nor cares nor frets,
But to her mother Nature all her care she lets. [17]

"Why then dost thou, O man! that of them all
Art lord, and eke of Nature sovereign,
Wilfully make thyself a wretched thrall,
And waste thy joyous hours in needless pain,
Seeking for danger and adventures vain?
What boots it all to have and nothing use?
Who shall him rue [18] that, swimming in the main,

1 Steer towards any particular point.
2 Talk.
3 Invent, fancy.
4 Dress, adorn.
5 Plaited.
6 Make.
7 From the Greek φαιδρος, joyous, jocund, or merry.
8 Countenance, demeanour.
9 Stream.
10 Bespake, desired.
11 Uninhabited, empty.
12 Shrub, or small tree.
13 Ditty, theme, of love.
14 The iris; French, "fleur-de-lis."
15 Conflict.
16 Lover.
17 Leaves.
18 Pity.

Will die for thirst, and water doth refuse?
Refuse such fruitless toil, and present pleasures choose."

Having lulled him fast asleep, and bathed his eyes in liquors strong, that he might not soon awake, she clove again in her boat "the slothful wave of that great greasy lake." On the farther shore she encountered Guyon, seeking for passage; she took the Knight aboard, but neither "for price nor prayers" would she receive the Palmer Reason; and Guyon, though all reluctant to leave him, was hurried off in the fleet bark, over "the dull billows thick as troubled mire, whom neither wind out of their seat could force, nor timely tides did drive out of their sluggish source." By the way "her merry fit she freshly gan to rear;" but the Knight, while partaking her honest mirth and pleasance, so soon as he saw "her pass the bounds of honest merrimake, her dalliance he despised and follies did forsake." Landing, Guyon knew that he had got astray, and upbraided the lady for misguiding him when he had trusted her.

"Fair Sir," quoth she, "be not displeas'd at all;
Who fares on sea may not command his way,
Nor wind and weather at his pleasure call;
The sea is wide, and easy for to stray;
The wind unstable, and doth never stay.
But here a while ye may in safety rest,
Till season serve new passáge to assay:
Better safe port than be in seas distrest."
Therewith she laugh'd, and did her earnest end in jest.

But he, half discontent, must nathëless
Himself appease, and issued forth on shore:
The joys whereof, and happy fruitfulness,
Such as he saw, she gan him lay before,
And all, though pleasant, yet she made much more.
The fields did laugh, the flow'rs did freshly spring,
The trees did bud, and early blossoms bore;
And all the quire of birds did sweetly sing,
And told that garden's pleasures in their carolling.

And she, more sweet than any bird on bough,
Would oftentimes amongst them bear a part,
And strive to pass[1] (as she could well enow)
Their native music by her skilful art:
So did she all, that might his constant heart
Withdraw from thought of warlike enterprise,
And drown in dissolute delights apart,
Where noise of arms, or view of martial guise,
Might not revive desire of knightly exercise.

But Guyon "was wise, and wary of her will, and ever held his hand upon his heart;" though he did not rudely reject the lady's attempts to please, yet he "ever her desirëd to depart;" while she, renewing her disports, "ever bade him stay till time the tide renewed." Meantime Cymochles woke out of his idle dream, and, stirred with shame extreme for his sloth in pursuit of vengeance, marched down to the strand. Meeting Sir Guyon with Phædria, he instantly challenged him to "let be that lady debonair," and prepare for battle. The knights waged a desperate conflict, until Guyon's angry blade cleft his opponent's crest in twain, and bared all his head to the bone—"wherewith astonish'd still he stood as senseless stone." Phædria, seizing the occasion, ran between them, piteously appealing for peace, "if ever love of lady did impierce their iron breasts, or pity could find place." She reproached herself as "the author of this heinous deed;" and continued—

"But, if for me ye fight, or me will serve,
Not this rude kind of battle, nor these arms
Are meet, the which do men in bale to sterve,[2]
And doleful sorrow heap with deadly harms:
Such cruel game my scarmoges[3] disarms.
Another war, and other weapons, I
Do love, where love does give his sweet alarms
Without bloodshéd, and where the enemy
Does yield unto his foe a pleasant victory.

"Debateful strife, and cruel enmity,
The famous name of knighthood foully shend;[4]
But lovely peace, and gentle amity,
And in amoúrs the passing hours to spend,
The mighty martial hands do most commend;
Of love they ever greater glory bore
Than of their arms: Mars is Cupído's friend,
And is for Venus' loves renownëd more
Than all his wars and spoils, the which he did of yore."

"Therewith she sweetly smil'd;" and—"such power have pleasing words! such is the might of courteous clemency in gentle heart!"—the knights ceased their strife. Guyon anew besought the damsel to let him depart; and now he found her "no less glad than he desirous was" of his departure, for she was disquieted when she saw him "a foe of folly and immodest toy," caring nothing for her joy and vain delight. She transported him to the farther strand, and there he spied Atin standing where Cymochles had left him. He assailed Guyon with bitter reviling, "as shepherd's cur, that in dark evening's shade hath tracëd out some salvage beastë's tread;" but the Knight, "though somewhat movëd in his mighty heart, yet with strong reason master'd passion frail," and passed unheeding on his way. Atin was left standing on the strand.

Whilst there the varlet stood, he saw from far
An armëd knight that toward him fast ran;
He ran on foot, as if in luckless war
His fórlorn[5] steed from him the victor wan:
He seemëd breathless, heartless, faint, and wan;
And all his armour sprinkled was with blood,
And soil'd with dirty gore, that no man can
Discern the hue thereof: he never stood,
But bent his hasty course towárd the Idle Flood.

1 Surpass.
2 Make men die in misery.

3 Skirmishes; from French "éscarmouche," Italian, "scaramuccia." 4 Disgrace. 5 Lost.

The varlet saw, when to the flood he came,
How without stop or stay he fiercely leapt,
And deep himself beduckëd in the same,
That in the lake his lofty crest was stept,[1]
Nor of his safety seemëd care he kept;
But with his raging arms he rudely flash'd
The waves about, and all his armour swept,
That all the blood and filth away was wash'd;
Yet still he beat the water, and the billows dash'd.

Drawing near, Atin recognised Pyrochles, and inquired what had befallen. "I burn, I burn, I burn," he cried aloud; "oh, how I burn with implacable fire." "Nor sea of liquor cold, nor lake of mire"—death alone—could quench his inly flaming side. Atin urged him not to think of laying hands on himself; but, called upon by his agonised lord to help his last hour, Atin rushed in to save him. He did not know the true nature of that sea, whose waves were so slow and sluggish, "engross'd with mud which did them foul agrise," that they bore up every weighty thing, and let nothing sink to the bottom.

While thus they struggled in that idle wave,
And strove in vain, the one himself to drown,
The other both from drowning for to save,
Lo! to that shore one in an ancient gown,
Whose hoary locks great gravity did crown,
Holding in hand a goodly arming sword,
By fortune came, led with the troublous soun':
Where drenchëd deep he found in that dull ford
The careful[2] servant striving with his raging lord.

Atin called to Archimago for help—for the new-comer was the enchanter, with the sword promised to Braggadocio; and Pyrochles was got out, still exclaiming against "that cursëd man, that cruel fiend of hell," Furor, whose deadly wounds within his liver swelled till, he said, "now I ween Jove's dreaded thunder light does scorch not half so sore, nor damnëd ghost in flaming Phlegethon does not so felly roast." Archimago knew at once his grief, and disarmed him, to search his secret wounds; then, with balms, and herbs, and mighty spells, he speedily restored Pyrochles to health.

CANTO VII.

Guyon finds Mammon in a delve,[3]
Sunning his treasure hoar;
Is by him tempted, and led down
To see his secret store.

As pilot well expert in perilous wave,
That to a steadfast star his course hath bent,
When foggy mists or cloudy tempests have
The faithful light of that fair lamp y-blent,[4]
And cover'd heaven with hideous dreariment;[5]
Upon his card and compass firms[6] his eye,
The masters of his long experiment,[7]
And to them does the steady helm apply,
Bidding his wingëd vessel fairly forward fly:

So, "having lost his trusty Guide," the Palmer, did Sir Guyon proceed on his way, through a wide wasteful desert, feeding himself with comfort "of his own virtues and praiseworthy deeds."

At last he came unto a gloomy glade,
Cover'd with boughs and shrubs from heaven's light
Where as he sitting found in secret shade
An uncouth, savage, and uncivil wight,
Of grisly hue[8] and foul ill-favour'd sight;
His face with smoke was tann'd, and eyes were blear'd;
His head and beard with soot were ill bedight;[9]
His coal-black hands did seem to have been sear'd
In smith's fire-spitting forge, and nails like claws appear'd.

His iron coat, all overgrown with rust,
Was underneath envelopëd with gold;
Whose glist'ning gloss, darken'd with filthy dust,
Well yet appearëd to have been of old
A work of rich entail[10] and curious mould,
Woven with antics[11] and wild imagery:
And in his lap a mass of coin he told,
And turnëd upside down, to feed his eye
And covetous desire with his huge treasury.

And round about him lay on ev'ry side
Great heaps of gold that never could be spent;
Of which some were rude ore, not purified
Of Mulciber's devouring element;[12]
Some others were new driven, and distent[13]
Into great ingots and to wedges square;
Some in round plates withouten moniment:[14]
But most were stamp'd, and in their metal bare
The antique shapes of Kings and Kaisers[15] strange and rare.

Soon as he Guyon saw, in great affright
And haste he rose, for to remove aside
Those precious hills from stranger's envious sight;
And down them pourëd through a hole full wide
Into the hollow earth, them there to hide:
But Guyon, lightly to him leaping, stay'd
His hand that trembled as one terrified;
And, though himself were at the sight dismay'd,
Yet him perforce restrain'd, and to him doubtful said;

"What art thou, man (if man at all thou art),

1 Steeped. 2 Sorrowful.
3 Dell, hollow place.
4 Blinded, bedimmed.
5 Darkness, dread. 6 Firmly fixes.
7 Experience. 8 Terror-striking aspect.
9 Disfigured. 10 Inlaid or engraved ornament.
11 Fantastic devices.

12 By fire: Vulcan had the name of "Mulciber," because he softened ("mulcebat") the metal in which he worked; and the Latin poets used "Mulciber" to signify fire. 13 Distended; beaten out.
14 Stamp, inscription.
15 Emperors; German, "Kaiser," from the Latin, "Cæsar."

That here in desert hast thine habitance,
And these rich hills of wealth dost hide apart
From the world's eye, and from her right usánce?"
Thereat, with staring eyes fixëd askance,
In great disdain he answer'd; "Hardy Elf,
That darest view my direful countenance!
I read[1] thee rash and heedless of thyself,
To trouble my still seat and heaps of precious pelf.

"God of the world and worldlings I me call,
Great Mammon, greatest god below the sky,
That of my plenty pour out unto all,
And unto none my graces do envý:[2]
Riches, renown, and principalitý,
Honour, estate, and all this worldë's good,
For which men swink[3] and sweat incessantlý,
From me do flow into an ample flood,
And in the hollow earth have their eternal brood."

If Guyon would deign to serve him, Mammon promised to place all these mountains, or ten times so much, at his command. But the Knight replied that his godhead's vaunt was vain and his offers were idle; for "regard of worldly muck doth foully blend and low abase the high heroic sprite;" and his delight was all in "fair shields, gay steeds, bright arms," the riches fit for an adventurous knight. Mammon told the "vainglorious Elf" that money could in the twinkling of an eye provide shields, steeds, and arms, and multiply crowns and kingdoms to him; for, he cried, "Do I not kings create, and throw the crown sometimes to him that low in dust doth lie, and him that reign'd into his room thrust down?"

"All otherwise," said he, "I riches read,[4]
And deem them root of all disquietness;
First got with guile, and then preserv'd with dread,
And after spent with pride and lavishness,
Leaving behind them grief and heaviness:
Infinite mischiefs of them do arise;
Strife and debate, bloodshed and bitterness,
Outrageous wrong and hellish covetise;
That noble heart as great dishonour doth despise.

"Nor thine be kingdoms, nor the sceptres thine;
But realms and rulers thou dost both confound,
And loyal truth to treason dost incline:
Witness the guiltless blood pour'd oft on ground;
The crownëd often slain; the slayer crown'd;
The sacred diadem in pieces rent,
And purple robe gorëd[5] with many a wound;
Castles surpris'd; great cities sack'd and brent:[6]
So mak'st thou kings, and gainest wrongful government!

"Long were to tell the troublous storms that toss
The private state, and make the life unsweet:
Who swelling sails in Caspian sea doth cross,
And in frail wood on Adrian gulf doth fleet,[7]
Doth not, I ween, so many evils meet."
Then Mammon waxing wroth; "And why then," said,
"Are mortal men so fond[8] and undiscreet,
So evil thing to seek unto their aid;
And, having not, complain: and, having it, upbraid?"

"Indeed," quoth he, "through foul intemperance
Frail men are oft captív'd to covetise:
But would they think with how small állowánce
Untroubled nature doth herself suffice,
Such superfluities they would despise,
Which with sad cares impeach[9] our native joys.
At the well-head the purest streams arise;
But mucky filth[10] his branching arms annoys,
And with uncomely weeds the gentle wave accloys.[11]

"The ántique world, in his first flow'ring youth,
Found no defect in his Creator's grace;
But with glad thanks, and unreprovëd[12] truth,
The gifts of sov'reign bounty did embrace:
Like angels' life was then men's happy case:
But later ages' pride, like corn-fed steed,
Abus'd her plenty and fat-swoll'n increase
To all licentious lust, and gan exceed
The measure of her mean[13] and natural first need.

"Then gan a cursed hand the quiet womb
Of his great grandmother with steel to wound,
And the hid treasures in her sacred tomb
With sacrilege to dig: therein he found
Fountains of gold and silver to abound,
Of which the matter of his huge desire
And pompous pride eftsoons he did compound;
Then Avarice gan through his veins inspire
His greedy flames, and kindled life-devouring fire."

"Son," said he then, "let be thy bitter scorn,
And leave the rudeness of that ántique age
To them that liv'd therein in state forlorn.
Thou, that dost live in later times, must wage[14]
Thy works for wealth, and life for gold engage.
If then thee list my offer'd grace to use,
Take what thou please of all this surplusage;
If thee list not, leave have thou to refuse:
But thing refusëd do not afterward accuse."

Guyon would receive nothing offered till he knew how it had been got—for he could not tell that Mammon had not won his treasures by force, or blood, or guile. Mammon answered that never yet had eye viewed, nor tongue told, nor hand handled them; but safe he had them

1 Judge, hold.
2 Begrudge.
3 Toil.
4 Regard.
5 Pierced.
6 Burnt.
7 Float. The "Adrian gulf" is the "Mare Adrianum," or, poetically, "Adria"—the Adriatic Sea, mentioned by Horace as a type of fickleness in love or in fortune." Odes, i. 33, 15; iii. 9, 23. Spenser must have thought of these and similar passages when penning the lines in the text.
8 Foolish.
9 Impede, destroy.
10 The filth of vile dross or pelf.
11 Clogs, encumbers.
12 Unreproached, blameless.
13 Moderate.
14 Pledge.

"kept in secret mew;" and he led the incredulous Knight through the thick covert, to a darksome way, deep descending through the hollow ground, "that was with dread and horror compassëd around."

At length they came into a larger space,
That stretch'd itself into an ample plain;
Through which a beaten broad highway did trace,[1]
That straight did lead to Pluto's grisly reign:
By that wayside there sat infernal Pain,
And fast beside him sat tumultuous Strife;
The one in hand an iron whip did strain,
The other brandishëd a bloody knife;
And both did gnash their teeth, and both did threaten life.

On th' other side in one consórt[2] there sate
Cruel Revenge, and rancorous Despite,
Disloyal Treason, and heart-burning Hate;
But gnawing Jealousy, out of their sight
Sitting alone, his bitter lips did bite;
And trembling Fear still to and fro did fly,
And found no place where safe he shroud him might:
Lamenting Sorrow did in darkness lie;
And Shame his ugly face did hide from living eye.

And over them sad Horror, with grim hue,
Did alway soar, beating his iron wings;
And after him owls and night-ravens flew,
The hateful messengers of heavy things,
Of death and dolour telling sad tidings;
While sad Celeno,[3] sitting on a clift,[4]
A song of bale[5] and bitter sorrow sings,
That heart of flint asunder could have rift;
Which having ended, after him she flieth swift.

All these before the gates of Pluto lay;
By whom they passing spake unto them naught.
But th' Elfin Knight with wonder all the way
Did feed his eyes, and fill'd his inner thought.
At last him to a little door he brought,
That to the gate of hell, which gapëd wide,
Was next adjoining, nor them parted aught:
Betwixt them both was but a little stride,
That did the House of Riches from hell-mouth divide.

Before the door sat self-consuming Care,
Day and night keeping wary watch and ward,
For fear lest Force or Fraud should unaware
Break in, and spoil the treasure there in guard:
Nor would he suffer Sleep once thitherward
Approach, although his drowsy den were next:
For next to Death is Sleep to be compar'd;
Therefore his house is unto his annext:
Here Sleep, there Riches, and Hell-gate them both betwixt.

So soon as Mammon there arriv'd, the door
To him did open and afforded way:
Him follow'd eke Sir Guyon evermore,
Nor darkness him nor danger might dismay.
Soon as he enter'd was, the door straightway
Did shut, and from behind it forth there leapt
An ugly fiend, more foul than dismal day;
The which with monstrous stalk[6] behind him stept,
And ever as he went due watch upon him kept.

Well hopëd he ere long that hardy guest,—
If ever covetous hand, or lustful eye
Or lips, he laid on thing that lik'd him best,
Or ever sleep his eye-strings did untie,—
Should be his prey: and therefore still on high
He over him did hold his cruel claws,
Threat'ning with greedy gripe to do[7] him die,
And rend in pieces with his ravenous paws,
If ever he transgress'd the fatal Stygian laws.

That House's form within was rude and strong,
Like a huge cave hewn out of rocky clift,
From whose rough vault the ragged breaches[8] hung
Emboss'd with massy gold of glorious gift,
And with rich metal loaded every rift,[9]
That heavy ruin they did seem to threat;
And over them Arachne[10] high did lift
Her cunning web, and spread her subtile net,
Enwrappëd in foul smoke and clouds more black than jet.

Both roof, and floor, and walls, were all of gold,
But overgrown with dust and old decay,
And hid in darkness, that none could behold
The hue thereof: for view of cheerful day
Did never in that House itself display,
But a faint shadow of uncertain light;
Such as a lamp, whose life does fade away;
Or as the moon, clothëd with cloudy night,
Does shew to him that walks in fear and sad affright.

In all that room was nothing to be seen
But huge great iron chests, and coffers strong,
All barr'd with double bands, that none could ween[11]
Them to enforce by violence or wrong;
On ev'ry side they placëd were along.
But all the ground with skulls was scatterëd,
And dead men's bones, which round about were flung;
Whose lives, it seemëd, whilom there were shed,
And their vile carcases now left unburiëd.

They forward pass; nor Guyon yet spoke word,
Till that they came unto an iron door,
Which to them open'd of his own accord,
And show'd of riches such exceeding store
As eye of man did never see before,
Nor ever could within one place be found,
Though all the wealth which is, or was of yore,
Could gather'd be through all the world around,
And that above were added to that under ground:

1 Pass, traverse.
2 All together, in one group.
3 Celæno, one of the Harpies.
4 Cliff.
5 Calamity.
6 Stride.
7 Make.
8 Rents or projecting points of the rock.
9 Crevice.
10 Arachne was a Lydian maiden, who excelled in weaving, and so enraged Minerva by the superior excellence of her work in a trial of skill, that the goddess rent the web in pieces. Arachne, in despair, hanged herself; and she was changed into a spider—the rope into the spider's thread.
11 Think.

The charge thereof unto a covetous sprite
Commanded was, who thereby did attend,
And warily awaited day and night,
From other covetous fiends it to defend,
Who it to rob and ransack did intend.[1]
Then Mammon, turning to that warrior, said;
"Lo, here the worldë's bliss! lo, here the end,
To which all men do aim, rich to be made!
Such grace now to be happy is before thee laid."

"Certes," said he, "I n'ill[2] thine offer'd grace,
Nor to be made so happy do intend!
Another bliss before mine eyes I place,
Another happiness, another end.
To them that list these base regards[3] I lend:
But I in arms, and in achievements brave,
Do rather choose my flitting hours to spend,
And to be lord of those that riches have,
Than them to have myself, and be their servile slave."

Thereat the Fiend his gnashing teeth did grate,
And griev'd so long to lack his greedy prey;[4]
For well he weenëd that so glorious bait
Would tempt his guest to take thereof assay:[5]
Had he so done, he had him snatch'd away
More light than culver[6] in the falcon's fist:
Eternal God thee save from such decay![7]
But when as Mammon saw his purpose miss'd,
Him to entrap unwares another way he wist.[8]

Thence forward he him led, and shortly brought
Unto another room, whose door forthright
To him did open as it had been taught:
Therein a hundred ranges[9] weren pight,[10]
A hundred furnaces all burning bright;
By every furnace many fiends did bide,
Deformëd creatures, horrible in sight;
And ev'ry fiend his busy pains applied
To melt the golden metal, ready to be tried.

One with great bellows gather'd filling air,
And with forc'd wind the fuel did inflame;
Another did the dying brands repair
With iron tongs, and sprinkled oft the same
With liquid waves, fierce Vulcan's[11] rage to tame,
Who, mast'ring them, renew'd his former heat:
Some scumm'd the dross that from the metal came;
Some stirr'd the molten ore with ladles great:
And ev'ry one did swink,[12] and ev'ry one did sweat.

But, when an earthly wight they present saw,
Glist'ning in arms and battailous array,
From their hot work they did themselves withdraw
To wonder at the sight; for, till that day,
They never creature saw that came that way:
Their staring eyes, sparkling with fervent fire,
And ugly shapes, did nigh the man dismay,
That, were it not for shame, he would retire;
Till that him thus bespake their sov'reign lord and sire:

"Behold, thou Faery's son, with mortal eye,
That living eye before did never see!
The thing that thou didst crave so earnestly,
To weet[13] whence all the wealth late show'd by me
Proceeded, lo! now is reveal'd to thee.
Here is the fountain of the worldë's good!
Now therefore, if thou wilt enrichëd be,
Advise[14] thee well, and change thy wilful mood;
Lest thou perhaps hereafter wish, and be withstood."

Guyon again refused the Money-god's offers; but Mammon, though much displeased, resolved to tempt him yet further.

He brought him, through a darksome narrow strait,
To a broad gate all built of beaten gold:
The gate was open; but therein did wait
A sturdy villain, striding stiff and bold,
As if the Highest God defy he wo'ld:
In his right hand an iron club he held,
But he himself was all of golden mould,
Yet had both life and sense, and well could weld[15]
That cursëd weapon, when his cruel foes he quell'd.

Disdain he callëd was, and did disdain
To be so call'd, and whoso did him call:
Stern was his look, and full of stomach[16] vain;
His portance[17] terrible, and stature tall,
Far passing th' height of men terrestrial;
Like a huge giant of the Titans' race;
That made him scorn all creatures great and small,
And with his pride all others' pow'r deface:
More fit amongst black fiends than men to have his place.

Soon as those glitt'ring arms he did espy,
That with their brightness made that darkness light,
His harmful club he gan to hurtle[18] high,
And threaten battle to the Faery Knight;
Who likewise gan himself to battle dight,[19]
Till Mammon did his hasty hand withhold,
And counsell'd him abstain from perilous fight;
For nothing might abash the villain bold,
Nor mortal steel empierce his miscreated mould.[20]

So having him with reason pacified,
And that fierce carl[21] commanding to forbear,
He brought him in. The room was large and wide,
As it some guild[22] or solemn temple were;
Many great golden pillars did upbear
The massy roof, and riches huge sustain;
And ev'ry pillar deckëd was full dear[23]

1 Strive, design. 2 Will not (have).
3 Objects of regard.
4 The prey for which he was greedy. 5 Trial.
6 Pigeon; from Anglo-Saxon, "culfre." 7 Ruin.
8 Contrived, (thought he) knew. 9 Grates.
10 Placed.
11 The name of the god is here used to signify his especial element, fire.
12 Labour hard.
13 Know. 14 Consider.
15 Wield. 16 Haughtiness, violence.
17 Carriage, port. 18 Shake, whirl.
19 Prepare. 20 Form, body.
21 Churl, rude fellow.
22 Hall in which a guild met.
23 Richly.

With crowns, and diadems, and titles vain,
Which mortal princes wore while they on earth did reign.

A rout of people there assembled were,
Of every sort and nation under sky,
Which with great uproar pressëd to draw near
To th' upper part, where was advancëd high
A stately siege [1] of sov'reign majesty;
And thereon sat a woman, gorgeous gay,
And richly clad in robes of royalty,
That never earthly prince in such array
His glory did enhance, and pompous pride display.

Her face right wondrous fair did seem to be,
That her broad beauty's beam great brightness threw
Through the dim shade, that all men might it see;
Yet was not that same her own native hue,
But wrought by art and counterfeited shew,
Thereby more lovers unto her to call;
Nathless most heav'nly fair in deed and view
She by creation was, till she did fall;
Thenceforth she sought for helps to cloak her crime withal.

There as in glist'ring glory she did sit,
She held a great gold chain y-linkëd well,
Whose upper end to highest heav'n was knit,
And lower part did reach to lowest hell;
And all that press did round about her swell
To catchen hold of that long chain, thereby
To climb aloft, and others to excel:
That was Ambition, rash desire to sty,[2]
And ev'ry link thereof a step of dignitý.

Some thought to raise themselves to high degree
By riches and unrightëous reward;
Some by close should'ring; some by flattery;
Others through friends; others for base regard;
And all, by wrong ways, for themselves prepar'd:[3]
Those that were up themselves, kept others low;
Those that were low themselves, held others hard,
Nor suffer'd them to rise or greater grow;
But ev'ry one did strive his fellow down to throw.

Guyon inquiring who the Lady was, Mammon answered that she was his daughter, from whom alone honour, dignity, and all worldly bliss, were derived.

"And fair Philotimé [4] she rightly hight,
The fairest wight that wonneth [5] under sky,
But that this darksome nether world her light
Doth dim with horror and deformity,
Worthy of heav'n and high felicity,
From whence the gods have her for envy thrust:
But, since thou hast found favour in mine eye,
Thy spouse I will her make, if that thou lust;[6]
That she may thee advance for works and merits just."

The Knight, with great thanks ("Gramercy"), declined the offered alliance, on the ground of inequality of condition, and a prior vow to another lady: "to change love causeless is reproach to warlike knight."

Mammon emmovëd was with inward wrath;
Yet, forcing it to feign,[7] him forth thence led
Through grisly shadows, by a beaten path,
Into a garden goodly garnishëd
With herbs and fruits, whose kinds might not be read:[8]
Not such as earth out of her fruitful womb
Throws forth to men, sweet and well savourëd,
But direful deadly black, both leaf and bloom,
Fit to adorn the dead and deck the dreary tomb.

There mournful cypress grew in greatest store;
And trees of bitter gall; and ebon sad;
Dead sleeping poppy; and black hellebore;
Cold coloquintida;[9] and tetra [10] mad;
Mortal samnitis;[11] and cicuta [12] bad,
With which th' unjust Athenians made to die
Wise Socrates, who, thereof quaffing glad,
Pour'd out his life and last philosophý
To the fair Critias, his dearest belamý! [13]

The Garden of Prosérpina this hight:
And in the midst thereof a silver seat,
With a thick arbour goodly overdight,[14]
In which she often us'd from open heat
Herself to shroud, and pleasures to entreat:[15]
Next thereunto did grow a goodly tree,
With branches broad dispread and body great,
Clothëd with leaves, that none the wood might see,
And loaden all with fruit as thick as it might be.

Their fruit were golden apples glist'ring bright,
That goodly was their glory to behold;
On earth like never grew, nor living wight
Like ever saw, but they from hence were sold;
For those, which Hercules with conquest bold
Got from great Atlas' daughters,[16] hence began,
And planted there did bring forth fruit of gold;

1 Seat; placed on the dais, or elevated portion of the hall at the upper end, where the lord and the honoured guests sat.
2 Soar, mount.
3 Consulted their own interest alone.
4 Love of honour or distinction; Greek, φιλοτιμια, ambition; from φιλεω, I love, and τιμη, honour.
5 Dwelleth.
6 Desire.
7 Making an effort to conceal it.
8 Declared, described.
9 Colocynth, or bitter apple.
10 Deadly nightshade.
11 Savin.
12 Hemlock.
13 Friend—French "bel ami." The poet refers to the dying discourse, reported in the "Phædo" of Plato, in which Socrates, reaching the noblest flight of Greek philosophy, argued for the immortality of the soul. The friend to whom Socrates "poured out his last philosophy," however, was not Critias, but Crito.
14 Overspread.
15 Court, enjoy.
16 Spenser accepts the mythology which makes the Hesperides the daughters of Atlas (called Hesperides from the name of their mother, Hesperis), and not of Hesperus. The maidens, aided by the unsleeping dragon, guarded the golden apples which the Goddess Earth (Gé) gave to Juno on her wedding-day.

And those, with which th' Eubœan young man[1] wan
Swift Atalanta, when through craft he her outran.

Here also sprang that goodly golden fruit,
With which Acontius got his lover true,
Whom he had long time sought with fruitless suit;[2]
Here eke that famous golden apple grew,
The which amongst the gods false Até threw;
For which th' Idæan Ladies disagreed,
Till partial Paris deem'd[3] it Venus' due,
And had of her fair Helen for his meed,
That many noble Greeks and Trojans made to bleed.

The warlike Elf much wonder'd at this tree,
So fair and great, that shadow'd all the ground;
And his broad branches, laden with rich fee,[4]
Did stretch themselves without the utmost bound
Of this great garden, compass'd with a mound:
Which overhanging, they themselves did steep
In a black flood, which flow'd about it round;
That is the river of Cocytus deep,
In which full many souls do endless wail and weep.

Which to behold he clomb up to the bank,
And, looking down, saw many damnëd wights
In those sad waves, which direful deadly stank,
Plungëd continually of[5] cruel sprites,
That with their piteous cries, and yelling shrights,[6]
They made the farther shore resounden wide:
Amongst the rest of those same rueful sights,
One cursëd creature he by chance espied,
That drenchëd[7] lay full deep under the garden side.

Deep was he drenchëd to the utmost chin,
Yet gapëd still as coveting to drink
Of the cold liquor which he waded in;
And, stretching forth his hand, did often think
To reach the fruit which grew upon the brink;
But both the fruit from hand, and flood from mouth,
Did fly aback, and made him vainly swink;[8]
The while he starv'd with hunger, and with drouth[9]
He daily died, yet never throughly dien couth.[10]

The Knight, him seeing labour so in vain,
Ask'd who he was, and what he meant thereby?
Who, groaning deep, thus answer'd him again;
"Most cursëd of all creatures under sky,
Lo, Tantalus, I here tormented lie!
Of whom high Jove wont whilom feasted be;
Lo, here I now for want of food do die!
But, if that thou be such as I thee see,[11]
Of grace I pray thee give to eat and drink to me!"

"Nay, nay, thou greedy Tantalus," the Knight replied, and bade him abide his fate, for an example to make those temperate who live in high degree. Tantalus broke out into revilings and blasphemy against Jove and heaven; while Guyon looked beyond, and saw another wretch, whose carcase was beneath the flood, but whose filthy hands, lifted up on high, seemed to wash themselves eternally, yet ever seemed fouler for the lost labour. Asked who he was, he answered, "I Pilate am, the falsest judge, alas, and most unjust!" who washed his hands in purity the while his soul was soiled with foul iniquity. An infinite number more the Knight saw also tormented there; but Mammon would not let him stay, roughly asking the "fearful fool" why he did not take of the golden fruit, and rest him on the silver stool. All this he did to make the Knight fall, "in frail intemperance, through sinful bait," and render him a prey to the dreadful fiend waiting behind; but Guyon was proof against all temptation.

And now he has so long remainëd there,
That vital pow'rs gan wax both weak and wan
For want of food and sleep, which two upbear,
Like mighty pillars, this frail life of man,
That none without the same enduren can:
For now three days of men were full outwrought
Since he this hardy enterprise began:
Forthy[12] great Mammon fairly he besought
Into the world to guide him back, as he him brought.

The god, though loth, yet was constrain'd t' obey;
For longer time than that no living wight
Below the earth might suffer'd be to stay:
So back again him brought to living light.
But all so soon as his enfeebled sprite
Gan suck this vital air into his breast,
As overcome with too exceeding might,
The life did flit away out of her nest,
And all his senses were with deadly fit opprest.

CANTO VIII.

Sir Guyon, laid in swoon, is by
Acrates' sons despoil'd;
Whom Arthur soon hath rescuëd,
And Paynim brethren foil'd.

And is there care in heav'n? And is there love
In heav'nly spirits to these creatures base,
That may compassion of their evils move?
There is: else much more wretched were the case
Of men than beasts: but O! th' exceeding grace
Of Highest God that loves his creatures so,

1 Hippomenes, the Bœotian (not Eubœan) youth who, dropping along the race-course the three golden apples with which Venus had furnished him, outstripped Atalanta in the race, the prize of which was her hand in marriage—the penalty of failure, death by her hand.

2 Acontius, having gone to Delos to the festival of Diana, fell in love with the beautiful Cydippe, and threw into her bosom an apple on which he had written a vow that she would wed him. The maiden pronounced the lines, in the presence of the goddess, and was therefore bound to wed her humble lover.

3 Decreed, adjudged. 4 Property, wealth.
5 By. 6 Shrieks.
7 Drowned, immersed. 8 Labour in vain.
9 Thirst. 10 Could never thoroughly, really, die.
11 As I judge thee by thine appearance.
12 Therefore.

And all his works with mercy doth embrace,
That blessed Angels he sends to and fro,
To serve to wicked man, to serve his wicked foe!

How oft do they their silver bowers leave
To come to succour us that succour want!
How oft do they with golden pinions cleave
The flitting skies, like flying pursuivant,
Against foul fiends to aid us militant!
They for us fight, they watch and duly ward,
And their bright squadrons round about us plant;
And all for love and nothing for reward:
O why should Heav'nly God to men have such
regard!

While Guyon abode in Mammon's House, the Palmer had found passage across the Lake; and he drew near the place where the Knight lay aswoon. Then he heard a voice that called long and clear, "'Come hither, come hither, oh! come hastily,' that all the fields resounded with the rueful cry." Following the voice, the Palmer came to the shady dell "where Mammon erst did sun his treasury;" and there, to his dismay, he found the good Guyon "slumbering fast in senseless dream."

Beside his head there sat a fair young man,
Of wondrous beauty and of freshest years,
Whose tender bud to blossom new began,
And flourish fair above his equal peers:
His snowy front, curlëd with golden hairs,
Like Phœbus' face adorn'd with sunny rays,
Divinely shone; and two sharp wingëd shears,[1]
Deckëd with diverse plumes, like painted jay's.
Were fixëd at his back, to cut his airy ways.

Like as Cupído on Idæan hill,[2]
When, having laid his cruel bow away,
And mortal arrows, wherewith he doth fill
The world with murderous spoils and bloody
prey,
With his fair mother he him dights[3] to play,
And with his goodly sisters, Graces three;
The goddess, pleasëd with his wanton play,
Suffers herself through sleep beguil'd to be,
The while the other ladies mind their merry
glee.

The Palmer was speechless through fear and wonder, till the child called him to behold this heavy sight—"but dread of death and dolour do away," for life should erelong to her home return. The Angel commended to the old man the charge of the Knight's dear safety, which God had allotted to him; with a warning to succour and defend him, for evil was at hand him to offend; "so having said, eftsoons he gan display his painted nimble wings, and vanish'd quite away"—leaving the astonished Palmer gazing after him, "as fowl escaped by flight." Turning to his charge, he found life not yet quite dislodged, and, much rejoicing, began to cover it tenderly, "as chicken newly hatched." But now he spied "two Paynim Knights all arm'd as bright as sky," with an aged sire beside, and far before a light-foot page, "that breathëd strife and troublous enmity." They were Pyrochles and Cymochles, whom Archimago, meeting on the Idle Strand, had informed that their conqueror was Guyon bold. The sons of Acrates, provoked by false Archimago and strifeful Atin, now sought revenge; and Pyrochles, with insulting words, called upon the Palmer to abandon soon the caitiff spoil of that false Knight's outcast carcase: "Lo! where he now inglorious doth lie, to prove he livëd ill, that did thus foully die." The Palmer fearlessly rebuked Pyrochles for blotting the honour of the dead; "vile is the vengeance on the ashes cold, and envy base to bark at sleeping frame." Cymochles, striking in, told the Palmer that he doted, and knew nothing about prowess or knighthood; that "gold all is not that doth golden seem;" that he should "the worth of all men by their end esteem;" and that he judged Guyon bad who thus lay dead on field. "Good or bad," cried Pyrochles fiercely, it mattered not to him, who had been baulked of his revenge; but, since he had no other way to wreak his spite, he would reave Guyon of his arms, "for why should a dead dog be deck'd in armour bright?" The Palmer vainly entreated the Paynims to "leave these relics of his living might to deck his hearse, and trap his tomb-black steed." "What hearse or steed," demanded Pyrochles, "should he have dight, but be entombëd in the raven or the kite?"

With that, rude hand upon his shield he laid,
And th' other brother gan his helm unlace;
Both fiercely bent to have him disarray'd;
Till that they spied where toward them did pace
An armëd knight, of bold and bounteous grace,
Whose squire bore after him an ebon lance
And cover'd shield: well kenn'd him so far
space[4]
Th' Enchanter by his arms and ámenánce,[5]
When under him he saw his Libyan steed to
prance;

The enchanter called on the brothers to rise immediately, and address themselves to battle; for yonder came "the prowest knight alive, Prince Arthur, flower of grace and nobiless, that hath to Paynim Knights wrought great distress." Upstarting furiously, they prepared for combat; and Pyrochles, lacking his own sword, asked of Archimago that which he bore. The enchanter would gladly have given it, but that he knew its power to be contrary to the work for which it was sought.

"For that same Knight's own sword this is, of
yore
Which Merlin made by his almighty art
For that his nursling, when he knighthood
swore,

1 Wings, with which he shears or cleaves the air.
2 Mount Ida, in ancient mythology celebrated as the scene of several triumphs of Love—such as the rape of Ganymede, and the judgment of Paris. Spenser, therefore, quite appropriately makes it the resort of Cupid.
3 Prepares.
4 Knew him so far off.
5 Carriage, bearing.

Therewith to do his foes eternal smart.
The metal first he mix'd with medæwart,[1]
That no enchantment from his dint might save;
Then it in flames of Etna wrought apart,
And sev'n times dippëd in the bitter wave
Of hellish Styx, which hidden virtue to it gave.

"The virtue is, that neither steel nor stone
The stroke thereof from entrance may defend;
Nor ever may be usëd by his fone;[2]
Nor forc'd his rightful owner to offend;
Nor ever will it break, nor ever bend;
Wherefore *Morddure*[3] it rightfully is hight.
In vain, therefóre, Pyrochles, should I lend
The same to thee, against his lord to fight;
For sure it would deceive thy labour and thy
 might."

But Pyrochles snatched the "virtuous steel" out of Archimago's hand, bound Guyon's shield about his wrist, and turned to face the new comer. Arthur, having saluted the brothers,—receiving in return only stern and disdainful words,—asked the Palmer what great misfortune had befallen the prostrate Knight, "in whose dead face he read great magnanimity." Informed that Guyon was only in a trance, and that the two knights who stood by would disarm him and treat him shamefully, Arthur appealed in gentle and courteous words for pardon for the carcase of him "whom fortune hath already laid in lowest seat." Cymochles, asking "What art thou that mak'st thyself his daysman," in arrogant and insolent language refused to forego his revenge; for "the trespass still doth live, although the person die."

"Indeed," then said the Prince, "the evil done
Dies not, when breath the body first doth leave;
But from the grandsire to the nephew's[4] son,
And all his seed, the curse doth often cleave,
Till vengeance utterly the guilt bereave:
So straitly[5] God doth judge. But gentle knight
That doth against the dead his hand uprear,
His honour stains with rancour and despite,
And great disparagement makes to his former
 might."

Pyrochles, in reply, calls Arthur "felon" and "partaker of his crime;" "therefore, by Termagaunt,[6] thou shalt be dead." He then strikes at Arthur with his own good sword Morddure; but the faithful steel, disdaining such treason, swerves aside. In the fierce combat that ensues, the Prince is unhorsed by Cymochles, and "in dangerous distress, wanting his sword when he on foot should fight;" both the brothers assail him, and on his shield, as thick as stormy shower, their strokes do rain. But he never quails nor shrinks backward, receiving the assault as a steadfast tower the unavailing double battery of the foe. He wounds Cymochles in the thigh; the spear-head is left in the wound, out of which "the red blood flowëd fresh, that underneath his feet soon made a purple plesh;"[7] and Pyrochles, weeping for very rage to see his brother's agony, strikes at Arthur with such fury as to pierce his right side. "Wide was the wound, and a large lukewarm flood, red as the rose, thence gushëd grievously;" and the Prince was in great perplexity, having no weapon but the truncheon of his headless spear.

Whom when the Palmer saw in such distress,
Sir Guyon's sword he lightly to him raught,[8]
And said; "Fair son, great God thy right hand
 bless,
To use that sword so well as he it ought!"[9]
Glad was the Knight, and with fresh courage
 fraught,
When as again he armëd felt his hond:
Then like a lion, which had long time sought
His robbëd whelps, and at the last them fond
Amongst the shepherd swains, then waxeth
 wood and yond:[10]

So fierce he laid about him, and dealt blows
On either side, that neither mail could hold
Nor shield defend the thunder of his throws:[11]
Now to Pyrochles many strokes he told;
Eft[12] to Cymochles twice so many fold;
Then, back again turning his busy hand,
Them both at once compell'd with courage bold
To yield wide way to his heart-thrilling[13] brand;
And though they both stood stiff, yet could not
 both withstand.

As savage bull, whom two fierce mastiffs bait,
When rancour doth with rage him once engore,[14]
Forgets with wary ward them to await,
But with his dreadful horns them drives afore,
Or flings aloft, or treads down in the floor,
Breathing out wrath, and bellowing disdain,
That all the forest quakes to hear him roar:
So rag'd Prince Arthur 'twixt his foemen twain,
That neither could his mighty puissánce sustain.

But ever at Pyrochles when he smit,
(Who Guyon's shield cast ever him before,
Whereon the Faery Queen's portráit was writ,[15])
His hand relented and the stroke forbore,
And his dear heart the picture gan adore;
Which oft the Paynim sav'd from deadly
 stowre:[16]
But him henceforth the same can save no more;
For now arrivëd is his fatal hour,
That no't[17] avoided be by earthly skill or pow'r.

Arthur soon cleaves the head of Cymochles, and dismisses his soul to the infernal shades. Pyrochles, seeing his brother's fall, is struck with stony fear, and, "as a man whom hellish fiends have fray'd, long trembling still he

1 Meadow-wort, meadow-sweet. 2 Foes.
3 The Hard Biter.
4 Grandson's; "to the third and fourth generations."
5 Strictly.
6 The Saracen deity Tervagant or Termagant. See note 26, page 147. 7 Plash, pool.
8 Reached.
9 As he to whom it belonged.

10 Furious and outrageous; "yond" is the same with "yonder" = beyond; and since the word outrage is derived from the Latin "ultra," beyond, the use of "yond" in the sense intended in the text is perfectly analogous. 11 Strokes.
12 Then, again. 13 Heart-piercing.
14 Penetrate. 15 Represented.
16 Calamity. 17 Cannot.

stood." Then, "all desperate, as loathing light, and with revenge desiring soon to die," he gathers all his strength, and rushes at Arthur, lashing outrageously, without reason or regard.

As when a windy tempest bloweth high,
That nothing may withstand his stormy stowre,[1]
The clouds, as things afraid, before him fly;
But, all so soon as his outrageous pow'r
Is laid, they fiercely then begin to show'r;
And, as in scorn of his spent stormy spite,
Now all at once their malice forth do pour:
So did Prince Arthur bear himself in fight,
And suffer'd rash Pyrochles waste his idle might.

At last when as the Saracen perceiv'd
How that strange sword refus'd to serve his need,
But, when he struck most strong, the dint deceiv'd,
He flung it from him; and, devoid of dread,
Upon him lightly leaping without heed,
'Twixt his two mighty arms engraspëd fast,
Thinking to overthrow and down him tread:
But him in strength and skill the Prince surpast,
And through his nimble sleight did under him down cast.

Naught booted it the Paynim then to strive;
For as a bittern in the eagle's claw,
That may not hope by flight to scape alive,
Still waits for death with dread and trembling awe;
So he, now subject to the victor's law,
Did not once move, nor upward cast his eye,
For vile disdain and rancour, which did gnaw
His heart in twain with sad melánchol ý;
As one that loathëd life, and yet despis'd to die.

Full of princely bounty and great mind, Arthur offered Pyrochles life if he would renounce his miscreance, and yield himself his true liegeman for aye; but Pyrochles disdained the boon, and Arthur, wroth yet sorrowful, struck off his head. Meantime Sir Guyon had wakened from his trance, and asked the Palmer what wicked hand had robbed him of his good sword and shield. The joyous Palmer told him all that had happened;

Which when he heard, and saw the tokens true,
His heart with great affection was embay'd,[2]
And to the Prince, with bowing rev'rence due,
As to the patron of his life, thus said;
"My lord, my liege, by whose most gracious aid
I live this day, and see my foes subdued,
What may suffice to be for meed repaid
Of so great graces as ye have me shew'd,
But to be ever bound"——

To whom the Infant[3] thus; "Fair Sir, what need
Good turns be counted, as a servile bond,
To bind their doers to receive their meed?
Are not all knights by oath bound to withstand
Oppressors' power by arms and puissant hand?
Suffice, that I have done my due in place."

[1] Shock, fury. [2] Bathed, soothed.
[3] Prince; from the Spanish "Infante"—although that title is not applied to the eldest son and heir apparent, but to the younger male royal children.

So goodly purpose[4] they together fand
Of kindness and of courtëous agrace;[5]
The while false Archimage and Atin fled apace.

CANTO IX.

The House of Temperance, in which
Doth sober Alma dwell,
Besieg'd of many foes, whom stranger knights to flight compel.

Of all God's works which do this world adorn,
There is no one more fair and excellent
Than is man's body, both for power and form,
While it is kept in sober government;
But none than it more foul and índecént,
Distemper'd through misrule and passions base;
It grows a monster, and incontinent[6]
Doth lose his dignity and native grace:
Behold, who list, both one and other in this place.

After the conquest of the Paynim brethren, the Prince and Guyon journey on together; and Arthur asks his companion why he bears on his shield the picture of that Lady's head. Guyon, launching out into praise of her mind's beauty, her virtue, and imperial power, says that

"She is the mighty Queen of Faëry,
Whose fair retrait[7] I in my shield do bear;
She is the flow'r of grace and chastity,
Throughout the world renownëd far and near,
My Life, my Liege, my Sovereign, my Dear,
Whose glory shineth as the morning star,
And with her light the earth illumines clear;
Far reach her mercies, and her praises far,
As well in state of peace, as puissánce of war."

"Thrice happy man," said then the Briton Knight,
"Whom gracious lot and thy great valiánce
Have made thee soldier of that Princess bright,
Which with her bounty and glad countenance
Doth bless her servants, and them high advance!
How may strange knight hope ever to aspire,
By faithful service and meet ámenánce,[8]
Unto such bliss? sufficient were that hire
For loss of thousand lives, to die at her desire."

Guyon answers that there is no meed so great, no grace of earthly prince so sovereign, that the Prince may not easily attain; and, if he were to enrol himself among the Knights of Maidenhead, he would gain high favour with that Queen. Arthur says that since his first devotion to arms and knighthood his whole desire has been to serve her; but he has sought her in vain, while the sun with his lamp-burning light hath walked round the world. But for the hard adventure that detains him, Guyon would himself guide the Prince through all Faery Land; and by request he relates the story "of false Acrasia,

[4] Discourse. [5] Favour.
[6] Immediately.
[7] Portrait; Italian, "ritratto," from "ritrarre," to "retrace," to draw. [8] Behaviour.

and her wicked wiles." So they talked, while "they wasted had much way, and measur'd many miles."

And now fair Phœbus gan decline in haste
His weary waggon to the western vale,
When as they spied a goodly Castle, plac'd
Foreby[1] a river in a pleasant dale;
Which choosing for that evening's hospitale,[2]
They thither march'd: but when they came in sight,
And from their sweaty coursers did avale,[3]
They found the gates fast barrëd long ere night,
And ev'ry loop[4] fast lock'd, as fearing foes' despite.

Which when they saw, they weenëd foul reproach
Was to them done, their entrance to forestall;[5]
Till that the squire gan nigher to approach,
And wind his horn under the Castle wall,
That with the noise it shook as it would fall.
Eftsoons forth lookëd from the highest spire
The watch, and loud unto the knights did call,
To weet[6] what they so rudely did require:
Who gently answerëd, they entrance did desire.

"Fly, fly, good Knights," said he, "fly fast away,
If that your lives ye love, as meet ye should;
Fly fast, and save yourselves from near decay;[7]
Here may ye not have entrance, though we would:
We would, and would again, if that we could;
But thousand enemies about us rave,
And with long siege us in this Castle hold:[8]
Sev'n years this wise they us besiegëd have,
And many good knights slain that have us sought to save."

Thus as he spoke, lo! with outrageous cry
A thousand villains round about them swarm'd
Out of the rocks and caves adjoining nigh;
Vile caitiff wretches, ragged, rude, deform'd,
All threat'ning death, all in strange manner arm'd;
Some with unwieldy clubs, some with long spears,
Some rusty knives, some staves in fiër warm'd:
Stern was their look; like wild amazëd steers,
Staring with hollow eyes, and stiff upstanding hairs.

Fiercely at first those Knights they did assail,
And drove them to recoil: but when again
They gave fresh charge, their forces gan to fail,
Unable their encounter to sustain;
For with such puissance and impetuous main[9]
Those champions broke on them, that forc'd them fly,
Like scatter'd sheep, when as the shepherd-swain
A lion and a tiger doth espy
With greedy pace forth rushing from the forest nigh.

A while they fled, but soon return'd again
With greater fury than before was found;
And evermore their cruel capitain
Sought with his rascal routs[10] t' enclose them round,
And, overrun, to tread them on the ground:
But soon the Knights, with their bright-burning blades,
Broke their rude troops, and orders did confound,
Hewing and slashing at their idle shades;
For though they bodies seem, yet substance from them fades.

As when a swarm of gnats at eventide
Out of the fens of Allan[11] do arise,
Their murmuring small trumpets sounden wide,
While in the air their clust'ring army flies,
That as a cloud doth seem to dim the skies;
Nor man nor beast may rest or take repast
For their sharp wounds and noyous[12] injuries,
Till the fierce northern wind with blust'ring blast
Doth blow them quite away, and in the ocean cast.

"That troublous rout dispers'd," the Knights returned to the Castle gate; and the Lady that dwelt there came forth to welcome them.

Alma[13] she callëd was; a virgin bright
That had not yet felt Cupid's wanton rage;
Yet was she woo'd of many a gentle knight,
And many a lord of noble parentage,
That sought with her to link in marriáge:
For she was fair, as fair might ever be,
And in the flow'r now of her freshest age;
Yet full of grace and goodly modesty,
That even heav'n rejoicëd her sweet face to see.

In robe of lily white she was array'd,
That from her shoulder to her heel down raught;[14]
The train whereof loose far behind her stray'd,
Branchëd with gold and pearl most richly wrought,
And borne of two fair damsels, which were taught
That service well: her yellow golden hair
Was trimly woven and in tresses wrought,
Nor other tire[15] she on her head did wear,
But crownëd with a garland of sweet rosiere.[16]

She brings the Knights into her Castle hall, and makes them gentle court and gracious delight, "with mildness virginal, showing herself both wise and liberal." When they have rested, they desire to see the Castle; and she grants the request:

First she them led up to the Castle[17] wall,
That was so high as foe might not it climb,
And all so fair and fencible[18] withal;
Not built of brick, nor yet of stone and lime,
But of thing like to that Egyptian slime
Whereof king Nine[19] whilóm built Babel tow'r:

1 Near. 2 Inn.
3 Alight, descend. 4 Loop-hole.
5 Prevent. 6 Learn.
7 Destruction.
8 "I have read, in the marvellous heart of man,
That strange and mystic scroll,
That an army of phantoms vast and wan
Beleaguer the human soul."
—LONGFELLOW; "The Beleaguered City."
9 Strength.

10 Base-born crowds.
11 The Bog of Allen, in Ireland.
12 Tormenting. 13 The Soul (Italian).
14 Reached. 15 Head-dress.
16 Rose-tree.
17 It is almost needless to say that the Castle is the body of man, inhabited by Alma, the Soul; and the allegorical description of the various parts and powers of the body, like most of Spenser's allegories, easily explains itself. 18 Defensible. 19 Ninus.

But O great pity, that no longer time
So goodly workmanship should not endure!
Soon it must turn to earth: no earthly thing is
sure.

The frame thereof seem'd partly circular,
And part triangular; O work divine!
Those two the first and last proportions are;
The one imperfect, mortal, feminine;
Th' other immortal, perfect, masculine;
And 'twixt them both a quadrate was the base,
Proportion'd equally by seven and nine;
Nine was the circle set in heaven's place:
All which compacted made a goodly diapase.[1]

Therein two gates were placëd seemly well:
The one before, by which all in did pass,
Did th' other far in workmanship excel;
For not of wood, nor of enduring brass,
But of more worthy substance fram'd it was:
Doubly disparted, it did lock and close,
That, when it lockëd, none might thorough pass,
And, when it open'd, no man might it close;
Still open'd to their friends, and closëd to their
foes.

Of hewen stone the porch was fairly wrought,
Stone more of value, and more smooth and fine,
Than jet or marble far from Ireland brought;
Over the which was cast a wand'ring vine,
Enchasëd[2] with a wanton ivy twine:
And over it a fair portcullis hung,
Which to the gate directly did incline
With comely compass and compacture strong,
Neither unseemly short, nor yet exceeding long.

Within the barbican[3] a porter sate,
Day and night duly keeping watch and ward;
Nor wight nor word might pass out of the gate,
But in good order, and with due regard;
Utt'rers of secrets he from thence debarr'd,
Babblers of folly, and blazers of crime:
His larum-bell might loud and wide be heard
When cause requir'd, but never out of time;
Early and late it rung, at ev'ning and at prime.

And round about the porch on ev'ry side
Twice sixteen warders sat, all armëd bright
In glist'ring steel, and strongly fortified:
Tall yeomen seemëd they and of great might,
And were enrangëd[4] ready still for fight.
By them as Alma passëd with her guests,
They did obeisance, as beseemëd right,
And then again returnëd to their rests:
The porter eke to her did lout with humble gests.[5]

Then she them brought into a stately hall,
Wherein were many tables fair dispread,
And ready dight with drapets festival,[6]
Against the viands should be minist'red.

At th' upper end there sat, y-clad in red
Down to the ground, a comely personage,
That in his hand a white rod managëd;
He steward was, hight Diet; ripe of age,
And in demeanour sober, and in counsel sage.

And through the hall there walkëd to and fro
A jolly yeoman, marshal of the same,
Whose name was Appetite; he did bestow
Both guests and meat, whenever in they came,
And knew them how to order without blame,
As him the steward bade. They both at one[7]
Did duty to their Lady, as became;
Who, passing by, forth led her guests anon
Into the kitchen room, nor spar'd for niceness[8]
none.

It was a vault y-built for great dispence,[9]
With many ranges[10] rear'd along the wall,
And one great chimney, whose long tunnel thence
The smoke forth threw; and in the midst of all
There placëd was a cauldron wide and tall,
Upon a mighty furnace, burning hot,
More hot than Etn', or flaming Mongiball:[11]
For day and night it burn'd, nor ceasëd not,
So long as any thing it in the cauldron got.

But to delay[12] the heat, lest by mischance
It might break out and set the whole on fire,
There added was by goodly ordinance
A huge great pair of bellows, which did stire[13]
Continually, and cooling breath inspire.
About the cauldron many cooks accoil'd[14]
With hooks and ladles, as need did require;
The while the viands in the vessel boil'd,
They did about their business sweat, and sorely
toil'd.

The master cook was call'd Concoctión;
A careful man, and full of comely guise:
The kitchen clerk, that hight Digestión,
Did order all th' achates[15] in seemly wise,
And set them forth, as well he could devise.
The rest had several offices assign'd;
Some to remove the scum as it did rise;
Others to bear the same away did mind;
And others it to use according to his kind.

But all the liquor which was foul and waste,
Not good nor serviceable else for aught,
They in another great round vessel plac'd,
Till by a conduit pipe it thence were brought;
And all the rest, that noyous[16] was and naught,
By secret ways, that none might it espy,
Was close convey'd, and to the back-gate brought,
That clepëd[17] was Port Esquiline,[18] whereby
It was avoided quite, and thrown out privily.

Which goodly order and great workman's skill

1 Diapason; concord.
2 Adorned, set round. 3 Watch-tower.
4 Arrayed in order. 5 Bow with humble gestures.
6 Prepared, covered, with festival drapery.
7 Together. 8 Delicacy, fastidiousness.
9 Lavish or liberal outlay.
10 Grates, furnaces.
11 Mongibello, or Monte Gibello, is the name by which Mount Etna is known to the Italians.
12 Temper, mitigate. 13 Stir.
14 Clustered, or bustled.
15 The purchases, or provisions; from the French, "acheter," to buy. Chaucer, in the Prologue to the Canterbury Tales, speaks of the Manciple as one

"Of which achatours mightë take ensample,
For to be wise in buying of vitaille."

The word seems to have had a special reference to the purchase of provisions; "cate," and "cater," have been derived from the same source.
16 Offensive, noxious. 17 Named.
18 Through the "Porta Esquilina," which led from the Esquiline Mount to the "Campus Esquilinus," the Romans led out their criminals to execution, and carried the bodies of the poor for burial; hence its appropriateness for Spenser's use in the text.

When as those Knights beheld, with rare delight
And gazing wonder they their minds did fill;
For never had they seen so strange a sight.
Thence back again fair Alma led them right,
And soon into a goodly parlour brought,
That was with royal arras richly dight,[1]
In which was nothing pórtrayëd nor wrought;
Not wrought nor pórtrayëd, but easy to be
thought:

And in the midst thereof, upon the floor,
A lovely bevy of fair Ladies[2] sate,
Courted of many a jolly paramour,
The which them did in modest wise amate,[3]
And each one sought his lady to aggrate.[4]
And eke amongst them little Cupid play'd
His wanton sports, being returnëd late
From his fierce wars, and having from him laid
His cruel bow, wherewith he thousands hath
dismay'd.

Divérse delights they found themselves to please;
Some sung in sweet consórt;[5] some laugh'd for
joy;
Some play'd with straws; some idly sat at ease;
But other some could not abide to toy,
All pleasance was to them grief and annoy:
This frown'd; that fawn'd; the third for shame
did blush;
Another seemëd envious, or coy;
Another in her teeth did gnaw a rush:
But at these strangers' presence ev'ry one did
hush.

Soon as the gracious Alma came in place,
They all at once out of their seats arose,
And to her homage made with humble grace:
Whom when the knights beheld, they gan dispose
Themselves to court, and each a damsel chose:
The Prince by chance did on a lady light,
That was right fair and fresh as morning rose,
But somewhat sad and solemn eke in sight,[6]
As if some pensive thought constrain'd her gentle
sprite.

In a long purple pall, whose skirt with gold
Was fretted[7] all about, she was array'd;
And in her hand a poplar branch did hold;
To whom the Prince in courteous manner said;
"Gentle Madáme, why be ye thus dismay'd,
And your fair beauty do with sadness spill?[8]
Lives any that you hath thus ill apaid?[9]
Or do you love, or do you lack your will?
Whatever be the cause, it sure beseems you ill."

The damsel answers, "half in disdainful wise," that she is pensive and sad in mind "through great desire of glory and of fame;" in which, she tells the Prince, he is no way behind, "that hath twelve months sought one, yet nowhere can her find." Inly moved at her speech, Arthur endeavours to hide the wound she has made, "now seeming flaming hot, now stony cold;" and he turns softly aside to inquire the lady's name—which, he is told, is Praise-desire. Meanwhile Guyon entertains another of that gentle crew, a maiden in blue attire, who often changes her native hue, whose garment is "close about her tuck'd with many a plait," and who bears an owl on her fist.

So long as Guyon with her communëd,
Unto the ground she cast her modest eye,
And ever and anon with rosy red
The bashful blood her snowy cheeks did dye,
That her became, as polish'd ivorý
Which cunning craftsman hand hath overlaid
With fair vermilion or pure lasterý.[10]
Great wonder had the Knight to see the maid
So strangely passionëd,[11]—

And gently inquired the cause of her troubled cheer, that he might try to ease her of her ill.

She answer'd naught, but more abash'd for
shame
Held down her head, the while her lovely face
The flashing blood with blushing did inflame,
And the strong passion[12] marr'd her modest
grace,
That Guyon marvell'd at her uncouth case;[13]
Till Alma him bespake; "Why wonder ye,
Fair Sir, at that which ye so much embrace?[14]
She is the fountain of your modesty;
You shamefast are, but Shamefastness itself is
she."

Thereat the Elf did blush in privity,
And turn'd his face away; but she the same
Dissembled fair, and feign'd to oversee.[15]
Thus they a while, with court and goodly game,
Themselves did solace each one with his dame,
Till that great Lady thence away them sought
To view her Castle's other wondrous frame:
Up to a stately turret[16] she them brought,
Ascending by ten steps of alabaster wrought.

That turret's frame most admirable was,
Like highest heaven compassëd around,
And lifted high above this earthly mass,
Which it surview'd,[17] as hills do lower ground:
But not on ground might like to this be found;
Not that, which antique Cadmus whilom built
In Thebes, which Alexander did confound;
Nor that proud tower of Troy, though richly gilt,
From which young Hector's[18] blood by cruel
Greeks was spilt.

The roof hereof was archëd overhead,
And deck'd with flow'rs and herbars[19] daintily;
Two goodly beacons, set in watches' stead,
Therein gave light and flam'd continually:
For they of living fire most subtilly
Were made, and set in silver sockets bright,
Cover'd with lids devis'd of substance sly,[20]

1 Furnished, adorned.
2 The Passions and Affections, housed in the "goodly parlour" of the Heart.
3 Bear them company.
4 Gratify, make himself agreeable to.
5 Accord, concert.
6 Aspect, air.
7 Embroidered, adorned.
8 Spoil.
9 Given you cause for such displeasure, or sadness.
10 A kind of red colour.
11 Moved.
12 Emotion.
13 Strange demeanour.
14 Of which you have yourself so large a share.
15 Not to observe.
16 The Head.
17 Overlooked.
18 Scamandrius, the son of Hector; whom, honouring the services of his father, the Trojans styled "Astyanax," lord or king of the city. When Troy was taken, the Greeks hurled him from the walls, that he might not restore the kingdom.
19 Plants.
20 Skilfully wrought.

That readily they shut and open might.
O who can tell the praises of that Maker's might!

Ne [1] can I tell, nor can I stay to tell,
This part's great workmanship and wondrous power,
That all this other world's work doth excel,
And likest is unto that heav'nly tower
That God hath built for his own blessed bower:
Therein were divers rooms, and divers stages;
But three the chiefest, and of greatest power,
In which there dwelt three honourable sages,
The wisest men, I ween, that livëd in their ages.

Not he [2] whom Greece, the nurse of all good arts,
By Phœbus' doom [3] the wisest thought alive,
Might be compar'd to these by many parts:
Nor that sage Pylian sire,[4] which did survive
Three ages, such as mortal men contrive,[5]
By whose advice old Priam's city fell,
With these in praise of policies might strive.
These three in these three rooms did sundry dwell,
And counsellëd fair Alma how to govern well.

The first of them could things to come foresee;
The next could of things present best advise,[6]
The third things past could keep in memory:[7]
So that no time nor reason could arise,
But that the same could one of these comprise.
Forthy [8] the first did in the fore-part sit,
That naught might hinder his quick prejudíce;[9]
He had a sharp foresíght and working wit
That never idle was, nor once would rest a whit.

His chamber was dispainted all within
With sundry colours, in the which were writ [10]
Infinite shapes of things dispersëd thin;
Some such as in the world were never yet,
Nor can devisëd be of mortal wit;
Some daily seen and knowen by their names,
Such as in idle fantasies do flit;
Infernal hags, centaurs, fiends, hippodames,[11]
Apes, lions, eagles, owls, fools, lovers, children, dames.

And all the chamber fillëd was with flies,
Which buzzëd all about, and made such sound
That they encumber'd [12] all men's ears and eyes;
Like many swarms of bees assembled round,
After their hives with honey do abound.
All those were idle thoughts and fantasies,
Devices, dreams, opiniōns unsound,
Shows, visiōns, sooth-says, and prophecies;
And all that feignëd is, as leasings, tales, and lies.

Amongst them all sate he which wonnëd [13] there,
That hight Phantastes [14] by his nature true;
A man of years yet fresh, as might appear,
Of swart complexion, and of crabbed hue,
That him full of melâncholy did shew;[15]
Bent hollow beetle brows, sharp staring eyes,
That mad or foolish seem'd: one by his view
Might deem him born with ill-disposëd skies,
When oblique [16] Saturn sate in th' house of agonies.[17]

Whom Alma having showëd to her guests,
Thence brought them to the second room, whose walls
Were painted fair with memorable gests [18]
Of famous wizards; and with picturals
Of magistrates, of courts, of tríbunâls,
Of commonwealths, of states, of policy,
Of laws, of judgments, and of décretâls,
All arts, all science, all philosophy,
And all that in the world was ay thought wittily.[19]

Of those that room was full; and them among
There sate a Man [20] of ripe and perfect age,
Who did them meditate all his life long,
That through continual practice and uságe
He now was grown right wise and wondrous sage:
Great pleasure had those stranger Knights to see
His goodly reason and grave personage,
That his disciples both desir'd to be:
But Alma thence them led to th' hindmost room of three.

That chamber seemëd ruinous and old,
And therefore was removëd far behind,
Yet were the walls, that did the same uphold,
Right firm and strong, though somewhat they declin'd;
And therein sat an old old Man,[21] half blind,
And all decrepit in his feeble corse,
Yet lively vigour rested in his mind,
And recompens'd them with a bitter scorse: [22]
Weak body well is chang'd for mind's redoubled force.

This man of infinite remembrance was,

[1] Neither.
[2] "The custom of Greece gave the title of Σοφος, or sage, to those who excelled their fellows in science, or moral worth. It is fabled, or perhaps the tale may be a fact, that a golden tripod having been drawn up in their nets by some fishermen of Miletus, a quarrel arose as to its possession. The oracle" of Apollo, or Phœbus, "at Delphi was consulted, and the dissension was allayed by its award of the tripod 'to the wisest.' The Milesians, by common consent, then offered it to their countryman Thales, who, with a laudable modesty, sent it on to Bias of Priene, who transferred it to Pittacus, and Pittacus to another yet, till it came seventhly to Solon, who, finding no other mortal worthy of it, dedicated it to Apollo, as the only wise."—"A Brief View of Greek Philosophy, up to the Age of Pericles," page 31.
[3] Judgment, decision. [4] Nestor.
[5] Three generations, such as mortal men live, or spend: from the Latin, "contero," "contrivi," I wear away; so Shakespeare speaks of "contriving an afternoon." [6] Consider.
[7] In the Tale of the Second Nun (page 175), Chaucer makes Cecilia say that
"—— A man hath sapiences three,
Memory, engine, and intellect also."
[8] Therefore. [9] Forejudgment. [10] Depicted.
[11] Hippopotami, river-horses. [12] Bewildered.
[13] Dwelt. [14] Fancy, Imagination.
[15] Chaucer, describing the love-sorrow of Arcita, says that his demeanour resembled mania—
"Engender'd of humours melâncholic
Before his head in his cell fântastic."
See note 1, page 31. [16] Unpropitious.
[17] Compare Saturn's own description of those "agonies," in the Knight's Tale, page 41.
[18] Deeds, feats. [19] Was ever thought wisely.
[20] The Judgment.
[21] Memory; called, a little afterwards, Eumnestes, or Well-remembering; ευμνηστος is used by Sophocles in that sense.
[22] Compensated his physical failings with a more than equivalent exchange.

And things foregone through many ages held,
Which he recorded still as they did pass,
Nor suffer'd them to perish through long eld,[1]
As all things else the which this world doth
weld;[2]
But laid them up in his immortal scrine,[3]
Where they for ever incorrupted dwell'd:
The wars he well remember'd of king Nine,[4]
Of old Assaracus,[5] and Inachus divine.[6]

The years of Nestor nothing were to his,
Nor yet Methusalem, though longest liv'd;
For he remember'd both their infancies:
No wonder then if that he were depriv'd
Of native strength, now that he them surviv'd.
His chamber all was hang'd about with rolls
And old records from ancient times deriv'd,
Some made in books, some in long parchment
scrolls,
That were all worm-eaten and full of canker holes.

Amidst them all he in a chair was set,
Tossing and turning them withouten end;
But, for[7] he was unable them to fet,[8]
A little boy did on him still attend,
To reach whenever he for aught did send:
And oft when things were lost, or laid amiss,
That boy them sought and unto him did lend:
Therefore he Anamnestes[9] clepëd[10] is;
And that old man Eumnestes, by their proper-
ties.

Having done him reverence due, the Knights began to examine his library. Prince Arthur found an ancient book, called "Briton Moniments," treating of this land's first conquest and final reduction to a single realm; while Sir Guyon chanced upon the "Antiquity of Faery Land," containing the genealogy of Elves and Fairies. "Burning both with fervent fire their country's ancestry to understand," they craved and obtained leave to read those books.

CANTO X.

A Chronicle of Briton Kings,
From Brute to Uther's reign;
And rolls of Elfin Emperors,
Till time of Gloriane.

WHO now shall give unto me words and sound
Equal unto this haughty[11] enterprise?
Or who shall lend me wings, with which from
ground
My lowly verse may loftily arise,
And lift itself unto the highest skies?
More ample spirit than hitherto was wont
Here needs me, while the famous ancestries
Of my most dreaded Sov'reign I recount,
By which all earthly princes she doth far sur-
mount.

Nor under sun that shines so wide and fair,
Whence all that lives does borrow life and light,
Lives aught that to her lineage may compare;
Which, though from earth it be derivëd right,
Yet doth itself stretch forth to heaven's height,
And all the world with wonder overspread;
A labour huge, exceeding far my might!
How shall frail pen, with fear disparagëd,
Conceive such sov'reign glory and great bounti-
head![12]

Argument worthy of Mæonian[13] quill;
Or rather worthy of great Phœbus' rote,[14]
Whereon the ruins of great Ossa hill,
And triumphs of Phlegræan Jove,[15] he wrote,[16]
That all the gods admir'd his lofty note.
But, if some relish of that heav'nly lay
His learnëd daughters would to me report,
To deck my song withal, I would assay
Thy name, O sov'reign Queen, to blazon far away.

Thy name, O sov'reign Queen, thy realm, and race,
From this renownëd Prince[17] derivëd are,
Who mightily upheld that royal mace[18]
Which now thou bear'st, to thee descended far
From mighty kings and conquerors in war,
Thy fathers and great-grandfathers of old,
Whose noble deeds above the northern star
Immortal Fame for ever hath enroll'd;
As in that Old Man's book they were in order
told.

The succeeding sixty-three stanzas of this canto are occupied by the "chronicle of Briton Kings from Brute to Uther's reign;" which is taken almost entirely from the fabulous history of Geoffrey of Monmouth, and may, without detriment to the poem or injustice to the poet, be presented in very brief outline. Britain, we are told, "in antique times was salvage wilderness, unpeopled, unmanur'd, unprov'd, unprais'd;" desolate and deserving no name "till that the venturous mariner that way learning his ship

1 Age.
2 Wield; possess or use.
3 Cabinet, document-chest.
4 Ninus, the mythical founder of Nineveh, about 2200 years before Christ.
5 King of Troy; the great-grandfather of Æneas, and thence taken as the original of the Roman people; which Virgil, in a passage that Spenser doubtless had in mind when he placed Assaracus among the oldest famous memories, calls "domus Assaraci" (Æneid, i. 284).
6 The first king of Argos, termed "divine" because, according to fable, he was born of the sea-gods Oceanus and Tethys. 7 Because. 8 Fetch.
9 Recollection; from the Greek, αναμιμνησκω, I remind; αναμνησις, the act of recollecting. Spenser follows the distinction drawn by Aristotle and Plato between αναμνησις and μνημη—recollection and memory; and our common phrase "to bring to memory" simply embodies in plain words the poet's allegory of recollection as the servant of memory.
10 Called. 11 Lofty. 12 Goodness, virtue.
13 Homeric. Homer was supposed to have been born in Mæonia, or Lydia; and Ovid calls the Muses "Mæonidæ," from the presumed birthplace of their greatest son.
14 In Moore's "Cyclopædia of Music," Rote is described as an old instrument generally supposed to have been the same as the English hurdy-gurdy, the tones of which are produced by the friction of a wheel; Latin, "rota." Here, of course, the word is used in the general sense of "lyre" or "harp." The "quill," in the preceding line, is the "plectrum" with which the player on stringed instruments struck the chords.
15 The giants, in that war with the gods during which they piled Mount Ossa on Mount Pelion to reach heaven, attacked their foes on the plain of Phlegra, in Macedonia, but were defeated by the aid of Hercules.
16 Described. 17 Arthur. 18 Sceptre.

from those white rocks to save" that lay all along the southern coast, made the same his sea-mark, and named it ALBION. Far inland dwelt a savage nation "of hideous giants, and half-beastly men that never tasted grace, nor goodness felt; but wild, like beasts, lurking in loathsome den, and flying fast as roebuck through the fen," all naked, living by the chase and by plunder. This abhorrent race of savages and giants was, after great battles, dispossessed by Brutus, anciently derived from royal stock of old Assarac's line—that is, from the kings of Troy.[1] Brutus was aided by Corineus, who gave the name of Cornwall to his province; by Devon, from whom Devonshire was named; and by Canute, whose portion was called Canutium—now Kent. Dying, Brutus left three sons, "born of fair Imogene of Italy," among whom he parted his realm, under the supreme sovereignty of Locrinus; Albanact having the northern part, which he called Albania (Albyn or Scotland), Camber the western part, and Logris the southern. A nation strange, with visage swart and courage fierce, invaded the north like Noah's great flood, but was overthrown by Locrinus at the Humber—so called from the opposing leader, drowned in the stream as he fled. Locrinus, puffed up by triumph, grew insolent, and lewdly loved fair Lady Estrild; withdrawing his heart from the faithful Guendolene, his wife, "the noble daughter of Corineus." The queen, not enduring to be thus disdained, encountered and vanquished her husband in battle; he was taken captive; Lady Estrild was slain on the spot; and "her daughter dear, begotten by her kingly paramour," the lovely Sabrina—"sad virgin, innocent of all, adown the rolling river she did pour, which of her name now Severn men do call." Guendoline ruled gloriously for her son Madan, till he grew to man's estate; then he reigned unworthily, succeeded by Memprise, "as unworthy of that place," and by Ebranck, who "salvëd both their infamies with noble deeds," made war on the German hero Brunechild, and by his twenty sons subdued all Germany. The second Brutus succeeded, who "with his victor sword first openëd the bowels of wide France, a forlorn dame," and paved the way to future conquests. Leill next "enjoy'd a heritage of lasting peace, and built Caerleill and built Caerleon strong." After pacific Huddibras, reigned Bladud the learned, of whose wondrous faculty the boiling baths at Caerbadon (Bath) are an ensample; but, striving to excel the might of men, he was dashed to pieces in an attempt to fly. Then comes the story of Lear, which, sixteen years after "The Faerie Queen" was published, Shakespeare, with important changes and far loftier power, took as the theme of his great tragedy.

Next him king Leir in happy peace long reign'd,
But had no issue male him to succeed,
But three fair daughters, which were well up-
train'd
In all that seemëd fit for kingly seed;
'Mongst whom his realm he equally decreed
To have divided: then, when feeble age
Nigh to his utmost date he saw proceed,
He call'd his daughters, and with speeches sage
Inquir'd which of them most did love her
parentage.

The eldest, Gonoril, gan to protest
That she much more than her own life him
lov'd;
And Regan greater love to him profest
Than all the world, whenever it were prov'd;
But Cordeill said she lov'd him as behov'd:
Whose simple answer, wanting colours fair
To paint it forth, him to displeasance mov'd,
That in his crown he counted her no heir,
But 'twixt the other twain his kingdom whole
did share.

So wedded th' one to Maglan king of Scots,
And th' other to the king of Cambria,
And 'twixt them shar'd his realm by equal lots;
But, without dower, the wise Cordelia
Was sent to Aganip of Celtica:
Their aged sire, thus easëd of his crown,
A private life led in Albania
With Gonoril, long had in great renown,
That naught him griev'd to be from rule deposëd
down.

But true it is, that, when the oil is spent,
The light goes out, and wick is thrown away;
So, when he had resign'd his regiment,[2]
His daughter gan despise his drooping day,
And weary wax of his continual stay:
Then to his daughter Regan he repair'd,
Who him at first well usëd every way;
But, when of his departure she despair'd,
Her bounty she abated, and his cheer impair'd.

The wretched man gan then advise[3] too late,
That love is not where most it is profest;
Too truly tried in his extremest state!
At last, resolv'd likewise to prove the rest,
He to Cordelia himself addrest,
Who with entire affection him receiv'd,
As for her sire and king her seemëd best;
And after all an army strong she leav'd,[4]
To war on those which him had of his realm
bereav'd.

Lear, restored to his crown, died at a ripe old age; succeeded by Cordelia, who, at last deposed and imprisoned by her sister's children, hanged herself in prison. Cundah, slaying his brother Morgan, reigned alone; then succeeded Rivall—"in whose sad time blood did from heaven rain"—great Gurgustus, fair Cæcily, Lago and Kinmarke, Gorbogud, and his rebellious sons "stout Ferrex and stern Porrex."

Here ended Brutus' sacred progeny,
Which had sev'n hundred years this sceptre
borne
With high renown and great felicity:

[1] See note 5, page 395.
[2] Government.
[3] Consider.
[4] Levied.

The noble branch from th' ántique stock was torn
Through discord, and the royal throne forlorn.[1]
Thenceforth this realm was into factions rent,
Whilst each of Brutus boasted to be born,
That in the end was left no monument
Of Brutus, nor of Britons' glory anciént.

Then up arose a man of matchless might,
And wondrous wit to manage high affairs,
Who, stirr'd with pity of the 'stressed plight
Of this sad realm, cut into sundry shares
By such as claim'd themselves Brute's rightful heirs,
Gather'd the princes of the people loose [2]
To taken counsel of their common cares;
Who, with his wisdom won, him straight did choose
Their king, and swore him fëalty to win or lose.

. . . .

Then made he sacred laws, which some men say
Were unto him reveal'd in visión;
By which he freed the traveller's high-way,
The Church's part, and ploughman's portión,
Restraining stealth and strong extortión;
The gracious Numa of great Brittany:[3]
For, till his days, the chief dominión
By strength was wielded without policy:
Therefore he first wore crown of gold for dignity.

The wise and good Donwallo, dying, left two sons of peerless prowess, as sacked Rome and ransacked Greece assayed—"Brennus and Belinus, kings of Brittany." Next came Gurgunt, Guitheline, Sifillus, Kimarus, Danius, Morindus, his five sons in turn, then all the sons of these five brethren, and all their grandsons—thrice eleven descents in the same family, till aged Hely by due heritage gained the crown. Lud, his eldest son, rebuilt the ruined walls "of Troynovant,[4] 'gainst force of enemy, and built that Gate which of his name is hight, by which he lies entombëd solemnly." Cassibelanus was chosen by the people to reign instead of Lud's young sons; and during his reign "warlike Cæsar, tempted with the name of this sweet Island never conquerëd," came hither with his Romans.

Yet twice they were repulsëd back again,
And twice enforc'd back to their ships to fly;
The while with blood they all the shore did stain,
And the gray ocean into purple dye:
Nor had they footing found at last, pardie,[5]
Had not Androgeus, false to native soil,
And envious of uncle's sov'reignty,
Betray'd his country unto foreign spoil.
Naught else but treason from the first this land did foil![6]

The chronicle now entered upon historical ground. After Cassibelanus reigned Tenantius; "then Kimbeline, what time th' Eternal Lord in fleshly slime enwombëd was, from wretched Adam's line to purge away the guilt of sinful crime." Slain by treachery in the invasion of Claudius, Kimbeline was succeeded by Arviragus, who compelled the Romans to seek peace, obtained the Emperor's daughter in marriage, and renounced the vassalage of Rome. Brought into subjection by Vespasian, he died; then reigned Marius, Coill, and "after him good Lucius, that first receivëd Christianity;" though long before that day Joseph of Arimathea had come hither, bringing the Holy Grail, and preaching the truth. The death of Lucius without children gave the Romans an opportunity of profiting by the divisions of the Britons; which seeing, Boadicea took arms and attacked the Romans, but was defeated, and slew herself rather than be made captive.

O famous monument of women's praise!
Matchable either to Semiramis,
Whom ántique history so high doth raise,
Or to Hypsipyl', or to Tomyris:[7]
Her host two hundred thousand number'd is;
Who, while good fortune favourëd her might,
Triumphëd oft against her enemies;
And yet, though overcome in hapless fight,
She triumphëd on death, in enemies' despite.

Fulgent, Carausius, Allectus, Asclepiodatus, interposed between Boadicea and Coill—the first crowned sovereign of the Britons since Lucius' time. Under Coill the realm began to "renew her passëd prime;" and "he of his name Coylchester built of stone and lime." He gave to Constantius his daughter Helena, most famous for her skill in music; and of her was begotten Constantine, afterwards Emperor of Rome. Octavius usurped the place of the absent Constantine, and gave his daughter to Maximian; during whose reign the Huns and Picts began to invade the land. The weary Britons were worn out by miseries under the new invaders, and gladly, "by consent of Commons and of Peers, they crown'd the second Constantine with joyous tears." He often vanquished in battle "the spoilful Picts, and swarming Easterlings," and pacified the realm; building, against the incursions of the Scots, "a mighty mound, which from Alcluid to Panwelt did that border bound." Vortigern usurped the crown during the pupilage of his two nephews—the sons of Constantine; and, fearing their attempts to reinstate themselves, he sent to Germany strange aid to rear. "Three hoys of Saxons," under Hengist and Horsus, arrived; and their leaders took advantage of the divisions of the Britons to drive Vortigern from the kingdom. Restored by the help of his son Vortimere, he received Hengist back into favour, through the fair face and flattering word of his daughter Rowena. But now the fugitive sons of Constantine, having

1 Left vacant. 2 Scattered, divided.
3 That is, in Britain he played the part that Numa Pompilius did in ancient Rome. 4 London.
5 Assuredly. 6 Defeat, baffle.
7 Queen of the Massagetæ, who marched against Cyrus when he threatened to invade her territory, overthrew and slew him, and ordered his severed head to be thrown into a vessel full of human blood—with the bitter exhortation to the dead prince to satiate himself with the gore for which he had thirsted.

attained ripe years, arrived to reclaim the crown; they slew Vortigern and Hengist, and Aurelius reigned peaceably "till that through poison stoppëd was his breath; so now entombëd lies at Stonehenge by the heath."

After him Uther,[1] which Pendragon hight,
Succeeding——There abruptly did it end,
Without full point, or other cesure[2] right;
As if the rest some wicked hand did rend,
Or th' author's self could not at last attend
To finish it: that so untimely breach
The Prince himself half seemëd to offend;
Yet secret pleasure did offence empeach,[3]
And wonder of antiquity long stopp'd his speech.

At last, quite ravish'd with delight to hear
The royal offspring of his native land,
Cried out; "Dear country! O how dearly dear
Ought thy remembrance and perpetual band
Be to thy foster child, that from thy hand
Did common breath and noriture[4] receive!
How brutish is it not to understand
How much to her we owe, that all us gave;
That gave unto us all whatever good we have!"

But Guyon all this while his book did read,
Nor yet had ended: for it was a great
And ample volume, that doth far exceed
My leisure so long leaves here to repeat:
It told how first Prometheus did create
A man, of many parts from beasts deriv'd,
And then stole fire from heav'n to animate
His work, for which he was by Jove depriv'd
Of life himself, and heart-strings of an eagle riv'd.[5]

That man so made he callëd Elf, to weet
Quick,[6] the first author of all Elfin kind;
Who, wand'ring through the world with weary feet,
Did in the gardens of Adonis find
A goodly creature, whom he deem'd in mind
To be no earthly wight, but either sprite,
Or angel, th' author of all woman kind;
Therefore a Fay he her according hight,
Of whom all Faeries spring, and fetch their lineage right.

Of these a mighty people shortly grew,
And puissant kings which all the world warray'd,[7]
And to themselves all nations did subdue:
The first and eldest, which that sceptre sway'd,
Was Elfin: him all India obey'd,
And all that now America men call:
Next him was noble Elfinan, who laid
Cleopolis' foundation first of all:
But Elfilin enclos'd it with a golden wall.

His son was Elfinell, who overcame
The wicked Gobbelins in bloody field:
But Elfant was of most renownëd fame,
Who all of crystal did Panthea build:

Then Elfar, who two brethren giants kill'd,
The one of which had two heads, th' other three:
Then Elfinor, who was in magic skill'd;
He built by art upon the glassy sea
A bridge of brass, whose sound heav'n's thunder seem'd to be.

He left three sons, the which in order reign'd,
And all their offspring, in their due descents;
Ev'n seven hundred princes, which maintain'd
With mighty deeds their sundry governments:
That were too long their infinite contents
Here to record, nor much material:
Yet should they be most famous monuments,
And brave ensample, both of martiál
And civil rule, to kings and states imperiál.

After all these Elficleos[8] did reign,
The wise Elficleos in great majesty,
Who mightily that sceptre did sustain,
And with rich spoils and famous victory
Did high advance the crown of Faëry:
He left two sons, of which fair Elferon,
The eldest brother, did untimely die;
Whose empty place the mighty Oberon
Doubly supplied, in spousal and dominión.

Great was his pow'r and glory over all
Which, him before, that sacred seat did fill,
That yet remains his wide memorial:
He, dying, left the fairest Tanaquill
Him to succeed therein, by his last will:
Fairer and nobler liveth none this hour,
Nor like in grace, nor like in learnëd skill;
Therefore they Glorian' call that glorious flow'r:
Long may'st thou, Glorian', live in glory and great pow'r!

Beguil'd thus with delight of novelties,
And natural desire of country's state,
So long they read in those antiquities,
That how the time was fled they quite forgate;[9]
Till gentle Alma, seeing it so late,
Perforce their studies broke, and them besought
To think how supper did them long await:
So half unwilling from their books them brought,
And fairly feasted as so noble knights she ought.

CANTO XI.

The enemies of Temperance
Besiege her dwelling-place;
Prince Arthur them repels, and foul
Maleger doth deface.[10]

What war so cruel, or what siege so sore,
As that which strong Affections do apply
Against the fort of Reason evermore,
To bring the Soul into captivitý?
Their force is fiercer through infirmitý
Of the frail flesh, relenting to their rage;

1 The father of Arthur. 2 *Cæsura*, stop.
3 Prevent. 4 Nurture.
5 Torn by an eagle. 6 That is to say, Alive.
7 Made war upon.
8 Elficleos is Henry VII.; Elferon, his eldest son Prince Arthur, who died young; mighty Oberon, Prince Henry—afterwards Henry VIII., who doubly supplied his brother's empty place, by succeeding to the throne and by marrying Catharine of Aragon, who had been affianced to Arthur; and Tanaquill, or Gloriana, is, of course, Queen Elizabeth.
9 Forgot. 10 Destroy.

And exercise most bitter tyranny
Upon the parts brought into their bondáge:
No wretchedness is like to sinful villenage.[1]

But in a body which doth freely yield
His parts to Reason's rule obedient,
And letteth her that ought the sceptre wield,
All happy peace and goodly government
Is settled there in sure establishment.
There Alma, like a Virgin Queen most bright,
Doth flourish in all beauty excellent;
And to her guests doth bounteous banquet dight,[2]
Attemper'd goodly well for health and for delight.

"Early, before the Morn, with crimson ray," had opened the windows of bright heaven, Guyon and the Palmer took their departure; at the ford, on the river's side, a ferryman instructed by Alma awaited them; when they were on board he launched his bark instantly, and was soon out of sight. Here the poet leaves Guyon, and returns to Arthur, who did a cruel fight that day.

For, all so soon as Guyon thence was gone
Upon his voyage with his trusty guide,
That wicked band of villains fresh begun
That Castle to assail on every side,
And lay strong siege about it far and wide.
So huge and infinite their numbers were,
That all the land they under them did hide;
So foul and ugly, that exceeding fear
Their visages impress'd, when they approachëd near.

Dividing them into twelve troops, their captain placed seven (the Cardinal or Deadly Sins) against the Castle gate, which they battered day and night; the other five troops were disposed against the five great bulwarks of the pile (the Five Senses). All accepted their charge with malicious zeal, "and planted there their huge artillery, with which they daily made most dreadful battery."

The first troop was a monstrous rabblement
Of foul misshapen wights, of which some were
Headed like owls, with beaks uncomely bent;
Others like dogs; others like griffins drear;
And some had wings, and some had claws to tear:
And ev'ry one of them had lynx's eyes;
And ev'ry one did bow and arrows bear:
All those were lawless Lusts, corrupt Envíes,
And covetous Aspécts, all cruel enemies.

Those same against the bulwark of the Sight
Did lay strong siege and battailous assault,
Nor once did yield it respite day nor night;
But, soon as Titan[3] gan his head exalt,
And soon again as he his light witholt,[4]
Their wicked engines they against it bent;
That is, each thing by which the eyes may fault.[5]
But two than all more huge and violent,
Beauty and Money, they that bulwark sorely rent.

1 The servitude of sin.
2 Prepare.
3 The Sun.
4 Withheld.
5 Fail, err.
6 Attack.
7 Falsehoods.

The second bulwark was the Hearing Sense,
'Gainst which the second troop designment[6] makes;
Deformëd creatures, in strange difference:
Some having heads like harts, some like to snakes,
Some like wild boars late rous'd out of the brakes;
Sland'rous Reproaches, and foul Infamies,
Leasings,[7] Backbitings, and vain-glorious Crakes,[8]
Bad Counsels, Praises, and false Flatteries:
All those against that fort did bend their batteries.

Likewise that same third fort, that is the Smell,
Of that third troop was cruelly assay'd;
Whose hideous shapes were like to fiends of hell,
Some like to hounds, some like to apes, dismade;[9]
Some, like to puttocks,[10] all in plumes array'd;
All shap'd according their conditións:
For by those ugly forms weren portray'd
Foolish Delights, and fond Abusións,[11]
Which do that Sense besiege with light illusións.

And that fourth band, which cruel battery bent
Against the fourth bulwárk, that is the Taste,
Was, as the rest, a greasy[12] rabblement;
Some mouth'd like greedy ostriches; some fac'd
Like loathly toads; some fashion'd in the waist
Like swine: for so deform'd is Luxury,
Surfeit, Misdiet, and unthrifty Waste,
Vain Feasts, and idle Superfluity:
All those this Sense's fort assail incessantly.

But the fifth troop, most horrible of hue
And fierce of force, is dreadful to report;
For some like snails, some did like spiders shew,
And some like ugly urchins[13] thick and short:
Cruelly they assailëd that fifth fort,
Armëd with darts of sensual Delight,
With stings of carnal Lust, and strong effórt
Of feeling Pleasures, with which day and night
Against that same fifth bulwark they continu'd fight.

The "restless siege" went on, and the "hideous ordinance" evermore cruelly played on the bulwarks of the Castle; till it began to threaten near decay. But the besieged garrison strongly repelled all attacks, mightily aided by the "two brethren giants," Arthur and his squire. Alma, however, grew "much dismayëd with that dreadful sight;" and the Prince, to reassure her, offered to go forth and fight for her defence against the carl "which was their chief and th' author of that strife." Soon, issuing through the unbarred gates, with his gay squire, he was espied by that unruly rabblement; who "reared a most outrageous dreadful yelling cry:"

And therewithal at once at him let fly
Their flutt'ring arrows, thick as flakes of snow,
And round about him flock impetuously,
Like a great water-flood, that tumbling low
From the high mountains, threats to overflow
With sudden fury all the fertile plain,

8 Boasts.
9 Mismade, misshapen.
10 Kites.
11 Foolish deceptions.
12 Filthy, gross.
13 Hedgehogs.

And the sad husbandman's long hope doth throw
Adown the stream, and all his vows make vain;
Nor bounds nor banks his headlong ruin may
sustain.

Upon his shield their heapëd hail he bore,
And with his sword dispers'd the rascal[1] flocks,
Which fled asunder, and him fell before;
As wither'd leaves drop from their driëd stocks,
When the wroth western wind does reave[2]
their locks:
And underneath him his courageous steed,
The fierce Spumador,[3] trod them down like
docks;
The fierce Spumador born of heav'nly seed;
Such as Laomedon of Phœbus' race did breed.

Which sudden horror and confusëd cry
When as their captain heard, in haste he yode[4]
The cause to weet,[5] and fault to remedy:
Upon a tiger swift and fierce he rode,
That as the wind ran underneath his load,
While his long legs nigh raught[6] unto the
ground:
Full large he was of limb, and shoulders broad;
But of such subtile substance and unsound,
That like a ghost he seem'd whose grave-clothes
were unbound:

And in his hand a bended bow was seen,
And many arrows under his right side,
All deadly dangerous, all cruel keen,
Headed with flint, and feathers bloody dy'd;
Such as the Indians in their quivers hide:
Those could he well direct, and straight as line,
And bid them strike the mark which he had ey'd;
Nor was there salve, nor was there medicine,
That might recure their wounds; so inly they
did tine.[7]

As pale and wan as ashes was his look;
His body lean and meagre as a rake;
And skin all wither'd like a driëd rook;[8]
Thereto[9] as cold and dreary as a snake;
That seem'd to tremble evermore and quake:
All in a canvas thin he was bedight,[10]
And girded with a belt of twisted brake:[11]
Upon his head he wore a helmet light,
Made of a dead man's skull, that seem'd a
ghastly sight:

Maleger[12] was his name: and after him
There follow'd fast at hand two wicked hags,
With hoary locks all loose, and visage grim;
Their feet unshod, their bodies wrapt in rags,
And both as swift on foot as chasëd stags;
And yet the one her other leg[13] had lame,
Which with a staff all full of little snags[14]
She did support, and Impotence her name:
But th' other was Impatience arm'd with raging
flame.

Felly pricking his beast towards the Prince, the carl shot at him a cruel shaft, which fell harmless on his shield. Arthur, couching his spear, rode fiercely at his assailant, to prevent the shower of arrows which he shot; but Maleger fled fast away, and Arthur could not approach him.

For as the wingëd wind his tiger fled,
That view of eye could scarce him overtake,
Nor scarce his feet on ground were seen to tread;
Through hills and dales he speedy way did make,
Nor hedge nor ditch his ready passage brake,
And in his flight the villain turn'd his face
(As wonts the Tartar by the Caspian Lake,
When as the Russian him in fight does chase),
Unto his tiger's tail, and shot at him apace.

"Apace he shot, and yet he fled apace," till Arthur resolved to follow him no more, but keep his stand, and avoid the arrows, until the perilous store was spent. Impotence, the lame hag, however, gathered up Maleger's shafts as fast as he shot them, and brought them to him again; and Arthur, dismounting, seized her and began to tie her hands. But Impatience, coming up in haste, threw him backward to the ground as he leaned over her sister; there, "with rude hands and grisly grapplement," they held him down till the villain came to their aid; and under their blows the Prince might have perished, but for the opportune onslaught of his gentle squire—who snatched off and held at bay the hags, while Arthur, pricked with reproachful shame, "united all his powers to purge himself from blame."

Like as a fire, the which in hollow cave
Hath long been underkept and down suppress,
With murmurous disdain doth inly rave
And grudge, in so strait prison to be prest,
At last breaks forth with furious unrest,
And strives to mount into his native seat;
All that did erst it hinder and molest,
It now devours with flames and scorching heat,
And carries into smoke with rage and horror
great.

So mightily the Briton Prince him rous'd
Out of his hold, and broke his caitive[15] bands;
And as a bear, whom angry curs have touz'd,[16]
Having off-shak'd them and escap'd their hands,
Becomes more fell, and all that him withstands
Treads down and overthrows. Now had the carl
Alighted from his tiger, and his hands
Dischargëd of his bow and deadly quar'l,[17]
To seize upon his foe flat lying on the marl.[18]

Maleger, disarmed and "far from his monstrous swarm," was taken at disadvantage; and Arthur, yet wrothful for his late disgrace, felled him to the ground with his iron mace. While Arthur fancied the field his own, his foe sprang up as if he had never been hurt, and snatched and threw at the Prince with exceeding sway "a

1 Base, depraved.
2 Strip off.
3 The Foamer.
4 Went.
5 Learn.
6 Reached.
7 Inflame, rankle.
8 Like a dried-up rick of corn or hay.
9 Besides.
10 Dressed.
11 Bracken, fern.
12 A name derived from Latin, "malum," evil, and "æger," sick; it signifies the disease produced by evil passions and indulgences.
13 Her left leg.
14 Knobs.
15 Captive.
16 Teased, harassed.
17 Arrows, bolts; called "quarrel" from the four-square form of the head.
18 Ground.

huge great stone, which stood upon one end, and had not been removëd many a day; some landmark seem'd to be, or sign of sundry way." Lightly leaping backward, Arthur avoided the blow; then he returned fiercely to the attack, "as a falcon fair, that once hath failëd of her souse full near, remounts again into the open air, and unto better fortune doth herself prepare." The Prince pierced Maleger's breast, "that half the steel behind his back doth rest," and, drawing back the blade, looked —but looked in vain—for the life-blood to flow, or the dead corpse to fall. Again the astonished Arthur struck him quite through both the sides, but with no more effect.

Thereat he smitten was with great affright,
And trembling terror did his heart appal;
Nor wist he what to think of that same sight,
Nor what to say, nor what to do at all:
He doubted lest it were some magical
Illusión that did beguile his sense,
Or wand'ring ghost that wanted funeral,
Or airy spirit under false pretence,
Or hellish fiend rais'd up through devilish
science.

His wonder far exceeded reason's reach,
That he began to doubt his dazzled sight,
And oft of error did himself appeach:[1]
Flesh without blood, a person without sprite,
Wounds without hurt, a body without might,
That could do harm, yet could not harmëd be,
That could not die, yet seem'd a mortal wight,
That was most strong in most infirmity;
Like did he never hear, like did he never see.

Throwing away his own good sword Morddure, that never failed at need till now, and his useless shield, Arthur seized Maleger in his arms, "and crush'd the carcase so against his breast," as to squeeze out the idle breath; then he cast "the lumpish corse unto the senseless ground," with such force that it rebounded aloft.

As when Jove's harness-bearing[2] bird from high
Stoops at a flying heron with proud disdain,
The stone-dead quarry[3] falls so forcibly,
That it rebounds against the lowly plain,
A second fall redoubling back again.
Then thought the Prince all peril sure was past,
And that he victor only did remain;
No sooner thought, than that the carl as fast
Gan heap huge strokes on him, as ere he down
was cast.

Arthur waxed nigh his wits' end; but
He then remember'd well, that had been said,
How th' Earth his mother was, and first him
bore;
She eke, so often as his life decay'd,
Did life with usury to him restore,
And rais'd him up much stronger than before,
So soon as he unto her womb did fall:
Therefore to ground he would him cast no more,
Nor him commit to grave terrestrial,
But bare him far from hope of succour usual.[4]

Then up he caught him 'twixt his puissant hands,
And having scruz'd[5] out of his carrion corse
The loathful life, now loos'd from sinful bands,
Upon his shoulders carried him perforce
Above three furlongs, taking his full course,
Until he came unto a standing lake;
Him thereinto he threw without remorse,
Nor stirr'd, till hope of life did him forsake:
So end of that carl's days and his own pains did
make.

Which when those wicked hags from far did spy,
Like to mad dogs they ran about the lands;
And th' one of them, with dreadful yelling cry,
Throwing away her broken chains and bands,
And having quench'd her burning fiër-brands,
Headlong herself did cast into that lake:
But Impotence with her own wilful hands
One of Maleger's cursëd darts did take,
So riv'd[6] her trembling heart, and wicked end
did make.

Faint with loss of blood, the conqueror was set on his steed by his squire, and brought to the castle, where many grooms and squires were ready to aid him; "and eke the fairest Alma met him there, with balm, and wine, and costly spicery, to comfort him in his infirmity." She caused her deliverer to be laid in sumptuous bed, "and, all the while his wounds were dressing, by him stay'd."

CANTO XII.

Guyon, by Palmer's governance,
Passing through perils great,
Doth overthrow the Bower of Bliss,
And Acrasy defeat.

GUYON, the Champion of Temperance, meanwhile approached the point of his adventure. He had sailed two days, after leaving the House of Alma, without beholding land, or living wight, or aught save peril. On the third morn they heard far off a hideous roaring, and saw the raging surges reared up to the skies. The boatman then urged the Palmer to steer aright and keep an even course: for on one side of the way by which they must pass was the Gulf of Greediness, "that deep engorgeth all this worldë's prey;" and on the other side a hideous overhanging rock of magnet stone, threatening ruin to passengers, who are drawn helpless towards it as they shun the Gulf's devouring jaws.

Forward they pass, and strongly he them rows,
Until they nigh unto that Gulf arrive,

1 Impeach, accuse. 2 Armour-bearing.
3 Prey.
4 It was thus that Hercules destroyed the giant Antæus, who received fresh life and strength so soon as he touched the ground, and whom the hero at last vanquished by raising him aloft and squeezing him to death in his arms.
5 Pressed. 6 Pierced.

Where stream more violent and greedy grows:
Then he with all his puissánce doth strive
To strike his oars, and mightily doth drive
The hollow vessel through the threatful wave;
Which, gaping wide to swallow them alive
In th' huge abyss of his engulfing grave,
Doth roar at them in vain, and with great terror rave.

They, passing by, that grisly[1] mouth did see
Sucking the seas into his entrails deep,
That seem'd more horrible than hell to be,
Or that dark dreadful hole of Tartarus steep
Through which the damnëd ghosts do often creep
Back to the world, bad livers to torment:
But naught that falls into this direful deep,
Nor that approacheth nigh the wide descent,
May back return, but is condemnëd to be drent.[2]

On th' other side they saw that perilous rock,
Threat'ning itself on them to ruinate,[3]
On whose sharp clifts the ribs of vessels broke,
And shiver'd ships which had been wreckëd late,
Yet stuck, with carcases exanimate[4]
Of such as, having all their substance spent
In wanton joys and lusts intemperate,
Did afterward make shipwreck violent
Both of their life and fame, for ever foully blent.[5]

Forthy[6] this hight the Rock of vile Reproach,
A dangerous and détestáble place,
To which nor fish nor fowl did once approach,
But yelling mews, with sea-gulls hoarse and base,
And cormorants, with birds of ravenous race,
Which still sat waiting on that wasteful clift
For spoil of wretches whose unhappy case,
After lost credit and consumëd thrift,
At last them driven hath to this despairful[7] drift.

. . . .

So forth they rowëd; and that ferryman
With his stiff oars did brush the sea so strong,
That the hoar waters from his frigate ran,
And the light bubbles dancëd all along,
While the salt brine out of the billows sprung.
At last far off they many islands spy
On ev'ry side floating the floods among:
Then said the Knight: "Lo! I the land descry;
Therefore, old Sire, thy course do thereunto apply."

That, the ferryman answered, would be ruin; for these were the Wandering Islands, which had often drawn many an unwary wight into most deadly danger:

"Yet well they seem to him, that far doth view,
Both fair and fruitful, and the ground dispread
With grassy green of délectáble hue;
And the tall trees with leaves apparellëd
Are deck'd with blossoms dy'd in white and red,
That might the passengers thereto allure;
But whosoever once hath fastenëd
His foot thereon, may never it recure,[8]
But wand'reth evermore uncertain and unsure:

As the isle of Delos "amid the Ægean Sea long time did stray," till Latona, flying from Juno's wrath, was there delivered of her fair twins (Diana and Apollo) "which afterward did rule the night and day." They hearkened to the ferryman's warning; and soon, passing one of the islands, "upon the bank they sitting did espy a dainty damsel dressing of her hair, by whom a little skippet[9] floating did appear.

She, them espying, loud to them gan call,
Bidding them nigher draw unto the shore,
For she had cause to busy them withal;
And therewith loudly laugh'd: but nathëmore
Would they once turn, but kept on as afore:
Which when she saw, she left her locks undight,[10]
And, running to her boat, withouten oar
From the departing land it launchëd light,
And after them did drive with all her power and might.

Whom overtaking, she in merry sort
Them gan to bord,[11] and purpose[12] diversely;
Now feigning dalliance and wanton sport,
Now throwing forth lewd words immodestly;
Till that the Palmer gan full bitterly
Her to rebuke for being loose and light:
Which not abiding, but more scornfully
Scoffing at him that did her justly wite,[13]
She turn'd her boat about, and from them rowëd quite.

"That was the wanton Phædria, which late did ferry him over the Idle Lake." The wary boatman now informed them that in front lay a perilous passage, "where many mermaids haunt, making false melodies;" and by the way there were a great quicksand and a whirlpool of hidden jeopardy, between which the way was very narrow. Scarce had he spoken, when "by the checkëd wave" they discerned "the Quicksand of Unthriftihead."

They, passing by, a goodly ship did see
Laden from far with precious merchandise,
And bravely furnishëd as ship might be,
Which through great disadventure, or misprise,[14]
Herself had run into that hazardise;[15]
Whose mariners and merchants with much toil
Labour'd in vain to have recur'd[16] their prize,
And the rich wares to save from piteous spoil;
But neither toil nor travail might her back recoil.

On th' other side they see that perilous pool,
That callëd was the Whirlpool of Decay;
In which full many had with hapless dool[17]
Been sunk, of whom no memory did stay:
Whose circled waters, rapt with whirling sway,
Like to a restless wheel, still running round,
Did covet, as they passëd by that way,

1 Terrible.
2 Drowned, sunk.
3 Fall in ruins.
4 Lifeless.
5 Disgraced.
6 Therefore.
7 Desperate.
8 Recover.
9 Shiplet, skiff.
10 Undressed, unbound.
11 Accost.
12 Speak.
13 Blame.
14 Mistake; French, "méprise."
15 Hazard.
16 Recovered, saved.
17 Dole, distress.

To draw their boat within the utmost bound
Of his wide labyrinth, and then to have them
drown'd.

Passing in safety, "sudden they see from midst of all the main the surging waters like a mountain rise."

The waves come rolling, and the billows roar
Outrageously, as they enragëd were,
Or wrathful Neptune did them drive before
His whirling chariot for exceeding fear;
For not one puff of wind there did appear;
That all the three thereat wox[1] much afraid,
Unweeting[2] what such horror strange did rear.[3]
Eftsoons they saw a hideous host array'd
Of huge sea-monsters, such as living sense dis-
may'd:

Most ugly shapes and horrible aspécts,
Such as Dame Nature's self might fear to see,
Or shame[4] that ever should so foul defects
From her most cunning hand escapëd be;
All dreadful portraits of deformity:
Spring-headed hydras;[5] and sea-should'ring
whales;
Great whirlpools,[6] which all fishes make to flee;
Bright scolopendras,[7] arm'd with silver scales;
Mighty monoceros[8] with unmeasúrëd tails;

The dreadful fish, that hath deserv'd the name
Of Death, and like him looks in dreadful hue;[9]
The grisly wasserman,[10] that makes his game
The flying ship with swiftness to pursue;
The horrible sea-satyr, that doth shew
His fearful face in time of greatest storm;
Huge ziffius,[11] whom mariners eschew
No less than rocks, as travellers inform;
And greedy rosmarines[12] with visages deform:

All these, and thousand thousands many more,
And more deformëd monsters thousand fold,
With dreadful noise and hollow rumbling roar
Came rushing, in the foamy waves enroll'd,
Which seem'd to fly for fear them to behold:
No wonder, if these did the Knight appal;
For all that here on earth we dreadful hold,
Be but as bugs[13] to fearen[14] babes withal,
Comparëd to the creatures in the sea's entrall.[15]

The Palmer counselled them to fear nothing, for these were only shapes sent by the witch Acrasia to deter them from proceeding; then he smote and calmed the sea with his virtuous staff, "and all that dreadful army fast gan fly into great Tethys' bosom, where they hidden lie." Soon they heard a rueful cry of wailing and weeping, and saw a seemly maiden, sitting by the shore, who appeared to lament some great misfortune, and called aloud to them for succour. Guyon wished to steer towards her, but the Palmer refused; telling him that hers was no real distress, "but only womanish fine forgery," meant to entangle him in ruin.

And now they nigh approachëd to the stead[16]
Where as those mermaids dwelt: it was a still
And calmy bay, on th' one side shelterëd
With the broad shadow of a hoary hill;
On th' other side a high rock tower'd still,
That 'twixt them both a pleasant port they made,
And did like a half theatre fulfil:[17]
There those five Sisters had continual trade,[18]
And us'd to bathe themselves in that deceitful
shade.

They were fair ladies, till they fondly striv'd
With th' Heliconian maids for mastery;[19]
Of whom they, over-comen, were depriv'd
Of their proud beauty, and th' one moiety
Transform'd to fish for their bold surquedry;[20]
But th' upper half their hue[21] retainëd still,
And their sweet skill in wonted melody;
Which ever after they abus'd to ill,
T' allure weak travellers, whom, gotten, they
did kill.

So now to Guyon, as he passëd by,
Their pleasant tunes they sweetly thus applied;
"O thou fair son of gentle Faëry,
That art in mighty arms most magnified
Above all knights that ever battle tried,
O turn thy rudder hitherward a while!
Here may thy storm-beat vessel safely ride;
This is the port of rest from troublous toil,
The world's sweet inn from pain and wearisome
turmoil."

With that the rolling sea, resounding soft,
In his big base them fitly answerëd;
And on the rock the waves breaking aloft
A solemn mean[22] unto them measurëd;
The while sweet Zephyrus loud whistelëd
His treble, a strange kind of harmony;
Which Guyon's senses softly tickelëd,
That he the boatman bade row easily,
And let him hear some part of their rare melody.

He was dissuaded from that vanity by the Palmer; and soon they descried the land they sought; when suddenly a gross fog overspread with his dull vapour all that desert, and made the universe seem but one confused mass. They were greatly dismayed, nor knew how to steer, when all at once an innumerable multitude of harmful birds came fluttering and crying about them, smiting them with their wicked wings,

1 Grew.
2 Ignorant.
3 Raise, cause.
4 Be ashamed.
5 As soon as one head of the fabulous Hydra was cut off, two sprang forth; and Spenser would seem to apply the epithet "spring-headed," from the notion that the monster had a "spring" or fountain of heads.
6 Huge fish of any kind, which produce the eddying effect of a whirlpool in their motion through the water.
7 The sea-scolopendra, a fish mentioned by Aristotle, which resembled the milliped.
8 Unicorns, or sword-fish; creatures with one horn —Greek, μονον, single, and κερας, a horn.
9 The Morse, or walrus (Latin, "Mors," death).
10 The "waterman," or merman; a fabulous being, like the sea-satyr mentioned just below.
11 The sword-fish (xiphias).
12 Sea-horses; German, "Ross," a horse. Another explanation derives the name from Latin "ros," dew, and makes the rosmarine an animal which fed upon the dew on the rocks.
13 Bugbears.
14 Frighten.
15 Entrails, depths.
16 Place.
17 Complete, form, an amphitheatre.
18 Resort.
19 See note 6, page 61.
20 Presumption.
21 Former or natural aspect.
22 Tenor.

and sore annoying them as they groped in that grisly night.

Ev'n all the nation of unfortunate
And fatal birds about them flockëd were,
Such as by nature men abhor and hate;
The ill-fac'd owl, death's dreadful messenger;
The hoarse night-raven, trump of doleful drear;[1]
The leather-wingëd bat, day's enemy̆;
The rueful screech,[2] still waiting on the bier;
The whistler shrill, that whoso hears doth die;
The hellish harpies, prophets of sad destiny̆:

All these, and all others that did horror breed, flew about them, filling their sails with fear; but still the voyagers pressed on, till the weather cleared, and the destined land began to show itself. Soon the Knight and the Palmer quitted the nimble boat, by which the ferryman remained; and they marched fairly forth, afraid of naught. "Ere long they heard a hideous bellowing of many beasts;" and by and by they confronted the horrid crowd, gaping greedily, with upstaring crests, to devour the unexpected guests. But the beasts were swiftly cowed into abject submission and fear by a fresh uplifting of the Palmer's "virtuous staff," that could all charms defeat.

Of that same wood it fram'd was cunningly,
Of which Caducëus whilóm was made,
Caducëus, the rod of Mercury,
With which he wonts[3] the Stygian realms invade
Through ghastly horror and eternal shade;
Th' infernal fiends with it he can assuage,
And Orcus tame, whom nothing can persuade,
And rule the Furies when they most do rage:
Such virtue in his staff had eke this Palmer sage.

Thence passing forth, they shortly do arrive
Where as the Bower of Bliss was situate;
A place pick'd out by choice of best alive
That nature's work by art can imitate:
In which whatever in this worldly state
Is sweet and pleasing unto living sense,
Or that may daintest fantasy aggrate,[4]
Was pourëd forth with plentiful dispence,[5]
And made there to abound with lavish affluence.

Goodly it was enclosëd round about,
As well their enter'd guests to keep within,
As those unruly beasts to hold without;
Yet was the fence thereof but weak and thin;
Naught fear'd their force that fortilage[6] to win,
But Wisdom's pow'r, and Temperance's might,
By which the mightiest things efforcëd bin:[7]
And eke the gate was wrought of substance light,
Rather for pleasure than for battery or fight.

It framëd was of precious ivory,
That seem'd a work of admirable wit;
And therein all the famous history
Of Jason and Medea was y-writ;
Her mighty charms, her furious loving fit;
His goodly conquest of the golden fleece;
His falsëd faith, and love too lightly flit;[8]
The wonder'd Argo, which in venturous piece[9]
First through the Euxine seas bore all the flow'r
of Greece.

Ye might have seen the frothy billows fry[10]
Under the ship as thorough them she went,
That seem'd the waves were into ivory,
Or ivory into the waves were sent;
And otherwhere the snowy substance sprent[11]
With vermeil,[12] like the boy's blood therein
shed,[13]
A piteous spectacle did represent;
And otherwhiles, with gold besprinkelëd,
It seem'd th' enchanted flame, which did Crëusa
wed.[14]

All this and more might in that goodly gate
Be read,[15] that ever open stood to all
Which thither came: but in the porch there sate
A comely personage of stature tall
And semblance pleasing, more than natural,
That travellers to him seem'd to entice;
His looser garment to the ground did fall,
And flew about his heels in wanton wise,
Not fit for speedy pace or manly exercise.

They in that place him Genius did call:—
Nŏt that celestial Power, to whom the care
Of life, and generatión of all
That lives, pertains in charge particular,
Who wondrous things concerning our welfáre,
And strange phantóms, doth let us oft foresee,
And oft of secret ills bids us beware:
That is our Self, whom though we do not see,
Yet each doth in himself it well perceive to be:

Therefore a god him sage Antiquity
Did wisely make, and good Agdistes call:
But this same was to that quite contrary,
The foe of life, that good envíes to all,
That secretly doth us procure to fall[16]
Through guileful semblants,[17] which he makes
us see:
He of this garden had the governal,[18]
And Pleasure's porter was devis'd to be,
Holding a staff in hand for more formality.

With diverse flowers he daintily was deck'd,
And strowëd round about; and by his side
A mighty mazer[19] bowl of wine was set,
As if it had to him been sacrified;
Wherewith all new-come guests he gratified:
So did he eke Sir Guyon passing by;
But he his idle courtesy defied,[20]

1 Sorrow. 2 Screech-owl, an omen of death.
3 Is accustomed.
4 Gratify the most delicate fancy.
5 Outlay, lavishness.
6 Fortalice or fortress; the meaning is, that those within the Bower had no fear that any would win the place by force—all coming to it gladly and eagerly—but Wisdom and Temperance.
7 Are conquered, forced. 8 Fleeted, fled.
9 Castle, or ship; "piece" signifies generally any structure made by the piecing or fitting together of parts. 10 Froth, seethe.
11 Sprinkled. 12 Vermilion.
13 The blood of Absyrtus, brother of Medea, whom she killed and threw in her father's way, to delay the pursuers, when she fled with Jason from Colchis.
14 Jason having proved unfaithful to Medea, and taken to wife Creusa, daughter of Creon, the king of Corinth, Medea sent to her supplanter an enchanted or poisoned garment, which consumed the wearer like a flame. 15 Seen, discerned.
16 Doth conspire, contrive, to make us fall.
17 Appearances, fancies. 18 Government.
19 Maple. 20 Contemned.

And overthrew his bowl disdainfullý,
And broke his staff, with which he charmëd[1]
semblants sly.[2]

Thus being enter'd, they behold around
A large and spacious plain, on ev'ry side
Strowëd with pleasance;[3] whose fair grassy
ground
Mantled with green, and goodly beautified
With all the ornaments of Flora's pride,
Wherewith her mother Art, as half in scorn
Of niggard Nature, like a pompous bride
Did deck her, and too lavishly adorn,
When forth from virgin bow'r she comes in th'
early morn.

Thereto the heavens, always jovial,
Look'd on them lovely, still in steadfast state,
Nor suffer'd storm nor frost on them to fall,
Their tender buds or leaves to violate;
Nor scorching heat, nor cold intemperate,
To afflict the creatures which therein did dwell;
But the mild air with season moderate
Gently attemper'd and dispos'd so well,
That still it breathëd forth sweet spirit[4] and
wholesome smell:

More sweet and wholesome than the pleasant hill
Of Rhodopé, on which the nymph, that bore
A giant babe, herself for grief did kill;
Or the Thessalian Tempé, where of yore
Fair Daphne Phœbus' heart with love did gore;[5]
Or Ida, where the gods lov'd to repair,[6]
Whenever they their heav'nly bow'rs forlore;[7]
Or sweet Parnass', the haunt of Muses fair;
Or Eden self, if aught with Eden might compare.

Much wonder'd Guyon at the fair aspéct
Of that sweet place, yet suffer'd no delight
To sink into his sense, nor mind affect;
But passëd forth, and look'd still forward right,
Bridling his will and mastering his might:
Till that he came unto another gate:
No gate, but like one, being goodly dight[8]
With boughs and branches, which did broad
dilate
Their clasping arms in wanton wreathings intri-
cate:

So fashionëd a porch with rare device,
Arch'd over head with an embracing vine,
Whose bunches hanging down seem'd to entice
All passers-by to taste their luscious wine,
And did themselves into their hands incline,
As freely off'ring to be gatherëd;
Some deep empurpled as the hyacine,[9]
Some as the ruby laughing sweetly red,
Some like fair emeralds, not yet well ripenëd:

And them amongst some were of burnish'd gold,
So made by art to beautify the rest,
Which did themselves amongst the leaves enfold,
As lurking from the view of covetous guest,
That the weak boughs with so rich load oppress
Did bow adown as overburdenëd.

Under that porch a comely dame did rest,
Clad in fair weeds, but foul disorderëd,
And garments loose that seem'd unmeet for
womanhead:

In her left hand a cup of gold she held,
And with her right the riper fruit did reach,
Whose sappy liquor, that with fulness swell'd,
Into her cup she scruz'd[10] with dainty breach[11]
Of her fine fingers, without foul empeach,[12]
That so fair winepress made the wine more sweet:
Thereof she us'd to give to drink to each
Whom passing by she happenëd to meet:
It was her guise all strangers goodly so to greet.

So she to Guyon offer'd it to tast;[13]
Who, taking it out of her tender hand,
The cup to ground did violently cast,
That all in pieces it was broken fand,[14]
And with the liquor stainëd all the land:
Whereat Excess exceedingly was wròth,
Yet n'ot[15] the same amend, nor yet withstand,
But suffer'd him to pass, all[16] were she loth;
Who, naught regarding her displeasure, forward
go'th.

There the most dainty paradise on ground
Itself doth offer to his sober eye,
In which all pleasures plenteously abound,
And none does other's happiness envý;
The painted flow'rs; the trees upshooting high;
The dales for shade; the hills for breathing space;
The trembling groves; the crystal running by;
And, that which all fair works doth most
aggrace,[17]
The art, which all that wrought, appearëd in
no place.[18]

One would have thought (so cunningly the rude
And scornëd parts were mingled with the fine),
That Nature had for wantonness ensued[19]
Art, and that Art at Nature did repine;
So, striving each th' other to undermine,
Each did the other's work more beautify;
So diff'ring both in wills, agreed in fine:[20]
So all agreed, through sweet diversitý,
This garden to adorn with all varietý.

And in the midst of all a fountain stood,
Of richest substance that on earth might be,
So pure and shiny that the silver flood
Through every channel running one might see;
Most goodly it with curious imagery
Was over-wrought, and shapes of naked boys,
Of which some seem'd with lively jollity
To fly about, playing their wanton toys,[21]
Whilst others did themselves embay[22] in liquid
joys.

And over all, of purest gold, was spread
A trail of ivy in his native hue;
For the rich metal was so colourëd,
That wight, who did not well advis'd[23] it view,
Would surely deem it to be ivy true:
Low his lascivious arms adown did creep,

1 Conjured up. 2 Skilful, cunning, apparitions.
3 Objects inspiring pleasure. 4 Breath.
5 Pierce. 6 See note 2, page 388.
7 Forsook. 8 Adorned.
9 Hyacinth. 10 Squeezed.
11 Pressure, fracture. 12 Injury.

13 Taste. 14 Found. 15 Could not.
16 Although. 17 Grace, make pleasing.
18 A paraphrase of the maxim, "Ars est celare artem"—the true art lies in concealing art.
19 Followed. 20 In end or aim. 21 Sports.
22 Bathe, delight. 23 Closely, attentively.

That, themselves dipping in the silver dew,
Their fleecy flow'rs they fearfully did steep,
Which drops of crystal seem'd for wantonness
to weep.

Infinite streams continually did well
Out of this fountain, sweet and fair to see,
The which into an ample laver fell,
And shortly grew to so great quantity,
That like a little lake it seem'd to be;
Whose depth exceeded not three cubits' height,
That through the waves one might the bottom
see,
All pav'd beneath with jasper shining bright,
That seem'd the fountain in that sea did sail
upright.

And all the margent[1] round about was set
With shady laurel trees, thence to defend
The sunny beams which on the billows bet,[2]
And those which therein bathëd might offend.
As Guyon happen'd by the same to wend,[3]
Two naked damsels he therein espied,
Which therein bathing seemëd to contend
And wrestle wantonly, nor car'd to hide
Their dainty parts from view of any which
them ey'd.

Sometimes the one would lift the other quite
Above the waters, and then down again
Her plunge, as over-masterëd by might,
Where both a while would coverëd remain,
And each the other from to rise[4] restrain;
The while their snowy limbs, as through a veil,
So through the crystal waves appearëd plain:
Then suddenly both would themselves unhele,[5]
And th' amorous sweet spoils to greedy eyes
reveal.

As that fair star, the messenger of morn,
His dewy face out of the sea doth rear:
Or as the Cyprian goddess, newly born
Of th' ocean's fruitful froth,[6] did first appear:
Such seemëd they, and so their yellow hair
Crystalline humour[7] droppëd down apace.
Whom such when Guyon saw, he drew him near,
And somewhat gan relent[8] his earnest pace;
His stubborn breast gan secret pleasance to
embrace.

The wanton maidens, him espying, stood
Gazing a while at his unwonted guise;[9]
Then th' one herself low duckëd in the flood,
Abash'd that her a stranger did advise:[10]
But th' other rather higher did arise,
And her two lily paps aloft display'd,
And all, that might his melting heart entice
To her delights, she unto him bewray'd;
The rest, hid underneath, him more desirous
made.

With that the other likewise up arose,
And her fair locks, which formerly were bound
Up in one knot, she low adown did loose,
Which, flowing long and thick, her cloth'd
around,
And th' ivory in golden mantle gown'd:[11]
So that fair spectacle from him was reft,
Yet that which reft it no less fair was found:
So, hid in locks and waves from looker's theft,
Naught but her lovely face she for his looking
left.

Withal she laughëd, and she blush'd withal,
That blushing to her laughter gave more grace,
And laughter to her blushing, as did fall.[12]
Now when they spied the Knight to slack his
pace,
Them to behold, and in his sparkling face
The secret signs of kindled lust appear,
Their wanton merriments they did increase,
And to him beckon'd to approach more near,
And show'd him many sights that courage cold
could rear:[13]

On which when gazing him the Palmer saw,
He much rebuk'd those wand'ring eyes of his,
And, counsell'd well, him forward thence did
draw.
Now are they come nigh to the Bower of Bliss,
Of her fond[14] favourites so nam'd amiss;
When thus the Palmer; "Now, Sir, well advise;[15]
For here the end of all our travail is:
Here wons[16] Acrasia, whom we must surprise,
Else she will slip away, and all our drift
despise."

Eftsoons they heard a most melodious sound
Of all that might delight a dainty ear,
Such as at once might not on living ground,
Save in this paradise, be heard elsewhere:
Right hard it was for wight which did it hear
To read[17] what manner music that might be;
For all that pleasing is to living ear
Was there consórted in one harmony;
Birds, voices, instruments, winds, waters, all
agree:

The joyous birds, shrouded in cheerful shade,
Their notes unto the voice attemper'd sweet;
Th' angelical soft trembling voices made
To th' instruments divine respondence meet;
The silver-sounding instruments did meet
With the base murmur of the waters' fall;
The waters' fall with difference discreet,
Now soft, now loud, unto the wind did call;
The gentle warbling wind low answerëd to all.

There, whence that music seemëd heard to be,
Was the fair Witch herself now solacing
With a new lover, whom through sorcery
And witchcraft she from far did thither bring:
There she had him now laid a-slumbering
In secret shade after long wanton joys;
Whilst round about them pleasantly did sing
Many fair ladies and lascivious boys,
That ever mix'd their song with light licentious
toys.[18]

1 Margin, edge. 2 Beat.
3 Go. 4 From rising.
5 Uncover, display; from Anglo-Saxon "hyllan," to cover, hide. 6 Venus Anadyomene.
7 Moisture. 8 Slacken.
9 Aspect. 10 Gaze upon, observe.
11 Robed. 12 Chance, happen.
13 Inspire. 14 Foolish.
15 Be well on your guard. 16 Dwells.
17 Tell. 18 Toyings, amorous sports.

And all that while right over him she hung,
With her false eyes fast fixëd in his sight,[1]
As seeking medicine whence she was stung,
Or greedily depasturing delight;
And oft inclining down, with kisses light,
For fear of waking him, his lips bedew'd,
And through his humid eyes did suck his sprite,
Quite molten into lust and pleasure lewd;
Wherewith she sighëd soft, as if his case she rued.[2]

The while some one did chant this lovely lay;
"*Ah! see, whoso fair thing dost fain to see,*
In springing flow'r the image of thy day![3]
Ah! see the virgin rose, how sweetly she
Doth first peep forth with bashful modesty,
That fairer seems the less ye see her may!
Lo! see soon after how more bold and free
Her barëd bosom she doth broad display;
Lo! see soon after how she fades and falls away!

So passeth, in the passing of a day,
Of mortal life the leaf, the bud, the flow'r;
Nor more doth flourish after first decay,
That erst was sought to deck both bed and bow'r
Of many a lady, and many a paramour!
Gather therefore the rose whilst yet is prime,
For soon comes age that will her pride deflow'r:
Gather the rose of love whilst yet is time,
Whilst loving thou may'st lovëd be with equal crime." [4]

He ceas'd; and then gan all the choir of birds
Their diverse notes t' attune unto his lay,
As in approvance of his pleasing words.
The constant[5] pair heard all that he did say,
Yet swervëd not, but kept their forward way
Through many covert groves and thickets close,
In which they creeping did at last display[6]
That wanton Lady, with her lover loose,
Whose sleepy head she in her lap did soft dispose.

Upon a bed of roses she was laid,
As faint through heat, or dight[7] to pleasant sin;
And was array'd, or rather disarray'd,
All in a veil of silk and silver thin,
That hid no whit her alabaster skin,
But rather shew'd more white, if more might be:
More subtile web Arachne cannot spin;
Nor the fine nets,[8] which oft we woven see
Of scorchëd dew, do not in th' air more lightly flee.

Her snowy breast was bare to ready spoil
Of hungry eyes, which n'ot[9] therewith be fill'd;
And yet, through languor of her late sweet toil,
Few drops, more clear than nectar, forth distill'd,
That like pure orient pearls adown it trill'd;[10]
And her fair eyes, sweet smiling in delight,
Moisten'd their fiery beams, with which she thrill'd
Frail hearts, yet quenchëd not; like starry light,
Which, sparkling on the silent waves, does seem more bright.

The young man sleeping by her seem'd to be
Some goodly swain of honourable place;[11]
That certes it great pity was to see
Him his nobility so foul deface:[12]
A sweet regard and amiable grace,
Mixëd with manly sternness, did appear,
Yet sleeping, in his well-proportion'd face;
And on his tender lips the downy hair
Did now but freshly spring, and silken blossoms bear.

His warlike arms, the idle instruments
Of sleeping praise, were hung upon a tree;
And his brave shield, full of old moniments,[13]
Was foully ras'd,[14] that none the signs might see;
Nor for them, nor for honour, carëd he,
Nor aught that did to his advancement tend;
But in lewd loves, and wasteful luxury,
His days, his goods, his body he did spend:
O horrible enchantment, that him so did blend![15]

The noble Elf and careful Palmer drew
So nigh them, minding naught but lustful game,
That sudden forth they on them rush'd, and threw
A subtile net, which only for that same
The skilful Palmer formally[16] did frame:
So held them under fast; the while the rest
Fled all away for fear of fouler shame.
The fair enchantress, so unwares opprest,
Tried all her arts and all her sleights thence out to wrest;[17]

And eke her lover strove; but all in vain:
For that same net so cunningly was wound,
That neither guile nor force might it distrain.[18]
They took them both, and both them strongly bound
In captive bands, which there they ready found:
But her in chains of adamant he tied;
For nothing else might keep her safe and sound:
But Verdant (so he hight) he soon untied,
And counsel sage in stead thereof to him applied.

But all those pleasant bow'rs, and palace brave,
Guyon broke down with rigour pitiless:
Nor aught their goodly workmanship might save
Them from the tempest of his wrathfulness,
But that their bliss he turn'd to balefulness;
Their groves he fell'd; their gardens did deface;
Their arbours spoil; their cabinets suppress;
Their banquet-houses burn; their buildings rase;
And of the fairest late now made the foulest place.

Then led they her away, and eke that knight
They with them led, both sorrowful and sad:
The way they came, the same return'd they right,
Till they arrivëd where they lately had
Charm'd those wild beasts that rag'd with fury mad;
Which, now awaking, fierce at them gan fly,
As in their mistress' rescue, whom they lad;[19]

1 Fixed on his face. 2 Pitied. 3 Life.
4 With equal fault—if fault it be; or, with equal occasion for love to that which thou thyself givest.
5 Resolute, steadfast. 6 Discover.
7 Prepared.
8 The gossamer web.
9 Could not. 10 Trickled.
11 Rank. 12 Disgrace.
13 Memorials. 14 Erased.
15 Blind, deceive. 16 Expressly, carefully.
17 Escape, wrench herself away.
18 Rend. 19 Led.

But them the Palmer soon did pacify.
Then Guyon ask'd, what meant those beasts
which there did lie.

Said he; "These seeming beasts are men in deed,
Whom this enchantress hath transformëd thus;
Whilóm her lovers, which her lusts did feed,
Now turnëd into figures hideous,
According to their minds like monstruous."
"Sad end," quoth he, "of life intemperate,
And mournful meed of joys delicious!
But, Palmer, if it might thee so aggrate,[1]
Let them returnëd be unto their former state."

Straightway he with his virtuous staff them
strook,
And straight of beasts they comely men became;
Yet, being men, they did unmanly look,
And starëd ghastly; some for inward shame,
And some for wrath to see their captive Dame:
But one above the rest in speciál,
That had a hog been late, hight Gryll by name,
Repinëd greatly, and did him miscall[2]
That had from hoggish form him brought to
natural.

Said Guyon; "See the mind of beastly man,
That hath so soon forgot the excellence
Of his creation, when he life began,
That now he chooseth, with vile difference,
To be a beast and lack intelligence!"
To whom the Palmer thus; "The dunghill kind
Delights in filth and foul incontinence:
Let Gryll be Gryll, and have his hoggish mind;
But let us hence depart, whilst weather serves
and wind."

THE THIRD BOOK

OF

THE FAERIE QUEEN:

CONTAINING

THE LEGEND OF BRITOMARTIS,[3] OR OF CHASTITY.

It falls me here to write of Chastity,
That fairest virtue, far above the rest:
For which what needs me fetch from Faëry
Foreign ensamples it to have exprest?
Since it is shrinëd in my Sov'reign's breast,
And form'd so lively in each perfect part,
That to all ladies, which have it profest,
Need but behold the portrait of her heart;
If pórtray'd it might be by any living art:

But living art may not least part express,
Nor life-resembling pencil it can paint:
All[4] were it Zeuxis or Praxiteles,
His dædal[5] hand would fail and greatly faint,
And her perfections with his error taint:
Nor poet's wit, that passeth painter far
In picturing the parts of beauty daint,[6]
So hard a workmanship adventure dare,
For fear through want of words her excellence
to mar.

How then shall I, apprentice of the skill
That whilom in divinest wits did reign,
Presume so high to stretch mine humble quill?
Yet now my luckless lot doth me constrain
Hereto perforce: but, O dread Sovereign!
Thus far forth pardon, since that choicest wit
Cannot your glorious portrait figure plain,
That I in colour'd shows may shadow it,
And ántique praises unto present persons fit.

But if in living colours, and right hue,
Thyself thou covet to see picturëd,
Who can it do more lively or more true
Than that sweet verse, with nectar sprinkelëd,
In which a gracious servant[7] picturëd
His Cynthia, his heaven's fairest light?
That, with his melting sweetness ravishëd,
And with the wonder of her beamës bright,
My senses lullëd are in slumber of delight.

But let that same delicious poet lend
A little leave unto a rustic Muse
To sing his Mistress' praise; and let him mend,
If aught amiss her liking may abuse:
Nor let his fairest Cynthia refuse
In mirrors more than one herself to see;
But either Gloriana let her choose,
Or in Belphœbe fashionëd to be;
In th' one her rule, in th' other her rare chastity.

CANTO I.

Guyon encount'reth Britomart:
Fair Florimell is chas'd:
Duessa's trains and Malecas-
ta's champions are defac'd.

Recovered in the House of Temperance from their fatigues and wounds, Prince Arthur and Guyon took leave of the fair Alma, and went

1 Please. 2 Abuse, upraid.

3 Britomartis (compound of the Greek words Βριτυς, sweet, and μαρτις, a maiden) was the name of a Cretan nymph, whom Minos vainly pursued with his love; at last, to avoid him, she leaped into the sea, and was changed into a goddess by Artemis or Diana. In Crete, the two divinities came to be identified, and the title of Britomartis was sometimes applied to Diana. The fitness of the name for Spenser's purpose in this book, which is devoted to the fortunes of a chaste and martial British maiden, is obvious; and so is the opportunity, which the poet does not neglect, of paying homage to the Virgin Queen on her pre-eminence in a virtue by which she set much store.

4 Although.

5 Skilful, cunning; from Greek, δαιδαλλω, I work cunningly. Daedalus was the name given to the Cretan artist who first separated the feet of his statues, to give them the appearance of motion.

6 Delicate, exquisite.

7 Sir Walter Raleigh, in his poem of "Cynthia."

forth together; the captive Acrasia, under strong guard, having been sent to Faery Court by another road. After long dangerous travel and many hard adventures, they came to an open plain, where they spied a knight, attended by an aged squire; and the stranger addressed himself to battle, displaying his shield, "that bore a lion passant in a golden field." Beseeching the Prince "to let him run that turn," Guyon spurred against the stranger; the two met in furious encounter; the Faery Knight was unhorsed, and "nigh a spear's length behind his crupper fell," though uninjured.

Great shame and sorrow of that fall he took;[1]
For never yet, since warlike arms he bore
And shiv'ring spear in bloody field first shook,
He found himself dishonourëd so sore.
Ah! gentlest knight that ever armour bore,
Let not thee grieve dismounted to have been,
And brought to ground, that never wast before;
For not thy fault, but secret pow'r unseen;
That spear enchanted was which laid thee on
the green!

But weenedst thou what wight thee overthrew,
Much greater grief and shamefuller regret
For thy hard fortune then thou wouldst renew,
That of a single damsel thou wert met
On equal plain, and there so hard beset:
Even the famous Britomart that was,
Whom strange adventure did from Britain fet.[2]
To seek her lover (love far sought, alas!)
Whose image she had seen in Venus' looking-
glass.

The wrathful Guyon would have continued the fight on foot; but the Palmer warned him against braving the death that "sat on the point of that enchanted spear;" and the Prince added his dissuasions, laying the blame of the fall, not on the Knight's carriage, but on his swerving steed and the imperfect buckling of his furnitures. "Thus reconcilement was between them knit," and they rode forward all in company.

O goodly usage of those ántique times!
In which the sword was servant unto right;
When not for malice and contentious crimes,
But all for praise, and proof of manly might,
The martial brood accustomëd to fight:
Then honour was the meed of victorý,
And yet the vanquishëd had no despite:
Let later age that noble use envý,
Vile rancour to avoid and cruel surquedrý![3]

Travelling long, they came to a wide forest, "whose hideous horror and sad trembling sound full grisly seem'd;" and there they rode long, finding no tracks but those of wild beasts.

All suddenly, out of the thickest brush,
Upon a milk-white palfrey all alone,
A goodly lady did foreby[4] them rush,
Whose face did seem as clear as crystal stone,
And eke, through fear, as white as whalë's bone:
Her garments all were wrought of beaten gold,
And all her steed with tinsel trappings shone,
Which fled so fast that nothing might him hold,
And scarce them leisure gave her passing to
behold.

Still, as she fled, her eye she backward threw,
As fearing evil that pursued her fast;
And her fair yellow locks behind her flew,
Loosely dispers'd with puff of every blast:
All as a blazing star doth far outcast
His hairy beams, and flaming locks dispread,
At sight whereof the people stand aghast;
But the sage wizard tells, as he has read,[5]
That it impórtunes[6] death and doleful dreari-
head.[7]

So as they gazëd after her a while,
Lo! where a grisly foster[8] forth did rush,
Breathing out beastly lust her to defile:
His tireling jade[9] he fiercely forth did push
Through thick and thin, both over bank and
bush,
In hope her to attain by hook or crook,
That from his gory sides the blood did gush:
Large were his limbs, and terrible his look,
And in his clownish hand a sharp boar-spear he
shook.

Seeing this outrage, the Knights instantly spurred after the lady, to rescue her; the "foul foster" was pursued by Timias (Prince Arthur's squire, whose name we now learn for the first time, and who is understood to represent Raleigh); while Britomart, after awaiting in vain for a certain space the return of the others, fearlessly held on her perilous way. At the issue from the wood, she spied a stately castle far away, and, on a fair green-mantled plain in front, six knights vehemently attacking one, who bravely resisted, so that none of them dared to attack him in front:

Like dastard curs, that, having at a bay
The salvage beast emboss'd[10] in weary chase,
Dare not adventure on the stubborn prey,
Nor bite before, but roam from place to place
To get a snatch when turnëd is his face.
In such distress and doubtful jeopardý
When Britomart him saw, she ran apace
Unto his rescue, and with earnest cry
Bade those same six forbear that single enemý.

The assailants paying no heed to her cry, Britomart pressed in, drove them off, and inquired the cause of strife. The single knight answered that the six would compel him to change his love, and love another dame; while he already loved "one, the truest one on ground," the Errant Damsel—for he is no other than the Redcross Knight.

"Certes," said she, "then be ye six to bláme,
To ween your wrong by force to justify:

1 The overthrow of Sir Guyon in the unprovoked encounter with Britomart, is supposed to refer to the futile presumption of the Earl of Essex, in his ambitious thought to match himself with Queen Elizabeth.
2 Fetch.
3 Arrogance, présumptuous self-conceit.
4 Near.
5 Divined.
6 Imports, portends.
7 Calamity.
8 Fórester.
9 Wearied horse.
10 Hard hunted, hunted down.

For knight to leave his lady were great shame,
That faithful is; and better were to die.
All loss is less, and less the infamy,
Than loss of love to him that loves but one:
Nor may love be compell'd by mastery;[1]
For, soon as mastery comes, sweet love anon
Taketh his nimble wings, and soon away is gone."[2]

One of the six explained that in the castle dwelt a lady of peerless beauty, who had ordained a law that every knight passing that way, if he had no lady or no love, should do her perpetual service; and if he had a love, "then must he her forego with foul defame," or maintain by his sword—as the Redcross was doing—that she was fairer than their fairest Dame. Britomart, asked to declare if she had a love, replied that she had certainly a love, though no lady, and refused to do service to their mistress. Then she attacked them, and laid three on ground, while a fourth succumbed to the Knight; the others, yielding themselves her liegemen, asked her "to enter in and reap the due reward" of their lady's favour. "Long were it to describe the goodly frame and stately port of Castle Joyous"—for so the pile was called—where the victors were brought into the presence of the Lady of Delight "through a chamber long and spacious."

But for to tell the sumptuous array
Of that great chamber should be labour lost;
For living wit, I ween, cannot display
The royal riches and exceeding cost
Of ev'ry pillar and of ev'ry post,
Which all of purest bullion framëd were,
And with great pearls and precious stones embost;
That the bright glister of their beamës clear
Did sparkle forth great light, and glorious did appear.

The stranger knights, struck with wonder, passed into an inner room far more richly royal:

The walls were round about apparellëd
With costly cloths of Arras and of Tour;[3]
In which with cunning hand was pórtrayëd
The love of Venus and her paramoúr,
The fair Adonis, turnëd to a flow'r;
A work of rare device and wondrous wit.
First did it show the bitter baleful stowre[4]
Which her assay'd with many a fervent fit,
When first her tender heart was with his beauty smit:

Then with what sleights and sweet allurements she
Entic'd the boy, as well that art she knew,
And wooëd him her paramour to be;
Now making garlands of each flow'r that grew,
To crown his golden locks with honour due;
Now leading him into a secret shade
From his beauperes,[5] and from bright heaven's view,
Where him to sleep she gently would persuade,
Or bathe him in a fountain by some covert glade:

And, whilst he slept, she over him would spread
Her mantle colour'd like the starry skies,
And her soft arm lay underneath his head,
And with ambrosial kisses bathe his eyes;
And, whilst he bath'd, with her two crafty spies[6]
She secretly would search each dainty limb,
And throw into the well sweet rosemaries,
And fragrant violets, and pansies trim;
And ever with sweet nectar she did sprinkle him.

So did she steal his heedless heart away,
And joy'd his love in secret unespied:
But, for[7] she saw him bent to cruel play,
To hunt the salvage beast in forest wide,
Dreadful of danger that might him betide,
She oft and oft advis'd him to refrain
From chase of greater beasts, whose brutish pride
Might breed him scath unwares: but all in vain;
For who can shun the chance that destiny doth ordain?

Lo! where beyond[8] he lieth languishing,
Deadly engorëd[9] of a great wild boar;
And by his side the goddess grovelling
Makes for him endless moan, and evermore
With her soft garment wipes away the gore
Which stains his snowy skin with hateful hue:
But, when she saw no help might him restore,
Him to a dainty flow'r she did transmue,[10]
Which in that cloth was wrought, as if it lively[11] grew.

So was that chamber clad in goodly wise:
And round about it many beds were dight,[12]
As whilom was the ántique worldë's guise,
Some for untimely ease, some for delight,
As pleasëd them to use that use it might:
And all was full of damsels and of squires,
Dancing and revelling both day and night,
And swimming deep in sensual desires;
And Cupid still amongst them kindled lustful fires.

And all the while sweet Music did divide
Her looser notes with Lydian harmony;
And all the while sweet birds thereto applied
Their dainty lays and dulcet melody,
Aye carolling of love and jóllity,
That wonder was to hear their trim consórt.[13]

1 Superior power, force.

2 These lines are almost literally taken from Chaucer, who, near the opening of The Franklin's Tale (page 122), says—

"Love will not be constrain'd by mastery.
When mastery comes, the god of love anon
Beateth his wings, and, farewell, he is gone.
Love is a thing as any spirit free."

The same idea and image are reproduced by Pope in the Epistle of Eloisa to Abelard, lines 73–76:

"How oft, when press'd to marriage, have I said,
Curse on all laws but those which love has made?
Love, free as air, at sight of human ties,
Spreads his light wings, and in a moment flies."

3 Tours, in France; where, as at Arras, the manufacture of tapestries and silk stuffs had attained great excellence.

4 Passion, pain of love.

5 Companions, fair peers or equals in age; like the Greek ἥλικες.

6 Her eyes.

7 Because.

8 Yonder.

9 Pierced, wounded.

10 He was transformed to an anemone.

11 Living.

12 Couches were arranged.

13 Pleasing concert.

Which when those knights beheld, with scornful eye
They sdeignëd[1] such lascivious disport,
And loath'd the loose demeanour of that wanton sort.[2]

Thence they were brought to that great Lady's view,
Whom they found sitting on a sumptuous bed
That glister'd all with gold and glorious shew,
As the proud Persian queens accustomëd:
She seem'd a woman of great bountihead[3]
And of rare beauty, saving that askance
Her wanton eyes (ill signs of womanhead)
Did roll too lightly, and too often glance,
Without regard of grace or comely ámenánce.[4]

Invited by the Lady, the Redcross Knight disarmed; but Britomart would only lift her visor.

As, when fair Cynthia, in darksome night,
Is in a noyous[5] cloud envelopëd,
Where she may find the substance thin and light,
Breaks forth her silver beams, and her bright head
Discovers to the world discomfited;[6]
Of the poor traveller that went astray
With thousand blessings she is heriëd:[7]
Such was the beauty and the shining ray,
With which fair Britomart gave light unto the day.

And eke those six, which lately with her fought,
Now were disarm'd, and did themselves present
Unto her view and company unsought;
For they all seemëd courteous and gent,[8]
And all six brethren, born of one parént,
Which had them train'd in all civility,
And goodly taught to tilt and tournament;
Now were they liegemen to this Lady free,
And her knight's-service ought,[9] to hold of her in fee.

The first of them by name Gardanté hight,
A jolly person, and of comely view;
The second was Parlanté, a bold knight;
And next to him Jocanté did ensue;
Basciantè did himself most courteous shew;
But fierce Bacchanté seem'd too fell and keen;
And yet in arms Noctanté[10] greater grew:
All were fair knights, and goodly well beseen;[11]
But to fair Britomart they all but shadows been.

For she was full of amiable grace
And manly terror mixëd therewithal;
That, as the one stirr'd up affections base,
So th' other did men's rash desires appal,
And hold them back that would in error fall:
As he that hath espied a vermeil rose,
To which sharp thorns and briars the way forestall,[12]
Dare not for dread his hardy hand expose,
But, wishing it far off, his idle wish doth lose.

Believing Britomart what she seemed, "a fresh and lusty knight," the Lady grew greatly enamoured, and soon burned in extreme desire; recklessly bursting into terms of open outrage, that plainly discovered her passionate nature—"not to love, but lust, inclin'd." The crafty glances of her false eyes aimed at the comely guest's heart, "and told her meaning in her countenance; but Britomart dissembled it with ignorance." A sumptuous supper was served; nothing lacked that was dainty and rare; "and aye the cups their banks did overflow, and aye between the cups" the Lady shot secret darts at the unmoved Maiden Knight. Having again vainly entreated Britomart to disarm, the Lady began to show her desire more openly, "with sighs, and sobs, and plaints, and piteous grief, the outward sparks of her in-burning fire;" and at last told her plainly, that if she did not show some pity, and do her some comfort, she must die. Britomart, credulously judging the other's "strong extremity" by her own secret passion—like a bird that, knowing not "the false fowler's call, into his hidden net full easily doth fall"—now entertained the Lady with fair countenance, while inwardly deeming "her love too light, to woo a wandering guest." The tables were removed; every knight and gentle squire "gan choose his dame with *basciomani*[13] gay;"

Some fell to dance; some fell to hazardry;[14]
Some to make love; some to make merriment;
As diverse wits to diverse things apply:
And all the while fair Malecasta[15] bent
Her crafty engines[16] to her close intent.[17]
By this th' eternal lamps, wherewith high Jove
Doth light the lower world, were half y-spent,
And the moist daughters of huge Atlas strove
Into the ocean deep to drive their weary drove.

The guests were lit to their chambers by long waxen torches; and the Britoness, when alone, "gan herself despoil, and safe commit to her soft feather'd nest," where she slept soundly.

Now when as all the world in silence deep
Y-shrouded was, and every mortal wight
Was drownëd in the depth of deadly sleep,
Fair Malecasta, whose engrievëd sprite[18]
Could find no rest in such perplexëd plight,
Lightly arose out of her weary bed,
And, under the black veil of guilty night,
Her with a scarlet mantle coverëd,
That was with gold and ermines fair envelopëd.

Then panting soft, and trembling ev'ry joint,
Her fearful feet towárd the bow'r[19] she mov'd,
Where she for secret purpose did appoint
To lodge the warlike Maid, unwisely lov'd;
And, to her bed approaching, first she prov'd
Whether she slept or wak'd: with her soft hand

1 Disdained. 2 Company. 3 Goodness.
4 Carriage, behaviour. 5 Gloomy, dismal.
6 Troubled, dejected (at her absence).
7 Honoured. 8 Gentle, noble.
9 Owed.
10 The names of the knights denote the stages in the progress of light love; they mean the Ogler, the Prattler, the Jester, the Kisser, the Drinker, and the Night Reveller or pursuer of nocturnal pleasures.
11 Well-arrayed. 12 Prevent.
13 Hand-kissings. 14 Gaming.
15 The Unchaste—the name of the Lady of Delight.
16 Wits, devices. 17 Secret purpose.
18 Wounded spirit. 19 Chamber.

She softly felt if any member mov'd,
And lent her wary ear to understand
If any puff of breath or sign of sense she fand.

Which when as none she found, with easy shift,[1]
For fear lest her unwares she should abraid,[2]
Th' embroider'd quilt she lightly up did lift,
And by her side herself she softly laid,
Of ev'ry finest finger's touch afraid;
Nor any noise she made, nor word she spake,
But inly sigh'd. At last the royal Maid
Out of her quiet slumber did awake,
And chang'd her weary side the better ease to take.

Where, feeling one close couchëd by her side,
She lightly leapt out of her filëd[3] bed,
And to her weapon ran, in mind to gride[4]
The loathëd lecher: but the Dame, half dead
Through sudden fear and ghastly drearihead,[5]
Did shriek aloud, that through the house it rung,
And the whole family,[6] therewith adread,[7]
Rashly[8] out of their rousëd couches sprung,
And to the troubled chamber all in arms did throng.

With the rest came, half-armed, the six knights, who found their Lady prostrate on the ground, and on the other side "the warlike Maid, all in her snow-white smock, with locks unbound, threat'ning the point of her avenging blade." They laid the Lady in comfortable couch, and reared her out of her frozen swound; then they began to upbraid the Maiden, but dared not approach her, restrained by the memory of the last day's loss, and by the presence of the Redcross Knight at her side.

But one of those six knights, Gardanté hight,
Drew out a deadly bow and arrow keen,
Which forth he sent with felonous[9] despite
And fell intent against the Virgin sheen:[10]
The mortal steel stay'd not till it was seen
To gore her side; yet was the wound not deep,
But lightly rasëd her soft silken skin,
That drops of purple blood thereout did weep,
Which did her lily smock with stains of vermeil steep.

Wherewith enrag'd she fiercely at them flew,
And with her flaming sword about her laid,
That none of them foul mischief could eschew,[11]
But with her dreadful strokes were all dismay'd:
Here, there, and everywhere, about her sway'd
Her wrathful steel, that none might it abide;
And eke the Redcross Knight gave her good aid,
Ay joining foot to foot, and side to side;
That in short space their foes they have quite terrified.

When all are put to shameful flight, the noble Britomartis arms herself, and, ere the morn, departs with the Redcross Knight from the haunt of "so loose life, and so ungentle trade."

1 Gentle movement.
2 Awake.
3 Defiled.
4 Pierce.
5 Terror.
6 Household.
7 Alarmed.
8 Hurriedly.
9 Cruel, villainous.
10 Bright, beautiful.

CANTO II.

The Redcross Knight to Britomart
Describeth Artegall:
The wondrous mirror, by which she
In love with him did fall.

HERE have I cause in men just blame to find,
That in their proper praise too partial be,
And not indifferent[12] to woman kind,
To whom no share in arms and chivalry
They do impart, nor maken memory
Of their brave gests[13] and prowess martial:
Scarce do they spare to one, or two, or three,
Room in their writs; yet the same writing small
Does all their deeds deface, and dims their glories all.

But by recórd of ántique times I find
That women wont in wars to bear most sway,
And to all great exploits themselves inclin'd,
Of which they still the garland bore away;
Till envious men, fearing their rule's decay,
Gan coin strait laws to curb their liberty:
Yet, since they warlike arms have laid away,
They have excell'd in arts and policy,
That now we foolish men that praise gin eke t' envý.[14]

The poet calls on Britomart to be the example of warlike puissance in ages past, and on Elizabeth to be the precedent of all wisdom; and proceeds to tell how, as they rode, her companion began to ask the Briton Maid "what uncouth wind brought her into those parts," and what enterprise made her disguise herself.

Thereat she, sighing softly, had no pow'r
To speak a while, nor ready answer make;
But with heart-thrilling throbs and bitter stowre,[15]
As if she had a fever fit, did quake,
And ev'ry dainty limb with horror shake;
And ever and anon the rosy red
Flash'd through her face, as it had been a flake
Of lightning through bright heaven fulminëd:
At last, the passion past, she thus him answerëd:

From her infancy she had been trained to arms, loving to confront death at point of foeman's spear, and loathing to lead her life "as ladies wont, in Pleasure's wanton lap, to finger the fine needle and nice thread." In quest of perils and adventures hard she had come, "withouten compass and withouten card," from her native Greater Britain (Wales) into Faery Land (England); and she asked the Knight if he could give her news of one called Artegall, on whom she wished to be revenged for foul dishonour and reproachful spite that he had done her. She would have unsaid the name, but the Knight, taking it up ere it fell, declared her unadvised to upbraid with unknightly blame a knight so gentle and famous in war as Artegall. Waxing

11 Escape.
12 Impartial.
13 Deeds.
14 Of course a compliment to Queen Elizabeth is here intended.
15 Emotion.

"inly wondrous glad to hear her love so highly magnified," the Maid still reviled Artegall, and demanded where he might be found. The Knight answered that he had no fixed abode, "but restless walketh all the world around," doing deeds of prowess and redress. More and more pleased at heart, Britomart still feigned gainsay ("so discord oft in music makes the sweetest lay"), and asked by what marks she might know Artegall if she encountered him. The Knight described him—all needlessly, for she knew him before in every part, "to her revealëd in a mirror plain."

By strange occasion she did him behold,
And much more strangely gan to love his sight,
As it in books hath written been of old.
In Deheubarth, that now South-Wales is hight,
What time king Ryence reign'd and dealëd right,
The great magician Merlin had devis'd,
By his deep science and hell-dreaded might,
A looking-glass, right wondrously aguis'd,[1]
Whose virtues through the wide world soon
were solemnis'd.

It virtue had to show in perfect sight
Whatever thing was in the world contain'd,
Betwixt the lowest earth and heaven's height,
So that it to the looker appertain'd:
Whatever foe had wrought, or friend had feign'd,
Therein discover'd was, nor aught might pass,
Nor aught in secret from the same remain'd;
Forthy[2] it round and hollow shapëd was,
Like to the world itself, and seem'd a world of
glass.

. . . . . .

One day it fortunëd fair Britomart
Into her father's closet to repair;
For nothing he from her reserv'd apart,
Being his only daughter and his heir;
Where when she had espied that mirror fair,
Herself a while therein she view'd in vain:[3]
Then, her advising[4] of the virtues rare
Which thereof spoken were, she gan again
Her to bethink of that might to herself pertain.

But, as it falleth, in the gentlest hearts
Imperious Love hath highest set his throne,
And tyrannizeth in the bitter smarts
Of them that to him buxom[5] are and prone:
So thought this maid (as maidens us'd to do'n)
Whom fortune for her husband would allot;
Not that she lusted after any one,
For she was pure from blame of sinful blot;
Yet wist her life at last must link in that same
knot.

Eftsoons there was presented to her eye
A comely knight, all arm'd in cómplete wise,
Through whose bright ventail[6] lifted up on high
His manly face, that did his foes agrise,[7]
And friends to terms of gentle truce entice,
Look'd forth, as Phœbus' face out of the east
Betwixt two shady mountains doth arise:
Portly his person was, and much increast
Through his heroic grace and honourable gest.[8]

His crest was cover'd with a couchant hound,
And all his armour seem'd of ántique mould,
But wondrous massy and assurëd sound,
And round about y-fretted all with gold,
In which there written was, with ciphers old,
Achilles' arms which Artegall did win:
And on his shield envelop'd sevenfold
He bore a crownëd little ermilin,[9]
That deck'd the azure field with her fair poul-
dred[10] skin.

The damsel well did view his personage,[11]
And likëd well; nor farther fasten'd[12] not,
But went her way; nor her unguilty age
Did ween, unwares, that her unlucky lot
Lay hidden in the bottom of the pot:
Of hurt unwist[13] most danger doth redound:
But the false archer, which that arrow shot
So slily that she did not feel the wound,
Did smile full smoothly at her weetless woeful
stound.[14]

Thenceforth the feather in her lofty crest,
Ruffëd of[15] love, gan lowly to avail;[16]
And her proud portance[17] and her princely gest,[8]
With which she erst triúmphëd, now did quail:
Sad, solemn, sour, and full of fancies frail,
She wox; yet wist she neither how, nor why;
She wist not, silly maid, what she did ail,
Yet wist she was not well at ease, pardie;[18]
Yet thought it was not love, but some melán-
choly.

So soon as Night had with her pallid hue
Defac'd the beauty of the shining sky,
And reft from men the world's desirëd view,
She with her nurse adown to sleep did lie;
But sleep full far away from her did fly:
Instead thereof sad sighs and sorrows deep
Kept watch and ward about her warily;
That naught she did but wail, and often steep
Her dainty couch with tears which closely[19] she
did weep.

And if, worn out, she slept, fantastic dreams made her start from her bed, to "renew her former smart, and think of that fair visage written in her heart." One night Glaucé, her ancient nurse, "feeling her leap out of her loathëd nest," caught her in her arms, and questioned her as to the cause of her changed manner; promising, if the cause was love, and that love worthy of her race and royal seed, to ease her grief and win her will. With many embraces, caresses, and assurances that "that blinded god, which hath ye blindly smit, another arrow hath your lover's heart to hit," Glaucé drew from Britomart the confession that she suffered from a hopeless passion for "the only shade and semblance of a knight," seen in the magic mirror. The aged nurse, relieved to find that no unlawful or unnatural desire preyed

1 Contrived, fashioned. 2 For that end.
3 Without any definite purpose or thought.
4 Bethinking. 5 Obedient.
6 Front of the helmet. 7 Terrify.
8 Demeanour. 9 Ermine.

10 Spotted. 11 Person.
12 Fixed her thoughts. 13 Unknown.
14 Unsuspected hurt. 15 Ruffled by.
16 Droop. 17 Carriage.
18 Assuredly. 19 Secretly.

on the Princess's mind, wished Britomart joy of her well-bestowed affection, and "upleaning on her elbow weak, her alabaster breast she soft did kiss; which all that while she felt to pant and quake, as it an earthquake were." Britomart, however, contended that her case was worse than that of Phasiphaé and other "shameful and unkind" lovers mentioned by Glaucé; for they at least "possessed their horrible intent;" while she, less fortunate and more foolish than Narcissus, beguiled with the love of his own face, loved a mere shade, and must feed on shadows while she died for food. Glaucé, maintaining that every shadow must have a body, promised, if Britomart could not overcome her passion, to compass her desire, and find that loved knight; and at last the maiden, somewhat comforted, sank to sleep, while the aged nurse "set her by to watch, and set her by to weep."

Early, the morrow next, before that Day
His joyous face did to the world reveal,
They both uprose and took their ready way
Unto the church, their prayers to appeal,[1]
With great devotion, and with little zeal:
For the fair damsel from the holy herse[2]
Her love-sick heart to other thoughts did steal;
And that old dame said many an idle verse,
Out of her daughter's heart fond fancies to reverse.[3]

Returnëd home, the royal Infant fell
Into her former fit; for why? no pow'r
Nor guidance of herself in her did dwell.
But th' aged nurse, her calling to her bow'r,
Had gather'd rue, and savin, and the flow'r
Of camphora, and calamint, and dill;
All which she in an earthen pot did pour,
And to the brim with coltwood did it fill,
And many drops of milk and blood through it did spill.

Then, taking thrice three hairs from off her head,
Them trebly braided in a threefold lace,
And round about the pot's mouth bound the thread;
And, after having whisperëd a space
Certain sad words with hollow voice and base,[4]
She to the Virgin said, thrice said she it;
"Come, daughter, come; come, spit upon my face;
Spit thrice upon me, thrice upon me spit;
Th' uneven number for this business is most fit."

That said, her round about she from her turn'd,
She turnëd her contrâry to the sun;
Thrice she her turn'd contrâry, and return'd
All cóntrary; for she the right did shun;
And ever what she did was straight undone.
So thought she to undo her daughter's love:
But love, that is in gentle breast begun,
No idle charms so lightly may remove;
That well can witness, who by trial it does prove.

Nor aught it might the noble Maid avail,
Nor slake the fury of her cruel flame,
But that she still did waste, and still did wail,
That, through long languor and heart-burning brame,[5]
She shortly like a pinëd ghost became
Which long hath waited by the Stygian strand:
That when old Glaucé saw, for fear lest blame
Of her miscarriage should in her be fand,
She wist not how t' amend, nor how it to withstand.

CANTO III.

Merlin bewrays[6] to Britomart
The state of Artegall:
And shows the famous progeny,
Which from them springen shall.

MOST sacred fire, that burnest mightily
In living breasts, y-kindled first above
Amongst th' eternal spheres and lamping[7] sky,
And thence pour'd into men, which men call Love;
Not that same, which doth base affections move
In brutish minds, and filthy lust inflame;
But that sweet fit that doth true beauty love,
And chooseth Virtue for his dearest Dame,
Whence spring all noble deeds and never-dying fame:

Well did Antiquity a god thee deem,
That over mortal minds hast so great might,
To order them as best to thee doth seem,
And all their actions to direct aright:
The fatal[8] purpose of divine foresight
Thou dost effect in destinëd descents,
Through deep impression of thy secret might,
And stirredst up th' heróës' high intents,
Which the late world admires for wondrous monuments.

But never was braver proof of Love's power, than when the royal British Maid sought "an unknown paramour, from the world's end, through many a bitter stowre." After invoking Clio's aid to recount his glorious Sovereign's goodly ancestry, the poet relates that Glaucé, finding all her charms and herbs unavailing to cure Britomart's grief, resolved to seek out Merlin himself, and ascertain from him "under what coast of heav'n the man did dwell" whose image had appeared in the magic mirror. "Forthwith themselves disguising both in strange and base attire," the Princess and her nurse took their way to Maridunum (Caermarthen), where Merlin dwelt "low underneath the ground, in a deep delve, far from the view of day."

And, if thou ever happen that same way
To travel, go to see that dreadful place:
It is a hideous hollow cave (they say)
Under a rock that lies a little space

1 Put up.
2 Service, rehearsal.
3 Drive away.
4 Low.
5 Fury, violence of love; the same word as "breme," which Chaucer uses to describe the fierceness of a combat.
6 Reveals.
7 Shining with lamps or stars.
8 Decreed by fate.

From the swift Barry, tumbling down apace
Amongst the woody hills of Dinevowr:[1]
But dare thou not, I charge, in any case,
To enter into that same baleful bow'r,[2]
For fear the cruel fiends should thee unwares devour:

But, standing high aloft, low lay thine ear,
And there such ghastly noise of iron chains
And brazen cauldrons thou shalt rumbling hear,
Which thousand sprites with long-enduring pains
Do toss, that it will stun thy feeble brains;
And oftentimes great groans, and grievous stounds,[3]
When too huge toil and labour them constrains;
And oftentimes loud strokes and ringing sounds
From under that deep rock most horribly rebounds.

The cause, some say, is this: A little while
Before that Merlin died, he did intend
A brazen wall in compass to compile
About Caermardin,[4] and did it commend
Unto these sprites to bring to perfect end:
During which work the Lady of the Lake,
Whom long he lov'd, for him in haste did send;
Who, thereby forc'd his workmen to forsake,
Them bound, till his return, their labour not to slake.[5]

In the mean time, through that false lady's train[6]
He was surpris'd, and buried under bier,
Nor ever to his work return'd again:
Nathless those fiends may not their work forbear,
So greatly his commandëment they fear,
But there do toil and travail day and night,
Until that brazen wall they up do rear.
For Merlin had in magic more insight
Than ever him before or after living wight:

For he by words could call out of the sky
Both sun and moon, and make them him obey;
The land to sea, and sea to mainland dry,
And darksome night he eke could turn to day:
Huge hosts of men he could alone dismay,
And hosts of men of meanest things could frame,
Whenso him list his enemies to fray:[7]
That to this day, for terror of his fame,
The fiends do quake when any him to them does name.

Entering the cave—not without fearful hesitation, which, "with Love to friend," Britomart first overcame—they found Merlin "writing strange characters in the ground," and all unmoved by their coming, of which he knew well beforehand. Glaucé at first pretended to be ignorant of the cause of the "sore evil" that afflicted Britomart; and Merlin, smiling softly at her smooth dissembling speeches, recommended that some physician should be consulted; for "who help may have elsewhere, in vain seeks wonders out of magic spell." Still disguising her knowledge, Glaucé said that the evil was beyond the power of leechcraft, and "either seems some cursëd witch's deed, or evil sprite." Bursting forth in laughter, the wizard, addressing his visitors by name, told them that he knew the cause of their coming.

The doubtful maid, seeing herself descried,
Was all abash'd, and her pure ivory
Into a clear carnation sudden dy'd;
As fair Aurora, rising hastily,
Doth by her blushing tell that she did lie
All night in old Tithonus' frozen bed,
Whereof she seems ashamëd inwardly:
But her old nurse was naught disheartenëd,
But vantage made of that which Merlin had aread;[8]

And said; "Since then thou knowest all our grief
(For what dost not thou know?) of grace I pray,
Pity our plaint, and yield us meet relief!"
With that the prophet still a while did stay,
And then his spirit thus gan forth display;
"Most noble Virgin, that by fatal lore
Hast learn'd to love, let no whit thee dismay
The hard begin[9] that meets thee in the door,
And with sharp fits thy tender heart oppresseth sore:

"For so must all things excellent begin;
And eke enrooted deep must be that tree,
Whose big embodied branches shall not lin[10]
Till they to heaven's height forth stretchëd be.
For from thy womb a famous progeny
Shall spring out of the ancient Trojan blood,
Which shall revive the sleeping memory
Of those same ántique peers, the heaven's brood,
Which Greek and Asian rivers stainëd with their blood.

"Renowned kings, and sacred emperors,
Thy fruitful offspring, shall from thee descend;
Brave captains, and most mighty warriors,
That shall their conquests through all lands extend,
And their decayëd kingdoms shall amend:
The feeble Britons, broken with long war,
They shall uprear, and mightily defend
Against their foreign foe that comes from far,
Till universal peace compound all civil jar."

No mere chance, "but the straight course of heav'nly destiny," had guided Britomart's glance into the charmed glass. Glaucé inquiring how the man might be found, Merlin answered that the destined spouse of Britomart was Artegall, who, though dwelling in Faery Land, was not of Faery birth or kindred; he had been stolen by false Faeries from his cradle, and believed that "he by an Elf was gotten of a Fay." He was really the son of Gorlois, brother to Cador, king of Cornwall; the renown of his

1 Dynevor Castle, near Caermarthen, the chief residence, in olden time, of the Princes of South Wales.
2 Abode; vault. 3 Noises.
4 Caermarthen. 5 Slacken.
6 Deceit, stratagem. The reader may remember how, in Tennyson's "Idylls of the King," Vivien cajoles Merlin into telling her the charm "of woven paces and of waving hands," and uses it to imprison him for ever in the hollow oak. The old "Morte d'Arthur," however, makes Merlin the importunate lover of the Lady of the Lake, who, to get rid of him, contrived to bury him under a great rock in Cornwall.
7 When he pleased to terrify his foes.
8 Declared. 9 Beginning. 10 Stop.

warlike feats stretched "from where the day out of the sea doth spring, until the closure of the evening;" and Britomart's destiny is to bring him back to his native soil, that he may aid his country against Paynim (Saxon) invaders. After long sway in arms, Artegall will be "too rath[1] cut off by practice criminal of secret foes;" but his son shall "living him in all activity" to her present, take from the head of his cousin Constantine the crown that was his father's right, and issue forth with dreadful might against his Saxon foes. "Like as a lion that in drowsy cave hath long time slept, himself so shall he shake," and overthrow the Mercians thrice in battle. The seer then sketched the reigns of Vortipore; of Malgo; of Careticus; the cruel invasion of great Gormond, who, having subdued Ireland and fixed his throne there, "like a swift otter, fell through emptiness, shall overswim the sea" with many of his Norsemen, to aid the Briton's foes; the overthrow of proud Ethelred by Cadwan; the mighty vengeance for all these wrongs taken by Cadwallin on his son Edwin; the slaughter of Edwin's sons "in battle upon Layburn plain;" Cadwallin's conquest of Northumbria; the death of Britons' reign with him, in spite of all the efforts of Cadwallader, his son—who, driven from his native land, shall live in wretched case in Armorica (Bretagne, or Lesser Britain, in France).

"Then woe, and woe, and everlasting woe,
Be to the Briton babe that shall be born,
To live in thraldom of his father's foe!
Late king, now captive; late lord, now forlorn;[2]
The world's reproach; the cruel victor's scorn;
Banish'd from princely bow'r to wasteful wood!
O! who shall help me to lament and mourn
The royal seed, the ántique Trojan blood,
Whose empire longer here than ever any stood!"

The Damsel was full deep impassionëd,
Both for his grief, and for her people's sake,
Whose future woes so plain he fashionëd;
And, sighing sore, at length him thus bespake;
"Ah! but will Heaven's fury never slake,
Nor vengeance huge relent itself at last?
Will not long misery late mercy make,
But shall their name for ever be defac'd,
And quite from off the earth their memory be ras'd?"

"Nay," answered Merlin; after twice four hundred years the Britons would be restored to former rule; and even in the period of their obscurity "their beams would oft break forth, that men them fair might see"—as in the careers of Roderick the Great, Howell Dha, and Griffith Conan. Nor should the Saxons enjoy all peaceably the crown wrested from the Britons; first a Raven, from the rising sun (the Danes) would "bid his faithless chickens overrun the fruitful plains;" and then a Lion (William of Normandy) would come roaring from the seaboard of Neustria, to rend from the head of the Danish tyrant (Harold) the usurped crown, and divide among his own hungry whelps the conquered land.

"Then, when the term is full accomplishëd,
There shall a spark of fire, which hath long while
Been in his ashes rakëd up and hid,
Be freshly kindled in the fruitful Isle
Of Mona, where it lurkëd in exíle;
Which shall break forth into bright burning flame,
And reach into the house that bears the style
Of royal majesty and sov'reign name:
So shall the Briton blood their crown again reclaim.[3]

"Thenceforth eternal union shall be made
Between the nations different afore,
And sacred Peace shall lovingly persuade
The warlike minds to learn her goodly lore,
And civil arms to exercise no more:
Then shall a Royal Virgin[4] reign, which shall
Stretch her white rod over the Belgic shore,
And the great Castle smite so sore withal,
That it shall make him shake, and shortly learn to fall:

"But yet the end is not"——"there Merlin stay'd, as overcomen of the spirit's power;" but soon he regained his cheerful looks, and reassured the two fearful women, who returned home with lighter hearts, "conceiving hope of comfort glad." They secretly took counsel how they might effect their hard enterprise; and at last Glaucé "in her foolhardy wit conceived a bold device." Good King Uther was then warring on the Paynim (Saxon) brethren Octa and Oza; and the nurse's plan was, that they should don armour and go to the wars—taking inspiration from the memory of many martial British royal dames, as Boadicea, Guendolene, Martia, and Emmelen, and also from the present example of a virgin who fought valiantly in the Saxon ranks—Angela, the leader of a martial and mighty people, the Angles, who were dreaded above all the other Saxons. Britomart gladly accepted the nurse's counsel, "her maid's attire to turn into a massy habergeon," and bade her put all things in readiness.

Th' old woman naught that needed did omit;
But all things did conveniently purvey.
It fortunëd (so time their turn did fit)
A band of Britons, riding on foráy
Few days before, had gotten a great prey
Of Saxon goods; amongst the which was seen
A goodly armour, and full rich array,

1 Soon; "rather" is the surviving comparative of this now obsolete word.

2 Ruined.

3 This refers to the pretended descent of the Tudors from King Arthur; in honour, or in vindication, of which, the first Tudor Monarch, Henry VII., gave to his eldest son the name of Arthur.

4 Queen Elizabeth; who protected and aided the Low Countries in their contest with Spain, and smote the pride and power of Castile in the overthrow of the Armada.

Which 'long'd to Angela, the Saxon queen,
All fretted round with gold, and goodly well
beseen.

The same, with all the other ornaments,
King Ryence causëd to be hangëd high
In his chief church, for endless monuments
Of his success and gladful victory:
Of which herself advising [1] readily,
In th' evening late old Glaucé thither led
Fair Britomart, and that same armoury
Down taking, her therein apparellëd
Well as she might, and with brave baldric [2]
garnishëd.

Beside those arms there stood a mighty spear,
Which Bladud made by magic art of yore,
And us'd the same in battle aye to bear;
Since which it had been here preserv'd in store,
For its great virtues provëd long afore:
For never wight so fast in sell [3] could sit,
But him perforce unto the ground it bore:
Both spear she took and shield which hung by
it;
Both spear and shiëld of great pow'r, for her
purpose fit.

Thus when she had the Virgin all array'd,
Another harness which did hang thereby
About herself she dight,[4] that the young maid
She might in equal arms accompanŷ,
And as her squire attend her carefullŷ:
Then to their ready steeds they clomb full light;
And through back ways, that none might them
espy,
Cover'd with secret cloud of silent night,
Themselves they forth convey'd, and passëd for-
ward right:

Nor rested until, following Merlin's directions, they came to Faery Land, and met the Redcross Knight; from whom, his way diverging, Britomart now took friendly leave.

CANTO IV.

Bold Marinell of [5] Britomart
Is thrown on the Rich Strand:
Fair Florimell of Arthur is
Long follow'd, but not fand.

After her parting with the Redcross Knight, with whom she bound "a friendly league of love perpetual," Britomart travelled on in pensive mood, turning over in her mind all the discourse of Artegall, and feeling the wound of love more deeply pierce her heart. Coming at last to the sea-coast,

There she alighted from her light-foot beast,
And, sitting down upon the rocky shore,
Bade her old squire unlace her lofty crest:
Then, having view'd a while the surges hoar
That 'gainst the craggy cliffs did loudly roar,
And in their raging surquedry [6] disdain'd
That the fast earth affronted them so sore,
And their devouring covetise restrain'd;
Thereat she sighëd deep, and after thus com-
plain'd:

"Huge sea of sorrow and tempestuous grief,
Wherein my feeble bark is tossëd long,
Far from the hopëd haven of relief,
Why do thy cruel billows beat so strong,
And thy moist mountains each on other throng,
Threat'ning to swallow up my fearful life?
O, do thy cruel wrath and spiteful wrong
At length allay, and stint [7] thy stormy strife,
Which in these troubled bowels reigns and
rageth rife!

"For else my feeble vessel, craz'd and crack'd
Through thy strong buffets and outrageous blows,
Cannot endure, but needs it must be wrack'd
On the rough rocks, or the sandy shallóws,
The while that Love it steers, and Fortune rows:
Love, my lewd pilot, hath a restless mind,
And Fortune, boatswain, no assurance knows,
But sail withouten stars 'gainst tide and wind:
How can they other do, since both are bold and
blind!

"Thou god of winds, that reignest in the seas,
That reignest also in the continent,
At last blow up some gentle gale of ease,
The which may bring my ship, ere it be rent,
Unto the gladsome port of her intent!
Then, when I shall myself in safety see,
A table,[8] for eternal monument
Of thy great grace and my great jeopardy,
Great Neptune, I avow to hallow unto thee!"

While Glaucé strove to assuage her secret grief, Britomart spied a horseman all in armour bright galloping towards her. Hastily donning her helmet and remounting her courser, she poured her sorrow into sudden wrath—like a foggy mist dissolving itself in a stormy shower when the watery south wind blows up from the sea-coast. Warned by the stranger knight, in stern words, to desist from the forbidden way, the Maid, thrilled with deep disdain, answered that "words fearen babes," and that she would pass or die. The two knights rode strongly against each other; Britomart, struck full on the breast by the stranger's spear, was made to "decline her head, and touch her crupper with her crown;" but, more unfortunate, her adversary received her spear through his left side, and was tumbled in a gory heap upon the sandy shore.

Like as the sacred ox that careless stands,
With gilden horns and flowery garlands crown'd,
Proud of his dying honour and dear bands,
While th' altars fume with frankincénse around,
All suddenly, with mortal stroke astound',
Doth grovelling fall, and with his streaming gore
Distains the pillars and the holy ground,
And the fair flow'rs that deckëd him afore:
So fell proud Marinell upon the Precious Shore.

[1] Bethinking. [2] Belt.
[3] Saddle. [4] Girt, put on.

[5] By. [6] Arrogance.
[7] Cease. [8] Votive tablet.

The martial Maid staid not him to lament,
But forward rode, and kept her ready way
Along the Strand; which as she over-went
She saw bestrowëd all with rich array
Of pearls and precious stones of great assay,[1]
And all the gravel mix'd with golden ore:
Whereat she wonder'd much, but would not stay
For gold, or pearls, or precious stones, an hour,
But them despisëd all; for all[2] was in her pow'r.

Tidings of her adversary's fall came to the ear of his mother, "the black-brow'd Cymoent, the daughter of great Nereus;" who, surprised by the earth-born Dumarin as she lay asleep in a secret place, had borne this boy and named him Marinell, fostering him up till he became a mighty man at arms, and kept the Rich Strand against all comers. To advance his fame and glory more, his mother had besought her sea-god sire to endow him with treasure and rich store above all the sons of men.

The god did grant his daughter's dear demand,
To do[3] his nephew[4] in all riches flow:
Eftsoons his heapëd waves he did command
Out of their hollow bosom forth to throw
All the huge treasure which the sea below
Had in his greedy gulf devourëd deep,
And him enrichëd through the overthrow
And wrecks of many wretches, which did weep
And often wail their wealth which he from them did keep.

Shortly upon that shore there heapëd was
Exceeding riches, and all precious things,
The spoil of all the world; that it did pass
The wealth of th' East, and pomp of Persian kings:
Gold, amber, ivory, pearls, owches,[5] rings,
And all that else was precïous and dear,
The sea unto him voluntary brings;
That shortly he a great lord did appear,
As was in all the Land of Faery, or elsewhere.

Seeing his valour, his mother feared lest it should bring him to woe, and often counselled him to forbear bloody battle and strife. She inquired of Proteus the destiny of her son, and was told "from womankind to keep him well; for of a woman he should have much ill; a virgin strange and stout him should dismay or kill." Therefore she daily warned him not to entertain the love of women; he obeyed the warning, "and ever from fair ladies' love did fly;" and though many ladies complained that they would die for love of him, "die whoso list for him, he was love's enemy." But, while his mother thought she had armed him, she had quite disarmed him; for she feared not woman's force, but woman's love; yet by the womanly force of Britomart—to whom Proteus' ambiguous prophecy referred—her son was brought to grief. Cymoent learned the news of his defeat where she play'd "amongst her watery sisters by a pond, gath'ring sweet daffodillies, to have made gay garlands, from the sun their foreheads fair to shade."

Eftsoons both flow'rs and garlands far away
She flung, and her fair dewy locks y-rent;
To sorrow huge she turn'd her former play,
And gamesome mirth to grievous dreariment:[6]
She threw herself down on the continent,[7]
Nor word did speak, but lay as in a swown,
While all her sisters did for her lament
With yelling outcries, and with shrieking soun';
And ev'ry one did tear her garland from her crown.

Soon as she up out of her deadly fit
Arose, she bade her chariot to be brought;
And all her sisters, that with her did sit,
Bade eke at once their chariots to be sought:
Then, full of bitter grief and pensive thought,
She to her waggon clomb; clomb all the rest,
And forth together went, with sorrow fraught:
The waves obedient to their behest
Them yielded ready passage, and their rage surceas'd.

Great Neptune stood amazëd at their sight,
While on his broad round back they softly slid;
And eke himself mourn'd at their mournful plight,
Yet wist not what their wailing meant, yet did,
For great compassion of their sorrow, bid
His mighty waters to them buxom[8] be:
Eftsoons the roaring billows still abid,[9]
And all the grisly monsters of the sea
Stood gaping at their gate,[10] and wonder'd them to see.

A team of dolphins rangëd in array
Drew the smooth chariot of sad Cymoent;
They were all taught by Triton to obey
To the long reins at her commandëment:
As swift as swallows on the waves they went,
That their broad flaggy fins no foam did rear,
Nor bubbling roundel[11] they behind them sent;
The rest of[12] other fishes drawen were,
Which with their finny oars the swelling sea did shear.[13]

Soon as they be arriv'd upon the brim
Of the Rich Strand, their chariot they forlore,[14]
And let their teamëd fishes softly swim
Along the margent of the foamy shore,
Lest they their fins should bruise, and surbate[15] sore
Their tender feet upon the stony ground:
And, coming to the place where, all in gore
And cruddy[16] blood enwallowëd, they found
The luckless Marinell lying in deadly swound,

Cymoent swooned at the sight. "But, soon as life recover'd had the rein" she made piteous lamentation—all her sister nymphs filling up

1 Value. 2 Although all. 3 Make. 4 Grandson. 5 Jewels, golden ornaments. 6 Sorrow. 7 Ground. 8 Yielding. 9 Abode.

10 Passage, progress. 11 Circle or eddy. 12 By. 13 Divide. 14 Left. 15 Bruise. 16 Curdled.

"her sobbing breaches with sad complement"—and reproached "fond[1] Proteus, father of false prophecies." "I fearëd love," she cried; "but they that love do live; but they that die do neither love nor hate." When all had sorrowed their fill, they softly searched his wound; disarming him, they spread on the ground "their watchet[2] mantles fring'd with silver round," wiped away the gelly (congealed) blood, and poured in sovereign balm and nectar good. Then the lily-handed Liàgore, who had learned leechcraft from Apollo, her lover, felt the pulse of Marinell, and gave his mother hope.

Then, up him taking in their tender hands,
They easily unto her chariot bear:
Her team at her commandment quiet stands,
While they the corse into her waggon rear,[3]
And strow with flow'rs the lamentable bier:
Then all the rest into their coaches climb,
And through the brackish waves their passage shear;
Upon great Neptune's neck they softly swim,
And to her watery chamber swiftly carry him.

Deep in the bottom of the sea, her bow'r
Is built of hollow billows heapëd high,
Like to thick clouds that threat a stormy show'r;
And vaulted all within, like to the sky
In which the gods do dwell eternally:
There they him laid in easy couch well dight;[4]
And sent in haste for Tryphon, to apply
Salves to his wounds, and medicines of might:
For Tryphon of sea-gods the sov'reign leech is hight.

The nymphs sat all around lamenting, while Cymoent, viewing his wide wound, oft cursed the hand that gave it. "But none of all those curses overtook the warlike Maid," who fairly thrived, though now pursued by Archimago, who had separated her from the Prince and Guyon. They, it will be remembered, had set out to rescue the lady on the white palfrey, pursued by the fierce lustful forester. "Through thick and thin, through mountains and through plains," the champions follow the fearful damsel; at a double way the Prince takes one path, Guyon the other; while Timias, Arthur's squire, still chases the forester. Arthur's chance was to take the way on which the damsel fled before; he caught sight of her, and vainly entreated her to stay; but still she fled as dove from hawk, for though she saw that the forester no longer pursued, she had equal terror of the unknown knight. But darkness came on, and the Prince had to abandon the chase, cursing his wicked fortune. Losing his way, he dismounted and laid himself down to sleep; but sleep refused to come; "instead thereof sad sorrow and disdain did of his hard hap vex his noble breast," and he was a prey to a thousand fancies, often wishing that the lady fair might be the Faery Queen after whom he complained, or that his Faery Queen were such as she; "and ever hasty Night be blamëd bitterly:"

"Night! thou foul mother of annoyance sad,
Sister of heavy Death, and nurse of Woe,
Which wast begot in heav'n, but for thy bad
And brutish shape thrust down to hell below,
Where, by the grim flood of Cocytus slow,
Thy dwelling is in Erebus' black house
(Black Erebus, thy husband, is the foe
Of all the gods), where thou ungracioús
Half of thy days dost lead in horror hideoús;

"What had th' Eternal Maker need of thee
The world in his continual course to keep,
That dost all things deface, nor lettest see
The beauty of his work? Indeed in sleep
The slothful body that doth love to steep
His lustless[5] limbs, and drown his baser mind,
Doth praise thee oft, and oft from Stygian deep
Calls thee his goddess, in his error blind,
And great Dame Nature's handmaid, cheering every kind.

"But well I wot that to a heavy heart
Thou art the root and nurse of bitter cares,
Breeder of new, renewer of old smarts:
Instead of rest thou lendest railing[6] tears;
Instead of sleep thou sendest troublous fears
And dreadful visions, in the which alive
The dreary image of sad Death appears:
So from the weary spirit thou dost drive
Desirëd rest, and men of happiness deprive.

"Under thy mantle black there hidden lie
Light-shunning Theft, and traitorous Intent,
Abhorrëd Bloodshed, and vile Felony,
Shameful Deceit, and Danger imminent,
Foul Horror, and eke hellish Dreariment:[7]
All these, I wot, in thy protection be,
And light do shun, for fear of being shent:[8]
For light alike is loath'd of them and thee:
And all that lewdness love do hate the light to see.[9]

"For Day discovers all dishonest ways,
And showeth each thing as it is in deed:
The praises of High God he fair displays,
And His large bounty rightly doth aread:[10]
Day's dearest children be the blessëd seed
Which Darkness shall subdue and heaven win:
Truth is his daughter; he her first did breed,
Most sacred virgin without spot of sin:
Our life is day; but death with darkness doth begin.

"O when will Day then turn to me again,
And bring with him his long-expected light!
O Titan! haste to rear thy joyous wain;
Speed thee to spread abroad thy beamës bright,
And chase away this too long ling'ring Night;
Chase her away, from whence she came, to hell:
She, she it is, that hath me done despite:
There let her with the damnëd spirits dwell,
And yield her room to Day, that can it govern well."

1 Foolish. 2 Light blue. 3 Raise. 4 Prepared. 5 Languid. 6 Flowing, streaming. 7 Sorrow. 8 Shamed.

9 John iii. 20: "For every one that doeth evil, hateth the light, neither cometh to the light, lest his deeds should be reproved."
10 Declare.

Outwearing the weary night in restless anguish and unquiet pain, ere morn the Prince arose and went forth with heavy look and lumpish pace, betraying the discomposure of his mind.

CANTO V.

Prince Arthur hears of Florimell:
Three fosters[1] *Timias wound;*
Belphœbe finds him almost dead,
And reareth out of swound.

Seeking an issue from the forest, the Prince met a dwarf, who seemed terrified and was all bescratched and lamed by running through the thick wood. He learned from the dwarf that his lady, Florimell, had quitted Faery Court, in great grief at the news that her only love, Marinell, the sea-nymph's son, had been slain by a foreign foe. All her delight was set on Marinell, though he set naught at all by Florimell; and she had vowed never to return till she found her love, alive or dead. The Prince, who recognised in the description of Florimell the lady whom he had pursued in vain, comforted the dwarf with the promise never to forsake him till he found tidings of his dame; and the two journeyed together—the Prince greatly lamenting the absence of his squire. Meanwhile, Timias had ridden fiercely after the forester foul, to take vengeance for the insult to the lady; but the villain escaped for the time, by the swiftness of his steed or his own knowledge of the wood-paths. Coming to his two brothers—"for they were three ungracious children of one graceless sire"—he stirred them up to aid him in revenge on the "foolhardy squire;" and the trio placed themselves in ambush for Timias in the thick wood, beside a covert glade, near a narrow ford. Timias rode unsuspectingly down to the ford; and when he was entangled in the water, the forester, who had formerly fled, appeared on the steep bank, and launched a javelin at him. Though unwounded, the squire could not mount the bank, from which the forester kept him off with his long boar-spear; while one of the brothers shot from the thicket "a cruel shaft headed with deadly ill, and featherëd with an unlucky quill," that sank deep into his thigh. Stung by wrath and vengeance, Timias struggled up the bank, when the third brother "drove at him with all his might and main" a forest-bill; but, avoiding the blow, the squire pierced both sides of his assailant with his spear, and tumbled him dead to the ground. Ere long the two others shared the same fate; the pursuer of Florimell had his head cleft to the chin; at the third, who sought to fly after discharging a useless arrow, Timias struck "with force so violent, that headless him into the ford he sent." But now he fell to earth in deadly swoon from his own wound; and death seemed at hand, if Providence had not sent to his aid the "noble huntress" Belphœbe, who had so affrighted Braggadocio.

She on a day, as she pursued the chase
Of some wild beast, which with her arrows keen
She wounded had, the same along did trace
By track of blood, which she had freshly seen
To have besprinkled all the grassy green;
By the great pérsue[2] which she there perceiv'd,
Well hopëd she the beast engor'd[3] had been,
And made more haste the life to have bereav'd:
But ah! her expectation greatly was deceiv'd.

Shortly she came where as that woeful squire,
With blood deformëd,[4] lay in deadly swound;
In whose fair eyes, like lamps of quenchëd fire,
The crystal humour stood congealëd round;
His locks, like faded leaves fallen to ground,
Knotted with blood in bunches rudely ran;
And his sweet lips, on which, before that stound,[5]
The bud of youth to blossom fair began,
Spoil'd of their rosy red, were waxen pale and wan.

Saw never living eye more heavy sight,
That could have made a rock of stone to rue,[6]
Or rive in twain: which when that Lady bright,
Beside all hope,[7] with melting eyes did view,
All suddenly abash'd she changëd hue,
And with stern horror backward gan to start:
But, when she better him beheld, she grew
Full of soft passion and unwonted smart:
The point of pity piercëd through her tender heart.

Stooping down, she felt by his pulse that life yet remained in his frozen members; then, undoing his armour, she "rubb'd his temples, and each trembling vein," and went hastily into the woods to seek remedial herbs, of which she had great knowledge. Returning with "the sovereign weed," she pounded and bruised it; with her lily hands she squeezed the juice into the wound, softening the flesh all around; and bound the wound with her scarf, to keep it from cold.

By this he had sweet life recur'd[8] again,
And, groaning inly deep, at last his eyes,
His watery eyes drizzling like dewy rain,
He up gan lift towárd the azure skies,
From whence descend all hopeless[9] remedies:
Therewith he sigh'd; and, turning him aside,
The goodly maid, full of divinities
And gifts of heavenly grace, he by him spied,
Her bow and gilden quiver lying him beside.

"Mercy! dear Lord," said he, "what grace is this
That thou hast showëd to me, sinful wight,
To send thine angel from her bow'r of bliss
To comfort me in my distressëd plight!
Angel, or goddess, do I call thee right?

1 Foresters.
2 Trail, continuous track, of blood, which she "pursued" in quest of the beast.
3 Pierced through.
4 Disfigured.
5 Misfortune.
6 Pity.
7 Beyond all expectation.
8 Recovered.
9 Unhoped for.

What service may I do unto thee meet,
That hast from darkness me return'd to light,
And with thy heav'nly salves and med'cines sweet
Hast dress'd my sinful wounds! I kiss thy blessëd feet."

Thereat she blushing said; "Ah! gentle squire,
Nor goddess I, nor angel; but the maid
And daughter of a woody nymph, desire
No service but thy safëty and aid;
Which if thou gain, I shall be well repaid.
We mortal wights, whose lives and fortunes be
To common accidents still open laid,
Are bound with common bond of frailty
To succour wretched wights whom we captívëd see."

Two of Belphœbe's damsels came up, and were sent to catch the squire's horse; on which the wounded youth was set, and forth with them conveyed.

Into that forest far they thence him led,
Where was their dwelling; in a pleasant glade
With mountains round about environëd
And mighty woods, which did the valley shade,
And like a stately theatre it made,
Spreading itself into a spacious plain;
And in the midst a little river play'd
Amongst the pumy[1] stones, which seem'd to plain[2]
With gentle murmur that his course they did restrain.

Beside the same a dainty place there lay,
Planted with myrtle trees and laurels green,
In which the birds sung many a lovely lay
Of God's high praise, and of their sweet love's teen,[3]
As it an earthly paradise had been:
In whose enclosëd shadow there was pight[4]
A fair pavilion, scarcely to be seen,
The which was all within most richly dight,[5]
That greatest princes living it might well delight.

Thither they brought that wounded squire, and laid
In easy couch his feeble limbs to rest.
He rested him a while; and then the maid
His ready wound with better salves new drest:
Daily she dressëd him, and did the best,
His grievous hurt to warish,[6] that she might;
That shortly she his dolour hath redrest,
And his foul sore reducëd to fair plight:
It she reducëd, but himself destroyëd quite.

O foolish physic, and unfruitful pain,[7]
That heals up one, and makes another wound!
She his hurt thigh to him recur'd again,
But hurt his heart, the which before was sound,
Through an unwary dart which did rebound
From her fair eyes and gracious countenance.
What boots it him from death to be unbound,
To be captívëd in endléss duránce[8]
Of sorrow and despair without aleggéance![9]

Still as his wound did gather, and grow whole,
So still his heart wox sore, and health decay'd:
Madness to save a part, and lose the whole!
Still when as he beheld the heav'nly maid,
While daily plasters to his wound she laid,
So still his malady the more increast,
The while her matchless beauty him dismay'd.
Ah God! what other could he do at least,
But love so fair a lady that his life releast!

Long while he strove in his courageous breast
With reason due the passion to subdue,
And love for to dislodge out of his nest:
Still when her excellencies he did view,
Her sov'reign bounty and celestial hue,
The same to love he strongly was constrain'd:
But, when his mean estate he did review,
He from such hardy boldness was restrain'd,
And of his luckless lot and cruel love thus plain'd:

"Unthankful wretch," said he, "is this the meed[10]
With which her sov'reign mercy thou dost quite?[11]
Thy life she savëd by her gracious deed;
But thou dost ween with villainous despite
To blot her honour and her heav'nly light:
Die; rather die than so disloyallý
Deem of her high desert, or seem so light:
Fair death it is, to shun more shame, to die.
Die; rather die than ever love disloyallý.

"But if, to love, disloyalty it be,
Shall I then hate her that from deathë's door
Me brought? ah! far be such reproach from me!
What can I less do than her love therefóre,
Since I her due reward cannot restore?
Die; rather die, and dying do her serve;
Dying her serve, and living her adore;
Thy life she gave, thy life she doth deserve:
Die; rather die than ever from her service swerve.

"But, foolish boy, what boots thy service base
To her, to whom the heav'ns do serve and sue?
Thou, a mean squire of meek and lowly place;
She, heav'nly born and of celestial hue.
How then? of all Love taketh equal view:
And doth not Highest God vouchsafe to take
The love and service of the basest crew?
If she will not, die meekly for her sake:
Die; rather die than ever so fair love forsake!"

Thus warrëd he long time against his will;
Till that through weakness he was forc'd at last
To yield himself unto the mighty ill,
Which, as a victor proud, gan ransack fast
His inward parts, and all his entrails waste,
That neither blood in face nor life in heart
It left, but both did quite dry up and blast;
As piercing levin,[12] which the inner part
Of ev'ry thing consumes and calcineth by art.[13]

Which seeing, fair Belphœbe gan to fear
Lest that his wound were inly not well heal'd,
Or that the wicked steel empoison'd were:

1 Pumice, porous; so, in "The Shepherd's Calendar" for March, Thomalin says, "Then pumie stones I hast'ly hent, and threw."
2 Complain.
3 Pain.
4 Placed, pitched.
5 Adorned, furnished.
6 Heal.
7 Pains.
8 Bondage.
9 Alleviation.
10 Reward.
11 Recompense.
12 Lightning.
13 By necessity.

Little she ween'd that love he close conceal'd.
Yet still he wasted, as the snow congeal'd
When the bright sun his beams thereon doth beat:
Yet never he his heart to her reveal'd;
But rather chose to die for sorrow great
Than with dishonourable terms her to intreat.

She, gracious lady, yet no pains did spare
To do him ease, or do him remedý:
Many restoratives of virtues rare,
And costly cordials, she did apply,
To mitigate his stubborn maladý:
But that sweet cordial, which can restore
A love-sick heart, she did to him envý;[1]
To him, and t' all th' unworthy world forlore,
She did envý that sov'reign salve in secret store.

That dainty rose, the daughter of her morn,
More dear than life she tenderëd, whose flow'r
The garland of her honour did adorn:
Nor suffer'd she the midday's scorching pow'r,
Nor the sharp northern wind, thereon to show'r;
But lappëd up her silken leaves most chare,[2]
Whenso the froward sky began to lour;
But, soon as calmëd was the crystal air,
She did it fair dispread and let to flourish fair.

Eternal God, in his almighty pow'r,
To make ensample of his heav'nly grace,
In Paradise whilóm did plant this flow'r;
Whence he it fetch'd out of her native place,
And did in stock of earthly flesh enrace,[3]
That mortal men her glory should admire.
In gentle ladies' breast and bounteous race
Of woman kind it fairest flow'r doth spire.[4]
And beareth fruit of honour and all chaste desire.

Fair imps[5] of beauty, whose bright shining beams
Adorn the world with like to heav'nly light,
And to your wills both royalties and reams[6]
Subdue, through conquest of your wondrous might;
With this fair flow'r your goodly garlands dight
Of chastity and virtue virginal,
That shall embellish more your beauty bright,
And crown your heads with heav'nly coronal,
Such as the angels wear before God's tribunâl!

To your fair selves a fair ensample frame
Of this fair Virgin, this Belphœbe fair;
To whom, in perfect love and spotless fame
Of chastity, none living may compare:
Nor pois'nous envy justly can impair
The praise of her fresh flow'ring maidenhead;
Forthy[7] she standeth on the highest stair
Of th' honourable stage of womanhead,
That ladies all may follow her ensample dead.[8]

In so great praise of steadfast chastity,
Nathless she was so courtëous and kind,
Temper'd with grace and goodly modesty,
That seemëd those two virtues strove to find
The higher place in her heroic mind:
So striving each did other more augment,
And both increas'd the praise of woman kind,
And both increas'd her beauty excellent:
So all did make in her a perfect complement.[9]

CANTO VI.

The birth of fair Belphœbe and
Of Amoret is told:
The Gardens of Adonis, fraught
With pleasures manifold.

THE poet sets out by meeting the wonder fair ladies must feel that "the noble damosel so great perfections in her did compile," since she dwelt in savage forests, "so far from Court and royal citadel, the great schoolmistress of all courtesy."

But to this fair Belphœbe in her birth
The heav'ns so favourable were and free,
Looking with mild aspéct upon the earth
In th' horoscope of her nativity,
That all the gifts of grace and chastity
On her they pourëd forth of plenteous horn:
Jove laugh'd on Venus from his sov'reign see,[10]
And Phœbus with fair beams did her adorn,
And all the graces rock'd her cradle being born.

"Her birth was of the womb of morning dew, and her conception of the joyous prime;" her whole creation showed her "pure and unspotted from all loathly crime that is ingenerate in fleshly slime." Her mother was the fair Chrysogoné, daughter of Amphisa; a Fairy born of high degree, who bore Belphœbe and Amoretta as twins, not borne and nurtured as other women's babes;

But wondrously they were begot and bred
Through influence of th' heaven's fruitful ray,
As it in ántique books is mentionëd.
It was upon a summer's shiny day,
When Titan[11] fair his beamës did display,
In a fresh fountain, far from all men's view,
She bath'd her breast the boiling heat t' allay;
She bath'd with roses red and violets blue,
And all the sweetest flow'rs that in the forest grew:

Till, faint through irksome weariness, adown
Upon the grassy ground herself she laid
To sleep, the while a gentle slumb'ring swown
Upon her fell all naked bare display'd:
The sunbeams bright upon her body play'd,
Being through former bathing mollified,
And pierc'd into her womb; where they embay'd[12]
With so sweet sense and secret pow'r unspied,
That in her pregnant flesh they shortly fructified.

Miraculous it may seem; but reason teaches that the seeds of all living things conceive life and are quickened "through impression of the sunbeams in moist complexion;" as, after the inundation of the Nile "infinite shapes of crea-

1 Begrudge, withhold from him.
2 Chary, vigilant.
3 Plant, enroot; French, "enraciner."
4 Shoot forth.
5 Daughters, children.
6 Realms.
7 Therefore.
8 The example which, dying, she will leave them.
9 Balance, completeness.
10 Seat.
11 The Sun.
12 Enclosed themselves.

tures men do find informëd in the mud on which the sun hath shin'd." Chrysogoné, smitten with wonder, shame, and foul disgrace, though conscious of innocence, fled into the wilderness, there to rear her unwieldy burden; then, as she rested after long travel, sleep overtook her.

It fortunëd, fair Venus having lost
Her little son, the wingëd god of love,
Who for some light displeasure, which him crost,
Was from her fled as fleet as airy dove,
And left her blissful bow'r of joy above
(So from her often he had fled away,
When she for aught him sharply did reprove,
And wander'd in the world in strange array,
Disguis'd in thousand shapes, that none might him bewray [1]);

Him for to seek, she left her heav'nly house,
The house of goodly forms and fair aspécts,
Whence all the world derives the glorioûs
Features of beauty, and all shapes select,
With which High God his workmanship hath deck'd;
And searchëd every way through which his wings
Had borne him, or his track she might detect:
She promis'd kisses sweet, and sweeter things,
Unto the man that of him tidings to her brings.

First she him sought in Court, where most he us'd
Whilóm to haunt, but there she found him not;
But many there she found which sore accus'd
His falsehood, and with foul infámous blot
His cruel deeds and wicked wiles did spot: [2]
Ladies and lords she everywhere might hear
Complaining, how with his empoison'd shot
Their woeful hearts he wounded had whilere,[3]
And so had left them languishing 'twixt hope and fear.

She then the cities sought from gate to gate,
And ev'ry one did ask, Did he him see?
And ev'ry one her answer'd, that too late
He had him seen, and felt the cruelty
Of his sharp darts and hot artillery:
And every one threw forth reproaches rife
Of his mischíevous deeds, and said that he
Was the disturber of all civil life,
The enemy of peace, and author of all strife.

Then in the country she abroad him sought,
And in the rural cottages inquir'd;
Where also many plaints to her were brought,
How he their heedless hearts with love had fir'd,
And his false venom through their veins inspir'd;
And eke the gentle shepherd swains, which sat
Keeping their fleecy flocks, as they were hir'd,
She sweetly heard complain both how and what
Her son had to them done; yet she did smile thereat.

But, when in none of all these she him got,
She gan advise [4] where else he might him hide:
At last she her bethought that she had not
Yet sought the salvage woods and forests wide,
In which full many lovely nymphs abide;
'Mongst whom might be that he did closely [5] lie,
Or that the love of some of them him tied:
Forthy [6] she thither cast her course t' apply,
To search the secret haunts of Dian's company.

Shortly unto the wasteful woods she came,
Where as she found the goddess with her crew,
After late chase of their embruëd [7] game,
Sitting beside a fountain in a rew; [8]
Some of them washing with the liquid dew
From off their dainty limbs the dusty sweat
And soil, which did deform their lively hue;
Others lay shaded from the scorching heat;
The rest upon her person gave attendance great.

She, having hung upon a bough on high
Her bow and painted quiver, had unlac'd
Her silver buskins from her nimble thigh,
And her lank [9] loins ungirt, and breasts unbrac'd,
After her heat the breathing cold to taste;
Her golden locks, that late in tresses bright
Embraided [10] were for hind'ring of her haste,
Now loose about her shoulders hung undight,[11]
And were with sweet ambrosia all besprinkled light.

Soon as she Venus saw behind her back,
She was asham'd to be so loose surpris'd;
And wox half wroth against her damsels slack,
That had not her thereof before advis'd,[12]
But suffer'd her so carelessly disguis'd
Be overtaken: soon her garments loose
Upgath'ring, in her bosom she compris'd
Well as she might, and to the goddess rose;
While all her nymphs did like a garland her enclose.

Goodly she gan fair Cytherea greet,
And shortly askëd her what cause her brought
Into that wilderness for her unmeet,
From her sweet bow'rs and beds with pleasures fraught:
That sudden change she strange adventure thought.
To whom half weeping she thus answerëd;
That she her dearest son Cupído sought,
Who in his frowardness from her was fled;
That she repented sore to have him angerëd.

Smiling "in scorn of her vain plaint," Diana scoffingly said that Venus might well be grieved for the loss of her gay son, that gave her so good aid to her disports; but Venus answered that it ill became her to upbraid, and, with her lofty crests, "to scorn the joy that Jove is glad to seek; we both are bound to follow heav'n's behests." Then the goddess of Love inquired if her son had not been heard to lurk among the cabins of Diana's nymphs, or disguise himself like one of them; "so saying, ev'ry nymph full narrowly she eyed."

But Phœbe therewith sore was angerëd,
And sharply said; "Go, Dame; go, seek your boy,
Where you him lately left, in Mars his bed:
He comes not here; we scorn his foolish joy,

1 Discover. 2 Blame, asperse.
3 Of late. 4 Consider.
5 Secretly. 6 Therefore.
7 Wet with blood. 8 Row.
9 Slender. 10 Braided.
11 Loose, undone. 12 Warned.

Nor lend we leisure to his idle toy:
But, if I catch him in this companý,
By Stygian lake I vow, whose sad annoy
The gods do dread, he dearly shall abye:[1]
I'll clip his wanton wings, that he no more shall fly."

Whom when as Venus saw so sore displeas'd,
She inly sorry was, and gan relent
What she had said: so her she soon appeas'd
With sugar'd words and gentle blandishment,
Which as a fountain from her sweet lips went
And wellëd goodly forth, that in short space
She was well pleas'd, and forth her damsels sent
Through all the woods, to search from place to place
If any track of him or tidings they might trace.

Diana herself went with Venus "to seek the fugitive both far and near;" and the pair came upon the fair Chrysogoné, who, in her sleep, "unwares had borne two babes as fair as spring-ing day." "Unwares she them conceiv'd, unwares she bore; she bore withouten pain, that she conceiv'd withouten pleasure." The goddesses, after an interval of speechless wonderment, agreed not to awake the sleeper, "but from her loving side the tender babes to take." Phœbe carried one to a nymph, "to be upbrought in perfect maidenhead," and named her Belphœbe; Venus took the other far áway, "to be upbrought in goodly womanhead," and called her Amoretta, to comfort herself for the absence of her little son.

She brought her to her joyous Paradise,[2]
Where most she wons[3] when she on earth does dwell,
So fair a place as Nature can devise:
Whether in Paphos, or Cithéron hill,
Or it in Cnidus be, I wot[4] not well;
But well I wot by trial, that this same
All other pleasant places doth excel,
And callëd is, by her lost lover's name,
The Garden of Adonis,[5] far renown'd by fame.

In that same garden all the goodly flow'rs
Wherewith Dame Nature doth her beautify,
And decks the garlands of her paramours,
Are fetch'd: there is the first seminarý
Of all things that are born to live and die,
According to their kinds. Long work it were
Here to account the endless progený
Of all the weeds[6] that bud and blossom there;
But so much as doth need must needs be counted[7] here.

It sited[8] was in fruitful soil of old,
And girt in with two walls on either side,
The one of iron, th' other of bright gold,
That none might thorough break, nor overstride:
And double gates it had which open'd wide,
By which both in and out men mighten pass;
Th' one fair and fresh, the other old and dried:
Old Genius the porter of them was,
Old Genius, the which a double nature has.[9]

He letteth in, he letteth out, to wend,[10]
All that to come into the world desire:
A thousand thousand naked babes attend
About him day and night, which do require
That he with fleshly weeds would them attire:
Such as him list, such as eternal fate
Ordainëd hath, he clothes with sinful mire,[11]
And sendeth forth to live in mortal state,
Till they again return back by the hinder gate.

After that they again returnëd been,
They in that Garden planted be again,
And grow afresh, as they had never seen
Fleshly corruptión nor mortal pain:
Some thousand years so do they there remain,
And then of him are clad with other hue,[12]
Or sent into the changeful world again,
Till thither they return where first they grew:
So, like a wheel, around they run from old to new.

Nor needs there gardener to set or sow,
To plant or prune; for of their own accord
All things, as they created were, do grow,
And yet remember well the mighty word
Which first was spoken by th' Almighty Lord,
That bade them to increase and multiply:
Nor do they need with water of the ford,[13]
Or of the clouds, to moisten their roots dry;
For in themselves eternal moisture they imply.[14]

Infinite shapes of creatures there are bred,
And úncouth forms, which none yet ever knew:
And ev'ry sort is in a sundry bed
Set by itself, and rank'd in comely rew;[15]
Some fit for reasonable souls t' indue;[16]
Some made for beasts, some made for birds to wear;
And all the fruitful spawn of fishes' hue[17]
In endless ranks along enrangëd were,
That seem'd the oceán could not contain them there.

Daily they grow, and daily forth are sent
Into the world, it to replenish more;
Yet is the stock not lessenëd nor spent,
But still remains in everlasting store
As it at first created was of yore:

1 Suffer for it.

2 The word is here used in its original sense of any garden or pleasure-ground; Greek, παραδεισος, representing the Sanscrit "paradesa."

3 Resides. 4 Know.

5 Adonis represents the reproductive principle of existence, the operation of which was typified in his alternate sojourn of half the year with Proserpine and half with Venus—half in the region of darkness and decay, half in the region of fructifying light and fertile life. The Garden of Adonis, or rather the Garden of Venus where Adonis lives in eternal bliss, is described as containing the seminal principle of all things—in harmony with the Lucretian philosophy, as indicated in the invocation to "Alma Venus," with which the first book "De Rerum Naturâ" opens.

6 To be here understood of plants generally, not merely of such as are noxious or useless.

7 Recounted. 8 Situated.

9 In the twelfth canto of the second book (page 404), the porter at the gate of Acrasia's Bower is also called Genius, but with express distinction from "that celestial Power, to whom the care of life, and generation of all that lives, pertains in charge particular." Genius here is the protecting deity of birth; from "geno," "gignere," to bring forth. 10 Go. 11 Clay.

12 Aspect, shape. 13 Stream. 14 Contain.

15 Row, order. 16 Put on. 17 Form, nature.

For in the wide womb of the world there lies,
In hateful darkness and in deep horrór,
A huge eternal Chaos, which supplies
The substances of Nature's fruitful progenies.

All things from thence do their first being fetch,
And borrow matter whereof they are made;
Which, when as form and feature it does ketch,[1]
Becomes a body, and doth then invade
The state of life out of the grisly shade.
That substance is etern, and bideth so;
Nor, when the life decays, and form does fade,
Doth it consume and into nothing go,
But changëd is, and often alter'd to and fro.

The substance is not chang'd nor alterëd,
But th' only[2] form and outward fashión;
For ev'ry substance is conditionëd
To change her hue, and sundry forms to don,
Meet for her temper and complexión:
For forms are variable, and decay
By course of kind[3] and by occasión;[4]
And that fair flow'r of beauty fades away,
As doth the lily fresh before the sunny ray.

Great enemy to it, and t' all the rest
That in the Garden of Adonis springs,
Is wicked Time; who, with his scythe addrest,[5]
Does mow the flow'ring herbs and goodly things,
And all their glory to the ground down flings,
Where they do wither and are foully marr'd:
He flies about, and with his flaggy wings
Beats down both leaves and buds without regard,
Nor ever pity may relent his malice hard.

Yet pity often did the gods relent,
To see so fair things marr'd and spoilëd quite:
And their great mother Venus did lament
The loss of her dear brood, her dear delight:
Her heart was pierc'd with pity at the sight,
When, walking through the garden, them she saw,
Yet n'ot[6] she find redress for such despite:
For all that lives is subject to that law:
All things decay in time, and to their end do draw.

But, were it not that Time their troubler is,
All that in this delightful Garden grows
Should happy be, and have immortal bliss:
For here all plenty and all pleasure flows;
And sweet Love gentle fits[7] amongst them throws,
Without fell rancour or fond jealousý:
Frankly each paramour his leman[8] knows;
Each bird his mate; nor any does envý
Their goodly merriment and gay felicitý.

There is continual spring, and harvest there
Continual, both meeting at one time:
For both the boughs do laughing blossoms bear,
And with fresh colours deck the wanton prime,[9]
And eke at once the heavy trees they climb,
Which seem to labour under their fruit's load:
The while the joyous birds make their pastíme
Amongst the shady leaves, their sweet abode,
And their true loves without suspicion tell abroad.

Right in the middest of that Paradise
There stood a stately mount, on whose round top
A gloomy grove of myrtle trees did rise,
Whose shady boughs sharp steel did never lop,
Nor wicked beasts their tender buds did crop;
But like a garland compassëd the height,
And from their fruitful sides sweet gum did drop,
That all the ground, with precious dew bedight,[10]
Threw forth most dainty odours and most sweet delight.

And in the thickest covert of that shade
There was a pleasant arbour, not by art,
But of the trees' own inclination, made,
Which, knitting their rank branches part to part,
With wanton ivy-twine entrail'd athwart,[11]
And eglantine and caprifole[12] among,
Fashion'd above within their inmost part,
That neither Phœbus' beams could through them throng,
Nor Æolus' sharp blast could work them any wrong.

And all about grew every sort of flow'r
To which sad lovers were transform'd of yore;
Fresh Hyacinthus, Phœbus' paramour
And dearest love;
Foolish Narciss', that likes the watery shore;
Sad Amaranthus, made a flow'r but late,
Sad Amaranthus, in whose purple gore
Me seems I see Amintas' wretched fate,[13]
To whom sweet poet's verse hath given endless date.

There wont fair Venus often to enjoy
Her dear Adonis' joyous company,
And reap sweet pleasure of the wanton boy:
There yet, some say, in secret he does lie,
Lappëd in flow'rs and precious spicerý,
By her hid from the world, and from the skill
Of Stygian gods, which do her love envý;
But she herself, whenever that she will,
Possesseth him, and of his sweetness takes her fill:

And sooth, it seems, they say; for he may not
For ever die, and ever buried be
In baleful night, where all things are forgot;
All[14] be he subject to mortality,
Yet is etern in mutability,
And by succession made perpetual,
Transformëd oft, and changëd diversely:
For him the father of all forms they call;
Therefore needs must he live, that living gives to all.

There now he liveth in eternal bliss,
Joying his goddess, and of her enjoy'd;

1 Catch, obtain.
2 Only the.
3 Nature.
4 Accident, force of circumstance.
5 Armed.
6 Knew not how, could not.
7 Emotions, impulses.
8 Mistress.
9 Spring.
10 Covered.
11 Twined across.
12 Woodbine; "caprifolium periclymenum."
13 Sir Philip Sydney, mortally wounded at Zutphen, is understood to be meant by Amintas; though the same title is applied to the Earl of Derby, in "Colin Clout's Come Home Again."
14 Although.

Nor feareth he henceforth that foe of his,
Which with his cruel tusk him deadly cloy'd:[1]
For that wild boar, the which him once annoy'd,
She firmly hath imprisonëd for aye
(That her sweet love his malice might avoid),
In a strong rocky cave, which is, they say,
Hewn underneath that mount, that none him
loosen may.

There now he lives in everlasting joy;
With many of the gods in company
Which thither haunt, and with the wingëd boy
Sporting himself in safe felicity:
Who, when he hath with spoils and cruelty
Ransack'd the world, and in the woeful hearts
Of many wretches set his triumphs high,
Thither resorts, and, laying his sad darts
Aside, with fair Adonis plays his wanton parts.

And his true love, fair Psyche, with him plays;
Fair Psyche to him lately reconcil'd,
After long troubles and unmeet upbrays,[2]
With which his mother Venus her revil'd,
And eke himself her cruelly exil'd:
But now in steadfast love and happy state
She with him lives, and hath him borne a child,
Pleasure, that doth both gods and men aggrate,[3]
Pleasure, the daughter of Cupíd and Psyche late.

Hither Venus brought Chrysogoné's younger daughter, committing her to Psyche, to be fostered and trained in true feminity; and Psyche tendered her charge no less carefully than her own daughter Pleasure, whom she made her companion. When Amoretta had grown to perfect ripeness, "of grace and beauty noble paragon," Psyche brought her forth into the world's view, "to be th' ensample of true love alone, and lodestar of all chaste affection," to all fair ladies. Coming to Faery Court, on Sir Scudamour alone her love she cast, and for his sake endured "sore sore trouble of a heinous enemy;" but the poet, on the plea that his reader must desire to know the fate of that fearful damsel Florimell, waives for the moment the story of Amoretta.

CANTO VII.

The witch's son loves Florimell:
She flies; he feigns to die.
Satyrane saves the Squire of Dames
From giant's tyranny.

As a solitary hind, that has escaped from a ravenous beast, "yet flies away of her own feet afear'd," her terror increased by every leaf that shakes with the least murmur of wind—so fled Florimell all night; and her white palfrey, having wrested the reins from her weary hand, carried her whither he pleased. At length, all jeopardy past, his strength failed, and he lay down motionless. Forced to alight and fare on foot, Florimell was now taught by need the lesson hard and rare, "That Fortune all in equal lance[4] doth sway; and mortal miseries doth make her play." At length the maiden reached a little valley, under a hill's side, all covered with thick woods; and through the tree-tops she descried "a little smoke, whose vapour thin and light reeking aloft uprollëd to the sky."

There in a gloomy hollow glen she found
A little cottage, built of sticks and reeds
In homely wise, and wall'd with sods around;
In which a witch did dwell, in loathly weeds[5]
And wilful want, all careless of her needs;
So choosing solitary to abide
Far from all neighbours, that her devilish deeds
And hellish arts from people she might hide,
And hurt far off unknown whomever she envíed.[6]

Entering, the damsel found the hag seemingly busy "about some wicked gin;"[7] but, at sight of the visitor, she "lightly upstarted from the dusty ground," and stared on her in speechless amazement. The prayer of the damsel for shelter from the storm checked the witch's fast-rising wrath; few trickling tears, "that like two orient pearls did purely shine upon her snowy cheek," completed the conquest; and the vile hag set about comforting and soothing the maid, who was "as glad of that small rest, as bird of tempest gone." When Florimell had arranged her rent garments and her loose locks, the hostess was so struck by her beauty, that, taking her for a goddess, or one of Diana's crew, she "thought her to adore with humble sprite; t' adore thing so divine as beauty were but right." "At undertime"[8] the witch's son, "a lazy loord,[9] for nothing fit to don," came home, and was dazzled by the beauty of the stranger, as one that has gazed on the bright sun unawares. His mother answered his questions with naught but ghastly looks; but the fair Virgin "to their senses vild[10] her gentle speech applied, that in short space she grew familiar in that desert place." The sluggish son, however, "conceiv'd affection base, and cast to love her in his brutish mind;" but he had not the courage to utter his desire, and strove to show his love by sighs, and signs, and kind attentions.

Oft from the forest wildings[11] he did bring,
Whose sides empurpled were with smiling red;
And oft young birds, which he had taught to sing
His mistress' praises sweetly carollëd:
Garlands of flow'rs sometimes for her fair head
He fine would dight;[12] sometimes the squirrel
wild
He brought to her in bands, as conquerëd

1 Pierced. 2 Upbraidings.
3 Gratify, charm.
4 Balance. 5 Garments.
6 Any one against whom she bore a grudge.
7 Charm, contrivance.

8 Time of "undern;" evening or dinner-time.
9 Debased, ignoble fellow; the word is akin to, or derived from, the French, "lourd," heavy, dull.
10 Vile, depraved. 11 Wild or crab apples.
12 Prepare.

To be her thrall, his fellow-servant vild:
All which she of him took with count'nance meek and mild.

But, after a time, for fear of mischief by the witch or her son, Florimell resolved to leave that desert mansion; and, secretly harnessing her now well-rested palfrey, she stole away ere the day broke. Great was the moan made by the witch and her son when they discovered her escape; but the son especially grieved, beating his breast and tearing his flesh, as if frenzy-stricken. Finding all her tears and charms ineffectual to comfort him, she "by her devilish arts thought to prevail to bring her back again, or work her final bale."[1]

Eftsoons out of her hidden cave she call'd
A hideous beast of horrible aspéct,
That could the stoutest courage have appall'd;
Monstrous, misshap'd, and all his back was speck'd
With thousand spots of colours quaint elect;[2]
Thereto[3] so swift that it all beasts did pass:
Like never yet did living eye detect;
But likest it to a hyena was,
That feeds on women's flesh as others feed on grass.

It forth she call'd, and gave it strait in charge
Through thick and thin her to pursue apace,
Nor once to stay to rest, or breathe at large,
Till her he had attain'd and brought in place,[4]
Or quite devour'd her beauty's scornful grace.
The monster, swift as word that from her went,
Went forth in haste, and did her footing trace
So sure and swiftly, through his perfect scent
And passing speed, that shortly he her overhent.[5]

Sore terrified, the damsel fled fast, till her fleet palfrey gave in, as she approached the sea-shore; then, lightly leaping from her dull horse, she continued the flight on foot.

Not half so fast the wicked Myrrha[6] fled
From dread of her revenging father's hand;
Nor half so fast, to save her maidenhead,
Fled fearful Daphne[7] on th' Ægean strand,
As Florimell fled from that monster yond,[8]
To reach the sea ere she of him were raught:[9]
For in the sea to drown herself she fand,[10]
Rather than of the tyrant to be caught:
Thereto fear gave her wings, and need her courage taught.

It fortunëd (High God did so ordain)
As she arrivëd on the roaring shore,
In mind to leap into the mighty main,
A little boat lay hoving[11] her before,
In which there slept a fisher old and poor,
The while his nets were drying on the sand:
Into the same she leapt, and with the oar
Did thrust the shallop from the floating strand:[12]
So safety found at sea, which she found not at land.

The baffled monster, to revenge himself, set upon Florimell's abandoned palfrey, "and slew him cruelly ere any rescue came;"

And after having him embowellëd,
To fill his hellish gorge, it chanc'd a knight
To pass that way, as forth he travellëd:
It was a goodly swain, and of great might,
As ever man that bloody field did fight;
But in vain shows, that wont young knights bewitch,
And courtly services, took no delight;
But rather joy'd to be than seemen sich:[13]
For both to be and seem to him was labour lich.[14]

It was, to wit, the good Sir Satyrane,
That rang'd abroad to seek adventures wild,
As was his wont, in forest and in plain:
He was all arm'd in rugged steel unfil'd,[15]
As in the smoky forge it was compil'd,[16]
And in his scutcheon bore a satyr's head:
He coming present, where the monster vild
Upon that milk-white palfrey's carcase fed,
Unto his rescue ran, and greedily[17] him sped.

Recognising the palfrey of Florimell, he was struck with fear lest any evil should have befallen that lady, whom he dearly loved; "besides, her golden girdle, which did fall from her in flight, he found, that did him sore appal." Fiercely he attacked the beast, but could not kill him; so, hurling his sword away, he lightly leapt upon the monster, that roared and raged to be underkept, and heaped strokes upon him.

As he that strives to stop a sudden flood,
And in strong banks his violence restrain,
Forceth it swell above his wonted mood,
And largely overflow the fruitful plain,
That all the country seems to be a main,[18]
And the rich furrows float, all quite fordone:[19]
The woeful husbandman doth loud complain
To see his whole year's labour lost so soon,
For which to God he made so many an idle boon.[20]

At last the beast submitted; and, since the witch's charms made steel powerless to slay him, Satyrane bound him with Florimell's golden girdle. "Thus as he led the beast along the way," Sir Satyrane spied a mighty giantess, on a courser dappled gray, flying fast from a bold knight; and lying athwart her horse was a doleful squire, bound hand and foot, "whom she did mean to make the thrall of her desire." Leaving his captive beast at liberty, Satyrane turned against the giantess, who, throwing aside her load, addressed herself to fight.

Like as a goshawk, that in foot doth bear

1 Cause her death.
2 Strangely chosen.
3 Besides.
4 To that place.
5 Overtook.
6 The mother of Adonis—who was the fruit of her unnatural passion for her father, Cinyras, King of Cyprus.
7 See note 12, page 37.
8 Furious. See note 10, page 389.
9 Reached.
10 Preferred.
11 Heaving.
12 Floating from the strand.
13 Seem such.
14 Like.
15 Unpolished.
16 Wrought.
17 Eagerly.
18 Sea.
19 Ruined.
20 Prayer.

A trembling culver,[1] having spied on height
An eagle that with plumy wings doth shear
The subtile air, stooping with all his might,
The quarry[2] throws to ground with fell despite,
And to the battle doth herself prepare:
So ran the giantess unto the fight;
Her fiery eyes with furious sparks did stare,
And with blasphémous banns[3] High God in pieces tare.

She caught in hand a huge great iron mace,
Wherewith she many had of life depriv'd;
But, ere the stroke could seize his aimëd place,[4]
His spear amids her sun-broad shield arriv'd;
Yet nathemore the steel asunder riv'd,
All[5] were the beam in bigness like a mast,
Nor her out of the steadfast saddle driv'd;
But, glancing on the temper'd metal, brast[6]
In thousand shivers, and so forth beside her past.

Her steed did stagger with that puissant stroke;
But she no more was movëd with that might,
Than it had lighted on an aged oak
Upon the top of mount Olympus' height,
Or on the marble pillar that is pight[7]
For the brave youthly champions to assay
With burning chariot wheels it nigh to smite;
But who that smites it mars his joyous play,
And is the spectacle of ruinous decay.[8]

The enraged giantess dealt her adversary such a blow on the helmet, that he was stunned, and reeled in his saddle; then she seized him by the collar, plucked him out of his wavering seat, laid him across her horse, and rode away. But the pressure of her original pursuer obliged her to drop the burden. By and by, Sir Satyrane came to his senses, and, after making moan for his misadventure, spied the helpless squire whom he had rescued.

To whom approaching, well he might perceive
In that foul plight a comely personage
And lovely face, made fit for to deceive
Frail ladies' hearts with love's consuming rage;
Now in the blossom of his freshest age:
He rear'd him up, and loos'd his iron bands,
And after gan inquire his parentage,
And how he fell into that giant's hands,
And who that was which chasëd her along the lands.

The squire informed him that the giantess was Arganté, begot, by incest, of the Titan Typhœus and his own mother Earth. Another babe she bore at the same birth, the mighty Olyphant,[9] with whom Arganté lived in sin; but, not content with this, she plunged into frightful profligacy, and sought all over the country for young men, whom she brought into a secret island, where they must either die in eternal bondage, or serve her pleasures. The squire, caught at vantage by Argantè, was being borne to her prison; but he would rather, he said, have died a thousand deaths, than break the vow he had plighted to fair Columbell. "As for my name, it mistereth not[10] to tell; call me the Squire of Dames; that me beseemeth well." The knight chasing the giantess was a fair virgin, famous in arms, named Palladine; and none might match that monster "but she, or such as she, that is so chaste a wight." Asked to tell what vow he had taken, the squire said that his lady had imposed on him, as a task by which he might gain her favour, the charge to wander through the world at will, doing everywhere service to gentle dames, whose names and pledges he was to bring back at the end of a year.

"So well I to fair ladies service did,
And found such favour in their loving hearts,
That, ere the year his course had compassëd,
Three hundred pledges for my good desarts,[11]
And thrice three hundred thanks for my good parts,
I with me brought, and did to her present:
Which when she saw, more bent to eke my smarts[12]
Than to reward my trusty true intent,
She gan for me devise a grievous punishment;

"To wit, that I my travel should resume,
And with like labour walk the world around,
Nor ever to her presence should presume,
Till I so many other dames had found,
The which, for all the suit I could propound,
Would me refuse their pledges to afford,
But did abide for ever chaste and sound."
"Ah! gentle Squire," quoth he, "tell, at one word,
How many found'st thou such to put in thy recórd?"

"Indeed, Sir Knight," said he, "one word may tell
All that I ever found so wisely staid,[13]
For only three they were dispos'd so well;
And yet three years I now abroad have stray'd,
To find them out." "Might I," then laughing said
The Knight, "inquire of thee what were those three,
The which thy proffer'd courtesy denay'd?[14]
Or ill they seemëd sure advis'd to be,
Or brutishly brought up, that ne'er did fashions see."

"The first which then refusëd me," said he,
"Certes was but a common courtisáne;
Yet flat refus'd to have ado with me,
Because I could not give her many a jane."[15]
(Thereat full heartily laugh'd Satyrane.)
"The second was a holy nun to choose,
Which would not let me be her chappellane,[16]

1 Pigeon. 2 Prey.
3 Curses. See note 3, page 135.
4 Attain its aim. 5 Although.
6 Broke.
7 Placed—as the goal in the Olympian chariot-races; Horace's "meta fervidis evitata rotis."
8 Defeat, injury.

9 See note 24, page 147; and canto xi. of the present book, page 437.
10 There is no occasion or need.
11 Deserts.
12 Add to my pain.
13 Steadfast, constant.
14 Denied.
15 A jane was a Genoese coin of small value; here the word is used generally for any coin.
16 Chaplain.

Because she knew, she said, I would disclose
Her counsel, if she should her trust in me repose.

"The third a damsel was of low degree,
Whom I in country cottage found by chance:
Full little weenëd I that chastity
Had lodging in so mean a maintenance;[1]
Yet was she fair, and in her countenance
Dwelt simple truth in seemly fashión:
Long thus I woo'd her with due óbservánce,
In hope unto my pleasure to have won;
But was as far at last, as when I first begun.

"Save her, I never any woman found
That chastity did for itself embrace,
But were for other causes firm and sound;
Either for want of handsome[2] time and place,
Or else for fear of shame and foul disgrace.
Thus am I hopeless ever to attain
My lady's love, in such a desperate case,
But all my days am like to waste in vain,
Seeking to match the chaste with th' unchaste ladies' train."[3]

"Pardie,"[4] said Satyrane, "thou Squire of Dames,
Great labour fondly[5] hast thou hent in hand,[6]
To get small thanks, and therewith many blames;
That may amongst Alcides' labours stand."
Thence back returning to the former land[7]
Where late he left the beast he overcame,
He found him not; for he had broke his band,
And was return'd again unto his dame,
To tell what tidings of fair Florimell became.

CANTO VIII.

The witch creates a snowy lady like to Florimell;
Who, wrong'd by Carl,[8] *by Proteus sav'd,*
Is sought by Paridell.

WHEN the malicious witch saw the beast return with Florimell's golden girdle, she rejoiced at the supposed destruction of the maiden, and ran with the token to her son, thinking to remove his grief by showing the hopelessness of his love. But the youth only sorrowed with fresh fury; and he would have slain his mother, "had she not fled into a secret mew,[9] where she was wont her sprites to entertain." Calling to her aid those "masters of her art," she conjured them to devise some means of healing for her son, whose senses were decayed; and by their advice and her own wicked wit she boldly took in hand to make "another Florimell, in shape and look so lively, and so like, that many it mistook."

The substance, whereof she the body made,
Was purest snow in massy mould congeal'd,
Which she had gather'd in a shady glade
Of the Rhipœan hills,[10] to her reveal'd
By errant sprites, but from all men conceal'd:
The same she temper'd with fine mercury
And virgin wax that never yet was seal'd,
And mingled them with perfect vermily;[11]
That like a lively sanguine it seem'd to the eye.

Instead of eyes two burning lamps she set
In silver sockets, shining like the skies,
And a quick moving spirit did arret[12]
To stir and roll them like two women's eyes:
Instead of yellow locks she did devise
With golden wire to weave her curlëd head:
Yet golden wire was not so yellow thrice[13]
As Florimell's fair hair: and, in the stead
Of life, she put a sprite to rule the carcase dead;

A wicked sprite, y-fraught with fawning guile
And fair resemblance above all the rest,
Which with the Prince of Darkness fell somewhile[14]
From heaven's bliss and everlasting rest:
Him needed not instruct which way were best
Himself to fashion likest Florimell,
Nor how to speak, nor how to use his gest;[15]
For he in counterfeasance[16] did excel,
And all the wiles of women's wits knew passing well.

Him shapëd thus she deck'd in garments gay,
Which Florimell had left behind her late;
That whoso then her saw, would surely say
It was herself whom it did imitate,
Or fairer than herself, if aught algate[17]
Might fairer be. And then she forth her brought
Unto her son, that lay in feeble state;
Who, seeing her, gan straight upstart, and thought
She was the lady's self whom he so long had sought.

Joyously embracing the fancied Florimell, the youth quickly recovered, and resumed his courtship—though, the better to seem what she was named, she "coyly rebutted his embracement light." On a day, as he walked the woods "with that his idol fair," he encountered "proud Braggadocio, that in vaunting vain his glory did repose and credit did maintain." Marvelling to see with that churl so fair a wight, he "thought that match a foul disparagement," and at spear's point compelled the silly clown to surrender the lady, whom the victor mounted on Trompart's steed and proudly led away. When safe from pursuit, Braggadocio began to woo her; but soon they met "an armëd knight upon a courser strong, whose trampling feet upon the hollow lay[18] seemëd to thunder." The stranger, "with bold words and bitter threat," bade Braggadocio surrender the lady,

1 Condition. 2 Convenient.
3 That is, to find a number of chaste ladies equal to the number of the unchaste. 4 Truly.
5 Foolishly. 6 Undertaken.
7 Place. 8 Churl; the witch's son.
9 Hiding-place, den.
10 A range of mountains in the remote north, of which the ancients knew but vaguely, and which they sometimes called the Mountains of the Hyperboreans.
11 Vermilion. 12 Appoint.
13 One-third so yellow. 14 Long before.
15 What deportment to use. 16 Counterfeiting.
17 In any way.
18 Lea, level land.

or else fight for her. The boaster, though quaking with fear, answered with words of vaunting defiance; and the stranger, waxing highly wroth, bade him turn his steed, on pain of death.

"Since, then," said Braggadocio, "needs thou wilt
Thy days abridge, through proof of puissánce,
Turn we our steeds; that both in equal tilt
May meet again, and each take happy chance."
This said, they both a furlong's mountenance[1]
Retir'd their steeds, to run in even race:
But Braggadocio with his bloody lance,
Once having turn'd, no more return'd his face,
But left his love to loss, and fled himself apace.

Disdaining to pursue, the knight took the dame from Trompart, and rode away with fairest Florimell; for so he deemed her, "and so herself did always to her tell; so made him think himself in heav'n, that was in hell."

But Florimell herself was far away,
Driven to great distress by fortune strange,
And taught the careful mariner to play,
Since late mischance had her compell'd to change
The land for sea, at random there to range:
Yet there that cruel Queen avengeress,[2]
Not satisfied so far her to estrange
From courtly bliss and wonted happiness,
Did heap on her new waves of weary wretchedness.

For, being fled into the fisher's boat
For refuge from the monster's cruelty,
Long so she on the mighty main did float,
And with the tide drove forward carelessly;
For th' air was mild, and clearëd was the sky,
And all his winds Dan[3] Æolus did keep
From stirring up their stormy enmity,
As pitying to see her wail and weep;
But all the while the fisher did securely sleep.

When, "drunk with drowsiness," he awoke, "and saw his drover[4] drive along the stream," he was dismayed; but other thoughts arose at sight of the lady. He began "to look on her fair face and mark her snowy skin;" and soon he rudely assaulted her honour. She struggled strongly both with hand and foot, till Heaven, out of "sovereign favour toward chastity," sent succour. As she stiffly strove, and importuned the wide sea with shrilling shrieks, "Proteus abroad did rove, along the foamy waves driving his finny drove."

Proteus is shepherd of the seas of yore,
And hath the charge of Neptune's mighty herd;
An aged sire with head all frowy[5] hoar,
And sprinkled frost upon his dewy beard:
Who, when those pitiful outcries he heard
Through all the seas so ruefully resound,
His chariot swift in haste he thither steer'd,
Which, with a team of scaly phocas[6] bound,
Was drawn upon the waves, that foamëd him around.

Coming to the boat, and seeing a sight that smote him with indignation and pity, Proteus haled the villain "from his hopëd prey," and beat him soundly with "his staff, that drives his herd astray." Florimell, all soiled and tear-stained, looked up at her deliverer, but "for shame, and more for fear of his grim sight, down in her lap she hid her face, and foully shright."[7]

Herself not savëd yet from danger dread
She thought, but chang'd from one to other fear:
Like as a fearful partridge, that is fled
From the sharp hawk which her attachëd near,[8]
And falls to ground to seek for succour there,
Where as the hungry spaniels she does spy
With greedy jaws her ready for to tear:
In such distress and sad perplexitý
Was Florimell, when Proteus she did see her by.

But Proteus, with speeches mild, strove to comfort and reassure her.

Her up betwixt his rugged hands he rear'd,
And with his frory[9] lips full softly kist,
While the cold icicles from his rough beard
Droppëd adown upon her ivory breast:
Yet he himself so busily addrest,
That her out of astonishment he wrought;
And, out of that same fisher's filthy nest
Removing her, into his chariot brought,
And there with many gentle terms her fair besought.

The "old lecher" he tied behind his chariot, dragging him through the waves, and afterwards casting him up upon the shore; "but Florimell with him unto his bower[10] he bore."

His bow'r is in the bottom of the main,
Under a mighty rock 'gainst which do rave
The roaring billows in their proud disdain,
That with the angry working of the wave
Therein is eaten out a hollow cave,
That seems rough mason's hand with engines keen
Had long while labourëd it to engrave:[11]
There was his won;[12] nor living wight was seen
Save one old nymph, hight Panopé, to keep it clean.

Thither he brought the sorry Florimell,
And entertainëd her the best he might
(And Panopé her entertain'd eke well),
As an immortal might a mortal wight,
To win her liking unto his delight:
With flatt'ring words he sweetly wooëd her,
And offerëd fair gifts t' allure her sight;
But she both offers and the offerer
Despis'd, and all the fawning of the flatterer.

Daily he tempted her with this or that,
And never suffer'd her to be at rest:
But evermore she him refusëd flat,
And all his feignëd kindness did detest;
So firmly she had sealëd up her breast.
Sometimes he boasted that a god he hight;

1 Distance. 2 Fate.
3 Lord; from Latin, "Dominus." 4 Boat.
5 Or "frowsy;" mossy, rugged, untidy.
6 Seals. 7 Shrieked.
8 Nearly seized. 9 Frozen.
10 Abode. 11 Cut out. 12 Dwelling.

But she a mortal creature lovëd best:
Then he would make himself a mortal wight;
But then she said she lov'd none but a Faery knight.

Then like a Faery knight himself he drest;
For ev'ry shape on him he could indue:
Then like a king he was to her exprest,
And offer'd kingdoms unto her in view,
To be his leman [1] and his lady true:
But, when all this he nothing saw prevail,
With harder means he cast [2] her to subdue,
And with sharp threats her often did assail;
So thinking for to make her stubborn courage quail.

To dreadful shapes he did himself transform:
Now like a giant; now like to a fiend;
Then like a centaur; then like to a storm
Raging within the waves: thereby he ween'd
Her will to win unto his wishëd end:
But when with fear, nor favour, nor with all
He else could do, he saw himself esteem'd,
Down in a dungeon deep he let her fall,
And threaten'd there to make her his eternal thrall.

Eternal thraldom was to her more lief [3]
Than loss of chastity, or change of love:
Die had she rather in tormenting grief,
Than any should of falseness her reprove,
Or looseness, that she lightly did remove.[4]
Most virtuous Virgin! glory be thy meed,
And crown of heav'nly praise with saints above,
Where most sweet hymns of this thy famous deed
Are still amongst them sung, that far my rhymes exceed.

"Fit song of angels carollëd to be!" exclaims the poet, as reluctantly he leaves the maiden in this woeful plight, to tell of Satyrane and the Squire of Dames. Having ended a long discourse of the Squire's adventures vain, "the which himself than ladies more defames," the pair returned from vain pursuit of the hyena, and met a knight whom Satyrane recognised as Sir Paridell, "both by the burning heart which on his breast he bare, and by the colours in his crest." Asked for tidings, Paridell answered that Faery Court had been thrown into mourning by "the late ruin of proud Marinell," and the sudden departure of Florimell, in quest of whom all the brave knights had gone. Satyrane then informed him that his labour all was lost, for Florimell might be accounted dead; and told how he had seen her palfrey slain by a monstrous beast, and had "found her golden girdle cast astray, distain'd with dirt and blood, as relic of the prey." Paridell admits that "the signs be sad," but will not forsake his quest "till trial do more certain truth bewray." Satyrane promises that he will not be behind the other searchers.

1 Mistress. 2 Designed, tried.
3 Preferable.
4 Change her affection. 5 Labour.
6 Restore. 7 Way.
8 In company. 9 Know.

"Ye noble knights," said then the Squire of Dames,
"Well may ye speed in so praiseworthy pain![5]
But, since the sun now gins to slake his beams
In dewy vapours of the western main,
And loose the team out of his weary wain,
Might not mislike you also to abate
Your zealous haste, till morrow next again
Both light of heav'n and strength of men relate:[6]
Which if ye please, to yonder castle turn your gate."[7]

That counsel pleasëd well; so all y-fere [8]
Forth marchëd to a castle them before;
Where soon arriving they restrainëd were
Of ready entrance, which ought evermore
To errant knights be common: wondrous sore
Thereat displeas'd they were, till that young Squire
Gan them inform the cause why that same door
Was shut to all which lodging did desire:
The which to let you weet [9] will farther time require.

CANTO IX.

Malbecco will no strange knights host,[10]
For peevish jealousy:
Paridell jousts with Britomart:
Both show their ancestry.

THE poet makes apology to the "redoubted knights and honourable dames," to whom he levels all his labour's end, for writing of a wanton lady; but reminds them that good more clearly appears by the contrast of evil, and that even in heaven a whole legion of angels fell. He proceeds to tell why the knights found so inhospitable reception at the castle. Therein, said the Squire of Dames, dwelt a cankered crabbed carl, uncourteous and heedless what men said of him, ill or well, and setting all his mind on mucky pelf. Yet was he linked to a lovely lass, wholly incompatible with him in years and dispositions, joying to play among her peers, hating hard restraints and jealous fears. Suspicious of her truth, her one-eyed husband mewed her closely up, and suffered nobody to approach her. "Malbecco [11] he, and Hellenore she hight, unfitly yok'd together in one team;" and the husband's jealousy denied admittance to all knights that came that way. Smiling, Satyrane pronounced the man extremely mad who thought "with watch and hard constraint to stay a woman's will which is disposed to go astray.[12]

"In vain he fears that which he cannot shun:
For who wots [13] not, that woman's subtilties

10 Entertain. 11 The Cuckold.
12 Chaucer, in the passage in The Manciple's Tale, which Spenser evidently follows, had declared the attempt "to keep a shrew" to be a "very nicety."
13 Knows.

Can guilen[1] Argus, when she list misdo'n?[2]
It is not iron bands, nor hundred eyes,
Nor brazen walls, nor many wakeful spies,
That can withhold her wilful-wand'ring feet;
But fast good will, with gentle courtesies,
And timely service to her pleasures meet,
May her perhaps contain[3] that else would algates fleet."[4]

But Paridell asked if he was not more mad who had sold himself to such service; "for sure a fool I do him firmly hold, that loves his fetters, though they were of gold." They resolved first to exhaust gentle means of gaining entrance, before resorting to force; and Paridell, knocking softly, requested admittance of "the goodman self, which then the porter play'd." He answered that all were gone to rest, and the keys were in the chamber of the master, whom he durst not awake. Threats were tried, to no purpose; and now a terrible storm of rain and hail drove the applicants to take shelter in a little swine-shed beside the gate. By and by, another knight, repelled from the inhospitable door of the castle, came also to the shed for shelter; but its occupants refused to admit the new comer. Enraged, he defied them all, till Paridell, overcoming his reluctance to fighting in the dark, issued forth to the combat, like a long-encaged wind that, escaping, "confounds both land and seas, and skies doth overcast." The two knights rode together with impetuous rage and force, and both were unhorsed. Paridell, though sore bruised, was eager to continue the fight on foot; but Satyrane made peace, and all combined against the castle's lord, to burn his gates with unquenchable fire, and slay himself.

Malbecco seeing them resolv'd in deed
To flame the gates, and hearing them to call
For fire in earnest, ran with fearful speed,
And, to them calling from the castle wall,
Besought them humbly him to bear withal,
As ignorant of servants' bad abuse
And slack attendance unto strangers' call.
The knights were willing all things to excuse,
Though naught believ'd, and entrance late did not refuse.

They be y-brought into a comely bow'r,
And serv'd of all things that might needful be;
Yet secretly their host did on them lour,
And welcom'd more for fear than charity;
But they dissembled what they did not see,
And welcomëd themselves. Each gan undight
Their garments wet, and weary armour free,
To dry themselves by Vulcan's flaming light,
And eke their lately bruisëd parts to bring in plight.[5]

And eke that stranger knight amongst the rest
Was for like need enforc'd to disarray:
Then, when as vailëd was her lofty crest,[6]
Her golden locks, that were in trammels[7] gay
Upbounden, did themselves adown display,
And raught[8] unto her heels; like sunny beams,
That in a cloud their light did long time stay,
Their vapour vaded,[9] show their golden gleams,
And through the persant air[10] shoot forth their azure streams.

She also doff'd her heavy habergeon,[11]
Which the fair feature of her limbs did hide;
And her well-plighted[12] frock, which she did won[13]
To tuck about her short when she did ride,
She low let fall, that flow'd from her lank[14] side
Down to her foot with careless modesty.
Then of them all she plainly was espied
To be a woman-wight, unwist[15] to be;
The fairest woman-wight that ever eye did see.

Like as Bellona (being late return'd
From slaughter of the giants conquerëd;
Where proud Encelade,[16] whose wide nostrils burn'd
With breathëd flames like to a furnace red,
Transfixëd with her spear down tumbled dead
From top of Hæmus by him heapëd high)
Hath loos'd her helmet from her lofty head,
And her Gorgonian[17] shield gins to untie
From her left arm, to rest in glorious victory.

All the rest were smitten with great amazement and admiration at the disclosure; their hungry view could not be satisfied, "but, seeing, still the more desired to see;" and, between her beauty and her prowess, "ev'ry one her lik'd, and ev'ry one her lov'd." Even Paridell was won out of his discontent for "his late fall and foul indignity." Soon supper was prepared; and all prayed Malbecco of courtesy that they might have the company of his wife.

But he, to shift their curious request,
Gan causen[18] why she could not come in place;[19]
Her crazëd[20] health, her late recourse to rest,
And humid evening ill for sick folk's case:
But none of those excuses could take place;[21]
Nor would they eat, till she in presence came:
She came in presence with right comely grace,
And fairly them saluted, as became,
And show'd herself in all a gentle courteous dame.

They sat to meat; and Satyrane his chance
Was her before, and Paridell beside;
But he himself[22] sat looking still askance
'Gainst Britomart, and ever closely ey'd
Sir Satyrane, that glances might not glide:
But his blind eye, that sided[23] Paridell,

1 Deceive.
2 Pleases to do wrong.
3 Restrain.
4 Would by whatever way, at any hazard, flee (in pursuit of her own will).
5 Heal.
6 When her helmet was taken off.
7 Braids.
8 Reached.
9 Gone, dispersed.
10 Piercing through the air.
11 Coat of mail.
12 Well-folded.
13 Was wont.
14 Slender.
15 (Formerly) unknown.
16 Enceladus; one of the Titans, who was killed by a thunderbolt of Zeus, or by Athena—not, as the poet says, by Bellona's spear.
17 Having upon it the Gorgon's head, which turned all beholders to stone. Spenser transfers its ownership from Athena to Bellona.
18 Began to explain, make excuses.
19 Be present.
20 Broken, impaired.
21 Have effect.
22 Malbecco.
23 Was on the side of.

All his demeanour from his sight did hide:
On her fair face so did he feed his fill,
And sent close[1] messages of love to her at will:

And ever and anon, when none was ware,
With speaking looks, that close embassage[2] bore,
He rov'd[3] at her, and told his secret care;
For all that art he learnëd had of yore:
Nor was she ignorant of that lewd lore,
But in his eye his meaning wisely read,
And with the like him answer'd evermore:
She sent at him one fiery dart, whose head
Empoison'd was with privy lust and jealous dread.

He from that deadly throw made no defence,
But to the wound his weak heart open'd wide:
The wicked engine, through false influence,
Pass'd through his eyes, and secretly did glide
Into his heart, which it did sorely gride.[4]
But nothing new to him was that same pain;
Nor pain at all; for he so oft had tried
The power thereof, and lov'd so oft in vain,
That thing of course he counted, love to entertain.

Thenceforth to her he sought to intimate
His inward grief, by means to him well known:
Now Bacchus' fruit out of the silver plate
He on the table dash'd, as overthrown,
Or of the fruitful liquor overflown;
And by the dancing bubbles did divine,
Or therein write to let his love be shown;
Which well she read out of the learned line:
A sacrament profane in mystery of wine.

And, whenso of his hand the pledge she raught,[5]
The guilty cup she feignëd to mistake,
And in her lap did shed her idle draught,
Showing desire her inward flame to slake.
By such close signs they secret way did make
Unto their wills, and one eye's watch escape:
Two eyes him needeth, for to watch and wake,
Who lovers will deceive. Thus was the ape,
By their fair handling, put into Malbecco's cape.[6]

"Now when of meats and drinks they had their fill," Hellenora requested the knights to tell their deeds of arms, their kindred and their names. Paridell, glad to commend himself to the dame, traced his descent from Paris, "most famous worthy of the world, by whom the war was kindled which did Troy inflame." Long before the siege, while yet a shepherd on Mount Ida, Paris "on fair Œnone got a lovely boy," whom she named Parius. He, after the ruin of the city, "gather'd the Trojan relics saved from flame, and, with them sailing thence, to th' isle of Paros came."

"That was by him call'd Paros, which before
Hight Nausa; there he many years did reign,
And built Nausiclé by the Pontic shore;
The which he, dying, left next in remain
To Paridas his son,
From whom I Paridell by kin descend:
But, for fair ladies' love and glory's gain,
My native soil have left, my days to spend
In suing[7] deeds of arms, my life's and labour's end."

Much moved by the story of the nation from which she was herself lineally extracted—"for noble Britons sprung from Trojans bold, and Troynovant[8] was built of old Troy's ashes cold"—Britomart asked Paridell to tell the fortunes of Æneas after his escape from the "city's woeful fire;" and Paridell related his wanderings and sufferings, before his arrival and settlement in Latium, and the foundation of the Roman realm.

"There, there," said Britomart, "afresh appear'd
The glory of the later world to spring,
And Troy again out of her dust was rear'd
To sit in second seat of sov'reign king
Of all the world, under her governing.
But a third kingdom yet is to arise
Out of the Trojans' scatterëd offspring,
That, in all glory and great enterprise,
Both first and second Troy shall dare to equalise.

"It Troynovant is hight, that with the waves
Of wealthy Thamis washëd is along,
Upon whose stubborn neck (whereat he raves
With roaring rage, and sore himself does throng,
That all men fear to tempt his billows strong),
She fasten'd hath her foot: which stands so high,
That it a wonder of the world is sung
In foreign lands; and all which passen by,
Beholding it from far do think it threats the sky.[9]

"The Trojan Brute did first that city found,
And High-gate made the meer[10] thereof by west,
And Overt-gate by north: that is the bound
Towárd the land; two rivers bound the rest.
So huge a scope[11] at first him seemëd best,
To be the compass of his kingdom's seat:
So huge a mind could not in lesser rest,
Nor in small meers contain his glory great,
That Albion had conquer'd first by warlike feat."

Paridell now, entreating the "fairest Lady-Knight" to pardon his heedless oversight, recited what he had once "heard tell from aged Mnemon:" that of the old Trojan stock there had grown "another plant, that raught[5] to wondrous height, and far abroad his mighty branches threw," even to the world's utmost corner. For that same Brute, Mnemon had said, was the son of Sylvius; who, having by accident slain his father, fled to sea with a youthly train, and, after many adventures, conquered Britain from its original inhabitants—"a huge nation of the giant's brood, that fed on living flesh, and drunk men's vital blood."

1 Secret.
2 Secret embassy.
3 Shot.
4 Wound, pierce.
5 Reached.
6 Hood. To put an ape into one's hood, upon one's head, is to befool him; the phrase is employed by Chaucer in the prologue to The Prioress's Tale (page 144).

7 Pursuing.
8 London; New Troy.
9 The reference may be either to the Tower of London, or—more probably—to Old London Bridge, and the lofty piles of building upon it.
10 Boundary.
11 Extent.

"His work great Troynovant, his work is eke
Fair Lincoln, both renownëd far away;
That who from East to West will endlong[1] seek,
Cannot two fairer cities find this day,
Except Cleopolis; so heard I say
Old Mnemon: therefore, Sir, I greet you well
Your country kin;[2] and you entirely pray
Of pardon for the strife, which late befell
Betwixt us both unknown." So ended Paridell.

But, all the while that he these speeches spent,
Upon his lips hung fair Dame Hellenore
With vigilant regard and due attent,[3]
Fashioning worlds of fancies evermore
In her frail wit, that now her quite forlore:[4]
The while unwares away her wond'ring eye
And greedy ears her weak heart from her bore:
Which he perceiving, ever privily,
In speaking, many false belgardes[5] at her let fly.

So long these knights discoursëd diversely
Of strange affairs, and noble hardiment,[6]
Which they had pass'd with mickle jeopardy,
That now the humid night was farforth spent,
And heav'nly lamps were halfendeal y-brent:[7]
Which th' old man seeing well, who too long thought
Ev'ry discourse, and ev'ry argument,
Which by the hours he measurëd, besought
Them go to rest. So all unto their bow'rs were brought.

CANTO X.

Paridell rapeth Hellenore;
Malbecco her pursues;
Finds amongst Satyrs, whence with him
To turn she doth refuse.

In the morning, Britomart and Satyrane left the castle; but Paridell, pleading the hurts received in his encounter with the Virgin Knight, stayed behind—much to the discontent of Malbecco, who did not let his wife out of his sight by night or by day.

But Paridell kept better watch than he,
A fit occasion for his turn to find.
False Love! why do men say thou canst not see,
And in their foolish fancy feign thee blind,
That with thy charms the sharpest sight dost bind,
And to thy will abuse? Thou walkest free,
And seest ev'ry secret of the mind;
Thou seest all, yet none at all sees thee:
All that is by the working of thy deity.

So perfect in that art was Paridell,
That he Malbecco's halfen eye[8] did wile;
His halfen eye he wilëd wondrous well,
And Hellenore's both eyes did eke beguile,
Both eyes and heart at once, during the while
That he there sojournëd his wounds to heal;
That Cupid self, it seeing, close[9] did smile
To weet[10] how he her love away did steal,
And bade that none their joyous treason should reveal.

The learned[11] lover lost no time nor tide
That least advantage might to him afford,
Yet bore so fair a sail, that none espied
His secret drift till he her laid aboard.
Whenso in open place and common board
He fortun'd her to meet, with common speech
He courted her; yet baited ev'ry word,
That his ungentle host n'ot[12] him appeach[13]
Of vile ungentleness or hospitage's breach.[14]

But when apart (if ever her apart
He found) then his false engines fast he plied,
And all the sleights unbosom'd in his heart:
He sigh'd, he sobb'd, he swoon'd, he pardie[15] died,
And cast himself on ground her fast beside:
Then, when again he him bethought to live,
He wept, and wail'd, and false laments belied,[16]
Saying, but if[17] she mercy would him give,
That he might algates[18] die, yet did his death forgive.

And other whiles with amorous delights
And pleasing toys he would her entertain;
Now singing sweetly to surprise her sprites,
Now making lays of love and lovers' pain,
Bransles,[19] ballads, virelays, and verses vain;
Oft purposes,[20] oft riddles, he devis'd,
And thousands like which flowëd in his brain,
With which he fed her fancy, and entic'd
To take to his new love, and leave her old despis'd.

And ev'ry where he might and ev'ry while
He did her service dutiful, and sued
At hand with humble pride and pleasing guile;
So closely yet, that none but she it view'd,
Who well perceivëd all, and all indued.[21]
Thus finely did he his false nets dispread,
With which he many weak hearts had subdued
Of yore, and many had alike misled:
What wonder then if she were likewise carriëd?

Soon Hellenora "her love and heart hath wholly sold" to the treacherous guest; and all is arranged for an elopement.

Dark was the ev'ning, fit for lovers' stealth,
When chanc'd Malbecco busy be elsewhere,
She to his closet went, where all his wealth
Lay hid; thereof she countless sums did rear,[22]
The which she meant away with her to bear;
The rest she fir'd, for sport or for despite:
As Helen, when she saw aloft appear
The Trojan flames, and reach to heaven's height,
Did clap her hands, and joyëd at that doleful sight;

1 From end to end.
2 On the relationship of your country with mine.
3 Attention.
4 Forsook.
5 Sweet looks.
6 Deeds of bravery.
7 Half burned out.
8 Single eye.
9 Secretly.
10 Know.
11 Skilful, practised.
12 Could not.
13 Accuse.
14 Violation of hospitality.
15 Truly.
16 Feigned.
17 Unless.
18 Certainly.
19 Airs for the dance called "bransel," "bransle," or "brawl," wherein a number of people joined hands and moved in a ring.
20 Conversations.
21 Accepted.
22 Lift take away.

The second Helen, fair Dame Hellenore,
The while her husband ran with sorry haste
To quench the flames which she had tin'd[1] before,
Laugh'd at his foolish labour spent in waste,[2]
And ran into her lover's arms right fast;
Where strait embracëd, she to him did cry
And call aloud for help, ere help were past;
For lo! that guest did bear her forcibly,
And meant to ravish her, that rather had to die!

The wretched man, hearing her call for aid,
And ready seeing him with her to fly,
In his disquiet mind was much dismay'd:
But when again he backward cast his eye,
And saw the wicked fire so furiously
Consume his heart, and scorch his idol's face,[3]
He was therewith distressëd diversely,
Nor wist he how to turn, nor to what place:
Was never wretched man in such a woeful case.

Ay when to him she cried, to her he turn'd,
And left the fire; love, money overcame:
But, when he markëd how his money burn'd,
He left his wife; money did love disclaim:
Both was he loth to lose his lovëd dame,
And loath to leave his liefest[4] pelf behind;
Yet, since he no't[5] save both, he sav'd that same
Which was the dearest to his dunghill mind,
The god of his desire, the joy of misers blind.

While all was in uproar, the lovers, under the safe-conduct of "Night, the patroness of love-stealth fair," fled at ease; leaving Malbecco to rave, and stamp, and cry, and chew the cud of inward grief. At last he resolved to hide part of his treasure, to bear the rest secretly with him, and, in the garb of a poor pilgrim, to seek his wife whereso she might be found. But all his search was vain; the "woman was too wise ever to come into his clutch again," and he too simple ever to surprise the jolly Paridell. In his wanderings he encountered Braggadocio and Trompart; and, by the display of his treasure, he induced the braggart, "the whole world's common remedy," to swear by Sanglamort his sword that the lady should be sent back and the ravisher chastised. Malbecco, deceived by the bombast of the pretentious pair, joyfully believed the thing as good as done; and the three travelled long together, "through many a wood and many an uncouth way"—Braggadocio and his crafty squire really seeking only an opportunity to deprive their companion of his treasure. At last they met Paridell himself, who, having filched the pleasures of the dame, had cast her up to the wide world, and let her fly alone; for he would not be clogged; "so had he servëd many one."

The gentle lady, loose at random left,
The green-wood long did walk, and wander wide
At wild adventure, like a fórlorn weft;[6]
Till on a day the Satyrs her espied
Straying alone withouten groom or guide:
Her up they took, and with them home her led,
With them as housewife ever to abide,
To milk their goats, and make them cheese and bread;
And ev'ry one as common good her handelëd:

So that she had soon forgotten both Malbecco and Paridell. When Malbecco saw the ravisher of his wife, "he fainted, and was almost dead with fear;" at last he summoned courage to inquire for Hellenora. But Paridell lightly answered, "I take no keep[7] of her; she wonneth[8] in the forest there before;" and forth he rode on new adventure—some convenient derangement in his horse's harness giving Braggadocio a pretext for letting him pass unpunished. Malbecco, greatly disquieted by the thought that his wife may be devoured by wild beasts, wished to enter the forest at once; but Trompart, working on his avarice by tales of robbers, induced him to leave his treasure behind, "buried in the ground for jeopardy."

Now when amid the thickest woods they were,
They heard a noise of many bagpipes shrill,
And shrieking hubbubs them approaching near,
Which all the forest did with horror fill:
That dreadful sound the boaster's heart did thrill
With such amazement, that in haste he fled,
Nor ever lookëd back for good or ill;
And after him eke fearful Trompart sped:
The old man could not fly, but fell to ground half dead:

Yet afterwards, close creeping as he might,
He in a bush did hide his fearful head.
The jolly Satyrs, full of fresh delight,
Came dancing forth, and with them nimbly led
Fair Hellenore, with garlands all bespread,
Whom their May-lady they had newly made:
She, proud of that new honour which they read,[9]
And of their lovely fellowship full glade,[10]
Danc'd lively, and her face did with a laurel shade.

The silly man, that in the thicket lay,
Saw all this goodly sport, and grievëd sore;
Yet durst he naught against it do or say,
But did his heart with bitter thoughts engore,[11]
To see th' unkindness of his Hellenore.
All day they dancëd with great lustihead,[12]
And with their hornëd feet the green grass wore;
The while their goats upon the browses[13] fed,
Till drooping Phœbus gan to hide his golden head.

Then up they gan their merry pipes to truss,[14]
And all their goodly herds did gather round;
But every Satyr first did give a buss[15]
To Hellenore; so busses did abound.
Now gan the humid vapour shed the ground
With pearly dew, and th' earthë's gloomy shade

1 Kindled.
2 Thrown away.
3 His wealth.
4 Best loved.
5 Could not.
6 Waif.
7 Heed, thought.
8 Dwelleth.
9 Showed.
10 Glad.
11 Pierce.
12 Pleasure.
13 Pasture, herbage.
14 Lift.
15 Kiss.

Did dim the brightness of the welkin round,
That ev'ry bird and beast awarnëd made[1]
To shroud[2] themselves, while sleep their senses did invade.

Which when Malbecco saw, out of the bush
Upon his hands and feet he crept full light,
And like a goat amongst the goats did rush;
That, through the help of his fair horns[3] on height,
And misty damp of misconceiving night,
And eke through likeness of his goatish beard,
He did the better counterfeit aright:
So home he march'd amongst the hornëd herd,
That none of all the Satyrs him espied or heard.

At night he saw his lovely wife lie among them, "embracëd of a Satyr rough and rude," who gave the husband cruel cause of jealousy. Creeping to her side when her companion slept, Malbecco sought to induce her to return with him, promising that all should be forgiven; but she flatly refused, and "chose amongst the jolly Satyrs still to won."[4]

He wooëd her till day-spring he espied;
But all in vain: and then turn'd[5] to the herd,
Who butted him with horns on ev'ry side,
And trod down in the dirt, where his hoar beard
Was foully dight,[6] and he of death afear'd.
Early, before the heaven's fairest light
Out of the ruddy East was fully rear'd,
The herds out of their folds were loosëd quite,
And he amongst the rest crept forth in sorry plight.

So soon as he the prison-door did pass,
He ran as fast as both his feet could bear,
And never lookëd who behind him was,
Nor scarcely who before: like as a bear,
That, creeping close amongst the hives to rear[7]
A honey-comb, the wakeful dogs espy,
And him assailing sore his carcase tear,
That hardly he with life away does fly,
Nor stays, till safe himself he see from jeopardy.

Nor stay'd he, till he came unto the place
Where late his treasure he entombëd had;
Where when he found it not (for Trompart base
Had it purloinëd for his master bad),
With éxtreme fury he became quite mad,
And ran away; ran with himself away:
That who so strangely had him seen bestad,[8]
With upstart hair and staring eyes dismay,[9]
From Limbo Lake him late escapëd sure would say.

High over hills and over dales he fled,
As if the wind him on his wings had borne;
Nor bank nor bush could stay him, when he sped
His nimble feet, as treading still on thorn:
Grief, and Despite, and Jealousy, and Scorn,
Did all the way him follow hard behind;
And he himself himself loath'd so forlorn,[10]
So shamefully forlorn of woman kind:
That, as a snake, still lurkëd in his wounded mind.

Still fled he forward, looking backward still;
Nor stay'd his flight nor fearful agony
Till that he came unto a rocky hill
Over the sea suspended dreadfully,
That living creature it would terrify
To look adown, or upward to the height:
From thence he threw himself dispiteously,
All desperate of his foredamnëd sprite,[11]
That seem'd no help for him was left in living sight.

But, through long anguish and self-murd'ring thought,
He was so wasted and forpinëd[12] quite,
That all his substance was consum'd to naught,
And nothing left but like an airy sprite;
That on the rocks he fell so flit[13] and light,
That he thereby receiv'd no hurt at all;
But chancëd on a craggy cliff to light;
Whence he with crooked claws so long did crawl,
That at the last he found a cave with entrance small:

Into the same he creeps, and thenceforth there
Resolv'd to build his baleful mansión,
In dreary darkness, and continual fear
Of that rock's fall, which ever and anon
Threats with huge ruin him to fall upon,
That he dare never sleep, but that one eye
Still ope he keeps for that occasión;
Nor ever rests he in tranquillity,
The roaring billows beat his bow'r[14] so boist'rously.

Nor ever is he wont on aught to feed
But toads and frogs, his pasture poisonous,
Which in his cold complexión do breed
A filthy blood, or humour rancorous,
Matter of doubt and dread suspicious,
That doth with cureless care consume the heart,
Corrupts the stomach with gall vicious,
Cross-cuts the liver with internal smart,
And doth transfix the soul with death's eternal dart.

Yet can he never die, but dying lives,
And doth himself with sorrow new sustain,
That death and life at once unto him gives,
And painful pleasure turns to pleasing pain.
There dwells he ever, miserable swain,
Hateful both to himself and ev'ry wight;
Where he, through privy grief and horror vain,
Is waxen so deform'd, that he has quite
Forgot he was a man, and Jealousy is hight.

1 Gave warning.
2 Shelter.
3 The badge of the cuckold.
4 Dwell.
5 Returned.
6 Soiled.
7 Carry away.
8 Bestead.
9 Dismayed.
10 Abandoned.
11 His spirit tormented before its time.
12 Pined away.
13 Fleeting, unsubstantial; so that he but skimmed the surface. To "fleet" milk, in some parts of England, is to skim off the cream.
14 Abode.

CANTO XI.

Britomart chaseth Olyphant;
Finds Scudamour distrest:
Assays the House of Busirane,
Where Love's spoils are exprest.

O HATEFUL hellish snake! what Fury first
Brought thee from baleful house of Próserpine,
Where in her bosom she thee long had nurst,
And foster'd up with bitter milk of tine;[1]
Foul Jealousy! that turnest love divine
To joyless dread, and mak'st the loving heart
With hateful thoughts to languish and to pine,
And feed itself with self-consuming smart;
Of all the passions in the mind thou vilest art!

O let him far be banishëd away,
And in his stead let Love for ever dwell!
Sweet Love, that doth his golden wings embay[2]
In blessëd nectar and pure pleasure's well,
Untroubled of vile fear or bitter fell.[3]
And ye, fair ladies, that your kingdoms make
In th' hearts of men, them govern wisely well,
And of fair Britomart ensample take,
That was as true in love as turtle to her make.[4]

Britomart and Satyrane, riding from Malbecco's house, espied a young man in hasty flight from the giant Olyphant, whose profligacy exceeded, if possible, that of his sister Argantë. They pricked against him, and he fled "swift as any roe," fearing not Satyrane, but Britomart, the flower of chastity; "for he the pow'r of chaste hands might not bear." The giant hid himself in a forest, into which his pursuers followed him; but in the search they were separated. Britomart by and by came to a fountain, beside which lay a knight "all wallowëd upon the grassy ground," with his armour cast aside, and "a little off his shield was rudely thrown, on which the wingëd boy[5] in colours clear depainted was." The Virgin shrank from awakening him out of seeming slumber; but soon she heard him groan, and sob, and break forth into bitter complaint for the captivity of Amoretta, his lady and his love, whom for seven months Busirane with wicked hand had cruelly penned in secret den. She was kept "in doleful darkness from the view of day," while her chaste breast was rent by torments, "and the sharp steel did rive her heart in tway," because she would not renounce the love of Scudamour. Struck with pity, Britomart touched him gently, and sought to comfort him by the promise of aid against the wicked felon who had outraged him and thralled his gentle mate. Scudamour replies that it is useless to bewail what cannot be redressed, "and sow vain sorrow in a fruitless ear;" then explains that his lady is in the hands of a tyrant, who, "by strong enchantments and black magic lear," has shut her close in a dungeon, guarded by many fiends. There she is tormented most terribly by night and by day with mortal pain; yet she cannot be constrained "love to conceive in her disdainful breast" for the enchanter. Britomart promises that she "will, with proof of last extremity deliver her from thence, or with her for you die;" and Scudamour is persuaded to reassume "his arms, which he had vowed to disprofess."[6] Soon the pair arrive before the castle of the enchanter, which is but a bowshot distant.

There they dismounting drew their weapons bold,
And stoutly came unto the castle gate,
Where as no gate they found them to withhold,
Nor ward to wait at morn and ev'ning late;
But in the porch, that did them sore amate,[7]
A flaming fire y-mix'd with smouldry smoke
And stinking sulphur, that with grisly hate
And dreadful horror did all entrance choke,
Enforcëd them their forward footing to revoke.[8]

Britomart was greatly dismayed and perplexed, and asked Scudamour, "What monstrous enmity provoke we here?" The Knight replied that the fire, by force of mighty enchantments, could not be quenched or removed away; and he besought the Maid to cease her fruitless pains. But Britomart held it shameful to abandon the enterprise on the mere show of peril.

Therewith, resolv'd to prove her utmost might,
Her ample shield she threw before her face,
And her sword's point directing forward right,
Assail'd the flame; the which eftsoons gave place,
And did itself divide with equal space,
That through she passëd; as a thunder-bolt
Pierceth the yielding air, and doth displace
The soaring clouds into sad show'rs y-molt;[9]
So to her yold[10] the flames, and did their force revolt.[11]

Scudamour vainly attempted to follow; the fire only burned more fiercely; and at last, giving up the enterprise, he threw himself on the grass in a paroxysm of impatient grief. Meanwhile the championess had entered "the outmost room, and pass'd the foremost door; the utmost room abounding with all precious store."

For, round about, the walls y-clothëd were
With goodly arras[12] of great majesty,
Woven with gold and silk so close and near,
That the rich metal lurkëd privily,
As feigning to be hid from envious eye;
Yet here, and there, and ev'rywhere, unwares
It show'd itself and shone unwillingly;
Like a discolour'd[13] snake, whose hidden snares
Through the green grass his long bright burnish'd back declares.

And in those tapets[14] weren fashionëd

1 Or "teen;" anguish, woe.
2 Bathe. 3 Gall, melancholy. 4 Mate.
5 Cupid. The Knight is Sir Scudamore, or Scudamour; the name signifying "the Shield of Love." See Scudamour's story in canto x., book iv.

6 Forswear. 7 Alarm, discomfit.
8 To retire. 9 Molten, melted.
10 Yielded. 11 Turn back.
12 Tapestry. 13 Parti-coloured.
14 Tapestry worked with figures.

Many fair portraits, and many a fair feat;
And all of love, and all of lustihead,[1]
As seemëd by their semblance, did entreat:[2]
And eke all Cupid's wars they did repeat,
And cruel battles, which he whilom fought
'Gainst all the gods, to make his empire great;
Besides the huge massácres which he wrought
On mighty Kings and Kaisers into thraldom
brought.

Therein was writ how often thund'ring Jove[3]
Had felt the point of his heart-piercing dart,
And, leaving heaven's kingdom, here did rove
In strange disguise, to slake his scalding smart;[4]
Now, like a ram, fair Helle to pervart,[5]
Now, like a bull, Europa[6] to withdraw:
Ah, how the fearful lady's tender heart
Did lively seem to tremble, when she saw
The huge seas under her t' obey her servant's
law!

Soon after that, into a golden shower
Himself he chang'd, fair Danaë[7] to view;
And through the roof of her strong brazen tower
Did rain into her lap a honey-dew;
The while her foolish guard, that little knew
Of such deceit, kept th' iron door fast barr'd,
And watch'd that none should enter nor issúe;
Vain was the watch, and bootless all the ward,
When as the god to golden hue himself trans-
ferr'd.[8]

Then was he turn'd into a snowy swan,
To win fair Leda[9] to his lovely trade:[10]
O wondrous skill, and sweet wit of the man,
That her in daffodillies sleeping made,
From scorching heat her dainty limbs to shade!
While the proud bird, ruffling his feathers wide,
And brushing his fair breast, did her invade,[11]
She slept; yet 'twixt her eyelids closely[12] spied
How toward her he rush'd, and smilëd at his
pride.

Then show'd it how the Theban Semelé,
Deceiv'd of jealous Juno,[13] did require
To see him in his sov'reign majesty,
Arm'd with his thunderbolts and lightning fire;
Whence dearly she with death bought her desire.
But fair Alcmena[14] better match did make,
Joying his love in likeness more entire:
Three nights in one they say that for her sake
He then did put, her pleasures longer to partake.

Twice was he seen in soaring eagle's shape,
And with wide wings to beat the buxom[15] air:
Once, when he with Asteria[16] did scape;
Again, when as the Trojan boy so fair[17]
He snatch'd from Ida hill, and with him bare:
Wondrous delight it was there to behold
How the rude shepherds after him did stare,
Trembling through fear lest down he fallen sho'ld,
And often to him calling to take surer hold.

In Satyr's shape Antiopé he snatch'd;
And like a fire, when he Ægin' assay'd:[18]
A shepherd, when Mnemosyne[19] he catch'd;
And like a serpent to the Thracian maid.[20]

1 Pleasure. 2 Treat.

3 Spenser's description of the tapestry in the House of Busirane is paraphrased from Ovid's account of the web woven by the Mæonian maid Arachne in her contest of skill with Minerva. (See note 10, page 384.) The passage may be cited for the sake of comparison:

"Mæonis elusam designat imagine tauri
Europen; verum taurum, freta vera putares.
Ipse videbatur terras spectare relictas,
Et comites clamare suas, tactumque vereri
Assilientis aquæ, timidasque reducere plantas.
Fecit et Asterien aquilâ luctante teneri;
Fecit olorinis Ledam recubare sub alis:
Addidit, ut satyri celatus imagine pulchram
Jupiter implerit gemino Nycteida fœtu;
Amphitryon fuerit, cum te, Tirynthia, cepit:
Aureus ut Danaen, Asopida luserit igneus:
Mnemosynen pastor: varius Deoïda serpens.
Te quoque mutatum torvo, Neptune, juvenco,
Virgine in Æoliâ posuit. Tu visus Enipeus
Gignis Aloidas: aries Bisaltida fallis.
Et te, flava comas, frugum mitissima mater,
Sensit equum: te sensit avem crinita colubris
Mater equi volucris: sensit Delphina Melantho.
Omnibus his faciemque suam, faciemque locorum
Reddidit. Est illic agrestis imagine Phœbus;
Utque modo accipitris pennas, modo terga leonis
Gesserit; ut pastor Macareida luserit Issen.
Liber ut Erigonen falsâ deceperit uvâ;
Ut Saturnus equo geminum Chirona crearit.
Ultima pars telæ, tenui circumdata limbo,
Nexilibus flores hederis habet intertextos."
—Metam., vi., 103-128.

4 Allay the burning pain of love.

5 Seduce, carry off. Helle, according to fable, was drowned in the sea now called the Hellespont, by falling off the golden-fleeced ram on which her mother Nephele was flying for refuge to Colchis with her two children, Helle and Phrixus. Spenser, by error or design, confounds the story of the golden ram with one of Jove's many transformations.

6 Daughter of Agenor king of Phœnicia; she was carried away to Crete by Jupiter, disguised in the form of a lovely and tame bull, on whose back Europa mounted as she was sporting with her maidens by the sea-shore. The story is beautifully told in Horace, Odes, iii. 27.

7 Danaë was the daughter of Acrisius, king of Argos; who confined her in a brazen tower, because an oracle had foretold that she would bear a son who would kill his father. But Jupiter obtained access to her prison, either by the transformation described in the text, or by the more prosaic method of bribing the guard; and the result was the birth of Perseus, who, grown to manhood, killed his grandfather at the public games by the accidental blow of his quoit.

8 Transformed to the semblance or shape of gold.

9 Wife of Tyndareus, king of Sparta; Jupiter courted her under the form of a swan, and she became the mother of Castor and Pollux.

10 Amorous commerce with him.

11 Approach, attack. 12 Secretly.

13 Juno, jealous of Semele, appeared to her under the form of her old nurse, and persuaded her to ask Jupiter to visit her in the same splendour and majesty in which his own queen knew him. Despite Jupiter's warning of her danger, Semele persisted, and her wish was granted; but she was consumed by the lightnings of the god—who, however, saved her son, Dionysus or Bacchus.

14 Wife of Amphitryon king of Thebes, and mother of Hercules. See note 28, page 261. 15 Yielding.

16 Sister of Latona and mother of Hecate; to escape from the love of Jupiter she changed herself into a quail, and threw herself down from heaven to earth.

17 Ganymede, brother of Assaracus the founder of the Trojan realm. He was the most beautiful of mortal men, and Zeus carried him off to be his cup-bearer.

18 Antiope and Ægina were daughters of the river-god Asopus, in Bœotia; the first became by Zeus the mother of Amphion and Zethus, the second of Æacus. Ægina was carried off to the island that now bears her name; and, as it was unpeopled, Zeus changed the abounding ants into men (Myrmidones), over whom Æacus might rule.

19 Daughter of Uranus (Heaven) and mother of the Muses. See note 4, page 357.

20 Deoïs, or Persephone (Proserpine), the daughter of Demeter (Δηω), is meant; but it is not easy to discover appropriateness in the epithet "Thracian."

While thus on earth great Jove these pageants play'd,
The wingëd boy did thrust into his throne,
And, scoffing, thus unto his mother said;
"Lo! now the heav'ns obey to me alone,
And take me for their Jove, while Jove to earth is gone."

And thou, fair Phœbus, in thy colours bright
Wast there enwoven, and the sad distress.
In which that boy thee plungëd, for despite
That thou betray'dst his mother's wantonness,
When she with Mars was meint[1] in joyfulness:
Forthy[2] he thrill'd thee with a leaden dart[3]
To love fair Daphne,[4] which thee lovëd less;
Less she thee lov'd than was thy just desart,
Yet was thy love her death, and her death was thy smart.

So lovedst thou the lusty Hyacinct;
So lovedst thou the fair Coronis dear:[5]
Yet both are of thy hapless hand extinct;
Yet both in flow'rs do live, and love thee bear,
The one a paunce,[6] the other a sweet-briar:
For grief whereof ye might have lively seen
The god himself rending his golden hair,
And breaking quite his garland ever green,
With other signs of sorrow and impatient teen.[7]

Both for those two, and for his own dear son,
The son of Clymené,[8] he did repent;
Who, bold to guide the chariot of the Sun,
Himself in thousand pieces fondly[9] rent,
And all the world with flashing fiër brent;[10]
So like, that all the walls did seem to flame.
Yet cruel Cupid, not herewith content,
Forc'd him eftsoons to follow other game,
And love a shepherd's daughter for his dearest dame.

He lovëd Issa[11] for his dearest dame,
And for her sake her cattle fed a while,
And for her sake a cowherd vile became:
The servant of Admetus, cowherd vile,
While that from heav'n he sufferëd exile.
Long were to tell each other lovely fit;[12]
Now, like a lion hunting after spoil;
Now, like a hag; now, like a falcon flit:[13]
All which in that fair arras was most lively writ.

Next unto him was Neptune picturëd,
In his divine resemblance wondrous like:
His face was rugged, and his hoary head
Droppëd with brackish dew; his threefork'd pike
He sternly shook, and therewith fierce did strike
The raging billows, that on ev'ry side
They trembling stood, and made a long broad dyke,
That his swift chariot might have passage wide,
Which four great hippodames[14] did draw, in team-wise tied.

His sea-horses did seem to snort amain,
And from their nostrils blow the briny stream,
That made the sparkling waves to smoke again
And flame with gold; but the white foamy cream
Did shine with silver, and shoot forth his beam:
The god himself did pensive seem and sad,
And hung adown his head as he did dream;
For privy love his breast empiercëd had,
Nor aught but dear Bisaltis[15] ay could make him glad.

He lovëd eke Iphimedia dear,
And Æolus' fair daughter, Arné hight,
For whom he turn'd himself into a steer,
And fed on fodder to beguile her sight.
Also, to win Deucalion's daughter bright,[16]
He turn'd himself into a dolphin fair;
And like a wingëd horse he took his flight
To snaky-lock[17] Medusa to repair,
On whom he got fair Pegasus that flitteth in the air.

Next Saturn was (but who would ever ween
That sullen Saturn ever ween'd to love?
Yet love is sullen, and Satúrnlike seen,
As he did for Erigoné[18] it prove),
That to a centaur did himself transmove.[19]
So prov'd it eke that gracious god of wine,
When, for to compass Philyra's hard love,
He turn'd himself into a fruitful vine,
And into her fair bosom made his grapes decline.

Long were to tell the amorous assays,
And gentle pangs, with which he makëd meek
The mighty Mars to learn his wanton plays;
How oft for Venus, and how often eke
For many other nymphs, he sore did shriek;
With womanish tears, and with unwarlike smarts,
Privily moistening his horrid cheek:

1 Mingled. In The Knight's Tale, Chaucer puts into the mouth of Arcita a reference to the incident. See note 18, page 40. 2 Therefore.

3 The golden darts of Cupid caused successful, the leaden unsuccessful love.

4 See note 12, page 37.

5 Hyacinthus, a beautiful Spartan youth, was beloved by Apollo and by Zephyrus; but the latter was not favoured, and in a fit of jealousy, when Apollo and Hyacinthus were playing at quoits, he blew the god's quoit with fatal force against the youth's head. From his blood sprang the flower called by his name. Coronis was the mother of Æsculapius by Apollo, who killed her to revenge the transference of her love to the Arcadian Ischys. She is the "Wife of Phœbus," of whom, following Ovid (Metam., ii. 531-632), Chaucer told the story in The Manciple's Tale.

6 Pansy. 7 Anguish. 8 Phaethon.

9 Foolishly. 10 Burned.

11 A Lesbian maiden, daughter of Macareus, whom Apollo wooed in the form of a shepherd. Spenser has chosen to couple with Apollo's love for Issa his servitude to Admetus, king of Pheræ, which was due to a quite different cause—to the judgment that he should serve for a year, as a mortal, a mortal man, in expiation of his murder of the Cyclopes.

12 Tale of love. 13 Fleet. 14 Sea-horses.

15 Theophane, daughter of Bisaltes; Neptune transformed her to a ewe.

16 Protogeneia was the daughter of Deucalion, but the mythology allots her to Zeus. In the passage quoted from Ovid, Melantho, the daughter of Poseidon, is named as the lady whom her own father wooed in the guise of a dolphin.

17 An exact translation of "crinita colubris." See note 3, page 438.

18 There is a singular error in this stanza; Erigone and Philyra are transposed; it was the first whom the "gracious god of wine" won "falsâ uvâ;" it was Philyra whom Saturn visited, in the form of a horse, and upon whom he begot the Centaur Chiron.

19 Transform.

There was he painted full of burning darts,
And many wide wounds lancëd through his inner parts.

Nor did he spare (so cruel was the elf)
His own dear mother (ah! why should he so!)
Nor did he spare sometimes to prick himself,
That he might taste the sweet consuming woe
Which he had wrought to many others mo'.
But to declare the mournful tragedies,
And spoils wherewith he all the ground did strow,—
More eath [1] to number with how many eyes
High heav'n beholds sad lovers' nightly thieveries.[2]

Kings, queens, lords, ladies, knights, and damsels gent,[3]
Were heap'd together with the vulgar sort,
And mingled with the rascal rabblement,
Without respect of person or of port,[4]
To show Dan Cupid's pow'r and great effórt:
And round about a border was entrail'd [5]
Of broken bows and arrows shiver'd short;
And a long bloody river through them rail'd [6]
So lively, and so like, that living sense it fail'd.[7]

And at the upper end of that fair room
There was an altar built of precious stone,
Of passing value and of great renowm,[8]
On which there stood an image all alone
Of massy gold, which with his own light shone;
And wings it had with sundry colours dight,[9]
More sundry colours than the proud pavone [10]
Bears in his boasted fan, or Iris bright,
When her discolour'd [11] bow she spreads through heaven bright.

Blindfold he was; and in his cruel fist
A mortal bow and arrows keen did hold,
With which he shot at random when him list;
Some headed with sad lead, some with pure gold;
(Ah! man, beware how thou those darts behold!)
A wounded dragon under him did lie,
Whose hideous tail his left foot did enfold,
And with a shaft was shot through either eye,
That no man forth might draw, nor no man remedý.

And underneath his feet was written thus,
Unto the victor of the gods this be:
And all the people in that ample house
Did to that image bow their humble knee,
And oft committed foul idolatry.
That wondrous sight fair Britomart amaz'd,
Nor seeing could her wonder satisfy,
But ever more and more upon it gaz'd,
The while the passing brightness her frail senses daz'd.

Then, as she backward cast her busy eye
To search each secret of that goodly stead,[12]
Over the door thus written she did spy,
Be bold: she oft and oft it over read,
Yet could not find what sense it figurëd:
But whatso were therein or writ or meant,
She was no whit thereby discouragëd
From prosecuting of her first intent,
But forward with bold steps into the next room went.

Much fairer than the former was that room,
And richlier, by many parts, array'd;
For not with arras made in painful loom,
But with pure gold it all was overlaid,
Wrought with wild antics,[13] which their follies play'd
In the rich metal, as they living were:
A thousand monstrous forms therein were made,
Such as false Love doth oft upon him wear;
For Love in thousand monstrous forms doth oft appear.

And, all about, the glist'ring walls were hung
With warlike spoils, and with victorious preys
Of mighty conquerors and captains strong,
Which were whilóm captívëd in their days
To cruel Love, and wrought their own decays:[14]
Their swords and spears were broke, and hauberks rent,
And their proud garlands of triumphant bays
Trodden in dust with fury insolent,
To show the victor's might and merciless intent.[15]

The warlike Maid marvelled much at the rich array of the place, but more that no trace of habitation or life appeared. Everywhere her eye encountered the inscription, "Be bold;" but at the upper end of the room was an iron door, and on it written, "Be not too bold." Those enigmatical counsels and cautions filled her with great perplexity. She waited until eventide without seeing any one; then, neither doffing her armour nor resigning herself to sleep, "she drew herself aside in sickerness."[16]

CANTO XII.

The Masque of Cupid, and the enchanted chamber are display'd;
Whence Britomart redeems fair Amoret, through charms decay'd.

THEN, when as cheerless Night y-cover'd had
Fair heaven with a universal cloud,
That ev'ry wight, dismay'd with darkness sad,
In silence and in sleep themselves did shroud,
She heard a shrilling trumpet sound aloud
Sign of nigh battle, or got victorý:
Naught therewith daunted was her courage proud,
But rather stirr'd to cruel enmitý,
Expecting ever when some foe she might descry.

With that, a hideous storm of wind arose,
With dreadful thunder and lightning atwixt,

1 Easy. 2 That is, it were easier to count the stars. 3 Noble. 4 Carriage, dignity. 5 Interwoven. 6 Flowed. 7 Deceived. 8 Written for "renown," for the sake of the rhyme; French, "renommée"

9 Set out, adorned. 10 Peacock. 11 Variegated, parti-coloured. 12 Place. 13 Fantastic devices. 14 Ruin. 15 Mind. 16 Into a position of safety.

And an earthquake, as if it straight would loose
The world's foundations from his centre fixt:
A direful stench of smoke and sulphur mixt
Ensued, whose noyance[1] fill'd the fearful stead
From the fourth hour of night until the sixt;
Yet the bold Britoness was naught y-dread,[2]
Though much enmov'd, but steadfast still persévered.

All suddenly a stormy whirlwind blew
Throughout the house, that clappëd ev'ry door;
With which that iron wicket open flew,
As it with mighty levers had been tore;
And forth issúed, as on the ready floor
Of some theátre, a grave personage
That in his hand a branch of laurel bore,
With comely 'haviour and count'nance sage,
Y-clad in costly garments fit for tragic stage.

Proceeding to the midst, he still did stand,
As if in mind he somewhat had to say;
And to the vulgar[3] beckoning with his hand,
In sign of silence, as to hear a play,
By lively actións he gan bewray[4]
Some argument of matter passionëd;
Which done, he back retirëd soft away,
And, passing by, his name discoverëd,
Ease, on his robe in golden letters cipherëd.

The noble Maid, still standing, all this view'd,
And marvell'd at his strange intendiment:[5]
With that a joyous fellowship[6] issúed
Of minstrels making goodly merriment,
With wanton bards, and rhymers impudent;
All which together sang full cheerfully
A lay of love's delight with sweet concent:[7]
After whom march'd a jolly company,
In manner of a masque, enrangëd orderly.

The while a most delicious harmony
In full strange notes was sweetly heard to sound,
That the rare sweetness of the melody
The feeble senses wholly did confound,
And the frail soul in deep delight nigh drown'd:
And, when it ceas'd, shrill trumpets loud did bray,
That their report did far away rebound;[8]
And, when they ceas'd, it gan again to play,
The while the masquers marchëd forth in trim array.

The first was Fancy, like a lovely boy
Of rare aspéct and beauty without peer,
Matchable either to that imp[9] of Troy,
Whom Jove did love and chose his cup to bear;
Or that same dainty lad, which was so dear
To great Alcides, that, when as he died,
He wailëd womanlike with many a tear,
And ev'ry wood and ev'ry valley wide
He fill'd with Hylas' name; the nymphs eke Hylas cried.

His garment neither was of silk nor say,[10]
But painted plumes in goodly order dight,
Like as the sunburnt Indians do array
Their tawny bodies in their proudest plight:
As those same plumes, so seem'd he vain and light,
That by his gait might easily appear;
For still he far'd as dancing in delight,
And in his hand a windy fan did bear,
That in the idle air he mov'd still here and there.

And him beside march'd amorous Desire,
Who seem'd of riper years than th' other swain,
Yet was that other swain this elder's sire,
And gave him being, common to them twain:
His garment was disguisëd very vain,[11]
And his embroider'd bonnet sat awry:
'Twixt both his hands few sparks he close did strain,
Which still he blew and kindled busily,
That soon they life conceiv'd, and forth in flames did fly.

Next after him went Doubt, who was y-clad
In a discolour'd[12] coat of strange disguise,
That at his back a broad cappuccio[13] had,
And sleeves dependent Albanesë-wise;[14]
He look'd askew with his mistrustful eyes,
And nicely trod, as thorns lay in his way,
Or that the floor to shrink he did advise;[15]
And on a broken reed he still did stay
His feeble steps, which shrank when hard thereon he lay.

With him went Danger, cloth'd in ragged weed
Made of bear's skin, that him more dreadful made;
Yet his own face was dreadful, nor did need
Strange horror[16] to deform his grisly shade:[17]
A net in th' one hand, and a rusty blade
In th' other was; this Mischief, that Mishap;
With th' one his foes he threaten'd to invade,
With th' other he his friends meant to enwrap:
For whom he could not kill he practis'd to entrap.

Next him was Fear, all arm'd from top to toe,
Yet thought himself not safe enough thereby,
But fear'd each shadow moving to or fro;
And, his own arms when glitt'ring he did spy,
Or clashing heard, he fast away did fly,
As ashes pale of hue, and wingëd-heel'd;
And evermore on Danger fix'd his eye,
'Gainst whom he always bent a brazen shield,
Which his right hand unarmëd fearfully did wield.

With him went Hope in rank, a handsome maid,
Of cheerful look and lovely to behold;
In silken samite[18] she was light array'd,
And her fair locks were woven up in gold:
She always smil'd, and in her hand did hold
A holy-water-sprinkle, dipt in dew,
With which she sprinkled favours manifold
On whom she list, and did great liking shew;
Great liking unto many, but true love to few.

1 Annoyance.
2 Terrified.
3 The crowd, the audience.
4 Reveal, unfold.
5 Meaning, design.
6 Company.
7 Harmony.
8 Re-echo.
9 Youth.
10 Thin silk stuff.
11 Fantastically fashioned or trimmed.
12 Many-coloured.
13 Capuchin, or hood; called after the Capuchin monks, from whose dress it was imitated.
14 Loose hanging sleeves in the Albanian fashion.
15 Perceive.
16 Any horror but its own, any foreign horror.
17 Appearance.
18 A light fine silk fabric.

And after them Dissemblance and Suspect[1]
March'd in one rank, yet an unequal pair;
For she was gentle and of mild aspéct,
Courteous to all and seeming debonair,[2]
Goodly adornëd and exceeding fair;
Yet was that all but painted and purloin'd,
And her bright brows were deck'd with borrow'd hair;
Her deeds were forgëd, and her words false coin'd,
And always in her hand two clews of silk she twin'd:

But he was foul, ill favourëd, and grim,
Under his eyebrows looking still askance;
And ever, as Dissemblance laugh'd on him,
He lour'd on her with dangerous[3] eye-glance,
Showing his nature in his countenance;
His rolling eyes did never rest in place,
But walk'd each where for fear of hid mischance;
Holding a lattice still before his face,
Through which he still did peep as forward he did pace.

Next him went Grief and Fury match'd y-fere;[4]
Grief all in sable sorrowfully clad,
Down hanging his dull head with heavy cheer,
Yet inly being more than seeming sad:
A pair of pincers in his hand he had,
With which he pinchëd people to the heart,
That from thenceforth a wretched life they lad,[5]
In wilful languor and consuming smart,
Dying each day with inward wounds of dolour's dart.

But Fury was full ill apparellëd
In rags, that naked nigh she did appear,
With ghastly looks and dreadful drearihead;[6]
And from her back her garments she did tear,
And from her head oft rent her snarlëd[7] hair:
In her right hand a firebrand she did toss
About her head, still roaming here and there;
As a dismayëd deer in chase embost,[8]
Forgetful of his safety, hath his right way lost.

After them went Displeasure and Pleasánce,
He looking lumpish and full sullen sad,
And hanging down his heavy countenance;
She cheerful, fresh, and full of joyance glad,
As if no sorrow she nor felt nor drad;[9]
That evil matchëd pair they seem'd to be:
An angry wasp th' one in a vial had,
Th' other in hers an honey lady-bee.
Thus marchëd these six couples forth in fair degree.

After all these there march'd a most fair Dame,[10]
Led of two greasy[11] villains, th' one Despite,
The other clepëd[12] Cruelty by name:
She, doleful lady, like a dreary sprite
Call'd by strong charms out of eternal night,
Had Death's own image figur'd in her face,
Full of sad signs, fearful to living sight;
Yet in that horror show'd a seemly grace,
And with her feeble feet did move a comely pace.

Her breast all naked, as net[13] ivory
Without adorn of gold or silver bright
Wherewith the craftsman wonts it beautify,
Of her due honour was despoilëd quite;
And a wide wound therein (O rueful sight!)
Entrenchëd deep with knife accursëd keen,
Yet freshly bleeding forth her fainting sprite,
(The work of cruel hand) was to be seen,
That dy'd in sanguine red her skin all snowy clean:

At that wide orifice her trembling heart
Was drawn forth, and in silver basin laid,
Quite through transfixëd with a deadly dart,
And in her blood yet steaming fresh embay'd.[14]
And those two villains (which her steps upstay'd,
When her weak feet could scarcely her sustain,
And fading vital powers gan to fade),
Her forward still with torture did constrain,
And evermore increasëd her consuming pain.

Next after her, the wingëd god himself
Came riding on a lion ravenous,
Taught to obey the menage[15] of that Elf
That man and beast with pow'r imperious
Subdueth to his kingdom tyrannous:
His blindfold eyes he bade a while unbind,
That his proud spoil of that same dolorous
Fair dame he might behold in perfect kind;[16]
Which seen, he much rejoicëd in his cruel mind.

Of which full proud, himself uprearing high,
He lookëd round about with stern disdain,
And did survey his goodly company;
And, marshalling the evil-order'd train,
With that the darts which his right hand did strain
Full dreadfully he shook, that all did quake,
And clapp'd on high his colour'd wingës twain,
That all his many[17] it afraid did make:
Then, blinding him again, his way he forth did take.

Behind him was Reproach, Repentance, Shame;
Reproach the first, Shame next, Repent behind:
Repentance feeble, sorrowful, and lame;
Reproach despiteful, careless, and unkind;
Shame most ill-favour'd, bestial, and blind:
Shame lour'd, Repentance sigh'd, Reproach did scold;
Reproach sharp stings, Repentance whips entwin'd,
Shame burning brand-irons in her hand did hold:
All three to each unlike, yet all made in one mould.

And after them a rude confusëd rout
Of persons flock'd, whose names is hard to read:[18]

1 Suspicion.
2 Gracious.
3 Suspicious.
4 Together.
5 Led.
6 Dismal, terrible air.
7 Matted, tangled.
8 Hard pressed.
9 Dreaded.
10 Amoretta.
11 Squalid, gross
12 Called.
13 Pure.
14 Bathed.
15 Management.
16 Manner.
17 Company.
18 Declare.

Amongst them was stern Strife; and Anger
stout;
Unquiet Care; and fond Unthriftihead;[1]
Lewd Loss of Time; and Sorrow seeming dead;
Inconstant Change; and false Disloyalty;
Consuming Riotise; and guilty Dread
Of heav'nly vengeance; faint Infirmity;
Vile Poverty; and, lastly, Death with infamy.

There were full many more like maladies,
Whose names and natures I n'ot readen well;[2]
So many more, as there be fantasies
In wavering women's wit, that none can tell,
Or pains in love, or punishments in hell:
All which disguisëd march'd in masking wise
About the chamber by the damosel;
And then returnëd, having marchëd thrice,
Into the inner room from whence they first did
rise.

So soon as they had entered, the door was closed, as it had been opened, by a blast of wind; and Britomart, issuing from her post of safety, vainly sought with force and with sleight to open it. She therefore resolved to wait till the masque appeared on the morrow; and when, on the second evening, the brazen door flew open, the Maiden entered fearlessly, "neither of idle shows nor of false charms aghast." Casting her eyes around, she found none of all the masquers; no living wight was there, save that same woeful lady, whose hands were bound fast, "and her small waist girt round with iron bands unto a brazen pillar, by the which she stands." Before her sat the vile enchanter, "figuring strange charácters of his art" in the living blood "dreadfully dropping from her dying heart," with the vain hope to charm her into loving him. Seeing Britomart, he overthrew his wicked books, and ran fiercely with a murderous knife to kill the lady true; but the Virgin Knight "his cursëd hand withheld, and masterëd his might." But now Busirane turned his wicked weapon against the deliverer, and "unwares it struck into her snowy chest, that little drops empurpled her fair breast." Wrathfully drawing her mortal blade, Britomart smote him to the ground half-dead; and she would have slain him outright, if Amoretta had not called on her to abstain, for he alone could undo the charm that wrought her pain. Britomart therefore spared his life, on condition that he should restore the captive dame immediately to her health and former state. The enchanter submitted;

And, rising up, gan straight to overlook
Those cursëd leaves, his charms back to reverse:
Full dreadful things out of that baleful book
He read, and measur'd many a sad verse,
That horror gan the Virgin's heart to perse,[3]
And her fair locks upstarëd stiff on end,
Hearing him those same bloody lines rehearse;
And, all the while he read, she did extend
Her sword high over him, if[4] aught he did offend.

Anon she gan perceive the house to quake,
And all the doors to rattle round about;
Yet all that did not her dismayëd make,
Nor slack her threatful hand for danger's doubt,
But still with steadfast eye and courage stout
Abode, to weet[5] what end would come of all:
At last that mighty chain, which round about
Her tender waist was wound, adown gan fall,
And that great brazen pillar broke in pieces
small.

The cruel steel, which thrill'd her dying heart,
Fell softly forth, as of its own accord;
And the wide wound, which lately did dispart
Her bleeding breast, and riven bowels gor'd,
Was closëd up, as it had not been sor'd;[6]
And ev'ry part to safëty full sound,
As she were never hurt, was soon restor'd:
Then, when she felt herself to be unbound
And perfect whole, prostráte she fell unto the
ground

Before Britomart, with eloquent utterances of praise and gratitude. Raising her up, the Maid replied that to have delivered her was sufficient reward, and bade her displace the memory of her past pain by the thought that "her gentle make[7] had no less grief endurëd for her gentle sake." Amoretta was much cheered by the mention of her lover; and Britomart then bound the enchanter with the same great chain that lately fastened his fair captive to the pillar.

Returning back, those goodly rooms, which erst
She saw so rich and royally array'd,
Now vanish'd utterly and clean subvers'd
She found, and all their glory quite decay'd;
That sight of such a change her much dismay'd.
Thence forth descending to that perilous porch,
Those dreadful flames she also found delay'd[8]
And quenchëd quite like a consumëd torch,
That erst all ent'rers wont so cruelly to scorch.

More easy issue now than entrance late
She found; for now that feignëd-dreadful flame,
Which chok'd the porch of that enchanted gate,
And passage barr'd to all that thither came,
Was vanish'd quite, as it were not the same,
And gave her leave at pleasure forth to pass.
Th' enchanter's self, which all that fraud did
frame
To have efforc'd the love of that fair lass,
Seeing his work now wasted, deep engrievëd was.

But, on arriving at the gate, they were astonished and grieved to find no Scudamour; for he had certainly believed that Britomart had perished in the flames, and, with the sorrowing Glaucé, he had ridden away in search of further aid.[10]

1 Foolish Unthrift. 2 I cannot well tell.
3 Pierce. 4 In case. 5 Learn.
6 As if it had never been inflicted.
7 Mate; Scudamour.
8 But a little while before. 9 Assuaged, stopped.
10 When the first three books of "The Faerie Queen" were printed, in 1590, seven stanzas not given in subsequent editions stood at the end of the third book, narrating the happy reunion of Scudamour and Amoret, and closing up their story in this wise:

"Thus do those lovers, with sweet countervail,
Each other of love's bitter fruit despoil.
But now my team begins to faint and fail,
All woxen weary of their journal toil;

THE FOURTH BOOK

OF

THE FAERIE QUEEN:

CONTAINING

THE LEGEND OF CAMBELL AND TRIAMOND, OR OF FRIENDSHIP.

THE rugged forehead,[1] that with grave foresight
Wields kingdoms' causes and affairs of state,
My looser rhymes, I wot, doth sharply wite,[2]
For praising love as I have done of late,
And magnifying lovers' dear debate;
By which frail youth is oft to folly led,
Through false allurement of that pleasing bait,
That better were in virtues disciplĕd,[3]
Than with vain poems' weeds to have their fancies fed.

Such ones ill judge of love, that cannot love,
Nor in their frozen hearts feel kindly flame:
Forthy[4] they ought not thing unknown reprove,
Nor natural affection faultless blame
For fault of few that have abus'd the same:
For it of honour and all virtue is
The root, and brings forth glorious flow'rs of fame,
That crown true lovers with immortal bliss,
The meed of them that love, and do not live amiss.

Which whoso list[5] look back to former ages,
And call to count[6] the things that then were done,
Shall find that all the works of those wise sages,
And brave exploits which great herŏës won,
In love were either ended or begun:
Witness the Father of Philosophy,[7]
Which to his Critias, shaded oft from sun,
Of love full many lessons did apply,
The which these Stoic censors cannot well deny.

To such therefŏre I do not sing at all;
But to that sacred Saint, my sov'reign Queen,
In whose chaste breast all bounty[8] natural
And treasures of true love enlockĕd be'n,[9]
'Bove all her sex that ever yet was seen;
To her I sing of love, that loveth best,
And best is lov'd of all alive, I ween;
To her this song most fitly is addrest,
The Queen of Love, and Prince of Peace from heaven blest.

Which that she may the better deign to hear,
Do thou, dread Infant,[10] Venus' darling dove,
From her high spirit chase imperious fear,[11]
And use of awful majesty remove:
Instead thereof with drops of melting love,
Dew'd with ambrosial kisses, by thee gotten
From thy sweet-smiling mother from above,
Sprinkle her heart, and haughty courage soften,
That she may hark to love, and read this lesson often.

CANTO I.

Fair Britomart saves Amoret:
Duessa discord breeds
'Twixt Scudamour and Blandamour:
Their fight and warlike deeds.

No more piteous story "of lovers' sad calamities of old" was ever told—so says the poet—"than that of Amoret's heart-binding chain, and this of Florimell's unworthy pain;" which he full often pities with tears, and wishes it had never been written. Amoret had "never joyĕd day" since Scudamour won her from twenty knights in battle, and with her the Shield of Love. On their wedding-day, the enchanter Busirane brought in that masque of Love which Britomart had seen; and, while the guests were heedless with wine, he had carried the bride away, as if in sport, to the place of torment whence the Virgin Knight had released her, after seven months' captivity. Now, riding beside her deliverer, Amoret "right fearful was and faint lest she with blame her honour should attaint;" for the "virgin wife" did not know the real sex of her companion; and her words trembled, her looks were coy and strange, "and ev'ry limb that touched her did quake." One evening the pair came to a castle at which a gay company was "assembled deeds of arms to see," and where it was the custom that whosoever had no love or leman present "should either win him one, or lie without the door." A jolly knight claimed Amoret for his love; but he was overthrown by Britomart—who, since he seemed valiant, cast in her mind how she might reconcile the admittance of the knight with the custom of the castle. She claimed Amoret as hers of right; then, as a lady, she claimed the knight for herself.

With that, her glist'ring helmet she unlaced;
Which doff'd, her golden locks, that were upbound
Still in a knot, unto her heels down traced,[12]

> Therefore I will their sweaty yokes assoil
> At this same furrow's end, till a new day;
> And ye, fair swains, after your long turmoil,
> Now cease your work, and at your pleasure play;
> Now cease your work; to-morrow is a holiday."

When, in 1596, Spenser reprinted the first three books with the first issue of the second three, he opened up again the story of Scudamour and Amoret, by substituting for the original seven closing stanzas the three in the text, and thus carrying forward into the new portion of his work the interest enlisted by the old.

1 Spenser is understood to refer to Burleigh, whose "censure grave" he had sought to conciliate in an introductory sonnet (page 307), but who had not been softened by the poet's flattering deprecation, and had treated the first three books of "The Faerie Queen" with much severity of judgment. "The rugged forehead," is not to be taken as a personal description; in the sonnet to Sir Christopher Hatton, Spenser had spoken of "the rugged brow of careful Policy."

2 Censure. 3 Disciplined. 4 Therefore.

5 Pleases (to). 6 To account, to memory.

7 Socrates. Here again the poet confounds Critias and Crito—both were disciples of Socrates, but the last was faithful to the teachings and the teacher to the end, while the first rendered himself odious by rapacity and cruelty in office. See note 13, page 386.

8 Goodness, virtue. 9 Are. 10 Cupid.

11 The imperious mood inspiring fear.

12 Went, flowed.

And like a silken veil in compass round
About her back and all her body wound:
Like as the shining sky in summer's night,
What time the days with scorching heat abound,
Is crested all with lines of fiery light,
That it prodigious seems in common people's
sight.

Such when those knights and ladies all about
Beheld her, all were with amazement smit,
And ev'ry one gan grow in secret doubt
Of this and that, according to each wit:
Some thought that some enchantment feignëd it;
Some, that Bellona in that warlike wise
To them appear'd, with shield and armour fit;
Some, that it was a masque of strange disguise:
So diversely each one did sundry doubts devise.

The young knight, now "doubly overcome," adored her; and Amoret, freed from fear, laid aside all her constraint. The pair spent all the night discoursing of their loves, and in the morning set out anew on their wanderings. At last they spied two armed knights riding towards them, each with a false but seeming-fair lady by his side: one of the dames the false Duessa in another of her many shapes; the other, no better than she, but more plainly showing what she was.

Her name was Até, mother of debate[1]
And all dissension which doth daily grow
Amongst frail men, that many a public state,
And many a private, oft doth overthrow.
Her false Duessa, who full well did know
To be most fit to trouble noble knights
Which hunt for honour, raisëd from below,
Out of the dwellings of the damnëd sprites,
Where she in darkness wastes her cursëd days
and nights.

Hard by the gates of hell her dwelling is;
There, where as all the plagues and harms
abound
Which punish wicked men that walk amiss:
It is a darksome delve[2] far under ground,
With thorns and barren brakes[3] environ'd round,
That none the same may easily out win;[4]
Yet many ways to enter may be found,
But none to issue forth when one is in:
For discord harder is to end than to begin.

And all within the riven walls were hung
With ragged monuments of times forepast,[5]
All which the sad effects of discord sung:
There were rent robes and broken sceptres
plac'd;
Altars defil'd, and holy things defac'd;
Disshiver'd spears, and shields y-torn in twain;
Great cities ransack'd, and strong castles ras'd;
Nations captivëd, and huge armies slain:
Of all which ruins there some relics did remain.

There was the sign[6] of ántique Babylon;
Of fatal Thebes; of Rome that reignëd long;
Of sacred Salem; and sad Ilion,
For memory of which on high there hung
The Golden Apple, cause of all their wrong,
For which the three fair goddesses did strive:[7]
There also was the name of Nimrod strong;
Of Alexander, and his princes five[8]
Which shar'd to them the spoils that he had got
alive:

And there the relics of the drunken fray,
The which amongst the Lapithæ befell;
And of the bloody feast, which sent away
So many Centaurs' drunken souls to hell,
That under great Alcides' fury fell:[9]
And of the dreadful discord, which did drive
The noble Argonauts to outrage fell,
That each of life sought others to deprive,
All mindless of the Golden Fleece, which made
them strive.

And eke of private persons many mo',
That were too long a work to count them all;
Some, of sworn friends that did their faith
forego;
Some, of born brethren prov'd unnatural;
Some, of dear lovers foes perpetual:
Witness their broken bands there to be seen,
Their garlands rent, their bow'rs despoilëd all;
The monuments whereof there biding be'n,[10]
As plain as at the first when they were fresh
and green.

Such was her house within; but all without
The barren ground was full of wicked weeds,
Which she herself had sowen all about,
Now growen great, at first of little seeds,
The seeds of evil words and factious deeds;
Which, when to ripeness due they growen are,
Bring forth an infinite increase, that breeds
Tumultuous trouble, and contentious jar,
The which most often end in bloodshed and in
war.

And those same cursëd seeds do also serve
To her for bread, and yield her living food:
For life it is to her, when others sterve[11]
Through mischievous debate[1] and deadly feud,
That she may suck their life and drink their
blood,
With which she from her childhood had been fed:
For she at first was born of hellish brood,

1 Strife Até was the divinity, among the ancient Greeks, who led men and gods into rash and heedless acts. In the second book of "The Faerie Queen," the same part is played by a masculine personage, named "Atin." See note 4, page 377."

2 Cave, hollow. 3 Brackens.

4 Find out. 5 Gone past. 6 Representation.

7 The goddess of Discord, Eris, enraged that she was not invited to the marriage of Peleus and Thetis, threw among the gods a golden apple, inscribed "to the fairest." When Hera, Athena, and Aphrodite, each claiming the apple, appeared to submit their charms to the judgment of Paris, the goddess of Love won the apple by promising the judge for his wife the fairest woman on earth—Helen, whose abduction led to the war of Troy.

8 Alexander's empire was divided among four of his generals—Cassander, Lysimachus, Seleucus Nicator, and Ptolemy Lagus—after the attempt of a fifth, Antigonus, to reign over the whole, had been frustrated.

9 The war of the Lapithæ and the Centaurs being terminated by a peace, the Centaurs were invited to the marriage-feast of Pirithous, king of the Lapithæ, and Hippodamia. The guests attempted to carry off the bride and the other women; and a bloody fight ensued, in which the Centaurs were defeated.

10 Are remaining.

11 Perish, die.

And by infernal Furies nourishëd;
That by her monstrous shape might easily be read.[1]

Her face most foul and filthy was to see,
With squinted eyes contrảry ways intended,[2]
And loathly mouth, unmeet a mouth to be,
That naught but gall and venom comprehended,
And wicked words that God and man offended:
Her lying tongue was in two parts divided,
And both the parts did speak, and both contended;
And as her tongue so was her heart discided,[3]
That never thought one thing, but doubly still was guided.

Als'[4] as she double spake, so heard she double,
With matchless[5] ears deformëd and distort',
Fill'd with false rumours and seditious trouble
Bred in assemblies of the vulgar sort,
That still are led with ev'ry light report:
And as her ears, so eke her feet were odd,
And much unlike; th' one long, the other short,
And both misplac'd; that, when th' one forward yode,[6]
The other back retirëd and contrảry trod.

Likewise unequal were her handës twain;
That one did reach, the other push'd away;
That one did make, the other marr'd again,
And sought to bring all things unto decay;
Whereby great riches gather'd many a day
She in short space did often bring to naught,
And their possessors often did dismay:[7]
For all her study was, and all her thought,
How she might overthrow the things that Concord wrought.

So much her malice did her might surpass,
That even th' Almighty's self she did malign,
Because to man so merciful he was,
And unto all his creatures so benign,
Since she herself was of his grace indign:[8]
For all this world's fair workmanship she tried
Unto its last confusión to bring,
And that great golden chain quite to divide,
With which it blessed Concord hath together tied.

Such was that hag, who, serving as Duessa's bawd, aided her in the malicious work of hurting good knights; for which end Duessa had assumed an aspect "as fresh and fragrant as the flower-de-luce." Her mate was the fickle-minded and inconstant Blandamour; and with him rode the false Sir Paridell. Seeing Britomart approach with Amoret, Blandamour incited Paridell to win the lady for his own; but Paridell, remembering his overthrow by Britomart before the castle of Malbecco, declined the encounter; whereupon Blandamour resigned to his companion his own lady, and pricked against the warlike Britoness, to challenge Amoret for his fee. But the Maid pitched her assailant out of his saddle, and rode disdainfully on, leaving him consumed with wondrous grief of mind and shame. Dissembling his vexation, he continued the journey with the rest of his company, and soon espied two knights approaching with speed. Blandamour was now more distressed than ever, discerning that one of the pair was Scudamour, "whom mortally he hated evermore;" and he besought Sir Paridell to repay him for his recent good turn, "and justify his cause on yonder knight"—since, through his wounds in the encounter with Britomart, he could not combat himself. Paridell consented; "myself will for you fight as you have done for me; the left hand rubs the right." Paridell then rushed against Scudamour; and both were unhorsed in the shock.

As when two billows in the Irish Sounds,
Forcibly driven with contrảry tides,
Do meet together, each aback rebounds
With roaring rage; and dashing on all sides,
That filleth all the sea with foam, divides
The doubtful current into diverse ways:
So fell those two in spite of both their prides;
But Scudamour himself did soon upraise,
And, mounting light, his foe for lying long upbrays.[9]

Paridell, however, all "rolled on a heap," lay still in swoon, till his companions ran to him, undid his helmet and mail, and at last restored him to consciousness. Blandamour meantime reviled Sir Scudamour for overthrowing "by sleight and foul advantage" a knight so much better than himself; and lamented that he was not himself in a condition to avenge the wrong done to his friend. Scudamour "little answered," though his mighty indignation plainly beclouded his face. The crafty Duessa now interposed, asking why they should strive so sore for ladies' love, and bidding Scudamour not be wroth that his lady "list love another knight; nor do yourself dislike a whit the more; for love is free, and led with self-delight, nor will enforcëd be with mastery of might." "Vile Até" reiterated in even broader terms the accusation of "false Duessa" against the honour of Amoret; and, conjured to tell what she had seen, she answered that she had seen a stranger knight, whose name she knew not, but in his shield he bore the heads of many broken spears:

"I saw him have your Amoret at will;
I saw him kiss; I saw him her embrace;
I saw him sleep with her all night his fill;
All, many nights; and many by in place
That present were to testify the case."
Which when as Scudamour did hear, his heart
Was thrill'd with inward grief: as when in chase
The Parthian strikes a stag with shiv'ring dart,
The beast astonish'd stands in middest of his smart;

So stood Sir Scudamour when this he heard,
Nor word he had to speak for great dismay,
But look'd on Glaucé grim, who wox afear'd
Of outrage for the words which she heard say,

1 Discerned. 2 Directed. 3 Cleft asunder. 4 Also. 5 Unmatched, dissimilar. 6 Went. 7 Overthrow, destroy. 8 Unworthy. 9 Upbraids.

Although untrue she wist them by assay.[1]
But Blandamour, when as he did espy
His change of cheer, that anguish did bewray,
He wox full blithe, as he had got[2] thereby,
And gan thereat to triumph without victory.

He taunted Scudamour on "the fruitless end of his vain boast, and spoil of love misgotten," assuring him that "all things not rooted well will soon be rotten;" while false Duessa chimed in with opprobrious and jeering words. Scudamour, for passing great despite, with difficulty restrained himself from slaying guiltless Glaucé; and he bitterly exclaimed against "discourteous, disloyal Britomart, untrue to God, and unto man unjust," who had "defiled the pledge committed to her trust"—for Scudamour is still unaware that Britomart is a maiden. Thrice, in his flaming fury, did the Knight raise his hand to kill the aged squire "whose lord had done his love this foul despite;" "and thrice he drew it back; so did at last forbear."

CANTO II.

Blandamour wins false[3] Florimell;
Paridell for her strives:
They are accorded:[4] Agapé
Doth lengthen her sons' lives.

FIREBRAND of hell, first tin'd[5] in Phlegethon
By thousand Furies, and from thence out thrown
Into this world, to work confusión,
And set it all on fire by force unknown,
Is wicked Discord; whose small sparks, once blown,
None but a god or godlike man can slake:
Such as was Orpheus, that, when strife was grown
Amongst those famous imps of Greece,[6] did take
His silver harp in hand, and shortly friends them make:

Or such as that celestial Psalmist was,
That, when the wicked fiend his lord[7] tormented,
With heav'nly notes, that did all other pass,
The outrage of his furious fit relented.[8]
Such music is wise words, with time concented,[9]
To moderate stiff minds dispos'd to strive:
Such as that prudent Roman[10] well invented;
What time his people into parts did rive,[11]
Them reconcil'd again, and to their homes did drive.

Such wise words did Glaucé use to calm the furious Sir Scudamour; while Blandamour and Paridell set her at naught. As they rode thus, they met the feigned or "snowy" Florimell, with the knight who had carried her off from Braggadocio, and who was called, as we now learn, "Sir Ferraugh." Blandamour, stung with desire to have the lovely lady—for his fancy light "was always flitting as the wav'ring wind after each beauty that appear'd in sight"—incited the dumpish Paridell to fight for her; but Paridell made "fair denial," and Blandamour spurred hotly against Ferraugh, whom with the sudden onset he unhorsed, and whose dame he vauntingly bore away. The snowy lady made semblance of love to her new lord, till "he seemëd brought to bed in paradise," so thoroughly did her deceits win his soul away. But Paridell envied him, "as seeming plac'd in sole felicity;" and Até, finding now fit opportunity to stir up strife, "did privily put coals into his secret fire." At last, Paridell reminds Blandamour of their covenant that every spoil or prey should be shared equally between them, and demands his part in the "lady bright." Blandamour answers with angry and taunting words; and the knights, forgetting all their friendship, ride against and unhorse each other.

As when two warlike brigantines at sea,
With murderous weapons arm'd to cruel fight,
Do meet together on the watery lea,[12]
They stem[13] each other with so fell despite,
That with the shock of their own heedless might
Their wooden ribs are shaken nigh asunder;
They which from shore behold the dreadful sight
Of flashing fire, and hear the ordnance thunder,
Do greatly stand amaz'd at such unwonted wonder.

But soon both start up in amaze, and fly at each other "like two mad mastiffs;" while their ladies, far from interposing, goad them on to fight with many provocative words. The poet thinks that they might be fighting yet, if the Squire of Dames had not come that way, and, first laying "on those ladies thousand blames" for fomenting the strife, humbly besought the knights to stay their hands. On their reluctant compliance, he inquires the cause of strife; and, being told that it is for the love of Florimell, he expresses his wonder how that could be, "and she so far astray, as none could tell." But Paridell angrily points out to him the lady there present; and the Squire, convinced that he beholds the true Florimell, instantly makes his obeisances—"for none alive but joy'd in Florimell." He then seeks to persuade the knights to join in friendship for her sake; and, to strengthen his counsel, tells them how Sir Satyrane had found the golden girdle of Florimell, "which for her sake he wore, as him beseemëd well."

"But when as she herself was lost and gone,
Full many knights, that lovëd her like[14] dear,
Thereat did greatly grudge, that he alone
That lost fair lady's ornament should wear,
And gan therefor close[15] spite to him to bear;

1 Experience. 2 As if he had gained.
3 The feigned. 4 Reconciled.
5 Kindled.
6 Youths or children of Greece; the Argonauts, whom Orpheus accompanied on their expedition to fetch the golden fleece.
7 Saul. See 1 Samuel, chap. xvi.
8 Softened, assuaged. 9 Harmonised.
10 Menenius Agrippa; who, when the Roman populace withdrew to the Mons Sacer, persuaded them to return by the well-known fable of the Belly and the Members, reproduced by Shakespeare in "Coriolanus," act i. scene i. 11 Divide. 12 Plain.
13 Strike against. 14 Equally. 15 Secret.

Which he to shun, and stop vile envy's sting,
Hath lately caus'd to be proclaim'd each where
A solemn feast, with public tourneying,
To which all knights with them their ladies are to bring:

"And of them all she that is fairest found
Shall have that golden girdle for reward;
And of those knights, who is most stout on ground,
Shall to that fairest lady be prefar'd.[1]
Since therefore she herself is now your ward,
To you that ornament of hers pertains,
Against all those that challenge it, to guard,
And save her honour with your venturous pains;
That shall you win more glory, than ye here find gains."

Hearing "the reason of his words," they abate their malice, swear new friendship, and ride forth together "in friendly sort, that lasted but a while; and of all old dislikes they made fair weather; yet all was forg'd and spread with golden foil, that under it hid hate and hollow guile." Thus marching all "in close disguise of feignëd love," they overtake two knights in close friendly conference, followed by "two ladies of most goodly hue," who, in courteous discourse with each other, are "unmindful both of that discordful crew." The overtaking company send forward the Squire of Dames to reconnoitre; and he returns with the news that they are two of the bravest knights in Faery Land, and those two ladies their two lovers dear; "Courageous Cambell, and stout Triamond, with Canacé and Cambine link'd in lovely bond."

Whilóm, as antique stories tellen us,
Those two were foes the felonest[2] on ground,
And battle made the dreadest dangerous
That ever shrilling trumpet did resound;
Though now their acts be nowhere to be found,
As that renownëd poet them compil'd
With warlike numbers and heroic sound,
Dan Chaucer, Well of English undefil'd,
On Fame's eternal beadroll worthy to be fil'd.

But wicked Time, that all good thoughts doth waste,
And works of noblest wits to naught outwear,
That famous monument hath quite defac'd,
And robb'd the world of treasure endless dear,
The which might have enrichëd all us here.
O cursed eld,[3] the canker-worm of writs![4]
How may these rhymes, so rude as doth appear,
Hope to endure, since works of heav'nly wits
Are quite devour'd, and brought to naught by little bits!

Then pardon, O most sacred happy spirit,
That I thy labours lost may thus revive,
And steal from thee the meed of thy due merit,
That none durst ever whilst thou wast alive,
And, being dead, in vain yet many strive:
Nor dare I like; but, through infusion sweet
Of thine own spirit which doth in me survive,
I follow here the footing of thy feet,
That with thy meaning so I may the rather meet.[5]

Cambello's sister was fair Canacé,
That was the learned'st lady in her days,
Well seen[6] in ev'ry science that might be,
And ev'ry secret work of nature's ways;
In witty riddles; and in wise soothsays;
In pow'r of herbs; and tunes of beasts and birds;
And, that augmented all her other praise,
She modest was in all her deeds and words,
And wondrous chaste of life, yet lov'd of knights and lords.

Full many lords and many knights her lov'd,
Yet she to none of them her liking lent,
Nor ever was with fond affection mov'd,
But rul'd her thoughts with goodly government,
For dread of blame and honour's blemishment;
And eke unto her looks a law she made,
That none of them once out of order went,
But, like to wary sentinels well stay'd,
Still watch'd on ev'ry side, of secret foes afraid.

So much the more as she refus'd to love,
So much the more she lovëd was and sought,
That oftentimes unquiet strife did move
Amongst her lovers, and great quarrels wrought;
That oft for her in bloody arms they fought.
Which when as Cambell, that was stout and wise,
Perceiv'd would breed great mischief, he bethought
How to prevent the peril that might rise,
And turn both him and her to honour in this wise.

One day, when all that troop of warlike wooers
Assembled were, to weet[7] whose she should be,
All mighty men and dreadful derring-doers[8]
(The harder it to make them well agree),
Amongst them all this end he did decree;
That, of them all which love to her did make,
They by consent should choose the stoutest three,
That with himself should combat for her sake,
And of them all the victor should his sister take.

Bold was the challenge, as himself was bold,
And courage full of haughty hardiment,[9]
Approvëd oft in perils manifold,
Which he achiev'd to his great ornament:
But yet his sister's skill unto him lent
Most confidence and hope of happy speed,
Conceivëd by a ring which she him sent,
That, 'mongst the many virtues which we read,
Had power to staunch all wounds that mortally did bleed.

Well was that ring's great virtue known to all;
That dread thereof, and his redoubted might,
Did all that youthly rout so much appal,
That none of them durst undertake the fight:
More wise they ween'd to make of love delight,

1 Preferred; she shall be bestowed upon him.
2 Fellest, cruelest.
3 Age.
4 Writings, manuscripts.
5 See note 18, page 121, on The Squire's Tale; which Chaucer left unfinished, and Spenser ventures to continue.
6 Skilled.
7 Learn.
8 Doers of daring deeds.
9 Hardihood, bravery.

Than life to hazard for fair lady's look:
And yet uncertain by such outward sight,
Though for her sake they all that peril took,
Whether she would them love, or in her liking brook.[1]

Amongst those knights there were three brethren bold,
Three bolder brethren never were y-born,
Born of one mother in one happy mould,
Born at one burden in one happy morn;
Thrice happy mother, and thrice happy morn,
That bore three such, three such not to be found!
Her name was Agapé, whose children wer'n[2]
All three as one; the first hight Priamond,
The second Diamond, the youngest Triamond.

Stout Priamond, but not so strong to strike;
Strong Diamond, but not so stout a knight;
But Triamond was stout and strong alike:
On horseback usëd Triamond to fight,
And Priamond on foot had more delight;
But horse and foot knew Diamond to wield:
With curtaxe[3] usëd Diamond to smite,
And Triamond to handle spear and shield,
But spear and curtaxe both us'd Priamond in field.

These three did love each other dearly well,
And with so firm affection were allied,
As if but one soul in them all did dwell,
Which did her pow'r into three parts divide;
Like three fair branches budding far and wide,
That from one root deriv'd their vital sap:
And like that root, that doth her life divide,
Their mother was; and had full blessed hap
These three so noble babes to bring forth at one clap.[4]

Their mother was a Fay, and had the skill
Of secret things, and all the pow'rs of Nature,
Which she by art could use unto her will,
And to her service bind each living creature,
Through secret understanding of their feature.[5]
Thereto she was right fair, whenso her face
She list[6] discover, and of goodly stature;
But she, as Fays are wont, in privy place
Did spend her days, and lov'd in forests wild to space.[7]

There on a day a noble youthly knight,
Seeking adventures in the salvage wood,
Did by great fortune get of her the sight,
As she sat careless by a crystal flood
Combing her golden locks, as seem'd her good;
And unawares upon her laying hold,
That strove in vain him long to have withstood,
Oppressëd[8] her, and there (as it is told)
Got these three lovely babes, that prov'd three champions bold:

Which she with her long foster'd in that wood,
Till that to ripeness of man's state they grew:
Then, showing forth signs of their father's blood,
They lovëd arms, and knighthood did ensue,[9]
Seeking adventures where they any knew.
Which when their mother saw, she gan to doubt
Their safety; lest by searching dangers new,
And rash provoking perils all about,
Their days might be abridgëd through their courage stout.

Therefore desirous th' end of all their days
To know, and them t' enlarge with long extent,
By wondrous skill and many hidden ways
To the Three Fatal Sisters'[10] house she went.
Far under ground from track of living went,
Down in the bottom of the deep Abyss,
Where Demogorgon[11] in dull darkness pent,
Far from the view of gods and heaven's bliss,
The hideous Chaos keeps, their dreadful dwelling is.

There she them found all sitting round about
The direful distaff standing in the mid,[12]
And with unwearied fingers drawing out
The lines of life, from living knowledge hid.
Sad Clotho held the rock,[13] the while the thread
By grisly Lachesis was spun with pain,
That cruel Atropos eftsoons undid,
With cursëd knife cutting the twist in twain:
Most wretched men, whose days depend on threads so vain!

She, them saluting there, by them sat still,
Beholding how the threads of life they span:
And when at last she had beheld her fill,
Trembling in heart, and looking pale and wan,
Her cause of coming she to tell began.
To whom fierce Atropos; "Bold Fay, that durst
Come see the secret of the life of man,
Well worthy thou to be of Jove accurst,
And eke thy children's threads to be asunder burst!"[14]

Whereat she sore afraid, yet her besought
To grant her boon, and rigour to abate,
That she might see her children's threads forth brought,
And know the measure of their utmost date
To them ordainëd by eternal fate:
Which Clotho granting, showëd her the same;
That when she saw, it did her much amate[15]
To see their threads so thin, as spiders frame,
And eke so short, that seem'd their ends out shortly came.

She then began them humbly to entreat
To draw them longer out, and better twine,
That so their lives might be prolongëd late:
But Lachesis thereat gan to repine,
And said; "Fond[16] Dame! that deem'st of things divine
As of humane, that they may alter'd be,
And chang'd at pleasure for those imps[17] of thine:
Not so; for what the Fates do once decree,
Not all the gods can change, nor Jove himself can free!"

1 Endure.
2 Were.
3 Also called "curtle-axe"—a cutlass.
4 At one blow—at one time.
5 Character.
6 Pleased (to).
7 Roam.
8 Ravished.
9 Pursue.
10 The Three Fates.
11 See note 3, page 314.
12 In the centre.
13 Distaff.
14 Broken.
15 Overcome, distress.
16 Foolish.
17 Children.

"Then since," quoth she, "the term of each man's life
For naught may lessen'd nor enlargëd be,
Grant this, that when ye shred with fatal knife
His line, which is the eldest of the three,
Which is of them the shortest, as I see,
Eftsoons his life may pass into the next;
And, when the next shall likewise ended be,
That both their lives may likewise be annext
Unto the third, that his may be so trebly wext."[1]

They granted it; and then that careful Fay
Departed thence with full contented mind;
And, coming home, in warlike fresh array
Them found all three, according to their kind;[2]
But unto them what destiny was assign'd,
Or how their lives were ek'd,[3] she did not tell;
But evermore, when she fit time could find,
She warnëd them to tend their safeties well,
And love each other dear, whatever them befell.

So did they surely during all their days,
And never discord did amongst them fall;
Which much augmented all their other praise:
And now, t' increase affection natural,
In love of Canacé they joinëd all:
Upon which ground this same great battle grew
(Great matter growing of beginning small),
The which, for length, I will not here pursue,
But rather will reserve it for a canto new.

CANTO III.

The battle 'twixt three brethren with
Cambell for Canacé:
Cambina with true friendship's bond
Doth their long strife agree.

O! WHY do wretched men so much desire
To draw their days unto the utmost date,
And do not rather wish them soon expire;
Knowing the misery of their estate,
And thousand perils which them still await,
Tossing them like a boat amid the main,
That ev'ry hour they knock at Deathë's gate!
And he that happy seems, and least in pain,
Yet is as nigh his end as he that most doth plain.[4]

Therefore the poet holds this Fay but foolish and vain, who, in seeking long life for her three children, did but "more prolong their pain." Yet while they lived they were happy, ennobled for their courtesy, and renowned for their chivalry. They took in hand the hardy challenge, "for Canacé with Cambell for to fight;" and on the day fixed they appeared in the lists, where six judges sat at one side, while at the other Canacé was placed on a stately stage. All the due ceremonial performed, Priamond came forward first of the three to fight; but after a cruel conflict, in which Cambell was severely wounded, though the magic power of the ring prevented his losing any blood, Priamond was slain by his own spearhead, fiercely thrown back at him by his antagonist, and cleaving his "weasand-pipe."

His weary ghost, assoil'd[5] from fleshly band,
Did not, as others wont, directly fly
Unto her rest in Pluto's grisly land;
Nor into air did vanish presentlÿ;
Nor changëd was into a star in sky;
But through traduction[6] was eftsoons deriv'd,[7]
Like as his mother pray'd the Destinÿ,
Into his other brethren that surviv'd,
In whom he liv'd anew, of former life depriv'd.

Diamond, the next brother, "stirr'd to vengeance and despite through secret feeling of his[8] generous sprite," now engaged Cambell in combat.

As when two tigers, prick'd with hunger's rage,
Have by good fortune found some beast's fresh spoil,
On which they ween[9] their famine to assuage,
And gain a feastful guerdon[10] of their toil;
Both falling out do stir up strifeful broil,
And cruel battle 'twixt themselves do make,
While neither lets the other touch the soil,[11]
But either 'sdains[12] with other to partake:
So cruelly those knights strove for that lady's sake.

Many strokes were interchanged and warded; till, growing impatient, Diamond concentrated his whole force in one mighty swing of his murderous axe. But Cambell nimbly swerved aside, and Diamond, missing his mark, slipped his right foot and almost fell.

As when a vulture, greedy of his prey,
Through hunger long, that heart[13] to him doth lend,
Strikes at a heron with all his body's sway,
That from his force seems naught may it defend;
The wary fowl, that spies him toward bend
His dreadful souse,[14] avoids it, shunning light,
And maketh him his wing in vain to spend;
That, with the weight of his own wieldless[15] might,
He falleth nigh to ground, and scarce recov'reth flight.

Seizing the fair chance, Cambell, ere his foe could recover himself, struck off his head; but the headless trunk stood still a while, much to the amazement of the spectators, who did not know the Fates' decree "for life's succession in the brethren three." Two souls possessed the body of Diamond; and though one was reft, the other would have remained, if the body had not been dismembered—"but, finding no fit seat, the lifeless corse it left."

It left; but that same soul which therein dwelt,
Straight ent'ring into Triamond, him fill'd

1 Waxed, increased. 2 Nature.
3 Augmented. 4 Complain.
5 Absolved, set free. 6 Transfer.
7 Communicated. 8 Priamond's.
9 Think.

10 Reward.
11 The prey, all soiled with the mud and dust of the chase. 12 Disdains.
13 Courage. 14 Swoop. See note 24, page 234.
15 Ungovernable.

With double life and grief; which when he felt,
As one whose inner parts had been y-thrill'd[1]
With point of steel that close[2] his heart-blood spill'd,
He lightly leap'd out of his place of rest,
And, rushing forth into the empty field,
Against Cambello fiercely him addrest;
Who, him affronting[3] soon, to fight was ready prest.[4]

Well might ye wonder how that noble knight,
After he had so often wounded been,
Could stand on foot now to renew the fight:
But had ye then him forth advancing seen,
Some newborn wight ye would him surely ween;
So fresh he seemëd, and so fierce in sight;
Like as a snake, whom weary winter's teen[5]
Hath worn to naught, now, feeling summer's might,
Casts off his ragged skin and freshly doth him dight.[6]

All was through virtue of the ring he wore;
The which not only did not from him let
One drop of blood to fall, but did restore
His weaken'd pow'rs, and dullëd spirits whet,
Through working of the stone therein y-set.
Else how could one of equal might with most,[7]
Against so many no less mighty met,
Once think to match three such on equal cost,[8]
Three such as able were to match a puissant host?

Triamond, nevertheless, fearless and hopeful of victory, fiercely assailed Cambell with blows "as thick as hail forth pourëd from the sky," so that Cambell found it prudent to yield ground, till his foe had spent his breath; then he forced Triamond to retreat in turn.

Like as the tide, that comes from th' ocean main,
Flows up the Shannon with contráry force,
And, overruling him in his own reign,
Drives back the current of his kindly[9] course,
And makes it seem to have some other source;
But when the flood is spent, then, back again
His borrow'd waters forc'd to redisburse,
He sends the sea his own with double gain,
And tribute eke withal, as to his sovëreign.

"Thus did the battle vary to and fro," till at last Triamond waxed faint and feeble through loss of blood.

But Cambell still more strong and greater grew,
Nor felt his blood to waste, nor pow'rs emperish'd,[10]
Through that ring's virtue, that with vigour new,
Still when as he enfeebled was, him cherish'd,
And all his wounds and all his bruises guerish'd:[11]
Like as a wither'd tree, through husband's[12] toil,
Is often seen full freshly to have flourish'd,
And fruitful apples to have borne a while,
As fresh as when it first was planted in the soil.

Through which advantage, in his strength he rose
And smote the other with so wondrous might,
That, through the seam which did his hauberk close,
Into his throat and life it piercëd quite,
That down he fell as dead in all men's sight:
Yet dead he was not; yet he sure did die,
As all men do that lose the living sprite:
So did one soul out of his body fly
Unto her native home from mortal misery.

But nathëless, whilst all the lookers-on
Him dead behight,[13] as he to all appear'd,
All unawáres he started up anon,
As one that had out of a dream been rear'd,
And fresh assail'd his foe; who, half afear'd
Of th' uncouth sight, as he some ghost had seen,
Stood still amaz'd, holding his idle sweard;[14]
Till, having often by him stricken been,
He forcëd was to strike and save himself from teen.[15]

Cambell now fought more warily, "as one in fear the Stygian gods t' offend;" and Triamond, thinking that his opponent's strength began to fail, heaved on high his mighty hand, to end him with one blow. Cambell anticipated the stroke by a thrust which pierced through both Triamond's sides. But the blow of Triamond in the same moment descended on Cambell's head; so that both, seeming dead, fell to the ground together. All believed that the battle was at an end; the judges rose; the lists were broken up; and Canacé began to wail her dearest friend. But, suddenly, the combatants started up anew, and continued to fight as before.

Whilst thus the case in doubtful balance hung,
Unsure to whether side it would incline,
And all men's eyes and hearts, which there among
Stood gazing, fillëd were with rueful tine,[16]
And secret fear to see their fatal fine;[17]
All suddenly they heard a troublous noise,
That seem'd some perilous tumult to design,[18]
Confus'd with women's cries and shouts of boys,
Such as the troubled theatres ofttimes annoys.

Thereat the champions both stood still a space,
To weeten[19] what that sudden clamour meant
Lo! where they spied, with speedy whirling pace,
One in a chariot of strange furniment[20]
Towárd them driving like a storm out sent.
The chariot deckëd was in wondrous wise
With gold and many a gorgeous ornament,
After the Persian monarchs' antique guise,
Such as the maker's self could best by art devise.[21]

And drawn it was (that wonder is to tell)
Of[22] two grim lions, taken from the wood,
In which their pow'r all others did excel;
Now made forget their former cruel mood,

1 Pierced.
2 Secretly.
3 Confronting.
4 Prepared.
5 Pain, affliction.
6 Dress, array.
7 Of ordinary strength.
8 Equal terms.
9 Natural.
10 Decayed, impaired.
11 Healed; French, "guérir," to cure.
12 Husbandman's.
13 Affirmed.
14 Sword.
15 Injury.
16 Same as "teen;" grief.
17 End.
18 Denote.
19 Learn.
20 Furnishing, equipment.
21 Describe.
22 By.

T' obey their rider's hest,[1] as seemëd good:
And therein sat a lady[2] passing fair
And bright, that seemëd born of angels' brood;
And, with her beauty, bounty did compare[3]
Whether of them in her should have the greater share.

Thereto[4] she learnëd was in magic lear,[5]
And all the arts that subtile wits discover,
Having therein been trainëd many a year,
And well instructed by the Fay her mother,
That in the same she far excell'd all other:
Who, understanding by her mighty art
Of th' evil plight in which her dearest brother
Now stood, came forth in haste to take his part,
And pacify the strife which caus'd so deadly smart.

And, as she passëd through th' unruly press
Of people thronging thick her to behold,
Her angry team, breaking their bonds of peace,
Great heaps of them, like sheep in narrow fold,
For haste did over-run in dust enroll'd;
That, thorough rude confusion of the rout,
Some fearing shriek'd, some being harmëd howl'd,
Some laugh'd for sport, some did for wonder shout,
And some, that would seem wise, their wonder turn'd to doubt.

In her right hand a rod of peace she bore,
About the which two serpents weren wound,
Entrailëd[6] mutually in lovely lore,[7]
And by the tails together firmly bound,
And both were with one olive garland crown'd
(Like to the rod which Maia's son[8] doth wield,
Wherewith the hellish fiends he doth confound);
And in her other hand a cup she held,
The which was with Nepenthe to the brim upfill'd.

Nepenthe is a drink of sov'reign grace,
Devisëd by the gods for to assuage
Heart's grief, and bitter gall away to chase
Which stirs up anguish and contentious rage:
Instead thereof sweet peace and quietage
It doth establish in the troubled mind.
Few men, but such as sober are and sage,
Are by the gods to drink thereof assign'd;
But such as drink eternal happiness do find.

Such famous men, such worthies of the earth,
As Jove will have advancëd to the sky,
And there made gods, though born of mortal birth,
For their high merits and great dignity,
Are wont, before they may to heaven fly,
To drink hereof; whereby all cares forepast[9]
Are wash'd away quite from their memory:
So did those old heróës hereof taste,
Before that they in bliss amongst the gods were plac'd.

Much more of price and of more gracious power
Is this, than that same water of Ardenne,[10]
The which Rinaldo drank in happy hour,
Describëd by that famous Tuscan pen:
For that had might to change the hearts of men
From love to hate, a change of evil choice:
But this doth hatred make in love to bren,[11]
And heavy heart with comfort doth rejoice.
Who would not to this virtue rather yield his voice?

At last, arriving by the listës' side,
She with her rod did softly smite the rail,
Which straight flew ope and gave her way to ride.
Eftsoons out of her coach she gan avail,[12]
And, passing fairly forth, did bid all hail
First to her brother whom she lovëd dear,
That so to see him made her heart to quail;
And next to Cambell, whose sad rueful cheer
Made her to change her hue, and hidden love t' appear.

They lightly her requit[13] (for small delight
They had as then her long to entertain),
And eft[14] them turnëd both again to fight:
Which when she saw, down on the bloody plain
Herself she threw, and tears gan shed amain;
Amongst her tears immixing prayers meek,
And with her prayers reasons, to restrain
From bloody strife; and blessed peace to seek,
By all that unto them was dear, did them beseek.[15]

But when as all might naught with them prevail,
She smote them lightly with her pow'rful wand:
Then suddenly, as if their hearts did fail,
Their wrathful blades down fell out of their hand,
And they, like men astonish'd, still did stand.
Thus whilst their minds were doubtfully distraught,
And mighty spirits bound with mightier band,
Her golden cup to them for drink she raught,[16]
Whereof, full glad for thirst, each drank a hearty draught:

Of which so soon as they once tasted had,
Wonder it is that sudden change to see:
Instead of strokes, each other kissëd glad,
And lovely hals'd,[17] from fear of treason free,
And plighted hands, for ever friends to be.
When all men saw this sudden change of things,
So mortal foes so friendly to agree,
For passing joy, which so great marvel brings,
They all gan shout aloud, that all the heaven rings.

The gentle Canacé in haste descended from her lofty chair, and greeted Cambina in lovely wise; all went homewards in joy and friendliness; and many days they spent feasting in perfect love. For Triamond had Canacé to wife,

1 Commandment.
2 Cambina, the sister of Triamond.
3 Her goodness or virtue competed.
4 Moreover.
5 Lore.
6 Interwoven.
7 Loving fashion.
8 Mercury; the rod is the "caduceus," the power of which is described at page 404.
9 Gone past.

10 In the first canto of the "Orlando Innamorata," Boiardo notices this fountain, prepared by Merlin to take away the love of Tristram for La Belle Isoude; the knight, however, never drank of its waters.
11 Burn.
12 Descend.
13 Saluted in return.
14 After; speedily.
15 Beseech.
16 Reached.
17 Lovingly embraced.

and Cambell took Cambina to his fere;[1] and never had such lovers been found elsewhere since their day.

CANTO IV.

Satyrane makes a tournament
For love of Florimell:
Britomart wins the prize from all,
And Artegall doth quell.

RETURNING from the retrospective episode in which he has shown the origin of the friendship between Cambell and Triamond, the poet takes up his story at the point where the friends and their ladies were overtaken by the "discordful crew" of which Duessa and Até were the inspiring members. Blandamour, thinking so to advance himself in the grace of the stranger ladies, began to insult and revile their knights; who would have sharply punished him, but that Cambina assuaged the fierceness of their mood. Then they all rode on in friendly converse; among other matters, of the great tourney which was to be held "for that rich girdle of fair Florimell, the prize of her which did in beauty most excel." All agreed to go thither and try their fortunes. On the way they were joined by Braggadocio, who recognised in the snowy Florimell the lady whom Sir Ferraugh had taken from him and Sir Blandamour from Ferraugh; and the boaster challenged her anew. Blandamour scornfully proposed that the hag Até should be set beside Florimell, and that whoever was beaten should have the hag, and always ride with her until he got another lady. Amid the merriment of the company, Braggadocio declared that he never thought to imperil his person in fight for such a hag; but if they had sought another lady alike fair and bright with Florimell, he would spend his life to justify his right. The revilings of Florimell, and the provocations of Até, were powerless to prompt him to fight; "for in base mind nor friendship dwells nor enmity." But Cambell "shut up all in jest," advising that all should keep themselves fresh and strong against the tournament, when their quarrel might be tried out. At last they reached the place of contest, where "many a brave knight and many a dainty dame" had already met; and there this brave crew divided—Blandamour with those of his company going on one side, the rest on the other, while Braggadocio, the better to attract notice, took his place alone.

Then first of all forth came Sir Satyrane,
Bearing that precious relic in an ark
Of gold, that bad eyes might it not profane;
Which drawing softly forth out of the dark,
He open show'd, that all men it might mark;
A gorgeous girdle, curiously embost
With pearl and precious stone, worth many a
 mark;[2]
Yet did the workmanship far pass the cost:
It was the same which lately Florimell had lost.

The same aloft he hung in open view,
To be the prize of beauty and of might;
The which, eftsoons discover'd, to it drew
The eyes of all, allur'd with close[3] delight,
And hearts quite robbèd[4] with so glorious sight,
That all men threw out vows and wishes vain.
Thrice happy lady, and thrice happy knight,
Them seem'd, that could so goodly riches gain,
So worthy of the peril, worthy of the pain.

Then took the bold Sir Satyrane in hand
A huge great spear, such as he wont to wield,
And, 'vancing[5] forth from all the other band
Of knights, address'd his maiden-headed shield,[6]
Showing himself all ready for the field:
'Gainst whom there singled from the other side
A Paynim knight that well in arms was skill'd,
And had in many a battle oft been tried,
Hight Bruncheval the bold, who fiercely forth
 did ride.

Furiously they met, "as two fierce bulls, that strive the rule to get of all the herd;" both were felled to the ground; and long they were unable to wield their idle spears. Espying this, the noble Ferramont pricked forth to aid Satyrane; and against him Blandamour rode with all his strength—only to fall to the earth, "tumbled horse and man." Paridell advanced to the rescue, but was likewise overthrown. Braggadocio, whose turn came next, lingered like a coward; then, all impatient, Triamond stepped forth, and bore Ferramont to ground. Sir Devon, Sir Douglas, and Sir Palimord, in succession went down beneath the strokes of Triamond. Meantime, Satyrane, recovering his senses, and perceiving the merciless affray which doughty Triamond had wrought "unto the noble Knights of Maidenhead," felt his mighty heart almost rent in two for very gall, and, gathering up his weapons, remounted his horse. Then, "like spark of fire that from the anvil glode,"[7] he rode forth where the valiant Triamond was driving all before him. Striking with his whole power at Triamond, Satyrane pierced him through the side so sorely that he had to withdraw out of the field; the challenging party had the best of the day, until at gloomy evening the trumpet bade them forbear; "so Satyrane that day was judg'd to bear the bell." Next day the tourney began anew; the hardy Satyrane, with all his noble crew, first appearing in place; but Triamond was detained from the field by his wound. Therefore Cambell, to save his friend's honour, assumed his arms and shield, and went forth to fight. He found Satyrane lord of the field, "triumphing in great joy and jollity;" and he rode at the victor of yesterday so fiercely, that both went to the ground. Rising, they betook themselves to their swords, and, to the amaze-

1 Companion, consort. 2 A coin. 3 Secret. 4 Carried away. 5 Advancing.

6 Bearing the head of the Maiden Queen. See the opening of canto ix., book ii., page 390. 7 Glanced.

ment of all the rest, fought "as two wild boars together grappling go, chafing, and foaming choler each against his foe." Satyrane's steed at last stumbled, and nigh cast his rider; Cambell, pursuing his advantage, tumbled him from his saddle by a blow on the head, and then leaped down to rend away, as the victor's meed, his arms and shield. But all at once a crowd of swords was laid upon him; a hundred knights beset him, hoping to rescue Satyrane, and take Cambell prisoner.

He with their multitude was naught dismay'd,
But with stout courage turn'd upon them all,
And with his brand-iron [1] round about him laid;
Of which he dealt large alms, as did befall:
Like as a lion, that by chance doth fall
Into the hunters' toil, doth rage and roar,
In royal heart disdaining to be thrall: [2]
But all in vain: for what might one do more?
They have him taken captive, though it grieve him sore.

Whereof when news to Triamond was brought,
There as he lay, his wound he soon forgot,
And, starting up, straight for his armour sought:
In vain he sought; for there he found it not;
Cambello it away before had got:
Cambello's arms therefore he on him threw,
And lightly issued forth to take his lot.
There he in troop found all that warlike crew
Leading his friend away, full sorry to his view.

Into the thickest of that knightly press
He thrust, and smote down all that was between,
Carried with fervent zeal; nor did he cease,
Till that he came where he had Cambell seen
Like captive thrall two other knights atween:
There he amongst them cruel havoc makes,
That they which lead him soon enforcëd be'n
To let him loose to save their proper stakes; [3]
Who, being freed, from one a weapon fiercely takes:

With that he drives at them with dreadful might,
Both in remembrance of his friend's great harm,
And in revengement of his own despite:
So both together give a new alarm,
As if but now the battle waxëd warm.
As when two greedy wolves do break by force
Into a herd, far from the husband [4] farm,
They spoil and ravin [5] without all remorse:
So did these two through all the field their foes enforce.

Fiercely they follow'd on their bold emprise,
Till trumpets' sound did warn them all to rest:
Then all with one consent did yield the prize
To Triamond and Cambell as the best:
But Triamond to Cambell it relest, [6]
And Cambell it to Triamond transferr'd;
Each labouring t' advance the other's gest, [7]
And make his praise before his own preferr'd:
So that the doom [8] was to another day deferr'd.

On the third day, Sir Satyrane excelled all the other knights in prowess, and "still the Knights of Maidenhead the better won" in the fierce jousts.

Till that there enter'd on the other side
A stranger knight, from whence no man could read, [9]
In quaint disguise, full hard to be descried:
For all his armour was like salvage weed, [10]
With woody moss bedight, [11] and all his steed
With oaken leaves attrap'd, [12] that seemëd fit
For salvage wight, and thereto well agreed
His word, [13] which on his ragged shield was writ,
Salvagesse sans finesse, [14] showing secret wit.

The new comer "charged his spear" at the first that appeared in his sight—the stout Sir Sanglier—and dismounted him; Sir Brianor shared the same fate:

Then, ere his hand he rear'd, he overthrew
Sev'n knights one after other as they came:
And, when his spear was burst, [15] his sword he drew,
The instrument of wrath, and with the same
Far'd like a lion in his bloody game,
Hewing and slashing shields and helmets bright,
And beating down whatever nigh him came,
That ev'ry one gan shun his dreadful sight
No less than death itself, in dangerous affright.

Much wonder'd all men what or whence he came,
That did amongst the troops so tyrannize;
And each of other gan inquire his name:
But, when they could not learn it by no wise,
Most answerable to his wild disguise
It seemëd, him to term the Salvage Knight;
But certes his right name was otherwise,
Though known to few, that Artegall he hight,
The doughtiest knight that liv'd that day, and most of might.

Thus was Sir Satyrane, with all his band,
By his sole manhood and achievement stout,
Dismay'd, [16] that none of them in field durst stand,
But beaten were and chasëd all about.
So he continu'd all that day throughout,
Till ev'ning that the sun gan downward bend:
Then rushëd forth out of the thickest rout
A stranger knight, that did his glory shend: [17]
So naught may be esteemëd happy till the end!

He at his entrance charg'd his pow'rful spear
At Artegall, in middest of his pride,
And therewith smote him on his umbriére [18]
So sore, that tumbling back he down did slide
Over his horse's tail above a stride; [19]
Whence little lust [20] he had to rise again.
Which Cambell seeing, much the same envied,
And ran at him with all his might and main;
But shortly was likewise seen lying on the plain.

Whereat full inly wroth was Triamond,
And cast [21] t' avenge the shame done to his friend:
But by [22] his friend himself eke soon he found,

1 Sword.
2 Enslaved.
3 Their own lives.
4 Husbandman's.
5 Make booty.
6 Released, resigned.
7 Achievement.
8 Decision.
9 Tell.
10 Savage or wild dress.
11 Adorned, trimmed.
12 Trapped, equipped.
13 Motto.
14 Wildness without art.
15 Broken.
16 Subdued.
17 Obscure, abase.
18 Visor of the helmet.
19 More than a stride—a considerable way.
20 Inclination.
21 Resolved, tried.
22 Beside.

In no less need of help than him he ween'd.[1]
All which when Blandamour from end to end
Beheld, he wox therewith displeasëd sore,
And thought in mind it shortly to amend:
His spear he feuter'd,[2] and at him it bore;
But with no better fortune than the rest before.

Full many others at him likewise ran;
But all of them likewise dismounted were:
Nor, certes, wonder; for no pow'r of man
Could bide[3] the force of that enchanted spear,
The which this famous Britomart did bear;
With which she wondrous deeds of arms achiev'd,
And overthrew whatever came her near,
That all those stranger knights full sore aggriev'd,
And that late weaker band of challengers reliev'd.

Like as in summer day, when raging heat
Doth burn the earth, and boilëd rivers dry,
That all brute beasts, forc'd to refrain from meat,
Do hunt for shade where shrouded they may lie,
And, missing it, fain[4] from themselves to fly;
All travellers tormented are with pain:
A watery cloud doth overcast the sky,
And poureth forth a sudden show'r of rain,
That all the wretched world recomforteth again:

So did the warlike Britomart restore
The prize to Knights of Maidenhead that day,
Which else was like to have been lost, and bore
The praise of prowess from them all away.
Then shrilling trumpets loudly gan to bray,
And bade them leave their labours and long toil
To joyous feast and other gentle play,
Where beauty's prize should win that precious
spoil:
Where I with sound of trump will also rest a
while.

CANTO V.

The ladies for the girdle strive
Of famous Florimell:
Scudamour, coming to Care's House,
Doth sleep from him expel.[5]

"After the proof of prowess ended well," came the contention of the ladies for the girdle of fair Florimell, which was to be awarded to her that most excelled in beauty's sovereign grace.

That girdle gave the virtue of chaste love
And wifehood true to all that did it bear;
But whosoever contrary doth prove
Might not the same about her middle wear,
But it would loose, or else asunder tear.
Whilóm it was (as Faeries wont report)
Dame Venus' girdle,[6] by her 'steemed[7] dear,
What time she us'd to live in wifely sort;
But laid aside whenso she us'd her looser sport.

Her husband Vulcan whilom for her sake,
When first he lovëd her with heart entire,
This precious ornament, they say, did make,
And wrought in Lemnos with unquenchëd fire:
And afterward did for her love's first hire
Give it to her, for ever to remain,
Therewith to bind lascivious desire,
And loose affections straitly to restrain;
Which virtue it for ever after did retain.

The same one day, when she herself dispos'd
To visit her belovëd paramoúr,
The god of War, she from her middle loos'd,
And left behind her in her secret bow'r
On Acidalian[8] mount, where many an hour
She with the pleasant Graces wont to play.
There Florimell in her first age's flow'r
Was foster'd by those Graces (as they say),
And brought with her from thence that goodly
belt away.

"That goodly belt was Cestus hight by name," and by its owner esteemed dear as her life; and many ladies sought to win it, "for peerless she was thought that did it bear." After due feasting, the judges "into the martial plain adown descended" to decide the doubtful case. But first they determined which of the knights had won the wager; and to Satyrane was given the credit of the first day, to Triamond that of the second, and to the Knight of the Ebon Spear —Britomart—the glory of the third and of all the three days; therefore to her the fairest lady was adjudged—at which Artegall much repined, and inwardly vowed vengeance. The knights now proceeded to bring forward their ladies, as competitors for the virtuous belt. First Cambell led forward Cambina; then Triamond his dear Canacé; then Paridell his false Duessa; then Ferramont his Lucida, "full fair and sheen;" and a hundred others, such, that no man had ever seen so many heavenly faces assembled in one place.

At last, the most redoubted Britoness
Her lovely Amoret did open shew;
Whose face, discover'd, plainly did express
The heav'nly portrait of bright angels' hue.
Well weenëd all, which her that time did view,
That she should surely bear the belt away;
Till Blandamour, who thought he had the true
And very Florimell, did her display:
The sight of whom, once seen, did all the rest
dismay.

For all before that seemëd fair and bright,
Now base and cóntemptíble did appear,
Compar'd to her that shone as Phœbé's light
Amongst the lesser stars in ev'ning clear.
All that her saw with wonder ravish'd were,
And ween'd no mortal creature she should be,
But some celestial shape that flesh did bear:
Yet all were glad there Florimell to see;
Yet thought that Florimell was not so fair as
she.

As guileful goldsmith that, by secret skill,
With golden foil doth finely overspread

1 Thought.
2 Put in the rest, made ready.
3 Abide, withstand.
4 Are fain or glad.
5 That is, "Care doth expel sleep from Scudamour."
6 The cestus of Venus, the text of some of Martial's epigrams: xiv. 206, 207.
7 Esteemed.
8 Venus was sometimes called "Acidalia," from the fountain on Mount Acidalius, where she used to bathe with the Graces. See canto x., book vi.

Some baser metal, which commend he will
Unto the vulgar for good gold instead,
He much more goodly gloss thereon doth shed
To hide his falsehood, than if it were true:
So hard this idol[1] was to be aread,[2]
That Florimell herself in all men's view
She seem'd to pass: so forgëd things do fairest
shew.

By the verdict of all, the golden belt was awarded to the false Florimell; it would, however, by no means meet "about her middle small"—but constantly loosened itself, "as feeling secret blame," to the general amazement. Many other ladies likewise tried to fasten it on themselves, but to no purpose.

Which when that scornful Squire of Dames did
view,
He loudly gan to laugh, and thus to jest;
"Alas! for pity that so fair a crew,
As like cannot be seen from east to west,
Cannot find one this girdle to invest![3]
Fy on the man that did it first invent,
To shame us all with this *Ungirt unblest!*
Let never lady to his love assent,
That hath this day so many so unmanly shent."[4]

"Thereat all knights gan laugh, and ladies lour," until Amoret's turn came; and then the girdle fitted her waist "without breach or let" —much to the envy of all the rest, especially of Florimell, who snatched the belt, and again vainly attempted to tie it on her body. Nevertheless the belt was adjudged to her, and she to Britomart; but Britomart would not forego her Amoret "for that strange dame, whose beauty's wonderment she less esteem'd than th' other's virtuous government." Florimell was then adjudged to the Salvage Knight; but he had already departed, "in great displeasure that he could not get her;" then to Triamond, "but Triamond lov'd Canacé and other none;" then to Satyrane, "who was right glad to gain so goodly meed." But Blandamour thereat greatly grudged; Paridell appealed from the decision of the judges to single combat; and many other knights, impelled by Até, advanced claims to Florimell. Among them was Braggadocio, whose claim Florimell herself confessed; much to the wrath of the knights, who were about to fight for her, when Satyrane interfered, and, reminding them that "sweet is the love that comes alone with willingness," proposed that the lady should herself choose her lover. All agreed, and each secretly prayed to Venus that she might fall to his lot; but she chose Braggadocio; and the boaster secretly stole away with her that same night, while the knights were quarrelling and fuming over their mortification. After the pair went all the remaining knights, in hope to save such a noble prey from a wight so unworthy: but Britomart, taking with her Amoret, rode forth on her first adventure—"to seek her lov'd, making blind Love her guide." Amoret "also sought her lover long miswent," the gentle Scudamour; to whose fortunes, after he had heard Até's false account of Amoret's infidelity, the poet now returns. Attended by Glaucé, the Knight went about to seek "revenge on blameless Britomart."

So as they travellëd, the drooping Night,
Cover'd with cloudy storm and bitter show'r,
That dreadful seem'd to ev'ry living wight,
Upon them fell, before her timely hour;[5]
That forcëd them to seek some covert bow'r,
Where they might hide their heads in quiet rest,
And shroud their persons from that stormy
stowre.[6]
Not far away, not meet for any guest,
They spied a little cottage, like some poor man's
nest.

Under a steep hill's side it placëd was,
There where the moulder'd earth had cav'd[7] the
bank;
And fast beside a little brook did pass
Of muddy water, that like puddle stank,
By which few crooked sallows[8] grew in rank;[9]
Whereto approaching nigh, they heard the sound
Of many iron hammers beating rank,[10]
And answering their weary turns around;[11]
That seemëd some blacksmith dwelt in that de-
sert ground.

There ent'ring in, they found the goodman's self
Full busily unto his work y-bent;
Who was, to wit, a wretched wearish[12] elf,
With hollow eyes and raw-bone cheeks forspent,[13]
As if he had in prison long been pent:
Full black and grisly did his face appear,
Besmear'd with smoke that nigh his eye-sight
blent;[14]
With rugged beard, and hoary shagged hair,
The which he never wont to comb, or comely
shear.

Rude was his garment, and to rags all rent;
Nor better had he, nor for better cared:
With blister'd hands amongst the cinders brent,[15]
And fingers filthy, with long nails unpared,
Right fit to rend the food on which he fared.
His name was Care; a blacksmith by his trade,
That neither day nor night from working spared,
But to small purpose iron wedges made;
Those be Unquiet Thoughts, that careful minds
invade.

In which his work he had six servants prest,[16]
About the anvil standing evermore
With huge great hammers, that did never rest
From heaping strokes which thereon sousëd[17]
sore:
All six strong grooms, but one than other more;
For by degrees they all were disagreed;

1 Image, imitation. 2 Detected.
3 Put on. 4 Disgraced.
5 Before her usual time.
6 Onset (of the elements). 7 Hollowed.
8 Willows. 9 In a row. 10 Violently.
11 Being beaten in measure. 12 Worn out, wasted.
13 Utterly spent or pined away.
14 Blinded. 15 Burnt.
16 Ready at hand; French, "prêt."
17 Struck, descended, forcibly.

So likewise did the hammers which they bore
Like bells in greatness orderly succeed,
That he, which was the last, the first did far
exceed.

He like a monstrous giant seem'd in sight,
Far passing Brontes or Pyracmon[1] great,
The which in Lipari do day and night
Frame thunderbolts for Jove's avengeful threat.
So dreadfully he did the anvil beat,
That seem'd to dust he shortly would it drive:
So huge his hammer, and so fierce his heat,
That seem'd a rock of diamond it could rive
And rend asunder quite, if he thereto list[2] strive.

Sir Scudamour, there ent'ring, much admir'd[3]
The manner of their work and weary pain;
And, having long beheld, at last inquir'd
The cause and end thereof; but all in vain;
For they for naught would from their work re-
frain,
Nor let his speeches come unto their ear.
And eke the breathful bellows blew amain,
Like to the northern wind, that none could hear;
Those Pensiveness did move; and Sighs the
bellows were.

Which when that warrior saw, he said no more,
But in his armour laid him down to rest:
To rest he laid him down upon the floor
(Whilóm for venturous knights the bedding best),
And thought his weary limbs to have redrest.[4]
And that old aged dame, his faithful squire,
Her feeble joints laid eke adown to rest;
That needed much her weak age to desire,
After so long a travel which them both did tire.

There lay Sir Scudamour long while expecting[5]
When gentle sleep his heavy eyes would close;
Oft changing sides, and oft new place electing,
Where better seem'd he might himself repose;
And oft in wrath he thence again uprose;
And oft in wrath he laid him down again.
But, wheresoe'er he did himself dispose,
He by no means could wishëd ease obtain:
So ev'ry place seem'd painful, and each changing
vain.

And evermore, when he to sleep did think,
The hammers' sound his senses did molest;
And evermore, when he began to wink,
The bellows' noise disturb'd his quiet rest,
Nor suffer'd sleep to settle in his breast.
And all the night the dogs did bark and howl
About the house, at scent of stranger guest:
And now the crowing cock, and now the owl
Loud shrieking, him afflicted to the very soul.

And, if by fortune any little nap
Upon his heavy eyelids chanc'd to fall,
Eftsoons one of those villains him did rap
Upon his head-piece with his iron mall;[6]
That he was soon awakëd therewithal,
And lightly started up as one afraid,
Or as if one him suddenly did call:
So oftentimes he out of sleep abraid,[7]
And then lay musing long on that him ill apaid.[8]

So long he musëd, and so long he lay,
That at the last his weary sprite, opprest
With fleshly weakness, which no creature may
Long time resist, gave place to kindly rest,
That all his senses did full soon arrest:
Yet, in his soundest sleep, his daily fear[9]
His idle brain gan busily molest,
And made him dream those two[10] disloyal were:
The things, that day most minds, at night do
most appear.

With that the wicked carl, the master smith,
A pair of red-hot iron tongs did take
Out of the burning cinders, and therewith
Under his side him nipp'd, that, forc'd to wake,
He felt his heart for very pain to quake,
And started up avengëd for to be
On him the which his quiet slumber brake:
Yet, looking round about him, none could see;
Yet did the smart remain, though he himself[11]
did flee.

In such disquiet and heart-fretting pain
He all that night, that too long night, did pass.
And now the day out of the ocean main
Began to peep above this earthly mass,
With pearly dew sprinkling the morning grass:
Then up he rose like heavy lump of lead,
That in his face, as in a looking-glass,
The signs of anguish one might plainly read,
And guess the man to be dismay'd with jealous
dread.

"Unto his lofty steed he clomb anon," and, accompanied by Glaucé, "forth upon his former voyage far'd."

1 Two of the Cyclopes.
2 Pleased (to).
3 Wondered at.
4 Restored.
5 Awaiting (the time).
6 Club, hammer.
7 Started.
8 On the subject which annoyed him.
9 The fear or care that occupied him by day.
10 Britomart and Amoret; Scudamour still believed Britomart a man.

CANTO VI.

Both Scudamour and Artegall
Do fight with Britomart:
He sees her face; doth fall in love,
And soon from her depart.

What equal torment to the grief of mind
And pining anguish hid in gentle heart,
That inly feeds itself with thoughts unkind,
And nourisheth her own consuming smart?
What medicine can any leach's art
Yield such a sore, that doth her grievance hide,
And will to none her malady impart![12]
Such was the wound that Scudamour did gride:[13]
For which Dan Phœbus' self[14] cannot a salve
provide.

Having quitted the House of Care, the Knight

11 The master smith, who had inflicted the smart.
12 This passage strongly recalls Shakespeare's "Canst thou not minister to a mind diseased?" &c.; "Macbeth," act iv. scene iii. "Macbeth" was written nine years after Spenser published his second three books.
13 Pierce.
14 Apollo was the god who afforded help, and therefore is sometimes made the god of the healing art—a position due strictly to his son Æsculapius.

rode on, full of melancholy, until he espied "an armëd knight under a forest side, sitting in shade beside his grazing steed." The stranger was about to attack Scudamour, who prepared to rencounter him in equal race; but suddenly the first lowered his spear, and, calling Scudamour by his name, craved pardon for the offence he had almost committed. In surprise, Scudamore inquired who he was; but was asked to excuse him from discovering his name aright, and call him "the Salvage Knight." A stranger knight had done him shame and dishonour; and he waited there to wreak on him that foul despite, whenever he might pass. Learning that the offending knight was he of the ebon spear (Britomart, yet unknown by name) Scudamour "swell'd in every part for fell despite," and related his own grievance against that knight, who had reft from him his love, "and eke defilëd with foul villainy the sacred pledge which in his faith was left." Both agreed to wreak their wraths on Britomart; and soon they saw her approach. By his own request, Scudamour first attacked; but the warlike Maid tumbled both horse and man to ground, where they lay. Artegall in turn attacked, and was unhorsed; but, lightly recovering, he assailed his enemy with his sword, so furiously that she had to give ground. A stroke of his sword, glancing down her back, cut her horse in two, compelling her also to alight and fight on foot:

Like as the lightning-brand from riven sky,
Thrown out by angry Jove in his vengeânce,
With dreadful force falls on some steeple high;
Which battering down, it on the church doth
glance,
And tears it all with terrible mischance.
Yet she no whit dismay'd her steed forsook;
And, casting from her that enchanted lance,
Unto her sword and shield her soon betook;
And therewithal at him right furiously she
strook.[1]

So furiously she struck in her first heat,
While with long fight on foot he breathless was,
That she him forcëd backward to retreat,
And yield unto her weapon way to pass:
Whose raging rigour neither steel nor brass
Could stay, but to the tender flesh it went,
And pour'd the purple blood forth on the grass;
That all his mail y-riv'd,[2] and plates y-rent,
Show'd all his body bare unto the cruel dent.[3]

At length, when as he saw her hasty heat
Abate, and panting breath begin to fail,
He through long sufferance[4] growing now more
great,
Rose in his strength, and gan her fresh assail,
Heaping huge strokes as thick as show'r of hail,
And lashing dreadfully at every part,
As if he thought her soul to disentrail.[5]
Ah! cruel hand, and thrice more cruel heart,
That work'st such wreck on her to whom thou
dearest art!

After a long contest, Artegall, still regaining strength as his adversary's declined, gathered all his forces for a final blow.

The wicked stroke upon her helmet chanc'd,
And with the force, which in itself it bore,
Her ventail[6] shear'd away, and thence forth
glanc'd
Adown in vain, nor harm'd her any more.
With that, her angel's face, unseen afore,
Like to the ruddy morn appear'd in sight,
Dewëd with silver drops through sweating sore;
But somewhat redder than beseem'd aright,
Through toilsome heat and labour of her weary
fight:

And round about the same her yellow hair,
Having through stirring loos'd their wonted
band,
Like to a golden border did appear,
Framëd in goldsmith's forge with cunning hand:
Yet goldsmith's cunning could not understand
To frame such subtile wire, so shiny clear;
For it did glister like the golden sand
The which Pactólus, with his waters sheer,[7]
Throws forth upon the rivage[8] round about him
near.

And as his hand he up again did rear,
Thinking to work on her his utmost wrack,[9]
His pow'rless arm, benumb'd with secret fear,
From his revengeful purpose shrunk aback,
And cruel sword out of his fingers slack
Fell down to ground, as if the steel had sense
And felt some ruth,[10] or sense his hand did lack,
Or both of them did think obedience
To do to so divine a beauty's excellence.

And he himself, long gazing thereupon,
At last fell humbly down upon his knee,
And of his wonder made religión,[11]
Weening some heav'nly goddess he did see,
Or else unweeting[12] what it else might be;
And pardon her besought his error frail,
That had done outrage in so high degree:
Whilst trembling horror did his sense assail,
And made each member quake, and manly heart
to quail.

Nathless she, full of wrath for that late stroke,
All that long while upheld her wrathful hand,
With fell intent on him to be y-wroke;[13]
And, looking stern, still over him did stand,
Threat'ning to strike unless he would with-
stand;[14]
And bade him rise, or surely he should die.
But, die or live, for naught he would upstand;
But her of pardon pray'd more earnestly̆,
Or wreak on him her will for so great injury̆.

Scudamour, recovering from his overthrow, now drew near, and, "turning fear to faint devotion," worshipped the Maid as some celestial vision. Glaucé also advanced, and persuaded her to grant to those warriors a truce. Then they lifted their beavers, and showed her their faces.

1 Struck. 2 Cloven. 3 Blow.
4 Patience. 5 Dislodge.
6 Front of the helmet. 7 Clear, pure.
8 Bank. 9 Wreck, destruction. 10 Pity.
11 Changed his wonder into worship.
12 Unknowing. 13 Revenged. 14 Resist.

When Britomart with sharp adviseful[1] eye
Beheld the lovely face of Artegall,
Temper'd with sternness and stout majesty,
She gan eftsoons it to her mind to call
To be the same which, in her father's hall,
Long since in that enchanted glass she saw:
Therewith her wrathful courage gan appall,
And haughty spirits meekly to adaw,[2]
That her enhancëd[3] hand she down gan soft withdraw.

Yet she it forc'd to have again upheld,
As feigning choler which was turn'd to cold:
But ever, when his visage she beheld,
Her hand fell down, and would no longer hold
The wrathful weapon 'gainst his count'nance bold:
But, when in vain to fight she oft assay'd,
She arm'd her tongue, and thought at him to scold:
Nathless her tongue not to her will obey'd,
But brought forth speeches mild when she would have missaid.[4]

Scudamour, inly glad to find that Até's tale of Amoret's infidelity was false, congratulated Sir Artegall by name on his submission to a lady, since he had been wont to despise them all:

Soon as she heard the name of Artegall,
Her heart did leap, and all her heart-strings tremble
For sudden joy and secret fear withal;
And all her vital powers, with motion nimble,
To succour it themselves gan there assemble;
That by the swift recourse of flushing blood
Right plain appear'd, though she it would dissemble,
And feignëd still her former angry mood,
Thinking to hide the depth by troubling of the flood.

When Glaucé thus gan wisely all upknit;
"Ye gentle knights, whom fortune here hath brought
To be spectators of this uncouth fit[5]
Which secret fate hath in this lady wrought
Against the course of kind,[6] ne marvel naught;
Nor thenceforth fear the thing that hitherto
Hath troubled both your minds with idle thought,
Fearing lest she your loves away should woo;
Fearëd in vain, since means ye see there wants thereto.

"And you, Sir Artegall, the Salvage Knight,
Henceforth may not disdain that woman's hand
Hath conquer'd you anew in second fight:
For whilom they have conquer'd sea, and land,
And heav'n itself, that naught may them withstand:
Nor henceforth be rebellious unto love,
That is the crown of knighthood and the band
Of noble minds, derivëd from above,
Which, being knit with virtue, never will remove.

"And you, fair Lady-Knight, my dearest Dame,
Relent the rigour of your wrathful will,
Whose fire were better turn'd to other flame;
And, wiping out remembrance of all ill,
Grant him your grace; but so that he fulfil
The penance which ye shall to him impart;[7]
For lovers' heav'n must pass by sorrow's hell."
Thereat full inly blushëd Britomart;
But Artegall, close-smiling,[8] joy'd in secret heart.

Yet durst he not make love so suddenly,
Nor think th' affection of her heart to draw
From one to other[9] so quite contrary:
Besides her modest countenance he saw
So goodly grave, and full of princely awe,
That it his ranging fancy did refrain,
And looser thoughts to lawful bounds withdraw;
Whereby the passion grew more fierce and fain,[10]
Like to a stubborn steed whom strong hand would restrain.

Scudamour now asked for news of his Amoret; but Britomart could give him none. She had done all in her power to preserve the lady from peril and fear, after they had quitted the scene of tournament:

"Till on a day, as through a desert wild
We travellëd, both weary of the way,
We did alight, and sat in shadow mild;
Where fearless I to sleep me down did lay:
But, when as I did out of sleep abray,[11]
I found her not where I her left whilére,[12]
But thought she wander'd was, or gone astray:
I call'd her loud, I sought her far and near;
But nowhere could her find, nor tidings of her hear."

The Knight, his heart thrilled with point of deadly fear, stood pale and senseless, and was to be comforted only by Britomart's assurance that she would not leave him till Amoret had been recovered or avenged. Then they all proceeded to a resting-place pointed out by Artegall, where they were handsomely entertained, until they recovered from their wounds and weariness.

In all which time Sir Artegall made way
Unto the love of noble Britomart,
And with meek service and much suit did lay
Continual siege unto her gentle heart;
Which, being whilom lanc'd with lovely dart,[13]
More eath[14] was new impression to receive;
However she her pain'd[15] with womanish art
To hide her wound, that none might it perceive:
Vain is the art that seeks itself for to deceive.

So well he woo'd her, and so well he wrought her,
With fair entreaty and sweet blandishment,

1 Observant.
2 Lower.
3 Uplifted.
4 Spoken harshly.
5 Strange passion.
6 Nature.
7 Apportion.
8 Secretly smiling.
9 From one extreme to the other—from hate to love.
10 Eager.
11 Awake.
12 A little while before.
13 Being long before pierced with the dart of love.
14 Easy.
15 Strove.

That at the length unto a bay he brought her,[1]
So as she to his speeches was content
To lend an ear, and softly to relent.
At last, through many vows which forth he pour'd,
And many oaths, she yielded her consent
To be his love, and take him for her lord,
Till they with marriage meet might finish that accord.[2]

At last Artegall saw that it was time to depart on a hard adventure yet before him, and came to take leave of her; but he found his mistress full loth to let him go, and could appease her only by the promise to return in three months. So, early on the morrow, the Knight rode forth, unattended save by his lady, who rode with him a while.

And by the way she sundry purpose [3] found
Of this or that, the time for to delay,
And of the perils whereto he was bound,
The fear whereof seem'd much her to affray:
But all she did was but to wear out day.
Full oftentimes she leave of him did take;
And eft [4] again devis'd somewhat to say,
Which she forgot, whereby excuse to make:
So loth she was his company for to forsake.

At last, when all her speeches she had spent,
And new occasion fail'd her more to find,
She left him to his fortune's government,
And back returnëd with right heavy mind
To Scudamour, whom she had left behind;
With whom she went to seek fair Amoret,
Her second care, though in another kind:
For virtue's only sake, which doth beget
True love and faithful friendship, she by her did set.[5]

CANTO VII.

Amoret rapt by greedy Lust
Belphœbe saves from dread:
The Squire her loves; and, being blam'd,
His days in dole doth lead.

TAKING up the story of Amoret, the poet relates that she and Britomart, after leaving the tournament for beauty's prize, travelled long, and at last alighted to rest in a forest. Sleep surprised the eyelids of Britomart, while fair Amoret walked unsuspectingly through the wood. Suddenly one who rushed forth out of the thickest weed, snatched her up from the ground, and bore her off, shrieking too feebly to break the slumber of the British Maid.

It was, to wit, a wild and salvage man;
Yet was no man, but only like in shape,
And eke in stature higher by a span;
All overgrown with hair, that could awhape [6]
A hardy heart; and his wide mouth did gape
With huge great teeth, like to a tuskëd boar;
For he liv'd all on ravin [7] and on rape
Of men and beasts; and fed on fleshly gore,
The sign whereof yet stain'd his bloody lips afore.

His nether lip was not like man nor beast,
But like a wide deep poke [8] down hanging low,
In which he wont the relics of his feast
And cruel spoil, which he had spar'd,[9] to stow:
And over it his huge great nose did grow,
Full dreadfully empurpled all with blood;
And down both sides two wide long ears did glow,
And raught[10] down to his waist when up he stood,
More great than th' ears of elephants by Indus flood.

His waist was with a wreath of ivy green
Engirt about, nor other garment wore;
For all his hair was like a garment seen;
And in his hand a tall young oak he bore,
Whose knotty snags were sharpen'd all afore,
And bath'd in fire for steel to be instead.
But whence he was, or of what womb y-bore,[11]
Of beasts, or of the earth, I have not read;
But certes was with milk of wolves and tigers fed.

This ugly creature in his arms her snatch'd,
And through the forest bore her quite away
With briers and bushes all to-rent and scratch'd;
Nor care he had, nor pity of the prey,
Which many a knight had sought for many a day:
He stayëd not, but, in his arms her bearing,
Ran till he came to th' end of all his way,
Unto his cave, far from all people's hearing,
And there he threw her in, naught feeling, nor naught fearing.

Awaking from her swoon, Amoret heard, through the darkness and dread horror of the place, some one sighing and sobbing sore; and inquired where she was and what would become of her. The sad voice foreshadowed a fate worse than death:

"This dismal day hath thee a captive made
And vassal to the vilest wretch alive;
Whose cursëd usage and ungodly trade
The heav'ns abhor, and into darkness drive:
For on the spoil of women he doth live,
Whose bodies chaste, whenever in his pow'r
He may them catch, unable to gainstrive,[12]
He with his shameful lust doth first deflow'r,
And afterwards themselves doth cruelly devour.

"Now twenty days, by which the sons of men
Divide their works, have pass'd through heaven sheen,[13]
Since I was brought into this doleful den;
During which space these sorry eyes have seen
Sev'n women by him slain and eaten clean:[14]
And now no more for him but I alone,
And this old woman, here remaining be'n,

1 He brought her to bay, or constrained her to surrender.
2 Agreement.
3 Conversation.
4 Soon.
5 Set any value by her.
6 Terrify.
7 Plunder.
8 Sack.
9 Saved.
10 Reached.
11 Born.
12 Resist, strive against him.
13 Bright.
14 Entirely.

Till thou cam'st hither to augment our moan;
And of us three to-morrow he will sure eat one."

Amoret asked who it was that unlucky lot had linked with her in the same chain; and her companion answered that she was "daughter unto a lord of high degree," and had loved a gentle swain, though but a squire of low degree, against the will of her father. But she had held faithfully to her love, and for him resolved "both sire and friends and all for ever to forego." All things were ready for flight with her lover; but in the grove where she had made tryst with him she found instead that "accursëd carl of hellish kind, the shame of men, and plague of womankind," who seized upon her and brought her to his den. There, as yet untouched, she remained "his wretched thrall, the sad Æmilia." "Thus of their evils as they did discourse," the villain himself rolled away the stone that closed the cave, came rushing rudely in, and began to prepare himself for his wonted sin; but Amoret, staying not to try the utmost end, ran forth in haste, pursued by the monster. "Full fast she flies, and far afore him goes, nor feels the thorns and thickets prick her tender toes."

Nor hedge, nor ditch, nor hill, nor dale she stays,[1]
But overleaps them all, like roebuck light,
And through the thickest makes her nighest ways;
And evermore, when with regardful sight
She looking back espies that grisly wight
Approaching nigh, she gins to mend her pace,
And makes her fear a spur to haste her flight;
More swift than Myrrh' or Daphne in her race,[2]
Or any of the Thracian Nymphs in salvage chase.

Long so she fled, and so he follow'd long;
Nor living aid for her on earth appears,
But if[3] the heav'ns help to redress her wrong,
Movëd with pity of her plenteous tears.
It fortunëd Belphœbe with her peers,[4]
The woody Nymphs, and with that lovely boy,[5]
Was hunting then the leopards and the bears
In these wild woods, as was her wonted joy,
To banish sloth that oft doth noble minds annoy.

Timias and his companions were separated in the chase; and the gentle squire came on the scene in time to intercept the monster as, with grinning laughter, he was carrying the overtaken Amoret back to his cave. Assailed by Timias, the carl defended himself with his "craggy club;" and made a buckler of the lady, laughing for delight whenever any little blow lighted on her. At last the squire "left the pikehead of his spear" in the monster's body; "a stream of coalblack blood thence gush'd amain," staining all Amoret's silken garments. Throwing her rudely to the earth, the ravisher laid both hands upon his club, and let drive at Timias so sorely, that he had to give ground. Fortunately, however, Belphœbe had heard "the hideous noise of their huge strokes," and came in view "with bow in hand, and arrows ready bent." At the sight the monster, knowing that in her he saw "his death's sole instrument," fled away in fear.

Whom seeing fly, she speedily pursued,
With wingëd feet, as nimble as the wind,
And ever in her bow she ready shew'd
The arrow to his deadly mark design'd:[6]
As when Latona's daughter,[7] cruel kind,
In vengement of her mother's great disgrace,
With fell despite her cruel arrows tin'd[8]
'Gainst woeful Niobe's unhappy race,
That all the gods did moan her miserable case.

So well she sped her and so far she ventur'd,
That, ere unto his hellish den he raught,[9]
Ev'n as he ready was there to have enter'd,
She sent an arrow forth with mighty draught,[10]
That in the very door him overcaught,
And, in his nape arriving, through it thrill'd
His greedy throat, therewith in two distraught,[11]
That all his vital spirits thereby spill'd,
And all his hairy breast with gory blood was fill'd.

Whom when on ground she grovelling saw to roll,
She ran in haste his life to have bereft;
But, ere she could him reach, the sinful soul,
Having his carrion corse quite senseless left,
Was fled to hell, surcharg'd with spoil and theft:
Yet over him she there long gazing stood,
And oft admir'd[12] his monstrous shape, and oft
His mighty limbs, whilst all with filthy blood
The place there overflown seem'd like a sudden flood.

Thenceforth she pass'd into his dreadful den,
Where naught but darksome dreariness she found,
Nor creature saw, but hearken'd now and then
Some little whisp'ring, and soft-groaning sound.
With that she ask'd, what ghosts there under ground
Lay hid in horror of eternal night;
And bade them, if so be they were not bound,
To come and show themselves before the light,
Now freed from fear and danger of that dismal wight.

Then forth the sad Æmilia issúed,
Yet trembling ev'ry joint through former fear;
And after her the hag there with her mew'd,[13]
A foul and loathsome creature, did appear;
A leman fit for such a lover dear:
That mov'd Belphœbe her no less to hate,
Than for to rue[14] the other's heavy cheer;
Of whom she gan inquire of her estate;[15]
Who all to her at large, as happen'd, did relate.

Thence she them brought toward the place where late
She left the gentle Squire with Amoret:
There she him found by that new lovely mate,
Who lay the while in swoon, full sadly set,

1 Stops for. 2 See note 6, page 427. 3 Unless. 4 Companions. 5 Timias, the squire of Prince Arthur, whom Belphœbe had rescued and taken to her abode after his conflict with the foresters; canto v. book iii.

6 Directed. 7 Diana. 8 Aimed. 9 Reached. 10 Drawn with mighty force. 11 Separated. 12 Wondered at. 13 Imprisoned. 14 Pity. 15 Condition.

From her fair eyes wiping the dowy wet,
Which softly still'd,[1] and kissing them atween,
And handling soft the hurts which she did get:
For of that carl she sorely bruis'd had been,
Als'[2] of his own rash hands one wound was to be seen.

Which when she saw with sudden glancing eye,
Her noble heart, with sight thereof, was fill'd
With deep disdain, and great indignity,
That in her wrath she thought them both have thrill'd[3]
With that self arrow which the carl had kill'd:
Yet held her wrathful hand from vengeance sore:
But, drawing nigh, ere he her well beheld,
"Is this the faith?"[4] she said—and said no more,
But turn'd her face, and fled away for evermore.

He, seeing her depart, arose up light,
Right sore aggrievëd at her sharp reproof,
And follow'd fast: but, when he came in sight,
He durst not nigh approach, but kept aloof,
For dread of her displeasure's utmost proof:
And evermore, when he did grace entreat,
And framëd speeches fit for his behoof,
Her mortal arrows she at him did threat,
And forc'd him back with foul dishonour to retreat.

At last, when long he follow'd had in vain,
Yet found no ease of grief nor hope of grace,
Unto those woods he turnëd back again,
Full of sad anguish and in heavy case:
And, finding there fit solitary place
For woeful wight, chose out a gloomy glade,
Where hardly eye might see bright heaven's face
For mossy trees, which cover'd all with shade
And sad melâncholy; there he his cabin made.

His wonted warlike weapons all he broke
And threw away, with vow to use no more,
Nor thenceforth ever strike in battle stroke,
Nor ever word to speak to woman more;
But in that wilderness, of men forlore,[5]
And of the wicked world forgotten quite,
His hard mishap in dolour to deplore,
And waste his wretched days in woeful plight:
So on himself to wreak his folly's own despite.

And eke his garment, to be thereto meet,
He wilfully did cut and shape anew;
And his fair locks, that wont with ointment sweet
To be embalm'd, and sweat out dainty dew,
He let to grow and grisly to concrue,[6]
Uncomb'd, uncurl'd, and carelessly unshed;
That in short time his face they overgrew,
And over all his shoulders did dispread,
That who he whilom was unneth was to be read.[7]

There he continued in this careful[8] plight,
Wretchedly wearing out his youthly years,
Through wilful penury[9] consumëd quite,
That like a pinëd ghost he soon appears:
For other food than that wild forest bears,
Nor other drink there did he ever taste
Than running water temper'd with his tears,
The more his weaken'd body so to waste:
That out of all men's knowledge he was worn at last.

For on a day, by fortune as it fell,
His own dear lord Prince Arthur came that way,
Seeking adventures where he might hear tell;
And, as he through the wand'ring wood did stray,
Having espied his cabin far away,
He to it drew, to weet[10] who there did won;[11]
Weening therein some holy hermit lay,
That did resort of sinful people shun;
Or else some woodman shrouded there from scorching sun.

Arriving there, he found this wretched man
Spending his days in dolour and despair,
And, through long fasting, waxing pale and wan,
All overgrown with rude and rugged hair;
That albeit his own dear Squire he were,
Yet he him knew not, nor advis'd[12] at all;
But like strange wight, whom he had seen nowhére,
Saluting him gan into speech to fall,
And pity much his plight, that liv'd like outcast thrall.

But to his speech he answerëd no whit,
But stood still mute as if he had been dumb,
Nor sign of sense did show, nor common wit,
As one with grief and anguish overcome;
And unto ev'rything did answer mum:
And ever, when the Prince unto him spake,
He louted[13] lowly, as did him become,
And humble homage did unto him make;
Midst sorrow showing joyous semblance for his sake.

At which his uncouth guise and usage quaint
The Prince did wonder much, yet could not guess
The cause of that his sorrowful constraint;
Yet ween'd, by secret signs of manliness
Which close appear'd in that rude brutishness,
That he whilóm some gentle swain had been,
Train'd up in feats of arms and knightliness;
Which he observ'd, by that he him had seen
To wield his naked sword, and try the edges keen;

And eke by that he saw on ev'ry tree
How he the name of one engraven had
Which likely was his liefest[14] love to be,
From whom he now so sorely was bestad;[15]
Which was by him BELPHŒBE rightly rad:[16]

1 Distilled. 2 Also. 3 Pierced.

4 In or shortly after the year 1592, Raleigh incurred the grave displeasure of Queen Elizabeth, by an amour which was discovered to exist between him and one of her maids of honour—Elizabeth, daughter of Sir Nicholas Throckmorton. Though he made reparation to the lady's honour by marrying her, still he was imprisoned for several months, and banished from the Queen's presence and Court. It is to this episode in the career of his friend Raleigh (whom, as it has been already stated, Timias represents) that Spenser refers in the not less bold than beautiful passage before us.

5 Abandoned. 6 Grow together.

7 That it was scarcely possible to tell who he formerly was. 8 Sorrowful. 9 Privation. 10 Learn. 11 Dwell. 12 Recognised. 13 Bowed. 14 Dearest.

15 Separated from whom he was so wretched. 16 Read.

Yet who was that Belphœbe he not wist;[1]
Yet saw he often how he waxëd glad
When he it heard, and how the ground he kist
Wherein it written was, and how himself he
blist.[2]

Then when he long had markëd his demeanour,
And saw that all he said and did was vain,
Nor aught might make him change his wonted
tenour,
Nor aught might cease to mitigate his pain;
He left him there in languor to remain,
Till time for him should remedy provide,
And him restore to former grace again:
Which, for it is too long here to abide,
I will defer the end until another tide.

CANTO VIII.

The gentle Squire recovers grace:
Slander her guests doth stain:
Corflambo chaseth Placidas,
And is by Arthur slain.

THE poet cites the saying of Solomon, "that the displeasure of the mighty is than death itself more dread and desperate;" and points the proverb by the sad case of Timias, "whose tender heart the fair Belphœbe had with one stern look so daunted," that his whole life was passed in sorrow and weeping, "as blasted bloom through heat doth languish and decay."

Till on a day, as in his wonted wise
His dool[3] he made, there chanc'd a turtle dove
To come, where he his dolours did devise,[4]
That likewise late had lost her dearest love,
Which loss her made like passion[5] also prove:[6]
Who seeing his sad plight, her tender heart
With dear compassion deeply did enmove,
That she gan moan his undeservëd smart,
And with her doleful accent bear with him a
part.

She sitting by him, as on ground he lay,
Her mournful notes full piteously did frame,
And thereof made a lamentable lay,
So sensibly compil'd,[7] that in the same
Him seemëd oft he heard his own right name.
With that he forth would pour so plenteous
tears,
And beat his breast, unworthy of such blame,
And knock his head, and rend his rugged hairs,
That could have pierc'd the hearts of tigers and
of bears.

Thus long this gentle bird to him did use,
Withouten dread of peril, to repair
Unto his won,[8] and with her mournful muse
Him to recomfort in his greatest care,
That much did ease his mourning and misfare:[9]
And ev'ry day, for guerdon of her song,
He part of his small feast to her would share;
That, at the last, of all his woe and wrong
Companion she became, and so continued long.

Upon a day, as she him sat beside,
By chance he certain moniments[10] forth drew,
Which yet with him as relics did abide
Of all the bounty which Belphœbe threw
On him, whilst goodly grace she did him shew:
Amongst the rest a jewel rich he found,
That was a ruby of right perfect hue,
Shap'd like a heart yet bleeding of the wound,
And with a little golden chain about it bound.

The same he took, and with a riband new,
In which his lady's colours were, did bind
About the turtle's neck, that with the view
Did greatly solace his engrievëd mind.
All unawares the bird, when she did find
Herself so deck'd, her nimble wings display'd,
And flew away as lightly as the wind:
Which sudden accident him much dismay'd;
And, looking after long, did mark which way
she stray'd;

But when as long he lookëd had in vain,
Yet saw her forward still to make her flight,
His weary eye return'd to him again,
Full of discomfort and disquiet plight,
That both his jewel he had lost so light,
And eke his dear companion of his care.
But that sweet bird departing flew forthright,
Through the wide region of the wasteful[11] air,
Until she came where wonnëd[12] his Belphœbe
fair.

There found she her (as then it did betide)
Sitting in covert shade of arbours sweet,
After late weary toil, which she had tried
In salvage chase, to rest as seem'd her meet.
There she, alighting, fell before her feet,
And gan to her her mournful plaint to make,
As was her wont, thinking to let her weet[13]
The great tormenting grief that for her sake
Her gentle Squire through her displeasure did
partake.

She, her beholding with attentive eye,
At length did mark about her purple breast
That precious jewel which she formerly
Had known right well, with colour'd ribands
drest:
Therewith she rose in haste, and her addrest
With ready hand it to have reft away:
But the swift bird obey'd not her behest,
But swerv'd aside, and there again did stay;
She follow'd her, and thought again it to assay.

And ever, when she nigh approach'd, the dove
Would flit a little forward, and then stay
Till she drew near, and then again remove:
So tempting her still to pursue the prey,
And still from her escaping soft away:
Till that at length into that forest wide
She drew her far, and led with slow delay:
In th' end, she her unto that place did guide
Where as that woeful man in languor did abide.

Eftsoons she flew unto his fearless hand,

1 Knew. 2 Blessed.
3 Lament. 4 Told his griefs.
5 Suffering. 6 Feel.

7 Constructed. 8 Dwelling.
9 Unhappiness. 10 Memorials.
11 Desert. 12 Dwelt. 13 Know.

And there a piteous ditty new devis'd,
As if she would have made him understand
His sorrow's cause, to be of her despis'd:
Whom when she saw in wretched weeds[1] disguis'd,
With hairy glib[2] deform'd, and meagre face,
Like ghost late risen from his grave agris'd,[3]
She knew him not, but pitied much his case,
And wish'd it were in her to do him any grace.

He, her beholding, at her feet down fell
And kiss'd the ground on which her sole did tread,
And wash'd the same with water which did well
From his moist eyes, and like two streams proceed;
Yet spake no word, whereby she might aread[4]
What mister wight[5] he was, or what he meant;
But, as one daunted with her presence dread,
Only few rueful looks unto her sent,
As messengers of his true meaning and intent.

Belphœbe does not understand his meaning, nor recognise his person; but she sees that he has been "some man of place," and, moved with pity, inquires what makes him thus wretched; calling on him not to despise the grace of his Creator, by wilful scorn of life. Breaking his long silence, Timias exclaims that Heaven has secretly consented with a cruel one, to cloud his days in doleful misery, and make him loathe both life and death:

"Nor any but yourself, O dearest Dread,[6]
Hath done this wrong, to wreak on worthless wight
Your high displeasure, through misdeeming[7] bred:
That, when your pleasure is to deem aright,
Ye may redress, and me restore to light!"
Which sorry words her mighty heart did mate[8]
With mild regard to see his rueful plight,
That her inburning wrath she gan abate,
And him receiv'd again to former favour's state.

In which he long time afterwards did lead
A happy life with grace and good accord,
Fearless of fortune's change or envy's dread,
And eke all mindless of his own dear lord
The noble Prince, who never heard one word
Of tidings, what did unto him betide,
Or what good fortune did to him afford;
But through the endless world did wander wide,
Him seeking evermore, yet nowhere him descried.

"Till on a day, as through that wood he rode," he found Æmilia and Amoret; the first yet weak from the hardships of her imprisonment, the other suffering grievously from the wound inflicted by Timias in the contest with the carl. Moved with pity especially for Amoret, the Prince bathed her wound with a few drops of that precious liquor[9] which he always carried about him, and soon restored her to health. He marvelled much at the story of their rescue, and greatly desired to know who was the Virgin that had delivered them; but since he could not learn, he set them on his horse, and walked beside on foot "to succour them from fear."

So when that forest they had passëd well,
A little cottage far away they spied,
To which they drew ere night upon them fell;
And, ent'ring in, found none therein abide,
But one old woman sitting there beside
Upon the ground in ragged rude attire,
With filthy locks about her scatter'd wide,
Gnawing her nails for fellness and for ire,
And thereout sucking venom to her parts entire.[10]

A foul and loathly creature sure in sight,[11]
And in conditions[12] to be loath'd no less:
For she was stuff'd with rancour and despite
Up to the throat, that oft with bitterness
It forth would break and gush in great excess,
Pouring out streams of poison and of gall
'Gainst all that truth or virtue do profess;
Whom she with leasings[13] lewdly[14] did miscall
And wickedly backbite: her name men Slander call.

Her nature is, all goodness to abuse,
And, causeless, crimes continually to frame,
With which she guiltless persons may accuse,
And steal away the crown of their good name:
Nor ever knight so bold, nor ever dame
So chaste and loyal liv'd, but she would strive
With forgëd cause them falsely to defame;
Nor ever thing so well was done alive,
But she with blame would blot, and of due praise deprive.

Her words were not, as common words are meant,
T' express the meaning of the inward mind,
But noisome breath, and pois'nous spirit sent
From inward parts, with canker'd malice lin'd,
And breathëd forth with blast of bitter wind;
Which, passing through the ears, would pierce the heart,
And wound the soul itself with grief unkind:
For, like the stings of asps that kill with smart,
Her spiteful words did prick and wound the inner part.

Bowing to necessity, the Prince and his companions patiently endured the cold and cheerless hunger of the place, and the scoldings and railings of the hag "for lodging there without her own consent." Anticipating the objections of some "rash-witted wight," who might deem those gentle ladies too light "for thus conversing with this noble knight," the poet admits that "now of days such temperance is rare, and hard to find," as that which restrains heat of youthful spirit from greed of pleasure; "more

1 Garments.
2 In his "View of the State of Ireland," Spenser says that the Irish, among other customs derived from the Scythians, have that of wearing "long glibs, which is a thick curled bush of hair, hanging down over their eyes and monstrously disguising them."
3 Terrified, confounded.
4 Discover.
5 Manner of man.
6 Object of reverent fear. See note 19, page 310.
7 Misjudgment.
8 Subdue.
9 Of which he had given a few drops to the Redcross Knight. See page 347.
10 Internal.
11 Aspect.
12 Qualities.
13 False speeches.
14 Wickedly.

hard for hungry steed t' abstain from pleasant lair."

But antique Age, yet in the infancy
Of time, did live then, like an innocent,
In simple truth and blameless chastity;
Nor then of guile had made experiment;
But, void of vile and treacherous intent,
Held virtue, for itself, in sov'reign awe:
Then loyal love had royal regiment,[1]
And each unto his lust[2] did make a law,
From all forbidden things his liking to withdraw.

The lion there did with the lamb consort,
And eke the dove sat by the falcon's side;
Nor each of other fearëd fraud or tort,[3]
But did in safe security abide,
Withouten peril of the stronger pride:
But when the world wax'd old, it wax'd warre[4] old
(Whereof it hight[5]), and, having shortly tried
The trains[6] of wit, in wickedness wax'd bold,
And darëd of all sins the secrets to unfold.

Then Beauty, which was made to represent
The great Creator's own resemblance bright,
Unto abuse of lawless lust was lent,
And made the bait of bestial delight:
Then fair grew foul, and foul grew fair in sight;
And that which wont to vanquish God and man
Was made the vassal of the victor's might;
Then did her glorious flow'r wax dead and wan,
Despis'd and trodden down of all that overran:

And now it is so utterly decay'd,
That any bud thereof doth scarce remain,
But if[7] few plants, preserv'd through heav'nly aid,
In prince's court do hap to sprout again,
Dew'd with her drops of bounty sovëreign,
Which from that goodly glorious flow'r[8] proceed,
Sprung of the ancient stock of princes' strain,[9]
Now th' only remnant of that royal breed
Whose noble kind at first was, sure, of heav'nly seed.

Soon as day dawned, the gentle crew continued their journey, in the same way as before; the "shameful hag, the slander of her sex," pursuing them with foul revilings, railing and raging, till she had spent all her poison.

At last, when they were passëd out of sight,
Yet she did not her spiteful speech forbear,
But after them did bark, and still backbite,
Though there were none her hateful words to hear:
Like as a cur doth felly bite and tear
The stone which passëd stranger at him threw;
So she, them seeing past the reach of ear,
Against the stones and trees did rail anew,
Till she had dull'd the sting which in her tongue's end grew.

1 Government, rule.
2 Will.
3 Wrong.
4 Worse.
5 Whence it takes its name.
6 Stratagems.
7 Unless.
8 Gloriana, or Queen Elizabeth.
9 Race.

Passing gently on their way, because of the great feebleness of Amoret, and the heavy armour which annoyed the Prince on foot, they spied at last, galloping towards them, a squire bearing before him on his steed a little dwarf who all the way cried for aid, "that seem'd his shrieks would rend the brazen sky." After them pursued, riding on a dromedary, a mighty man "of stature huge, and horrible of hue," from whose fearful eyes two fiery beams, sharper than points of needles, proceeded, powerful to kill as glances of the basilisk. He threw many angry curses and threats at the squire, who, when he saw the Prince, called aloud to him for rescue. Arthur, causing the ladies to alight, mounted his steed; and just as the pursuer aimed a dreadful blow at the squire, the Prince interposed:

Who, thrusting boldly 'twixt him and the blow,
The burden of the deadly brunt did bear
Upon his shield, which lightly he did throw
Over his head, before the harm came near:
Nathless it fell with so dispiteous drear[10]
And heavy sway, that hard unto his crown
The shield it drove, and did the covering rear:[11]
Therewith both squire and dwarf did tumble down
Unto the earth, and lay long while in senseless swoon.

Whereat the Prince, full wroth, his strong right hand
In full avengement heavëd up on high,
And struck the Pagan with his steely brand
So sore, that to his saddle-bow thereby
He bowëd low, and so a while did lie:
And, sure, had not his massy iron mace
Betwixt him and his hurt been happily,
It would have cleft him to the girding place;[12]
Yet, as it was, it did astonish[13] him long space.

But, when he to himself return'd again,
All full of rage he gan to curse and swear,
And vow by Mahound[14] that he should be slain.
With that his murd'rous mace he up did rear,
That seemëd naught the souse[15] thereof could bear,
And therewith smote at him with all his might:
But, ere that it to him approachëd near,
The royal Child,[16] with ready quick foresight,
Did shun the proof thereof, and it avoided light.

But, ere his hand he could recure[17] again
To ward his body from the baleful stound,[18]
He smote at him with all his might and main
So furiously, that, ere he wist, he found
His head before him tumbling on the ground;
The while his babbling tongue did yet blaspheme
And curse his god that did him so confound;
The while his life ran forth in bloody stream,
His soul descended down into the Stygian ream.[19]

Glad was the squire, and bitterly sorry the

10 Terror.
11 Removed the cover—which veiled the blinding brightness of the shield.
12 To the belt, or waist.
13 Stun.
14 Mahomet.
15 Forcible descent.
16 Youth.
17 Recover.
18 Blow.
19 Realm.

dwarf, to see the giant's fall; and Arthur began to inquire of the first what he was whose eyes did flame with fire. The squire replied that the mighty man whom the Prince had slain was bred of a huge giantess, and had won to himself command of many kingdoms, not by armies nor by bloody fight, "but by the power of his infectious sight," which killed whoever saw him. Never had he been vanquished, for no man could match him; while no woman was so fair that he did not make her captive to his thought, and waste her unto naught, by casting secret flakes of lustful fire into her heart from his false eyes. "Therefore Corflambo [1] was he call'd aright;" and he had left one daughter, Pæana, outwardly as fair as living eye had ever seen, but inwardly given to vain delight, "and eke too loose of life, and eke of love too light." As it fell, a gentle squire loved a lady of high parentage—Æmilia—who had resolved to fly with him; but as he went to the trysting-place, he was caught by Corflambo, and thrown into his dungeon, where he remained "of all unsuccoured and unsought." The giant's daughter, coming "in her joyous glee" to gaze on the captives, fell in love with "the squire of low degree," whose name was Amyas, and promised him liberty for his love; "he granted love, but with affection cold, to win her grace his liberty to get;" still she detained him a captive, fearing that, if freed, he would quit her. Yet sometimes he had the favour of walking about her pleasure-garden, with the dwarf as his keeper, who held the keys of every prison door. The squire whom Arthur had rescued, and who was called Placidas, for zealous love of the prisoner went to search the place of his captivity; there he was discovered by the dwarf, who, deceived by his strong resemblance to Amyas, told his mistress that her squire of low degree secretly stole out of his prison; and, being taken and brought before Pæana, Placidas was reproached for his untruth and desire to escape, and driven away by the dwarf to the dungeon where his faithful friend languished "in heavy plight and sad perplexity." The captive, however, was only the more grieved by the captivity of his friend; for his sole joy in his distress was the freedom of his Placidas and his Æmilia. But the new prisoner insisted upon the other's consent to a scheme for deliverance, through taking advantage of the resemblance between the two.

"The morrow next, about the wonted hour,
The dwarf call'd at the door of Amyas
To come forthwith unto his lady's bow'r:
Instead of whom forth came I, Placidas,
And undiscernëd forth with him did pass.
There with great joyance and with gladsome glee
Of fair Pæana I receivëd was,
And oft embrac'd, as if that I were he,
And with kind words acoy'd,[2] vowing great love to me.

"Which I, that was not bent to former love,
As was my friend that had her long refus'd,
Did well accept, as well it did behove,
And to the present need it wisely us'd.
My former hardness [3] first I fair excus'd;
And, after, promis'd large amends to make.
With such smooth terms her error I abus'd,
To my friend's good more than for mine own sake,
For whose sole liberty I love and life did stake.

"Thenceforth I found more favour at her hand;
That to her dwarf, which had me in his charge,
She bade to lighten my too heavy band,
And grant more scope to me to walk at large.
So on a day, as by the flow'ry marge
Of a fresh stream I with that elf did play,
Finding no means how I might us enlarge,
But if [4] that dwarf I could with me convey,
I lightly snatch'd him up, and with me bore away.

"Thereat he shriek'd aloud, that with his cry
The tyrant self came forth with yelling bray,
And me pursued; but nathëmore would I
Forego the purchase [5] of my gotten prey,
But have perforce him hither brought away."
Thus as they talkëd, lo! where nigh at hand
Those ladies two, yet doubtful through dismay,
In presence came, desirous t' understand
Tidings of all which there had happen'd on the land.

Where soon as sad Æmilia did espy
Her captive lover's friend, young Placidas;
All mindless of her wonted modesty
She to him ran, and, him with strait embras[6]
Enfolding, said; "And lives yet Amyas?"
"He lives," quoth he, "and his Æmilia loves."
"Then less," said she, "by all the woe I pass,[7]
With which my weaker patience Fortune proves:
But what mishap thus long him from myself removes?"

Then gan he all this story to renew,
And tell the course of his captivity;
That her dear [8] heart full deeply made to rue [9]
And sigh full sore to hear the misery
In which so long he merciless did lie.
Then, after many tears and sorrows spent,
She dear besought the Prince of remedy:
Who thereto did with ready will consent,
And well perform'd; as shall appear by his event.

CANTO IX.

The squire of low degree, releas'd,
Pæana takes to wife:
Britomart fights with many knights;
Prince Arthur stints [10] their strife.

Hard is the doubt, and difficult to deem,[11]
When all three kinds of love together meet
And do dispart [12] the heart with pow'r extreme,

1 The Inflamer of Hearts.
2 Caressed, enticed. 3 Indifference.
4 Unless. 5 Acquisition. 6 Close embrace.
7 Less do I consider all the woe.
8 Loving. 9 Pity.
10 Stops. 11 Decide, judge. 12 Divide.

Whether shall weigh the balance down ; to weet,
The dear affection unto kindred sweet,
Or raging fire of love to womankind,
Or zeal of friends combin'd with virtues meet.
But of them all the band of virtuous mind,
Me seems, the gentle heart should most assurëd
bind.

For natural affection soon doth cease,
And quenchëd is with Cupid's greater flame ;
But faithful friendship doth them both suppress,
And them with mast'ring discipline doth tame,
Through thoughts aspiring to eternal fame.
For as the soul doth rule the earthly mass,
And all the service of the body frame,
So love of soul doth love of body pass,
No less than perfect gold surmounts the meanest
brass.

All which who list by trial to assay,[1]
Shall in this story find approvëd plain ;
In which these squires true friendship more
did sway
Than either care of parents could refrain,
Or love of fairest lady could constrain.
For though Pæana were as fair as morn,
Yet did this trusty squire with proud disdain,
For his friend's sake, her offer'd favours scorn ;
And she herself her sire of whom she was y-born.

Considering how he might best achieve the enterprise of succouring Amyas, Arthur resolved to set the body of Corflambo, "having imp'd the head to it again," upon the dromedary ; before the dead but live-seeming giant he laid Placidas, as if he were a captive ; and he made the dwarf lead the beast to the castle—where the watch unsuspectingly admitted the corpse and the Prince together.

There did he find, in her delicious bow'r,
The fair Pæana playing on a rote,[2]
Complaining of her cruel paramoúr,
And singing all her sorrow to the note,
As she had learnëd readily by rote ;
That with the sweetness of her rare delight
The Prince half rapt began on her to dote ;
Till, better him bethinking of the right,
He her unwares attach'd,[3] and captive held by
might.

Pæana called, but vainly, on her father for aid ; then, seeing that she had been betrayed, she began to weep, and wail, and charge the squire with treason. But Arthur, unheeding, made the dwarf open the prison doors ; and above a score of knights and ladies were released —among them, full weak and wan, the squire of low degree. Placidas and Æmilia ran to embrace him ; while Pæana, gnawed with envy, cursed them both, and wept bitterly. By and by, however, she began to doubt which of the two squires was the man with whom she had been in love—so like were they in person ; and her doubt and wonder were shared by the Prince and all present. Ransacking the castle, the Prince found much ill-gotten treasure, on which he seized ; he rested some time there to recruit the weaker ladies after their weary toil ; and he liberated Pæana—who, however, would not "show gladsome countenance nor pleasant glee," for grief at the loss of her father, her lordship, and "her new love, the hope of her desire." By degrees, Arthur softened away the foul rudeness of the lady ; while he counselled Placidas to "accept her to his wedded wife"—offering to "make him chief of all her land and lordship during life." Placidas consented, and all went happily.

From that day forth in peace and joyous bliss
They liv'd together long without debate ;
Nor private jar, nor spite of enemies,
Could shake the safe assurance of their state :
And she, whom nature did so fair create
That she might match the fairest of her days,
Yet with lewd loves and lust intemperate
Had it defac'd, thenceforth reform'd her ways,
That all men much admir'd her change, and
spake her praise.

Having settled Amyas and Æmilia, Placidas and Pæana, in peace and rest, Arthur set out on his former quest (after the Faery Queen), taking with him Amoret, now fearless for her safety, but fearful of her honour—though cause of fear she had none, for while she rode by the self-controlling Arthur, "she was as safe as in a sanctuary."

At length they came where as a troop of knights
They saw together skirmishing, as seem'd :
Six they were all, all full of fell despite,
But four of them the battle best beseem'd,[4]
That which of them was best might not be
deem'd.
These four were they from whom false Florimell
By Braggadocio lately was redeem'd ;[5]
To wit, stern Druon, and lewd Claribell,
Love-lavish Blandamour, and lustful Paridell.

Druon's delight was all in single life,
And unto ladies' love would lend no leisure :
The more was Claribell engagëd rife[6]
With fervent flames, and lovëd out of measure :
So eke lov'd Blandamour, but yet at pleasure
Would change his liking, and new lemans[7]
prove :
But Paridell of love did make no treasure,[8]
But lusted after all that him did move :
So diversely these four disposëd were to love.

But those two others, which beside them stood,
Were Britomart and gentle Scudamour ;
Who all the while beheld their wrathful mood,
And wonder'd at their ímplacáble stowre,[9]
Whose like they never saw till that same hour :
So dreadful strokes each did at other drive,
And laid on load with all their might and pow'r,
As if that ev'ry dint the ghost would rive
Out of their wretched corses, and their lives
deprive.

1 Who chooses to test by experiment.
2 See note 14, page 395.
3 Seized.
4 Seemed fit for.
5 At the tournament of Satyrane. See canto v. of the present book.
6 Frequently.
7 Mistresses.
8 Hold no account.
9 Conflict.

As when Dan Æolus, in great displeasure
For loss of his dear love by Neptune hent,[1]
Sends forth the winds out of his hidden treasure,[2]
Upon the sea to wreak his full intent;
They, breaking forth with rude unruliment
From all four parts of heav'n, do rage full sore,
And toss the deeps, and tear the firmament,
And all the world confound with wide uproar;
As if instead thereof they Chaos would restore.

It may be remembered that, after Sir Satyrane's tournament (in canto iv. of this book) the "discordful crew" with whom Duessa and Até travelled, had set out in quest of "the snowy maid," the false Florimell; and now they had all met, and were fighting confusedly, provoked "through lewd upbraid" of the two strifeful dames in their company. Ever changing sides and opponents, they continued the battle with ever new fury; proving the truth of the saying, that "faint friends when they fall out most cruel foemen be." While they fought, Scudamour and Britomart had come in sight, inspiring them all with new rancour—for the Maid had put them all to shame in the late tourney. All now turned their cruel blades from themselves, against the new comers, who bore themselves bravely, and repaid the assailants their own with usury.

Full oftentimes did Britomart assay
To speak to them, and some emparlance[3] move;
But they for naught their cruel hands would stay,
Nor lend an ear to aught that might behove.
As when an eager mastiff once doth prove
The taste of blood of some engorëd[4] beast,
No words may rate,[5] nor rigour him remove
From greedy hold of that his bloody feast:
So, little did they hearken to her sweet behest.

Whom when the Briton Prince afar beheld
With odds of so unequal match opprest,
His mighty heart with indignation swell'd,
And inward grudge fill'd his heroic breast:
Eftsoons himself he to their aid addrest,
And, thrusting fierce into the thickest press,
Divided them, however loth to rest;
And would them fain from battle to surcease,
With gentle words persuading them to friendly peace:

But they so far from peace or patience were,
That all at once at him gan fiercely fly,
And lay on load, as they him down would bear:
Like to a storm which hovers under sky,
Long here and there and round about doth sty,[6]
At length breaks down in rain, and hail, and sleet,
First from one coast, till naught thereof be dry;
And then another, till that likewise fleet;[7]
And so from side to side till all the world it weet.[8]

At last, on the intercession of Scudamour and Britomart, the Prince granted a truce, and asked the combatants to tell the cause of their cruel heat. They began to repeat all that had passed, telling how Britomart had foiled them in open tourney, and beguiled them of their loves. Britomart, in a passage not quite reconcileable with what goes before, defended herself from the charge, showing that she had not carried Amoret away by force, but of her own liking.

To whom the Prince thus goodly well replied;
"Certes, Sir Knights, ye seemen much to blame
To rip up wrong that battle once hath tried;
Wherein the honour both of arms ye shame,
And eke the love of ladies foul defame;
To whom the world this franchise[9] ever yielded,
That of their loves' choice they might freedom claim,
And in that right should by all knights be shielded:
'Gainst which, me seems, this war ye wrongfully have wielded."

"And yet," quoth she, "a greater wrong remains:
For I thereby my former love have lost;
Whom seeking ever since with endless pains
Hath me much sorrow and much travail cost:
Ah me, to see that gentle maid so tost!"
But Scudamour then sighing deep thus said;
"Certes her loss ought me to sorrow most,
Whose right she is, wherever she be stray'd,
Through many perils won, and many fortunes weigh'd:[10]

"For from the first that I her love profest,
Unto this hour, this present luckless hour,
I never joyëd happiness nor rest:
But thus turmoil'd from one to other stowre[11]
I waste my life, and do my days devour
In wretched anguish and incessant woe,
Passing the measure of my feeble pow'r;
That, living thus a wretch and loving so,
I neither can my love nor yet my life forego."

Then good Sir Claribell him thus bespake;
"Now were it not, Sir Scudamour, to you
Dislikeful[12] pain so sad a task to take,
Might we entreat you, since this gentle crew
Is now so well accorded all anew,
That, as we ride together on our way,
Ye will recount to us in order due
All that adventure which ye did assay
For that fair lady's love: past perils well apay."[13]

All the rest, especially Britomart, made the same request; and, glad to satisfy the Maid, Scudamour spoke as the next canto reports.

1 Neptune was said to have carried off Arne, one of the daughters of Æolus. 2 Storehouse.
3 Parley, treaty for peace. 4 Wounded.
5 Chide off. 6 Move.
7 Float. 8 Wet.
9 Privilege, liberty. 10 Endured.
11 Conflict, trouble. 12 Disagreeable.
13 The recollection of perils past is well pleasing.

CANTO X.

Scudamour doth his conquest tell
Of virtuous Amoret:
Great Venus' Temple is describ'd;
And lovers' life forth set.

"TRUE he it said, whatever man it said,
That love with gall and honey doth abound:[1]
But if the one be with the other weigh'd,
For every dram of honey therein found
A pound of gall doth over it redound;
That I too true by trial have approv'd;
For since the day that first with deadly wound
My heart was lanc'd, and learnëd to have lov'd,
I never joyëd hour, but still with care was mov'd.

"And yet such grace is giv'n them from above,
That all the cares and evil which they meet
May naught at all their settled minds remove,
But seem, 'gainst common sense, to them most sweet;
As boasting in their martyrdom unmeet.
So all that ever yet I have endur'd
I count as naught, and tread down under feet,
Since of my love at length I rest assur'd
That to disloyalty she will not be allur'd.

"Long were to tell the travail and long toil
Through which the Shield of Love I late have won,
And purchasëd this peerless beauty's spoil;
That harder may be ended than begun:
But since ye so desire, your will be done.
Then hark, ye gentle knights and ladies free,
My hard mishaps that ye may learn to shun;
For though sweet love to conquer glorious be,
Yet is the pain thereof much greater than the fee.

"What time the fame of this renownëd prize
Flew first abroad, and all men's ears possest;
I, having arms then taken, gan advise[2]
To win me honour by some noble gest,[3]
And purchase me some place amongst the best.
I boldly thought (so young men's thoughts are bold),
That this same brave emprise for me did rest,
And that both shield and she whom I behold
Might be my lucky lot; since all by lot we hold.

"So on that hard adventure forth I went,
And to the place of peril shortly came:
That was a temple fair and ancient,
Which of great mother Venus bare the name,
And far renownëd through exceeding fame;
Much more than that which was in Paphos built,
Or that in Cyprus,[4] both long since[5] this same,
Though all the pillars of the one were gilt,
And all the other's pavement were with ivory spilt.[6]

"And it was seated in an island strong,
Abounding all with délicés[7] most rare,
And wall'd by nature 'gainst invaders' wrong,
That none might have accéss, nor inward fare,[8]
But by one way that passage did prepare.
It was a bridge y-built in goodly wise
With curious corbs[9] and pendants graven fair,
And archëd all with porches did arise
On stately pillars fram'd after the Doric guise:

"And for defence thereof on th' other end
There rearëd was a castle fair and strong,
That warded all which in or out did wend,
And flankëd both the bridge's sides along
'Gainst all that would it fain[10] to force or wrong:
And therein wonnëd[11] twenty valiant knights;
All twenty tried in war's experience long;
Whose office was against all manner wights[12]
By all means to maintain that castle's ancient rights.

"Before that castle was an open plain,
And in the midst thereof a pillar plac'd;
On which this shield, of many sought in vain,
THE SHIELD OF LOVE, whose guerdon me hath grac'd,
Was hang'd on high, with golden ribands lac'd;
And in the marble stone was written this,
With golden letters goodly well enchas'd;
Blessëd the man that well can use this bliss:
Whose ever be the shield, fair Amoret be his.

"Which when I read, my heart did inly yearn,
And pant with hope of that adventure's hap:
Nor stayëd further news thereof to learn,
But with my spear upon the shield did rap,
That all the castle ringëd with the clap.
Straight forth issûed a knight all arm'd to proof,
And bravely mounted to his most mishap:
Who, staying not to question from aloof,
Ran fierce at me, that fire glanc'd from his horse's hoof.

"Whom boldly I encounter'd (as I co'ld),
And by good fortune shortly him unseated.
Eftsoons outsprang two more of equal mould;
But I them both with equal hap defeated:
So all the twenty I likewise entreated,
And left them groaning there upon the plain.
Then, pressing to the pillar, I repeated
The read[13] thereof for guerdon of my pain,
And, taking down the shield, with me did it retain.

"So forth without impediment I past,
Till to the bridge's outer gate I came;
The which I found sure lock'd and chainëd fast.
I knock'd, but no man answer'd me by name;
I call'd, but no man answer'd to my claim:[14]
Yet I persëver'd still to knock and call;
Till at the last I spied within the same
Where one stood peeping through a crevice small,
To whom I call'd aloud, half angry therewithal.

1 Chaucer has put into the mouth of Rigour, in "The Court of Love," the statement that women "be bound by nature to deceive, and spin, and weep, and sugar strew on gall;" page 205.
2 Bethink myself.
3 Achievement.
4 The two were really the same; the famous temple of Venus stood at Paphos, a town on the west coast of the island of Cyprus.
5 After.
6 Inlaid.
7 Delights.
8 Pass, go.
9 Corbels.
10 Desire.
11 Dwelt.
12 Manner of persons.
13 Motto, inscription.
14 Call; the literal meaning of "claim," from Latin, "clamo."

"That was, to wit, the porter of the place,
Unto whose trust the charge thereof was lent:[1]
His name was Doubt, that had a double face,
Th' one forward looking, th' other backward bent,
Therein resembling Janus anciént
Which hath in charge the ingate[2] of the year:
And evermore his eyes about him went,
As if some provëd peril he did fear,
Or did misdoubt some ill whose cause did not appear.

"On th' one side he, on th' other sat Delay,
Behind the gate, that none her might espy;
Whose manner was, all passengers to stay
And entertain with her occasions sly;[3]
Through which some lost great hope unheedilý,
Which never they recover might again;
And others, quite excluded forth, did lie
Long languishing there in unpitied pain,
And seeking often entrance afterwards in vain.

"Me when as he[4] had privily espied
Bearing the shield which I had conquer'd late,
He kenn'd[5] it straight, and to me open'd wide:
So in I pass'd, and straight he clos'd the gate.
But being in, Delay in close await
Caught hold on me, and thought my steps to stay,
Feigning full many a fond[6] excuse to prate,
And time to steal, the treasure of man's day,
Whose smallest minute lost no riches render[7] may.

"But by no means my way I would forslow[8]
For aught that ever she could do or say;
But, from my lofty steed dismounting low,
Pass'd forth on foot, beholding all the way
The goodly works, and stones of rich assay,
Cast into sundry shapes by wondrous skill,
That like on earth nowhere I reckon may;
And, underneath, the river rolling still
With murmur soft, that seem'd to serve the workman's will.

"Thence forth I passëd to the second gate,
The Gate of Good Desert, whose goodly pride
And costly frame were long here to relate:
The same to all stood always open wide;
But in the porch did evermore abide
A hideous giant, dreadful to behold,
That stopp'd the entrance with his spacious stride,
And with the terror of his count'nance bold
Full many did affray, that else fain enter wo'ld:

"His name was Danger, dreaded over all;
Who day and night did watch and duly ward
From fearful cowards entrance to forestall[9]
And faint-heart fools, whom show of peril hard
Could terrify from fortune's fair award:
For oftentimes faint hearts, at first espial
Of his grim face, were from approaching scar'd:
Unworthy they of grace, whom one denial
Excludes from fairest hope withouten farther trial.

"Yet many doughty warriors, often tried
In greater perils to be stout and bold,
Durst not the sternness of his look abide;
But, soon as they his count'nance did behold,
Began to faint, and feel their courage cold.
Again, some other, that in hard assays
Were cowards known, and little count did hold,[10]
Either through gifts, or guile, or such like ways,
Crept in by stooping low, or stealing of the keys.

"But I, though meanest man of many mo',
Yet much disdaining unto him to lout,[11]
Or creep between his legs, so in to go,
Resolv'd him to assault with manhood stout,
And either beat him in, or drive him out.
Eftsoons, advancing that enchanted shield,
With all my might I gan to lay about:
Which when he saw, the glaive[12] which he did wield
He gan forthwith t' avale,[13] and way unto me yield.

"So as I enter'd, I did backward look,
For fear of harm that might lie hidden there;
And lo! his hind-parts, whereof heed I took,
Much more deformëd, fearful, ugly were,
Than all his former parts did erst[14] appear:
For Hatred, Murder, Treason, and Despite,
With many more, lay in ambúshment there,
Awaiting to entrap the wareless[15] wight
Which did not them prevent with vigilant foresíght.

"Thus having pass'd all peril, I was come
Within the compass of that island's space;
The which did seem, unto my simple doom,[16]
The only pleasant and delightful place
That ever trodden was of footing's trace:
For all that Nature by her mother wit
Could frame in earth, and form of substance base,
Was there; and all that Nature did omit,
Art, playing second Nature's part, suppliëd it.

"No tree, that is of count, in greenwood grows,
From lowest juniper to cedar tall;
No flow'r in field, that dainty odour throws,
And decks his branch with blossoms over all,
But there was planted, or grew natural:
Nor sense of man so coy and curious nice,
But there might find to please itself withal;
Nor heart could wish for any quaint device,
But there it present was, and did frail sense entice.

"In such luxurious plenty of all pleasure,
It seem'd a second Paradise, I guess,
So lavishly enrich'd with Nature's treasure,
That if the happy souls which do possess
Th' Elysian fields, and live in lasting bliss,
Should happen this with living eye to see,
They soon would loathe their lesser happiness,
And wish to life return'd again to be,
That in this joyous place they might have joyance free.

1 Given. 2 Entrance, beginning. 3 Plausible pretexts. 4 The porter, Doubt 5 Knew. 6 Idle. 7 Restore. 8 Delay, retard, my progress. 9 Prevent.

10 Were held in small esteem. 11 Stoop. 12 Sword. 13 Lower. 14 Formerly. 15 Unwary. 16 Judgment.

"Fresh shadows, fit to shroud from sunny ray;
Fair lawns, to take the sun in season due;
Sweet springs, in which a thousand nymphs did play;
Soft-rumbling brooks, that gentle slumber drew;
High-rearëd mounts, the lands about to view;
Low-looking dales, disloin'd[1] from common gaze;
Delightful bow'rs, to solace lovers true;
False labyrinths, fond runners' eyes to daze;
All which, by Nature made, did Nature's self amaze.

"And all without were walks and alleys dight[2]
With divers trees enrang'd in even ranks;
And here and there were pleasant arbours pight,[3]
And shady seats, and sundry flow'ring banks,
To sit and rest the walkers' weary shanks:
And therein thousand pairs of lovers walk'd,
Praising their god, and yielding him great thanks,
Nor ever aught but of their true loves talk'd,
Nor ever for rebuke or blame of any balk'd.[4]

"All these together by themselves did sport
Their spotless pleasures and sweet love's content;
But, far away from these, another sort
Of lovers linkëd in true hearts' consent;
Which lovëd not as these for like intent,
But on chaste virtue grounded their desire,
Far from all fraud or feignëd blandishment;
Which, in their spirits kindling zealous fire,
Brave thoughts and noble deeds did evermore aspire.[5]

"Such were great Hercules, and Hylas dear;
True Jonathan, and David trusty tried;
Stout Theseus, and Pirithöus his fere;[6]
Pylades, and Orestes by his side;
Mild Titus, and Gesippus without pride;
Damon and Pythias, whom death could not sever:
All these, and all that ever had been tied
In bands of friendship, there did live for ever;
Whose lives although decay'd, yet loves decayëd never.

"Which when as I, that never tasted bliss
Nor happy hour, beheld with gazeful eye,
I thought there was none other heav'n than this;
And gan their endless happiness envý,
That, being free from fear and jealousý,
Might frankly there their love's desire possess;
Whilst I, through pains and perilous jeopardý,
Was forc'd to seek my life's dear patroness:
Much dearer be the things which come through hard distress.

"Yet all those sights, and all that else I saw,
Might not my steps withhold, but that forthright
Unto that purpos'd place I did me draw,
Where as my love was lodgëd day and night,—
The temple of great Venus, that is hight
The queen of Beauty, and of Love the mother,
There worshippëd of ev'ry living wight;
Whose goodly workmanship far pass'd all other
That ever were on earth, all[7] were they set together.

"Not that same famous temple of Diane,
Whose height all Ephesus did oversee,
And which all Asia sought with vows profane,
One of the world's Sev'n Wonders said to be,
Might match with this by many a degrée.
Nor that, which that wise King of Jewry[8] fram'd
With endless cost to be th' Almighty's see;[9]
Nor all that else through all the world is nam'd
To all the heathen gods, might like to this be claim'd.

"I, much admiring that so goodly frame,
Unto the porch approach'd, which open stood;
But therein sat an amiable Dame,
That seem'd to be of very sober mood,
And in her semblant[10] show'd great womanhood:
Strange was her tire;[11] for on her head a crown
She wore, much like unto a Danish hood,
Powder'd with pearl and stone; and all her gown
Enwoven was with gold, that raught[12] full low adown.

"On either side of her two young men stood,
Both strongly arm'd, as fearing one another;
Yet were they brethren both of half the blood,
Begotten by two fathers of one mother,
Though of contráry natures each to other:
The one of them hight Love, the other Hate;
Hate was the elder, Love the younger brother;
Yet was the younger stronger in his state
Than th' elder, and him master'd still in all debate.

"Nathless that Dame so well them temper'd both,
That she them forcëd hand to join in hand,
All be[7] that Hatred was thereto full loth,
And turn'd his face away, as he did stand,
Unwilling to behold that lovely band:
Yet she was of such grace and virtuous might,
That her commandment he could not withstand,
But bit his lip, for felonous despite,
And gnash'd his iron tusks at that displeasing sight.

"Concord she callëd was in common read,[13]
Mother of blessed Peace and Friendship true;
They both her twins, both born of heav'nly seed,
And she herself likewise divinely grew;
The which right well her works divine did shew:
For strength and wealth and happiness she lends,
And strife and war and anger does subdue;
Of little much, of foes she maketh friends,
And to afflicted minds sweet rest and quiet sends.

"By her the heav'n is in his course contain'd,
And all the world in state unmovëd stands,
As their Almighty Maker first ordain'd,
And bound them with inviolable bands;

1 Far removed.
2 Prepared, constructed.
3 Placed, pitched.
4 Turned aside.
5 Aspire towards.
6 Companion.
7 Although.
8 Solomon.
9 Seat, habitation.
10 Air, aspect.
11 Attire.
12 Reached.
13 Discourse, speech.

Else would the waters overflow the lands,
And fire devour the air, and hele [1] them quite;
But that she holds them with her blèssed hands.
She is the nurse of pleasure and delight,
And unto Venus' grace the gate doth open right.

"By her I ent'ring half dismayëd was;
But she in gentle wise me entertain'd,
And 'twixt herself and Love did let me pass;
But Hatred would my entrance have restrain'd,
And with his club me threaten'd to have brain'd,
Had not the Lady with her pow'rful speech
Him from his wicked will unneth [2] refrain'd;
And th' other eke his malice did impeach, [3]
Till I was throughly past the peril of his reach.

"Into the inmost temple thus I came,
Which fuming all with frankincénse I found,
And odours rising from the altars' flame.
Upon a hundred marble pillars round
The roof up high was rearëd from the ground,
All deck'd with crowns, and chains, and garlands gay,
And thousand precious gifts worth many a pound,
The which sad lovers for their vows did pay;
And all the ground was strow'd with flowers as fresh as May.

"A hundred altars round about were set,
All flaming with their sacrifices' fire,
That with the steam thereof the temple sweat,
Which, roll'd in clouds, to heaven did aspire,
And in them bore true lovers' vows entire:
And eke a hundred brazen caldrons bright,
To bathe in joy and amorous desire,
Ev'ry of which was to a damsel hight; [4]
For all the priests were damsels in soft linen dight. [5]

"Right in the midst the goddess' self did stand,
Upon an altar of some costly mass,
Whose substance was unneth [6] to understand:
For neither precious stone, nor dureful [7] brass,
Nor shining gold, nor mould'ring clay it was;
But much more rare and precious to esteem,
Pure in aspéct, and like to crystal glass;
Yet glass was not, if one did rightly deem;
But, being fair and brittle, likest glass did seem.

"But it in shape and beauty did excel
All other idols which the heath'n adore,
Far passing that which by surpassing skill
Phidias did make in Paphos isle of yore,
With which that wretched Greek, that life forlore, [8]
Did fall in love: yet this much fairer shin'd,
But cover'd with a slender veil afore;
And both her feet and legs together twin'd
Were with a snake, whose head and tail were fast combin'd. [9]

"The cause why she was cover'd with a veil
Was hard to know, for that her priests the same
From people's knowledge labour'd to conceal:
But sooth it was not sure for womanish shame,
Nor any blemish which the work might blame;
But for (they say) she hath both kinds [10] in one,
Both male and female, both under one name:
She sire and mother is herself alone,
Begets and eke conceives, nor needeth other none.

"And all about her neck and shoulders flew
A flock of little Loves, and Sports, and Joys,
With nimble wings of gold and purple hue;
Whose shapes seem'd not like to terrestrial boys,
But like to angels playing heav'nly toys [11]
The whilst their eldest brother was away;—
Cupid, their eldest brother: he enjoys
The wide kingdom of Love with lordly sway,
And to his law compels all creatures to obey.

"And all about her altar scatter'd lay
Great sorts [12] of lovers piteously complaining,
Some of their loss, some of their love's delay,
Some of their pride, some paragons' disdaining, [13]
Some fearing fraud, some fraudulently feigning,
As ev'ry one had cause of good or ill.
Amongst the rest some one, through love's constraining
Tormented sore, could not contain it still,
But thus brake forth, that all the temple it did fill;

"'Great Venus! queen of beauty and of grace, [14]
The joy of gods and men, that under sky
Dost fairest shine, and most adorn thy place;
That with thy smiling look dost pacify
The raging seas, and mak'st the storms to fly;
Thee, goddess, thee the winds, the clouds do fear;
And, when thou spread'st thy mantle forth on high,
The waters play, and pleasant lands appear,
And heavens laugh, and all the world shows joyous cheer:

"'Then doth the dædal [15] earth throw forth to thee
Out of her fruitful lap abundant flow'rs;
And then all living wights, soon as they see
The Spring break forth out of his lusty bow'rs,
They all do learn to play the paramoúrs:
First do the merry birds, thy pretty pages,
Privily prickëd with thy lustful pow'rs,
Chirp loud to thee out of their leafy cages,
And thee their mother call to cool their kindly [16] rages.

"'Then do the salvage beasts begin to play
Their pleasant frisks, and loathe their wonted food:
The lions roar; the tigers loudly bray;
The raging bulls rebellow through the wood,
And breaking forth dare tempt the deepest flood
To come where thou dost draw them with desire:
So all things else, that nourish vital blood,

1 Conceal, cover.
2 With difficulty.
3 Hinder.
4 Intrusted.
5 Dressed.
6 Difficult.
7 Enduring.
8 Forsook, lost.
9 Firmly united.
10 Sexes.
11 Sports.
12 Troops.
13 The disdain of their companions or rivals.
14 The four stanzas that follow are imitated from the invocation of Venus with which Lucretius opens his poem; and they may be compared with the "Second Song of Troilus," in Chaucer's "Troilus and Cressida," page 262.
15 Productive.
16 Natural.

Soon as with fury thou dost them inspire,
In generation seek to quench their inward fire.

"'So all the world by thee at first was made,
And daily yet thou dost the same repair:
Nor aught on earth that merry is and glad,
Nor aught on earth that lovely is and fair,
But thou the same for pleasure didst prepare:
Thou art the root of all that joyous is:
Great god of men and women, queen of th' air,
Mother of laughter, and well-spring of bliss,
O grant that of my love at last I may not miss!'

"So did he say: but I, with murmur soft,
That none might hear the sorrow of my heart,
Yet inly groaning deep and sighing oft,
Besought her to grant ease unto my smart,
And to my wound her gracious help impart.
Whilst thus I spake, behold! with happy eye
I spied where, at the Idol's feet apart,
A bevy of fair damsels close did lie,
Waiting when as the anthem should be sung on high.

"The first of them did seem of riper years
And graver countenance than all the rest;
Yet all the rest were eke her equal peers,
Yet unto her obeyëd all the best:
Her name was Womanhood; that she exprest
By her sad semblant [1] and demeanour wise:
For steadfast still her eyes did fixëd rest;
Nor rov'd at random, after gazers' guise,
Whose luring baits ofttimes do heedless hearts entice.

"And next to her sat goodly Shamefastness,
Nor ever durst her eyes from ground uprear,
Nor ever once did look up from her dess,[2]
As if some blame of evil she did fear,
That in her cheeks made roses oft appear:
And her against sweet Cheerfulness was plac'd,
Whose eyes, like twinkling stars in ev'ning clear,
Were deck'd with smiles that all sad humours chas'd,
And darted forth delights the which her goodly grac'd.

"And next to her sat sober Modesty,
Holding her hand upon her gentle heart;
And her against sat comely Courtesy,
That unto ev'ry person knew her part;
And her before was seated overthwart [3]
Soft Silence, and submiss [4] Obedience,
Both link'd together never to dispart; [5]
Both gifts of God not gotten but from thence;
Both garlands of his saints against their foes' offence.

"Thus sat they all around in seemly rate: [6]
And in the midst of them a goodly Maid
(Ev'n in the lap of Womanhood) there sate,
The which was all in lily white array'd,
With silver streams amongst the linen stray'd;
Like to the Morn, when first her shining face
Hath to the gloomy world itself bewray'd:
That same was fairest Amoret in place,
Shining with beauty's light and heav'nly virtue's grace.

"Whom soon as I beheld, my heart gan throb,
And weigh'd in doubt what best were to be done:
For sacrilege me seem'd the church to rob;
And folly seem'd to leave the thing undone
Which with so strong attempt I had begun.
Then, shaking off all doubt and shamefast fear,
Which ladies' love I heard had never won
'Mongst men of worth, I to her steppëd near,
And by the lily hand her labour'd up to rear.[7]

"Thereat that foremost matron [8] me did blame,
And sharp rebuke for being overbold;
Saying it was to knight unseemly shame
Upon a récluse virgin to lay hold,
That unto Venus' services was sold.[9]
To whom I thus; 'Nay, but it fitteth best
For Cupid's man with Venus' maid to hold;
For ill your goddess' services are drest
By virgins, and her sacrifices let to rest.'

"With that my shield I forth to her did show,
Which all that while I closely had conceal'd;
On which when Cupid with his killing bow
And cruel shafts emblazon'd she beheld,
At sight thereof she was with terror quell'd,
And said no more: but I, which all that while
The pledge of faith, her hand, engagëd held
(Like wary hind within the weedy soil),
For no intreaty would forego so glorious spoil.

"And evermore upon the goddess' face
Mine eye was fix'd, for fear of her offence:
Whom when I saw with amiable grace
To laugh on me, and favour my pretence,
I was embolden'd with more confidence;
And, naught for niceness nor for envy sparing,
In presence of them all forth led her thence,
All looking on, and like astonish'd staring,
Yet to lay hand on her not one of all them daring.

"She often pray'd, and often me besought,
Sometime with tender tears, to let her go,
Sometime with witching smiles: but yet, fo naught
That ever she to me could say or do,
Could she her wishëd freedom from me woo;
But forth I led her through the temple gate,
By which I hardly pass'd with much ado:
But that same lady,[10] which me friended late
In entrance, did me also friend in my retrate.[11]

"No less did Danger threaten me with dread,
When as he saw me, maugré [12] all his pow'r,
That glorious spoil of beauty with me lead,
Than Cerberus, when Orpheus did recour [13]
His leman [14] from the Stygian prince's bow'r.
But evermore my shield did me defend
Against the storm of ev'ry dreadful stowre: [15]
Thus safely with my love I thence did wend."
So ended he his tale, where I this canto end.

1 Grave aspect.
2 Writing-table, desk.
3 Opposite.
4 Submissive.
5 Separate.
6 Arrangement, order.
7 Raise.
8 Womanhood.
9 Devoted.
10 Concord.
11 Withdrawal.
12 In spite of.
13 Recover.
14 His mistress, Eurydice.
15 Assault, peril.

CANTO XI.

Marinell's former wound is heal'd;
He comes to Proteus' hall,
Where Thamës doth the Medway wed,
And feasts the sea-gods all.

But ah! for pity that I have thus long
Left a fair lady languishing in pain!
Now well-away! that I have done such wrong,
To let fair Florimell in bands remain,
In bands of love, and in sad thraldom's chain;
From which unless some heav'nly power her free
By miracle not yet appearing plain,
She longer yet is like captív'd to be;
That ev'n to think thereof it inly pities me.

Here need you to remember, how erewhile[1]
Unlovely Proteus, missing[2] to his mind
That virgin's love to win by wit or wile,
Her threw into a dungeon deep and blind,[3]
And there in chains her cruelly did bind,
In hope thereby her to his bent to draw:
For, when as neither gifts nor graces kind
Her constant mind could move at all he saw,
He thought her to compel by cruelty and awe.

Deep in the bottom of a huge great rock
The dungeon was, in which her bound he left,
That neither iron bars, nor brazen lock,
Did need to guard from force or secret theft
Of all her lovers which would her have reft;
For wall'd it was with waves, which rag'd and roar'd
As they the cliff in pieces would have cleft;
Besides, ten thousand monsters foul abhorr'd
Did wait about it, gaping grisly, all begor'd.[4]

And in the midst thereof did Horror dwell,
And Darkness dread that never viewëd day,
Like to the baleful house of lowest hell,
In which old Styx her aged bones alway
(Old Styx the grandame of the gods) doth lay.
There did this luckless maid sev'n months abide,
Nor ever evening saw, nor morning's ray,
Nor ever from the day the night descried,
But thought it all one night, that did no hours divide.

And all this was for love of Marinell,
Who her despis'd (ah! who would her despise!)
And women's love did from his heart expel,
And all those joys that weak mankind entice.
Nathless his pride full dearly he did price;[5]
For of[6] a woman's hand it was y-wroke,[7]
That of the wound he yet in languor lies,
Nor can be curëd of that cruel stroke
Which Britomart him gave, when he did her provoke.

Yet far and near the nymph, his mother, sought,
And many salves did to his sore apply,
And many herbs did use: but when as naught
She saw could ease his rankling malady,
At last to Tryphon she for help did hie[8]
(This Tryphon is the sea-gods' surgeon hight),
Whom she besought to find some remedy:
And for his pains a whistle him behight,[9]
That of a fish's shell was wrought with rare delight.

So well that leach did hark to her request,
And did so well employ his careful pain,
That in short space his hurts he had redrest,[10]
And him restor'd to healthful state again:
In which he long time after did remain
There with the nymph his mother, like her thrall;[11]
Who sore against his will did him retain,
For fear of peril which to him might fall
Through his too venturous prowess provëd over all.

It fortun'd then, a solemn feast was there
To all the sea-gods and their fruitful seed,
In honour of the spousals which then were
Betwixt the Medway and the Thames agreed.
Long had the Thames (as we in records read)
Before that day her wooëd to his bed;
But the proud nymph would for no worldly meed,[12]
Nor no entreaty, to his love be led;
Till now at last relenting she to him was wed.

So both agreed that this their bridal feast
Should for the gods in Proteus' house be made;
To which they all repair'd, both most and least,[13]
As well which in the mighty ocean trade,[14]
As that in rivers swim, or brooks do wade:
All which, not if a hundred tongues to tell,
And hundred mouths, and voice of brass I had,
And endless memory that might excel,
In order as they came could I recount them well.

Help therefore, O thou sacred imp[15] of Jove,
The nursling of Dame Memory his dear,
To whom those rolls, laid up in heav'n above,
And records of antiquity appear,
To which no wit of man may comen near;
Help me to tell the names of all those Floods
And all those Nymphs, which then assembled were
To that great banquet of the watery gods,
And all their sundry kinds, and all their hid abodes.

First came great Neptune, with his three-fork'd mace,[16]
That rules the seas and makes them rise or fall;
His dewy locks did drop with brine apace
Under his diadem imperiál:
And by his side his queen with coronal,
Fair Amphitrite, most divinely fair,
Whose ivory shoulders weren cover'd all,
As with a robe, with her own silver hair,
And deck'd with pearls which th' Indian seas for her prepare.

1 Formerly. See canto viii. of the third book.
2 Failing.
3 Dark.
4 Stained with gore.
5 Pay for.
6 By.
7 Revenged; by the hand of Britomart, as told in canto iv. of the third book.
8 Haste.
9 Promised.
10 Healed.
11 As if he were her slave.
12 Gift, reward.
13 Greatest and smallest.
14 Resort, have their abode.
15 Child. Clio, the historic Muse, daughter of Jupiter and Mnemosyne or Memory.
16 Sceptre; the trident.

These marchëd far before the other crew:
And all the way before them, as they went,
Triton his trumpet shrill before them blew,
For goodly triumph and great jolliment,[1]
That made the rocks to roar as they were rent.
And after them the royal issue came,
Which of them sprung by lineal descent:
First the sea-gods, which to themselves do claim
The pow'r to rule the billows, and the waves to tame:

Phorcys, the father of that fatal brood
By whom those old heröës won such fame;[2]
And Glaucus, that wise soothsays understood;
And tragic Ino's son, the which became
A god of seas through his mad mother's blame,[3]
Now hight Palæmon, and is sailors' friend;
Great Brontes; and Astræus, that did shame
Himself with incest of his kin unkenn'd;[4]
And huge Orion, that doth tempests still portend;

The rich Cteatus; and Eurytus long;
Neleus and Pelias, lovely brethren both;
Mighty Chrysaor; and Caïcus strong;
Eurypylus, that calms the waters wroth;
And fair Euphœmus, that upon them go'th
As on the ground, without dismay or dread;
Fierce Eryx; and Alebius, that know'th
The waters' depth, and doth their bottom tread;
And sad Asopus, comely with his hoary head.

There also some most famous founders were
Of puissant nations, which the world possest,
Yet sons of Neptune, now assembled here:
Ancient Ogyges, ev'n the ancientest:
And Inachus renown'd above the rest;
Phœnix; and Aon; and Pelasgus old;
Great Belus; Phœax; and Agenor best;
And mighty Albion, father of the bold
And warlike people which the Britain Islands hold:

For Albion the son of Neptune was;
Who, for the proof of his great púissánce,
Out of his Albion did on dry-foot pass
Into old Gaul, that now is callëd France,
To fight with Hercules, that did advance
To vanquish all the world with matchless might;
And there his mortal part by great mischance
Was slain; but that which is th' immortal sprite
Lives still, and to this Feast with Neptune's seed was dight.[5]

But what do I their names seek to rehearse,
Which all the world have with their issue fill'd?
How can they all in this so narrow verse
Containëd be, and in small compass held?
Let them record them that are better skill'd,
And know the monuments of passëd age:
Only what needeth shall be here fulfill'd,
T' express some part of that great equipage
Which from great Neptune do derive their parentage.

Next came the aged Ocean and his Dame
Old Tethys, th' oldest two of all the rest;
For all the rest of those two parents came,
Which afterward both sea and land possest;
Of all which Nereus, th' eldest and the best,
Did first proceed; than which none more upright
Nor more sincere in word and deed profest;
Most void of guile, most free from foul despite,
Doing himself and teaching others to do right:

Thereto he was expert in prophecies,
And could the leden[6] of the gods unfold;
Through which, when Paris brought his famous prize,
The fair Tyndarid lass,[7] he him foretold
That her all Greece with many a champion bold
Should fetch again, and finally destroy
Proud Priam's town: so wise is Nereus old,
And so well skill'd: nathless he takes great joy
Ofttimes amongst the wanton nymphs to sport and toy.

And after him the famous Rivers came,
Which do the earth enrich and beautify:
The fertile Nile, which creatures new doth frame;
Long Rhodanus, whose scurce springs from the sky;[8]
Fair Ister,[9] flowing from the mountains high;
Divine Scamander, purpled yet with blood
Of Greeks and Trojans which therein did die;
Pactólus glist'ring with his golden flood;
And Tigris fierce, whose streams of none may be withstood;

Great Ganges; and immortal Eúphrates;
Deep Indus; and Mæander intricate;
Slow Peneus; and tempestuous Phasides;[10]
Swift Rhine; and Alpheus still immaculate;[11]
Araxes, fearëd for great Cyrus' fate;
Tibris,[12] renownëd for the Romans' fame;
Rich Orinoco, though but knowen late;
And that huge river, which doth bear his name
Of[13] warlike Amazons who do possess the same.

Joy on those warlike women, which so long
Can from all men so rich a kingdom hold!
And shame on you, O men, which boast your strong
And valiant hearts, in thoughts less hard and bold,
Yet quail in conquest of that land of gold![14]
But this to you, O Britons, most pertains,
To whom the right hereof itself hath sold;
The which, for sparing little cost or pains,
Lose so immortal glory, and so endless gains.

1 Pleasure.
2 He was fabled to be the father of the Grææ, the Gorgons, the Hesperian dragon, the Hesperian maids, and Scylla.
3 Driven mad by Hera, to punish her love for Athamas, Ino threw herself into the sea with her son; and both became marine deities.
4 Unknown.
5 Prepared.
6 Language. See note 28, page 119.
7 Helen, daughter of Tyndarus, king of Sparta.
8 The Rhone, springing from its lofty glacier, at the foot of Mount Furca, 5470 feet above the sea.
9 The Danube; one of whose sources, in the castle-yard of Donaueschingen, in Baden, is about 3000 feet above sea level.
10 The Phasis, a river in Colchis.
11 After its junction with the Eurotas, the Alpheus flowed on side by side with its muddier companion without mingling its waters.
12 Tiber.
13 From.
14 The contest with Spain in the New World, the "land of gold," was the great task of the Elizabethan heroes and navigators, whom the poet here urges on to new efforts.

Then was there heard a most celestial sound
Of dainty music, which did next ensue[1]
Before the spouse: that was Arion crown'd;[2]
Who, playing on his harp, unto him drew
The ears and hearts of all that goodly crew;
That even yet the dolphin, which him bore
Through the Ægean seas from pirates' view,
Stood still by him astonish'd at his lore,[3]
And all the raging seas for joy forgot to roar.

So went he playing on the watery plain:
Soon after whom the lovely bridegroom came,
The noble Thames, with all his goodly train.
But him beforé there went, as best became,
His ancient parents,[4] namely th' ancient Thame;
But much more aged was his wife than he,
The Ouse, whom men do Isis rightly name;
Full weak and crooked creature seemëd she,
And almost blind through eld,[5] that scarce her way could see.

Therefore on either side she was sustain'd
Of two small grooms, which by their names were hight
The Churn and Cherwell, two small streams, which pain'd
Themselves her footing to direct aright,
Which failëd oft through faint and feeble plight:
But Thame was stronger, and of better stay;
Yet seem'd full agëd by his outward sight,
With head all hoary, and his beard all gray,
Dewëd with silver drops that trickled down alway:

And eke he somewhat seem'd to stoop afore
With bowëd back, by reason of the load
And ancient heavy burden which he bore
Of that fair City,[6] wherein make abode
So many learnëd imps,[7] that shoot abroad,
And with their branches spread all Brittany,
No less than do her elder sister's[8] brood.
Joy to you both, ye double nursery
Of arts! but, Oxford, thine doth Thame most glorify.

But he their son[9] full fresh and jolly was,
All deckëd in a robe of watchet hue.[10]
On which the waves, glitt'ring like crystal glass,
So cunningly enwoven were, that few
Could weenen[11] whether they were false or true:
And on his head like to a coronet
He wore, that seemëd strange to common view,
In which were many tow'rs and castles set,
That it encompass'd round as with a golden fret.[12]

Like as the mother of the gods, they say,
In her great iron chariot wonts to ride
When to Jove's palace she doth take her way,
Old Cybelé, array'd with pompous pride,
Wearing a diadem embattled wide
With hundred turrets, like a turribant.[13]
With such an one was Thamës beautified;
That was, to wit, the famous Troynovant,[14]
In which her kingdom's throne is chiefly resiant.[15]

And round about him many a pretty page
Attended duly, ready to obey;
All little rivers which owe vassalage
To him, as to their lord, and tribute pay:
The chalky Kennet; and the Thetis gray;
The moorish Colne; and the soft-sliding Brean;
The wanton Lea, that oft doth lose his way;
And the still Darent, in whose waters clean
Ten thousand fishes play and deck his pleasant stream.

Then came his neighbour floods which nigh him dwell,
And water all the English soil throughout;
They all on him this day attended well,
And with meet service waited him about;
Nor none disdainëd low to him to lout:[16]
No, not the stately Severn grudg'd at all,
Nor storming Humber, though he lookëd stout;
But both him honour'd as their principal,
And let their swelling waters low before him fall.

There was the speedy Tamar, which divides
The Cornish and the Devonish confines;
Through both whose borders swiftly down it glides,
And, meeting Plym, to Plymouth thence declines:
And Dart, nigh chok'd with sands of tinny mines:
But Avon marchëd in more stately path,
Proud of his adamants[17] with which he shines
And glisters wide, as als'[18] of wondrous Bath,
And Bristol fair, which on his waves he builded hath.

And there came Stour with terrible aspéct,
Bearing his six deformëd heads on high,
That doth his course through Blandford plains direct,
And washeth Wimborne meads in season dry.
Next him went Wileyburn with passage sly,
That of his wiliness his name doth take,
And of himself doth name the shire[19] thereby:
And Mole, that like a nousling[20] mole doth make
His way still under ground till Thames he overtake.

Then came the Rother, deckëd all with woods
Like a wood god, and flowing fast to Rye;
And Stour, that parteth with his pleasant floods
The Eastern Saxons from the Southern nigh,[21]
And Clare and Harwich both doth beautify:
Him follow'd Yare, soft washing Norwich wall,
And with him brought a present joyfully
Of his own fish unto their festival,
Whose like none else could shew, the which they ruffins call.

Next these the plenteous Ouse came far from land,
By many a city and by many a town,

1 Follow. 2 See note 21, page 237. 3 Skill.
4 The Thames, according to the common opinion in Spenser's days, was formed by the junction of the Thame and the Isis.
5 Old age. 6 Oxford. 7 Children.
8 Cambridge, called the "elder sister" of Oxford, because the traditions of its University's foundation carry it back to a period 150 years earlier than that of Oxford's—though more authentic records give the palm of antiquity to the latter. 9 The Thames.
10 Blue. 11 Judge. 12 Band.
13 Turban. 14 London.
15 Resident. 16 Bend.
17 The crystals known as Bristol stones.
18 Also. 19 Wiltshire. 20 Burrowing.
21 Dividing Essex and Suffolk.

And, many rivers taking underhand
Into his waters as he passeth down
(The Cle, the Were, the Grant, the Stour, the Rowne),
Thence doth by Huntingdon and Cambridge flit,
My mother Cambridge,[1] whom as with a crown
He doth adorn, and is adorn'd of it
With many a gentle Muse and many a learned wit.

And after him the fatal Welland went,
That if old saws prove true (which God forbid !)
Shall drown all Holland [2] with his excrement,
And shall see Stamford, though now homely hid,
Then shine in learning more than ever did
Cambridge or Oxford, England's goodly beams.
And next to him the Nen down softly slid;
And bounteous Trent, that in himself enseams [3]
Both thirty sorts of fish and thirty sundry streams.

Next these came Tyne, along whose stony bank
That Roman monarch built a brazen wall,
Which might the feebled Britons strongly flank
Against the Picts that swarmëd over all;
Which yet thereof Gualsever [4] they do call:
And Tweed, the limit betwixt Logris [5] land
And Albany: [5] and Eden, though but small,
Yet often stain'd with blood of many a band
Of Scots and English both, that tinëd [6] on his strand.

Then came those six sad brethren, like forlorn,
That whilom were, as ántique fathers tell,
Six valiant knights of one fair nymph y-born,
Which did in noble deeds of arms excel,
And wonnëd [7] there where now York people dwell;
Still Ure, swift Wharf, and Ouse the most of might,
High Swale, unquiet Nidd, and troublous Skell;
All whom a Scythian king, that Humber hight,
Slew cruelly, and in the river drownëd quite:

But pass'd not long, ere Brutus' warlike son,
Locrinus, them aveng'd, and the same date [8]
Which the proud Humber unto them had done,
By equal doom repaid on his own pate:
For in the self-same river where he late
Had drenchëd them, he drownëd him again;
And nam'd the river of his wretched fate: [9]
Whose bad condition yet it doth retain,
Oft tossëd with his storms which therein still remain.

These after came the stony shallow Lone,[10]
That to old Lancaster his name doth lend:
And following Dee, which Britons long y-gone
Did call divine, that doth by Chester tend;
And Conway, which out of his stream doth send
Plenty of pearls to deck his dames withal;
And Lindus, that his pikes doth most commend,
Of which the ancient Lincoln men do call:
All these together marchëd toward Proteus' hall.

Nor thence the Irish rivers absent were;
Since no less famous than the rest they be,
And join in neighbourhood of kingdom near,
Why should they not likewise in love agree,
And joy likewise this solemn day to see?
They saw it all, and pleasant were in place;
Though I them all, according their degree,
Cannot recount, nor tell their hidden race,
Nor read [11] the savage countries thorough which they pace.

There was the Liffey rolling down the lea;
The sandy Slane; [12] the stony Aubrion;
The spacious Shannon spreading like a sea;
The pleasant Boyne; the fishy fruitful Bann;
Swift Awniduff, which of the Englishman
Is call'd Blackwater; and the Liffar deep;
Sad Trowis, that once his people overran;
Strong Allo tumbling from Slievelogher steep;
And Mulla mine, whose waves I whilom taught to weep.[13]

And there the three renownëd brethren were,
Which that great giant Blomius begot
Of the fair nymph Rheüsa wand'ring there:
One day, as she to shun the season hot
Under Slievebloom in shady grove was got,
This giant found her and by force deflow'r'd;
Whereof conceiving, she in time forth brought
These three fair sons, which being thence forth pour'd
In three great rivers ran, and many countries scour'd.

The first the gentle Suir, that, making way
By sweet Clonmell, adorns rich Waterford;
The next, the stubborn Nore, whose waters gray
By fair Kilkenny and Rosseponté board;
The third, the goodly Barrow, which doth hoard
Great heaps of salmons in his deep bosóm:
All which, long sunder'd, do at last accord [14]
To join in one, ere to the sea they come; [15]
So, flowing all from one, all one at last become.

There also was the wide embayëd Mare; [16]
The pleasant Bandon, crown'd with many a wood;
The spreading Lee that like an island fair,
Encloseth Cork with his divided flood;
And baleful Oure, late stain'd with English blood:
With many more whose names no tongue can tell.
All which that day in order seemly good
Did on the Thames attend, and waited well
To do their dueful service, as to them befell.

Then came the bride, the lovely Medway came,
Clad in a vesture of unknowen gear [17]

1 Spenser was a student at Pembroke Hall, in Cambridge University.
2 The south-eastern part of the county of Lincoln is called Holland.
3 Contains or comprehends; "fattens" is the old explanation, but it could apply to the fish alone; for the Trent can scarcely be said to "fatten" a stream which swells its own bulk.
4 Wall of Severus.
5 England and Scotland. See page 396.
6 Were slain, perished.
7 Dwelled.
8 The same gift, or fate, of death.
9 See page 396.
10 The Lune.
11 Declare.
12 Slaney.
13 Spenser's Irish residence, Kilcolman Castle, stood near the banks of the Mulla, in county Cork; there he probably wrote his poem of "Astrophel"—a lament for the death of Sir Philip Sidney—and his "Tears of the Muses."
14 Agree.
15 In Waterford Harbour.
16 Broadening into Kenmare River or Bay.
17 Material.

And uncouth[1] fashion, yet her well became,
That seem'd like silver sprinkled here and there
With glitt'ring spangs[2] that did like stars appear,
And wav'd upon, like water chamelot,[3]
To hide the metal, which yet ev'rywhere
Bewray'd itself, to let men plainly wot[4]
It was no mortal work, that seem'd and yet was not.

Her goodly locks adown her back did flow
Unto her waist, with flow'rs bescatterëd,
The which ambrosial odours forth did throw
To all about, and all her shoulders spread
As a new spring; and likewise on her head
A chapëlet of sundry flow'rs she wore,
From under which the dewy humour shed
Did trickle down her hair, like to the hoar
Congealëd little drops which do the morn adore.[5]

On her two pretty handmaids did attend,
One call'd the Theise, the other call'd the Crane;
Which on her waited things amiss to mend,
And both behind upheld her spreading train;
Under the which her feet appearëd plain,
Her silver feet, fair wash'd against this day;
And her before there pacëd pages twain,
Both clad in colours like and like array,
The Doune and eke the Frith, both which prepar'd her way.

And after these the sea-nymphs marchëd all,
All goodly damsels, deck'd with long green hair,
Whom of their sire Neréïdes men call,
All which the Ocean's daughter to him bare,
The gray-ey'd Doris; all which fifty are;
All which she there on her attending had:
Swift Proto; mild Eucraté; Thetis fair;
Soft Spio; sweet Endoré; Sao sad;
Light Doto; wanton Glaucé; and Galené glad;

White-hand Eunica; proud Dynamené;
Joyous Thalía; goodly Amphitrite;
Lovely Pasithee; kind Eulimené;
Light-foot Cymothoë; and sweet Melite;
Fairest Pherusa; Phao lily white;
Wonder'd[6] Agavé; Poris; and Nesæa;
With Erato that doth in love delight;
And Panopé; and wise Protomedæa;
And snowy-neck'd Doris; and milk-white Galatæa;

Speedy Hippothoë; and chaste Actea;
Large Lisianassa; and Pronœa sage;
Euagoré; and light Pontoporea;
And, she that with her least word can assuage
The surging seas when they do sorest rage,
Cymodocé; and stout Autonoë;
And Neso; and Eioné well in age;
And, seeming still to smile, Glauconomé;
And, she that hight of many hests, Polynomé;[7]
Fresh Alimeda, deck'd with garland green;
Hyponoo, with salt-bedewëd wrists;
Laomedia, like the crystal sheen;[8]
Liagoré, much prais'd for wise behests;
And Psamathé for her broad snowy breasts;
Cymo; Eupompé; and Themisté just;
And, she that virtue loves and vice detests,
Euarna; and Menippé true in trust;
And Nemertea learnëd well to rule her lust.[9]

All these the daughters of old Nereus were,
Which have the sea in charge to them assign'd,
To rule his tides, and surges to uprear,
To bring forth storms, or fast them to upbind,
And sailors save from wrecks of wrathful wind.
And yet besides three thousand more there were
Of th' Ocean's seed, both Jove's and Phœbus' kind;
The which in floods and fountains do appear,
And all mankind do nourish with their waters clear.

The which, more eath[10] it were for mortal wight
To tell the sands, or count the stars on high,
Or aught more hard, than think to reckon right.
But well I wot[11] that these, which I descry,[12]
Were present at this great solemnity:
And there, amongst the rest, the mother was
Of luckless Marinell, Cymodocé;[13]
Which, for[14] my Muse herself now tirëd has,
Unto another canto I will overpass.

CANTO XII.

Marin, for love of Florimell,
In languor wastes his life:
The Nymph, his mother, getteth her,
And gives to him for wife.

O WHAT an endless work have I in hand,
To count the Sea's abundant progený,
Whose fruitful seed far passeth those in land,
And also those which won[15] in th' azure sky!
For much more eath[10] to tell the stars on high,
All be[16] they endless seem in estimation,
Than to recount the Sea's posteritý:
So fertile be the floods in generation,
So huge their numbers, and so numberless their nation.

Therefore the antique wizards well invented
That Venus of the foamy sea was bred;
For that the seas by her are most augmented.
Witness th' exceeding fry[17] which there are fed,
And wondrous shoals which may of none be read.[18]
Then blame me not if I have err'd in count
Of gods, of nymphs, of rivers, yet unread:[19]
For though their numbers do much more surmount,
Yet all those same were there which erst I did recount.

1 Strange, rare. 2 Spangles. 3 Camlet. 4 Know. 5 Adorn. 6 Admired. 7 Of many laws. 8 Bright. 9 Will. 10 Easy.

11 Know. 12 Describe. 13 Called Cymoent in the fourth canto of the fourth book. 14 Because. 15 Dwell. 16 Although. 17 Swarm, host. 18 Told. 19 Unmentioned.

All those were there, and many other more,
Whose names and nations were too long to tell,
That Proteus' house they fill'd ev'n to the door;
Yet were they all in order, as befell,
According their degrees disposëd well.
Amongst the rest was fair Cymodocé,
The mother of unlucky Marinell,
Who thither with her came, to learn and see
The manner of the gods when they at banquet be.

But, for he was half mortal, being bred
Of mortal sire, though of immortal womb,
He might not with immortal food be fed,
Nor with th' eternal gods to banquet come;
But walk'd abroad, and round about did roam
To view the building of that uncouth place,
That seem'd unlike unto his earthly home:
Where, as he to and fro by chance did trace,[1]
There unto him betid a disadventurous[2] case.

Under the hanging of a hideous cliff
He heard the lamentable voice of one
That piteously complain'd her careful[3] grief,
Which never she before disclos'd to none,
But to herself her sorrow did bemoan:
So feelingly her case she did complain,
That ruth[4] it movëd in the rocky stone,
And made it seem to feel her grievous pain,
And oft to groan with billows' beating from the
main:

It is Florimell, who bewails her hard hap, the hard heart of her captor, and the indifference of her lover, that lets her die when he might have delivered her by arms. Having wept a space, she begins anew, calling on the gods of sea, "if any gods at all have care of right or ruth of wretches' wrong," to set her free, or grant her death, or make her lover the companion of her captivity. But then she falls to rebuking her own vain judgment; for Marinell, she says, "where he list goes loose, and laughs at me." "So ever loose, so ever happy be!" she cries, and calls on her lover to know that her sorrow is all for him.

All which complaint when Marinell had heard,
And understood the cause of all her care
To come of him, for using her so hard;
His stubborn heart, that never felt misfare,[5]
Was touch'd with soft remorse and pity rare;
That ev'n for grief of mind he oft did groan,
And inly wish that in his power it were
Her to redress: but, since he means found none,
He could no more but her great misery bemoan.

Thus whilst his stony heart with tender ruth
Was touch'd, and mighty courage mollified,
Dame Venus' son, that tameth stubborn youth
With iron bit, and maketh him abide
Till like a victor on his back he ride,
Into his mouth his mast'ring bridle threw,
That made him stoop, till he did him bestride:
Then gan he make him tread his steps anew,
And learn to love by learning lover's pains to
rue.

1 Pass, roam.
2 Lamentable, unhappy.
3 Sorrowful.
4 Pity.
5 Misfortune.

In his grieved mind he began to devise how he might free the lady from that dungeon; whether by making fair and humble petition to Proteus, or taking her by force with sword and targe, or stealing her away. Each plan has too many difficulties; so he finds no resource but to reproach himself for despising so chaste and fair a dame, and bringing to such misery her who for his sake "refus'd a god that had her sought to wife."

In this sad plight he walkëd here and there,
And roamëd round about the rock in vain,
As he had lost himself he wist not where;
Oft list'ning if he might her hear again;
And still bemoaning her unworthy pain;
Like as a hind whose calf is fall'n unwares
Into some pit, where she him hears complain,
A hundred times about the pit-side fares,
Right sorrowfully mourning her bereavëd cares.[6]

And now by this the feast was throughly ended,
And ev'ry one gan homeward to resort:
Which seeing, Marinell was sore offended
That his departure thence should be so short,[7]
And leave his love in that sea-wallëd fort:
Yet durst he not his mother disobey;
But, her attending in full seemly sort,
Did march amongst the many all the way;
And all the way did inly mourn, like one astray.

Being returnëd to his mother's bow'r,
In solitary silence, far from wight,[8]
He gan record the lamentable stowre[9]
In which his wretched love lay day and night,
For his dear sake, that ill deserv'd that plight:
The thought whereof empierc'd his heart so
deep,
That of no worldly thing he took delight;
Nor daily food did take, nor nightly sleep,
But pin'd, and mourn'd, and languish'd, and
alone did weep;

That in short space his wonted cheerful hue
Gan fade, and lively spirits deaded quite:
His cheek-bones raw, and eye-pits hollow grew,
And brawny arms had lost their knowen might;
That nothing like himself he seem'd in sight.
Ere long so weak of limb, and sick of love,
He wox, that longer he not[10] stand upright,
But to his bed was brought, and laid above,
Like rueful ghost, unable once to stir or move.

His mother, sore grieved at his inexplicable sickness; wept over and tended him night and day; Tryphon, again summoned, assured her that it was no old wound which now troubled him, but some other malady or grief unknown, which he could not discern; and the attempts of the nymph to extract the truth from Marinell himself were unavailing—he "still her answer'd, there was naught."

Nathless she rested not so satisfied;
But, leaving watery gods, as booting naught,
Unto the shiny heav'n in haste she hied,
And thence Apollo king of leaches brought.

6 The object of her cares, of which she has been deprived.
7 Soon.
8 From any mortal.
9 Affliction.
10 Could not.

Apollo came; who, soon as he had sought
Through his disease, did by and by out find
That he did languish of some inward thought,
The which afflicted his engrievëd mind;
Which love he read[1] to be, that leads each living kind.

Which when he had unto his mother told,
She gan thereat to fret and greatly grieve;
And, coming to her son, gan first to scold
And chide at him that made her misbelieve:
But afterward she gan him soft to shrieve,[2]
And woo with fair entreaty, to disclose
Which of the nymphs his heart so sore did meve:[3]
For sure she ween'd it was some one of those
Which he had lately seen, that for his love he chose.

Now less she fearëd that same fatal read,[4]
That warnëd him of women's love beware:
Which, being meant of mortal creature's seed,
For love of nymphs she thought she need not care,
But promis'd him, whatever wight she were,
That she her love to him would shortly gain:
So he her told: but soon as she did hear
That Florimell it was which wrought his pain,
She gan afresh to chafe, and grieve in ev'ry vein.

Yet, since she saw the strait extremity
In which his life unluckily was laid,
It was no time to scan the prophecy,
Whether old Proteus true or false had said,
That his decay should happen by a maid;
(It 's late, in death, of danger to advise,[5]
Or love forbid him that is life denay'd;[6])
But rather gan in troubled mind devise
How she that lady's liberty might enterprise.

To Proteus' self to sue she thought it vain,
Who was the root and worker of her woe;
Nor unto any meaner to complain;
But unto great King Neptune's self did go,
And, on her knee before him falling low,
Made humble suit unto his majesty
To grant to her her son's life, which his foe,
A cruel tyrant, had presumptuously
By wicked doom condemn'd a wretched death to die.

To whom god Neptune, softly smiling, thus;
"Daughter, me seems of double wrong ye plain,
'Gainst one that hath both wrongëd you and us:
For death t' award I ween'd did appertain
To none but to the sea's sole sovëreign;
Read[7] therefore who it is which this hath wrought,
And for what cause; the truth discover plain:
For never wight so evil did or thought,
But would some rightful cause pretend, though rightly naught."

To whom she answer'd; "Then it is by name
Proteus, that hath ordain'd my son to die;
For that a waif, the which by fortune came
Upon your seas, he claim'd as property:
And yet nor his, nor his in equity,
But yours the waif by high prerogative:
Therefore I humbly crave your majesty
It to replevy,[8] and my son reprive:[9]
So shall you by one gift save all us three alive."

He granted it: and straight his warrant made,
Under the sea-god's seal authentical,
Commanding Proteus straight t' enlarge the maid
Which, wand'ring on his seas imperial,
He lately took, and sithens[10] kept as thrall.
Which she receiving with meet thankfulness,
Departed straight to Proteus therewithal:
Who, reading it with inward loathfulness,
Was grievëd to restore the pledge he did possess.

Yet durst he not the warrant to withstand,
But unto her deliver'd Florimell:
Whom she receiving by the lily hand,
Admir'd her beauty much, as she might well,
For she all living creatures did excel;
And was right joyous that she gotten had
So fair a wife for her son Marinell.
So home with her she straight the virgin lad,[11]
And showëd her to him, then being sore bestad.[12]

Who, soon as he beheld that angel's face,
Adorn'd with all divine perfection,
His cheerëd heart eftsoons away gan chase
Sad death, revivëd with her sweet inspection,
And feeble spirit inly felt refection;[13]
As wither'd weed, through cruel winter's tine,[14]
That feels the warmth of sunny beams' reflection,
Lifts up his head, that did before decline,
And gins to spread his leaf before the fair sunshíne.

Right so himself did Marinell uprear,
When he in place his dearest love did spy;
And though his limbs could not his body bear,
Nor former strength return so suddenly,
Yet cheerful signs he showëd outwardly.
Nor less was she in secret heart affected,
But that she maskëd it with modesty,
For fear she should of lightness be detected:
Which to another place I leave to be perfected.

1 Perceived. 2 Question, confess. 3 Move. 4 Declaration. 5 Consider. 6 Denied. 7 Declare.
8 Replevy, or replevin, is a law term, meaning to take possession of property claimed, giving security at the same time to submit the question, of property to a legal tribunal within a given time.
9 Reprieve, rescue from death. 10 Since. 11 Led. 12 Bestead, distressed. 13 Refreshment. 14 Affliction, injury.

THE FIFTH BOOK
OF
THE FAERIE QUEEN:
CONTAINING
THE LEGEND OF ARTEGALL, OR OF JUSTICE.

So oft as I with state of present time
The image of the ántique world compare,
When as man's age was in his freshest prime,
And the first blossom of fair virtue bare;
Such odds I find 'twixt those, and these which are,
As that, through long continuance of his course,
Me seems the world is run quite out of square
From the first point of his appointed source;
And, being once amiss, grows daily worse and worse:

For from the golden age, that first was nam'd,
It 's now at erst [1] become a stony one;
And men themselves, the which at first were fram'd
Of earthly mould, and form'd of flesh and bone,
Are now transformëd into hardest stone;
Such as behind their backs (so backward bred)
Were thrown by Pyrrha and Deucalion:
And if than those may any worse be read,[2]
They into that ere long will be degenderëd.[3]

Let none then blame me, if, in discipline
Of virtue and of civil use's lore,
I do not form them to the common line
Of present days which are corrupted sore;
But to the antique use [4] which was of yore,
When good was only for itself desir'd,
And all men sought their own, and none no more;
When Justice was not for most meed out-hir'd,
But simple Truth did reign, and was of all admir'd.

For that which all men then did Virtue call,
Is now call'd Vice; and that which Vice was hight,
Is now hight Virtue, and so us'd of all:
Right now is wrong, and wrong that was is right;
As all things else in time are changëd quite.
Nor wonder; for the heavens' revolution
Is wander'd far from where it first was pight,[5]
And so do make contráry constitution
Of all this lower world towárd his dissolution.

For whoso list into the heavens look,
And search the courses of the rolling spheres,
Shall find that from the point where they first took
Their setting forth, in these few thousand years
They all are wander'd much;[6] that plain appears:

For that same golden fleecy ram, which bore
Phrixus and Hellé [7] from their stepdame's fears,
Hath now forgot where he was plac'd of yore,
And shoulder'd hath the bull which fair Europa bore:

And eke the bull hath, with his bow-bent horn,
So hardly butted those two twins of Jove,
That they have crush'd the crab, and quite him borne
Into the great Nemean lion's grove.
So now all range, and do at random rove
Out of their proper places far away,
And all this world with them amiss do move,
And all his creatures from their course astray;
Till they arrive at their last ruinous decay.

Nor is that same great glorious lamp of light,
That doth enlumine all these lesser fires,
In better case, nor keeps his course more right,
But is miscarried with the other spheres:
For since the term of fourteen hundred years,
That learned Ptolemy his height did take,
He is declinëd from that mark of theirs
Nigh thirty minutes to the southern lake;[8]
That makes me fear in time he will us quite forsake.

And if to those Egyptian wizards old
(Which in star-read [9] were wont have best insíght)
Faith may be given, it is by them told
That since the time they first took the sun's height,
Four times his place he shifted hath in sight,
And twice hath risen where he now doth west,
And wested twice where he ought rise aright.
But most is Mars amiss of all the rest;
And next to him old Saturn, that was wont be best.

For during Saturn's ancient reign it 's said
That all the world with goodness did abound;
All lovëd virtue, no man was afraid
Of force, nor fraud in wight was to be found;
No war was known, no dreadful trumpet's sound;
Peace universal reign'd 'mongst men and beasts:
And all things freely grew out of the ground:
Justice sat high ador'd with solemn feasts,
And to all people did divide her dread behests:[10]

Most sacred Virtue she of all the rest,
Resembling God in his imperial might;
Whose sov'reign pow'r is herein most exprest,
That both to good and bad he dealeth right,
And all his works with justice hath bedight.[11]
That power he also doth to princes lend,
And makes them like himself in glorious sight,
To sit in his own seat, his cause to end,
And rule his people right, as he doth recommend.

Dread sov'reign Goddess,[12] that dost highest sit
In seat of judgment in th' Almighty's stead,

1 At length. 2 Discovered.
3 Degenerated. 4 Usage. 5 Fixed.
6 The allusion is to the precession of the equinoxes, through which the stars that a century before Christ were in the sign Aries are now in Taurus, those in Taurus now in Gemini, and so on.

7 See note 5, page 438.
8 This refers to the diminution of the obliquity of the ecliptic, by which the sun recedes from the pole, and approaches the equator.
9 Knowledge or reading of the stars.
10 Commands, decrees. 11 Adorned. 12 Elizabeth.

And with magnific might and wondrous wit
Dost to thy people righteous doom aread,[1]
That farthest nations fills with awful dread,
Pardon the boldness of thy basest thrall,
That dare discourse of so divine a read[2]
As thy great justice praisëd over all;
The instrument whereof, lo! here thy Artegall.[3]

CANTO I.

Artegall train'd in Justice' lore;
Irena's quest pursued;
He doth avenge on Sanglier
His lady's blood embrued.

THOUGH virtue were held in highest price in the old times of which the poet treats, yet, he says, the seeds of vice sprang and grew great, beating with their boughs the gentle plants. "But evermore some of the virtuous race rose up, inspirëd with heroic heat," and cropped the base branches. Such first was Bacchus, who established right in the East, before his time untamed; and next, Hercules, in the West, subdued monstrous tyrants with the club of justice. Such also was "the champion of true justice, Artegall;" who, when he quitted Britomart (as told at the end of canto vi., book iv.), went forth to succour a distressed dame, unjustly held in bondage by a strong tyrant named Grantorto,[4] who withheld her from her heritage. Irena,[5] the dame in question, had besought redress from the Faery Queen; and Gloriana had entrusted the task to Artegall, "for that to her he seem'd best skill'd in righteous lore." He had been brought up in justice from his infancy, and taught "all the depth of rightful doom" by Astræa while she dwelt on earth. She had taken him from among his youthful peers, and nursed and trained him "in a cave from company exil'd."

There she him taught to weigh both right and wrong
In equal balance with due recompense,
And equity to measure out along
According to the line of consciénce,
Whenso it needs with rigour to dispense:
Of all the which, for want there of mankind,
She causëd him to make experience
Upon wild beasts, which she in woods did find
With wrongful pow'r oppressing others of their kind.

Thus she him trainëd, and thus she him taught
In all the skill of deeming[6] wrong and right,
Until the ripeness of man's years he raught;[7]
That ev'n wild beasts did fear his awful sight,
And men admir'd his over-ruling might;
Nor any liv'd on ground that durst withstand
His dreadful hest,[8] much less him match in fight,
Or bide the horror of his wreakful[9] hand,
Whenso he list in wrath lift up his steely brand:

Which steely brand, to make him dreaded more,
She gave unto him, gotten by her sleight
And earnest search, where it was kept in store
In Jove's eternal house, unwist[10] of wight,
Since he himself it us'd in that great fight
Against the Titans, that whilóm rebell'd
'Gainst highest heav'n; Chrysaor[11] it was hight;
Chrysaor, that all other swords excell'd,
Well prov'd in that same day when Jove those giants quell'd:

For of most perfect metal it was made,
Temper'd with adamant amongst the same,
And garnish'd all with gold upon the blade
In goodly wise, whereof it took its name;
And was of no less virtue than of fame:
For there no substance was so firm and hard,
But it would pierce or cleave whereso it came;
Nor any armour could its dint out ward;[12]
But wheresoever it did light, it throughly shar'd.[13]

Now when the world with sin gan to abound,
Astræa, loathing longer here to space[14]
'Mongst wicked men, in whom no truth she found,
Return'd to heaven, whence she deriv'd her race;
Where she hath now an everlasting place
'Mongst those twelve signs, which nightly we do see
The heav'ns' bright-shining baldric[15] to enchase;[16]
And is the Virgin, sixth in her degree,[17]
And next herself her righteous Balance[18] hanging be.

But when she parted hence she left her groom,[19]
An Iron Man, which did on her attend
Always to execute her steadfast doom,
And willëd him with Artegall to wend,[20]
And do whatever thing he did intend:
His name was Talus,[21] made of iron mould,
Immovable, resistless, without end;

1 Judgment declare. 2 Theme.
3 Artegall (called Arthegall, by the original editions, in the earlier books of the poem) is understood to represent Arthur, Lord Grey of Wilton, who was Lord Lieutenant of Ireland for two years from July 1580. Spenser was his secretary; and the events in Ireland during his government, which included the suppression of the rebellion of Earl Desmond, are shadowed forth in the present book. The name of the hero is obviously compounded of "Arthur," and "egal," equal or just.
4 Great Wrong.
5 Ireland; anciently called Ierné, modern Irish, Erin.
6 Judging. 7 Reached.
8 Command, will. 9 Avenging.
10 Unknown. 11 Golden-sword.
12 Keep out. 13 Sheared, cleaved.
14 Dwell, roam. 15 Belt; the Milky Way.
16 Adorn.
17 Reckoning from March, in which month the year at Spenser's day began, August—the month in which the sun enters Virgo—was the sixth.
18 The sign Libra, following Virgo in the Zodiac.
19 Servant.
20 Go.
21 Talos, in the ancient mythology, was a brazen man given by Vulcan to Minos, king of Crete; he protected the island by walking round it thrice daily. Spenser has modified the fable, making Talus the personification of the inflexible and unpitying power that must accompany Justice.

Who in his hand an iron flail did hold,
With which he thresh'd out falsehood, and did truth unfold.

Talus attended Artegall on his enterprise; and the twain were on their way, when they descried a squire in squalid garb, weeping and lamenting bitterly. Approaching, they saw a headless lady lie beside him, wallowing in her blood; and Artegall, flaming with zeal of vengeance, asked who had so cruelly treated the lady. The sad squire said that the malefactor was a knight, who, accompanied by the now headless dame, had come upon him as he sat in solace with a fair love whose loss he deplored. The knight insisted on exchanging ladies; and, throwing down his own dame from his courser, took up on his steed the squire's love, to bear her away by force. But his own lady followed him, entreating him not to forsake her, but rather to slay her; and he, wrathfully drawing his sword, "at one stroke cropp'd off her head with scorn," and rode away. He had "pricked over yonder plain;" and in his shield he bore "a broken sword within a bloody field." Artegall instantly sent his iron page after the profligate and cruel knight (supposed to indicate Shan O'Neal, leader of the Irish rebellion of 1567, who was conspicuous for his profligacy); and soon Talus, who was "swift as swallow in her flight, and strong as lion in his lordly might," overtook and brought back to his master the knight—who was called Sir Sanglier—and the lady whom he had carried off. Artegall gently asked the captive what had taken place between him and the squire; but Sir Sanglier sternly and proudly answered, that he was guiltless, for he had not shed the lady's blood, nor taken away the squire's love, "but his own proper good." Knowing himself too weak to meet the knight's defiance in the field, the squire rather chose to confess himself guilty; but Artegall plainly perceived the truth, and contrived a method of getting at the facts. Exacting a promise that they would abide by his judgment, he proposed that the living and the dead lady should be divided between the knight and the squire in equal shares; and that whosoever dissented from his judgment should bear for twelve months the lady's head, "to witness to the world that she by him is dead."

Well pleasëd with that doom was Sanglier,
And offer'd straight the lady to be slain:
But that same squire, to whom she was more dear,
When as he saw she should be cut in twain,
Did yield she rather should with him remain
Alive, than to himself be sharëd dead;
And, rather than his love should suffer pain,
He chose with shame to bear that lady's head:
True love despiseth shame when life is call'd in dread.[1]

Whom when so willing Artegall perceiv'd,
"Not so, thou Squire," he said; "but thine I deem
The living lady, which from thee he reav'd:[2]
For worthy thou of her dost rightly seem.
And you, Sir Knight, that love so light esteem
As that ye would for little leave the same,
Take here your own, that doth you best beseem,
And with it bear the burden of defame;[3]
Your own dead lady's head, to tell abroad your shame."

But Sanglier disdainëd much his doom,
And sternly gan repine at his behest;[4]
Nor would for aught obey, as did become,
To bear that lady's head before his breast;
Until that Talus had his pride represt,
And forcëd him, malgré,[5] it up to rear.
Who when he saw it bootless to resist,
He took it up, and thence with him did bear;
As rated spaniel takes his burden up for fear.

The squire, much admiring the great justice of Artegall, offered him perpetual service; but the Knight would have no attendant save Talus; with whom he passed on his way—"they two enough t' encounter a whole regiment."

CANTO II.

Artegall hears of Florimell;
Does with the Pagan fight:
Him slays; drowns Lady Munera;
Does raze her castle quite.

As he journeyed, Artegall met Dony, the dwarf of Florimell, hasting to the wedding-feast, which was to take place in three days at the Castle of the Strand—but fearful lest his progress should be arrested "a little there beyond" by a cursed cruel Saracen, who kept the passage of a bridge by the strong hand, and had there brought to ruin many errant knights. He was "a man of great defence, expert in battle and in deeds of arms;" and all the more emboldened by the wicked charms with which his daughter aided him. He had gained great property by his extortions, and daily increased his wrongs, letting none go by, rich or poor, that did not pay his passage-penny. To poll and pill the poor, he kept "a groom of evil guise, whose scalp is bare, that bondage doth bewray;" but he himself tyrannised over the rich. His name was Pollenté; and he was accustomed to fight on a narrow bridge, exceeding long, and full of trap-doors, through which riders often fell. Beneath the bridge ran a swift and deep river, in which, through practice, he could easily manage his steed, and overthrow the confused enemy; then he took the victims' spoil at will, and brought it to his daughter Munera, who dwelt at hand. Not only was she surprisingly rich with his gifts won by wrong; but, Dony adds,

1 Placed in doubt.
2 Took by force.
3 Disgrace.
4 Rebel against his command.
5 Against his will.

"Thereto[1] she is full fair, and rich attir'd,
With golden hands and silver feet beside,
That many lords have her to wife desir'd;
But she them all despiseth for great pride."
"Now by my life," said he,[2] "and God to guide,
None other way will I this day betake,
But by that bridge where as he doth abide:
Therefore me thither lead." No more he spake,
But thitherward forthright his ready way did make.

Unto the place he came within a while,
Where on the bridge he ready armëd saw
The Saracen, awaiting for some spoil:
Who as they to the passage gan to draw,
A villain to them came with skull all raw,[3]
That passage-money did of them require,
According to the custom of their law:
To whom he answer'd wroth, "Lo! there thy hire;"
And with that word him struck, that straight he did expire.

The Pagan thereat waxed wroth, and addressed himself to fight; Artegall was not behind; and as they met in combat on the bridge, a trap gave way, and both were soon struggling in the flood.

As when a dolphin and a seal are met
In the wide champaign of the ocean plain,
With cruel chafe their couragës they whet,
The masterdom of each by force to gain,
And dreadful battle 'twixt them do darrain;[4]
They snuff, they snort, they bounce, they rage, they roar,
That all the sea, disturbëd with their train,
Doth fry with foam above the surges hoar:
Such was betwixt these two the troublesome uproar.

The Saracen, forced to quit his horse's back, found Artegall a match for him as a swimmer, and better breathed—so that he became irresistible, and struck off Pollenté's head just as he began to raise it a little above the brink to tread upon the land. His body was carried down the stream; but Artegall, for a warning to all mighty men not to abuse their power to the oppression of the feeble, pitched the blasphemous head upon a pole, where it remained many years. Then he turned against the castle, where he was met by blasphemies and showers of stones, so that he was forced to commit to Talus the task of its reduction.

Eftsoons his page drew to the castle gate,
And with his iron flail at it let fly,
That all the warders it did sore amate,[5]
The which erewhile spake so reproachfully,
And made them stoop, that lookëd erst so high.
Yet still he beat and bounc'd upon the door,
And thunder'd strokes thereon so hideously,
That all the piece[6] he shakëd from the floor,
And fillëd all the house with fear and great uproar.

With noise whereof the lady forth appear'd
Upon the castle wall; and when she saw
The dangerous state in which she stood, she fear'd
The sad effect of her near overthrow;
And gan entreat that Iron Man below
To cease his outrage, and him fair besought;
Since neither force of stones which they did throw,
Nor pow'r of charms which she against him wrought,
Might otherwise prevail, or make him cease for aught.

But, when as yet she saw him to proceed
Unmov'd with prayers or with piteous thought,
She meant him to corrupt with goodly meed;
And caus'd great sacks, with endless riches fraught,
Unto the battlement to be upbrought,
And pourëd forth over the castle wall,
That she might win some time, though dearly bought,
Whilst he to gath'ring of the gold did fall;
But he was nothing mov'd nor tempted therewithal:

He continued to "lay on load" with his huge iron flail, till he broke open the gate for his master's entrance. All fled and hid for fear; Talus, after long search, found Munera concealed under a heap of gold, and dragged her out by the hair; then remorselessly he cut off her hands of gold and feet of silver, "which sought unrighteousness, and justice sold." Finally, he threw her over the wall into the flood; poured after her all her wealth, after it had been burnt to ashes; razed the castle; and defaced all its hewn stones, that it might never be rebuilt. Then Artegall undid the evil fashion, reformed the wicked custom of the bridge, and pursued his former journey. Drawing nigh to the sea, they saw before them, far as they could view, a vast crowd of people; and, wondering at the great assembly, they drew near to learn its cause and object.

There they beheld a mighty giant stand
Upon a rock, and holding forth on high
A huge great pair of balance in his hand,
With which he boasted in his surquedry[7]
That all the world he would weigh equally,
If aught he had the same to counterpoise:
For want whereof he weighëd vanity,
And fill'd his balance full of idle toys:
Yet was admirëd much of fools, womën, and boys.

He said that he would all the earth uptake,
And all the sea, divided each from either:
So would he of the fire one balance make,
And one of th' air, without or wind or weather:
Then would he balance heav'n and hell together,
And all that did within them all contain;
Of all whose weight he would not miss a feather:
And look what surplus did of each remain,
He would to his own part restore the same again.

1 Besides, in addition. 2 Artegall. 3 Bare.
4 Wage. 5 Terrify. 6 Building. 7 Presumption.

For why, he said, they all unequal were,
And had encroachëd upon other's share;
Like as the sea (which plain he showëd there)
Had worn the earth; so did the fire the air;
So all the rest did others' parts impair:
And so were realms and nations run awry.
All which he undertook for to repair,
In sort as they were formëd anciently;
And all things would reduce unto equality.

Therefore the vulgar did about him flock,
And cluster thick unto his leasings [1] vain,
Like foolish flies about a honey-crock,
In hope by him great benefit to gain,
And uncontrollëd freedom to obtain.
All which when Artegall did see and hear,
How he misled the simple people's train,
In sdeignful [2] wise he drew unto him near,
And thus unto him spake, without regard or fear;

"Thou, that presum'st to weigh the world anew,
And all things to an equal to restore,
Instead of right me seems great wrong dost shew,
And far above thy force's pitch to soar:
For, ere thou limit what is less or more
In ev'ry thing, thou oughtest first to know
What was the poise [3] of ev'ry part of yore:
And look, then, how much it doth overflow
Or fail thereof, so much is more than just to trow.[4]

"For at the first they all created were
In goodly measure [5] by their Maker's might;
And weighëd out in balances so near,
That not a dram was missing of their right:
The earth was in the middle centre pight,[6]
In which it doth immovable abide,
Hemm'd in with waters like a wall in sight,
And they with air, that not a drop can slide:
All which the heav'ns contain, and in their courses guide.

"Such heav'nly justice doth among them reign,
That ev'ry one do know their certain bound;
In which they do these many years remain,
And 'mongst them all no change hath yet been found:
But if thou now shouldst weigh them new in pound,[7]
We are not sure they would so long remain:
All change is perilous, and all chance unsound.
Therefore leave off to weigh them all again,
Till we may be assur'd they shall their course retain."

"Thou foolish Elf," said then the giant wroth,
"Seest not how badly all things present be,
And each estate quite out of order go'th?
The sea itself dost thou not plainly see
Encroach upon the land there under thee?
And th' earth itself how daily it's increast
By all that, dying, to it turnëd be?
Were it not good that wrong were then surceast,[8]
And from the most that some were given to the least?

"Therefore I will throw down these mountains high,
And make them level with the lowly plain;
These tow'ring rocks, which reach unto the sky,
I will thrust down into the deepest main,
And, as they were, them equalise again.
Tyrants, that make men subject to their law,
I will suppress, that they no more may reign;
And lordlings curb that commons overawe;
And all the wealth of rich men to the poor will draw."

"Of things unseen how canst thou deem aright,"
Then answerëd the righteous Artegall,
"Since thou misdeem'st so much of things in sight?
What though the sea with waves continual
Do eat the earth, it is no more at all;
Nor is the earth the less, or loseth aught:
For whatsoever from one place doth fall
Is with the tide unto another brought:
For there is nothing lost, that may be found if sought.

"Likewise the earth is not augmented more
By all that, dying, into it do fade;
For of the earth they formëd were of yore:
However gay their blossom or their blade
Do flourish now, they into dust shall vade.[9]
What wrong then is it if that, when they die,
They turn to that whereof they first were made?
All in the power of their great Maker lie:
All creatures must obey the voice of the Most High.

"They live, they die, like as He doth ordain,
Nor ever any asketh reason why.
The hills do not the lowly dales disdain;
The dales do not the lofty hills envy.
He maketh kings to sit in sovereignty;
He maketh subjects to their pow'r obey;
He pulleth down, He setteth up on high;
He gives to this, from that He takes away:
For all we have is His: what He list do, He may.

"Whatever thing is done, by Him is done,
Nor any may His mighty will withstand;
Nor any may His sov'reign power shun,
Nor loose that He hath bound with steadfast band:
In vain therefóre dost thou now take in hand
To call to count, or weigh His works anew,
Whose counsels' depth thou canst not understand;
Since of things subject to thy daily view
Thou dost not know the causes nor their courses due.

"For take thy balance, if thou be so wise,
And weigh the wind that under heav'n doth blow;
Or weigh the light that in the east doth rise;
Or weigh the thought that from man's mind doth flow:
But if the weight of these thou canst not show,

1 Falsehoods. 2 Disdainful. 3 Weight, proportion. 4 Believe. 5 Proportion. 6 Placed. 7 Anew in the balance. 8 Ended. 9 Go.

Weigh but one word which from thy lips doth fall:
For how canst thou those greater secrets know,
That dost not know the least thing of them all?
Ill can he rule the great that cannot reach the small."

Therewith the giant much abashëd, said
That he of little things made reckoning light;
Yet the least word that ever could be laid
Within his balance he could weigh aright.
"Which is," said he, "more heavy then in weight,
The right or wrong, the false or else the true?"
He answerëd that he would try it straight:
So he the words into his balance threw;
But straight the wingëd words out of his balance flew.

Wroth wax'd he then, and said that words were light,
Nor would within his balance well abide:
But he could justly weigh the wrong or right.
"Well then," said Artegall, "let it be tried:
First in one balance set the true aside."
He did so first, and then the false he laid
In th' other scale; but still it down did slide,
And by no mean could in the weight be stay'd:
For by no means the false will with the truth be weigh'd.

"Now take the right likewise," said Artegale,
"And counterpoise the same with so much wrong."
So first the right he put into one scale;
And then the giant strove with puissance strong
To fill the other scale with so much wrong:
But all the wrongs that he therein could lay
Might not it poise; yet did he labour long,
And sweat, and chaf'd, and provëd[1] ev'ry way:
Yet all the wrongs could not a little right down weigh.

Which when he saw, he greatly grew in rage,
And almost would his balances have broken:
But Artegall him fairly gan assuage,
And said, "Be not upon thy balance wroken;[2]
For they do naught but right or wrong betoken;
But in the mind the doom[3] of right must be:
And so likewise of words the which be spoken,
The ear must be the balance, to decree
And judge whether with truth or falsehood they agree.

"But set the truth and set the right aside,
For they with wrong or falsehood will not fare,
And put two wrongs together to be tried,
Or else two falses,[4] of each equal share,
And then together do them both compare:
For truth is one, and right is ever one."
So did he; and then plain it did appear
Whether of them the greater were at one:[5]
But right sat in the middest of the beam alone.

But he the right from thence did thrust away;
For it was not the right which he did seek:
But rather strove extremities to weigh;
Th' one to diminish, th' other for to eke:[6]
For of the mean[7] he greatly did misleke.[8]
Whom when so lewdly[9] minded Talus found,
Approaching nigh unto him cheek by cheek
He shoulder'd him from off the higher ground,
And down the rock him throwing, in the sea him drown'd.

Like as a ship, whom cruel tempest drives
Upon a rock with horrible dismay,
Her shatter'd ribs in thousand pieces rives,
And, spoiling all her gears[10] and goodly ray,[11]
Does make herself misfortune's piteous prey:
So down the cliff the wretched giant tumbled;
His batter'd balances in pieces lay,
His timber'd[12] bones all broken rudely rumbled:
So was the high-aspiring with huge ruin humbled.

That when the people, which had there about
Long waited, saw his sudden desolation,
They gan to gather in tumultuous rout,
And mutining to stir up civil faction
For certain loss of so great expectation:
For well they hopëd to have got great good
And wondrous riches by his innovation:
Therefore resolving to revenge his blood,
They rose in arms, and all in battle order stood.

Which lawless multitude him coming to
In warlike wise when Artegall did view,
He much was troubled, nor wist what to do;
For loth he was his noble hands t' embrue
In the base blood of such a rascal crew;
And otherwise, if that he should retire,
He fear'd lest they with shame would him pursue:
Therefore he Talus to them sent t' inquire
The cause of their array, and truce for to desire.

But soon as they him nigh approaching spied,
They gan with all their weapons him assay,
And rudely struck at him on every side;
Yet naught they could him hurt, nor aught dismay:
But when at them he with his flail gan lay,
He like a swarm of flies them overthrew:
Nor any of them durst come in his way,
But here and there before his presence flew,
And hid themselves in holes and bushes from his view;

As when a falcon hath with nimble flight
Flown at a flush of ducks foreby[13] the brook,
The trembling fowl, dismay'd with dreadful sight
Of death, the which them almost overtook,
Do hide themselves from her astonying[14] look
Amongst the flags and covert round about.
When Talus saw they all the field forsook,
And none appear'd of all that rascal rout,
To Artegall he turn'd, and went with him throughout.

1 Tried. 2 Revenged. 3 Judgment.
4 Falsehoods. 5 At once. 6 Increase.
7 Moderation, the medium. 8 Dislike.
9 Wickedly. 10 Equipments.
11 Array. 12 Massive, like timbers.
13 Near. 14 Confounding.

CANTO III.

The spousals of fair Florimell,
Where tourney many knights:
There Braggadocio is uncas'd
In all the ladies' sights.

"AFTER long storms and tempests overblown," the sun breaks forth; so must some blissful hours appear when Fortune has exhausted her spite; and so did Florimell experience, whose bridal feast was prepared in Faery Land, infinite great store of lords and ladies, and all the brave knights, resorting thither from every side. The splendid feast over, deeds of arms ensued; and Marinell issued forth with six knights, who undertook to maintain against all comers the peerless excellence of Florimell. Against them came all that chose to joust, "from ev'ry coast and country under sun;" but all the first day Marinell won the greatest praise; and also on the second day the trumpets proclaimed that Marinell had best deserved. On the third day, he still performed great deeds of valour; but, pressing too far among his enemies, his retreat was cut off, and he was made prisoner. Just then Artegall chanced to come into the tilt-yard, along with Braggadocio and the false Florimell, whom he had met on the way; and, learning what had befallen Marinell, he borrowed the boaster's shield, to be the better hid. Then, overtaking the crowd of knights who were leading Marinell away, Artegall rescued the captive, and, with his help, chased the captors utterly out of the field. The deliverer then restored to Braggadocio the borrowed shield; the judges rose; and all came into the open hall to hear the decision on that day's tourneying. Thither also came fair Florimell, to congratulate each knight on his prize of valour; and loud calls arose for the stranger knight, who should gain the garland of that day. Artegall came not forth; but instead came Braggadocio, "and did show his shield, which bore the sun broad blazëd in a golden field." The trumpets sounded his triumph thrice, and Florimell advanced to greet and thank him; but the boaster, with proud disdain, declared that what he had done that day he had done not for her, but for his own dear lady's sake—whom on his peril he undertook to excel both her and all others. Much confounded and ashamed by his uncourteous and vaunting words, the true Florimell turned aside. "Then forth he brought his snowy Florimell," whom Trompart had in keeping, covered with a veil; and all the crowd, amazed, cried that it was either Florimell, or one that excelled her in beauty.

Which when as Marinell beheld likewise,
He was therewith exceedingly dismay'd;[1]
Nor wist he what to think, or to devise:
But, like as one whom fiends had made afraid,
He long astonish'd stood, nor aught he said,
Nor aught he did, but with fast fixëd eyes
He gazëd still upon that snowy maid;
Whom ever as he did the more advise,[2]
The more to be true Florimell he did surmise.

As when two suns appear in th' azure sky,
Mounted in Phœbus' chariot fiery bright,
Both darting forth fair beams to each man's eye,
And both adorn'd with lamps of flaming light;
All that behold so strange prodigious sight,
Not knowing Nature's work, nor what to ween,
Are rapt with wonder and with rare affright:
So stood Sir Marinell when he had seen
The semblant[3] of this false by his fair beauty's queen.

All which when Artegall, who all this while
Stood in the press close cover'd, well adview'd,
And saw that boaster's pride and graceless guile,
He could no longer bear, but forth issúed,
And unto all himself there open shew'd,
And to the boaster said; "Thou losel[4] base,
That hast with borrow'd plumes thyself indued,
And others' worth with leasings[5] dost deface,
When they are all restor'd thou shalt rest in disgrace.

"That shield, which thou dost bear, was it indeed
Which this day's honour sav'd to Marinell;
But not that arm, nor thou the man, I read,[6]
Which didst that service unto Florimell:
For proof, show forth thy sword, and let it tell
What strokes, what dreadful stowre,[7] it stirr'd this day:
Or show the wounds which unto thee befell;
Or show the sweat with which thou diddest sway
So sharp a battle, that so many did dismay.

"But this the sword which wrought those cruel stounds,[8]
And this the arm the which that shield did bear,
And these the signs" (so showëd forth his wounds),
"By which that glory gotten doth appear.
As for this lady, which he showeth here,
Is not (I wager) Florimell at all;
But some fair franion,[9] fit for such a fere,[10]
That by misfortune in his hand did fall."
For proof whereof he bade them Florimell forth call.

So forth the noble lady was y-brought,
Adorn'd with honour and all comely grace:
Whereto her bashful shamefastness y-wrought
A great increase in her fair blushing face;
As roses did with lilies interlace:
For of those words, the which that boaster threw,
She inly yet conceivëd great disgrace:
Whom when as all the people such did view,
They shouted loud, and signs of gladness all did shew.

Then did he set her by that snowy one,
Like the true saint beside the image set;

1 Disturbed, amazed. 2 Regard. 3 Resemblance. 4 Loose, worthless fellow. 5 Falsehoods. 6 Declare. 7 Conflict. 8 Blows. 9 Loose woman. 10 Companion.

Of both their beauties to make paragon[1]
And trial, whether should the honour get.
Straightway, so soon as both together met,
Th' enchanted damsel vanish'd into naught:
Her snowy substance melted as with heat,
Nor of that goodly hue[2] remainëd aught
But th' empty girdle which about her waist was wrought.

As when the daughter of Thaumantes fair[3]
Hath in a watery cloud displayëd wide
Her goodly bow, which paints the liquid air,
That all men wonder at her colours' pride;
All suddenly, ere one can look aside,
The glorious picture vanisheth away,
Nor any token doth thereof abide:
So did this lady's goodly form decay,
And into nothing go, ere one could it bewray.

All were stricken with great astonishment; and Braggadocio himself, for grief and despair, stood "like a living corpse, immoveable."

But Artegall that golden belt uptook,
The which of all her spoil was only left;
Which was not hers, as many it mistook,
But Florimell's own girdle, from her reft
While she was flying, like a weary weft,[4]
From that foul monster which did her compel
To perils great; which he unbuckling eft[5]
Presented to the fairest Florimell;
Who round about her tender waist it fitted well.

Full many ladies often had assay'd
About their middles that fair belt to knit;
And many a one suppos'd to be a maid:
Yet it to none of all their loins would fit,
Till Florimell about her fasten'd it.
Such power it had, that to no woman's waist
By any skill or labour it would fit,
Unless that she were continent and chaste;
But it would loose or break, that many had disgrac'd.

Now came forth Sir Guyon from the press, to claim his own good steed, which the braggart had stolen when its owner left it to go to the relief of Amavia (see canto i., book ii.); and after "great hurly-burly" in the hall had been appeased by Artegall, the Knight of Temperance related the circumstances under which he had lost the horse, and vainly challenged the cowardly thief to combat. Artegall—though pronouncing that Braggadocio's refusal to fight was sufficient proof that he was in the wrong—asked Guyon what privy tokens the steed bore; and he answered that "within his mouth a black spot doth appear, shap'd like a horse's shoe, who list to seek it there."

Whereof to make due trial one did take
The horse in hand, within his mouth to look:
But with his heels so sorely he him strake,
That all his ribs he quite in pieces broke,
That never word from that day forth he spoke.
Another, that would seem to have more wit,
Him by the bright embroider'd headstall took:
But by the shoulder him so sore he bit,
That he him maimëd quite, and all his shoulder split.

Nor he his mouth would open unto wight,
Until that Guyon's self unto him spake,
And callëd Brigadore (so was he hight);
Whose voice so soon as he did undertake,[6]
Eftsoons he stood as still as any stake,
And suffer'd all his secret mark to see;
And, when as he him nam'd, for joy he brake
His bands, and follow'd him with gladful glee,
And frisk'd, and flung aloft, and louted[7] low on knee.

Artegall therefore adjudged the steed to Guyon, and told the braggart to fare on foot till he had gained a horse. Braggadocio, however, foully reviled the judge and disdained his judgment; and Artegall was about to draw sword upon him, when Guyon restrained the Knight with the reflection that it would ill become the judge of their equity to wreak his wrath on such a churl, whose open shame was his sufficient punishment.

So did he mitigate Sir Artegall;
But Talus by the back the boaster hent,[8]
And, drawing him out of the open hall,
Upon him did inflict this punishment:
First he his beard did shave, and foully shent;[9]
Then from him reft his shield, and it reverst,
And blotted out his arms with falsehood blent;[10]
And himself baffled,[11] and his arms unherst;[12]
And broke his sword in twain, and all his armour sperst.[13]

The while his guileful groom[14] was fled away;
But vain it was to think from him to fly:
Who overtaking him did disarray,
And all his face deform'd with infamy,
And out of court him scourgëd openly.
So ought all faitours,[15] that true knighthood shame,
And arms dishonour with base villainy,
From all brave knights be banish'd with defame:[16]
For oft their lewdness[17] blotteth good deserts with blame.

Much mirth arose over the unmasking of these counterfeits; and the poet leaves all the company in pleasure and repast—"taking usury of time forepast" with all rare delights—to follow Artegall.

1 Comparison. 2 Form, aspect.
3 Iris, or the rainbow; the daughter of Thaumas.
4 Waif. 5 Quickly.
6 Hear.
7 Bended. 8 Seized.
9 Disgraced. 10 Stained.
11 Treated with ignominy. 12 Defaced.
13 Scattered. 14 Trompart.
15 Deceivers. 16 Infamy.
17 Wickedness.

CANTO IV.

Artegall dealeth right betwixt
Two brethren that do strive;
Saves Terpine from the gallows tree,
And doth from death reprive.

SETTING out with some reflections on the necessity that whoso would divide true justice to the people should have mighty hands to fulfil the judgment he has given—"for Power is the right hand of Justice truly hight"—the poet resumes the story of Artegall's adventure. Quitting the Castle of the Strand, attended by Talus only, he encountered on the sea-shore two comely squires, brothers, who strove together; and by them stood two seemly damsels, seeking, now by fair words and now by threats, to assuage their ire. Between them, seeming to be the object of their strife, "stood a coffer strong fast bound on ev'ry side with iron bands," that had suffered much injury either by being wrecked upon the sands, or by being carried far from foreign lands. The squires were ready for the combat, with sword in hand, when Artegall arrived, and inquired the cause of strife. The elder replied that their father, Milesio, had equally divided his lands between himself and a younger brother—two islands not far off, one of which was now "but like a little mount of small degree," the sea having washed away the most of the elder brother's, and thrown it up to the younger's share. The elder had before that time loved "that farther maid, hight Philtera the fair," who had a goodly dower; while the younger, Amidas, loved the other damsel, Lucy bright, who had but little wealth. But Philtera, seeing the lands of Bracidas (the elder brother) decay, eloped to Amidas, who received her and left his own love to go astray. Lucy, in despair, threw herself into the sea; and as she wavered between life and death, having half seen the ugly visage of the latter, but not relishing the sight, she lighted upon the coffer, and, catching hold of it, at last came ashore on the diminished island of Bracidas—to whom, in recompense for her salvation, she presented the coffer, "together with herself in dowry free." But Philtera claimed the coffer, and the treasure which it contained, as her property, lost by shipwreck on the way to her new husband; while Bracidas declared his intention to hold his own—for though his brother had won away his land, and then his love, he should not likewise make a prey of his good luck. Amidas maintained that Philtera's claim to the coffer could be proved "by good marks and perfect good espial;" but both brothers agreed to accept Artegall's decision, and laid their swords under his foot.

Then Artegall thus to the younger said:
"Now tell me, Amidas, if that ye may,
Your brother's land, the which the sea hath laid
Unto your part, and pluck'd from his away,
By what good right do you withhold this day?"
"What other right," quoth he, "should you esteem,
But that the sea it to my share did lay?"
"Your right is good," said he, "and so I deem
That what the sea unto you sent your own should seem."

Then turning to the elder, thus he said:
"Now, Bracidas, let this likewise be shown;
Your brother's treasure, which from him is stray'd,
Being the dowry of his wife well known,
By what right do you claim to be your own?"
"What other right," quoth he, "should you esteem,
But that the sea hath it unto me thrown?"
"Your right is good," said he, "and so I deem
That what the sea unto you sent your own should seem.

"For equal right in equal things doth stand:
For what the mighty sea hath once possest,
And pluckëd quite from all possessors' hand,
Whether by rage of waves that never rest,
Or else by wreck that wretches hath distrest,
He may dispose by his imperial might,
As thing at random left, to whom he list.
So, Amidas, the land was yours first hight;[1]
And so the treasure yours is, Bracidas, by right."

"So was their discord by this doom appeas'd, and each one had his right." Prosecuting his journey, Artegall espied "a rout of many people far away," whom, on drawing near, he found to be a troop of armed women, leading along, amid taunts and reproaches, a knight with both his hands pinioned behind him, and a halter round his neck, groaning inwardly that he should die so base a death at women's hands. The Amazons would have laid hands on Artegall also; but he drew back, and, ashamed to raise his own mighty hand against womankind, sent Talus to disperse the crowd with a few blows of his flail. They left behind them their captive—whom, brought to him by Talus, Artegall recognised as Sir Terpine, and interrogated as to the cause of his disgraceful plight. Much ashamed and confounded, Terpine laid the blame on fate, and continued:

"Being desirous (as all knights are wont)
Through hard adventures deeds of arms to try,
And after fame and honour for to hunt,
I heard report that far abroad did fly,
That a proud Amazon did late defy
All the brave knights that hold of Maidenhead,
And unto them wrought all the villainy
That she could forge in her malicious head,
Which some hath put to shame, and many done be dead.[2]

"The cause, they say, of this her cruel hate,
Is for the sake of Bellodant the bold,
To whom she bore most fervent love of late,
And wooëd him by all the ways she co'ld:
But, when she saw at last that he not wo'ld
For aught or naught be won unto her will,

[1] Called, declared.

[2] Slain.

She turn'd her love to hatred manifold,
And for his sake vow'd to do all the ill
Which she could do to knights; which now she
doth fulfil.

"For all those knights, the which by force or
guile
She doth subdue, she foully doth entreat:
First, she doth them of warlike arms despoil,
And clothe in women's weeds; and then with
threat
Doth them compel to work, to earn their meat,
To spin, to card, to sew, to wash, to wring;
Nor doth she give them other thing to eat
But bread and water or like feeble thing;
Them to disable from revenge adventuring.

"But if, through stout disdain of manly mind,
Any her proud observance will withstand,
Upon that gibbet, which is there behind,
She causeth them be hang'd up out of hand;
In which condition I right now did stand:
For, being overcome by her in fight,
And put to that base service of her band,
I rather chose to die, in life's despite,[1]
Than lead that shameful life, unworthy of a
knight."

The name of that Amazonian queen is Radigund, "in arms well tried and sundry battles." Artegall, vowing that he will not rest till he has tried her might, bids Sir Terpine throw aside the badges of reproach which he wears, and aid him in his enterprise. Soon they came to the dwelling of the Amazon, "a goodly city and a mighty one, the which, of her own name, she callëd Radigone."

Where they arriving, by the watchmen were
Descriëd straight; who all the city warn'd
How that three warlike persons did appear,
Of which the one him seem'd a knight all
arm'd,
And th' other two well likely to have harm'd.
Eftsoons the people all to harness ran,
And like a sort of bees in clusters swarm'd:
Ere long their queen herself, half like a man,
Came forth into the rout, and them t' array
began.

And now the knights, being arrivëd near,
Did beat upon the gates to enter in;
And at the porter, scorning them so few,
Threw many threats, if they the town did win,
To tear his flesh in pieces for his sin:
Which when as Radigund their coming heard,
Her heart for rage did grate, and teeth did
grin:[2]
She bade that straight the gates should be un-
barr'd,
And to them way to make with weapons well
prepar'd.

The knights pressed in, but were met by a shower of arrows, which made them halt; while the enemy heaped strokes and hailed arrows on them so thick that they could not abide. Radigund, inflamed with fury to see the late captive Terpine "so cruel dole among her maids divide," to avenge his shame, flew at him like a fell lioness, and smote him senseless to the ground.

Soon as she saw him on the ground to grovel,
She lightly to him leap'd; and, in his neck
Her proud foot setting, at his head did level,
Weening at once her wrath on him to wreak,
And his contempt, that did her judgment break
As when a bear hath seiz'd her cruel claws
Upon the carcase of some beast too weak,
Proudly stands over, and awhile doth pause
To hear the piteous beast pleading her plaintive
cause.

Whom when as Artegall in that distress
By chance beheld, he left the bloody slaughter
In which he swam, and ran to his redress:
There her assailing fiercely fresh he raught[3] her
Such a huge stroke, that it of sense distraught[4]
her;
And, had she not it warded warily,
It had depriv'd her mother of a daughter:
Nathless, for all the pow'r she did apply,
It made her stagger oft, and stare with ghastly
eye.

Like to an eagle in his kingly pride,
Soaring through his wide empire of the air
To weather his broad sails, by chance hath spied
A goshawk, which hath seizëd for her share
Upon some fowl that should her feast prepare;
With dreadful force he flies at her belive,[5]
That with his souce,[6] which none enduren dare,
Her from the quarry he away doth drive,
And from her griping pounce the greedy prey
doth rive.

But, soon as she her sense recover'd had,
She fiercely toward him herself gan dight,[7]
Through vengeful wrath and sdeignful[8] pride
half mad;
For never had she suffer'd such despite:
But, ere she could join hand with him to fight,
Her warlike maids about her flock'd so fast,
That they disparted them, maugré[9] their might,
And with their troops did far asunder cast:
But 'mongst the rest the fight did until evening
last.

And ev'ry while that mighty Iron Man
With his strange weapon, never wont[10] in war,
Them sorely vex'd, and cours'd, and overran,
And broke their bows, and did their shooting
mar,
That none of all the many once did dare
Him to assault, nor once approach him nigh;
But, like a sort of sheep dispersed far,
For dread of their devouring enemy,
Through all the fields and valleys did before
him fly.

Night falling, Radigund gave the signal to retire; and all her people entered the city. Artegall pitched his rich pavilion in open sight

1 Contempt.
2 Grind.
3 Reached, dealt.
4 Deprived.
5 Immediately.
6 Swoop.
7 Prepare.
8 Disdainful.
9 Despite.
10 Used.

before the gate, and rested, with Terpine; while Talus kept watch. But Radigund, full of heart-gnawing grief at her defeat, tossed in her troubled mind how she might revenge herself. At last she called a trusty maid, named Clarin, or Clarinda, and sent her forth to challenge the Faery Knight to single combat on the morrow.

"But these conditions do to him propound;
That, if I vanquish him, he shall obey
My law, and ever to my lore[1] be bound;
And so will I, if me he vanquish may;
Whatever he shall like to do or say:
Go straight, and take with thee to witness it
Six of thy fellows of the best array,
And bear with you both wine and junkets[2] fit,
And bid him eat: henceforth he oft shall hungry sit."

The challenge was duly delivered and accepted; then Artegall betook himself to rest, "that he might fresher be against the next day's fight."

CANTO V.

Artegall fights with Radigund,
And is subdu'd by guile:
He is by her imprisonëd,
But wrought by Clarin's wile.

So soon as Day, forth dawning from the east,
Night's humid curtain from the heav'ns withdrew,
And, early calling forth both man and beast,
Commanded them their daily works renew;
These noble warriors, mindful to pursue
The last day's purpose of their vowëd fight,
Themselves thereto prepar'd in order due;
The Knight, as best was seeming for a knight,
And th' Amazon, as best it lik'd herself to dight.[3]

All in a camis[4] light of purple silk
Woven upon with silver, subtly wrought,
And quilted upon satin white as milk;
Trailëd[5] with ribands diversely distraught,[6]
Like as the workmen had their courses taught;
Which was short tuckëd for light motión
Up to her ham; but, when she list, it raught[7]
Down to her lowest heel; and thereupon
She wore for her defence a mailëd habergeon.

And on her legs she painted buskins wore,
Basted[8] with bands of gold on ev'ry side,
And mails between, and lacëd close before;
Upon her thigh her scimitar was tied
With an embroider'd belt of mickle pride;
And on her shoulder hung her shield, bedeckt
Upon the boss with stones that shinëd wide,
As the fair moon in her most full aspéct;
That to the moon it might be like in each respect.

So forth she came out of the city-gate,
With stately port and proud magnificence,
Guarded with many damsels, that did wait
Upon her person for her sure defence,
Playing on shalms and trumpets, that from hence
Their sound did reach unto the heaven's height:
Só forth into the field she marchëd thence,
Where was a rich pavilion ready pight[9]
Her to receive, till time they should begin the fight.

Artegall came forth out of his tent; and when both combatants had entered, the lists were closed, "the trumpets sounded, and the field began." In a long and furious encounter, Artegall shears away half of Radigund's shield; she wounds him in the thigh with her scimitar; and he responds with two blows, the first shattering the remainder of her shield, the second, delivered upon her helmet, felling her to the ground in senseless swoon. Leaping to her with dreadful look, the Knight unlaces her helmet, intending to cut off her head.

But, when as he discover'd had her face,
He saw, his senses' strange astonishment,
A miracle of Nature's goodly grace
In her fair visage, void of ornament,
But bath'd in blood and sweat together ment;[10]
Which, in the rudeness of that evil plight,
Bewray'd the signs of feature excellent:
Like as the moon, in foggy winter's night,
Doth seem to be herself, though darken'd be her light.

At sight thereof his cruel-minded heart
Empiercëd was with pitiful regard,
That his sharp sword he threw from him apart,
Cursing his hand that had that visage marr'd:
No hand so cruel, nor no heart so hard,
But ruth[11] of beauty will it mollify.
By this, upstarting from her swoon, she star'd
A while about her with confusëd eye;
Like one that from his dream is wakëd suddenly.

Soon as the Knight she there by her did spy
Standing with empty hands all weaponless,
With fresh assault upon him she did fly,
And gan renew her former cruelness:
And though he still retir'd, yet nathëless
With huge redoubled stroke she on him laid;
And more increas'd her outrage merciless
The more that he with meek entreaty pray'd
Her wrathful hand from greedy vengeance to have stay'd.

Like as a puttock,[12] having spied in sight
A gentle falcon sitting on a hill,
Whose other wing, now made unmeet for flight,
Was lately broken by some fortune ill;
The foolish kite, led with licentious will,
Doth beat upon the gentle bird in vain,
With many idle stoops her troubling still:
Ev'n so did Radigund with bootless pain
Annoy this noble Knight, and sorely him constrain.

He is at last compelled to deliver up his shield, and submit to the conditions of the contest—

1 Instructions, commands. 2 Dainties. 3 Array. 4 Dress of thin stuff. 5 Adorned. 6 Disposed. 7 Reached. 8 Sowed. 9 Placed. 10 Mingled. 11 Compassion. 12 Kite.

for, though he had first won the victory, he had wilfully lost it by abandoning his weapon. Striking him with the flat of her sword, Radigund took him as her vassal; but Terpine she ordered to be hanged straightway; while Talus, thundering with his iron flail among those who sought to bar his path, made his escape—not once attempting to rescue his lord, but thinking it just to obey the conditions of the battle.

Then took the Amazon this noble Knight,
Left to her will by his own wilful blame,
And causëd him to be disarmëd quite
Of all the ornaments of knightly name
With which whilóm he gotten had great fame:
Instead whereof she made him to be dight[1]
In woman's weeds, that is to manhood shame,
And put before his lap an apron white,
Instead of curiets and bases[2] fit for fight.

So being clad she brought him from the field,
In which he had been trainëd many a day,
Into a long large chamber, which was ceil'd
With monuments of many knights' decay,
By her subduëd in victorious fray:
Amongst the which she caus'd his warlike arms
Be hang'd on high, that might his shame bewray;
And broke his sword, for fear of farther harms,
With which he wont to stir up battailous alarms.

There enter'd in, he round about him saw
Many brave knights whose names right well he knew,
There bound t' obey that Amazon's proud law,
Spinning and carding all in comely rew,[3]
That his big heart loath'd so uncomely view:
But they were forc'd, through penury and pine,
To do those works to them appointed due:
For naught was given them to sup or dine,
But what their hands could earn by twisting linen twine.

Amongst them all she placëd him most low,
And in his hand a distaff to him gave,
That he thereon should spin both flax and tow;
A sordid office for a mind so brave:
So hard it is to be a woman's slave!
Yet he took it in his own self's despite,
And thereto did himself right well behave
Her to obey, since he his faith had plight
Her vassal to become, if she him won in fight.

Who had him seen, imagine might thereby
That[4] whilom hath of Hercules been told,
How for Iola's[5] sake he did apply
His mighty hands the distaff vile to hold,
For his huge club, which had subdued of old
So many monsters which the world annoy'd;
His lion's skin chang'd to a pall[6] of gold,
In which, forgetting wars, he only joy'd
In combats of sweet love, and with his mistress toy'd.

Such is the cruelty of womenkind,
When they have shaken off the shamefast band
With which wise nature did them strongly bind
T' obey the hests of man's well-ruling hand,
That then all rule and reason they withstand,
To purchase a licentious liberty:
But virtuous women wisely understand
That they were born to base[7] humility,
Unless the heav'ns them lift to lawful sov'reignty.

Thus Artegall long continued to serve Radigund with due subjection; while the royal Amazon conceived love for her captive, and was tormented day and night by her anguish, which ever increased the more she strove against it. At last she began to stoop "to meek obeisance of Love's mighty reign;" and, calling secretly to her the handmaid whom she most did trust, told her that she must now test her friendship in greatest need.

With that she turn'd her head, as half abash'd,
To hide the blush which in her visage rose
And through her eyes like sudden lightning flash'd,
Decking her cheek with a vermilion rose:
But soon she did her countenance compose,
And, to her turning, thus began again;
"This grief's deep wound I would to thee disclose,
Thereto compellëd through heart-murd'ring pain;
But dread of shame my doubtful lips doth still restrain."

Encouraged by the handmaid to say on and be bold, Radigund confesses that the Faery Knight has won her heart, and that she would fain "by his freedom get his free goodwill, yet so as bound to me he may continue still," by the bands of "sweet love and sure benevolence." The queen entreats Clarinda to try if she can win him any way, without discovering her mistress's mind;

"Which that thou may'st the better bring to pass,
Lo! here this ring, which shall thy warrant be
And token true to old Eumenias,
From time to time, when thou it best shall see,
That in and out thou may'st have passage free.
Go now, Clarinda; well thy wits advise,
And all thy forces gather unto thee,
Armies of lovely looks, and speeches wise,
With which thou canst ev'n Jove himself to love entice."

Clarinda comforted Radigund with sure promise of her best endeavour, and thenceforth sought by all the means she might to curry favour with the Elfin Knight; proving him with wide-glancing words, drawing dark pictures of his captive future, and kindling in his mind the thought of deliverance. Having led him to the admission that the man were unworthy of better day who did not take the offer of good hope, she spoke thus:

"Then why dost not, thou ill-advisëd man,
Make means to win thy liberty forlorn,[8]
And try if thou by fair entreaty can

1 Dressed.
2 Cuirass and armour for the legs.
3 Row.
4 That which.
5 Not Iola, but Omphale, is intended.
6 Cloak.
7 Lowly.
8 Lost.

Move Radigund? who though she still have worn [1]
Her days in war, yet (weet thou) was not born
Of bears and tigers, nor so savage minded
As that, all be [2] all love of men she scorn,
She yet forgets that she of men was kinded: [3]
And sooth oft seen that proudest hearts base love hath blinded."

"Certes, Clarinda, not of canker'd will,"
Said he, "nor obstinate disdainful mind,
I have forbore this duty to fulfil:
For well I may this ween, by that I find,
That she, a queen, and come of princely kind,
Both worthy is for to be sued unto,
Chiefly by him whose life her law doth bind,
And eke of pow'r her own doom to undo,
And als' [4] of princely grace to be inclin'd thereto.

"But want of means hath been mine only let [5]
From seeking favour where it doth abound;
Which if I might by your good office get,
I to yourself should rest for ever bound,
And ready to deserve what grace I found."
She, feeling him thus bite upon the bait,
Yet doubting lest his hold was but unsound
And not well fasten'd, would not strike him straight,
But drew him on with hope, fit leisure to await.

But, foolish maid, while heedless of the hook
She thus ofttimes was beating off and on,
Through slippery footing fell into the brook,
And there was caught to her confusión:
For, seeking thus to salve [6] the Amazon,
She wounded was with her deceit's own dart,
And gan thenceforth to cast affectión,
Conceivëd close in her beguilëd heart,
To Artegall, through pity of his causeless smart.

But she dared disclose to none "her fancy's wound," and thought it best to await fit time, meanwhile dissembling her sad thoughts' unrest. One day Radigund asked her how her mission was succeeding; and Clarinda, overcoming a momentary confusion, began to tell what she had done, and how she had found Artegall "obstinate and stern," resolved to die in misery rather than entertain his foe's love; "his resolution was, both first and last, his body was her thrall, his heart was freely plac'd." Enraged "to be so scornëd of a base-born thrall, whose life did lie in her least eyelid's fall," Radigund at first vowed to deprive him of life; but, relenting her mood, she said that she would bear awhile with his first folly, till Clarinda had "tried again, and tempted him more near."

"Say and do all that may thereto prevail;
Leave naught unpromis'd that may him persuade;
Life, freedom, grace, and gifts of great avail, [7]
With which the gods themselves are milder made:
Thereto add art, ev'n women's witty trade,
The art of mighty words, that men can charm;
With which in case thou canst him not invade,
Let him feel hardness of thy heavy arm:
Who will not stoop with good shall be made stoop with harm.

"Some of his diet do from him withdraw;
For I him find to be too proudly fed:
Give him more labour, and with straiter law,
That he with work may be forweariëd: [8]
Let him lodge hard, and lie in strawen bed,
That may pull down the courage of his pride;
And lay upon him, for his greater dread,
Cold iron chains with which let him be tied;
And let whatever he desires be him denied.

"When thou hast all this done, then bring me news
Of his demean; [9] thenceforth not like a lover,
But like a rebel stout, I will him use:
For I resolve this siege not to give over,
Till I the conquest of my will recover."
So she departed, full of grief and sdain, [10]
Which inly did to great impatience move her:
But the false maiden shortly turn'd again
Unto the prison, where her heart did thrall remain.

There all her subtle nets she did unfold,
And all the engines of her wit display;
In which she meant him wareless [11] to enfold,
And of his innocence to make her prey.
So cunningly she wrought her craft's assay,
That both her Lady, and herself withal,
And eke the Knight, at once she did betray;
But most the Knight, whom she with guileful call
Did cast [12] for to allure into her trap to fall.

As a bad nurse, which, feigning to receive
In her own mouth the food meant for her child,
Withholds it to herself, and doth deceive
The infant, so for want of nurture spoil'd;
Even so Clarinda her own Dame beguil'd,
And turn'd the trust, which was in her affied, [13]
To feeding of her private fire, which boil'd
Her inward breast, and in her entrails fried,
The more that she it sought to cover and to hide.

To the Knight she feigned that Radigund had sternly met her earnest entreaties for his freedom, by commands to augment his misery and load him with iron bands—which the handmaid forebore to do, for love of him; and she promised, if she found favour in his eyes, to devise how he might be enlarged out of prison. The Knight, glad to gain his freedom, gave her great thanks, and, "to feed the humour of her malady," entertained her with promises that he would by all good means deserve such grace. So daily he showed her fair semblance, yet never meaning to be untrue to his own absent love; while Clarinda never found in her false heart to unbind his bondage, ever telling Radigund that he defied her love, and Artegall that "her Dame his freedom did deny."

1 Spent. 2 Although. 3 Begotten.
4 Also. 5 Obstacle.
6 Heal. 7 Value.

8 Utterly wearied. 9 Demeanour.
10 Disdain. 11 Unwary.
12 Contrive. 13 Reposed.

Yet thus much friendship she to him did show,
That his scarce diet somewhat was amended,
And his work lessen'd, that his love might grow:
Yet to her Dame him still she discommended,
That she with him might be the more offended.
Thus he long while in thraldom there remain'd,
Of both belovëd well, but little friended;
Until his own true love his freedom gain'd:
Which in another canto will be best contain'd.

CANTO VI.

Talus brings news to Britomart
Of Artegall's mishap:
She goes to seek him; Dolon meets,
Who seeks her to entrap.

Britomart had waited for the return of her knight beyond the appointed term of three months, and now began "to cast in her misdoubtful mind a thousand fears"—chiefly apprehensive "lest some new love had him from her possest." Spending her time in fears, and jealous fancies, and irresolute resolves to seek him out—finding ease nowhere—one day she came to a window that opened west, "towards which coast her love his way addrest." She "sent her wingëd thoughts more swift than wind to bear unto her love the message of her mind." Looking long, she spied one advancing with hasty speed; and soon she discerned that it was Talus, Artegall's squire. Filled at once with hope and dread, she met him in the door, and impatiently asked where was his lord. The Iron Man, although he wanted "sense and sorrow's feeling," did yet inly chill and quake with consciousness of his ill tidings, and stood mute, till again called upon to tell whatever news he had, or good or bad. Then he said that his lord, her love, by hard mishap did lie in wretched bondage, woefully bestead. "And is he vanquish'd by his tyrant enemy?" cried Britomart.

"Not by that tyrant, his intended foe;
But by a tyranness," he then replied,
"That him captivëd hath in hapless woe."
"Cease, thou bad news-man; badly dost thou hide
Thy master's shame, in harlot's bondage tied;
The rest myself too readily can spell."
With that in rage she turn'd from him aside,
Forcing in vain the rest to her to tell;
And to her chamber went like solitary cell.

There she began to make mournful plaint against her knight for being so untrue; blamed herself for yielding so easily to a stranger's love; and cast in her wrathful will how to revenge the blot of honour stained—"to fight with him, and goodly die her last." Now she walked and chafed; now she threw herself on her bed, and lamented, not loudly, as women wont, but with deep sighs and few sobs.

Like as a wayward child, whose sounder sleep
Is broken with some fearful dream's affright,
With froward will doth set himself to weep,
Nor can be still'd for all his nurse's might,
But kicks, and squalls, and shrieks for fell despite;
Now scratching her, and her loose locks misusing,
Now seeking darkness, and now seeking light,
Then craving suck, and then the suck refusing:
Such was this lady's fit in her love's fond accusing.

Having thus long afflicted herself in vain, she returned to Talus, and began to inquire of him in milder mood the certain cause of Artegall's detention. Informed that he lay in wretched thraldom, not compelled by strong hand, "but his own doom, that none can now undo," she declared anew that the story was "a thing compact" between master and squire to deceive her of faith plighted to her. But when Talus had told the whole story, she was distracted with grief and wrath, and, donning her armour and mounting her steed straightway, bade Talus guide her on.

So forth she rode upon her ready way,
To seek her knight, as Talus her did guide:
Sadly she rode, and never word did say,
Nor good nor bad, nor ever look'd aside,
But still right down; and in her thought did hide
The fellness[1] of her heart, right fully bent
To fierce avengement of that woman's pride,
Which had her lord in her base prison pent,
And so great honour with so foul reproach had blent.[2]

So as she thus meláncholic did ride,
Chewing the cud of grief and inward pain,
She chanc'd to meet towárd the eventide
A knight, that softly pacëd on the plain,
As if himself to solace he were fain;
Well shot[3] in years he seem'd, and rather bent
To peace than needless trouble to constrain;
As well by view of that his vestiment,
As by his modest semblant,[4] that no evil meant.

Gently saluting her, he strove to enter into conversation; but, her mind filled with one great thought, she was little disposed to talk of aught. Noticing her constrained manner, the stranger ceased to trouble her with speech, but besought her, "since shady damp had dimm'd the heaven's reach," to lodge with him that night. The championess consenting, they soon reached his dwelling, and were received and entertained in seemly wise. The time of rest being come, Britomart was taken to a chamber, where grooms waited to disarm her; but she refused to doff her armour, on the plea that she had vowed never to do so until she had taken vengeance upon a mortal foe for a late wrong. The host grew right discontent in mind, lest by the Maid's refusal he should miss his secret purpose; but he took leave of her, and departed,

1 Fierceness, fury. 2 Stained. 3 Advanced. 4 Appearance.

leaving Britomart restless, comfortless, and sleepless—reproving her eyes if they betrayed any inclination to close.

"Ye guilty eyes," said she, "the which with guile
My heart at first betray'd, will ye betray
My life now too, for which a little while
Ye will not watch? false watches, well-away!
I wot [1] when ye did watch both night and day
Unto your loss; and now needs will ye sleep?
Now ye have made my heart to wake alway,
Now will ye sleep? ah! wake, and rather weep
To think of your Knight's want, that should ye waking keep."

Thus did she watch, and wear the weary night
In wailful plaints, that none was to appease;
Now walking soft, now sitting still upright,
As sundry change her seemëd best to ease.
Nor less did Talus suffer sleep to seize
His eyelids sad, but watch'd continually,
Lying without her door in great disease; [2]
Like to a spaniel waiting carefully
Lest any should betray his lady treach'rously.

What time the native bellman of the night,
The bird that warnëd Peter of his fall,
First rings his silver bell t' each sleepy wight,
That should their minds up to devotion call,
She heard a wondrous noise below the hall:
All suddenly the bed, where she should lie,
By a false trap was let adown to fall
Into a lower room, and by and by
The loft [3] was rais'd again, that no man could it spy.

Though much dismayed at the discovery that treason was meant, she kept her place with courage confident; and soon, hearing the sound of armed men coming towards her chamber, she caught up her sword and shield. Two armed knights, followed by a rascal crowd, appeared at the door; but Talus, espying them, sprang from the ground, and with his rude iron flail drove all the assailants to flight. Though wondrous wroth at the treason, and burning for revenge, Britomart had to abide till day in the place, but with careful guard against further guile. The goodman of the place, it appeared, was Dolon, "a man of subtile wit and wicked mind," that had in his youth been a knight, but had got little good and honour by warlike life; for he was nothing valorous, but undermined all noble knights with sly shifts and wiles. He had three sons, of whom one was named Guizor—the "groom of evil guise" who had helped Pollente to maintain the evil custom of the bridge, destroyed by Artegall. To avenge his son, Dolon and his surviving sons had entrapped Britomart—whom, from her attendant, Talus, they took for Artegall—and meant to have slain him; "but by God's grace, and her good heediness," she had escaped their wiles. At dawn next day, the vengeful Britomart sought Dolon and his sons throughout the house in vain; but, as she proceeded on her way, she encountered the two false brethren on the bridge on which Pollente and Artegall had fought. "Strait was the passage, like a ploughëd ridge, that, if two met, the one must needs fall o'er the ledge."

There they did think themselves on her to wreak
Who as she nigh unto them drew, the one
These vile reproaches gan unto her speak;
"Thou recreant false traitor, that with loan [4]
Of arms hast knighthood stol'n, yet knight art none,
No more shall now the darkness of the night
Defend thee from the vengeance of thy fone: [5]
But with thy blood thou shalt appease the sprite
Of Guizor, by thee slain, and murder'd by thy sleight."

Strange were the words in Britomartis' ear;
Yet stay'd she not for them, but forward far'd,
Till to the perilous bridge she came; and there
Talus desir'd that he might have prepar'd
The way to her, and those two losels scar'd:
But she thereat was wroth, that for despite
The glancing sparkles through her beaver glar'd,
And from her eyes did flash out fiery light,
Like coals that through a silver censer sparkled bright.

She stay'd not to advise which way to take;
But, putting spurs unto her fiery beast,
Thorough the midst of them she way did make.
The one of them, which most her wrath increast,
Upon her spear she bore before her breast,
Till to the bridge's farther end she past;
Where falling down his challenge he releast:
The other overside the bridge she cast
Into the river, where he drunk his deadly last.

As when the flashing levin [6] haps to light
Upon two stubborn oaks, which stand so near
That way betwixt them none appears in sight;
The engine, fiercely flying forth, doth tear
The one from th' earth, and through the air doth bear;
The other it with force doth overthrow
Upon one side, and from his roots doth rear:
So did the championess those two there strow,
And to their sire their carcases left to bestow.

CANTO VII.

Britomart comes to Isis' church, [7]
Where she strange visions sees:
She fights with Radigund, her slays,
And Artegall thence frees.

NAUGHT is on earth more sacred or divine,
That gods and men do equally adore,
Than this same virtue that doth right define: [8]
For th' heav'ns themselves, whence mortal men implore
Right in their wrongs, are rul'd by righteous lore
Of highest Jove, who doth true justice deal

[1] Know. [2] Uneasiness. [3] Floor. [4] Borrowing. [5] Foes. [6] Lightning. [7] Temple. [8] Justice.

To his inferior gods, and evermore
Therewith contains [1] his heav'nly commonweal:
The skill whereof to princes' hearts he doth
reveal.

Well, therefore, did the antique world invent [2]
That Justice was a god of sov'reign grace,
And altars unto him and temples lent,
And heav'nly honours in the highest place;
Calling him great Osiris, of the race
Of th' old Egyptian kings that whilom were;
With feignëd colours shading [3] a true case;
For that Osiris, whilst he lived here,
The justest man alive and truest did appear.

His wife was Isis; whom they likewise made
A goddess of great pow'r and sov'reignty,
And in her person cunningly did shade [4]
That part of Justice which is Equity,
Whereof I have to treat here presently:
Unto whose temple when as Britomart
Arrivëd, she with great humility
Did enter in, nor would that night depart;
But Talus might not be admitted to her part.[5]

There she receivëd was in goodly wise
Of many priests, which duly did attend
Upon the rites and daily sacrifice,
All clad in linen robes [6] with silver hemm'd;
And on their heads, with long locks comely
kem'd [7]
They wore rich mitres shapëd like the moon,
To show that Isis doth the moon portend;
Like as Osiris signifies the sun:
For that they both like [8] race in equal justice
run.

The championess them greeting, as she co'ld,[9]
Was thence by them into the temple led;
Whose goodly building when she did behold
Borne upon stately pillars, all dispread
With shining gold, and archëd over head,
She wonder'd at the workman's passing skill,
Whose like before she never saw nor read;
And thereupon long while stood gazing still,
But thought that she thereon could never gaze
her fill.

Thenceforth unto the idol they her brought;
The which was framëd all of silver fine,
So well as could with cunning hand be wrought,
And clothëd all in garments made of line,[10]
Hemm'd all about with fringe of silver twine:
Upon her head she wore a crown of gold,
To show that she had pow'r in things divine:
And at her feet a crocodile was roll'd,
That with her wreathëd tail her middle did
enfold.

One foot was set upon the crocodile,
And on the ground the other fast did stand;
So meaning to suppress both forgëd guile
And open force: and in her other hand
She stretchëd forth a long white slender wand.
Such was the goddess: whom when Britomart
Had long beheld, herself upon the land [11]
She did prostrâte, and with right humble heart
Unto herself her silent prayers did impart.

To which the idol, as it were inclining
Her wand, did move with amiable look,
By outward show her inward sense designing: [12]
Who, well perceiving how her wand she shook,
It as a token of good fortune took.
By this the day with damp was overcast,
And joyous light the house of Jove [13] forsook:
Which when she saw, her helmet she unlac'd,
And by the altar's side herself to slumber plac'd.

For other beds the priests there usëd none,
But on their mother Earth's dear lap did lie,
And bake [14] their sides upon the cold hard stone,
T' inure themselves to sufferance thereby,
And proud rebellious flesh to mortify:
For, by the vow of their religiön,
They tiëd were to steadfast chastitŷ
And continence of life; that, all foregone,[15]
They might the better tend to their devotiön.

Therefore they might not taste of fleshly food,
Nor feed on aught the which doth blood contain,
Nor drink of wine; for wine, they say, is blood,
Even the blood of giants, which were slain
By thund'ring Jove in the Phlegræan plain; [16]
For which the Earth (as they the story tell),
Wroth with the gods, which to perpetual pain
Had damn'd [17] her sons which 'gainst them did
rebel,
With inward grief and malice did against them
swell:

And of their vital blood, the which was shed
Into her pregnant bosom, forth she brought
The fruitful vine; whose liquor bloody red,
Having the minds of men with fury fraught,
Might in them stir up old rebellious thought,
To make new war against the gods again:
Such is the pow'r of that same fruit, that
naught
The fell contagion may thereof restrain,
Nor within reason's rule her madding [18] mood
contain.

There did the warlike maid herself repose,
Under the wings of Isis, all that night;
And with sweet rest her heavy eyes did close,
After that long day's toil and weary plight:
Where, whilst her earthly parts with soft delight
Of senseless sleep did deeply drownëd lie,
There did appear unto her heav'nly sprite
A wondrous vision, which did close imply [19]
The course of all her fortune and posteritŷ.

Her seem'd, as she was doing sacrifice
To Isis, deck'd with mitre on her head,
And linen stole,[20] after those priestës' guise,[21]
All suddenly she saw transfigurëd

1 Controls. 2 Feign, suppose.
3 Shadowing forth. 4 Represent.
5 That part to which she was admitted.
6 The Romans called Isis herself "linigera," because her priests and servants wore linen garments.
7 Combed, kempt. 8 The same.
9 As she well could do.
10 Linen.
11 Ground. 12 Signifying.
13 The heaven. 14 Harden.
15 Everything quite renounced.
16 See note 15, page 395. 17 Condemned.
18 Maddening. 19 Secretly contain.
20 Robe. 21 Fashion.

Her linen stole to robe of scarlet red,
And moon-like mitre to a crown of gold;
That even she herself much wonderëd
At such a change, and joyëd to behold
Herself adorn'd with gems and jewels manifold.

And, in the midst of her felicity,
A hideous tempest seemëd from below
To rise through all the temple suddenly,
That from the altar all about did blow
The holy fire, and all the embers strow
Upon the ground; which, kindled privily,
Into outrageous flames unwares did grow,
That all the temple put in jeopardy
Of flaming, and herself in great perplexity.

With that the crocodile, which sleeping lay
Under the idol's feet in fearless bow'r,
Seem'd to awake in horrible dismay,
As being troubled with that stormy stowre;[1]
And, gaping greedy wide, did straight devour
Both flames and tempest; with which growen great,
And swoll'n with pride of his own peerless pow'r,
He gan to threaten her likewise to eat;
But that the goddess with her rod him back did beat.

Then, turning all his pride to humbless[2] meek,
Himself before her feet he lowly threw,
And gan for grace and love of her to seek:
Which she accepting, he so near her drew,
That of his game[3] she soon enwombëd grew,
And forth did bring a lion of great might,
That shortly did all other beasts subdue:
With that she wakëd, full of fearful fright,
And doubtfully dismay'd through that so uncouth sight.

So thereupon long while she musing lay,
With thousand thoughts feeding her fantasy:
Until she spied the lamp of lightsome day
Uplifted in the porch of heaven high:
Then up she rose, fraught with melancholy,
And forth into the lower parts did pass,
Where as the priests she found full busily
About their holy things for morrow mass;[4]
Whom she saluting fair, fair resaluted was.

"But, by the change of her uncheerful look," they perceived that she was ill at ease; and one, who seemed "to be the wisest and the gravest wight," hinted that the evil rest of last night had annoyed her. She told to him her vision; at the recital, through great astonishment, his long locks stood up stiffly; and, "fill'd with heav'nly fury, thus he her behight"[5]—betraying his knowledge of her real sex:

"Magnific Virgin, that in quaint disguise
Of British arms dost mask thy royal blood,
So to pursue a perilous emprise;
How couldst thou ween, through that disguisëd hood,[6]
To hide thy state from being understood?
Can from th' immortal gods aught hidden be?
They do thy lineage, and thy lordly brood,
They do thy sire lamenting sore for thee,
They do thy love forlorn in women's thraldom, see.

"The end whereof, and all the long event,
They do to thee in this same dream discover:
For that same crocodile doth represent
The righteous Knight that is thy faithful lover,
Like to Osiris in all just endeavour:
For that same crocodile Osiris is,
That under Isis' feet doth sleep for ever;
To show that clemence[7] oft, in things amiss,
Restrains those stern behests and cruel dooms[8] of his.

"That Knight shall all the troublous storms assuage,
And raging flames, that many foes shall rear[9]
To hinder thee from the just heritage
Of thy sire's crown, and from thy country dear.
Then shalt thou take him to thy lovëd fere,[10]
And join in equal portion of thy realm:
And afterwards a son to him shalt bear,
That lion-like shall show his power extreme.
So bless thee God, and give thee joyance of thy dream!"

All which when she unto the end had heard,
She much was easëd in her troublous thought,
And on those priests bestowëd rich reward;
And royal gifts of gold and silver wrought
She for a present to their goddess brought.
Then, taking leave of them, she forward went
To seek her love, where he was to be sought,
Nor rested till she came, without relent,[11]
Unto the land of Amazons, as she was bent.

At the tidings of her arrival, Radigund was "fill'd with courage and with joyous glee," though somewhat taken aback by the news that the Iron Man, who lately had slain her people, attended the new-comer. Britomart pitched her pavilion before the city gate, and rested all night under the guard of Talus; while "they of the town in fright upon their wall good watch and ward did keep." In the morning, the Amazon queen issued forth to fight, and first sought to impose on Britomart the "strait conditions" on which she encountered her foes. But Britomart disdained all terms that were not prescribed by the laws of chivalry; and the battle began, with great fury—neither warlike lady sparing "their dainty parts, which nature had created so fair and tender, without stain or spot," for far other uses.

As when a tiger and a lioness
Are met at spoiling of some hungry prey,
Both challenge[12] it with equal greediness:
But first the tiger claws thereon did lay,
And therefore, loth to lose her right away,
Doth in defence thereof full stoutly stand:
To which the lion strongly doth gainsay,
That she to hunt the beast first took in hand;
And therefore ought it have wherever she it fand.[13]

1 Trouble, peril. 2 Humility. 3 Through his sport. 4 Morning service. 5 Addressed. 6 Dress.

7 Clemency. 8 Judgments. 9 Raise. 10 Consort, husband. 11 Delay. 12 Dispute, claim. 13 Found.

Long and stoutly they fought, till they trod in gore, "and on the ground their lives did strow, like fruitless seed, of which untimely death should grow." At last Radigund let drive at her opponent with dreadful might, telling her to bear that token to the man she loved so dear. The stroke pierced to Britomart's shoulder-bone, and made a grisly wound; but, stung by furious pain, the Britoness struck the Amazon on the helmet with such force as to pierce her brain and throw her proud person prostrate on the ground—where with another blow the victor "both head and helmet cleft." At the sight of their mistress's fall all Radigund's train fled fast into the town;

But yet so fast they could not home retrate,[1]
But that swift Talus did the foremost win;
And, pressing through the press unto the gate,
Pell-mell with them at once did enter in:
There then a piteous slaughter did begin;
For all that ever came within his reach
He with his iron flail did thresh so thin,
That he no work at all left for the leach;[2]
Like to a hideous storm, which nothing may
empeach.[3]

Entering the city, Britomart was struck with pity at the havoc of Talus, and restrained his hand, "else he sure had left not one alive." Then breaking open the prison of the degraded knights, and seeing "that loathly uncouth sight of men disguis'd in womanish attire," her heart began to grudge for deep despite "of so unmanly mask in misery misdight."[4] Coming to her own lover, she had to turn aside her head for secret shame, and dismissed all her former jealous suspicions.

Not so great wonder and astonishment
Did the most chaste Penelope possess,
To see her lord, that was reported drent[5]
And dead long since in dolorous distress,
Come home to her in piteous wretchedness,
After long travel of full twenty years;
That she knew not his favour's likeliness,[6]
For many scars and many hoary hairs;
But stood long staring on him 'mongst uncertain
fears.

"Ah! my dear lord, what sight is this," quoth
she;
"What May-game hath misfortune made of you?
Where is that dreadful manly look? where be
Those mighty palms, the which ye wont t' embrue
In blood of kings, and great hosts to subdue?
Could aught on earth so wondrous change have
wrought,
As to have robb'd you of that manly hue?[7]
Could so great courage stoopëd have to aught?
Then farewell, fleshly force; I see thy pride is
naught!"

1 Retreat, retire.
2 For the surgeon: that is, he killed them outright.
3 Hinder.
4 Disfigured.
5 Drenched, drowned.
6 The likeness of his countenance.
7 Aspect.
8 Chamber.
9 To take off those vile, unseemly, garments.

Thenceforth she straight into a bow'r[8] him
brought,
And caus'd him those uncomely weeds undight;[9]
And in their stead for other raiment sought,
Whereof there was great store, and armours
bright,
Which had been reft from many a noble knight,
Whom that proud Amazon subduëd had
Whilst fortune favour'd her success in fight:
In which when as she him anew had clad,
She was reviv'd, and joy'd much in his sem-
blance[10] glad.

So there a while they afterwards remain'd,
Him to refresh, and her late wounds to heal:
During which space she there as Princess reign'd;
And, changing all that form of commonweal,
The liberty of women did repeal,
Which they had long usurp'd; and, them restor-
ing
To men's subjection, did true justice deal:
That all they, as a goddess her adoring,
Her wisdom did admire, and hearken'd to her
loring.[11]

She made the captive knights magistrates of the city, gave them great property, and obliged them to swear fealty to Artegall; who, much to the sorrow of his lady—sorrow repressed at the thought of what his honour required—soon set out on his adventure to redeem Irena. Britomart continued at the city for a time; then she set out to seek change of air and place, hoping that thereby her pain would be changed and her sorrow eased.

CANTO VIII.

Prince Arthur and Sir Artegall
Free Samient from fear:
They slay the Soldan; drive his wife
Adicia to despair.

NAUGHT under heav'n so strongly doth allure
The sense of man, and all his mind possess,
As beauty's lovely bait, that doth procure
Great warriors oft their rigour to repress,
And mighty hands forget their manliness;
Drawn with the pow'r of a heart-robbing eye,
And wrapt in fetters of a golden tress,
That can with melting pleasance mollify
Their harden'd hearts, inur'd to blood and
cruelty.

So whilom learn'd that mighty Jewish swain,[12]
Each of whose locks did match a man in might,
To lay his spoils before his leman's train:
So also did that great Œtean knight[13]
For his love's sake his lion's skin undight:[14]
And so did warlike Antony neglect
The world's whole rule for Cleopatra's sight.

10 Appearance.
11 Teaching, lore.
12 Samson.
13 Hercules, who burned himself to death on Mount Œta, in Thessaly.
14 Put off: when the hero was at the court of Omphale.

Such wondrous pow'r hath women's fair aspéct
To captive men, and make them all the world
reject.

"Yet could it not stern Artegall restrain" from the adventure committed to his trust by Gloriana; and after leaving Britomart he rested idly neither night nor day. As he travelled, attended by Talus alone, he saw a damsel fleeing fast, "carried with wings of fear, like fowl aghast," and chased fiercely by two knights; who in their turn, as in the game of base, were chased by a third knight. One of the pursuers of the lady was forced to turn against the single knight; but the other still followed the lady, who gladly fled towards Sir Artegall for protection. The persecutor continuing the chase, Artegall pitched him more than two spear's lengths out of his saddle, upon his head, so that his neck was broken, and he lay there dead. Meantime the single knight, who had slain the second pursuer of the lady, came up, and ran with spear in rest against Sir Artegall, not staying to discriminate. The Knight met his antagonist in the same fashion; both spears were shivered; and both warriors drew their swords. But the lady called on them to stay their cruel hands, for both her Paynim persecutors were slain—or, if they fought about her, to end on her their revenge. The knights stop, and raise their ventails; the stranger is found to be Prince Arthur; and the pair interchange apologies, courtesies, and assurances of friendship. Artegall inquires of the Prince who the two dead knights were; but the Prince does not know, having only encountered them by chance; and both seek an explanation from the damsel. She says that she serves a queen who dwells not far away, "a princess of great pow'r and majesty, famous through all the world, and honour'd far and nigh."

"Her name Mercilla [1] most men use to call;
That is a Maiden Queen of high renown
For her great bounty,[2] knowen over all,
And sov'reign grace, with which her royal
crown
She doth support, and strongly beateth down
The malice of her foes, which her envý
And at her happiness do fret and frown;
Yet she herself the more doth magnify,
And even to her foes her mercies multiply.

"'Mongst many which malign her happy state,
There is a mighty man, which wons [3] hereby,
That with most fell despite and deadly hate
Seeks to subvert her crown and dignitý,
And all his power doth thereunto apply:
And her good knights (of which so brave a
band
Serves her as any princess under sky),
He either spoils, if they against him stand,
Or to his part allures, and bribeth underhand.

"Nor him sufficeth all the wrong and ill
Which he unto her people does each day;
But that he seeks by traitorous trains to spill [4]
Her person, and her sacred self to slay:
That, O ye heav'ns, defend! and turn away
From her unto the miscreant himself;
That neither hath religión nor fay,[5]
But makes his God of his ungodly pelf,
And idols serves: so let his idols serve the elf!

"To all which cruel tyranny, they say,
He is provok'd, and stirr'd up day and night,
By his bad wife, that hight Adicia; [6]
Who counsels him, through confidence of might,
To break all bonds of law and rules of right:
For she herself professeth mortal foe
To Justice, and against her still doth fight,
Working, to all that love her, deadly woe,
And making all her knights and people to do
so."

Mercilla had sent the damsel to mediate with Adicia for final peace and fair reconcilement; but the haughty dame had thrust the envoy out of doors like a dog, miscalling her by many a bitter name; and, that no shame might be wanting, had also sent in pursuit of her the two knights whom Arthur and Artegall had just slain, to be by them dishonoured and disgraced. The two friends, having heard the story of Samient (for so the damsel was named), resolved, in wrath, to take vengeance on the Soldan and his Lady; and they agreed that, to make their design the easier of success, Artegall should array himself in the armour of one of the two dead Knights, and take Samient, as if she were a prisoner, unto the Soldan's Court. The plan was executed; the Soldan's Lady, seeing, as she thought, her Paynim knight returning, sent a page to guide him to his appointed place; and meantime Prince Arthur appeared without, demanding of the Soldan, with bold defiance, the release of the captive damsel.

Wherewith the Soldan, all with fury fraught,
Swearing and banning [7] most blasphémously,
Commanded straight his armour to be brought;
And, mounting straight upon a chariot high
(With iron wheels and hooks arm'd dreadfully,
And drawn of cruel steeds, which he had fed
With flesh of men, whom through fell tyranny
He slaughter'd had, and ere they were half
dead
Their bodies to his beasts for provender did
spread);

So forth he came all in a coat of plate
Burnish'd with bloody rust; while on the green
The Briton Prince him ready did await,
In glist'ring arms right goodly well beseen,
That shone as bright as doth the heaven sheen; [8]
And by his stirrup Talus did attend,
Playing his page's part, as he had been
Before directed by his lord; to th' end
He should his flail to final execution bend.

Like to the Thracian tyrant,[9] who, they say,

1 The Merciful; Queen Elizabeth. 2 Virtue.
3 Dwells. The "mighty man," or the "Soldan," is the King of Spain, Philip II.

4 Destroy. 5 Faith.
6 Injustice. 7 Cursing.
8 Clear. 9 Diomedes.

Unto his horses gave his guests for meat,
Till he himself was made their greedy prey,
And torn in pieces by Alcides great;
So thought the Soldan, in his folly's threat,
Either the Prince in pieces to have torn
With his sharp wheels, in his first rage's heat,
Or under his fierce horses' feet have borne,
And trampled down in dust his thoughts' disdainëd scorn.

Arthur leapt aside before the chariot's swift advance, shunning also a dart which the Paynim threw at him. Vainly the Prince tried with his spear point to reach his enemy, seated so high and whirled so fast by his coursers; and he was wounded by a more successful dart launched by the Soldan.

Much was he grievëd with that hapless throe,
That open'd had the well-spring of his blood;
But much the more, that to his hateful foe
He might not come to wreak his wrathful mood:
That made him rave, like to a lion wood,[1]
Which, being wounded of the huntsman's hand,
Cannot come near him in the covert wood,
Where he with boughs hath built his shady stand,
And fenc'd himself about with many a flaming brand.

At last, despairing of attaining the Soldan by natural or human means, the Prince resorted to supernatural;[2] he drew from his shield the cover that always veiled its dazzling brightness, and, coming full before his enemy's horses, showed the shield to them.

Like lightning flash that hath the gazer burn'd,
So did the sight thereof their sense dismay,
That back again upon themselves they turn'd,
And with their rider ran perforce away:
Nor could the Soldan them from flying stay
With reins or wonted rule, as well he knew:
Naught fearëd they what he could do or say,
But th' only fear that was before their view;
From which like mazëd deer dismayfully they flew.

Fast did they fly as them their feet could bear,
High over hills, and lowly over dales,
As they were follow'd of their former fear:
In vain the Pagan bans, and swears, and rails,
And back with both his hands unto him hales
The resty[3] reins, regarded now no more:
He to them calls and speaks, yet naught avails;
They hear him not, they have forgot his lore,
But go which way they list; their guide they have forlore.[4]

As when the fiery-mouthëd steeds, which drew
The Sun's bright wain to Phaethon's decay,
Soon as they did the monstrous Scorpion view,
With ugly craples[5] crawling in their way,
The dreadful sight did them so sore affray,
That their well-knowen courses they forwent;[6]
And, leading th' ever burning lamp astray,
This lower world nigh all to ashes brent,[7]
And left their scorchëd path[8] yet in the firmament.

Such was the fury of these headstrong steeds,
Soon as the Infant's[9] sunlike shield they saw,
That all obedience both to words and deeds
They quite forgot, and scorn'd all former law:
Through woods, and rocks, and mountains they did draw
The iron chariot, and the wheels did tear,
And toss'd the Paynim without fear or awe;
From side to side they toss'd him here and there,
Crying to them in vain that n'ould[10] his crying hear.

Yet still the Prince pursued him close behind,
Oft making offer him to smite, but found
No easy means according to his mind:
At last they have all overthrown to ground
Quite topside-turvy, and the Pagan hound,
Amongst the iron hooks and grapples keen,
Torn all to rags, and rent with many a wound;
That no whole piece of him was to be seen,
But scatter'd all about, and strow'd upon the green.

Like as the cursed son of Theseus,[11]
That, following his chase in dewy morn,
To fly his stepdame's love outragëous,
Of his own steeds was all to pieces torn,
And his fair limbs left in the woods forlorn;
That for his sake Diana did lament,
And all the woody nymphs did wail and mourn:
So was this Soldan rapt and all to-rent,
That of his shape appear'd no little monument.[12]

Only his shield and armour, which there lay,
Though nothing whole, but all to-bruis'd and broken,
He up did take, and with him brought away,
That might remain for an eternal token
To all 'mongst whom this story should be spoken,
How worthily, by Heaven's high decree,
Justice that day of wrong herself had wroken;[13]
That all men, which that spectacle did see,
By like ensample might for ever warnëd be.

Arthur hanged the arms on a tree before the tyrant's door; and at sight of them the tyrant's Lady, wild with rage, ran with knife in hand to revenge herself on the maiden messenger, Samient, still a prisoner.

Like raging Ino, when with knife in hand
She threw her husband's murder'd infant out;
Or fell Medea, when on Colchic strand
Her brother's bones she scatter'd all about;
Or as that madding mother, 'mongst the rout
Of Bacchus' priests, her own dear flesh did tear:
Yet neither Ino, nor Medea stout,
Nor all the Mænades so furious were
As this bold woman, when she saw that damsel there.

1 Furious.
2 An admission that the defeat of King Philip's Armada might not have been achieved, but for the supernatural aid of the winds and waves.
3 Restive.
4 Lost.
5 Claws.
6 Forsook, strayed from.
7 Burned.
8 The Milky Way.
9 Prince's. See note 3, page 390.
10 Would not.
11 Hippolytus. See page 331.
12 Not even the least memorial.
13 Avenged.

But Artegall stayed in time her cruel hand, and wrested the weapon from her grasp; whereon she ran madly forth by a postern door into the wild woods, and there she was, as it is said, transformed to a tiger. Then Artegall, discovering himself, issued forth and overcame all the adherents of the Soldan and Adicia; after which he caused the castle gates to be opened wide, and entertained Prince Arthur as victor of the day, presenting him with all the rich array and royal pomp, "purchas'd through lawless power and tortious wrong of that proud Soldan." Having stayed a little time in the castle, to rest, the two Knights took their journey, with Samient, to the court of Mercilla.

CANTO IX.

Arthur and Artegall catch Guile,
Whom Talus doth dismay:
They to Mercilla's palace come,
And see her rich array.

WHAT tiger, or what other salvage wight,
Is so exceeding furious and fell
As Wrong, when it hath arm'd itself with might;
Not fit 'mongst men that do with reason mell,[1]
But 'mongst wild beasts and salvage woods, to dwell;
Where still the stronger doth the weak devour,
And they that most in boldness do excel
Are dreaded most, and fearëd for their pow'r;
Fit for Adicia there to build her wicked bow'r.[2]

As Arthur and Artegall, invited by Samient, journeyed to the court of Mercilla, their companion told them of a wicked villain, bold and stout, that dwelt in a rock not far away, and took to his inaccessible den the pillage of all the country round.

Thereto both his own wily wit, she said,
And eke the fastness of his dwelling-place,
Both unassailable, gave him great aid:
For he so crafty was to forge and face,[3]
So light of hand, and nimble of his pace,
So smooth of tongue, and subtile in his tale,
That could deceive one looking in his face:
Therefore by name Malengine[4] they him call,
Well knowen by his feats, and famous over all.[5]

Through these his sleights he many doth confound:
And eke the rock, in which he wonts to dwell,
Is wondrous strong and hewn far under ground,
A dreadful depth, how deep no man can tell;
But some do say it goeth down to hell:
And, all within, it full of windings is
And hidden ways, that scarce a hound by smell
Can follow out those false footsteps of his,
Nor none can back return that once are gone amiss.

Determined "to understand that villain's dwelling-place," the knights induced Samient to lead them thither. Arriving near the rock, they agreed to send the damsel to weep and wail near the mouth of the den, as if deploring some calamity; their plan being to attract the caitiff carl forth, and snare him ere he could get back to his den. Samient accordingly, throwing herself on the ground, began to lament aloud.

The cry whereof, ent'ring the hollow cave,
Eftsoons brought forth the villain, as they meant,
With hope of her some wishful boot[6] to have.
Full dreadful wight he was as ever went
Upon the earth, with hollow eyes deep pent,
And long curl'd locks that down his shoulders shagg'd,
And on his back an uncouth vestiment
Made of strange stuff, but all to-worn and ragg'd,
And underneath his breech was all to-torn and jagg'd.

And in his hand a huge long staff he held,
Whose top was arm'd with many an iron hook,
Fit to catch hold of all that he could weld,[7]
Or in the compass of his clutches took;
And ever round about he cast his look:
Als'[8] at his back a great wide net he bore,
With which he seldom fishëd at the brook,
But us'd to fish for fools on the dry shore,
Of which he in fair weather wont to take great store.

Him when the damsel saw fast by her side,
So ugly creature, she was nigh dismay'd;
And now for help aloud in earnest cried:
But, when the villain saw her so afraid,
He gan with guileful words her to persuade
To banish fear; and with Sardonian smile
Laughing on her, his false intent to shade,
Gan forth to lay his bait her to beguile,
That from herself unwares he might her steal the while.

Like as the fowler on his guileful pipe
Charms to the birds full many a pleasant lay,
That they the while may take less heedy keep[9]
How he his nets doth for their ruin lay:
So did the villain to her prate and play,
And many pleasant tricks before her show,
To turn her eyes from his intent away:
For he in sleights and juggling feats did flow,[10]
And of legérdemain the mysteries did know.

To which whilst she lent her attentive mind,
He suddenly his net upon her threw,
That overspread her like a puff of wind;
And snatching her soon up, ere well she knew,
Ran with her fast away unto his mew,[11]
Crying for help aloud: but when as nigh

1 That meddle with or possess reason.
2 Dwelling.
3 Dissemble.
4 Guile, Evil Ingenuity.
5 Everywhere.
6 Booty.
7 Wield, carry.
8 Also.
9 Attention.
10 Abound.
11 Den.

He came unto his cave, and there did view
The armëd knights stopping his passage by,
He threw his burden down, and fast away did fly.

But Artegall him after did pursue;
The while the Prince there kept the entrance still:
Up to the rock he ran, and thereon flew
Like a wild goat, leaping from hill to hill,
And dancing on the craggy cliffs at will;
That deadly danger seem'd in all men's sight
To tempt such steps, where footing was so ill:
Nor aught availëd for the armëd Knight
To think to follow him that was so swift and light.

Which when he saw, his Iron Man he sent
To follow him; for he was swift in chase:
He him pursued wherever that he went;
Both over rocks, and hills, and ev'ry place
Whereso he fled, he follow'd him apace:
So that he shortly forc'd him to forsake
The height, and down descend unto the base:
There he him cours'd afresh, and soon did make
To leave his proper form, and other shape to take.

Into a fox himself he first did turn;
But he him hunted like a fox full fast:
Then to a bush himself he did transform;
But he the bush did beat, till that at last
Into a bird it chang'd, and from him past,
Flying from tree to tree, from wand to wand:
But he then stones at it so long did cast,
That like a stone it fell upon the land;
But he then took it up, and held fast in his hand.

So he it brought with him unto the knights,
And to his lord Sir Artegall it lent,
Warning him hold it fast for fear of sleights:[1]
Who whilst in hand it griping hard he hent,[2]
Into a hedgehog all unwares it went,
And prick'd him so that he away it threw:
Then gan it run away incontinent,
Being returnëd to his former hue;
But Talus soon him overtook, and backward drew.

But, when as he would to a snake again
Have turn'd himself, he with his iron flail
Gan drive at him with so huge might and main,
That all his bones as small as sandy grail[3]
He broke, and did his bowels disentrail,[4]
Crying in vain for help, when help was past;
So did deceit the self deceiver fail:[5]
There they him left a carrion out cast
For beasts and fowls to feed upon for their repast.

Passing forth, they came to the stately palace of Samient's mistress, Mercilla; "most sacred wight, most debonair and free," that ever was seen on earth or crowned with diadem.

There they alighting, by that damsel were
Directed in, and showëd all the sight;
Whose porch, that most magnific did appear,
Stood open wide to all men day and night;
Yet warded well by one of mickle might,
That sat thereby, with giant-like resemblance,
To keep out guile, and malice, and despite,
That, under show ofttimes of feignëd semblance,
Are wont in princes' courts to work great scathe and hindrance:

His name was Awe; by whom they passing in
Went up the hall, that was a large wide room,
All full of people making troublous din
And wondrous noise, as if that there were some
Which unto them was dealing righteous doom:[6]
By whom they passing through the thickest press,
The marshal of the hall to them did come,
His name hight Order; who, commanding peace,
Them guided through the throng, that did their clamours cease.

They ceas'd their clamours upon them to gaze;
Whom seeing all in armour bright as day,
Strange there to see, it did them much amaze,
And with unwonted terror half affray:
For never saw they there the like array;
Nor ever was the name of war there spoken,
But joyous peace and quietness alway
Dealing just judgments, that might not be broken
For any bribes, or threats of any to be wroken.[7]

There, as they enter'd at the screen, they saw
Some one, whose tongue was for his trespass vile
Nail'd to a post, adjudgëd so by law;
For that therewith he falsely did revile
And foul blaspheme that Queen for forgëd guile,
Both with bold speeches which he blazëd had,
And with lewd poems which he did compile;
For the bold title of a poet bad
He on himself had ta'en, and railing rhymes had sprad.[8]

Thus there he stood, whilst high over his head
There written was the purport of his sin,
In ciphers strange, that few could rightly read,
Bonfont;[9] but *Bon*, that once had written been,
Was rasëd out,[10] and *Mal* was now put in:
So now *Malfont*[11] was plainly to be read;
Either for th' evil which he did therein,
Or that he liken'd was to a wellhead
Of evil words and wicked slanders by him shed.

They, passing by, were guided by degree
Unto the presence of that gracious Queen;
Who sat on high, that she might all men see,
And might of all men royally be seen,
Upon a throne of gold full bright and sheen,[12]
Adornëd all with gems of endless price,
As either might for wealth have gotten been,
Or could be fram'd by workman's rare device;
And all emboss'd with lions and with fleur-de-lice.[13]

All over her a cloth of state was spread,

1 Tricks. 2 Held, grasped.
3 Gravel. 4 Dash out, dislodge.
5 Deceive the deceiver himself.
6 Judgment. 7 Revenged.

8 Spread. 9 Fount of Good.
10 Erased. 11 Fount of Evil. 12 Shining.
13 The royal flower of France, shown in the royal shield of England.

Not of rich tissue, nor of cloth of gold,
Nor of aught else that may be richest read,[1]
But like a cloud, as likest may be told,
That her broad-spreading wings did wide unfold;
Whose skirts were border'd with bright sunny beams,
Glist'ring like gold amongst the plights[2] enroll'd,
And here and there shooting forth silver streams,
'Mongst which crept little angels through the glitt'ring gleams.

Seemëd those little angels did uphold
The cloth of state, and on their purpled wings
Did bear the pendants through their nimbless[3] bold;
Besides, a thousand more of such as sings
Hymns to High God, and carols heavenly things,
Encompassëd the throne on which she sate;
She, angel-like, the heir of ancient kings
And mighty conquerors, in royal state;
Whilst Kings and Kaisers at her feet did them prostrâte.

In her hand was a sceptre, the "sacred pledge of peace and clemency;" and at her feet was laid her sword, rusted with long rest, though when foes enforced, or friends sought aid, "she could it sternly draw, that all the world dismay'd."

And round about before her feet there sate
A bevy of fair virgins clad in white,
That goodly seem'd t' adorn her royal state;
All lovely daughters of high Jove, that hight
Litæ,[4] by him begot in love's delight
Upon the righteous Themis; those, they say,
Upon Jove's judgment-seat wait day and night;
And, when in wrath he threats the world's decay,
They do his anger calm and cruel vengeance stay.

They also do, by his divine permission,
Upon the thrones of mortal Princes tend,
And often treat for pardon and remission
To suppliants through frailty which offend:
Those did upon Mercilla's throne attend,
Just Dice,[5] wise Eunomie,[6] mild Eirene;[7]
And them amongst, her glory to commend,
Sat goodly Temperance in garments clean,
And sacred Reverence, y-born of heav'nly strene.[8]

Underneath Mercilla's feet was a huge great lion, "with a strong iron chain and collar bound," so that he could not stir, but only "murmur with rebellious sound," when "savage choler gan redound." The two Knights made lowly reverence to the Queen, who received them with mild and cheerful air; and soon she returned to the business that occupied her when they arrived—"the trial of a great and weighty case"—for their better understanding of which she took them up into her throne, and set them one on each side. And now, under the allegory of the trial of Duessa, who unexpectedly turns up, we have a most remarkable statement of the case between Elizabeth and Mary Queen of Scots—whose head had fallen at Fotheringay nearly ten years before this passage was published.

Then was there brought, as prisoner to the bar,
A lady of great countenance and place,
But that she it with foul abuse did mar;
Yet did appear rare beauty in her face,
But blotted with condition vile and base,
That all her other honour did obscure,
And titles of nobility deface:
Yet, in that wretched semblant,[9] she did sure
The people's great compassion unto her allure.

Then up arose a person of deep reach
And rare insight hard matters to reveal;
That well could charm his tongue, and time his speech
To all essays;[10] his name was callëd Zeal:
He gan that Lady strongly to appeal[11]
Of many heinous crimes by her enur'd;[12]
And with sharp reasons rang her such a peal,
That those, whom she to pity had allur'd,
He now t' abhor and loathe her person had procur'd.

First gan he tell how this, that seem'd so fair
And royally array'd, Duessa hight;
That false Duessa, which had wrought great care[13]
And mickle mischief unto many a knight,
By her beguilëd and confounded quite:
But not for those she now in question came,
Though also those might question'd be aright,
But for vile treasons and outrageous shame,
Which she against the dread Mercilla oft did frame.

For she whilóm (as ye might yet right well
Remember) had her counsels false conspir'd
With faithless Blandamour and Paridell[14]
(Both two her paramours, both by her hir'd,
And both with hope of shadows vain inspir'd),
And with them practis'd, how for to deprive
Mercilla of her crown, by her aspir'd,[15]
That she might it unto herself derive,
And triumph in their blood whom she to death did drive.

But through high heaven's grace, which favour not
The wicked drifts of traitorous designs
'Gainst loyal princes, all this cursëd plot,
Ere proof it took,[16] discover'd was betimes,
And th' actors won the meed meet for their crimes:
Such be the meed of all that by such mean[17]
Unto the type of kingdom's title climbs!
But false Duessa, now untitled Queen,
Was brought to her sad doom, as here was to be seen.

1 Described, discovered.
2 Folds, plaits.
3 Nimbleness.
4 Prayers.
5 Justice.
6 Making of good laws.
7 Peace.
8 Stock, race.
9 Appearance.
10 Undertakings.
11 Impeach.
12 Committed.
13 Trouble.
14 The Earls of Northumberland and Westmoreland, leaders of the Northern Insurrection of 1569, are believed to be signified under these names.
15 Aspired to (by Duessa).
16 Ere it was put in execution.
17 Means.

Strongly did Zeal her heinous fact enforce,
And many other crimes of foul defame[1]
Against her brought, to banish all remorse,
And aggravate the horror of her blame:
And with him, to make part against her, came
Many grave persons that against her pled.
First was a sage old sire,[2] that had to name
The Kingdom's Care, with a white silver head,
That many high regards and reasons 'gainst her read.

Then gan Authority her to oppose
With peremptory power, that made all mute;
And then the Law of Nations 'gainst her rose,
And reasons brought, that no man could refute;
Next gan Religion 'gainst her to impute
High God's behest, and pow'r of holy laws;
Then gan the People's Cry, and Commons' Suit,
Importune care of their own public cause;
And lastly Justice chargëd her with breach of laws.

But then, for her, on the contrâry part,
Rose many advocates for her to plead:
First there came Pity, with full tender heart;
And with her join'd Regard of Womanhead;
And then came Danger, threat'ning hidden dread
And high alliance unto foreign pow'r;[3]
Then came Nobility of Birth, that bred
Great ruth[4] through her misfortune's tragic stowre;[5]
And lastly Grief did plead, and many tears forth pour.

With the near touch whereof in tender heart
The Briton Prince[6] was sore empassionate,
And wox inclinëd much unto her part,
Through the sad terror of so dreadful fate,
And wretched ruin of so high estate;
That for great ruth his corage[7] gan relent:
Which when as Zeal perceivëd to abate,
He gan his earnest fervour to augment,
And many fearful objects to them to present.

He gan t' enforce the evidence anew,
And new accusements to produce in place:
He brought forth that old hag of hellish hue,
The cursed Até, brought her face to face,
Who privy was and party in the case:
She, glad of spoil and ruinous decay,
Did her impeach; and, to her more disgrace,
The plot of all her practice did display,
And all her trains[8] and all her treasons forth did lay.

Then brought he forth with grisly grim aspéct
Abhorrëd Murder, who, with bloody knife
Yet dropping fresh in hand, did her detect,
And there with guilty bloodshed chargëd rife:
Then brought he forth Sedition, breeding strife
In troublous wits, and mutinous uproar:
Then brought he forth Incontinence of life,
Ev'n foul Adultery her face before,
And lewd Impiety, that her accusëd sore.

All which when as the Prince had heard and seen,
His former fancy's ruth[9] he gan repent,
And from her party eftsoons was drawn clean:
But Artegall, with constant firm intent
For zeal of Justice, was against her bent:
So was she guilty deemëd of them all.
Then Zeal began to urge her punishment,
And to their Queen for judgment loudly call,
Unto Mercilla mild, for Justice 'gainst the thrall.

But she, whose princely breast was touchëd near
With piteous ruth of her so wretched plight,
Though plain she saw, by all that she did hear,
That she of death was guilty found by right,
Yet would not let just vengeance on her light;
But rather let, instead thereof, to fall
Few pearling drops from her fair lamps of light;
The which she, cov'ring with her purple pall,
Would have the passion hid, and up arose withal.

CANTO X.

Prince Arthur takes the enterprise
For Belgé for to fight:
Geryoneo's Seneschal
He slays in Belgé's right.

SOME clerks[10] do doubt in their deviceful art
Whether this heav'nly thing whereof I treat,
To weeten[11] Mercy, be of Justice part,
Or drawn forth from her by divine extreat:[12]
This well I wot, that sure she is as great,
And meriteth to have as high a place,
Since in th' Almighty's everlasting seat
She first was bred, and born of heav'nly race;
From thence pour'd down on men by influence of grace.

For if that virtue be of so great might,
Which from just verdict will for nothing start,
But, to preserve inviolated right,
Oft spills[13] the principal to save the part;
So much more, then, is that of pow'r and art
That seeks to save the subject of her skill,
Yet never doth from doom[14] of right depart;
As it is greater praise to save than spill,
And better to reform than to cut off the ill.

The poet continues to praise the clemency of Mercilla, who moderated the judgment against Duessa "without grief or gall," until enforced thereto by strong constraint; even then pitying "her wilful fall with more than needful natural remorse, and yielding the last honour to her wretched corse." While Arthur and Artegall were entertained at court, "approving daily to their noble eyes royal examples of her mercies rare, and worthy patterns of her clemencies," two youths came from a foreign land, sent by their widowed mother to seek Mercilla's aid against a strong tyrant, who had invaded her land, and slain her children.

1 Disgrace.
2 Lord Treasurer Burleigh.
3 France.
4 Pity.
5 Assault.
6 The Earl of Leicester is supposed to be represented in Prince Arthur; he was believed to have been disposed towards the cause of Mary.
7 Heart.
8 Stratagems.
9 Pity.
10 Learned men.
11 To wit.
12 Extraction.
13 Ruins.
14 Judgment.

Her name was Belgé; who, in former age,
A lady of great worth and wealth had been,
And mother of a fruitful heritage,
Ev'n sev'nteen goodly sons;[1] which who had seen
In their first flow'r, before this fatal teen[2]
Them overtook, and their fair blossoms blasted,
More happy mother would her surely ween
Than famous Niobé, before she tasted
Latona's children's wrath, that all her issue wasted.

But this fell tyrant,[3] through his tortious[4] power,
Had left her now but five[5] of all that brood:
For twelve of them he did by times devour,
And to his idols sacrifice their blood,
Whilst he of none was stoppëd nor withstood:
For soothly[6] he was one of matchless might,
Of horrible aspéct and dreadful mood,
And had three bodies in one waist empight,[7]
And th' arms and legs of three to succour him in fight.

He was the son of Geryon—the three-bodied giant whose oxen Hercules carried away from Spain; and, when his father fell under Alcides' club, he fled from Spain to the land where Belgé dwelt, a new-made widow, flourishing in all wealth and happiness. Taking advantage of her widowhood and yet fresh woes, Geryoneo offered his services against foreign enemies, and by careful diligence he induced her to commit to him everything. From that time he began to create strife and trouble; giving the children of Belgé one by one to a dreadful monster to devour, "and setting up an idol of his own, the image of his monstrous parent Geryon." The woeful widow had no resource but to appeal for aid to Mercilla; and her two eldest sons had just arrived to seek that succour. All the other knights hung back from undertaking the enterprise; but Prince Arthur (still representing the Earl of Leicester, who in 1585 went to the Netherlands as Captain-General) accepted the adventure, and next morning set out with Belgé's two sons.

It was not long till that the Prince arriv'd
Within the land where dwelt that Lady sad;
Whereof that tyrant had her now depriv'd,
And into moors and marshes banish'd had,
Out of the pleasant soil and cities glad
In which she wont to harbour happily:
But now his cruelty so sore she drad,[8]
That to those fens for fastness[9] she did fly,
And there herself did hide from his hard tyranny.

"There he her found in sorrow and dismay, all solitary without living wight," and alarmed at the view of an armed stranger, till she saw her two sons, and understood that they brought succour. Embracing them with tears, she told them that already she felt her spirits recover, and already Fortune's wheel began to turn; then she thanked the Prince, that had taken such toilsome pain "for wretched woman, miserable wight." Much moved by her distress, he sought to comfort her, and asked her to go with him to some place where they might rest and feed, and she might regain her heart and hope.

"Ah me!" said she, "and whither shall I go?
Are not all places full of foreign pow'rs?
My palaces possessëd of my foe,
My cities sack'd, and their sky-threat'ning tow'rs
Razëd and made smooth fields now full of flow'rs?
Only these marishes and miry bogs,
In which the fearful efts do build their bow'rs,
Yield me an hostry[10] 'mongst the croaking frogs,
And harbour here in safety from those ravenous dogs."

"Nathless," said he, "dear Lady, with me go;
Some place shall us receive and harbour yield;
If not, we will it force, maugré[11] your foe,
And purchase it to us with spear and shield:
And if all fail, yet farewell[12] open field!
The Earth to all her creatures lodging lends."
With such his cheerful speeches he doth wield[13]
Her mind so well, that to his will she bends;
And, binding up her locks and weeds,[14] forth with him wends.[15]

They came unto a city far up land,
The which whilóm that Lady's own had been;
But now by force extort[16] out of her hand
By her strong foe, who had defacëd clean
Her stately tow'rs and buildings sunny sheen,[17]
Shut up her haven, marr'd her merchants' trade,
Robbëd her people that full rich had been,
And in her neck a castle[18] huge had made,
The which did her command without needing persuade.

That castle was the strength of all that State,
Until that State by strength was pullëd down;
And that same city, so now ruinate,
Had been the key of all that kingdom's crown;
Both goodly castle, and both goodly town,
Till that th' offended heavens list to lour
Upon their bliss, and baleful fortune frown.
When those 'gainst states and kingdoms do conjure,[19]
Who then can think their headlong ruin to recure![20]

But he had brought it now in servile bond,
And made it bear the yoke of Inquisition,
Striving long time in vain it to withstand;
Yet glad at last to make most base submission,
And life enjoy for any composition:

1 The seventeen provinces of the Netherlands.
2 Affliction.
3 The King of Spain.
4 Wrongous.
5 The five northern provinces (Holland, Zealand, Utrecht, Guelderland, and Friesland) which in 1579 asserted their independence against Spain, and, by the Union of Utrecht, formed themselves into a separate republic, that subsequently took the name of Holland.
6 Truly.
7 Contained in one waist.
8 Dreaded.
9 Security.
10 Hostelry, lodging.
11 Despite.
12 Welfare, welcome.
13 Influence.
14 Garments.
15 Goes.
16 Extorted.
17 Bright.
18 The city is Antwerp, the great seat of Netherlandish commerce; which was strongly fortified, and made a splendid resistance to the Prince of Parma in 1585.
19 Conspire.
20 Recover.

So now he hath new laws and orders new
Impos'd on it with many a hard condition,
And forcëd it, the honour that is due
To God, to do unto his idol most untrue.

To him he hath before this castle green
Built a fair chapel, and an altar fram'd
Of costly ivory full rich beseen,
On which that cursëd idol, far proclaim'd,
He hath set up, and him his god hath nam'd;
Off'ring to him in sinful sacrifice
The flesh of men, to God's own likeness fram'd,
And pouring forth their blood in brutish wise,
That any iron eyes to see it would agrise.[1]

And, for more horror and more cruelty,
Under that cursëd idol's altar-stone
A hideous monster[2] doth in darkness lie,
Whose dreadful shape was never seen of none
That lives on earth; but unto those alone
The which unto him sacrificëd be:
Those he devours, they say, both flesh and bone;
What else they have is all the tyrant's fee:[3]
So that no whit of them remaining one may see.

There also he had placed a strong garrison, and a seneschal[4] of dreaded might (Prince Alexander of Parma, Regent of the Netherlands), who first vanquished and then shamed all venturous knights. Belgé counsels Prince Arthur to shun the place; but, naught regarding her fearful speeches, he sends by the guard a challenge to their tyrant's seneschal—who soon comes riding forth to fight with courage fierce. "They both encounter in the middle plain;" the seneschal's spear is shivered on Arthur's shield, while Arthur's spear transfixes and slays his opponent. The Prince then advances to the castle, but three knights issue forth and attack him simultaneously, like "three great culverins[5] for battery bent, and levell'd all against one certain place." Never even swerving in his saddle under their shock, Arthur drives his spear through the body of him that rides in the midst. The two others fly; but the pursuer slays one in the threshold, the other in the hall; then all that are in the castle flee away through a postern door. Finding none to oppose him, the Prince went to lead the delighted Lady into the castle, with her two beloved sons; "and all that night themselves they cherishëd."

CANTO XI.

Prince Arthur overcomes the great
Geryoneo in fight;
Doth slay the monster, and restore
Belgé unto her right.

At the news that Lady Belgé had found a champion, who had overthrown his seneschal, and threatened to confound himself, Geryoneo "gan burn in rage, and freeze in fear, doubting sad end of principle unsound." Nevertheless he armed himself in haste, and came to the castle, demanding that the Prince should "deliver him his own, ere yet too late." Coming forth prepared for battle, the Prince asked if he was the same that had done all that wrong to the woeful dame. The tyrant boldly answered that he stood there "that would his doings justify with his own hand." Then with his great iron axe he flew at Arthur furiously; and so great advantage had he from "his three double hands thrice multiplied," that the Prince was forced to fight a wary and defensive battle. By a swift counterstroke, he smote off one of the monster's arms; and Geryoneo responded with a blow that, lighting on the head of the Prince's horse, stunned him and compelled his rider to dismount. Before long Arthur shore away two more of his adversary's arms, that fell "like fruitless branches, which the hatchet's sleight hath prunëd from the native tree and croppëd quite." With that the tyrant grew all mad and furious, "like a fell mastiff through enraging heat," cursing and blaspheming most horribly, and fighting furiously at random. Taking advantage of a blow in which Geryoneo overreached himself, Arthur smote him through all the three bodies, and tumbled him on the plain "biting the earth for very death's disdain." Seeing the tyrant's fall, Belgé went forth in haste to greet and thank the Prince; prostrating herself, with her sons, at his feet, in presence of all the people on the city walls, and offering to him as guerdon of his pain the realm which he had saved. The Prince, taking her up by the lily hand, assured her that the truth and right of her cause had really fought for her that day, and he needed no other reward than that which virtue always yields—"that is, the virtue's self, which her reward doth pay." Humbly thanking him for that wondrous grace, she entreated him not to stay his victorious arm till he had rooted out all the relics of that vile tyrant race. He asked what yet remained; and she answered:

"Then wot[6] you, Sir, that in this church hereby
There stands an idol of great note and name,
The which this giant rearëd first on high,
And of his own vain fancy's thought did frame:
To whom, for endless horror of his shame,
He offer'd up for daily sacrifice
My children and my people, burnt in flame
With all the tortures that he could devise,
The more t' aggrate[7] his god with such his bloody guise.

"And underneath this idol there doth lie
A hideous monster, that doth it defend,
And feeds on all the carcases that die
In sacrifice unto that cursëd fiend:
Whose ugly shape none ever saw, nor kenn'd,[8]
That ever scap'd: for of a man, they say,
It has the voice, that speeches forth doth send,

1 Horrify.
2 The Inquisition.
3 Property.
4 Steward, governor.
5 Cannons.
6 Know.
7 Gratify.
8 Knew.

Even blasphémous words, which she doth bray
Out of her poisonous entrails fraught with dire
decay."[1]

Which when the Prince heard tell, his heart gan
yearn
For great desire that monster to assay;
And pray'd the place of her abode to learn:
Which being show'd, he gan himself straightway
Thereto address, and his bright shield display.
So to the church he came, where it was told
The monster underneath the altar lay;
There he that idol saw of massy gold
Most richly made, but there no monster did
behold.

Upon the image with his naked blade
Three times, as in defiance, there he strook;[2]
And, the third time, out of a hidden shade
There forth issúed from under th' altar's smook[3]
A dreadful fiend with foul deformëd look,
That stretch'd itself as it had long lain still;
And her long tail and feathers strongly shook,
That all the temple did with terror fill;
Yet him naught terrified that fearëd nothing ill.

A huge great beast it was, when it in length
Was stretchëd forth, that nigh fill'd all the place,
And seem'd to be of infinite great strength;
Horrible, hideous, and of hellish race,
Born of the brooding of Echidna base,
Or other like infernal Fury's kind:
For of a maid she had the outward face,
To hide the horror which did lurk behind,
The better to beguile whom she so fond[4] did
find.

Thereto[5] the body of a dog she had,
Full of fell ravin[6] and fierce greediness,
A lion's claws, with pow'r and rigour clad,
To rend and tear whatso she can oppress;
A dragon's tail, whose sting without redress
Full deadly wounds whereso it is empight;[7]
An eagle's wings, for scope and speediness,
That nothing may escape her reaching might,
Whereto she ever list to make her hardy flight.

Much like in foulness and deformity
Unto that monster,[8] whom the Theban knight,[9]
The father of that fatal progeny,
Made kill herself for very heart's despite
That he had read her riddle, which no wight
Could ever loose,[10] but suffer'd deadly dool:[11]
So also did this monster use like sleight
To many a one which came unto her school,
Whom she did put to death deceivëd like a fool.

When the beast beheld the Prince, she would have fled, but he forced her to turn and fight. She griped his shield with all her strength; but "her lion's claws he from her feet away did wipe;" then, casting forth foul blasphemous speeches and bitter curses, she struck at him with her huge tail, and made him stagger:

As when the mast of some well-timber'd hulk
Is with the blast of some outrageous storm
Blown down, it shakes the bottom of the bulk,
And makes her ribs to crack as they were torn;
Whilst still she stands astonish'd and forlorn;
So was he stunn'd with stroke of her huge tail:
But, ere that it she back again had borne,
He with his sword it struck, that without fail
He jointed it, and marr'd the swinging of her
flail.

Crying much louder than before, the fiend reared herself on her wide great wings, and flew at the Prince's head; but, thrusting his fatal sword under her belly, he made a way for her entrails to gush forth. "Then down to ground fell that deformëd mass;" and Arthur, all his tasks and dangers over, "went forth his gladness to partake" with Belgé. Great laud and rejoicing attended his victory over the beast, and his subsequent destruction of the idol; and the Prince stayed for a while with Belgé, "making great feast and joyous merriment," until he had securely re-established her in her kingdom. Then, taking leave of the Lady, he set out afresh on "his first emprise"—his quest after Gloriana.

"But turn we now to noble Artegall," who, attended only by Talus, had gone forth from the court of Mercilla, to deliver Irena and punish Grantorto. As he travelled, he met the aged man, Sergis, who had attended Irena when she came to Faery Court to ask aid; and the Knight sought of him news of his mistress. Sergis answered that she lived sure and sound, though bound in wretched thraldom by the tyrant;

"For she, presuming on th' appointed tide[12]
In which ye promis'd, as ye were a knight,
To meet her at the Salvage Island's[13] side,
And then and there, for trial of her right,
With her unrighteous enemy to fight,
Did thither come; where she, afraid of naught,
By guileful treason and by subtíle sleight
Surprisëd was, and to Grantorto brought,
Who her imprison'd hath, and her life often
sought.

"And now he hath to her prefix'd a day,
By which if that no champion do appear
Which will her cause in battailous array
Against him justify, and prove her clear
Of all those crimes that he 'gainst her doth rear,[14]
She death shall sure aby."[15] Those tidings sad
Did much abash Sir Artegall to hear,
And grievëd sore, that through his fault she had
Fallen into that tyrant's hand and usage bad.

Artegall calls on heaven to witness that he is "clear from blame of this upbraid," having been prevented from keeping his time by his own captivity; and, learning that the tyrant has allowed ten days of grace, the Knight vows that if he lives till those ten days have end she shall have aid, though he should die for her. As he proceeds on his way with Sergis, Artegall

1 Destruction. 2 Struck. 3 Smoke. 4 Foolish. 5 Moreover. 6 Ravenousness. 7 Infixed. 8 The Sphinx.

9 Œdipus. 10 Solve. 11 Misfortune. 12 Time. 13 Ireland's. 14 Assert. 15 Suffer.

sees before him a crowd of people flocking confusedly together, as if there were some tumultuous affray.

To which as they approach'd the cause to know,
They saw a knight [1] in dangerous distress
Of a rude rout [2] him chasing to and fro,
That sought with lawless pow'r him to oppress,
And bring in bondage of their brutishness:
And far away, amid their rakehell bands,
They spied a lady [3] left all succourless,
Crying, and holding up her wretched hands
To him for aid, who long in vain their rage withstands.

Yet still he strives, nor any peril spares,
To rescue her from their rude violence;
And like a lion wood [4] amongst them fares,
Dealing his dreadful blows with large dispence,[5]
'Gainst which the pallid death finds no defence:
But all in vain; their numbers are so great,
That naught may boot to banish them from thence;
For, soon as he their outrage back doth beat,
They turn afresh, and oft renew their former threat.

And now they do so sharply him assay,
That they his shield in pieces batter'd have,
And forcëd him to throw it quite away,[6]
From dangers dread his doubtful life to save;
All be [7] that it most safety to him gave,
And much did magnify his noble name:
For from the day that he thus did it leave,
Amongst all knights he blotted was with blame,
And counted but a recreant knight with endless shame.

Artegall went to the knight's aid; but the "rude rout" boldly assailed him and his companions, and fled only when the Iron Man had brought his huge flail into play. The rescued knight drew near to thank his deliverer; and Artegall inquired the whole occasion of his recent evil plight, and who he and his pursuers were. His name, he answered, was Burbon, heretofore far renowned, until by late mischief his former praise had all been sorely blemished. The Lady was Fleur-de-lis, his own love, though she had abandoned him; "whether withheld from him by wrongful might, or with her own good will," he could not tell. She had at first plighted her faith to him, till a tyrant, Grantorto (not the Grantorto of Irena—who is an abstraction of Wrong—but here signifying the King of Spain) had enticed her away "with golden gifts and many a guileful word;" and since that time she had abhorred her former lord. Grantorto had now sent a troop of villains to carry her off by open force; and it was while Burbon strove against great odds to retain her, that Artegall had come up.

"But why have ye," said Artegall, "forborne
Your own good shield in dangerous dismay?
That is the greatest shame and foulest scorn
Which unto any knight behappen may,
To lose the badge that should his deeds display."
To whom Sir Burbon, blushing half for shame;
"That shall I unto you," quoth he, "bewray;[8]
Lest ye therefor might happily [9] me blame,
And deem it done of will, that through enforcement came.

"True is, that I at first was dubbëd knight
By a good knight, the Knight of the Redcross;
Who, when he gave me arms in field to fight,
Gave me a shield, in which he did endoss [10]
His dear Redeemer's badge upon the boss:
The same long while I bore, and therewithal
Fought many battles without wound or loss;
Therewith Grantorto's self I did appal,
And made him oftentimes in field before me fall.

"But for [11] that many did that shield envy,
And cruel enemies increasëd more,
To stint all strife and troublous enmity,
That bloody scutcheon, being batter'd sore,
I laid aside, and have of late forbore;
Hoping thereby to have my love obtain'd:
Yet can I not my love have nathëmore;
For she by force is still from me detain'd,
And with corruptful bribes is to untruth mistrain'd." [12]

To whom thus Artegall; "Certes, Sir Knight,
Hard is the case the which ye do complain;
Yet not so hard (for naught so hard may light [13]
That it to such a strait might you constrain)
As to abandon that which doth contain
Your honour's style, that is, your warlike shield.
All peril ought be less, and less all pain,
Than loss of fame in disadventurous field:
Die, rather than do aught that might dishonour yield!"

"Not so," quoth he; "for yet, when time doth serve,
My former shield I may resume again:
To temporize is not from truth to swerve,
Nor for advantage term to entertain,
When as necessity doth it constrain."
"Fie on such forgery," said Artegall,
"Under one hood to shadow faces twain:
Knights ought be true, and truth is one in all;
Of all things, to dissemble, foully may befall!" [14]

Burbon nevertheless entreated the Knight, of his courtesy, to aid him against those peasants and free his love from their hands; after an arduous battle the flail of Talus had its usual effect; and the troop of villains was scattered to all the winds.

1 Henry Bourbon of Navarre, or Henry IV. of France.
2 The rebellious Roman Catholics, under the name of the League.
3 France; or the French crown.
4 Furious.
5 Lavish abundance.
6 The shield is the Protestant religion, which, under the pressure of his and its enemies, Henry IV. renounced in 1593.
7 Although.
8 Reveal.
9 Haply.
10 Endorse, inscribe.
11 Because.
12 Misled.
13 Chance.
14 Foul or evil hap befall those who dissemble!

At last they came where as that Lady bode,[1]
Whom now her keepers had forsaken quite
To save themselves, and scatter'd were abroad:
Her half dismay'd they found in doubtful plight,
As neither glad nor sorry for their sight;
Yet wondrous fair she was, and richly clad
In royal robes, and many jewels dight;[2]
But that those villains, through their usage bad,
Them foully rent and shamefully defacëd had.

But Burbon, straight dismounting from his steed,
Unto her ran with greedy great desire,
And catching her fast by her ragged weed[3]
Would have embracëd her with heart entire:[4]
But she, backstarting with disdainful ire,
Bade him avaunt, nor would unto his lore[5]
Allurëd be for prayer nor for meed:[6]
Whom when those knights so froward and forlore[7]
Beheld, they her rebukëd and upbraided sore.

Said Artegall; "What foul disgrace is this
To so fair Lady, as ye seem in sight,
To blot your beauty, that unblemish'd is,
With so foul blame as breach of faith once plight,
Or change of love for any world's delight?
Is aught on earth so precïous or dear
As praise and honour? or is aught so bright
And beautiful as glory's beams appear,
Whose goodly light than Phœbus' lamp doth shine more clear?

"Why then will ye, fond[8] Dame, attempted[9] be
Unto a stranger's love, so lightly plac'd,
For gifts of gold or any worldly glee,
To leave the love that ye before embrac'd,
And let your fame with falsehood be defac'd?
Fie on the pelf for which good name is sold,
And honour with indignity debas'd!
Dearer is love than life, and fame than gold;
But dearer than them both your faith once plighted hold."

Much was the Lady in her gentle mind
Abash'd at his rebuke, that bit her near;
Nor aught to answer thereunto did find:
But, hanging down her head with heavy cheer,[10]
Stood long amaz'd as she amated[11] were:
Which Burbon seeing, her again assay'd;
And, clasping 'twixt his arms, her up did rear
Upon his steed, while she no whit gainsaid:
So bore her quite away, nor well nor ill apaid.[12]

Nathless the Iron Man did still pursue
That rascal many with unpitied spoil;
Nor ceasëd not, till all their scatter'd crew
Into the sea he drove quite from that soil,
The which they troubled had with great turmoil:
But Artegall, seeing his cruel deed,
Commanded him from slaughter to recoil,[13]
And to his voyage gan again proceed;
For that the term, approaching fast, requirëd speed.

CANTO XII.

Artegall doth Sir Burbon aid,
And blames for changing shield:[14]
He with the great Grantorto fights,
And slayeth him in field.

O SACRED[15] hunger of ambitious minds,
And impotent[16] desire of men to reign!
Whom neither dread of God, that devils binds,
Nor laws of men, that commonweals contain,[17]
Nor bands of naturé, that wild beasts restrain,
Can keep from outrage and from doing wrong,
Where they may hope a kingdom to obtain:
No faith so firm, no trust can be so strong,
No love so lasting then, that may enduren long.

"Witness may Burbon be," whom love of lordship and of lands made "most faithless and unsound;" witness also Geryoneo, who oppressed fair Belgé, and Grantorto, "who no less than all the rest burst out to all outrageousness." Prosecuting his enterprise against Grantorto, Artegall comes to the sea-shore, finds a ship all ready, and in one day reaches the desired coast —which is occupied by great hosts of men, ranked to prevent his landing. But soon the foes are routed by Talus, and fly like doves affrighted by an eagle; fresh forces brought against the newcomers by the tyrant are also scattered by the terrible flail, till they lie over all the land "as thick as doth the seed after the sower's hand;" and the tyrant gladly hails the message of Artegall, that he has come not for such slaughter's sake, but to try with him in single fight the right of fair Irena's cause. Grantorto fixes the combat for the next day, and draws off his people. Artegall spends the night in his tent, pitched on the open plain; supplied with needful entertainment by secret friends of Irena, who disregard the tyrant's command that none should entertain the strangers.

The morrow next, that was the dismal day
Appointed for Irena's death before,
So soon as it did to the world display
His cheerful face, and light to men restore,
The heavy maid, to whom none tidings bore
Of Artegall's arrival her to free,
Look'd up with eyes full sad and heart full sore,
Weening her life's last hour then near to be;
Since no redemption nigh she did nor hear nor see.

Then up she rose, and on herself did dight[18]
Most squalid garments, fit for such a day;
And with dull count'nance and with doleful sprite
She forth was brought in sorrowful dismay
For to receive the doom of her decay:[19]
But coming to the place, and finding there
Sir Artegall in battailous array,
Waiting his foe, it did her dead heart cheer,
And new life to her lent in midst of deadly fear.

1 Abode. 2 Adorned. 3 Robe. 4 Sincere. 5 Wishes. 6 Reward, bribe. 7 Devoid of propriety. 8 Foolish. 9 Tempted. 10 Mien. 11 Subdued, overawed. 12 Satisfied. 13 Return.
14 The first limb of this argument is erroneously prefixed to this canto, to the contents of which it bears no relation. It agrees with the contents of the preceding canto. 15 Cursed. 16 Violent, uncontrollable. 17 Restrain. 18 Dress. 19 Destruction.

Like as a tender rose in open plain,
That with untimely drought nigh wither'd was,
And hung the head, soon as few drops of rain
Thereon distil and dew her dainty face,
Gins to look up, and with fresh wonted grace
Dispreads the glory of her leavës gay;
Such was Irena's count'nance, such her case,
When Artegall she saw in that array,
There waiting for the tyrant till it was far day:

Who came at length with proud presumptuous gait
Into the field, as if he fearless were,
All armëd in a coat of iron plate
Of great defence to ward the deadly fear;
And on his head a steel-cap he did wear
Of colour rusty-brown, but sure and strong;
And in his hand an huge poleaxe did bear,
Whose stele[1] was iron-studded, but not long,
With which he wont to fight, to justify his wrong.

Of stature huge and hideous he was,
Like to a giant for his monstrous height,
And did in strength most sorts of men surpass,
Nor ever any found his match in might;
Thereto[2] he had great skill in single fight:
His face was ugly and his count'nance stern,
That could have fray'd one with the very sight,
And gapëd like a gulf when he did gern;[3]
That whether man or monster one could scarce discern.

Artegall, nothing daunted by his opponent's frightful aspect, buckled himself to fight; but Grantorto's blows were so fast and furious, that he had to shun them, as a skilful mariner shuns the peril of a storm by striking his sails. At last, just as Grantorto reared high his hand to smite him mortally, Artegall pierced the giant's side; but the blow nevertheless descended with such force that the battle-axe stuck fast in the shield which the Knight had interposed. In his efforts to release the axe, the giant dragged Artegall all about the field; till the Knight let go the shield, and, while the giant was encumbered with it, smote him on the head with his sword; Chrysaor following up the stroke, till Grantorto fell to the ground, and the conqueror cut off his head. All the people shouted for joy of his success, and threw themselves at the feet of Irena, whom they adored as their true liege and princess natural; Artegall led her to the royal palace, and established her in her kingdom; then he punished all the adherents of the dead tyrant, so that while he stayed with her "not one was left that durst her once have disobey'd."

During which time that he did there remain,
His study was true justice how to deal,
And day and night employ'd his busy pain
How to reform that ragged commonweal:
And that same Iron Man, which could reveal
All hidden crimes, through all that realm he sent
To search out those that us'd to rob and steal,
Or did rebel 'gainst lawful government;
On whom he did inflict most grievous punishment.[4]

But, ere he could reform it thoroughly,
He through occasion callëd was away
To Faery Court, that of necessity
His course of justice he was forc'd to stay,
And Talus to revoke from the right way,
In which he was that realm for to redress:
But Envy's cloud still dimmeth Virtue's ray!
So, having freed Irena from distress,
He took his leave of her there left in heaviness.

Then as he back returnëd from that land,
And there arriv'd again whence forth he set,
He had not passëd far upon the strand,
When as two old ill-favour'd hags he met,
By the wayside being together set;
Two grisly creatures; and, to that their faces
Most foul and filthy were, their garments yet,
Being all ragg'd and tatter'd, their disgraces[5]
Did much the more augment, and made most ugly cases.

The one of them, that elder did appear,
With her dull eyes did seem to look askew,
That her misshape much help'd;[6] and her foul hair
Hung loose and loathsomely; thereto[7] her hue
Was wan and lean, that all her teeth a-rew[8]
And all her bones might through her cheeks be read;[9]
Her lips were, like raw leather, pale and blue:
And as she spake, therewith she slaverëd;
Yet spake she seldom; but thought more, the less she said:

Her hands were foul and dirty, never wash'd
In all her life, with long nails over-raught[10]
Like puttock's[11] claws; with th' one of which she scratch'd
Her cursëd head, although it itchëd naught;
The other held a snake with venom fraught,
On which she fed and gnawëd hungrily,
As if that long she had not eaten aught;
That round about her jaws one might descry
The bloody gore and poison dropping loathsomely.

Her name was Envy, knowen well thereby;
Whose nature is to grieve and grudge at all
That ever she sees done praiseworthily;
Whose sight to her is greatest cross may fall,[12]
And vexeth so, that makes her eat her gall:
For, when she wanteth other thing to eat,
She feeds on her own maw unnatural,
And of her own foul entrails makes her meat;
Meat fit for such a monster's monsterous dieat:[13]

1 Handle. 2 Also. 3 Grin, yawn.
4 Spenser describes here the features of Lord Grey's government of Ireland; his severity aroused against him great outcry in England, and exposed him to those attacks of envy and malice of which the poet goes on to speak.
5 Deformity.
6 Much increased her ugliness.
7 Moreover.
8 In a row.
9 Perceived.
10 Over-reached.
11 Kite's.
12 That may happen.
13 Diet.

And if she happ'd of any good to hear
That had to any happily betid,[1]
Then would she inly fret, and grieve, and tear
Her flesh for fellness [2] which she inward hid:
But if she heard of ill that any did,
Or harm that any had, then would she make
Great cheer, like one unto a banquet bid;
And in another's loss great pleasure take,
As she had got thereby and gainëd a great stake.

The other nothing better was than she,
Agreeing in bad will and canker'd kind;[3]
But in bad manner they did disagree:
For whatso Envy good or bad did find,
She did conceal, and murder her own mind;
But this, whatever evil she conceiv'd,
Did spread abroad and throw in th' open wind:
Yet this in all her words might be perceiv'd,
That all she sought was men's good name to have bereav'd.

For whatsoever good by any said
Or done she heard, she would straightways invent
How to deprave or sland'rously upbraid,
Or to miscónstrue of a man's intent,
And turn to ill the thing that well was meant:
Therefore she usëd often to resort
To common haunts, and companies frequent,
To hark what any one did good report,
To blot the same with blame, or wrest in wicked sort:

And if that any ill she heard of any,
She would it eke,[4] and make much worse by telling,
And take great joy to publish it to many;
That ev'ry matter worse was for her melling:[5]
Her name was hight Detraction, and her dwelling
Was near to Envy, ev'n her neighbour next;
A wicked hag, and Envy's self excelling
In mischief; for herself she only vext,
But this same both herself and others eke perplext.

Her face was ugly, and her mouth distort,
Foaming with poison round about her gills,
In which her cursëd tongue full sharp and short
Appear'd, like aspë's sting, that closely [6] kills,
Or cruelly does wound whomso she wills:
A distaff in her other hand she had,
Upon the which she little spins, but spills;[7]
And fains [8] to weave false tales and leasings [9] bad,
To throw amongst the good which others had disprad.[10]

These two now had themselves combin'd in one,
And link'd together 'gainst Sir Artegall;
For whom they waited as his mortal fone,[11]
How they might make him into mischief fall,
For freeing from their snares Irena thrall:
Besides, unto themselves they gotten had
A monster, which the Blatant Beast [12] men call,
A dreadful fiend, of gods and men y-drad,[13]
Whom they by sleights allur'd and to their purpose lad.[14]

Such were these hags, and so unhandsome drest:
Who when they nigh approaching had espied
Sir Artegall return'd from his late quest,[15]
They both arose, and at him loudly cried,
As it had been two shepherd's curs had 'scried [16]
A ravenous wolf amongst the scatter'd flocks:
And Envy first, as she that first him eyed,
Towárd him runs, and with rude flaring locks
About her ears, does beat her breast and forehead knocks.

Then from her mouth the gobbet she does take,
The which whilere [17] she was so greedily
Devouring, even that half-gnawen snake,
And at him throws it most despitefully:
The cursëd serpent, though she hungrily
Erst [18] chew'd thereon, yet was not all so dead,
But that some life remainëd secretly;
And, as he pass'd afore withouten dread,
Bit him behind, that long the mark was to be read.[19]

Then th' other, coming near, gan him revile,
And foully rail, with all she could invent;
Saying that he had, with unmanly guile
And foul abusion, both his honour blent,[20]
And that bright sword, the sword of Justice lent,
Had stainëd with reproachful cruelty
In guiltless blood of many an innocent:
As for Grantorto, him with treachery
And trains having surpris'd, he foully did to die.

Thereto the Blatant Beast, by them set on,
At him began aloud to bark and bay
With bitter rage and fell contentión;
That all the woods and rocks nigh to that way
Began to quake and tremble with dismay;
And all the air rebellowëd again,
So dreadfully his hundred tongues did bray:
And evermore those hags themselves did pain [21]
To sharpen him, and their own cursed tongues did strain.

And, still among, most bitter words they spake,
Most shameful, most unrighteous, most untrue,
That they the mildest man alive would make
Forget his patience, and yield vengeance due
To her, that so false slanders at him threw:
And more to make them pierce and wound more deep,
She with the sting which in her vile tongue grew
Did sharpen them, and in fresh poison steep:
Yet he pass'd on, and seem'd of them to take no keep.[22]

But Talus, hearing her so lewdly [23] rail,
And speak so ill of him that well deserv'd,
Would her have chástis'd with his iron flail,
If her Sir Artegall had not preserv'd,

1 Happened. 2 Fury.
3 Nature. 4 Increase.
5 Meddling. 6 Secretly.
7 Spoils. 8 Delights.
9 Falsehoods. 10 Spread, diffused. 11 Foes.
12 The bellowing beast; Calumny, or popular clamour.

13 Dreaded. 14 Led.
15 Enterprise. 16 Descried.
17 Just before. 18 Before.
19 Perceived. 20 Stained.
21 Exert. 22 Heed.
23 Wickedly

And him forbidden, who his hest[1] observ'd:
So much the more at him still did she scold,
And stones did cast; yet he for naught would swerve
From his right course, but still the way did hold
To Faery Court; where what him fell shall else be told.

THE SIXTH BOOK

OF

THE FAERIE QUEEN:

CONTAINING

THE LEGEND OF SIR CALIDORE, OR OF COURTESY.

THE ways through which my weary steps I guide,
In this delightful land of Faëry,
Are so exceeding spacïous and wide,
And sprinkled with such sweet variety
Of all that pleasant is to ear or eye,
That I, nigh ravish'd with rare thoughts' delight,
My tedious travail do forget thereby;
And, when I gin to feel decay of might,
It strength to me supplies, and cheers my dullëd sprite.

Such secret comfort and such heav'nly pleasures,
Ye sacred Imps,[2] that on Parnassus dwell,
And there the keeping have of Learning's treasures
Which do all worldly riches far excel,
Into the minds of mortal men do well,[3]
And goodly fury[4] into them infuse;
Guide ye my footing, and conduct me well
In these strange ways where never foot did use,[5]
Nor none can find but who was taught them by the Muse:

Reveal to me the sacred nursery
Of Virtue, which with you doth there remain,
Where it in silver bow'r does hidden lie
From view of men and wicked world's disdain;
Since it at first was by the gods with pain[6]
Planted in earth, being deriv'd at first
From heav'nly seeds of bounty sovëreign,[7]
And by them long with careful labour nurst,
Till it to ripeness grew, and forth to honour burst.

Amongst them all grows not a fairer flow'r
Than is the bloom of comely Courtesy;
Which though it on a lowly stalk do bow'r,[8]
Yet brancheth forth in brave nobility,
And spreads itself through all civility:
Of which though present age do plenteous seem,
Yet, being match'd with plain antiquity,
Ye will them all but feignëd shows esteem,
Which carry colours fair that feeble eyes misdeem:[9]

But, in the trial of true Courtesy,
It's now so far from that which then it was,
That it indeed is naught but forgery,
Fashion'd to please the eyes of them that pass,
Which see not perfect things but in a glass:
Yet is that glass so gay that it can blind
The wisest sight, to think gold that is brass:[10]
But Virtue's seat is deep within the mind,
And not in outward shows but inward thoughts defin'd.

But where shall I in all antiquity
So fair a pattern find, where may be seen
The goodly praise of princely Courtesy,
As in yourself, O sov'reign Lady Queen?
In whose pure mind, as in a mirror sheen,[11]
It shows, and with her brightness doth inflame
The eyes of all which thereon fixëd be'n;
But meriteth indeed a higher name:
Yet so, from low to high, uplifted is your name.

Then pardon me, most dreaded Sovëreign,
That from yourself I do this Virtue bring,
And to yourself do it return again:
So from the Ocëan all rivers spring,
And tribute back repay as to their king:
Right so from you all goodly virtues well
Into the rest which round about you ring,[12]—
Fair Lords and Ladies which about you dwell,
And do adorn your Court where courtesies excel.

CANTO I.

Calidore saves from Maleffórt
A damsel usëd vild:[13]
Doth vanquish Crudor · and doth make
Briana wax more mild.

OF Court, it seems, men Courtesy do call,
For that it there most useth to abound;
And well beseemeth that in prince's hall
That Virtue should be plentifully found,
Which of all goodly manners is the ground,
And root of civil conversatión:
Right so in Faery Court it did redound,
Where courteous Knights and Ladies most did won[14]
Of all on earth, and made a matchless paragon.

But 'mongst them all was none more courteous knight
Than Calidore,[15] belovëd over all:

1 Command.
2 Children (of Jove); the Muses.
3 Cause to flow.
4 Poetic frenzy.
5 Frequent, use to go.
6 Difficulty.
7 Supreme goodness or virtue.
8 Abide, grow.
9 Misjudge, are misled by.

10 To think that golden which is but of brass.
11 Shining, clear.
12 Encircle.
13 Vilely.
14 Dwell.
15 Calidore—from the Greek καλος, beautiful, and διδωμι, I give—means the man gifted with beautiful qualities (Callidoros), and represents Sir Philip Sidney.

In whom it seems that gentleness of sprite [1]
And manners mild were planted natural;
To which he adding comely guise withal
And gracious speech, did steal men's hearts away:
Nathless thereto [2] he was full stout and tall,
And well approv'd in battailous affray,
That him did much renown, and far his fame
display.

Nor was there knight nor was there lady found,
In Faery Court, but him did dear embrace [3]
For his fair usage and conditions [4] sound,
The which in all men's liking gainëd place,
And with the greatest purchas'd greatest grace;
Which he could wisely use, and well apply,
To please the best, and th' evil to embase: [5]
For he loath'd leasing [6] and base flattery;
And lovëd simple truth and steadfast honesty.

Now, travelling in earnest pursuit of a hard adventure, he met Sir Artegall returning "half sad" from his late conquest of Grantorto; and Artegall, who was an old friend, related his whole exploit. Calidore, congratulating him, said that where the other had ended he was about to begin; for his enterprise was to chase the Blatant Beast through the world, till it should be subdued; but he knew not where to find the monster. Artegall asked what that Blatant Beast was; and Calidore replied that it was "a monster bred of hellish race," which had often annoyed and destroyed good knights and ladies true.

"Of Cerberus whilóm he was begot
And fell Chimæra, in her darksome den,
Through foul commixture of his filthy blot;
Where he was foster'd long in Stygian fen,
Till he to perfect ripeness grew; and then
Into this wicked world he forth was sent
To be the plague and scourge of wretched men:
Whom with vile tongue and venomous intent
He sore doth wound, and bite, and cruelly tor-
ment."

"Then, since the Salvage Island [7] I did leave,"
Said Artegall, "I such a Beast did see,
The which did seem a thousand tongues to have,
That all in spite and malice did agree,
With which he bay'd and loudly bark'd at me,
As if that he at once would me devour:
But I, that knew myself from peril free,
Did naught regard his malice nor his pow'r;
But he the more his wicked poison forth did
pour."

Calidore gladly and hopefully recognised in the description the monster whom he sought; and, after goodly leave-taking, the knights pursued their respective ways. Soon Calidore came upon a comely squire tied to a tree, whom he loosed, and then asked how he came into that dangerous and disgraceful plight. Not through misdesert, but through misfortune, the squire replied:

"Not far from hence, upon yon rocky hill,
Hard by a strait there stands a castle strong,
Which doth observe a custom lewd [8] and ill,
And it hath long maintain'd with mighty
wrong:
For may no knight nor lady pass along
That way (and yet they needs must pass that
way,
By reason of the strait, and rocks among),
But they that lady's locks do shave away,
And that knight's beard, for toll which they for
passage pay."

"A shameful use [9] as ever I did hear,"
Said Calidore, "and to be overthrown.
But by what means did they at first it rear, [10]
And for what cause? Tell, if thou have it
known."
Said then that squire; "The lady which doth
own
This castle is by name Briana hight;
Than which a prouder lady liveth none:
She long time hath dear lov'd a doughty knight,
And sought to win his love by all the means she
might.

"His name is Crudor; who, through high dis-
dain
And proud despite of his self-pleasing mind,
Refusëd hath to yield her love again,
Until a mantle she for him do find
With beards of knights and locks of ladies lin'd:
Which to provide, she hath this castle dight, [11]
And therein hath a seneschal assign'd,
Call'd Maleffórt, [12] a man of mickle might,
Who executes her wicked will with worse
despite.

"He, this same day as I that way did come
With a fair damsel, my belovëd dear,
In execution of her lawless doom
Did set upon us, flying both for fear;
For little boots against him hand to rear:
Me first he took, unable to withstond, [13]
And, while he her pursuëd ev'rywhere,
Till his return unto this tree he bound;
Nor wot I surely whether he her yet have
found."

While they spoke, they heard a loud and rueful shriek, and saw the carl, Maleffort, with hand unblest, "hauling that maiden by the yellow hair," nigh tearing her garments from her snowy breast and her locks from her head. Calidore at once hastened towards him, and demanded that he should let go that "misgotten weft." The seneschal, turning fiercely against Calidore, tauntingly asked him whether for that maid he would give his beard, "though it but little be;" and he laid on hideous strokes with such importune might, that the Knight staggered, and had to fight on the defensive, till his adversary grew wearied. Then,

Like as a water-stream, whose swelling source

1 Nobility of spirit.
2 Also.
3 Esteem.
4 Qualities.
5 Disgrace, abase.
6 Falsehood.
7 The island of Irena—Ireland.
8 Wicked, vile.
9 Usage.
10 Establish.
11 Erected.
12 Evil Effort or Strength.
13 Withstand.

Shall drive a mill, within strong banks is pent,
And long restrainëd of his ready course;
So soon as passage is unto him lent,
Breaks forth, and makes his way more violent;
Such was the fury of Sir Calidore:
When once he felt his foeman to relent,
He fiercely him pursued, and pressëd sore;
Who as he still decay'd, so he increasëd more.

Unable to withstand "the heavy burden of his dreadful might," Maleffort fled to the castle, "for dread of death" calling aloud to the warder to open the gate hastily; but Calidore pursued so closely, that just as the gate was opened he cleft the flying foe to the chin, and the carcase, tumbling down within the door, "did choke the entrance with a lump of sin." Calidore entered, and slew the porter:

With that the rest the which the castle kept
About him flock'd, and hard at him did lay;
But he them all from him full lightly swept,
As doth a steer, in heat of summer's day,
With his long tail the brizes[1] brush away.
Thence passing forth into the hall he came,
Where of the Lady's self in sad dismay
He was y-met, who with uncomely shame
Gan him salute, and foul upbraid with faulty
blame:

"False traitor Knight," said she, "no knight at
all,
But scorn of arms! that hast with guilty hand
Murder'd my men, and slain my seneschal;
Now comest thou to rob my house unmann'd,[2]
And spoil myself, that cannot thee withstand?
Yet doubt thou not, but that some better knight
Than thou, that shall thy treason understand,
Will it avenge, and pay thee with thy right:
And if none do, yet shame shall thee with shame
requite."

Much was the Knight abashëd at that word;
Yet answer'd thus; "Not unto me the shame,
But to the shameful doer it afford.
Blood is no blemish; for it is no blame
To punish those that do deserve the same;
But they that break bands of civility,
And wicked customs make, those do defame
Both noble arms and gentle courtesy:
No greater shame to man than inhumanity."

Calidore therefore exhorted the lady, "for dread of shame," to forego the evil custom which she maintained; but she wrathfully disdained his courteous lore, and, on her love's behalf, bade him be defied. Calidore held it no indignity to take defiance at her word; and declared that, were any there who would abet the lady's cause with his sword, "he might it dear abide." Briana sent to Crudor a dwarf bearing a gold ring, "a privy token which between them past," desiring him to come to her rescue; and meantime the discourteous lady treated her unwelcome guest with scornful pride and foul indignity. But he well endured her womanish disdain, which became the more bitter when, in the morning, the dwarf returned with the promise of Crudor that before he tasted bread he would succour her, and "alive or dead her foe deliver up into her hand." Calidore issued forth to meet his enemy, whom he soon descried pricking fast towards the castle; and, without pause or parley, they "met in middest of the plain with so fell fury and dispiteous force," that horses and men all rolled to ground together. It was some time before they recovered from the shock: but then they commenced a furious conflict on foot. After long tracing and traversing to and fro, and many grievous wounds on both sides, Calidore anticipated a stroke of his adversary by a blow on the helmet, which, vigorously followed up, cast him grovelling to the ground. The Knight would have instantly slain his prostrate foe, but that Crudor entreated mercy.

With that his mortal hand a while he stay'd:
And, having somewhat calm'd his wrathful
heat
With goodly patience, thus he to him said;
"And is the boast of that proud Lady's threat,
That menacëd me from the field to beat,
Now brought to this? By this now may ye
learn
Strangers no more so rudely to entreat;
But put away proud look and usage stern,
The which shall naught to you but foul dishonour earn.

"For nothing is more blameful to a knight,
That court'sy doth as well as arms profess,
However strong and fortunate in fight,
Than the reproach of pride and cruelness:
In vain he seeketh others to suppress,
Who hath not learn'd himself first to subdue:
All flesh is frail and full of fickleness,
Subject to Fortune's chance, still changing new;
What haps to-day to me, to-morrow may to
you.

"Who will not mercy unto others shew,
How can he mercy ever hope to have?
To pay each with his own is right and due:
Yet since ye mercy now do need to crave,
I will it grant, your hopeless life to save,
With these conditions which I will propound:
First, that ye better shall yourself behave
Unto all errant knights, whereso on ground;
Next, that ye ladies aid in ev'ry stead and
stound."[3]

Crudor gladly promised to obey these injunctions; and Calidore, suffering him to rise, made him swear "by his own sword, and by the cross thereon," to take Briana, without dower or condition, for his wife. Then he called forth "the sad Briana, which all this beheld," and cheered her with news of the agreement to which he had compelled Crudor.

Whereof she now more glad than sorry erst,[4]
All overcome with infinite affect[5]
For his exceeding courtesy, that pierc'd

[1] Breeze-flies, gadflies.
[2] Undefended by men.

[3] In every place and at every time.
[4] Before.
[5] Affection.

Her stubborn heart with inward deep effect,
Before his feet herself she did project;[1]
And, him adoring as her life's dear lord,
With all due thanks and dutiful respect,
Herself acknowledg'd bound for that accord[2]
By which he had to her both life and love restor'd.

"So all returning to the castle glad," were most joyfully entertained by Briana; who freely gave Sir Calidore that castle for his pain. But he would retain "nor land nor fee for hire of his good deed;" giving them to the squire and the lady whom he had lately freed from the seneschal; and, when his wounds were healed, "to his first quest[3] he passèd forth along."

CANTO II.

Calidore sees young Tristram slay
A proud discourteous knight:
He makes him squire, and of him learns
His state and present plight.

WHAT virtue is so fitting for a knight,
Or for a lady whom a knight should love,
As Courtesy; to bear themselves aright
To all of each degree as should behove?
For whether they be placèd high above
Or low beneath, yet ought they well to know
Their good;[4] that none them rightly may reprove
Of rudeness for not yielding what they owe:
Great skill it is such duties timely to bestow.

Thereto great help Dame Nature's self doth lend:
For some so goodly gracious are by kind,[5]
That ev'ry action doth them much commend,
And in the eyes of men great liking find;
Which others that have greater skill in mind,
Though they enforce themselves, cannot attain:
For ev'ry thing, to which one is inclin'd,
Doth best become and greatest grace doth gain:
Yet praise likewise deserve good thews enforc'd with pain.[6]

That well in courteous Calidore appeared, whose every act and deed was like enchantment, stealing away the heart through the eyes and the ears. Pursuing his quest, he spied a tall young man fighting on foot against a mounted knight; and beside them stood a lady fair in foul array. Before he could come up, Calidore saw, to his great wonder, the knight killed by the youth.

Him steadfastly he mark'd, and saw to be
A goodly youth of amiable grace,
Yet but a slender slip, that scarce did see
Yet sev'nteen years, but tall and fair of face,
That sure he deem'd him born of noble race:
All in a woodman's jacket he was clad
Of Lincoln green, belaid[7] with silver lace;
And on his head a hood with aiglets[8] sprad,[9]
And by his side his hunter's horn he hanging had.

Buskins he wore of costliest cordwain,[10]
Pink'd upon gold,[11] and palèd part per part,[12]
As then the guise[13] was for each gentle swain:
In his right hand he held a trembling dart,
Whose fellow he before had sent apart;
And in his left he held a sharp boar-spear,
With which he wont to lance the salvage heart
Of many a lion and of many a bear,
That first unto his hand in chase did happen near.

Calidore inquired of the "gentle swain," why, being no knight, he had embrued his too bold hand in the blood of a knight. The youth replied that, though loth to have broken the law of arms, he would break it again, rather than let himself be struck while he had two arms to avenge himself. Not he, but the dead knight, had given the first offence; for as he was ranging the forest in pursuit of game, he had met the knight, on horseback, while his lady "on her fair feet by his horse-side did pass through thick and thin, unfit for any dame;" and, if she lagged, her lord would thump her forward with his spear. Moved with indignation, the young huntsman said, he had blamed the knight for such cruelty to a lady, whom with kind usage he should rather have taken up behind. The knight had angrily threatened to chastise the remonstrant, "as doth t' a child pertain;" and, finding his scornful taunts flung back in his teeth, had struck the youth with his spear. The youth had responded by throwing, "not in vain," a slender dart, the fellow of the one he bore, which smote the knight underneath the heart, so that he soon died. Hearing the youth's tale,

Much did Sir Calidore admire his speech,
Temper'd so well; but more admir'd the stroke
That through the mails had made so strong a breach
Into his heart, and had so sternly wroke[14]
His wrath on him that first occasion broke:[15]
Yet rested not, but farther gan inquire
Of that same lady, whether what he spoke
Were soothly[16] so, and that th' unrighteous ire
Of her own knight had given him his own due hire.[17]

She could deny nothing, and cleared the stripling of the imputed blame; while Sir Calidore also released him from all censure, for what he had spoken, he had spoken to save her, what he had done, he had done to save himself; and against both the dead knight had wrought unknightly shame, "for knights and all men this by nature have, toward all womenkind

1 Throw. 2 Agreement.
3 Enterprise.
4 Their proper and seemly deportment.
5 Nature.
6 Good manners or qualities exercised with difficulty.
7 Adorned. 8 Aiguillettes, tags.
9 Covered. 10 Cordovan leather.
11 Worked with gold in small holes.
12 Intersected with "pales" or stripes.
13 Fashion. 14 Wreaked.
15 First provoked the quarrel.
16 Truly. 17 Retribution.

them kindly to behave." Calidore then asked the lady to tell what had caused the cruel conduct of her knight; and, though full loth "to raise a living blame against the dead," she complied. As they rode together, she said, they had found in a forest glade a lady and a knight "in joyous jolliment." Her own knight had coveted the other lady, and, finding his own dame an encumbrance, had bidden her alight; but when she showed reluctance to leave her love so suddenly, he had thrown her from his steed by force, and ridden hard against the other knight. He, though all disarmed, for gentle dalliance with his lady, had refused to quit his love, and demanded time to don his arms, that he might fight for her. But the dead knight, fierce and hot, had given him no time, but pierced him with his spear. Meanwhile the other lady had hidden herself in the grove; the triumphant aggressor had sought her in vain; and, forced at last to abandon the search and continue his journey with his own lady, he had, to gratify his rage, bestowed upon her the unknightly usage for which the young huntsman had taken vengeance. Calidore then pronounced that what had befallen the dead knight clearly befell him by his own fault:

Then turning back unto that gentle boy,
Which had himself so stoutly well acquit;
Seeing his face so lovely stern and coy,
And hearing th' answers of his pregnant wit,
He prais'd it much, and much admirëd it;
That sure he ween'd[1] him born of noble blood,
With whom those graces did so goodly fit:
And, when he long had him beholding stood,
He burst into these words, as to him seemëd good;

"Fair gentle swain, and yet as stout as fair,
That in these woods amongst the nymphs dost
won,[2]
Which daily may to thy sweet looks repair,
As they are wont unto Latona's son[3]
After his chase on woody Cynthus[4] done;
Well may I certes such an one thee read,[5]
As by thy worth thou worthily hast won,
Or surely born of some heroic seed,
That in thy face appears and gracious goodli-
head.[6]

"But, should it not displease thee it to tell
(Unless thou in these woods thyself conceal
For love amongst the woody gods to dwell),
I would thyself require thee to reveal;
For dear affection and unfeignëd zeal
Which to thy noble personage I bear,
And wish thee grow in worship[7] and great weal:
For, since the day that arms I first did rear,[8]
I never saw in any greater hope appear."

The youth replies that he is a Briton born, son of a king, though through fate or fortune he has lost his country and his crown.

"And Tristram is my name; the only heir
Of good king Meliogras, which did reign
In Cornwall till that he, through life's despair,
Untimely died, before I did attain
Ripe years of reason, my right to maintain:
After whose death his brother, seeing me
An infant, weak a kingdom to sustain,
Upon him took the royal high degree,
And sent me, where him list, instructed for
to be.

"The widow queen my mother, which that hight
Fair Emmeline, conceiving then great fear
Of my frail safety, resting in the might
Of him that did the kingly sceptre bear,
Whose jealous dread, enduring not a peer,
Is wont to cut off all that doubt may breed,
Thought best away me to remove somewhere
Into some foreign land, where as no need
Of dreaded danger might his doubtful[9] humour
feed.

"So, taking counsel of a wise man read,[10]
She was by him advis'd to send me quite
Out of the country wherein I was bred,
The which the fertile Lioness[11] is hight,
Into the Land of Faery, where no wight
Should weet[12] of me, nor work me any wrong:
To whose wise read[13] she heark'ning, sent me
straight
Into this land, where I have wonn'd[14] thus long
Since I was ten years old, now grown to stature
strong.

"All which my days I have not lewdly[15] spent,
Nor spilt[16] the blossom of my tender years
In idleness; but, as was cónveniént,
Have trainëd been with many noble feres[17]
In gentle thews and such like seemly leres:[18]
'Mongst which my most delight hath always been
To hunt the salvage chase, amongst my peers,[19]
Of all that rangeth in the forest green,
Of which none is to me unknown that e'er was
seen.

"Nor there is hawk which mantleth[20] her on
perch,
Whether high tow'ring or accosting[21] low,
But I the measure of her flight do search,
And all her prey and all her diet know:
Such be our joys which in these forests grow:
Only the use of arms, which most I joy,
And fitteth most for noble swain to know,
I have not tasted yet; yet past a boy,
And being now high time these strong joints to
employ."

Therefore Tristram entreats Calidore to make him a squire without delay, and give him the spoil of the dead knight, "these goodly gilden

1 Thought.
2 Dwell.
3 Apollo.
4 Mount Cynthus, in the island of Delos, where Apollo and Diana were born; hence these deities were respectively termed "Cynthius" and "Cynthia."
5 Declare, believe.
6 Comeliness.
7 Honour.
8 Assume.
9 Suspicious.
10 A man esteemed sage.
11 A country represented in the old British legends as once contiguous to Cornwall, and extending from the Land's End to the Scilly Isles, but long ago submerged.
12 Know.
13 Counsel.
14 Dwelt.
15 Viciously, unprofitably.
16 Wasted.
17 Companions.
18 Lessons, arts.
19 Fellows, equals.
20 Rests with outspread wings.
21 Stooping.

arms which I have won in fight." Sir Calidore, admiringly and joyfully, grants the request:

There him he caus'd to kneel, and made to swear
Faith to his knight, and truth to ladies all,
And never to be recreant for fear
Of peril, or of aught that might befall:
So he him dubbëd, and his squire did call.
Full glad and joyous then young Tristram grew;
Like as a flow'r, whose silken leavës small,
Long shut up in the bud from heaven's view,
At length breaks forth, and broad displays his smiling hue.

After long converse, Calidore "betook him to depart;" and Child Tristram prayed that he might attend him on his adventure. The Knight was greatly delighted by the request, but had to refuse it, since he had vowed to his dread Sovereign to pursue his enterprise alone. He entrusted, however, to the new-made squire the care of the desolate lady, which he joyfully accepted; "and Calidore forth passëd to his former pain."

But Tristram then, despoiling that dead knight
Of all those goodly implements of praise,
Long fed his greedy eyes with the fair sight
Of the bright metal shining like sun rays;
Handling and turning them a thousand ways:
And, after having them upon him dight,[1]
He took that lady, and her up did raise
Upon the steed of her own late dead knight:
So with her marchëd forth, as she did him behight.[2]

Before he had travelled many a mile, Calidore found the unarmed knight, who had been wounded by Tristram's discourteous adversary, weltering in his blood; and by him, lamenting, sat his woeful lady. The Knight, struck with sorrow, sought to comfort the lady, and drew from her the tale of her grief.

When Calidore this rueful story had
Well understood, he gan of her demand
What manner wight he was, and how y-clad,
Which had this outrage wrought with wicked hand.
She then, like as she best could understand,
Him thus describ'd, to be of stature large,
Clad all in gilden arms, with azure band
Quarter'd athwart, and bearing in his targe
A lady on rough waves row'd in a summer barge.

Calidore knew that it was the same knight whom Tristram had slain; bade the lady be glad that the worker of her lover's pain was fully punished; and besought her to cast aside her grief and think how her lover might be cured. Embarrassed as to the means by which he might be carried thence, she was set at ease by the proposal of the Knight, that each should bear a part of the burden.

So off he did his shield, and downward laid
Upon the ground, like to a hollow bier;
And pouring balm, which he had long purvey'd,
Into his wounds, him up thereon did rear,
And 'twixt them both with parted[3] pains did bear,
'Twixt life and death, not knowing what was done:
Thence they him carried to a castle near,
In which a worthy ancient knight did won:[4]
Where what ensued shall in next canto be begun.

CANTO III.

Calidore brings Priscilla home;
Pursues the Blatant Beast:
Saves Sérena, whilst Calepine
By Turpine is opprest.

True is, that whilom that good poet[5] said,
The gentle mind by gentle deeds is known:
For a man by nothing is so well bewray'd
As by his manners; in which plain is shown
Of what degree and what race he is grown:
For seldom seen a trotting stallion get
An ambling colt, that is his proper own:
So seldom seen that one in baseness[6] set
Doth noble courage show with courteous manners met.

But evermore the contrary has been experienced, "that gentle blood will gentle manners breed;" witness the courteous deed of Calidore, who bore the wounded knight on his back to the castle, the owner of which, Aldus, was the father of the luckless man. In his day he had been a brave knight; and now, though weak age had dimmed his candlelight, still he was courteous to every wight, "and lovëd all who did to arms incline." Great was his wailing over his "sorry boy," that brought such hope to his hoary hair, and turned his expected joy to such sad annoy.

"Such is the weakness of all mortal hope;
So tickle[7] is the state of earthly things;
That, ere they come unto their aimëd scope,
They fall too short of our frail reckonings,
And bring us bale and bitter sorrowings,
Instead of comfort which we should embrace:
This is the state of Kaisers and of Kings!
Let none, therefóre, that is in meaner place,
Too greatly grieve at any his unlucky case!"

The good old knight, however, suppressed his sorrow to entertain and cheer his guests; but the lady would be comforted by naught, sighing and sorrowing for her lover dear, and afflicting herself by the thought of the dishonour of her name.

For she was daughter to a noble lord

1 Girt, dressed. 2 Direct. 3 Divided. 4 Dwell.
5 Chaucer, in The Wife of Bath's Tale (page 81):—
"Look who that is most virtuous alway,
Prive and apert, and most intendeth ay
To do the gentle deedës that he can;
And take him for the greatest gentleman."
6 Low estate.
7 Fickle, unstable.

Which dwelt thereby, who sought her to affy[1]
To a great peer; but she did disaccord,[2]
Nor could her liking to his love apply,
But lov'd this fresh young knight who dwelt her
nigh,
The lusty Aladine, though meaner born
And of less livehood and hability,[3]
Yet full of valour, the which did adorn
His meanness[4] much, and make her th' other's
riches scorn.

So, having both found fit occasión,
They met together in that luckless glade;
Where that proud knight, in his presumptión,
The gentle Aladine did erst invade,[5]
Being unarm'd and set in secret shade.
Whereof she now bethinking, gan t' advise
How great a hazard she at erst had made
Of her good fame; and farther gan devise
How she the blame might salve with colourëd
disguise.

Calidore did his utmost to comfort her, and the old knight seconded his efforts; until time came for rest, and the wearied Knight, brought to his chamber, slept soundly all night. Far otherwise was it with the fair Priscilla (so the lady was called), who all night watched her wounded love, and washed his wounds so well in her tears, that at last she drove away the peril of death which hung over him. Then, with mutual tears, they consulted how the lady's hazarded good name might be preserved; "for which the only help now left them last seem'd to be Calidore; all other helps were past."

Him they did deem, as sure to them he seem'd,
A courteous knight, and full of faithful trust;[6]
Therefore to him their cause they best esteem'd
Whole to commit, and to his dealing just.
Early, so soon as Titan's beams forth brust[7]
Through the thick clouds, in which they steepëd
lay
All night in darkness, dull'd with iron rust,
Calidore, rising up as fresh as day,
Gan freshly him address unto his former way.

But first he visited the wounded knight, who seized the occasion to "break to him the fortunes of his love and all his disadventures to unfold." Calidore in the end pledged his honour as a knight to conduct the lady safe to her father's castle; and by and by he passed forth with her in fair array, "fearless who aught did think or aught did say, since his own thought he knew most clear from wite."[8] As they went on their way, he devised this stratagem, to give colour to the lady's story:

Straight to the carcase of that knight he went
(The cause of all this evil, who was slain
The day before, by just avengëment
Of noble Tristram), where it did remain;
There he the neck thereof did cut in twain,
And took with him the head, the sign of shame.
So forth he passëd thorough that day's pain,
Till to that lady's father's house he came;
Most pensive man, through fear what of his
child became.

There Calidore presented the lady to her father, "most perfect pure, and guiltless innocent of blame, as he did on his knighthood swear," since he had freed her from fear of a discourteous knight, who was bearing her away by force, and whose head he adduced in proof that the theft had been punished. The father overflowed with joy and thanks; and Calidore made a brief stay in the castle, after which he prosecuted his first adventure. Erelong he came upon a jolly knight resting unarmed in covert shade beside his lady: and after courteous apologies for the interruption of their quiet love's delight, the two knights sat down to relate to each other their adventures:

Of which whilst they discoursëd both together,
The fair Serena (so his[9] lady hight),
Allur'd with mildness of the gentle weather,
And pleasance of the place, the which was dight[10]
With divers flow'rs distinct with rare delight,
Wander'd about the fields, as liking led
Her wavering lust[11] after her wand'ring sight,
To make a garland to adorn her head,
Without suspect[12] of ill or danger's hidden dread.

All suddenly, out of the forest near,
The Blatant Beast, forth rushing unaware,
Caught her, thus loosely wand'ring here and
there,
And in his wide great mouth away her bare,
Crying aloud to show her sad misfare[13]
Unto the knights, and calling oft for aid;
Who, with the horror of her hapless care,[14]
Hastily starting up, like men dismay'd,
Ran after fast to rescue the distressëd maid.

The Beast, with their pursuit incited more,
Into the wood was bearing her apace
For to have spoilëd her;[15] when Calidore,
Who was more light of foot and swift in chase,
Him overtook in middest of his race;
And, fiercely charging him with all his might,
Forc'd to forego his prey there in the place,
And to betake himself to fearful flight;
For he durst not abide with Calidore to fight.

Who nathëless, when he the lady saw
There left on ground, though in full evil plight,
Yet knowing that her knight now near did draw,
Stay'd not to succour her in that affright,
But follow'd fast the monster in his flight:
Through woods and hills he follow'd him so fast,
That he n'ould[16] let him breathe nor gather
sprite,[17]
But forc'd him gape and gasp, with dread aghast,
As if his lungs and lights were nigh asunder
brast.[18]

Sir Calepine—so the stranger knight was called—came up by and by, to find Serena lying on

1 Affiance.
2 Dissent from the arrangement.
3 Smaller revenue and possession.
4 Humble estate.
5 A little while ago attack.
6 Trustworthiness.
7 Burst, broke.
8 Blame.
9 The stranger knight's.
10 Adorned.
11 Inclination.
12 Suspicion.
13 Misfortune.
14 Affliction.
15 Made a prey of her.
16 Would not.
17 Breath.
18 Burst.

the ground, all bloody and wounded from the monster's teeth. Lifting her in his arms, he restored her to consciousness, set her on his steed, and went on foot beside her in quest of some place of safety where she might remain till her wounds were healed. At nightfall he spied a pleasant place "down in a dale foreby a river's side;" but, making wearily thitherward in hope, he found the intervening river hardly passable on foot, and lingered a while in perplexity. Meantime an armed knight rode up, accompanied by a lady; and, as they were about to pass the ford, Calepine courteously besought the knight, "for safe conducting of his sickly dame," to take him up behind him on his steed. But the other, with rude revilings, bade Calepine,—"thou peasant knight,"—since he had lost his steed with shame, bear the lady on his back with pleasing pain, and prove his manhood on the billows vain. The lady of the rude knight reproved his speech, and would have taken Calepine on her own palfrey, but that, in his inward wrath, he refused the offer with thanks, and carelessly into the river went—through which, with one hand staying his lady up, with the other staying himself by the end of his spear, he safely won his way to the farther side. Meantime the churlish knight stood on the bank taunting him as he struggled with the flood; and no sooner had Calepine reached the safe shore, than he defied the "unknightly knight, the blemish of that name, and blot of all that arms upon them take," to combat on foot. But the dastard only laughed out the challenge, and, heedless of Calepine's fury, rode away to the castle, of which he was the lord. To the same place Calepine bent his steps, and at the gate mildly entreated lodging for his sick charge. But the prayer was churlishly refused; for the lord of the castle, Sir Turpine, was "terrible and stern in all assays to ev'ry errant knight, because of one that wrought him foul despite." Calepine marvelled why, if he was so valiant, he should be so stern to strangers; "for seldom yet did living creature see that courtesy and manhood ever disagree."

"But go thy ways to him, and from me say
That here is at his gate an errant knight,
That house-room craves; yet would be loth t' assay
The proof of battle now in doubtful night,
Or courtesy with rudeness to requite:
Yet, if he needs will fight, crave leave till morn,
And tell withal the lamentable plight
In which this lady languisheth forlorn,
That pity craves, as he of woman was y-born."

But Sir Turpine, "sitting with his lady then at board," rejected the challenge, and reviled the challenger and his love; heedless of the entreaties of his lady, named Blandina, that the strangers might at least be lodged for that night. Calepine had no alternative but to swallow his rage, and lay his lady "underneath a bush to sleep cover'd with cold, and wrapt in wretchedness;" while all night he wept and kept wary watch by her side.

The morrow next, so soon as joyous day
Did show itself in sunny beams bedight,[1]
Serena, full of dolorous dismay,
'Twixt darkness dread and hope of living light,
Uprear'd her head to see that cheerful sight.
Then Calepine, however inly wroth,
And greedy to avenge that vile despite,
Yet for the feeble lady's sake, full loth
To make there longer stay, forth on his journey go'th.

He go'th on foot all armëd by her side,
Upstaying still herself upon her steed,
Being unable else alone to ride;
So sore her sides, so much her wounds did bleed:
Till that at length, in his extremest need,
He chanc'd far off an armëd knight to spy
Pursuing him apace with greedy speed;
Whom well he wist[2] to be some enemy,
That meant to make advantage of his misery.

Calepine awaited his approach, and soon recognised the man who yesterday had abused and shamed him with such scornful pride; and he had but time to place himself on his guard, when Turpine ran fiercely against him, pursuing him from place to place, "with full intent him cruelly to kill." Calepine could only shelter himself behind his lady, who continually besought the assailant "to spare her knight, and rest with reason pacified." But Turpine, only the more enraged, now took Calepine at an advantage, and struck him through the shoulder with his spear. The knight's life was in the utmost jeopardy from his cowardly foe's pursuit, when he was rescued by a wondrous chance; "such chances oft exceed all human thought!"

CANTO IV.

Calepine by a Salvage Man
From Turpine rescued is;
And, whilst an Infant from a bear
He saves, his Love doth miss.

LIKE as a ship, with dreadful storm long tost,
Having spent all her masts and her ground-hold,[3]
Now far from harbour, likely to be lost,
At last some fisher-bark doth near behold,
That giveth comfort to her courage cold;
Such was the state of this most courteous Knight,
Being oppressëd by that faitour[4] bold,
That he remainëd in most perilous plight,
And his sad lady left in pitiful affright:

Till that, by fortune passing all foresight,
A Salvage Man, which in those woods did won,[5]
Drawn with that lady's loud and piteous shright,[6]

1 Bedecked. 2 Knew.
3 Ground-tackle; cables and anchors.
4 Traitor, malefactor. 5 Dwell.
6 Shrieking.

Towârd the same incessantly did run
To understand what there was to be done:
There he this most discourteous craven found
As fiercely yet, as when he first begun,
Chasing the gentle Calepine around,
Nor sparing him the more for all his grievous wound.

The Salvage Man, that never till this hour
Did taste of pity, neither gentless knew,
Seeing his sharp assault and cruel stowre,[1]
Was much emmovëd at his peril's view,
That ev'n his ruder heart began to rue,[2]
And feel compassion of his evil plight,
Against his foe that did him so pursue;
From whom he meant to free him, if he might,
And him avenge of that so villainous despite.

Yet arms or weapon had he none to fight,
Nor knew the use of warlike instruments,
Save such as sudden rage him lent to smite;
But naked, without needful vestiments
To clad his corpse with meet habiliments,
He carëd not for dint of sword nor spear,
No more than for the stroke of straws or bents:[3]
For from his mother's womb, which him did bear,
He was invulnerable made by magic lear.[4]

Staying not to think which way were best to assail his foe, the Wild Man rushed furiously against Turpine; who smote him on the breast with his spear, making him recoil, yet without drawing blood or inflicting wound. "Like to a tiger that hath miss'd his prey," the Wild Man flew again at Turpine with fresh rage, and fixed upon his shield a tenacious grip. After long struggle, the knight was forced to forsake both spear and shield, and flee for sheer terror, shrieking under the close pursuit of the savage. At last the pursuer saw his labour vain, and returned to Serena and Calepine; finding the knight bleeding sorely, and the lady "fearfully aghast," both by the sharpness of her rankling wound, and through fear of the Salvage Man, against whom she was now defenceless. Serena could only recommend herself "to God's sole grace, whom she did oft implore to send her succour, being of all hope forlore."

But the Wild Man, contrâry to her fear,
Came to her creeping like a fawning hound;
And by rude tokens made to her appear
His deep compassion of her doleful stound;[5]
Kissing his hands, and crouching to the ground;
For other language had he none, nor speech,
But a soft murmur and confusëd sound
Of senseless words (which Nature did him teach
T' express his passions) which his reason did empeach:[6]

And coming likewise to the wounded Knight,
When he beheld the streams of purple blood
Yet flwoing fresh, as movëd with the sight,
He made great moan after his salvage mood;
And, running straight into the thickest wood,
A certain herb from thence unto him brought,
Whose virtue he by use well understood;
The juice whereof into his wound he wrought,
And stopp'd the bleeding straight, ere he it stanchëd thought.

Then, taking up that recreant's shield and spear,
Which erst he left,[7] he signs unto them made
With him to wend unto his wonning[8] near;
To which he easily did them persuade.
Far in the forest, by a hollow glade
Cover'd with mossy shrubs, which, spreading broad,
Did underneath them make a gloomy shade,
Where foot of living creature never trod,
Nor scarce wild beasts durst come, there was this wight's abode.

Thither he brought these unacquainted guests;
To whom fair semblance,[9] as he could, he show'd
By signs, by looks, and all his other gests:[10]
But the bare ground, with hoary moss bestrow'd,
Must be their bed; their pillow was unsow'd;
And the fruits of the forest was their feast:
For their bad steward neither plough'd nor sow'd,
Nor fed on flesh, nor ever of wild beast
Did taste the blood, obeying Nature's first behest.[11]

Yet, howsoever base[12] and mean it were,
They took it well, and thankëd God for all,
Which had them freëd from that deadly fear,
And sav'd from being to that caitiff thrall.
Here they of force (as fortune now did fall)
Compellëd were themselves a while to rest,
Glad of that easement, though it were but small;
That, having there their wounds a while redrest,
They might the abler be to pass unto the rest.

During which time that Wild Man did apply
His best endeavour, and his daily pain,[13]
In seeking all the woods both far and nigh
For herbs to dress their wounds; still seeming fain[14]
When aught he did, that did their liking gain.
So as ere long he had that Knightë's wound
Recurëd well, and made him whole again:
But that same lady's hurt no herb he found
Which could redress, for it was inwardly unsound.

One day, when Calepine, now grown strong, had gone forth unarmed "to take the air and hear the thrush's song," he saw a cruel bear which bore an infant betwixt his blood-besprinkled jaws. The loud and shrill cries of the child, filling all the woods with piteous plaints, drew Calepine to pursue the beast—all the more nimbly, that he had left his armour behind, and felt like a hawk that is freed from bells and jesses;[15] so that "him seem'd his feet

1 Calamity. 2 Feel pity. 3 Dried-up grass.
4 Skill, lore. 5 Grief, calamity.
6 Obstruct, obscure.
7 Which he had lately abandoned. 8 Dwelling.

9 Demeanour. 10 Acts, gestures. 11 Commandment.
12 Lowly. 13 Labour. 14 Glad.
15 Straps, thongs, by which a hawk was attached to the wrist.

did fly, and in their speed delight." At last he overtook the weary bear, which dropped its prey, and turned upon him; gaping full wide "with greedy force and fury."

But the bold Knight, no whit thereat dismay'd,
But catching up in hand a ragged stone
Which lay thereby (so Fortune did him aid)
Upon him ran, and thrust it all at one[1]
Into his gaping throat, that made him groan
And gasp for breath, that he nigh chokëd was,
Being unable to digest that bone;
Nor could it upward come, nor downward pass,
Nor could he brook the coldness of the stony mass.

Whom when as he thus cumber'd did behold,
Striving in vain, that nigh his bowels brast,[2]
He with him clos'd, and, laying mighty hold
Upon his throat, did gripe his gorge so fast,
That wanting breath him down to ground he cast;
And, then oppressing him with urgent pain,
Ere long enforc'd to breathe his utmost blast,[3]
Gnashing his cruel teeth at him in vain,
And threat'ning his sharp claws, now wanting pow'r to strain.

Taking in his arms the little babe, the Knight found it unharmed by the teeth of the beast, and then sought, but in vain, the way back to the Wild Man's abode. All day he wandered about in idle search, "with weary travel and uncertain toil;" while the infant, "crying for food, him greatly did offend." But about sunset he got out of the forest, into the open champaign; and, while looking about for "some place of succour to content his mind," he heard the voice of a woman, complaining of fate and reviling fortune. Approaching, Calepine learned from the unfortunate lady, Matilda by name, that she was the wife of bold Sir Bruin, who had lately conquered all that land from the giant Cormorant, in three great battles—but who, now possessed of the land, was grievously afflicted by the fact that he was childless.

"But most my lord is grievëd herewithal,
And makes exceeding moan, when he does think
That all this land unto his foe shall fall,
For which he long in vain did sweat and swink,[4]
That now the same he greatly doth forthink.[5]
Yet was it said, '*There should to him a son*
Be gotten, not begotten; which should drink
And dry up all the water which doth run
In the next brook, by whom that fiend should be fordone.'[6]

"Well hop'd he then, when this was prophesied,
That from his sides some noble child should rise,
The which through fame should far be magnified,
And this proud giant should with brave emprise
Quite overthrow, who now gins to despise
The good Sir Bruin, growing far in years,
Who thinks from me his sorrow all doth rise.
Lo! this my cause of grief to you appears;
For which I thus do mourn, and pour forth ceaseless tears."

1 At once. 2 Burst. 3 His last breath.
4 Toil. 5 Regret, think sorrowfully upon.

Inly touched with pity for her unmerited grief, Calepine, after a little thought, began to "conceive a fit relief for all her pain." "If," he says—

"If that the cause of this your languishment
Be lack of children to supply your place,
Lo! how good fortune doth to you present
This little babe, of sweet and lovely face,
And spotless spirit, in which ye may enchase[7]
Whatever forms ye list thereto apply,
Being now soft and fit them to embrace;
Whether ye list him train in chivalry,
Or nursle up[8] in lore of learn'd philosophy.

"And, certes, it hath oftentimes been seen
That of the like, whose lineage was unknown,
More brave and noble knights have raisëd been
(As their victorious deeds have often shown,
Being with fame through many nations blown),
Than those which have been dandled in the lap.
Therefore some thought that those brave imps were sown
Here by the gods, and fed with heav'nly sap,
That made them grow so high t' all honourable hap."

"Hearkening to his senseful speech," the lady took the babe, and "having over it a little wept, she bore it thence, and ever as her own it kept." Calepine was not less glad to be rid of the youthful burden—which Matilda palmed off on the old knight as his own, and brought up so well in all goodly thews, that the babe "became a famous knight well known, and did right noble deeds; the which elsewhere are shown." Calepine, meantime, left alone "under the greenwood's side in sorry plight," weaponless, steedless, and houseless, threw himself on the cold ground, and tossed all night in anguish, vowing that he would never lie in bed or at ease, "till that his lady's side he did attain," or learn that she was in safety.

CANTO V.

The Salvage serves Serena well,
Till she Prince Arthur find:
Who her, together with his Squire,
With th' Hermit leaves behind.

O WHAT an easy thing is to descry
The gentle blood, however it be wrapt
In sad misfortune's foul deformity,
And wretched sorrows, which have often hapt!
For howsoever it may grow misshapt,
Like this Wild Man being undisciplin'd,
That to all virtue it may seem unapt;
Yet will it show some sparks of gentle mind,
And at the last break forth in its own proper kind.

That plainly may in this Wild Man be read,[9]
Who, though he were still in this desert wood,

6 Undone, ruined. 7 Engrave, imprint.
8 Train, educate. 9 Perceived.

'Mongst salvage beasts, both rudely born and bred,
Nor ever saw fair guise, nor learnëd good,
Yet show'd some token of his gentle blood
By gentle usage of that wretched dame:
For certes he was born of noble blood,
However by hard hap he hither came;
As ye may know, when time shall be to tell the same.

Waxing exceeding sorrowful and sad at the absence of Sir Calepine, the Wild Man went forth into the forest, and sought him far and near in vain. Then, returning to Serena, he expressed his sorrow "by speaking signs, as he could best them frame;" now wringing his hands, "now beating his hard head upon a stone." The lady understood his meaning, and threw herself on the ground in a passion of grief; regardless of her wounds, that still bled copiously. Seeing her so sorely distressed, the savage raised her up, and did his best to "stanch the bleeding of her dreary wound;" but she could not be comforted for the loss of her knight; and at last, abandoning hope of his return, she mounted his steed, and rode forth, "though feeble and forlorn." Her rude host, however, would not let her go alone; he awkwardly donned the arms which Calepine had left behind, and attended her on foot. "So forth they travell'd, an uneven pair;" the Salvage Man most carefully and faithfully serving the lady, "withouten thought of shame or villainy; nor ever showëd sign of foul disloyalty." One day, some of the furniture of her steed chanced to become disordered; and her groom, laying aside his cumbrous arms, applied himself to amend what was amiss. While he was busied thus, Prince Arthur and his squire Timias—who had met again by strange occasion—came riding thitherward. The poet suspends the story of Serena to tell us that, after Timias had regained the favour of Belphœbe (as related in canto viii., book iv.), he lived, "neither of envy nor of change afear'd," in her sovereign liking evermore; though many foes maligned him, "and with unjust detraction him did beard."

But, of them all which did his ruin seek,
Three mighty enemies did him most despite;
Three mighty ones, and cruel-minded eke,
That him not only sought by open might
To overthrow, but to supplant by sleight:
The first of them by name was call'd Despetto,[1]
Exceeding all the rest in pow'r and height;
The second, not so strong, but wise, Decetto;[2]
The third, nor strong nor wise, but spitefulest, Defetto.[3]

Ofttimes their sundry pow'rs they did employ,
And several deceits, but all in vain;
For neither they by force could him destroy,
Nor yet entrap in treason's subtile train:
Therefore, conspiring all together plain,
They did their counsels now in one compound:
Where single forces fail, conjoin'd may gain.
The Blatant Beast the fittest means they found
To work his utter shame, and throughly him confound.

Upon a day, as they the time did wait
When he did range the wood for salvage game,
They sent that Blatant Beast to be a bait
To draw him from his dear belovëd dame
Unwares into the danger of defame:[4]
For well they wist that squire to be so bold,
That no one beast in forest, wild or tame,
Met him in chase, but he it challenge wo'ld,
And pluck the prey ofttimes out of their greedy hold.

Timias, "seeing the ugly monster passing by," set upon him without fear, and forced him to fly—though not till the victor had been bitten by "his tooth impure." Leading his pursuer through thick woods and brakes and briars, to weary him and waste his breath, the Beast brought Timias at last to a woody glade, where his enemies awaited him. Assailed by all three at once, the wearied squire set his back to a tree, and warily warded off their heaped strokes.

Like a wild bull, that, being at a bay,
Is baited of a mastiff and a hound
And a cur-dog, that do him sharp assay
On ev'ry side, and beat about him round;
But most that cur, barking with bitter sound,
And creeping still behind, doth him encumber,
That in his chafe[5] he digs the trampled ground,
And threats his horns, and bellows like the thunder:
So did that squire his foes disperse and drive asunder.

Him well behovëd so; for his three foes
Sought to encompass him on ev'ry side,
And dang'rously did round about enclose:
But, most of all, Defetto him annoy'd,
Creeping behind him still to have destroy'd;
So did Decetto eke him circumvent;
But stout Despetto in his greater pride
Did front him, face to face against him bent:
Yet he them all withstood, and often made relent.

At last, however, worn out with his former chase and his present exertions, the squire began to shrink and give way a little; when in the nick of time the neighing of a horse sounded through the forest, and a knight, entering upon the scene, at once flew to the squire's rescue. The three assailants of Timias did not wait for the near approach of the stranger; and, holding it useless to pursue them, Prince Arthur—for it was he—joyfully recognised and embraced Timias, "his lief, his life's desire." After many affectionate greetings and gracious speeches, the Prince and the squire mounted

1 Malice, Despite; Italian, "dispetto."
2 Deceit.
3 Defamation; Italian, "difetto," defect, flaw, or lack; thus Chaucer makes Troilus praise and "lack" such ladies as he chose in the temple where he first saw Cressida (page 233)—that is, praise and disparage or speak slightingly of them.
4 Disgrace.
5 Angry passion.

their steeds, "and forth together rode, a comely couplement." Now, having arrived in sight of the Wild Man, busied about the sad Serena, "with those brave armours lying on the ground," they fancy that the "hilding hound"[1] has made a spoil of some worthy knight; Timias advances to take up the armour, but is sternly resisted by the savage.

Gnashing his grinded teeth with grisly look,
And sparkling fire out of his furious eyne,
Him with his fist unwares upon th' head he strook,[2]
That made him down unto the earth incline;
Whence soon upstarting, much he gan repine,
And, laying hand upon his wrathful blade,
Thought therewithal forthwith him to have slain;
Who it perceiving, hand upon him laid,
And, greedily him griping, his avengement stay'd.

Serena now interposes, calling on the Prince to separate the combatants; Arthur complies; then, answering the inquiries of the Prince, Serena relates her misfortunes, and the gentle behaviour of the Wild Man, for whom she entreats gentleness and forbearance "since he cannot express his simple mind, nor yours conceive, nor but by tokens speak." Her fair words assuage all heat, so "that they to pity turn'd their former rage;" and, having made all things right about Serena's horse, they proceed together in search of some place where the wounds inflicted on Serena and Timias by the Blatant Beast may be healed—for both the sufferers are now in extreme pain and weakness, and the lady's hurts begin to breed corruption. By the way, Serena narrates to Arthur "the foul discourtesies and unknightly parts" lately showed her by Turpine; and the Prince vows that, so soon as he returns, he will avenge the abuses of that proud and shameful knight. Towards evening, they came to a plain "by which a little hermitage there lay, far from all neighbourhood, the which annoy it may."

And nigh thereto a little chapel stood,
Which being all with ivy overspread,
Deck'd all the roof, and, shadowing the rood,[3]
Seem'd like a grove fair branchëd over head:
Therein the hermit, which his life here led
In strait observance of religious vow,
Was wont his hours and holy things to bed;[4]
And therein he likewise was praying now,
When as these knights arriv'd, they wist not where nor how.

They stay'd not there, but straightway in did pass:
Whom when the hermit present saw in place,
From his devotion straight he troubled was;
Which breaking off he toward them did pace
With stayëd steps and grave beseeming grace:
For well it seem'd that whilom he had been
Some goodly person, and of gentle race,
That coud his good[5] to all; and well did ween
How each to entertain with court'sy well beseen:[6]
And soothly it was said by common fame,
So long as age enabled him thereto,
That he had been a man of mickle name,
Renownëd much in arms and derring-do:[7]
But being agëd now, and weary too
Of war's delight and world's contentious toil,
The name of knighthood he did disavow;
And, hanging up his arms and warlike spoil,
From all this world's encumbrance did himself assoil.[8]

He thence them led into his hermitage,
Letting their steeds to graze upon the green;
Small was his house, and like a little cage,
For his own turn; yet inly neat and clean,
Deck'd with green boughs and flowers gay beseen;
Therein he them full fair did entertain,
Not with such forgëd shows, as fitter be'n
For courting fools that courtesies would feign,
But with entire affection and appearance plain.

Yet was their fare but homely, such as he
Did use his feeble body to sustain;
The which full gladly they did take in gree,
Such as it was, nor did of want complain;
But, being well suffic'd, them rested fain:[9]
But fair Serene all night could take no rest,
Nor yet that gentle squire, for grievous pain
Of their late wounds, the which the Blatant Beast
Had given them, whose grief through suff'rance[10] sore increast.

So all that night they pass'd in great disease,[11]
Till that the morning, bringing early light
To guide men's labours, brought them also ease,
And some assuagement of their painful plight.
Then up they rose, and gan themselves to dight[12]
Unto their journey; but that squire and dame
So faint and feeble were, that they ne might
Endure to travel, nor one foot to frame:
Their hearts were sick; their sides were sore; their feet were lame.

Therefore the Prince, urged to depart by "great affairs in mind," left them in the good hermit's care, and rode away, attended by the Wild Man; who, "seeing his royal usage and array, was greatly grown in love of that brave peer."

CANTO VI.

The Hermit heals both Squire and Dame
Of their sore maladies;
He[13] *Turpine doth defeat and shame*
For his late villainies.

No wound, which warlike hand of enemy
Inflicts with dint of sword, so sore doth light,

1 Base, paltry dog. 2 Struck.
3 Cross. 4 To bid; to pray.
5 Knew his proper deportment.
6 Becoming. 7 Daring deeds.
8 Absolve, free. 9 Gladly.
10 Endurance, neglect. 11 Discomfort, pain.
12 Prepare.
13 Prince Arthur.

As doth the poisonous sting which infamy
Infixeth in the name of noble wight:
For by no art, nor any leach's might,
It ever can recurëd be again;
Nor all the skill, which that immortal sprite
Of Podairius[1] did in it retain,
Can remedy such hurts; such hurts are hellish pain.

Such were the wounds the which that Blatant Beast
Made in the bodies of that squire and dame;
And, being such, were now much more increast
For want of taking heed unto the same,
That now corrupt and cureless[2] they became:
Howbe that careful hermit did his best,
With many kinds of medicines meet, to tame
The pois'nous humour which did most infest
Their rankling wounds, and ev'ry day them duly drest.

For he right well in leach's craft was seen;[3]
And, through the long experience of his days,
Which had in many fortunes tossëd been,
And pass'd through many perilous assays,
He knew the diverse went[4] of mortal ways,
And in the minds of men had great insight;
Which with sage counsel, when they went astray,
He could inform, and them reduce aright;
And all the passions heal, which wound the weaker sprite.

For whilom he had been a doughty knight,
As any one that livëd in his days,
And provëd oft in many a perilous fight,
In which he grace and glory won always,
And in all battles bore away the bays:
But, being now attack'd with timely age,
And weary of this world's unquiet ways,
He took himself unto this hermitage,
In which he liv'd alone, like careless bird in cage.

One day, as he was searching of their wounds,
He found that they had fester'd privily;
And, rankling inward with unruly stounds,[5]
The inner parts now gan to putrefy,
That quite they seem'd past help of surgery;
And rather needed to be disciplin'd
With wholesome read[6] of sad sobriety,
To rule the stubborn rage of passion blind:
Give salves to every sore, but counsel to the mind.

So, taking them apart into his cell,
He to that point fit speeches gan to frame,
As he the art of words knew wondrous well,
And eke could do as well as say the same:
And thus he to them said; "Fair Daughter Dame,
And you, fair Son, which here thus long now lie
In piteous languor since ye hither came,
In vain of me ye hope for remedy,
And I likewise in vain do salves to you apply:

"For in yourself your only help doth lie
To heal yourselves, and must proceed alone
From your own will to cure your malady.
Who can him cure that will be cur'd of none?
If therefore health ye seek, observe this one:
First learn your outward senses to refrain
From things that stir up frail affectión;[7]
Your eyes, your ears, your tongue, your talk restrain
From that they most affect, and in due terms contain.

"For from those outward senses, ill affected,
The seed of all this evil first doth spring,
Which at the first, before it had infected,
Might easy be suppress'd with little thing:
But, being growen strong, it forth doth bring
Sorrow, and anguish, and impatient pain
In th' inner parts; and lastly, scattering
Contagious poison close[8] through ev'ry vein,
It never rests till it have wrought his final bane.

"For that Beast's teeth, which wounded you tofore,[9]
Are so exceeding venomous and keen,
Made all of rusty iron rankling sore,
That, where they bite, it booteth not to ween
With salve, or antidote, or other mean,
It ever to amend: nor marvel aught;
For that same beast was bred of hellish strene,[10]
And long in darksome Stygian den upbrought,
Begot of foul Echidna, as in books is taught.

"Echidna is a monster, direful dread,
Whom gods do hate, and heav'ns abhor to see;
So hideous is her shape, so huge her head,
That ev'n the hellish fiends affrighted be
At sight thereof, and from her presence flee:
Yet did her face and former[11] parts profess[12]
A fair young maiden, full of comely glee;
But all her hinder parts did plain express
A monstrous dragon, full of fearful ugliness.

"To her the gods, for her so dreadful face,
In fearful darkness, farthest from the sky
And from the earth, appointed have her place
'Mongst rocks and caves, where she enroll'd doth lie
In hideous horror and obscurity,
Wasting the strength of her immortal age:
There did Typhaon[13] with her company;
Cruel Typhaon, whose tempestuous rage
Makes th' heavens tremble oft, and him with vows assuage.

"Of that commixtion they did then beget
This hellish dog, that hight the Blatant Beast;
A wicked monster, that his tongue doth whet
'Gainst all, both good and bad, both most[14] and least,
And pours his poisonous gall forth to infest
The noblest wights with notable defame:
Nor ever knight that bore so lofty crest,

1 The son of Æsculapius; who, with his brother Machaon, inherited his father's skill in the healing art.
2 Difficult of cure.
3 Skilled.
4 Course, tendency.
5 Pangs.
6 Counsel.
7 Passion.
8 Secretly.
9 Before.
10 Strain, stock.
11 Front, foremost.
12 Present the appearance of; declare.
13 Typhoeus, a huge giant, son of Titan and Terra, who fought against the gods, but was struck down by Jove's thunderbolt, and buried under Mount Etna. Sometimes—as in the text—his name is confounded with that of Typhon, a giant produced from the earth by a blow of Juno's hand.
14 Greatest.

Nor ever lady of so honest name,
But he them spotted with reproach or secret shame.

"In vain therefore it were with medicine
To go about to salve such kind of sore,
That rather needs wise read[1] and discipline
Than outward salves that may augment it more."
"Aye me!" said then Serena, sighing sore,
"What hope of help doth then for us remain,
If that no salves may us to health restore!"
"But since we need good counsel," said the swain,
"Aread,[2] good Sire, some counsel that may us sustain."

"The best," said he, "that I can you advise,
Is to avoid th' occasion of the ill:
For when the cause, whence evil doth arise,
Removëd is, th' effect surceaseth still.
Abstain from pleasure, and restrain your will;
Subdue desire, and bridle loose delight;
Use scanted diet, and forbear your fill;
Shun secrecy, and talk in open sight:
So shall you soon repair your present evil plight."

Following these wise counsels, Timias and Serena were soon entirely healed; and, taking leave of the hermit, they went on their way together—the lady fearing to go alone, the squire too courteous to leave her. As they travelled, they met a fair maiden clad in mourning, "upon a mangy jade unmeetly set, and a lewd fool her leading thorough dry and wet." But the poet leaves to another time the explanation of her sorry plight, and follows Prince Arthur and the Wild Man to the castle of the discourteous Turpine.

Arriving there, as did by chance befall,
He found the gate wide ope, and in he rode,
Nor stay'd till that he came into the hall;
Where soft dismounting, like a weary load,
Upon the ground with feeble feet he trod,
As he unable were for very need
To move one foot, but there must make abode;
The while the Salvage Man did take his steed,
And in some stable near did set him up to feed.

Ere long to him a homely groom there came,
That in rude wise him askëd what he was,
That durst so boldly, without let[3] or shame,
Into his lord's forbidden hall to pass:
To whom the Prince, him feigning to embase,[4]
Mild answer made, he was an errant knight,
The which was fall'n into this feeble case
Through many wounds, which lately he in fight
Receivëd had, and pray'd to pity his ill plight.

But the porter, waxing the more outrageous and bold, sternly bade him begone, and laid rude hand on him, to thrust him out of doors. Beholding this, the Salvage Man, who had now entered, grew enraged, and "like a fell lion" fiercely flew at the churlish porter, whom he tore all to pieces with teeth and nails. Summoned by the hapless wretch's cries, the people of the house rushed to the spot, and fell furiously on Arthur and his companion; but the Prince mightily resisted their attack, killed many of them, and drove the few survivors to flight. Learning from these what had happened, Turpine came forth in haste, and, seeing the havoc wrought among his people, taunted Arthur with treason vile for slaying his men in that unmanly manner. Then he and his forty attendant yeomen addressed themselves together to battle against the Prince, with boisterous strokes "that on his shield did rattle like to hail in a great tempest;" while the craven coward Turpine waited at his back for a chance of slaying him unawares. Turning upon the coward—like a fierce bull, beset by many foes, that turns felly upon some cur biting his heels—the Prince, with heavy strokes, drove him through the press, and chased him from room to room, to the chamber of Blandina, every joint quaking for fear. Arthur now felled the base knight to the ground with a blow of his sword; but the lady, covering him with her garment, besought mercy, which Arthur granted. Even yet, however, Turpine "did lie as dead, and quake and quiver;" and his lady's aid was required before he was raised to his feet. Then the Prince bitterly rebuked him for knightless cowardice, which aggravated the shame of the wicked custom that he had enforced against errant knights and ladies—whom, when he could, he was wont to spoil of their arms or their upper garments. But since he had promised his life to his lady, the Prince bade him "live in reproach and scorn;" taking away, however, the goodly arms which he had disgraced. Then, bethinking him of the Salvage Man, Arthur descended to the hall, and found his attendant, environed with dead bodies, laying about vehemently on the survivors, who fled like scattered sheep. At the Prince's signal, the Wild Man stopped his murderous play; and, "all things well in peace ordained," Arthur rested there that night, courteously entertained by Blandina, who was well acquainted with the art of winning the good will of others "through tempering of her words and looks by wondrous skill."

Yet were her words and looks but false and feign'd,
To some hid end to make more easy way,
Or to allure such fondlings,[5] whom she train'd[6]
Into her trap, unto their own decay:
Thereto,[7] when needed, she could weep and pray,
And when her listed she could fawn and flatter;
Now smiling smoothly like to summer's day,
Now glooming sadly, so to cloak her matter;
Yet were her words but wind, and all her tears but water.

Whether such grace were given her by kind,[8]
As women wont their guileful wits to guide;

[1] Advice.
[2] Declare, unfold.
[3] Delay, hesitation.
[4] Humble himself.
[5] Fools.
[6] Allured.
[7] Moreover.
[8] Nature.

Or learn'd the art to please, I do not find:
This well I wot, that she so well applied
Her pleasing tongue, that soon she pacified
The wrathful Prince, and wrought her husband's peace:
Who nathëless, not therewith satisfied,
His rancorous despite did not release,
Nor secretly from thought of fell revenge surcease.

All night, while the Prince rested unsuspectingly, Turpine watched with weapons ready to kill him; but for very cowardice he let the night pass without acting; and early in the morning the Prince "pass'd forth to follow his first enterprise."

CANTO VII.

Turpine is baffled; his two knights
Do gain their treason's meed.
Fair Mirabella's punishment
For Love's disdain decreed.

The first half of this canto is devoted to a recital of Turpine's devices to wreak, by proxy, vengeance on Prince Arthur; and of his failure and punishment. Following the Prince at safe distance, Turpine met two young knights, whom he incited to attack his chastiser, by stories of great discourtesy suffered at his hands, and offers of rich reward. The credulous knights pursued and attacked Arthur, who speedily killed one outright, and compelled the other to offer to reveal the treason if his life were saved. The victor held his hand, listened to the tale of Turpine's treachery, and made the knight swear to bring back the wretch that had hired him to do the wicked deed. Returning to Turpine, the baffled youth assured him that his enemy was dead, and led him to the place where the Prince lay alone and slumbering. Turpine vainly sought to tempt his companion to slay Arthur in his sleep; and the opportune arrival of the Wild Man, who had gone to gather fruit, awakened the Prince and saved him from farther peril. Turpine speedily found his adversary's foot set on his neck, in token of thraldom; and Arthur finally hanged him by the heels upon a tree, for greater infamy, and left him to the scorn of all that passed that way. Then the poet returns to the story of that lady "whom late we left riding upon an ass, led by a carl and fool[1] which by her side did pass."

She was a lady of great dignity,[2]
And lifted up to honourable place,
Famous through all the Land of Faëry:
Though of mean parentage and kindred base,
Yet deck'd with wondrous gifts of Nature's grace,
That all men did her person much admire,
And praise the feature of her goodly face;
The beams whereof did kindle lovely fire[3]
In th' hearts of many a knight, and many a gentle squire:

But she thereof grew proud and insolent,
That none she worthy thought to be her fere,[4]
But scorn'd them all that love unto her meant;
Yet was she lov'd of many a worthy peer:
Unworthy she to be belov'd so dear,
That could not weigh[5] of worthiness aright:
For beauty is more glorious bright and clear,
The more it is admir'd of many a wight,
And noblest she that servëd is of noblest knight.

But this coy damsel thought, contráriwise,
That such proud looks would make her praisëd more;
And that, the more she did all love despise,
The more would wretched lovers her adore.
What carëd she who sighëd for her sore,
Or who did wail or watch the weary night?
Let them that list their luckless lot deplore;
She was born free, not bound to any wight,
And so would ever live, and love her own delight.

Through such her stubborn stiffness and hard heart,
Many a wretch for want of remedý
Did languish long in life-consuming smart,
And at the last through dreary dolour die:
Whilst she, the lady of her libertý,
Did boast her beauty had such sov'reign might,
That with the only twinkle of her eye
She could or save or spill[6] whom she would hight:[7]
What could the gods do more, but do it more aright?

But lo! the gods, that mortal follies view,
Did worthily revenge this maiden's pride;
And, naught regarding her so goodly hue,
Did laugh at her that many did deride,
Whilst she did weep, of no man mercified:[8]
For on a day, when Cupid kept his court,
As he is wont at each Saint Valentide,
Unto the which all lovers do resort,
That of their love's success they there may make report;

It fortun'd then, that, when the rolls were read
In which the names of all Love's folk were fil'd,[9]
That many there were missing; which were dead,
Or kept in bands, or from their loves exil'd,
Or by some other violence despoil'd.
Which when as Cupid heard, he waxëd wroth;
And, doubting to be[10] wrongëd or beguil'd,
He bade his eyes to be unblindfold both,
That he might see his men, and muster them by oath.

[1] Only the fool, and not the carl, is mentioned at the lady's first introduction to us in the preceding canto.

[2] This lady, Mirabella, is supposed to represent that "Rosalind"—"the widow's daughter of the glen," as Spenser had called her in "The Shepherd's Calendar"—whom the poet loved and courted, and whose rejection of his suit rankled long in his mind.

[3] The fire of love.

[4] Companion, consort.

[5] Estimate.

[6] Destroy.

[7] Name, choose.

[8] Pitied.

[9] Registered.

[10] Suspecting that he was.

Then found he many missing of his crew,
Which wont do suit and service to his might;
Of whom what was becomen no man knew.
Therefore a jury was empanell'd straight,
T' enquire of them, whether by force, or sleight,
Or their own guilt, they were away convey'd:
To whom foul Infamy and fell Despite
Gave evidence, that they were all betray'd
And murder'd cruelly by a rebellious maid.

Fair Mirabella was her name, whereby
Of all those crimes she there indicted was:
All which when Cupid heard, he by and by
In great displeasure will'd a capias[1]
Should issue forth t' attach that scornful lass.
The warrant straight was made, and therewithal
A bailiff errant forth in post did pass,
Whom they by name there Portamour[2] did call;
He which doth summon lovers to Love's Judgment Hall.

The damsel was attach'd,[3] and shortly brought
Unto the bar, where as she was arraign'd:
But she thereto n'ould[4] plead, nor answer aught,
Even for stubborn pride, which her restrain'd:
So judgment pass'd, as is by law ordain'd
In cases like: which when at last she saw,
Her stubborn heart, which love before disdain'd,
Gan stoop; and, falling down with humble awe,
Cried mercy, to abate th' extremity of law.

The son of Venus, who is mild by kind,[5]
But[6] where he is provok'd with peevishness,
Unto her prayers piteously inclin'd,
And did the rigour of his doom repress;
Yet not so freely, but that nathëless
He unto her a penance did impose,
Which was, that through this world's wide wilderness
She wander should in company of those,[7]
Till she had sav'd so many loves as she did lose.

So now she had been wand'ring two whole years
Throughout the world, in this uncomely case,
Wasting her goodly hue in heavy tears,
And her good days in dolorous disgrace;
Yet had she not, in all these two years' space,
Savëd but two; yet in two years before,
Through her dispiteous pride, whilst love lack'd place,
She had destroyëd two and twenty more.
Ah me, how could her love make half amends therefor!

And now she was upon the weary way,
When as the gentle squire, with fair Serene,
Met her in such misseeming[8] foul array;
The while that mighty man did her demean[9]
With all the evil terms and cruel mean[10]
That he could make; and eke that angry fool
Which follow'd her, with cursëd hands unclean
Whipping her horse, did with his smarting tool[11]
Oft whip her dainty self, and much augment her dool.[12]

Nor aught it might avail her to entreat
The one or th' other better her to use;
For both so wilful were and obstinate,
That all her piteous plaint they did refuse,
And rather did the more her beat and bruise:
But most the former villain, which did lead
Her tireling jade,[13] was bent her to abuse;
Who, though she were with weariness nigh dead,
Yet would not let her light, nor rest a little stead:[14]

For he was stern and terrible by nature,
And eke of person huge and hideous,
Exceeding much the measure of man's stature,
And rather like a giant monstruous:
For sooth he was descended of the house
Of those old giants which did wars darrain[15]
Against the Heav'n in order battailous;
And sib[16] to great Orgoglio, which was slain
By Arthur, when as Una's knight he did maintain.[17]

His looks were dreadful, and his fiery eyes,
Like two great beacons, glarëd bright and wide,
Glancing askew,[18] as if his enemies
He scornëd in his overweening pride;
And stalking stately, like a crane, did stride
At ev'ry step upon the tiptoes high;
And, all the way he went, on ev'ry side
He gaz'd about and starëd horribly,
As if he with his looks would all men terrify.

He wore no armour, nor for none did care,
As no whit dreading any living wight;
But in a jacket, quilted richly rare
Upon checklaton,[19] he was strangely dight;[20]
And on his head a roll of linen plight,[21]
Like to the Moors of Malabar, he wore,
With which his locks, as black as pitchy night,
Were bound about and voided[22] from before;
And in his hand a mighty iron club he bore.

This was Disdain, who led that lady's horse
Through thick and thin, through mountains and through plains;
Compelling her, where she would not, by force,
Hauling her palfrey by the hempen reins:
But that same fool, which most increas'd her pains,
Was Scorn; who, having in his hand a whip,
Her therewith yerks;[23] and still, when she complains,

1 Writ of arrest.
2 Carrier or Messenger of Love.
3 Arrested.
4 Would not.
5 Nature.
6 Except.
7 Her two companions, afterwards described—Disdain and Scorn.
8 Unseemly.
9 Abase, degrade.
10 Means.
11 Weapon, implement (his whip).
12 Sorrow.
13 Her weary beast.
14 While.
15 Wage.
16 Related.
17 When he kept Una's Knight a prisoner. See canto viii., book i., page 343.
18 Askance, sideways.
19 Cloth of silk and gold. See note 5, page 147.
20 Arrayed.
21 Folded.
22 Removed.
23 Lashes sharply.

The more he laughs, and does her closely quip,[1]
To see her sore lament and bite her tender lip.

Whose cruel handling when that squire beheld,
And saw those villains her so vilely use,
His gentle heart with indignation swell'd,
And could no longer bear so great abuse
As such a lady so to beat and bruise;
But, to him stepping, such a stroke him lent,
That forc'd him th' halter from his hand to loose,
And, maugré[2] all his might, back to relent:[3]
Else had he surely there been slain, or foully shent.[4]

The villain, wroth for greeting him so sore,
Gather'd himself together soon again,
And with his iron baton, which he bore,
Let drive at him so dreadfully amain,
That for his safety he did him constrain
To give him ground, and shift to ev'ry side,
Rather than once his burden[5] to sustain:
For bootless thing him seemëd to abide
So mighty blows, or prove the puissance of his pride.

Like as a mastiff having at a bay
A savage bull, whose cruel horns do threat
Desperate danger, if he them assay,
Traceth[6] his ground, and round about doth beat,
To spy where he may some advantage get,
The while the beast doth rage and loudly roar;
So did the squire, the while the carle did fret
And fume in his disdainful mind the more,
And oftentimes by Termagant[7] and Mahound[8] swore.

Nathless so sharply still he him pursued,
That at advantage him at last he took,
When his foot slipp'd (that slip he dearly rued),
And with his iron club to ground him strook;[9]
Where still he lay, nor out of swoon awook,[10]
Till heavy hand the carl upon him laid,
And bound him fast; then when he up did look
And saw himself captív'd, he was dismay'd,
Nor pow'r had to withstand, nor hope of any aid.

Then up he made him rise, and forward fare,
Led in a rope which both his hands did bind;
Nor aught that fool for pity did him spare,
But with his whip him following behind
Him often scourg'd, and forc'd his feet to find:
And otherwhiles with bitter mocks and mows[11]
He would him scorn, that to his gentle mind
Was much more grievous than the other's blows:
Words sharply wound, but greatest grief of scorning grows.

Serena, seeing Timias fall under the club of Disdain, thought him slain, and fled away with all the speed she might—to encounter many perils, before she rejoined Sir Calepine.

1 Jeer.
2 In spite of.
3 Retire.
4 Maltreated, disgraced.
5 The weight of his club.
6 Traverseth.

CANTO VIII.

Prince Arthur overcomes Disdain:
Quits Mirabell from Dread:
Serena, found of savages,
By Calepine is freed.

YE gentle Ladies, in whose sov'reign power
Love hath the glory of his kingdom left,
And th' hearts of men, as your eternal dow'r,
In iron chains, of liberty bereft,
Deliver'd hath unto your hands by gift;
Be well aware how ye the same do use,
That pride do not to tyranny you lift;
Lest, if men you of cruelty accuse,
He from you take that chiefdom which ye do abuse.

And as ye soft and tender are by kind,[12]
Adorn'd with goodly gifts of beauty's grace,
So be ye soft and tender eke in mind;
But cruelty and hardness from you chase,
That all your other praises will deface,
And from you turn the love of men to hate:
Ensample take of Mirabella's case,
Who from the high degree of happy state
Fell into wretched woes, which she repented late.

Mirabella, "touchëd with compassion entire," much lamented the calamity into which the gentle squire had fallen for her sake; but her entreaties on his behalf only made the captors the more cruel. Passing on their way, they met Prince Arthur, with Sir Enias (for such was the name of the knight who had exposed to him the treachery of Turpine), and augmented their cruelty, as if to grieve the new comers. Timias, seeing his lord the witness of his disgrace—"ashamed that with a hempen cord he like a dog was led in captive case," hung down his head. Sir Enias besought leave of the Prince to deliver the two captives; then, receiving his companion's assent, he dismounted, and challenged the captors to free their victims from their loathly hands. Disdain replied only by a swift and terrible blow of his club, which would have been fatal, if Enias had not lightly slipped aside; and he requited the carl by a cruel stroke with his sword. But, as the knight's arm was raised for a second blow, Disdain met the sword in mid-air with his club, shivered it to pieces, hurled Enias to the ground, and set his foot on his neck with fell disdain. Scorn now came running in, and held the knight down, while Disdain proceeded to bind and thrall him.

As when a sturdy ploughman with his hind
By strength have overthrown a stubborn steer,
They down him hold, and fast with cords do bind,
Till they him force the buxom yoke to bear:
So did these two this knight oft tug and tear.

7 A Saracenic deity. See note 26, page 147.
8 Mahomet.
9 Struck.
10 Awoke.
11 Insulting grimaces.
12 Nature.

Which when the Prince beheld, there standing by,
He left his lofty steed to aid him near;
And, buckling soon himself, gan fiercely fly
Upon that carl, to save his friend from jeopardy.

Leaving Timias to the tender mercies of his mate, Disdain vehemently attacked the Prince, who yielded for a while to the blows of his club; at last, when the caitiff had put forth all his strength in what he meant to be a mortal blow, Arthur anticipated him, "under his club with wary boldness went, and smote him on the knee, that never yet was bent."

It never yet was bent, nor bent it now,
All be the stroke so strong and puissant were,
That seem'd a marble pillar it could bow;
But all that leg, which did his body bear,
It crack'd throughout (yet did no blood appear),
So as it was unable to support
So huge a burden on such broken gear,
But fell to ground like to a lump of dirt;
Whence he essay'd to rise, but could not for his hurt.

The Prince nimbly stepped to him, meaning to strike the head from his shoulders; but the lady interposed to save his life—since by his death her life would have lamentable end. Staying his hand, Arthur inquired the meaning of those strange words from the lips of one whom, in default of men, the very heavens would rescue and redress.

Then bursting forth in tears, which gushëd fast
Like many water-streams, a while she stay'd,
Till, the sharp passion being overpast,
Her tongue to her restor'd, then thus she said;
"Nor heav'ns, nor men, can me, most wretched maid,
Deliver from the doom of my desart,[1]
The which the god of Love hath on me laid,
And damnëd to endure this direful smart,
For penance of my proud and hard rebellious heart.

"In prime of youthly years, when first the flow'r
Of beauty gan to bud, and bloom delight,
And Nature me endued with plenteous dow'r
Of all her gifts, that pleas'd each living sight;
I was belov'd of many a gentle knight,
And sued and sought with all the service due:
Full many a one for me deep groan'd and sight,[2]
And to the door of death for sorrow drew,
Complaining *out on me* that would not on them rue.[3]

"But let them love that list, or live or die,
Me list not die for any lover's dool:[4]
Nor list me leave my lovëd liberty
To pity him that list to play the fool:
To love myself I learnëd had in school.
Thus I triúmphëd long in lovers' pain,
And, sitting careless on the scorner's stool,
Did laugh at those that did lament and plain:
But all is now repaid with interest again.

"For lo! the wingëd god, that woundeth hearts,
Caus'd me be callëd to account therefor;
And, for revengement of those wrongful smarts,
Which I to others did inflict before,
Addeem'd[5] me to endure this penance sore;
That in this wise, and this unmeet array,
With these two lewd[6] companions, and no more,
Disdain and Scorn, I through the world should stray,
Till I have sav'd so many as I erst[7] did slay."

"Certes," said then the Prince, "the god is just,
That taketh vengeance of his people's spoil:[8]
For were no law in love, but all that lust[9]
Might them oppress, and painfully turmoil,
His kingdom would continue but a while.
But tell me, Lady, wherefore do you bear
This bottle thus before you with such toil,
And eke this wallet at your back arrear,[10]
That for these carls to carry much more comely were?"

"Here in this bottle," said the sorry maid,
"I put the tears of my contritión,
Till to the brim I have it full defray'd:[11]
And in this bag, which I behind me don,
I put repentance for things past and gone.
Yet is the bottle leak,[12] and bag so torn,
That all which I put in falls out anon,
And is behind me trodden down of Scorn,
Who mocketh all my pain, and laughs the more I mourn."

Much wondering at Cupid's wise judgments, that could so subject proud hearts, the Prince suffered Disdain to arise; which he did with difficulty, by the aid of Scorn.

But, being up, he look'd again aloft,
As if he never had receivëd fall;
And with stern eye-brows starëd at him[13] oft,
As if he would have daunted him withal:
And standing on his tiptoes, to seem tall,
Down on his golden feet he often gaz'd,
As if such pride the other could appal;
Who was so far from being aught amaz'd,
That he his looks despisëd, and his boast disprais'd.[14]

Turning back to unbind the captive squire, who all the while sought to shun observation, the Prince was amazed and delighted to discover his own true groom, Timias; but the embraces of the pair were interrupted by the cry of Mirabella, entreating the Prince to stay the Wild Man's vehement assault upon Scorn, whom he was scourging to death with his own whip. The Prince put an end to the savage's assault, and offered Mirabella her choice between being set free from her attendants, and being left as she was; but she said she must by all means fulfil

1 Desert, offence.
2 Sighed.
3 Have pity.
4 Grief.
5 Adjudged.
6 Base.
7 Before.
8 For the destruction of his servants.
9 Pleased.
10 Behind.
11 Filled, completed.
12 Leaky.
13 Prince Arthur.
14 Disparaged.

Love's penance, and prosecuted her journey with her former companions; while the Prince went on his way with Enias and the Wild Man. The poet now returns to Serena, whom he left flying in fear, after Timias, her protector, had been beaten down and bound by Disdain. "Through hills and dales, through bushes and through briars," she fled long, till she thought herself beyond peril; then, alighting and sitting down on the plain, she blamed Sir Calepine as the author of all her sorrow—although never was turtle truer to his mate, than he to his lady bright, for whose sake he endured great peril and took restless pains. By and by she laid herself to sleep on the grass; and while she lay securely in Morpheus' bosom, "false Fortune did her safëty betray unto a strange mischance, that menac'd her decay."

In these wild deserts, where she now abode,
There dwelt a salvage nation, which did live
Of stealth and spoil, and making nightly road[1]
Into their neighbours' borders; nor did give
Themselves to any trade (as for to drive
The painful plough, or cattle for to breed,
Or by adventurous merchandise to thrive),
But on the labours of poor men to feed,
And serve their own necessities with others' need.

"Thereto[2] they us'd one most accursëd order;[3]
To eat the flesh of men, whom they might find,
And strangers to devour which on their border
Were brought by error or by wreckful wind:
A monstrous cruelty 'gainst course of kind![4]
They, towards ev'ning, wand'ring ev'ry way
To seek for booty, came by fortune blind
Where as this lady, like a sheep astray,
Now drownëd in the depth of sleep all fearless lay.

Soon as they spied her, Lord! what gladful glee
They made amongst themselves! but when her face
Like the fair ivory shining they did see,
Each gan his fellow solace and embrace,
For joy of such good hap by heav'nly grace.
Then gan they to devise what course to take;
Whether to slay her there upon the place,
Or suffer her out of her sleep to wake,
And then her eat at once, or many meals to make.

The best advisement[5] was, of bad, to let her
Sleep out her fill without encumberment;[6]
For sleep, they said, would make her battel[7] better:
Then, when she wak'd, they all gave one consent
That, since by grace of God she there was sent,
Unto their god they would her sacrifice,
Whose share, her guiltless blood they would present;
But of her dainty flesh they did devise
To make a common feast, and feed with gourmandise.

So round about her they themselves did place
Upon the grass, and diversely dispose,
As each thought best to spend the lingering space:
Some with their eyes the daintiest morsels chose;
Some praise her paps; some praise her lips and nose;
Some whet their knives, and strip their elbows bare;
The priest himself a garland doth compose
Of finest flow'rs, and with full busy care
His bloody vessels wash and holy fire prepare.

The damsel wakes; then all at once upstart,
And round about her flock, like many flies,
Whooping and halloing on ev'ry part,
As if they would have rent the brazen skies.
Which when she sees with ghastly grieffful eyes,
Her heart does quake, and deadly pallid hue
Benumbs her cheeks: then out aloud she cries,
Where none is nigh to hear that will her rue,[8]
And rends her golden locks, and snowy breasts embrue.[9]

But all boots not; they hands upon her lay;
And first they spoil her of her jewels dear,
And afterwards of all her rich array;
The which amongst them they in pieces tear,
And of the prey each one a part doth bear.
Now being naked, to their sordid eyes
The goodly treasures of natúre appear:
Which as they view with lustful fantasies,
Each wisheth to himself, and to the rest envíes.

Her ivory neck; her alabaster breast;
Her paps, which like white silken pillows were
For Love in soft delight thereon to rest;
Her tender sides; her belly white and clear,
Which like an altar did itself uprear
To offer sacrifice divine thereon;
Her goodly thighs, whose glory did appear
Like a triumphal arch, and thereupon
The spoils of princes hang'd which were in battle won.

Those dainty parts, the darlings of delight,
Which might not be profan'd of common eyes,
Those villains view'd with loose lascivious sight,
And closely tempted with their crafty spies;[10]
And some of them gan 'mongst themselves devise
Thereof by force to take their beastly pleasure:
But them the priest rebuking did advise
To dare not to pollute so sacred treasure
Vow'd to the gods: religion held even thieves in measure.[11]

So, being stay'd, they her from thence directed
Unto a little grove not far aside,
In which an altar shortly they erected
To slay her on. And now the Eventide
His broad black wings had through the heavens wide
By this dispread, that was the time ordain'd
For such a dismal deed, their guilt to hide:
Of few green turfs an altar soon they feign'd,[12]
And deck'd it all with flow'rs which they nigh hand obtain'd.

1 Inroad. 2 Moreover. 3 Custom. 4 Nature. 5 Counsel. 6 Annoyance, hindrance.

7 Batten, grow fat and tender. 8 Pity. 9 Stains with blood. 10 Glances, eyes. 11 Restraint. 12 Constructed.

Then, when as all things ready were aright,
The damsel was before the altar set,
Being already dead with fearful fright:
To whom the priest, with naked arms full net,[1]
Approaching nigh, and murderous knife well whet,
Gan mutter close a certain secret charm,
With other devilish ceremonies met: [2]
Which done, he gan aloft t' advance his arm,
Whereat they shouted all, and made a loud alarm.

Then gan the bagpipes and the horns to shrill
And shriek aloud, that, with the people's voice
Confusëd, did the air with terror fill,
And made the wood to tremble at the noise:
The while she wail'd, the more they did rejoice.
Now might ye understand that to this grove
Sir Calepine, by chance more than by choice,
The selfsame evening Fortune hither drove,
As he to seek Serena through the woods did rove.

Long had he sought her, and through many a soil
Had travell'd still on foot in heavy arms,
Nor aught was tirëd with his endless toil,
Nor aught was fearëd of [3] his certain harms:
And now, all weetless [4] of the wretched storms
In which his love was lost, he slept full fast;
Till, being wakëd with these loud alarms,
He lightly started up like one aghast,
And, catching up his arms, straight to the noise forth past.

There, by th' uncertain gleams of starry night,
And by the twinkling of their sacred fire,
He might perceive a little dawning sight
Of all which there was doing in that quire: [5]
'Mongst whom a woman spoil'd of all attire
He spied lamenting her unlucky strife,[6]
And groaning sore from grievëd heart entire:
Eftsoons he saw one with a naked knife
Ready to lance her breast, and let out lovëd life.

With that he thrusts into the thickest throng;
And, ev'n as his right hand adown descends,
He him preventing lays on earth along,
And sacrificeth to th' infernal fiends:
Then to the rest his wrathful hand he bends;
Of whom he makes such havoc and such hew,[7]
That swarms of damnëd souls to hell he sends:
The rest, that scape his sword and death eschew,[8]
Fly like a flock of doves before a falcon's view.

From them returning to that lady back,
Whom by the altar he doth sitting find,
Yet fearing death, and next to death the lack
Of clothes to cover what she ought by kind;[9]
He first her hands beginneth to unbind,
And then to question of her present woe,
And afterwards to cheer with speeches kind;
But she, for naught that he could say or do,
One word durst speak, or answer him a whit thereto.

So inward shame of her uncomely case
She did conceive, through care of womanhood,
That, though the night did cover her disgrace,
Yet she in so unwomanly a mood
Would not bewray the state in which she stood:
So all that night to him unknown she past:
But day, that doth discover bad and good,
Ensuing, made her known to him at last:
The end whereof I 'll keep until another cast.[10]

CANTO IX.

Calidore hosts[11] with Melibee,
And loves fair Pastorell:
Corydon envies him, yet he
For ill rewards him well.

Now turn again my team, thou jolly swain,[12]
Back to the furrow which I lately left;
I lately left a furrow one or twain
Unplough'd, the which my coulter had not cleft;
Yet seem'd the soil both fair and fruitful eft,[13]
As I it pass'd; that were too great a shame,
That so rich fruit should be from us bereft;
Besides the great dishonour and defame
Which should befall to Calidore's immortal name.

So sharply he the monster did pursue,[14]
That day nor night he suffer'd him to rest,
Nor rested he himself (but nature's due)
For dread of danger not to be redrest,[15]
If he for sloth forslack'd[16] so famous quest.
Him first from court he to the cities cours'd,
And from the cities to the towns him press'd,
And from the towns into the country forc'd,
And from the country back to private farms he scors'd.[17]

From thence into the open fields he fled,
Where as the herds were keeping of their neat,[18]
And shepherds singing, to their flocks that fed,
Lays of sweet love and youth's delightful heat:
Him thither eke, for all his fearful threat,
He follow'd fast, and chasëd him so nigh,
That to the folds, where sheep at night do seat,
And to the little cots, where shepherds lie
In winter's wrathful time, he forcëd him to fly.

One day, as he pursued the chase, he spied a company of shepherds piping and carolling, while their beasts fed beside them in the budded brooms, and nipped the tender blooms. Calidore asked them if they had seen such a beast as he pursued; but they answered in the negative, and offered him refreshments, which he courteously accepted. Sitting among them, he saw a fair damsel, wearing a crown of flowers, and "clad in home-made green that her own hands had dyed."

1 Clean. 2 Joined.
3 Frightened, deterred, by.
4 Ignorant. 5 Crowd.
6 Calamity. 7 Hewing.
8 Avoid. 9 Nature.
10 Occasion. 11 Dwells as a guest.

12 Cupid—whom the poet had invoked as his guide in the opening of the first book. 13 Also.
14 The Blatant Beast, which, in canto iii. of the present book, Calidore is left chasing.
15 Repaired. 16 Slackened, delayed.
17 Made to change his course. 18 Cattle.

Upon a little hillock she was plac'd,
Higher than all the rest, and round about
Environ'd with a garland, goodly grac'd,
Of lovely lasses; and them all without
The lusty shepherd swains sat in a rout,[1]
The which did pipe and sing her praises due,
And oft rejoice, and oft for wonder shout,
As if some miracle of heav'nly hue [2]
Were down to them descended in that earthly
view.

And soothly sure she was full fair of face,
And perfectly well shap'd in ev'ry limb,
Which she did more augment with modest grace
And comely carriage of her count'nance trim,
That all the rest like lesser lamps did dim:
Who, her admiring as some heav'nly wight,
Did for their sov'reign goddess her esteem,
And, carolling her name both day and night,
The fairest Pastorella her by name did hight.[3]

Nor was there herd, nor was there shepherd's
swain,
But her did honour; and eke many a one
Burn'd in her love, and with sweet pleasing pain
Full many a night for her did sigh and groan:
But most of all the shepherd Corydon
For her did languish, and his dear life spend;
Yet neither she for him nor other none
Did care a whit, nor any liking lend:
Though mean her lot, yet higher did her mind
ascend.

Her while Sir Calidore there viewëd well,
And mark'd her rare demeanour, which him
seem'd
So far the mien of shepherds to excel,
As that he in his mind her worthy deem'd
To be a prince's paragon [4] esteem'd,
He was unwares surpris'd in subtle bands
Of the Blind Boy; [5] nor thence could be re-
deem'd
By any skill out of his cruel hands;
Caught like the bird which gazing still on others
stands.

So stood he still long gazing thereupon,
Nor any will had thence to move away,
Although his quest [6] were far afore him gone:
But, after he had fed, yet did he stay
And sate there still, until the flying day
Was farforth spent, discoursing diversely
Of sundry things, as fell, to work delay:
And evermore his speech he did apply
To th' herds, but meant them to the damsel's
fantasy.

By this the moisty Night, approaching fast,
Her dewy humour gan on th' earth to shed,
That warn'd the shepherds to their homes to
hast [7]
Their tender flocks, now being fully fed,
For fear of wetting them before their bed: [8]
Then came to them a good old aged sire,
Whose silver locks bedeck'd his beard and head,
With shepherd's hook in hand, and fit attire,
That will'd the damsel rise; the day did now
expire.

He was, to wit, by common voice esteem'd
The father of the fairest Pastorell,
And of herself in very deed so deem'd;
Yet was not so; but, as old stories tell,
Found her by fortune, which to him befell,
In th' open fields an infant left alone;
And, taking up, brought home and nursëd well
As his own child; for other he had none;
That she in tract [9] of time accounted was his
own.

She at his bidding meekly did arise,
And straight unto her little flock did fare:
Then all the rest about her rose likewise,
And each his sundry sheep with several care
Gather'd together, and them homeward bare:
Whilst ev'ry one with helping hands did strive
Amongst themselves, and did their labours
share,
To help fair Pastorella home to drive
Her fleecy flock; but Corydon most help did
give.

But Melibee (so hight that good old man),
Now seeing Calidore left all alone,
And night arrivëd hard at hand, began
Him to invite unto his simple home;
Which, though it were a cottage clad with
loam,[10]
And all things therein mean, yet better so
To lodge than in the salvage fields to roam.
The Knight full gladly soon agreed thereto,
Being his heart's own wish; and home with
him did go.

There he was welcom'd of that honest sire,
And of his aged beldame, homely well;
Who him besought himself to disattire,
And rest himself till supper time befell;
By which home came the fairest Pastorell,
After her flock she in their fold had tied;
And, supper ready dight,[11] they to it fell
With small ado, and nature satisfied,
The which doth little crave contented to abide.

Then, when they had their hunger slakëd well,
And the fair maid the table ta'en away,
The gentle Knight, as he that did excel
In courtesy, and well could do and say,
For so great kindness as he found that day
Gan greatly thank his host and his good wife;
And, drawing thence his speech another way,
Gan highly to commend the happy life
Which shepherds lead, without debate or bitter
strife.

"How much," said he, "more happy is the state
In which ye, father, here do dwell at ease,

1 Company.
2 Aspect, form.
3 Pastorella represents Frances, the daughter of Sir Francis Walshingham, and wife of Sir Philip Sidney—whose portrait, as already noticed, is painted in Sir Calidore. In "The Ruins of Time," a poem published some years previously, Spenser had already spoken of Sir Francis Walshingham as "old Melibee;" and under the same designation he is introduced a little farther on in the present canto.
4 Companion, equal.
5 Love.
6 The object of his pursuit.
7 Hasten.
8 Before they were housed for the night.
9 Course.
10 Clay.
11 Prepared.

Leading a life so free and fortunate
From all the tempests of these worldly seas,
Which toss the rest in dangerous disease ;[1]
Where wars, and wrecks, and wicked enmitý
Do them afflict, which no man can appease!
That certes I your happiness envý,
And wish my lot were plac'd in such felicitý!"

"Surely, my son," then answer'd he again,
"If happy, then it is in this intent,
That, having small, yet do I not complain
Of want, nor wish for more it to augment,
But do myself, with that I have, content;
So taught of Nature, which doth little need
Of foreign helps to life's due nourishment:
The fields my food, my flock my raiment breed;
No better do I wear, no better do I feed.

"Therefore I do not any one envý,
Nor am envíed of any one therefor:
They that have much, fear much to lose thereby,
And store of cares doth follow riches' store.
The little that I have grows daily more
Without my care, but only to attend it;
My lambs do ev'ry year increase their score,
And my flock's father daily doth amend it.
What have I, but to praise th' Almighty that doth send it!

"To them that list, the world's gay shows I leave,
And to great ones such follies do forgive ;[2]
Which oft through pride do their own peril weave,
And through ambition down themselves do drive
To sad decay, that might contented live.
Me no such cares nor cumbrous thoughts offend,
Nor once my mind's unmovëd quiet grieve;
But all the night in silver sleep I spend,
And, all the day, to what I list I do attend.

"Sometimes I hunt the fox, the vowëd foe
Unto my lambs, and him dislodge away;
Sometimes the fawn I practise from the doe,
Or from the goat her kid, how to convey;
Another while I baits and nets display,
The birds to catch, or fishes to beguile;
And, when I weary am, I down do lay
My limbs in ev'ry shade to rest from toil;
And drink of ev'ry brook, when thirst my throat doth boil.

"The time was once, in my first prime of years,
When pride of youth forth prickëd my desire,
That I disdain'd amongst mine equal peers
To follow sheep and shepherd's base attire;
For farther fortune then I would inquire:
And, leaving home, to royal court I sought,
Where I did sell myself for yearly hire,
And in the Prince's garden daily wrought:
There I beheld such vainness as I never thought.

"With sight whereof soon cloy'd, and long deluded
With idle hopes which them[3] do entertain,
After I had ten years myself excluded
From native home, and spent my youth in vain,
I gan my follies to myself to plain,[4]
And this sweet peace, whose lack did then appear:
Then back returning to my sheep again,
I from thenceforth have learn'd to love more dear
This lowly quiet life which I inherit here."

Whilst thus he talk'd, the Knight with greedy ear
Hung still upon his melting mouth attent;[5]
Whose senseful words empierc'd his heart so near,
That he was rapt with double ravishment,
Both of his speech, that wrought him great content,
And also of the object of his view,[6]
On which his hungry eye was always bent;
That 'twixt his pleasing tongue, and her fair hue,
He lost himself, and like one half-entrancëd grew.

Yet to occasion means to work his mind,
And to insinuate his heart's desire,
He thus replied; "Now surely, Sire, I find
That all this world's gay shows which we admire
Be but vain shadows to this safe retire[7]
Of life, which here in lowliness ye lead,
Fearless of foes, or Fortune's wrackful ire,
Which tosseth states, and under foot doth tread
The mighty ones afraid of ev'ry change's dread.

"That even I, which daily do behold
The glory of the great 'mongst whom I won,[8]
And now have prov'd what happiness ye hold
In this small plot of your dominión,
Now loathe great lordship and ambitión;
And wish the heav'ns so much had gracëd me,
As grant me live in like conditión;
Or that my fortunes might transposëd be
From pitch of higher place unto this low degree."

"In vain," said then old Melibee, "do men
The heavens of their fortune's fault accuse;
Since they know best what is the best for them:
For they to each such fortune do diffuse,
As they do know each can most aptly use.
For not that which men covet most, is best;
Nor that thing worst, which men do most refuse;
But fittest is, that all contented rest
With that they hold: each hath his fortune in his breast.

"It is the mind that maketh good or ill,
That maketh wretch or happy, rich or poor:
For some, that hath abundance at his will,
Hath not enough, but wants in greatest store;
And other, that hath little, asks no more,
But in that little is both rich and wise;
For wisdom is most riches: fools therefóre
They are, which fortunes do by vows devise;[9]
Since each unto himself his life may fortunise."[10]

"Since then in each man's self," said Calidore,
"It is to fashion his own life's estate,
Give leave a while, good Father, in this shore
To rest my bark, which hath been beaten late
With storms of fortune and tempestuous fate,

1 Trouble. 2 Resign. 3 Those at court. 4 Lament. 5 Attentive.

6 Pastorella. 7 Retirement. 8 Dwell. 9 Seek to attain. 10 Make fortunate, or otherwise.

In seas of troubles and of toilsome pain;
That, whether quite from them for to retrate[1]
I shall resolve, or back to turn again,
I may here with yourself some small repose obtain."

He will be content with their simple fare and lowly cabin, and he offers much gold for recompense; but the good man, "naught tempted with the offer of his rich mould," thrusts it away lest it should "impair his peace with danger's dread," and makes the Knight welcome to share their humble life. So there he long remained, "daily beholding the fair Pastorell, and feeding on the bait of his own bane;" entertaining the maiden "with all kind courtesies he could invent," and every day accompanying her to the field. But she, unused to the ways of court, "had ever learn'd to love the lowly things;" and she "carëd more for Colin's carollings," than for all Calidore could do; "his lays, his loves, his looks, she did them all despise."

Which Calidore perceiving, thought it best
To change the manner of his lofty look,
And, doffing his bright arms, himself addrest
In shepherd's weed; and in his hand he took,
Instead of steel-head spear, a shepherd's hook;
That who had seen him then, would have bethought
On Phrygian Paris by Plexippus' brook,
When he the love of fair Œnone[2] sought,
What time the Golden Apple was unto him brought.

So being clad, unto the fields he went
With the fair Pastorella ev'ry day,
And kept her sheep with diligent attent,
Watching to drive the ravenous wolf away,
The whilst at pleasure she might sport and play;
And ev'ry evening helping them to fold:
And otherwhiles, for need, he did essay
In his strong hand their rugged teats to hold,
And out of them to press the milk: love so much co'ld.

Corydon, who had long loved Pastorella, was rendered intensely jealous by the stranger's proceedings; he scowled, and pouted, and complained to his comrades of the maiden's fickleness; and whenever he came in company with Calidore, his demeanour gave plain proof of his self-consuming jealousy. But Calidore, far from bearing malice or envy, did all he could to promote Corydon in the favour of their mistress.

And oft, when Corydon unto her brought
Or little sparrows stolen from their nest,
Or wanton squirrels in the woods far sought,
Or other dainty thing for her addrest,[3]
He would commend his gift, and make the best:
Yet she no whit his presence did regard,
Nor him could find to fancy in her breast:
This new-come shepherd had his market marr'd.
Old love is little worth when new is more prefar'd.

One day, when as the shepherd swains together
Were met to make their sports and merry glee,
As they are wont in fair sunshiny weather,
The while their flocks in shadows shrouded be,
They fell to dance: then did they all agree
That Colin Clout should pipe, as one most fit;
And Calidore should lead the ring, as he
That most in Pastorella's grace did sit:
Thereat frown'd Corydon, and his lip closely bit.

But Calidore, of courteous inclination,
Took Corydon and set him in his place,
That he should lead the dance, as was his fashion;
For Corydon could dance and trimly trace;[4]
And when as Pastorella, him to grace,
Her flow'ry garland took from her own head,
And plac'd on his, he did it soon displace,
And did it put on Corydon's instead:
Then Corydon wox frolic, that erst[5] seemëd dead.

Another time, when as they did dispose
To practise games and masteries to try,
They for their judge did Pastorella choose;
A garland was the meed of victory:
There Corydon, forth stepping, openly
Did challenge Calidore to wrestling game;
For he, through long and perfect industry,
Therein well practis'd was, and in the same
Thought sure t' avenge his grudge, and work his foe great shame.

But Calidore he greatly did mistake;
For he was strong and mightily stiff pight,[6]
That with one fall his neck he almost brake;
And, had he not upon him fallen light,
His dearest joint he sure had broken quite.
Then was the oaken crown by Pastorell
Given to Calidore as his due right;
But he, that did in courtesy excel,
Gave it to Corydon, and said he won it well.

Bearing himself thus, the Knight won the commendation of his rivals—"for courtesy among the rudest breeds good will and favour;" and he gained also the love of fair Pastorella; but the poet reserves to another place the story of the strange fortunes that befell him "ere he attain'd the point by him intended."

CANTO X.

Calidore sees the Graces dance
To Colin's melody:
The while his Pastorell is led
Into captivity.

"WHO now does follow the foul Blatant Beast, while Calidore does follow that fair maid?" For Calidore, unmindful of his vow to pursue

1 Retire.
2 Œnone, the wife of Paris, before the contest of the goddesses for the golden apple diverted his heart to Helen. Tennyson has in beautiful language and with rare melody woven into a poem the lament of the deserted Œnone.
3 Intended.
4 Move gracefully.
5 Just before.
6 Firmly fixed.

the monster without ceasing, and entangled in the toils of love, means to prosecute the quest no more; he has another game in view, and will rather rest among the rustic sort, than hunt after shadows vain "of courtly favour, fed with light report of ev'ry blast, and sailing always in the port."[1] Nor does the poet think that the Knight is greatly to be blamed for stooping from so high to so low a step; for who, having once tasted the happy peace of humility, and proved the perfect pleasures which grow among poor swains, would ever delight in the painted show of false bliss, set in courts "for stales[2] t'entrap unwary fools in their eternal bales?"[3]

For what hath all that goodly glorious gaze
Like to one sight which Calidore did view?
The glance whereof their dimmëd eyes would daze,[4]
That never more they should endure the shew
Of that sunshíne that makes them look askew:[5]
Nor aught, in all that world of beauties rare,
(Save only Gloriana's heav'nly hue,
To which what can compare?) can it compare;
The which, as cometh now by course, I will declare.

One day, as he did range the fields abroad,
Whilst his fair Pastorella was elsewhere,
He chanc'd to come, far from all people's trode,[6]
Unto a place whose pleasance did appear
To pass all others on the earth which were:
For all that ever was, by Nature's skill,
Devis'd to work delight, was gather'd there,
And there by her were pourëd forth at fill,
As if, this to adorn, she all the rest did pill.[7]

It was a hill plac'd in an open plain,
That round about was border'd with a wood
Of matchless height, that seem'd th' earth to disdain;
In which all trees of honour stately stood,
And did all winter as in summer bud,
Spreading pavilions for the birds to bower,[8]
Which in their lower branches sung aloud
And in their tops the soaring hawk did tower,
Sitting like king of fowls in majesty and power:

And, at the foot thereof, a gentle flood
His silver waves did softly tumble down,
Unmarr'd with ragged moss or filthy mud;
Nor might wild beasts, nor might the ruder clown,
Thereto approach; nor filth might therein drown:
But Nymphs and Faeries by the banks did sit
In the woods' shade which did the waters crown,
Keeping all noisome things away from it,
And to the water's fall tuning their accents fit.

And on the top thereof a spacious plain
Did spread itself, to serve to all delight,
Either to dance, when they to dance would fain,
Or else to course about their bases light;[9]
Nor aught there wanted which for pleasure might
Desirëd be, or thence to banish bale;[10]
So pleasantly the hill with equal height
Did seem to overlook the lowly vale;
Therefore it rightly callëd was Mount Acidale.[11]

They say that Venus, when she did dispose
Herself to pleasance, usëd to resort
Unto this place, and therein to repose
And rest herself as in a gladsome port,
Or with the Graces there to play and sport;
That ev'n her own Cytheron,[12] though in it
She usëd most to keep her royal court
And in her sov'reign majesty to sit,
She in regard hereof refus'd and thought unfit.

Unto this place when as the Elfin Knight
Approach'd, him seemëd that the merry sound
Of a shrill pipe he playing heard on height,
And many feet fast thumping th' hollow ground,
That through the woods their echo did rebound.
He nigher drew to weet[13] what might it be:
There he a troop of ladies dancing found
Full merrily, and making gladful glee,
And in the midst a shepherd piping he did see.

He durst not enter into th' open green,
For dread of them unwares to be descried,
For breaking of their dance, if he were seen;
But in the covert of the wood did bide,
Beholding all, yet of them unespied.
There he did see that[14] pleasëd much his sight,
That even he himself his eyes envíed;
A hundred naked maidens lily white
All rangëd in a ring and dancing in delight.

All they without were rangëd in a ring,
And dancëd round; but in the midst of them
Three other ladies did both dance and sing,
The whilst the rest them round about did hem,
And like a garland did in compass stem:[15]
And in the midst of thóse same three was plac'd
Another damsel, as a precious gem
Amidst a ring most richly well enchas'd,
That with her goodly presence all the rest much grac'd.

Look! how the crown, which Ariadne wore
Upon her ivory forehead, that same day
That Theseus her unto his bridal bore,
When the bold Centaurs made that bloody fray
With the fierce Lapiths, which did them dismay,[16]
Being now placëd in the firmament,
Through the bright heaven doth her beams display,
And is unto the stars an ornament,
Which round about her move in order excellent.

1 Obliged, even while apparently safe in the port (of office or favour), to make all the efforts and practise all the vigilance that would be needed on the open sea.
2 Decoys. 3 Ruin.
4 Dazzle. 5 Askance.
6 Path, thoroughfare.
7 Spoil, pillage; French, "piller."
8 Inhabit.
9 To sport at the game called prison-base, or prison-bars.
10 Sorrow. 11 See note 8, page 455.
12 The island of Cythera is meant; but Spenser follows his great exemplar, Chaucer, in confounding Mount Cithæron with the isle of Cythera. See note 2, page 36; and note 23, page 201. 13 Learn.
14 That which. 15 Enclosed in a circle. 16 Defeat.

Such was the beauty of this goodly band,
Whose sundry parts were here too long to tell:
But she, that in the midst of them did stand,
Seem'd all the rest in beauty to excel,
Crown'd with a rosy garland that right well
Did her beseem: and ever, as the crew
About her danc'd, sweet flow'rs that far did smell
And fragrant odours they upon her threw;
But, most of all, those three did her with gifts endue.

Those were the Graces, daughters of delight,
Handmaids of Venus, which are wont to haunt
Upon this hill, and dance there day and night:
Those three to men all gifts of grace do grant;
And all that Venus in herself doth vaunt
Is borrowëd of them: but that fair one,
That in the midst was placëd paravant,[1]
Was she to whom that shepherd pip'd alone;
That made him pipe so merrily as never none.

She was, to wit, that jolly shepherd's lass,
Which pipëd there unto that merry rout;
That jolly shepherd, which there pipëd, was
Poor Colin Clout (who knows not Colin Clout?)
He pip'd apace, whilst they him danc'd about.
Pipe, jolly shepherd, pipe thou now apace
Unto thy love that made thee low to lout;[2]
Thy love is present there with thee in place;
Thy love is there advanc'd to be another Grace![3]

Much wonder'd Calidore at this strange sight,
Whose like before his eye had never seen;
And standing long astonishëd in sprite,
And rapt with pleasance, wist not what to ween;[4]
Whether it were the train of Beauty's Queen,
Or Nymphs, or Faeries, or enchanted show
With which his eyes might have deluded been.
Therefore, resolving what it was to know,
Out of the wood he rose, and toward them did go.

But, soon as he appearëd to their view,
They vanish'd all away out of his sight,
And clean were gone, which way he never knew;
All save the shepherd, who, for fell despite
Of that displeasure, broke his bagpipe quite,
And made great moan for that unhappy turn:
But Calidore, though no less sorry wight
For that mishap, yet seeing him to mourn,
Drew near, that he the truth of all by him might learn:

And, first him greeting, thus unto him spake;
"Hail, jolly shepherd, which thy joyous days
Here leadest in this goodly merry-make,
Frequented of these gentle Nymphs always,
Which to thee flock to hear thy lovely lays!
Tell me, what might these dainty damsels be
Which here with thee do make their pleasant plays?
Right happy thou that may'st them freely see!
But why, when I them saw, fled they away from me?"

"Not I so happy," answer'd then that swain,
"As thou unhappy, which them thence did chase,
Whom by no means thou canst recall again;
For, being gone, none can them bring in place,
But whom they of themselves list so to grace."
"Right sorry I," said then Sir Calidore,
"That my ill fortune did them hence displace:
But since things passëd none may now restore,
Tell me what were they all, whose lack thee grieves so sore."

Then gan that shepherd thus for to dilate;
"Then wot, thou shepherd, whatsoe'er thou be,
That all those ladies which thou sawest late
Are Venus' damsels, all within her fee,[5]
But differing in honour and degree:
They all are Graces which on her depend;
Besides a thousand more which ready be
Her to adorn, whenso she forth doth wend;
But those three in the midst do chief on her attend.

"They are the daughters of sky-ruling Jove,
By him begot of fair Eurynomé,
The Ocean's daughter, in this pleasant grove,
As he, this way coming from feastful glee
Of Thetis' wedding with Æacidee,[6]
In summer's shade himself here rested weary:
The first of them hight mild Euphrosyné,
Next fair Aglaia, last Thalia merry;
Sweet Goddesses all three, which me in mirth do cherry!"[7]

"These three on men all gracious gifts bestow
Which deck the body or adorn the mind,
To make them lovely or well-favour'd show;
As comely carriage, entertainment kind,
Sweet semblance,[8] friendly offices that bind,
And all the complements of courtesy:
They teach us how to each degree and kind
We should ourselves demean, to low, to high,
To friends, to foes; which skill men call Civility.

"Therefore they always smoothly seem to smile,
That we likewise should mild and gentle be;
And also naked are, that without guile
Or false dissemblance all them plain may see,
Simple and true, from covert malice free;
And eke themselves so in their dance they bore,
That two of them still froward[9] seem'd to be,
But one still towards show'd herself afore;
That good should from us go, than come, in greater store.[10]

"Such were those Goddesses which ye did see;
But that fourth Maid, which there amidst them trac'd,[11]
Who can aread[12] what creature might she be,
Whether a creature, or a goddess grac'd

1 In front, conspicuously.
2 Bend.
3 Colin Clout being the poet himself, his "love," in this passage, considering the dates, must be understood as representing the Irish lady whom he married.
4 Knew not what to think.
5 In her service.
6 Æacides—Peleus, the son of Æacus.
7 Cherish; French, "chérir."
8 Demeanour.
9 At a distance—or, directed away from (the spectator).
10 To show that good should go out from us in more liberal measure than it comes to us.
11 Moved.
12 Declare.

With heav'nly gifts from heaven first enrac'd![1]
But whatso sure she was, she worthy was
To be the fourth with those three other plac'd:
Yet was she certes but a country lass;
Yet she all other country lasses far did pass:

"So far as doth the Daughter of the Day[2]
All other lesser lights in light excel;
So far doth she in beautiful array
Above all other lasses bear the bell;
Nor less in virtue that beseems her well
Doth she exceed the rest of all her race;
For which the Graces, that here wont to dwell,
Have for more honour brought her to this place,
And gracëd her so much to be another Grace.

"Another Grace she well deserves to be,
In whom so many graces gather'd are,
Excelling much the mean[3] of her degree;
Divine resemblance, beauty sov'reign rare,
Firm chastity, that spite ne blemish dare:
All which she with such courtesy doth grace,
That all her peers cannot with her compare,
But quite are dimmëd when she is in place:
She made me often pipe, and now to pipe apace.

"Sun of the world, great glory of the sky,
That all the earth doth lighten with thy rays,
Great Gloriana, greatest Majesty!
Pardon thy shepherd, 'mongst so many lays
As he hath sung of thee in all his days,
To make one minim[5] of thy poor handmaid,
And underneath thy feet to place her praise;
That, when thy glory shall be far display'd
To future age, of her this mention may be made!"

When the shepherd had ended his speech, Calidore asked pardon that, in rashly seeking what he might not see, he had by his "luckless breach" bereft the other of his love's dear sight. The twain then spent long time in pleasant discourses; and the Knight, charmed with the speech of the shepherd and the pleasure of the place, would fain have made his dwelling there. But the envenomed sting deep fixed in his heart began afresh to rankle sore; and there was no remedy for the wound, save return to her that inflicted it—"like as the wounded whale to shore flies from the main." "So, taking leave of that same gentle swain," Calidore returned to his rustic dwelling, to his constant and pure-minded courtship of Pastorella, to his rivalry with Corydon in carolling as they kept their sheep, in exercising games, or in presenting to their mistress the results of their labours. One day, when they had all three gone into the woods to gather strawberries, a tiger rushed out of the covert, and, with fell claws "and greedy mouth wide-gaping like hell-gate," ran at Pastorella. Hearing her cries for help, Corydon first hastened up; but, at sight of the beast, "through coward fear he fled away as fast." But Calidore, enraged instead of frightened when he saw the danger of his love, smote the monster to the ground with the only weapon he had—his shepherd's hook; then, hewing off the head, he presented it to Pastorella, receiving a thousand thanks for her life preserved. From that day forth Calidore quite displaced in her heart the coward Corydon, "fit to keep sheep, unfit for love's content;" yet the Knight did not utterly despise his rival, but used his fellowship as a means of cloaking his own successful love for Pastorella:

So well he woo'd her, and so well he wrought her,
With humble service, and with daily suit,
That at the last unto his will he brought her;
Which he so wisely well did prosecute,
That of his love he reap'd the timely fruit,
And joyëd long in close[6] felicity:
Till Fortune, fraught with malice blind and brute,
That envies lovers' long prosperity,
Blew up a bitter storm of foul adversity.

It fortunëd one day, when Calidore
Was hunting in the woods, as was his trade,
A lawless people, Brigands hight of yore,
That never us'd to live by plough nor spade,
But fed on spoil and booty, which they made
Upon their neighbours which did nigh them border,
The dwelling of these shepherds did invade;
And spoil'd their houses, and themselves did murder,
And drove away their flocks; with other much disorder.

Among the rest, they spoiled old Melibee of all he had, and carried him off under shade of night to their dwelling, along with all his people, with Pastorella, and Corydon. The den of the marauders was in a little island, covered with shrubby woods, in which no way appeared, nor could any footing be found "for overgrowen grass:"

For underneath the ground their way was made
Through hollow caves, that no man might discover
For the thick shrubs, which did them always shade
From view of living wight and cover'd over;
But darkness dread and daily night[7] did hover
Through all the inner parts wherein they dwelt;
Nor lighten'd was with window, nor with lover,[8]
But with continual candle-light, which dealt
A doubtful sense of things, not so well seen as felt.

Here the Brigands kept their prey, meaning to sell them to certain merchants, who either held them in hard bondage, or sold them again. The poet refers to another canto the tale of Pastorella's sorrow and terror, and of what befell her in that "thievish won—"[9] where she thought herself in hell, and day and night, by

1 Implanted. 2 The Moon.
3 Measure. 4 Rank.
5 A little, trifling song; properly, a short note in music.
6 Secret. 7 Night by day.

8 "Louvre," or "lover," (from the French, "l'ouvert," the open place), was an opening in the roof, to let out smoke, to admit light, or—as Fuller uses the word in his "Worthies"—to let the pigeons fly out of a dovecote. 9 Dwelling.

lamentation, wasted her goodly beauty, which did fade "like to a flow'r that feels no heat of sun which may her feeble leaves with comfort glad."

CANTO XI.

The thieves fall out for Pastorell,
Whilst Melibee is slain:
Her Calidore from them redeems,
And bringeth back again.

The joys of love, if they should ever last
Without affliction or disquietness
That worldly chances do amongst them cast,
Would be on earth too great a blessedness,
Liker to heav'n than mortal wretchedness:
Therefore the wingëd god, to let men weet[1]
That here on earth is no sure happiness,
A thousand sours hath temper'd with one sweet,
To make it seem more dear and dainty, as is meet.

So did it now befall to Pastorella: Fortune, not content with making her a captive among thieves, in dreadful darkness, threw on her greater mischief; for the captain of the band, one day viewing the prisoners, beheld with lustful eyes that lovely guest, "fair Pastorella, whose sad mournful hue like the fair morning clad in misty fog did shew." His barbarous heart was fired with love; in his own mind, he allotted her to himself as his part of the prey; and from that day he sought, by kindness and threats combined, to win her to his will. But all that he could do did not one whit affect her constancy and purity; though at last, fearing lest he might take by force what she denied, she granted him some little show of favour, in the hope that either she might be set free, or her captivity eased: "a little well is lent that gaineth more withal." The captain, however, was only stimulated to more eager urging of his suit; till the maiden found no means to bar him, but to feign a sudden sickness, during which he could approach her only when others were present. While Pastorella lay sick, a company of merchants arrived at the island in quest of slaves, and were met by some of the thieves. Conducting the new-comers to the captain, as he sat "by his fair patient's side with sorrowful regret," the men asked that the captives might be sold, and the price equally shared among the band. Though "much appalled" by the request, the captain could not but comply; Melibee, Corydon, and the rest, were brought forth and shown to the merchants; but before any bargain was concluded, some of the gang inquired for the fair shepherdess who had been taken along with the others, and began to extol her beauty, "the more t' augment her price through praise of comeliness."

To whom the captain in full angry wise
Made answer, that the maid of whom they spake
Was his own purchase and his only prize;
With which none had to do, nor aught partake,
But he himself which did that conquest make;
Little for him to have one silly[2] lass;
Besides, through sickness now so wan and weak,
That nothing meet in merchandise to pass:
So shew'd them her, to prove how pale and weak she was.

The sight of whom, though now decay'd and marr'd,
And eke but hardly seen by candle-light,
Yet, like a diamond of rich regard,[3]
In doubtful shadow of the darksome night,
With starry beams about her shining bright,
These merchants' fixëd eyes did so amaze,
That what through wonder, and what through delight,
A while on her they greedily did gaze,
And did her greatly like, and did her greatly praise.

At last when all the rest them offer'd were,
And prices to them placëd at their pleasure,
They all refusëd in regard of her;[4]
Nor aught would buy, however pric'd with measure,[5]
Withouten her, whose worth above all treasure
They did esteem, and offer'd store of gold:
But then the captain, fraught with more displeasure,
Bade them be still; his love should not be sold;
The rest take if they would; he her to him would hold.

Some of the chief robbers bade him forbear such insolent language—for, let it grieve him ever so much, the maid should be sold with the rest, to enhance their price. The captain drew his sword and dared any to lay hand on her; soon they fell to blows; "and the mad steel about doth fiercely fly," making way for Death to walk in a thousand dreadful shapes "in the horror of the grisly night"—the candles having been quenched.

Like as a sort[6] of hungry dogs, y-met
About some carcase by the common way,
Do fall together, striving each to get
The greatest portion of the greedy prey;
All on confusëd heaps themselves assay,
And snatch, and bite, and rend, and tug, and tear;
That who them sees would wonder at their fray,
And who sees not would be afraid to hear:
Such was the conflict of those cruel Brigands there.

But first of all the robbers slew the captives, lest they should join against the weaker side, or rise against the surviving remnant; Corydon alone escaping craftily in the darkness. All

1 Know. 2 Simple. 3 Value.
4 In comparison with her.
5 However moderate the price set upon them.
6 Troop, crowd.

this while Pastorella was defended by the captain, who minded more her safety than himself; but at last he was slain and laid on ground, yet holding fast in his arms the maiden, whom the wound that ended his life had pierced through the arm, and thrown into deadly swoon. The captain dead, the fray ceased, and the candles were relit.

Their captain there they cruelly found kill'd,
And in his arms the dreary dying maid,
Like a sweet angel 'twixt two clouds uphild;[1]
Her lovely light was dimmëd and decay'd
With cloud of death upon her eyes display'd;
Yet did the cloud make even that dimm'd light
Seem much more lovely in that darkness laid;
And 'twixt the twinkling of her eyelids bright
To spark out little beams, like stars in foggy
night.

Finding her still alive, the robbers busily applied themselves "to call the soul back to her home again;" at last they restored the maiden to a sense of her desolate and perilous position, bereaved of all her friends and left a second spoil in the hands of those who had "renew'd her death by timely death denying;" and they left her in charge of one of their number, "the best of many worst," who much molested her with unkind disdain and cruel rigour, scarcely yielding her due food or timely rest, or suffering her painful festered wound to be dressed. Meantime Calidore had suffered the direst agony since the day on which, returning from the chase, he found his cottage spoiled and his love reft away; "he chaf'd, he griev'd, he fretted, and he sigh'd," and fared like a furious wild bear whose whelps are stolen in her absence.

Nor wight he found to whom he might complain,
Nor wight he found of whom he might inquire;
That more increas'd the anguish of his pain:
He sought the woods, but no man could see
there;
He sought the plains, but could no tidings hear:
The woods did naught but echoes vain rebound;
The plains all waste and empty did appear;
Where wont the shepherds oft their pipes resound,
And feed a hundred flocks, there now not one
he found.

At last, "with ragged weeds, and locks upstaring high," Corydon came in view, and soon had told all the sad story of the robbers' cavern—nay, more, confidently affirming that Pastorella was dead; for what could her defender, the captain, do against them all alone: "it could not boot; needs must she die at last!" For a while Calidore's heart was deadened and his wit distracted by the tidings; but when his grief had spent itself in beatings of his head and breast, in cursings of heaven and wishes that he had been near to his mistress in her peril, the Knight began to devise means of avenging Pastorella's death, if she were dead; or saving her life, if life yet lasted; or dying with her, if he could not save her. With great difficulty he persuaded the coward Corydon to guide him to the thievish abode; and then both set out disguised as shepherds, though Calidore wore his arms under his garments. Approaching the robbers' isle, they saw flocks and shepherds, to whom they drew near to make inquiries; but to their surprise they found that the flocks were their own, kept by some of the robbers themselves, for want of herds. Corydon recognised with tears his own sheep, and besought Calidore to slay the robbers—who slept soundly in the shade of the bushes—and take away the spoil. But Calidore had secretly made in his mind "a farther purpose," and would not slay them, "but, gently waking them, gave them the time of day."[2]

Then, sitting down by them upon the green,
Of sundry things he purpose[3] gan to feign,
That he by them might certain tidings ween
Of Pastorell, were she alive or slain:
'Mongst which the thieves them questionëd again,
What mister men,[4] and eke from whence, they
were.
To whom they answer'd, as did appertain,
That they were poor herdgrooms, the which
whilere[5]
Had from their masters fled, and now sought
hire elsewhere.

Whereof right glad they seem'd, and offer made
To hire them well if they their flocks would
keep:
For they themselves were evil grooms, they said,
Unwont with herds to watch, or pasture sheep,
But to foráy the land, or scour the deep.
Thereto they soon agreed, and earnest took
To keep their flocks for little hire and cheap;
For they for better hire did shortly look:
So there all day they bode, till light the sky
forsook.

When towards darksome night it drew, the thieves brought the new shepherds to their hellish den; and soon the strangers became acquainted with all the secrets of the band, learning, greatly to Calidore's joy, that Pastorella still lived. At dead of night, when all the thieves were buried in sleep, Calidore armed himself with "a sword of meanest sort," which he had obtained by diligent search; and he went "straight to the captain's nest." They found the cave fast; but Calidore, with resistless might, burst open the door, awakening the thief who guarded Pastorella—and who, running to the entrance, was instantly slain. Almost dead with fear at the new uproar, Pastorella heard Calidore calling on her name, recognised his voice, and was suddenly revived and thrilled with wondrous joy; like a tempest-tost mariner, looking into the very jaws of death, who "at length espies at hand the happy coast."

Her gentle heart, that now long season past
Had never joyance felt nor cheerful thought,
Began some smack of comfort new to taste,

1 Upheld. 2 Saluted them.

3 Conversation. 4 What manner of men. 5 Lately.

Like lifeful heat to numbëd senses brought,
And life to feel that long for death had sought:
Nor less in heart rejoicëd Calidore
When he her found; but, like to one distraught
And robb'd of reason, toward her him bore;
A thousand times embrac'd, and kiss'd a thousand more.

But now by this, with noise of late uproar,
The hue and cry was raisëd all about;
And all the Brigands flocking in great store
Unto the cave gan press, naught having doubt[1]
Of that was done, and enter'd in a rout.
But Calidore in th' entry close did stand,
And, entertaining them with courage stout,
Still slew the foremost that came first to hand;
So long, till all the entry was with bodies mann'd.[2]

Then, when no more could nigh to him approach,
He breath'd his sword, and rested him till day;
Which when he spied upon the earth t' encroach,
Through the dead carcases he made his way,
'Mongst which he found a sword of better say,[3]
With which he forth went into th' open light,
Where all the rest for him did ready stay,
And, fierce assailing him, with all their might
Gan all upon him lay: there gan a dreadful fight.

How many flies in hottest summer's day
Do seize upon some beast whose flesh is bare,[4]
That all the place with swarms do overlay,
And with their little stings right felly fare:[5]
So many thieves about him swarming are,
All which do him assail on ev'ry side,
And sore oppress, nor any him doth spare;
But he doth with his raging brand divide
Their thickest troops, and round about him scatt'reth wide.

Like as a lion, 'mongst a herd of deer,
Disperseth them to catch his choicest prey;
So did he fly amongst them here and there,
And all that near him came did hew and slay,
Till he had strow'd with bodies all the way;
That none his danger daring to abide
Fled from his wrath, and did themselves convey
Into their caves, their heads from death to hide,
Nor any left that victory to him envíed.[6]

Then, back returning to his dearest dear,
He her gan to recomfort all he might
With gladful speeches and with lovely cheer;
And, forth her bringing to the joyous light,
Whereof she long had lack'd the wishful sight,
Devis'd all goodly means from her to drive
The sad remembrance of her wretched plight:
So her unneth[7] at last he did revive,
That long had laïn dead, and made again alive.

This done, into those thievish dens he went,
And thence did all the spoils and treasures take,
Which they from many long had robb'd and rent,
But Fortune now the victor's meed did make:
Of which the best he did his love betake;[8]
And also all those flocks, which they before
Had reft from Melibee and from his make,[9]
He did them all to Corydon restore:
So drove them all away, and his love with him bore.

CANTO XII.

Fair Pastorella by great hap
Her parents understands.
Calidore doth the Blatant Beast
Subdue, and bind in bands.

LIKE as a ship, that through the Ocean wide
Directs her course unto one certain coast,
Is met of many a counter wind and tide,
With which her wingëd speed is let[10] and crost,
And she herself in stormy surges tost;
Yet, making many a board and many a bay,[11]
Still winneth way, nor hath her compass lost;
Right so it fares with me in this long way,
Whose course is often stay'd, yet never is astray.

For nothing has been wasted or missaid of all that has prevented Calidore from following his first quest, since it has shown "the courtesy by him profest even unto the lowest and the least." But now the poet comes back into his course, to the "achievement of the Blatant Beast," which all this time roamed unrestrained. Calidore, when he had rescued Pastorella, brought her to the Castle of Belgard, belonging to the good Sir Bellamour, who in youth had been "a lusty knight as ever wielded spear," and had fought many a battle for a lady dear and fair. Claribell was her name; and her father, the Lord of Many Islands, thought to have wedded her to the Prince of Pictland. But she loved Bellamour, and secretly married him; her father discovered the marriage, and threw them both into dungeons deep but separate; yet, by bribing the keepers, Bellamour gained access to the lady, and in time she bore a maiden child. The babe was given to Claribella's handmaid, to be brought up under some strange attire.

The trusty damsel bearing it abroad
Into the empty fields, where living wight
Might not bewray[12] the secret of her load,
She forth gan lay unto the open light
The little babe, to take thereof a sight:
Whom whilst she did with watery eyne behold,
Upon the little breast, like crystal bright,
She might perceive a little purple mold,[13]
That like a rose her silken leaves did fair unfold.

Much as she pitied the babe, the handmaid could not remedy its wretched case, but had to

1 Suspicion.
2 Blocked up; filled (as a ship with her crew).
3 Assay, temper.
4 Appears through a raw or wound.
5 Cruelly behave.
6 Disputed with him.
7 With difficulty.
8 Bestow upon.
9 Mate, wife.
10 Hindered.
11 Many a tack, and many a bend or curve. "A board" is defined in "Young's Nautical Dictionary" as "the stretch which a vessel makes on each tack in beating to windward."
12 Discover.
13 Mole.

leave it there—stealing behind the bushes, to know the little one's fate. Led by the infant's cries, a shepherd drew near, pitied the babe, and took it home to his honest wife, who nurtured and named it as her own. Meantime, Claribell and Bellamour lingered in captivity, till the lady's father died, and left unto them all; so they dwelt secure from the storms of Fortune, in perfect confidence and love, till Calidore brought Pastorella thither. Struck with shame for the negligence with which he had pursued the enterprise entrusted to him by the Faery Queen, Calidore now resolved, all peril being past, to leave his love with Claribell, while he sought the monster through the world. "So, taking leave of his fair Pastorell," he went forth on his quest. The poet lingers, to tell the story of the maiden; on whose snowy breast, one morning while she was dressing, Melissa—the handmaid who had exposed her—espied "the rosy mark, which she remember'd well." Straightway she ran to her mistress, to assure her that "the heavens had her grac'd, to save her child, which in Misfortune's mouth was plac'd." A few words were sufficient to set Claribella's maternal feelings all in flame:

The matron stay'd no longer to enquire,
But forth in haste ran to the stranger maid;
Whom catching greedily, for great desire
Rent up her breast, and bosom open laid,
In which that rose she plainly saw display'd:
Then, her embracing 'twixt her armës twain,
She long so held, and softly weeping said;
"And livest thou, my daughter, now again?
And art thou yet alive, whom dead I long did feign?"[1]

Then farther asking her of sundry things,
And times comparing with their accidents,
She found at last, by very certain signs,
And speaking marks of passëd monuments,
That this young maid, whom chance to her presents,
Is her own daughter, her own infant dear.
Then, wond'ring long at those so strange events,
A thousand times she her embracëd near,
With many a joyful kiss and many a melting tear.

Whoever is the mother of one child,
Which, having thought long dead, she finds alive,
Let her, by proof of that which she hath fild[2]
In her own breast, this mother's joy descrive:[3]
For other none such passion can contrive[4]
In perfect form, as this good lady felt,
When she so fair a daughter saw survive
As Pastorella was; that nigh she swelt[5]
For passing joy, which did all into pity melt.

Running to her loved lord, she recounted to him all that had happened; and he joyfully acknowledged fair Pastorella for his own. All this time Calidore had been pursuing the Blatant Beast "by the trace of his outrageous spoil."

Through all estates[6] he found that he had past,
In which he many massacres had left,
And to the Clergy now was come at last;
In which such spoil, such havoc, and such theft
He wrought, that thence all goodness he bereft,
That endless were to tell. The Elfin Knight,
Who now no place besides unsought had left,
At length into a monast'ry did light,
Where he him found despoiling all with main and might.

Into their cloisters now he broken had,
Through which the monks he chasëd here and there,
And them pursued into their dortours[7] sad,[8]
And searchëd all their cells and secrets near;
In which what filth and ordure did appear,
Were irksome to report; yet that foul Beast,
Naught sparing them, the more did toss and tear,
And ransack all their dens from most to least,
Regarding naught religion nor their holy heast.[9]

From thence into the sacred church he broke,
And robb'd the chancel, and the desks down threw,
And altars foulëd, and blasphémy spoke,
And th' images, for all their goodly hue,
Did cast to ground, whilst none was them to rue;[10]
So all confounded and disorder'd there:
But, seeing Calidore, away he flew,
Knowing his fatal hand by former fear;
But he him fast pursuing soon approachëd near.

Him in a narrow place he overtook,
And, fierce assailing, forc'd him turn again:
Sternly he turn'd again, when he him strook[11]
With his sharp steel, and ran at him amain
With open mouth, that seemëd to contain
A full good peck within the outmost brim,
All set with iron teeth in ranges twain,
That terrified his foes, and armëd him,
Appearing like the mouth of Orcus[12] grisly grim:

And therein were a thousand tongues empight,[13]
Of sundry kinds and sundry quality;
Some were of dogs, that barkëd day and night;
And some of cats, that wrawling[14] still did cry;
And some of bears, that groin'd[15] continually;
And some of tigers, that did seem to gren[16]
And snarl at all that ever passëd by:
But most of them were tongues of mortal men,
Which spake reproachfully, not caring where nor when.

And them amongst were mingled here and there
The tongues of serpents, with three-forkëd stings,
That spat out poison, and gore-bloody gear,[17]
At all that came within his ravenings;
And spake licentious words and hateful things
Of good and bad alike, of low and high;

1 Imagine. 2 Felt.
3 Describe. 4 Conceive.
5 Fainted. 6 Ranks, orders of society.
7 Dormitories; French, "dortoirs."
8 Gloomy, sombre.

9 Office, duty (as those who had taken vows).
10 Lament. 11 Struck.
12 Hell; the Lower World.
13 Placed, infixed. 14 Mewing, wauling.
15 Growled. 16 Grin. 17 Matter.

Nor Kaisers sparëd he a whit, nor Kings;
But either blotted them with infamy,
Or bit them with his baneful teeth of injury.

But Calidore, thereof no whit afraid,
Rencounter'd him with so impetuous might,
That th' outrage of his violence he stay'd,
And beat aback, threat'ning in vain to bite,
And spitting forth the poison of his spite
That foamëd all about his bloody jaws:
Then rearing up his former[1] feet on height,[2]
He ramp'd[3] upon him with his ravenous paws,
As if he would have rent him with his cruel claws.

But he right well aware, his rage to ward,
Did cast his shield atween; and, therewithal
Putting his puissance forth, pursued so hard,
That backward he enforcëd him to fall;
And, being down, ere he new help could call,
His shield he on him threw, and fast down held;
Like as a bullock, that in bloody stall
Of butcher's baleful hand to ground is fell'd,
Is forcibly kept down, till he be throughly quell'd.

Full cruelly the Beast did rage and roar
To be down held, and master'd so with might,
That he gan fret and foam out bloody gore,
Striving in vain to rear himself upright:
For still, the more he strove, the more the Knight
Did him suppress, and forcibly subdue;
That made him almost mad for fell despite;
He grinn'd, he bit, he scratch'd, he venom threw,
And farëd like a fiend right horrible in hue:

Or like the hell-born Hydra, which they feign
That great Alcides whilom overthrew,
After that he had labour'd long in vain
To crop his thousand heads, the which still new
Forth budded, and in greater number grew.
Such was the fury of this hellish Beast,
Whilst Calidore him under him down threw;
Who nathëmore his heavy load releast,
But ay, the more he rag'd, the more his pow'r increast.

Then, when the Beast saw he might naught avail
By force, he gan his hundred tongues apply,
And sharply at him to revile and rail
With bitter terms of shameful infamy;
Oft interlacing many a forgëd lie,
Whose like he never once did speak, nor hear,
Nor ever thought thing so unworthily:
Yet did he naught, for all that, him forbear,
But strainëd him so straitly that he chok'd him near.

At last, when as he found his force to shrink
And rage to quail, he took a muzzle strong
Of surest iron made with many a link;
Therewith he murëd[4] up his mouth along,
And therein shut up his blasphémous tongue,
For never more defaming gentle knight
Or unto lovely lady doing wrong:
And thereunto a great long chain he tight,[5]
With which he drew him forth, ev'n in his own despite.

Like as whilóm that strong Tirynthian swain[6]
Brought forth with him the dreadful dog of hell,
Against his will fast bound in iron chain,
And, roaring horribly, did him compel
To see the hateful sun, that he might tell
To grisly Pluto what on earth was done,
And to the other damnëd ghosts which dwell
For ay in darkness which day-light doth shun:
So led this Knight his captive with like conquest won.

Yet greatly did the Beast repine at those
Strange bands, whose like till then he never bore,
Nor ever any durst till then impose;
And chafëd inly, seeing now no more
Him liberty was left aloud to roar:
Yet durst he not draw back, nor once withstand
The provëd pow'r of noble Calidore;
But trembled underneath his mighty hand,
And like a fearful dog him follow'd through the land.

Him through all Faery Land he follow'd so
As if he learnëd had obedience long,
That all the people, whereso he did go,
Out of their towns did round about him throng,
To see him lead that Beast in bondage strong;
And, seeing it, much wonder'd at the sight:
And all such persons as he erst[7] did wrong
Rejoicëd much to see his captive plight,
And much admir'd[8] the Beast, but more admir'd the Knight.

Thus was this monster by the mast'ring might
Of doughty Calidore suppress'd and tam'd,
That never more he might endamage wight
With his vile tongue, which many had defam'd,
And many causeless causëd to be blam'd:
So did he eke long after this remain,
Until that (whether wicked fate so fram'd,
Or fault of men) he broke his iron chain,
And got into the world at liberty again.

Thenceforth more mischief and more scath he wrought
To mortal men than he had done before;
Nor ever could, by any, more be brought
Into like bands, nor master'd any more:
All be[9] that, long time after Calidore,
The good Sir Pelleas him took in hand;
And after him Sir Lamorac of yore,
And all his brethren born in Britain land:
Yet none of them could ever bring him into band.

So now he rangeth through the world again,
And rageth sore in each degree and state;[10]

1 Fore.
2 Aloft.
3 Sprang.
4 Shut.
5 Tied, attached.
6 Hercules; of whose famous twelve labours the bringing of Cerberus from the lower world was the last and the most arduous. Tiryns was an ancient town of Argolis, where Hercules was brought up, and from which he obtained the epithet "Tirynthius."
7 Before.
8 Wondered at.
9 Although.
10 Rank and condition.

Nor any is that may him now restrain,
He growen is so great and strong of late,
Barking and biting all that him do bait,[1]
All be they[2] worthy blame, or clear of crime;
Nor spareth he most learned wits to rate,
Nor spareth he the gentle poet's rhyme;
But rends without regard of person or of time.

Nor may this homely verse, of many meanest,
Hope to escape his venomous despite,
More than my former writs, all[3] were they cleanest
From blameful blot, and free from all that wite[4]
With which some wicked tongues did it backbite,
And bring into a mighty Peer's[5] displeasure,
That never so deservëd to endite.[6]
Therefore do you, my rhymes, keep better measure,
And seek to please; that now is counted wise men's treasure.

TWO CANTOS OF

MUTABILITY:

WHICH, BOTH FOR FORM AND MATTER, APPEAR TO BE PARCEL OF SOME FOLLOWING BOOK OF

THE FAERIE QUEEN,

UNDER

THE LEGEND OF CONSTANCY.[7]

CANTO VI.

Proud Change (not pleas'd in mortal things
Beneath the moon to reign)
Pretends as well of gods as men
To be the Sovëreign.

WHAT man that sees the ever-whirling wheel
Of Change, the which all mortal things doth sway,
But that thereby doth find, and plainly feel,
How Mutability in them doth play
Her cruel sports to many men's decay?[8]
Which that to all may better yet appear,
I will rehearse, that whilom I heard say,
How she at first herself began to rear
'Gainst all the gods, and th' empire sought from them to bear.

But first here falleth fittest to unfold
Her ántique race and lineage anciént,
As I have found it register'd of old
In Faery Land 'mongst records permanent.
She was, to wit, a daughter by descent
Of those old Titans that did whilom strive
With Saturn's son for heaven's regiment;[9]
Whom though high Jove of kingdom did deprive,
Yet many of their stem long after did survive:
And many of them afterwards obtain'd
Great pow'r of Jove, and high authority:
As Hecaté, in whose almighty hand
He plac'd all rule and principality,
To be by her disposëd diversely
To gods and men, as she them list divide;
And dread Bellona, that doth sound on high
Wars and alarums unto nations wide,
That makes both heav'n and earth to tremble at her pride.

So likewise did this Titaness aspire
Rule and dominion to herself to gain;
That as a goddess men might her admire,
And heav'nly honours yield, as to them twain:[10]
And first on earth she sought it to obtain;
Where she such proof and sad examples shew'd
Of her great pow'r, to many one's great pain,
That not men only (whom she soon subdued),
But eke all other creatures her bad doings rued.[11]

For she the face of earthly things so chang'd,
That all which Nature had establish'd first
In good estate, and in meet order rang'd,
She did pervert, and all their statutes burst:[12]
And all the world's fair frame (which none yet durst

1 Molest, attack.
2 Whether they be.
3 Although.
4 Blameworthiness, censure.
5 The Lord Treasurer, Burleigh, who had severely handled the earlier books of "The Faerie Queen." See note 1, page 444.
6 That never had good cause to indict or censure it so.
7 The two cantos called "Of Mutability," and two stanzas of a third canto, were not published during Spenser's lifetime. They first appeared with the third edition of "The Faerie Queen," published in 1609, which contains no preface or explanation; thus, although they are usually set down as belonging to the seventh book, there is no actual warrant for that assumption. The internal evidence leaves no doubt that they were the work of Spenser; and, the peculiar characteristics of the poet quite apart, they are more majestically and musically Spenserian than many cantos of the earlier books. They are here presented without curtailment.
8 Ruin.
9 Rule.
10 That is, as to Hecate and Bellona.
11 Deplored.
12 Broke.

Of gods or men to alter or misguide)
She alter'd quite; and made them all accurst
That God had bless'd, and did at first provide
In that still happy state for ever to abide.

Nor she the laws of Nature only brake,
But eke of Justice and of Policy;
And wrong of right, and bad of good, did make,
And death for life exchangëd foolishly:
Since which all living wights have learn'd to die,
And all this world is waxen daily worse.
O piteous work of Mutability,
By which we all are subject to that curse,
And death, instead of life, have suckëd from our nurse!

And now, when all the earth she thus had brought
To her behest, and thrallëd to her might,
She gan to cast in her ambitious thought
T' attempt the empire of the heaven's height,
And Jove himself to shoulder from his right.
And first she pass'd the region of the air
And of the fire, whose substance thin and slight
Made no resistance, nor could her contrair,[1]
But ready passage to her pleasure did prepare.

Thence to the circle of the Moon she clamb,[2]
Where Cynthia reigns in everlasting glory,
To whose bright shining palace straight she came,
All fairly deck'd with heaven's goodly story;
Whose silver gates (by which there sat a hoary
Old aged sire, with hower-glass[3] in hand,
Hight Time) she enter'd were he lief or sorry;[4]
Nor stay'd till she the highest stage had scann'd,[5]
Where Cynthia did sit, that never still did stand.

Her sitting on an ivory throne she found,
Drawn of two steeds, th' one black, the other white,
Environ'd with ten thousand stars around,
That duly her attended day and night;
And by her side there ran her page, that hight
Vesper, whom we the evening-star intend;[6]
That with his torch, still twinkling like twilight,
Her lighten'd all the way where she should wend,
And joy to weary wand'ring travellers did lend:

That when the hardy Titaness beheld
The goodly building of her palace bright,
Made of the heaven's substance, and upheld
With thousand crystal pillars of huge height,
She gan to burn in her ambitious sprite,
And t' envy her that in such glory reign'd.
Eftsoons she cast by force and tortious[7] might
Her to displace, and to herself t' have gain'd
The kingdom of the Night, and waters by her wan'd.[8]

Boldly she bid the goddess down descend
And let herself into that ivory throne;
For she herself more worthy thereof wend,[9]
And better able it to guide alone;
Whether to men, whose fall she did bemoan,
Or unto gods, whose state she did malign,
Or to th' infernal pow'rs her need give loan[10]
Of her fair light and bounty most benign,
Herself of all that rule she deemëd most condign.[11]

But she, that had to her that sov'reign seat
By highest Jove assign'd, therein to bear
Night's burning lamp, regarded not her threat,
Nor yielded aught for favour or for fear;
But with stern count'nance and disdainful cheer,[12]
Bending her hornëd brows, did put her back;
And, boldly blaming her for coming there,
Bade her at once from heaven's coast to pack,
Or at her peril bide the wrathful thunder's wrack.

Yet nathëmore the giantess forbare;
But, boldly pressing on, raught[13] forth her hand
To pluck her down perforce from off her chair;
And, therewith lifting up her golden wand,
Threaten'd to strike her if she did withstand:
Whereat the Stars, which round about her blaz'd,
And eke the Moon's bright waggon, still did stand,
All being with so bold attempt amaz'd,
And on her uncouth habit and stern look still gaz'd.

Meanwhile the Lower World, which nothing knew
Of all that chancëd here, was darken'd quite;
And eke the heav'ns, and all the heav'nly crew
Of happy wights, now unpurvey'd of[14] light,
Were much afraid, and wonder'd at that sight;
Fearing lest Chaos broken had his chain,
And brought again on them eternal night;
But chiefly Mercury, that next doth reign,
Ran forth in haste unto the King of Gods to plain.[15]

All ran together with a great outcry
To Jove's fair palace fix'd in heaven's height;
And, beating at his gates full earnestly,
Gan call to him aloud with all their might
To know what meant that sudden lack of light.
The Father of the Gods, when this he heard,
Was troubled much at their so strange affright,
Doubting lest Typhon were again uprear'd,[16]
Or other his old foes that once him sorely fear'd.

Eftsoons the son of Maia[17] forth he sent
Down to the circle of the Moon, to know
The cause of this so strange astonishment,
And why she did her wonted course forslow;[18]
And, if that any were on earth below
That did with charms or magic her molest,
Him to attach, and down to hell to throw;

1 Withstand. 2 Climbed.
3 Hour-glass. 4 Willing or unwilling.
5 Climbed, ascended; Latin, "scando," I climb.
6 Name; understand to be. 7 Wrongful.
8 Diminished; by the moon's influence in producing the tides.
9 Weened, believed.
10 She needed to lend. There is an allusion to Diana's threefold sovereignty, in earth, in heaven, and in hell. See note 23, page 39.
11 Worthy.
12 Demeanour. 13 Reached.
14 Unprovided with. 15 Complain.
16 Typhoeus, whom Jupiter had buried under Mount Etna. See note 13, page 524.
17 Mercury; or, as the Greeks called him, Hermes.
18 Neglect, slacken.

But if from heav'n it were, then to arrest
The author, and him bring before his presence
prest.[1]

The wing'd-foot god so fast his plumes did beat,
That soon he came where as the Titaness
Was striving with fair Cynthia for her seat;
At whose strange sight and haughty hardiness
He wonder'd much, and fearëd her no less:
Yet, laying fear aside to do his charge,
At last he bade her, with bold steadfastness,
Cease to molest the Moon to walk at large,
Or come before high Jove her doings to discharge.[2]

And therewithal he on her shoulder laid
His snaky-wreathëd mace,[3] whose awful pow'r
Doth make both gods and hellish fiends afraid:
Whereat the Titaness did sternly lour,
And stoutly answer'd, that in evil hour
He from his Jove such message to her brought,
To bid her leave fair Cynthia's silver bow'r;
Since she his Jove and him esteemëd naught,
No more than Cynthia's self; but all their
kingdoms sought.

The heaven's herald stay'd not to reply,
But pass'd away his doings to relate
Unto his lord; who now, in th' highest sky,
Was placëd in his principal estate,[4]
With all the gods about him congregate:
To whom when Hermes had his message told,
It did them all exceedingly amate,[5]
Save Jove; who, changing naught his count'-
nance bold,
Did unto them at length these speeches wise
unfold;

"Hearken to me a while, ye heav'nly Pow'rs:
Ye may remember since th' Earth's cursëd seed
Sought to assail the heav'ns' eternal tow'rs,
And to us all exceeding fear did breed;
But how we then defeated all their deed
Ye all do know, and them destroyëd quite;
Yet not so quite, but that there did succeed
An offspring of their blood, which did alight
Upon the fruitful earth, which doth us yet
despite.

"Of that bad seed is this bold woman bred,
That now with bold presumption doth aspire
To thrust fair Phœbe from her silver bed,
And eke ourselves from heaven's high empíre,
If that her might were match to her desire.
Wherefore it now behoves us to advise[6]
What way is best to drive her to retire;
Whether by open force, or counsel wise:
Aread,[7] ye Sons of God, as best ye can devise."

So having said, he ceas'd; and with his brow
(His black eye-brow, whose doomful dreaded
beck
Is wont to wield the world unto his vow,
And ev'n the highest pow'rs of heav'n to check)
Made sign to them in their degrees to speak;
Who straight gan cast their counsel grave and
wise.
Meanwhile th' Earth's daughter, though she
naught did reck
Of Hermes' message, yet gan now advise
What course were best to take in this hot bold
emprize.

Eftsoons she thus resolv'd: that, whilst the
gods
(After return of Hermes' embassy)
Were troubled, and amongst themselves at
odds,
Before they could new counsels re-ally,[8]
To set upon them in that ecstasy,[9]
And take what fortune, time and place would
lend.
So forth she rose, and through the purest sky
To Jove's high palace straight cast to ascend,
To prosecute her plot; good onset bodes good
end.

She there arriving, boldly in did pass;
Where all the gods she found in counsel close,
All quite unarm'd, as then their manner was.
At sight of her they sudden all arose
In great amaze, nor wist what way to choose:
But Jove, all fearless, forc'd them to aby,[10]
And in his sov'reign throne gan straight dispose
Himself, more full of grace and majesty,
That might encheer[11] his friends, and foes might
terrify.

That when the haughty Titaness beheld,
All[12] were she fraught with pride and impu-
dence,
Yet with the sight thereof was almost quell'd;
And, inly quaking, seem'd as reft of sense
And void of speech in that dread audience;
Until that Jove himself herself bespake:
"Speak, thou frail woman, speak with confi-
dence;
Whence art thou, and what dost thou here now
make?[13]
What idle errand hast thou earth's mansion to
forsake?"

She, half confusëd with his great command,
Yet gath'ring spirit of her nature's pride,
Him boldly answer'd thus to his demand;
"I am a daughter, by the mother's side,
Of her that is grandmother magnified
Of all the gods, great Earth, great Chaos' child:
But by the father's, be it not envíed,
I greater am in blood, whereon I build,[14]
Than all the gods, though wrongfully from
heav'n exil'd.

"For Titan, as ye all acknowledge must,
Was Saturn's elder brother by birthright;
Both sons of Uranus; but by unjust
And guileful means, through Corybantes'
sleight,

1 Quickly.
2 Defend, give an account of.
3 The Caduceus. See page 404.
4 Supreme rank or dignity.
5 Terrify.
6 Consult, consider.
7 Declare.
8 Before they could form new plans.
9 Surprise, unsettlement.
10 Abide.
11 Encourage.
12 Although.
13 What meanest thou by coming here?
14 Found my claim.

The younger thrust the elder from his right:
Since which thou, Jove, injuriously hast held
The heaven's rule from Titan's sons by might;
And them to hellish dungeons down hast fell'd:
Witness, ye heav'ns, the truth of all that I have tell'd."[1]

Whilst she thus spake, the gods, that gave good ear
To her bold words, and markëd well her grace
(Being of stature tall as any there
Of all the gods, and beautiful of face
As any of the goddesses in place),
Stood all astonied; like a sort[2] of steers,
'Mongst whom some beast of strange and foreign race
Unwares is chanc'd, far straying from his peers:
So did their ghastly gaze bewray their hidden fears.

Till, having paus'd a while, Jove thus bespake;
"Will never mortal thoughts cease to aspire
In this bold sort to heaven claim to make,
And touch celestial seats with earthly mire?
I would have thought that bold Procrustes' hire,
Or Typhon's fall, or proud Ixion's pain,
Or great Prometheus tasting of our ire,[3]
Would have suffic'd the rest for to restrain,
And warn'd all men by their example to refrain:

"But now this off-scum of that cursed fry
Dares to renew the like bold enterprise,
And challengè th' heritage of this our sky;
Whom what should hinder, but that we likewise
Should handle as the rest of her allies,
And thunder-drive to hell?" With that he shook
His nectar-dewëd locks, with which the skies
And all the world beneath for terror quook,
And eft[4] his burning levin-brand[5] in hand he took.

But when he lookëd on her lovely face,
In which fair beams of beauty did appear
That could the greatest wrath soon turn to grace
(Such sway doth beauty ev'n in heaven bear),
He stay'd his hand; and, having chang'd his cheer,[6]
He thus again in milder wise began;
"But ah! if gods should strive with flesh y-fere,[7]
Then shortly should the progeny of man
Be rooted out, if Jove should do still what he can!

"But thee, fair Titan's child, I rather ween
Through some vain error, or inducement light,
To see that mortal eyes have never seen;
Or through ensample of thy sister's might,
Bellona, whose great glory thou dost spite,[8]
Since thou hast seen her dreadful pow'r below,
'Mongst wretched men (dismay'd with her affright),
To bandy crowns, and kingdoms to bestow:
And sure thy worth no less than hers doth seem to show.

"But wot thou this, thou hardy Titaness,
That not the worth of any living wight
May challenge aught in heaven's interess;[9]
Much less the title of old Titan's right:
For we by conquest of our sov'reign might,
And by eternal doom of Fates' decree,
Have won the empire of the heavens bright;
Which to ourselves we hold, and to whom we
Shall worthy deem partakers of our bliss to be.

"Then cease thy idle claim, thou foolish girl;
And seek by grace and goodness to obtain
That place, from which by folly Titan fell:
Thereto[10] thou may'st perhaps, if so thou fain,[11]
Have Jove thy gracious lord and sovëreign."
So having said, she thus to him replied,
"Cease, Saturn's son, to seek by proffers vain
Of idle hopes t' allure me to thy side,
For to betray my right before I have it tried.

"But thee, O Jove, no equal[12] judge I deem
Of my desert, or of my dueful right;
That in thine own behalf may'st partial seem:
But to the highest him, that is behight[13]
Father of Gods and men by equal might,
To wit, the God of Nature, I appeal."
Thereat Jove waxëd wroth, and in his sprite
Did inly grudge, yet did it well conceal;
And bade Dan Phœbus scribe her appellation[14] seal.

Eftsoons the time and place appointed were,
Where all, both heav'nly pow'rs and earthly wights,
Before great Nature's presence should appear,
For trial of their titles and best rights;
That was, to wit, upon the highest heights
Of Arlo-hill[15] (who knows not Arlo-hill?)
That is the highest head, in all men's sights,
Of my old Father Mole, whom shepherd's quill
Renownëd hath with hymns fit for a rural skill.

And, were it not ill fitting for this file[16]
To sing of hills and woods 'mongst wars and knights,
I would abate the sternness of my style,
'Mongst these stern stounds[17] to mingle soft delights:
And tell how Arlo, through Diana's spites
(Being of old the best and fairest hill
That was in all this Holy Island's[18] heights),

1 Told. 2 Herd.
3 Typhon (rather, Typhoeus) and Prometheus, are correctly enough reckoned among those who aspired to the sovereignty of heaven; and though Ixion was not a Titan, but only king of the Lapithæ—not a rival, but only a treacherous guest, of Zeus—his introduction in such company may be excused, in despite of mythochronological record. But Procrustes—the Attican robber-chief whose exacting bed is even yet famous, and of whom Theseus rid the country—belongs to a totally distinct category and period from those in which he is here mentioned.
4 Then, also.
5 Thunder-bolt.
6 Countenance. 7 Together.
8 Envy, begrudge. 9 Interest.
10 Besides. 11 Desire.
12 Impartial. 13 Called. 14 Appeal.
15 Now named Galty More, the loftiest summit in the eastern range of the Ballyhoura hills, called the mountains of Mole in the passage before us, and in "Colin Clout's Come Home Again." A defile of Galty More, it is said, is still known as the "Glen of Aharlow." Arlo is also mentioned by Spenser in his "View of the Present State of Ireland;" so that the name is not merely a poetic fiction.
16 Record, narrative. 17 Alarms, assaults.
18 Ireland's.

Was made the most unpleasant and most ill:
Meanwhile, O Clio, lend Calliopé thy quill.

Whilom when Ireland flourishëd in fame
Of wealth and goodness far above the rest
Of all that bear the British Islands' name,
The gods then us'd, for pleasure and for rest,
Oft to resort thereto, when seem'd them best:
But none of all therein more pleasure found
Than Cynthia,[1] that is sov'reign Queen profest
Of woods and forests, which therein abound,
Sprinkled with wholesome waters more than most on ground:

But 'mongst them all, as fittest for her game,—
Either for chase of beasts with hound or bow,
Or for to shroud in shade from Phœbus' flame,
Or bathe in fountains that do freshly flow
Or from high hills or from the dales below,—
She chose this Arlo; where she did resort
With all her nymphs enrangëd on a row,
With whom the woody gods did oft consort;
For with the Nymphs the Satyrs love to play and sport:

Amongst the which there was a nymph that hight
Molanna; daughter of old Father Mole,
And sister unto Mulla fair and bright:[2]
Unto whose bed false Bregog whilom stole,
That Shepherd Colin dearly did condole,
And made her luckless loves well known to be:
But this Molanna, were she not so shoal,[3]
Were no less fair and beautiful than she;
Yet, as she is, a fairer flood may no man see.

For, first, she springs out of two marble rocks,
On which a grove of oaks high-mounted grows,
That as a garland seems to deck the locks
Of some fair bride, brought forth with pompous shows
Out of her bow'r, that many flowers strows:
So through the flow'ry dales she tumbling down
Through many woods and shady coverts flows,
That on each side her silver channel crown,
Till to the plain she come, whose valleys she doth drown.

In her sweet streams Diana usëd oft,
After her sweaty chase and toilsome play,
To bathe herself; and, after, on the soft
And downy grass her dainty limbs to lay
In covert shade, where none behold her may;
For much she hated sight of living eye.
Foolish god Faunus, though full many a day
He saw her clad, yet longëd foolishly
To see her naked 'mongst her nymphs in privity.

No way he found to compass his desire,
But to corrupt Molanna, this her maid,
Her to discover for some secret hire:[4]
So her with flatt'ring words he first assay'd;
And, after, pleasing gifts for her purvey'd,[5]
Queen-apples, and red cherries from the tree,
With which he her allurëd, and betray'd
To tell what time he might her Lady see
When she herself did bathe, that he might secret be.

Thereto[6] he promis'd, if she would him pleasure
With this small boon, to quit[7] her with a better;
To wit, that whereas she had out of measure
Long lov'd the Fanchin,[8] who by naught did set her,[9]
That he would undertake for this to get her
To be his love, and of him likëd well:
Besides all which, he vow'd to be her debtor
For many more good turns than he would tell,
The least of which this little pleasure should excel.

The simple maid did yield to him anon;
And eft[10] him placëd where he close[11] might view
That never any saw, save only one,[12]
Who, for his hire to so fool-hardy due,[13]
Was of his hounds devour'd in hunter's hue.[14]
Then, as her manner was on sunny day,
Diana, with her nymphs about her, drew
To this sweet spring; where, doffing her array,
She bath'd her lovely limbs, for Jove a likely prey.

There Faunus saw that pleasëd much his eye,
And made his heart to tickle in his breast,
That, for great joy of somewhat he did spy,
He could him not contain in silent rest;
But, breaking forth in laughter, loud profest
His foolish thought: a foolish Faun, indeed,
That couldst not hold thyself so hidden blest,
But wouldest needs thine own conceit aread![15]
Babblers unworthy be of so divine a meed.

The Goddess, all abashëd with that noise,
In haste forth started from the guilty brook;
And, running straight where as she heard his voice,
Enclos'd the bush about, and there him took
Like darred lark,[16] not daring up to look
On her whose sight before so much he sought.
Thence forth they drew him by the horns, and shook
Nigh all to pieces, that they left him naught;
And then into the open light they forth him brought.

Like as a housewife, that with busy care
Thinks of her dairy to make wondrous gain,
Finding where as some wicked beast unware

1 Diana.

2 The poetical title given by Spenser to the river Awbeg, near his residence of Kilcolman Castle. In "Colin Clout's Come Home Again," he describes himself as "keeping his sheep amongst the cooly shade of the green alders by the Mulla's shore;" and he relates the love-story of the Mulla and the Bregog.

3 Shallow. The Molanna, now called the Brackbawn, flows out of the western range of the Ballyhoura hills.

4 Reward.

5 Provided.

6 Moreover.

7 Recompense.

8 A stream now called the Funcheon.

9 Naught esteemed or cared for her.

10 Soon after.

11 Secretly.

12 Actæon.

13 The reward earned by his foolhardy conduct.

14 Form, appearance.

15 Declare.

16 Like a lark dazzled by the glare of the "darring-glass," or mirror used in catching that bird.

That breaks into her dair'-house, there doth drain
Her creaming pans, and frustrate all her pain,
Hath, in some snare or gin set close behind,
Entrappëd him, and caught into her train,[1]
Then thinks what punishment were best assign'd,
And thousand deaths deviseth in her vengeful mind:

So did Diana and her maidens all
Use silly Faunus, now within their bail:[2]
They mock and scorn him, and him foul miscall;
Some by the nose him pluck'd, some by the tail,
And by his goatish beard some did him hale:
Yet he (poor soul!) with patience all did bear;
For naught against their wills might countervail:
Nor aught he said, whatever he did hear;
But, hanging down his head, did like a mome[3] appear.

At length, when they had flouted him their fill,
They gan to cast what penance him to give.
Some would have gelt him; but that same would spill[4]
The wood-gods' breed, which must for ever live:
Others would through the river him have drive
And duckëd deep; but that seem'd penance light:
But most agreed, and did this sentence give,
Him in deer's skin to clad, and in that plight
To hunt him with their hounds, himself save how he might.

But Cynthia's self, more angry than the rest,
Thought not enough to punish him in sport,
And of her shame to make a gamesome jest;
But gan examine him in straiter sort,
Which of her nymphs, or other close consórt,[5]
Him thither brought, and her to him betray'd?
He, much afear'd, to her confessëd short
That 'twas Molanna which her so bewray'd.
Then all at once their hands upon Molanna laid.

But him (according as they had decreed)
With a deer's skin they cover'd, and then chas'd
With all their hounds, that after him did speed;
But he, more speedy, from them fled more fast
Than any deer; so sore him dread aghast.[6]
They after follow'd all with shrill outcry,
Shouting as they the heavens would have brast;[7]
That all the woods and dales, where he did fly,
Did ring again, and loud re-echo to the sky.

So they him follow'd till they weary were;
When, back returning to Molann' again,
They, by commandment of Diana, there
Her whelm'd with stones: yet Faunus, for her pain,
Of her belovëd Fanchin did obtain
That her he would receive unto his bed.
So now her waves pass through a pleasant plain,
Till with the Fanchin she herself do wed,
And, both combin'd, themselves in one fair river spread.

Nathless Diana, full of indignation,
Thenceforth abandon'd her delicious brook;
In whose sweet stream, before that bad occasion,
So much delight to bathe her limbs she took:
Nor only her, but also quite forsook
All those fair forests about Arlo hid;
And all that mountain, which doth overlook
The richest champaign that may else be rid;[8]
And the fair Shure, in which are thousand salmons bred.

Them all, and all that she so dear did weigh,[9]
Thenceforth she left; and, parting from the place,
Thereon a heavy hapless curse did lay;
To wit, that wolves, where she was wont to space,[10]
Should harbour'd be and all those woods deface,
And thieves should rob and spoil that coast around.
Since which, those woods, and all that goodly chase,
Doth to this day with wolves and thieves a-bound:
Which too too true that land's indwellers since have found!

CANTO VII.

'Pealing[11] from Jove to Nature's bar,
Bold Alteration pleads
Large evidence: but Nature soon
Her righteous doom areads.[12]

AH! whither dost thou now, thou greater Muse,[13]
Me from these woods and pleasing forests bring,
And my frail spirit, that doth oft refuse
This too high flight, unfit for her weak wing,
Lift up aloft, to tell of heaven's king
(Thy sov'reign sire) his fortunate success;
And victory in bigger notes to sing
Which he obtain'd against that Titaness,
That him of heaven's empire sought to dispossess?

Yet, since I needs must follow thy behest,
Do thou my weaker wit with skill inspire,
Fit for this turn; and in my feeble breast
Kindle fresh sparks of that immortal fire
Which learnëd minds inflameth with desire
Of heav'nly things: for who but thou alone,
That art y-born of heav'n and heav'nly sire,
Can tell things done in heav'n so long y-gone,
So far past memory of man that may be known?

Now, at the time that was before agreed,
The gods assembled all on Arlo Hill;
As well those that are sprung of heav'nly seed,
As those that all the other world do fill,
And rule both sea and land unto their will:

1 Snare. 2 Custody.
3 A speechless and senseless blockhead.
4 Destroy. 5 Companion.
6 Confounded, terrified.
7 Burst, rent. 8 For "read;" discovered.

9 Value. 10 Roam.
11 Appealing. 12 Pronounces.
13 Clio now retakes from Calliope—the historic from the epic Muse—the quill which was lent her to describe the fate of sad Molanna.

Only th' infernal pow'rs might not appear;
As well for horror of their count'nance ill,
As for th' unruly fiends which they did fear;
Yet Pluto and Proserpina were present there.

And thither also came all other creatures,
Whatever life or motion do retain,
According to their sundry kinds of features,
That Arlo scarcely could them all contain,
So full they fillëd ev'ry hill and plain;
And had not Nature's Sergeant (that is Order)
Them well disposëd by his busy pain,
And rangëd far abroad in ev'ry border,
They would have causëd much confusion and disorder.

Then forth issüed (great Goddess) great Dame Nature,
With goodly port and gracious majesty,
Being far greater and more tall of stature
Than any of the gods or pow'rs on high;
Yet, certes, by her face and physnomy,[1]
Whether she man or woman inly[2] were,
That could not any creature well descry;
For with a veil, that wimpled ev'rywhere,[3]
Her head and face was hid, that might to none appear.

That, some do say, was so by skill devis'd
To hide the terror of her úncouth hue
From mortal eyes, that should be sore agris'd;[4]
For that her face did like a lion shew,
That eye of wight could not endure to view:
But others tell that it so beauteous was,
And round about such beams of splendour threw,
That it the sun a thousand times did pass,
Nor could be seen but like an image in a glass.

That well may seemen true; for well I ween
That this same day, when she on Arlo sat,
Her garment was so bright and wondrous sheen,[5]
That my frail wit cannot devise to what
It to compare, nor find like stuff to that:
As those three sacred saints, though else most wise,
Yet on Mount Tabor quite their wits forgat,
When they their glorious Lord in strange disguise
Transfigur'd saw; his garments so did daze[6] their eyes.

In a fair plain upon an equal hill
She placëd was in a pavilión;
Not such as craftsmen by their idle skill
Are wont for princes' states[7] to fashión;
But th' Earth herself, of her own motión,
Out of her fruitful bosom made to grow
Most dainty trees, that, shooting up anon,
Did seem to bow their blooming heads full low
For homage unto her, and like a throne did show.

So hard it is for any living wight
All her array and vestiments to tell,
That old Dan Geoffrey[8] (in whose gentle sprite
The pure well-head of poesy did dwell)
In his *Fowls' Parley*[9] durst not with it mell,[10]
But it transferr'd to Alane,[11] who he thought
Had in his *Plaint of Kind* describ'd it well:
Which who will read set forth so as it ought,
Go seek he out that Alane where he may be sought.

And all the earth far underneath her feet
Was dight[12] with flow'rs, that voluntary grew
Out of the ground, and sent forth odours sweet;
Ten thousand mores[13] of sundry scent and hue,
That might delight the smell, or please the view,
The which the nymphs from all the brooks thereby
Had gatherëd, they at her foot-stool threw;
That richer seem'd than any tapëstry
That princes' bow'rs adorn with painted imag'ry.

And Mole himself, to honour her the more,
Did deck himself in freshest fair attire;
And his high head, that seemeth always hoar
With harden'd frosts of former winters' ire,
He with an oaken garland now did tire;[14]
As if the love of some new nymph, late seen,
Had in him kindled youthful fresh desire,
And made him change his gray attire to green:
Ah! gentle Mole, such joyance hath thee well beseen.[15]

Was never so great joyance since the day
That all the gods whilóm assembled were
On Hæmus[16] hill, in their divine array,
To celebrate the solemn bridal cheer
'Twixt Peleus and Dame Thetis' pointed[17] there:
Where Phœbus' self, that god of poets hight,
They say, did sing the spousal hymn full clear,
That all the gods were ravish'd with delight
Of his celestial song, and music's wondrous might.

This great grandmother of all creatures bred,
Great Nature, ever young, yet full of eld;
Still moving, yet unmovëd from her stead;[18]
Unseen of any, yet of all beheld;
Thus sitting in her throne, as I have tell'd,[19]
Before her came Dame Mutability;
And, being low before her presence fell'd[20]
With meek obeisance and humility,
Thus gan her plaintive plea with words to amplify:

"To thee, O greatest Goddess, only great!
A humble suppliant, lo! I lowly fly,
Seeking for right, which I of thee entreat,
Who right to all dost deal indiff'rently,[21]
Damning[22] all wrong and tortious[23] injury

1 Physiognomy, countenance. 2 Really, wholly.
3 Was closely drawn all around her.
4 Terrified. 5 Shining. 6 Dazzle.
7 Canopies or pavilions. Chaucer, in "The Court of Love," describes the king and queen "under the cloth of their estate." See reference in note 6, page 202.
8 Chaucer.
9 "The Assembly of Fowls," or Parliament of Birds.
10 Meddle.
11 See note 8, page 220. The lines in Chauce are,
"And right as Alain, in his Plaint of Kind,
Deviseth Nature of such array and face,
In such array men mightë her there find."
12 Decked.
13 Roots, plants; the word, surviving in provincial dialects, may be traced to the Anglo-Saxon, "myrran," to spread. 14 Attire. 15 Beseemed.
16 Spenser is here again at fault; the nuptials of Peleus and Thetis were celebrated on Mount Pelion.
17 Appointed. 18 Place.
19 Told. 20 Fallen prostrate.
21 Impartially. 22 Condemning. 23 Wrongful.

Which any of thy creatures do to other,
Oppressing them with pow'r unequally;
Since of them all thou art the equal mother,
And knittest each to each, as brother unto brother.

"To thee therefore of this same Jove I plain,[1]
And of his fellow gods that feign to be,
That challenge[2] to themselves the whole world's reign,
Of which the greatest part is due to me,
And heav'n itself by heritage in fee:
For heav'n and earth I both alike do deem,
Since heav'n and earth are both alike to thee;
And gods no more than men thou dost esteem:
For ev'n the gods to thee, as men to gods, do seem.

"Then weigh, O sov'reign goddess, by what right
These gods do claim the world's whole sov'-reignty;
And that[3] is only due unto thy might,
Arrogate to themselves ambitiously:
As for the gods' own principality,
Which Jove usurps unjustly, that to be
My heritage Jove's self cannot deny,
From my great grandsire Titan unto me
Deriv'd by due descent; as is well known to thee.

"Yet maugré[4] Jove, and all his gods beside,
I do possess the world's most regiment;[5]
As, if ye please it into parts divide,
And ev'ry part's inholders[6] to convent,[7]
Shall to your eyes appear incontinent.[8]
And first, the Earth (great mother of us all),
That only seems unmov'd and permanent,
And unto Mutability not thrall,
Yet is she chang'd in part, and eke in general:

"For all that from her springs, and is y-bred,
However fair it flourish for a time,
Yet see we soon decay; and, being dead,
To turn again unto their earthly slime:
Yet out of their decay and mortal crime[9]
We daily see new creatures to arise,
And of their winter spring another prime,[10]
Unlike in form, and chang'd by strange disguise:
So turn they still about, and change in restless wise.

"As for her tenants, that is, man and beasts,
The beasts we daily see massácred die
As thralls and vassals unto men's behests;[11]
And men themselves do change continually,
From youth to eld, from wealth to poverty,
From good to bad, from bad to worst of all:
Nor do their bodies only flit and fly,
But eke their minds (which they immortal call,
Still change, and vary thoughts, as new occasions fall.

"Nor is the water in more constant case;
Whether those same on high, or these below:
For th' ocean moveth still from place to place;
And ev'ry river still doth ebb and flow;
Nor any lake that seems most still and slow,
Nor pool so small, that can his smoothness hold
When any wind doth under heaven blow;
With which the clouds are also toss'd and roll'd,
Now like great hills, and straight like sluices them unfold.

"So likewise are all watery living wights
Still toss'd and turnëd with continual change,
Never abiding in their steadfast plights:
The fish, still floating, do at random range,
And never rest, but evermore exchange
Their dwelling places, as the streams them carry:
Nor have the watery fowls a certain grange[12]
Wherein to rest, nor in one stead do tarry;
But flitting still do fly, and still their places vary.

"Next is the air; which who feels not by sense
(For of all sense it is the middle mean[13])
To flit still, and with subtile influence
Of his thin spirit all creatures to maintain
In state of life? O weak life! that does lean
On thing so tickle[14] as th' unsteady air,
Which ev'ry hour is chang'd, and alter'd clean
With ev'ry blast that bloweth, foul or fair:
The fair doth it prolong; the foul doth it impair.

"Therein the changes infinite behold,
Which to her creatures ev'ry minute chance;
Now boiling hot; straight freezing deadly cold;
Now fair sunshíne, that makes all skip and dance;
Straight bitter storms, and baleful countenance,
That makes them all to shiver and to shake:
Rain, hail, and snow do pay them sad penánce,
And dreadful thunder-claps (that make them quake)
With flames and flashing lights that thousand changes make.

"Last is the fire; which, though it live for ever,
Nor can be quenchëd quite, yet ev'ry day
We see his parts, so soon as they do sever,
To lose their heat and shortly to decay;
So makes himself his own consuming prey:
Nor any living creatures doth he breed,
But all that are of others bred doth slay,
And with their death his cruel life doth feed;
Naught leaving but their barren ashes without seed.

"Thus all these four (the which the ground-work be
Of all the world and of all living wights)
To thousand sorts of change we subject see:
Yet are they chang'd by other wondrous sleights
Into themselves, and lose their native mights;
The fire to air, and th' air to water sheer,[15]
And water into earth; yet water fights
With fire, and air with earth, approaching near;
Yet all are in one body, and as one appear.

"So in them all reigns Mutability;
However these, that gods themselves do call,

1 Complain.
2 Claim.
3 That which.
4 In spite of.
5 The rule of the greater part of the world.
6 Inhabitants.
7 Convene.
8 Immediately.
9 Fault; or, doom.
10 Spring.
11 Commands.
12 Dwelling.
13 The medium of communication between the senses and their objects.
14 Uncertain.
15 Clear.

Of them do claim the rule and sov'reignty;
As Vesta, of the fire ethereal;
Vulcan, of this with us so usual;
Ops, of the earth; and Juno, of the air;
Neptune, of seas; and Nymphs, of rivers all:
For all those rivers to me subject are;
And all the rest, which they usurp, be all my share.

"Which to approven true, as I have told,
Vouchsafe, O Goddess! to thy presence call
The rest which do the world in being hold;
As Times and Seasons of the year that fall:
Of all the which demand in general,
Or judge thyself by verdict of thine eye,
Whether to me they are not subject all."
Nature did yield thereto; and by and by
Bade Order call them all before her majesty.

So forth issued the Seasons of the year.
First, lusty Spring, all dight[1] in leaves of flow'rs,
That freshly budded and new blooms did bear,
In which a thousand birds had built their bow'rs,
That sweetly sung to call forth paramours;
And in his hand a javelin he did bear,
And on his head (as fit for warlike stowres[2])
A gilt engraven morion[3] he did wear;
That as some did him love, so others did him fear.

Then came the jolly Summer, being dight
In a thin silken cassock colour'd green,
That was unlinëd all, to be more light:
And on his head a garland well beseen
He wore, from which, as he had chafëd[4] been,
The sweat did drop; and in his hand he bore
A bow and shafts, as he in forest green
Had hunted late the leopard or the boar,
And now would bathe his limbs, with labour heated sore.

Then came the Autumn, all in yellow clad,
As though he joyëd in his plenteous store,
Laden with fruits that made him laugh, full glad
That he had banish'd hunger, which before
Had by the belly oft him pinchëd sore:
Upon his head a wreath, that was enroll'd
With ears of corn of ev'ry sort, he bore;
And in his hand a sickle he did hold,
To reap the ripen'd fruits the which the earth had yold.[5]

Lastly came Winter, clothëd all in frieze,
Chatt'ring his teeth for cold that did him chill;
Whilst on his hoary beard his breath did freeze,
And the dull drops, that from his purpled bill[6]
As from a limbec did adown distill:
In his right hand a tippëd staff he held,
With which his feeble steps he stayëd still;
For he was faint with cold, and weak with eld;
That scarce his loosëd limbs he able was to weld.[7]

These, marching softly, thus in order went;
And after them the Months all riding came.
First, sturdy March,[8] with brows full sternly bent,
And armëd strongly, rode upon a Ram,[9]
The same which over Hellespontus swam;[10]
Yet in his hand a spade he also hent,[11]
And in a bag all sorts of seeds y-sam,[12]
Which on the earth he strowëd as he went,
And fill'd her womb with fruitful hope of nourishment.

Next came fresh April, full of lustihead,
And wanton as a kid whose horn new buds:
Upon a Bull he rode, the same which led
Europa floating through th' Argolic floods;
His horns were gilden all with golden studs,
And garnishëd with garlands goodly dight[13]
Of all the fairest flow'rs and freshest buds
Which th' earth brings forth; and wet he seem'd in sight
With waves, through which he waded for his love's delight.

Then came fair May, the fairest maid on ground,
Deck'd all with dainties of her season's pride,
And throwing flow'rs out of her lap around:
Upon two brethren's shoulders she did ride,
The Twins of Leda;[14] which on either side
Supported her like to their sov'reign queen:
Lord! how all creatures laugh'd when her they spied,
And leap'd and danc'd as they had ravish'd been!
And Cupid's self about her flutter'd all in green.

And after her came jolly June, array'd
All in green leaves, as he a player were;
Yet in his time he wrought as well as play'd,
That by his plough-irons might right well appear:
Upon a Crab he rode, that him did bear
With crooked crawling steps an uncouth pace,
And backward yode,[15] as bargemen wont to fare,
Bending their force contrary to their face;
Like that ungracious crew which feigns demurest grace.

Then came hot July, boiling like to fire,
That all his garments he had cast away:
Upon a Lion raging yet with ire
He boldly rode, and made him to obey.
(It was the beast that whilom did foray
The Nemean forest, till th' Amphytrionide[16]
Him slew, and with his hide did him array.)
Behind his back a scythe, and by his side
Under his belt he bore a sickle circling wide.

The sixth was August, being rich array'd
In garment all of gold down to the ground:
Yet rode he not, but led a lovely maid
Forth by the lily hand, the which was crown'd
With ears of corn, and full her hand was found:
That was the righteous Virgin,[17] which of old
Liv'd here on earth, and plenty made abound;

1 Clad. 2 Conflicts. 3 Helmet.
4 Heated. 5 Yielded.
6 Nose. 7 Wield, use.
8 Which, under the Old Style (in England, until 1752), began the year.
9 Each Month is mounted on or attended by the personification of that sign of the zodiac which the sun enters during its course.
10 See note 5, page 438. 11 Held, grasped.
12 Together; German, "zusammen."
13 Prepared. 14 Castor and Pollux.
15 Went.
16 Hercules, so called from Amphytrion; the husband of his mother Alcmena.
17 Astræa. See the opening stanzas of canto i., book v., page 482.

But, after wrong was lov'd, and justice sold,
She left th' unrighteous world, and was to heav'n extoll'd.[1]

Next him September marchëd, eke on foot;
Yet was he heavy laden with the spoil
Of harvest's riches, which he made his boot,[2]
And him enrich'd with bounty of the soil:
In his one hand, as fit for harvest's toil,
He held a knife-hook; and in th' other hand
A Pair of Weights,[3] with which he did assoil[4]
Both more and less, where it in doubt did stand,
And equal gave to each as Justice duly scann'd.

Then came October, full of merry glee;
For yet his noule[5] was totty[6] of the must[7]
Which he was treading in the wine-fats' sea,
And of the joyous oil, whose gentle gust[8]
Made him so frolic and so full of lust:[9]
Upon a dreadful Scorpion he did ride,
The same which by Diana's doom unjust
Slew great Orion; and eke by his side
He had his ploughing-share and coulter ready tied.

Next was November; he full gross and fat
As fed with lard, and that right well might seem;
For he had been a-fatting hogs of late,
That yet his brows with sweat did reek and steam,
And yet the season was full sharp and breme;[10]
In planting eke he took no small delight.
Whereon he rode, not easy was to deem;
For it a dreadful Centaur was in sight,
The seed of Saturn and fair Nais,[11] Chiron hight.

And after him came next the chill December:
Yet he, through merry feasting which he made
And great bonfires, did not the cold remember;
His Saviour's birth his mind so much did glad.
Upon a shaggy-bearded Goat he rode,
The same wherewith Dan Jove in tender years,
They say, was nourish'd by th' Idæan maid;[12]
And in his hand a broad deep bowl he bears,
Of which he freely drinks a health to all his peers.

Then came old January, wrappëd well
In many weeds to keep the cold away;
Yet did he quake and quiver like to quell,[13]
And blow his nails to warm them if he may;
For they were numb'd with holding all the day
A hatchet keen, with which he fellëd wood
And from the trees did lop the needless spray:[14]
Upon a huge great earth-pot stone[15] he stood,
From whose wide mouth there flowëd forth the Roman flood.[16]

And lastly came cold February, sitting
In an old waggon, for he could not ride,
Drawn of two Fishes, for the season fitting,
Which through the flood before did softly slide
And swim away; yet had he by his side
His plough and harness fit to till the ground,
And tools to prune the trees, before the pride
Of hasting Prime[17] did make them burgeon[18] round.
So pass'd the twelve Months forth, and their due places found.

And after these there came the Day and Night,
Riding together both with equal pace;
Th' one on a palfrey black, the other white:
But Night had cover'd her uncomely face
With a black veil, and held in hand a mace,[19]
On top whereof the moon and stars were pight,[20]
And Sleep and Darkness round about did trace:[21]
But Day did bear upon his sceptre's height
The goodly sun encompass'd all with beamës bright.

Then came the Hours, fair daughters of high Jove
And timely Night; the which were all endued
With wondrous beauty, fit to kindle love;
But they were virgins all, and love eschew'd,
That might forslack[22] the charge to them foreshew'd[23]
By mighty Jove; who did them porters make
Of heaven's gate (whence all the gods issúed)
Which they did daily watch, and nightly wake
By even turns, nor ever did their charge forsake.

And after all came Life; and lastly Death:
Death with most grim and grisly visage seen,
Yet is he naught but parting of the breath;
Nor aught to see, but like a shade to ween,
Unbodiëd, unsoul'd, unheard, unseen:
But Life was like a fair young lusty boy,
Such as they feign Dan Cupid to have been,
Full of delightful health and lively joy,
Deck'd all with flow'rs and wings of gold fit to employ.

When these were past, thus gan the Titaness;
"Lo! mighty Mother, now be judge, and say
Whether in all thy creatures more or less
CHANGE doth not reign and bear the greatest sway:
For who sees not that Time on all doth prey?
But times do change and move continually:
So nothing here long standeth in one stay:
Wherefore this lower world who can deny
But to be subject still to Mutability?"

Then thus gan Jove; "Right true it is, that these
And all things else that under heaven dwell
Are chang'd of Time, who doth them all disseise[24]
Of being: but who is it (to me tell)

1 Elevated. 2 Booty.
3 Denoting the constellation Libra.
4 Determine. 5 Pate, noddle.
6 Dizzy. 7 New wine.
8 Flavour. 9 Pleasure.
10 Piercing, inclement.
11 Naïs, or Chariclo, was the *wife* of Chiron; it was of Saturn and Philyra that he was born. See note 18, page 439.
12 Jupiter was brought up on Mount Dicte, in Crete, by the nymphs Adrastia and Ida, and nourished with the milk of the goat Amalthea. Probably enough the word Idæan in the text (Iæan, as the old editions have it), results from a confusion between the name of the nymph Ida, and the name of Mount Ida, also in Crete.
13 Quail, perish. 14 Branch.
15 Vessel, urn, of stone.
16 From the watering-pot of Aquarius flowed the constellation Eridanus—which is the Greek name for the River Po, the greatest Italian stream.
17 Spring. 18 Bud.
19 Sceptre. 20 Fixed.
21 Move. 22 Cause neglect of.
23 Intrusted beforehand. 24 Dispossess.

That Time himself doth move, and still compel
To keep his course? Is not that namely We,
Which pour that virtue from our heav'nly cell
That moves them all, and makes them changëd be?
So them We gods do rule, and in them also thee."

To whom thus Mutability; "The things
Which we see not how they are mov'd and sway'd,
Ye may attribute to yourselves as kings,
And say, they by your secret pow'r are made:
But what we see not, who shall us persuade?
But were they so, as ye them feign to be,
Mov'd by your might, and order'd by your aid,
Yet what if I can prove, that even Ye
Yourselves are likewise chang'd, and subject unto Me?

"And first, concerning her that is the first,
Ev'n you, fair Cynthia; whom so much ye make
Jove's dearest darling, she was bred and nurst
On Cynthus hill, whence she her name did take;
Then is she mortal born, howso ye crake:[1]
Besides, her face and count'nance ev'ry day
We changëd see, and sundry forms partake,
Now horn'd, now round, now bright, now brown and gray;
So that 'as changeful as the moon' men use to say.

"Next Mercury; who, though he less appear
To change his hue, and always seem as one,
Yet he his course doth alter ev'ry year,
And is of late far out of order gone.
So Venus eke, that goodly paragon,
Though fair all night, yet is she dark all day:
And Phœbus' self, who lightsome is alone,
Yet is he oft eclipsëd by the way,
And fills the darken'd world with terror and dismay.

"Now Mars, that valiant man, is changëd most;
For he sometimes so far runs out of square,
That he his way doth seem quite to have lost,
And clean without his usual sphere to fare;
That even these star-gazers 'stonish'd are
At sight thereof, and damn their lying books:
So likewise grim Sir Saturn oft doth spare
His stern aspéct, and calm his crabbëd looks:
So many turning cranks these have, so many crooks.

"But you, Dan Jove, that only constant are,
And king of all the rest, as ye do claim,
Are you not subject eke to this misfare?[2]
Then let me ask you this withouten blame:
Where were ye born? Some say in Crete by name,
Others in Thebes, and others otherwhere;
But, wheresoever they comment[3] the same,
They all consent that ye begotten were
And born here in this world; nor other can appear.

"Then are ye mortal born, and thrall to me;
Unless the kingdom of the sky ye make
Immortal and unchangeable to be:
Besides, that pow'r and virtue which ye spake,
That ye here work, doth many changes take,
And your own natures change: for each of you,
That virtue have or this or that to make,
Is check'd and changëd from his nature true
By others' opposition or obliquid[4] view.

"Besides, the sundry motions of your spheres,
So sundry ways and fashions as clerks[5] feign,
Some in short space, and some in longer years,
What is the same but alteration plain?
Only the starry sky doth still remain:
Yet do the stars and signs therein still move,
And ev'n itself is mov'd, as wizards sayn:[6]
But all that moveth doth mutation love:
Therefore both you and them to me I subject prove.

"Then since within this wide great Universe
Nothing doth firm and permanent appear,
But all things toss'd and turnëd by transvérse;
What then should let,[7] but I aloft should rear
My trophy, and from all the triumph bear?
Now judge then, O thou greatest Goddess true,
According as thyself dost see and hear,
And unto me addoom[8] that is my due;
That is, the rule of all; all being rul'd by you."

So having ended, silence long ensued;
Nor Nature to or fro spake for a space,
But with firm eyes affix'd the ground still view'd.
Meanwhile all creatures, looking in her face,
Expecting th' end of this so doubtful case,
Did hang in long suspense what would ensue,
To whether side should fall the sov'reign place:
At length she, looking up with cheerful view,
The silence brake, and gave her doom[9] in speeches few:

"I well consider all that ye have said;
And find that all things steadfastness do hate
And changëd be; yet, being rightly weigh'd,[10]
They are not changëd from their first estate;
But by their change their being do dilate;
And, turning[11] to themselves at length again,
Do work their own perfection so by fate:
Then over them Change doth not rule and reign:
But they reign over Change, and do their states maintain.

"Cease, therefore, Daughter, farther to aspire,
And thee content thus to be rul'd by me:
For thy decay[12] thou seek'st by thy desire:
But time shall come that all shall changëd be,
And from thenceforth none no more change shall see!"
So was the Titaness put down and whist,[13]
And Jove confirm'd in his imperial see.[14]
Then was that whole assembly quite dismist,
And Nature's self did vanish, whither no man wist.

1 Boast. 2 Misfortune.
3 Falsely relate, or pretend; like "glose," as used by Chaucer. 4 Oblique.
5 Scholars. 6 As sages say.
7 Hinder. 8 Adjudge.
9 Judgment. 10 Examined, considered.
11 Returning. 12 Ruin.
13 Silenced, hushed. 14 Seat.

CANTO VIII. (IMPERFECT.)

WHEN I bethink me on that speech whilere[1]
Of Mutability, and well it weigh ;
Me seems, that though she all unworthy were
Of th' heavens' rule, yet, very sooth to say,
In all things else she bears the greatest sway :
Which makes me loathe this state of life so tickle,[2]
And love of things so vain to cast away ;
Whose flow'ring pride, so fading and so fickle,
Short Time shall soon cut down with his consuming sickle !

Then gin I think on that which Nature said,
Of that same time when no more change shall be,
But steadfast rest of all things, firmly stay'd
Upon the pillars of Eternity,
That is contráir to Mutability :
For all that moveth doth in change delight :
But thenceforth all shall rest eternally
With Him that is the God of Sabaoth hight :
Oh ! that great Sabaoth God, grant me that Sabbath's sight !

. . . . . .

1 Lately

2 Unstable.

THE END OF THE FAERIE QUEEN.

THE SHEPHERD'S CALENDAR:

CONTAINING

TWELVE ECLOGUES,

PROPORTIONABLE TO THE TWELVE MONTHS.

ENTITLED

TO THE NOBLE AND VIRTUOUS GENTLEMAN, MOST WORTHY OF ALL TITLES, BOTH OF LEARNING AND CHIVALRY,

MASTER PHILIP SIDNEY.

[1579.][1]

TO HIS BOOK.

Go, little Book! thyself present,
As child whose parent is unkent,[2]
To him that is the president
Of Nobless and of Chivalry:
And if that Envy bark at thee,
As sure it will, for succour flee
Under the shadow of his wing.
And, askèd who thee forth did bring,
A shepherd's swain, say, did thee sing,
All as his straying flock he fed:
And, when his Honour has thee read,
Crave pardon for my hardihead.
But, if that any ask thy name,
Say, thou wert base-begot with blame,
Forthy[3] *thereof thou takest shame.*
And, when thou art past jeopardy,
Come tell me what was said of me,
And I will send more after thee.—IMMERITO.

TO THE MOST EXCELLENT AND LEARNED,
BOTH ORATOR AND POET,

MASTER GABRIEL HARVEY,

HIS VERY SPECIAL AND SINGULAR GOOD FRIEND E. K.[4] COMMENDETH THE GOOD LIKING OF THIS HIS GOOD LABOUR, AND THE PATRONAGE OF THE NEW POET.

"UNCOUTH, unkiss'd," said the old famous poet Chaucer:[5] whom for his excellency and wonderful skill in making,[6] his scholar Lydgate, a worthy scholar of so excellent a master, calleth the lodestar of our language: and whom our Colin Clout in his Æglogue calleth Tityrus the god of shepherds, comparing him to the worthiness of the Roman Tityrus, Virgil. Which proverb, mine own good friend M. Harvey, as in that good old poet it served well Pandar's purpose for the bolstering of his bawdy brocage,[7] so very well taketh place in this our new Poet,

1 "The Shepherd's Calendar," the greatest pastoral poem in the English language, was registered on the books of the Stationers' Company on 5th December 1579, and published, in small quarto, by Hugh Singleton, "dwelling in Creed Lane, near unto Ludgate." who chose the means of an introductory epistle, general and particular arguments, and a glossary, to make such explanations of his meaning as the rustic style of the work required, or as he deemed convenient to give respecting the persons and circumstances dealt with. The author's name was not attached to "The Shepherd's Calendar."

2 Unknown.

3 Therefore.

4 "E. K." is generally understood to have been one Edmund Kirke, or Kerke, who was a University friend of the poet's, and apparently entrusted in the fullest confidence not only with his works before their publication, but with the knowledge of his purposes and his meaning. There are not wanting, however, believers in the theory that "E. K." really was the poet himself,

5 In the first book of "Troilus and Cressida;" where, endeavouring to encourage his friend to declare his love for Cressida, Pandarus says to Troilus, "Unknown, unkist, and lost that is unsought."

6 Writing poetry. See note 10, page 273.

7 Pimping.

who for that he is uncouth (as said Chaucer) is unkiss'd, and, unknown to most men, is regarded but of a few. But I doubt not, so soon as his name shall come into the knowledge of men, and his worthiness be sounded in the trump of Fame, but that he shall be not only kiss'd, but also beloved of all, embraced of the most, and wonder'd at of the best. No less, I think, deserveth his wittiness in devising, his pithiness in uttering, his complaints of love so lovely, his discourses of pleasure so pleasantly, his pastoral rudeness, his moral wiseness, his due observing of decorum everywhere, in personages, in seasons, in matter, in speech; and generally, in all seemly simplicity of handling his matters and framing his words: the which, of many things which in him be strange, I know will seem the strangest, the words themselves being so ancient, the knitting of them so short and intricate, and the whole period and compass of speech so delightsome for the roundness, and so grave for the strangeness. And first of the words to speak, I grant they be something hard, and of most men unused, yet both English, and also used of most excellent authors and most famous poets. In whom when as this our Poet hath been much travailed and throughly read, how could it be (as that worthy orator said) but that walking in the sun, although for other cause he walks, yet needs he must be sunburnt; and, having the sound of those ancient poets still ringing in his ears, he must needs, in singing, hit out some of their tunes. But whether he useth them by such casualty and custom, or of set purpose and choice, as thinking them fittest for such rustical rudeness of shepherds, either for that their rough sound would make his rhymes more ragged and rustical, or else because such old and obsolete words are most used of country folk, sure I think, and think I think not amiss, that they bring great grace, and, as one would say, authority to the verse. For all be, amongst many other faults, it specially be objected of Valla[1] against Livy, and of other against Sallust, that with over much study they affect antiquity, as coveting thereby credence and honour of elder years; yet I am of opinion, and eke the best learned are of the like, that those ancient solemn words are a great ornament, both in the one and in the other: the one labouring to set forth in his work an eternal image of antiquity, and the other carefully discoursing matters of gravity and importance. For, if my memory fail not, Tully, in that book wherein he endeavoureth to set forth the pattern of a perfect orator,[2] saith that ofttimes an ancient word maketh the style seem grave, and as it were reverend, no otherwise than we honour and reverence gray hairs for a certain religious regard which we have of old age. Yet neither everywhere must old words be stuffed in, nor the common dialect and manner of speaking so corrupted thereby, that, as in old buildings, it seem disorderly and ruinous. But all as in most exquisite pictures they use to blaze and portray not only the dainty lineaments of beauty, but also round about it to shadow the rude thickets and craggy cliffs, that, by the baseness of such parts, more excellency may accrue to the principal: for ofttimes we find ourselves, I know not how, singularly delighted with the show of such natural rudeness, and take great pleasure in that disorderly order. Even so do those rough and harsh terms enlumine, and make more clearly to appear, the brightness of brave and glorious words. So oftentimes a discord in music maketh a comely concordance: so great delight took the worthy poet Alcæus to behold a blemish in the joint of a well-shaped body. But, if any will rashly blame such his purpose in choice of old and unwonted words, him may I more justly blame and condemn, or[3] of witless headiness in judging, or of heedless hardiness in condemning: for, not marking the compass of his bent, he will judge of the length of his cast: for in my opinion it is one especial praise of many, which are due to this Poet, that he hath laboured to restore, as to their rightful heritage, such good and natural English words as have been long time out of use, and almost clean disherited. Which is the only cause that our mother tongue, which truly of itself is both full enough for prose, and stately enough for verse, hath long time been counted most bare and barren of both. Which default when as some endeavoured to salve and recure, they patched up the holes with pieces and rags of other languages, borrowing here of the French, there of the Italian, everywhere of the Latin; not weighing how ill those tongues accord with themselves, but much worse with ours: So now they have made our English tongue a gallimaufrey, or hodge-podge of all other speeches. Other some, not so well seen[4] in the English tongue as perhaps in other languages, if they happen to hear an old word, albeit very natural and significant, cry out straightway, that we speak no English, but gibberish, or rather such as in old time Evander's mother[5] spake: whose first shame is, that they are not ashamed, in their own mother tongue, to be counted strangers and aliens. The second shame no less than the first, that whatso they understand not, they straightway deem to be senseless, and not at all to be understood. Much like to the mole in Æsop's fable, that, being blind herself, would in no wise be persuaded that any beast could see. The last, more shameful than both, that of their own country and natural speech, which together with their nurse's milk they sucked, they have so base regard and bastard judgment, that they will not only themselves not labour to garnish and beautify it, but also repine that of other it should be embellished. Like to the dog in the manger, that himself can eat no hay, and yet barketh at the hungry bullock, that so

1 Laurence Valla, a celebrated Italian philologer, who lived in the first half of the fifteenth century, and made important contributions to the revival of learning.

2 Cicero, "De Oratore." 3 Either. 4 Instructed.

5 Carmentis, who fled with her son from Arcadia to Latium, and uttered oracles on the Capitoline Hill.

fain would feed: whose currish kind, though it cannot be kept from barking, yet I can them thank that they refrain from biting.

Now, for the knitting of sentences, which they call the joints and members thereof, and for all the compass of the speech, it is round without roughness, and learned without hardness, such indeed as may be perceived of the least, understood of the most, but judged only of the learned. For what in most English writers useth to be loose, and as it were ungirt, in this Author is well grounded, finely framed, and strongly trussed up together. In regard whereof, I scorn and spue out the rakehelly rout of our ragged rhymers (for so themselves use to hunt the letter) which without learning boast, without judgment jangle, without reason rage and foam, as if some instinct of poetical spirit had newly ravished them above the meanness of common capacity. And being in the midst of all their bravery, suddenly, either for want of matter or rhyme, or having forgotten their former conceit, they seem to be so pained and travailed in their remembrance, as it were a woman in childbirth, or as that same Pythia, when the trance came upon her. "*Os rabidum fera corda domans*," &c.

Nathless, let them a God's name feed on their own folly, so they seek not to darken the beams of others' glory. As for Colin, under whose person the Author's self is shadowed, how far he is from such vaunted titles and glorious [1] shows, both himself showeth, where he saith:

> "Of Muses, Hobbin, I conne no skill."

And

> "Enough is me to paint out my unrest," &c.

And also appeareth by the baseness of the name, wherein it seemeth he chose rather to unfold great matter of argument covertly, than, professing it, not suffice thereto accordingly. Which moved him rather in Æglogues than otherwise to write, doubting perhaps his ability, which he little needed, or minding to furnish our tongue with this kind, wherein it faulteth; [2] or following the example of the best and most ancient poets, which devised this kind of writing, being both so base for the matter, and homely for the manner, at the first to try their abilities; and as young birds, that be newly crept out of the nest, by little first prove their tender wings, before they make a greater flight. So flew Theocritus, as you may perceive he was already full fledged. So flew Virgil, as not yet well feeling his wings. So flew Mantuan, [3] as not being full summed. [4] So Petrarch. So Boccaccio. So Marot, Sanazarius, and also divers other excellent both Italian and French poets, whose footing this Author everywhere followeth: yet so as few, but they be well scented, [5] can trace him out. So finally flieth this our new Poet as a bird whose principals [6] be scarce grown out, but yet as one that in time shall be able to keep wing with the best.

Now, as touching the general drift and purpose of his Æglogues, I mind not to say much, himself labouring to conceal it. Only this appeareth, that his unstaid youth had long wandered in the common labyrinth of love; in which time, to mitigate and allay the heat of his passion, or else to warn (as he saith) the young shepherds, his equals and companions, of his unfortunate folly, he compiled these twelve Æglogues, which, for that they be proportioned to the state of the twelve months, he termeth the *Shepherd's Calendar*, applying an old name to a new work. [7] Hereunto have I added a certain gloss, or scholion, for the exposition of old words and harder phrases; which manner of glossing and commenting, well I wot, will seem strange and rare in our tongue: yet, for so much as I knew many excellent and proper devices, both in words and matter, would pass in the speedy course of reading either as unknown, or as not marked; and that in this kind, as in other, we might be equal to the learned of other nations; I thought good to take the pains upon me, the rather for that by means of some familiar acquaintance I was made privy to his counsel and secret meaning in them, as also in sundry other works of his. Which albeit I know he nothing so much hateth as to promulgate, yet thus much have I adventured upon his friendship, himself being for long time far estranged; hoping that this will the rather occasion him to put forth divers other excellent works of his, which sleep in silence; as his *Dreams*, his *Legends*, his *Court of Cupid*, and sundry others, whose commendation to set out were very vain, the things, though worthy of many, yet being known to few. These my present pains, if to any they be pleasurable or profitable, be you judge, mine own good Master Harvey, to whom I have, both in respect of your worthiness generally, and otherwise upon some particular and special considerations, vowed this my labour, and the maidenhead of this our common friend's poetry; himself having already in the beginning dedicated it to the noble and worthy gentleman, the right worshipful Master Philip Sidney, a special favourer and maintainer of all kind of learning. Whose

1 Vainglorious.

2 Is deficient.

3 Virgil, from his birthplace, was called the "Mantuan;" and "E. K." does not reflect much credit on his classical training by treating the local appellation as the name of some other poet. On the other hand, if we understand "Mantuan" to mean the greater Tasso—whose father for thirty years was in the service of the Duke of Mantua—the instance is false, for his epic "Rinaldo" was published many years before his idyll "Aminta." Besides, Tasso was contemporary with Spenser; and, even if his works had been familiarly known to "E. K.," the enumeration of him before Petrarch and Boccaccio would not have been natural.

4 Not having the feathers full-grown.

5 Keen of scent.

6 The "principals" of a hawk are the longest wing-feathers.

7 "The Boke of Shephearde's Kalender," says Mr Craik, was the title of an old manual of the nature of an almanac, supposed to have been first printed by Wynkyn de Worde. Reference is made in note 20, p. 186, to a French "Calendrier des Bergiers," which probably formed the original of the English "Kalender."

cause I pray you, Sir, if envy shall stir up any wrongful accusation, defend with your mighty rhetoric and other your rare gifts of learning, as you can, and shield with your good will, as you ought, against the malice and outrage of so many enemies, as I know will be set on fire with the sparks of his kindled glory. And thus recommending the Author unto you, as unto his most special good friend, and myself unto you both, as one making singular account of two so very good and so choice friends, I bid you both most heartily farewell, and commit you and your commendable studies to the tuition of the Greatest.

Your own assuredly to be commanded,

E. K.

P.S.—Now I trust, M. Harvey, that upon sight of your special friend's and fellow poet's doings, or else for envy of so many unworthy Quidams, which catch at the garland which to you alone is due, you will be persuaded to pluck out of the hateful darkness those so many excellent English poems of yours which lie hid, and bring them forth to eternal light. Trust me, you do both them great wrong, in depriving them of the desired sun; and also yourself, in smothering your deserved praises; and all men generally, in withholding from them so divine pleasures, which they might conceive of your gallant English verses, as they have already done of your Latin poems, which, in my opinion, both for invention and elocution, are very delicate and super-excellent. And thus again I take my leave of my good M. Harvey. From my lodging at London this tenth of April, 1579.

THE GENERAL ARGUMENT OF THE WHOLE BOOK.

Little, I hope, needeth me at large to discourse the first original of Æglogues, having already touched the same. But, for the word Æglogues I know is unknown to most, and also mistaken of some of the best learned (as they think), I will say somewhat thereof, being not at all impertinent to my present purpose.

They were first of the Greeks, the inventors of them, called Æglogai, *as it were,* Ægon, or Æginomon logi,[1] *that is, Goatherds' tales. For although in Virgil and others the speakers be more shepherds than goatherds, yet Theocritus, in whom is more ground of authority than in Virgil, this specially from that deriving, as from the first head and wellspring, the whole invention of these Æglogues, maketh goatherds the persons and authors of his tales. This being, who seeth not the grossness of such as by colour of learning would make us believe that they are more rightly termed* Eclogai, *as they would say, extraordinary discourses of unnecessary matter: which definition all be in substance and meaning it agree with the nature of the thing, yet no whit answereth with the analysis and interpretation of the word. For they be not termed* Eclogues, *but* Æglogues; *which sentence this Author very well observing, upon good judgment, though indeed few goatherds have to do herein, nevertheless doubteth*[2] *not to call them by the used and best known name. Other curious discourses hereof I reserve to greater occasion.*

These twelve Æglogues, everywhere answering to the seasons of the twelve months, may be well divided into three forms or ranks. For either they be plaintive, as the first, the sixth, the eleventh, and the twelfth; or recreative, such as all those be which contain matter of love, or commendation of special personages; or moral, which for the most part be mixed with some satirical bitterness: namely, the second, of reverence due to old age; the fifth, of coloured deceit; the seventh and ninth, of dissolute shepherds and pastors; the tenth, of contempt of poetry and pleasant wits. And to this division may everything herein be reasonably applied; a few only except, whose special purpose and meaning I am not privy to. And thus much generally of these twelve Æglogues. Now will we speak particularly of all, and first of the first, which he calleth by the first month's name, January: wherein to some he may seem foully to have faulted,[3] *in that he erroneously beginneth with that month, which beginneth not the year. For it is well known, and stoutly maintained with strong reasons of the learned, that the year beginneth in March; for then the sun reneweth his finished course, and the seasonable spring refresheth the earth, and the pleasance thereof, being buried in the sadness of the dead winter now worn away, reliveth.*[4]

This opinion maintain the old Astrologers and Philosophers, namely, the reverend Andalo, and Macrobius in his "Holy Days of Saturn;" which account also was generally observed both of Grecians and Romans. But, saving the leave of such learned heads, we maintain a custom of counting the seasons from the month January, upon a more special cause than the heathen Philosophers ever could conceive; that is, for the Incarnation of our mighty Saviour and Eternal Redeemer the Lord Christ, who, as then renewing

1 More correctly, "Aigon, or Aigonomon logoi"—Αἰγὼν or Αἰγονόμων λόγοι—the discourses or words of goat-herds. But the word "Eclogue" is really derived from ἐκλέγω, I select; ἐκλογή, a selection, or the thing selected as best; and means that which the author has chosen to put forth as his best work.

2 Hesitateth.

3 Erred.

4 In the procession of the months, in the second canto of Mutability, the order is observed the departure from which is here defended.

the state of the decayed world, and returning the compass of expired years to their former date and first commencement, left to us his heirs a memorial of his birth in the end of the last year and beginning of the next. Which reckoning, besides that eternal monument of our salvation, leaneth also upon good proof of special judgment.

For albeit that in elder times, when as yet the count of the year was not perfected, as afterward it was by Julius Cæsar, they began to tell[1] *the months from March's beginning, and according to the same, God (as is said in Scripture) commanded the people of the Jews to count the month* Abib, *that which we call March, for the first month, in remembrance that in that month he brought them out of the land of Egypt: yet, according to tradition of latter times, it hath been otherwise observed, both in government of the Church and rule of mightiest realms. For from Julius Cæsar, who first observed the leap year, which he called* Bissextilem Annum, *and brought into a more certain course the odd wandering days which of the Greeks were called* Hyperbainontes, *of the Romans* Intercalares *(for in such matter of learning I am forced to use the terms of the learned), the months have been numbered twelve, which in the first ordinance of Romulus were but ten, counting but* 304 *days in every year, and beginning with March. But Numa Pompilius, who was the father of all the Roman ceremonies and religion, seeing that reckoning to agree neither with the course of the sun nor the moon, thereunto added two months, January and February; wherein it seemeth, that wise king minded upon good reason to begin the year at January, of him therefore so called* tanquam janua anni, *the gate and entrance of the year; or of the name of the god* Janus, *to which god for that the old Paynims*[2] *attributed the birth and beginning of all creatures new coming into the world, it seemeth that he therefore to him assigned the beginning and first entrance of the year. Which account*[3] *for the most part hath hitherto continued: notwithstanding that the Egyptians begin their year at September; for that, according to the opinion of the best Rabbins and very purpose of the Scripture itself, God made the world in that month, that is called of them* Tisri. *And therefore he commanded them to keep the feast of Pavilions in the end of the year, in the fifteenth day of the seventh month, which before that time was the first.*

But our Author, respecting neither the subtilty of the one part, nor the antiquity of the other, thinketh it fittest, according to the simplicity of common understanding, to begin with January; weening it perhaps no decorum that shepherds should be seen[4] *in matter of so deep insight, or canvass a case of so doubtful judgment. So therefore beginneth he, and so continueth he throughout.*

THE SHEPHERD'S CALENDAR.

JANUARY.

ÆGLOGA PRIMA.—ARGUMENT.

In this first Æglogue Colin Clout, a shepherd's boy, complaineth him of his unfortunate love, being but newly (as seemeth) enamoured of a country lass called Rosalind: with which strong affection being very sore travailed, he compareth his careful case[5] *to the sad season of the year, to the frosty ground, to the frozen trees, and to his own winter-beaten flock. And, lastly, finding himself robbed of all former pleasance and delights, he breaketh his pipe in pieces, and casteth himself to the ground.*

Colin Clout.[6]

A SHEPHERD'S boy (no better do him call),
When winter's wasteful spite was almost spent,
All in a sunshine day, as did befall,
Led forth his flock, that had been long y-pent:[7]
So faint they wox, and feeble in the fold,
That now unnethes[8] their feet could them uphold.

All as the sheep, such was the shepherd's look;
For pale and wan he was (alas the while!)
May seem he lov'd, or else some care he took;
Well couth he[9] tune his pipe and frame his style:
Then to a hill his fainting flock he led,
And thus him plain'd, the while his sheep there fed:

"Ye gods of love! that pity lovers' pain
(If any gods the pain of lovers pity),
Look from above, where you in joys remain,
And bow your ears unto my doleful ditty:
And, Pan! thou shepherds' god, that once didst love,
Pity the pains that thou thyself didst prove.

"Thou barren ground, whom winter's wrath hath wasted,
Art made a mirror to behold my plight:
Whilom thy fresh spring flow'r'd, and after hasted

1 Reckon.
2 Pagans.
3 Way of reckoning.
4 Skilled, instructed.
5 Sorrowful plight.
6 "Under which name this poet secretly shadoweth himself, as sometimes did Virgil under the name of Tityrus."—*E. K.*
7 Pent up, confined.
8 Hardly.
9 Could he—had he skill to.

Thy summer proud, with daffodillies dight;
And now is come thy winter's stormy state,
Thy mantle marr'd wherein thou maskedst late.

"Such rage as winter's reigneth in my heart,
My life-blood freezing with unkindly cold;
Such stormy stours[1] do breed my baleful smart,
As if my year were waste and waxen old;
And yet, alas! but now my spring begun,
And yet, alas! it is already done.

"You naked trees, whose shady leaves are lost,
Wherein the birds were wont to build their bow'r,
And now are cloth'd with moss and hoary frost,
Instead of blossoms, wherewith your buds did flow'r;
I see your tears that from your boughs do rain,
Whose drops in dreary icicles remain.

"All so my lustful leaf is dry and sear,
My timely buds with wailing all are wasted;
The blossom which my branch of youth did bear
With breathëd sighs is blown away and blasted;
And from mine eyes the drizzling tears descend,
As on your boughs the icicles depend.

"Thou feeble flock! whose fleece is rough and rent,
Whose knees are weak through fast and evil fare,
May'st witness well, by thy ill government,
Thy master's mind is overcome with care:
Thou weak, I wan; thou lean, I quite forlorn:
With mourning pine I; you with pining mourn.

"A thousand siths[2] I curse that careful hour
Wherein I long'd the neighbour town to see,
And eke ten thousand siths I bless the stour[3]
Wherein I saw so fair a sight as she:
Yet all for naught: such sight hath bred my bane.
Ah, God! that love should breed both joy and pain!

"It is not Hobbinol[4] wherefor I plain,
All be my love he seek with daily suit;
His clownish gifts and court'sies I disdain,
His kids, his cracknels, and his early fruit.
Ah, foolish Hobbinol! thy gifts be vain;
Colin them gives to Rosalind[5] again.

"I love that lass (alas! why do I love?)
And am forlorn (alas! why am I lorn?)
She deigns not my good will, but doth reprove,
And of my rural music holdeth scorn.
Shepherd's device she hateth as the snake,
And laughs the songs that Colin Clout doth make.

"Wherefore, my pipe, all be rude Pan thou please,
Yet for thou pleasest not where most I would;
And thou, unlucky Muse, that wont'st to ease
My musing mind, yet canst not when thou should;
Both pipe and Muse shall sore the while aby."[6]
So broke his oaten pipe, and down did lie.

By that the welkëd Phœbus[7] gan avail[8]
His weary wain; and now the frosty Night
Her mantle black through heav'n gan overhale:[9]
Which seen, the pensive boy, half in despite,
Arose, and homeward drove his sunnëd sheep,
Whose hanging heads did seem his careful case to weep.

COLIN'S EMBLEM:

Ancora speme. (Hope is my anchor.)

1 Attacks, calamities.
2 Times.
3 Occasion, chance.
4 Under this name is understood to be represented Spenser's University companion, Gabriel Harvey.
5 "Rosalind is a feigned name, which, being well ordered, will bewray the very name of his love and mistress, whom by that name he coloureth."—*E. K.*

6 Abide, suffer.
7 The waning sun.
8 Bring down.
9 Draw over.

FEBRUARY.

ÆGLOGA SECUNDA.—ARGUMENT.

This Æglogue is rather moral and general, than bent to any secret or particular purpose. It specially containeth a discourse of old age, in the person of Thenot, an old shepherd, who, for his crookedness and unlustiness, is scorned of Cuddie, an unhappy herdman's boy. The matter very well accordeth with the season of the month, the year now drooping, and as it were drawing to his last age. For as in this time of year, so then in our bodies, there is a dry and withering cold, which congealeth the curdled blood, and freezeth the weather-beaten flesh, with storms of Fortune and hoar-frosts of Care. To which purpose the old man telleth a tale of the Oak and the Briar, so lively, and so feelingly, as, if the thing were set forth in some picture before our eyes, more plainly could not appear.

Cuddie. Thenot.

C. Ah for pity! will rank winter's rage
These bitter blasts never gin t' assuage?
The keen cold blows through my beaten hide,
All as I were through the body gride:[10]
My ragged ronts[11] all shiver and shake,
As do high towers in an earthquake:
They wont in the wind wag their wriggle tails
Perk[12] as a peacock; but now it avails.[13]
T. Lewdly[14] complainest, thou lazy lad,
Of winter's wrack for making thee sad.
Must not the world wend in his common course,
From good to bad, and from bad to worse,
From worse unto that is worst of all,
And then return to his former fall?[15]
Who will not suffer the stormy time,
Where will he live till the lusty prime?[16]
Self have I worn out thrice thirty years,

10 Pierced.
11 Young bullocks.
12 Pert, lively.
13 Droops.
14 Foolishly, ignorantly.
15 State.
16 Spring.

Some in much joy, many in many tears,
Yet never complainëd of cold nor heat,
Of summer's flame, nor of winter's threat;
Nor ever was to Fortúne foemán,
But gently took that ungently came;
And ever my flock was my chief care;
Winter or summer they might well fare.
C. No marvel, Thenot, if thou can bear
Cheerfully the winter's wrathful cheer;
For age and winter accord full nigh,
This chill, that cold; this crookëd, that wry;
And as the louring weather looks down,
So seemest thou like Good Friday to frown:
But my flow'ring youth is foe to frost,
My ship unwont in storms to be tost.
T. The sov'reign of seas he blames in vain,
That, once sea-beat, will to sea again:
So loitering live you little herdgrooms,[1]
Keeping your beasts in the budded brooms;[2]
And, when the shining sun laugheth once,
You deemen the spring is come at once;
Then gin you, fond[3] flies! the cold to scorn,
And, crowing in pipes made of green corn,
You thinken to be lords of the year;
But eft,[4] when ye count you freed from fear,
Comes the breme[5] Winter with chamfred[6] brows,
Full of wrinkles and frosty furrόws,
Drearily shooting his stormy dart,
Which curdles the blood and pricks the heart:
Then is your careless courage accoy'd,[7]
Your careful herds with cold be annoy'd:
Then pay you the price of your surquedry[8]
With weeping, and wailing, and misery.
C. Ah! foolish old man! I scorn thy skill,
That wouldst me my springing youth to spill:[9]
I deem thy brain emperishëd be
Through rusty eld that hath rotted thee;
Or sicker thy head very totty[10] is,
So on thy corb[11] shoulder it leans amiss.
Now thyself hath lost both lop[12] and top,
Als' my budding branch thou wouldest crop;
But were thy years green, as now be mine,
To other delights they would incline:
Then wouldest thou learn to carol of love,
And hery[13] with hymns thy lass's glove;
Then wouldest thou pipe of Phyllis' praise;
But Phyllis is mine for many days;
I won her with a girdle of gelt,[14]
Emboss'd with bugle[15] about the belt:
Such an one shepherds would make full fain;
Such an one would make thee young again.
T. Thou art a fon,[16] of thy love to boast;
All that is lent to love will be lost.
C. Seëst how brag[17] yond bullock bears,
So smirk,[18] so smooth, his prickëd ears?
His horns be as broad as rainbow bent,
His dewlap as lithe as lass of Kent:
See how he venteth[19] into the wind;
Weenest of love is not his mind?[20]
Seemeth thy flock thy counsel can,[21]
So lustless[22] be they, so weak, so wan;
Clothëd with cold, and hoary with frost,
Thy flock's father his courage hath lost.
Thy ewes, that wont to have blowen bags,
Like wailful widows hangen their crags;[23]
The rather[24] lambs be starv'd with cold,
All for their master is lustless and old.
T. Cuddie, I wot thou ken'st[25] little good,
So vainly t' advance thy heedlesshood;[26]
For youth is a bubble blown up with breath,
Whose wit is weakness, whose wage is death,
Whose way is wilderness, whose inn penánce
And stoop-gallant[27] Age, the host of Grievánce.
But shall I tell thee a tale of truth,
Which I conn'd[28] of Tityrus[29] in my youth,
Keeping his sheep on the hills of Kent?
C. To naught more, Thenot, my mind is bent
Than to hear novels of his devise;[30]
They be so well thewëd,[31] and so wise,
Whatever that good old man bespake.
T. Many meet tales of youth did he make,
And some of love, and some of chivalrý;
But none fitter than this to apply.
Now listen a while and hearken the end.
"There grew an aged tree on the green,
A goodly Oak sometime had it been,
With arms full strong and largely display'd,
But of their leaves they were disarray'd:
The body big, and mightily pight,[32]
Throughly rooted, and of wondrous height;
Whilom had been the king of the field,
And mochel[33] mast to the husband[34] did yield,
And with his nuts larded[35] many swine:
But now the gray moss marrëd his rine;[36]
His barëd boughs were beaten with storms,
His top was bald, and wasted with worms,
His honour decayëd, his branches sear.
"Hard by his side grew a bragging Brere,
Which proudly thrust into th' element,[37]
And seemëd to threat the firmament:
It was embellish'd with blossoms fair,
And thereto ay wonted to repair
The shepherds' daughters to gather flow'rs,
To paint their garlands with his colóurs;
And in his small bushes us'd to shroud
The sweet nightingale singing so loud;
Which made this foolish Briar wax so bold,
That on a time he cast him to scold
And sneb[38] the good Oak, for he was old.
"'Why stand'st there,' quoth he, 'thou brutish block?

1 Shepherd boys.
2 These two lines are almost literally taken from Chaucer's "House of Fame." See page 237 (note 30).
3 Foolish.
4 Quickly.
5 Bitter.
6 Wrinkled, knitted.
7 Daunted.
8 Presumption.
9 Waste.
10 Tottering, dizzy.
11 Crooked, curved. French, "courbe."
12 Branch.
13 Celebrate.
14 Gold; German, "Geld."
15 Beads.
16 Fool.
17 Proudly.
18 Smart, neat.
19 Snuffeth.
20 Thinkest thou his thought is not of love?
21 Know.
22 Languid, listless.
23 Necks.
24 Earlier-born.
25 Knowest.
26 Heedlessness.
27 Making its gallantry stoop.
28 Learned.
29 E. K. supposes "Tityrus" here to mean Chaucer, and the reference to Kent so far sanctions the supposition; but the story is not any more in Chaucer's manner, than the verse in which it is told. See note 1, page 607.
30 Tales of his invention.
31 Of such excellent quality.
32 Strongly fixed.
33 Much.
34 Husbandman.
35 Fattened.
36 Rind.
37 The air.
38 "Snub," revile.

Nor for fruit nor for shadow serves thy stock;
Seëst how fresh my flowers be spread,
Dy'd in lily white and crimson red,
With leaves engrainëd in lusty green;
Colours meet to clothe a maiden queen?
Thy waste bigness but cumbers the ground,
And dirks [1] the beauty of my blossoms round:
The mouldy moss, which thee accloyeth,[2]
My cinnamon smell too much annoyeth:
Wherefore soon I read [3] thee hence remove,
Lest thou the price of my displeasure prove.'
So spake this bold Briar with great disdain:
Little him answer'd the Oak again,
But yielded, with shame and grief adaw'd,[4]
That of a weed he was overcraw'd.[5]
"It chancëd after, upon a day,
The husbandman's self to come that way,
Of custom for to surview his ground,
And his trees of state in compass round:
Him when the spiteful Briar had espied,
Causeless complainëd, and loudly cried
Unto his lord, stirring up stern strife:
'O my liege lord! the god of my life,
Pleaseth you ponder your suppliant's plaint,
Causëd of wrong and cruel constraint
Which I your poor vassal daily endure;
And, but [6] your goodness the same recure,[7]
Am like for desperate dool [8] to die,
Through felonous force of mine enemý.'
"Greatly aghast with this piteous plea,
Him rested the goodman on the lea,
And bade the Briar in his plaint proceed.
With painted words then gan this proud weed
(As most usen ambitïous folk)
His colourëd crime with craft to cloak.
"'Ah, my sovëreign! lord of creatures all,
Thou placer of plants both humble and tall,
Was not I planted of thine own hand,
To be the primrose [9] of all thy land;
With flow'ring blossoms to furnish the prime,[10]
And scarlet berries in summer time?
How falls it then that this faded Oak,
Whose body is sear, whose branches broke,
Whose naked arms stretch unto the fire,[11]
Unto such tyranny doth aspire;
Hind'ring with his shade my lovely light,
And robbing me of the sweet sun's sight?
So beat his old boughs my tender side,
That oft the blood springeth from woundës wide;
Untimely my flowers forc'd to fall,
That be the honoúr of your coronal:
And oft he lets his canker-worms light
Upon my branches, to work me more spite;
And oft his hoary locks [12] down doth cast,
Wherewith my fresh flow'rets be defac'd.
For this, and many more such outráge,
Craving your goodlihead to assuage
The rancorous rigour of his might,
Naught ask I, but only to hold my right;
Submitting me to your good suff'ránce,
And praying to be guarded from grievánce.'
"To this the Oak cast him to reply
Well as he could; but his enemý
Had kindled such coals of displeasure,
That the goodman n'ould [13] stay his leisure,
But home him hasted with furious heat,
Increasing his wrath with many a threat:
His harmful hatchet he hent [14] in hand
(Alas! that it so ready should stand!)
And to the field alone he speedeth
(Ay little help to harm there needeth!)
Anger n'ould let him speak to the tree,
Enauntre [15] his rage might coolëd be;
But to the root bent his sturdy stroke,
And made many wounds in the waste Oak.
The axe's edge did oft turn again,
As half unwilling to cut the grain;
Seemëd the senseless iron did fear,
Or to wrong holy eld did forbear;
For it had been an ancïent tree,
Sacred with many a mystery,
And often cross'd with the priestës' crew,
And often hallów'd with holy-water dew:
But such fancies were foolery,
And brought this Oak to this misery;
For naught might they quitten [16] him from decay,
For fiercely the goodman at him did lay:
The blóck oft groanëd under the blow,
And sigh'd to see his near overthrow.
In fine, the steel had piercëd his pith,
Then down to the earth he fell forthwith.
His wondrous weight made the ground to quake,
Th' earth shrunk under him, and seemëd to shake:—
There lieth the Oak, pitiëd of none!
"Now stands the Briar like a lord alone,
Puff'd up with pride and vain pleasánce;
But all this glee had no continuánce:
For eftsoons winter gan to approach;
The blustering Boreas did encroach,
And beat upon the solitáry Brere;
For now no succour was seen him near.
Now gan he repent his pride too late;
For, naked left and disconsolate,
The biting frost nippëd his stalk dead,
The watery wet weigh'd down his head,
And heapëd snow burden'd him so sore,
That now upríght he can stand no more;
And, being down, is trod in the dirt
Of cattle, and bruis'd, and sorely hurt.
Such was th' end of this ambitious Brere,
For scorning eld"—
C. Now I pray thee, shepherd, tell it not forth:
Here is a long tale, and little worth.
So long have I listen'd to thy speech,
That graffëd to the ground is my breech;
My heart-blood is well nigh frorn [17] I feel,
And my galage [18] grown fast to my heel;

1 Obscures, darkens.
2 Encumbereth.
3 Counsel.
4 Confounded.
5 Overcrowed.
6 Unless.
7 Redress.
8 Grief.
9 The chief flower.
10 Spring.
11 Are fit only for firewood.
12 Withered leaves.
13 Would not.
14 Seized.
15 "In adventure," like "parauntre" for "peradventure;" in case that.
16 Deliver.
17 Frozen; German, "gefroren."
18 E. K. explains this as "a start-up, or clownish shoe;" French, "galoche."

But little ease of thy lewd[1] tale I tasted:
Hie thee home, shepherd, the day is nigh wasted.

THENOT'S EMBLEM:

Iddio, perche è vecchio,
Fa suoi al suo essempio.
(God, because He is old, makes His own like to Himself.)

CUDDIE'S EMBLEM:

Niuno vecchio
Spaventa Iddio.
(No old man fears God.)

MARCH.

ÆGLOGA TERTIA.—ARGUMENT.

In this Æglogue two shepherds' boys, taking occasion of the season, begin to make purpose[2] of love, and other pleasance which to spring-time is most agreeable. The special meaning hereof is, to give certain marks and tokens, to know Cupid the poets' god of Love. But more particularly, I think, in the person of Thomalin is meant some secret friend, who scorned Love and his knights so long, till at length himself was entangled, and unwares wounded with the dart of some beautiful regard, which is Cupid's arrow.

Willy. Thomalin.

W. THOMALIN, why sitten we so,
As weren overwent[3] with woe,
Upon so fair a morrow?
The joyous time now nigheth fast
That shall allegge[4] this bitter blast,
And slake the winter sorrow.
T. Sicker, Willy, thou warnest well;
For winter's wrath begins to quell,[5]
And pleasant spring appeareth:
The grass now gins to be refresh'd,
The swallow peeps out of her nest,
And cloudy welkin[6] cleareth.
W. Seëst not this same hawthorn stud,[7]
How bragly[8] it begins to bud,
And utter[9] his tender head?
Flora now calleth forth each flower,
And bids make ready Maia's bower,
That new is uprist from bed:
Then shall we sporten in delight,
And learn with Lettice[10] to wax light,
That scornfully looks askance;
Then will we little Love awake,
That now sleepeth in Lethe Lake,
And pray him leaden our dance.
T. Willy, I ween thou be assot;[11]
For lusty Love still sleepeth not,
But is abroad at his game.
W. How ken'st[12] thou that he is awoke?
Or hast thyself his slumber broke?
Or made privy to the same?
T. No; but happily[13] I him spied,
Where in a bush he did him hide,
With wings of purple and blue;
And, were not that my sheep would stray,
The privy marks I would bewray[14]
Whereby by chance I him knew.
W. Thomalin, have no care forthy;[15]
Myself will have a double eye,
Alike to my flock and thine;
For, alas! at home I have a sire,
A stepdame eke, as hot as fire,
That duly a-days[16] counts mine.
T. Nay, but thy seeing will not serve,
My sheep for that may chance to swerve,
And fall into some mischief:
For sithens[17] is but the third morrow
That I chanc'd to fall asleep, with sorrow,
And wakëd again with grief;
The while this same unhappy ewe,
Whose clouted[18] leg her hurt doth shew,
Fell headlong into a dell,
And there unjointed both her bones:
Might her neck been jointed at once,[19]
She should have need no more spell;[20]
Th' elf was so wanton and so wood[21]
(But now I trow can better good[22]),
She might ne gang[23] on the green.
W. Let be, as may be, that is past;
That is to come, let be forecast:
Now tell us what thou hast seen.
T. It was upon a holiday,
When shepherds' grooms have leave to play,
I cast to go a shooting;
Long wand'ring up and down the land,
With bow and bolts in either hand,
For birds in bushes tooting,[24]
At length within the ivy tod[25]
(There shrouded was the little god),
I heard a busy bustling;
I bent my bolt against the bush,
List'ning if anything did rush,
But then heard no more rustling.
Then, peeping close into the thick,
Might see the moving of some quick,[26]
Whose shape appearëd not;
But were it fairy, fiend, or snake,
My courage yearn'd it to awake,
And manfully thereat shot:
With that sprang forth a naked swain,
With spotted wings like peacock's train,
And laughing lope[27] to a tree;
His gilden quiver at his back,
And silver bow, which was but slack,
Which lightly he bent at me:
That seeing, I levell'd again,
And shot at him with might and main,
As thick as it had hail'd.
So long I shot, that all was spent;
Then pumy[28] stones I hast'ly hent,
And threw; but naught avail'd:

1 Foolish. 2 Conversation.
3 As if we were overcome. 4 Allay.
5 Abate. 6 Sky, heaven.
7 Trunk, stock. 8 Proudly, bravely.
9 Put forth.
10 "The name of some country lass."—*E. K.*
11 Stupid, besotted. 12 Knowest.
13 By chance, haply. 14 Declare.
15 For that cause. 16 Daily.
17 Since. 18 Mended, bound up.
19 At the same time.
20 Charm to preserve or recover health.
21 Wild. 22 She knows better.
23 She could not go. 24 Searching.
25 Thick bush. 26 Some living thing.
27 Leaped. 28 Pumice.

He was so wimble and so wight,[1]
From bough to bough he leapëd light,
And oft the pumies latchëd:[2]
Therewith afraid I ran away;
But he, that erst[3] seem'd but to play,
A shaft in earnest snatchëd,
And hit me, running, in the heel:
For then[4] I little smart did feel,
But soon it sore increasëd;
And now it rankleth more and more,
And inwardly it fest'reth sore,
Nor wot I how to cease it.
W. Thomalin, I pity thy plight,
Pardie,[5] with Love thou diddest fight;
I know him by a token:
For once I heard my father say,
How he him caught upon a day
(Whereof he will be wroken[6]),
Entangled in a fowling net,
Which he for carrion crows had set
That in our pear-tree haunted:
Then said, he was a wingëd lad,
But bow and shafts as then none had,
Else had he sore been daunted.
But see, the welkin thicks apace,
And stooping Phœbus steeps his face;
It's time to haste us homeward.

WILLY'S EMBLEM:

To be wise and eke to love,
Is granted scarce to gods above.

THOMALIN'S EMBLEM:

Of honey and of gall in love there is store;
The honey is much, but the gall is more.

APRIL.

ÆGLOGA QUARTA.—ARGUMENT.

This Æglogue is purposely intended to the honour and praise of our most gracious Sovereign, Queen Elizabeth. The speakers herein be Hobbinol and Thenot, two shepherds: the which Hobbinol, being before mentioned greatly to have loved Colin, is here set forth more largely, complaining him of that boy's great misadventure in love; whereby his mind was alienated and withdrawn not only from him, who most loved him, but also from all former delights and studies, as well in pleasant piping, as cunning rhyming and singing, and other his laudable exercises. Whereby he taketh occasion, for proof of his more excellency and skill in poetry, to record a song, which the said Colin sometime made in honour of her Majesty, whom abruptly he termeth Elisa.

Thenot. Hobbinol.

T. TELL me, good Hobbinol, what gars thee greet?[7]
What! hath some wolf thy tender lambs y-torn?
Or is thy bagpipe broke, that sounds so sweet?
Or art thou of thy lovëd lass forlorn?
Or be thine eyes attemper'd to the year,
Quenching the gasping furrows' thirst with rain?
Like April show'r, so stream the trickling tears
Adown thy cheek, to quench thy thirsty pain.
H. Nor this, nor that, so much doth make me mourn,
But for[8] the lad, whom long I lov'd so dear,
Now loves a lass that all his love doth scorn:
He, plung'd in pain, his tressëd locks doth tear;
Shepherds' delights he doth them all forswear;
His pleasant pipe, which made us merriment,
He wilfully hath broke, and doth forbear
His wonted songs wherein he all outwent.[9]
T. What is he for a lad[10] you so lament?
Is love such pinching pain to them that prove?
And hath he skill to make[11] so excellent,
Yet hath so little skill to bridle love?
H. Colin thou ken'st,[12] the southern shepherd's boy;
Him Love hath wounded with a deadly dart:
Whilom on him was all my care and joy,
Forcing with gifts to win his wanton heart.
But now from me his madding mind is start,
And wooes the widow's daughter of the glen;
So now fair Rosalind hath bred his smart;
So now his friend is changëd for a fren.[13]
T. But if his ditties be so trimly dight,
I pray thee, Hobbinol, record[14] some one,
The while our flocks do graze about in sight,
And we close shrouded in this shade alone.
H. Contented I: then will I sing his lay
Of fair Elisa, queen of shepherds all,
Which once he made as by a spring he lay,
And tunëd it unto the waters' fall.

"Ye dainty Nymphs, that in this blessëd brook
Do bathe your breast,
Forsake your watery bow'rs, and hither look,
At my request.
And eke you Virgins, that on Parnass' dwell,
Whence floweth Helicon, the learnëd well,
Help me to blaze
Her worthy praise,
Which in her sex doth all excel.

"Of fair Elisa be your silver song,
That blessëd wight,
The flow'r of virgins; may she flourish long
In princely plight!
For she is Syrinx' daughter without spot,
Which Pan,[15] the shepherds' god, of her begot:
So sprung her grace
Of heav'nly race,
No mortal blemish may her blot.

"See, where she sits upon the grassy green
(O seemly sight!)

[1] So nimble and active. [2] Caught. [3] Before. [4] At the time. [5] Of a surety. [6] Revenged. [7] What makes thee weep? [8] Because. [9] Excelled.
[10] What sort of lad is he? The idiom is that of the Germans, "Was für ein Junge ist er?"
[11] Versify. [12] Knowest.
[13] A stranger; otherwise "frem" or "fremd;" German, "Fremde." [14] Call to mind, rehearse.
[15] "By Pan is here meant the most famous and victorious king, her Highness's father, late of worthy memory, King Henry the Eighth."—*E. K.* Syrinx, therefore, must signify Anne Boleyn.

Y-clad in scarlet, like a maiden queen,
And ermines white:
Upon her head a crimson coronet,
With damask roses and daffodillies set;
Bay leaves between,
And primroses green,
Embellish the sweet violet.

"Tell me, have ye seen her angelic face,
Like Phœbe fair?
Her heav'nly 'haviour, her princely grace,
Can you well compare?
The red rose medled[1] with the white y-fere,[2]
In either cheek depainten[3] lively cheer:
Her modest eye,
Her majesty,
Where have you seen the like but there?

"I saw Phœbus thrust out his golden head,
Upon her to gaze;
But, when he saw how broad her beams did spread,
It did him amaze.
He blush'd to see another sun below,
Nor durst again his fiery face out show.
Let him, if he dare,
His brightness compare
With hers, to have the overthrow.

"Shew thyself, Cynthia, with thy silver rays,
And be not abash'd:
When she the beams of her beauty displays,
O how art thou dash'd!
But I will not match her with Latona's seed;
Such folly great sorrow to Niobé did breed.
Now she is a stone,
And makes daily moan,
Warning all other to take heed.

"Pan may be proud that ever he begot
Such a bellibone;[4]
And Syrinx rejoice, that ever was her lot
To bear such an one.
Soon as my younglings cryen for the dam,
To her will I offer a milk-white lamb;
She is my goddess plain,
And I her shepherd's swain,
All be forswonk and forswat I am.[5]

"I see Calliope speed her to the place
Where my goddess shines;
And after her the other Muses trace,[6]
With their violins.
Be they not bay-branches which they do bear,
All for Elisa in her hand to wear?
So sweetly they play,
And sing all the way,
That it a heaven is to hear.

"Lo, how finely the Graces can it foot
To the instrument:
They dancen deftly, and singen swoot,[7]
In their merriment.
Wants not a fourth Grace, to make the dance even?
Let that room to my Lady be given.
She shall be a Grace,
To fill the fourth place,
And reign with the rest in heaven.

"And whither runs this bevy of ladies bright,
Rangëd in a row?
They be all Ladies of the Lake behight,[8]
That unto her go.
Chloris, that is the chiefest nymph of all,
Of olive branches bears a coronal:
Olives be for peace,
When wars do surcease:
Such for a princess be principal.

"Ye shepherds' daughters, that dwell on the green,
Hie you there apace:
Let none come there but that virgins be'n
To adorn her grace:
And, when you come where as she is in place,
See that your rudeness do not you disgrace:
Bind your fillets fast,
And gird in your waist,
For more fineness, with a tawdry lace.[9]

"Bring hither the pink and purple columbine,
With gillyflow'rs;
Bring coronatïons, and sops-in-wine,[10]
Worn of paramoűrs:[11]
Strow me the ground with daffodowndillies,
And cowslips, and kingcups, and lov'd lilies:
The pretty paunce,[12]
And the chevisance,
Shall match with the fair flow'r délice.[13]

"Now rise up, Elisa, deckëd as thou art
In royal array;
And now ye dainty damsels may depart
Each one her way.
I fear I have troubled your troops too long;
Let Dame Elisa thank you for her song:
And, if you come hither
When damsons I gather,
I will part them all you among."

T. And was this same song of Colin's own making?
Ah! foolish boy! that is with love y-blent;[14]
Great pity is, he be in such taking,
For naught caren that be so lewdly[15] bent.
H. Sicker I hold him for a greater fon,[16]
That loves the thing he cannot purchase.[17]
But let us homeward, for night draweth on,
And twinkling stars the daylight hence chase.

1 Mingled. 2 Together. 3 Picture.
4 "Belle et bonne"—a lovely and good maiden; otherwise "bonnibelle."
5 Although I am overtoiled and spent with heat.
6 Go, walk. 7 Sweetly. 8 Called.
9 A lace or girdle bought at the fair of Saint Ethelred, vulgarly called Saint Audrey.
10 "A flower in colour much like to a coronation (carnation), but differing in smell and quantity."—*E. K.*
11 Lovers. 12 Pansy.
13 Flower-de-luce, or iris; "being in Latin," says E. K., "called *flos delitiarum*," flower of delights.
14 Blinded. 15 Foolishly.
16 Fool. 17 Obtain.

THENOT'S EMBLEM:

O quam te memorem, Virgo! (O! what shall I call thee, Virgin!)

HOBBINOL'S EMBLEM:

O Dea certe![1] (O! assuredly a Goddess!)

MAY.

ÆGLOGA QUINTA.—ARGUMENT.

In this fifth Æglogue, under the person of two shepherds, Piers and Palinode, be represented two forms of Pastors or Ministers, or the Protestant and the Catholic; whose chief talk standeth in reasoning, whether the life of the one must be like the other; with whom having showed that it is dangerous to maintain any fellowship, or give too much credit to their colourable and feigned good-will, he telleth him a tale of the Fox, that, by such a counterpoint of craftiness, deceived and devoured the credulous Kid.

Palinode. Piers.

Pal. Is not this the merry month of May,
When love-lads masken in fresh array?
How falls it, then, we no merrier be'n,
Like as others, girt in gaudy green?
Our blonket liveries[2] be all too sad
For this same season, when all is y-clad
With pleasance; the ground with grass, the woods
With green leaves, the bushes with blooming buds.
Youth's folk now flocken in ev'rywhere,
To gather May-buskets[3] and smelling brere;[4]
And home they hasten the posts to dight,[5]
And all the kirk-pillars, ere daylight,
With hawthorn buds, and sweet eglantine,
And garlands of roses and sops-in-wine.
Such merry-make holy saints doth queme,[6]
But we here sitten as drown'd in dream.
Piers. For younkers, Palinode, such follies fit,
But we two be men of elder wit.
Pal. Sicker[7] this morrow, no longer ago,
I saw a shoal of shepherds outgo
With singing, and shouting, and jolly cheer:
Before them yode a lusty tabrere,[8]
That to the many a horn-pipe play'd,
Whereto they dancen each one with his maid.
To see those folks make such jovisance[9]
Made my heart after the pipe to dance:
Then to the green wood they speeden them all,
To fetchen home May with their musical;[10]
And home they bringen in a royal throne,
Crownëd as king; and his queen at one[11]
Was Lady Flora, on whom did attend
A fair flock of fairies, and a fresh bend[12]
Of lovely nymphs. (O that I were there,
To helpen the ladies their May-bush bear!)
Ah! Piers, be not thy teeth on edge, to think
How great sport they gainen with little swink?[13]
Piers. Pardie! so far am I from envy,
That their fondness[14] inly I pity:
Those faitours[15] little regarden their charge,
While they, letting their sheep run at large,
Passen their time, that should be sparely spent,
In lustihead and wanton merriment.
These same be shepherds for the devil's stead,
That playen while their flocks be unfed:
Well it is seen their sheep be not their own,
That letten them run at random alone:
But they be hirëd, for little pay,
Of other that caren as little as they
What fallen the flock, so they have the fleece,
And get all the gain, paying but a piece.
I muse, what account both these will make,—
The one for the hire, which he doth take,
And th' other for leaving his Lord's task,—
When great Pan[16] account of shepherds shall ask.
Pal. Sicker,[7] now I see thou speakest of spite,
All for thou lackest somedeal[17] their delight.
I (as I am) had rather be envíed,
All were it of my foe, than fonly[18] pitíed;
And yet, if need were, pitied would be,
Rather than other should scorn at me;
For pitied is mishap that n' has remedy,
But scornëd be deeds of fond[19] foolery.
What shoulden shepherds other things tend,
Than, since their God his good does them send,
Reapen the fruit thereof, that is pleasure,
The while they here liven at ease and leisure.
For, when they be dead, their good is y-go,
They sleepen in rest, well as other mo':
Then with them wends what they spent in cost,[20]

1 "This poesy is taken out of Virgil, and there of him used in the person of Æneas to his mother Venus, appearing to him in likeness of one of Diana's damsels; being there most divinely set forth."—*E. K.*

2 "Gray coats."—*E. K.*

3 Bunches or little bushes of hawthorn.

4 Briar.

5 To dress the May-poles.

6 Please.

7 Certain.

8 Went a jolly tabourer or drummer.

9 Joyance.

10 Music.

11 At the same time.

12 Band.

13 Toil.

14 Folly.

15 Vagabonds.

16 "Great Pan is Christ, the very God of all shepherds, which calleth himself the great and good shepherd. The name is most rightly (methinks) applied to him; for Pan signifieth all, or omnipotent, which is only the Lord Jesus." So says E. K., and proceeds to apply to Christ Eusebius' story of the voice which cried on the sea that the great Pan was dead.

17 Somewhat.

18 Foolishly.

19 Foolish.

20 "*Then with them* doth imitate the epitaph of the riotous king Sardanapalus, which he caused to be written on his tomb in Greek: which verses be thus translated by Tully:

'Hæc habui quæ edi, quæque exsaturata libido
Hausit, at illa manent multa ac præclara relicta.'

Which may thus be turned into English,

'All that I eat did I joy, and all that I greedily gorged:
As for those many goodly matters left I for others.'

Much like the epitaph of a good old Earl of Devonshire, which though much more wisdom bewrayeth than Sardanapalus, yet hath a smack of his sensual delights and beastliness: the rhymes be these:

'Ho, ho! who lies here?
I the good Earle of Devonshere,
And Maulde my wife that was ful deare:
We lived together lv. yeare.
That we spent, we had:
That we gave, we have:
That we lefte, we lost.'"—*E. K.*

But what they left behind them is lost.
Good is no good, but if [1] it be spend;
God giveth good for none other end.
Piers. Ah! Palinode, thou art a world's child:
Who touches pitch, must needs be defil'd;
But shepherds (as Algrind [2] us'd to say)
Must not live alike as men of the lay.[3]
With them it sits [4] to care for their heir,
Enauntre [5] their heritage do impair:
They must provide for means of maintenance,
And to continue their wont countenance:
But shepherd must walk another way,
Such worldly souvenance [6] he must forsay.[7]
The son of his loins why should he regard
To leave enrichëd with that he hath spar'd?
Should not thilk [8] God, that gave him that good,
Eke cherish his child, if in his ways he stood?
For if he mislive in lewdness and lust,
Little boots all the wealth and the trust
That his father left by inheritance;
All will be soon wasted with misgovernance:
But through this, and other their miscreance,[9]
They maken many a wrong chevisance,[10]
Heaping up waves of wealth and woe,
The floods whereof shall them overflow.
Such men's folly I cannot compare
Better than to the ape's foolish care,
That is so enamour'd of her young one
(And yet, God wot, such cause had she none),
That with her hard hold, and strait émbracíng,
She stoppeth the breath of her younglíng.
So oftentimes, when as good is meant,
Evil ensueth of wrong intent.
The time was once, and may again return
(For aught may happen, that hath been beforn),
When shepherds had none inheritance,
Nor of land, nor fee in sufferance,
But what might arise of the bare sheep
(Were it more or less) which they did keep.
Well, y-wis, was it with shepherds then:
Naught having, naught fearëd they to forgo;[11]
For Pan himself was their inheritance,[12]
And little them serv'd for their maintenance.
The shepherds' God so well them guided,
That of naught they were unprovided;
Butter enough, honey, milk, and whey,
And their flocks' fleeces them to array:
But tract of time, and long prósperitý
(That nurse of vice, this of ínsolencý),
Lull'd the shepherds in such security,
That, not content with loyal obeisánce,
Some gan to gape for greedy governánce,[13]
And match themselves with mighty potentates,
Lovers of lordship, and troublers of states:
Then gan shepherds' swains to look aloft,
And leave to live hard, and learn to lig [14] soft:
Then, under colour of shepherds, somewhile
There crept in wolves, full of fraud and guile,
That often devourëd their own sheep,
And often the shepherds that did them keep:
This was the first source of shepherds' sorrow,
That now n'ill [15] be quit with bail nor borrow.[16]
Pal. Three things to bear be very burdenous,
But the fourth to forbear is oútrageous:
Women, that of love's longing once lust,
Hardly forbearen, but have it they must:
So when choler is inflamëd with rage,
Wanting revenge, is hard to assuage:
And who can counsel a thirsty soul
With patience to forbear the offer'd bowl?
But of all burdens that a man can bear,
Most is a fool's talk to bear and to hear.
I ween the giant [17] has not such a weight,
That bears on his shoulders the heaven's height.
Thou findest fault where n' is [18] to be found,
And buildest strong work upon a weak ground:
Thou railest on right withouten reason,
And blamest them much for small encheason.[19]
How shoulden shepherds live, if not so?
What? should they pinen in pain and woe?
Nay, say I thereto, by my dear borrow,[20]
If I may rest, I n'ill [15] live in sorrow.
Sorrow ne need to be hastened on,
For he will come, without calling, anon.
While times enduren of tranquillity,
Usen we freely our felicity;
For, when approachen the stormy stours,[21]
We must with our shoulders bear off the sharp show'rs;
And, sooth to sayn, naught seemeth [22] such strife,
That shepherds so witen [23] each other's life,
And layen their faults the worlds beforn,
The while their foes do each of them scorn.
Let none mislike of that may not be mended;
So conteck [24] soon by concórd might be ended.
Piers. Shepherd, I list no accordance make
With shepherd that does the right way forsake;
And of the twain, if choice were to me,
Had lever [25] my foe than my friend he be;
For what concórd have light and dark sam? [26]
Or what peace has the lion with the lamb?
Such faitours,[27] when their false hearts be hid,
Will do as did the Fox by the Kid.[28]
Pal. Now, Piers, of fellowship, tell us that saying;
For the lad can keep both our flocks from straying.

1 Unless.
2 Grindal, Archbishop of Canterbury, conspicuous for his leaning to the puritanical party in the Reformed Church.
3 Laity.
4 It beseems them.
5 Lest.
6 Remembrance.
7 Forsake.
8 The same.
9 Misbelief.
10 Bargain.
11 Lose.
12 "Pan himself; God; according as is said in Deuteronomy, that, in division of the land of Canaan, to the tribe of Levi no portion of heritage should be allotted, for God himself was their inheritance."—*E. K.*
13 "Meant of the Pope, and his Antichristian prelates, which usurp a tyrannical dominion in the Church, &c."—*E. K.*
14 Lie.
15 Will not.
16 Pledge or surety.
17 Atlas.
18 None is.
19 Occasion.
20 "By my Saviour," whom E. K. calls "the common pledge of all men's debt to death."
21 The assaults of storm.
22 Ill beseems.
23 Blame.
24 Strife.
25 Rather.
26 Together.
27 Ill-doers.
28 "By the Kid may be understood the simple sort of the faithful and true Christians. By his dam, Christ, that hath already with careful watchwords (as here doth the Goat) warned her little ones to beware of such doubling deceit. By the Fox, the false and faithless Papists, to whom is no credit to be given, nor fellowship to be used."—*E. K.*

Piers. This same Kid (as I can well devise)
Was too very foolish and unwise;
For on a time, in summer seasón,
The Goat her dam, that had good reasón,
Yode[1] forth abroad unto the green wood,
To browze, or play, or what she thought good:
But, for she had a motherly care
Of her young son, and wit to beware,
She set her youngling before her knee,
That was both fresh and lovely to see,
And full of favour as kid might be.
His velvet head began to shoot out,
And his wreathëd horns gan newly sprout;
The blossoms of lust to bud did begin,
And spring forth rankly under his chin.
"My son," quoth she; and with that gan weep;
For careful thoughts in her heart did creep;
"God bless thee, poor orphan! as he might me,
And send thee joy of thy jollity.
Thy father" (that word she spake with pain,
For a sigh had nigh rent her heart in twain),
"Thy father, had he livëd this day,
To see the branch of his body display,
How would he have joyëd at this sweet sight?
But, ah! false Fortune such joy did him spite,[2]
And cut off his days with untimely woe,
Betraying him into the trains[3] of his foe.
Now I, a wailful widow behight,[4]
Of my old age have this one delight,
To see thee succeed in thy father's stead,
And flourish in flowers of lustihead;
For ev'n so thy father his head upheld,
And so his haughty horns did he weld."[5]
Then, marking him with melting eyes,
A thrilling throb[6] from her heart did arise,
And interrupted all her other speech
With some old sorrow that made a new breach;
Seemëd she saw in her youngling's face
The old lineaments of his father's grace.
At last her sullen[7] silence she broke,
And gan his new-budded beard to stroke.
"Kiddie," quoth she, "thou ken'st[8] the great care
I have of thy health and thy welfáre,
Which many wild beasts liggen[9] in wait
For to entrap in thy tender state:
But most the Fox, master of collusion;[10]
For he has vowëd thy last confusion.
Forthy,[11] my Kiddie, be rulëd by me,
And never give trust to his treachery;
And, if he chance come when I am abroad,
Sperr[12] the gate fast, for fear of fraud;
Nor for all his worst, nor for his best,
Open the door at his request."
So schoolëd the Goat her wanton son,
That answer'd his mother, all should be done.
Then went the pensive dam out of door,
And chanc'd to stumble at the threshold floor;
Her stumbling step somewhat her amaz'd
(For such, as signs of ill luck, be disprais'd);
Yet forth she yode,[1] thereat half aghast;
And Kiddie the door sperr'd after her fast.
It was not long after she was gone,
But the false Fox came to the door anon;
Not as a fox, for then he had been kenn'd,[13]
But all as a poor pedlar he did wend,
Bearing a truss[14] of trifles at his back,
As bells, and babes, and glasses, in his pack:[15]
A biggen[16] he had got about his brain,
For in his headpiece he felt a sore pain:
His hinder heel was wrapt in a clout,
For with great cold he had got the gout:
There at the door he cast me down his pack,
And laid him down, and groanëd, "Alack! alack!
Ah! dear Lord! and sweet Saint Charity!
That some good body would once pity me!"
Well heard Kiddie all this sore constraint,
And long'd to know the cause of his complaint;
Then, creeping close behind the wicket's clink,[17]
Privily he peepëd out through a chink,
Yet not so privily but the Fox him spied;
For deceitful meaning is double-eyed.
"Ah! good young master" (then gan he cry),
"Jesus bless that sweet face I espy,
And keep your corse from the careful stounds[18]
That in my carrion carcase abounds."
The Kid, pitying his heaviness,
Askëd the cause of his great distress,
And also who and whence that he were.
Then he, that had well y-conn'd his lear,[19]
Thus medled[20] his talk with many a tear:
"Sick, sick, alas! and little lack of dead,[21]
But I be relievëd by your beastlihead.[22]
I am a poor sheep, all be my colour dun,
For with long travel I am burnt in the sun;
And if that my grandsire me said be true,
Sicker I am very sib[23] to you;
So be your goodlihead do not disdain
The base kindred of so simple swain.
Of mercy and favour then I you pray,
With your aid to forestall my near decay."[24]
Then out of his pack a glass he took,
Wherein while Kiddie unwares did look,
He was so enamourëd with the newell,[25]
That naught he deemëd dear for the jewel:
Then openëd he the door, and in came
The false Fox, as he were stark lame:
His tail he clapp'd betwixt his legs twain,
Lest he should be descried by his train.
Being within, the Kid made him good glee,[26]
All for the love of the glass he did see.
After his cheer, the pedlar gan chat,
And tell many leasings[27] of this and that,
And how he could show many a fine knack;[28]
Then showëd his ware and open'd his pack,

1 Went.
2 Begrudge. 3 Snares.
4 Called. 5 Wield, bear.
6 A piercing sigh. 7 Mournful.
8 Knowest. 9 Lie. 10 Guile.
11 Therefore. 12 Bar, shut.
13 Recognised. 14 Bundle.
15 "By such trifles are noted the relics and rags of Popish superstition, which put no small religion in bells, and babies or idols, and glasses or paxes, and such like trumperies."—*E. K.* 16 Cap.
17 The key-hole. 18 Sorrowful pangs.
19 Conned, learned, his lesson. 20 Mingled.
21 Little short of being dead.
22 By your beastship. 23 Closely related.
24 To prevent my approaching destruction.
25 Novelty. 26 Gladly entertained him.
27 Lies. 28 Toy, nick-nack.

All save a bell, which he left behind
In the basket for the Kid to find;
Which when the Kid stoop'd down to catch,
He popp'd him in, and his basket did latch;
Nor stay'd he once the door to make fast,
But ran away with him in all haste.
Home when the doubtful Dam had her hied,
She might see the door stand open wide;
All aghast, loudly she gan to call
Her Kid; but he n'ould[1] answer at all:
Then on the floor she saw the merchandise
Of which her son had set too dear a price.[2]
What help? her Kid she knew well was gone:
She weepëd, and wailëd, and made great moan.
Such end had the Kid, for he n'ould warn'd be
Of craft, colourëd with simplicity;
And such end, pardie, does all them remain,
That of such falsers'[3] friendship be fain.[4]
Pal. Truly, Piers, thou art beside thy wit,
Farthest from the mark, weening it to hit.
Now, I pray thee, let me thy tale borrow
For our Sir John,[5] to say to-morrow
At the kirk when it is holyday;
For well he means, but little can say.
But an' if foxes be so crafty as so,
Much needeth all shepherds them to know.
Piers. Of their falsehood more could I recount;
But now the bright sun ginneth to dismount;
And, for the dewy night now doth nigh,
I hold it best for us home to hie.

PALINODE'S EMBLEM:

Πᾶς μὲν ἄπιστος ἀπιστεῖ. (Every one without faith is distrustful.)

PIERS HIS EMBLEM:

Τὶς δ'αρα πίστις ἀπίστῳ; (What faith, then, is to be placed in the faithless?)

JUNE.

ÆGLOGA SEXTA.—ARGUMENT.

This Æglogue is wholly vowed[6] to the complaining of Colin's ill success in his love. For being (as is aforesaid) enamoured of a country lass Rosalind, and having (as seemeth) found place in her heart, he lamenteth to his dear friend Hobbinol, that he is now forsaken unfaithfully, and in his stead Menalcas, another shepherd, received disloyally. And this is the whole Argument of this Æglogue.

Hobbinol. Colin Clout.

H. Lo! Colin, here the place whose pleasant site
From other shades hath wean'd my wand'ring mind;
Tell me, what wants me here to work delight?
The simple air, the gentle warbling wind,
So calm, so cool, as nowhere else I find;
The grassy ground with dainty daisies dight,
The bramble bush, where birds of ev'ry kind
To the waters' fall their tunes attemper[7] right.

C. O happy Hobbinol! I bless thy state,
That Paradise hast found which Adam lost:
Here wander may thy flock early or late,
Withouten dread of wolves to be y-tost;[8]
Thy lovely lays here may'st thou freely boast:
But I, unhappy man! whom cruel Fate
And angry gods pursue from coast to coast,
Can nowhere find to shroud my luckless pate.

H. Then, if by me thou list advisëd be,
Forsake the soil that so doth thee bewitch;
Leave me those hills where harbour n' is to see,[9]
Nor holly-bush, nor briar, nor winding ditch;
And to the dales resort, where shepherds rich,
And fruitful flocks, be ev'rywhere to see:
Here no night-ravens lodge, more black than pitch,
Nor elvish ghosts, nor ghastly owls do flee;

But friendly Fairies, met with many Graces,
And lightfoot Nymphs, can chase the lingering Night
With heydeguys,[10] and trimly trodden traces,
Whilst Sisters Nine, which dwell on Parnass' height,
Do make them music for their more delight;
And Pan himself, to kiss their crystal faces,
Will pipe and dance when Phœbe shineth bright:
Such peerless pleasures have we in these places.

C. And I, whilst youth, and course of careless years,
Did let me walk withouten links of love,
In such delights did joy amongst my peers;
But riper age such pleasures doth reprove:
My fancy eke from former follies move
To stayëd steps; for time in passing wears
(As garments do, which waxen old above),
And draweth new delights with hoary hairs.

Then could I sing of love, and tune my pipe
Unto my plaintive pleas in verses made;
Then would I seek for queen-apples unripe,
To give my Rosalind; and in summer shade
Dight[11] gaudy garlands was my common trade,
To crown her golden locks; but years more ripe,
And loss of her whose love as life I weigh'd,[12]
Those weary wanton toys away did wipe.

H. Colin, to hear thy rhymes and roundelays,
Which thou wert wont on wasteful[13] hills to sing,
I more delight than lark in summer days;
Whose echo made the neighbour groves to ring,
And taught the birds, which in the lower spring[14]
Did shroud in shady leaves from sunny rays,
Frame to thy song their cheerful chirruping,
Or hold their peace for shame of thy sweet lays.

1 Would not.
2 For which her son had paid so dear—with his life.
3 Deceivers.
4 Glad, desirous.
5 The taunting or disrespectful title applied to a Popish priest; so the Host addresses the Nun's Priest in The Canterbury Tales. See note 1, page 165.

6 Devoted.
7 Modulate.
8 Harassed.
9 Where no shelter is to be seen.
10 Country dances.
11 To prepare.
12 Valued.
13 Desert.
14 In the young trees.

I saw Calliope, with Muses mo',
Soon as thy oaten pipe began to sound,
Their ivory lutes and tambourines forego,
And from the fountain, where they sat around,
Run after hastily thy silver sound;
But, when they came where thou thy skill didst show,
They drew aback, as half with shame confound
Shepherd to see them in their art outgo.

C. Of Muses, Hobbinol, I con no skill,
For they be daughters of the highest Jove,
And holden scorn of homely shepherd's quill;
For since I heard that Pan with Phœbus strove,
Which him to much rebuke and danger drove,
I never list presume to Parnass' hill;
But, piping low in shade of lowly grove,
I play to please myself, albeit ill.

Naught weigh[1] I who my song doth praise or blame,
Nor strive to win renown or pass the rest:
With shepherd sits not[2] follow flying Fame,
But feed his flock in fields where falls them best.
I wot my rhymes be rough, and rudely drest;
The fitter they my careful case[3] to frame:
Enough is me to paint out my unrest,
And pour my piteous plaints out in the same.

The god of shepherds, Tityrus, is dead,
Who taught me homely, as I can, to make:[4]
He, whilst he livëd, was the sov'reign head
Of shepherds all that be with love y-take;[5]
Well could he wail his woes, and lightly slake
The flames which love within his heart had bred,
And tell us merry tales to keep us wake,
The while our sheep about us safely fed.

Now dead he is, and lieth wrapt in lead
(O! why should Death on him such outrage show?)
And all his passing skill with him is fled,
The fame whereof doth daily greater grow.
But, if on me some little drops would flow
Of that the spring was in his learned head,
I soon would learn these woods to wail my woe,
And teach the trees their trickling tears to shed.

Then should my plaints, caus'd of discourtesy,
As messengers of this my plainful[6] plight,
Fly to my love, wherever that she be,
And pierce her heart with point of worthy wite,[7]
As she deserves that wrought so deadly spite.
And thou, Menalcas! that by treachery
Didst underfong[8] my lass to wax so light,
Shouldst well be known for such thy villainy.

But since I am not as I wish I were,
Ye gentle shepherds! which your flocks do feed,
Whether on hills, or dales, or otherwhere,
Bear witness all of this so wicked deed;
And tell the lass, whose flower is wox a weed,
And faultless faith is turn'd to faithless fear,
That she the truest shepherd's heart made bleed
That lives on earth, and lovëd her most dear.

H. O careful[9] Colin! I lament thy case;
Thy tears would make the hardest flint to flow!
Ah! faithless Rosalind, and void of grace,
That art the root of all this ruthful[10] woe!
But now is time, I guess, homeward to go:
Then rise, ye blessëd flocks! and home apace,
Lest night with stealing steps do you forslow,[11]
And wet your tender lambs that by you trace.[12]

COLIN'S EMBLEM:

Gia speme spenta. (Now hope is extinct.)

JULY.

ÆGLOGA SEPTIMA.—ARGUMENT.

This Æglogue is made in the honour and commendation of good shepherds, and to the shame and dispraise of proud and ambitious pastors: such as Morrell is here imagined to be.

Thomalin. Morrell.[13]

T. Is not this same a goatherd proud,
 That sits on yonder bank,
Whose straying herd themselves do shroud
 Among the bushes rank?
M. What, ho! thou jolly shepherd's swain,
 Come up the hill to me;
Better is than the lowly plain,
 Als'[14] for thy flock and thee.
T. Ah! God shield,[15] man, that I should climb,
 And learn to look aloft;
This read[16] is rife,[17] that oftentime
 Great climbers fall unsoft.
In humble dales is footing fast,
 The trode[18] is not so tickle,[19]
And though one fall through heedless haste,
 Yet is his miss not mickle.
And now the Sun hath rearëd up
 His fiery-footed team,
Making his way between the Cup
 And golden Diademe;
The rampant Lion[20] hunts he fast
 With Dogs of noisome breath,
Whose baleful barking brings in haste
 Pain, plagues, and dreary death.
Against his cruel scorching heat
 Where hast thou coverture?
The wasteful hills unto his threat
 Is a plain overture:[21]
But, if thee list to holden chat
 With seely[22] shepherd swain,

1 Care. 2 It befits not (to).
3 Unhappy condition.
4 To make poetry. 5 Overtaken.
6 Lamentable. 7 Merited blame.
8 Seduce; "undermine and deceive by false suggestions."—*E. K.*
9 Sorrowful. 10 Pitiable.
11 Retard. 12 Go.
13 Morrell—though E. K. gives no authority for the supposition—is understood to be the Bishop of London, Elmer or Aylmer, a prominent upholder of the High Church party, as Grindal was of the Low.
14 Both. 15 God forbid.
16 Saying, proverb. 17 Frequent, familiar.
18 Footing, path. 19 Uncertain.
20 The sun enters Leo in July; at which time the sultry influences of the Dogstar are at their height.
21 Lie fully open. 22 Simple.

Come down, and learn the little what[1]
  That Thomalin can sayn.
M. Sicker thou's but a lazy loord,[2]
  And recks much of thy swink,[3]
That with fond[4] terms, and witless words,
  To blear mine eyes[5] dost think.
In evil hour thou hent'st[6] in hand
  Thus holy hills to blame,
For sacred unto saints they stand,
  And of them have their name.
St Michael's Mount who does not know,
  That wards the Western coast?
And of St Bridget's Bow'r I trow
  All Kent can rightly boast:
And they that con of Muses' skill
  Say most-what that they dwell
(As goatherds wont) upon a hill,
  Beside a learned well.
And wonnëd[7] not the great god Pan[8]
  Upon Mount Olivet,
Feeding the blessed flock of Dan,[9]
  Which did himself beget?
T. O blessed Sheep! O Shepherd great!
  That bought his flock so dear,
And them did save with bloody sweat
  From wolves that would them tear.
M. Besides, as holy Fathers sayn,
  There is a holy place[10]
Where Titan riseth from the main
  To run his daily race,
Upon whose top the stars be stay'd,
  And all the sky doth lean;
There is the cave where Phœbe laid
  The shepherd[11] long to dream.
Whilom there usëd shepherds all
  To feed their flocks at will,
Till by his folly one did fall,
  That all the rest did spill.;[12]
And, sithens[13] shepherds be forsaid[14]
  From places of delight:
Forthy[15] I ween thou be afraid
  To climb this hillë's height.
Of Sinai can I tell thee more,
  And of our Lady's Bow'r;
But little needs to strow my store;
  Suffice this hill of our.
Here have the holy Fauns recourse,
  And Sylvans haunten rathe;[16]
Here has the salt Medway his source,
  Wherein the Nymphs do bathe;
The salt Medway, that trickling streams
  Adown the dales of Kent,
Till with his elder brother Thames
  His brackish waves be ment.[17]
Here grows melampode[18] ev'rywhere,
  And terebinth,[19] good for goats;
The one my madding kids to smear,
  The next to heal their throats.
Hereto,[20] the hills be nigher heaven,
  And thence the passage eath;[21]
As well can prove the piercing levin,[22]
  That seldom falls beneath.
T. Sicker thou speaks like a lewd lorel,[23]
  Of heav'n to deemen so;
How be I am but rude and borel,[24]
  Yet nearer ways I know.
To kirk the narre, from God more far,[25]
  Has been an old-said saw;
And he that strives to touch a star
  Oft stumbles at a straw.
As soon may shepherd climb to sky,
  That leads in lowly dales,
As goatherd proud, that, sitting high,
  Upon the mountain sails.
My seely sheep like well below,
  They need not melampode;
For they be hale enough, I trow,
  And liken their abode:
But, if they with thy goats should yede,[26]
  They soon might be corrupted,
Or like not of the frowy[27] feed,
  Or with the weeds be glutted.
The hills where dwellëd holy saints
  I reverence and adore,
Not for themselves, but for the saints
  Which have been dead of yore.
And now they be to heav'n forewent,[28]
  Their good is with them go;
Their sample[29] only to us lent,
  That als' we might do so.
Shepherds they weren of the best,
  And liv'd in lowly leas;
And, since their souls be now at rest,
  Why do we them disease?[30]
Such one he was (as I have heard
  Old Algrind often sayn)
That whilom was the first shephérd,[31]
  And liv'd with little gain:
And meek he was, as meek might be,
  Simple as simple sheep;
Humble, and like in each degree
  The flock which he did keep.
Often he usëd of his keep[32]
  A sacrifice to bring,
Now with a kid, now with a sheep,
  The altars hallowing.
So louted[33] he unto his Lord,
  Such favour could he find,
That never sithens[13] was abhorr'd
  The simple shepherds' kind.
And such, I ween, the brethren were
  That came from Canaän,

1 Matter.
2 See note 9, page 426.
3 Toil.
4 Foolish.
5 To cajole or beguile me. See note 26, page 54.
6 Takest.
7 Dwelt.
8 "Christ."—*E. K.*
9 Of Israel; one tribe being put for the whole nation.
10 Mount Ida.
11 Endymion; though not on Ida, but on Latmos, was the cave in which the favoured shepherd was laid to his perpetual sleep by Diana.
12 Ruin. E. K. interprets this to apply to Adam in Paradise; but it more obviously applies to Paris, who brought destruction on the dwellers in Troy.
13 Since.
14 Banished.
15 Therefore.
16 Early.
17 Mingled.
18 Black hellebore.
19 The turpentine tree.
20 Moreover.
21 Easy.
22 Lightning.
23 Ignorant, worthless fellow; losel.
24 Clownish, unlearned.
25 "The nearer the church, the farther from grace," is the modern form of this proverb.
26 Go.
27 Musty, mossy.
28 Gone before.
29 Example.
30 Disturb.
31 Abel.
32 Charge, flock.
33 Did honour.

The brethren Twelve, that kept y-fere[1]
The flocks of mighty Pan.
But nothing such that shepherd was
Whom Ida hill did bear,[2]
That left his flock to fetch a lass,
Whose love he bought too dear.
For he was proud, that ill was paid[3]
(No such must shepherds be!)
And with lewd lust was overlaid:
Two things do ill agree.
But shepherd must be meek and mild,
Well ey'd, as Argus was,[4]
With fleshly follies undefiled,
And stout as steed of brass.
Such one (said Algrind) Moses was,
That saw his Maker's face,
His face, more clear than crystal glass,
And spake to him in place.
This had a brother[5] (his name I knew),
The first of all his cote,[6]
A shepherd true, yet not so true[7]
As he that erst I hote.[8]
Whilom all these were low and lief,[9]
And lov'd their flocks to feed;
They never stroven to be chief,
And simple was their weed:[10]
But now (thankëd be God therefor!)
The world is well amend,
Their weeds be not so nighly[11] wore;
Such simpless might them shend![12]
They be y-clad in purple and pall,[13]
So hath their God them blist;
They reign and rulen over all,
And lord it as they list;
Y-girt with belts of glittering gold
(Might they good shepherds be'n!)
Their Pan[14] their sheep to them has sold;
I say as some have seen.
For Palinode (if thou him ken)
Yode[15] late on pilgrimage
To Rome (if such be Rome), and then
He saw this misuságe;
For shepherds (said he) there do lead
As lords do otherwhere;
Their sheep have crusts, and they the bread;
The chips,[16] and they the cheer:
They have the fleece, and eke the flesh
(O seely[17] sheep the while!)
The corn is theirs, let others thresh,
Their hands they may not file.[18]
They have great store and thrifty stocks,
Great friends and feeble foes;
What need them caren for their flocks,
Their boys can look to those.
These wizards[19] welter in wealth's waves,
Pamper'd in pleasures deep;
They have fat kerns,[20] and leany knaves,[21]
Their fasting flocks to keep.
Such mister men[22] be all misgone,[23]
They heapen hills of wrath;
Such surly shepherds have we none,
They keepen all the path.
M. Here is a great deal of good matter
Lost for lack of telling;
Now sicker I see thou dost but clatter;
Harm may come of melling.[24]
Thou meddlest more than shall have thank,
To witen[25] shepherds' wealth;
When folk be fat, and riches rank,
It is a sign of health.
But say me, what is Algrind, he
That is so oft benempt?[26]
T. He is a shepherd great in gree,[27]
But hath been long y-pent:[28]
One day he sat upon a hill,
As now thou wouldest me;
But I am taught, by Algrind's ill,
To love the low degree;
For, sitting so with barëd scalp,
An eagle soarëd high,
That, weening his white head was chalk,
A shell-fish down let fly;
She ween'd the shell-fish to have broke,
But therewith bruis'd his brain;
So now, astonied[29] with the stroke,
He lies in lingering pain.
M. Ah! good Algrind! his hap was ill,
But shall be better in time.
Now farewell! shepherd, since this hill
Thou hast such doubt to climb.

THOMALIN'S EMBLEM:

In medio virtus. (Virtue dwells in the middle place.)

MORRELL'S EMBLEM:

In summo felicitas. (Happiness in the highest.)

AUGUST.

ÆGLOGA OCTAVA.—ARGUMENT.

In this Æglogue is set forth a delectable controversy, made in imitation of that in Theocritus: whereto also Virgil fashioned his third and seventh Æglogue. They choose, for umpire of their strife, Cuddie, a neatherd's boy; who, having ended their cause, reciteth also himself a proper song, whereof Colin, he saith, was author.

Willie. Perigot. Cuddie.

W. Tell me, Perigot, what shall be the game
Wherefor with mine thou dare thy music match?

1 Together. 2 Paris. 3 Discontented.
4 Vigilant, like the hundred-eyed Argus.
5 Aaron. 6 Sheepfold.
7 For, while Moses was absent on Sinai, he led the people of Israel in their worship of the golden calf.
8 That I mentioned before. 9 Beloved.
10 Dress. 11 Not nearly so much worn. 12 Disgrace.
13 "Spoken of the Popes and Cardinals, which use such tyrannical colours and pompous painting."—*E. K.*
14 "The Pope, whom they count their God and greatest shepherd."—*E. K.*
15 Went. 16 Fragments.
17 Simple. 18 Defile, soil.
19 Learned men. 20 Farmers.
21 Servants. 22 Kind of men.
23 Gone astray. 24 Meddling.
25 Censure. 26 Named.
27 Degree, rank.
28 Confined. In 1578, Archbishop Grindal was, by an order of the Star Chamber, confined to his house and suspended from his duty for six months, because he had written a letter to the Queen in advocacy of his Low Church views.
29 Stunned.

Or be thy bagpipes run far out of frame?
  Or hath the cramp thy joints benumb'd with ache?
P. Ah! Willie, when the heart is ill assay'd,[1]
How can bagpipe or joints be well apaid?[2]
W. What the foul evil hath thee so bestad?[3]
  Whilom thou was peregall[4] to the best,
And wont to make the jolly shepherds glad,
  With piping and dancing didst pass the rest.
P. Ah! Willie, now I have learn'd a new dance;
My old music marr'd by a new mischance.
W. Mischief might to that mischance befall,
  That so hath reft us of our merriment;
But read[5] me what pain doth thee so appall;
  Or lovest thou, or be thy younglings miswent?[6]
P. Love hath misled both my younglings and me;
I pine for pain, and they my pain to see.
W. Pardie, and well-away! ill may they thrive;
  Never knew I lover's sheep in good plight:
But an' if in rhymes with me thou dare strive,
  Such fond fantasies shall soon be put to flight.
P. That shall I do, though mochel[7] worse I far'd:
Never shall be said that Perigot was dar'd.[8]
W. Then lo! Perigot, the pledge which I plight,
  A mazer[9] y-wrought of the maple warre,[10]
Wherein is enchasëd[11] many a fair sight
  Of bears and tigers, that maken fierce war;
And over them spread a goodly wild vine,
Entrail'd[12] with a wanton ivy twine.
Thereby is a lamb in the wolfë's jaws;
  But see, how fast runneth the shepherd swain
To save the innocent from the beast's paws,
  And here with his sheephook hath him slain.
Tell me, such a cup hast thou ever seen?
Well might it beseem any harvest queen.
P. Thereto[13] will I pawn yonder spotted lamb;
  Of all my flock there n' is[14] such another,
For I brought him up without the dam;
  But Colin Clout reft me of his brother,
That he purchas'd of me in the plain field;
Sore against my will was I forc'd to yield.
W. Sicker, make like account of his brother:
  But who shall judge the wager won or lost?
P. That shall yonder herdgroom, and none other,
  Which over the pease hitherward doth post.
W. But, for the sunbeam so sore doth us beat,
Were not better to shun the scorching heat?
P. Well agreed, Willie: then set thee down, swain;
  Such a song never heardest thou but Colin sing.
C. Gin, when ye list, ye jolly shepherds twain;
  Such a judge as Cuddie were for a king.
P. It fell upon a holy eve,
W.   Hey, ho, holyday!
P. When holy Fathers wont to shrieve;[15]
W.   Now ginneth this roundelay.
P. Sitting upon a hill so high,
W.   Hey, ho, the high hill!
P. The while my flock did feed thereby;
W.   The while the shepherd self did spill;[16]
P. I saw the bouncing bellibone,
W.   Hey, ho, bonnibell!
P. Tripping over the dale alone;
W.   She can trip it very well.
P. Well deckëd in a frock of gray,
W.   Hey, ho, gray is greet![17]
P. And in a kirtle of green say,[18]
W.   The green is for maidens meet.
P. A chaplet on her head she wore,
W.   Hey, ho, chapëlet!
P. Of sweet violets therein was store;
W.   She sweeter than the violet.
P. My sheep did leave their wonted food,
W.   Hey, ho, seely[19] sheep!
P. And gaz'd on her as they were wood,[20]
W.   Wood as he that did them keep.
P. As the bonny lass passed by,
W.   Hey, ho, bonny lass!
P. She rov'd[21] at me with glancing eye,
W.   As clear as the crystal glass:
P. All as the sunny beam so bright,
W.   Hey, ho, the sunny beam!
P. Glanceth from Phœbus' face forthright,
W.   So love into thy heart did stream:
P. Or as the thunder cleaves the clouds,
W.   Hey, ho, the thunder!
P. Wherein the lightsome levin[22] shrouds,
W.   So cleaves thy soul asunder:
P. Or as Dame Cynthia's silver ray,
W.   Hey, ho, the moonlight!
P. Upon the glittering wave doth play,
W.   Such play is a piteous plight.
P. The glance into my heart did glide,
W.   Hey, ho, the glider!
P. Therewith my soul was sharply gride,[23]
W.   Such wounds soon waxen wider.
P. Hasting to wrench the arrow out,
W.   Hey, ho, Perigot!
P. I left the head in my heart-root,
W.   It was a desperate shot.
P. There it rankleth, ay more and more,
W.   Hey, ho, the arrow!
P. Nor can I find salve for my sore;
W.   Love is a cureless sorrow.
P. And though my bale with death I bought,
W.   Hey, ho, heavy cheer!
P. Yet should that lass not from my thought,
W.   So you may buy gold too dear.
P. But whether in painful love I pine,
W.   Hey, ho, pinching pain!
P. Or thrive in wealth, she shall be mine,
W.   But if thou can her obtain.
P. And if for graceless grief I die,
W.   Hey, ho, graceless grief!
P. Witness she slew me with her eye,
W.   Let thy folly be the prief.[24]
P. And you, that saw it, simple sheep,
W.   Hey, ho, the fair flock!
P. For prief[24] thereof, my death shall weep,
W.   And moan with many a mock.

1 Affected.
2 In good condition. 3 Disposed.
4 Equal. 5 Tell.
6 Gone astray. 7 Much.
8 Frightened; perhaps "darred" should be read. See note 16, page 547. 9 Drinking-bowl.
10 Ware. 11 Engraved.
12 Interwoven. 13 Against it (the cup).
14 Is not. 15 Here confession.
16 Was ruined, brought to mischief.
17 Mourning, sorrow. 18 Silk.
19 Simple. 20 Mad.
21 Shot. 22 Lightning.
23 Pierced. 24 Proof.

P. So learn'd I love on a holy eve,
W. Hey, ho, holyday!
P. That ever since my heart did grieve;
W. Now endeth our roundelay.
C. Sicker, such a roundel never heard I none;
Little lacketh Perigot of the best,
And Willie is not greatly overgone,[1]
So weren his undersongs well addrest.
W. Herdgroom, I fear me thou have a squint eye;
Aread[2] uprightly who has the victory.
C. Faith of my soul, I deem each have gain'd;
Forthy[3] let the lamb be Willie his own;
And, for Perigot so well hath him pain'd,[4]
To him be the wroughten mazer alone.
P. Perigot is well pleasëd with the doom,[5]
Nor can Willie wite[6] the witeless[7] herdgroom.
W. Never deem'd more right of beauty, I ween,
The shepherd of Ida,[8] that judg'd Beauty's queen.
C. But tell me, shepherds, should it not y-shend[9]
Your roundels fresh, to hear a doleful verse
Of Rosalind (who knows not Rosalind?)
That Colin made? ilk[10] can I you rehearse.
P. Now say it, Cuddie, as thou art a lad;
With merry thing it 's good to medle[11] sad.
W. Faith of my soul, thou shalt y-crownëd be
In Colin's stead, if thou this song aread;[12]
For never thing on earth so pleaseth me
As him to hear, or matter of his deed.[13]
C. Then listen each unto my heavy lay,
And tune your pipes as ruthful as ye may:

"Ye wasteful Woods! bear witness of my woe,
Wherein my plaints did oftentimes resound;
Ye careless Birds are privy to my cries,
Which in your songs were wont to make a part:
Thou, pleasant Spring, hast lull'd me oft asleep,
Whose streams my trickling tears did oft augment!

"Resort of people doth my griefs augment;
The wallëd towns do work my greater woe;
The forest wide is fitter to resound
The hollow echo of my careful cries:
I hate the house, since thence my love did part,
Whose wailful want debars mine eyes of sleep.

"Let streams of tears supply the place of sleep;
Let all, that sweet is, void;[14] and all, that may augment
My dole,[15] draw near! More meet to wail my woe
Be the wild woods, my sorrows to resound,
Than bed, or bow'r, both which I fill with cries
When I them see so waste, and find no part

"Of pleasure past. Here will I dwell apart
In ghastful[16] grove therefóre, till my last sleep
Do close mine eyes; so shall I not augment,
With sight of such as change, my restless woe.
Help me, ye baneful Birds! whose shrieking sound
Is sign of dreary death, my deadly cries

"Most ruthfully to tune: and as my cries
(Which of my woe cannot bewray least part)
You hear all night, when Nature craveth sleep,
Increase, so let your irksome yells augment.
Thus all the nights in plaints, the day in woe,
I vowëd have to waste, till safe and sound

"She home return, whose voice's silver sound
To cheerful songs can change my cheerless cries.
Hence with the Nightingale will I take part,
That blessëd bird, that spends her time of sleep
In songs and plaintive pleas, the more t' augment
The memory of his misdeed that bred her woe.[17]

"And you that feel no woe,
When as the sound
Of these my nightly cries
Ye hear apart,
Let break your sounder sleep,
And pity augment."

P. O Colin, Colin! the shepherds' joy,
How I admire each turning of thy verse;
And Cuddie, fresh Cuddie, the liefest[18] boy,
How dolefully his dole thou didst rehearse!
C. Then blow your pipes, shepherds, till you be at home;
The night nigheth fast, it 's time to be gone.

PERIGOT HIS EMBLEM:

Vincenti gloria victi. (To the conqueror belongs the glory of the conquered.)

WILLIE'S EMBLEM:

Vinto non vitto. (Conquered, not overcome.)

CUDDIE'S EMBLEM:

Felice chi puo. (He is happy who can.[19])

SEPTEMBER.

ÆGLOGA NONA.—ARGUMENT.

Herein Diggon Davie is devised to be a shepherd that, in hope of more gain, drove his sheep into a far country. The abuses whereof, and loose living of Popish prelates, by occasion of Hobbinol's demand, he discourseth at large.

Hobbinol. Diggon Davie.

H. DIGGON DAVIE! I bid her good-day;
Or[20] Diggon her is, or I missay.

1 Surpassed. 2 Tell.
3 Therefore. 4 Striven.
5 Judgment. 6 Blame.
7 Blameless. 8 Paris.
9 Disparage. 10 The same.
11 Mingle. 12 Repeat.
13 Doing. 14 Depart.
15 Sorrow. 16 Dreary.
17 See note 5, page 252. 18 Dearest.

19 "The meaning [of these emblems] is very ambiguous: for Perigot by his poesy claiming the conquest, and Willie not yielding, Cuddie, the arbiter of their cause and patron of his own, seemeth to challenge it as his due, saying, that he is happy which can; so abruptly ending: but he meaneth either him, that can win the best, or moderate himself being best, and leave off with the best."—*E. K.*

20 Either.

D. Her was her, while it was daylight,
But now her is a most wretched wight:
For day, that was, is wightly[1] past,
And now at erst[2] the dark night doth haste.
H. Diggon, aread[3] who has thee so dight;[4]
Never I wist thee in so poor a plight.
Where is the fair flock thou wast wont to lead?
Or be they chaffer'd,[5] or at mischief dead?[6]
D. Ah! for love of that is to thee most lief,[7]
Hobbinol, I pray thee gall not my old grief;
Such question rippeth up cause of new woe,
For one, openëd, might unfold many mo'.
H. Nay, but sorrow close shrouded in heart,
I know, to keep is a burdenous smart:
Each thing imparted is more eath[8] to bear:
When the rain is fallen, the clouds waxen clear.
And now, sithens[9] I saw thy head last,
Thrice three moons be fully spent and past;
Since when thou hast measurëd much ground,
And wander'd, I ween, about the world round,
So as thou can many things relate;
But tell me first of thy flock's estate.
D. My sheep be wasted (woe is me therefor!)
The jolly shepherd that was of yore
Is now nor jolly, nor shepherd more.
In foreign coasts men said was plentý;
And so there is, but all of miserý:
I deem'd there much to have ekëd[10] my store,
But such eking hath made my heart sore.
In those countries, where as I have been,
No being for those that truly mean;
But for such as of guile maken gain,
No such country as there to remain;
They setten to sale their shops of shame,
And maken a mart of their good name:
The shepherds there robben one another,
And layen baits to beguile their brother;
Or they will buy his sheep out of the cote,
Or they will carven[11] the shepherd's throat.
The shepherd's swain you cannot well ken,[12]
But[13] it be by his pride, from other men;
They looken big as bulls that be bate,[14]
And bearen the crag[15] so stiff and so state,[16]
As cock on his dunghill crowing crank.[17]
H. Diggon, I am so stiff and so stank,[18]
That uneath[19] may I stand any more;
And now the western wind bloweth sore,
That now is in his chief sovereignty,
Beating the witherëd leaf from the tree;
Sit we down here under the hill;
Then may we talk and tellen our fill,
And make a mock at the blustering blast:
Now say on, Diggon, whatever thou hast.
D. Hobbin, ah Hobbin! I curse the stound[20]
That ever I cast to have lorn[21] this ground:
Well-away the while I was so fond[22]
To leave the good, that I had in hand,
In hope of better that was uncouth![23]
So lost the dog the flesh in his mouth.
My silly sheep (ah! silly sheep!)
That hereby there I whilom us'd to keep,
All[24] were they lusty as thou didst see,
Be all starvëd with pine and penury;
Hardly myself escapëd thilk[25] pain,
Driven for need to come home again.
H. Ah, fon![26] now by thy loss art taught
That seldom change the better brought:
Content who lives with triëd state,
Need fear no change of frowning Fate;
But who will seek for unknown gain,
Oft lives by loss, and leaves with pain.
D. I wot not, Hobbin, how I was bewitch'd
With vain desire and hope to be enrich'd:
But, sicker, so it is, as the bright star
Seemeth ay greater when it is far:
I thought the soil would have made me rich,
But now I wot it is nothing sich;[27]
For either the shepherds be idle and still,
And led of their sheep what way they will,
Or they be false, and full of covetise,
And casten to compass many wrong emprise:
But the more be fraught with fraud and spite,
Nor in good nor goodness taken delight,
But kindle coals of conteck[28] and ire,
Wherewith they set all the world on fire;
Which when they thinken again to quench,
With holy water they do them all drench.
They say they con[29] to heav'n the highway,
But by my soul I dare undersay[30]
They never set foot in that same trode,[31]
But balk[32] the right way, and strayen abroad.
They boast they have the devil at command,
But ask them therefor what they have pawn'd:
Marry! that great Pan bought with dear borrow,[33]
To quit[34] it from the black bower of sorrow.[35]
But they have sold that same long ago;
Forthy[36] woulden draw with them many mo'.
But let them gang[37] alone a God's name;
As they have brewëd, so let them bear blame.
H. Diggon, I pray thee speak not so dirk;[38]
Such mister saying[39] me seemeth too mirk.[40]
D. Then, plainly to speak of shepherds most-
what,[41]
Bad is the best (this English is flat);
Their ill 'havïour gars[42] men missay[43]
Both of their doctrine and their fay.[44]
They say the world is much warre[45] than it wont,
All for her shepherds be beastly and blunt.[46]
Other say, but how truly I n'ot,[47]
All for they holden shame of their cote:

1 Quickly, suddenly.
2 At once.
3 Explain, relate.
4 Treated.
5 Sold.
6 Or dead by mischance.
7 Dear.
8 Easy.
9 Since.
10 Increased.
11 Out.
12 Recognise.
13 Unless.
14 Baited, well-fed.
15 Neck.
16 Stoutly.
17 Vigorously, merrily.
18 Weary.
19 Scarcely.
20 Hour; German, "Stunde."
21 Left.
22 Foolish.
23 Unknown.
24 Although.
25 The same.
26 Fool.
27 Nothing of the kind.
28 Strife.
29 Know.
30 Say in contradiction.
31 Path.
32 Swerve from.
33 That which Christ redeemed with great pledge *i.e.*, their souls.
34 Deliver.
35 From Hell.
36 Therefore.
37 Go.
38 Darkly.
39 Such kind of speech.
40 Obscure.
41 Generally.
42 Makes, causes.
43 Say evil.
44 Faith.
45 Worse; Scotticé, "waur."
46 Unpolished, uneducated.
47 Know not.

Some stick not to say (hot coal on their tongue !)
That such mischief grazeth them among,
All for they casten too much of world's care,
To deck their dame, and enrich their heir;
For such encheason,[1] if you go nigh,
Few chimneys reeking you shall espy.
The fat ox, that wont lig[2] in the stall,
Is now fast stall'd in their crumenall.[3]
Thus chatten the people in their steads,
Alike as a monster of many heads:
But they, that shooten nearest the prick,[4]
Say, others the fat from their beards do lick:
For big bulls of Bashan brace[5] them about,
That with their horns butten the more stout,
But the lean souls treaden under foot;
And to seek redress might little boot;[6]
For liker be they to pluck away more,
Than aught of the gotten good to restore:
For they be like foul quagmires overgrass'd,[7]
That, if thy galage[8] once sticketh fast,
The more to wind it out thou dost swink,[9]
Thou must ay deeper and deeper sink.
Yet better leave off with a little loss,
Than by much wrestling to lose the gross.[10]
H. Now, Diggon, I see thou speakest too plain;
Better it were a little to feign,
And cleanly cover that cannot be cur'd;
Such ill, as is forc'd, must needs be endur'd.
But of such pastors how do the flocks creep?
D. Such as the shepherds, such be their sheep,
For they n' ill[11] listen to the shepherd's voice
But if he call them at their good choice;
They wander at will and stay at pleasure,
And to their folds go at their own leisure.
But they had be better come at their call;
For many have into mischief fall,
And been of ravenous wolves y-rent,
All for they n' ould[12] be buxom and bent.[13]
H. Fie on thee, Diggon, and all thy foul leasing![14]
Well is known that, since the Saxon king,[15]
Never was wolf seen, many nor some,
Nor in all Kent, nor in Christendom;
But the fewer wolves (the sooth to sayn)
The more be the foxes that here remain.
D. Yes, but they gang[16] in more secret wise,
And with sheeps' clothing do them disguise.
They walk not widely as they were wont,
For fear of rangers and the great hunt,[17]
But privily prowling to and fro,
Enauntre[18] they might be inly know.
H. Or privy or pert[19] if any bin,[20]
We have great bandogs will tear their skin.
D. Indeed thy Ball is a bold big cur,
And could make a jolly hole in their fur:
But not good dogs them needeth to chase,
But heedy shepherds to discern their face;
For all their craft is in their countenance,
They be so grave and full of maintenance.[21]
But shall I tell thee what myself know
Chancëd to Roffin not long ago?
H. Say it out, Diggon, whatever it hight,[22]
For naught but well might him betight:[23]
He is so meek, wise, and merciable,[24]
And with his word his work is convenable.[25]
Colin Clout, I ween, be his self[26] boy
(Ah, for Colin! he whilom my joy):
Shepherds such God might us many send,
That doen so carefully their flocks tend!
D. This same shepherd might I well mark,
He has a dog to bite or to bark;
Never had shepherd so keen a cur,
That waketh and if but a leaf stir.
Whilom there wonnëd[27] a wicked wolf,
That with many a lamb had glutted his gulf,
And ever at night wont to repair
Unto the flock, when the welkin shone fair,
Y-clad in clothing of silly sheep,
When the good old man usëd to sleep;
Then at midnight he would bark and bawl
(For he had eft[28] learnëd a currë's call),
As if a wolf were among the sheep:
With that the shepherd would break his sleep,
And send out Lowder (for so his dog hote[29])
To range the fields with wide open throat.
Then, when as Lowder was far away,
This wolfish sheep would catchen his prey,
A lamb, or a kid, or a weanel wast;[30]
With that to the wood would he speed him fast.
Long time he usëd this slippery prank,
Ere Roffy could for his labour him thank.
At end, the shepherd his practice spied
(For Roffy is wise, and as Argus ey'd),
And, when at even he came to the flock,
Fast in their folds he did them lock,
And took out the wolf in his counterfeit coat,
And let out the sheep's blood at his throat.
H. Marry, Diggon, what should him affray
To take his own wherever it lay?
For, had his weasand been a little wider,
He would have devour'd both hidder and shidder.[31]
D. Mischief light on him, and God's great curse!
Too good for him had been a great deal worse;
For it was a perilous beast above all,
And eke had he conn'd[32] the shepherd's call,
And oft in the night came to the sheep-cote,
And callëd Lowder, with a hollow throat,
As if it the old man's self had been:
The dog his master's voice did it ween,
Yet half in doubt he open'd the door,
And ran out as he was wont of yore.
No sooner was out, but, swifter than thought,
Fast by the hide the wolf Lowder caught;

1 Occasion. 2 Lie.
3 Purse; Latin "crumena." 4 Mark.
5 Compass, embrace. 6 Avail.
7 Overgrown with grass. 8 Shoe.
9 Labour. 10 Whole.
11 Will not. 12 Would not.
13 Yielding and obedient. 14 Falsehood.
15 King Edgar, during whose reign (957-975) all the wolves are said to have been destroyed in England, through the payment of money rewards for their heads.
16 Go.
17 "Executing of laws and justice."—*E. K.*
18 Lest. 19 Secret or open.
20 Be. 21 Behaviour.
22 Purports. 23 Betide.
24 Merciful. 25 Conformable.
26 His own. 27 Dwelt.
28 Quickly. 29 Was called.
30 Weaned youngling.
31 Male and female; him and her. 32 Learned.

And, had not Roffy run to the steven,[1]
Lowder had been slain that same even.
H. God shield, man, he should so ill have thrive,
All for he did his devoir belive![2]
If such be wolves, as thou hast told,
How might we, Diggon, them behold?
D. How, but, with heed and watchfulness,
Forstallen[3] them of their wiliness:
Forthy[4] with shepherd sits not[5] play,
Or sleep, as some doen, all the long day;
But ever liggen[6] in watch and ward,
From sudden force their flocks for to guard.
H. Ah! Diggon, that same rule were too strait,
All the cold season to watch and wait:
We be of flesh, men as others be,
Why should we bound to such misery?
Whatever thing lacketh changeable rest,
Must needs decay, when it is at best.
D. Ah! but, Hobbinol, all this long tale
Naught easeth the care that doth me forhale;[7]
What shall I do? what way shall I wend,[8]
My piteous plight and loss to amend?
Ah! good Hobbinol, might I thee pray
Of aid or counsel in my decay?[9]
H. Now by my soul, Diggon, I lament
The hapless mischief that has thee hent;[10]
Nathless thou seëst my lowly sail,
That froward Fortune doth ever avail:[11]
But, were Hobbinol as God might please,
Diggon should soon find favour and ease:
But if to my cottage thou wilt resort,
So as I can I will thee comfórt;
There may'st thou lig[6] in a vetchy bed,[12]
Till fairer Fortune show forth her head.
D. Ah, Hobbinol, God may it thee requite!
Diggon on few such friends did ever light.

DIGGON'S EMBLEM:

Inopem me copia fecit. (Plenty has made me poor.)

OCTOBER.

ÆGLOGA DECIMA.—ARGUMENT.

In Cuddie is set out the perfect pattern of a Poet, which, finding no maintenance of his state and studies, complaineth of the contempt of Poetry, and the causes thereof: specially having been in all ages, and even amongst the most barbarous, always of singular account and honour, and being indeed so worthy and commendable an art; or rather no art, but a divine gift and heavenly instinct, not to be gotten by labour and learning, but adorned with both; and poured into the wit by a certain Enthousiasmos *and celestial inspiration, as the Author hereof elsewhere at large discourseth in his book called* The English Poet, *which book being lately come to my hands, I mind also by God's grace, upon farther advisement, to publish.*

Piers. Cuddie.

P. CUDDIE, for shame, hold up thy heavy head,
And let us cast with what delight to chase
And weary this long ling'ring Phœbus' race.
Whilom thou wont the shepherds' lads to lead
In rhymes, in riddles, and in bidding base;[13]
Now they in thee, and thou in sleep, art dead.

C. Piers, I have pipëd erst[14] so long with pain,
That all mine oaten reeds be rent and wore,
And my poor Muse hath spent her sparëd store,
Yet little good hath got, and much less gain.
Such pleasance makes the grasshopper so poor,
And lig so laid,[15] when winter doth her strain.

The dapper[16] ditties, that I wont devise
To feed youth's fancy and the flocking fry,
Delighten much; what I the bet forthy?[17]
They have the pleasure, I a slender price:
I beat the bush, the birds to them do fly:
What good thereof to Cuddie can arise?

P. Cuddie, the praise is better than the price,
The glory eke much greater than the gain:
O what an honour is it, to restrain
The lust of lawless youth with good advice,
Or prick them forth with pleasance of thy vein,
Whereto thou list their trainëd wills entice!

Soon as thou gin'st to set thy notes in frame,
O how the rural routs to thee do cleave!
Seemeth thou dost their soul of sense bereave,
All as the shepherd[18] that did fetch his dame
From Pluto's baleful bow'r withouten leave;
His music's might the hellish hound did tame.

C. So praisen babes the peacock's spotted train,
And wonder at bright Argus' blazing eye;
But who rewards him e'er the more forthy,[4]
Or feeds him once the fuller by a grain?
Such praise is smoke, that sheddeth in the sky;
Such words be wind, and wasten soon in vain.

P. Abandon then the base and viler clown;
Lift up thyself out of the lowly dust,
And sing of bloody Mars, of wars, of giusts;[19]
Turn thee to those that wield the awful crown,
To doubted[20] knights, whose woundless[21] armour rusts,
And helms unbruisëd waxen daily brown.

There may thy Muse display her fluttering wing,
And stretch herself at large from east to west;
Whether thou list in fair Elisa[22] rest,
Or, if thee please in bigger notes to sing,
Advance the Worthy[23] whom she loveth best,
That first the White Bear to the stake did bring.

1 Noise, cry.
2 Promptly did his duty.
3 Hinder, balk.
4 Therefore.
5 It befits not (to).
6 Lie.
7 Distress, distract.
8 Go, turn.
9 Ruin, calamity.
10 Seized upon.
11 Lower.
12 A bed of pease straw.
13 At the game of prison base.
14 Before.
15 Lie so faint.
16 Pretty.
17 What am I the better on that account?
18 Orpheus.
19 Tournaments, jousts.
20 Redoubted.
21 Unwounded.
22 Queen Elizabeth.
23 The Earl of Leicester, whose cognizance was the bear and ragged staff; he is represented in "The Faerie Queen" by Prince Arthur.

And, when the stubborn stroke of stronger stounds[1]
Has somewhat slack'd the tenor of thy string,
Of love and lustihead then may'st thou sing,
And carol loud, and lead the Miller's round,[2]
All[3] were Elisa one of that same ring;
So might our Cuddie's name to heav'n sound.

C. Indeed the Romish Tityrus,[4] I hear,
Through his Mæcenas left his oaten reed,
Whereon he erst had taught his flocks to feed,
And labour'd lands to yield the timely ear,
And eft[5] did sing of wars and deadly dread,
So as the heav'ns did quake his verse to hear.

But ah! Mæcenas is y-clad in clay,
And great Augustus long ago is dead,
And all the worthies liggen[6] wrapt in lead
That matter made for poets on to play:
For ever, who in derring-do[7] were dread,
The lofty verse of them was lovëd ay.

But after Virtue gan for age to stoop,
And mighty Manhood brought a bed of ease,
The vaunting poets found naught worth a pease
To put in press among the learnëd troop;[8]
Then gan the streams of flowing wits to cease,
And sunbright honour penn'd in shameful coop.

And if that any buds of Poesy,
Yet, of the old stock, gan to shoot again,
Or it men's follies must be forc'd to feign,
And roll with rest in rhymes of ribaldry;
Or, as it sprung, it wither must again:
Tom Piper makes us better melody.

P. O peerless Poesy! where is then thy place?
If nor in prince's palace thou dost sit
(And yet is prince's palace the most fit),
Nor breast of baser birth doth thee embrace,
Then make thee wings of thine aspiring wit,
And, whence thou cam'st, fly back to heav'n apace.

C. Ah! Percy, it is all too weak and wan
So high to soar, and make so large a flight;
Her piecëd[9] pinions be not so in plight:
For Colin fits such famous flight to scan;
He, were he not with love so ill bedight,[10]
Would mount as high and sing as sweet as swan.

P. Ah! fon;[11] for Love does teach him climb so high,
And lifts him up out of the loathsome mire;
Such immortal mirror, as he doth admire,
Would raise one's mind above the starry sky,
And cause a caitiff corage[12] to aspire;
For lofty love doth loathe a lowly eye.

C. All otherwise the state of Poet stands;
For lordly Love is such a tyrant fell,
That, where he rules, all pow'r he doth expel;
The vaunted verse a vacant head demands,

1 Efforts. 2 A kind of dance.
3 Although. 4 Virgil.
5 Soon afterwards. 6 Lie. 7 Daring deeds.
8 The poets found no deeds worthy to be advanced or celebrated by the Muses. 9 Imperfect.
10 Bestead. 11 Fool. 12 A base mind.
13 Knowest. 14 Strange. 15 Therefore.

Nor wont with crabbed Care the Muses dwell:
Unwisely weaves, that takes two webs in hand.

Who ever casts to compass weighty prize,
And thinks to throw out thundering words of threat,
Let pour in lavish cups and thrifty bits of meat,
For Bacchus' fruit is friend to Phœbus wise;
And, when with wine the brain begins to sweat,
The numbers flow as fast as spring doth rise.

Thou ken'st[13] not, Percie, how the rhyme should rage;
O if my temples were distain'd with wine,
And girt in garlands of wild ivy twine,
How I could rear the Muse on stately stage,
And teach her tread aloft in buskin fine,
With quaint[14] Bellona in her equipage!

But ah! my courage cools ere it be warm:
Forthy[15] content us in this humble shade,
Where no such troublous tides[16] have us assay'd;
Here we our slender pipes may safely charm.[17]
P. And, when my goats shall have their bellies laid,
Cuddie shall have a kid to store his farm.

CUDDIE'S EMBLEM:

Agitante calescimus illo, &c.[18]

NOVEMBER.

ÆGLOGA UNDECIMA.—ARGUMENT.

In this eleventh Æglogue he bewaileth the death of some maiden of great blood, whom he calleth Dido. The personage is secret, and to me altogether unknown, albeit of himself I often required the same. This Æglogue is made in imitation of Marot his song, which he made upon the death of Loyes the French Queen; but far passing his reach, and in mine opinion all other the Æglogues of this Book.

Thenot. Colin.

T. COLIN, my dear, when shall it please thee sing,
As thou wert wont, songs of some jovisance?[19]
Thy Muse too long slumb'reth in sorrowing,
Lullëd asleep through Love's misgovernance.
Now somewhat sing whose endless souvenance[20]
Among the shepherds' swains may ay remain,
Whether thee list thy lovëd lass advance,
Or honour Pan with hymns of higher vein.
C. Thenot, now n'is[21] the time of merry-make,
Nor Pan to hery,[22] nor with Love to play;
Such mirth in May is meetest for to make,
Or summer shade, under the cockëd hay.
But now sad winter welkëd[23] hath the day,
And Phœbus, weary of his yearly task,

16 Times, seasons. 17 Attune.
18 "Hereby is meant, as also in the whole course of this Æglogue, that Poetry is a divine instinct, and unnatural rage, passing the reach of common reason."—*E. K.* 19 Joyousness. 20 Memory.
21 Is not. 22 Celebrate.
23 Shortened.

Y-stabled hath his steeds in lowly lay,[1]
And taken up his inn[2] in Fishes' hask:[3]
This sullen season sadder plight doth ask,
And loatheth such delights as thou dost praise:
The mournful Musé in mirth now list not mask,
As she was wont in youth and summer days;
But, if thou algate lust light virelays,
And looser songs of love, to underfong,[4]
Who but thyself deserves such poets' praise?
Relieve thy oaten pipes that sleepen long.
T. The nightingale is sovëreign of song,
Before him sits[5] the titmouse silent be;
And I, unfit to thrust in skilful throng,
Should Colin make judge of my foolery.
Nay, better learn of them that learnëd be,
And have been water'd at the Muses' well;
The kindly dew drops from the higher tree,
And wets the little plants that lowly dwell:
But if sad winter's wrath, and season chill,
Accord not with thy Muse's merriment,
To sadder times thou may'st attune thy quill,
And sing of sorrow and death's dreariment;
For dead is Dido, dead, alas! and drent,[6]
Dido! the great shephérd[7] his daughter sheen:[8]
The fairest May[9] she was that ever went,
Her like she has not left behind, I ween:
And, if thou wilt bewail my woeful teen,[10]
I shall thee give yond cosset[11] for thy pain;
And, if thy rhymes as round and rueful be'n
As those that did thy Rosalind complain,
Much greater gifts for guerdon thou shalt gain,
Than kid or cosset, which I thee benempt:[12]
Then up, I say, thou jolly shepherd swain,
Let not my small demand be so contempt.[13]
C. Thenot, to that I choose thou dost me tempt;
But ah! too well I wot my humble vein,
And how my rhymes be rugged and unkempt;[14]
Yet, as I con, my conning I will strain.[15]

"Up, then, Melpomené! the mournful'st Muse of Nine,
Such cause of mourning never hadst afore;
Up, grisly ghosts! and up my rueful rhyme!
Matter of mirth now shalt thou have no more;
For dead she is, that mirth thee made of yore.
Dido, my dear, alas! is dead,
Dead, and lieth wrapt in lead.
O heavy herse![16]
Let streaming tears be pourëd out in store;
O careful[17] verse!

"Shepherds, that by your flocks on Kentish downs abide,
Wail ye this woeful waste of Nature's wark;[18]
Wail we the wight, whose presence was our pride;
Wail we the wight, whose absence is our cark;[19]
The sun of all the world is dim and dark;
The earth now lacks her wonted light,
And all we dwell in deadly night.
O heavy herse!
Break we our pipes, that shrill'd as loud as lark;
O careful verse!

"Why do we longer live (ah! why live we so long?)
Whose better days Death hath shut up in woe?
The fairest flow'r our garland all among
Is faded quite, and into dust y-go.
Sing now, ye shepherds' daughters, sing no mo'
The songs that Colin made you in her praise;
But into weeping turn your wanton lays.
O heavy herse!
Now is time to die: nay, time was long ago:
O careful verse!

"Whence is it, that the flow'ret of the field doth fade,
And lieth buried long in Winter's bale;[20]
Yet, soon as Spring his mantle hath display'd,
It flow'reth fresh, as it should never fail?
But thing on earth that is of most avail,[21]
As virtue's branch and beauty's bud,
Reliven[22] not for any good.
O heavy herse!
The branch once dead, the bud eke needs must quail;[23]
O careful verse!

"She, while she was (that 'was' a woeful word to sayn!)
For beauty's praise and pleasance had no peer;
So well she could the shepherds entertain
With cakes and cracknels, and such country cheer:
Nor would she scorn the simple shepherd's swain;
For she would call him often heam,[24]
And give him curds and clouted cream.
O heavy herse!
Als' Colin Clout she would not once disdain;
O careful verse!

"But now such happy cheer is turn'd to heavy chance,
Such pleasance now displac'd by dolor's dint;[25]
All music sleeps, where Death doth lead the dance,
And shepherds' wonted solace is extinct.
The blue in black, the green in gray, is tinct;[26]
The gaudy garlands deck her grave,
The faded flowers her corse embrave.[27]
O heavy herse!
Mourn now, my Muse, now mourn with tears besprint;[28]
O careful verse!

"O thou great shepherd, Lobbin, how grea is thy grief!

1 Plain; referring to the sun's declinature towards the south as winter approaches. 2 Abode.
3 In the fishes' basket: the sun enters the constellation Pisces in November.
4 If, however, you choose to undertake light virelays and looser songs of love. 5 It befits.
6 Drowned.
7 "Dido" and "the great shepherd" are believed to signify real personages; but no clue to their identification remains. 8 Bright, lovely.
9 Maid. 10 Affliction.
11 A lamb brought up without the ewe.
12 Mentioned, promised. 13 Contemned.
14 Uncombed, unpolished. 15 Exert my ability.
16 "The solemn obsequy in funerals."—*E. K.*
17 Sorrowful. 18 Work.
19 Care, grief. 20 Ruin.
21 Value. 22 Live again. 23 Perish.
24 Home; after the north country pronunciation.
25 The stroke or wound of grief.
26 Dyed. 27 Adorn.
28 Besprinkled.

Where be the nosegays that she dight[1] for thee?
The colour'd chapëlets wrought with a chief,[2]
The knotted rush-rings, and gilt rosemary?
For she deemëd no thing too dear for thee.
Ah! they be all y-clad in clay;
One bitter blast blew all away.
O heavy herse!
Thereof naught remains but the memory;
O careful verse!

"Ah me! that dreary Death should strike so mortal stroke,
That can undo Dame Nature's kindly course;
The faded locks[3] fall from the lofty oak,
The floods do gasp, for driëd is their source,
And floods of tears flow in their stead perforce:
The mantled meadows mourn,
Their sundry colours turn.
O heavy herse!
The heav'ns do melt in tears without remorse;
O careful verse!

"The feeble flocks in field refuse their former food,
And hang their heads as they would learn to weep;
The beasts in forest wail as they were wood,[4]
Except the wolves, that chase the wand'ring sheep,
Now she is gone that safely did them keep:
The turtle on the barëd branch
Laments the wound that Death did launch.
O heavy herse!
And Philomel her song with tears doth steep;
O careful verse!

"The water nymphs, that wont with her to sing and dance,
And for her garland olive branches bear,
Now baleful boughs of cypress do advance;
The Muses, that were wont green bays to wear,
Now bringen bitter elder-branches sear;
The Fatal Sisters eke repent
Her vital thread so soon was spent.
O heavy herse!
Mourn now, my Muse, now mourn with heavy cheer;
O careful verse!

"O trustless state of earthly things, and slipper[5] hope
Of mortal men, that swink[6] and sweat for naught,
And, shooting wide, do miss the markëd scope;
Now have I learn'd (a lesson dearly bought)
That n' is[7] on earth assurance to be sought;
For what might be in earthly mould,
That did her buried body hold.
O heavy herse!
Yet saw I on the bier when it was brought
O careful verse!

"But maugré[8] Death, and dreaded Sisters' deadly spite,
And gates of Hell, and fiery Furies' force,
She hath the bonds broke of eternal night,
Her soul unbodied of the burdenous corse.
Why then weeps Lobbin so without remorse?
O Lobb! thy loss no longer lament;
Dido n' is[7] dead, but into heaven hent.[9]
O happy herse!
Cease now, my Muse, now cease thy sorrows' source;
O joyful verse!

"Why wail we then? why weary we the gods with plaints,
As if some evil were to her betight?[10]
She reigns a goddess now among the saints,
That whilom was the saint of shepherds' light,
And is installëd now in heaven's height.
I see thee, blessed soul! I see
Walk in Elysian fields so free.
O happy herse!
Might I once come to thee (O that I might!)
O joyful verse!

"Unwise and wretched men, to weet what's good or ill,
We deem of death as doom of ill desert;
But knew we, fools, what it us brings until,
Die would we daily, once it to expert![11]
No danger there the shepherd can astert;[12]
Fair fields and pleasant lays[13] there be'n;
The fields ay fresh, the grass ay green.
O happy herse!
Make haste, ye shepherds, thither to revert.
O joyful verse!

"Dido is gone afore (whose turn shall be the next?)
There lives she with the blessëd gods in bliss;
There drinks she nectar with ambrosia mixt,
And joys enjoys that mortal men do miss.
The honour now of highest gods she is,
That whilom was poor shepherd's pride,
While here on earth she did abide.
O happy herse!
Cease now, my song, my woe now wasted is;
O joyful verse!"

T. Ah! frank shephérd, how be thy verses meint[14]
With doleful pleasance, so as I not wot
Whether rejoice or weep for great constraint!
Thine be the cosset, well hast thou it got.
Up, Colin, up, enough thou mournëd hast;
Now gins to mizzle,[15] hie we homeward fast.

COLIN'S EMBLEM:

La mort ny mord. (Death doth not bite.)

DECEMBER.

ÆGLOGA DUODECIMA.—ARGUMENT.

This Æglogue (even as the first began) is ended with a complaint of Colin to god Pan; wherein, as weary

1 Dressed.
2 Wrought into a head, like a nosegay.
3 Withered leaves.
4 Mad.
5 Slippery.
6 Labour.
7 Is not.
8 Despite.
9 Taken, received.
10 Betided, happened.
11 Experience.
12 Befall unawares, startle.
13 Leas, plains.
14 Mingled.
15 It begins to rain a little.

of his former ways, he proportioneth his life to the four seasons of the year; comparing his youth to the spring time, when he was fresh and free from love's folly. His manhood to the summer, which, he saith, was consumed with great heat and excessive drouth, caused through a comet or blazing star, by which he meaneth love; which passion is commonly compared to such flames and immoderate heat. His riper years he resembleth to an unseasonable harvest, wherein the fruits fall ere they be ripe. His latter age to winter's chill and frosty season, now drawing near to his last end.

THE gentle shepherd sat beside a spring,
All in the shadow of a bushy brere,[1]
That Colin hight, which well could pipe and sing,
For he of Tityrus his song did lear:[2]
There as he sat in secret shade alone,
Thus gan he make of love his piteous moan.

"O sov'reign Pan! thou god of shepherds all,
Which of our tender lambkins takest keep,[3]
And, when our flocks into mischance might fall,
Dost save from mischief the unwary sheep,
Als' of their masters hast no less regard
Than of the flocks, which thou dost watch and ward;

"I thee beseech (so be thou deign to hear
Rude ditties, tun'd to shepherd's oaten reed,
Or if I ever sonnet sung so clear,
As it with pleasance might thy fancy feed),
Hearken a while, from thy green cabinet,
The rural song of careful Colinet.

"Whilom in youth, when flower'd my joyful Spring,
Like swallow swift I wander'd here and there;
For heat of heedless lust me so did sting,
That I of doubted danger had no fear:
I went the wasteful woods and forest wide,
Withouten dread of wolves to be espied.

"I wont to range amid the mazy thicket,
And gather nuts to make my Christmas-game,
And joyëd oft to chase the trembling pricket,[4]
Or hunt the heartless hare till she were tame.
What reckëd I of wintry age's waste?
Then deemëd I my spring would ever last.

"How often have I scal'd the craggy oak,
All to dislodge the raven of her nest?
How have I wearièd, with many a stroke,
The stately walnut-tree, the while the rest
Under the tree fell all for nuts at strife?
For like to me was liberty and life.

"And, for I was in those same looser years
(Whether the Muse so wrought me from my birth,
Or I too much believ'd my shepherd peers),
Somedeal y-bent[5] to song and music's mirth,
A good old shepherd, Wrenock was his name,
Made me by art more cunning in the same.

"From thence I durst in derring-do[6] compare
With shepherd's swain whatever fed in field;
And, if that Hobbinol right judgment bare,
To Pan his own self pipe I need not yield:
For, if the flocking nymphs did follow Pan,
The wiser Muses after Colin ran.

"But, ah! such pride at length was ill repaid;
The shepherds' god (pardie! god was he none)
My hurtless pleasance did me ill upbraid;
My freedom lorn,[7] my life he left to moan.
Love they him callëd that gave me checkmate,
But better might they have behote[8] him Hate.

"Then gan my lovely Spring bid me farewell,
And Summer season sped him to display
(For Love then in the Lion's house[9] did dwell)
The raging fire that kindled at his ray.
A comet stirr'd up that unkindly heat,
That reignëd (as men said) in Venus' seat.

"Forth was I led, not as I wont afore,
When choice I had to choose my wand'ring way,
But whither luck and love's unbridled lore
Would lead me forth on Fancy's bit to play:
The bush my bed, the bramble was my bow'r;
The woods can witness many a woeful stour.[10]

"Where I was wont to seek the honey-bee,
Working her formal rooms in waxen frame,
The grisly toadstool grown there might I see,
And loathëd paddocks[11] lording on the same:
And where the chanting birds lull'd me asleep,
The ghastly owl her grievous inn[12] doth keep.

"Then, as the Spring gives place to elder time,
And bringeth forth the fruit of Summer's pride;
All so my age, now passëd youthly prime,
To things of riper season self applied,
And learn'd of lighter timber cotes to frame,
Such as might save my sheep and me from shame.

"To make fine cages for the nightingale,
And baskets of bulrushes, was my wont:
Who to entrap the fish in winding sale[13]
Was better seen,[14] or hurtful beasts to hunt?
I learnëd als' the signs of heav'n to ken,[15]
How Phœbus fails,[16] where Venus sets, and when.

"And triëd time yet taught me greater things;
The sudden rising of the raging seas,
The sooth[17] of birds by beating of their wings,
The pow'r of herbs, both which can hurt and ease,
And which be wont t'enrage the restless sheep,
And which be wont to work eternal sleep.

"But, ah! unwise and witless Colin Clout,
That kid'st[18] the hidden kinds of many a weed,
Yet kid'st not one to cure thy sore heart-root,

1 Briar.
2 Learn. 3 Care.
4 Buck. 5 Somewhat inclined.
6 Deeds of daring. 7 Lost. 8 Called.
9 E. K. says: "He imagineth simply that Cupid, which is Love, had his abode in the hot sign Leo, which is the midst of summer; a pretty allegory" designed to imply the heat of Colin's passion.
10 Affliction. 11 Toads. 12 Abode.
13 Net of sallow or wicker-work. 14 Skilled.
15 Know. 16 How the moon wanes.
17 Soothsaying, omens. 18 Knewest.

Whose rankling wound as yet does rifely[1] bleed.
Why liv'st thou still, and yet hast thy death's wound?
Why diest thou still, and yet alive art found?

"Thus is my Summer worn away and wasted,
Thus is my Harvest hasten'd all too rathe;[2]
The ear that budded fair is burnt and blasted,
And all my hopëd gain is turn'd to scathe.
Of all the seed that in my youth was sown,
Was none but brakes and brambles to be mown.

"My boughs, with blooms that crownëd were at first,
And promisëd of timely fruit such store,
Are left both bare and barren now at erst;[3]
The flattering fruit is fall'n to ground before,
And rotted ere they were half mellow ripe;
My harvest, waste, my hope away did wipe.

"The fragrant flow'rs, that in my garden grew,
Be wither'd, as they had been gather'd long:
Their roots be driëd up for lack of dew,
Yet dew'd with tears they have been ever among.[4]
Ah! who has wrought my Rosalind this spite,
To spoil the flow'rs that should her garland dight?[5]

"And I, that whilom wont to frame my pipe
Unto the shifting of the shepherd's foot,
Such follies now have gather'd as too ripe,
And cast them out as rotten and unswoot.[6]
The looser lass I cast to please no more;
One if I please, enough is me therefóre.

"And thus of all my harvest-hope I have
Naught reapëd but a weedy crop of care;
Which, when I thought have thresh'd in swelling sheave,
Cockle for corn, and chaff for barley, bare:
Soon as the chaff should in the fan be fin'd,[7]
All was blown away of the wav'ring wind.

"So now my year draws to his latter term,
My Spring is spent, my Summer burnt up quite;
My Harvest hastes to stir up Winter stern,
And bids him claim with rigorous rage his right:
So now he storms with many a sturdy stour;[8]
So now his blust'ring blast each coast doth scour.

"The careful cold[9] hath nipp'd my rugged rind,
And in my face deep furrows eld hath pight:[10]
My head besprent[11] with hoary frost I find,
And by mine eye the crow his claw doth write:
Delight is laid abed, and pleasure past;
No sun now shines; clouds have all overcast.

"Now leave, ye shepherds' boys, your merry glee;
My Muse is hoarse and weary of this stound:[12]
Here will I hang my pipe upon this tree;
Was never pipe of reed did better sound:
Winter is come, that blows the bitter blast,
And after Winter dreary death does haste.

"Gather together, ye my little flock,
My little flock, that was to me so lief;[13]
Let me, ah! let me in your folds ye lock,
Ere the breme[14] winter breed you greater grief.
Winter is come, that blows the baleful breath,
And after Winter cometh timely death.

"Adieu, delights, that lullëd me asleep;
Adieu, my dear, whose love I bought so dear;
Adieu, my little lambs and lovëd sheep;
Adieu, ye woods, that oft my witness were:
Adieu, good Hobbinol, that was so true;
Tell Rosalind, Colin bids her adieu."

COLIN'S EMBLEM:

Vivitur ingenio: cætera mortis erunt. (The creations of genius live; all other things shall be the prey of death.)

EPILOGUE.

Lo! I have made a Calendar for ev'ry year,
That steel in strength, and time in durance, shall outwear;
And, if I markëd well the stars' revolution,
It shall continue till the world's dissolution,
To teach the ruder shepherd how to feed his sheep,
And from the falser's fraud his folded flock to keep.
Go, little Calendar! thou hast a free passpórt;
Go but a lowly gait amongst the meaner sort:
Dare not to match thy pipe with Tityrus[15] his style,
Nor with the Pilgrim that the Ploughman play'd a while;[16]
But follow them far off, and their high steps adore
The better please, the worse despise; I ask no more.

MERCE NON MERCEDE.

(For recompense, but not for hire.)

1 Abundantly. 2 Early.
3 At last. 4 Ever and anon.
5 Adorn. 6 Unsweet.
7 Sifted. 8 Assault.
9 "For care is said to cool the blood."—*E. K.* See note 2, page 169.
10 Set, marked. 11 Besprinkled.
12 Effort. 13 Dear.
14 Bitter. 15 Virgil.
16 Probably Chaucer—among whose "Canterbury Tales" formerly stood a poem of great length, full of attacks on the clergy like those made in Spenser's fifth, seventh and ninth Eclogues, and called The Ploughman's Tale. Its authenticity is now doubted, and it is rejected from modern editions; but in Spenser's day it was probably considered genuine, and its burthen and tone may naturally have given it an especial prominence at a time when the great and bitter controversy between Catholicism and Protestantism was by no means at an end in England.

THE RUINS OF TIME.

[1591.]

DEDICATION

TO THE RIGHT NOBLE AND BEAUTIFUL LADY,

THE LADY MARY,

COUNTESS OF PEMBROKE.

Most honourable and bountiful Lady, there be long since deep sowed in my breast the seeds of most entire love and humble affection unto that most brave Knight, your noble brother deceased;[1] which, taking root, began in his life-time somewhat to bud forth, and to show themselves to him, as then in the weakness of their first spring; and would in their riper strength (had it pleased High God till then to draw out his days) spired forth[2] fruit of more perfection. But since God hath disdeigned[3] the world of that most noble spirit, which was the hope of all learned men, and the patron of my young Muses; together with him both their hope of any farther fruit was cut off, and also the tender delight of those their first blossoms nipped and quite dead. Yet, since my late coming into England, some friends of mine (which might much prevail with me, and indeed command me), knowing with how strait bands of duty I was tied to him, as also bound unto that noble house (of which the chief hope then rested in him), have sought to revive them by upbraiding me, for that I have not showed any thankful remembrance towards him or any of them, but suffer their names to sleep in silence and forgetfulness. Whom chiefly to satisfy, or else to avoid that foul blot of unthankfulness, I have conceived this small poem, intituled by a general name of *The World's Ruins;* yet specially intended to the renowning of that noble race, from which both you and he sprung, and to the eternising of some of the chief of them late deceased. The which I dedicate unto your Ladyship, as whom it most specially concerneth; and to whom I acknowledge myself bounden by many singular favours and great graces. I pray for your honourable happiness; and so humbly kiss your hands.

Your Ladyship's ever humbly at command,

E. S.

It chancëd me one day beside the shore
Of silver streaming Thamesis to be,
Nigh where the goodly Ver'lam[4] stood of yore,
Of which there now remains no memory,
Nor any little monument to see,
By which the traveller, that fares that way,
"This once was she," may warnëd be to say.

There, on the other side, I did behold
A woman sitting sorrowfully wailing,
Rending her yellow locks, like wiry gold
About her shoulders carelessly down trailing,
And streams of tears from her fair eyes forth railing:[5]
In her right hand a broken rod she held,
Which toward heav'n she seem'd on high to weld.[6]

Whether she were one of that river's nymphs,
Which did the loss of some dear love lament,
I doubt; or one of those three fatal Imps[7]
Which draw the days of men forth in extent;
Or th' ancient Genius of that city brent:[8]
But, seeing her so piteously perplex'd,
I (to her calling) ask'd what her so vex'd.

"Ah! what delight," quoth she, "in earthly thing,
Or comfort can I, wretched creature, have?
Whose happiness the heavens envying,
From highest stair to lowest step me drave,
And have in mine own bowels made my grave,
That of all nations now I am forlorn,
The world's sad spectacle, and fortune's scorn."

Much was I movëd at her piteous plaint,
And felt my heart nigh riven in my breast
With tender ruth to see her sore constraint;
That, shedding tears a while, I still did rest,
And, after, did her name of her request.
"Name have I none," quoth she, "nor any being,
Bereft of both by Fate's unjust decreeing.

"I was that city which the garland wore
Of Britain's pride, deliver'd unto me
By Roman victors, which it won of yore;
Though naught at all but ruins now I be,
And lie in mine own ashes, as ye see:
Ver'lam I was: what boots it that I was,
Since now I am but weeds and wasteful grass?

"O vain world's glory! and unsteadfast state
Of all that lives on face of sinful earth!
Which, from their first until their utmost date,
Taste no one hour of happiness or mirth;
But like as at the ingate[9] of their birth
They crying creep out of their mother's womb,
So wailing back go to their woeful tomb.

1 Sir Philip Sidney. 2 Put forth.
3 Counted unworthy.
4 Verolamium, or Verulam, was a Roman town, near St Alban's, in Hertfordshire, some remains of which are still visible. 5 Flowing. 6 Wield, lift.
7 The Fates. 8 Burnt. 9 Entrance.

"Why then doth flesh, a bubble-glass of breath,
Hunt after honour and advancement vain,
And rear a trophy for devouring death,
With so great labour and long-lasting pain,
As if his days for ever should remain?
Since all that in this world is great or gay
Doth as a vapour vanish and decay.

"Look back, who list, unto the former ages,
And call to count what is of them become:
Where be those learnëd wits and ántique sages
Which of all wisdom knew the perfect sum?
Where those great warriors, which did overcome
The world with conquest of their might and main,
And made one meer[1] of th' earth and of their reign?

"What now is of th' Assyrian lioness,
Of whom no footing now on earth appears?
What of the Persian bear's outrageousness,
Whose memory is quite worn out with years?
Who of the Grecian leopard[2] now aught hears,
That overran the East with greedy power,
And left his whelps their kingdoms to devour?

"And where is that same great sev'n-headed Beast
That made all nations vassals of her pride,
To fall before her feet at her behest,
And on the neck of all the world did ride?
Where doth she all that wondrous wealth now híde?
With her own weight down pressëd now she lies,
And by her heaps her hugeness testifies.

"O Rome, thy ruin I lament and rue,
And in thy fall my fatal overthrow,
That whilom was, whilst heav'ns with equal view
Deign'd to behold me, and their gifts bestow,
The picture of thy pride in pompous show:
And of the whole world as thou wast the empress,
So I of this small northern world was princess.

"To tell the beauty of my buildings fair,
Adorn'd with purest gold and precious stone;
To tell my riches and endowments rare,
That by my foes are now all spent and gone;
To tell my forces, matchable to none;
Were but lost labour, that few would believe,
And with rehearsing would me more aggrieve.

"High tow'rs, fair temples, goodly theatres,
Strong walls, rich porches, princely palaces,
Large streets, brave houses, sacred sepulchres,
Sure gates, sweet gardens, stately galleries
Wrought with fair pillars and fine imageries;
All those (O pity!) now are turn'd to dust,
And overgrown with black oblivion's rust.

"Thereto for warlike pow'r, and people's store,
In Brittany was none to match with me,
That many often did aby full sore:
Nor Troynovant,[3] though elder sister she,
With my great forces might comparëd be;
That stout Pendragon[4] to his peril felt,
Who in a siege sev'n years about me dwelt.

"But, long ere this, Bonduca,[5] Britoness,
Her mighty host against my bulwarks brought;
Bonduca! that victorious conqueress,
That, lifting up her brave heroic thought
'Bove women's weakness, with the Romans fought,
Fought, and in field against them thrice prevail'd:
Yet was she foil'd, when as she me assail'd.

"And though at last by force I conquer'd were
Of hardy Saxons, and became their thrall;
Yet was I with much bloodshed bought full dear,
And pric'd[6] with slaughter of their General:
The monument of whose sad funeral,
For wonder of the world, long in me lasted;
But now to naught, through spoil of time, is wasted.

"Wasted it is, as if it never were;
And all the rest, that me so honour'd made,
And of the world admirëd ev'rywhere,
Is turn'd to smoke, that doth to nothing fade;
And of that brightness now appears no shade,
But grisly shades, such as do haunt in hell
With fearful fiends, that in deep darkness dwell.

"Where my high steeples whilom us'd to stand,
On which the lordly falcon wont to tow'r,
There now is but a heap of lime and sand
For the screech-owl to build her baleful bow'r:
And where the nightingale wont forth to pour
Her restless plaints, to comfort wakeful lovers,
There now haunt yelling mews and whining plovers.

"And where the crystal Thamis wont to slide
In silver channel, down along the lea,
About whose flow'ry banks on either side
A thousand nymphs, with mirthful jollity,
Were wont to play, from all annoyance free;
There now no river's course is to be seen,
But moorish fens, and marshes ever green.

"Seems, that that gentle River, for great grief
Of my mishaps, which oft I to him plain'd,—
Or for to shun the horrible mischief,
With which he saw my cruel foes me pain'd,
And his pure streams with guiltless blood oft stain'd,—
From my unhappy neighbourhood far fled,
And his sweet waters away with him led.

"There also, where the wingëd ships were seen
In liquid waves to cut their foamy way,
And thousand fishers number'd to have been,
In that wide lake looking for plenteous prey
Of fish, which they with baits us'd to betray,
Is now no lake, nor any fisher's store,
Nor ever ship shall sail there any more.

"They all are gone, and all with them is gone!
Nor aught to me remains, but to lament
My long decay, which no man else doth moan,

1 Boundary.
2 Alexander the Great.
3 London.
4 The father of King Arthur—Uther Pendragon.
5 Boadicea.
6 Purchased.

And mourn my fall with doleful dreariment.
Yet it is comfort, in great languishment,
To be bemoanëd with compassion kind,
And mitigates the anguish of the mind.

"But me no man bewaileth, but in game,
Nor sheddeth tears from lamentable eye:
Nor any lives that mentioneth my name
To be remember'd of posterity,
Save one, that maugré Fortune's injury,
And Time's decay, and Envy's cruel tort,[1]
Hath writ my record in true-seeming sort.

"Camden![2] the norice[3] of antiquity,
And lantern unto late succeeding age,
To see the light of simple verity
Buried in ruins, through the great outráge
Of her own people led with warlike rage:
Camden! though time all monuments obscure,
Yet thy just labours ever shall endure.

"But why (unhappy wight!) do I thus cry,
And grieve that my remembrance quite is ras'd
Out of the knowledge of posterity,
And all my antique monuments defac'd?
Since I do daily see things highest plac'd,
So soon as Fates their vital thread have shorn,
Forgotten quite as they were never born.

"It is not long since these two eyes beheld
A mighty prince,[4] of most renownëd race,
Whom England high in count of honour held,
And greatest ones did sue to gain his grace;
Of greatest ones he, greatest in his place,
Sat in the bosom of his Sovëreign,
And *Right and Loyal* did his word maintain.

"I saw him die, I saw him die, as one
Of the mean people, and brought forth on bier;
I saw him die, and no man left to moan
His doleful fate, that late him lovëd dear:
Scarce any left to close his eyelids near;
Scarce any left upon his lips to lay
The sacred sod, or requiem to say.

"O trustless state of miserable men!
That build your bliss on hope of earthly thing,
And vainly think yourselves half happy then,
When painted faces with smooth flattering
Do fawn on you, and your wide praises sing;
And, when the courting masker louteth low,
Him true in heart and trusty to you trow!

"All is but feignëd, and with ochre dy'd,
That ev'ry shower will wash and wipe away;
All things do change that under heav'n abide,
And after death all friendship doth decay.
Therefore, whatever man bear'st worldly sway,
Living, on God and on thyself rely;
For, when thou diest, all shall with thee die.

"He now is dead, and all is with him dead,
Save what in heaven's storehouse he uplaid:
His hope is fail'd, and come to pass his dread,
And evil men now, dead, his deeds upbraid:
Spite bites the dead, that living never bay'd.
He now is gone, the while the fox is crept
Into the hole the which the badger swept.

"He now is dead, and all his glory gone,
And all his greatness vapourëd to naught,
That as a glass upon the water shone,
Which vanish'd quite, so soon as it was sought:
His name is worn already out of thought,
Nor any poet seeks him to revive;
Yet many poets honour'd him alive.

"Nor doth his Colin, careless Colin Clout,[5]
Care now his idle bagpipe up to raise,
Nor tell his sorrow to the list'ning rout
Of shepherd grooms, which wont his songs to praise:
Praise whoso list, yet I will him dispraise,
Until he quit him of this guilty blame:
Wake, shepherd's boy, at length awake for shame.

"And whoso else did goodness by him gain,
And whoso else his bounteous mind did try,[6]
Whether he shepherd be, or shepherd's swain
(For many did, which do it now deny),
Awake, and to his song a part apply:
And I, the whilst you mourn for his decease,
Will with my mourning plaints your plaint increase.

"He died, and after him his brother[7] died,
His brother prince, his brother noble peer,
That whilst he livëd was of none envíed,
And dead is now, as living, counted dear;
Dear unto all that true affection bear:
But unto thee most dear, O dearest Dame,
His noble spouse, and paragon of fame.

"He, whilst he livëd, happy was through thee,
And, being dead, is happy now much more;
Living, that linkëd chanc'd with thee to be,
And dead, because him dead thou dost adore
As living, and thy lost dear love deplore.
So whilst that thou, fair flow'r of chastity,
Dost live, by thee thy lord shall never die.

"Thy lord shall never die, the while this verse
Shall live, and surely it shall live for ever:
For ever it shall live, and shall rehearse
His worthy praise, and virtues dying never,
Though death his soul do from his body sever:
And thou thyself herein shalt also live;
Such grace the heav'ns do to my verses give.

"Nor shall his sister, nor thy father, die;
Thy father, that good Earl of rare renown,
And noble patron of weak poverty!
Whose great good deeds, in country and in town,
Have purchas'd him in heav'n a happy crown:
Where he now liveth in eternal bliss,
And left his son t' ensue[8] those steps of his.

"He, noble bud, his grandsire's lively heir,
Under the shadow of thy countenance

1 Wrong.
2 William Camden, the famous antiquarian, the first edition of whose "Britannia" had appeared in 1586, with a dedication to Lord Burleigh.
3 Nurse.
4 The Earl of Leicester, who died at Cornbury, in Oxfordshire, in September 1588. Spenser takes a poetic licence in making his illustrious patron die at St Alban's.
5 The author himself.
6 Experience.
7 Ambrose Dudley, Earl of Warwick, elder brother of Leicester, who died in February 1589. His "spouse" was Anne, eldest daughter of Francis Russell, Earl of Bedford.
8 Follow.

Now gins to shoot up fast, and flourish fair
In learnëd arts, and goodly governance,
That him to highest honour shall advance.
Brave imp[1] of Bedford, grow apace in bounty,
And count of wisdom more than of thy county!

"Nor may I let thy husband's sister[2] die,
That goodly lady, since she eke did spring
Out of his stock and famous family,
Whose praises I to future age do sing;
And forth out of her happy womb did bring
The sacred brood of learning and all honour;
In whom the heav'ns pour'd all their gifts upon
her.

"Most gentle spirit, breathëd from above
Out of the bosom of the Maker's bliss,
In whom all bounty and all virtuous love
Appearëd in their native properties,
And did enrich that noble breast of his
With treasure passing all this worldë's worth;
Worthy of heav'n itself, which brought it forth.

"His blessëd spirit, full of pow'r divine
And influence of all celestial grace,
Loathing this sinful earth and earthly slime,
Fled back too soon unto his native place;
Too soon for all that did his love embrace;
Too soon for all this wretched world, whom he
Robb'd of all right and true nobility.

"Yet, ere his happy soul to heaven went
Out of this fleshly gaol, he did devise
Unto his heav'nly Maker to present
His body as a spotless sacrifice;
And chose that guilty hands of enemies
Should pour forth th' off'ring of his guiltless
blood:
So life exchanging for his country's good.

"O noble spirit, live there ever bless'd,
The world's late wonder, and the heav'ns' new
joy;
Live ever there, and leave me here distress'd
With mortal cares and cumbrous world's annoy!
But, where thou dost that happiness enjoy,
Bid me, O! bid me quickly come to thee,
That happy there I may thee always see!

"Yet, whilst the Fates afford me vital breath,
I will it spend in speaking of thy praise;
And sing to thee, until that timely death
By heaven's doom do end my earthly days:
Thereto do thou my humble spirit raise,
And into me that sacred breath inspire
Which thou there breathest perfect and entire.

"Then will I sing; but who can better sing
Than thine own sister,[3] peerless lady bright,
Which to thee sings with deep heart's sorrowing,
Sorrowing temperëd with dear delight,
That her to hear I feel my feeble sprite
Robbëd of sense, and ravishëd with joy;
O sad joy, made of mourning and annoy!

"Yet will I sing; but who can better sing,
Than thou thyself, thine own self's valiance,
That, whilst thou livedst, mad'st the forests ring,
And fields resound, and flocks to leap and dance,
And shepherds leave their lambs unto mis-
chance,
To run thy shrill Arcadian pipe to hear?
O happy were those days, thrice happy were!

"But now more happy thou, and wretched we,
Which want the wonted sweetness of thy voice,
While thou now in Elysian fields so free,
With Orpheus, and with Linus,[4] and the choice
Of all that ever did in rhymes rejoice,
Conversest, and dost hear their heav'nly lays,
And they hear thine, and thine do better praise.

"So there thou livest, singing evermore,
And here thou livest, being ever sung
Of us, which living lovëd thee afore,
And now thee worship 'mongst that blessëd
throng
Of heav'nly poets and heröës strong.
So thou both here and there immortal art,
And ev'rywhere through excellent desart.[5]

"But such as neither of themselves can sing,
Nor yet are sung of others for reward,
Die in obscure oblivion, as the thing
Which never was; nor ever with regard
Their names shall of the later age be heard,
But shall in rusty darkness ever lie,
Unless they mention'd be with infamy.

"What booteth it to have been rich alive?
What to be great? what to be gracïous?
When after death no token doth survive
Of former being in this mortal house,
But sleeps in dust, dead and inglorious,
Like beast whose breath but in his nostrils is,
And hath no hope of happiness or bliss.

"How many great ones may remember'd be,
Which in their days most famously did flourish;
Of whom no word we hear, nor sign now see,
But as things wip'd out with a sponge do perish,
Because they living carëd not to cherish
No gentle wits, through pride or covetise,
Which might their names for ever memorise!

"Provide therefore, ye princes, whilst ye live,
That of the Muses ye may friended be,
Which unto men eternity do give;
For they be daughters of Dame Memory
And Jove, the father of Eternity,
And do those men in golden thrones repose,
Whose merits they to glorify do choose.

"The sev'nfold iron gates of grisly Hell,
And horrid house of sad Proserpina,
They able are with pow'r of mighty spell
To break, and thence the souls to bring away
Out of dread darkness to eternal day,
And them immortal make which else would die
In foul forgetfulness, and nameless lie.

"So whilom raisëd they the puissant brood[6]

1 Shoot, scion.
2 Lady Mary Sidney, the mother of Sir Philip.
3 Mary, Countess of Pembroke, who published her brother's "Arcadia;" to her "The Ruins of Time" is dedicated.
4 Fabled to have been the son of Apollo and Calliope, or of Amphimarus and Urania; and to have been killed by Apollo, with whom he ventured on a musical contest, or by Hercules, to whom he taught the use of the lyre.
5 Merit.
6 Hercules, who burned himself to death on Mount Œta, in Thessaly.

Of golden-girt Alcmena, for great merit,
Out of the dust, to which the Œtæan wood
Had him consum'd, and spent his vital spirit,
To highest heav'n, where now he doth inherit
All happiness in Hebe's silver bow'r,
Chosen to be her dearest paramour.

"So rais'd they eke fair Leda's warlike twins,[1]
And interchangëd life unto them lent,
That, when th' one dies, the other then begins
To shew in heav'n his brightness orient;
And they, for pity of the sad waimént[2]
Which Orpheus for Eurydicé did make,
Her back again to life sent for his sake.

"So happy are they, and so fortunate,
Whom the Pierian sacred Sisters love,
That, freed from bands of ímplacáble Fate,
And pow'r of death, they live for ay above,
Where mortal wreaks[3] their bliss may not remove:
But with the gods, for former virtue's meed,
On nectar and ambrosia do feed.

"For deeds do die, however nobly done,
And thoughts of men do as themselves decay:
But wise words, taught in numbers for to run,
Recorded by the Muses, live for ay;
Nor may with storming showers be wash'd away;
Nor bitter-breathing winds, with harmful blast,
Nor age, nor envy, shall them ever waste.

"In vain do earthly princes then, in vain,
Seek with pyramidës to heav'n aspir'd,
Or huge colosses built with costly pain,
Or brazen pillars, never to be fir'd,
Or shrines made of the metal most desir'd,
To make their memories for ever live:
For how can mortal immortality give?

"Such one Mausolus[4] made, the world's great wonder,
But now no remnant doth thereof remain:
Such one Marcellus, but was torn with thunder:
Such one Lysippus, but is worn with rain:
Such one King Edmund, but was rent for gain.
All such vain monuments of earthly mass,
Devour'd of Time, in time to naught do pass.

"But Fame with golden wings aloft doth fly,
Above the reach of ruinous decay,
And with brave plumes doth beat the azure sky,
Admir'd of base-born men from far away:
Then whoso will with virtuous deeds assay
To mount to heav'n, on Pegasus must ride,
And with sweet poets' verse be glorified.

"For not to have been dipt in Lethe Lake
Could save the son of Thetis[5] from to die;
But that blind Bard[6] did him immortal make
With verses dipt in dew of Castalie:
Which made the Eastern conqueror[7] to cry,
'O fortunate young man! whose virtue found
So brave a trump, thy noble acts to sound!'

"Therefore in this half happy I do read[8]
Good Melibee,[9] that hath a poet got
To sing his living praises being dead,
Deserving never here to be forgot,
In spite of envy that his deeds would spot:
Since whose decease learning lies unregarded,
And men of arms do wander unrewarded.

"Those two be those two great calamities
That long ago did grieve the noble sprite
Of Solomon with great indignities;
Who whilom was alive the wisest wight:
But now his wisdom is disprovëd quite;
For he, that now wields all things at his will,
Scorns th' one and th' other in his deeper skill.

"O grief of griefs! O gall of all good hearts!
To see that virtue should despisëd be
Of him that first was rais'd for virtuous parts,
And now, broad spreading like an aged tree,
Lets none shoot up that nigh him planted be.
O let the man, of whom the Muse is scorn'd,
Nor alive nor dead be of the Muse adorn'd![10]

"O vile world's trust! that with such vain illusion
Hath so wise men bewitch'd and overkest,[11]
That they see not the way of their confusion:
O vainness! to be added to the rest,
That do my soul with inward grief infest:
Let them behold the piteous fall of me,
And in my case their own ensample see.

"And whoso else that sits in highest seat
Of this world's glory, worshippëd of all,
Nor feareth change of time, nor fortune's threat.
Let him behold the horror of my fall,
And his own end unto remembrance call;
That of like ruin he may warnëd be,
And in himself be mov'd to pity me."

Thus having ended all her piteous plaint,
With doleful shrieks she vanishëd away,
That I, through inward sorrow waxen faint,
And all astonishëd with deep dismay
For her departure, had no word to say;
But sat long time in senseless sad affright,
Looking still, if I might of her have sight.

Which when I missëd, having lookëd long,
My thought returnëd grievëd home again,
Renewing her complaint, with passion strong,
For ruth of that same woman's piteous pain;
Whose words recording in my troubled brain,
I felt such anguish wound my feeble heart,
That frozen horror ran through ev'ry part.

So inly grieving in my groaning breast,
And deeply musing at her doubtful speech,
Whose meaning much I labour'd forth to wrest,
Being above my slender reason's reach;

1 Castor and Pollux. 2 Lamentation.
3 Revenges, violences.
4 Not Mausolus, but Artemisia, his widow. See note 4, page 129.
5 Achilles.
6 Homer.
7 Alexander, the conqueror of the East.
8 Declare.
9 Sir Francis Walshingham, who had died in 1590, is Melibee. See note 3, page 532. The poet referred to is Thomas Watson.
10 These bitter lines are pointed against Burleigh, who on more than one occasion had put forth his influence to the disadvantage of the poet; and not least conspicuously in regard to the first three books of "The Faerie Queen," which had been published the year before the volume wherein "The Ruins of Time" appeared. See note 1, page 444.
11 Overcast.

At length, by demonstration me to teach,
Before mine eyes strange sights presented were,
Like tragic pageants seeming to appear.

I.

I SAW an Image, all of massy gold,
Placëd on high upon an altar fair,
That all, which did the same from far behold,
Might worship it, and fall on lowest stair.
Not that great idol might with this compare,
To which th' Assyrian tyrant would have made
The holy brethren falsely to have pray'd.

But th' altar, on the which this image stay'd,
Was (O great pity !) built of brittle clay,
That shortly the foundatïon decay'd,
With show'rs of heav'n and tempests worn away;
Then down it fell, and low in ashes lay,
Scornëd of ev'ry one which by it went;
That I, it seeing, dearly did lament.

II.

Next unto this a stately Tow'r appear'd,
Built all of richest stone that might be found,
And nigh unto the heav'ns in height uprear'd,
But placëd on a plot of sandy ground:
Not that great Tow'r, which is so much renown'd
For tongues' confusïon in Holy Writ,
King Ninus' work, might be compar'd to it.

But O! vain labours of terrestrial wit,
That builds so strongly on so frail a soil,
As with each storm does fall away, and flit,
And gives the fruit of all your travail's toil
To be the prey of Time, and Fortune's spoil!
I saw this tow'r fall suddenly to dust,
That nigh with grief thereof my heart was brust.

III.

Then did I see a pleasant Paradise,
Full of sweet flow'rs and daintiest delights,
Such as on earth man could not more devise,
With pleasures choice to feed his cheerful sprites:
Not that which Merlin by his magic sleights
Made for the gentle Squire, to entertain
His fair Belphœbe, could this garden stain.

But O short pleasure, bought with lasting pain!
Why will hereafter any flesh delight
In earthly bliss, and joy in pleasures vain,
Since that I saw this garden wasted quite,
That where it was scarce seemëd any sight?
That I, which once that beauty did behold,
Could not from tears my melting eyes withhold.

IV.

Soon after this a Giant came in place,
Of wondrous pow'r, and of exceeding stature,
That none durst view the horror of his face;
Yet was he mild of speech, and meek of nature:
Not he, which in despite of his Creator
With railing terms defied the Jewish host,
Might with this mighty one in hugeness boast;

For from the one he could to th' other coast
Stretch his strong thighs, and th' ocean overstride,
And reach his hand into his enemies' host.
But see the end of pomp and fleshly pride!
One of his feet unwares from him did slide,
That down he fell into the deep abyss,
Where drown'd with him is all his earthly bliss.

V.

Then did I see a Bridge, made all of gold,
Over the sea from one to other side,
Withoúten prop or pillar it t' uphold,
But like the colour'd rainbow archëd wide:
Not that great arch which Trajan edified,
To be a wonder to all age ensuing,
Was matchable to this in equal viewing.

But ah! what boots it to see earthly thing
In glory or in greatness to excel,
Since time doth greatest things to ruin bring?
This goodly bridge, one foot not fasten'd well,
Gan fail, and all the rest down shortly fell,
Nor of so brave a building aught remain'd,
That grief thereof my spirit greatly pain'd.

VI.

I saw two Bears,[1] as white as any milk,
Lying together in a mighty cave,
Of mild aspéct, and hair as soft as silk,
That salvage nature seemëd not to have,
Nor after greedy spoil of blood to crave:
Two fairer beasts might not elsewhere be found,
Although the compass[2] world were sought around.

But what can long abide above this ground
In state of bliss, or steadfast happiness?
The cave, in which these bears lay sleeping sound,
Was but of earth, and with her weightiness
Upon them fell, and did unwares oppress;
That, for great sorrow of their sudden fate,
Henceforth all world's felicity I hate.

Much was I troubled in my heavy sprite
At sight of these sad spectacles forepast,
That all my senses were bereavëd quite,
And I in mind remainëd sore aghast,
Distraught 'twixt fear and pity; when at last
I heard a voice, which loudly to me call'd,
That with the sudden shrill I was appall'd.

"Behold," said it, "and by ensample see,
That all is vanity and grief of mind,
Nor other comfort in this world can be,
But hope of heav'n, and heart to God inclin'd;
For all the rest must needs be left behind:"
With that it bade me to the other side
To cast mine eye, where other sights I spied.

I.

UPON that famous river's farther shore
There stood a snowy Swan, of heav'nly hue,
And gentle kind as ever fowl afore;
A fairer one in all the goodly crew
Of white Strymonian brood might no man view:
There he most sweetly sung the prophecy
Of his own death in doleful elegy.

At last, when all his mourning melody
He ended had, that both the shores resounded,
Feeling the fit that him forewarn'd to die,
With lofty flight above the earth he bounded,
And out of sight to highest heaven mounted,

[1] The Earls of Leicester and Warwick.

[2] Round.

Where now he is become a heav'nly sign;
There now the joy is his, here sorrow mine.

II.

Whilst thus I lookëd, lo! adown the lee
I saw a Harp strung all with silver twine,
And made of gold and costly ivory,
Swimming, that whilom seemëd to have been
The harp on which Dan Orpheus was seen
Wild beasts and forests after him to lead,
But was th' harp of Philisides [1] now dead.

At length out of the river it was rear'd,
And borne above the clouds to be divin'd, [2]
Whilst all the way most heav'nly noise was heard
Of the strings, stirrëd with the warbling wind,
That wrought both joy and sorrow in my mind:
So now in heav'n a sign it doth appear,
The Harp well known beside the Northern Bear.

III.

Soon after this I saw, on th' other side,
A curious Coffer made of ebon wood,
That in it did most precious treasure hide,
Exceeding all this baser worldë's good:
Yet through the overflowing of the flood
It almost drownëd was, and done to naught,
That sight thereof much griev'd my pensive thought.

At length, when most in peril it was brought,
Two angels, down descending with swift flight,
Out of the swelling stream it lightly caught,
And 'twixt their blessëd arms it carried quite
Above the reach of any living sight:
So now it is transform'd into that star
In which all heav'nly treasures lockëd are.

IV.

ooking aside I saw a stately Bed,
Adornëd all with costly cloth of gold,
That might for any prince's couch be read, [3]
And deck'd with dainty flowers, as if it sho'ld
Be for some bride her joyous night to hold:
Therein a goodly Virgin sleeping lay;
A fairer wight saw never summer's day.

I heard a voice that callëd far away,
And her awaking bade her quickly dight,
For lo! her bridegroom was in ready ray [4]
To come to her, and seek her love's delight:
With that she started up with cheerful sight,
When suddenly both bed and all was gone,
And I in languor left there all alone.

[1] Sir Philip Sidney. [2] Made divine.
[3] Recognised. [4] Array.

V.

Still as I gazëd, I beheld where stood
A Knight all arm'd, upon a wingëd steed,
The same that bred was of Medusa's blood,
On which Dan Perseus, born of heav'nly seed,
The fair Andromeda from peril freed:
Full mortally this knight y-wounded was,
That streams of blood forth flowëd on the grass:

Yet was he deck'd (small joy to him, alas!)
With many garlands for his victories,
And with rich spoils, which late he did purchâse
Through brave achievements from his enemies:
Fainting at last through long infirmities,
He smote his steed, that straight to heav'n him bore,
And left me here his loss for to deplore.

VI.

Lastly I saw an Ark of purest gold
Upon a brazen pillar standing high,
Which th' ashes seem'd of some great prince to hold, [5]
Enclos'd therein for endless memory
Of him whom all the world did glorify:
Seemëd the heav'ns with th' earth did disagree,
Whether should of those ashes keeper be.

At last me seem'd wing-footed Mercury,
From heav'n descending to appease their strife,
The ark did bear with him above the sky,
And to those ashes gave a second life,
To live in heav'n, where happiness is rife:
At which the earth did grieve exceedingly,
And I for dole [6] was almost like to die.

L'Envoy.

Immortal spirit of Philisides,
Which now art made the heavens' ornament,
That whilom wast the worldë's chief'st richéss,
Give leave to him that lov'd thee to lament
His loss, by lack of thee to heaven hent, [7]
And with last duties of this broken verse,
Broken with sighs, to deck thy sable hearse!

And ye, fair Lady! th' honour of your days,
And glory of the world your high thoughts scorn;
Vouchsafe this monument of his last praise
With some few silver-dropping tears t' adorn;
And as ye be of heav'nly offspring born,
So unto heav'n let your high mind aspire,
And loathe this dross of sinful world's desire!

[5] Sir Philip Sidney's corpse, which was brought home from the Netherlands to England.
[6] Grief. [7] Taken.

PROSOPOPOIA:

OR,

MOTHER HUBBERD'S TALE.

[1591.]

DEDICATION

TO THE RIGHT HONOURABLE

THE LADY COMPTON AND MOUNTEAGLE.[1]

MOST fair and virtuous Lady; having often sought opportunity by some good means to make known to your Ladyship the humble affection and faithful duty which I have always professed, and am bound to bear to that house from whence ye spring, I have at length found occasion to remember the same, by making a simple present to you of these my idle labours; which having long since composed in the raw conceit of my youth, I lately amongst other papers lighted upon, and was by others, which liked the same, moved to set them forth. Simple is the device, and the composition mean, yet carrieth some delight, even the rather because of the simplicity and meanness thus personated. The same I beseech your Ladyship take in good part, as a pledge of that profession which I have made to you; and keep with you until, with some other more worthy labour, I do redeem it out of your hands, and discharge my utmost duty. Till then, wishing your Ladyship all increase of honour and happiness, I humbly take leave.

Your Ladyship's ever humbly,

ED. SP.

IT was the month in which the righteous Maid,[2]
That for disdain of sinful world's upbraid
Fled back to heav'n, whence she was first conceiv'd,
Into her silver bow'r the sun receiv'd;
And the hot Syrian Dog on him awaiting,
After the chafëd Lion's cruel baiting,
Corrupted had th' air with his noisome breath,
And pour'd on th' earth plague, pestilence, and death.
Amongst the rest a wicked malady
Reign'd amongst men, that many did to die,
Depriv'd of sense and ordinary reason,
That it to leaches seemëd strange and geason.[3]
My fortune was, 'mongst many others mo',
To be partaker of their common woe;
And my weak body, set on fire with grief,
Was robb'd of rest and natural relief.
In this ill plight there came to visit me
Some friends, who, sorry my sad case to see,
Began to comfort me in cheerful wise,
And means of gladsome solace to devise.
But seeing kindly sleep refuse to do
His office, and my feeble eyes forego,
They sought my troubled sense how to deceive
With talk that might unquiet fancies reave;
And, sitting all in seats about me round,
With pleasant tales (fit for that idle stound[4])
They cast in course to waste the weary hours:
Some told of ladies, and their paramours;
Some of brave knights, and their renownëd squires;
Some of the fairies and their strange attires;
And some of giants, hard to be believ'd;
That the delight thereof me much reliev'd.
Amongst the rest a good old woman was,
Hight Mother Hubberd, who did far surpass
The rest in honest mirth, that seem'd her well.
She, when her turn was come her tale to tell,
Told of a strange adventure that betided
Betwixt the Fox and th' Ape by him misguided;
The which, for that my sense it greatly pleased,
All were my spirit heavy and diseased,
I'll write in terms as she the same did say,
So well as I her words remember may.
No Muse's aid me needs hereto to call;
Base[5] is the style, and matter mean withal.
Whilom (said she) before the world was civil,
The Fox and th' Ape, disliking of their evil
And hard estate, determinëd to seek
Their fortunes far abroad, like with his like:
For both were crafty and unhappy witted;
Two fellows might nowhere be better fitted.
The Fox, that first this cause of grief did find,
'Gan first thus plain his case with words unkind.
"Neighbour Ape, and my gossip eke beside
(Both two sure bands in friendship to be tied),
To whom may I more trustily complain
The evil plight, that doth me sore constrain,
And hope thereof to find due remedy?

1 Anne, fifth daughter of Sir John Spencer of Althorpe. See note 10, page 612.

2 Astræa; placed in the Zodiac as the sign Virgo, which the sun enters in August.
3 Uncommon. 4 Occasion, hour. 5 Humble.

Hear, then, my pain and inward agony.
Thus many years I now have spent and worn,
In mean regard, and basest fortune's scorn,
Doing my country service as I might,
No less, I dare say, than the proudest wight;
And still I hopëd to be up advanc'd
For my good parts; but still it has mischanc'd.
Now therefore that no longer hope I see,
But froward fortune still to follow me,
And losels[1] lifted high, where I did look,
I mean to turn the next leaf of the book.
Yet, ere that any way I do betake,
I mean my gossip privy first to make."
"Ah! my dear gossip," answer'd then the Ape,
"Deeply do your sad words my wits awhape,[2]
Both for because your grief doth great appear,
And eke because myself am touchëd near:
For I likewise have wasted much good time,
Still waiting to preferment up to climb,
Whilst others always have before me stept,
And from my beard the fat away have swept;
That now unto despair I gin to grow,
And mean for better wind about to throw.
Therefore to me, my trusty friend, aread[3]
Thy counsel; two is better than one head."
"Certes," said he, "I mean me to disguise
In some strange habit, after uncouth wise,
Or like a pilgrim, or a limiter,[4]
Or like a gipsy, or a juggeler,
And so to wander to the worldë's end,
To seek my fortune where I may it mend:
For worse than that I have I cannot meet.
Wide is the world, I wot, and ev'ry street
Is full of fortunes and adventures strange,
Continually subject unto change.
Say, my fair brother now, if this device
Doth like you, or may you to like entice."
"Surely," said th' Ape, "it likes me wondrous well;
And, would ye not poor fellowship expel,
Myself would offer you t' accompany
In this adventure's chanceful jeopardy:
For to wax old at home in idleness
Is disadventurous, and quite fortuneless;
Abroad, where change is, good may gotten be."
The Fox was glad, and quickly did agree:
So both resolv'd, the morrow next ensuing,
So soon as day appear'd to people's viewing,
On their intended journey to proceed;
And over night, whatso thereto did need,
Each did prepare, in readiness to be.
The morrow next, so soon as one might see
Light out of heaven's windows forth to look,
Both their habiliments unto them took,
And put themselves (a God's name) on their way;
When as the Ape, beginning well to weigh
This hard adventure, thus began t' advise:
"Now read,[5] Sir Reynold, as ye be right wise,
What course ye ween is best for us to take,
That for ourselves we may a living make.
Whether shall we profess some trade or skill?
Or shall we vary our device at will,
Even as new occasïon appears?
Or shall we tie ourselves for certain years
To any service, or to any place?
For it behoves, ere that into the race
We enter, to resolve first hereupon."
"Now surely, brother," said the Fox anon,
"Ye have this matter motionëd in season:
For ev'ry thing that is begun with reason
Will come by ready means unto his end;
But things miscounsellëd must needs miswend.[6]
Thus therefore I advise upon the case,
That not to any certain trade or place,
Nor any man, we should ourselves apply;
For why should he that is at liberty
Make himself bond? since then we are free-born,
Let us all servile base subjection scorn;
And, as we be sons of the world so wide,
Let us our father's heritage divide,
And challenge to ourselves our portions due
Of all the patrimony, which a few
Now hold in hugger-mugger[7] in their hand,
And all the rest do rob of good and land.
For now a few have all, and all have naught,
Yet all be brethren alike dearly bought:
There is no right in this partitión,
Nor was it so by institutión
Ordainëd first, nor by the law of Nature,
But that she gave like blessing to each creature,
As well of worldly livelod[8] as of life,
That there might be no difference nor strife,
Nor aught call'd mine or thine: thrice happy then
Was the conditïon of mortal men.
That was the golden age of Saturn old,
But this might better be the world of gold;
For without gold now nothing will be got,
Therefore (if please you) this shall be our plot:
We will not be of any occupation;
Let such vile vassals, born to base vocation,
Drudge in the world, and for their living droil,[9]
Which have no wit to live withouten toil.
But we will walk about the world at pleasure,
Like two free men, and make our ease our treasure.
Free men some beggars call, but they be free;
And they which call them so more beggars be:
For they do swink[10] and sweat to feed the other,
Who live like lords of that which they do gather,
And yet do never thank them for the same,
But as their due by nature do it claim.
Such will we fashion both ourselves to be,
Lords of the world; and so will wander free
Where so us listeth, uncontroll'd of any:
Hard is our hap, if we (amongst so many)
Light not on some that may our state amend;
Seldom but some good cometh ere the end."
Well seem'd the Ape to like this ordinance:
Yet, well considering of the circumstance,
As pausing in great doubt, a while he stay'd,
And afterwards with grave advisement said;
"I cannot, my lief[11] brother, like but well
The purpose of the complot which ye tell:
For well I wot (compar'd to all the rest
Of each degree) that beggars' life is best;

1 Base, worthless persons.
2 Confound.
3 Declare.
4 A friar licensed to beg within a certain district.
5 Tell.
6 Go wrong.
7 Secretly.
8 Livelihood, means of living.
9 Work slavishly.
10 Toil.
11 Dear.

And they, that think themselves the best of all,
Ofttimes to begging are content to fall:
But this I wot withal, that we shall run
Into great danger, like to be undone,
Wildly to wander thus in the world's eye,
Withouten passport or good warranty,
For fear lest we like rogues should be reputed,
And for ear-markëd beasts abroad be bruited;
Therefore I read,[1] that we our counsels call,
How to prevent this mischief ere it fall,
And how we may, with most security,
Beg amongst those that beggars do defy."[2]
"Right well, dear gossip, ye advisëd have,"
Said then the Fox, "but I this doubt will save:
For ere we farther pass I will devise
A passport for us both in fittest wise,
And by the names of Soldiers us protect;
That now is thought a civil begging sect.
Be you the soldier, for you likest are
For manly semblance and small skill in war:
I will but wait on you, and, as occasion
Falls out, myself fit for the same will fashion."
The passport ended, both they forward went;
The Ape clad soldierlike, fit for th' intent,
In a blue jacket with a cross of red
And many slits, as if that he had shed
Much blood through many wounds therein receiv'd,
Which had the use of his right arm bereav'd;
Upon his head an old Scotch cap he wore,
With a plume feather all to pieces tore:
His breeches were made after the new cut,
Al Portuguese, loose like an empty gut;
And his hose broken high above the heeling,
And his shoes beaten out with travelling.
But neither sword nor dagger he did bear;
Seems that no foe's revengement he did fear;
Instead of them a handsome bat[3] he held,
On which he leanëd, as one far in eld.[4]
Shame light on him, that through so false illusion
Doth turn the name of Soldiers to abusion,
And that, which is the noblest mystery,[5]
Brings to reproach and common infamy!
Long they thus travellëd, yet never met
Adventure which might them a-working set:
Yet many ways they sought, and many tried;
Yet for their purposes none fit espied.
At last they chanc'd to meet upon the way
A simple husbandman in garments gray;
Yet, though his vesture were but mean and base,
A good yeoman he was, of honest place,
And more for thrift did care than for gay clothing:
Gay without good is good heart's greatest loathing.
The Fox, him spying, bade the Ape him dight[6]
To play his part, for lo! he was in sight
That (if he err'd not) should them entertain,
And yield them timely profit for their pain.
Eftsoons the Ape himself gan up to rear,
And on his shoulders high his bat to bear,
As if good service he were fit to do
(But little thrift for him he did it to!)
And stoutly forward he his steps did strain,
That like a handsome swain it him became:
When as they nigh approachëd, that good man,
Seeing them wander loosely, first began
T' inquire, of custom, what and whence they were?
To whom the Ape: "I am a Soldïer,
That late in wars have spent my dearest blood,
And in long service lost both limbs and good;
And now, constrain'd that trade to overgive,
I driven am to seek some means to live:
Which might it you in pity please t' afford,
I would be ready, both in deed and word,
To do you faithful service all my days.
This iron world"—that same he weeping says—
"Brings down the stoutest hearts to lowest state:
For misery doth bravest minds abate,
And make them seek for that they wont to scorn,
Of fortune and of hope at once forlorn."
The honest man, that heard him thus complain,
Was griev'd, as he had felt part of his pain;
And, well dispos'd him some relief to show,
Ask'd if in husbandry he aught did know,
To plough, to plant, to reap, to rake, to sow,
To hedge, to ditch, to thrash, to thatch, to mow?
Or to what labour else he was prepar'd?
For husband's[7] life is labourous and hard.
When as the Ape him heard so much to talk
Of labour, that did from his liking balk,[8]
He would have slipp'd the collar handsomely,
And to him said: "Good Sir, full glad am I
To take what pains may any living wight:
But my late maimëd limbs lack wonted might
To do their kindly services as needeth:
Scarce this right hand the mouth with diet feedeth,
So that it may no painful work endure,
Nor to strong labour can itself inure.
But if that any other place you have,
Which asks small pains, but thriftiness to save,
Or care to overlook, or trust to gather,
Ye may me trust as your own ghostly father."
With that the husbandman gan him advise,
That it for him were fittest exercise
Cattle to keep, or grounds to oversee;
And askëd him, if he could willing be
To keep his sheep, or to attend his swine,
Or watch his mares, or take his charge of kine?
"Gladly," said he, "whatever such-like pain
Ye put on me, I will the same sustain:
But gladliest I of your fleecy sheep
(Might it you please) would take on me the keep.[9]
For ere that unto arms I me betook,
Unto my father's sheep I us'd to look,
That yet the skill thereof I have not lost:
Thereto right well this cur-dog, by my cost"—

1 Advise.
2 Distrust.
3 Staff, baton.
4 Far advanced in age.
5 Profession.
6 Prepare.
7 Husbandman's.
8 Was at variance with his liking.
9 Care, charge.

Meaning the Fox—"will serve my sheep to gather,
And drive to follow after their bellwether."
  The husbandman was meanly [1] well content
Trial to make of his endeavourment;
And, home him leading, lent to him the charge
Of all his flock, with liberty full large,
Giving account of th' annual increase
Both of their lambs, and of their woolly fleece.
Thus is the Ape become a shepherd swain,
And the false Fox his dog (God give them pain!)
For ere the year have half his course outrun,
And do return from whence he first begun,
They shall him make an ill account of thrift.
Now when as Time, flying with wingës swift,
Expirëd had the term that these two javels [2]
Should render up a reckoning of their travails
Unto their master, which it of them sought,
Exceedingly they troubled were in thought,
Nor wist what answer unto him to frame,
Nor how to scape great punishment or shame
For their false treason and vile thievery:
For not a lamb of all their flock's supply
Had they to shew; but, ever as they bred,
They slew them, and upon their fleshes fed;
For that disguisëd dog lov'd blood to spill,
And drew the wicked shepherd to his will.
So 'twixt them both they not a lambkin left;
And, when lambs fail'd, the old sheep's lives they reft;
That how t' acquit themselves unto their lord
They were in doubt, and flatly set abord.[3]
The Fox then counsell'd th' Ape for to require
Respite till morrow t' answer his desire;
For time's delay new hope of help still breeds.
The good man granted, doubting naught their deeds,
And bade next day that all should ready be.
But they more subtile meaning had than he;
For the next morrow's meed [4] they closely meant,
For fear of afterclaps,[5] for to prevent:
And that same ev'ning, when all shrouded were
In careless sleep, they without care or fear
Cruelly fell upon their flock in fold,
And of them slew at pleasure what they wo'ld.
Of which when as they feasted had their fill,
For a full complement of all their ill,
They stole away, and took their hasty flight,
Carried in clouds of all-concealing night.
  So was the husbandman left to his loss,
And they unto their fortune's change to toss.
After which sort they wanderëd long while,
Abusing many through their cloakëd guile;
That at the last they gan to be descried
Of ev'ry one, and all their sleights espied.
So as their begging now them failëd quite,
For none would give, but all men would them wite;[6]
Yet would they take no pains to get their living,
But seek some other way to gain by giving,
Much like to begging, but much better nam'd;
For many beg which are thereof asham'd.
And now the Fox had gotten him a gown,
And th' Ape a cassock sidelong hanging down;
For they their occupation meant to change,
And now in other state abroad to range:
For since their soldier's pass no better sped,
They forg'd another, as for clerks book-read.
Who passing forth, as their adventures fell,
Through many haps which needs not here to tell,
At length chanc'd with a formal priest to meet,
Whom they in civil manner first did greet,
And after ask'd an alms for God's dear love.
The man straightway his choler up did move,
And with reproachful terms gan them revile
For following that trade so base and vile;
And ask'd what license or what pass they had?
"Ah!" said the Ape, as sighing wondrous sad,
"It's a hard case, when men of good deserving
Must either driven be perforce to sterving,[7]
Or askëd for their pass by ev'ry squib [8]
That list at will them to revile or snib:[9]
And yet (God wot) small odds I often see
'Twixt them that ask, and them that askëd be.
Nathless, because you shall not us misdeem,
But that we are as honest as we seem,
Ye shall our passport at your pleasure see,
And then ye will (I hope) well movëd be."
Which when the priest beheld, he view'd it near,
As if therein some text he studying were,
But little else (God wot) could thereof skill:
For read he could not evidence, nor will,
Nor tell a written word, nor write a letter,
Nor make one title worse, nor make one better:
Of such deep learning little had he need,
Nor yet of Latin, nor of Greek, that breed
Doubts 'mongst divines, and difference of texts,
From whence arise diversity of sects,
And hateful heresies, of God abhorr'd:
But this good Sir [10] did follow the plain word,
Nor meddled with their controversies vain;
All his care was, his service well to sayn,
And to read homilies upon holidays:
When that was done, he might attend his plays;
An easy life, and fit High God to please.
  He, having overlook'd their pass at ease,
Gan at the length them to rebuke again,
That no good trade of life did entertain,
But lost their time in wand'ring loose abroad;
Seeing the world, in which they bootless bode,[11]
Had ways enough for all therein to live;
Such grace did God unto his creatures give.
Said then the Fox; "Who hath the world not tried,
From the right way full eath [12] may wander wide.
We are but novices, new come abroad,
We have not yet the track of any trode,
Nor on us taken any state of life,
But ready are of any to make prief.[13]
Therefore might please you, which the world have prov'd,
Us to advise, which forth but lately mov'd,
Of some good course that we might undertake,
Ye shall for ever us your bondmen make."
The priest gan wax half proud to be so pray'd,
And thereby willing to afford them aid,

1 Tolerably, middling.
2 Worthless fellows.
3 Adrift; at a loss.
4 Reward, retribution.
5 Future mishaps.
6 Blame.
7 Starving, perishing.
8 Insignificant fellow.
9 Snub.
10 See note 1, page 165.
11 Dwelt unprofitably.
12 Easily.
13 Proof, trial.

"It seems," said he, "right well that ye be clerks,[1]
Both by your witty words, and by your works.
Is not that name enough to make a living,
To him that hath a whit of Nature's giving?
How many honest men see ye arise
Daily thereby, and grow to goodly price;[2]
To Deans, to Archdeacons, to Commissaries,
To Lords, to Principals, to Prebendaries?
All jolly Prelates, worthy rule to bear,
Whoever them envý: yet spite bites near.
Why should ye doubt, then, but that ye likewise
Might unto some of those in time arise?
In the meantime to live in good estate,
Loving that love, and hating those that hate;
Being some honest curate, or some vicar,
Content with little in condition sicker."[3]
"Ah! but," said th' Ape, "the charge is wondrous great,
To feed men's souls, and hath a heavy threat."
"To feed men's souls," quoth he, "is not in man:
For they must feed themselves, do what we can.
We are but charg'd to lay the meat before:
Eat they that list, we need to do no more.
But God it is that feeds them with His grace,—
The bread of life pour'd down from heav'nly place.
Therefore said he that with the budding rod
Did rule the Jews, *All shall be taught of God.*
That same hath Jesus Christ now to him raught,[4]
By whom the flock is rightly fed and taught:
He is the Shepherd, and the Priest is he;
We but his shepherd swains ordain'd to be.
Therefore herewith do not yourselves dismay;
Nor is the pain so great, but bear ye may;
For not so great, as it was wont of yore,
It 's now-a-days, nor half so strait and sore:
They whilom usëd duly ev'ry day
Their service and their holy things to say,
At morn and ev'n, besides their Anthems sweet,
Their penny Masses, and their Complines meet,
Their Diriges, their Trentals, and their Shrifts,[5]
Their memories,[6] their singings, and their gifts.
Now all those needless works are laid away;
Now once a week, upon the Sabbath day,
It is enough to do our small devotion,
And then to follow any merry motion.
Nor are we tied to fast but when we list;
Nor to wear garments base of woollen twist,
But with the finest silks us to array,
That before God we may appear more gay,
Resembling Aaron's glory in his place:
For far unfit it is that person base
Should with vile clothes approach God's majestý,
Whom no uncleanness may approachen nigh:
Or that all men, which any master serve,
Good garments for their service should deserve;
But he that serves the Lord of Hosts Most High,
And that in highest place, t' approach him nigh,
And all the people's prayers to present
Before his throne, as on embassage sent
Both to and fro, should not deserve to wear
A garment better than of wool or hair.
Besides, we may have lying by our sides
Our lovely lasses, or bright shining brides;
We be not tied to wilful chastity,
But have the Gospel of free liberty."
By that he ended had his ghostly sermon,
The Fox was well induc'd to be a parson;
And of the priest eftsoons 'gan to inquire
How to a benefice he might aspire.
"Marry, there," said the priest, "is art indeed:
Much good deep learning one thereout may read;
For that the groundwork is and end of all,
How to obtain a beneficïal.
First, therefore, when ye have in handsome wise
Yourself attirëd, as you can devise,
Then to some nobleman yourself apply,
Or other great one in the worldë's eye,
That hath a zealous dispositión
To God, and so to his religión:
There must thou fashion eke a godly zeal,
Such as no carpers may contrair reveal:
For each thing feignëd ought more wary be.
There thou must walk in sober gravity,
And seem as saintlike as Saint Radegund:
Fast much, pray oft, look lowly on the ground,
And unto ev'ry one do court'sy meek:
These looks (naught saying) do a benefice seek;
And be thou sure one not to lack ere long.
But if thee list unto the Court to throng,
And there to hunt after the hopëd prey,
Then must thou thee dispose another way:
For there thou needs must learn to laugh, to lie,
To face,[7] to forge, to scoff, to companý,
To crouch, to please, to be a beetle-stock
Of thy great master's will, to scorn, or mock:
So may'st thou chance mock out a benefice,
Unless thou canst one conjure by device,
Or cast a figure for a Bishopric;
And if one could, it were but a school trick.
These be the ways by which, without reward,
Livings in Court be gotten, though full hard;
For nothing there is done without a fee:
The courtier needs must recompensëd be
With a benevolence, or have in gage
The primitias[8] of your parsonage:
Scarce can a Bishopric forpass them by,
But that it must be gilt in privity.
Do not thou therefore seek a living there,
But of more private persons seek elsewhere,
Where as thou may'st compound a better penny;
Nor let thy learning question'd be of any.
For some good gentleman, that hath the right
Unto his church for to present a wight,
Will cope[9] with thee in reasonable wise;
That if the living yearly do arise
To forty pound, that then his youngest son
Shall twenty have, and twenty thou hast won:
Thou hast it won, for it is of frank gift,
And he will care for all the rest to shift,
Both that the Bishop may admit of thee,
And that therein thou may'st maintainëd be.
This is the way for one that is unlearn'd
Living to get, and not to be discern'd.[10]

1 Scholars. 2 Esteem. 3 Secure.
4 Reached, taken. 5 Confessions.
6 Memorial services for the dead. 7 Dissemble.

8 First-fruits; the first year's whole profits of a benefice. Latin, "primitiæ."
9 Make a bargain. 10 Detected.

But they that are great clerks have nearer ways
For learning's sake to living them to raise:
Yet many eke of them (God wot) are driv'n
T' accept a benefice in pieces riv'n.
How say'st thou, friend? have I not well discours'd
Upon this common-place, though plain, not worst?
Better a short tale than a bad long shriving:[1]
Needs any more to learn to get a living?"
"Now sure, and by my halidom," quoth he,
"Ye a great master are in your degree:
Great thanks I yield you for your discipline,
And do not doubt but duly to incline
My wits thereto, as ye shall shortly hear."
The priest him wish'd good speed, and well to fare:
So parted they, as either's way them led.
But th' Ape and Fox erelong so well them sped,
Through the priest's wholesome counsel lately taught,
And through their own fair handling wisely wrought,
That they a benefice 'twixt them obtain'd;
And crafty Reynold was a priest ordain'd,
And th' Ape his Parish Clerk procur'd to be.
Then made they revel rout and goodly glee.
But, ere long time had passëd, they so ill
Did order their affairs, that th' evil will
Of all their parish'ners they had constrain'd;
Who to the Ordinary of them complain'd,
How foully they their offices abus'd,
And them of crimes and heresies accus'd;
That pursuivants he often for them sent.
But they, neglecting his commandëment,
So long persisted obstinate and bold,
Till at the length he publishëd to hold
A visitation, and them cited thither:
Then was high time their wits about to gather;
What did they then, but made a composition
With their next neighbour priest for light condition,
To whom their living they resignëd quite
For a few pence, and ran away by night?
So passing through the country in disguise,
They fled far off, where none might them surprise,
And after that long strayëd here and there,
Through ev'ry field and forest far and near;
Yet never found occasion for their turn,
But, almost starv'd, did much lament and mourn.
At last they chanc'd to meet upon the way
The Mule, all deck'd in goodly rich array,
With bells and bosses that full loudly rung,
And costly trappings that to ground down hung.
Lowly they him saluted in meek wise;
But he, through pride and fatness, gan despise
Their meanness; scarce vouchsaf'd them to requite.[2]
Whereat the Fox, deep groaning in his sprite,
Said: "Ah! sir Mule, now blessëd be the day
That I see you so goodly and so gay
In your attires, and eke your silken hide
Fill'd with round flesh, that ev'ry bone doth hide.
Seems that in fruitful pastures ye do live,
Or fortune doth you secret favour give."
"Foolish Fox!" said the Mule, "thy wretched need
Praiseth the thing that doth thy sorrow breed.
For well I ween, thou canst not but envý
My wealth, compar'd to thine own miserý,
That art so lean and meagre waxen late,
That scarce thy legs uphold thy feeble gait."
"Ah me!" said then the Fox, "whom evil hap
Unworthy[3] in such wretchedness doth wrap,
And makes the scorn of other beasts to be!
But read,[4] fair Sir, of grace, from whence come ye,
Or what of tidings you abroad do hear;
News may perhaps some good unweeting[5] bear."
"From royal Court I lately came," said he,
"Where all the bravery that eye may see,
And all the happiness that heart desire,
Is to be found; he nothing can admire
That hath not seen that heaven's portraiture;
But tidings there is none, I you assure,
Save that which common is, and known to all,
That courtiers as the tide do rise and fall."
"But tell us," said the Ape, "we do you pray,
Who now in Court doth bear the greatest sway;
That, if such fortune do to us befall,
We may seek favour of the best of all."
"Marry," said he, "the highest now in grace
Be the wild beasts, that swiftest are in chase;
For in their speedy course and nimble flight
The Lion now doth take the most delight;
But chiefly joys on foot them to behold,
Enchas'd[6] with chain and circulet of gold:
So wild a beast so tame y-taught to be,
And buxom[7] to his bands, is joy to see;
So well his golden circlet him beseemeth.
But his late chain his Liege unmeet esteemeth;
For so brave beasts she[8] loveth best to see
In the wild forest ranging fresh and free.
Therefore, if fortune thee in Court to live,
In case thou ever there wilt hope to thrive,
To some of these thou must thyself apply;
Else, as a thistledown in th' air doth fly,
So vainly shalt thou to and fro be tost,
And lose thy labour and thy fruitless cost.
And yet full few which follow them, I see,
For virtue's bare regard advancëd be,
But either for some gainful benefit,
Or that they may for their own turns be fit.
Nathless perhaps ye things may handle so,
That ye may better thrive than thousands mo'."
"But," said the Ape, "how shall we first come in,
That after we may favour seek to win?"
"How else," said he, "but with a good bold face,
And with big words, and with a stately pace,
That men may think of you, in general,
That to be in you which is not at all:
For not by that which is the world now deemeth
(As it was wont), but by that same that seemeth.

1 Confession. 2 To return their salutation. 3 Undeservedly. 4 Tell.

5 Unknowing. 6 Embellished. 7 Submissive. 8 The Queen.

Nor do I doubt but that ye well can fashion
Yourselves thereto, according to occasion:
So fare ye well; good courtiers may ye be!"
So, proudly neighing, from them parted he.
Then 'gan this crafty couple to devise
How for the Court themselves they might aguise:[1]
For thither they themselves meant to address,
In hope to find their happier success.
So well they shifted, that the Ape anon
Himself had clothëd like a gentleman,
And the sly Fox as like to be his groom,
That to the Court in seemly sort they come;
Where the fond[2] Ape, himself uprearing high
Upon his tiptoes, stalketh stately by,
As if he were some great Magnifico,
And boldly doth amongst the boldest go;
And his man Reynold, with fine counterfeasánce,[3]
Supports his credit and his countenance.
Then gan the courtiers gaze on ev'ry side,
And stare on him, with big looks basin-wide,[4]
Wond'ring what mister wight he was, and whence:
For he was clad in strange accoutrements,
Fashion'd with quaint devices never seen
In Court before, yet there all fashions be'n;
Yet he them in newfangleness did pass:
But his behaviour altogether was
Alla Turchesca, much the more admir'd;
And his looks lofty, as if he aspir'd
To dignity, and 'sdain the low degree;
That all, which did such strangeness in him see,
By secret means gan of his state inquire,
And privily his servant thereto hire:
Who, throughly arm'd against such coverture,
Reported unto all, that he was, sure,
A noble gentleman of high regard,
Which through the world had with long travel far'd,
And seen the manners of all beasts on ground;
Now here arriv'd, to see if like he found.
Thus did the Ape at first him credit gain,
Which afterwards he wisely did maintain
With gallant show, and daily more augment
Through his fine feats and courtly complement;
For he could play, and dance, and vault, and spring,
And all that else pertains to revelling,
Only through kindly[5] aptness of his joints.
Besides, he could do many other points,
The which in Court him servëd to good stead:
For he 'mongst ladies could their fortunes read
Out of their hands, and merry leasings[6] tell,
And juggle finely, that became him well:
But he so light was at legérdemain,
That what he touch'd came not to light again;
Yet would he laugh it out, and proudly look,
And tell them that they greatly him mistook.
So would he scoff them out with mockery,
For he therein had great felicity;
And with sharp quips joy'd others to deface,
Thinking that their disgracing did him grace:
So whilst that other like vain wits he pleas'd,
And made to laugh, his heart was greatly eas'd.
But the right gentle mind would bite his lip,
To hear the javel[7] so good men to nip:
For, though the vulgar yield an open ear,
And common courtiers love to gibe and fleer
At ev'rything which they hear spoken ill,
And the best speeches with ill meaning spill;[8]
Yet the brave Courtier,[9] in whose beauteous thought
Regard of honour harbours more than aught,
Doth loathe such base condition, to backbite
Any's good name for envy or despite:
He stands on terms of honourable mind,
Nor will be carried with the common wind
Of Court's inconstant mutability,
Nor after ev'ry tattling fable fly;
But hears and sees the follies of the rest,
And thereof gathers for himself the best:
He will not creep, nor crouch with feignëd face,
But walks upright with comely steadfast pace,
And unto all doth yield due courtesy;
But not with kissëd hand below the knee,
As that same apish crew is wont to do:
For he disdains himself t' embase thereto.
He hates foul leasings, and vile flattery,
Two filthy blots in noble gentery;
And loathful idleness he doth detest,
The canker-worm of ev'ry gentle breast;
The which to banish with fair exercise
Of knightly feats he daily doth devise:
Now managing the mouths of stubborn steeds,
Now practising the proof of warlike deeds,
Now his bright arms assaying, now his spear;
Now the nigh aimëd ring away to bear.
At other times he casts to sue[10] the chase
Of swift wild beasts, or run on foot a race,
T' enlarge his breath (large breath in arms most needful),
Or else by wrestling to wax strong and heedful;
Or his stiff arms to stretch with yewen bow,
And manly legs still passing to and fro,
Without a gownëd beast him fast beside,
A vain ensample of the Persian pride;
Who, after he had won th' Assyrian foe,
Did ever after scorn on foot to go.
Thus when this courtly gentleman with toil
Himself hath wearied, he doth recoil[11]
Unto his rest, and there with sweet delight
Of music's skill revives his toilëd sprite;
Or else with loves and ladies' gentle sports,
The joy of youth, himself he recomfórts:
Or, lastly, when the body list to pause,
His mind unto the Muses he withdraws;
Sweet Lady Muses, Ladies of delight,
Delights of life, and ornaments of light!
With whom he close confers with wise discourse,
Of Nature's works, of heav'n's continual course,
Of foreign lands, of people different,
Of kingdoms' change, of diverse government,
Of dreadful battles of renownëd Knights,

1 Equip. 2 Foolish.
3 Counterfeiting. 4 Widely extended.
5 Natural. 6 Lies.
7 Worthless rascal.
8 Spoil.
9 In the passage that follows, Spenser pays a noble tribute to his friend Sir Philip Sidney.
10 Follow. 11 Retire.

With which he kindleth his ambitious sprites
To like desire and praise of noble fame,
The only upshot whereto he doth aim:
For all his mind on honour fixëd is,
To which he levels all his purposes,
And in his Prince's service spends his days,
Not so much for to gain, or for to raise
Himself to high degree, as for his grace,
And in his liking to win worthy place,
Through due deserts and comely carriáge,
In whatso please employ his personage,
That may be matter meet to gain him praise;
For he is fit to use in all assays,
Whether for arms and warlike amenance,[1]
Or else for wise and civil governance;
For he is practis'd well in policy,
And thereto doth his courting[2] most apply;
To learn the enterdeal[3] of princes strange,
To mark th' intent of counsels, and the change
Of States, and eke of private men somewhile,
Supplanted by fine falsehood and fair guile;
Of all the which he gath'reth what is fit
T' enrich the storehouse of his pow'rful wit,
Which through wise speeches and grave conference
He daily ekes,[4] and brings to excellence.
Such is the rightful Courtier in his kind.
But unto such the Ape lent not his mind;
Such were for him no fit companións;
Such would descry his lewd conditións:
But the young lusty gallants he did choose
To follow, meet to whom he might disclose
His witless pleasance, and ill pleasing vain.
A thousand ways he them could entertain
With all the thriftless games that may be found;
With mumming and with masking all around,
With dice, with cards, with billiards far unfit,
With shuttlecocks, misseeming[5] manly wit,
With courtesans, and costly riotise,
Whereof still somewhat to his share did rise;
Nor, them to pleasure, would he sometimes scorn
A pandar's coat (so basely was he born).
Thereto he could fine loving verses frame,
And play the poet oft. But ah, for shame!
Let not sweet poets' praise, whose only pride
Is virtue to advance, and vice deride,
Be with the work of losels' wit defam'd,
Nor let such verses poetry be nam'd!
Yet he the name on him would rashly take,
Maugré[6] the sacred Muses, and it make
A servant to the vile affectión
Of such as he depended most upon;
And with the sugary sweet thereof allure
Chaste ladies' ears to fantasies impure.
To such delights the noble wits he led
Which him reliev'd, and their vain humours fed
With fruitless follies and unsound delights.
But if perhaps into their noble sprites
Desire of honour or brave thought of arms
Did ever creep, then with his wicked charms
And strong conceits he would it drive away,
Nor suffer it to house there half a day.
And whenso love of letters did inspire
Their gentle wits, and kindle wise desire,
That chiefly doth each noble mind adorn,
Then he would scoff at learning, and eke scorn
The sectaries[7] thereof, as people base,
And simple men, which never came in place
Of world's affairs, but, in dark corners mew'd,
Mutter'd of matters as their books them shew'd,
Nor other knowledge ever did attain,
But with their gowns their gravity maintain.
From them he would his impudent lewd speech
Against God's holy ministers oft reach,
And mock divines and their professión:
What else then did he, by progressión,
But mock high God himself, whom they profess?
But what car'd he for God or godliness?
All his care was himself how to advance,
And to uphold his courtly countenance
By all the cunning means he could devise;
Were it by honest ways, or otherwise,
He made small choice: yet sure his honesty
Got him small gains, but shameless flattery,
And filthy brocage,[8] and unseemly shifts,
And borrow[9] base, and some good ladies' gifts:
But the best help, which chiefly him sustain'd
Was his man Reynold's purchase which he gain'd.
For he was school'd by kind[10] in all the skill
Of close conveyance, and each practice ill
Of cozenage[11] and cleanly[12] knavery,
Which oft maintain'd his master's bravery.[13]
Besides, he us'd another slippery sleight,
In taking on himself, in common sight,
False personages fit for every stead,[14]
With which he thousands cleanly[15] cozenëd:
Now like a merchant, merchants to deceive,
With whom his credit he did often leave
In gage for his gay master's hopeless debt:
Now like a lawyer, when he land would let,
Or sell fee-simples in his master's name,
Which he had never, nor aught like the same;
Then would he be a broker, and draw in
Both wares and money, by exchange to win:
Then would he seem a farmer, that would sell
Bargains of woods, which he did lately fell,
Or corn, or cattle, or such other ware,
Thereby to cozen men not well aware:
Of all the which there came a secret fee
To th' Ape, that he his countenance might be.
Besides all this, he us'd oft to beguile
Poor suitors, that in Court did haunt some while:
For he would learn their business secretly,
And then inform his master hastily,
That he by means might cast them to prevent,
And beg the suit, the which the other meant.
Or otherwise false Reynold would abuse
The simple suitor, and wish him to choose
His master, being one of great regard
In Court, to compass any suit not hard,
In case his pains were recompens'd with reason.
So would he work the silly man by treason
To buy his master's frivolous good will,

1 Behaviour.
2 Attendance at court.
3 Negotiations, dealings.
4 Increases.
5 Unbecoming.
6 Despite.
7 Followers.
8 Pimping.
9 Usury.
10 Nature.
11 Fraud.
12 Skilful.
13 Proud show.
14 Situation.
15 Skilfully, deftly.

That had not pow'r to do him good or ill.
So pitiful a thing is suitor's state!
Most miserable man, whom wicked fate
Hath brought to court, to sue for had y-wist,[1]
That few have found, and many one hath mist!
Full little knowest thou, that hast not tried,
What hell it is in suing long to bide:
To lose good days that might be better spent;
To waste long nights in pensive discontent;
To speed[2] to-day, to be put back to-morrow;
To feed on hope; to pine with fear and sorrow;
To have thy Prince's grace, yet want her peers';
To have thy asking, yet wait many years;
To fret thy soul with crosses and with cares;
To eat thy heart through comfortless despairs:
To fawn, to crouch, to wait, to ride, to run,
To spend, to give, to want, to be undone.
Unhappy wight, born to disastrous end,
That doth his life in so long tendance spend!
Who ever leaves sweet home, where mean estate,
In safe assurance, without strife or hate,
Finds all things needful for contentment meek;
And will to Court for shadows vain to seek,
Or hope to gain, himself will a daw try:[3]
That curse God send unto mine enemy!
For none but such as this bold Ape unblest
Can ever thrive in that unlucky quest;
Or such as hath a Reynold to his man,
That by his shifts his master furnish can.
But yet this Fox could not so closely hide
His crafty feats, but that they were descried
At length by such as sat in justice' seat,
Who for the same him foully did entreat;
And, having worthily him punishĕd,
Out of the Court for ever banishĕd.
And now the Ape, wanting his huckster man,
That wont provide his necessaries, gan
To grow into great lack, nor could uphold
His countenance in those his garments old;
Nor new ones could he easily provide,
Though all men him uncasĕd gan deride,
Like as a puppet placĕd in a play,
Whose part once past, all men bid take away:
So that he driven was to great distress,
And shortly brought to hopeless wretchedness.
Then closely[4] as he might he cast to leave
The Court, not asking any pass or leave;
But ran away in his rent rags by night,
Nor ever stay'd in place, nor spake to wight,
Till that the Fox his copesmate[5] he had found,
To whom complaining his unhappy stound,[6]
At last again with him in travel join'd,
And with him far'd some better chance to find.
So in the world long time they wanderĕd,
And mickle want and hardness sufferĕd;
That them repented much so foolishly
To come so far to seek for misery,
And leave the sweetness of contented home,
Though eating hips,[7] and drinking watery foam.
Thus as they them complainĕd to and fro,
Whilst through the forest reckless they did go,
Lo! where they spied how, in a gloomy glade,
The Lion sleeping lay in secret shade,
His crown and sceptre lying him beside,
And having doff'd for heat his dreadful hide:
Which when they saw, the Ape was sore afraid,
And would have fled, with terror all dismay'd.
But him the Fox with hardy words did stay,
And bade him put all cowardice away;
For now was time (if ever they would hope)
To aim their counsels to the fairest scope,
And them for ever highly to advance,
In case the good, which their own happy chance
Them freely offer'd, they would wisely take.
Scarce could the Ape yet speak, so did he quake;
Yet, as he could, he ask'd how good might grow
Where naught but dread and death do seem in show.
"Now," said he, "while the Lion sleepeth sound,
May we his crown and mace take from the ground,
And eke his skin, the terror of the wood,
Wherewith we may ourselves (if we think good),
Make kings of beasts, and lords of forests all,
Subject unto that power imperial."
"Ah! but," said th' Ape, "who is so bold a wretch,
That dare his hardy hand to those outstretch,
When as he knows his meed, if he be spied,
To be a thousand deaths, and shame beside?"
"Fond[8] Ape!" said then the Fox, "into whose breast
Never crept thought of honour nor brave gest,[9]
Who will not venture life a king to be,
And rather rule and reign in sov'reign see[10]
Than dwell in dust inglorious and base,
Where none shall name the number of his place?
One joyous hour in blissful happiness,
I choose before a life of wretchedness.
Be therefore counsellĕd herein by me,
And shake off this vile-hearted cowardry.
If he awake, yet is not death the next,
For we may colour it with some pretext
Of this, or that, that may excuse the crime:
Else we may fly; thou to a tree may'st climb,
And I creep under ground, both from his reach:
Therefore be rul'd to do as I do teach."
The Ape, that erst[11] did naught but chill and quake,
Now gan some courage unto him to take,
And was content t' attempt that enterprise,
Tickled with glory and rash covetise.
But first gan question, whether[12] should essay
Those royal ornaments to steal away?
"Marry, that shall yourself," quoth he thereto,
"For ye be fine and nimble it to do;
Of all the beasts which in the forests be,
Is not a fitter for this turn than ye:
Therefore, mine own dear brother, take good heart,

1 To sue in vain expectation of a benefit which will be only a subject of vain regret—or of continual declarations that "had I wist" (if I had known all that I know now), "I would never have entered on the useless pursuit."

2 To seem to succeed.

3 Will prove or discover himself to be a daw, a fool.

4 Secretly.

5 Comrade.

6 Plight, disaster.

7 Dog-berries.

8 Foolish.

9 Achievement.

10 Seat.

11 But a little ago.

12 Which of the two.

And ever think a kingdom is your part."
Loth was the Ape, though praisëd, to adventure,
Yet faintly gan into his work to enter,
Afraid of ev'ry leaf that stirr'd him by,
And ev'ry stick that underneath did lie:
Upon his tiptoes nicely he up went,
For making noise, and still his ear he lent
To ev'ry sound that under heaven blew;
Now went, now stept, now crept, now backward drew,
That it good sport had been him to have eyed:
Yet at the last (so well he him applied),
Through his fine handling, and his cleanly[1] play,
He all those royal signs had stol'n away,
And with the Fox's help them borne aside
Into a secret corner unespied.
Whither when as they came, they fell at words,
Whether of them should be the lord of lords:
For th' Ape was strifeful and ambitious,
And the Fox guileful and most covetous;
That neither pleasëd was to have the reign
'Twixt them divided into even twain,
But either algates [2] would be lord alone:
For love and lordship bide no paragon.
"I am most worthy," said the Ape, "since I
For it did put my life in jeopardý:
Thereto I am in person and in stature
Most like a man, the lord of every creature,
So that it seemeth I was made to reign,
And born to be a kingly Sovëreign."
"Nay," said the Fox, "Sir Ape, you are astray;
For though to steal the diadem away
Were the work of your nimble hand, yet I
Did first devise the plot by policý;
So that it wholly springeth from my wit:
For which also I claim myself more fit
Than you to rule; for government of State
Will without wisdom soon be ruinate.
And where ye claim yourself for outward shape
Most like a man, man is not like an Ape
In his chief parts, that is, in wit and spirit;
But I, therein most like to him, do merit,
For my sly wiles and subtile craftiness,
The title of the kingdom to possess.
Nathless, my brother, since we passëd are
Unto this point, we will appease our jar;
And I with reason meet will rest content,
That ye shall have both crown and government,
Upon condition that ye rulëd be
In all affairs and counsellëd by me;
And that ye let none other ever draw
Your mind from me, but keep this as a law:
And hereupon an oath unto me plight."
The Ape was glad to end the strife so light,
And thereto swore; for who would not oft swear,
And oft unswear, a diadem to bear?
Then freely up those royal spoils he took,
Yet at the Lion's skin he inly quook;
But it dissembled, and upon his head
The crown, and on his back the skin, he did,
And the false Fox him helpëd to array.
Then, when he was all dight,[3] he took his way
Into the forest, that he might be seen
Of the wild beasts in his new glory sheen.[4]
There the two first whom he encounter'd were
The Sheep and th' Ass, who, stricken both with fear
At sight of him, gan fast away to fly;
But unto them the Fox aloud did cry,
And in the King's name bade them both to stay,
Upon the pain that thereof follow may.
Hardly, nathless, were they restrainëd so,
Till that the Fox forth toward them did go,
And there dissuaded them from needless fear,
For that the King did favour to them bear;
And therefore dreadless bade them come to Court:
For no wild beasts should do them any tort,[5]
There or abroad, nor would his Majesty
Use them but well, with gracious clemency,
As whom he knew to him both fast and true:
So he persuaded them, with homage due,
Themselves to humbly to the Ape prostráte,
Who, gently to them bowing in his gate,[6]
Receivëd them with cheerful entertain.[7]
Thenceforth proceeding with his princely train,
He shortly met the Tiger and the Boar,
Which with the simple Camel ragëd sore
In bitter words, seeking to take occasion
Upon his fleshly corse to make invasion:
But, soon as they this mock-King did espy,
Their troublous strife they stinted by and by,[8]
Thinking indeed that it the Lion was:
He then, to prove whether his pow'r would pass
As current, sent the Fox to them straightway,
Commanding them their cause of strife bewray;
And, if that wrong on either side there were,
That he should warn the wronger to appear
The morrow next at Court, it to defend;
In the meantime upon the King t' attend.
The subtile Fox so well his message said,
That the proud beasts him readily obey'd:
Whereby the Ape in wondrous stomach wox,[9]
Strongly encourag'd by the crafty Fox;
That King indeed himself he shortly thought,
And all the beasts him fearëd as they ought,
And followëd unto his palace high;
Where taking congé, each one by and by
Departed to his home in dreadful awe,
Full of the fearëd sight which late they saw.
The Ape, thus seized of the regal throne,
Eftsoons by counsel of the Fox alone
Gan to provide for all things in assurance,
That so his rule might longer have endurance.
First to his gate he 'pointed a strong guard,
That none might enter but with issue hard:
Then, for the safeguard of his personage,
He did appoint a warlike equipage
Of foreign beasts, not in the forest bred,
But part by land and part by water fed;
For tyranny is with strange aid supported.
Then unto him all monstrous beasts resorted,
Bred of two kinds, as Griffons, Minotaurs,
Crocodiles, Dragons, Beavers, and Centaurs:

1 Skilful.
2 At all events.
3 Equipped.
4 Bright.
5 Wrong.
6 Walk, progress.
7 Entertainment.
8 Stopped immediately.
9 Grew wondrous haughty.

With those himself he strengthen'd mightily,
That fear he need no force of enemy.
Then gan he rule and tyrannise at will,
Like as the Fox did guide his graceless skill;
And all wild beasts made vassals of his pleasures,
And with their spoils enlarg'd his private treasures.
No care of justice, nor no rule of reason,
No temperance, nor no regard of season,
Did thenceforth ever enter in his mind;
But cruelty, the sign of currish kind,
And 'sdainful pride, and wilful arrogance;
Such follows those whom fortune doth advance.
But the false Fox most kindly[1] play'd his part:
For whatsoever mother-wit or art
Could work, he put in proof: no practice sly,
No counterpoint of cunning policy,
No reach, no breach, that might him profit bring,
But he the same did to his purpose wring.
Naught suffer'd he the Ape to give or grant,
But through his hand alone must pass the fiant.[2]
All offices, all leases, by him leapt,
And of them all whatso he lik'd he kept.
Justice he sold injustice for to buy,
And for to purchase for his progeny.
Ill might it prosper that ill gotten was;
But, so he got it, little did he pass.[3]
He fed his cubs with fat of all the soil,
And with the sweat of others' sweating toil;
He crammëd them with crumbs of benefices,
And fill'd their mouths with meeds of malefices;[4]
He clothëd them with all coloúrs, save white,
And loaded them with lordships and with might,
So much as they were able well to bear,
That with the weight their backs nigh broken were;
He chaffer'd[5] chairs in which Churchmen were set,
And breach of laws to privy farm did let:
No statute so establishëd might be,
Nor ordinance so needful, but that he
Would violate, though not with violence,
Yet under colour of the confidence
The which the Ape repos'd in him alone,
And reckon'd him the kingdom's corner stone.
And ever, when he aught would bring to pass,
His long experience the platform was:
And when he aught not pleasing would put by,
The cloak was care of thrift, and husbandry,
For to increase the common treasure's store;
But his own treasure he increasëd more,
And lifted up his lofty tow'rs thereby,
That they began to threat the neighbour sky;
The while the Prince's palaces fell fast
To ruin (for what thing can ever last?)
And whilst the other peers, for poverty,
Were forc'd their ancient houses to let lie,
And their old castles to the ground to fall,
Which their forefathers, famous over all,
Had founded for the kingdom's ornament,

1 Naturally, natural. 2 Fiat, decree.
3 Care. 4 Rewards of evil deeds.
5 Sold.

And for their memories' long monument.
But he no count made of nobility,
Nor the wild beasts whom arms did glorify,
The realm's chief strength and garland of the crown.
All these through feignëd crimes he thrust adown,
Or made them dwell in darkness of disgrace:
For none, but whom he list, might come in place.
Of men of arms he had but small regard,
But kept them low, and strainëd very hard.
For men of learning, little he esteem'd;
His wisdom he above their learning deem'd.
As for the rascal commons, least he car'd;
For not so common was his bounty shar'd:
"Let God," said he, "if please, care for the many;
I for myself must care before else any."
So did he good to none, to many ill,
So did he all the kingdom rob and pill,[6]
Yet none durst speak, nor none durst of him plain;
So great he was in grace, and rich through gain.
Nor would he any let to have accéss
Unto the Prince, but by his own address:
For all that else did come, were sure to fail.
Yet would he further none but for avail:[7]
For on a time the Sheep, to whom of yore
The Fox had promisëd of friendship store
What time the Ape the kingdom first did gain,
Came to the Court, her case there to complain;
How that the Wolf, her mortal enemy,
Had sithence[8] slain her Lamb most cruelly;
And therefore crav'd to come unto the King,
To let him know the order of the thing.
"Soft, Goody Sheep!" then said the Fox; "not so:
Unto the King so rash ye may not go;
He is with greater matter busiëd
Than a Lamb, or the Lamb's own mother's head.
Nor, certes, may I take it well in part,
That ye my cousin Wolf so foully thwart,
And seek with slander his good name to blot:
For there was cause, else do it he would not:
Therefore surcease, good Dame, and hence depart."
So went the Sheep away with heavy heart:
So many more, so ev'ry one was used,
That to give largely to the box refused.
Now when high Jove, in whose almighty hand
The care of kings and pow'r of empires stand,
Sitting one day within his turret high,
From whence he views, with his black-lidded eye,
Whatso the heav'n in his wide vault contains,
And all that in the deepest earth remains,
And troubled kingdom of wild beasts beheld,
Whom not their kindly[1] Sovëreign did weld,[9]
But an usurping Ape, with guile suborn'd,
Had all subvers'd; he 'sdainfully it scorn'd
In his great heart, and hardly did refrain,
But that with thunderbolts he had him slain,

6 Plunder.
7 Profit, advantage, to himself.
8 Since that time. 9 Wield, rule.

And driven down to hell, his duest meed:
But, him advising,[1] he that dreadful deed
Forbore, and rather chose with scornful shame
Him to avenge, and blot his brutish name
Unto the world, that never after any
Should of his race be void of infamy;
And his false counsellor, the cause of all,
To damn to death or dole [2] perpetual,
From whence he never should be quit nor stal'd.[3]
Forthwith he Mercury unto him call'd,
And bade him fly with never-resting speed
Unto the forest, where wild beasts do breed,
And there, inquiring privily, to learn
What did of late chance to the Lion stern,
That he rul'd not the empire, as he ought;
And whence were all those plaints unto him brought
Of wrongs and spoils by salvage beasts committed:
Which done, he bade the Lion be remitted
Into his seat, and those same traitors vile
Be punishëd for their presumptuous guile.
The son of Maia, soon as he receiv'd
That word, straight with his azure wings he cleav'd
The liquid clouds and lucid firmament;
Nor stay'd, till that he came with steep descent
Unto the place where his prescript [4] did show.
There stooping, like an arrow from a bow,
He soft arrivëd on the grassy plain,
And fairly pacëd forth with easy pain,
Till that unto the palace nigh he came.
Then gan he to himself new shape to frame;
And that fair face, and that ambrosial hue,
Which wonts to deck the gods' immortal crew,
And beautify the shiny firmament,
He doff'd, unfit for that rude rabblement.
So, standing by the gates in strange disguise,
He gan inquire of some in secret wise
Both of the King, and of his government,
And of the Fox, and his false blandishment:
And evermore he heard each one complain
Of foul abuses both in realm and reign;
Which yet to prove more true, he meant to see,
And an eye-witness of each thing to be.
Then on his head his dreadful hat he dight,[5]
Which maketh him invisible in sight,
And mocketh th' eyes of all the lookers on,
Making them think it but a visión.
Through pow'r of that, he runs through enemies' swerds;
Through pow'r of that, he passeth through the herds
Of ravenous wild beasts, and doth beguile
Their greedy mouths of the expected spoil;
Through pow'r of that, his cunning thieveries
He wonts to work, that none the same espies;
And through the pow'r of that he putteth on
What shape he list in apparitión.
That on his head he wore, and in his hand
He took Caduceus, his snaky wand,
With which the damnëd ghosts he governeth,
And furies rulës, and Tartare tempereth.[6]
With that he causeth sleep to seize the eyes,
And fear the hearts, of all his enemies;
And, when him list, an universal night
Throughout the world he makes on every wight;
As when his sire with Alcumena lay.[7]
Thus dight,[8] into the Court he took his way,
Both through the guard, which never him descried,
And through the watchmen, who him never spied:
Thenceforth he pass'd into each secret part,
Where as he saw, that sorely griev'd his heart,
Each place abounding with foul injuries,
And fill'd with treasure rack'd with robberies;
Each place defil'd with blood of guiltless beasts
Which had been slain to serve the Ape's behests;
Gluttony, malice, pride, and covetise,
And lawlessness reigning with riotise;
Besides the infinite extortións
Done through the Fox's great oppressións,
That the complaints thereof could not be told.
Which when he did with lothful eyes behold,
He would no more endure, but came his way,
And cast to seek the Lion where he may,
That he might work th' avengement for this shame
On those two caitiffs which had bred him blame:
And, seeking all the forest busily,
At last he found, where sleeping he did lie.
The wicked weed, which there the Fox did lay,
From underneath his head he took away,
And then, him waking, forced up to rise.
The Lion, looking up, gan him advise,[9]
As one late in a trance, what had of long
Become of him: for fantasy is strong.
"Arise," said Mercury, "thou sluggish beast!
That here liest senseless, like the corse deceast,
The whilst thy kingdom from thy head is rent,
And thy throne royal with dishonour blent:[10]
Arise, and do thyself redeem from shame,
And be aveng'd on those that breed thy blame."
Thereat enragëd, soon he gan upstart,
Grinding his teeth, and grating[11] his great heart;
And, rousing up himself, for his rough hide
He gan to reach; but nowhere it espied:
Therewith he gan full terribly to roar,
And chaf'd at that indignity right sore.
But when his crown and sceptre both he wanted,[12]
Lord! how he fum'd, and swell'd, and rag'd, and panted;
And threaten'd death, and thousand deadly dolours,
To them that had purloin'd his princely honours.
With that in haste, disrobëd as he was,
He toward his own palace forth did pass;
And all the way he roarëd as he went,
That all the forest with astonishment
Thereof did tremble, and the beasts therein
Fled fast away from that so dreadful din.

1 Bethinking. 2 Suffering.
3 Released nor taken away (stolen).
4 Orders; warrant. 5 Placed.
6 Controls.

7 See note 28, page 261.
8 Equipped. 9 Consider.
10 Stained. 11 Chafing.
12 Missed, found wanting.

At last he came unto his mansión,
Where all the gates he found fast lock'd anon,
And many warders round about them stood:
With that he roar'd aloud, as he were wood,[1]
That all the palace quakëd at the stound,[2]
As if it quite were riven from the ground,
And all within were dead and heartless left;
And th' Ape himself, as one whose wits were reft,
Fled here and there, and ev'ry corner sought,
To hide himself from his own fearëd thought.
But the false Fox, when he the Lion heard,
Fled closely forth, straightway of death afear'd,
And to the Lion came, full lowly creeping,
With feignëd face, and watery eyne half weeping,
T' excuse his former treason and abusion,
And turning all unto the Ape's confusion:
Nathless the Royal Beast forbore believing,
But bade him stay at ease till farther preving.[3]
Then, when he saw no entrance to him granted,
Roaring yet louder, that all hearts it daunted,
Upon those gates with force he fiercely flew,
And, rending them in pieces, felly slew
Those warders strange, and all that else he met.
But th' Ape, still flying, he nowhere might get:
From room to room, from beam to beam, he fled,
All breathless, and for fear now almost dead:
Yet him at last the Lion spied, and caught,
And forth with shame unto his judgment brought.
Then all the beasts he caus'd assembled be,
To hear their doom, and sad ensample see:
The Fox, first author of that treachery,
He did uncase, and then away let fly.
But th' Ape's long tail (which then he had) he quite
Cut off, and both ears parëd of their height;
Since which, all apes but half their ears have left,
And of their tails are utterly bereft.
So Mother Hubberd her discourse did end:
Which pardon me, if I amiss have penn'd;
For weak was my remembrance it to hold,
And bad her tongue that it so bluntly told.

MUIOPOTMOS;

OR,

THE FATE OF THE BUTTERFLY.

[1590.]

DEDICATION

TO THE RIGHT WORTHY AND VIRTUOUS LADY,

THE LADY CAREY.[4]

MOST brave and bountiful Lady; for so excellent favours as I have received at your sweet hands, to offer these few leaves as in recompense, should be as to offer flowers to the gods for their divine benefits. Therefore I have determined to give myself wholly to you, as quite abandoned from myself, and absolutely vowed to your services: which in all right is ever held for full recompense of debt or damage, to have the person yielded. My person I wot well how little worth it is. But the faithful mind and humble zeal which I bear unto your Ladyship may perhaps be more of price, as may please you to account and use the poor service thereof; which taketh glory to advance your excellent parts and noble virtues, and to spend itself in honouring you; not so much for your great bounty to myself, which yet may not be unminded; nor for name or kindred's sake by you vouchsafed, being also regardable; as for that honourable name, which ye have by your brave deserts purchased to yourself, and spread in the mouths of all men: with which I have also presumed to grace my verses, and, under your name, to commend to the world this small Poem. The which beseeching your Ladyship to take in worth, and of all things therein according to your wonted graciousness to make a mild construction, I humbly pray for your happiness.

Your Ladyship's ever humbly,

E. S.

I SING of deadly dolorous debate,
Stirr'd up through wrathful Nemesis' despite,
Betwixt two mighty ones of great estate,[5]

1 Mad. 2 Alarm.

3 Proving, testing, of his story.

4 Second daughter of Sir John Spencer of Althorpe; her husband, Sir George Carey, became Lord Hunsdon by the death of his father in 1596. She is believed to be the same with "Lady Carew," to whom the poet addressed one of the recommendatory sonnets prefixed to "The Faerie Queen;" page 310.

5 It is probable that this poem allegorises some actual event or court episode of Spenser's day; but all clue to the real occasion is lost. Mr Craik, after quoting the two opening stanzas, pronounces the opinion that "the narrative thus solemnly introduced can hardly be a mere story of a spider and a fly;" and the singularly personal character that pervades the poetry of Spenser powerfully countenances the opinion.

Drawn into arms, and proof of mortal fight,
Through proud ambition and heart-swelling hate,
Whilst neither could the other's greater might
And 'sdainful scorn endure; that from small jar
Their wraths at length broke into open war.

The root whereof and tragical effect,
Vouchsafe, O thou the mournful'st Muse of Nine,[1]
That wont'st the tragic stage for to direct,
In funeral complaints and wailful tine,[2]
Reveal to me, and all the means detect,
Through which sad Clarion did at last decline
To lowest wretchedness: And is there then
Such rancour in the hearts of mighty men?

Of all the race of silver-wingëd Flies
Which do possess the empire of the air,
Betwixt the centred earth and azure skies,
Was none more favourable nor more fair,
Whilst heav'n did favour his felicities,
Than Clarion, the eldest son and heir
Of Muscaroll; and in his father's sight
Of all alive did seem the fairest wight.

With fruitful hope his aged breast he fed
Of future good, which his young toward years,
Full of brave courage and bold hardihead,
Above th' ensample of his equal peers,
Did largely promise, and to him fore-read[3]
(Whilst oft his heart did melt in tender tears),
That he in time would sure prove such an one
As should be worthy of his father's throne.

The fresh young Fly, in whom the kindly fire
Of lustful youth began to kindle fast,
Did much disdain to súbject his desire
To loathsome sloth, or hours in ease to waste;
But joy'd to range abroad, in fresh attire,
Through the wide compass of the airy coast;
And, with unwearied wings, each part t' inquire
Of the wide rule of his renownëd sire.

For he so swift and nimble was of flight,
That from this lower tract he dar'd to sty[4]
Up to the clouds, and thence with pinions light
To mount aloft unto the crystal sky,
To view the workmanship of heaven's height:
Whence down descending he along would fly
Upon the streaming rivers, sport to find;
And oft would dare to tempt the troublous wind.

So on a summer's day, when season mild
With gentle calm the world had quieted,
And high in heav'n Hyperion's fiery child
Ascending did his beams abroad dispread,
While all the heav'ns on lower creatures smil'd;
Young Clarion, with vauntful lustihead,
After his guise did cast[5] abroad to fare;
And thereto gan his furnitures prepare.

His breastplate first, that was of substance pure,
Before his noble heart he firmly bound,
That might his life from iron death assure,
And ward his gentle corse from cruel wound:
For it by art was framëd to endure
The bite of baleful steel and bitter stound,[6]
No less than that which Vulcan made, to shield
Achilles' life from fate of Trojan field.

And then about his shoulders broad he threw
A hairy hide of some wild beast, whom he
In salvage forest by adventure slew,
And reft the spoil his ornament to be;
Which, spreading all his back with dreadful view,
Made all, that him so horrible did see,
Think him Alcides with the lion's skin,
When the Nemean conquest he did win.

Upon his head his glistering burganet,[7]
The which was wrought by wonderous device,
And curiously engraven, he did set:
The metal was of rare and passing price;
Not Bilbo[8] steel, nor brass from Corinth fet,[9]
Nor costly orichalch[10] from strange Phœnice;
But such as could both Phœbus' arrows ward,
And th' hailing darts of heaven beating hard.

Therein two deadly weapons fix'd he bore,
Strongly outlancëd toward either side,
Like two sharp spears, his enemies to gore:
Like as a warlike brigantine, applied
To fight, lays forth her threatful pikes afore,
The engines which in them sad death do hide:
So did this Fly outstretch his fearful horns,
Yet so as him their terror more adorns.

Lastly his shiny wings, as silver bright,
Painted with thousand colours passing far
All painter's skill, he did about him dight:
Not half so many sundry colours are
In Iris' bow; nor heav'n doth shine so bright,
Distinguishëd with many a twinkling star;
Nor Juno's bird in her eye-spotted train
So many goodly colours doth contain.

Nor (may it be withouten peril spoken)
The Archer God, the son of Cytheree,
That joys on wretched lovers to be wroken,[11]
And heapëd spoils of bleeding hearts to see,
Bears in his wings so many a changeful token.
Ah! my liege Lord, forgive it unto me
If aught against thine honour I have told;
Yet sure those wings were fairer manifold.

Full many a lady fair, in Court full oft
Beholding them, him secretly envíed,
And wish'd that two such fans, so silken soft
And golden fair, her love would her provide;
Or that, when them the gorgeous Fly had doff'd,
Some one, that would with grace be gratified,
From him would steal them privily away,
And bring to her so precïous a prey.

Report is, that Dame Venus, on a day
In spring, when flow'rs do clothe the fruitful ground,
Walking abroad with all her nymphs to play,
Bade her fair damsels, flocking her around,
To gather flow'rs her forehead to array:

1 Melpomene.
2 "Teen;" affliction, sorrow.
3 Foretold.
4 Soar.
5 Resolve.
6 Blow.
7 Helmet.
8 Bilbao, a Biscayan town famous for the temper of its steel; there rapiers were first made.
9 Fetched.
10 A kind of brass—literally "mountain brass."
11 Revenged.

Amongst the rest a gentle nymph was found,
Hight Asterie, excelling all the crew
In courteous usage and unstainëd hue.

Who, being nimbler jointed than the rest,
And more industrious, gatherëd more store
Of the fields' honour than the others best;
Which they in secret hearts envýing sore,
Told Venus, when her as the worthiest
She prais'd, that Cupid (as they heard before)
Did lend her secret aid, in gathering
Into her lap the children of the Spring.

Whereof the goddess gath'ring jealous fear—
Not yet unmindful how not long ago
Her son to Psyche secret love did bear,
And long it close conceal'd, till mickle woe
Thereof arose, and many a rueful tear,—
Reason with sudden rage did overgo;
And, giving hasty credit to th' accuser,
Was led away of them that did abuse her.

Eftsoons that damsel, by her heav'nly might,
She turn'd into a wingëd butterfly,
In the wide air to make her wand'ring flight;
And all those flow'rs, with which so plenteously
Her lap she fillëd had, that bred her spite,
She placëd in her wings, for memory
Of her pretended crime, though crime none were:
Since which that fly them in her wings doth bear.

Thus the fresh Clarion, being ready dight,
Unto his journey did himself address,
And with good speed began to take his flight:
Over the fields, in his frank lustiness,
And all the champaign o'er, he soarëd light;
And all the country wide he did possess,
Feeding upon their pleasures bounteously,
That none gainsaid, nor none did him envý.

The woods, the rivers, and the meadows green,
With his air-cutting wings he measur'd wide;
Nor did he leave the mountains bare unseen,
Nor the rank grassy fens' delights untried.
But none of these, however sweet they be'n,
Might please his fancy, nor him cause t' abide:
His choiceful sense with ev'ry change doth flit;
No common things may please a wavering wit.

To the gay gardens his unstaid desire
Him wholly carried, to refresh his sprites:
There lavish Nature, in her best attire,
Pours forth sweet odours and alluring sights;
And Art, with her contending, doth aspire
T' excel the natural with made delights:
And all, that fair or pleasant may be found,
In riotous excess doth there abound.

There he arriving, round about doth fly,
From bed to bed, from one to other border;
And takes survey, with curious busy eye,
Of ev'ry flow'r and herb there set in order;
Now this, now that, he tasteth tenderly;
Yet none of them he rudely doth disorder,
Nor with his feet their silken leaves deface;
But pastures on the pleasures of each place.

And evermore, with most variety
And change of sweetness (for all change is sweet),
He casts[1] his glutton sense to satisfy;
Now sucking of the sap of herb most meet,
Or of the dew which yet on them does lie;
Now in the same bathing his tender feet:
And then he percheth on some branch thereby,
To weather him, and his moist wings to dry.

And then again he turneth to his play,
To spoil the pleasures of that Paradise;
The wholesome saulge,[2] and lavender still gray,
Rank-smelling rue, and cummin good for eyes,
The roses reigning in the pride of May,
Sharp hyssop good for green wounds' remedies,
Fair marigolds, and bees-alluring thyme,
Sweet marjoram, and daisies decking Prime:[3]

Cool violets, and orpine growing still,
Embathëd balm, and cheerful galingale,
Fresh costmary, and breathful camomill,
Dull poppy, and drink-quick'ning setuale,
Vein-healing vervain, and head-purging dill,
Sound savory, and bazil hearty-hale,
Fat colworts, and comfórting perseline,
Cold lettuce, and refreshing rosmarine.

And whatso else of virtue good or ill
Grew in this garden, fetch'd from far away,
Of ev'ry one he takes, and tastes at will,
And on their pleasures greedily doth prey.
Then when he hath both play'd, and fed his fill,
In the warm sun he doth himself embay,[4]
And there him rests in riotous suffisance[5]
Of all his gladfulness, and kingly joyance.

What more felicity can fall to creature
Than to enjoy delight with liberty,
And to be lord of all the works of Nature,
To reign in th' air from th' earth to highest sky,
To feed on flow'rs and weeds of glorious feature,
To take whatever thing doth please the eye?
Who rests not pleasëd with such happiness,
Well worthy he to taste of wretchedness!

But what on earth can long abide in state?
Or who can him assure of happy day?
Since morning fair may bring foul ev'ning late,
And least mishap the most bliss alter may!
For thousand perils lie in close await
About us daily to work our decay;
That none, except a god, or God him guide,
May them avoid, or remedy provide.

And whatso heavens in their secret doom
Ordainëd have, how can frail fleshly wight
Forecast but it must needs to issue come?
The sea, the air, the fire, the day, the night,
And th' armies of their creatures all and some,
Do serve to them, and with impórtune might
War against us, the vassals of their will.
Who then can save what they dispose to spill?[6]

Not thou, O Clarion, though fairest thou
Of all thy kind, unhappy happy Fly,
Whose cruel fate is woven even now
Of Jove's own hand, to work thy misery!
Nor may thee help the many hearty vow
Which thine old sire, with sacred piety,

1 Contrives. 2 Sage. 3 Spring. 4 Bathe, bask. 5 Contentment. 6 Destroy.

Hath pourëd forth for thee, and th' altars sprent:[1]
Naught may thee save from heav'ns' avengëment!

It fortunëd (as heavens had behight[2])
That, in this garden where young Clarion
Was wont to solace him, a wicked wight,
The foe of fair things, th' author of confusión,
The shame of Nature, the bondslave of Spite,
Had lately built his hateful mansión;
And, lurking closely, in await now lay
How he might any in his trap betray.

But when he spied the joyous Butterfly
In this fair plot dispacing[3] to and fro,
Fearless of foes and hidden jeopardý,
Lord! how he gan for to bestir him tho,[4]
And to his wicked work each part apply!
His heart did yearn against his hated foe,
And bowels so with rankling poison swell'd,
That scarce the skin the strong contagion held.

The cause why he this Fly so malicëd[5]
Was (as in stories it is written found)
For that his mother, which him bore and bred,
The most fine-finger'd workwoman on ground,
Arachné, by his means was vanquishëd
Of Pallas, and in her own skill confound,
When she with her for excellence contended,
That wrought her shame and sorrow never ended.

For the Tritonian goddess,[6] having heard
Her blazëd fame, which all the world had fill'd,
Came down to prove the truth, and due reward
For her praiseworthy workmanship to yield:
But the presumptuous damsel rashly dar'd
The goddess' self to challenge to the field,
And to compare[7] with her in curious skill
Of works with loom, with needle, and with quill.[8]

Minerva did the challenge not refuse,
But deign'd with her the paragon[9] to make:
So to their work they sit, and each doth choose
What story she will for her tapet[10] take.
Arachné figur'd how Jove did abuse
Europa like a bull, and on his back
Her through the sea did bear; so lively seen,
That it true sea, and true bull, ye would ween.

She seem'd still back unto the land to look,
And her play-fellows' aid to call, and fear
The dashing of the waves, that up she took
Her dainty feet, and garments gather'd near:
But, Lord! how she in every member shook
When as the land she saw no more appear,
But a wild wilderness of waters deep:
Then gan she greatly to lament and weep.

Before the bull she pictur'd wingëd Love,
With his young brother Sport, light fluttering
Upon the waves, as each had been a dove;
The one his bow and shafts, the other spring[11]
A burning tead[12] about his head did move,
As in their sire's new love both triumphing:
And many Nymphs about them flocking round,
And many Tritons which their horns did sound.

And, round about, her work she did empale[13]
With a fair border wrought of sundry flow'rs,
Enwoven with an ivy-winding trail:
A goodly work, full fit for kingly bow'rs;
Such as Dame Pallas, such as Envy pale,
That all good things with venomous tooth devours,
Could not accuse.[14] Then gan the goddess bright
Herself likewise unto her work to dight.

She made the story of the old debate
Which she with Neptune did for Athens try:
Twelve gods do sit around in royal state,
And Jove in midst with awful majesty,
To judge the strife between them stirrëd late:
Each of the gods, by his like physnomy,[15]
Eath[16] to be known; but Jove above them all,
By his great looks and pow'r imperial.

Before them stands the god of seas in place,
Claiming that sea-coast city as his right,
And strikes the rocks with his three-forkëd mace;
Whenceforth issúes a warlike steed in sight,
The sign by which he challengeth the place;
That all the gods, which saw his wondrous might,
Did surely deem the victory his due:
But seldom seen[17] forejudgment proveth true.

Then to herself she gives her Ægide shield,
And steel-head spear, and morion[18] on her head,
Such as she oft is seen in warlike field:
Then sets she forth, how with her weapon dread
She smote the ground, the which straight forth did yield
A fruitful olive-tree, with berries spread,
That all the gods admir'd; then all the story
She compass'd with a wreath of olives hoary.

Amongst these leaves she made a butterfly,
With excellent device and wondrous sleight,
Flutt'ring among the olives wantonlý,
That seem'd to live, so like it was in sight:
The velvet nap which on his wings doth lie,
The silken down with which his back is dight,
His broad outstretchëd horns, his hairy thighs,
His glorious colours, and his glistering eyes.

Which when Arachné saw, as overlaid
And masterëd with workmanship so rare,
She stood astonied long, nor aught gainsaid;
And with fast fixëd eyes on her did stare,

1 Sprinkled. 2 Ordained.
3 Roaming. 4 Then.
5 Bore such malice against this fly.
6 Athena or Minerva; called "Trito," or "Tritogeneia," because brought up by the sea-god Triton. See note 3, page 249. 7 Compete.
8 Needle; any sharp-pointed instrument; hence "quilt," a cloth wrought by such means.
9 Comparison, rivalry.
10 Figured work, tapestry.
11 Springal, youth. 12 Torch. 13 Enclose.

14 "Non illud Pallas, non illud carpere Livor
Possit opus."—Ovid, "Metam.," vi. 129, 130.
These words immediately follow the passage quoted in note 3, page 438; but Spenser has not farther followed his original. Ovid makes the beaten and jealous goddess rend the web and smite the face of her rival—who, unable to brook the insult, hangs herself, and is by the compunctious Athena changed into a spider. Spenser makes the goddess the victor, and Arachne destroy herself out of envy and rage. 15 Countenance.
16 Easy. 17 It is seldom seen that. 18 Helmet.

And by her silence, sign of one dismay'd,
The victory did yield her as her share;
Yet did she inly fret and felly burn,
And all her blood to poisonous rancour turn:

That shortly, from the shape of womanhead,
Such as she was when Pallas she attempted,[1]
She grew to hideous shape of drearihead,[2]
Pinëd with grief of folly late repented:
Eftsoons her white straight legs were alterëd
To crooked crawling shanks, of marrow emptiëd;
And her fair face to foul and loathsome hue,
And her fine corse t' a bag of venom grew.

This cursëd creature,[3] mindful of that old
Enfested grudge, the which his mother felt,
So soon as Clarion he did behold,
His heart with vengeful malice inly swelt;
And, weaving straight a net with many a fold
About the cave in which he lurking dwelt,
With fine small cords about it stretchëd wide,
So finely spun, that scarce they could be spied.

Not any damsel, which her vaunteth most
In skilful knitting of soft silken twine;
Nor any weaver, which his work doth boast
In diaper, in damask, or in line;[4]
Nor any skill'd in workmanship embost;
Nor any skill'd in loops of fingering fine;
Might in their divers cunning ever dare
With this so curious network to compare.

Nor do I think that that same subtile gin,
The which the Lemnian god fram'd craftily,
Mars sleeping with his wife to compass in,[5]—
That all the gods with common mockery
Might laugh at them, and scorn their shameful
sin,—
Was like to this. This same he did apply
For to entrap the careless Clarion,
That rang'd eachwhere without suspición.

Suspicïon of friend, nor fear of foe,
That hazarded his health, had he at all,
But walk'd at will, and wander'd to and fro,
In the pride of his freedom principal:
Little wist he his fatal future woe,
But was secure; the liker he to fall.
He likest is to fall into mischance,
That is regardless of his governance.

Yet still Aragnoll (so his foe was hight)
Lay lurking covertly him to surprise;
And all his gins,[6] that him entangle might,
Dress'd in good order as he could devise.
At length the foolish Fly, without foresight,
As he that did all danger quite despise,
Toward those parts came flying carelessly,
Where hidden was his hateful enemy.

Who, seeing him, with secret joy therefor
Did tickle inwardly in ev'ry vein;
And his false heart, fraught with all treason's
store,
Was fill'd with hope his purpose to obtain:
Himself he close upgather'd more and more
Into his den, that his deceitful train[7]
By his there being might not be bewray'd;
Nor any noise nor any motion made.

Like as a wily fox, that, having spied
Where on a sunny bank the lambs do play,
Full closely creeping by the hinder side,
Lies in ambúshment of his hopëd prey,
Nor stirreth limb; till, seeing ready tide,[8]
He rusheth forth, and snatcheth quite away
One of the little younglings unawares:
So to his work Aragnoll him prepares.

Who now shall give unto my heavy eyes
A well of tears, that all may overflow?
Or where shall I find lamentable cries
And mournful tunes enough my grief to show?
Help, O thou Tragic Muse! me to devise
Notes sad enough t' express this bitter throe:
For lo! the dreary stound[9] is now arriv'd,
That of all happiness hath us depriv'd.

The luckless Clarion, whether cruel Fate
Or wicked Fortune faultless[10] him misled,
Or some ungracious blast, out of the gate
Of Æole's reign, perforce him drove on head,[11]
Was (O sad hap! and hour unfortunate!)
With violent swift flight forth carriëd
Into the cursëd cobweb, which his foe
Had framëd for his final overthrow.

There the fond Fly entangled, struggled long
Himself to free thereout; but all in vain.
For, striving more, the more in laces strong
Himself he tied, and wrapt his wingës twain
In limy snares the subtile loops among;
That in the end he breathless did remain,
And, all his youthly forces idly spent,
Him to the mercy of th' avenger lent.

Which when the grisly tyrant did espy,
Like a grim lion rushing with fierce might
Out of his den, he seizëd greedily
On the resistless prey; and, with fell spite,
Under the left wing struck his weapon sly
Into his heart, that his deep-groaning sprite
In bloody streams forth fled into the air,
His body left the spectacle of care.

1 Challenged, assailed. 2 Wretchedness, terror.
3 Aragnoll. 4 Linen.
5 See note 18, page 40; and note 31, page 201.
6 Engines, crafty contrivances. 7 Stratagem
8 The appropriate moment. 9 Hour.
10 Without any blame of his. 11 Forward, ahead.

COLIN CLOUT'S COME HOME AGAIN.

[1595.]

TO THE RIGHT WORTHY AND NOBLE KNIGHT

SIR WALTER RALEIGH,

CAPTAIN OF HER MAJESTY'S GUARD, LORD WARDEN OF THE STANNARIES, AND LIEUTENANT OF THE COUNTY OF CORNWALL.

SIR,—That you may see that I am not always idle as ye think, though not greatly well occupied, nor altogether undutiful, though not precisely officious, I make you present of this simple Pastoral, unworthy of your higher conceit for the meanness of the style, but agreeing with the truth in circumstance and matter. The which I humbly beseech you to accept in part of payment of the infinite debt, in which I acknowledge myself bounden unto you for your singular favours, and sundry good turns, showed to me at my late being in England; and with your good countenance protect against the malice of evil mouths, which are always wide open to carp at and misconstrue my simple meaning. I pray continually for your happiness. From my house of Kilcolman, the 27th of December, 1591.

Yours very humbly,

ED. SP.

THE Shepherd's Boy (best knowen by that name)
That after Tityrus[1] first sung his lay,—
Lays of sweet love, without rebuke or blame,—
Sat (as his custom was) upon a day,
Charming[2] his oaten pipe unto his peers,[3]
The shepherd swains that did about him play:
Who all the while, with greedy listful[4] ears,
Did stand astonish'd at his curious skill,
Like heartless deer, dismay'd with thunder's sound.
At last, when as he pipëd had his fill,
He rested him: and, sitting then around,
One of those grooms[5] (a jolly groom was he,
As ever pipëd on an oaten reed,
And lov'd this shepherd dearest in degree,
Hight Hobbinol,[6] gan thus to him aread.[7]
"Colin, my lief,[8] my life, how great a loss
Had all the shepherds' nation by thy lack!
And I, poor swain, of many, greatest cross!
That, since thy Muse first since thy turning back
Was heard to sound as she was wont on high,
Hast made us all so blessëd and so blithe.
Whilst thou wast hence, all dead in dole[9] did lie:
The woods were heard to wail full many a sithe,[10]
And all their birds with silence to complain:
The fields with faded flow'rs did seem to mourn,
And all their flocks from feeding to refrain:
The running waters wept for thy return,
And all their fish with languor did lament:
But now both woods and fields and floods revive,
Since thou art come, their cause of merriment,
That us, late dead, hast made again alive:
But, were it not too painful to repeat
The passëd fortunes which to thee befell
In thy late voyage, we thee would entreat
Now at thy leisure them to us to tell."
To whom the shepherd gently answer'd thus;
"Hobbin, thou temptest me to that[11] I covet:
For of good passëd newly[12] to discuss,
By double usury doth twice renew it.
And since I saw that Angel's[13] blessëd eye,
Her world's bright sun, her heaven's fairest light,
My mind, full of my thoughts' satiety,
Doth feed on sweet contentment of that sight:
Since that same day in naught I take delight,
Nor feeling have in any earthly pleasure,
But in remembrance of that glory bright,
My life's sole bliss, my heart's eternal treasure.
Wake then, my pipe; my sleepy Muse, awake!
Till I have told her praises lasting long:
Hobbin desires, thou may'st it not forsake;
Hark then, ye jolly shepherds, to my song."
With that they all gan throng about him near,
With hungry ears to hear his harmony:
The while their flocks, devoid of danger's fear,
Did round about them feed at liberty.
"One day," quoth he, "I sat (as was my trade[14])
Under the foot of Mole,[15] that mountain hoar,

1 "Tityrus" would appear to signify, *not* Chaucer, according to some explanations, but Virgil—who is by Propertius, in the thirty-fourth elegy of his second book, called "Tityrus," from the name of the shepherd that figures in the Eclogues—and "after" whom, in whose manner or pastoral vein, Spenser had "first" tried the powers of his Muse, in "The Shepherd's Calendar."

2 Modulating, playing; the Latin "carmen," a song or tune, is the original of our "charm."

3 Companions.

4 Listening, attentive.

5 Shepherds. The word "groom," in its original sense, means generally an attendant or keeper of anything—horses, sheep, &c.

6 As in "The Shepherd's Calendar," Hobbinol represents the poet's friend, Gabriel Harvey.

7 Speak.

8 Loved friend.

9 Grief.

10 Time.

11 The thing which.

12 Anew.

13 Queen Elizabeth's.

14 Custom, vocation.

15 The Ballyhoura Hills, which rose at a short distance from Kilcolman Castle, Spenser's Irish residence. See note 15, page 546.

Keeping my sheep amongst the cooly shade
Of the green alders by the Mulla's[1] shore:
There a strange shepherd chanc'd to find me out,
Whether allurëd with my pipe's delight,
Whose pleasing sound y-shrillëd far about,
Or thither led by chance, I know not right:
Whom when I askëd from what place he came,
And how he hight, himself he did y-clepe[2]
The Shepherd of the Ocëan[3] by name,
And said he came far from the main-sea deep.
He, sitting me beside in that same shade,
Provokëd me to play some pleasant fit;[4]
And, when he heard the music which I made,
He found himself full greatly pleas'd at it:
Yet, æmuling[5] my pipe, he took in hand
My pipe, before that æmulëd of many,
And play'd thereon (for well that skill he conn'd[6]);
Himself as skilful in that art as any.
He pip'd, I sung; and when he sung, I pip'd;
By change of turns, each making other merry;
Neither envÿing other, nor envíed,
So pipëd we, until we both were weary."
  There interrupting him, a bonny swain,
That Cuddy hight, him thus atween bespake:
"And should it not thy ready course restrain,
I would request thee, Colin, for my sake,
To tell what thou didst sing when he did play;
For well, I ween, it worth recounting was,
Whether it were some hymn, or moral lay,
Or carol made to praise thy lovëd lass."
  "Nor of my love, nor of my lass," quoth he
"I then did sing, as then occasion fell:
For love had me forlorn, forlorn of me,
That made me in that desert choose to dwell.
But of my river Bregog's[7] love I sung,
Which to the shiny Mulla he did bear,
And yet doth bear, and ever will, so long
As water doth within his banks appear."
  "Of fellowship," said then that bonny boy,
"Record to us that lovely lay again:
The stay whereof[8] shall naught these ears annoy,
Who all that Colin makes do covet fain."
  "Hear, then," quoth he, "the tenor of my tale,
In sort as I it to that shepherd told:
No leasing[9] new, nor grandam's fable stale,
But ancient truth confirm'd with credence old.
  "Old Father Mole (Mole hight that mountain gray
That walls the north side of Armulla dale),
He had a daughter fresh as flow'r of May,
Which gave that name unto that pleasant vale;
Mulla, the daughter of old Mole, so hight
The Nymph which of that water-course has charge,
That, springing out of Mole, doth run down right
To Buttevant, where, spreading forth at large,
It giveth name unto that ancient city
Which Kilnemullah callëd is of old;
Whose ragged ruins breed great ruth and pity
To travellers which it from far behold.
Full fain she lov'd, and was belov'd full fain
Of her own brother river, Bregog hight;
So hight because of this deceitful train
Which he with Mulla wrought to win delight.
But her old sire, more careful of her good,
And meaning her much better to prefer,
Did think to match her with the neighbour flood,
Which Allo[10] hight, Broadwater callëd far;
And wrought so well with his continual pain,
That he that river for his daughter won:
The dower agreed, the day assignëd plain,
The place appointed where it should be done.
Nathless the Nymph her former liking held;
For love will not be drawn, but must be led;
And Bregog did so well her fancy weld,[11]
That her good will he got her first to wed.
But for[12] her father, sitting still on high,
Did warily still watch which way she went,
And eke from far observ'd, with jealous eye,
Which way his course the wanton Bregog bent;
Him to deceive, for all his watchful ward,
The wily lover did devise this sleight:
First into many parts his stream he shar'd,[13]
That, whilst the one was watch'd, the other might
Pass unespied to meet her by the way;
And then, besides, those little streams so broken
He under ground so closely[14] did convey,
That of their passage doth appear no token,
Till they into the Mulla's water slide.
So secretly did he his love enjoy:
Yet not so secret, but it was descried,
And told her father by a shepherd's boy.
Who, wondrous wroth for that so foul despite,
In great revenge did roll down from his hill
Huge mighty stones, the which encumber might
His passage, and his water courses spill.[15]
So of[16] a river, which he was of old,
He none was made, but scatter'd all to naught;
And, lost among those rocks into him roll'd,
Did lose his name: so dear his love he bought."
  Which having said, him Thestylis bespake;
"Now, by my life, this was a merry lay,
Worthy of Colin's self that did it make.
But read[17] now eke, of friendship I thee pray,
What ditty did that other shepherd sing:
For I do covet most the same to hear,
As men use most to covet foreign thing."
  "That shall I eke," quoth he, "to you declare:
His song was all a lamentable lay

1 The river Awbeg, which Spenser poetically called Mulla, after the mountain in which it had its source. See note 13, page 477.
2 Call.
3 Sir Walter Raleigh; who visited Spenser at Kilcolman in the latter part of 1589; and with whom the poet—bearing in manuscript and ready for the press the first three books of "The Faerie Queen"—proceeded to England before the close of the same year.
4 Strain.
5 Emulating.
6 Knew.
7 The Irish name of the river means "false" or "sly;" the stream, which rises in the Ballyhoura Hills, runs for some distance under ground.
8 The delay caused by the recital of which.
9 Falsehood.
10 Among the Irish rivers enumerated in canto xi., book iv., of "The Faerie Queen" (page 477), as attending the marriage of the Thames and the Medway, are—

"Strong Allo tumbling from Slievelogher steep,
  And Mulla mine, whose waves I whilom taught to weep."

11 Wield, govern.
12 Because.
13 Divided.
14 Secretly.
15 Spoil.
16 From being.
17 Tell.

Of great unkindness, and of usage hard,
Of Cynthia,[1] the Lady of the Sea,
Which from her presence faultless him debarr'd.
And ever and anon, with singulfs rife,[2]
He criëd out, to make his undersong;
'Ah! my love's queen, and goddess of my life,
Who shall me pity, when thou dost me wrong?'"
Then gan a gentle bonny lass to speak,
That Marin hight; "Right well he sure did plain,
That could great Cynthia's sore displeasure break,
And move to take him to her grace again.
But tell on farther, Colin, as befell
'Twixt him and thee, that thee did hence dissuade."
"When thus our pipes we both had wearied well,"
Quoth he, "and each an end of singing made,
He gan to cast great liking to my lore,
And great disliking to my luckless lot,
That banish'd had myself, like wight forlore,
Into that waste, where I was quite forgot.
The which to leave thenceforth he counsell'd me,
Unmeet for man in whom was aught regardful,
And wend with him his Cynthia to see;
Whose grace was great, and bounty most rewardful.
Besides her peerless skill in making[3] well,
And all the ornaments of wondrous wit,
Such as all womankind did far excel;
Such as the world admir'd, and praisëd it:
So, what with hope of good, and hate of ill,
He me persuaded forth with him to fare.
Naught took I with me but mine oaten quill:[4]
Small needments else need shepherd to prepare.
So to the sea we came; the sea, that is
A world of waters heapëd up on high,
Rolling like mountains in wide wilderness,
Horrible, hideous, roaring with hoarse cry."
"And is the sea," quoth Corydon, "so fearful?"
"Fearful much more," quoth he, "than heart can fear:
Thousand wild beasts with deep mouths gaping direful
Therein still wait poor passengers to tear.
Who life doth loathe, and longs death to behold,
Before he die, already dead with fear,
And yet would live with heart half stony cold,
Let him to sea, and he shall see it there.
And yet as ghastly dreadful as it seems,
Bold men, presuming life for gain to sell,
Dare tempt that gulf, and in those wand'ring streams
Seek ways unknown, ways leading down to hell.
For, as we stood there waiting on the strand,
Behold, a huge great vessel to us came,
Dancing upon the water's back to land,
As if it scorn'd the danger of the same;
Yet was it but a wooden frame and frail,
Gluëd together with some subtile matter.
Yet had it arms and wings, and head and tail,
And life to move itself upon the water.
Strange thing! how bold and swift the monster was,
That neither car'd for wind, nor hail, nor rain,
Nor swelling waves, but thorough them did pass
So proudly, that she made them roar again.
The same aboard us gently did receive,
And without harm us far away did bear,
So far that land, our mother, us did leave,
And naught but sea and heav'n to us appear.
Then heartless quite, and full of inward fear,
That shepherd I besought to me to tell
Under what sky, or in what world, we were,
In which I saw no living people dwell.
Who, me recomforting all that he might,
Told me that that same was the regiment[5]
Of a great shepherdess, that Cynthia hight,
His liege, his lady, and his life's regënt.
'If then,' quoth I, 'a shepherdess she be,
Where be the flocks and herds which she doth keep?
And where may I the hills and pastures see,
On which she useth for to feed her sheep?'
'These be the hills,' quoth he, 'the surges high,
On which fair Cynthia her herds doth feed:
Her herds be thousand fishes with their fry,
Which in the bosom of the billows breed.
Of them the shepherd which hath charge in chief
Is Triton,[6] blowing loud his wreathëd horn:
At sound whereof they all for their relief
Wend to and fro at ev'ning and at morn.
And Proteus eke with him does drive his herd
Of stinking seals and porpoises together,
With hoary head and dewy dropping beard,
Compelling them which way he list, and whither.
And I, among the rest, of many least,
Have in the Ocean charge to me assign'd;
Where I will live or die at her behest,
And serve and honour her with faithful mind.
Besides, a hundred nymphs all heav'nly born,
And of immortal race, do still attend
To wash fair Cynthia's sheep, when they be shorn,
And fold them up, when they have made an end.
Those be the shepherds which my Cynthia serve
At sea, besides a thousand more at land:
For land and sea my Cynthia doth deserve
To have in her commandëment at hand.'
"Thereat I wonder'd much, till, wond'ring more
And more, at length we land far off descried:
Which sight much gladded me; for much afore
I fear'd lest land we never should have ey'd:
Thereto our ship her course directly bent,
As if the way she perfectly had known.
We Lundy[7] pass; by that same name is meant
An island which the first to west was shown.
From thence another world of land we kenn'd,[8]
Floating amid the sea in jeopardy,

1 Queen Elizabeth; some court disgrace of Raleigh's not connected with the Throckmorton affair (see note 4, page 462), appears to be referred to in the lines that follow.

2 Abundant sighs.

3 Poetising. See note 10, page 273.

4 Pipe, reed.

5 Realm.

6 Signifying Howard of Effingham, Lord High Admiral of England, and conqueror of the Armada.

7 Lundy Island, which lies in the opening of the Bristol Channel.

8 Discerned.

And round about with mighty white rocks hemm'd,
Against the sea's encroaching cruelty.
Those same, the shepherd told me, were the fields
In which Dame Cynthia her land-herds fed;
Fair goodly fields, than which Armulla yields
None fairer, nor more fruitful to be read.[1]
The first, to which we nigh approachëd, was
A high headlánd [2] thrust far into the sea,
Like to a horn, whereof the name it has,
Yet seem'd to be a goodly pleasant lea:
There did a lofty mount at first us greet,
Which did a stately heap of stones uprear,
That seem'd amid the surges for to fleet,[3]
Much greater than that frame which us did bear:
There did our ship her fruitful womb unlade,
And put us all ashore on Cynthia's land."
"What land is that thou mean'st," then Cuddy said,
"And is there other than whereon we stand?"
"Ah! Cuddy," then quoth Colin, "thou 's a fon,[4]
Thou hast not seen least part of Nature's work:
Much more there is unkenn'd[5] than thou dost con,[6]
And much more that does from men's knowledge lurk.
For that same land much larger is than this,
And other men and beasts and birds doth feed:
There fruitful corn, fair trees, fresh herbage is,
And all things else that living creatures need.
Besides, most goodly rivers there appear,
No whit inferior to thy Fanchin's praise,
Or unto Allo, or to Mulla clear:
Naught hast thou, foolish boy, seen in thy days."
"But if that land be there," quoth he, "as here,
And is their heaven likewise there all one?
And, if like heav'n, be heav'nly graces there,
Like as in this same world where we do won?"[7]
"Both heav'n and heav'nly graces do much more,"
Quoth he, "abound in that same land than this.
For there all happy peace and plenteous store
Conspire in one to make contented bliss:
No wailing there nor wretchedness is heard,
No bloody issues nor no leprosies,
No grisly famine, nor no raging sweard,[8]
No nightly bordrags,[9] nor no hue and cries;
The shepherds there abroad may safely lie,
On hills and downs, withouten dread or danger:
No ravenous wolves the goodman's hope destroy,
Nor outlaws fell affray the forest ranger.
There learnëd arts do flourish in great honour,
And poets' wits are had in peerless price:
Religion hath lay power to rest upon her,[10]
Advancing virtue and suppressing vice.
For end,[11] all good, all grace there freely grows,
Had people grace it gratefully to use:
For God his gifts there plenteously bestows,
But graceless men them greatly do abuse."
"But say on farther," then said Corylas,
"The rest of thine adventures, that betided."
"Forth on our voyage we by land did pass,"
Quoth he, "as that same shepherd still us guided,
Until that we to Cynthia's presence came:
Whose glory, greater than my simple thought,
I found much greater than the former fame;
Such greatness I can not compare to aught:
But if I her like aught on earth might read,[12]
I would her liken to a crown of lilies
Upon a virgin bride's adornëd head,
With roses dight[13] and golds[14] and daffodillies;
Or like the circlet of a turtle true,
In which all colours of the rainbow be;
Or like fair Phœbe's garland shining new,
In which all pure perfection one may see.
But vain it is to think, by paragon[15]
Of earthly things, to judge of things divine:
Her pow'r, her mercy, and her wisdom, none
Can deem,[16] but who the Godhead can define.
Why then do I, base shepherd, bold and blind,
Presume the things so sacred to profane?
More fit it is t' adore, with humble mind,
The image of the heav'ns in shape humane."
With that Alexis broke his tale asunder,
Saying; "By wond'ring at thy Cynthia's praise,
Colin, thyself thou mak'st us more to wonder,
And, her upraising, dost thyself upraise.
But let us hear what grace she showëd thee,
And how that shepherd strange thy cause advanc'd."
"The Shepherd of the Ocëan," quoth he,
"Unto that Goddess' grace me first enhanc'd,
And to mine oaten pipe inclin'd her ear,
That she thenceforth therein gan take delight,
And it desir'd at timely hours to hear,
All[17] were my notes but rude and roughly dight;
For not by measure of her own great mind,
And wondrous worth, she mote[18] my simple song,
But joy'd that country shepherd aught could find
Worth hearkening to amongst the learnëd throng."
"Why?" said Alexis then, "what needeth she
That is so great a shepherdess herself,
And hath so many shepherds in her fee,
To hear thee sing, a simple silly elf?
Or be the shepherds which do serve her lazy,
That they list not their merry pipes apply?
Or be their pipes untunable and crazy,
That they can not her honour worthily?"
"Ah! nay," said Colin, "neither so, nor so:
For better shepherds be not under sky,
Nor better able, when they list to blow
Their pipes aloud, her name to glorify.
There is good Harpalus,[19] now waxen agëd

1 Discovered.
2 Cornwall; Latin, "cornu," a horn.
3 Float.
4 "Thou art a fool." "Ill hail, Alain, by God, thou is a fonne"—or "fon"—is a line in Chaucer's Reeve's Tale; page 57.
5 Unknown.
6 Know.
7 Dwell.
8 Sword.
9 Border forays.
10 The lay or civil power is based upon, supported by, religion.
11 To sum up; in fine.
12 Declare.
13 Decked.
14 Marigolds.
15 Comparison.
16 Estimate.
17 Although.
18 Meted, judged.
19 Barnaby Googe, a retainer of Cecil's, who published in 1563 a collection of "Eclogues, Epitaphs, and Sonnets."

In faithful service of fair Cynthia:
And there is Corydon,[1] though meanly wagëd,
Yet ablest wit of most I know this day.
And there is sad Alcyon,[2] bent to mourn,
Though fit to frame an everlasting ditty,
Whose gentle sprite for Daphne's death doth turn
Sweet lays of love to endless plaints of pity.
Ah! pensive boy, pursue that brave conceit
In thy sweet Eglantine of Meriflure;[3]
Lift up thy notes unto their wonted height,
That may thy Muse and mates to mirth allure.
There eke is Palin,[4] worthy of great praise,
All be[5] he envy at my rustic quill:
And there is pleasing Alcon,[6] could he raise
His tunes from lays to matter of more skill.
And there is old Palemon,[7] free from spite,
Whose careful[8] pipe may make the hearer rue:[9]
Yet he himself may ruëd be more right,
That sung so long until quite hoarse he grew.
And there is Alabaster,[10] throughly taught
In all this skill, though knowen yet to few;
Yet, were he known to Cynthia as he ought,
His Eliseïs would be read anew.
Who lives that can match that heroic song,
Which he hath of that mighty Princess made?
O dreaded Dread,[11] do not thyself that wrong,
To let thy fame lie so in hidden shade:
But call it forth, O call him forth to thee,
To end thy glory which he hath begun:
That, when he finish'd hath as it should be,
No braver poem can be under sun.
Nor Po nor Tiber's swans so much renown'd,
Nor all the brood of Greece so highly prais'd,
Can match that Muse when it with bays is crown'd,
And to the pitch of her perfection rais'd.
And there is a new shepherd late upsprung,
The which doth all afore him far surpass;
Appearing well in that well tunëd song
Which late he sung unto a scornful lass.
Yet doth his trembling Muse but lowly fly,
As daring not too rashly mount on height,
And doth her tender plumes as yet but try
In love's soft lays and looser thoughts' delight.
Then rouse thy feathers quickly, Daniel,[12]
And to what course thou please thyself advance:
But most, me seems, thy accent will excel
In tragic plaints and passionate mischance.
And there that Shepherd of the Ocean[13] is,
That spends his wit in love's consuming smart;
Full sweetly temper'd is that Muse of his,
That can empierce a Prince's mighty heart.
There also is—ah no, he is not now!
But since I said he is, he quite is gone,
Amyntas[14] quite is gone, and lies full low,
Having his Amaryllis left to moan.
Help, O ye shepherds, help ye all in this,
Help Amaryllis this her loss to mourn!
Her loss is yours, your loss Amyntas is,
Amyntas, flower of shepherds' pride forlorn:
He whilst he livëd was the noblest swain
That ever pipëd in an oaten quill:
Both did he others, which could pipe, maintain,
And eke could pipe himself with passing skill.
And there, though last not least, is Aetion;[15]
A gentler shepherd may nowhére be found:
Whose Muse, full of high thoughts' invention,
Doth like himself heroically sound.
All these and many others more remain,
Now, after Astrophel[16] is dead and gone:
But, while as Astrophel did live and reign,
Amongst all these was none his paragon.
All these do flourish in their sundry kind,
And do their Cynthia immortal make:
Yet found I liking in her royal mind,
Not for my skill, but for that shepherd's sake."[17]
Then spake a lovely lass, hight Lucida;
"Shepherd, enough of shepherds thou hast told
Which favour thee, and honour Cynthia:
But of so many nymphs which she doth hold
In her retínue thou hast nothing said;
That seems, with none of them thou favour foundest,
Or art ungrateful to each gentle maid,
That none of all their due deserts resoundest."
"Ah, far be it," quoth Colin Clout, "from me,
That I of gentle maids should ill deserve!
For that myself I do profess to be
Vassal to one whom all my days I serve;
The beam of beauty sparkled from above,
The flow'r of virtue and pure chastity,
The blossom of sweet joy and perfect love,
The pearl of peerless grace and modesty:
To her my thoughts I daily dedicate,
To her my heart I nightly martyrize:
To her my love I lowly do prostráte,
To her my life I wholly sacrifice:
My thought, my heart, my love, my life is she,
And I hers ever only, ever one:
One ever I all vowëd hers to be,
One ever I, and other's never none."[18]
Then thus Melissa said; "Thrice happy maid,

1 Abraham Fraunce, a friend of Sir Philip Sidney's, who was the author of "The Lamentation of Corydon for the Love of Alexis," published in 1588.

2 Sir Arthur Gorges; in honour of whose dead wife, Douglas Howard, daughter and heir of Henry Lord Howard, Viscount Byndon, Spenser wrote his elegy entitled "Daphnaïda." In the present passage, Daphne is, of course, the deceased lady.

3 Probably an unpublished poem of Sir Arthur's.

4 Thomas Chaloner, a pastoral poet; or George Peele, the dramatist.

5 Although.

6 Thomas Watson, who published in 1591 a collection of sonnets.

7 Thomas Churchyard, a prolific poet of the day.

8 Sorrowful.

9 Feel pity.

10 William Alabaster, a scholar and poet of the period; his "Eliseïs" was, of course, in eulogy of the Queen.

11 Queen Elizabeth. See note 10, page 306.

12 Samuel Daniel, a poet and dramatist of considerable reputation, who, on the death of Spenser, succeeded him as Poet-Laureate.

13 Raleigh.

14 Ferdinando, Earl of Derby, who died in April 1594, while the poem was still in Spenser's hands.

15 It is almost beyond doubt that under this name Spenser pays a tribute to his greater contemporary, William Shakespeare.

16 Sir Philip Sidney.

17 Spenser owed his first introduction to Queen Elizabeth to the persuasions and good offices of his visitor and travelling companion, Raleigh.

18 When this was written, Spenser was probably courting the lady to whom he dedicated his Sonnets, and whom he had wedded—before "Colin Clout" was published—in June 1594.

Whom thou dost so enforce[1] to deify:
That woods, and hills, and valleys thou hast made
Her name to echo unto heaven high.
But say, who else vouchsafëd thee of grace?"
"They all," quoth he, "me gracëd goodly well,
That all I praise; but, in the highest place,
Urania,[2] sister unto Astrophel,
In whose brave mind, as in a golden coffer,
All heav'nly gifts and riches lockëd are;
More rich than pearls of Ind, or gold of Ophir,
And in her sex more wonderful and rare.
Nor less praiseworthy I Theana[3] read,[4]
Whose goodly beams, though they be overdight[5]
With mourning stole of careful widowhead,
Yet through that darksome veil do glister bright;
She is the well of bounty and brave mind,
Excelling most in glory and great light:
She is the ornament of womankind,
And Court's chief garland, with all virtues dight.
Therefore great Cynthia her in chiefest grace
Doth hold, and next unto herself advance,
Well worthy of so honourable place,
For her great worth and noble governance.
Nor less praiseworthy is her sister dear,
Fair Marian,[6] the Muses' only darling:
Whose beauty shineth as the morning clear,
With silver dew upon the roses pearling.
Nor less praiseworthy is Mansilia,[7]
Best known by bearing up great Cynthia's train:
That same is she to whom Daphnaïda
Upon her niece's death I did complain:
She is the pattern of true womanhead,
And only mirror of feminity:
Worthy next after Cynthia to tread,
As she is next her in nobility.
Nor less praiseworthy Galathea seems
Than best of all that honourable crew,
Fair Galathea with bright shining beams,
Inflaming feeble eyes that her do view.
She there then waited upon Cynthia,
Yet there is not her won;[8] but here with us,
About the borders of our rich Coshma,
Now made of Maa the nymph delicious.
Nor less praiseworthy fair Neæra is,
Neæra ours, not theirs, though there she be;
For of the famous Shure the nymph she is,
For high desert advanc'd to that degree.
She is the blossom of grace and courtesy,
Adornëd with all honourable parts:
She is the branch of true nobility,
Belov'd of high and low with faithful hearts.
Nor less praiseworthy Stella[9] do I read,
Though naught my praises of her needed are,
Whom verse of noblest shepherd lately dead
Hath prais'd and rais'd above each other star.
Nor less praiseworthy are the sisters three,
The honour of the noble family
Of which I meanest boast myself to be,
And most that unto them I am so nigh:
Phyllis, Charyllis, and sweet Amaryllis.[10]
Phyllis, the fair, is eldest of the three:
The next to her is bountiful Charyllis:
But th' youngest is the highest in degree.
Phyllis, the flower of rare perfection,
Fair spreading forth her leaves with fresh delight,
That, with their beauty's amorous reflexion,
Bereave of sense each rash beholder's sight.
But sweet Charyllis is the paragon
Of peerless price, and ornament of praise,
Admir'd of all, yet enviëd of none,
Through the mild temperance of her goodly rays.
Thrice happy do I hold thee, noble swain,
The which art of so rich a spoil possest,
And, it embracing dear without disdain,
Hast sole possession in so chaste a breast:
Of all the shepherds' daughters which there be,
And yet there be the fairest under sky,
Or that elsewhere I ever yet did see,
A fairer nymph yet never saw mine eye;
She is the pride and primrose of the rest,
Made by the Maker's self to be admired;
And like a goodly beacon high addrest,[11]
That is with sparks of heav'nly beauty fired.
But Amaryllis,—whether fortunate,
Or else unfortunate, may I aread,[12]
That freëd is from Cupid's yoke by fate,
Since which she doth new bands' adventure dread?—
Shepherd, whatever thou hast heard to be
In this or that prais'd diversely apart,
In her thou may'st them all assembled see,
And seal'd up in the treasure of her heart.
Nor thee less worthy, gentle Flavia,
For thy chaste life and virtue I esteem:
Nor thee less worthy, courteous Candida,[13]

1 Endeavour.

2 Mary, Countess of Pembroke, sister of Sir Philip Sidney; to whom Spenser dedicated "The Ruins of Time," and addressed one of the recommendatory sonnets prefixed to "The Faerie Queen;" page 309.

3 Anne, widow of Ambrose Dudley, Earl of Warwick, whom the poet has also eulogised in "The Ruins of Time" (page 585).

4 Declare, consider.

5 Covered over, veiled.

6 Margaret, Countess of Cumberland.

7 Helena, Marchioness of Northampton, to whom Spenser dedicated his "Daphnaïda."

8 Dwelling.

9 Lady Penelope Devereux, daughter of the Earl of Essex, whom Sir Philip Sidney celebrated in his "Arcadia" under the name of "Philoclea," and under that of "Stella" in his poems of Astrophel; she had married Lord Rich, but was at this time a widow.

10 Three of the six daughters of Sir John Spencer of Althorpe, from whom sprang the noble houses of Spencer and Marlborough. Phyllis represents Elizabeth, the second daughter, who married Sir George Carey, the son of Lord Hunsdon—to which title he succeeded in 1596; Spenser addressed to her one of the recommendatory sonnets prefixed to "The Faerie Queen," and dedicated to her "Muiopotmos." Charyllis is Anne, the fifth daughter, who successively married Lord Mounteagle, Lord Compton, and Lord Buckhurst (Earl of Dorset in 1608); to her was dedicated "Mother Hubberd's Tale." Amaryllis is the sixth and youngest daughter, Alice, to whom—as Lady Strange—the poet inscribed "The Tears of the Muses," and who was now the widowed Countess of Derby, Lord Strange having succeeded to the earldom in 1592, and died two years afterwards. Not merely in the lines in the text, but in all the three dedications which have been mentioned, does the poet advance his claim to kindred with the high-connected Spencers.

11 Placed, prepared.

12 Pronounce.

13 Of Galathea, Neæra, Flavia, and Candida, nothing is known farther than that the first two were Irish ladies.

For thy true love and loyalty I deem.
Besides yet many more that Cynthia serve,
Right noble nymphs, and high to be commended:
But, if I all should praise as they deserve,
This sun would fail me ere I half had ended.
Therefore, in closure[1] of a thankful mind,
I deem it best to hold eternally
Their bounteous deeds and noble favours shrin'd,
Than by discourse them to indignify."
So having said, Aglaura him bespake:
"Colin, well worthy were those goodly favours
Bestow'd on thee, that so of them dost make,
And them requitest with thy thankful labours.
But of great Cynthia's goodness, and high grace,
Finish the story which thou hast begun."
"More eath,"[2] quoth he, "it is in such a case
How to begin, than know how to have done.
For ev'ry gift, and ev'ry goodly meed,
Which she on me bestow'd, demands a day;
And ev'ry day, in which she did a deed,
Demands a year it duly to display.
Her words were like a stream of honey fleeting,[3]
The which doth softly trickle from the hive,
Able to melt the hearer's heart unweeting,[4]
And eke to make the dead again alive.
Her deeds were like great clusters of ripe grapes,
Which load the branches of the fruitful vine;
Off'ring to fall into each mouth that gapes,
And fill the same with store of timely wine.
Her looks were like beams of the morning sun,
Forth looking through the windows of the east,
When first the fleecy cattle have begun
Upon the pearlëd grass to make their feast.
Her thoughts are like the fume of frankincénse,
Which from a golden censer forth doth rise,
And, throwing forth sweet odours, mounts from thence
In rolling globes up to the vaulted skies.
There she beholds, with high aspiring thought,
The cradle of her own creation,
Amongst the seats of angels heav'nly wrought,
Much like an angel in all form and fashion."
"Colin," said Cuddy then, "thou hast forgot
Thyself, me seems, too much, to mount so high:
Such lofty flight base shepherd seemeth not,[5]
From flocks and fields to angels and to sky."
"True," answer'd he, "but her great excellence
Lifts me above the measure of my might:
That, being fill'd with furious insolence,
I feel myself like one y-rapt in sprite.
For when I think of her, as oft I ought,
Then want I words to speak it fitly forth:
And, when I speak of her what I have thought,
I cannot think according to her worth.
Yet will I think of her, yet will I speak,
So long as life my limbs doth hold together;
And, when as death these vital bands shall break,
Her name recorded I will leave for ever.
Her name in ev'ry tree I will endorse,
That, as the trees do grow, her name may grow:
And in the ground eachwhere will it engross,[6]
And fill with stones, that all men may it know.
The speaking woods, and murmuring waters' fall,
Her name I'll teach in knowen terms to frame:
And eke my lambs, when for their dams they call,
I'll teach to call for Cynthia by name.
And, long while after I am dead and rotten,
Amongst the shepherds' daughters dancing round,
My lays made of her shall not be forgotten,
But sung by them with flow'ry garlands crown'd.
And ye, whoso ye be, that shall survive,
When as ye hear her memory renew'd,
Be witness of her bounty here alive,
Which she to Colin her poor shepherd shew'd."
Much was the whole assembly of those herds
Mov'd at his speech, so feelingly he spake:
And stood a while astonish'd at his words,
Till Thestylis at last their silence brake,
Saying; "Why, Colin, since thou found'st such grace
With Cynthia and all her noble crew,
Why didst thou ever leave that happy place,
In which such wealth might unto thee accrue,
And back returnëdst to this barren soil,
Where cold and care and penury do dwell,
Here to keep sheep with hunger and with toil?
Most wretched he, that is, and cannot tell."
"Happy indeed," said Colin, "I him hold,
That may that blessëd presence still enjoy,
Of fortune and of envy uncontroll'd,
Which still are wont most happy states t' annoy:
But I, by that which little while I prov'd,
Some part of those enormities did see
The which in Court continually hov'd,[7]
And follow'd those which happy seem'd to be.
Therefore I, silly man, whose former days
Had in rude fields been altogether spent,
Durst not adventure such unknowen ways,
Nor trust the guile of Fortune's blandishment;
But rather chose back to my sheep to turn,
Whose utmost hardness I before had tried,
Than, having learn'd repentance late, to mourn
Amongst those wretches which I there descried."
"Shepherd," said Thestylis, "it seems of spite
Thou speakest thus 'gainst their felicity,
Which thou envíest, rather than of right
That aught in them blameworthy thou dost spy."
"Cause have I none," quoth he, "of canker'd will
To quite[8] them ill that me demean'd so well:[9]
But self-regard of private good or ill
Moves me of each, so as I found, to tell,
And eke to warn young shepherds' wand'ring wit,
Which, through report of that life's painted bliss,
Abandon quiet home to seek for it,
And leave their lambs, to loss misled amiss.
For, sooth to say, it is no sort of life
For shepherd fit to lead in that same place,

1 Within the enclosure.
2 Easy.
3 Flowing.
4 Unconsciously.
5 Beseems not lowly shepherd.
6 Engrave.
7 Hovered, abode.
8 Requite.
9 Behaved, demeaned, themselves so well to me.

Where each one seeks with malice and with strife
To thrust down others into foul disgrace,
Himself to raise: and he doth soonest rise
That best can handle his deceitful wit
In subtile shifts, and finest sleights devise,
Either by sland'ring his well-deemëd name
Through leasings lewd[1] and feignëd forgery;
Or else by breeding him some blot of blame,
By creeping close into his secrecy;
To which him needs a guileful hollow heart,
Maskëd with fair dissembling courtesy,
A filëd[2] tongue, furnish'd with terms of art,
No art of school, but courtiers' schoolery.
For arts of school have there small countenance,
Counted but toys to busy idle brains;
And there professors find small maintenance,
But to be instruments of others' gains.
Nor is there place for any gentle wit,
Unless to please itself it can apply;
But shoulder'd is, or out of door quite shut,
As base, or blunt, unmeet for melody.
For each man's worth is measur'd by his weed,[3]
As harts by horns, or asses by their ears:
Yet asses be not all whose ears exceed,
Nor yet all harts that horns the highest bears.
For highest looks have not the highest mind,
Nor haughty words most full of highest thoughts;
But are like bladders blowen up with wind,
That, being prick'd, do vanish into naughts.
Ev'n such is all their vaunted vanity,
Naught else but smoke, that fumeth soon away:
Such is their glory, that in simple eye
Seem greatest when their garments are most gay.
So they themselves for praise of fools do sell,
And all their wealth for painting on a wall;
With price whereof they buy a golden bell,
And purchase highest rooms in bow'r and hall:
While single Truth and simple Honesty
Do wander up and down despis'd of all;
Their plain attire such glorious gallantry
Disdains so much, that none them in doth call."
"Ah! Colin," then said Hobbinol, "the blame
Which thou imputest is too general,
As if not any gentle wit of name,
Nor honest mind, might there be found at all.
For well I wot, since I myself was there,
To wait on Lobbin[4] (Lobbin well thou knew'st),
Full many worthy ones then waiting were,
As ever else in prince's court thou view'st.
Of which among you many yet remain,
Whose names I cannot readily now guess:
Those that poor suitors' papers do retain,
And those that skill of medicine profess,
And those that do to Cynthia expound
The leden[5] of strange languages in charge:
For Cynthia doth in sciences abound,
And gives to their professors stipends large.
Therefore unjustly thou dost wite[6] them all,
For that which thou mislikedst in a few."
"Blame is," quoth he, "more blameless general,
Than that which private errors doth pursue;
For well I wot that there amongst them be
Full many persons of right worthy parts,
Both for report of spotless honesty,
And for profession of all learnëd arts,
Whose praise hereby no whit impairëd is,
Though blame do light on those that faulty be;
For all the rest do most-what[7] fare amiss,
And yet their own misfaring[8] will not see:
For either they be puffëd up with pride,
Or fraught with envy, that their galls do swell,
Or they their days to idleness divide,[9]
Or drownëd lie in pleasure's wasteful well,
In which like moldwarps nousling[10] still they lurk,
Unmindful of chief parts of manliness;
And do themselves, for want of other work,
Vain votaries of lazy Love profess,
Whose service high so basely they ensue,[11]
That Cupid's self of them ashamëd is,
And, must'ring all his men in Venus' view,
Denies them quite for servitors of his."
"And is Love then," said Corylas, "once known
In Court, and his sweet lore professëd there?
I weenëd sure he was our god alone,
And only wonn'd[12] in fields and forests here."
"Not so," quoth he; "Love most aboundeth there;
For all the walls and windows there are writ
All full of love, and love, and love my dear,
And all their talk and study is of it.
Nor any there doth brave or valiant seem,
Unless that some gay mistress' badge he bears:
Nor any one himself doth aught esteem,
Unless he swim in love up to the ears.
But they of Love, and of his sacred lere[13]
(As it should be), all otherwise devise
Than we poor shepherds are accustom'd here,
And him do sue and serve all otherwise.
For with lewd speeches, and licentious deeds,
His mighty mysteries they do profane,
And use his idle name to other needs,
But as a complement for courting vain.
So him they do not serve as they profess,
But make him serve to them for sordid uses:
Ah! my dread Lord, that dost liege hearts possess,
Avenge thyself on them for their abuses!
But we poor shepherds, whether rightly so,
Or through our rudeness into error led,
Do make religion how we rashly go[14]
To serve that god, that is so greatly dread;[15]
For him the greatest of the gods we deem,
Born without sire or couples of one kind;
For Venus' self doth solely couples seem,
Both male and female through commixture join'd:

1 Wicked lies. 2 Smooth. 3 Dress.
4 Supposed to mean the Earl of Leicester.
5 Dialect. See note 28, page 119.
6 Blame. 7 For the most part.
8 Misdoing. 9 Allot, give up.

10 Like moles burrowing. 11 Follow.
12 Dwelt. 13 Lore.
14 That is, we have such true religion, we so truly fear the god, that we are very careful how we serve him.
15 Dreaded.

So pure and spotless Cupid forth she brought,
And in the gardens of Adonis nurst:
Where growing, he his own perfection wrought,
And shortly was of all the gods the first.
Then got he bow and shafts of gold and lead,[1]
In which so fell and púissánt he grew,
That Jove himself his pow'r began to dread,
And, taking up to heav'n, him godded[2] new.
From thence he shoots his arrows ev'rywhere
Into the world, at random as he will,
On us frail men, his wretched vassals here,
Like as himself us pleaseth save or spill.[3]
So we him worship, so we him adore
With humble hearts to heav'n uplifted high,
That to true loves he may us evermore
Prefer, and of their grace us dignify:[4]
Nor is there shepherd, nor yet shepherd's swain,
Whatever feeds in forest or in field,
That dare with evil deed or leasing[5] vain
Blaspheme his pow'r, or terms unworthy yield."
"Shepherd, it seems that some celestial rage
Of love," quoth Cuddy, "is breath'd into thy breast,
That poureth forth these oracles so sage
Of that high pow'r wherewith thou art possest.
But never wist I till this present day,
All be[6] of Love I always humbly deem'd,
That he was such an one as thou dost say,
And so religiously to be esteem'd.
Well may it seem, by this thy deep insight,
That of that god the priest thou shouldest be:
So well thou wot'st[7] the mystery of his might,
As if his godhead thou didst present see."
"Of Love's perfection perfectly to speak,
Or of his nature rightly to define,
Indeed," said Colin, "passeth reason's reach,
And needs his priest t' express his pow'r divine.
For long before the world he was y-bore,
And bred above in Venus' bosom dear:
For by his pow'r the world was made of yore,
And all that therein wondrous doth appear.
For how should else things so far from at one,[8]
And so great enemies as of them be,
Be ever drawn together into one,
And taught in such accordance to agree?
Through him the cold began to covet heat,
And water fire; the light to mount on high,
And th' heavy down to pese;[9] the hungry t' eat,
And voidness to seek full satiety.
So, being former foes, they waxëd friends,
And gan by little learn to love each other:
So, being knit, they brought forth other kinds
Out of the fruitful womb of their great mother.
Then first gan heaven out of darkness dread
For to appear, and brought forth cheerful day:
Next gan the earth to show her naked head
Out of deep waters which her drown'd alway:
And, shortly after, ev'ry living wight
Crept forth like worms out of her slimy nature.
Soon as on them the Sun's life-giving light
Had pourëd kindly heat and formal feature,
Thenceforth they gan each one his like to love,
And like himself desire for to beget:
The lion chose his mate, the turtle dove
Her dear, the dolphin his own dolphinet;
But man, that had the spark of reason's might
More than the rest to rule his passion,
Chose for his love the fairest in his sight,
Like as himself was fairest by creation:
For Beauty is the bait which with delight
Doth man allure for to enlarge his kind;
Beauty, the burning lamp of heaven's light,
Darting her beams into each feeble mind:
Against whose pow'r nor God nor man can find
Defence, nor ward the danger of the wound;
But, being hurt, seek to be medicin'd
Of her that first did stir that mortal stound.[10]
Then do they cry and call to Love apace,
With prayers loud impórtuning the sky,
Whence he them hears; and, when he list show grace,
Does grant them grace that otherwise would die.
So Love is lord of all the world by right,
And rules the creatures by his pow'rful saw:[11]
All being made the vassals of his might,
Through secret sense which thereto doth them draw.
Thus ought all lovers of their lord to deem,
And with chaste heart to honour him alway:
But whoso else doth otherwise esteem,
Are outlaws, and his lore do disobey.
For their desire is base, and doth not merit
The name of love, but of disloyal lust:
Nor 'mongst true lovers they shall place inherit,
But as exiles out of his court be thrust."
So having said, Melissa spake at will;
"Colin, thou now full deeply hast divin'd[12]
Of Love and Beauty; and, with wondrous skill,
Hast Cupid's self depainted in his kind.[13]
To thee are all true lovers greatly bound,
That dost their cause so mightily defend:
But most, all women are thy debtors found,
That dost their bounty still so much commend."
"That ill," said Hobbinol, "they him requite;
For, having lovëd ever one most dear,
He is repaid with scorn and foul despite,
That irks each gentle heart which it doth hear."
"Indeed," said Lucid, "I have often heard
Fair Rosalind of divers foully blam'd
For being to that swain too cruel hard;
That her bright glory else hath much defam'd.
But who can tell what cause had that fair maid
To use him so, that usëd her so well?
Or who with blame can justly her upbraid
For loving not? for who can love compel?
And, sooth to say, it is foolhardy thing
Rashly to witen[14] creatures so divine;
For demigods they be, and first did spring
From heav'n, though graff'd in frailness feminine.
And well I wot, that oft I heard it spoken,
How one, that fairest Helen did revile,
Through judgment of the gods to be y-wroken,[15]
Lost both his eyes, and so remain'd long while,
Till he recanted had his wicked rhymes,

1 See note 8, page 210.
2 Deified.
3 Destroy.
4 Make us worthy of their favour.
5 Falsehood.
6 Although.
7 Knowest.
8 From being in harmony.
9 Poise, weigh.
10 Pain, hurt.
11 Saying, decree.
12 Reasoned, discoursed.
13 Nature.
14 Blame.
15 Revenged.

And made amends to her with treble praise.
Beware therefore, ye grooms, I read,[1] betimes,
How rashly blame of Rosalind ye raise."
"Ah! shepherds," then said Colin, "ye ne weet [2]
How great a guilt upon your heads ye draw,
To make so bold a doom,[3] with words unmeet,
Of thing celestial which ye never saw.
For she is not like as the other crew
Of shepherds' daughters which amongst you be,
But of divine regard and heav'nly hue,
Excelling all that ever ye did see.
Not then to her, that scornëd thing so base,
But to myself the blame that look'd so high:
So high her thoughts as she herself have place,
And loathe each lowly thing with lofty eye.
Yet so much grace let her vouchsafe to grant
To simple swain, since her I may not love:
Yet that I may her honour paravant,[4]
And praise her worth, though far my wit above.
Such grace shall be some guerdon[5] for the grief
And long affliction which I have endur'd:
Such grace sometimes shall give me some relief,
And ease of pain which cannot be recur'd.
And ye, my fellow shepherds, which do see
And hear the languors of my too long dying,
Unto the world for ever witness be,
That hers I die, naught to the world denying
This simple trophy of her great conquést."
So having ended, he from ground did rise;
And after him uprose eke all the rest:
All loth to part, but that the glooming skies
Warn'd them to draw their bleating flocks to rest.

AMORETTI; OR SONNETS.[6]

[1595.]

I.

HAPPY, ye leaves! when as those lily hands,
Which hold my life in their dead-doing might,
Shall handle you, and hold in love's soft bands,
Like captives trembling at the victor's sight.
And happy lines! on which, with starry light,
Those lamping eyes will deign sometimes to look,
And read the sorrows of my dying sprite,
Written with tears in heart's close-bleeding book.
And happy rhymes! bath'd in the sacred brook
Of Helicon, whence she derivëd is;
When ye behold that Angel's blessed look,
My soul's long-lackëd food, my heaven's bliss;
Leaves, lines, and rhymes, seek her to please alone,
Whom if ye please, I care for other none!

IV.

New Year, forth looking out of Janus' gate,
Doth seem to promise hope of new delight:
And, bidding th' old adieu, his passëd date
Bids all old thoughts to die in dumpish[7] sprite:
And, calling forth out of sad Winter's night
Fresh Love, that long hath slept in cheerless bow'r,
Wills him awake, and soon about him dight
His wanton wings and darts of deadly pow'r.
For lusty Spring now in his timely hour
Is ready to come forth, him to receive;
And warns the Earth with diverse-colour'd flow'r
To deck herself, and her fair mantle weave.
Then you, fair flower! in whom fresh youth doth reign,
Prepare yourself new love to entertain.

IX.

Long-while I sought to what I might compare
Those pow'rful eyes, which lighten my dark sprite:
Yet find I naught on earth, to which I dare
Resemble th' image of their goodly light.
Not to the sun; for they do shine by night;
Nor to the moon; for they are changëd never;
Nor to the stars; for they have purer sight;
Nor to the fire; for they consume not ever;
Nor to the lightning; for they still persévor;
Nor to the diamond; for they are more tender;
Nor unto crystal; for naught may them sever;
Nor unto glass; such baseness might offend her.
Then to the Maker's self they likest be,
Whose light doth lighten all that here we see.

XV.

Ye tradeful merchants, that with weary toil
Do seek most precious things to make your gain,
And both the Indias of their treasure spoil,
What needeth you to seek so far in vain?
For lo! my Love doth in herself contain
All this world's riches that may far be found:

1 Counsel. 2 Ye know not.
3 Judgment. 4 Publicly; before all others.
5 Recompense.
6 Spenser's "Amoretti," published in 1595, along with the "Epithalamion," are a series of eighty-eight Sonnets, reflecting the fortunes of the poet's courtship of his second love and only wife—an Irish lady, regarding whom nothing positive is known; for Spenser's own hints as to the lowliness of her birth, both in the Sonnets and in "The Faerie Queen" (canto x., book vi., where she is introduced as a fourth Grace) are no more to be taken *au pied de la lettre*, than the similar indications regarding Rosalind, in "The Shepherd's Calendar." The Sonnets begin about the close of 1592, and extend to nearly the date of the poet's marriage, in June 1594. Of the eighty-eight, thirty-one have been selected for the present edition, representing as fairly as possible the various phases of the poet's passion and love-fortunes.
7 Sad.

If sapphires, lo! her eyes be sapphires plain;
If rubies, lo! her lips be rubies sound;
If pearls, her teeth be pearls, both pure and round;
If ivory, her forehead ivory ween;
If gold, her locks are finest gold on ground;
If silver, her fair hands are silver sheen:
But that which fairest is, but few behold,—
Her mind adorn'd with virtues manifold.

XVIII.

The rolling wheel, that runneth often round,
The hardest steel in tract of time doth tear:
And drizzling drops, that often do redound,
The firmest flint doth in continuance wear:
Yet cannot I, with many a dropping tear
And long entreaty, soften her hard heart;
That she will once vouchsafe my plaint to hear,
Or look with pity on my painful smart.
But, when I plead, she bids me play my part;
And, when I weep, she says, tears are but water;
And, when I sigh, she says, I know the art;
And, when I wail, she turns herself to laughter.
So do I weep, and wail, and plead in vain,
While she as steel and flint doth still remain.

XIX.

The merry Cuckoo, messenger of Spring,
His trumpet shrill hath thrice already sounded,
That warns all lovers wait upon their king,
Who now is coming forth with garland crownëd.
With noise whereof the choir of birds resounded
Their anthems sweet, devisëd of Love's praise,
That all the woods their echoes back rebounded,
As if they knew the meaning of their lays.
But 'mongst them all, which did Love's honour raise,
No word was heard of her that most it ought;
But she his precept proudly disobeys,
And doth his idle message set at naught.
Therefore, O Love, unless she turn to thee
Ere Cuckoo end, let her a rebel be!

XXVI.

Sweet is the rose, but grows upon a brere;
Sweet is the juniper, but sharp his bough;
Sweet is the eglantine, but pricketh near;
Sweet is the fir-bloom, but his branches rough;
Sweet is the cypress, but his rind is tough;
Sweet is the nut, but bitter is his pill;
Sweet is the broom-flower, but yet sour enough;
And sweet is moly, but his root is ill.
So ev'ry sweet with sour is temper'd still,
That maketh it be coveted the more:
For easy things, that may be got at will,
Most sorts of men do set but little store.
Why then should I account of little pain,
That endless pleasure shall unto me gain?

XXVII.

Fair Proud! now tell me, why should fair be proud,
Since all world's glory is but dross unclean,
And in the shade of death itself shall shroud,
However now thereof ye little ween!
That goodly idol, now so gay beseen,
Shall doff her flesh's borrow'd fair attire,
And be forgot as it had never been,
That many now much worship and admire!
Nor any then shall after it inquire,
Nor any mention shall thereof remain,
But what this verse, that never shall expire,
Shall to you purchase with her thankless pain!
Fair! be no longer proud of that shall perish;
But that, which shall you make immortal, cherish.

XXVIII.

The laurel-leaf,[1] which you this day do wear,
Gives me great hope of your relenting mind:
For since it is the badge which I do bear,
Ye, bearing it, do seem to me inclin'd:
The pow'r thereof, which oft in me I find,
Let it likewise your gentle breast inspire
With sweet infusion, and put you in mind
Of that proud maid, whom now those leaves attire:
Proud Daphne, scorning Phœbus' lovely fire,
On the Thessalian shore from him did fly:
For which the gods, in their revengeful ire,
Did her transform into a laurel tree.
Then fly no more, fair Love, from Phœbus' chase,
But in your breast his leaf and love embrace.

XXIX.

See! how the stubborn damsel doth deprave
My simple meaning with disdainful scorn;
And by the bay, which I unto her gave,
Accounts myself her captive quite forlorn.
The bay, quoth she, is of the victors borne,
Yielded them by the vanquish'd as their meeds,
And they therewith do Poets' heads adorn,
To sing the glory of their famous deeds.
But since she will the conquest challenge needs,
Let her accept me as her faithful thrall;
That her great triumph, which my skill exceeds,
I may in trump of fame blaze over all.
Then would I deck her head with glorious bays,
And fill the world with her victorious praise.

XL.

Mark when she smiles with amiable cheer,
And tell me whereto can ye liken it;
When on each eyelid sweetly do appear
A hundred Graces as in shade to sit.
Likest it seemeth, in my simple wit,
Unto the fair sunshine in summer's day;
That, when a dreadful storm away is flit,
Through the broad world doth spread his goodly ray;
At sight whereof, each bird that sits on spray,
And ev'ry beast that to his den was fled,
Comes forth afresh out of their late dismay,
And to the light lift up their drooping head.
So my storm-beaten heart likewise is cheer'd
With that sunshine, when cloudy looks are clear'd.

LIV.

Of this world's theatre in which we stay,
My Love like the spectator idly sits;
Beholding me, that all the pageants play,
Disguising diversely my troubled wits.

[1] Spenser, apparently, had presented to his mistress the wreath with which he was crowned Poet-Laureate.

Sometimes I joy when glad occasion fits,
And mask in mirth like to a comedy:
Soon after, when my joy to sorrow flits,
I wail, and make my woes a tragedy.
Yet she, beholding me with constant eye,
Delights not in my mirth, nor rues my smart:
But, when I laugh, she mocks; and, when I cry,
She laughs, and hardens evermore her heart.
What then can move her? if nor mirth, nor moan,
She is no woman, but a senseless stone.

LV.

So oft as I her beauty do behold,
And therewith do her cruelty compare,
I marvel of what substance was the mould
The which her made at once so cruel fair.
Not earth; for her high thoughts more heav'nly are:
Not water; for her love doth burn like fire:
Not air; for she is not so light or rare:
Not fire; for she doth freeze with faint desire.
Then needs another element inquire
Whereof she might be made; that is, the sky.
For to the heav'n her haughty looks aspire;
And eke her love is pure immortal high.
Then, since to heav'n ye liken'd are the best,
Be like in mercy as in all the rest.

LVI.

Fair be ye sure, but cruel and unkind,
As is a tiger, that with greediness
Hunts after blood; when he by chance doth find
A feeble beast, doth felly him oppress.
Fair be ye sure, but proud and pitiless,
As is a storm, that all things doth prostráte;
Finding a tree alone all comfortless,
Beats on it strongly, it to ruinate.
Fair be ye sure, but hard and obstinate,
As is a rock amidst the raging floods;
'Gainst which a ship, of succour desolate,
Doth suffer wreck both of herself and goods.
That ship, that tree, and that same beast, am I,
Whom ye do wreck, do ruin, and destroy.

LX.[1]

They, that in course of heav'nly spheres are skill'd,
To ev'ry planet point his sundry year,
In which her circle's voyage is fulfill'd;
As Mars in threescore years doth run his sphere.
So, since the wingëd god his planet clear
Began in me to move, one year is spent:
The which doth longer unto me appear
Than all those forty which my life out-went.
Then by that count, which lovers' books invent,
The sphere of Cupid forty years contains:
Which I have wasted in long languishment,
That seem'd the longer for my greater pains.
But let my Love's fair planet short her ways,
This year ensuing, or else short my days.

LXII.

The weary year his race now having run,
The new begins his compast[2] course anew:
With show of morning mild he hath begun,
Betokening peace and plenty to ensue.
So let us, which this change of weather view,
Change eke our minds, and former lives amend;
The old year's sins forepast let us eschew,
And fly the faults with which we did offend.
Then shall the new year's joy forth freshly send
Into the glooming world his gladsome ray:
And all these storms, which now his beauty blend,[3]
Shall turn to calms, and timely clear away.
So, likewise, Love! cheer you your heavy sprite,
And change old year's annoy to new delight.

LXIII.

After long storms and tempests' sad assay,
Which hardly I endurëd heretofore,
In dread of death, and dangerous dismay,
With which my silly bark was tossëd sore,
I do at length descry the happy shore,
In which I hope ere long for to arrive:
Fair soil it seems from far, and fraught with store
Of all that dear and dainty is alive.
Most happy he! that can at last achive[4]
The joyous safety of so sweet a rest;
Whose least delight sufficeth to deprive
Remembrance of all pains which him opprest.
All pains are nothing in respect of this;
All sorrows short that gain eternal bliss.

LXIV.

Coming to kiss her lips (such grace I found),
Me seem'd, I smell'd a garden of sweet flow'rs,
That dainty odours from them threw around,
For damsels fit to deck their lovers' bow'rs.
Her lips did smell like unto gilliflow'rs;
Her ruddy cheeks, like unto roses red;
Her snowy brows, like budded bellamours;
Her lovely eyes, like pinks but newly spread;
Her goodly bosom, like a strawberry bed;
Her neck, like to a bunch of columbines;
Her breast, like lilies ere their leaves be shed;
Her nipples, like young blossom'd jessamines:
Such fragrant flow'rs do give most odorous smell;
But her sweet odour did them all excel.

LXV.

The doubt which ye misdeem, fair Love, is vain,
That fondly fear to lose your liberty;
When, losing one, two liberties ye gain,
And make him bond that bondage erst[5] did fly.
Sweet be the bands the which true love doth tie
Without constraint, or dread of any ill:
The gentle bird feels no captivity
Within her cage, but sings, and feeds her fill.
There pride dare not approach, nor discord spill[6]
The league 'twixt them that loyal love hath bound:
But simple truth, and mutual good will,
Seeks, with sweet peace, to salve each other's wound:

1 By this Sonnet the poet's birth has been ascertained to have taken place in 1552; for these lines were written in 1593, and in that year, he says, he was forty-one years old. As the new year is mentioned in the next Sonnet but one, the date of the poet's birth was probably late in 1552.

2 Round.

3 Obscure.

4 Achieve, attain.

5 Formerly.

6 Destroy.

There Faith doth fearless dwell in brazen tow'r,
And spotless Pleasure builds her sacred bow'r.

LXVII.

Like as a huntsman after weary chase,
Seeing the game from him escap'd away,
Sits down to rest him in some shady place,
With panting hounds beguilëd of their prey:
So, after long pursuit and vain assay,
When I all weary had the chase forsook,
The gentle deer return'd the selfsame way,
Thinking to quench her thirst at the next brook:
There she, beholding me with milder look,
Sought not to fly, but fearless still did bide;
Till I in hand her yet half trembling took,
And with her own good will her firmly tied.
Strange thing, me seem'd, to see a beast so wild
So goodly won, with her own will beguil'd.

LXVIII.

Most glorious Lord of life! that on this day[1]
Didst make thy triumph over death and sin;
And, having harrow'd hell,[2] didst bring away
Captivity thence captive, us to win:
This joyous day, dear Lord, with joy begin;
And grant that we, for whom thou diddest die,
Being with thy dear blood clean wash'd from sin,
May live for ever in felicity!
And that thy love we weighing worthily,
May likewise love thee for the same again;
And for thy sake, that all like dear didst buy,
With love may one another entertain!
So let us love, dear Love, like as we ought:
Love is the lesson which the Lord us taught.

LXX.

Fresh Spring, the herald of love's mighty king,
In whose coat-armour richly are display'd
All sorts of flow'rs, the which on earth do spring,
In goodly colours gloriously array'd;
Go to my love, where she is careless laid,
Yet in her winter's bow'r not well awake;
Tell her the joyous time will not be stay'd,
Unless she do him by the forelock take;
Bid her therefóre herself soon ready make
To wait on Love amongst his lovely crew;
Where ev'ry one that misseth then her make[3]
Shall be by him amerc'd with penance due.
Make haste therefóre, sweet love, while it is prime;
For none can call again the passëd time.

LXXI.

I joy to see how, in your drawen work,
Yourself unto the Bee ye do compare;
And me unto the Spider, that doth lurk
In close await, to catch her unaware:
Right so yourself were caught in cunning snare
Of a dear foe, and thrallëd to his love;
In whose strait bands ye now captívëd are
So firmly, that ye never may remove.
But as your work is woven all about
With woodbine flow'rs and fragant eglantine;
So sweet your prison you in time shall prove,
With many dear delights bedeckëd fine.
And all thenceforth eternal peace shall see
Between the Spider and the gentle Bee.

LXXIV.

Most happy letters! fram'd by skilful trade,
With which that happy name was first design'd,
The which three times thrice happy hath me made,
With gifts of body, fortune, and of mind.
The first my being to me gave by kind,
From mother's womb deriv'd by due descent:
The second is my sov'reign Queen most kind,
That honour and large riches to me lent:
The third, my love, my life's last ornament,
By whom my spirit out of dust was rais'd:
To speak her praise and glory excellent,
Of all alive most worthy to be prais'd.
Ye three ELIZABETHS! for ever live,
That three such graces did unto me give.

LXXV.

One day I wrote her name upon the strand;
But came the waves, and washëd it away:
Again I wrote it with a second hand;
But came the tide, and made my pains his prey.
Vain man, said she, that dost in vain assay
A mortal thing so to immortalise;
For I myself shall like to this decay,
And eke my name be wipëd out likewise.
Not so, quoth I; let baser things devise
To die in dust, but you shall live by fame:
My verse your virtues rare shall éternise,
And in the heavens write your glorious name.
Where, when as death shall all the world subdue,
Our love shall live, and later life renew.

LXXVI.

Fair bosom! fraught with virtue's richest treasure,
The nest of love, the lodging of delight,
The bow'r of bliss, the paradise of pleasure,
The sacred harbour of that heav'nly sprite;
How was I ravish'd with your lovely sight,
And my frail thoughts too rashly led astray!
While, diving deep through amorous insíght,
On the sweet spoil of beauty they did prey;
And 'twixt her paps (like early fruit in May,
Whose harvest seem'd to hasten now apace)
They loosely did their wanton wings display,
And there to rest themselves did boldly place.
Sweet thoughts! I envy your so happy rest,
Which oft I wish'd, yet never was so blest.

LXXVII.

Was it a dream, or did I see it plain?
A goodly table of pure ivory,
All spread with junkets, fit to entertain
The greatest prince with pompous royalty:
'Mongst which, there in a silver dish did lie
Two golden apples of unvalúed price;
Far passing those which Hercules came by,
Or those which Atalanta did entice;
Exceeding sweet, yet void of sinful vice;
That many sought, yet none could ever taste;
Sweet fruit of pleasure, brought from Paradise

[1] Good Friday. [2] See note 11, page 51.

[3] Has failed to find a mate.

By Love himself, and in his garden plac'd.
Her breast that table was, so richly spread;
My thoughts the guests, which would thereon have fed.

LXXX.

After so long a race as I have run
Through Faery Land, which those six books compile,[1]
Give leave to rest me, being half fordone,
And gather to myself new breath a while.
Then, as a steed refreshëd after toil,
Out of my prison I will break anew;
And stoutly will that second work assoil,[2]
With strong endeavour and attention due.
Till then give leave to me in pleasant mew[3]
To sport my Muse, and sing my Love's sweet praise;
The contemplation of whose heav'nly hue
My spirit to a higher pitch will raise.
But let her praises yet be low and mean,
Fit for the handmaid of the Faery Queen.

LXXXI.

Fair is my Love, when her fair golden hairs
With the loose wind ye waving chance to mark;
Fair, when the rose in her red cheeks appears;
Or in her eyes the fire of love does spark.
Fair, when her breast, like a rich laden bark,
With precious merchandise, she forth doth lay;
Fair, when that cloud of pride, which oft doth dark
Her goodly light, with smiles she drives away.
But fairest she, whenso she doth display
The gate with pearls and rubies richly dight,
Through which her words so wise do make their way
To bear the message of her gentle sprite.
The rest be works of Nature's wonderment;
But this the work of heart's astonishment.

LXXXII.

Joy of my life! full oft for loving you
I bless my lot, that was so lucky plac'd:
But then the more your own mishap I rue,
That are so much by so mean love embas'd.
For, had the equal[4] heav'ns so much you grac'd
In this as in the rest, ye might invent
Some heav'nly wit, whose verse could have enchas'd
Your glorious name in golden monument.
But since ye deign'd so goodly to relent
To me your thrall, in whom is little worth,
That little, that I am, shall all be spent
In setting your immortal praises forth:
Whose lofty argument, uplifting me,
Shall lift you up unto a high degree.

LXXXIII.

Let not one spark of filthy lustful fire
Break out, that may her sacred peace molest;
Nor one light glance of sensual desire
Attempt to work her gentle mind's unrest:
But pure affections bred in spotless breast,
And modest thoughts breath'd from well-temper'd sprites,
Go visit her in her chaste bower of rest,
Accompanied with ángelic delights.
There fill yourself with those most joyous sights,
The which myself could never yet attain:
But speak no word to her of these sad plights
Which her too constant stiffness doth constrain.
Only behold her rare perfectión,
And bless your fortune's fair electión.[5]

EPITHALAMION.[6]

[1595.]

YE learnëd Sisters, which have oftentimes
Been to me aiding, others to adorn
Whom ye thought worthy of your graceful rhymes,
That ev'n the greatest did not greatly scorn
To hear their names sung in your simple lays,
But joyëd in their praise;
And when ye list your own mishaps to mourn,
Which death, or love, or fortune's wreck did raise,
Your string could soon to sadder tenor turn,
And teach the woods and waters to lament
Your doleful dreariment:
Now lay those sorrowful complaints aside;

1 In the thirty-third Sonnet, Spenser, addressing his friend Lodowick Briskett, had apologised for the great wrong done to Queen Elizabeth in "not finishing her Queen of Faery, that might enlarge her living praises, dead;" the poet's excuse being, that his wit was "lost through troublous fit of a proud love." That Sonnet was probably written in the spring of 1593; the eightieth in the spring of 1594.

2 Absolve, discharge; he refers to the second half of his great poem.

3 Retirement.

4 Just.

5 Five Sonnets complete the series; the first defends the poet against the charge that his praises of his mistress are overstrained; the second vehemently dooms to "all the plagues and horrid pains of hell" some "venomous tongue" that has stirred in his true love coals of ire, and broken his own sweet peace; and the other three bewail a temporary withdrawal of the light of his mistress's presence. But this parting wail is quickly drowned in the jubilant melody of the "Epithalamion."

6 Written in honour of the poet's own marriage, which took place on St Barnabas' Day, the 11th (now the 22d) of June, 1594.

And, having all your heads with garlands crown'd,
Help me mine own love's praises to resound;
Nor let the same of any be envied:
So Orpheus did for his own bride!
So I unto myself alone will sing;
The woods shall to me answer, and my echo ring.

Early, before the world's light-giving lamp
His golden beam upon the hills doth spread,
Having dispers'd the night's uncheerful damp,
Do ye awake; and, with fresh lustihead,
Go to the bow'r of my belovëd love,
My truest turtle dove;
Bid her awake; for Hymen is awake,
And long since ready forth his masque to move,
With his bright tead[1] that flames with many a flake;
And many a bachelor to wait on him,
In their fresh garments trim.
Bid her awake therefóre, and soon her dight,[2]
For lo! the wishëd day is come at last,
That shall, for all the pains and sorrows past,
Pay to her usury of long delight:
And, whilst she doth her dight,
Do ye to her of joy and solace sing,
That all the woods may answer, and your echo ring.

Bring with you all the Nymphs that you can hear,
Both of the Rivers and the Forests green,
And of the Sea that neighbours to her near;
All with gay garlands goodly well beseen.
And let them also with them bring in hand
Another gay garlánd,
For my fair love, of lilies and of roses,
Bound true-love wise, with a blue silk ribánd.
And let them make great store of bridal posies,
And let them eke bring store of other flowers,
To deck the bridal bowers.
And let the ground where as her foot shall tread,
For fear the stones her tender foot should wrong,
Be strow'd with fragrant flowers all along,
And diaper'd like the discolour'd mead.
Which done, do at her chamber door await,
For she will waken straight;
The while do ye this song unto her sing,
The woods shall to you answer, and your echo ring.

Ye Nymphs of Mulla, which with careful heed
The silver scaly trouts do tend full well,
And greedy pikes which use therein to feed
(Those trouts and pikes all others do excel);
And ye likewise, which keep the rushy lake,
Where none do fishes take;
Bind up the locks the which hang scatter'd light,
And in his waters, which your mirror make,
Behold your faces as the crystal bright,
That when you come where as my love doth lie,
No blemish she may spy.
And eke, ye lightfoot maids, which keep the door,
That on the hoary mountain used to tow'r;
And the wild wolves, which seek them to devour,
With your steel darts do chase from coming near;
Be also present here,
To help to deck her, and to help to sing,
That all the woods may answer, and your echo ring.

Wake now, my love, awake; for it is time;
The rosy Morn long since left Tithon's bed,
All ready to her silver coach to climb;
And Phœbus gins to show his glorious head.
Hark! how the cheerful birds do chant their lays,
And carol of love's praise.
The merry lark her matins sings aloft;
The thrush replies; the mavis descant plays;
The ouzel shrills; the ruddock[3] warbles soft;
So goodly all agree, with sweet concent,
To this day's merriment.
Ah! my dear love, why do ye sleep thus long,
When meeter were that ye should now awake,
T' await the coming of your joyous make,[4]
And hearken to the birds' love-learnëd song,
The dewy leaves among!
For they of joy and pleasance to you sing,
That all the woods them answer, and their echo ring.

My love is now awake out of her dreams,
And her fair eyes, like stars that dimmëd were
With darksome cloud, now show their goodly beams,
More bright than Hesperus his head doth rear.
Come now, ye damsels, daughters of delight,
Help quickly her to dight:
But first come, ye fair Hours, which were begot
In Jove's sweet Paradise, of Day and Night;
Which do the seasons of the year allot,
And all, that ever in this world is fair,
Do make and still repair:
And ye three handmaids[5] of the Cyprian Queen,
The which do still adorn her beauty's pride,
Help to adorn my beautifulest bride:
And, as ye her array, still throw between
Some graces to be seen;
And, as ye use to Venus, to her sing,
The while the woods shall answer, and your echo ring.

Now is my love all ready forth to come:
Let all the virgins therefore well await;
And ye fresh boys, that tend upon her groom,
Prepare yourselves; for he is coming straight.
Set all your things in seemly good array,
Fit for so joyful day:
The joyful'st day that ever sun did see.
Fair Sun! show forth thy favourable ray,
And let thy lifeful heat not fervent be,
For fear of burning her sunshiny face,
Her beauty to disgrace.
O fairest Phœbus! Father of the Muse!
If ever I did honour thee aright,
Or sing the thing that might thy mind delight,
Do not thy servant's simple boon refuse;
But let this day, let this one day, be mine;
Let all the rest be thine.

1 Torch. 2 Array. 3 Redbreast. 4 Mate. 5 The Graces.

Then I thy sov'reign praises loud will sing,
That all the woods shall answer, and their echo ring.

Hark! how the minstrels gin to shrill aloud
Their merry music that resounds from far,
The pipe, the tabor, and the trembling croud,[1]
That well agree withouten breach or jar.
But, most of all, the damsels do delight,
When they their timbrels smite,
And thereunto do dance and carol sweet,
That all the senses they do ravish quite;
The while the boys run up and down the street,
Crying aloud with strong confusëd noise,
As if it were one voice,
"Hymen, Iö Hymen, Hymen!" they do shout;
That even to the heav'ns their shouting shrill
Doth reach, and all the firmament doth fill;
To which the people standing all about,
As in approvance, do thereto applaud,
And loud advance her laud;
And evermore they "Hymen, Hymen!" sing,
That all the woods them answer, and their echo ring.

Lo! where she comes along with portly pace,
Like Phœbe, from her chamber of the East,
Arising forth to run her mighty race,
Clad all in white, that seems a virgin best.
So well it her beseems, that ye would ween
Some angel she had been.
Her long loose yellow locks, like golden wire,
Sprinkled with pearl, and pearling flowers atween,
Do like a golden mantle her attire;
And, being crownëd with a garland green,
Seem like some maiden queen.
Her modest eyes, abashëd to behold
So many gazers as on her do stare,
Upon the lowly ground affixëd are;
Nor dare lift up her countenance too bold,
But blush to hear her praises sung so loud,
So far from being proud.
Nathless do ye still loud her praises sing,
That all the woods may answer, and your echo ring.

Tell me, ye merchants' daughters, did ye see
So fair a creature in your town before;
So sweet, so lovely, and so mild as she,
Adorn'd with beauty's grace and virtue's store?
Her goodly eyes like sapphires shining bright,
Her forehead ivory white,
Her cheeks like apples which the sun hath rudded,[2]
Her lips like cherries charming men to bite,
Her breast like to a bowl of cream uncrudded,[3]
Her paps like lilies budded,
Her snowy neck like to a marble tower;
And all her body like a palace fair,
Ascending up, with many a stately stair,
To honour's seat and chastity's sweet bower.
Why stand ye still, ye virgins, in amaze,
Upon her so to gaze,
While ye forget your former lay to sing,
To which the woods did answer, and your echo ring?

[1] Violin. [2] Made ruddy. [3] Uncurdled.

But if ye saw that which no eyes can see,—
The inward beauty of her lively sprite,
Garnish'd with heav'nly gifts of high degree,—
Much more then would ye wonder at that sight,
And stand astonish'd like to those which read[4]
Medusa's mazeful[5] head.
There dwells sweet Love, and constant Chastity,
Unspotted Faith, and comely Womanhead,
Regard of Honour, and mild Modesty;
There Virtue reigns as queen in royal throne,
And giveth laws alone,
The which the base affections do obey,
And yield their services unto her will;
Nor thought of things uncomely ever may
Thereto approach, to tempt her mind to ill.
Had ye once seen these her celestial treasures,
And unrevealëd pleasures,
Then would ye wonder, and her praises sing,
That all the woods should answer, and your echo ring.

Open the temple gates unto my love,
Open them wide that she may enter in,
And all the posts adorn as doth behove,
And all the pillars deck with garlands trim,
For to receive this saint with honour due,
That cometh in to you.
With trembling steps, and humble reverence,
She cometh in, before th' Almighty's view:
Of her, ye virgins, learn obedience,
When so ye come into those holy places,
To humble your proud faces:
Bring her up to th' high altar, that she may
The sacred ceremonies there partake,
The which do endless matrimony make;
And let the roaring organs loudly play
The praises of the Lord in lively notes;
The while, with hollow throats,
The choristers the joyous anthem sing,
That all the woods may answer, and their echo ring.

Behold, while she before the altar stands,
Hearing the holy priest that to her speaks,
And blesseth her with his two happy hands,
How the red roses flush up in her cheeks,
And the pure snow with goodly vermeil stain,
Like crimson dy'd in grain:
That ev'n the angels, which continually
About the sacred altar do remain,
Forget their service, and about her fly,
Oft peeping in her face, that seems more fair
The more they on it stare.
But her sad eyes, still fasten'd on the ground,
Are governëd with goodly modesty,
That suffers not one look to glance awry,
Which may let in a little thought unsound.
Why blush ye, Love, to give to me your hand,
The pledge of all our band!
Sing, ye sweet angels, Alleluia sing!
That all the woods may answer, and your echo ring.

Now all is done: bring home the bride again;
Bring home the triumph of our victory;
Bring home with you the glory of her gain;
With joyance bring her and with jollity.

[4] Saw. [5] Wonderful, astounding.

Never had man more joyful day than this,
Whom heav'n would heap with bliss.
Make feast therefore now all this livelong day;
This day for ever to me holy is.
Pour out the wine without restraint or stay,
Pour not by cups, but by the belly full,
Pour out to all that wull,[1]
And sprinkle all the posts and walls with wine,
That they may sweat, and drunken be withal.
Crown ye god Bacchus with a coronal,
And Hymen also crown with wreaths of vine;
And let the Graces dance unto the rest,
For they can do it best:
The while the maidens do their carol sing,
To which the woods shall answer, and their echo
ring.

Ring ye the bells, ye young men of the town,
And leave your wonted labours for this day:
This day is holy; do ye write it down,
That ye for ever it remember may.
This day the sun is in his chiefest height,
With Barnaby the bright,
From whence declining daily by degrees,
He somewhat loseth of his heat and light,
When once the Crab behind his back he sees.
But for this time it ill ordainëd was
To choose the longest day in all the year,
And shortest night, when longest fitter were:
Yet never day so long, but late would pass.
Ring ye the bells, to make it wear away,
And bonfires make all day;
And dance about them, and about them sing,
That all the woods may answer, and your echo
ring.

Ah! when will this long weary day have end,
And lend me leave to come unto my love?
How slowly do the Hours their numbers spend!
How slowly does sad Time his feathers move!
Haste thee, O fairest Planet, to thy home
Within the western foam!
Thy tirëd steeds long since have need of rest.
Long though it be, at last I see it gloom,
And the bright Ev'ning Star, with golden crest,
Appear out of the East.
Fair child of beauty! glorious lamp of love!
That all the host of heav'n in ranks dost lead,
And guidest lovers through the night's sad dread,
How cheerfully thou lookest from above,
And seem'st to laugh atween thy twinkling light,
As joying in the sight
Of these glad many which for joy do sing,
That all the woods them answer, and their echo
ring!

Now cease, ye damsels, your delights forepast;
Enough it is that all the day was yours:
Now day is done, and night is nighing fast,
Now bring the bride into the bridal bow'rs.
The night is come, now soon her disarray,
And in her bed her lay;
Lay her in lilies and in violets,
And silken curtains over her display,
And odour'd sheets, and Arras coverlets.

Behold how goodly my fair love does lie,
In proud humility!
Like unto Maia, when as Jove her took
In Tempé, lying on the flow'ry grass,
'Twixt sleep and wake, after she weary was
With bathing in the Acidalian brook.
Now it is night, ye damsels may be gone,
And leave my love alone;
And leave likewise your former lay to sing:
The woods no more shall answer, nor your echo
ring.

Now welcome, Night! thou night so long expected,
That long day's labour dost at last defray,
And all my cares, which cruel Love collected,
Hast summ'd in one, and cancellëd for ay:
Spread thy broad wing over my love and me,
That no man may us see;
And in thy sable mantle us enwrap,
From fear of peril and foul horror free.
Let no false treason seek us to entrap,
Nor any dread disquiet once annoy
The safety of our joy;
But let the night be calm and quietsome,
Without tempestuous storms or sad affray:
Like as when Jove with fair Alcmena lay,
When he begot the great Tirynthian groom:[2]
Or like as when he with thyself did lie,
And begot Majesty.
And let the maids and young men cease to
sing;
Nor let the woods them answer, nor their echo
ring.

Let no lamenting cries, nor doleful tears,
Be heard all night within, nor yet without:
Nor let false whispers, breeding hidden fears,
Break gentle sleep with misconceivëd doubt.
Let no deluding dreams, nor dreadful sights,
Make sudden sad affrights;
Nor let house-fires, nor lightning's helpless
harms,
Nor let the pouk,[3] nor other evil sprites,
Nor let mischievous witches with their charms,
Nor let hobgoblins, names whose sense we see
not,
Fray us with things that be not:
Let not the screech-owl nor the stork be heard,
Nor the night-raven, that still deadly yells;
Nor damnëd ghosts, call'd up with mighty
spells,
Nor grisly vultures, make us once afear'd:
Nor let th' unpleasant choir of frogs still croaking
Make us to wish their choking.
Let none of these their dreary accents sing;
Nor let the woods them answer, nor their echo
ring.

But let still Silence true night-watches keep,
That sacred Peace may in assurance reign,
And timely Sleep, when it is time to sleep,
May pour his limbs forth on your pleasant
plain;

1 Will.
2 Hercules. See note 28, page 261.
3 Puck, or Robin Goodfellow, a mischievous night-goblin.

The while a hundred little wingëd Loves,
Like diverse-feather'd doves,
Shall fly and flutter round about the bed,
And in the secret dark, that none reproves,
Their pretty stealths shall work, and snares shall spread
To filch away sweet snatches of delight,
Conceal'd through covert night.
Ye sons of Venus, play your sports at will!
For greedy Pleasure, careless of your toys,
Thinks more upon her Paradise of joys,
Than what ye do, albeit good or ill.
All night, therefore, attend your merry play,
For it will soon be day:
Now none doth hinder you, that say or sing;
Nor will the woods now answer, nor your echo ring.

Who is the same, which at my window peeps?
Or whose is that fair face that shines so bright?
Is it not Cynthia, she that never sleeps,
But walks about high heaven all the night?
Oh! fairest goddess, do thou not envy
My love with me to spy:
For thou likewise didst love, though now unthought,
And for a fleece of wool, which privily
The Latmian shepherd[1] once unto thee brought,
His pleasures with thee wrought.
Therefore to us be favourable now;
And since of women's labours thou hast charge,
And generation goodly dost enlarge,[2]
Incline thy will t' effect our wishful vow,
And the chaste womb inform with timely seed,
That may our comfort breed:
Till which we cease our hopeful hap to sing;
Nor let the woods us answer, nor our echo ring.

And thou, great Juno! which with awful might
The laws of wedlock still dost patronise;
And the religion of the faith first plight
With sacred rites hast taught to solemnise;
And eke for comfort often callëd art

1 Endymion.
2 See note 17, page 37.

Of women in their smart;[2]
Eternally bind thou this lovely band,
And all thy blessings unto us impart.
And thou, glad Genius![3] in whose gentle hand
The bridal bow'r and genial bed remain,
Without blemish or stain;
And the sweet pleasures of their love's delight
With secret aid dost succour and supply,
Till they bring forth the fruitful progeny;
Send us the timely fruit of this same night.
And thou, fair Hebe! and thou, Hymen free!
Grant that it may so be.
Till which we cease your farther praise to sing;
Nor any woods shall answer, nor your echo ring.

And ye, high heav'ns, the temple of the gods,
In which a thousand torches flaming bright
Do burn, that to us wretched earthly clods
In dreadful darkness lend desirëd light;
And all ye Pow'rs which in the same remain,
More than we men can feign![4]
Pour out your blessing on us plenteously,
And happy influence upon us rain,
That we may raise a large posterity,
Which from the earth, which they may long possess
With lasting happiness,
Up to your haughty palaces may mount;
And, for the guerdon of their glorious merit,
May heav'nly tabernacles there inherit,
Of blessëd saints for to increase the count.
So let us rest, sweet love, in hope of this,
And cease till then our timely joys to sing:
The woods no more us answer, nor our echo ring!

Song! made in lieu of many ornaments,
With which my love should duly have been deck'd,
Which cutting off through hasty accidents,
Ye would not stay your due time to expect,
But promis'd both to recompense;
Be unto her a goodly ornament,
And for short time an endless monument!

3 See "The Faerie Queen," canto vi., book iii., page 424 (note 9).
4 Imagine.

THE END.

PRINTED BY BALLANTYNE AND COMPANY
EDINBURGH AND LONDON

CATALOGUE

OF

Popular and Standard Books

PUBLISHED BY

WILLIAM P. NIMMO,

EDINBURGH,

AND SOLD BY ALL BOOKSELLERS.

EDINBURGH.
1869.

11.69.

NIMMO'S
LARGE PRINT UNABRIDGED
LIBRARY EDITION OF THE BRITISH POETS,
FROM CHAUCER TO COWPER.

In Forty-eight Vols. Demy 8vo, Pica Type, Superfine Paper, Elegant Binding, price 4s. each Volume.

THE TEXT EDITED BY
CHARLES COWDEN CLARKE.

With Authentic Portraits Engraved on Steel.

The following Works are comprised in the Series:—

	Vols.		Vols.
WYATT,	1	CHURCHILL,	1
SPENSER,	5	BEATTIE, BLAIR, FALCONER,	1
SHAKESPEARE, SURREY,	1	BURNS,	2
HERBERT,	1	COWPER,	2
WALLER, DENHAM,	1	BOWLES,	2
MILTON,	2	SCOTT,	3
BUTLER,	2	CHAUCER'S CANTERBURY TALES,	3
DRYDEN,	2	CRAWSHAW, QUARLES' EMBLEMS,	1
PRIOR,	1	ADDISON, GAY'S FABLES, SOMERVILLE'S CHASE,	1
THOMSON,	1	YOUNG'S NIGHT THOUGHTS,	1
JOHNSON, PARNELL, GRAY, SMOLLETT,	1	PERCY'S RELIQUES OF ANCIENT ENGLISH POETRY,	3
POPE,	2	SPECIMENS, WITH LIVES, OF THE LESS KNOWN BRITISH POETS,	3
SHENSTONE,	1	H. K. WHITE AND J. GRAHAME'S POETICAL WORKS,	1
AKENSIDE,	1		
GOLDSMITH, COLLINS, T. WARTON,	1		
ARMSTRONG, DYER, GREEN,	1		

Any of the Works may be had separately, Price 4s. per Volume.

Nimmo's Large Print Unabridged Library Edition of the British Poets—*continued.*

OPINIONS OF THE PRESS.

'This edition issued by Mr. Nimmo is remarkable even in this age of cheap literature, and will go far to supply what has been long needed,—an accurate, elegant, and cheap edition of the Poets. . . . . The editor's temperament involves some of the choicest elements of poetic impressions, while his critical canons are for the most part sound and trustworthy.'—*Eclectic Review.*

'A truly valuable, correct, and cheap edition of the British Poets.'—*Globe.*

'Large handsome type, fitted even for ancient eyes, with liberal margin for the loving pencils of students. As reprints, they are the cheapest and handsomest we can name.'—*Leader.*

'This edition of the Poets is one of the very best and cheapest that has ever appeared.'—*Daily News.*

'Most assuredly the work itself, no less than the price at which it is proposed to be issued, must commend the plan to all lovers of literature.'—*Bell's Weekly Messenger.*

'Even in this age of cheap books, such a bargain has never been presented.'—*Christian News.*

'The critical remarks, like all that the editor writes, are vigorous in conception, and generally felicitous in phrase. The volumes are handsome and tasteful.'—*Scotsman.*

'The biographies are well and carefully condensed. . . . . Few publications can be so strongly recommended.'—*Art Journal.*

'This is one of the most magnificent enterprises of modern times. We know of no one who would compare with the editor in competency for the work he has undertaken.'—*Homilist.*

'An ornament to any library.'—*Atlas.*

'This series is beyond impeachment on the score of careful accuracy; and the books are quite a glory of typography, unsurpassed in that respect by the most costly edition ever produced.'—*Nonconformist.*

'To the editor the task seems a labour of love. . . . . Mr. Nimmo has well done his part, and supplied solid paper and excellent print.'—*Economist.*

'The series has, in fact, been continued and completed with the same painstaking regard to the convenience of the reader with which it was commenced, and it now presents to the public—by the combined efforts of printer, publisher, and editor—an edition of the poetry of Spenser, elegant in all the extrinsic equipments of a book, accurate in text, and with all the difficulties of an old writer cleared away.'—*The Bookseller.*

From the Right Honourable Earl Russell, K.G., etc. etc.

'I have had an opportunity of consulting some, and looking at the rest, of the volumes of your Library Edition of British Poets. I think it exceedingly well executed,—the type clear, the printing correct; and the whole Lives display a taste and judgment which are rarely to be found. I hope this edition will circulate widely, for I should like to see our great Poets not only on the shelf, but in the hands of our reading public.'

From the Right Honourable Bulwer Lytton, Bart.

'I think your Library Edition of the British Poets, as far as I have had leisure to look into the volumes published, exceedingly well executed. While cheap and acceptable to the mass of the public, it is in form a handsome library work, and is got up with literary taste and scholarship. It has one very valuable merit not common in popular works—viz. a large, clear, and intelligible letterpress. I sincerely trust the work will meet all the encouragement it well deserves.'

HUGH MILLER'S WORKS.

CHEAP POPULAR EDITIONS,

In crown 8vo, cloth extra, price 5s. each.

I.

Thirteenth Edition,

My Schools and Schoolmasters; or, The Story of my Education.

'A story which we have read with pleasure, and shall treasure up in memory for the sake of the manly career narrated, and the glances at old-world manners and distant scenes afforded us by the way.'—*Athenæum.*

A cheaper edition of 'My Schools and Schoolmasters' is also published, bound in limp cloth, price 2s. 6d.

II.

Thirty-fourth Thousand,

The Testimony of the Rocks; or, Geology in its Bearings on the Two Theologies, Natural and Revealed. *Profusely Illustrated.*

'The most remarkable work of perhaps the most remarkable man of the age. . . . A magnificent epic, and the Principia of Geology.'—*British and Foreign Evangelical Review.*

III.

Ninth Edition,

The Cruise of the Betsey; or, a Summer Ramble among the Fossiliferous Deposits of the Hebrides. With Rambles of a Geologist; or, Ten Thousand Miles over the Fossiliferous Deposits of Scotland.

IV.

Sketch-Book of Popular Geology.

V.

Ninth Edition,

First Impressions of England and its PEOPLE.

'This is precisely the kind of book we should have looked for from the author of the "Old Red Sandstone." Straightforward and earnest in style, rich and varied in matter, these "First Impressions" will add another laurel to the wreath which Mr. Miller has already won for himself.'—*Westminster Review.*

A cheaper edition of 'First Impressions of England' is also published, bound in limp cloth, price 2s. 6d.

HUGH MILLER'S WORKS.

NEW CHEAP RE-ISSUE.

IN announcing a NEW CHEAP EDITION of the WORKS OF HUGH MILLER, the Publisher does not consider it necessary to add anything by way of commendation. The fame of Hugh Miller is securely established throughout the world, and his works, by universal consent, take rank among the highest in English Literature.

To the higher and more cultivated classes of society he appeals by the purity and elegance of his style, as well as by his remarkable powers of description, and his profound knowledge of the marvels of nature. To the humbler classes and the working man, the story of his life—himself originally a working man in the strictest sense of the word, pushing his way upward to the distinguished position which he attained—must possess a peculiar charm, and to them his writings cannot fail to prove of special value.

At the present time, the works of Hugh Miller, one of the most gifted of our self-taught and self-made men, are peculiarly suited to exercise a most powerful influence in promoting the great cause of the progress of Education; and this new Edition, while elegant enough to command a place in the libraries of the rich, is cheap enough to be within the reach of the student and the working man.

Although many of his books have already attained an immense sale, notwithstanding their high price, the Publisher feels assured that they only require to be offered to the general public at a moderate rate to ensure for them a very widely increased circulation.

OPINIONS OF THE PRESS.

'This effort to bring the works of so distinguished an author within the reach of all classes, cannot fail to be universally appreciated.'—*Morning Star.*

'Hugh Miller's writings have long passed the period of criticism, and taken rank among standard works. From the times of the British Essayists and Oliver Goldsmith, no literary man has shown a greater mastery of the English language than the author of *The Old Red Sandstone.* The size of the page and the letterpress are suitable for the library, while the price is a third less than the original edition.'—*Daily Review.*

'The moderate price at which the series is now offered, however, will enable thousands of readers to acquire for themselves those volumes which they have hitherto only found accessible by means of the circulating library. From the pure, manly, and instructive character of his writings—whether social, moral, or scientific—and from the fascinating attractions of his style, we do not know any works better deserving of a vast circulation than those of Hugh Miller. The edition is clearly printed, and altogether well got up.'—*Glasgow Herald.*

'This cheap re-issue by Mr. Nimmo will enable tens of thousands who have yet only heard of Hugh Miller soon to learn to appreciate and admire him.'—*Bell's Messenger.*

'This cheap edition of Hugh Miller's works deserves, and will doubtless secure, a very extended public support. No one knew better than Hugh Miller how to combine amusement with instruction; and all his works exhibit this most important combination.'—*Public Opinion.*

'The works of Hugh Miller cannot be too widely known or studied; and the publisher deserves our thanks for his cheap re-issue of them.'—*The Standard.*

'A new cheap issue of Hugh Miller's admirable works will be hailed with pleasure by all who desire to possess a really valuable collection of books.'—*The Observer.*

NIMMO'S CARMINE GIFT-BOOKS.

I.

Small 4to, beautifully printed within red lines on superior paper, handsomely bound in cloth extra, bevelled boards, gilt edges, price 7s. 6d.,

ROSES AND HOLLY:

A Gift-Book for all the Year. With Original Illustrations by eminent Artists.

'This is really a collection of art and literary gems—the prettiest book, take it all in all, that we have seen this season.'—*Illustrated Times.*

II.

Uniform with the above, price 7s. 6d.,

PEN AND PENCIL PICTURES FROM THE POETS.

With Choice Illustrations by the most eminent Artists.

III.

Uniform with the above, 7s. 6d.,

GEMS OF LITERATURE:

Elegant, Rare, and Suggestive. Illustrated by distinguished Artists.

'For really luxurious books, Nimmo's "Pen and Pencil Pictures from the Poets" and "Gems of Literature" may be well recommended. They are luxurious in the binding, in the print, in the engravings, and in the paper.'—*Morning Post.*

IV.

Uniform with the above, price 7s. 6d.,

THE BOOK OF ELEGANT EXTRACTS.

Profusely Illustrated by the most eminent Artists.

'This is one of the most attractive and beautiful books which we have seen for some time, and is really worthy of a place on any drawing-room table.'—*Herald.*

V.

Uniform with the above, price 7s. 6d.,

THE GOLDEN GIFT.

A Book for the Young. Profusely Illustrated with Original Engravings on Wood by eminent Artists.

'The editor of this elegant gift-book has set himself the task of filling up the gap which undoubtedly exists in the illustrations for the young of those stories of English literature, for which at the later period of life they find the greatest possible enjoyment. He has been ably seconded by artists whom he has called to his aid in the accomplishment of this very desirable work. We have thus a book which, while it forms an acceptable gift to the young, will be turned to and read with pleasure even when they have passed into the sere and yellow leaf of age.'—*The Examiner.*

Four Volumes, crown 8vo, cloth, price 18s.,

THE PEOPLE'S EDITION OF

TYTLER'S HISTORY OF SCOTLAND.

'The most brilliant age of Scotland is fortunate in having found a historian whose sound judgment is accompanied by a graceful liveliness of imagination. We venture to predict that this book will soon become, and long remain, the standard History of Scotland.'—*Quarterly Review.*

'The want of a complete History of Scotland has been long felt; and from the specimen which the volume before us gives of the author's talents and capacity for the task he has undertaken, it may be reasonably inferred that the deficiency will be very ably supplied. The descriptions of the battles are concise, but full of spirit. The events are themselves of the most romantic kind, and are detailed in a very picturesque and forcible style.'—*Times.*

Demy 8vo, cloth, price 10s. 6d.,

JAMIESON'S SCOTTISH DICTIONARY.

Abridged from the Dictionary and Supplement (in 4 vols. 4to) by JOHN JOHNSTONE. An entirely New Edition, Revised and Enlarged, by JOHN LONGMUIR, A.M., LL.D., formerly Lecturer in King's College and University, Aberdeen.

COMPLETION OF THE COPYRIGHT EDITION OF

WILSON'S TALES OF THE BORDERS.

EDITED BY ALEXANDER LEIGHTON,

One of the Original Editors and Contributors.

In announcing the completion of the Copyright Edition of the BORDER TALES, the Publisher does not consider it necessary to say anything in recommendation of a work which has stood the test of a general competition, and which has increased in public favour with its years. Equally suited to all classes of readers, it has been received with delight in the school-room, the drawing-room, the parlour, and the village reading-room. Many of the Tales have been publicly read. The high tone of its morality renders it an admirable small library for young members of the family.

The new Copyright Edition will contain four additional Volumes, now first published, which will complete the work. It will be issued in Twenty-four Monthly Volumes, price 1s. each, sewed in elegant wrapper, commencing March 1st, 1869. But at the same time the entire work will be kept on sale, so that all who desire to possess it—either complete, or any separate volume thereof—can be supplied at once. Each volume is complete in itself, forming an independent collection of stories. The work may also be had in Twelve Double Volumes, handsomely bound in cloth, price 3s. each, or in Roxburgh, gilt top, for libraries, etc., 4s. 6d. each.

Those who already possess the first twenty Volumes are recommended to complete their sets by purchasing the four New Volumes, the last of which will contain a Steel Portrait of the Editor and principal contributor, Alexander Leighton, with a copious Glossary.

Second Edition, crown 8vo, cloth extra, price 3s. 6d.,

FAMILY PRAYERS

FOR

FIVE WEEKS,

WITH PRAYERS FOR SPECIAL OCCASIONS, AND A TABLE FOR READING THE HOLY SCRIPTURES THROUGHOUT THE YEAR.

BY WILLIAM WILSON, MINISTER OF KIPPEN.

'This is an excellent compendium of family prayers. It will be found invaluable to parents and heads of families. The prayers are short, well expressed, and the book, as a whole, does the author great credit.'—*Perth Advertiser.*

Crown 8vo, cloth extra, price 3s.,

TRIUMPH:

THE CHRISTIAN MORE THAN CONQUEROR.

BY THE REV. GEORGE PHILIP, M.A., FREE ST. JOHN'S CHURCH, EDINBURGH.

'Mr. Philip is the successor in the pulpit of Dr. Guthrie and Dr. Hanna, and he now follows them in the press—rather heavy metal, it must be avowed, to cope with either way. If, however, we are to judge of Mr. Philip's pulpit qualifications from his first attempt at book-making, we must set him down as a worthy successor of both of his immediate predecessors.'—*London Weekly Review.*

A NEW TALE BY HARRIET MILLER DAVIDSON.

Crown 8vo, cloth extra, price 6s.,

CHRISTIAN OSBORNE'S FRIENDS.

A TALE

BY MRS. HARRIET MILLER DAVIDSON,

Author of 'Isobel Jardine's History.'

'There is an entire absence of cant in the book; the principal heroine (for there are two), Mercy Lester, reminds us of Dinah in "Adam Bede," and occasionally of Currer Bell's "Shirley." She unites in her person some of the qualities which distinguish both; and while we would not imply that Mrs. Davidson occupies so high a position as George Eliot or Currer Bell, we must admit that she possesses in a minor degree some of the qualities which have made their writings so remarkably successful.'—*The Nonconformist.*

'It may interest many to learn that the authoress is the daughter of one of Scotland's most gifted sons, the lamented Hugh Miller. The story is well constructed, the style good, and the moral unexceptional. We can commend "Christian Osborne's Friends" to the friendship of all who love a good book.'—*The Morning Advertiser.*

NIMMO'S
Library Edition of Standard Works.

In large Demy 8vo, with Steel Portrait and Vignette, handsomely bound, Roxburgh style, gilt tops, price 5s. each.

I.

The Complete Works of William SHAKESPEARE. With a Biographical Sketch by MARY COWDEN CLARKE, a Copious Glossary, and numerous Illustrations.

II.

The Complete Poetical and Prose Works of ROBERT BURNS. With Life and Variorum Notes, and numerous Illustrations, by eminent Artists.

III.

The Miscellaneous Works of Oliver GOLDSMITH.

IV.

The Poetical Works of Lord Byron. Illustrated by eminent Artists.

V.

Josephus: The Whole Works of Flavius JOSEPHUS, the Jewish Historian. Translated by WHISTON.

VI.

The Arabian Nights' Entertainments. Translated from the Arabic. An entirely New Edition. Illustrated with upwards of 100 original Engravings on Wood.

VII.

The Works of Jonathan Swift, D.D. Carefully selected, with Life of the Author, and original and authentic Notes.

VIII.

The Works of Daniel Defoe. Carefully selected from the most authentic sources; with Life of the Author.

IX.

The Works of Tobias Smollett. Carefully selected from the most authentic sources, with copious Original Notes, and Life of the Author.

X.

The Canterbury Tales and Faerie Queen: With other Poems of CHAUCER and SPENSER. Edited for Popular Perusal, with current Illustrative and Explanatory Notes.

*** *The above Works may also be had elegantly bound in half-calf extra, gilt back, price 8s. each.*

NIMMO'S

Handy Books of Useful Knowledge.

Foolscap 8vo, uniformly bound in cloth extra.

PRICE ONE SHILLING EACH.

I.

THE EARTH'S CRUST: A Handy Outline of Geology. With numerous Illustrations. Third Edition. By DAVID PAGE, LL.D., F.R.S.E., F.G.S., Author of 'Text-Books of Geology and Physical Geography,' etc.

'Such a work as this was much wanted,—a work giving in clear and intelligible outline the leading facts of the science, without amplification or irksome details. It is admirable in arrangement, and clear, easy, and, at the same time, forcible in style. It will lead, we hope, to the introduction of geology into many schools that have neither time nor room for the study of large treatises.'—*The Museum.*

II.

POULTRY AS A MEAT SUPPLY: Being Hints to Henwives how to Rear and Manage Poultry Economically and Profitably. Fourth Edition. By the Author of 'The Poultry Kalendar.'

'The author's excellent aim is to teach henwives how to make the poultry-yard a profitable as well as pleasant pursuit, and to popularize poultry-rearing among the rural population generally.' —*The Globe.*

III.

HOW TO BECOME A SUCCESSFUL ENGINEER: Being Hints to Youths intending to adopt the Profession. Third Edition. By BERNARD STUART, Engineer.

'Parents and guardians, with youths under their charge destined for the profession, as well as youths themselves who intend to adopt it, will do well to study and obey the plain curriculum in this little book. Its doctrine will, we hesitate not to say, if practised, tend to fill the ranks of the profession with men conscious of the heavy responsibilities placed in their charge.'—*Practical Mechanic's Journal.*

IV.

RATIONAL COOKERY: Cookery made Practical and Economical, in connection with the Chemistry of Food. Fifth Edition. By HARTELAW REID.

VI.

DOMESTIC MEDICINE: Plain and Brief Directions for the Treatment requisite before Advice can be obtained. Second Edition. By OFFLEY BOHUN SHORE, Doctor of Medicine of the University of Edinburgh, etc. etc. etc.

'This is one of the medicine books that ought to be published. It is from the pen of Dr. Shore, an eminent physician, and it is dedicated, by permission, to Sir James Y. Simpson, Bart., one of the first physicians of the age. We can recommend it to the attention of heads of families and to travellers.'—*The Standard.*

VII.

DOMESTIC MANAGEMENT: Hints on the Training and Treatment of Children and Servants. By Mrs. CHARLES DOIG.

VIII.

FREE-HAND DRAWING: A Guide to Ornamental, Figure, and Landscape Drawing. By an ART STUDENT, Author of 'Ornamental and Figure Drawing.' Profusely Illustrated.

IX.

THE METALS USED IN CONSTRUCTION: Iron, Steel, Bessemer Metal, etc. etc. By FRANCIS HERBERT JOYNSON. Illustrated.

OTHER VOLUMES IN PREPARATION.

Popular Works by the Author of 'Heaven our Home.'

Aggregate sale of the following popular works, **157,000** *copies.*

I.

Crown 8vo, cloth antique, **One Hundredth Thousand,** price 3s. 6d.,

HEAVEN OUR HOME.

'The author of the volume before us endeavours to describe what heaven is, as shown by the light of reason and Scripture; and we promise the reader many charming pictures of heavenly bliss, founded upon undeniable authority, and described with the pen of a dramatist, which cannot fail to elevate the soul as well as to delight the imagination. . . . . Part Second proves, in a manner as beautiful as it is convincing, the DOCTRINE OF THE RECOGNITION OF FRIENDS IN HEAVEN,—a subject of which the author makes much, introducing many touching scenes of Scripture celebrities meeting in heaven and discoursing of their experience on earth. Part Third DEMONSTRATES THE INTEREST WHICH THOSE IN HEAVEN FEEL IN EARTH, AND PROVES, WITH REMARKABLE CLEARNESS, THAT SUCH AN INTEREST EXISTS NOT ONLY WITH THE ALMIGHTY AND AMONG THE ANGELS, BUT ALSO AMONG THE SPIRITS OF DEPARTED FRIENDS. We unhesitatingly give our opinion that this volume is one of the most delightful productions of a religious character which has appeared for some time; and we would desire to see it pass into extensive circulation.'—*Glasgow Herald.*

A CHEAP EDITION OF 'HEAVEN OUR HOME,'

In crown 8vo, cloth limp, price 1s. 6d., is also published.

II.

Crown 8vo, cloth antique, **Twenty-ninth Thousand,** price 3s. 6d.,

MEET FOR HEAVEN.

'The author, in his or her former work, "Heaven our Home," portrayed a SOCIAL HEAVEN, WHERE SCATTERED FAMILIES MEET AT LAST IN LOVING INTERCOURSE AND IN POSSESSION OF PERFECT RECOGNITION, to spend a never-ending eternity of peace and love. In the present work the individual state of the children of God is attempted to be unfolded, and more especially the state of probation which is set apart for them on earth to fit and prepare erring mortals for the society of the saints. . . . . The work, as a whole, displays an originality of conception, a flow of language, and a closeness of reasoning rarely found in religious publications. . . . The author combats the pleasing and generally accepted belief, that DEATH WILL EFFECT AN ENTIRE CHANGE ON THE SPIRITUAL CONDITION OF OUR SOULS, and that all who enter into bliss will be placed on a common level.'—*Glasgow Herald.*

A CHEAP EDITION OF 'MEET FOR HEAVEN,'

In crown 8vo, cloth limp, price 1s. 6d., is also published.

III.

Crown 8vo, cloth antique, **Twenty-first Thousand,** price 3s. 6d.,

LIFE IN HEAVEN.

THERE, FAITH IS CHANGED INTO SIGHT, AND HOPE IS PASSED INTO BLISSFUL FRUITION.

'This is certainly one of the most remarkable works which have been issued from the press during the present generation; and we have no doubt it will prove as acceptable to the public as the two attractive volumes to which it forms an appropriate and beautiful sequel.'—*Cheltenham Journal.*

A CHEAP EDITION OF 'LIFE IN HEAVEN,'

In crown 8vo, cloth limp, price 1s. 6d., is also published.

IV.

Crown 8vo, cloth antique, **Seventh Thousand,** price 3s. 6d.,

CHRIST'S TRANSFIGURATION;

OR, TABOR'S TEACHINGS.

'The main subjects discussed in this new work are, Christ's glory and eternal intercourse with his people. These are developed with great power of thought, and great beauty of language. The book is sure to meet with as flattering a reception as the author's former works.'—*The Newsman.*

A CHEAP EDITION OF 'CHRIST'S TRANSFIGURATION,'

In crown 8vo, cloth limp, price 1s. 6d., is also published.

www.ingramcontent.com/pod-product-compliance
Lightning Source LLC
LaVergne TN
LVHW021055110826
845150LV00001B/82

* 9 7 8 1 4 2 5 5 6 6 9 0 6 *